REVIEWS OF UNITED KINGDOM STATISTICAL SOURCES

Volume XXVIII

THE FOOD INDUSTRIES

REVIEWS OF UNITED KINGDOM STATISTICAL SOURCES

Other volumes in this series published by Chapman & Hall

XXIII	*Agriculture*, G. H. Peters
XXIV	*Local Government*, J. M. Gillespie
XXV	*Family Planning*, P. F. Selman
XXVI	*International Aspects of UK Economic Activities*, P. Buckley and R. D. Pearce
XXVII	*Research and Development*, D. L. Bosworth, R. A. Wilson and A. Young
XXVIII	*The Food Industries*, J. Mark and R. Strange
XXIX	*Distribution*, C. Moir and J. A. Dawson

Available from Chapman & Hall 2–6 Boundary Row, London SE1 8HN
Telephone 071-522-9966

REVIEWS OF UNITED KINGDOM STATISTICAL SOURCES

Edited by M. C. FLEMING
Professor of Economics,
Loughborough University

Volume XXVIII

THE FOOD INDUSTRIES

JOHN MARK

and

ROGER STRANGE

The Management Centre,
King's College London
University of London

with contributions by Jim Burns
Department of Agricultural Economics and Management
University of Reading

CRC Press is an imprint of the
Taylor & Francis Group, an **informa** business
A CHAPMAN & HALL BOOK

First published 1993 by Chapman and Hall
First edition 1993

Published 2019 by CRC Press
Taylor & Francis Group
6000 Broken Sound Parkway NW, Suite 300
Boca Raton, FL 33487-2742

First issued in paperback 2019

ISBN 13: 978-0-367-44995-7 (pbk)
ISBN 13: 978-0-412-35660-5 (hbk)

Visit the Taylor & Francis Web site at
http://www.taylorandfrancis.com

and the CRC Press Web site at
http://www.crcpress.com

Typeset at Oxford University Computing Service

A catalogue record for this book is available from the British Library

Library of Congress Cataloging-in-Publication data available

CONTENTS OF VOLUME XXVIII

FOREWORD

The Sources and Nature of the Statistics of the United Kingdom, produced under the auspices of the Royal Statistical Society and edited by Maurice Kendall, filled a notable gap on the library shelves when it made its appearance in the early post-war years. Through a series of critical reviews by many of the foremost national experts, it constituted a valuable contemporary guide to statisticians working in many fields as well as a bench-mark to which historians of the development of statistics in this country are likely to return again and again. The Social Science Research Council (now the Economic and Social Research Council) and the Society were both delighted when Professor Maunder came forward with the proposal that a revised version should be produced, indicating as well his willingness to take on the onerous task of editor (a task in which he was assisted from 1985 to 1987 by Professor Fleming who then took over the editorship). The two bodies were more than happy to act as co-sponsors of the project and to help in its planning through a joint steering committee. The result, we are confident, will be judged a worthy successor to the previous volumes by the very much larger 'statistics public' that has come into being in the intervening years.

W. SOLESBURY
Secretary
Economic and Social Research Council

D. A. LIEVESLEY
Honorary Secretary
Royal Statistical Society

MEMBERSHIP OF JOINT STEERING COMMITTEE

(December 1987)

Chairman: Miss S. V. Cunliffe

Representing the Royal Statistical Society:

Mr M. C. Fessey

Dr S. Rosenbaum

Mrs E. J. Snell

Representing the Economic and Social Research Council:

Mr I. Maclean

Miss J. Morris

Secretary: Mr D. E. Allen

EDITORIAL INTRODUCTION

The series of *Reviews of United Kingdom Statistical Sources* is meant to serve a dual purpose: first, to provide an authoritative guide to statistical sources in the United Kingdom (both official and unofficial) and, secondly, to provide a critical appraisal of the nature and limitations of the available data. To maximise its usefulness as a source of reference, each volume in the series follows a standard format which incorporates a number of features designed to meet the varied needs of different users. A detailed guide for users follows this introduction.

This review of the *Food Industries* covers the diverse range of industries concerned with the supply and *processing* of food in the United Kingdom. It does not cover agriculture, which is the subject of a separate review in the series (Volume XXIII). There is a clear division between the two volumes: *Agriculture* covers all sources of data relating to food production in the United Kingdom up to 'the farm gate'. This volume covers sources relating to subsequent production and processing, including foodstuffs supplied from abroad, and also fish supply and processing. Thus it may be said that it takes over where the other volume left off. But industries concerned with drink and tobacco, sectors which are grouped together with food in the official *Standard Industrial Classification*, are not covered here.

For the purpose of this volume some ten separate industries are defined: organic oils and fats; slaughtering of animals and production of meat and by-products; preparation of milk and milk products; processing of fruit and vegetables; fish processing; grain milling and bread, biscuits and flour confectionery; sugar and sugar by-products; ice-cream, cocoa, chocolate and sugar confectionery; tea and coffee; starch and miscellaneous foods. The volume of information available for this range of industries is very large and comes from both official and non-official (national and international) sources; indeed the latter are particularly numerous in this sector of the economy. The size of this volume is a reflection of the diverse range of information available as well as the fact that coverage is not confined to a single industry.

The fact that coverage extends to several industries has raised some difficult issues concerning the best way to organize the volume so as to meet the needs of users. It was felt that the overriding advantage lay with an arrangement in which the volume was sub-divided according to industry rather than subject (as in most other volumes in the series). The general principle followed, therefore, has been to treat each industry in a separate chapter of its own, but to preserve the advantages of an arrangement by subject by arranging the material within each chapter by subject, following, as far as possible, a common format. However, most official statistics are common to all industries and thus to treat the official sources in detail in each chapter would have involved considerable repetition. These sources, therefore, are treated together in a single chapter — Chapter 2 — coupled with cross-references in each industry chapter as appropriate.

Regrettably, this volume will be one of the last to appear under the joint sponsorship of the Royal Statistical Society and the ESRC. The series received the generous financial support of the ESRC (and the former SSRC — the Social Science Research Council) from its inception around 1969 until the end of 1987. During that time work on 25 volumes covering 43 review topics was completed (although three of these volumes were not published until 1988). Several reviews were then abandoned, but progress on four other volumes was sufficiently far advanced to make their completion seem feasible in a short space of time without further financial support. Unfortunately, this optimism was misplaced. Although it has proved possible to avoid abandoning these volumes, progress has been slow and has only been maintained with the aid of *ad hoc* funding obtained from time to time to support either the authors', or the editorial, work.

Until the end of 1987, the series was directed by a Joint Steering Committee of the Royal Statistical Society and the ESRC. It only remains here to express gratitude to the members of the committee, who directed the overall strategy with as admirable a mixture of guidance and forbearance as any editors of such a series could desire. At the same time they bear no responsibility for shortcomings in execution. Especial thanks are due to David Allen, the Secretary of the Committee, who was involved with the project almost as long and almost as closely as anybody. One must also pay tribute to the work done by Professor W.F.Maunder as editor throughout the whole period to 1987. A very great deal is owed to him both for the development of the original idea and for his perseverance and determination in bringing so many volumes through to completion, as well as for helping to initiate work on so many others (including this volume). Statistics-users owe him a great debt.

The authors of this volume join me in thanking all those who gave up their time to attend the seminar which was held to discuss the first draft of the review and which contributed materially to improving the final version. We are also most grateful to Chapman and Hall Limited for their support and in particular to their Production Department, who put all the pieces together. Special thanks are also due to Mr Ray Burnley of the Social Studies Data Processing Unit at the University of Exeter, who again has masterminded our use of the Lasercomp System at Oxford University Computing Service, and to the latter for the use of this facility. Finally, we also wish to record our appreciation of the permission granted us to reproduce crown copyright material by the Central Statistical Office and the Ministry of Agriculture, Fisheries and Food, and other copyright material by Blackwell Scientific Publications Limited, the Federation of UK Milk Marketing Boards, E.D.&F. Man Cocoa Ltd., the Meat and Livestock Commission and the Seed Crushers' and Oil Processors' Association.

Michael C. Fleming

Loughborough University

GUIDE TO THE SERIES AND HOW TO USE IT

The Scope and Nature of the Series

The purpose of the series is twofold. The primary aim is to act as an authoritative work of reference to the sources of statistical material of all kinds, both official and unofficial, in the United Kingdom. The intention here is to enable the user to discover what data are available on the subject in which he or she is interested and from where they may be obtained. Secondly, it seeks to provide a critical appraisal of the nature and limitations of the available data so that the user is able to interpret them safely and avoid pitfalls in their use.

Data are regarded as available not only if published in the normal printed format but also if they are likely to be released to a *bona fide* enquirer in any other form, such as duplicated documents, computer print-out or even magnetic tape. On the other hand, no reference is made to material which, even if it is known to exist, is not accessible to the general run of potential users. The distinction, of course, is not clear-cut and mention of a source is not to be regarded as a guarantee that data will be released; in particular cases it may very well be a matter for negotiation. The latter caution applies with particular force to the question of obtaining computer print-outs of custom-specified tabulations.

The intention is that the source for each topic should be reviewed in detail, and the brief supplied to authors calls for comprehensive coverage at the level of 'national interest'. This term does not denote any necessary restriction to statistics collected on a national basis (still less, of course, to national aggregates) but it means that sources of a purely local character, without wider interest in either content or methodology, are excluded. Indeed, the mere task of identifying all material of this latter kind is an impossibility. The interpretation of the brief has obviously involved discretion and it is up to the users of these reviews to say what unreasonable gaps become apparent to them. They are cordially invited to do so by communicating with the editor.

The Format and Content of Reviews

To facilitate the use of the series as a work of reference, a common format is adopted for each review. This involves the incorporation of six standard features:

1. Text
2. Quick Reference List (QRL)

3. QRL Key to Publications
4. Bibliography
5. Subject Index
6. Specimen Forms and Questionnaires

Each of these is described in turn below.

1. *The Text.* This is designed, in so far as varying subject matter permits, to follow a standard form of arrangement, covering introductory material on the activity covered and its organisation, core material on the available sources and a discussion of desirable improvements.

The introductory material is meant to give a clear background understanding of how data are collected, what is being measured, the stage at which measurements are made, what the reporting units are, the channels through which returns are routed and where they are processed, coupled with a discussion of specific problems of definition and measurement. This is followed by core sections or chapters on available sources. Wherever possible these are arranged according to subject (rather than source). But in practice they may be arranged, at the author's discretion, by origin, by subject subdivision, or by type of data, as there is too much heterogeneity between topics to permit any imposition of complete uniformity on all authors. A final chapter is devoted to a discussion of general shortcomings and possibly desirable improvements. In case a contrary expectation should be aroused, it should be said that authors have not been asked to produce a comprehensive plan for the reform of statistical reporting in the whole of their field. However, a review of existing sources is a natural opportunity to make some suggestions for future policy on the collection and publication of statistics within the scope of their review and authors have been encouraged to take full advantage of it.

2. *The Quick Reference List (QRL).* This provides a detailed list of all the categories of data that are available and, again, is generally arranged according to subject. It also includes cross-references to the sections of the text in which the data are discussed and to the publication sources listed in the *QRL Key*. Each publication shown as a data source is given a serial number and the prefix 'QRL'.

3. *The QRL Key to Publications.* This gives full details of the publications shown as *data sources* in the QRL.

4. *The Bibliography.* This gives references to works discussing wider aspects of the topic under review and the statistics relating to it, including methodology. These publications are identified by a serial number and the prefix 'B'.

5. *The Subject Index.* This acts as a conventional line of enquiry on textual references. Considerable detail is given, including different variants of any one entry, in order to facilitate search. The references given relate to the numbered sections into which the text is divided, not page numbers, and are given down to the 4-digit level, as appropriate.

6. *Specimen Forms and Questionnaires.* Finally, specimen copies of the more important returns or forms used in data collection are reproduced, as appropriate, as appendices so that it may be seen what tabulations it is possible to make as well as helping to clarify the basis of those actually available.

How to Use the Series

As we have indicated, the standard format adopted for each review in the series was designed expressly to facilitate its use for reference purposes. The features which it incorporates provide three possible "ways in" for the user. These are:

1. The Contents List.
2. The Quick Reference List.
3. The Subject Index.

For users most interested in discovering quickly whether or not a particular sort of data is available and where it is published, the Quick Reference List should be the most useful feature to consult first. As noted above, included within the list are cross-references to the numbered sections of the text in which the data are discussed and references to the publication sources for the data (QRL references). To facilitate its speedy use, it is arranged by subject as far as possible and the list is itself preceded by its own summary contents list.

The main Contents list at the front of the book provides, of course, a summary indication of the subject matter of each chapter but it also shows the main sub-divisions into which it is divided. It is useful, therefore, for anyone interested in locating material in the book on broad subject areas, rather than more specific statistical sources.

The subject index provides an alternative means of locating information but one which is intermediate between the Quick Reference List and the Contents list. It gives references to the subject matter at a more detailed level than the contents list, but it does not duplicate the degree of detail for particular categories of statistical data, given in the QRL.

46: THE FOOD INDUSTRIES

JOHN MARK

Senior Lecturer in Economics
The Management Centre,
King's College, London
University of London

and

ROGER STRANGE

Head of The Management Centre,
and Lecturer in Economics
The Management Centre,
King's College, London
University of London

with contributions by

JIM BURNS

Lecturer in Food Economics and Marketing
Department of Agricultural Economics and Management
University of Reading

REFERENCE DATE OF SOURCES REVIEWED

This review is believed to represent the position, broadly speaking, as it obtained in mid-1989, but a few minor revisions have been made to update the main text during the proof-reading stage in mid-1991. Major changes are noted in the Addenda which are included towards the end of the volume immediately preceding the Subject Index.

CONTENTS OF REVIEW 46

List of Tables in the Text

List of Figures

List of Tables

ABBREVIATIONS AND ACRONYMS

AA	The Advertising Association
ABF	Associated British Foods
ACARD	Advisory Council for Applied Research and Development
ACP	African, Caribbean and Pacific States
AEU	Amalgamated Engineering Union
AFRC	Agriculture and Food Research Council
AGB	Audits of Great Britain
AGB/TCA	Audits of Great Britain Television Consumer Audit
AH	Activity Heading
APEX	Association of Professional, Executive, Clerical and Computer Staff
ASSILEC	Association de l'Industrie Laitière de la CÉÉ
ASTMS	Association of Scientific, Technical and Managerial Staffs
[B]	Bibliography Identification
BACH	La Banque de Données Harmonisées sur les Comptes d'Enterprises
BAG	Bread Advisory Group
BCCCA	Biscuit, Cake, Chocolate and Confectionery Alliance
BFAWU	Bakers, Food and Allied Workers' Union
BFMIRA	British Food Manufacturing Industries Research Association
BIBRA	British Industrial Biological Research Association
BoT	Board of Trade
BRAD	British Rate and Data
BSC	British Sugar Corporation
BSO	Business Statistics Office
BTN	Brussels Tariff Nomenclature
CADOS	Catalogue for CRONOS
CAOBISCO	Association of the Chocolate, Biscuit and Confectionery Industries of the EEC
CAP	Common Agricultural Policy
CBA	Cake and Biscuit Alliance
CBI	Confederation of British Industry
CCCA	Cocoa, Chocolate and Confectionery Alliance
CCCN	Customs Cooperation Council Nomenclature
CD-ROMS	Compact Disc - Read Only Memory System
CÉÉ	Communauté Économique Européenne
CCT	Common Customs Tariff
CFP	Common Fisheries Policy
CFPRA	Campden Food Preservation Research Association
cif	cost including insurance and freight

CLIO	Conversational Language for Input-output
CMS	Commodity Market Services
CN	Combined Nomenclature of the European Communities
CNC	Combined Nomenclature Committee
COGECA	Comité Générale de la Cooperation Agricole de la CÉÉ
COMEXT	EUROSTAT Database for External Trade Statistics
CPC	CPC (United Kingdom) Ltd.
CPCCOM	Central Product Classification for the Communities
CRB	Commodity Research Bureau
CRONOS	EUROSTAT Databank
CR5	Five-firm Concentration Ratio
CSA	Commonwealth Sugar Agreement
CSF	Cadbury Schweppes Foods
CSO	Central Statistical Office
CTN	Confectioners, Tobacconists and Newsagents
CWP	Coordinating Working Party (on Atlantic Fishery Statistics)
DAE	Department of Applied Economics (Cambridge)
DAFS	Department of Agriculture and Fisheries for Scotland
DANI	Department of Agriculture for Northern Ireland
DDS	Donovan Data Systems
DE	Department of Employment
DES	Department of Education and Science
DG	Directorate General
DSIR	Department of Scientific and Industrial Research
DTI	Department of Trade and Industry
EAEC	European Atomic Energy Community (EURATOM)
EAGGF	European Agricultural Guidance and Guarantee Fund
EC	European Community
ECSC	European Coal and Steel Community
ECSS	European Community Statistical System
ECU	European Currency Unit
EDC	Economic Development Committee
EEC	European Economic Community
EEPTU	Electrical, Electronic, Telecommunication and Plumbing Union
EFTA	European Free Trade Area
EIU	Economist Intelligence Unit
ESA	European System of Integrated Economic Accounts
ESRC	Economic and Social Research Council
EUA	European Units of Account
EURATOM	European Atomic Energy Community
EURONET	European Telecommunication Network for Scientific, Technical, Social and Economic Information (a Data Transmissions Network Inaugurated in 1979)
EUROSTAT	Statistical Office of the European Communities
FAO	Food and Agriculture Organisation
FAST	Forecasting and Assessment in Science and Technology (EC-supported Programme)
FERU	Fishery Economics Research Unit

FES	Family Expenditure Survey
FESU	Fisheries Economics and Statistics Unit
FIRS	Fonds d'Intervention et de Régularisation du Marché du Sucre
FMBRA	Flour Milling and Baking Research Association
fob	free on board
FOMAD	Food Market Awareness Databank
FOSFA	Federation of Oils, Seeds and Fats Associations
FOX	Futures and Options Exchange (London)
GAFTA	The Grain and Feed Trade Association
GATT	General Agreement on Tariffs and Trade
GB	Great Britain
GDP	Gross Domestic Product
GLC	Greater London Council
GMB	General Municipal Boilermakers' Union
GMBATU	General, Municipal, Boilermakers and Allied Trades Union
GSS	Government Statistical Service
HC	Henderson Crosthwaite
HCIC	Horticultural Crop Intelligence Committee
HFCS	High Fructose Corn Syrup
HGCA	Home-Grown Cereals Authority
HMSO	Her Majesty's Stationery Office
HS	Harmonised Commodity Description and Coding System
IBAP	Intervention Board for Agricultural Produce
ICA	International Cocoa Agreement 1986 and International Coffee Agreement 1982
ICC	Inter-Company Comparisons Ltd.
ICCH	International Commodity Clearing House
ICI	Imperial Chemical Industries
ICCO	International Cocoa Organisation
ICES	International Council for the Exploration of the Sea
ICO	International Coffee Organisation
IDC	Income Data Services
IGD	Institute of Grocery Distribution
ILO	International Labour Organisation
IMF	International Monetary Fund
IMS	Institute of Manpower Studies
IOCCC	International Office of Cocoa, Chocolate and Sugar Confectionery
ISIC	International Standard Industrial Classification of All Economic Activities
ISO	International Sugar Organisation
ISSCFC	International Standard Statistical Classification of Fishery Commodities
ITCA	Independent Television Companies Association
JIC	Joint Industrial Council
KAU	Kind of Activity Unit
KVI	Known Value Item
LCE	London Commodity Exchange
LDP	London Daily Price

LFS	Labour Force Survey
LMC	Landell Mills Commodities
LWE	Landed Weight Equivalent
MA	prefix to the Annual Business Monitors in the Miscellaneous Series
MAFF	Ministry of Agriculture, Fisheries and Food
MCA	Monetary Compensatory Amounts
MEAL	Media Expenditure Analysis Ltd.
MEALINK	MEAL Database
MLC	Meat and Livestock Commission
MLH	Minimum List Headings
MM	prefix to the Monthly Business Monitors in the Miscellaneous Series
MMA	Millers' Mutual Association
MMB	Milk Marketing Board
MMC	Monopolies and Mergers Commission
MO	prefix to the Occasional Business Monitors in the Miscellaneous Series
MQ	prefix to the Quarterly Business Monitors in the Miscellaneous Series
MSI	Marketing Strategies for Industry
NABIM	National Association of British and Irish Millers
NACE	Nomenclature Générale des Activités Économiques dans les Communautés Européennes
NADOR	Notification of Accidents and Dangerous Occurences Regulations
NAMBCC	National Association of Master Bakers, Confectioners and Caterers
NBPI	National Board for Prices and Incomes
NEDO	National Economic Development Office
NERC	Natural Environment Research Council
nes	not elsewhere specified
NES	New Earnings Survey
NFS	National Food Survey
NIESR	National Institute of Economic and Social Research
NIG	National Industry Groups
NIMEXE	Nomenclature of Goods for the External Trade Statistics of the European Community
NIPRO	Common Nomenclature of Industrial Products
NJC	National Joint Committee
NJNC	National Joint Negotiating Committee
NOMIS	National On-line Manpower Information System
NOP	National Opinion Poll
NPC	National Ports Council
ODA	Overseas Development Association
OECD	Organisation for Economic Co-operation and Development
OPCS	Office of Population Censuses and Surveys
PA	prefix to the Annual Business Monitors in the Production Series
PAF	(Small Users) Postcode Address File
PAS	prefix to the Annual Business Monitors in the Production Annual Series
PBR	Payment By Results
PFMA	Pet Food Manufacturers' Association
PGRO	Processors and Growers' Research Association

PMB Potato Marketing Board
PO prefix to the Occasional Business Monitors in the Production Series
POA Price On Application
PQ prefix to the Quarterly Business Monitors in the Production Series
PTP Production Target Price
[QRL] Quick Reference List Identification of Source Publication
QSI Quarterly Sales Inquiry
RAs Research Associations
R&D Research and Development
RHM Rank Hovis MacDougall
RI Research Institute
RMP Representative Market Price
RPI Retail Prices Index
RPIAC Retail Prices Index Advisory Committee
RSS Royal Statistical Society
SABINE System of Databanks for Classifications
SAD Single Administrative Document
SCOPA Seed Crushers and Oil Processors' Association
SDA préfix to thé Annual Businéss Monitors in thé Sérvicé and Distributivé Series
SDO prefix to the Occasional Business Monitors in the Service and Distributive Series
SET Selective Employment Tax
SFIA Sea Fish Industry Authority
SGM Standard Gross Margin
SIC Standard Industrial Classification
SIC(1968) 1968 Revision of the Standard Industrial Classification
SIC(1980) 1980 Revision of the Standard Industrial Classification
SIR Scientific Information and Retrieval
SITC Standard International Trade Classification
SITC(R2) Revision 2 of the Standard International Trade Classification
SITC(R3) Revision 3 of the Standard International Trade Classification
SMMB Scottish Milk Marketing Board
SNA United Nations' System of National Accounts
SNACMA Snack, Nut and Crisp Manufacturers' Association Ltd
SOEC Statistical Office of the European Communities
SSAP Statement of Standard Accounting Practice
SUC Statistics Users' Conference
TAC Total Allowable Catches
TARIC Integrated Tariff of the European Communities
TCA Television Consumer Audit
TGWU Transport & General Workers' Union
TUC Trades Union Congress
UB United Biscuits (UK) Ltd.
UHT Ultra High Temperature
UK United Kingdom
UN United Nations
UNCTAD United Nations Conference on Trade and Development

US	United States of America
USA	United States of America
USDA	United States Department of Agriculture
USDAW	Union of Shop, Distributive and Allied Workers
USM	Unlisted Securities Market
VAT	Value Added Tax
VRA	Voluntary Restraint Agreement
WHO	World Health Organisation
WSE	White Sugar Equivalent

ACKNOWLEDGEMENTS

A volume which is as necessarily wide-ranging as this one draws upon the expertise and goodwill of many people who are deeply involved in the collection processes. They are inevitably the most knowledgeable about both statistical sources and methods and we would therefore like to record the invaluable help they have given.

David Lewis and Roger Norton and many of their staff at the Business Statistics Office, Newport provided both information and suggestions for our approach to the many facets of business statistics. Dr John Slater, John Watson, Paul Roberts and their staff at the Ministry of Agriculture, Fisheries and Food provided valuable guidance on aspects of the MAFF inquiries. The advice provided by both the Business Statistics Office (now part of the Central Statistical Office) and the Ministry of Agriculture, Fisheries and Food are central to a number of the issues tackled in Chapter 2. John Bowles of the Department of Trade and Industry commented on the Research and Development section of Chapter 2. Robin Lynch of the Department of Trade and Industry made some observations on the minutiae of input-output statistics. David Rees of the Advertising Association contributed careful observations on the draft of the Advertising section. The Department of Employment furnished detailed material on the collection of labour statistics much of which has been incorporated. Jonathan Green of the Monopolies and Mergers Commission scrutinised parts of the Official Investigations section of Chapter 2. Brian Newson and his staff at Eurostat have checked over the materials assembled in the European Community section.

The subject chapters have also benefited from the advice of experts in these particular fields. We acknowledge the comments of Roland Williams and the staff of the Milk Marketing Board towards Chapter 4 on Milk and Milk Products. Dr Martin Palmer of the Meat and Livestock Commission made suggestions for the approach towards Chapter 5 on Meat and Meat Products. Neil McKellar and his staff at the Sea Fish Industry Authority provided continual support on the niceties and sources of fisheries statistics for Chapter 7 on Fish Processing and Keith Morgan of the MAFF gave pertinent observations on the collection process. Sylvia Claydon of MAFF and John Taylor of the Potato Marketing Board commented on the draft of Chapter 6 on the Processing of Fruit and Vegetables. Simon Harris of Berisford International made some suggestions for Chapter 9 on Sugar and Sugar By-products. Wilfrid Newman, Statistics Services Secretary of the Biscuit, Cake, Chocolate and Confectionery Alliance (BCCCA), provided the most careful comments on Chapter 10 on Ice-cream, Cocoa, Chocolate and Sugar Confectionery and afforded every assistance his organisation could give. Henry Jason of the International Cocoa Organisation (ICCO) facilitated the work on the cocoa section of Chapter 10, Pablo Dubois of the International Coffee Organisation (ICO) made observations on points of detail regarding coffee statistics and Peter Abel of the International Tea Committee checked through the materials of Chapter 12 with respect to tea.

The Royal Statistical Society and the Economic and Social Research Council organised a seminar for this Review when the participants scrutinised the first draft. Of those not already acknowledged, the late Andrew Ashby took considerable trouble to read through the entire first draft and to make many points of detail. Professor George Peters of the University of Oxford did likewise and offered most pertinent suggestions on the whole approach at this stage. This was particularly valuable in the light of his experience in preparing the complementary volume on Agriculture published in 1988. Professor Derek Maunder of the University of Exeter gave the tactful impetus for us to make a start on what has been a massive project throughout the four years to final draft and the six years to the finished product. His successor, Professor Michael Fleming of Loughborough University, has provided not only sharp comments on points of detail but, in the light of his own substantial contribution to this Series, has given the continued benefit of his own expertise as well as moral support during what has seemed at times an interminable voyage on the sea of statistics.

The major responsibility for the navigation and writing of Chapters 1, 2, 6, 7, 9, 10, 12, 13, the Addenda and the construction of the Quick Reference List has been that of John Mark who provided the sustained effort with respect to the creation and design of the entire book. Jim Burns of Reading University has been mainly responsible for writing Chapters 8 and 11. Roger Strange has written Chapters 3, 4 and 5, and revised and redrafted all the other chapters. He has also been responsible for the detailed organisation of the whole volume.

Many past students of the former Queen Elizabeth College and present King's College, London, have provided research help in greater or lesser measure, in particular Christopher Ellis. We mention also Dr Robert Nurick of Sussex University, Neil Bramwell and Margaret Antoniou. Dr Gail Mulvey of the University of the West of England, Bristol, and Audrey Taylor of Boston University also gave assistance at critical stages of the first draft.

Much of the final draft was completed and the concluding chapter written during the six months that John Mark spent on sabbatical leave in 1989 at Queen Elizabeth House, University of Oxford. The enormous job of organising the references and bibliography was begun during this period and the congenial and stimulating atmosphere of Queen Elizabeth House was of major support during the performance of this daunting task.

Invaluable and consistent service has been provided throughout by Veronica Clarke of King's College, London, who has patiently typed the bulk of the manuscript, both on typewriter and on the mainframe computer at King's College, which she most spiritedly mastered. The computing staff of the College have given advice and guidance, particularly on computer programs which have assisted in the alphabetical ordering of the references and bibliography. Due thanks are given to Mark George and Dr Jean Davey.

Many other people have commented on points of detail at many stages and their contributions should not go unacknowledged. But, unlike film credits, there is a limit to which one can go. But it always remains to be said that none of those named can be held responsible for any errors which remain in the text. However, given that the text is held at King's College on computer file, the wherewithal exists to bring out revised editions of this work.

Most authors acknowledge the patience of their families during the gestation of major projects, not only in relation to the long periods of seclusion in libraries, but also to the obsessive drive without which many books remain unfinished. Heartfelt salutations are thus made to Sara, Justine, Hugh and Jeffrey Mark and to Elizabeth Bowey, Emma and Tom.

We have drawn upon considerable library resources during the last five years and indeed it is tempting to provide a guide to libraries as well as to statistics. We highlight here the excellence of the British Library of Political and Economic Science at the London School of Economics and the expertise and courtesy provided there by John Pinfold and other librarians. In London, the Science Reference Library for market research reports, the Department of Trade and Industry Library in Victoria Street, the Department of Employment Library in Tothill Street, the City Business Library, the MAFF Libraries at Whitehall Place and Horseferry Road, the Advertising Association Library and the libraries of London Business School and King's College must be acknowledged. At Oxford, the Bodleian, the libraries at Queen Elizabeth House and Templeton College and the library of the Institute of Economics and Statistics were all of significant use.

One concluding point needs to be made. For many years, Queen Elizabeth College has been at the centre of research and teaching activities in Food Science and Nutrition. In 1985, Queen Elizabeth College became part of King's College, London. This volume, written by economists of the Management Centre, both reflects the traditions of Queen Elizabeth College and looks forward to the future in its focus on sources of statistics for economics and business as well as for food.

CHAPTER 1

INTRODUCTION AND PLAN OF BOOK

This chapter contains the following sections:

1.1 The Food Industries

The Food industries comprise one of the most important collections of industries in the United Kingdom. A wealth of statistical information is published relating to these industries, but the data are dispersed among a variety of different publications. The aim of this book is to supply a guide to such statistical sources, not only by identifying them but also by providing some appraisal of their content. In 1968, the National Economic Development Office (NEDO) published *Food Statistics: A Guide to the Major Official and Unofficial UK Sources* [B.283] which set out to provide a simple index of sources of statistics, together with an indication of their coverage. The NEDO guide did not, however, provide any analysis or discussion of the statistics themselves.

Our concern in this book is with that group of industries responsible for food manufacturing and processing. We do not cover the agriculture sector — this is the subject of a separate Review in this series [B.144]. The Food industries are an important component of the entire Food sector. It has been estimated by Slater [B.165] that in 1985 food from domestic farmers, the sea and imports from abroad, which together cost £16 billion in 1985, was transformed into products sold by domestic retailers, or exported abroad, valued at £42 billion. In terms of value added to all inputs (rather than just food), the Food sector (including drink) contributed over 9 per cent of Gross Domestic Product, employed over 2.5 million people, and thus accounted for 9.5 per cent of the employed labour force in the United Kingdom. Figure 1.1, prepared by the Economics and Statistics (Food) Division of the MAFF, illustrates the food chain in the UK in 1986 and gives estimates of the size of key components of it. These estimates are the latest available at the time of writing — mid-1989.

This Review covers that part of the Food sector from the input of raw material supplies to the output of the final product to the retailer, and which accounts for about half the value added cited in the last paragraph. The Food industries refer to those industries involved in the treatment and transformation of the raw food

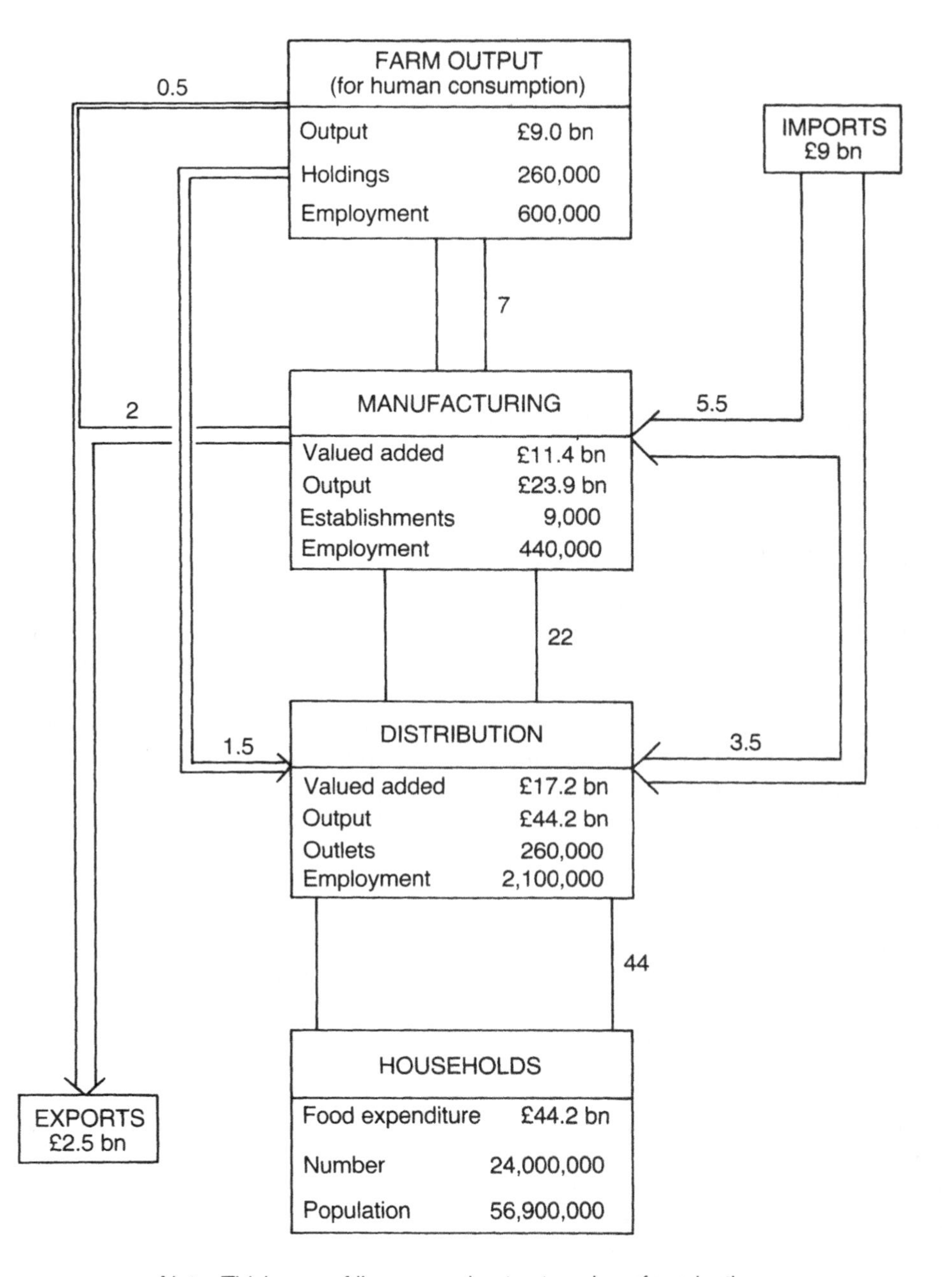

Figure 1.1 The UK Food Chain, 1986 (£ billion).
Source: Economics and Statistics (Food) Division, Ministry of Agriculture, Fisheries and Food, © Crown Copyright.

materials into a form suitable for sale to the customer. The industries so defined should not be confused with the food production of domestic farmers, the cull of the sea, nor food distribution to consumers. In theory, the Food industries are concerned with the manufacture and processing of food, and are distinct from both agriculture and distribution. In practice, however, the boundaries between these activities may be somewhat blurred at times, and there will inevitably be some overlap between the contents of this volume and those of two other volumes in this series, viz: *Agriculture* [B.144] by G.H. Peters, and *Distribution* [B.125] by C. Moir and J. Dawson.

1.2 The Standard Industrial Classification

A Standard Industrial Classification (SIC) was first introduced in the United Kingdom in 1948. Its purpose was to provide a framework for the collection, presentation and analysis of data about the performance of the economy. The classification was subsequently revised in 1958, in 1968 and, most recently in 1980, to take account of changes in the organisation of a number of industries, and to distinguish industries not separately identified previously.

Prior to the 1980 revision, the general principles followed in the SIC were those laid down in the United Nations International Standard Industrial Classification of all Economic Activities (ISIC). For the 1980 revision, however, the attempt has been made to align the UK classification as closely as is practicable with the activity classification of the Statistical Office of the European Communities (EUROSTAT) — i.e. with the Nomenclature Générale des Activités Économiques dans les Communautés Européennes (NACE). The 1980 revision will thus enable easier comparison of UK data with data from other EC countries.

The 1980 revision of the Standard Industrial Classification — SIC(1980) — is described in many places. For a full description see [B.232], but for a concise summary, see the article by Bowditch [B.21] in the November 1979 issue of *Statistical News* [B.381]. The 1968 classification — SIC(1968) — divided the full range of economic activities into 27 Orders, each of which was subdivided into a number of "Minimum List Headings" (MLH). SIC(1980) divides economic activities into 10 broad Divisions (each denoted by a single digit from 0 to 9), viz:

Division 0 Agriculture, forestry and fishing
Division 1 Energy and water supply industries
Division 2 Extraction of minerals and ores other than fuels: manufacture of metals, mineral products and chemicals
Division 3 Metal goods, engineering and vehicles industries
Division 4 Other manufacturing industries
Division 5 Construction
Division 6 Distribution, hotels and catering; repairs
Division 7 Transport and communication
Division 8 Banking, finance, insurance, business services and leasing
Division 9 Other services

Each Division is in turn divided into Classes (each denoted by a two digit number): e.g. Class 41/42 "Food, drink and tobacco manufacturing industries". Each Class is then divided into Groups (each denoted by a three digit number). e.g.

Group 411 Organic oils and fats

Group 412 Slaughtering of animals and production of meat and by-products
Group 413 Preparation of milk and milk products
Group 414 Processing of fruit and vegetables
Group 415 Fish processing
Group 416 Grain milling
Group 418 Starch
Group 419 Bread, biscuits and flour confectionery
Group 420 Sugar and sugar by-products
Group 421 Ice-cream, cocoa, chocolate and sugar confectionery
Group 422 Animal feeding stuffs
Group 423 Miscellaneous foods

Finally, each Group is divided into a number of Activity Headings (each denoted by a four digit number). e.g.

Activity Heading 4121 Slaughterhouses
Activity Heading 4122 Bacon curing and meat processing
Activity Heading 4123 Poultry slaughter and processing
Activity Heading 4126 Animal by-product processing

There are 10 Divisions, 60 Classes, 222 Groups and 334 Activity Headings in total in SIC(1980). The Food industries are defined as those industries falling into Groups 411 to 423 inclusive (as listed above).

The Groups and Activity Headings of SIC(1980) do not correspond exactly to the MLH of SIC(1968) as there has been some reclassification of a number of industries. A detailed reconciliation of SIC(1980) and SIC(1968) is provided in [B.379]. Information on specific Groups is provided in the following chapters, and is summarised in Appendix A. One major change which is of importance is that "Slaughtering" is included with the Food industries in SIC(1980) instead of with wholesale distribution as in SIC(1968).

1.3 Organisation of the Review

It should be clear from section 1.2 that the Food industries are not one homogeneous industry, but that they comprise several quite distinct industrial sectors. These sectors differ widely in terms of the capital intensity of production, the degree of processing, the variety of their outputs and the nature of their markets. This heterogeneity, together with the interdependence of the various sectors, poses severe problems for the organisation of a Review of this nature. One possible solution would have been to arrange the material by data source — i.e. to describe the relevant contents of, for example, the *Annual Abstract of Statistics* [QRL.37], the *Employment Gazette* [QRL.186], *Business Monitor MM20: Overseas Trade Statistics of the United Kingdom* [QRL.85], and so on, one at a time. An alternative would have been to adopt an arrangement by type of data — i.e. data on output for all industries, on employment, on prices etc. We felt, however, that both such arrangements would not be very helpful to the reader who was interested in one particular industrial sector. That reader would have to sift through many irrelevant references and types of data before alighting on those that were of use and interest. At the other extreme, a separate discussion of each and every food product would have been a fascinating yet quite impossible task.

We have accordingly adopted a middle course and decided to devote a chapter to each of Groups 411 to 423 in SIC(1980). There are four exceptions to this general plan. First, Chapter 8 contains a joint review for Group 416 "Grain milling", Group 419 "Bread, biscuits and flour confectionery" and "Breakfast cereals" from Group 423 "Miscellaneous foods". Our rationale is that these Groups are so closely related, and share so many common statistical sources, that to discuss them separately would not be sensible. Second, we have devoted a complete chapter (Chapter 12) to statistical sources on "Tea and coffee", rather than discussing them together with other "Miscellaneous foods" in Chapter 11. Third, we have combined the remainder (excluding tea, coffee and breakfast cereals) of Group 423 "Miscellaneous foods" with Group 418 "Starch" in Chapter 11. Fourth, we have excluded Group 422 "Animal feeding stuffs" on the grounds that we want to concentrate on human food. One might argue that many pet foods are fit for human consumption, and should not therefore be excluded. However, pet foods are not produced primarily for human consumption so we feel that our decision is justified. Readers who are interested in data on pet foods should contact the Petfood Manufacturers Association whose address is provided in Appendix B.

The chapter arrangement does, nevertheless, still have its idiosyncrasies. There are cases where unrelated food products are classified to the same Group, no more so than in Group 423 "Miscellaneous foods". Pasta production, infant and dietetic foods, and cake mixtures are all quite different. The difficulties of this Group will be discussed and resolved in Chapter 11. There are other instances where particular products are classified to different Groups, but where those products might more logically have been discussed together. For instance, margarine is classified to Group 411 "Organic oils and fats" whereas butter is classified to Group 413 "Preparation of milk and milk products". Tea and coffee are treated together in Chapter 12, but cocoa is left with Group 421 "Ice-cream, cocoa, chocolate and sugar confectionery". Bakehouses attached to retail shops are excluded completely from this Review, yet "foods" such as tea, coffee and ice lollies are all included. However, the arrangement here, arbitrary though it may be, does have the advantage that very many statistical publications (e.g. the Business Monitors) use the same SIC(1980) classification and many other publications (e.g. ICC Business Ratio reports) organise their material around SIC(1980). The basis we have chosen is better than any other alternative.

In the interests of uniformity and ease of reference, each chapter is organised in the same format, viz:

Section 1: Introduction

This includes the definition of the Group as provided in SIC(1980) and also outlines the main products and their uses. Any changes in coverage from previous Standard Industrial Classifications are discussed.

Section 2: Industry Structure

This provides a description of the structure and development of the industry, and discusses the role of the various trade organisations etc., within it, particularly those which publish statistics, so as to place their contribution in context. This section is particularly useful as there exists no one reference work which details the structure of the various industries within the Food sector.

Section 3: The European Community

This examines the influence of the European Community on both UK methods of statistical collection and economic structure. The system of intervention prices, national production quotas etc. for sugar, for instance, affects the structure of the industry and the statistics collected by the Intervention Board.

Section 4: Output

This provides sources of statistics on output in both physical and monetary units.

Section 5: Current Inputs other than Labour

This section contains information on the various sources of data on raw material inputs to the Food industries. Domestic inputs only are considered — imports are covered in section 8. In addition, sources of input-output data are discussed.

Section 6: Labour

This provides sources of statistics not only on employment but also on unemployment, labour costs, wage rates, industrial stoppages and accidents, labour productivity etc.

Section 7: Capital

This considers sources of statistics on capital expenditure, the stock of fixed capital, and capital productivity. Sources of data on financial capital and overseas capital transactions are discussed in sections 13 and 8 respectively.

Section 8: International Transactions

This provides details of the main sources of trade — export and import — statistics, as well as information on international capital movements and food aid.

Section 9: Stocks

This gives sources of information not only on stocks of raw materials, but also on stocks of finished goods.

Section 10: Consumption

This section focuses on the data on the consumption of food provided in the National Food Survey and the Family Expenditure Survey.

Section 11: Supplies and Disposals

Various measures are used to describe the overall food position of the nation. This section details the different sources.

Section 12: Prices

This provides sources of statistics on retail prices, wholesale prices, producer prices, other input prices (other than labour) etc.

Section 13: Financial Information

This section contains sources of information on costs, profits and margins, and details of both official and commercial coverage.

Section 14: Advertising and Market Research
This section appraises the major sources of statistics on advertising expenditure including, for example, those provided by Media Expenditure Analysis Ltd. (MEAL). The section also contains details of various independent reviews of the industry, such as those published by the Economist Intelligence Unit in *Retail Business* [QRL.432] and by Mintel in *Market Intelligence* [QRL.339].

Section 15: Research and Development
This section contains details of R&D activity within the industry.

Section 16: Official Investigations
This section contains reports by bodies such as the Price Commission, the Monopolies and Merger Commission etc.

Section 17: Improvements and Comments
This suggests ways in which the present statistical publications might be improved to make them more helpful and/or intelligible to the user.

Chapters 3 to 12 on individual industrial Groups are preceded by Chapter 2 on "General Statistical Sources". This chapter covers sources which refer to the "Food industries" (Groups 411–423) in aggregate, and sources on the "Food, drink and tobacco manufacturing industries" (Class 41/42) combined. The primary sources which are particular to a given Group — e.g. *United Kingdom Dairy Facts & Figures* [QRL.503], *Scottish Sea Fisheries Statistical Tables* [QRL.449] — are covered in the specialist chapters.

Moreover, Chapter 2 also contains detailed discussion of many of the main official statistical inquiries, the process of data collection in each, and the government department responsible. It is thus recommended that the reader should consult the general chapter along with the chapter which refers to the particular industry which is of interest. For example, sources of statistics on the export performance of the dairy industry may be found in section 2.8.2 as well as in section 5.8.2.

Two publications summarise concisely the agencies involved in the collection of official statistics — *Government Statistics: A Brief Guide to Sources* [B.295], and John Slater's more specialist "Statistics of food supplies and consumption" [B.164]. For the present, we simply present a short list which cover the main types of data collected:

Output and production —	Business Statistics Office
Agricultural inputs, stocks and consumption —	Ministry of Agriculture, Fisheries and Food
Exports and imports —	HM Customs and Excise
Employment and prices —	Department of Employment
Financial and R&D information —	Department of Trade and Industry
Scotland —	Scottish Office
Wales —	Welsh Office
Northern Ireland —	Northern Ireland Departments

For most of the period under consideration in this Review, these government departments collected the considerable volume of basic data, and the Central

Statistical Office (CSO) coordinated the whole system. However some changes in organisation in 1989, involving the enlarged CSO, are discussed in Chapter 13.

It must be stressed that a direct benefit of this form of organisation is that Chapter 2 will prove useful as a guide to statistical sources for any industry, whether it be concerned with food or not. The Food industries draw from many facets of economic data hence Chapter 2 will be useful to *any* industrial economist wishing to penetrate back to the original sources. Since it has been necessary to draw on such a wide range of statistical sources, cross reference is made at appropriate points to other volumes in this series — e.g. Andrew Dean's *Wages and Earnings* [B.44] in the section on Labour.

All the statistical publications cited in this book are given a serial identification — e.g. *Annual Abstract of Statistics* [QRL.37] — and are catalogued in the Quick Reference List Key. The aim of the Quick Reference List is to give direct reference to data of a specific nature, and the arrangement is more by type of data (e.g. output, exports) than by industry. The Quick Reference List and the Quick Reference List Key to titles tie together the statistical sources of these diverse industries. All other general works discussing sources, problems of definition and measurement, methodology etc. are given a serial identification — e.g. *Business Monitor PA1001: Introductory Notes* [B.214] — in the Bibliography.

CHAPTER 2

GENERAL STATISTICAL SOURCES FOR THE FOOD INDUSTRIES

2.1 Introduction

This chapter concentrates on statistical sources for the Food industries in aggregate, i.e. Groups 411 to 423 in SIC(1980). Many of the sources also include statistics for the constituent Groups, hence the material in this chapter should be read in conjunction with the relevant specialist chapter for the Group of interest. It should be noted that some sources do not provide statistics for the Food industries alone but only for the Food, drink and tobacco manufacturing industries combined — Class 41/42 in SIC(1980). Useful secondary sources and their derivation are also discussed. The following sections are separately identified:

2.1.1 *Business Statistics Office Inquiries*

The Business Statistics Office (BSO) is the government's main agency for collecting and processing official business statistics. Approximately 400,000 inquiry forms are sent out each year (for instance 384,000 forms were sent out in 1988) to selected firms across the whole spectrum of UK industry, asking detailed questions about production, sales, employment and investment etc. This information is published in a series of Business Monitors — a detailed list of which is provided in [B.219]. The main inquiries are outlined below.

2.1.1.1 The Census of Production

An annual Census of Production has been conducted since 1970 by the Business Statistics Office (see section 2.1.1.6 for details of previous censuses). Despite its name, it is not a true "census". It is in fact a sample inquiry. Forms are sent under the Statistics of Trade Act 1947 to all businesses with an employment of 100 or more and to a sample of those with employment between 20 and 99. Most of the Groups in SIC(1980) are the subject of an annual Production Monitor, identified by the prefix PA. For the Food industries, the relevant Monitors are:

Business Monitor PA411: Organic Oils and Fats [QRL.105]
Business Monitor PA412: Slaughtering of Animals and Production of Meat and By-products [QRL.106]
Business Monitor PA413: Preparation of Milk and Milk Products [QRL.107]
Business Monitor PA414: Processing of Fruit and Vegetables [QRL.108]
Business Monitor PA415: Fish Processing [QRL.109]
Business Monitor PA416: Grain Milling [QRL.110]
Business Monitor PA419: Bread, Biscuits and Flour Confectionery [QRL.111]
Business Monitor PA420: Sugar and Sugar By-products [QRL.112]
Business Monitor PA421: Ice-cream, Cocoa, Chocolate and Sugar Confectionery [QRL.113]
Business Monitor PA423: Starch and Miscellaneous Foods [QRL.114]

These Monitors provide considerable information on total purchases, total sales, stocks, work-in-progress, capital expenditure, operating ratios, employment, wages, net output and gross value added, as well as analyses of output and costs, of business units by size, and of net capital expenditure. Individual Monitors will be discussed in more detail in the specialist chapters to which they refer. Summary tabulations are however provided in *Business Monitor PA1002: Summary Volume* [QRL.93] and encompass data on output and costs, purchases, capital expenditure, stocks and work-in-progress, and operating ratios. Data on employment, wages and salaries, output, capital expenditure, stocks and work-in-progress etc. are cross-classified by employment size and a regional distribution of employment, capital expenditure, output etc. is shown.

Detailed information about collection methods, coverage and the interpretation of figures from the Census of Production is given in *Business Monitor PA1001: Introductory Notes* [B.214]. The increased use of sampling over recent years has led to a fall in the number of forms mailed. For 1984, however, a benchmark census was conducted, resulting in more forms being mailed. 1989 was also a benchmark year.

2.1.1.2 The Quarterly Sales Inquiry

The Quarterly Sales Inquiries have been developed under an integrated system of industrial statistics since 1969. The results are published in a series of quarterly Business Monitors, identified by the prefix PQ, and appear about three months after the quarter to which they relate. They characteristically provide data for the latest eight quarters and the past six years, though with some variation. The most recently published quarterly and annual data are usually provisional and revised in later Monitors. In some instances, quantity detail is shown for the numbers of products sold as well as their total sales value. The PQ Monitors aim to provide valuable short term market indicators and usually contain information on overseas trade (exports and imports), producer prices, employment and an index of output. Some Monitors have additional series of particular relevance to the industry in question. The list of PQ Monitors which refer to the Food industries are as follows:

Business Monitor PQ4115: Margarine and Compound Cooking Fats [QRL.128]
Business Monitor PQ4116: Organic Oils and Fats [QRL.129]
Business Monitor PQ4122: Bacon Curing and Meat Products [QRL.130]
Business Monitor PQ4123: Poultry and Poultry Products [QRL.131]
Business Monitor PQ4126: Animal By-products [QRL.132]
Business Monitor PQ4147: Fruit and Vegetable Products [QRL.133]
Business Monitor PQ4150: Fish Products [QRL.134]
Business Monitor PQ4180: Starch [QRL.135]
Business Monitor PQ4196: Bread and Flour Confectionery [QRL.136]
Business Monitor PQ4197: Biscuits and Crispbread [QRL.137]
Business Monitor PQ4213: Ice-cream [QRL.138]
Business Monitor PQ4239: Miscellaneous Foods [QRL.139]

Industrial establishments are classified to the Activity Heading to which the greatest part of their turnover relates, but they may also produce commodities which are principal products of other industries. The benefit of this integrated quarterly system is in the treatment of those products sold by establishments classified to other industries. The Business Monitor for each industry gives estimates of total principal product sales which includes sales of those products by establishments classified to other industries as well as sales by establishments classified to that industry.

An example is needed to clarify this. If a computer firm happened to make "Biscuits and crispbread" as a sideline, then these values would be found in *Business Monitor PQ4197* [QRL.137]. Conversely, if the biscuit firm dabbled in computers, any values would be assigned to the relevant computer PQ Monitor.

Although it is discussed in more detail later (See section 2.3.3.1), we note here briefly that from 1987 the reporting unit became the "business" rather than the "establishment".

Each Quarterly Sales Inquiry (QSI) is thus industry-based and, prior to 1981, establishments with 25 or more employees were generally required to provide data. But from the beginning of 1981, the number of contributors to the quarterly inquiries was reduced by generally raising the employment threshold or "cut-off" levels selectively for different industries. Prior to that time, cut-off was set at 25 for all but a dozen industries. In 1988 only 33 industries had a cut-off of 25 (or lower). Other cut-offs used are 35, 50, 75, 100, 150, 200 and 300. There are 148 industries with cut-offs below 100 and 45 industries with a cut-off of 100 or more. Methodology is summarised in *Business Monitor PO1001: Guide to Short Term Statistics of Manufacturers' Sales* [B.216] and any changes are noted in the individual PQ Monitors.

One corollary was that six food manufacturing industries were dropped altogether from the quarterly inquiries — see section 2.1.1.3 for further details.

Further rationalisation of inquiries followed the *Review of DTI Statistics* [B.367] as explained in Chapter 13. Of the PQ Monitors particular to the food sector, only *Business Monitor PQ4122: Bacon Curing and Meat Products* [QRL.130] and *Business Monitor PQ4213: Ice-cream* [QRL.138] survived after Autumn 1989.

2.1.1.3 The Topping-up Inquiry

When the employment thresholds were raised in 1981, it was recognised that a topping-up inquiry would need to be undertaken periodically in order to collect product sales information from those businesses dropped from the Quarterly Sales Inquiries. The first such inquiry was conducted for 1985 and covered 28 selected industries where the raising of the employment threshold in 1981 rendered acute the problem of data reliability. In addition the six food manufacturing industries dropped from the 1981 quarterly inquiries were included. The following Activity Headings (AH) in the Food industries were covered:

AH4130	Preparation of milk and milk products
AH4160	Grain milling
AH4196	Bread and flour confectionery (included because the employment threshold was raised significantly)
AH4200	Sugar and sugar by-products
AH4214	Cocoa, chocolate and sugar confectionery.
AH4221	Compound animal feeds
AH4222	Pet foods and non-compound animal feeds

The results of the 1985 inquiry are available on application to the BSO Library, Newport with the exception of "Sugar and sugar by-products". The sheets carrying these data are collated together in papers entitled *Inquiry into Sales of Industry 1985: Introductory Notes and Results Tables for the 1985 Topping-up Inquiry into Product Sales in Selected Manufacturing Industries* [QRL.285].

2.1.1.4 The Purchases Inquiry

Purchases inquiries have been carried out at five-year intervals in 1974, 1979 and 1984 and are another important aspect of the work of the Business Statistics Office. They are separate inquiries of industry purchases at the Activity Heading level and are further discussed in section 2.5. *Business Monitor PA1002.1: 1979 Census of Production and Purchases Inquiry* [QRL.94] carries the results for 1979. More recently *Business Monitor PO1008: Purchases Inquiry 1984* [QRL.116] carries data for 1984. The Purchases Inquiry for 1989 is being conducted at the time of writing and the results are to be published in 1992.

2.1.1.5 Register analyses

Business Monitor PO1007: Classified List of Manufacturing Businesses 1984 [B.217] is issued in six parts, including one part devoted to Food, drink and tobacco. It contains a list of selected companies which participate in the integrated work of the BSO. The list is compiled from the register of manufacturing businesses in the United Kingdom maintained by the BSO primarily for conducting statistical inquiries. The classified list of manufacturing businesses is confined to local units classified to manufacturing for whom the parent establishments exceed the 50 employment size threshold and for whom consent for inclusion in the list has been given through the Annual Census of Production form. Thus the published list is a subset of the register itself which contains lists of local manufacturing sites belonging to companies sent forms for the Annual Census of Production.

The register is a live register which can be updated according to the births and deaths of firms, using data derived from the administration of Value Added Tax (VAT) and by the despatch of proving letters which ask for details of local sites and the activity of businesses. The integrated register includes both production and non-production legal units. The former are generally classified by the SIC(1980) Activity Heading whilst the latter are generally based upon SIC(1968). The confidentiality of individual register units is governed both by the Statistics of Trade Act of 1947 and by the VAT Act 1983. Thus the published list itself is a restricted sample of consenting firms. Another version, also in six parts, has been produced for 1989, catalogued as *Business Monitor PO1007: The UK Directory of Manufacturing Businesses* [B.218].

The register of production units throughout the United Kingdom is held on the BSO computer. It identifies the unit's eligibility for inclusion, its relationship with other units in common ownership, its classification in SIC(1980), the nationality of its parent company and location details for regional analysis. The Annual Census of Production, the Quarterly Sales Inquiry and the Purchases Inquiry, which together form a comprehensive system of industrial statistics, are themselves sources of information for updating and checking the register on which they are based. The food companies registered are classified by name, address etc. in [B.217] and [B.218]. The 1984 version was the first to use SIC(1980). Special geographical and alphabetical analyses in the form of computer printouts are available for users looking for a regional or local sorting of businesses. A magnetic tape version of the list is also available.

2.1.1.6 Historical data

The Census of Production Act of 1906 laid upon the Board of Trade the obligation to take a census in 1908 relating to the year 1907, and subsequently to undertake censuses at such intervals as might be determined. In 1911 an Order was made that a census should be taken in 1913 (for 1912) and "thereafter in every successive fifth year". The results of the 1912 census were still being examined at the outbreak of World War I and no seperate report was published; available results were included for comparison in the report on the third census taken in 1925 (for 1924). Two other censuses (for 1930 and 1935) were taken before the outbreak of World War II.

Since the end of World War II, the detailed census years have been 1948, 1951, 1954, 1958, 1963 and 1968 prior to the introduction of the annual exercises in 1970 except for the slimline inquiry in 1974–1975. A full list is now given for ease of reference.

First Census of Production of the United Kingdom (1907) [QRL.219]
Final Report on the Third Census of Production of the United Kingdom (1924) [QRL.213]
Final Report on the Fourth Census of Production (1930) [QRL.216]
Final Report on the Fifth Census of Production and the Import Duties Act Inquiry 1935 [QRL.215]
Final Report on the Census of Production for 1948 [QRL.214]
The Report on the Census of Production for 1949 [QRL.420]
The Report on the Census of Production for 1950 [QRL.421]
Censuses of Production for 1950, 1949, and 1948. Summary Tables Part 1 [QRL.151]
The Report on the Census of Production for 1951 [QRL.422]

The Report on the Censuses of Production for 1952 and 1953 [QRL.426]
The Report on the Census of Production for 1954 [QRL.423]
The Report on the Census of Production for 1958 [QRL.424]
The Report on the Censuses of Production for 1959, 1960, 1961 and 1962 [QRL.427]
Report on the Census of Production 1963 [QRL.417]
The Report on the Censuses of Production for 1964, 1965, 1966 and 1967 [QRL.428]
Report on the Census of Production 1968 [QRL.418]
Report on the Censuses of Production 1974 & 1975 [QRL.425] (slimline inquiry)

A concise guide to the many changes (up to 1970) in the coverage is given in the *Historical Record of the Census of Production 1907 to 1970* [QRL.264]. This is a convenient summary of the many census volumes already listed and compiled by the Board of Trade from 1907 to 1963; by the Department of Trade and Industry for 1964, 1965, 1966 and 1967; and by the Business Statistics Office of the Department of Trade and Industry from 1968 onwards. Unfortunately the *Historical Record* [QRL.264] is now out of print. However photocopies may be obtained from the BSO library at Newport and copies are held in a selection of reference and university libraries.

It is worth stressing that the coverage of the census has been subject to change. Thus the introductory notes to the relevant reports merit careful study. The conceptual framework of the first Census of Production in 1907 appears to picture output as a function of material inputs, the number of people employed and some index of a motive power input. This simple notion has not subsequently been maintained. Nor, as consumer demand has changed and food technology has progressed, could the industrial classification remain immutable. For example, "cured, smoked and salted fish" were of far greater import in 1907, than in Group 415 of the current SIC(1980).

The *Historical Record* [QRL.264] carries data on net output in value terms often with separate coverage for England, Wales, Scotland, Northern Ireland and the United Kingdom in total for various census years. But the historical coverage varies according to industry although the series are complete from 1958. The time series go right back to 1907 for some products (e.g. grain milling and sugar) but start at a later date for others (e.g. milk and milk products). A shorter time series (1958, 1963, 1968 and 1970) is provided for SIC(1968) Order III "Food, drink and tobacco" in aggregate. The *Historical Record* [QRL.264] also summarises sales and work done and gross output of particular products from each MLH. Sales and work done is sometimes subdivided into more product detail with a variety of initial dates from 1907 onwards for the larger establishments. A reasonable comparison can be made over time for many of the food products (e.g. flour confectionery, cocoa products, margarine), all too numerous to list here. The footnotes to the tables in the *Historical Record* [QRL.264] need careful scrutiny since there are gaps and inconsistencies in coverage between the various censuses.

Finally, it is worth briefly comparing the last complete quinquennial Census of Production in 1968 with the activities of the Business Statistics Office. Even in 1968, the Census of Production was a misnomer because the nature of the inquiry was much more the measurement of total productive activity rather than the enumeration of physical production and its value that the title implies. The coverage incorporated output, fine detail of product sales, statistics on labour and capital inputs and analyses of purchases. Thus it can be seen that what used to be published in one Census report became the five BSO components of the Annual Census of Production, the Quarterly Sales Inquiries, the Topping-up Inquiry, the quinquennial Purchases inquiry, and the compilation and revision of the Classified List of Manufacturing Businesses.

2.1.2 *The Census of Production in Northern Ireland*

The *Report on the Census of Production and Construction in Northern Ireland* [QRL.419] is carried out under the Statistics of Trade and Employment (Northern Ireland) Order 1988 by the Department of Economic Development. Since 1973, the Northern Ireland census has been aligned with that undertaken in Great Britain by the Business Statistics Office in an attempt to achieve comparability for the United Kingdom as a whole. Since 1980, the reports have been produced on the basis of the SIC(1980). Census returns are required from businesses employing 20 or more persons on average during the year of the return. In general, the inquiries are carried out by the Department of Economic Development for Northern Ireland and the BSO compiles results for the United Kingdom.

The information is summarised at Class level for the Food, drink and tobacco manufacturing industries in aggregate. A further breakdown is available as follows:-

Meat and fish products (Groups 412 and 415)
Milk and milk products (Group 413)
Bread, biscuits and flour confectionery (Group 419)
Other foods, drink and tobacco (other Groups except 412, 413, 415 and 419)

Data are collected for similar items as in the BSO inquiries: output and costs, purchases, capital expenditure, stocks and work-in-progress, employment, wages and salaries etc. As with the work of the BSO and its predecessors, the coverage of the census has not been consistent over time. Early censuses were taken in Northern Ireland for the years 1907, 1912, 1924, 1930 and 1935 under the provisions of the Census of Production Act 1906, amended by the Census of Production Act 1912. The 1907 and 1912 studies covered production in Ireland as a whole. The censuses from 1949 onwards have been done under the aegis of the Statistics of Trade Act (Northern Ireland) 1949.

The censuses since 1949 have exhibited varying detail for the Food industries, with a tendency over time towards less disaggregated data. In 1949, "Food, drink and tobacco" was divided into the following: grain milling; bread or flour confectionery; biscuits; bacon curing and sausage; milk products; sugar confectionery; preserved fruit and vegetables; miscellaneous preserved foods; mineral waters; wholesale bottling; miscellaneous. Subsequent censuses in the years 1951, 1954, 1958, 1963 and 1968 were more extensive inquiries. The census of 1968, for example, covered firms of all sizes engaged in the production industries and followed SIC(1968) in separately treating the following: grain milling and animal feed compounding; bread; biscuits and flour confectionery; bacon curing, meat and fish products; milk products; fruit and vegetable products; soft drinks, wine and cider; and miscellaneous food, drink and tobacco trades. These categories were maintained until 1973–1975, from when the headings covered became: grain milling, bread and flour confectionery; bacon curing; meat and fish products; milk and milk products; fruit and vegetable products;

animal and poultry foods; and soft drinks. These distinctions held until the SIC(1980) which had fewer subdivisions.

Thus it can be seen that the industry detail has diminished over time. As always, the introductory notes to the volumes summarise major changes in coverage. Despite the variations, a picture can be built up of output, employment and capital expenditure throughout.

2.1.3 *The National Accounts*

The *United Kingdom National Accounts* [QRL.506] — the CSO "Blue Book" — contains estimates of the domestic and national product, income and expenditure for the United Kingdom. This volume, published annually since 1984, was formerly called *National Income and Expenditure* [QRL.374] and is prepared by the CSO in collaboration with other government departments and the Bank of England. A general description of the statistics given in this publication, together with a detailed description of the definitions, sources and methods used in making the estimates, is given in *United Kingdom National Accounts: Sources and Methods. Third Edition* [B.395]. This edition, published in 1985, is a revised and updated version of the 1968 publication, *National Accounts Statistics: Sources and Methods* [B.122]. A further source of reference is *The National Accounts — A Short Guide* [B.339], which contains a broad description of the national income and expenditure accounts and comments on the significance of some of the items.

From the 1984 issue of [QRL.506], the tables which contain industry analyses are based as far as possible on SIC(1980). Hence, Groups 411–423 inclusive are defined as "Food", and Groups 411–429 inclusive as "Food, drink and tobacco". Disaggregated data for both are provided as follows:

- gross domestic product in the "Food" industry
- income from employment in the "Food" industry
- gross domestic product at constant factor cost in the "Food" industry: output-based measure
- household expenditure at current prices on the following food products: bread and cereals; meat and bacon; fish; milk, cheese and eggs; oils and fats; fruit; potatoes; vegetables; sugar; preserves and confectionery; coffee, tea and cocoa; soft drinks; other manufactured food
- household expenditure at constant prices on the above food products
- gross domestic fixed capital formation in the "Food" industry by type of asset: vehicles, ships and aircraft; plant and machinery; and new buildings and works
- gross capital stock in the "Food" industry at constant replacement cost by type of asset: vehicles; plant and machinery; buildings
- change in the book value of assets in the "Food, drink and tobacco" industry
- value of the physical increase in stocks in the "Food, drink and tobacco" industry at current prices
- value of the physical increase in stocks in the "Food, drink and tobacco" industry at constant prices
- index numbers of production at constant factor cost for the "Food, drink and tobacco" industry

The data cover the latest eleven years. Some of the more recent figures may be provisional and will be revised at a later date. Further details on reliability are given in *United Kingdom National Accounts: Sources and Methods. Third Edition* [B.395]. Monthly estimates of many of the above items are published in the *Monthly Digest of Statistics* [QRL.362]. Moreover, a computer-readable Blue Book data set was released during October 1987, as part of the CSO Databank service. This Blue Book data set contains annual series only, and the time period covered is the same as in the Blue Book itself. A limited number of series cover a longer time-span.

The CSO Databank service provides macroeconomic time series data on magnetic tape. Details of the service offered and the schedule of charges may be obtained from the Databank manager at the CSO (address and telephone number provided in the current issue of the Blue Book). The CSO does not offer direct on-line access for these data but a list of host bureaux offering such a facility is available on request from the CSO.

2.1.4 *Comments*

This section has emphasised the work of the BSO on the Annual Census of Production, the Quarterly Sales Inquiry, the Purchases Inquiry, the Topping-up Inquiry and Register analyses. It has also mentioned Northern Ireland coverage. Although it will be discussed further, the work of the Ministry of Agriculture, Fisheries and Food (MAFF) as summarised by Barnett [B.12] and Slater [B.164] should also be referred to here. The MAFF monitors the utilisation of some basic foodstuffs and, until 1969, data on supplies from the UK food processing industry came from various short period inquiries conducted by the Ministry. In 1981, as part of the review of the government statistical services, it was decided to reduce the number of short period inquiries so that each industry should be covered by just one inquiry whether conducted by the BSO, MAFF or a trade association. Details of the range of inquiries are given in Appendix C. MAFF sponsor the Quarterly Sales Inquiries of the BSO and itself carries out the complementary inquiries in the production of some processed foods published initially in the various MAFF Statistical Notices and then in the *Monthly Digest of Statistics* [QRL.362] and the *Annual Abstract of Statistics* [QRL.37].

2.2 Industry Structure

First of all, useful guides to statistics are noted before a listing of general statistical sources. These references which cover descriptions of economic structure precede more specific data sources on industrial concentration and mergers and acquisitions.

2.2.1 *Guides to Sources*

2.2.1.1 Guides to official sources

The Central Statistical Office have periodically published a *Guide to Official Statistics* [B.298] from the first issue in 1976 to the sixth, and latest, issue in 1990. It is a well indexed source with a good bibliography. Two useful earlier references are the MAFF guide to *Agricultural and Food Statistics* [B.197], published in 1974, and the NEDO publication *Food Statistics* [B.283], which emerged in 1968. The former has more of an agricultural emphasis but the latter refers to official and business sources throughout the food chain.

2.2.1.2 Guides to commercial sources

Sources of Unofficial UK Statistics [B.130] lists a number of unofficial publications including those produced by trade associations and companies. It also includes a list of market research organisations with a percentage figure for the proportion of their sources which are primary and which result from their own work. The latter is the result of a questionnaire survey by the authors and there is no explanation of statistical methodology. Many but not all sources are covered.

Information Sources in Management and Business [B.179] contains a couple of essays which are of interest. Joan Harvey provides a good introductory guide on statistical publications for business and management. David King provides a useful review of market research reports, but does not include any significant discussion of their methodology.

Paul Norkett has written a *Guide to Company Information in Great Britain* [B.137] which reviews sources of information ranging from Business Monitors to data bases. Addresses and telephone numbers are included which inevitably need periodic updating. Its emphasis is primarily financial with sections on how to assess company performance, how to read accounts and how to use financial data bases. This work is further referred to in section 2.10.2.

James Tudor has compiled the *Macmillan Directory of Business Information Sources* [B.175] which uses the SIC(1980) Activity Headings to arrange this guide to finding business information whether official, commercial or on line. An alphabetical index to SIC(1980) is provided and a list of British trade publications, editorial offices, addresses etc. is given. Patricia Millard provides a useful guide in *Trade Associations and Professional Bodies of the United Kingdom* [B.124] which lists, and indexes under various product headings, all the trade associations in the United Kingdom. The inevitable problem of updating is partially tackled in *Business Information Sourcebook* [B.211] which has periodic loose leaf supplements.

There are a number of directories pertaining to the Food sector which are periodically revised. The most recent edition of the *European Food Trades Directory formerly Food Trades Directory & Food Buyer's Yearbook* [B.259] was published in 1989 and was the twenty-first issue in the series formerly entitled *Food Trades Directory & Food Buyers' Yearbook* [B.285]. These biennial publications show the broad nexus of the Food sector. They give MAFF personnel, trade associations, professional bodies, food suppliers and processors with name of company and address, food products and ingredients from information supplied by companies. The *Food Industry Directory* [B.282] provides information on companies, products and brand names which relate to plant and materials used by manufacturers and distributors. Classified product indexes comprise 30,000 entries under more than 1700 categories. The *Food Industry Directory* [B.282] is available as a separate book, but is also provided as part of [B.285]. Company names and addresses are derived from a computer data base created by the publishers from questionnaire respondents. *Binsted's Directory of Food Trade Marks and Brand Names* [B.203] in its various editions gives brand names, the nature of the product and the company responsible.

2.2.2 *General Statistical Sources*

There are a number of well known volumes which collate statistics from the many government departments and which appear repeatedly throughout this Review because they cover a variety of topics. The *Monthly Digest of Statistics* [QRL.362] and the *Annual Abstract of Statistics* [QRL.37], are prime examples. Frequent mention is also made of *Economic Trends* [QRL.181] and *British Business* [QRL.66].

Comparable sources which provide regional coverage for the countries of the United Kingdom are the *Scottish Abstract of Statistics* [QRL.446], the *Scottish Economic Bulletin* [QRL.447], the *Digest of Welsh Statistics* [QRL.177], *Welsh Economic Trends* [QRL.517] and the *Northern Ireland Annual Abstract of Statistics* [QRL.377]. The *Isle of Man Digest of Economic and Social Statistics* [QRL.295] gives a comprehensive picture of economic trends on the Isle of Man.

All the above publications contain statistics on all industries. More specialist contributions which refer specifically to the Food industries include the NEDO *Food and Drink Statistics Data Bank* [QRL.232] which draws together data from many official publications with the sources duly acknowledged. *The Food Industry Statistics Digest* [QRL.237] published by the Institute of Grocery Distribution and updated monthly incorporates figures derived mostly from primary official sources. Both the above mainly focus on the Food industries whereas the two volumes of *Food Focus* [QRL.235] have a more agricultural and horticultural emphasis, as does the *Statistical Handbook of UK Agriculture* [QRL.5].

2.2.3 *Descriptions of Economic Structure*

The Food industries cover a range of industries which are discussed in detail in the chapters on individual Groups of SIC(1980). These heterogeneous industries exhibit a large degree of interdependence. Many large firms have substantial activities in more than one industry Group. The activities of some firms are limited to the Food, drink and tobacco manufacturing industries, but some are conglomerates and holding companies active in other commercial sectors. Some firms transcend national boundaries. The activities of some food processing firms — for instance in grain milling, starch and sugar — are close to agricultural commodity processing. Such first stage processors, as they are sometimes known, sell much of their output to second stage manufacturers of more highly processed foods (e.g. bread, biscuits, confectionery).

It is thus not surprising that there is no single authoritative reference on the Food industries as a whole. However, Jordan Information Services attempt a description of the industry in *Britain's Food Processing Industry* [B.150], developed within the framework of SIC(1980). The economic analysis and narrative is supported by statistical tables, and financial profiles of the major firms. But Peter Maunder's contributions in both editions of the *Structure of British Industry* [B.117] and [B.120] are both more accessible and more concise. Both are devoted to food manufacturing as defined first in SIC(1968), and second in SIC(1980), with illustrative statistics of market structure, behaviour and performance.

A number of other publications describe the structure of the Food industries, together with the many interrelationships of the entire Food sector, and also provide illustrative statistical data. They are listed below with the most recent contributions first:

"The food sector in the UK" [B.165] by John Slater of MAFF was compiled in 1987 and gives a statistical overview of current issues and past developments with accompanying figures and tables.

Review of the Food and Drink Manufacturing Industry [B.370] was published by NEDO and describes developments in the industry, supported by statistical appendices from official sources.

The Future of the Agriculture and Food System [B.74] is a background study published in 1986 by the University of Reading. It provides an overview of the Food sector and gives selected statistics in the text.

Structural Change and Public Policy in the European Food Industry [B.43], sponsored by the European Community (1986), reviews trends in the manufacturing sector.

"The food sector in the context of the UK economy" [B.126], by R.E. Mordue, covers the entire food chain but also contains a concise section with detailed statistical illustrations devoted to food manufacturing in the context of SIC(1968). This paper was published in a book entitled *The Food Industry: Economics and Policies* [B.31] which also contains other papers of interest.

"The UK food chain with particular reference to the inter-relations between manufacturers and distributors" [B.30], by Jim Burns, described food manufacturing, market structure and the balance with food distribution.

Structural Adjustments in the Food Industries: Adjustment in the United Kingdom Food Manufacturing Industry over the Past Twenty Years [B.184], by B.G.A. Watts, contains a statistical annex covering the years 1960–1979.

A Study in the Evolution of Concentration in the Food Industry for the United Kingdom [B.384] is a two-part European Commission Study. Part 1 is a general food industry survey that mentions many of the statistical problems, particularly with official data. Part 2 is in two volumes covering various product markets. Manufactured milk; infant foods; ice-cream; grain milling and biscuits; are in Volume 1. Margarine; sugar; canned, frozen and dehydrated foods; dietetic and health foods; and the summary and conclusions are in Volume 2.

"Britain's food manufacturing industry" [B.4], by A.W. Ashby, is another important earlier (1978) overall source.

2.2.4 *Numbers of Firms and Legal Units*

The annual *Report of the Commissioners of Her Majesty's Customs and Excise* [QRL.408] has often enumerated the number of registered persons in each industry Class in SIC(1980). But *Business Monitor PA1003: Size Analyses of United Kingdom Businesses* [QRL.96] gives much more detail, recording the number of legal units (production industries) for the latest year for SIC(1980) Activity Headings by turnover sizeband. The total for each Activity Heading covered and a Class total are also given. The number of legal units in manufacturing industries according to SIC(1980) Class are further cross-classified according to employment size band. Since this source is significant for the size analyses of employment, it is further discussed in section 2.6.1.2 where the distinction between legal unit (usually tax units for VAT purposes) and local unit (i.e. site or factory) is made. The local unit analyses give the number of local units in manufacturing industries according to SIC(1980) Class for a five-year run. The further cross-classification of Class data by employment size band gives the local units in each employment size band. Thus both the local unit and the legal unit analyses provide information on the structure of industry at a specific time.

2.2.5 *Industrial Concentration*

The summary volume *Business Monitor PA1002* [QRL.93] identifies the five largest enterprises by employment size. Then the ratio of the share of the five largest enterprises thus identified to the total for the industry is calculated for many economic dimensions: gross output, net output, total sales and work done, employment, net capital expenditure, wages and salaries and gross value added at factor cost. An example of these data is found in Table 13 of the 1986 *Business Monitor PA1002* [QRL.93]. The calculations are carried out for most Groups in the Food industries. There is no information for the highly concentrated "Sugar and sugar by-products" because of disclosure difficulties.

Business Monitor PO1006: Statistics of Product Concentration of UK Manufacturers [QRL.115] is now discontinued. The last issue gave concentration data for 1975, 1976 and 1977 based on SIC(1968). Previous issues covered 1963 and 1968. It is worth noting that the treatment in the Census of Production differs from what is available in [QRL.115]. The census measures (output share etc.) are based on the percentage of each component attributable to the five enterprises with the largest employment in the industry. In contrast, the size of the enterprise used for ranking purposes was the sales of the product or product group for one of the tables and sales within industry for the other. In addition, the data in *Business Monitor PO1006* [QRL.115] related solely to establishments within the scope of the Quarterly Sales Inquiry (i.e. those employing 25 or more) whereas the annual census includes estimates for all manufacturers within an industry.

Concentration is a complex matter and these are simple ratios. Watts [B.184] is most important in discussing both methodology and details. He summarises five-firm concentration ratios for employment from 1958 to 1978 and uniquely presents a sales-based five-firm concentration ratio adjusted for foreign trade using MAFF estimates based on UK trade figures. Finer definitions of product markets tend to be drawn in market research reports — e.g. *Retail Business* [QRL.432] — and reports of the Monopolies and Mergers Commission. Burns [B.30] quotes some results for the share of the largest firms in many diverse markets.

2.2.6 *Mergers and Acquisitions*

Business Monitor MQ7: Acquisitions and Mergers by Industrial and Commercial Companies [QRL.92] analyses acquisitions and mergers based on financial press reports and special Department of Trade and Industry (DTI) inquiries into the form, value and timing of acquisitions. For the Food industries, data are provided on companies making acquisitions, the number of companies being acquired, and the amount paid. This Monitor is published about six weeks after each quarter and at the same time a short summary appeared in *British Business* [QRL.66]. Data are usually supplied for the latest five quarters with the most recent figures being provisional. Sales of subsidiaries between company groups in the United Kingdom are similarly reported at Class level but there is no such breakdown for foreign acquisitions by UK companies or for UK companies acquired by overseas interests. The *Annual Abstract of Statistics* [QRL.37] reports the expenditure by industry Group of acquiring company and the number of companies acquired for the previous eight years.

The *Annual Report of the Director General of Fair Trading* [QRL.48] records all acquisition proposals, but not consummated mergers, including those in the financial sector for British and non British companies involving assets in excess of a certain level (£15m to 1984 and £30m subsequently). There is a breakdown by SIC(1980) Class of the number, assets, and average assets and nationality of target companies. But the main purpose of the *Annual Report* [QRL.48] is to report what the Office of Fair Trading and Monopolies and Mergers Commission have been doing during the year, noting dates of merger referrals to the Commission, and merger reports by named company.

Acquisitions Monthly [QRL.14], which was first published in 1985, carries sectoral analyses which summarise acquisitions completed in the previous quarter. The same data are reviewed annually. Detail is provided on the names and activities of the selling and buying firms, the price paid and the date of purchase. Companies are classified by Activity Heading in SIC(1980). Every month, statistical information is published on management buyouts; new UK public bids, both pending and completed; completed acquisitions of UK private companies; UK divestments; UK acquisitions of US companies; other US acquisitions; and UK acquisitions of foreign companies. The statistics are compiled from the Acquisitions Monthly data base, and subscribers to the data base can extract more up-to-date information. This private sector source relies upon data supplied by banks, companies etc. and others involved in these continual economic struggles.

2.2.7 *Comments*

In the light of the continual interest in industrial concentration, it is to be regretted that the specialist and occasional *Business Monitor PO1006* [QRL.115] has been discontinued. *Business Monitor MQ7* [QRL.92] only provides aggregate data on mergers and acquisitions for food processing and manufacture as a whole. *Business Monitor PA1002* [QRL.93] does provide five-firm concentration ratios for Groups. But the limitations of the simple concentration index as an indication of market power are well-known. The arbitrary delineations relating to the SIC mean a supply-sided and process-based classification. The coverage of small firms is not consistent. Adjustments should be made to account for overseas competition, as noted by Watts [B.184]. Limited inferences on the structure of, the level of concentration and the extent of conglomeration in, the food industry may be gleaned from the available raw data.

Official data are thus limited both from the point of view of statistical coverage and as regards the more general purposes of assessing market structure, power and industrial performance. We note in section 2.16 and elsewhere the valuable role played by the reports of the Monopolies and Mergers Commission in repairing some of these deficiencies, but events have moved on by the time they are published. There are also, particularly on the financial side as catalogued in section 2.13, a host of stockbrokers' reports, market research work (by the Economist Intelligence Unit, Intercompany Comparisons etc.) and press information which may all be used alongside primary official data in order that a fuller picture may be obtained.

Thus the existence of many publications which attempt to repair these conceptual and practical deficiencies must be noted. Hannah and Kay [B.67], Hart, Utton and Walshe [B.72] and Sawyer [B.157] are a selection of books which explain more complex concentration measures as well as reporting some statistics. Utton [B.178] looks at the degree of specialisation in "Food, drink and tobacco". But since the major companies are quite diversified across these and other sectors, a better notion of economic power may be gained by interpreting the statistics at a more aggregate level. *The Evolution of Giant Firms in Britain* [B.146], by S.J. Prais, makes thorough use of available Census of Production information to give an overview of the importance of the UK's largest 100 private companies in food processing. *Big Business; Theoretical and Empirical Aspects of Concentration and Mergers in the UK* [B.158], by M.C. Sawyer and S. Aaronovitch, ploughs a similar furrow. *The Structure of Industry in the EEC* [B.57], by K.D. George and T. Ward, is also important in its analysis of methodology and intra-European comparisons.

Business Monitor PA1002 [QRL.93] and *Business Monitor MQ7* [QRL.92] thus provide a flow of fairly aggregate information which always must be supplemented for it cannot be expected that the enlarged CSO, the BSO and other DTI statistical divisions can provide data for all purposes. Academic research, whether in the form of books or specialist articles, fills out the picture but inevitably becomes dated. The private market continually provides a host of information in many forms ranging from the well known *Times 1000* [QRL.486] to stockbrokers' reports which are sometimes available only to clients.

Indeed, many private sources seek to provide information on economic and market structure, mergers and acquisitions and the latest company news. As such, they are drawn upon, sometimes extensively, in the Industry Structure sections at the beginning of each of the following chapters. A good example is the many reports of *Retail Business* [QRL.432] and *Market Intelligence* [QRL.339] used in Chapter 6 to give a description of the many segments of the fruit and vegetables processing nexus. Thus these reports do more than summarise official sources. They seek to give a flow of both data and commentary which may help in assessing the changing balance of economic power in the Food industries.

2.3 The European Community

The Treaty of Rome in 1957 heralded the formation of the European Community (EC). The initial signatories were France, Belgium, the Netherlands, Luxembourg, Italy and the Federal Republic of Germany. In 1973, Denmark and the United Kingdom left the European Free Trade Area (EFTA) and, together with the Irish Republic, joined the Community. Subsequently, Greece became a member in 1981, and membership was extended to twelve countries with the accession of Spain and Portugal in 1986. These developments have had far-reaching effects on the United Kingdom, and the progress towards the Single European Market from 1992 and subsequent developments may well have a further profound impact.

As regards this Review, three points should be made about the accession of the United Kingdom to the Community. First, membership has had an economic influence upon the structure of the UK Food industries. References which address this subject are provided in section 2.3.1. Second, the Community itself coordinates many series of statistics through its own Statistical Office (EUROSTAT). These are outlined briefly in section 2.3.2. Third, and most important for this Review, membership has had an effect on the scope and methods of statistical collection in the United Kingdom. This topic will be addressed in section 2.3.3.

2.3.1 *The Economic Influence of the Community*

In this section, we detail various general references which describe or analyse the economic influence of accession to the Community on the UK Food industries. Clearly, the Common Agricultural Policy (CAP) and the Common Fisheries Policy have marked and particular effects on individual Food industries, and these will be discussed in more detail in the appropriate chapters.

The Impact of the EEC on the UK Food Industry [B.135] was published in 1978, and remarked upon the many publications on agriculture and the economy in general. The contrast with the sparse coverage of the Food industries was clear. This publication aimed to fill some of this gap. Indeed it attempted to compare the panorama prior to UK accession with that of five years later. An overview was provided of the UK Food industries, and sectoral analyses were presented for the following: breakfast cereals; bread and flour; cakes and biscuits; processed meat; processed fish; dairy products; sugar; chocolate and sugar confectionery; processed fruit and vegetables; non alcoholic beverages; other food products; alcoholic drinks and tobacco products. The method involved the analysis of company reports, interviews with trade associations, and the completion of detailed case studies of companies. The accompanying case studies appeared separately in *Case Studies on the Effects of the EEC on the UK Food and Drink Industry* [B.136]. It must be stressed however that the impact of UK entry cannot be easily isolated, as other economic factors change concomitantly.

The Food and Farm Policies of the European Community [B.71] was published in 1983. Besides a coverage of the main aspects of the CAP, this book examines the interaction between the CAP and the Food industries in the Community. In particular, it contains a chapter on the impact of farm policies on the Food industries. This included a statistical illustration of the relative shares of agriculture and the Food industries in gross value added at market prices, comparing the United Kingdom with Germany, France, Italy, the Netherlands and Belgium.

It is worth noting that, with the deficiency payments system which applied in the United Kingdom prior to EC entry, the UK Government made most, but not all, payments direct to farmers. In contrast, intervention buying in the Community is usually available for products which have undergone some transformation — e.g. butter, skim milk powder, white sugar, beef carcases — and hence offers a potential output for the first stage processors, not the farmers. Since many of the price support mechanisms of the CAP operate through the Food industries, the first stage agricultural processors have often had a privileged position with a guaranteed and unlimited outlet for production, a known price and the benefit of a built in "cost plus" margin. This aspect of the CAP has obviously influenced the Food industries, and it is discussed at length. This reference also includes an overview of food legislation, but does not attempt to cover the complexities of fisheries nor competition policy.

The EEC and the Food Industries [B.173] was published in 1984. It carries a collection of conference papers on many aspects of the Community. These include an analysis of the CAP with respect to the Food industries. First stage processors are again distinguished from second stage processors, as the former may have guaranteed processing margins whereas the latter may have the problem of paying administered prices to first stage processors and then selling on under normal commercial pressures to retailers. The influence of EEC Food Law (e.g. legislation on harmonising additives) is considered, and a useful list is provided of EC Directives. Cross references to the *Official Journal of the European Communities* [B.341] are presented. EC structural and competition policy is surveyed in separate contributions and a Commission view given. The overall summary includes a statistical demonstration of the significance of food and drink processing in the Community. *The EEC and the Food Industries* [B.173] thus demonstrates the influence on the Food industries of many aspects of EC membership; in particular the CAP, food legislation, structural policy and competition policy. Sources are identified, and mechanisms explained, which are helpful when updated statistics are required.

Structural Change and Public Policy in the European Food Industry: Part I [B.43] became available in 1986 as an occasional publication from the Community-supported experimental programme on Forecasting and Assessment in Science and Technology (FAST). Food processing came under Theme 3 (Strategic Industrial Systems) of FAST, whose objectives are to identify long-term priorities for joint research and development, and to examine the possible effects on society and the economy. *Structural Change and Public Policy* [B.43] profiles trends in manufacturing. Moreover, it gives a structural survey of the European food manufacturing industries, as well as analysing trends in distribution and the relationships in the food chain.

The Single European Market and the Food and Drink Industry: Political Myth or Market Opportunity [B.374] appeared in 1988 as a guide to prospects for 1992 and is mentioned given the importance of this topic. There are other more general guides. *European File* [B.258] has frequent summaries of Community events and publications with yearly indexes. *European Access* [B.256] is a quarterly guide which catalogues community developments and publications under many headings including "Trade and Industry" and "Agriculture/Fisheries".

The *General Report of the Activities of the European Communities* [QRL.248], *The Agricultural Situation in the Community* [QRL.28] and the *Report on Competition Policy* [QRL.410] are all important examples of annual reports of the Commission of the European Communities. They give comprehensive annual reviews of events and issues with selected statistical data which can be used to update the basic information.

2.3.2 *EUROSTAT and Community Statistics*

The Statistical Office of the European Communities (EUROSTAT or SOEC) is a service organisation within the European Commission. Its task is to coordinate the output of the various national statistical services to ensure that the Commission has, at its disposal, whatever statistical information it needs as background for its policy decisions. The first statistical service of the Community was established in 1953 to serve the High Authority of the European Coal and Steel Community (ECSC). In 1958, a joint decision was taken by the executive bodies of the European Economic Community (EEC), the European Atomic Energy Community (EAEC or EURATOM), and the ECSC to form the Statistical Office of the European Communities.

EUROSTAT is housed with other Commission services in the Jean Monnet Building in Luxembourg. Data are received from various sources and, if harmonised, may be used for comparing the UK Food industries with those of other countries, as well as being an alternative, but not usually original, fount of UK data. Coverage has changed over time, and with the increased membership. The *Eurostat Catalogue: Publications and Electronic Services* [B.261] of 1988 summarises the various publications under a scheme which serves to place each title within one of eight subject themes:

Theme 1 General statistics (midnight blue covers)
Theme 2 Economy and finance (violet covers)
Theme 3 Population and social conditions (yellow covers)
Theme 4 Energy and industry (blue covers)
Theme 5 Agriculture, forestry and fisheries (green covers)
Theme 6 Foreign trade (red covers)
Theme 7 Services and transport (orange covers)
Theme 9 Miscellaneous (brown covers)

Each theme may then incorporate publications in the following series:

Series A General yearbooks
Series B Short-term trends
Series C Accounts, surveys and statistics
Series D Studies and analyses
Series E Methods
Series F Rapid reports

In the cases where the statistics are available in other forms, an indication is given by a sign in the adjacent column. This covers at present on-line information, magnetic tapes and diskettes.

The work of EUROSTAT is fully described in the *Introductory Course for Officials of the National Statistical Services* [B.322], compiled in February 1987 by the heads of the various departments. *Eurostat News* [B.262] is an analogous source of information to that provided for the United Kingdom by *Statistical News* [B.381]. An annual article reviews the work of EUROSTAT in the previous year. Other articles discuss aspects of EEC statistics, and outline forthcoming developments. A yellow page insert in the final issue of each year gives the availability of current titles, specifying both Themes and Series.

The basic data are generally collected by member countries, but the processing and dissemination are complex and are explained at length in the *Introductory Course* [B.322]. EUROSTAT is the creator of a whole range of numerical data banks. The coverage is explained in a 1986 issue of *Eurostat News* [B.262]. The CRONOS data bank is the largest. It carries most of the time series broken down into 23 domains, covering industrial statistics, agricultural data etc. CADOS is a documentary statistical catalogue devised to allow users to find out whether data on a particular subject exists in CRONOS. A separate data bank, COMEXT, has been created for the external trade statistics of the Community, and statistics of trade between Member States. The SABINE system of data banks is used for the storage and management of classifications of all kinds (e.g. NACE, SITC). Access is provided through commercial on-line information. Privileged users (mostly the suppliers of the data) have direct access.

Some other useful guides to the statistical output of the Community exist. *A Guide to the Official Publications of the European Communities* [B.89] provides an historical description and listings of EUROSTAT publications. The editions of 1978 and 1981 are followed, in 1989, by *The Documentation of the European Communities: A Guide* [B.174]. Detailed accounts by Maria Collins on "Statistical sources of the European Communities" and Simon D.A. O'Sullivan on "Agricultural policy and its information sources" were published in 1985 in *European Communities Information: Its Use and Users* [B.82].

The *Eurostat Index* [B.151] is another valuable aid which facilitates the use of EUROSTAT statistics. The keyword subject index locates the relevant titles whose contents are described in the text. For example, the keyword "Frozen fish" leads to:

- "Family Budget", properly titled as *Family Budgets; Comparative Tables: Germany, France, Italy, United Kingdom* [QRL.203] under "Domestic Expenditure".
- "Consumer Prices in the EC" titled *Consumer Prices in the EC 1980* [QRL.164] and "Yearbook of Agricultural Statistics" which since 1986 is *Agriculture: Statistical Yearbook* [QRL.34] under "Prices", and
- "Analytical Tables of Foreign Trade" now *External Trade Analytical Tables* [QRL.196] under "Trade".

An appendix gives an alphabetical listing of EUROSTAT titles included in the text. No attempt is made to index internal EUROSTAT publications, or statistical publications issued by the Directorate General of the Commission of the European Communities. In its third (1986) edition, the *Eurostat Index* [B.151] covers publications up to December 1985. New serial titles published since the last edition are noted, occasional titles are listed, and serial titles which have ceased publication or changed title since the last edition are recorded.

Given the march of events, with the introduction of new titles as well as the changes in existing ones, no guide can be completely accurate. *Statistics Europe: Sources for Social, Economic and Market Research* [B.75] is another reference. It includes the work of EUROSTAT along with the central statistical offices of many countries, Particularly useful is the alphabetical titles index which refers to a numbered description in the text.

A catalogue and critique of the burgeoning bank of EUROSTAT sources is not in our remit since EUROSTAT is, in general, not an original fount of UK data. But nevertheless, the reader should be aware of these sources, given the importance of the EC. Thus we have provided a wherewithal to locate and update them. The importance of *Eurostat News* [B.262] in this last respect should be emphasised as it provides a service somewhat akin to *Statistical News* [B.381].

We also must mention the catalogues produced by the Office for Official Publications of the European Community itself. The quarterly *Publications of the*

European Communities [B.357] is usefully divided into three parts. Part 1 is the classified list which provides a subject classification of titles under 22 headings, each of which are divided into subheadings. "Statistics" merits a separate heading given the numerous monographs, series and periodicals which are available. Part II presents full details of each current Community periodical, listed alphabetically. Part III gives the indexes of titles and series alphabetically and cross refers to the entries in Part I of the catalogue in which the bibliographic information appears. These indexes cumulate throughout the year. The year-end *Publications of the European Communities* [B.357] cumulates information for the year.

Complementary to [B.357] are the Office of Official Publications of the European Communities *Documents* [B.241] catalogues. These are conceived of as monthly lists which provide a thematic classified index but which are married with cumulative catalogues published every three months and annually. The quarterly and annual catalogues both add to the monthly classified index the alphabetical index comprising keywords based on the Eurovoc thesaurus (i.e. multilingual list of Community terminology) and the numerical index comprising all documents in ascending numerical order. Thus we can have readily at hand details of statistical data and a documentary guide to the many reports of the Commission of the European Communities, the reports of the European Parliament etc. A more compact single source is the annual *The European Community as a Publisher* [B.257] which essentially abridges the information in *Publications of the European Communities* [B.357]. Finally, *British Business* [QRL.66] used to, and *Statistical News* [B.381] does occasionally, review developments in EUROSTAT. They also note how European links have affected UK statistical thinking and methods, to which we now turn.

2.3.3 *The Influence of the Community on the Collection of UK Statistics*

New commitments in the context of the European Community were not the first experience for the UK Government Statistical Service (GSS) of international cooperation, as has been pointed out by Sir Claus A. Moser and I.B. Beesley in "United Kingdom official statistics and the European Communities" [B.132]. GSS links with the United Nations Statistical Commission, with the International Labour Office (ILO), the World Health Organisation (WHO), the Food and Agricultural Organisation (FAO) and other United Nations (UN) bodies, with the International Monetary Fund (IMF) and the Organisation for Economic Cooperation and Development (OECD), and with Commonwealth statisticians predate EEC ties.

Much emphasis at EUROSTAT has been necessarily placed on the basic task of organising the collection of the material from the Member States in such a way that the data can be used for Community purposes. With each new Member State, this task begins afresh. The harmonisation of statistics at the Community level has been a major concern of EUROSTAT from the beginning. However, a clear distinction needs to be made between information which is needed domestically in the United Kingdom, and information which is substantially for Community purposes. Changes of emphasis result because of the establishment and implementation of common policies. For instance, the adoption of a classification scheme, or the specification of a survey, may well be undertaken through instruments of secondary legislation, i.e.

legal obligations of the original treaties creating the Community. Here we should distinguish between EC Regulations and Directives. The former are generally applicable, and are binding in every respect with the direct force of law in every Member State. The latter are binding in the Member State(s), to which they are addressed, as far as the results to be achieved, but delegate the means to the discretion of the national authorities.

The influence of the Community on the collection of UK statistics extends to many of the economic dimensions (e.g. production, labour, trade) separately discussed in this chapter, and also affects the government bodies responsible for the primary collection of the data. The major developments are now summarised, as they relate to the Food industries.

2.3.3.1 Production statistics

Classification schemes are at the heart of statistical collection. Every statistical survey requires the classification of data. Different industrial structures mean many national classifications. The SIC for the United Kingdom (see section 1.2 for further details) provides a framework for classifying business establishments by type of economic activity, and for the collection, tabulation, presentation and analysis of data. It follows the same general principles as the United Nations International Standard Industrial Classification of All Economic Activities (ISIC), but differences occur in detail because the ISIC provides a generalised framework for economic structures across the world as a whole, rather than for those in a particular country.

In the 1980 revision of the SIC — SIC(1980), the attempt was made to align the UK classification as closely as was practicable with the activity classification of EUROSTAT — i.e. with the Nomenclature Général des Activitiés Économiques dans les Communautés Européennes (NACE). NACE is broadly comparable with ISIC, but differs in detail to allow for use by the industrialised economies of Western Europe. A further refinement of NACE is the Common Nomenclature of Industrial Products (NIPRO), which is a classification of industrial products constructed according to the NACE framework. A clear and detailed exposition of NIPRO, and of both NACE and NIMEXE (see section 2.3.3.5), is found in the introduction to the *Common Nomenclature of Industrial Products: NIPRO* [B.229]. Akin to this for the United Kingdom is the considerable detail in the classification list found in *Business Monitor PO1000: Index of Commodities* [B.215]. In fact, a new product classification is being developed alongside the revised NACE, as was reported in the February 1988 issue of *Statistical News* [B.381], although the SIC(1980) itself is primarily an Activity and not strictly a Commodity classification as such. This new scheme is the Central Product Classification for the Communities (CPCCOM), which has the objective of describing the principal products of each of the Activity Headings in such a way that goods can be defined in terms of the Harmonised System (HS) that was introduced for classifying overseas trade in January 1988. Indeed one of the purposes is to render an improved comparability between the overseas trade and the production statistics. Further discussions of classification schemes may be found in Moser and Beesley [B.131], Berman [B.16], Bowditch [B.21] and Collins [B.82], while proposed future changes may be always traced in *Statistical News* [B.381].

The SIC is a formidable structure in itself. Yet it reflects as far as practicable the structure of NACE with voluntary harmonisation as far as possible. Moser and

Beesley [B.131] and Berman [B.16] outlined the major changes envisaged in statistical collection in articles published in our first year of membership. Many of these issues are also summarised in the February 1973 issue of *Statistical News* [B.381]. In fact developments are discussed not only in special articles but also noted in the current developments section of *Statistical News* [B.381].

The legal basis for the collection of general industrial statistics may be found in the following Council Directives:

- Directive no. 64 *475* EEC (30th July 1964) on the annual survey of investment by industrial undertakings
- Directive no. 72 *221* EEC (6th June 1972) on the annual and five yearly surveys on the structure and activity of industrial undertakings
- Directive no. 72 *211* EEC (30th May 1972) on industrial business statistics

These Directives have legal force in member countries, as has been already noted. Previously (up to the the end of 1980) Census of Production returns in the United Kingdom were only required from establishments employing 25 or more persons. But the EC practice is to require units employing 20 or more persons to complete a questionnaire. As noted in section 2.1.1, the UK practice from the beginning of 1981 has been to sample those units with an employment of 20 to 99 etc. The statistical aim is to move towards the requirements of the EC Directive subject to suitable decisions on resource availability.

The EUROSTAT publication *Structure and Activity of Industry: Main Results* [QRL.468] exemplifies the difficulties in collating data forwarded by national authorities in standard NACE form. Although it was possible to realign and reclassify to NACE as far as practicable with the introduction of SIC(1980), more difficulty was encountered with the standardisation of the statistical unit. The statistical unit used in the United Kingdom remained the "establishment" up to the 1987 Census of Production. This was defined as the "smallest unit which can supply the data normally required in an economic inquiry, such as employment, value of purchases, turnover etc." This provided a problem of comparability since the two statistical units used by EUROSTAT are (a) the enterprise, defined as the smallest legally autonomous unit and (b) the Kind of Activity Unit (KAU). Kind of activity units are those enterprises or parts thereof (whether spatially separated or not) that carry on a single activity characterised by the nature of the goods or services produced or by the essential identity of the production process employed.

Thus the results provided by the BSO based on the establishment have appeared in *Structure and Activity of Industry: Main Results* [QRL.468] both under the headings for data by enterprises, and under those containing data by KAU. Information on employment, labour costs, sales, stocks etc. are all brought together. The 18 variables and 8 ratios for enterprises and 4 variables for KAUs are coded at the end of the volume. It is thus necessary, and rather cumbersome, to have to turn to the coding table to ascertain the name of the variable.

Industrial Production: Quarterly Statistics [QRL.274] places the production data for the Activity Headings of the Food industries in the section on non-harmonised statistics, rather than the section on harmonised statistics. Quarterly and annual data are provided for many foodstuffs.

Structure and Activity of Industry: Data by Size of Enterprises [QRL.467] furnish summary size distribution data for NACE 41/42. The components covered are the number of enterprises; the number of persons employed; turnover; gross value added at factor cost.

Structure and Activity of Industry: Data by Regions [QRL.466] provides regional data for NACE 41/42 for the numbers of units; number of persons employed; gross wage and salaries; total of investment.

The closer correspondence dating from the 1987 Census of Production (when the reporting unit was mostly changed from the "establishment" to "businesses" with the aim of a greater company emphasis) will eventually work its way through into the derivative EUROSTAT publications. These changes were also reflected in the PQ Monitors from the first quarter of 1987. More prominence is given to the company unit in determining the coverage of the QSI returns. Under the new arrangements, most returns are completed for a single company but for a limited number of the larger mixed activity companies returns had to remain on the existing establishment basis. These changes are also noted in section 2.3.3.2 which draws on John Perry's article in the August 1985 issue of *Statistical News* [B.142].

A comparison of SIC(1980) and NACE shows a large degree of correspondence between SIC(1980) Class 41/42 "Food, drink and tobacco manufacturing industries" and NACE 41/42 "Food, drink and tobacco". At Group level, there are minor variations in title, as shown below. The one major difference is that there is no heading in SIC(1980) corresponding to NACE 417 "Spaghetti, macaroni and similar products". The degree of correspondence at Activity Heading level (and below) is not so great.

	NACE		SIC(1980)
411	Vegetable and animal oils and fats	411	Organic oils and fats
412	Products of slaughtering, preparation and preserves of meat	412	Slaughtering of animals and production of meat and by-products
413	Dairy products	413	Preparation of milk and milk products
414	Processed and preserved fruit and vegetables	414	Processing of fruit and vegetables
415	Processed or preserved fish and other sea foods, fit for human consumption	415	Fish processing
416	Products of grain milling	416	Grain milling
417	Spaghetti, macaroni and similar products		
418	Starch and starch products	418	Starch
419	Products of bread and flour confectionery	419	Bread, biscuits and flour confectionery
420	Products of sugar manufacture and refining	420	Sugar and sugar by-products
421	Cocoa, chocolate and sugar confectionery products	421	Ice-cream, cocoa, chocolate and sugar confectionery
422	Animal and poultry foods (including fish meat and flour)	422	Animal feeding stuffs
423	Other food products	423	Miscellaneous foods

Finally, *Indexes to the Standard Industrial Classification Revision 1980* [B.317] carries a numerical index which lists each heading of SIC(1980), followed by a list of characteristic activities. A second index arranges these activities in alphabetical order. Alongside each entry are the headings to which the activity is classified in SIC(1968), SIC(1980) and NACE. For example:

Fish fingers (frozen) manufacturing	SIC(1968)	MLH214.2
	SIC(1980)	AH4150.1
	NACE	415.1

2.3.3.2 Value added tax statistics

Value Added Tax (VAT) was imposed under section 1 of the Finance Act 1972, and was introduced on 1 April 1973. It replaced purchase tax and selective employment tax. VAT is a broadly based tax on goods and services supplied in the course of business in the United Kingdom, and on imports of goods. The incentive for the United Kingdom to adopt VAT was closely related to its use by existing EC members — see Horsman [B.83]. The programme of fiscal harmonisation entails the adoption of the same sorts of taxes, even if VAT rates diverge between member countries.

It is a fair assumption that the United Kingdom would not have adopted VAT so readily but for accession to the Community. Thus the introduction of the new tax may certainly be said to be part of any Community influence on the collection of UK statistics. Section 155 of the Finance Act 1973 gave powers to HM Customs and Excise to transfer information about units registered for VAT to the BSO for the purpose of compiling a central register of businesses, and for undertaking any statistical survey. The powers to supply VAT registration number, name, trading style, address, legal status, trade classification and turnover were re-affirmed in the Value Added Tax Act 1983, as noted in "The development of a new register of businesses" [B.142].

Registers are an essential part of the BSO inquiries for the Census of Production, the Quarterly Sales Inquiries, the Purchases Inquiry and the Topping-up Inquiries described in section 2.1.1. It was always anticipated — see Berman [B.16] — that the VAT system would provide additional detailed information, as it embraces all businesses trading in the United Kingdom, with the exception of those with turnovers below a fixed threshold. A source which is regularly and consistently updated is the ideal basis for a central register. Once the VAT-based register had proved its usefulness for the inquiries into the distributive and service trades, the extension to the production industries was considered. The resulting integrated register was created towards the end of 1984. It combines the legal unit (companies, sales proprietors, partnerships, etc.) yielding data from VAT sources, with the local unit information from the earlier production register. The new register has more establishments than the previous production register, and is updated each week with information from HM Customs and Excise covering new registrations, de-registrations, and changes to existing registrations. It is this integrated register which is now used for the annual Census of Production, the Quarterly Sales Inquiries, the Purchases Inquiry and the Inquiry into research and development expenditure.

A direct example of the impact of the integrated register of businesses may be found in the changed coverage for the years from 1985 in *Business Monitor PA1003:*

Size Analyses of United Kingdom Businesses [QRL.96]. Businesses within each Activity Heading and Class are analysed by size of turnover. Data are available for units with employment below 20 persons, and the lowest range of turnover considered is £20,000 to £50,000. The highest range is above £5 million. Data for each Class are also analysed by size of employment and by region and country. A summary of the methodology is given in *Business Monitor PA1003* [QRL.96], and a more extensive description is provided in "The development of a new register of businesses" [B.142].

The integrated register provided the spur which led to enhanced prominence of the company unit in the main BSO production inquiries, which were based upon establishments until the end of 1986 as already explained. This enabled the United Kingdom to get closer to meeting the requirements of the relevant EC Directives concerning statistical units, already mentioned in section 2.3.3.1. Another advantage of this change was that more statistical data would become available at the company level.

The disadvantages of these changes were fully discussed in "The development of a new register of businesses" [B.142]. One of the main difficulties was envisaged as the substantial loss of intra-sales data, i.e. sales between establishments owned by a single company. However, simulation studies showed that these distortions could be reduced to acceptable levels by the retention of establishments as reporting units for some 500 large mixed companies as reported in [B.142] which presaged the actual compromise reached. The compromise involved the retention of establishments as reporting units for these some 500 large mixed companies, and the introduction of the scheme of company reporting for other units. These changes thus partly stemmed from the requirements of the European Community, and partly from the influence of the VAT register. Finally, with regard to additional statistics collected, the annual *Report of the Commissioners of Her Majesty's Customs and Excise* [QRL.408] carries VAT registrations and tax payable for Class 41/42 in the section on manufacturing industries. Statistics on the approximate number of registered persons at 31st March, tax due on imported goods and goods from bonded warehouses, other tax due, tax deductible other than on imported goods and goods from bonded warehouses, and net tax payable or repayable, are separately itemised. As previously noted, VAT was introduced on 1 April 1973 under the provisions of the Finance Act 1972, which also abolished purchase tax after 31st March 1973. Consequently, the annual statistics on the yield of purchase tax ceased after the end of the financial year ending 31st March 1973. As regards the interpretation of the VAT data, it should be noted that food and drink, other than dutiable alcoholic drinks, petfood, ice-cream, chocolate and sugar confectionery products and food and drink supplied in the course of catering, are zero rated.

2.3.3.3 National accounts statistics

National Accounts statistics are published by EUROSTAT for the Community countries in accordance with the European System of Integrated Economic Accounts (ESA). ESA is the Community version of the United Nations' System of National Accounts (SNA). ESA has more detail than SNA since the former is more closely defined in a manner suitable for industrial economies, whereas the SNA must also cater for the economies of less developed countries. The UK system of national accounts is thoroughly described in *United Kingdom National Accounts Statistics: Sources and Methods, Third Edition* [B.395], where it is remarked that the concepts closely follow the recommendations of both the SNA and the ESA. Any changes in concepts and definitions are included as notes in the annual *United Kingdom National Accounts* [QRL.506]. The coverage for the Food industries has already been described in section 2.1.3.

When the ESA was first produced, it was hoped that countries would introduce the ESA definitions into their own national accounts. However, as Moser and Beesley [B.132] remarked, there was a reluctance to abandon the well-established statistical presentation in the UK National Accounts. Moreover, there was a desire to retain continuity with past data. Hence, membership of the EC has meant that the UK authorities now have to recalculate the figures in accordance with ESA definitions after the national data have been compiled. These harmonised data are then forwarded on standardised questionnaire forms 9–12 months after the end of the year.

In the ESA, the economy is broken down in different ways for different purposes. For the detailed analyses of the production and use of goods and services, the economy is split into "branches" which are groups of units of homogeneous production each engaged in a single activity. The data are stored in the time series data base CRONOS, which is available for consultation via EURONET. Statistics are also published in the EUROSTAT series "National Accounts ESA" in five parts, viz: aggregates; detailed tables by branch; detailed tables by sector; general government accounts and statistics; and input-output tables.

National Accounts ESA: Detailed Tables by Branch [QRL.370] gives international comparisons of various national accounts components in the structural tables based on purchasing power parity. Further national data include gross value added at market prices, share of employee compensation, yearly change of value added per head, and gross fixed capital formation. All are given by the branch of " Food, beverages and tobacco." In addition, data are presented of the final consumption of a range of foodstuffs e.g. bread and cereals, meat, fish etc.

National data converted at market exchange rates do not give a true comparison of the actual volume of goods and services produced in different countries. To adjust for price differences, purchasing power parities are calculated based on harmonised price surveys covering consumption and gross fixed capital formation in the Member States. For example, the data for 1986 yield a set of parities (or relative price levels) for the countries at differing aggregate levels of expenditure — e.g. total consumption, consumption of food, consumption of bread etc. Using these parities, extrapolated back to earlier years with national accounts price indices, better comparisons between countries have been obtained. These are published in successive issues of *National Accounts ESA: Aggregates* [QRL.369], for long time series (e.g. 1960–1985), and are treated in *National Accounts ESA: Detailed Tables by Branch* [QRL.370]. The basic criteria governing the selection of the approx 2500 products in the sample are discussed at length in the *Introductory Course* [B.322].

Another example of the influence of the Community is the requirement for data for input-output tables, harmonised in accordance with the ESA. EUROSTAT assembles the input-output tables in 44 branches, and distinguishes domestically produced goods from imports. These tables are published for every fifth year (1970, 1975, 1980 and 1985) in *National Accounts ESA: Input-output Tables* [QRL.371]. These sources are of limited use, however, as the tables only cover the 44 branches of economic activity defined in NACE/CLIO, and the figures are published after a long time lag. CLIO is the acronym for Conversational Language for Input-output. The 1980 edition of *National Accounts ESA: Input-output Tables* [QRL.371] was published in 1986. The tables simply contain a harmonised, but more aggregate, treatment of the 1979 data available in *Business Monitor PA1004: Input-output Tables for the United Kingdom 1979* [QRL.101] published in 1983. The input-output tables are available on magnetic tape, or computer print-out, on request from EUROSTAT.

2.3.3.4 Labour statistics

As early as 1960, EUROSTAT organised the first Community labour force survey in the six original Member States. Annual surveys were subsequently carried out in most countries in the years 1968 to 1971. Since then, a biennial programme was established with surveys in 1973, 1975, 1977, 1979 and 1981. The more recent intention, given the higher levels of unemployment in the 1980s, has been to hold a survey every year. Results have been published annually from 1983.

Although the three new members of the Community were not required to take part in the 1973 survey, the United Kingdom did so. EUROSTAT is responsible for the contents of the survey, the size of the sample, the compilation of the list of questions, and the implementation of the system of common coding. In the United Kingdom, the *Labour Force Survey* [QRL.309] is conducted by the Office of Population Censuses and Surveys (OPCS), the General Register Office for Scotland, and the Department of Economic Development in Northern Ireland, on behalf of the Department of Employment and the European Community.

It should be noted that other questions, not required by the EC, are included in the UK surveys in order to obtain information about topics of pertinent interest to government departments. As noted in section 2.6, coverage varies over time, and the estimates for various Classes and Activity Headings are often available only on application to the Department of Employment. The emphasis is more on occupation, employment status, unemployment, job mobility etc. The background and methodology are explained in the introduction to the *Labour Force Survey* [QRL.309]. The EUROSTAT publication, *Labour Force Sample Survey: Methods and Definitions* [B.324] outlines the main methodological characteristics. Subsequent changes are noted in *Labour Force Survey: Results* [QRL.310] since, in addition to the standard questions, the opportunity is usually taken to add supplementary questions of current concern. Membership of the EC from 1973 had the effect that data for Great Britain was combined with that for Northern Ireland to give UK coverage. It did not preclude the UK initiative of undertaking an annual survey since 1984.

The first comprehensive survey of labour costs in Great Britain was carried out by the Department of Employment and Productivity in 1964, and was published in *Labour Costs in Great Britain in 1964* [QRL.307]. This early survey gave detailed analyses by industry (grain milling etc.) and by category of labour costs. Results for a later survey by the Department of Employment were published in *Labour Costs in Great Britain 1968* [QRL.306], when a parallel survey was carried out for Northern Ireland.

The results for the third comprehensive survey in 1973 appeared in the September 1975 issue of the *Employment Gazette* [QRL.186], where it was noted that this survey was carried out at the request of the EC. The questionnaire was based on the EC model, and the United Kingdom has since participated in the triennial EC surveys carried out for 1975, 1978, 1981 and 1984. The 1975 results are available in the four EUROSTAT volumes of *Labour Costs in Industry 1972–1975* [QRL.308]. Subsequent results are to be found in the two volume triennial *Labour Costs* [QRL.305].

It must be stressed that in the EUROSTAT publications, as distinct from the *Employment Gazette* [QRL.186] that data for Great Britain are amalgamated with the parallel survey for Northern Ireland to provide estimates for the United Kingdom as a whole. The most recent survey at the time of writing is for 1988. As the Labour Costs Survey has now become quadrennial, the most recent results published in *Labour Costs* [QRL.305] are for 1988. The next survey is planned for 1992. Labour costs are also discussed in section 2.6.11.

Methods and definitions were discussed in Volume 1 of *Labour Costs in Industry 1972–1975* [QRL.308] and the survey questionaire used was shown in an appendix. Explanations are also given in Volume 1 of *Labour Costs* [QRL.305]. Both volumes of [QRL.305] carry a host of tables and the contents draw attention to the further tables carried on the microfiche *Labour Costs* [QRL.304] as for instance for 1981. The considerable coverage of wages and salary expenditures and related employers' costs, composition of employees, hours worked, numbers of employees etc., compiled according to NACE, enables country comparisons to be attempted. This more recent microfiche format enables more tables to be published. It must be remembered, for purposes of comparison, that UK data relate to the financial year, not the calendar year and that the data are expressed in European Units of Account (EUA), now European Currency Units (ECU).

2.3.3.5 International trade statistics

Membership of the European Community has had a profound effect not only on UK trade but also on the scope and methodology of the collection of UK trade statistics.

(Virtually) all tariffs on trade between the United Kingdom and the other Member States of the Community were abolished on 1st July 1977 when the United Kingdom adopted the final stage of the common external tariff on trade with non-Community countries. Thereafter, the United Kingdom, along with the other EC members, has operated a common tariff on imports from non-members, while trade between the member countries has been free of customs duties. The rates of duty were initially specified with reference to the Common Customs Tariff (CCT), managed by the Administration of the Customs Union of the European Commission. The CCT has been amended to a minor degree each year, and these amendments were published in the *Official Journal of the European Communities* [B.341] towards the end of each year, with the changes becoming effective from the beginning of the following year. Groupings in the CCT were usually based on the material from which the goods were made. The commodity detail was based principally on the Customs

Cooperation Council Nomenclature (CCCN), formerly known as the Brussels Tariff Nomenclature (BTN). The CCT included the 4-digit main headings of the CCCN, and also duty/levy subheadings.

With the Council Regulation on the CCT, adopted on 28th June 1968, and the Regulation on the nomenclature of goods for external trade statistics, adopted on 24th April 1972, the Community and its Member States had been using two compatible but distinct product nomenclatures for the separate purposes of tariffs and statistics. The statistical nomenclature NIMEXE — the Nomenclature of Goods for the External Trade Statistics of the European Community — was used by EUROSTAT for the classification of statistics in its various compendiums — see section 2.8.2.5. Each NIMEXE heading corresponded either to a heading of the CCCN, or to a subheading of the CCT nomenclature, and had a code number made up of six digits. Of these, the first four were those of the CCCN heading, and the last two identified the NIMEXE item. For example:

Grapefruit, fresh or dried NIMEXE code 08.02–70

Amendments to NIMEXE were published annually in the *Official Journal of the European Communities* [B.341].

On 1st January 1988, a single nomenclature of goods, known as the Combined Nomenclature (CN) of the European Community, replaced both the CCT and NIMEXE. The CN is based on the Harmonised Commodity Description and Coding System, or Harmonised System (HS) for short, which is an internationally agreed system of goods classification for Customs, freight and commercial use as well as for statistical purposes — see section 2.8.1.1. The HS is broadly comparable with the CCCN which formed the basis of NIMEXE, but it is more detailed and up-to-date both in structure and content. As well as the European Commission and its Member States, other major trading nations (including the United States and Canada) are adopting the HS. Eventually it is intended to be used worldwide and will enable comparisons of international trade statistics to be made more easily.

In the United Kingdom, a single integrated classification — the HM Customs and Excise Tariff and Overseas Trade Classification — had been in existence since 1st January 1970 both for Duty purposes and for export and import statistics. The Tariff was based principally on the CCCN, and contained some 9000 commodity descriptions, each uniquely identified by an 8-digit code number: the first four digits indicated the chapter and main heading of the Tariff; the 5th and 6th digits indicated the heading of NIMEXE to which it correlated; and the 7th and 8th digits were reserved for national statistical subdivisions. For example,

Grapefruit, fresh or dried	Tariff code	0802 7000
	NIMEXE code	08.02–70
	SITC(R2) heading	057.22

The full text of each description was published in the annual *Guide to the Classification for Overseas Trade Statistics* [B.213], together with the corresponding heading in the Standard International Trade Classification (SITC) — see section 2.8.1.2 for further details. The SITC(R2) provided headings which corresponded directly with those of the CCCN; the order in which the articles were grouped differed, however, between the two classifications. Whereas the CCCN grouped all products obtained from the same substance and pertaining to the same industries, the SITC draws a distinction between raw materials, semi-manufactured goods, and finished articles.

The adoption of the CN has led to the replacement of the 8-digit Tariff code with a new 9-digit Commodity code number. The former 4-digit CCCN heading has been updated by the HS, and gives a higher degree of detail at the 6-digit level. Many of the CCT duty subheadings are subsumed by the HS. The next two digits (7 and 8) identify the CN subheadings, wherein many national subdivisions are subsumed at EC level. Member States were encouraged to reduce the number of their remaining national subdivisions (from two digits to one), and these are now recorded as the 9th digit. This "national code" takes the value of zero for imports from third countries.

In addition, two further digits (10 and 11) are often added. These denote the subheadings of the Integrated Tariff of the European Communities (TARIC), and are used to indicate tariff-related measures such as duty suspensions and quotas for all imports from non-EC members, and for some trade with accessionary Member States. The TARIC subheadings are set equal to zero for exports, and for all intra-EC trade. Exceptionally, an additional TARIC code of four digits may be used for the application of specific Community measures which are not coded, or not entirely coded, in the 10th and 11th digits. The basic formats of the 8-digit Tariff code (to 1987), and the 9-digit Commodity code (from 1988) are shown below:

	8-digit Tariff code (to 1987)		*9-digit Commodity code* (from 1988)
Digit		Digit	
1+2	CCCN chapter	1+2	HS chapter
3+4	CCCN heading	3+4	HS main heading
		5+6	HS structured heading
5+6	NIMEXE heading	7+8	CN subheading
7+8	National subdivision	9	National subdivision
		10+11	TARIC subheading

The CN thus brings together the duty and statistical nomenclatures of the Community. Just as the CCT and NIMEXE were based on the CCCN, so the CN is based on the HS. Statistics users will find the full list of Council and Commission Regulations, constituting the body of Community statistical legislation on international trade, in the third edition of the EUROSTAT *External Trade Statistics: User's Guide* [B.267], published in 1988.

It should be noted that considerable divergences have arisen at subheading level between the CN and the formerly used NIMEXE, giving rise to a break in the goods-related time series between 1987 and 1988. Up to December 1987, EUROSTAT publications used SITC(R2), which was worked out using the 6-digit NIMEXE, while from January 1988, they use SITC(R3), which has been drawn up using the 8-digit subheadings of the CN. The headings of SITC(R3) correspond directly with those of the CN, except that the order in which the articles are grouped differs between the two classifications. For example:

Grapefruit, fresh or dried	SITC(R3) heading	057.22
	Commodity code	080540 00 0

As an aid to the interpretation of the statistics, EUROSTAT have published *External Trade Nomenclature of Goods, Correlation Tables NIMEXE 1988 to CN 1987* [B.266].

Moreover, the 1988 edition of the *Guide to the Classification of Overseas Trade Statistics: Correlation Tables* [B.299] provides correlations between SITC(R2) and SITC(R3), and also gives guidance on the relationships between the SITCs and the more detailed commodity codes. Detailed descriptions of each commodity heading in HS, and notes on each Chapter, are provided in the four volumes of *Harmonized Commodity Description and Coding System: Explanatory Notes* [B.301].

The drive behind the introduction by the Community of the HS and TARIC was the requirement that all imported and exported goods should be declared on the Single Administrative Document (SAD). Overall, the SAD has replaced approximately 100 import, export and Community Transit forms in the Member States. A very thorough publicity and education campaign was mounted in the United Kingdom with the aim of ensuring that declarants were as fully conversant with the changes as possible. Many trade sectors also held their own seminars which were supported by Customs representation. It was claimed that few problems were encountered in understanding the new procedures and codes, and HM Customs and Excise regard the project as a success. Although some errors have inevitably arisen, these were no worse than were anticipated beforehand.

Accession to the Community has had other effects, apart from those of classification, on UK trade statistics. Special customs export and import procedures are operated under the Common Agricultural Policy (CAP). Under EEC Regulations, agricultural levies are chargeable on a wide range of basic and processed agricultural products imported from non-EC sources. The European Communities Act 1972 provided for these levies to be collected as though they were customs duties, and applied to them the legal provisions relating to customs generally. HM Customs and Excise collect most of the duties and levies, and share the management of CAP work with the Intervention Board for Agricultural Produce (IBAP). HM Customs and Excise apply the physical and documentary controls at import and export, and are responsible for collecting agricultural levies and other charges (e.g. Monetary Compensation Amounts) at import. IBAP collects charges due at export and looks after any payments returned to traders.

The yearly *Report of the Commissioners of Her Majesty's Customs and Excise* [QRL.408] provides data and information which differ with respect to the year in question. For instance, the 78th Report provides an analysis of imports of "food and live animals" (SITC(R2) Section 0) from the EC and from the whole world in 1986, showing dutiable status and duty charged. The geographical detail used to be greater up to the 71st Report for the year ended 31st March 1980. Analyses were provided of imports of goods:

- from the whole world
- originating in the EC; and EFTA
- originating in the Commonwealth; and the rest of the world
- originating in the Generalised System of Preference countries; the African, Caribbean and Pacific States and Overseas Countries or Territories; and the Mediterranean agreement countries

Moreover, up to the 72nd Report for the year ended 31st March 1981, customs duty receipts used to be analysed by Tariff chapter. Moreover, in recent years, [QRL.408] has reflected the preoccupation with such matters as the economic background, detention and search statistics etc. on top of the usual statistics of taxes and duties. The analysis of imports of "food and live animals" is no longer a feature.

Member States' influence on the EC is exercised by participation in the Community's meetings, which are convened under the auspices of the European Commission. UK delegates from HM Customs and Excise and the DTI attend meetings of the Committee on External Trade Statistics, and the Combined Nomenclature Committee (CNC), in Luxembourg. Meetings of the former committee deal principally with statistical methodology; that is; policy for the collection, compilation and transmission of trade statistics in the Community. At the CNC, Commission proposals and any generated by Member States are tabled, discussed and voted upon. The UK delegates' line on any topic is influenced by the consensus views of interested government departments and the UK trade, who are consulted as appropriate.

The requirements and methods of collection of intra-Community trade statistics after 1992 have been continually addressed since 1988/89. Discussion centres on the removal of frontier controls between the Member States, and consequently on the need for alternative arrangements for collecting trade statistics. Possible solutions include a link with the VAT system for the collection of statistics, statistical surveys, or a combination of the two methods. The current Customs entry system will be maintained for the purposes of external trade.

2.3.3.6 Statistics on intervention prices and stocks

The Common Agricultural Policy (CAP) is a complex arrangement, which differs in many ways from previous UK agricultural policy. Its significance is such that it takes around two thirds of the Community budget. A substantial number of Community Regulations are concerned with agriculture and fisheries. Much agricultural activity, and part of the food processing industry, now works within the framework of detailed legislation from the European Community.

In section 2.3.1, we noted the many price support mechanisms which operate on first stage food processors. We emphasise here that a direct and major statistical consequence is the collection and publication of the wide range of data contained in the *Intervention Board for Agricultural Produce: Annual Report* [QRL.293]. The very accession of the UK to the Community made it necessary to set up the Board, which became operational on 1st February 1973 when the CAP came into effect within the United Kingdom. The annual reports, from 1973 to present, furnish a range of statistics on intervention prices and other aspects of agricultural support payments.

A simplified picture is that, under the previous deficiency payments system, the UK imported and consumed foodstuffs at world prices, and subsidised UK farmers out of general taxation. Under the CAP, the pivot of the system is the range of target prices, which are fixed annually. If the market price does not reach this target (if there is an excess of supply over demand), an intervention price is set at a guaranteed minimum to buy any surplus into intervention store. To prevent imports undermining internal Community prices, a threshold price is set at a level such that the imported commodity will sell at around the target price after transport costs have been taken into account. An import levy is then charged on the importers' price in order to bring it up to the threshold price. Conversely, for exports, if there is a surplus in the Community, an export refund may be made to Community producers so that they can sell their produce at the lower prices prevailing in world markets.

A selection of textbooks summarise these major features: for example, Marsh and Swanney [B.110], Fennell [B.52], Harris, Swinbank and Wilkinson [B.71], and Swann

[B.170]. It is worth stressing, however, that the description in the previous paragraph is a very simplified picture. Practices vary over time and according to commodity. Hence the *CAP Monitor* [B.220] should be noted as it provides a comprehensive picture of the regime for each commodity. It gives practical and up-to-date details of how and when the various prices and aids are calculated, with reference to the Regulations which govern each aspect of the regime. Each commodity section is usefully updated by loose-leaf amendments as significant changes occur. *The Agricultural Situation in the Community* [QRL.28] provides a statistically backed summary of the year in question, with a comprehensive review of the situation in the many agricultural markets.

The influence of EC membership on the collection of statistics is discussed in the chapters on individual industries, but the broad coverage of the *Intervention Board: Annual Report* [QRL.293] may be summarised here. The statistical tables have changed over the years from 1973 to present as support systems have been modified, but UK intervention prices have usually been published for cereals; milk products; beef; and oilseed rape. Thus [QRL.293] is an additional source of price and other information for these Food industries.

The analysis of UK expenditure born by the European Agricultural Guidance and Guarantee Fund in the 1986 *Report of the Intervention Board* [QRL.293] included the following major areas; cereals; dehydrated fodder; peas, field beans, sweet lupins; rice; milk and milk products; oils and fats; sugar; beef and veal; pigmeat; sheepmeat; eggs; poultry; fish; fruit and vegetables; wine; seeds; flax; hops; bee keeping; and processed goods not included in Annex II of the Treaty of Rome. The summary of expenditure born by the UK Exchequer showed the importance of intervention buying notably for cereals; skimmed milk powder; butter; and beef.

Indeed the *Report of the Intervention Board* [QRL.293] publishes more than just data on prices and financial costs. Information is also presented on quantities denatured (e.g. wheat and skimmed milk) and, from the outset, on stocks (e.g. intervention buying of butter). Moreover, the Board issues guides to trading regimes both in general and for particular commodities in a series of "External market" leaflets.

2.3.3.7 Supply balance sheets

The variety of supply balance sheets prepared for most basic agricultural products and for some important processed products (e.g. wheat flour and starch) is described in section 2.11. We note here that supply balance sheets have been constructed by MAFF for many years, but that EUROSTAT now issues standardised balance sheet questionnaires to all Member States for completion on the basis of methodology agreed by the *ad hoc* Working Group of the Agricultural Statistics Committee — see Slater [B.164]. The results are published in *Agriculture: Statistical Yearbook* [QRL.34]. These EUROSTAT tables may be compared with the tables published in the *Annual Review of Agriculture* [QRL.51]. Results for the sectors of interest are also published by EUROSTAT in *Crop Production* [QRL.167] and in *Animal Production* [QRL.36].

2.3.3.8 Product balance sheets

In 1986, EUROSTAT began work on arrangements to collect statistics on the processing of agricultural produce, especially in the agro-food industries. The objective is to trace the processing chain for each product, or group of products, in both quantity and value terms. These chains will be accompanied by product balance sheets. Input-output tables will eventually be drawn up, and statistics compiled, on the technical production structure and regional distribution. The aim is to complement the information provided by industrial statistics.

2.3.3.9 Comments

The major statistical influence of the European Community has been the demand for harmonised data. EUROSTAT provides a range of statistical sources which enable economic comparisons to be made, and which provide background information for policy deliberations. In some instances, Member States now have to prepare two sets of statistics (e.g. for the national accounts statistics).

There are also areas where the Community has had a more direct influence on UK statistical activities. One example of this is the work of the Intervention Board for Agricultural Produce. Another is the impetus to collect data for the United Kingdom as a whole (e.g. the Labour Force Survey), and for the calendar rather than the financial year. In addition, it can be claimed that the introduction of VAT has both inspired more statistical activity, and in some instances extended the coverage of industrial statistics to smaller units. The impact of revised classification schemes on both industrial statistics, and external trade statistics, must also be emphasised. These schemes have been complicated because EC requirements must be married to UN developments with ISIC and SITC. The influence of the Community on the scope and methodology of UK statistics may not have been dramatic, but the overall effect is cumulative. For example, the supply balance sheets (see section 2.3.3.7) will reflect the HS (Harmonised system) in the treatment of exports and imports.

However, this is not to conclude that the future impact of EC membership will not be very significant. An extreme view is that the formation of the single market in 1992 reduces the need for much intra-EC trade data. Indeed, Mr. Francis Maude, when Secretary of State for Corporate Affairs, likened the EC, after the formation of the single market, to the United States of America and questioned the need for intra-EC trade data at the Statistics Users' Conference (SUC). The proceedings of this 1988 conference on UK International Trade Statistics are summarised in the February 1989 issue of *Statistical News* [B.381]. This extreme extension of the Rayner Doctrine "that the Government should not be responsible for the provision of statistics for private sector use" would indeed affect the coverage of the *Business Monitor MM20: Overseas Trade Statistics of the United Kingdom* [QRL.85] if implemented. So, perhaps in the light of this non-interventionist attitude, a significant effect of our EC membership may be that statistical coverage will be retained because of the EC requirements. So it could well be that we will in the end "be saved by EUROSTAT!".

The organisational structure of the European Commissions' Statistical System (ECSS) is described by Clarke [B.36]. In addition, he remarks, contrary to Rayner, that the information collected is regarded as a public good when private users will generally be required to pay at most the marginal costs of making the information available in the required form.

The spirit of the Treaty of Rome is to lay the foundations of an ever closer union among the peoples of Europe. It is envisaged that the streamlining and coordination of statistical activities within the Member States will facilitate the process of integration at Community level. The daily contribution of EUROSTAT is the long-term task of helping the national statistical systems to move closer to each other. But, as noted in "Life with Eurostat: a personal view" [B.36], harmonisation, interactive classifications and the rapid international exchange of statistical data are at present the most prominent effects.

2.4 Output

Many different agencies publish data on the output of the Food industries. Moreover, the measures of output they produce tend to be different. This section thus describes the measures used in the various BSO and MAFF inquiries, and the approach adopted in the National Accounts statistics. In addition, we detail the various indicators of output for the regions of the United Kingdom.

2.4.1 *Output, Sales and Value Added*

2.4.1.1 Business Statistics Office inquiries

The collection of data on output is an important part of the extensive work of the Business Statistics Office (BSO), as has already been outlined in section 2.1.1. The annual Business Monitor for the industry Groups, and *Business Monitor PA1002: Summary Volume* [QRL.93] provide four major output measures viz: total sales and work done; gross output; net output; and gross value added at factor cost. Total sales and work done covers more than the sales of goods produced as it includes amounts charged for other work carried out. Gross output is the adjustment of total sales and work done by the change during the year of work-in-progress and goods on hand for sale. Net output is the traditional census measure arrived at by deducting the cost of purchase of materials etc. from the gross output figure. Gross value added at factor cost is calculated by deducting from net output the cost of non-industrial services received, rates and the cost of motor vehicles. Gross value added at factor cost thus is the closest to the value added concept in National Accounts statistics.

The annual Monitors for each industry Group provide data on the four measures of output for the latest five years. All four components are also analysed by employment size for all UK businesses classified to the industry. In addition, there is the regional analysis of net output and gross output at factor cost. These figures are expressed in money terms for the standard regions and the countries of the United Kingdom and Great Britain plus a measure of their percentage contribution to the UK global total. An example of this typical coverage is found in *Business Monitor PA415: Fish Processing* [QRL.109].

Business Monitor PA1002 [QRL.93] provides data on these output measures for the latest five years by Group and usually contains other details as follows. In the

1986 Summary Volume establishment analyses, these components were detailed according to employment size. The net output and gross value added at factor cost measures were presented for the standard regions for Class 41/42. The enterprise analyses gave the four measures cross-classified for employment size.

The quarterly Monitors give information on commodity sales (in value and, when appropriate, quantities) and production in volume terms up to Autumn 1989. For example, *Business Monitor PQ4150: Fish Products* [QRL.134] provides sales data for a variety of fish products for the latest five quarters, and most recent two years, and production figures of certain fish products by UK manufacturers under various sub-headings over the same periods. It is worth noting here that the availability of physical production data compares well with the non food industries. However the coverage is not uniform across Groups and is supplemented for some by the Topping-up Inquiry (see section 2.1.1.3).

Past data on these output measures may be found in previous issues of the relevant Business Monitors. Alternatively, as has been described in section 2.1.1.6, and rather more easily, the *Historical Record of the Census of Production* [QRL.264] provides data on net output for various industries back to 1907 and up to 1970.

2.4.1.2 Ministry of Agriculture, Fisheries and Food inquiries

The basic data collected by the Ministry (MAFF) covers much of both the Agricultural and Food industries. These embrace many parts of the food chain as efficiently described by Barnett [B.12] and Slater [B.164]. MAFF provides many statistics relevant to this volume; ranging from processed output, which is the concern of this section, to supply balance sheets, consumption, stocks, disposals and current inputs both of agricultural commodities and first-processed products. The coverage is summarised in Appendix C from Slater [B.164] and cuts across several industries. Data on supplies from the UK food processing and manufacturing industry came from many short period MAFF inquiries up to 1979. Since the *Review of Government Statistical Services: Report to the Prime Minister* [B.368] by Sir Derek Rayner in December 1980, the aim has been to reduce the number of short-period inquiries such that a given industry would be covered by either the BSO, by MAFF, or by a trade association (such as the Biscuit, Cake, Chocolate and Confectionery Alliance). Barnett [B.12] describes the various series and collecting agencies, and these are further discussed in the relevant industry chapters. But it is to be noted here that some processed outputs — e.g. organic oils produced, animals slaughtered, volume of grain milled — are inputs for secondary processing. Other surveys catalogue the output of final products — e.g. coffee production, fruit and vegetable canning and bottling, sales by value and volume of chocolate and sugar confectionery.

Slater [B.164] and Barnett [B.12] both summarise the picture in 1986. The earlier MAFF guide to *Agricultural and Food Statistics* [B.197] codified the title, frequency and publication phase of the inquiries which existed in 1974 as well as other statistical information. An earlier publication in this series by W.D. Stedman Jones on *Food Statistics* [B.167] traces the genesis of many of these inquiries which were widened in World War II to monitor the overall food position of the nation.

Much of the current information is published in MAFF Statistical Notices. Both the *Annual Abstract of Statistics* [QRL.37] and the *Monthly Digest of Statistics*

[QRL.362] give details for many foods using data from MAFF sources. The *Annual Abstract of Statistics* [QRL.37] contains a table entitled "Processed food and animal feeding stuffs: production" which details the physical output for the UK for the latest eleven years of a wide range of foods. The following is a selection of the activities covered: flour milling; oat milling; seed crushing; production of home-killed meat; production of poultry meat; production of bacon and ham; production of milk products; production of sugar from home-grown sugar-beet; production of compound fats; and production of other processed foods (e.g. jam and marmalade; soups; breakfast cereals; sugar confectionery; chocolate confectionery). The MAFF inquiries are more wide-ranging than this summary list, and yield data on many food products through the various stages of production and processing. Further details are provided in the specialist chapters. Some data are reproduced in the *Monthly Digest of Statistics* [QRL.362], usually giving monthly averages in physical terms for up to the latest sixteen months and last seven years. The main groups covered are: cereals; sugar; jams; meats; fish; milk etc.; canned fruit; vegetables and soups; cocoa; chocolate; tea; coffee etc. Both the *Annual Abstract of Statistics* [QRL.37] and the *Monthly Digest of Statistics* [QRL.362] summarise statistics on physical outputs from otherwise widely dispersed and specialised sources.

2.4.1.3 The national accounts

The *United Kingdom National Accounts* [QRL.506] provide estimates of gross domestic product (GDP) in current prices for the "Food" industry (Groups 411–423 inclusive). Data are provided for the latest eleven years. They refer to the contribution of the industry to GDP before depreciation, but after providing for stock appreciation. The estimates are derived from data on gross value added from the BSO Census of Production. The methodology is thoroughly discussed in *United Kingdom National Accounts: Sources and Methods, Third Edition* [B.395], published in 1985. The reliability of the estimates is determined by the reliability of the basic data from the annual censuses of production, and are liable to the conceptual limitations noted in [B.395]. Nevertheless, the GDP estimates are stated to be correct within a margin of plus or minus three per cent.

2.4.2 *Index Numbers of Output*

The *United Kingdom National Accounts* [QRL.506] provide an output-based measure of gross domestic product (GDP) in the "Food" industry (Groups 411–423 inclusive) at constant factor cost. Index numbers are provided for the latest eleven years. Prior to the 1987 edition, data were only available for "Food, drink and tobacco" in aggregate — and this heading excluded grain milling, starch, compound animal feeds, and processing organic oils and fats, which were classified as intermediate rather than consumer goods.

Detailed discussion of the methodology adopted in the construction of this series may be found in chapter 5 of *United Kingdom National Accounts: Sources and Methods, Third Edition* [B.395]. The index is a base-weighted (Laspeyres) index compiled by the CSO as the weighted mean of 329 component series, each representing the output of an individual industry or part of an industry. In most cases these component series are built up from some 700 activity indicators, each derived by other government departments. They form part of the annual index of output, but also provide valuable information about trends in the different industries. To combine the individual production series, each industry has been given a weight proportional to the distribution of net output in 1980, as derived from the 1980 Census of Production.

The general methodology of the construction of index numbers is explained in many good statistics textbooks. However, the relative performance of each industry changes over time, and hence there are periodic reviews of the weights used in the construction of the series. Since September 1983, the index of output has been based on 1980 weights. Its construction is explained by J.A. Perry in "The rebased estimate of the index of the output of the production industries" [B.141]. Perry describes the effect of rebasing index numbers, and contrasts the weights of, and movements in, the 1980-based and 1975-based indices of production for the "Food" industry (Groups 411–423 inclusive). The commodity indicators used in the calculation of the index are continually under review. The CSO publishes a stream of information. Three useful references are:

- *Series and Weights Used in the Index of Output of the Production Industries — 1980 Base* [B.372], published in 1983.
- *Series and Weights Used in the Output-based Estimates of Gross Domestic Product at Factor Cost (1980=100)* [B.373], published in 1984.
- *Supplementary Analysis of Series Used in the Index of the Output of the Production Industries — 1980 Base* [B.385], published in 1984.

Mention should also be made of successive CSO publications:

- *The Index of Industrial Production* [B.315], published in 1952.
- *The Index of Industrial Production: Method of Compilation* [B.314], published in 1959.
- *The Index of Industrial Production and Other Output Measures* [B.316], published in 1970.
- *The Measurement of Changes in Production. The Index of Industrial Production and the Output-based Measures of Gross Domestic Product* [B.330], published in 1976.

The *Monthly Digest of Statistics* [QRL.362] provides estimates of the index of output for the "Food" industry as well as for "Food, drink and tobacco". Seasonally adjusted data are provided for the latest twenty months, and twenty four quarters. Unadjusted data may be obtained direct from the CSO. The seasonally adjusted data were also reproduced in *British Business* [QRL.66]. Further detail for the various Activity Headings within the Food industries may be found in the respective quarterly Business Monitors in the PQ series — see section 2.1.1.2 for details.

Finally, the *Annual Abstract of Statistics* [QRL.37] furnishes two series of index numbers on output. First, it gives index numbers of output in the "Food" industry at constant factor cost for the latest eleven years. Second, it provides selected component indices which are used to derive the aggregate index of output. Data for the past eleven years are provided for Groups 413, 419, 421, 422 and 423 individually — these are reproduced from the appropriate Business Monitors in the PQ series up to late 1989.

2.4.3 *Regional Coverage*

It is important to clarify in this section the whole approach to regional coverage of statistics. We thus give below the definitions of the standard regions which now apply, reproduced from the 1987 version of *Business Monitor PA1001* [B.214].

South East: Greater London, Bedfordshire, Berkshire, Buckinghamshire, East Sussex, Essex, Hampshire, Hertfordshire, Isle of Wight, Kent, Oxfordshire, Surrey, West Sussex.

East Anglia: Cambridgeshire, Norfolk, Suffolk.

South West: Avon, Cornwall, Devon, Dorset, Gloucestershire, Somerset, Wiltshire.

West Midlands: West Midlands*, Hereford and Worcester, Shropshire, Staffordshire, Warwickshire.

East Midlands: Derbyshire, Leicestershire, Lincolnshire, Northamptonshire, Nottinghamshire.

Yorkshire and Humberside: South Yorkshire*, West Yorkshire*, Humberside, North Yorkshire.

North West: Greater Manchester*, Merseyside*, Cheshire, Lancashire.

North: Tyne and Wear*, Cleveland, Cumbria, Durham, Northumberland.

Wales: Clwyd, Dyfed, Gwent, Gwynedd, Mid Glamorgan, Powys, South Glamorgan, West Glamorgan.

Scotland: Borders, Central, Dumfries and Galloway, Fife, Grampian, Highland, Lothian, Strathclyde, Tayside and the Orkney Islands, Shetland Islands and the Western Isles.

Northern Ireland: Antrim, Armagh, Belfast CB, Down, Fermanagh, Londonderry, Londonderry CB, Tyrone.

* = metropolitan counties.

The standard regions of England are typically covered in the PA Business Monitors and the summary tables of *Business Monitor PA1002* [QRL.93]. The global results in the PQ Business Monitors refer to the United Kingdom in entirety. The typical coverage in the PA Business Monitors is to give results for the standard regions of England and then a total for England. Separate tables for Wales and Scotland are given before a figure for Great Britain is arrived at. When the figure for Northern Ireland is added in, then the global total for the United Kingdom is arrived at.

Even though the BSO coordinates, and indeed supervises, the collection of data, specific publications are obviously angled to cover the individual countries of the United Kingdom. We now summarise some of the major collections. The proud Englishman may be surprised that these do not yet include any *English Abstract of Statistics!*

As explained in section 2.1.2, the Northern Ireland census is now aligned with that carried out for the United Kingdom by the BSO. The *Report on the Census of Production and Construction in Northern Ireland* [QRL.419] currently reports data on total sales and work done, gross output, net output and gross value added at factor cost plus net output per head and gross value added at factor cost per head for Class 41/42 in aggregate. More disaggregated data, as outlined in section 2.1.2, are also provided in both the current, and earlier, censuses.

The *Northern Ireland Annual Abstract of Statistics* [QRL.377] provides an index of production for the "Food" industry (Groups 411–423 inclusive) in Northern Ireland.

Annual data are given for the most recent eight years, and six quarters, all seasonally adjusted. Much of the information used in the compilation of the index relates to sales rather than production during the period. Normally this will not affect interpretation, but where sales are drawn from stocks of finished goods as well as production, some distortions may result. Adjustments are made for the closure of manufacturing units and the opening of new manufacturing units.

The earlier biannual publication, *Digest of Statistics: Northern Ireland* [QRL.176] provided an index of production for SIC(1968) Order III "Food, drink and tobacco". Quarterly data were given for the latest twenty four quarters — the statistics were averages of the monthly figures — and lengthy annual series were also provided.

The *Scottish Abstract of Statistics* [QRL.446] usually reports gross output and gross value added, both in aggregate and per employee, for the latest available year by Class. The figures are derived from data collected by the BSO, but the estimate of gross value added is only an approximation. When a census return covers addresses in Scotland and other parts of the United Kingdom, an estimate of gross value added attributable to Scotland is made on the assumption that it is proportional to employment in Scotland. The *Scottish Economic Bulletin* [QRL.447] has provided both the main quarterly and annual series of economic statistics since the first issue in Summer 1971, as well as carrying statistically illustrated articles. It often repeats the gross value added results annually for the latest three years, and like the *Scottish Abstract of Statistics* [QRL.446] expresses Scottish output as a percentage of total output for the UK Food, drink and tobacco manufacturing industries, for purposes of comparison.

The former *Digest of Scottish Statistics* [QRL.175] used to draw from both MAFF and Department of Agriculture and Fisheries sources to give data on output of the following processed foods for the most recent six years: wheat milled; oats processed; refined sugar from beet and imported raws respectively; chocolate and sugar confectionery; jam and marmalade; biscuits; margarine; compound cooking fat; canned foods listing fruit, vegetables, fish and soups separately; pickles and sauces; kippered, pickled, cured and canned fish; smoked and canned white fish. The same table also carried data on the production of the following foods which are typically inputs to the final processing phase: animals slaughtered separating cattle, calves, sheep and lambs; pigs and bacon factories; eggs sold through packing stations; milk sold through marketing schemes for liquid consumption and otherwise; milk products including butter, cheese, condensed milk, milk powder; bacon and ham; and quick frozen fish as an input.

The *Scottish Economic Bulletin* [QRL.447] provides an index of production for the "Food" industries (Groups 411–423 inclusive) in Scotland. Seasonally adjusted data are provided quarterly for the most recent ten years. The July 1984 edition contained an article by J.A. Polley entitled "Index of industrial production for Scotland: reclassification and rebasing" [B.145] which described the new series and weightings after the adoption of SIC(1980) as the basis for classification. [QRL.447] also gives the gross domestic product output based measure by industry at constant factor cost from the national accounts. The *Scottish Abstract of Statistics* [QRL.446] reproduces the same index, providing annual data for the latest seven years.

Welsh Economic Trends [QRL.517] provides data on net output, and net output per employee, in Wales for Class 41/42, and also gives comparative data for

Scotland; the North of England; the West Midlands; the South East of England; and the United Kingdom. The 1987 issue carries statistics for 1983 which are taken from the BSO Census of Production for that year. The results include estimates for non-respondents and establishments with less than twenty employees which are exempted from the censuses. As with the Scottish figures in the *Scottish Abstract of Statistics* [QRL.446], estimates are made by the BSO of net output attributable to each region by reference to employment in that region.

Welsh Economic Trends [QRL.517] also provides an index of production for Class 41/42 in Wales. Seasonally adjusted data are given for the most recent twelve quarters, and latest six years. Revisions to the series are normally made each quarter to take account both of more recent information and improved seasonal factors. The same data are also published in the *Digest of Welsh Statistics* [QRL.177], though for the most recent twenty four quarters and eight years.

Regional Trends [QRL.401] provides data on gross value added in Class 41/42 for the United Kingdom and its standard regions, again using data from the BSO Census of Production. The 1987 issue carries figures for 1984 but the 1988 edition contained no Class 41/42 breakdown.

2.4.4 *Comments*

Thus many dimensions of output are measured including the physical, monetary and financial. The agencies responsible embrace the BSO, the MAFF and the CSO. However, those seeking additional data for named companies may have to consult the many company reports and the output of some market research organisations.

2.5 Current Inputs other than Labour

The Food industries use raw materials from the land and the sea, converting them into products demanded by the consumer. These products are then sold on through the wholesaling and retailing networks. In this section, we are concerned with statistical sources on current domestic inputs, and on input-output relationships. Imports provide a further provenance of current inputs to the Food industries, but sources of statistics on UK imports will be discussed, together with sources on UK exports, in section 2.8. Furthermore, data on inputs are often cited in calculations of product supplies and disposals — see section 2.11 for further details.

2.5.1 *Domestic Inputs*

Part of agricultural output is destined for final consumption but much constitutes an input to the food processing industries. The richness of the statistical sources on agriculture is shown by G.H. Peters in his companion volume in this series, *Reviews of United Kingdom Statistical Sources — Agriculture* [B.144]. Nevertheless, it is important to note the major sources of statistical information on agricultural output in this section. Sources specific to particular industries will be discussed, where appropriate, in the following chapters.

2.5.1.1 Ministry of Agriculture, Fisheries and Food inquiries

The Ministry of Agriculture, Fisheries and Food (MAFF) collates and publishes a wide range of statistics on agricultural output. Much of this is first disseminated in a series of press notices which bear the generic title "MAFF Statistics". The data are then subsequently reproduced in a variety of compendia.

MAFF Statistics — Agricultural Returns: England and Wales, Regions and Counties [QRL.316] is published in the Spring and contains the main results of the agricultural census from the previous summer. Provisional results are published in August. The annual publication *Agricultural Statistics: United Kingdom* [QRL.32] appears later and records the main figures from the annual agricultural censuses and the regular surveys of agricultural prices. Most of the physical statistics collated in the annual census are summarised for each of the four countries of the United Kingdom. Five-year runs of figures are given for the production and yield of selected main crops, and for livestock on agricultural holdings. The separate horticulture section provides details of land devoted to particular types of vegetables and fruit. Much of the output is naturally marketed directly, but some passes to the food processing industries. In some instances (e.g. brussel sprouts, beetroot and peas) separate figures are provided for each category.

As its title suggests, *Output and Utilisation of Farm Produce in the United Kingdom* [QRL.382] furnished rather more apposite information for this Review. This annual publication used to be compiled by MAFF in conjunction with the Agricultural Departments for Scotland, Northern Ireland and Wales. Estimated total supplies, utilisation and output from home crop are provided for the main farm crops (wheat; barley; oats; mixed corn; all cereals). The wheat statistics, for example, show utilisation in milling (distinguishing the home-grown components); cereal breakfast foods; malting, flaking and roasting; starch and glucose; animal feed; and seed and waste on farms and in distribution. Data on supplies of potatoes, and production and utilisation of sugar beet are also given. In the horticulture section, data are provided on the gross yield, gross production, marketed output, and value of marketed output of about twenty types of vegetable and ten types of fruit. Figures on slaughterings; chicken and turkey hatchings; packing station throughput of chicken and fowl; and concentrated feedingstuffs are also provided — again after first being published in one of the "MAFF Statistics" press notices. However, [QRL.382] ceased to be published in 1988, when the last year covered was normally 1987. Some of the information subsequently appears in the *Annual Review of Agriculture* [QRL.51] and *Agriculture in the United Kingdom*.

The *Annual Review of Agriculture* [QRL.51] appeared under that title from the accession of the UK to the European Community in 1973. Its previous title (1951–1972) was the *Annual Review and Determination of Guarantees* [QRL.50]. Recently, there have been further changes in title and coverage which are noted here, recorded in the QRL Key to this volume and further discussed in the Addenda. For 1988 alone, both the last issue of [QRL.51] and the first issue of *Agriculture in the United Kingdom* appeared. But from 1989 onwards, *Agriculture in the United Kingdom* became the major publication, taking over the mantle of both the *Annual Review of Agriculture* [QRL.51] and *Output and Utilisation* [QRL.382].

Both the *Annual Review of Agriculture* [QRL.51] and *Output and Utilisation* [QRL.382] do more than show how UK agricultural output provides inputs for the food processing industries. A complete picture is provided of the balance between home output, imports and exports, and stock changes which is more fully discussed in section 2.11. Supply balance sheets are compiled by MAFF from their many farm and processor surveys, details of which are concisely summarised by Slater [B.164]. Thus as well as home output, statistics are also derived for cereal supplies; oilseed rape supplies; potato supplies; sugar supplies; supplies of various horticultural products; meat supplies; milk product supplies; and egg supplies. The exact treatment differs from product to product but home production as a percentage of total new supply is usually calculated. Statistics are provided in volume terms, with a forecast for the latest year, actual figures for the previous four years and some averages for earlier years. A short statistically illustrated summary of commodity trends is also given. Full details are also stored in the EUROSTAT CRONOS data bank (see section 2.3) and are published quarterly by EUROSTAT.

The *Monthly Digest of Statistics* [QRL.362] draws on data from the Agricultural Departments to provide annual figures on land use and crop areas in the United Kingdom; yields and production of the main agricultural and horticultural crops; and six monthly figures on livestock. The *Annual Abstract of Statistics* [QRL.37] presents similar data though for longer time periods, and also publishes data on the output of farm crops; vegetables; and fruit in both current and constant prices.

2.5.1.2 Business Statistics Office inquiries

A more specific picture of industry purchases of inputs is featured in the quinquennial purchases inquiry conducted by the BSO and published as *Business Monitor PO1008: Purchases Inquiry 1984* [QRL.116]. The results of the 1984 inquiry were published in 1987. The aggregate value of purchases in the survey year, other than purchases for merchanting or factoring, are given for all establishments classified by Activity Heading in SIC(1980). The detailed breakdown varies according to the Activity Heading, but the classification of inputs is presented in standard format. The materials for use in production are mainly the farm inputs, the unprocessed and intermediate agricultural products, and sometimes vitamin concentrates, chemicals etc. Expenditure on stationery and printed matter, packaging materials, and replacement parts and consumable tools are the other headings. The latter covers tyres and vehicle spare parts, replacement parts for machinery, all other materials etc. Each component is expressed as a percentage of total expenditure and aggregated to give the total value of all materials. Fuel, electricity etc. have a separate breakdown into derv fuel and motor spirit; gas/diesel oil; electricity; and all other fuel.

The introductory notes to *Business Monitor PO1008* [QRL.116] explain the methodology. For each Activity Heading, only establishments whose employment was greater than a given "cut-off" (either 50 or 100) were surveyed. The response rate with respect to total employment was 73 per cent in 1984, compared to 68 per cent for the 1979 inquiry. The effective response rate was also calculated for each Activity Heading. Deficient returns are adjusted according to the commodity purchases of other comparable establishments. The results were matched with the 1984 Census of Production, and credibility checks were carried out by comparing the sum of the component figures with the total figures requested on the inquiry form.

The previous inquiry — also based on SIC(1980) — covered the year 1979 and the broadly comparable results were published in *Business Monitor PA1002.1: 1979*

Census of Production and Purchases Inquiry [QRL.94] in 1983. The 1974 inquiry was carried out as a supplement to the Census of Production and the results — based on SIC(1968) — were published in the Production Monitors for each Minimum List Heading (MLH) for 1974 and 1975. Data for 1963 and 1968 were also provided in the Census of Production for those years. The notes on the Purchases Inquiry always merit careful study since the employment "cut-off" varies for different MLHs, and from inquiry to inquiry.

In recent years, a summary picture may be found in the annual Production Monitors for each industry Group (see section 2.1.1.1 for those that relate to the Food industries). A single statistic describes the purchases of materials for use in production, packaging and fuel. Data are given for the latest five years on hire of vehicles, plant and machinery; rents of industrial and commercial buildings; commercial insurance premiums; rates, excluding water rates etc. A conscious effort is made to distinguish such current inputs from capital inputs. These data are largely replicated in *Business Monitor PA1002* [QRL.93].

Other Production Monitors cover industries, part of whose output may be regarded as inputs to firms in the Food industries. *Business Monitor PA251: Basic Industrial Chemicals* [QRL.102] provides output data *inter alia* on chemically defined organic compounds; vegetable tannins; and dyeing extracts. *Business Monitor PA256: Specialised Chemical Products Mainly for Industrial and Agricultural Purposes* [QRL.103] includes output data on essential oils; natural and artificial flavourings; and industrial gases. It should be said, however, that such Monitors are of limited use as sources of input data because the output figures are aggregate values and, moreover, export sales are also included.

2.5.1.3 Historical data

Considerable progress has been made since June 8th 1864 when the House of Commons voted £10,000 for the collection of agricultural statistics, despite the opposition of many country gentlemen. An invaluable compendium is *A Century of Agricultural Statistics: Great Britain 1866–1966* [QRL.1] which also contains a commentary by A.H. Baines. Annual production and yield per acre in England and Wales; Scotland; and Great Britain are given (usually for 1886–1966) for wheat; barley; oats; potatoes; hay; sugar beet (1921–1966 only); and turnips and swedes (1884–1966 only). Estimated production of meat and livestock products, and milk and egg yields, may also be found together with a wide range of other data.

2.5.1.4 Regional coverage

The *Economic Report on Scottish Agriculture* [QRL.180] carries annual data in volume terms on output and utilisation of the principal crops, livestock and horticulture. The first edition was issued in 1980 and succeeded *Agricultural Statistics: Scotland* [QRL.31] which ceased publication in 1978. Basic information for 1979 was contained in the 1980 edition of [QRL.180]. A statistically illustrated commentary is carried in *Agriculture in Scotland* [QRL.33]. Furthermore, the *Scottish Abstract of Statistics* [QRL.446] reproduces some annual data from Department of Agriculture and Fisheries (DAFS) sources on the output of the main cereals, animals and fish.

The *Statistical Review of Northern Ireland Agriculture* [QRL.460] performs a similar service for the province, providing detailed results from the latest annual agricultural census, and time series data usually for the latest five years. *Northern Ireland Agriculture* [QRL.376] is an annual report from the Department of Agriculture for Northern Ireland (DANI) which includes data and statistical appendices on output and utilisation. The *Northern Ireland Annual Abstract of Statistics* [QRL.377] carries compilations from DANI sources of the output of the land and the sea.

Welsh Agricultural Statistics [QRL.515] provides annual data for Wales on the physical output of crops; milk utilisation; animals slaughtered; meat production etc. The *Digest of Welsh Statistics* [QRL.177] gives annual data on crop production and sales of farm produce and fatstock using Welsh Office sources. These sources also provide data on the output of crops and numbers of livestock for *Welsh Economic Trends* [QRL.517].

2.5.1.5 Comments

Data on domestic inputs thus come from two main sources — MAFF and the BSO — though the two are rarely combined. An exception is *Structural Adjustment in the United Kingdom Food Manufacturing Industry Over the Past Twenty Years* [B.184] by B.G.A. Watts, which is a useful reference work on the relationship between agricultural materials and other inputs. Watts provides data for food manufacturing on the input costs of agricultural raw materials; packaging; fuel; and a weighted all-inputs index for 1960, 1965, 1970, 1975, 1979 and 1980, and the percentage changes over the period 1960–1980. The latter changes are compared with those for manufacturing (excluding food, drink and tobacco) as a whole. Constant (1975) price figures were also calculated. The data cited in the study were based on DTI and MAFF estimates, and were prepared for an OECD symposium. Current published sources are insufficient to update it.

2.5.2 *Input-output Analysis*

2.5.2.1 United Kingdom

The intermediate transactions between industries are outlined in *Input-output Tables for the United Kingdom 1984* [QRL.284]. This latest edition at the time of writing was published in 1988 and presented data for 1984 using SIC(1980) as the basis for classification — the data are consistent with the National Accounts for 1984 published in the 1987 edition of [QRL.506]. The input-output tables add an extra dimension to the National Accounts. The latter are concerned with the value and composition of goods and services purchased by final expenditure, and with the factor incomes and value added which are generated in their production. In contrast, input-output tables focus on the transactions between industries which form part of the process of supplying final demand. They highlight the purchases of goods and services for use in the production process, such as the purchase of sugar by the confectionery industry.

The input-output tables adopt the same names to denote industries and commodities, yet there is a clear distinction between the two concepts. An industry is defined as an aggregation of production establishments, and the major part of its sales consist of goods and services which are regarded as characteristic of the industry and are called its principal products. A commodity is defined as the principal product of an industry, and there are as many industries as there are commodities. Many production establishments also produce and sell products characteristic of other industries. The figures for industries in the tables shows the purchases and sales relating to the total activities of each industry, and so include the sales of principal and non-principal products. The figures for commodities analyse totals for the relevant products in whatever industries they are produced.

One hundred and one separate industry/commodity groups are identified in the 1984 tables, of which the following relate to the Food industries:

Industry/commodity group		Activity Headings of SIC(1980)
57	Oils and fats	4115, 4116
58	Slaughtering and meat processing	4121, 4122, 4123, 4126
59	Milk and milk products	4130
60	Fruit, vegetables and fish processing	4147, 4150
61	Grain milling and starch	4160, 4180
62	Bread, biscuits and flour confectionery	4196, 4197
63	Sugar	4200
64	Confectionery	4213, 4214
65	Animal feeding stuffs	4221, 4222
66	Miscellaneous foods	4239

(Agriculture (AH0100) and Forestry and fishing (AH0200, 0300) are classified as industry/commodity groups 1 and 2 respectively.)

The 1984 input-output tables contain three basic tables (1 to 3), and eight derived tables (4 to 11), viz:

1. the "make" matrix shows the value of sales of each commodity produced in the United Kingdom, analysed by the industries which produced it.
2. the "domestic use" matrix shows how commodities produced in the United Kingdom are purchased by industries and by final demand.
3. the "imports use" matrix gives a commodity breakdown of imports purchased by each industry and by final demand.
4. the commodity by commodity domestic use matrix.
5. the "Leontief inverse" shows the total input requirements of each industry per unit of final output.
6. the commodity by commodity imports-use matrix.
7. the composition of final expenditure in terms of net output.
8. the commodity analysis of consumers' expenditure by function.
9. the commodity analysis of general government final consumption.
10. the commodity analysis of gross domestic fixed capital formation.
11. output of principal products of each industry group as a percentage of the industry group's total output, and output produced as principal products as a percentage of the total output of each commodity group.

The number of tables provided in the 1984 edition is rather fewer than in previous publications wherein were also shown the industry by industry equivalents of the commodity by commodity derived tables set out above. In contrast, the number of industry/commodity groups separately identified in the Food industries has tended to increase over the years. The first official input-output tables for the United Kingdom were published in 1961, and related to the year 1954 as indicated in the title of [QRL.281]. Separate figures were only provided for food, drink and tobacco; agriculture, forestry and fishing; cereal foodstuffs; and other manufactured foods.

Before 1954, tables had been prepared by T. Barna for the year 1935 and published as part of an article [QRL.4] on the interdependence of the British economy where the food processing sector was identified. A further study [QRL.11] was prepared by the Department of Applied Economics in Cambridge for the year 1948. Since then tables have been published at approximately five-yearly intervals for the years 1963 [QRL.282], 1968 [QRL.283], 1974 [QRL.100], 1979 [QRL.101], and now 1984 [QRL.284]. The 1974 and 1979 tables were both published as Business Monitors. Additional "updated" tables were also published as *Business Monitor PA1004* [QRL.97], [QRL.98], and [QRL.99] for the years 1970–1972, but this more frequent and less detailed series has now been discontinued.

The original classic essay on input-output analysis is that by Leontief [B.102] but there are specific methodological explanations applicable to the United Kingdom in the tables themselves. The 1984 edition of *Input-output Tables for the United Kingdom* [QRL.284] carries an useful introduction explaining the principles of the tables. A full description of the sources and methods used to compile the 1984 tables became available in 1989 along with a set of tables for 1985, updated from the 1984 benchmark tables. The extensive introductions to [QRL.283], [QRL.282] and [QRL.281] contain invaluable summaries of the historical background, basic concepts and methods of construction of input-output tables. Later references which provide guidance on the general methodology include *Input-output Tables and Analysis* [B.319], *Input-output Analysis in Developing Countries* [B.28], and *Readings in Input-output Analysis* [B.166]. The latter is a comprehensive collection of many important papers written over the past fifty years, and was published in 1986.

2.5.2.2 Regional coverage

The *Input-output Tables for Scotland: 1973* [QRL.280] were prepared on the basis of SIC(1968) and were available in the form of a wallchart. "Agriculture" and "Forestry and fishing" were distinguished as primary inputs. The food industry was analysed in aggregate, but disaggregated data were also provided for bakery products; meat and fish; and sugar and confectionery. The remaining Food industries were subsumed within "other food products", thus concealing much of the intra-sector dependency.

The *Scottish Input-output Tables for 1979* [QRL.448] were constructed on the basis of SIC(1980) and represent a more thorough treatment. "Agriculture" and "Fishing" are again the primary inputs. The food industry is analysed in aggregate, but is also subdivided into meat products (comprising bacon curing and meat processing; poultry slaughter and processing; and animal by-product processing); slaughterhouses; fish; bread, biscuits and flour confectionery (combining bread and flour confectionery, and biscuits and crisp bread); sugar confectionery (comprising sugar and sugar by-products, and cocoa, chocolate and sugar confectionery); and the remaining industries subsumed under the heading "other food products and tobacco". The exercise was carried out in some detail and is contained in five volumes which were published at different times. There are both industry by industry, and commodity by commodity, domestic use matrices. The commodity analyses of imports from the rest of the United Kingdom, and from the rest of the world measure the respective interdependencies. Comparisons are also presented with the 1973 figures, and with data for the United Kingdom in 1979.

The *Inter-regional Input-output Tables for Wales and the Rest of the United Kingdom: 1968* [QRL.7] reported industry by industry, and commodity by commodity analyses wherein the Agriculture and Food industries were separately identified. The interdependency between Wales and the rest of the United Kingdom is statistically explored. Many of the examples provided to illustrate the use of the tables are couched in terms of "Food, drink and tobacco".

The *Input-output Tables for Northern Ireland: 1963* [QRL.279] were based on the Census of Production for that year, and were the first and last such tables to be published for the Northern Ireland economy. The nine tables were compiled at three levels. "Food" is included in the most aggregate 22x22 tables. It is subsequently subdivided into milling; bread and biscuits; and miscellaneous food, drink and tobacco in the 38x38 table. Finally, the most detailed 62x62 analysis is performed on the basis of the MLH in SIC(1968) and the following headings are identified: grain milling; fruit and vegetable products; animal and poultry foods; bread and biscuits; chocolate and sweets; bacon curing, meat and fish preparations; milk products; and starch and miscellaneous foods. There is no analysis of the interdependency between Northern Ireland and the rest of the United Kingdom.

2.5.2.3 Comments

Some general remarks are now in order. Input-output tables seek to bridge the gap between detailed analyses of individual industries and the macroeconomic picture given in the National Accounts. In principle, they present an illuminating perspective on the structure of the economy but, in practice, they suffer from a number of limitations. First, much of the statistical material is difficult to collect, and any published data must be consistent with that in other sources such as the *United Kingdom National Accounts* [QRL.506]. This invariably slows down the preparation of the tables and the 1984 tables, for example, were not published until 1988. Similar delays may be noted in the publication of tables for Scotland, Wales and Northern Ireland. Second, the time lag is also important in that technical change may well affect the size of the input-output coefficients. Third, a more complete picture could be obtained if more disaggregated detail were available. Once again, however, this would entail the collation of more material and exacerbate the publication lag.

As regards the Food industries, there are a number of observations to be made about the input-output tables. The distinction has already been made between direct food production in agriculture and horticulture (e.g. potatoes), and food produced for processing by the Food industries — Class 41/42 in SIC(1980). A further distinction might also be made within the Food industries between primary and secondary processors. Primary processors take the basic agricultural produce and may process it for direct sale to the consumer (e.g. sugar beet into white sugar). Or they may supply other food manufacturers (the secondary processors) with fundamental ingredients such as dairy fats and proteins, glucose syrup, liquid sugar, and flour for use in the production of soups, cakes, confectionery, ice-cream etc. These secondary processors too may supply other food manufacturers, so one might envisage a tertiary stage. Milk is an input in butter manufacture. Butter in turn is one of the ingredients in cake and biscuit manufacture. Beet is an input in sugar manufacture. Sugar in turn is an input for many other Food industries such as jams and marmalade. This all emphasises the point made by Mordue [B.126] that the Food industries purchase a sizeable proportion of their inputs from themselves. Moreover, the interdependencies are much more complex than may be ascertained from the input-output tables.

"Oils and fats" and "Milk and milk products" both furnish not only final outputs, but also provide inputs for the same industry Groups and for other food processors. "Slaughtering and meat processing" includes the output of slaughterhouses which constitutes an input into the bacon curing and meat processing industries. "Grain milling" and "Starch" are combined, and produce inputs for "Bread, biscuits and flour confectionery" and the many "Miscellaneous foods". "Sugar" yields final products, and also provides inputs for many other industries notably "Confectionery". "Fruit, vegetables and fish processing" draw their inputs from the land and the sea. Some of the "Miscellaneous foods" producers purchase inputs from other domestic Food industries, but products such as tea and coffee are often processed after being imported from abroad. In short, input-output analysis only provides limited insights about the interactions of the various Food industries.

2.6 Labour

The wide range of statistical information on the labour force means that this input into the food manufacturing process is treated separately. Wages and salaries, although they are strictly prices, are dealt with in this section. Andrew Dean in *Wages and Earnings* [B.44] (an earlier volume in this series) gives a guide to sources in this area. N.K. Buxton and D.I. MacKay focus more on employment in their book *British Employment Statistics* [B.33]. Walsh, Izatt and Pearson [B.182] give much useful information both on sources of labour information and in their directory of labour market information. Even though this Institute of Manpower Studies (IMS) work entitled *The UK Labour Market* [B.182] was published in 1980, it is still a good starting point. Marsden and Redlbacher [B.109] provide a more recent guide on wage statistics in the European Community together with a separate chapter on UK sources. Walsh and Pearson [B.183] have also written a reference book on labour market information. The major continuous source, however, is the *Employment Gazette* [QRL.186].

This Review focuses on the sources for the Food, drink and tobacco manufacturing industries, detailing in particular where the data are further disaggregated for the Food industries alone or for the constituent Groups and Activity Headings.

It must be stressed at the outset that there are basically three official agencies responsible for collecting the statistics. The Department of Employment runs the

Census of Employment and other inquiries. The Business Statistics Office collects employment data as part of the Census of Production. The Office of Population Census and Surveys is responsible for the decennial Census of Population which also contains data on the labour force.

Employment Statistics: Sources and Definitions [B.254] is a useful catalogue of many of the regular Government Statistical Services sources of employment data. Coverage, description, methodology of inquiry and availability of data are summarised.

The *Employment Gazette* [QRL.186] is the best single source on the many statistical dimensions of the labour market and it also provides notes on the many changes. Each issue carries a substantial section on labour market data, together with an index to regularly published statistics. There have been variations in title in the past, including the *Department of Employment Gazette* (1971–1979), the *Employment and Productivity Gazette* (1968–1970) and the *Ministry of Labour Gazette* (1922–1967).

The *British Journal of Industrial Relations* [B.209], first published in 1963, usefully includes a Chronicle section for the four-month period preceding each issue. This summarises recent influences on the labour market. The sections on government policies and activities, labour market policies, the employers, the trades unions, and major agreements and negotiations, are often statistically illustrated.

The *British Labour Statistics Historical Abstract* 1886–1968 [QRL.67], and the *British Labour Statistics Yearbook* [QRL.68], which ran from 1969 to 1976, collected together the main statistics covering the many dimensions of the labour market. They are no longer compiled but provide a convenient source of past data.

2.6.1 *Employment*

The work force in employment is made up of the employees in employment plus HM forces, the self-employed and participants in work-related government training programs. Statistical data on employees in employment are forthcoming from various Department of Employment and Business Statistics Office inquiries, and the Census of Population. These are discussed in turn in the following sections. Sources of statistics on the self-employed are discussed separately in section 2.6.1.6.

2.6.1.1 Department of Employment inquiries

Data published by the Department of Employment (DE) on employees in employment come from the Census of Employment, annual Labour Force surveys, and a series of monthly and quarterly sample inquiries of employers. The lynchpin of this system of reporting is the Census of Employment which provides accurate national and regional "benchmark" figures. Monthly and quarterly estimates for later dates are obtained by using data from sample surveys of employers to estimate proportionate changes in the number of employees since the last census. The results of successive censuses have shown, however, that such short-term estimates underestimate the number of employees. Results from the annual Labour Force Survey (LFS) are therefore used to calculate allowances for undercounting, and these are included in the estimates of the number of employees. It should be noted, however, that the LFS sample is too small to provide bias corrections disaggregated by industry, so that the adjustments that are incorporated in the quarterly estimates for individual industries are necessarily more uncertain than those made at the aggregate level. Further details are provided in the January 1987 issue of the *Employment Gazette* [QRL.186].

Prior to 1971, estimates of the number of employees were based on counts of national insurance cards. Since 1971, detailed statistics of employees (not the self-employed), analysed by industry and area covering virtually the whole economy, have been provided by the Censuses of Employment. The only sectors excluded are HM Forces and employees in private domestic service; also, to avoid duplication of inquiries, the figures for agriculture are based on data provided by MAFF and DAFS. The censuses were conducted annually in June, from 1971 to 1978. The *Review of Government Statistical Services: Report to the Prime Minister* [B.368] by Sir Derek Rayner recommended that the census should normally be conducted triennially. Hence censuses have subsequently been taken in 1981, 1984, 1987 and 1989. The September 1991 census is in progress. The methodology and coverage of the census have also been subject to frequent changes, and these are discussed in various articles in the *Employment Gazette* [QRL.186]. For example, two articles in the December 1983 and July 1984 issues describe how the data from the sample surveys of employers are used to estimate the changes in the number of employees since the last census. An article in the January 1987 issue explains that the relatively small sample sizes (and large sampling errors) in the monthly and quarterly surveys have led to the decision to reduce the extent of industry detail which is regularly published. From that issue onwards, two series of data on employees in employment have been regularly published:

- a quarterly series providing figures for both male and female employees (with part-time employees separately enumerated). Figures are published for one month (March, June, September or December) in the quarter, together with comparable figures for three months earlier, and for the same month in the previous year. Separate detail is forthcoming for meat and meat products, organic oils and fats (Groups 411/412); bread, biscuits and flour confectionery (419); alcoholic and soft drink manufacture (424–428); all other Food, drink and tobacco manufacture (413–418/420–423/429); and Food, drink and tobacco (41/42) in aggregate.
- a monthly series providing figures for both male and female employees, but with no separate enumeration of part-time employees. Figures are published for the latest month available, together with data for the previous two months, and revised figures for the comparable month in the previous year. The level of industrial detail is rather less as the monthly survey is based on a sample half the size of that for the quarterly inquiry. Separate figures are only provided for meat and meat products, organic oils and fats (411/412); alcoholic and soft drink manufacture (424–428); all other Food, drink and tobacco manufacture (413–423/429); and Food, drink and tobacco (41/42) in aggregate.

Up to the December 1986 issue of the *Employment Gazette* [QRL.186], the level of industrial detail published for both series was much greater, with fourteen headings identified under Food, drink and tobacco in the quarterly series, and eight in the monthly series. More detailed estimates of the later data are, however, available on request from Statistics Branch C2 of the Department of Employment. There may be a charge for this service, and the estimates will be provided in writing with the warning that they are subject to above-average estimation error.

The contribution of the annual Labour Force Survey has already been explained in the first paragraph of this section. However, we note here that the Labour Force Survey is a survey of households in the United Kingdom. It is carried out by the Social Survey Division of the Office of Population Censuses and Surveys (OPCS) on behalf of the Department of Employment. The first LFS in the United Kingdom was conducted in 1973, under the terms of a Regulation derived from the Treaty of Rome, and was carried out biennially from 1973 to 1983. From 1984, the LFS has been carried out annually.

Details of the various Censuses of Employment (more central to our discussion) may be traced in past issues of the *Employment Gazette* [QRL.186]. The first results of the September 1981 Census were published as *Occasional Supplement No. 1* in the May 1983 issue, and the final results as *Occasional Supplement No. 2* in the December 1983 issue of the *Employment Gazette* [QRL.186]. An article in the January 1987 issue of the *Employment Gazette* [QRL.186] presents and discusses the results of the 1984 Census. The September 1987 issue incorporated figures from the 1984 Census of Employment for Northern Ireland, provided by the Department of Economic Development, and thus produced data for the United Kingdom.

Other supplements have been periodically published, and these function as convenient sources for long time series of the Department's statistics. *Historical Supplement No. 1* was first published in the August 1984 issue of the *Employment Gazette* [QRL.186], but was superseded by a revised version in the April 1985 issue. The latter provides a disaggregated quarterly series from December 1981 to September 1984, a quarterly series for Class 41/42 back to September 1977, and an annual series back to June 1971. *Historical Supplement No. 2* was published in the October 1987 issue of the *Employment Gazette* [QRL.186] and extends the disaggregated series from December 1984 to September 1986, and the quarterly series for Class 41/42 to March 1987. The data prior to 1981 are derived from information collected on the basis of the 181 MLHs of SIC(1968). Conversion and reclassification of this data to the 334 Activity Headings of SIC(1980) were carried out by the Department of Employment. Only the aggregate time series should really be considered to be consistent, and the majority of the less aggregate figures are not too reliable.

In general, it should be stressed that the employment statistics are subject to frequent and continual revision. For example, the results of the 1984 Census led to a revision of the estimates of employees in employment since the 1981 Census. As explained in the January 1987 issue of the *Employment Gazette* [QRL.186], a comparison of the 1981 and 1984 results showed coding errors for larger establishments in 1981. Second, as already noted above, the results of the LFS are used to calculate allowances for undercounting. And third, it is a normal problem with statistical series that provisional results will later be revised in the light of new information.

Finally, mention should be made of other publications which carry statistics from the Department of Employment. The *Annual Abstract of Statistics* [QRL.37] carries data for Class 41/42 for both Great Britain and the United Kingdom, and also more disaggregated industry detail as featured in the *Employment Gazette* [QRL.186]. The figures relate to June each year, and five years annual data is provided, though with a two-year time lag before publication. Given the constant revision of the estimates mentioned above, these statistics may often be out-of-date even though this source is particularly convenient. The *Monthly Digest of Statistics* [QRL.362] reports the total number of employees in employment at Class level for the United Kingdom. Monthly data for the past two years (with a two-month publication lag), plus annual data for the previous five years, are provided.

2.6.1.2 Business Statistics Office inquiries

We have so far discussed employment data generated by the Department of Employment. We now turn to the provision of employment data as an important component of the Census of Production carried out by the Business Statistics Office. As explained in section 2.1.1.1 the BSO generally despatch forms to businesses with 100 or more employed and to samples of those with employment between 20 and 99. The results are reported in the summary tables of *Business Monitor PA1002* [QRL.93] as well as in the individual PA Monitors. The establishment (and now businesses) analyses at Class level give a breakdown for the standard regions and countries of the United Kingdom with figures for the respective percentages of UK employment. Data for both Class and Activity Headings are provided for the latest five years. The employment size distribution is published for both Class and Group in the enterprise tables.

Analyses by Activity Headings can also be located in the individual (PA) Monitors in the Production series. All these BSO estimates of employment differ from those of the Department of Employment itself. The DE codes separately each work place covered by a single PAYE scheme which are usually much smaller than the legal units used by the BSO. In theory, the DE Census of Employment should lead to more accurate identification of individual activities but, in practice, the Business Monitors now have data for the Activity Headings which are no longer published in the *Employment Gazette* [QRL.186] apart from the detailed triennial Census of Employment results.

Longer time series can be found for employment, and employment size distributions, with country analyses for establishments in the United Kingdom in the *Historical Record of the Census of Production* [QRL.264]. The data are classified according to the Minimum List Headings of SIC(1968).

The BSO also produces *Business Monitor PA1003: Size Analyses of United Kingdom Businesses* [QRL.96]. This has provided annual data on employment in a similar format since the 1985 issue. The coverage may be summarised as follows:

- Analysis of the number of legal units in manufacturing industries cross-classified by SIC(1980) Class by employment sizeband.
- Analysis of the number of local units in manufacturing industries cross-classified by SIC(1980) Class by employment sizeband.
- Analysis of the number of local units in manufacturing industries by SIC(1980) Activity Heading by employment sizeband.
- Analysis of the number of local units in manufacturing industries according to region and country by SIC(1980) Class by employment sizeband.

All sets of data run from the low employment size classes of 1–9 and 10–19 through 20–49, 50–99, 100–199, 200–499, 500–999, 1000 and over, plus a global total. The numbers of legal and local units in the 1988 issue of [QRL.96] refer to 1988 but the SIC(1980) Class and Activity Headings employment sizebands refer to 1986, which are lagged two years in general.

Although the coverage of *Business Monitor PA1003* [QRL.96] is explained in the summary in each report, we may stress the following points. First of all, the inclusion of units with employment below 20 provides more detailed coverage of manufacturing industry than is available elsewhere. Secondly, as explained by J.A. Perry [B.142] in the August 1985 issue of *Statistical News*, the coverage since 1985 has been made possible by the integration of the two main BSO registers which took place towards the end of 1984. Thus the *legal* unit information available from VAT sources is combined with the *local* unit information on the earlier production register. The BSO register of business comprises legal units (companies, partnerships, sole proprietors, public authorities, central government departments, local authorities and non-profit making bodies). The register is maintained from information obtained by Customs and Excise in the administration of value added tax and passed to the BSO under Section 44 of the Value Added Tax Act 1983. The legal units are thus usually the tax units for VAT purposed as explained in the notes to [QRL.96]. In the production industries, each local unit (i.e. site or factory) is linked with its parent VAT legal unit. Further regional analysis is possible because the local unit register data includes the full address for each site down to SIC Class. This contrasted with the legal unit tables which were not produced up to 1988 on a regional basis since nationally-based companies operate sites in many regions. But since 1989 regional analyses were provided for legal units.

Business Monitor PA1003 [QRL.96] gives coverage back to 1971. Its original title was *Business Monitor PA1003: Analyses of United Kingdom Manufacturing (Local) Units by Employment Size* [QRL.95]. It ran as such from 1971–1984 — excluding 1974, 1980 and 1981. It characteristically did employment size analysis by SIC Class and Activity Headings, beginning with an employment size group of 20–49. The country and standard region analyses were performed by SIC Class. Foreign-owned manufacturing units with 20 or more employees were enumerated and expressed as a percentage of the total employment.

The present *Business Monitor PA1003: Size Analyses of United Kingdom Businesses* [QRL.96] was introduced from 1985, featuring new tables giving counts of VAT legal units analysed by turnover (see also section 2.2.4) and dropping the foreign-owned data. As previously explained in this section, it did however incorporate data on units with employment size below 20. It does give additional data on the structure of industry, analysed by employment and turnover. The analysis for local units is predominantly by employment which is our primary concern here. The analysis for legal units is mainly by turnover (see also section 2.2.4). Indeed, rather unusually, besides the other usual Activity Headings, the level of disaggregation does enable us to contrast the few large local units and their extensive employment in "Sugar" (AH4200) with for instance the many local units and their employees in "Bread and flour confectionery" (AH4196). We instance this as a rare example of official coverage of AH4200.

Finally, the change from SIC(1968) to SIC(1980) and the revision in standard regions needs to be noted. Further, the timing of the actions involved in registration and de-registration concerning VAT may obscure the underlying changes from year to year. It should also be stressed that the legal units may be engaged not only in manufacturing but also non-manufacturing activities such as retailing. However, it is the *local* unit analyses which gives us the clearest statistical picture of employment in manufacturing industry, both by Class and Activity Heading. For example, in 1989 there was employment of 548,689 in local units in manufacturing industry in Class 41/42 "Food, drink and tobacco manufacturing industries". This ranked second to Class 32 Mechanical enginering. Thus the data in [QRL.96] confirms that Class 41/42 "Food, drink and tobacco manufacturing industries" made a significant contribution to the total manufacturing employment of 4,805,857 in 1989. This confirms that "Food, drink and tobacco" is one of the foremost manufacturing industries in the United Kingdom.

2.6.1.3 The Census of Population

The Department of Employment produces statistics on a regular monthly, quarterly and annual basis and the Business Statistics Office renders yearly data. But this third major source (the Census of Population run by the Office of Population Censuses and Surveys) may claim to be the most complete. The modern Census of Population attempts to give a complete record of the population of the nation at a particular moment of time. For Great Britain, this has been every ten years since 1801 except 1941. The methodology of the 1981 Census is summarized in *Census 1981: Definitions, Great Britain* [B.222]. This is an economical account compared with the extensive volumes of *Census 1981: User Guide* [B.223]. With such a massive documentation, the *Census 1981: User Guide Catalogue* [B.224] usefully gives numerical listings of user guides, subjects and indexes of user guide numbers by topic. *Guide to Census Reports: Great Britain 1801–1966* [B.296] provides listings of previous reports, describes significant developments in the scope and organisation of the census since 1801, furnishes questions and schedules used, details selected subjects of census inquiries etc. Indeed the coverage has differed over time. However, there is also Buxton and MacKay [B.33] which is a guide to sources, methods and content which may appeal to the economist.

The census approach is unique in its range of detail. Many other dimensions of the labour force are covered over and above our preoccupation with industrial statistics. *OPCS Census Guide 3: 1981 Census: Britain's Workforce* [B.347] summarises much of what is available. The working population is portrayed according to occupation, employment status and economic position etc. as well as industry. Much data are available on historical trends, geographical distribution, jobs, social class, qualifications, unemployment, mobility and migration, place of work, journey to work and so on.

Yet of the many volumes of the 1981 Census for Great Britain, the *Census 1981: Economic Activity: Great Britain* [QRL.148] volume is the most relevant for this Review as it contains employment statistics classified according to industry as well as occupation. Total numbers in employment for each Activity Heading are given by sex and full-time/part-time for Great Britain. Data for industry Classes are cross-classified by area of work place for Great Britain, England and Wales, the regions of England, metropolitan counties, Wales, Scotland and regions etc. The industry Class data by age last birthday and male/female are presented for Great Britain only.

There are separate volumes for Scotland and Northern Ireland. The 1981 Report for Scotland, *Census 1981: Scotland Economic Activity (10% Sample)* [QRL.149] gave details for the total in employment separately enumerated by sex and by full-time/part-time. The industry Class data are cross-classified by age, sex, area of work place and social class. The actual numbers, and proportions per 10,000 in employment attributable to the Food, drink and tobacco manufacturing industries are computed. *The Northern Ireland Census 1981: Economic Activity Report* [QRL.378] yields industry Class data cross-classified by sex, area of work place and age. The Great Britain and Scottish volumes are grossed up from a 10 per cent sample.

2.6.1.4 Regional coverage

The separate *Report on the Census of Production and Construction in Northern Ireland* [QRL.419] is based upon the same definitions as *Business Monitor PA1002* [QRL.93]. Average employment is given at Class level for the Census year and also detailed for the following: meat (excluding slaughterhouses) and fish products; milk and milk products; bread, biscuits and flour confectionery; and other foods, grain milling, animal feeding stuffs, drink and tobacco. The *Northern Ireland Annual Abstract of Statistics* [QRL.377] summarises employment data from the main primary sources which are the Census of Employment since 1971 and the supplementation since 1977 by the less detailed Quarterly Employment Enquiry. Yearly figures are given separately for males and females for the latest ten years plus an overall total. The male/female and full-time/part-time distinctions are reported from the September 1984 Census of Population. Quarterly data for male/female are given for the latest ten quarters in the 1988 issue of [QRL.377]. All data are by SIC(1980) Class.

The *Digest of Welsh Statistics* [QRL.177] yielded Class data for the male/female distinction still based on SIC(1968) for the years 1977, 1978 and 1981 in the 1987 issue. But the 1988 issue according to SIC(1980) does not retain this Class distinction. Previous issues sometimes gave some Minimum List Headings detail. The 1986 issue of *Welsh Economic Trends* [QRL.517] reports September 1981 Class data for the male/female full-time/part-time distinctions but this series is not maintained by Class in the 1987 issue nor in its supplement.

The *Scottish Abstract of Statistics* [QRL.446] gives the number of employees for Class 41/42 "Food, drink and tobacco", together with size bands according to numbers of employees. Cross-classifications by sex and female part-time are made. The more detailed information down to Activity Headings is also reproduced.

Given the interest in regional data, there is an obvious need for more consistency in the statistical series reproduced from issue to issue in these collections together with clearer explanations of original sources. However, coverage of the English standard regions is of course featured in the Business Monitors along with the usual countries of the United Kingdom.

2.6.1.5 Occupational analyses

The *Employment Gazette* [QRL.186] carries Class data with the twofold occupational breakdown given by sex as well as an overall total. The two broad categories are operatives; and administrative, technical and clerical staff together. The latter are defined to cover such groups as directors (except those paid by fee only); managers, superintendents and works or general foremen (i.e. foremen with other foremen under their control); professional, scientific, technical and design staff; draughtsmen and tracers; sales representatives and salesmen; and office (including works office) staff. All other employees are regarded as operatives. This Class level data for Great Britain is reported for September of the current year with comparative revised figures for the two previous years. Administrative, technical and clerical staff are expressed as a percentage of all employees in total and analysed by sex. This percentage is also given in the *Annual Abstract of Statistics* [QRL.37] without the male/female split but with numbers for the most recently available six years.

Business Monitor PA1002 [QRL.93] contains a similar analysis of operatives, and others, by industry Group, usually for the most recently available five years. The employment size distribution is given for these two categories at Class level for the Census year. The enterprise tables summarise the employment size distribution at Class and Group level too. Separate analyses are typically included in the individual (PA) Monitors in the Production series. The employment size distribution is provided for operatives; administrative, technical and clerical staff; and a total including working proprietors. Data for selected years between 1907 and 1970 can be traced back for SIC(1968) Orders and Minimum List Headings in the *Historical Record of the Census of Production* [QRL.264]. The two-way split for operatives and others gives average employment for the business units classified.

The *Report on the Census of Production and Construction in Northern Ireland* [QRL.419] makes a tripartite breakdown of average employment by operatives; administrative, technical and clerical staff; and working proprietors and directors. These data are summarised at Class level but separately disaggregated for the four most important groupings, viz: meat and fish products; milk and milk products; bread, biscuits and flour confectionery; and, other foods, grain milling, animal feeding stuffs, drink and tobacco.

However, it is the Census of Population which furnishes the most detailed occupational breakdown, although the data are only provided for every tenth year. For the 1981 Census for Great Britain, the *Census 1981: Economic Activity: Great Britain* [QRL.148] volume gives both industry divisions and activities by employment status and by sex. The employment status data cross-classifies employees by Activity Heading according to whether they are managers (both large and small establishments); foremen and supervisors (both manual and non-manual), apprentices and articled trainees; professional employees and other employees. A much more detailed occupational analysis is done for industry Classes by age and by sex. These 17 occupation orders and 162 groups are described in the *Classification of Occupations and Coding Index 1980* [B.227]. The same analysis of employment status by Activity Heading and by sex is reported for 1981 for Scotland in the *Census 1981: Scotland Economic Activity (10% Sample)* [QRL.149] volume which also contains the occupation orders and groups for classes by sex. *The Northern Ireland Census 1981: Economic Activity Report* [QRL.378] carries the more aggregated Class analysis by employment status, by the more detailed occupation orders and groups, and by sex.

2.6.1.6 The self-employed

Both the Census of Employment and the Census of Production are primarily concerned with those people in employment. But the major statistical source for the self-employed is the Census of Population. The tables in the volume on *Census 1981: Economic Activity: Great Britain* [QRL.148] yield the numbers of self-employed for each Activity Heading by sex. The distinction is made between those without employees and those with employees; the latter being further divided into large (over 25 employees) and small establishments. The industry Class tables show the numbers of self-employed by age, sex and areas of Great Britain. Activity Heading by sex data are given for 1981 in the *Census 1981: Scotland Economic Activity* [QRL.149] volume for Scotland. The same distinctions between the self-employed are made for Northern Ireland in 1981 but for Class level only cross-classified by sex in *The Northern Ireland Census 1981 Economic Activity Report* [QRL.378].

Both the Great Britain and Scotland Census for 1981 processed the data on the self-employed at both the 10 per cent and 100 per cent level. The 100 per cent figures were derived from form fillers' self assessment of their employment status, but the 10 per cent figures were more rigorously coded. The methodology is discussed both in the introductory note to *Census 1981: Economic Activity: Great Britain* [QRL.148], and in the February 1983 issue of the *Employment Gazette* [QRL.186]. Whatever the shortcomings, the Census of Population provides benchmark figures for the self-employed. The Labour Force Survey (see section 2.6.1.1) also provides estimates of the annual change in the number of self-employed. These are used to update the benchmark figures provided by the Census of Population. One can keep track of the latest information and the amount of detail available by consulting the special feature articles in the *Employment Gazette* [QRL.186].

2.6.2 *Unemployment*

Detailed industrial analyses of the unemployed used to be carried out monthly and were published monthly from 1948 to June 1976 in the predecessors in title of the *Employment Gazette* [QRL.186]. The statistics reported the numbers of men and women unemployed at the middle of the previous month for all Minimum List Headings. Subsequently, the analyses became quarterly (August, November, February and May) until May 1982 — see the July 1982 issue of the *Employment Gazette* [QRL.186] — when this industrial analysis for Great Britain and the United Kingdom ceased.

An article on the compilation of the unemployment statistics in the September 1982 issue of the *Employment Gazette* [QRL.186] discussed the change from the previous method of basing the unemployment count on the number of people registering for work with the employment services (job centres or careers offices). Registration for employment is now voluntary and the records on which the new count is based relate solely to claimants who make regular declarations of their unemployment at Benefit Offices for the purpose of receiving National Insurance credits. Industrial analyses are now discontinued and the best to be hoped for at the moment is that figures for broad industrial sectors will be available from surveys.

W.R. Garside [B.56] carries an appraisal of industrial unemployment statistics. He observes that the industry to which a wholly unemployed person was assigned was that in which he or she was most recently employed for more than three days. It could be argued that the classification of unemployed registrants by the industry of their last jobs need not necessarily have been their usual employment and was not necessarily the industry they wanted to enter again. However, in the case of new labour market entrants, they may have specified the industry which they considered most suitable. But it is nevertheless to be regretted that the industrial detail has diminished, particularly at times of high levels of unemployment. But when more detail was available, both the definitional changes and the various revisions of the SIC affected the statistics recorded. Comparisons over time must be made with caution.

Past time-series of the numbers of persons registered as wholly unemployed in the United Kingdom were presented in the *British Labour Statistics Historical Abstract 1886–1968* [QRL.67], and analysed by SIC(1968) Order. These statistics ran from 1948 to 1968, and included a male/female breakdown. *Statistics on Incomes, Prices, Employment and Production* [QRL.464] carried a multitude of data from 1962 to 1969, derived from the same Ministry of Labour sources. The registered wholly unemployed were enumerated for "Food, drink and tobacco" but "Bread and Flour Confectionery" were separated from the total for "Other Food Industries". The data were cross-classified by sex, age (under 18 and over 18), country and region plus special analyses of young people entering employment analysed by SIC(1968) Order for the regions, with boy apprentices separately enumerated. When *Statistics on Incomes, Prices, Employment and Production* [QRL.464] ceased publication, the issues of the *British Labour Statistics Yearbook* [QRL.68] carried quarterly data for both SIC(1968) Orders and Minimum List Headings for both Great Britain and the United Kingdom from 1969 to 1976.

The Census of Population, the General Household Survey and the Labour Force Survey are other inquiries into the unemployed but all give little industrial detail. However, the *Northern Ireland Abstract of Statistics* [QRL.377] gives unemployment by broad industry Class and travel to work area. Separate data are given for males and females. All results are for June in the latest available year and are claimant based.

2.6.3 *Vacancies*

Statistics on unfilled vacancies at job centres etc. at Class level were reported quarterly in the *Employment Gazette* [QRL.186] up to August 1985. Subsequent data have been collected quarterly and reported on the National On-line Manpower Information System (NOMIS). It is estimated that only about one third of all vacancies are notified to job centres.

Vacancies used to be analysed in a little more detail, according to sex, age and placings. This is reflected in back issues of the *Employment Gazette* [QRL.186] and its predecessors in title. The *British Labour Statistics Yearbook* [QRL.68] carried a breakdown by industry between employment offices and careers offices, and according to the standard regions and countries of the United Kingdom. *Statistics on Incomes, Prices, Employment and Production* [QRL.464] contained results by region, sex and age. The data for "Food, drink and tobacco" were subdivided into "Bread and Flour confectionery" and "Other Food Industries". There is much more occupational and regional detail on vacancies than analysis by industry.

2.6.4 *Labour Turnover*
Labour turnover statistics at Class level are currently published in the *Employment Gazette* [QRL.186] for Great Britain. The engagement rate and the leaving rate show the number of engagements and discharges (and other losses) respectively in four week periods as percentages of the numbers employed at the beginning of the period. SIC(1968) was used as the basis of classification up to the November 1983 issue of the *Employment Gazette* [QRL.186], and finer detail for each Minimum List Heading was provided.

2.6.5 *Redundancies*
Confirmed redundancies are published monthly in the *Employment Gazette* [QRL.186] at Class level for Great Britain. Figures are given for the latest three months with usually a two month time lag for the most recent observations. The most recent two months are provisional statistics. The previous five quarters and the past two years are given for comparison.

The statistics are based on administrative procedures arising from the employment protection and redundancy payments legislation dating from 1965, but have been available on a consistent basis only since 1977. The Department of Employment collects three series of statistics on redundancies. Firstly there are advance notifications under the Employment Protection Act 1975 which requires employers to notify the DE of impending redundancies involving ten or more employees in any establishment. Secondly the Manpower Services Commission follows up with data on the redundancies due to occur. Thirdly, there are statistics relating to the number of employees (not restricted to groups of ten or more) receiving redundancy payments under the Employment Act 1978 and earlier legislation. The methodology of collection, and redundancy statistics from June 1977 to June 1982 for each SIC(1968) Order, were published in a special feature in the June 1983 issue of the *Employment Gazette* [QRL.186]. The annual special feature in the *Employment Gazette* [QRL.186] usually cross-classifies Class data by the standard regions of England, and the countries of Great Britain. Any changes in legislation and statistical coverage are summarised in [QRL.186].

The *Northern Ireland Annual Abstract of Statistics* [QRL.377] reported the number of redundancies (payments cases only) at Class level with a male/female breakdown, and totals for the most recently available two years until January 1987.

2.6.6 *Industrial Stoppages*
Each month statistics at Class level related to stoppages at work owing to industrial disputes are published in the *Employment Gazette* [QRL.186]. These give the number of stoppages, workers involved, and working days lost to date in the current year. Data for the comparable period in the previous year are also given.

A special annual feature analyses stoppages caused by industrial disputes in the previous year. This usually appears in the July or August issue of the *Employment Gazette* [QRL.186]. The technical notes are worth consulting because work-to-rule and go-slows are not included in the statistics, nor are stoppages involving fewer than ten workers, or lasting less than one day, unless the number of working days lost in the dispute is greater than 100. Incidence rates from stoppages of work for the latest two years are given per 1000 employees. A cross-classification is made for stoppages resulting in a loss of 5,000 or more working days, giving the time period of the stoppage, the number of workers involved, the number of working days lost, the type of worker involved and the cause or object of the stoppage.

Up to and including the special feature for 1982 in the July 1983 issue of the *Employment Gazette* [QRL.186], the stoppages were more finely analysed in the annual review presenting "Grain milling", "Bread and flour confectionery", and "Biscuits" on their own. The remaining Orders were collected together under "All other food industries". An article in the March 1983 issue of the *Employment Gazette* [QRL.186] concisely describes the changes brought about by the introduction of SIC(1980) and pinpoints the impact on statistics of industrial disputes. Instead of the finer annual breakdown in terms of 50 SIC(1968) categories, both the annual and monthly data are now only provided for 30 industry groupings from SIC(1980). Nevertheless, statistics on stoppages are still coded by industry Group so further unpublished detail may be available from the Department of Employment.

Data on industrial stoppages for the countries of the United Kingdom are sparse. However, the *Northern Ireland Annual Abstract of Statistics* [QRL.377] gives Class data for the most recent six years, showing the number of stoppages and enumerating the days lost.

Strikes in Britain [QRL.10] uses Department of Employment data to probe both more deeply econometrically and more finely statistically. Data for each SIC(1968) Order are analysed according to strike incidence ranked for plant size, with respect to stoppage numbers, working days lost and employment in percentage terms and strike frequency per employee by size of plant. The years covered are 1971–1973 for Great Britain. Further statistical tables used as a basis for the report include annual figures (1970–1975) and averages for the number of stoppages per 100,000 employees analysed both by Order and by Minimum List Heading for the United Kingdom. Minimum List Heading details are given for the number of working days lost per 1000 employees (1970–1975) and the proportion of plants free of stoppages (1971–1973) by employment size. This occasional study is more revealing than the *Employment Gazette* [QRL.186], because the data collected are not all regularly published.

2.6.7 *Index of Average Earnings*

The sources noted in this section are discussed more fully in Dean's *Wages and Earnings* [B.44] but our focus is more narrowly industrial. The monthly index of average earnings (which is periodically rebased) is published for all employees in Great Britain (not seasonally adjusted) in the *Employment Gazette* [QRL.186]. The data for each Class (e.g. Class 41/42) pertain to the latest available month (usually with a four-month publication lag). Comparable monthly data for the latest four years, and annual averages for the previous three years, are usually also given.

This same information may also be found in the *Monthly Digest of Statistics* [QRL.362], where monthly data are provided for the last four years and annual data for the previous eight years. The *Annual Abstract of Statistics* [QRL.37] also carries the same statistics, but only cites monthly data for the previous year and annual averages for the latest seven years. These figures are for Great Britain and are based on SIC(1980). Although the monthly earnings index can be traced back in previous issues of the *Employment Gazette* [QRL.186] and predecessors in title, care must be exercised in making historical comparisons. Besides the changes in SIC and base year, the "new" series which runs from January 1976 has a more comprehensive coverage than the "old series" which was begun in January 1963 by the then Ministry of Labour. The new series extended coverage from what was mainly the production industries to encompass the major distribution activities, as explained in the April 1976 issue of the *Employment Gazette* [QRL.186].

The *British Labour Statistics Historical Abstract 1886–1968* [QRL.67] carries the monthly index from 1963–1968 and the *British Labour Statistics Yearbook* [QRL.68] summarised the results for a four year period.

2.6.8 *Earnings and Hours of Work*

Earnings and hours of work are linked, so they will be discussed together in this section. Many of the sources noted were also appraised by Dean [B.44]. His treatment is updated here where necessary.

2.6.8.1 The New Earnings Survey

A major source is the *New Earnings Survey* [QRL.375] which is a 1 per cent sample inquiry conducted by the Department of Employment of the earnings of employees in April of each year. Employees in all sizes of business are covered but the self-employed are excluded. The survey is carried out under the Statistics of Trade Act 1947. The extensive nature of this survey may be illustrated from the results of the 1986 New Earnings Survey. These were published in six parts as follows:

Part A Streamlined analyses and key analyses by agreement
Part B Report, summary analyses and other analyses by agreement
Part C Analyses by industry
Part D Analyses by occupation
Part E Analyses by region and age group
Part F Hours, Earnings of part-time women employees, Size of organisation

The methodology of the New Earnings Survey (NES) is described in Part B. There are an impressive number of tables (190 in total), but it is the data in Part C which are of particular interest here. For example, Tables 54–57 provide data on the following:

- Average gross weekly earnings (divided into pay affected and unaffected by absence)
- average gross hourly earnings (divided into including and excluding overtime pay and overtime hours)
- average weekly hours (total, normal basic and overtime)
- number in sample
- standard error as percentage of the average for weekly earnings and hourly earnings

The level of industry detail provided varies with the type of worker considered and is also determined by sample size. For example, taking the 1986 edition of [QRL.375]:

- Table 54: Full-time manual males on adult rates
    - Slaughtering of animals and production of meat and by-products (412)
    - Preparation of milk and milk products (413)
    - Bread, biscuits and flour confectionery (419)
    - Bread and flour confectionery (4196)
    - Ice-cream, cocoa, chocolate and sugar confectionery (421)
    - Cocoa, chocolate and sugar confectionery (4214)
    - Food (Groups 411–423 inclusive)
    - Food, drink and tobacco (Class 41/42)
- Table 55: Full-time non-manual males on adult rates
    - Food
    - Food, drink and tobacco
- Table 56: Full-time manual females on adult rates
    - Slaughtering of animals and production of meat and by-products (412)
    - Food
    - Food, drink and tobacco
- Table 57: Full-time non-manual females on adult rates
    - Food
    - Food, drink and tobacco
- Tables 58–61 provide data on the increase in average earnings between April 1985 and April 1986, both weekly and hourly, including and excluding overtime, with the associated standard errors. Separate figures are given for each of the four types of worker above, and for the same level of industry detail.
- Tables 62 to 65 report percentage increases for the same measures.
- Tables 66 to 69 give the cumulative distribution of gross weekly earnings.
- Tables 70 to 73 give the cumulative percentages for hourly earnings for the same four categories.
- Tables 74 to 77 classify gross weekly and hourly earnings into lowest and highest deciles, median, and lower and upper quartiles.
- Tables 79 to 82 decompose average gross weekly earnings into total pay, overtime pay, payments by results (PBR) etc., shift etc. premium payments, and all other pay. These components are converted into percentages of the totals. The percentage of employees who received overtime pay, PBR etc. payments, and shift etc. premium payments, is calculated.
- Tables 83 and 84 carry out further overtime analyses for all employees.

It can be seen that data are not provided for some Activity Headings (e.g. fish processing; processing of fruit and vegetables; starch; miscellaneous foods). The reason is that the sample sizes are not sufficiently large although information could possibly be supplied by the Department of Employment if the survey results were considered reliable enough. The following industrial detail from the other parts must be noted.

Part A: This contains similar detailed analyses for those parts of the Food, drink and tobacco manufacturing industries which have national agreements in the private sector. These include the Baking Industry National Joint Committee (NJC) for England and Wales, the Food manufacturing Joint Industrial Council (JIC), and the Milk products/milk processing and distribution National Joint Negotiating Committee (NJNC) for England and Wales.

Part B: This also contains further details of national wage agreements.

Part D: There is coverage of occupational earnings, both male and female, at Class level.

Part F: The section on hours of work yields data for both full-time males and full-time females.

Data are provided for the Activity Headings/Groups identified above, for the Food industries (Groups 411–423), and for the Food, drink and tobacco manufacturing industries in aggregate (Class 41/42). The hourly earnings of part-time females in the Food industries, and the Food, drink and tobacco manufacturing industries are also reported.

Thus the analyses of the different groups of workers by industry are extensive. Fortunately Tables 4–7 in Part A summarise much of the data for the four categories of workers. Hence, the reader who does not wish to scrutinise all six Parts can find here average figures for gross weekly pay; the breakdown into overtime, PBR, and shift payments; the size distribution of weekly pay; average weekly hours; and so on. Summary results of the Parts as they emerge are featured in special articles in the *Employment Gazette* [QRL.186].

Despite the amount of detail, the six Part format has been fairly standard since the NES for 1974. Any changes in coverage are detectable from the brief introduction in Part A, and the methodological section in Part B. The major change since Dean [B.44] has been the introduction of SIC(1980) in the 1983 NES. This means that the industry data are not strictly comparable before and after that date. The industry detail provided under SIC(1968) was bread and flour confectionery; bacon curing; meat and fish products; milk and milk products; cocoa, chocolate and sugar confectionery; and fruit and vegetable products. This may be contrasted with the detail under SIC(1980) above. Sample sizes are insufficient to present data for the other three categories, i.e. full-time manual females, full-time non-manual females and full-time non-manual males. Finally, despite the multiplicity and what can easily be confusing quantities of data, the user often finds that the table numbers remain the same from year to year. For example the distribution of gross weekly earnings for full-time manual males on adult rates may be compared in Table 66 from 1974 to the present day.

2.6.8.2 The October Earnings Survey

Distinct from the annual New Earnings Survey which takes place in April, there is a voluntary October Earnings Survey of manual workers which is also conducted by the Department of Employment. The results of the previous October enquiry are usually summarised in the February (sometimes March) issue of the *Employment Gazette* [QRL.186]. This survey of earnings and hours is one of the major sources of such information at detailed industry level. The dimensions reported are: average weekly earnings; average hours worked; and average hourly earnings for each SIC(1980) Group. The categories of male, female, and part-time female, as well as the total, are identified for manual employees on adult rates. Data are also reported for full-time males and females (manual employees) on other rates.

Dean [B.44] covers the historical origins and limitations so these will not be repeated here. But it should be noted that the October 1984 survey was the first to be based on SIC(1980). The February 1985 issue of the *Employment Gazette* [QRL.186] attempted to link together the series by reanalysing the results of the October 1983 survey according to the SIC(1980) and presenting data for both October 1983 and October 1984 on a comparable basis. As explained in the technical notes (always worth consulting) of the February 1986 issue of the *Employment Gazette* [QRL.186], a response rate of about 85 per cent was achieved from the 12,000 firms approached. Samples were taken of establishments in Great Britain employing less than 100 manual workers, but for Northern Ireland all establishments with more than ten employees were covered.

2.6.8.3 Other sources publishing data from the New Earnings Survey and the October Earnings Survey

Other publications often incorporate data from the New Earnings Survey and the October Earnings Survey. The *Monthly Digest of Statistics* [QRL.362] reports data from the October Earnings Survey at Class level on the average weekly earnings of manual workers for the latest four years, for full-time males and females, and all full-time workers on adult rates. It is stressed that these statistics represent average earnings, including bonus and overtime payments etc. before the deduction of income tax and insurance contributions. The data relate to one week in October, and are compiled from employers' returns.

The *British Labour Statistics Historical Abstract 1886–1968* [QRL.67] summarises the various sources prior to reporting data on earnings and hours actually worked in fifty two statistical tables. Without cataloguing the considerable detail, it is worth noting that data on average weekly earnings and average weekly hours are collected together as far back as 1886 for the many component parts of the Food industries. This task was continued in the massive reporting of data, predominantly from the NES and the October Survey, in successive issues of the *British Labour Statistics Yearbook* [QRL.68]. Historical data on wages and hours were also reported in *Statistics on Incomes, Prices, Employment and Production* [QRL.464].

The interdependence of earnings, hours of work and wage rates is obvious. Thus the sources in section 2.6.9 "Wage Rates and Conditions of Work" should also be consulted. Many of these sources record minimum earnings levels as well as providing abundant data on wage rates.

2.6.8.4 Regional coverage

The *Scottish Abstract of Statistics* [QRL.446] draws on the same sources as the *Monthly Digest of Statistics* [QRL.362], reporting average male weekly earnings at Class level for the latest available five years. Coding is now undertaken according to SIC(1980) and Scottish earnings as a percentage of total UK earnings are computed using the latest annual data. The *Digest of Welsh Statistics* [QRL.177] compared the Department of Employment results for Wales and the United Kingdom for two years in the 1986 issue, reporting average weekly earnings, average hours worked and average hourly earnings (in pence) for male manual workers on adult rates. But more recently, annual data for Wales alone are supplied. The *Northern Ireland Annual Abstract of Statistics* [QRL.377] reports average weekly earnings, and hours worked, for both full-time adult male and female manual workers at Class level for the latest year. Both the Welsh and the Northern Ireland sources code according to SIC(1980).

2.6.9 *Wage Rates and Conditions of Work*

2.6.9.1 Official sources

Time Rates of Wages and Hours of Work [QRL.483] is now a regularly (monthly) updated loose-leaf folder available on subscription from the Department of Employment. It aims to set out the basic (or standard) rates of wages, or minimum wage entitlements, of workers in the United Kingdom which have been laid down in wages orders made by statutory Wages Boards and Councils. It also covers the wage rates etc. stipulated in many of the national collective wage agreements made between organisations of employees and organisations of workers, or by Joint Industrial Councils and similar bodies. Data on the basic rates and hours of work are always given but details of the guaranteed week; minimum entitlements for piece workers, shift workers, night workers and other special categories; overtime rates; wage rates for young workers; and paid holiday entitlements etc. are available depending on the form of the agreement orders.

The coverage of the Food industries is quite extensive. Since the coverage does not precisely correspond to SIC(1980), and since there is varying geographical coverage, the industrial groupings included in *Time Rates of Wages and Hours of Work* [QRL.483] are now listed:

Corn trade	Great Britain
Flour milling	Great Britain
Sugar confectionery and food preserving	Northern Ireland
Baking	England and Wales, Scotland, and Northern Ireland
Biscuit manufacture	Great Britain
Bacon curing	Great Britain
Milk product manufacture and processing	England and Wales
Milk processing	Northern Ireland
Food manufacturing industry	Great Britain
Seed crushing, compounds and provender manufacture	United Kingdom

As an illustration of the information available, we take an example from a page issued in September 1991 relating to seed crushing, compound and provender manufacture in the United Kingdom. Class of worker is given (e.g. General labourers, 18 years and over) and the standard weekly rate. Hours of work are defined and piece work rates specified. Details of allowances for shift workers are given. Young workers (i.e. those 17 and 16 years old) are paid a proportion of adult rates. Appendices cover rates of pay for young workers, overtime rates of pay and holidays with pay. Estimates of the numbers of workers covered by principal national collective agreements in the United Kingdom (including flour milling, baking, biscuit manufacture, dairy industry, milk processing, food manufacturing and grain distilling and ancillary trades) are provided in a separate appendix.

The attempt is made to cover standard terms and conditions of service which go beyond the recording of a standard weekly rate and hours of work. It should be emphasised that the rates recorded are minimum rates and do not reflect supplementary local agreements.

Since the *Rayner Review* [B.368], however, information on wage rates and hours of work has become less accessible. The monthly loose-leaf folder on *Time Rates of Wages and Hours of Work* [QRL.483] is only available on subscription. The 550 or so subscribers are serviced by a government employee using word processing facilities to update information each month. Previously, *Time Rates of Wages and Hours of Work* [QRL.484] was published each year and it provided comprehensive yearly summaries of collective agreements as at April until its last issue in 1982. The complementary monthly information sheet *Changes in Rates of Wages and Hours of Work* [QRL.153] reported the latest changes up to December 1982. The loose leaf folder *Time Rates of Wages and Hours of Work* [QRL.483] has replaced them both in the interests of economy. However, to continue the yearly information for posterity, there is the ring binder "brown book" also entitled *Time Rates of Wages and Hours of Work* [QRL.485]. This collects together the data in [QRL.483] up to the end of April of each year.

It must also be stressed that the detail of coverage has diminished as free collective bargaining at company or plant level has become more prevalent. This is reflected in the size of [QRL.483] which has become slimmer month by month. This tendency towards a reduction in coverage is unlikely to diminish in the near future, due both to the trend away from national bargaining and given legislation typified by the Wages Act 1986. Wage Council orders no longer apply to workers aged under 21, and Wage Councils are limited to setting one basic hourly rate of pay, an overtime rate, and a limit on charges for any accommodation the employer provides.

With *Time Rates of Wages and Hours of Work* [QRL.483] no longer widely available, the more accessible *Employment Gazette* [QRL.186] becomes doubly important. Yet recent issues only reflect the diminished amount of data made public. An annual article still details changes in hours and holiday entitlements featured in national collective agreements or in wages orders made by Wages Councils, listing details for the Food industries where they occur. In the past, however, the *Employment Gazette* [QRL.186] gave monthly summaries of settlements, and ran an annual article on wages rates, hours of work and holiday entitlements etc. summarising the information from *Time Rates of Wages and Hours of Work* [QRL.484]. In addition, *British Labour Statistics Yearbook* [QRL.68] repeated details of basic weekly rates set out in selected collective agreements or statutory orders (men and women separately) and reported changes in wage rates and normal hours of manual workers by industry. Longer runs for various trades are reported in the *British Labour Statistics Historical Abstract 1886–1968* [QRL.67]. This gives the data on basic weekly rates for men in selected collective agreements or statutory orders from 1947–1968. Thus, for example, rates for "biscuit manufacture etc." are recorded back to 1st April 1947. Adult workers in the baking trade are covered from 1914–1938. Finally, official sources usually note the number of employees covered by the agreements. This information is usually given in one of the appendices in *Time Rates of Wages and Hours of Work* [QRL.483].

2.6.9.2 Commercial and trades union sources

Given the limitations of official sources, it is more than ever essential to refer to union and commercial data. Various sources monitor the many agreements on pay and conditions for the company or plant, and are evidently not confined to national collective agreements and Wages Councils. They tend to cover the complete package of the work contract system, often containing many more dimensions than wage rates and hours of work.

IDS Report [QRL.271] catalogues all agreements, as well as national bargaining etc., which have become known in the past fortnight. Some of this information has appeared in the Press and official publications, but this is a private subscription service run by Incomes Data Services (IDS). Use of the fortnightly reports to identify food companies is facilitated by the annual *Incomes Data Index* [B.313] and the IDS computerised data base service. Old weekly rates, new rates, future rates, total increases and percentage total increases, are reported for the grades of workers covered. The parties to the agreement are listed as well as all relevant details. For instance, Report 495 (April 1987) covered the agreement between Lyons Bakery Ltd. and the Bakers, Food and Allied Workers Union. This particular example featured data on pay structure, sick pay and shift payments. The treatment is not standard but as much detail as possible of a given settlement is recorded. [QRL.271] is an important source for both plant and company agreements.

Incomes Data Services also publishes a series entitled *IDS Study* [QRL.272] which goes into further detail on particular pay and conditions of work arrangements. For example, Study 142 (March 1977) entitled "Food Manufacturing" is an example of an in-depth examination which describes the local and national bargaining procedures and the role of the Joint Industrial Councils (JIC). The concluding section lists company agreements and national agreements together with data on basic weekly rates, overtime, holidays, seasonal earnings variations etc. according to the individual settlement. It would be useful if these occasional studies were undertaken more regularly so that company agreements and national agreements could be found in one place.

The *Industrial Relations Review and Report* [QRL.275] is produced twice monthly by another private organisation, Industrial Relations Services. The reports, which began in 1971, now have three distinct sections, viz: Pay and Benefits Bulletin; Industrial Relations Legal Information Bulletin; and, Health and Safety Information Bulletin. Surveys, case studies and reports/reviews are summarised on the back page update. The yearly *Industrial Relations Review and Report Index* [B.318] identifies those issues which report on the food manufacturing industries, and settlements in food companies, whether from national negotiations or company agreements. Settlements in "Food, drink and tobacco" are regularly summarised with illustrative statistics on basic pay, increases etc. The *Industrial Relations Review and Report* [QRL.275] is, however, more of a commentary, compared with the *IDS Report* [QRL.271] which is much more statistical.

Given the diversity of information, a useful service is provided by the Labour Research Department which is financed by affiliation fees and the sale of its publications. The present affiliates include over fifty national unions covering over four-fifths of Trades Union Congress (TUC) membership. Information on agreements is published in *Bargaining Report* [QRL.60], which appears eleven times a year. For Class 41/42, each party to the settlement is named, and precise information recorded on the numbers of manual workers covered, date of settlement, lowest weekly rates and the percentage change, basic hours, basic holidays, and annual hours, plus any other comments on conditions distinctive to the particular firm and agreement. Sometimes the data refer to the particular industry covered (e.g. "slaughtering"). A weekly *Fact Service* [QRL.201] provides updates. In the Autumn, *Bargaining Report* [QRL.60] includes a review of the year. More continuous information is available to affiliates through the Labour Research Database.

Of the many trades unions with members in food companies, the following may be distinguished. First, there are unions which organise manual workers which cut across many industrial boundaries (e.g. the Transport and General Workers' Union (TGWU), the General Municipal and Boilermakers' Union (GMB), the Union of Shop, Distributive and Allied Workers (USDAW) etc.) Second, unions such as the Association of Scientific, Technical and Managerial Staffs (ASTMS) and the Association of Professional, Executive, Clerical and Computer Staff (APEX) are involved with technical, clerical and managerial employees. Third, organisations like the Bakers, Food and Allied Workers represent a particular industry. Fourth, craft unions as exemplified by the the Electrical, Electronic, Telecommunication and Plumbing Union (EETPU) and the Amalgamated Engineering Union (AEU) have members in a diversity of food manufacturing industries. Some, but not all trades unions, publish information on settlements. Usually the research section is willing to give information to inquirers, filling out what may be found in the press on various settlements (see Appendix B for the addresses of the main trades unions).

The TGWU *Report and Accounts* [QRL.404] includes an extensive report on the industrial scene for the Food, drink and tobacco manufacturing industries. It summarises rates of pay for many workers, including overtime rates, shift rates and minimum wage rates. In the 1986 issue, the settlements for named companies are classified to the following categories:

Chocolate/confectionery
Frozen and chilled foods
General food manufacturing
Fruit and vegetables
Food manufacturing NJIC
Ice-cream
Meat products
Milling industries

The retail food and drink subsection is also relevant for it covers pay rates and conditions of service in food distribution. There is a shorter section from the Agricultural and Allied Workers' Group, which includes data on basic weekly pay from the Poultry Workers' National Advisory Committee. The Committee embraces membership throughout the industry from hatcheries, farms, processing through to egg packing.

A major and expanding source, unique of its kind and unmatched by other union publications, is the *UK Food and Drink Industry Wages and Conditions Survey* [QRL.495]. The 1986 issue exemplifies the comprehensive nature of the coverage of these "Blue Books" collated by the General, Municipal and Boilermakers' Union (the GMB).The information gathered from shop stewards and officials in the firms is now stored, analysed and processed by computer. These invaluable data banks of firms in the Food industries give the names and addresses of the employer or parent company, and the main products manufactured or services provided. The following dimensions of pay and conditions are recorded in the summary of replies from 115 workplaces:

- the annual settlement date
- the standard hours of work per week
- the current lowest basic rate for weekly hours expressed as a percentage of the skilled rate
- the current skilled rate for weekly hours
- the number of grades
- the job evaluation standards
- whether bonus schemes exist and to whom the bonus schemes apply, with examples of average bonus earnings
- overtime premiums
- shift premiums
- holiday entitlement
- holiday pay formula applied
- paid paternity/maternity leave
- bereavement leave
- sick pay
- stand by and call out payments
- overnight stay and first aid allowances
- details of free issues of clothing

These data are presented in four parts:

Part A: Food and food manufacturing
Part B: Biscuits, cocoa, chocolate and sugar confectionery
Part C: Brewing, distilling and soft drinks
Part D: Cold storage

Details of any abnormal conditions and allowances, and whether there is a guaranteed week, are also included. This Survey is obviously dependent on the work of the officials on the ground, and accurate data-processing, but it is evidently a rich source on wages and conditions of service for this sector. There is continuing pressure to maximise the number of returns for the annual conference and the rising size of the sample suggests that the Survey is an increasingly important source.

In principle, the research departments of the trades unions should be able to provide information even though the Annual Reports to conference concentrate more on finance and membership details. One notable source, besides the TGWU *Report and Accounts* [QRL.404] is the *Annual Report* [QRL.43] of the Union of Shop, Distributive and Allied Workers (USDAW). It names the company involved in a settlement, usually giving old and new weekly rates for various grades and operatives, plus other information on holiday entitlements when part of the agreement.

Data on wages and conditions are thus diverse. There are many commercial and trades union sources which supplement as well as reproduce official statistics.

2.6.9.3 Index of wage rates

Indices of wage rates of manual workers combine the details of wage rates in individual agreements into one aggregate index. Since World War Two, the rates used in compiling this index have been restricted to those quoted in national agreements and wages orders. The compilation of the index and historical data were discussed in Dean [B.44]. The series has now been discontinued following the *Rayner Review* [B.368] of statistical services in 1979. This decision was noted in the May 1981 issue of the *Employment Gazette* [QRL.186]. The series was published for the last time in the April 1984 issue of the *Employment Gazette* [QRL.186]. It gave indices of basic weekly wage rates for manual workers, and a separate series of basic wage rates adjusted for changes in normal weekly hours. The information was given for the latest twenty four months and also expressed as an annual average for the latest five years. Data for "Food, drink and tobacco" were reported, together with its weighting in the overall index (1972 = 100). Whilst it existed, the index did not in general take account of changes determined by local negotiations. It also reflected the limitations of wage rate data noted in section 2.6.9 above.

2.6.10 *Salaries and Remunerations Packages*

2.6.10.1 Official sources

A salary is a "fixed payment made by an employer, often monthly, for professional or office work". In practice, however, it is often difficult to isolate data on salary payments from that on earnings, wages, and other labour costs.

The Labour Costs Survey conducted periodically by the Department of Employment (see section 2.6.11) collects data on wages and salaries at Class level. "Wages and salaries" comprise the gross amount before deductions. For firms employing 100 or more employees, it includes bonuses, and wages and salaries of full-time trainees. The results of the 1984 survey were presented in the June 1986 issue of the *Employment Gazette* [QRL.186], and provided figures for wages and salaries as a percentage of all labour costs per hour. This 1984 survey differed from earlier surveys as firms were asked to treat both manual and non-manual employees as a single category.

Wages and salaries are also taken together in the Census of Production inquiries. The summary volume, *Business Monitor PA1002* [QRL.93], records these data for both Class 41/42 and Activity Headings for the latest five years. The individual (PA) Business Monitors have a similar coverage. The figures represent amounts paid during the year to administrative, technical and clerical employees all taken together and to operatives separately. The amounts embrace overtime payments, bonuses, commissions, holiday pay and redundancy payments, less amounts reimbursed for this purpose from government sources. Payments to working proprietors, payments in kind, travelling expenses, lodging allowances etc. are not included nor are employers' national insurance contributions. Separate figures are provided for payments to operatives, and to the administrative, technical and clerical staff, and in so far as these correlate with the distinction between wages and salaries, some appropriate inferences may be made.

The *Report on the Census of Production and Construction in Northern Ireland* [QRL.419] makes similar distinctions, giving figures for Class 41/42 and the industrial groupings (see section 2.1.2) therein. In addition, the *New Earnings Survey* [QRL.375] (see section 2.6.8) has extensive data on non-manual males and females.

The data on average gross hourly earnings reflect what may be regarded as salary payments and other remuneration components.

2.6.10.2 Commercial sources

A very large number of surveys of salaries and remuneration packages exist. The annual *Directory of Salary Surveys* [B.240], by the IDS Top Pay Unit, is a convenient compendium for the majority of what is published. Much of the information concerns executive functions (marketing, finance, production etc.), levels of responsibility, emoluments at various layers of management etc., but there are some industrial analyses of salaries and conditions of service. The twice monthly *IDS Report* [QRL.271], as noted in section 2.6.9.2, concentrates more on weekly-paid operatives. Nevertheless, the reports from company agreements, including food companies, may also include data on agreements for the salaries of staff employees. For example, pay changes, pay structure (e.g. clerical), and job evaluation payments etc., at Reckitt & Colman were featured in the April 1987 issue, which also gave a month by month commentary on settlements in the Food industries over the past year. The companies are named, the numbers of employees recorded, and the pay increases for the past two years presented. Similar comments apply to the *Industrial Relations Review and Report* [QRL.275]. The focus here is more on manual workers, yet there is also information on supervisors on salary scales, and staff grades (clerical, administrative, technical and sales) in the named firms in the Food sector. This is featured in the regular food section of the report.

Reward: The Management Salary Survey [QRL.440], by the Reward Group, bases its statistical coverage on information provided by companies. The median basic salary in the Food, drink and tobacco manufacturing industries is calculated, together with figures for the lower and upper quartiles, the variation on the median, and the sample size. An analysis of median salary by size of company (£m turnover) is undertaken for the following ranks: director; senior manager or senior specialist; senior, middle manager; junior, middle manager; junior manager; supervisor and senior technician; and senior clerical and technician. The Reward Group also furnishes other reports on the regions, and on specific functions, viz: directors' rewards; sales and marketing rewards; financial and accounting rewards; clerical and operative rewards; research and development; consulting engineers; local salary and wage surveys. The companies are coded by Class, and further information is available from the Reward Group.

Inbucon's *Survey of UK Executive Salaries Benefits* [QRL.478] is based upon a questionnaire. Top, senior and middle management are placed into six ranks, and an index of salary differentials and increases is calculated. The industry categories include "Food, drink and tobacco", "Food" and "Drink".

Hay Management Consultants publish *Hay Remuneration Comparison* [QRL.257] and *Hay Survey of Employee Benefits* [QRL.258]. Information on base salary, cash, bonus, regional allowances, plus incentives and benefits (i.e. pensions and company cars) can be found. All the data reflect total net benefits received. Shorter supplements are available where sixteen industrial sectors and over sixty functional job groupings are analysed. Hay claim to have over 11 per cent coverage from the Food industries.

Remuneration Economics Survey of Financial Functions [QRL.402] is another source which quotes "Food, drink and tobacco" as one of the most frequently represented sectors.

Charterhouse and Monks take their data from two different sources in *Charterhouse Top Management Remuneration* [QRL.154]. First, information is extracted from over 1200 company annual reports in order to identify data on salaries and conditions for named food companies. Second, the data from the company reports are combined with a sample survey of some 400 companies to yield information on base salary, total earnings etc. in the Food, drink and tobacco manufacturing industries. A separate publication, *Monks Guide to Board and Senior Management in Companies up to £20m Turnover* [QRL.361], repeats the exercise for smaller (£1m to £20m) companies. "Food, drink and tobacco" is one of the ten industry sectors. *Sales and Marketing Remuneration in Fast Moving Consumer Goods* [QRL.443] was another survey of fifteen different positions which identified data for Class 41/42 but was discontinued after 1988.

Hence there exists a variety of subscription sources which examine the various dimensions of remuneration packages. This is the market response to executives wanting information, and companies needing to know the going rates. There are also some "club" surveys which are confidential to the interested companies which commission them, as well as the more generally available sources mentioned in this section. The *Survey of Executive Compensation among Consumer-packaged Goods Companies in the United Kingdom* [QRL.476], by Hewitt Associates, is an example of a private survey which covers the major UK food companies. They calculate the cash equivalent of remuneration schemes, covering base salary, bonuses, and benefits (e.g. company car, stock option plans). The same organisation produces a *Survey of Remuneration in Levels of Senior UK Managers and Headquarters and Operating Unit Levels* [QRL.477] which is of more general interest. Many private organisations collect information from different samples and/or summarise information from company reports. Some of these surveys can be purchased, but some are confidential to the participants. Some organisations (e.g Hewitt Associates) make a charge for extracts from their data banks. What can be divulged may be subject to the nature of the inquiry in the ebb and flow of these markets.

2.6.11 *Labour Costs*

Wages and salaries are the major, but not exclusive, component of labour costs. Thus reference must also be made to statistical sources which give a much more complete picture of total labour costs. The first comprehensive survey of labour costs in Great Britain was carried out by the Department of Employment in 1964, and was followed by a second in 1968. The 1973 survey was carried out at the request of the European Community. A parallel inquiry for the year was pursued by the (now) Department of Economic Development in Northern Ireland. Another survey was carried out for 1975, which brought the United Kingdom into line with the EC, and subsequently surveys have been conducted in 1978, 1981, 1984 and 1988. These are further discussed in section 2.3.3.4.

Thus data are available on total labour costs for 1964, 1968, 1973, 1975, 1978, 1981, 1984 and 1988. The survey was triennial (1975, 1978, 1981 and 1984) but subsequently became quadriennial (1988 and 1992). The definitive coverage, methodology and results of the 1984 Labour Costs Survey are explained in a special feature article in the June 1986 issue of the *Employment Gazette* [QRL.186]. As shown in [QRL.186], these results for Great Britain cover the full range of labour costs as examplified in the results for labour costs per hour presented for Class 41/42. Labour costs per hour are given in total and then broken down into average expenditure per employee as a percentage of total labour costs into the following categories: wages and salaries; statutory national insurance contributions; provision for redundancy; voluntary social welfare payments; training excluding wages; liability insurance benefits in kind and subsidised services; and government contributions (i.e. negative costs). Another table presents Class results for average contribution per employee per hour in total plus a breakdown and percentage contribution for the following: holidays and other time off with pay; sickness, injury or maternity pay; periodical bonuses and wages and salaries of apprentices and full-time trainees. The 1988 Labour Costs Survey is reported in roughly comparable detail in the September 1990 issue of the *Employment Gazette* [QRL.186]. It must be stressed that these special features in [QRL.186] report for Great Britain and have a time lag of about two years.

As comparable surveys are carried out in Northern Ireland by the Department of Economic Development, results for the United Kingdom can also be compiled. These results are supplied to the European Community. Thus results for the United Kingdom, along with those for other EC countries, are published in EUROSTAT'S *Labour Costs* [QRL.305]. Volume I presents principal results. Volume II gives results by size classes and regions. The latter presents results for aggregate labour costs, both in ECU and in national currencies, both monthly and hourly for both manual and non-manual workers by Class. The time lag before publication is about three years.

A more detailed breakdown by Activity Headings, which clearly identifies the costs of wages and salaries to industry, is published in *Business Monitor PA1002* [QRL.93]. Statistics are presented for operatives, separately from administrative, technical and clerical employees. Per capita labour costs are given for each category. Employers' national insurance contributions appear in total. It must be stressed that the results of these data from the BSO Census of Production are for the United Kingdom. All statistics are for the latest available five years. An analysis of wages and salaries by size of businesses is also presented for Class 41/42 in *Business Monitor PA1002* [QRL.93], and also for Groups and for Activity Headings where they coincide with Groups in the SIC(1980) in the relevant Business Monitors in the PA series.

The *Report on the Census of Production and Construction in Northern Ireland* [QRL.419] summarises the same information for Class 41/42, and for the industrial groupings listed in section 2.1.2.

A complete picture of labour costs cannot be gathered from the work of the Labour Costs Survey of the Department of Employment and the work of the Business Statistics Office discussed in this section. One needs also to draw upon the sources on wage rates and conditions of work and salaries and remuneration packages as described in sections 2.6.9 and 2.6.14.

2.6.12 *Labour Productivity*

Indices of output per person employed are published quarterly for Class 41/42 in the *Employment Gazette* [QRL.186]. However, an unpublished breakdown for the Food industries only is available from the Central Statistical Office. The quarterly data for Class 41/42 are presented for the past five years, and annually for the latest eight years. The most recent figures relate to about two quarters prior to the publication date, and estimates are subject to revision, particularly new estimates of employment.

Given the importance of this item, it may be a little surprising that measures of productivity are not calculated in more detail to show a trend. Only very approximate estimates may be made by using data from the Census of Production to derive output figures for the Activity Headings, and then dividing through by the numbers of employees in employment. *Business Monitor PA1002* [QRL.93] provides ratios of gross output per head, net output per head, and gross value added per head. Figures are usually reported for five years, and five years' data are given in the PA Business Monitors for the individual Groups. A similar exercise is carried out for net output per head, and gross value added at factor cost per head, for Northern Ireland in the *Report on the Census of Production and Construction in Northern Ireland* [QRL.419].

An improvement on this simplistic approach are the computations of total factor productivity carried out by R.E. Mordue and J.D. Marshall [B.127] and B.G.A. Watts [B.184] (see section 2.7.3). The comparisons between the growth of total factor productivity, output, labour input and capital input, using official data for 1968 to 1976 mean that a measure of labour productivity can be inferred for each MLH in SIC(1968). An earlier study by Bateman [B.13] calculated the percentage changes in labour productivity from the Census of Production Reports for 1954, 1958 and 1963. The periods 1954/1958 to 1958/1963 were compared, and the statistical relationships between productivity and associated variables assessed.

In all these exercises, changes in the labour input are simply measured as changes in numbers employed. This ignores changes in hours worked, and changes in labour force quality. A more sophisticated study was carried out by R. Wragg and J. Robertson [B.189]. They drew upon Census of Production statistics from 1963 to 1973 to identify the annual average compound rate of growth in output per head, and output per operative, in selected industries. They also provided statistics on unit wage and salary costs, unit salary costs, unit wage costs, unit gross margin costs, and unit material costs, as performance indicators.

2.6.13 *Trades Union Membership*

The *Employment Gazette* [QRL.186] carries an annual article (usually in February) giving statistics of trades union membership for the latest year. Since 1975, the statistics relate to organisations falling within the definition of "trade union" as specified in section 28 of the Trade Unions and Labour Relations Act 1974. The basic data are collected by the Certification Office established under section 7 of the Employment Protection Act 1975. The annual return for a trades union requests figures on the number of members (male, female and total), for Great Britain, Northern Ireland, the Irish Republic and elsewhere abroad (including the Channel Islands).

Since 1976, statistics have been summarized in the *Annual Report of the Certification Officer* [QRL.46]. Section 7 of the Employment Protection Act 1975 transferred to the Certification Officer certain functions relating to trades unions and employers' associations which were previously carried out by the Chief Registrar of Friendly Societies under other legislation. The transferred functions included the responsibilities of maintaining lists of trades unions and employers' associations under the Trade Unions and Labour Relations Act 1974. Figures are presented on the number of members, income by source, breakdown of expenditure, total funds and assets etc., for each trades union with more than 100,000 members. Totals for these categories are shown for other listed trades unions with less than 100,000 members, for unlisted trades unions, and for all trades unions. The *Annual Report* [QRL.46] has usually been published in the April following the year to which the data refer. At the time of writing there is no industrial breakdown. However the top twenty four trades unions include the TGWU, GMB, ASTMS, and USDAW which all have a significant food industry membership. Both lists and returns can be inspected at the Certification Office. In the case of organisations having their head office in Scotland, there is a second office in Edinburgh. Northern Ireland has the separate *Report of the Registrar of Friendly Societies: Northern Ireland* [QRL.409], but the *Annual Report* [QRL.46] has UK coverage.

The information collected by the Certification Office provides the main basis for updating the biannual *Directory of Employees' Associations, Trade Unions, Joint Organisations etc.* [B.238], all classified according to SIC(1980). The Office also compiles the annual statistics of numbers, and membership, of trades unions as published in the *Employment Gazette* [QRL.186]. The *Directory* [B.238] gives the names of the trades unions, addresses, telephone numbers, names of secretaries etc. Some industrial breakdown could be obtained by examining the branch records of the trades unions, since employees are shown by their SIC code. This method was used by G.S. Bain and R.J. Price [B.7] to give statistics for each Class. It is laborious. Any future attempt at industrial classification of membership would be helped if the Certification Office were to ask for a standardised system of reporting the industry of the membership. But this would be more difficult to achieve for large trades unions with members in many industries. Further data and finer classification by industry are really only obtainable by examination of branch records and the annual reports of the trades union. However, the double counting of an employee belonging to more than one trades union is always a possibility, and the accuracy of the results would also depend upon the efficiency of the branch officials.

A later article by R.J. Price and G.S. Bain [B.149] in 1983 entitled "Union growth in Britain: retrospect and prospect" contains further analyses of unionisation by sector and industry. Numbers and percentages unionised were given for 1948, 1968 and 1979 for "Food and drink" and the changes over 1949–1968 and 1969–1979 calculated. Some data can also be found in *Profiles of Union Growth* [B.8] by the same authors.

Before 1976 and the subsequent coverage of the *Annual Report of the Certification Officer* [QRL.46] data on trades union membership etc. were published in the trades unions' section of the *Report of the Chief Registrar of Friendly Societies* [QRL.406]. Indeed these reports gave more industrial detail than now available, see, for example, the 1974 issue of [QRL.406]. A breakdown by Class (Food, drink and tobacco) of total membership was given, with the number of trades unions listed and submitting returns. Information on average annual contributions and expenditure per member overall were detailed, the latter split into unemployment benefit, dispute benefits, all benefits and administration expenses etc. Political fund transactions were analysed for the grouping of "Food, drink and tobacco". Indeed, more information is now published in the *Annual Report* [QRL.46] than could be gleaned from the annual returns to the Chief Registrar. Coverage evidently depends upon the prevailing legislation in force. The 1970 report gave a concise history of the Registry of Friendly Societies, showing the role of the Registrars in the information collection process. However, as previously mentioned, Section 7 of the Employment Protection Act 1975 transferred to the Certification Officer the functions previously carried out by the Chief Registrar of Friendly Societies under other legislation.

2.6.14 *Industrial Training*

The various issues of the *Annual Report and Accounts* [QRL.44] of the Food Drink and Tobacco Industry Training Board for 1973 to 1983 gave statistical details of the Board's activities. The coverage differed from that of the SIC(1980). The industrial groupings separately identified were: meat and meat products; biscuits and cakes; flour and bakery products; chocolate and sweets; dairy; fish; fresh produce; and general food processing. The training in each sector is described in the text. Statistics on levy points, the number of included establishments, and the number of employees covered, were given. Levy points by country were detailed and levy exemptions enumerated. Data on the disbursement of training levy were summarised. The grants paid for training in industrial relations and industrial training courses, together with the number of employees and students involved, were also presented. The information was reported in [QRL.44] according to the Board's statutory returns until the Board was abolished in 1983.

2.6.15 *Industrial Accidents*

The HM Factory Inspectorate became a component part of the Health and Safety Executive as a consequence of the Health and Safety at Work Act 1974. Information before that date thus flows from the work of the Inspectorate, whereas subsequently it is the responsibility of the Executive.

The changes in title of the various publications are quoted in the QRL Key, but are worth stressing here. From 1880 to 1974, data and commentary were carried in the *Annual Report of the Chief Inspector of Factories* [QRL.47], which was succeeded by a sole (1975) issue of *Industries and Services* [QRL.277]. From 1976 to 1984, *Manufacturing and Service Industries Report* [QRL.338] was the title of the annual report of HM Factories Inspectorate, before this gave way to *Health and Safety at Work: Report by HM Chief Inspector of Factories* [QRL.259]. Although the successors to the *Annual Report of the Chief Inspector of Factories* [QRL.47] have carried statistics in varying detail, the annual publication *Health and Safety Statistics* [QRL.261] is the statistical source which has run from 1975 with minor variations in title.

Up to and including the 1981–1982 issue, *Health and Safety Statistics* [QRL.261] gave data for the number of fatal accidents, the total number of reported accidents, and the incidence rate, for each MLH in SIC(1968). Annual data were typically provided, with selected figures reported for earlier years. Recent coverage has been confined to Class data for fatal and major injuries, and incidence rates reported to enforcement authorities by industry. The accompanying commentary has tended to grow and the statistical detail diminish. Caution must be exercised when using the data because of the number of changes in legislation and reporting procedures which are all noted in the reports. Data, based on census material from the Department of Employment and updated by the quarterly Employment and annual Labour Force surveys, are used to calculate the incidence rates. Ignorance of the requirement to report as specified by the Notification of Accidents and Dangerous Occurrences Regulations 1980 (NADOR) will limit the reliability of reported data.

The *Manufacturing and Service Industries Report* [QRL.338], and the one issue of *Industries and Services* [QRL.277], were the annual reports of the Chief Inspector of Factories and were produced by the Health and Safety Executive. The coverage reflects injuries to employees reportable to the Inspectorate. Data were provided for each MLH for fatal and major accidents, numbers and incidence rates for the latest two years. The later publication, *Health and Safety at Work: Report by HM Chief Inspector of Factories* [QRL.259], is primarily a commentary since the statistics are concentrated in *Health and Safety Statistics* [QRL.261]. But the 1986/87 edition of *Health and Safety at Work: Report by HM Chief Inspector of Factories* [QRL.259] features a chapter on "Food — Safety, Health and Hygiene" and quotes data on accidents in the baking industry (1984–1985) involving slips, trips or falls. There has been a sister publication entitled *Health and Safety Commission Report* [QRL.260] which since 1982/1983 has contained a statistical appendix which has quoted data on fatal injuries, major injuries and incidence rates for Class 41/42. Separate figures are provided for the self-employed and non-employees.

Since the Health and Safety at Work Act 1974, therefore, there have been a multiplicity of publications, all of which succeeded the previous coverage of the *Annual Report of HM Chief Inspector of Factories* [QRL.47]. The last issue (1974) usefully summarises the history of the Factory Inspectorate since the Factories Act of 1833. The statistical appendices usually carried total reported accidents, fatal accidents, and incidence rates for the Minimum List Headings of SIC(1968). A long historical picture can be built up since 1880 but the totality of the detail is too great to report here. Reported accidents in individual industries used to be analysed by process and primary cause (see appendix II of the 1960 report), and by age and sex (see appendix II of the 1951 report).

Another route to accident statistics is through the Department of Health and Social Security data derived from the administration of industrial injury benefit and industrial death benefit claims. *Social Security Statistics* [QRL.455] contains data for the latest two years, analysing the initial assessments of industrial disablement benefit and enumerating the number of accidents and prescribed diseases by Class. Deaths which attracted awards of benefits during the year are analysed by Class for the latest five years with comparative data for 1971 and 1976. These illustrations are drawn from the 1987 issue of [QRL.455]. This information (analysed by Class) is generally more reliable than that in *Health and Safety Statistics* [QRL.261]. A complete survey of cases is carried out for the actual payments of the benefits results from the verification of accident and death. For example, the industrial death benefit statistics by Class are based on a 100 per cent collection. There is also earlier coverage of the lengths of spells of certified incapacity terminated during the period considered resulting from industrial accidents (see the issues of [QRL.455] from 1972 to 1982). The number of spells of certified incapacity commencing in the statistical year resulting from fresh industrial accidents with a male/female breakdown ran from 1972 to 1984. Even though there are changes in coverage, this can be detected more easily through the good organisation of [QRL.455]. A conscious effort is made to retain the same numerical code for the tables. Gaps in the numbering of sections and of tables within sections permit the identification of any additions and deletions of tables.

Given the need to relate accidents to working conditions, the occasional review of *Food and Packaging Health and Safety* [B.279] is a most valuable source for the Food industries. It resulted from the collaboration of the Factory Inspectorate with the Food and Packaging National Industry Groups (NIG), which coordinated working parties from well over two hundred trade associations in the Food industries, and interested trades union parties. The result is an analysis of risks to health and safety common to most sectors, and those which result from transport and refrigeration. Concise descriptions of structure, technological development, and possible risk areas, are given for the following: animal by product industry; bakers; butter and cheese packing; cake and biscuits; confectionery; the dairy industry; the edible oil industry; flour milling; fruit and vegetable canning; grain handling; poultry processing; provender milling; and vegetable grading and packing. This useful guide to many of the processes of the Food industries is followed by convenient statistical tables in the appendix. Data on fatal accidents, all reported accidents, and incidence rates for each MLH were collated for 1977–1982 from HM Factory Inspectorate and the Health and Safety Executive. The number of legal prosecutions for 1977–1980 are given for each MLH. The 1977–1982 issue presents a table on "bacon curing, meat and fish products" which identifies accidents during 1978–1980 involving hand tools, both powered and non-powered, and detailed by accident type. The cooperation of the many trade associations with the Factory Inspectorate, and with the Health and Safety Executive as a spur to prevention, has thus provided valuable information on industrial accidents.

Finally, it must be noted that the most precise detail is sometimes found in trades union sources. The *Annual Report* [QRL.42] of the Bakers, Food and Allied Workers' Union (BFAWU) gives statistics of accident settlements agreed from each district, listing the company, the types of injury, the persons injured and the compensation paid.

2.6.16 *Comments*

Many observations have been made in this section, and we draw together the major points below:

Employment: The Census of Employment, the Census of Production and the Census of Population are the three major sources. The industrial breakdown for Activity Headings is to be found in the individual Business Monitors in the PA series. The available employment data generated by the Department of Employment are unfortunately less detailed. The less frequent Census of Population is the major source for the self-employed, and gives the most detailed occupational breakdown. We have sought to clarify the coverage of these three major sources, and think that the relationship between the various sources should be made clear to the users in the notes.

Unemployment: We note here the diminution in industrial coverage. This important gap in the statistics can only be made good by detailed industrial surveys.

Vacancies, Turnover, Redundancies, Industrial Stoppages, Index of Average Earnings: Most of the data under these headings are published at Class level only.

Earnings and Hours of Work: The *New Earnings Survey* [QRL.375] has been described in detail. Some of the SIC(1980) Activity Headings are consolidated, but more information may possibly be available from the Department of Employment.

Index of Wage Rates: This has been discontinued following the *Rayner Report* [B.368] as noted in section 2.6.9.3

Wage Rates and Conditions of Work: The same comment applies with respect to Rayner. The loose-leaf folder on *Time Rates of Wages and Hours of Work* [QRL.483] is less detailed than the previous publication under the same name, and is moreover only available on subscription. This limitation of the official sources is partly balanced however by the existence of commercial and union data.

Salaries and Remuneration Packages: The official work on wages and salaries as reported in the Business Monitor PA series is filled out by commercial sources which seek to cover the whole of the remuneration package.

Labour Costs: Details are given of the many components of labour costs in 2.6.11, defined more broadly than "Wages and Salaries". But one could not claim that the data cover all perquisites and factor payments. One should also doubtless consult the rich economic literature on the informal economy.

Labour Productivity: Despite the intense interest in this dimension, disaggregated data are difficult to find. The only realistic solution is to have detailed analyses and comparisons of different plants and firms in the Food industries.

Trades Union Membership: Official information is collected by the Certification Office. Further industrial breakdown can only be obtained by examining the branch records of the unions, or approaching the unions themselves.

Industrial Training: The Food, Drink and Tobacco Industry Training Board was abolished in 1983 and its publication *Annual Report and Accounts* [QRL.44] was discontinued. Information, if required, must be obtained directly from the firms themselves.

Industrial Accidents: Many sources exist but the level of detail used to be much greater in the past, as exemplified by the *Annual Report of HM Chief Inspector of Factories* [QRL.47].

Our preoccupation has been predominantly industrial given our need to monitor coverage of these major dimensions according to the SIC. We have drawn together the various strands, supplementing official data with trades union and commercial sources. Much data are available but dispersed among many publications. Time could indeed be saved if a labour market collection drew many of these series together. If the coverage were of both official and commercial sources, then this would be a worthy successor to the *British Labour Statistics Yearbook* [QRL.68].

2.7 Capital

In this section, we consider sources of statistics on capital expenditure, the stock of fixed capital and capital productivity. Sources of data on financial capital and overseas capital transactions are discussed in section 2.10.

2.7.1 *Capital Expenditure*

In this section we consider additions to the stock of physical assets used in the food industry.

2.7.1.1 Business Statistics Office inquiries

Statistics on capital expenditure are an important component of the Annual Censuses of Production carried out by the BSO (see section 2.1.1.1 for details). The results are published for each Activity Heading in Class 41/42 in the relevant annual Business Monitor in the PA series and are summarised in *Business Monitor PA1002: Summary Volume* [QRL.93]. These Business Monitors all provide precise definitions of the term "capital expenditure" as used in the BSO inquiries. A slightly expanded explanation, together with a sample inquiry form, is given in *Business Monitor PA1001: Introductory Notes* [B.214]. In essence, "capital expenditure" is made up of expenditure on new building work; land and existing buildings; plant and machinery; and vehicles. It should be noted that the capital expenditure figures are inclusive of any amounts received or expected to be received in grants and/or allowances from government sources, statutory bodies or local authorities. Where expenditure is spread over more than one census year, payments are included in the years in which they were made. The value of any assets acquired in the takeover of existing businesses is excluded, but capital expenditure in respect of production units where production had not started before the end of the year is included, as is the value of capital goods produced for the businesses' own use by their own staff. The definition of "net" capital expenditure simply refers to expenditure net of any disposals, but the figures are still gross in the sense that no allowance is made for depreciation, amortisation or obsolescence. Care should be taken to avoid confusion with the gross/net distinction used in the National Accounts (see section 2.7.1.3).

Business Monitor PA1002 [QRL.93] provides data on the following:

- gross capital expenditure on new building work; acquisitions and disposals of land and existing buildings; acquisitions and disposals of plant and equipment; and acquisitions and disposals of vehicles; for each Group. Data are provided for the most recent five years.
- net capital expenditure for Class 41/42 analysed by size (employment) of establishment. Data are provided for the most recent year only.
- net capital expenditure on land and buildings, and in total, for Class 41/42, analysed by standard region of the United Kingdom. Data are provided for the most recent year only.
- net capital expenditure for Class 41/42 analysed by country, standard region and assisted area. Data are provided for the most recent year only.
- net capital expenditure per head, and net capital expenditure as a percentage of gross value added, for each Group. Data are provided for the most recent five years.
- net capital expenditure for each Activity Heading. Data are provided for the most recent five years.

- net capital expenditure for each Group analysed by size (employment) of enterprise. Data are provided for the most recent year only. The share provided by the five largest enterprises in the industry is also calculated.
- net capital expenditure for Class 41/42 by the private sector's 100 largest enterprises defined by size of employment. Data are provided for the most recent year only.
- net capital expenditure for Class 41/42 by the private sector's 100 largest enterprises defined by size of net output. Data are provided for the most recent year only.
- net capital expenditure for Class 41/42 by the private sector's 100 largest enterprises defined by size of total sales and work done. Data are provided for the most recent year only.
- gross acquisitions, gross disposals, and net capital expenditure for Class 41/42 by private sector enterprises of foreign nationality. Data are provided for the most recent year only.

The *Historical Record of the Census of Production* [QRL.264] carries a summary analysis of capital expenditure by establishments classified to SIC(1968) Order III "Food, drink and tobacco", and to each MLH therein. Data on net capital expenditure, and for the gross components, are provided for 1948–1970.

The BSO provides further data on capital expenditure from the results of a voluntary quarterly inquiry and these are reported in *British Business* [QRL.66] up to September 1989. The net figures given cover acquisitions less disposals of vehicles and plant and machinery and expenditure on new building work. Spending on land and existing buildings is excluded from these figures. These seasonally adjusted statistics on fixed capital expenditure cover the "Food" industry (Groups 411–423 inclusive). Separate figures are provided for "Drink and Tobacco" (Groups 424–429). The revised results are published within one quarter of the end of the quarter to which they relate, following the provisional results which are usually published three weeks earlier. Comparative quarterly data are presented for the preceding four years, and annual data for the preceding eight years. The survey now takes account of the leasing of assets to manufacturers from the financial sector, since leasing has become an important form of investment in capital inputs. However, at the time of writing, an analysis of leased assets by user industry within manufacturing is not available, so it is not known how much of this expenditure is attributable to the Food industries. The figures from this inquiry are more up-to-date than those from the annual census, but they are also more aggregated and approximate. The data from the voluntary inquiry are, however, checked against, and reconciled with, those from the statutory annual inquiry.

The results of the quarterly inquiry are also published in the *Monthly Digest of Statistics* [QRL.362], again itemising capital expenditure for the "Food" industry separately from "Drink and Tobacco". The quarterly figures at current values are revalued at constant prices and are then seasonally adjusted. In recent editions, quarterly data have been given for the latest available twenty quarters, both in current prices and seasonally adjusted. Annual data are presented for the most recent seven years, both in current and constant (1985) prices.

2.7.1.2 Department of Trade and Industry inquiries

One of the problems of the Census of Production has been the emphasis on establishments. A new system of company reporting was introduced in 1987 (see section 2.3.3.1) and the establishment bias has been partially resolved by the analyses of a representative sample of consolidated annual accounts of companies which are published in *Business Monitor MA3: Company Finance* [QRL.81]. Much of the information is of a financial nature and will be discussed in more detail in section 2.13. However, data are provided on expenditure on fixed assets for companies classified to the Food industries (Groups 411 to 423 inclusive), further broken down into tangible assets, intangible assets and acquisition of subsidiaries. The coverage of the sample survey varies over time, and details are provided in the introductory notes to each issue. In the nineteenth issue published in 1988, information for 1982–1985 (final), and 1986 (provisional), is confined to large companies, defined as those whose capital employed is more than £2.9 million. Information is also given for smaller companies for 1982–1985 (final).

Earlier coverage and methodology was described by S.J. Penneck in "The top 1500 industrial and commercial companies" [B.140] and, for small and medium-sized companies, by Clive Lewis in "Constructing a sampling frame of industrial and commercial companies" [B.103]. The coverage and methodology of the new sample of companies for use in the DTI Company Accounts analysis are described by John Knight in "Top companies in the DTI company accounts analysis" [B.97] and by John Knight and Graham Jenkinson in "Smaller companies in the DTI company accounts analysis" [B.98]. Any changes in coverage are usually noted in *Statistical News* [B.381].

Prior to the tenth issue, [QRL.81] had been published as *Business Monitor M3* [QRL.79]. Due to changes in coverage etc., limited historical comparison of capital expenditure may be derived from this source. However, a long series for "Food" and other industries has been constructed by A.W. Goudie and G. Meeks [QRL.6]. Expenditure on fixed tangible assets can be traced through from 1959 to 1977 in the sources and uses of funds tables.

2.7.1.3 The national accounts

Another obvious and major source is the *United Kingdom National Accounts* [QRL.506] — see section 2.1.3 — which provides data on gross domestic fixed capital formation. Figures for the "Food" industry (Groups 411–423) are provided for the most recent eleven years broken down by type of asset: vehicles, ships and aircraft; plant and machinery; and new buildings and works. The definitions, methodology and sources are discussed in chapter 12 of *United Kingdom National Accounts: Sources and Methods, Third Edition* [B.395]. It should be noted that these estimates of fixed capital formation depend heavily upon the statistics collected by the BSO in the annual censuses of production and in the quarterly capital expenditure inquiries.

2.7.1.4 Suppliers of machinery to the food industry

Data on capital inputs to the food processing and manufacturing industries may also be inferred from output data of machinery suppliers. *Business Monitor PA324:*

Machinery for the Food, Chemical and Related Industries; Process Engineering Contractors [QRL.104] gives the value of sales of goods produced for the latest five years, some of which is to food firms. But more valuable is the information in *Business Monitor PQ3244: Food, Drink and Tobacco Processing Machinery; Packaging and Bottling Machinery* [QRL.127] up to 1989 on the value, and sometimes quantity, of sales for the latest five quarters and past two years. The overall total for food and drink processing machinery is composed of many categories as this selective summary of the list shows: dairy machinery and plant; bakery and biscuit ovens; bakery, biscuit and flour confectionery machinery; sugar confectionery making machinery; slaughterhouse and meat processing machinery; machinery for grain milling etc. The total for "packaging and bottling machinery" includes labelling machinery; filling, closing, sealing and capsuling machinery for bottles, cans, boxes, bags, sacks, sachets etc; packing and wrapping machines etc. *Business Monitor PQ3244* [QRL.127] also contains the value and occasionally the number of many machines imported and thus used in food processing. The considerable breakdown into dairy machinery; bakery and biscuit machinery; machinery for cereal food manufacture; machinery for the confectionery industry; machinery for sugar manufacture; machinery for the preparation of meat; machinery for the preparation of fish; machinery and plant for the edible oils and fats industry; machinery for processing tea and coffee; must also be mentioned.

2.7.1.5 Regional coverage

The *Scottish Economic Bulletin* [QRL.447] usually gives statistics for net capital expenditure, and net capital expenditure per employee, in the Food, drink and tobacco manufacturing industries in Scotland for the latest three years. Net capital expenditure in Scotland as a percentage of that in the United Kingdom is also computed. The data are taken from *Business Monitor PA1002* [QRL.93] and are reproduced again for Scotland in the *Scottish Abstract of Statistics* [QRL.446], where figures are provided for the latest four years.

The *Digest of Welsh Statistics* [QRL.177] provides statistics for net capital expenditure in the Food, drink and tobacco manufacturing industries in Wales, and also the percentage share taken by Wales of the UK total.

The *Report on the Census of Production and Construction in Northern Ireland* [QRL.419] yields capital expenditure data for Class 41/42 and the disaggregated Groups as described in section 2.1.2. Data are provided for the latest year and, unlike in the Scottish and Welsh sources, the figures for total net capital expenditure are broken down into land and buildings; vehicles; and plant and machinery; together with an enumeration of acquisitions and disposals. The coverage of the census is aligned with that carried out for the United Kingdom by the BSO.

Regional data for England, and its standard regions as well as the countries of the United Kingdom are found for net capital expenditure in the Business Monitor PA series. These are also covered in *Business Monitor PA1002* [QRL.93] for the Activity Headings.

2.7.2 *Stock of Fixed Capital*

Annual data on gross capital stock at constant replacement cost in the Food industries (Groups 411–423 inclusive) are provided for the most recent eleven years in *United Kingdom National Accounts* [QRL.506], and broken down by vehicles; plant and machinery; and buildings. Figures for net capital stock are only analysed by sector (personal; industrial and commercial companies; financial companies and institutions; public corporations; central government; local authorities) and type of asset. Statistics on retirements, capital consumption, and net domestic fixed capital formation are only provided for manufacturing as a whole. These various measures all have slightly different meanings. Retirements are estimated as part of the calculation of gross capital stock — the difference between gross capital stock at the end of one year and the next is the annual gross domestic fixed capital formation less retirements. The figures for retirements provide estimates of withdrawals of fixed capital which are different in concept from the 'capital consumption' estimates, which relate to the depreciation of the capital stock. Net domestic fixed capital formation is defined as gross domestic fixed capital formation less capital consumption. In essence, gross capital stock assumes that the original value of fixed assets is maintained until the year of retirement, whereas net capital stock assumes that the value of assets declines gradually over their useful service lives.

Further discussion of the methodology is found in two articles by Tom Griffin, "Revised estimates of the consumption and stock of fixed capital" [B.61] and "The stock of fixed assets in the United Kingdom: how to make best use of the statistics" [B.62]. The former describes how the capital stock, consumption and retirement estimates are derived from capital expenditure survey data together with the expected life lengths of fixed assets. The latter includes length of life estimates for fixed capital stock in various manufacturing industries, including "Food, drink and tobacco", in SIC(1968).

Data on tangible fixed assets owned by food processing and manufacturing companies may, of course, be gleaned from their respective Annual Reports and Accounts. A summary of this information is published annually in *Business Monitor MA3: Company Finance* [QRL.81]. Such data will be expressed in net book values, and will thus reflect any revaluations of the assets and also depend upon the depreciation methods adopted by the companies concerned. Net tangible assets, intangible assets and investments in unconsolidated subsidiaries are identified.

2.7.3 *Capital Productivity*

One of the uses of capital series is to provide an approximate idea of the rate of investment. Another is to measure the productivity of capital. These issues are addressed by R.E. Mordue and J.D. Marshall in "Changes in total factor productivity in UK food and drink manufacturing" [B.127]. This paper generated estimates for the capital input to each MLH in SIC(1968). The growth rate of gross capital stock in the food industry is provided for the years 1960–1977. Similar data are also given for the constituent MLHs for the period 1968–1976. In both instances, the changes in capital inputs were measured by changes in gross capital stock at constant prices. Estimates were subsequently obtained for the growth in output by reference to the appropriately weighted growth rates of capital and labour — total factor productivity is the residual.

This research was originally carried out for the Economic Development Committee (EDC) for Food and Drink Manufacturing and arrived at estimates of productivity change. The Food and Drink Manufacturing EDC also produced estimates of output per unit of capital in *Productivity Growth in UK Food and Drink Manufacturing Industries* [B.355], published in 1978. The data were calculated by MAFF from CSO and Department of Employment information, and show the change in output per unit of capital over the period 1960 to 1975, and the annual change over the period 1970 to 1975. Other indicators of productivity were also calculated: capital input; output per head; and output per unit of labour and capital. Total value added, value added per head and the percentage changes from 1968 to 1975 were compared across the United Kingdom, the United States and West Germany. A comparison was also made of investment at 1970 prices in food manufacturing for these three countries using data derived from primary statistical sources.

A subsequent (1982) Food and Drink Manufacturing EDC paper *Improving Productivity in the Food and Drink Manufacturing Industry: The Case for a Joint Approach* [B.312] also used primary data to estimate productivity change. It is worth stressing here that productivity is a complex issue. Labour productivity, capital productivity and technical progress are interconnected. The emphasis has usually been on labour productivity (output per employee, per person per hour, or per unit of labour cost etc.) but it is sensible to regard productivity change in the broad sense of the change in value added in relation to all the company's resources. Value added per head is associated with the level of capital intensity and it is legitimate to examine several indicators of productivity. Firstly, data on fixed capital expenditure at 1975 prices in the food industry are given and compared with expenditure in the drink and tobacco industries, and in all manufacturing. Secondly, a comparison of investment per worker in "Food, drink and tobacco" over the period 1970–1978 is made for the United Kingdom, France, Italy, West Germany, the Netherlands, Belgium and the United States. Thirdly, indices of value added, employment, and labour productivity for "Food, drink and tobacco" are also compared. Incremental capital-output ratios are also computed for 1970–1978.

Statistics for the growth of output and productivity, contrasting food and all manufacturing between 1960 and 1980 are presented by Watts [B.184]. The total change for the whole period and the annual change is given for labour input; output per head; capital input; output per unit of capital; and output per unit of labour and capital. These statistics, and the inference of the partial substitution of capital for labour over this period, are derived from MAFF data. Indeed many productivity studies combine different series of primary statistics and present the results for capital and labour productivity together.

2.7.4 *Comments*

Figures on capital expenditure and the stock of fixed capital come from the work of the BSO, the CSO and the DTI. The companies themselves are the original source of data. *Business Monitor MA3* [QRL.81] is the resultant of the sampling of these data and provides a summary picture for the "Food" industry despite its conglomerate and multinational nature. Coverage is summarised in the introductory notes to [QRL.81] and subject to change.

On the face of it, it is surprising that little information outside that noted in section 2.7.3 can be found on capital productivity. The internal assessments of food companies themselves and/ or any studies they commission from economic consultants must be the most precise sources. As such, these data are likely to be closely held. Thus it is difficult to obtain up-to-date information which relates to capital productivity, statistical cost analyses relating to the economics of plant or indeed economies of scale from the multi-plant operations of a given business enterprise.

2.8 International Transactions

Sources of statistics on the international transactions of the United Kingdom are covered in detail by Buckley and Pearce in the companion volume in this series, *International Aspects of UK Economic Activities* [B.27]. In this Review, we simply provide guidance to the main sources. First, we outline various schemes adopted for the classification of trade statistics. Then we provide details of the main sources of trade statistics — considering exports and imports together, as most sources give data on both. Lastly, we supply information about international capital movements, and about food aid.

2.8.1 *Classification Schemes for Trade Statistics*

2.8.1.1 The Harmonised Commodity Description and Coding System

Until the end of 1987, the scheme used by EUROSTAT for the classification of overseas trade statistics was the EC Nomenclature of Goods for the External Trade Statistics of the Community and Statistics of Trade between Member States (NIMEXE). On 1st January 1988, the Combined Nomenclature (CN) of the European Community was introduced and this replaced not only NIMEXE, as the basis of statistical classification, but also the Common Customs Tariff (CCT). These developments are outlined in more detail in section 2.3.3.5.

The CN is based on the Harmonised Commodity Description and Coding System, or Harmonised System (HS) for short, which is an internationally agreed system of goods classification. Each commodity in the HS is allocated a 6-digit code number which reflects its classification to a particular Section and Chapter. For the Food industries, the relevant Sections are:

Section I — Live animals; animal products
Section II — Vegetable products
Section III — Animal or vegetable fats and oils and their cleavage products; prepared edible fats; animal or vegetable waxes
Section IV — Prepared foodstuffs; beverages, spirits and vinegar; tobacco and manufactured tobacco substitutes

These Sections are then divided into the following Chapters:

Section I

Chapter 1 — Live animals
Chapter 2 — Meat and edible meat offal
Chapter 3 — Fish and crustaceans, molluscs and other aquatic invertebrates
Chapter 4 — Dairy produce; birds' eggs; natural honey; edible products of animal origin, not elsewhere specified or included

Chapter 5	Products of animal origin, not elsewhere specified or included
Section II	
Chapter 6	Live trees and other plants; bulbs, roots and the like; cut flowers and ornamental foliage
Chapter 7	Edible vegetables and certain roots and tubers
Chapter 8	Edible fruit and nuts; peel of citrus fruit or melons
Chapter 9	Coffee, tea, mate and spices
Chapter 10	Cereals
Chapter 11	Products of the milling industry; malt; starches; inulin; wheat gluten
Chapter 12	Oil seeds and oleaginous fruits; miscellaneous grains, seeds and fruit; industrial or medicinal plants; straw and fodder
Chapter 13	Lac; gums, resins and other vegetable saps and extracts
Chapter 14	Vegetable plaiting materials; vegetable products not elsewhere specified or included
Section III	
Chapter 15	Animal or vegetable fats and oils and their cleavage products; prepared edible fats; animal or vegetable waxes
Section IV	
Chapter 16	Preparations of meat, of fish or of crustaceans, molluscs or other aquatic invertebrates
Chapter 17	Sugars and sugar confectionery
Chapter 18	Cocoa and cocoa preparations
Chapter 19	Preparations of cereals, flour, starch or milk; pastrycooks' products
Chapter 20	Preparations of vegetables, fruit, nuts or other parts of plants
Chapter 21	Miscellaneous edible preparations
Chapter 22	Beverages, spirits and vinegar
Chapter 23	Residues and waste from the Food industries; prepared animal fodder
Chapter 24	Tobacco and manufactured tobacco substitutes

These Chapters are further divided into 4-digit headings, and finally into 6-digit HS codes. Full details of these codes are beyond the scope of this Review, but an example may prove helpful:

Section II	Vegetable products
Chapter 8	Edible fruit and nuts; peel of citrus fruit or melons
Main Heading 08.05	Citrus fruit, fresh or dried
HS code 0805.40	Grapefruit, fresh or dried

2.8.1.2 The Standard International Trade Classification

The HM Customs and Excise Integrated Tariff of the United Kingdom contains about 10,500 commodity headings which cover the overseas trade of the United

Kingdom. The Tariff is based on the Harmonised System (HS), within which the Tariff incorporates the subheadings of the Combined Nomenclature (CN). The description of each heading is uniquely identified by a 9-digit Commodity code number in the Tariff: the first six digits indicate the Chapter and Main Heading within the HS; the 7th and 8th digits indicate the subheading of the CN to which it correlates; and the 9th digit is the UK code. Both the number and scope of headings in the Tariff have changed extensively with the introduction of HS on 1st January 1988. Details of the full text of each trade description, together with their code numbers, are published in the *Business Monitor MA21: Guide to the Classification for Overseas Trade Statistics* [B.213].

While trade statistics are compiled on the basis of the headings that appear in the Tariff, they are detailed in many publications (see section 2.8.2.1) under the headings of the Standard International Trade Classification (SITC). The SITC was introduced by the United Nations in 1950 to succeed the "Minimum List of Commodities for International Trade Statistics" published in 1938 by the League of Nations. The SITC was subsequently revised in 1960 to bring it into line with the 1955 Tariff Nomenclature (CCCN) of the Customs Cooperation Council, revised for a second time — SITC(R2) — in 1975, and for a third time in January 1988. The third, and current, revision — SITC(R3) — classifies commodities to one of the following ten Sections:

Section 0	Food and live animals
Section 1	Beverages and tobacco
Section 2	Crude materials, inedible, except fats
Section 3	Mineral fuels, lubricants and related materials
Section 4	Animal and vegetable oils, fats and waxes
Section 5	Chemicals and related products, not elsewhere specified
Section 6	Manufactured goods classified chiefly by material
Section 7	Machinery and transport equipment
Section 8	Miscellaneous manufactured articles
Section 9	Commodities and transactions not classified elsewhere in the SITC

Each Section is then further divided into a number of Divisions, of which the following are the most relevant for this Review:

Division 00	Live animals other than animals of Division 3
Division 01	Meat and meat preparations
Division 02	Dairy products and birds' eggs
Division 03	Fish, (not marine mammals), crustaceans, molluscs, and aquatic invertebrates and preparations thereof
Division 04	Cereals and cereal preparations
Division 05	Vegetables and fruit
Division 06	Sugar, sugar preparations and honey
Division 07	Coffee, tea, cocoa, spices, and manufactures thereof
Division 08	Feeding stuff for animals (not including unmilled cereals)
Division 09	Miscellaneous edible products and preparations
Division 22	Oil seeds and oleaginous fruit
Division 41	Animal oils and fats
Division 42	Fixed vegetable fats and oils; crude, refined or fractionated
Division 43	Animal and vegetable oils and fats, processed, and waxes of animal or vegetable origin; inedible mixtures or preparations of

animal or vegetable fats and oils nes.

Details of the SITC(R3) headings within these Divisions will be provided, where appropriate, in the following chapters. One example only is given here:

Section 0	Food and live animals
Division 05	Vegetables and fruit
SITC(R3) heading 057.22	Grapefruit, fresh or dried
Commodity code 080540 00 0	Grapefruit, fresh or dried

SITC(R3) provides headings corresponding directly to those of the Harmonised system, which forms the basis of the CN; however, the order in which articles are grouped differs between the two classifications.

2.8.1.3 The National Ports Council Commodity Classification

Until 1981, the National Ports Council (NPC) used to collect statistics on the foreign traffic of British ports. This responsibility has now passed to the Department of Transport. The statistics are obtained for the most part from the records maintained by each port authority of the dues levied on goods passing through the port area. In some cases port authorities have supplemented their own records with figures supplied by shipowners, shippers, stevedores, private wharfingers and HM Customs and Excise. These statistics are analysed according to the NPC common commodity classification, which is based on SITC(R2) at the time of writing, and which is detailed in an appendix to *Port Statistics* [QRL.383]. The codes which are relevant for this Review are:

NPC code	Commodity class	SITC(R2) code
1.11	Meat and meat preparations	01
1.12	Dairy products and eggs	02
1.131	Unmilled cereals	041 to 045
1.132	Milled cereals and cereal preparations	046 to 048
1.141	Fresh fruit and vegetables	05
1.142	Fruit and vegetables, other than fresh	05
1.15	Animal feeding stuffs	08
1.2	Sugar and sugar preparations	06
1.4	Other foodstuffs and tobacco	03,07,09,12
2.521	Oil seeds and nuts	22
2.522	Animal and vegetable oils and fats	41,42,43
5.2	Live animals	00,94

Publications using the NPC code will be outlined in section 2.8.2.2.

2.8.2 *International Trade*

Data on the international trade of the United Kingdom are available in a wide range of statistical publications. In this section, we group these publications as to whether they give commodity analyses using data provided by HM Customs and Excise, or data provided by the port authorities, or whether they provide analyses of trade by industrial sector. Moreover, we detail a number of European and international publications which are secondary sources only, but which are convenient compendia for cross-country comparisons. As a general rule, these secondary sources are published much later than the UK sources. At the time of writing this section, the latest editions of most of them still presented data analysed by SITC(R2).

2.8.2.1 HM Customs and Excise records

As befits a major trading nation, the collection of both export and import data for the United Kingdom by HM Customs and Excise has a long history, and the detail available is considerable. The primary source is the monthly *Business Monitor MM20: Overseas Trade Statistics of the United Kingdom* [QRL.85], published before January 1989 as *Overseas Trade Statistics of the United Kingdom* [QRL.85]. These provide monthly data, and cumulative data for the current year, on the following:

- imports in value terms, analysed by country of origin and by Division of SITC(R3),
- imports in both value and volume terms of some 3100 commodity headings in SITC(R3), analysed by countries accounting for significant amounts of trade,
- imports in both value and volume terms of every 9-digit trade description in the HM Customs and Excise Integrated Tariff,
- exports in value terms, analysed by country of destination and by Division of SITC(R3),
- exports in both value and volume terms of some 3100 commodity headings in SITC(R3), analysed by countries accounting for significant amounts of trade,
- exports in both value and volume terms of every 9-digit trade description in the HM Customs and Excise Integrated Tariff.

Further information for any of the 10,500 commodity headings, and for the 216 areas and countries distinguished, may normally be obtained from any of the marketing agents appointed by HM Customs and Excise — details are given in [QRL.85].

An annual edition of *Overseas Trade Statistics of the United Kingdom* [QRL.80] is also published, usually mid-year, and this contains updated information taking into account corrections notified to the HM Customs and Excise Statistical Office after the monthly figures have been compiled. From 1990, this is published as *Business Monitor MA20: Overseas Trade Statistics of the United Kingdom* [QRL.80]. The figures for exports and imports form the starting point of the estimates of visible trade on a balance of payments basis, which were published monthly in *British Business* [QRL.66]. They appear annually in *United Kingdom Balance of Payments* [QRL.502]. The latter provides eleven years' data on exports, imports and the visible balance for "Food, Beverages and Tobacco" — Sections 0 and 1 in the SITC(R3).

There is a continual demand for up-to-date information on trade flows to which the CSO and the Department of Trade and Industry (DTI) respond by issuing monthly press notices. The DTI also publish a *Monthly Review of External Trade Statistics* [QRL.364] which gives monthly, quarterly and annual commodity analyses of visible trade for Sections 0 and 1 of the SITC(R3). A quarterly document, *UK External Trade: Area x Commodity Analysis* [QRL.494], formerly *United Kingdom Trade with European Countries* [QRL.508], was available up to 1987 and may be restored in the future. They gave annual data for Divisions in value terms for exports, imports, exports less imports and the percentage of exports over imports by specified trading country and bloc. All three use data from computer printouts furnished by HM Customs and Excise.

"Food from Britain" is an organisation whose promotional work includes the presention of trade statistics in a more digestible form. *UK Food & Drink Trade Statistics* [QRL.496] is prepared each month. It gives the value of UK food and drink imports, exports and the trade balance for the latest six months. Some commodity breakdown for types of product is available. The *United Kingdom Food and Drink Trade: Annual Statistics* [QRL.505] provides annual value data for exports and imports with more detailed product breakdown according to trading partners (France, Holland etc.) A third digest, *United Kingdom Food and Drink Exports: Priority Markets* [QRL.504], collects together annual export data featuring the following: beef and veal; lamb; pork; bacon; poultry-duck; fish; shellfish; dairy products; cheese; confectionery; cakes; biscuits; crispbreads; jams and marmalades; tea; beer; gin and whisky. There are further subdivisions within these sections. Although [QRL.496], [QRL.505] and [QRL.504] are strictly secondary and derive from Customs and Excise, they provide a useful service to the Food industries.

Mention should also be made of the *Monthly Digest of Statistics* [QRL.362] and the *Annual Abstract of Statistics* [QRL.37], both of which make use of HM Customs and Excise data. For instance, the *Annual Abstract of Statistics* [QRL.37] carries annual value data of exports and imports analysed by sections and divisions. Finally, the reworking by the BSO of Customs and Excise data for the PQ Business Monitors is discussed in section 2.8.2.3.

2.8.2.2 Port statistics

The *Digest of Port Statistics* [QRL.174] was published annually from 1966 to 1973 by the National Ports Council — each issue providing data for the previous year. In 1973, the Digest was substantially revised and expanded. The new *Annual Digest of Port Statistics* [QRL.39] was published in two volumes for the years from 1973 to 1979 — the year in the title now referring to the year to which the statistics relate rather than the year of publication. In 1981, the National Ports Council was abolished and all its statistical publications discontinued.

A new series of statistical publications concerning ports was started, published jointly by the Department of Transport and the British Ports Association. The annual *Port Statistics* [QRL.383] was based on volume 1 of [QRL.39] though with less detail. It provides an analysis of imports and exports of the various commodity classes in the NPC classification for the latest four years. Moreover, it provides an analysis of the imports and exports of these commodity classes through forty one selected ports for the most recent year. Two other publications of the British Ports Association, the quarterly *Statistical Abstract of the UK Ports Industry* [QRL.457] and the annual *Statistical Abstract of the UK Ports Industry* [QRL.458], have recently been discontinued.

In general, the number of publications containing port statistics has been rationalised considerably in recent years. Details of extinct volumes may be traced through the various editions of [QRL.383] and its predecessors.

The *Scottish Economic Bulletin* [QRL.447] provides HM Customs and Excise data on imports and exports through Scottish ports of Sections 0 and 1 in SITC(R3).

Figures are provided for the latest eight years. Similar data are provided in the *Scottish Abstract of Statistics* [QRL.446].

2.8.2.3 Industry analyses of trade

In 1975, R. Sellwood of the Department of Industry wrote an article entitled "New statistical series analysing commodities imported and exported according to the industries of which they are the principal products" [B.160]. The article provided an analysis of UK overseas trade expressed in terms of industries, as defined by SIC(1968). This arrangement complemented the normal presentation based on the SITC. The general principle used in the construction of the series was that each of the 8-digit code numbers in the SITC (see section 2.8.1.1) was classified to the industry (MLH) in which the product was principally manufactured. The series for each industry was thus obtained by summing the trade for those 8-digit code numbers so classified.

Sellwood discusses the various problems inherent in the interpretation of the series. For instance, exports of commodities requiring several processing stages in their manufacture were wholly allocated to the industry to which they were classified in the final form in which they were exported. Thus, for example, exports of bread were classified to MLH212 "Bread and flour confectionery" and no allocation was made to MLH211 "Grain milling". Sellwood also provides import and export data for 1970–1973 classified according to MLH in SIC(1968). Quarterly data for each MLH subsequently appeared in *Business Monitor M10: Overseas Trade Analysed in Terms of Industries* [QRL.77] until the end of 1978. From 1979 onwards, the series has been published quarterly in *Business Monitor MQ10: Overseas Trade Analysed in Terms of Industries* [QRL.90]. No issues were published in 1981 due to industrial action, and it was not until the first quarter issue for 1983 that the statistics were classified according to SIC(1980). Data are now provided for each Activity Heading in SIC(1980), and for many sub-activity headings. The statistics appear about one quarter after the quarter to which they refer, and data are provided for the latest five quarters and two years. A brief preview of the contents of [QRL.90] used to be available rather earlier in *British Business* [QRL.66] but data were only provided for Class 41/42 in aggregate.

The quarterly Business Monitors in the PQ series publish data on exports and imports for many of the products designated within the Activity Headings — see the following chapters for further details. Moreover, they also provide details of the HM Customs and Excise Tariff/Trade code numbers corresponding to each of the products identified within the PQ Monitors for the industry in question. It is useful that the BSO rework Customs and Excise data such that the consequent groupings relate more closely to the comparable groups used for UK sales data.

Business Monitor MQ12: Import Penetration and Export Sales Ratios for Manufacturing Industry [QRL.91] presents four ratios relating overseas trade in the goods produced by virtually every sector of manufacturing to domestic production and apparent consumption of those goods. SIC(1980) has been used since the first quarter of 1983, and figures are currently provided for each Group and Activity Heading (except AH4121) within Class 41/42, and for the Class in aggregate. The ratios were first introduced by Wells and Imber in a 1977 article entitled "The home and export performance of United Kingdom industries" [B.185] which described the conceptual and methodological problems involved in measuring such variables as "import penetration". The article also published ratios at MLH level for the years 1968 to 1976. Annual ratios at MLH level for the years 1970 to 1979 were presented in the 1980 article by Alan Hewer on "Manufacturing industry in the seventies: an assessment of import penetration and export performance" [B.78]. Data for 1975 to 1977 were also published in the first issue of *Business Monitor M12: Import Penetration and Export Sales Ratios for Manufacturing Industry* [QRL.78], which appeared in May 1978. The final issue of [QRL.78] was published in August 1978 and provided data for March of that year, after which it was succeeded by *Business Monitor MQ12* [QRL.91], the first issue of which provided data for September 1978. However, after the *Review of DTI Statistics* [B.367], quarterly sales data are much diminished. Consequently, the second quarter 1989 issue of *Business Monitor MQ12* [QRL.91] is the last in this format, with data up to the second quarter of 1989.

The four ratios calculated relate to twelve-month periods at quarterly intervals, and are defined as follows:

(1) imports/home demand
 (home demand = manufacturers' sales + imports − exports)
(2) imports/home demand + exports
(3) exports/manufacturers' sales
(4) exports/manufacturers' sales + imports

Ratio (1) is the measure commonly used when describing import penetration of a home market, purporting to measure the share of the home market captured by imports. It takes no account, however, of the extent of the domestic industry's involvement in export markets, a high level of which might be deemed to compensate for a high level of imports. Allowance is made for this in ratio (2), which reduces as exports increase. Similarly while ratio (3) is the measure usually adopted to relate exports to total sales by UK manufacturers, and indeed it is the one against which individual manufacturers might reasonably attempt to compare their own export to sales ratio, it ignores the extent to which imports of the same product are finding their way into the United Kingdom. This is allowed for in ratio (4). A further advantage of ratios (2) and (4) is that they have the same denominator (home demand plus exports equals manufacturers' sales plus imports) and thus the difference between the two measures also has some meaning as an indicator of the trade gap. Ratios (2) and (4), moreover, also circumvent any distortion caused when goods are imported for subsequent re-export.

The sales figures used in the preparation of these ratios relate to UK manufacturers' sales of the principal products of the industry concerned, excluding, where possible, waste products and work done. Generally these are derived from the appropriate Business Monitor in the PQ series, whilst the overseas trade series used are based on the figures compiled for *Business Monitor MQ10* [QRL.90]. *British Business* [QRL.66] published the ratios for Class 41/42 in aggregate rather earlier than [QRL.90]. The ratios for Class 41/42 are also reproduced for twelve-month periods at quarterly intervals in the *Monthly Digest of Statistics* [QRL.362], and annually for the latest eleven years in the *Annual Abstract of Statistics* [QRL.37].

It should be noted that the ratios suffer from certain deficiencies. First, there is no exact correspondence between the production-based SIC and the commodity-based

SITC. Second, timing differences in reporting the different transactions may produce distortions, particularly in short-period calculations. Third, quarterly sales data often suffer from erratic and seasonal movements. An article by David Elis-Williams [B.47] discusses methods of seasonal adjustment of the overseas trade figures. Fourth, the provision of finer industrial detail would be welcomed by users, yet would be difficult to accomplish without costly specific market surveys. Yet the statistics have been used by many authors to draw conclusions about the Food industries. Wells and Imber [B.185] commented on the success of food manufacturing in reducing import penetration and increasing export sales from 1968 to 1976. Hewer [B.78] identified bacon curing, meat and fish products; milk and milk products; and oils and fats in SIC(1968) as industries which were especially successful at reducing import penetration and improving export performance between 1970 and 1979.

2.8.2.4 Index numbers of volumes and unit values

The *Monthly Review of External Trade Statistics* [QRL.364] is the primary source on volume and unit value index numbers for exports and imports. The volume indices set out to show movements in imports and exports after eliminating variations due to price changes. They are prepared by estimating the value of goods in the current period at base year prices. The unit value index numbers are intended as guides to changes in the prices of exports and imports. The unit values are obtained by dividing the value of trade recorded in the month for each heading by a corresponding quantity (numbers, tonnes etc.). The indices are then constructed by weighting the growth in unit values by the value of trade in the base year. The indices are thus called unit value rather than price indices. The methodology is outlined in *United Kingdom Balance of Payments* [QRL.502] — the CSO 'Pink Book' — and in the *Monthly Digest of Statistics Supplement: Definitions and Explanatory Notes* [B.337], and is appraised by Buckley and Pearce [B.27].

Export volume indices are presented for "Food, beverages and tobacco" (SITC(R3) codes 0+1), and "Animal and vegetable oils and fats" (4), under the heading of non-manufactured goods. Further indices are also published for "food and live animals" (0), "beverages" (11), and "beverages and tobacco" (1). These indices are seasonally adjusted, and monthly figures are provided for the latest two years, quarterly figures for the latest three years, and annual figures for the latest ten years. The level of detail for unit value indices is similar.

The *Monthly Review of External Trade Statistics* [QRL.364] is also the primary source for import volume, and unit value, indices. Again, "Food, beverages and tobacco" (0+1) and "Animal and vegetable oils and fats" (4) are identified under non-manufactured goods, but more commodity breakdown is provided. Separate indices are presented for "meat and meat preparations" (01), "dairy products and eggs" (02), "cereals and animal feeding stuffs" (04+08), "fruit and vegetables" (05), and "food and live animals" (0). The treatment of unit value indices is similar (to that for exports) with monthly, quarterly and annual data.

The *Monthly Review of External Trade Statistics: Annual Supplement* [QRL.365] provides longer time series of annual and quarterly data, available for all series covered in the *Monthly Review of External Trade Statistics* [QRL.364]. Data are also to be found in the *Monthly Review of External Trade Statistics: Mid-year Supplement*

[QRL.366]. The *Monthly Digest of Statistics* [QRL.362] repeats the export and import volume and unit value index numbers for "Food, beverages and tobacco", providing monthly, quarterly and annual figures.

2.8.2.5. European and international sources

As noted in section 2.8.2, most of the publications cited in this section did not, at the time of writing, present statistics classified according to the HS and SITC(R3). Hence, we describe here the treatment of the data up to the end of 1987, in the expectation that the new treatment will not differ significantly.

The Statistical Office of the European Communities (EUROSTAT) provides a variety of publications which cite statistics on the trade performance of the United Kingdom, and the other Member States of the European Community. These sources containing foreign trade statistics are identified as "Theme 6" (red covers) in the classification of EUROSTAT publications (see section 2.3.2). Information on EUROSTAT's external trade publications, together with a detailed description of the methods used, can be found in *External Trade Statistics: User's Guide* [B.267]. For the purposes of this Review, the following volumes are of particular interest.

In the *External Trade Analytical Tables* [QRL.196], EUROSTAT publishes detailed annual data on the Community's external trade and trade between Member States down to the 6-digit level of the NIMEXE classification. Two sets of thirteen volumes are published: one set for imports, and one set for exports. Volume A in both sets covers chapters 1–24 of NIMEXE, wherein lie most of the food products of interest for this Review. In Volume Z (both sets), the data on trade with individual partner countries are published in aggregate form at the 2-digit (chapter heading) level. Quarterly data are available on microfiche for all levels of the NIMEXE and SITC.

The predecessor of [QRL.196] was the *Analytical Tables of Foreign Trade* [QRL.35]. This publication was based on the SITC up to 1983, and was divided into six volumes. Volume II covered Sections 0–4 of SITC(R2) and provided data on the trade of the Community and its Member States broken down at the 5-digit level, and by trading partners. In 1984, the NIMEXE classification system was adopted and [QRL.35] was published in thirteen volumes, but it was not until 1985 that the name was changed to its present title [QRL.196].

These publications are complemented by *External Trade Monthly Statistics* [QRL.195] which provides monthly, quarterly and annual trends in the external trade of the Member States, broken down by Sections of SITC(R2). The *External Trade Analytical Tables: Glossarium* [B.264] and the *External Trade Monthly Statistics: Glossarium* [B.265] both provide useful background material on the scope and methodology used.

A number of other international agencies also provide statistical compendia. Here we will consider a selection. The *International Trade Statistics Yearbook* [QRL.292] is published in two volumes by the United Nations. Volume I provides trade data in both weight and value terms for each country analysed by Division of SITC(R2). Figures are provided for the latest four years. Volume II provides analyses of world trade by country for each subgroup (4-digit) and item (5-digit) of SITC(R2). Figures are provided for the latest five years. Commodity matrix tables are also given which show the 22 major exporting countries, and 20 major importing countries, ranked by value for each group (3-digit) level of SITC(R2). Another United Nations publication, *Commodity Trade Statistics* [QRL.156], provides annual figures on world commodity trade by regions and trading partners of provenance and destination. Data are provided for each item (5-digit) in SITC(R2).

The Food and Agriculture Organisation (FAO) reported trade data over the latest eleven quarters for major exporting and importing countries in the *FAO Monthly Bulletin of Statistics* [QRL.205]. Data were only provided for certain products each month — see the cumulative index on the back page for details of the contents — from 1989 the *FAO Quarterly Bulletin of Statistics* [QRL.206] has had similar coverage but quarterly. The *FAO Trade Yearbook* [QRL.207], (known as *FAO Trade Commerce* [QRL.207] since 1987), provides trade data for the latest three years for each food item (5-digit) in SITC(R2), analysed by country. In addition, tables are published of trade in agricultural requisites: tractors; crude fertilizers; manufactured fertilizers; and pesticides; analysed by country. Trade data for each country are also given for the past six years, analysed by Division in SITC(R2).

Other international organizations — e.g. the Organization for Economic Cooperation and Development (OECD), the United Nations Conference on Trade and Development (UNCTAD) — also publish statistical compendia. Our objective here, however, is not to provide a comprehensive survey of such works, but just to give a few examples. One last publication which is worthy of note is the annual review of *International Trade* [QRL.291] by the GATT (General Agreement on Tariffs and Trade) organization. This contains not only statistical information taken from the above references, but also a commentary on developments in world food trade.

2.8.3 *International Capital Movements*

In addition to trade flows, mention should also be made of capital movements into and out of the United Kingdom. These are chronicled annually in *Business Monitor MA4: Overseas Transactions* [QRL.82]. Data are provided on both outward and inward net direct investment by companies classified to Class 41/42 "Food, drink and tobacco", analysed by area and main country. Moreover, data are also given for net earnings by such companies from both outward and inward direct investment, analysed by area and main country. For both investment and earnings, statistics are provided for the latest five years. Finally, figures are also given of receipts and expenditure of overseas royalties and similar transactions, again for "Food, drink and tobacco" in aggregate.

The estimates of direct investment are derived from statistical inquiries conducted by the Department of Trade and Industry (DTI), the Bank of England, and the Association of British Insurers. Direct investment, as defined in these inquiries, is a financial concept and is not the same as capital expenditure on fixed assets, or the growth in companies' net assets. Direct investment covers the money investment in a related concern by a parent company, which need not necessarily be used for the purchase of fixed assets. Further details are provided in the introduction to [QRL.82].

Business Monitor MA4 [QRL.82] appears about eighteen months after the end of the year to which the data refer. A preview of the main results was published, together with a commentary, some months earlier in *British Business* [QRL.66]. In general, the figures for both net investment and for net earnings, analysed by industrial activity and country, are inexact and should only be used as guidelines to trends.

To complement the analysis in [QRL.82], there is *Business Monitor MO4: Census of Overseas Assets* [QRL.76] which focuses on the book value of UK net direct investment overseas, and overseas net direct investment in the United Kingdom. Data are provided on the book value of outward direct investment in "Food, drink and tobacco" analysed by country; the book value of inward direct investment in "Food, drink and tobacco" analysed by country; and the book value of outward direct investment analysed by industry of UK enterprise and industry of overseas affiliate — again "Food, drink and tobacco" is separately identified.

The data result from inquiries carried out triennially by the DTI since 1962. *Business Monitor MO4* [QRL.76] was first published in 1987, and carried data for the end of 1984. Prior to this, the results had been published as *Business Monitor MA4 Supplement: Census of Overseas Assets* [QRL.83]. Summary data were available in *British Business* [QRL.66], and more disaggregated information may be obtained for the "Food" industry alone on application to the DTI.

2.8.4 *Food Aid*

Annual statistics on food aid in value terms to selected recipient countries are published for the latest five years in *British Aid Statistics: Statistics of UK Economic Aid to Developing Countries* [QRL.65]. A comprehensive data base of food aid flows is maintained by the Food and Agriculture Organization (FAO). The FAO continuously monitors food aid flows and developments, and publishes relevant up-to-date information in its monthly *Food Outlook* [QRL.239] and the periodic *Food Aid Bulletin* [QRL.230]. *Food Aid in Figures* [QRL.231] complements the information presented in these publications by providing further details on food aid flows by commodities, donors and recipients, and by covering a longer time period. Flows of the following commodities are analysed by donor and by recipient: cereals; wheat; rice; coarse grains; skimmed milk powder; other dairy products; vegetable oil; and butteroil. Shipments of each of these types of food aid by the United Kingdom to over 100 recipient countries may be identified.

2.8.5 *Comments*

Some observations may now be made on the wide variety of sources of trade statistics. First, it should be clear that the major source is *Business Monitor MM20: Overseas Trade Statistics of the United Kingdom* [QRL.85], and that this publication provides considerable commodity detail. Electronic improvements in data collection, handling and processing should enable faster access to the available information. Second, many other sources reproduce data first published in [QRL.85]. It would be helpful if these derivations could be more clearly indicated in many of the publications. Third, the lack of an exact correspondence between the SIC and the SITC is unavoidable, but does lead to certain difficulties in extracting data relevant to the Food industries from [QRL.85]. It is sometimes not easy to identify the separate items in SITC(R3) which relate to farm foodstuffs, semi-processed goods, and fully-processed products. Here the various industrial analyses outlined in section 2.8.2.3 prove invaluable. Fourth, changes in classifications do lead to some discontinuities. For instance, the adoption by HM Customs and Excise of the Harmonised Commodity Description and Coding System (HS) has the aims of providing a more up-to-date classification of goods and of improving international comparisons. Yet there are discontinuities between the series collected after January 1988 and previous data based on the earlier classification. Fifth, the individual chapters provide further sources of trade statistics for the relevant industries, but often these do little more than rework the data from HM Customs and Excise records.

These are, however, minor comments compared with the prospects for 1992 and beyond, which has brought into question the need for disaggregated data, especially with respect to trade with other members of the European Community. These matters are discussed in the February 1989 issue of *Statistical News* [B.381] and fully covered in the papers and proceedings of the 1988 Statistics Users' Conference on UK International Trade Statistics.

2.9 Stocks

The concept of stocks embraces stocks of raw materials and semi-processed goods, stocks of finished products, and stocks in the distribution chain. Data are available in a wide variety of sources.

2.9.1 *Ministry of Agriculture, Fisheries and Food Inquiries*

There are many MAFF reports which yield data on stocks; some are unpublished and some are for official use only. The coverage ranges from stocks of inputs into further processing (e.g. stocks of cereals, and vegetable fats and oils) to stocks of products for final consumption (e.g. stocks of tea, and sugar). Slater [B.164] provides a catalogue of these inquiries, and a list is provided in Appendix C. The inquiries are also outlined in the commodity statistics section of Barnett [B.12].

These sources are discussed in detail in the relevant chapters which follow, but many of the main results are collected together in the *Monthly Digest of Statistics* [QRL.362]. The foodstuffs listed are a mixture of primary, intermediate and processed products. The specific MAFF inquiry which generated the data is often cited in the footnotes, and these merit attention. Stocks of the following are usually reported, although there is some variation in coverage at times: wheat and flour; oats; barley; animal feeding stuffs (maize; oilcake and meal; wheat milling offals); potatoes; sugar; oilseeds and nuts; vegetable oil; marine oil; butter; cheese; condensed and evaporated milk; full-cream milk powder; skimmed milk powder; canned and bottled fruit; canned vegetables; chocolate and sugar confectionery; tea; and raw coffee. The data are provided in physical terms for the end of the latest five years. End-of-month figures are also provided for the latest year, and often longer.

The *Annual Abstract of Statistics* [QRL.37] carries a table of recorded stocks, including stocks held in bond or held by the main processors. The figures relate to the end of December in each year, and are provided for the latest twelve years. The food products separately identified are: wheat and flour; barley; maize; oil cake and meal; oilseeds and nuts; vegetable oil; marine oil; butter; imported meat and offal; raw coffee; tea; sugar; chocolate and sugar confectionery. Both the *Monthly Digest of Statistics* [QRL.362] and the *Annual Abstract of Statistics* [QRL.37] usefully summarise diverse information from the many MAFF inquiries.

2.9.2 *Business Statistics Office Inquiries*

Statistics on stocks and work-in-progress are collected by the BSO as part of the Census of Production. The results for the Food industries are published in the relevant annual Production Monitors, as listed in section 2.1.1.1 and discussed in the following chapters, and in the summary volume *Business Monitor PA1002* [QRL.93]. The annual Production Monitors provide data on stocks of goods on hand for sale; stocks of materials, stores and fuel; and work-in-progress. The value of goods on hand for sale includes goods for merchanting or factoring, and together with the value of materials, stores and fuel covers stocks held by businesses coming within the scope of the Census of Production whether the stocks are held in the United Kingdom or abroad. Values include any duty payable but exclude VAT. Work-in-progress represents materials which have been partially processed and are awaiting further processing before being sold or transferred. Progress payments made to sub-contractors are excluded and progress payments received from other organisations are not deducted. The value of materials, stores and fuel; work in progress; goods on hand for sale; and the total are usually given for the latest year. Changes in value during the latest five years are detailed for these components and the total. The employment size distribution is done for the total at year end and the ratio of gross output to stocks calculated. It is thus the aggregate value of stocks which is reported rather than the volume of individual items as provided by the MAFF inquiries.

Business Monitor PA1002 [QRL.93] pulls this information from the Monitors for the individual industry Groups and presents a more complete picture. The following data on stocks are provided for the Food industries:

- the value of stocks of goods on hand for sale; of stocks of materials, stores and fuel; and of work-in-progress at the end of the year. Data are provided for each industry Group (411–423) for the latest five years,
- the value of the increase in work-in-progress and goods on hand for sale; and of the increase in stocks of materials, stores and fuel; during the year. Data are provided for each industry Group (411–423) for the latest five years,
- the increase in total stocks and work-in-progress during the year, and the value at the end of the year, analysed by size of employment of establishments. Data are provided for Class 41/42 for the latest year only,
- the increase in total stocks and work-in-progress during the year, and the value at the end of the year, analysed by size of employment of enterprises. Data are provided for Class 41/42 for the latest year only,
- the increase in total stocks and work-in-progress during the year, and the value at the end of the year, analysed for the private sector's 100 largest enterprises defined by size of employment. Data are provided for Class 41/42 for the latest year only,

- the increase in total stocks and work-in-progress during the year, and the value at the end of the year, analysed for the private sector's 100 largest enterprises defined by size of net output. Data are provided for Class 41/42 for the latest year only,
- the increase in total stocks and work-in-progress during the year, and the value at the end of the year, analysed for the private sector's 100 largest enterprises defined by size of total sales and work done. Data are provided for Class 41/42 for the latest year only.

Data for past years may be traced back in the various Production Monitors and in early reports on the Census of Production. The *Historical Record of the Census of Production 1907–1970* [QRL.264] contains time series data over the period 1948–1970 for the change in stocks during the year, and the value of the three elements of total stocks at the end of each year. Data for the Food industries in aggregate are similarly covered for the period 1959–1970.

2.9.3 *The National Accounts*

The *United Kingdom National Accounts* [QRL.506] provide data on the changes in the book value of stocks, and the value of the physical increase in stocks in both current and constant prices. Separate figures for the latest eleven years are provided for materials and fuel; work-in-progress; and finished goods in the Food, drink and tobacco manufacturing industries (Class 41/42 in aggregate). Food stocks held by wholesalers, retailers or the catering trades are impossible to identify (see section 2.9.4). Aggregate figures only are given for wholesale distribution etc. (Class 61–63, except AH6148); retailing and repairing (Classes 64, 65 and 67 except for Groups 651, 652 and 671); and other industries (which includes hotel and catering trades).

A full description of the methods of calculation of the estimates is given in chapter 13 of *United Kingdom National Accounts: Sources and Methods. Third Edition* [B.395] which also details the statistical sources used. As regards the Food industries, initial estimates of changes in stock levels are provided by the Quarterly Inquiry into Manufacturers' Stocks conducted by the BSO. The Annual Census of Production with its fuller coverage and greater industrial detail is then used to benchmark the information collected by the Quarterly Inquiry. As the Census of Production allows companies to report for a twelve month period covering their financial year, it is necessary to adjust the information to a calendar basis before comparing it with the corresponding figures in the Quarterly Inquiry. Once the level of stocks at the beginning and end of the calendar year have been estimated, the Quarterly results are used to derive a quarterly path over the year. The reliability of the annual estimates of the book value of stocks is thought to be in the range ± three to ten per cent.

2.9.4 *Stocks at Wholesalers, Retailers and Caterers*

The BSO carries out sample inquiries into wholesaling, retailing and catering. We touch on them here because of the importance of stocks in the distribution chain although Moir and Dawson [B.125] provide a more complete discussion. The results of the inquiries are published in a series of Business Monitors covering the service and distributive trades and identified by the prefix SD.

The main sources of information on stocks held by food retailers are a series of annual inquiries carried out by the BSO. "Full" inquiries were carried out annually from 1976 to 1980, but only every two years since then with "slimline" inquiries in the alternate years. From 1987, a new intermediate inquiry was introduced for the subsequent years, and a full inquiry is taken in respect of 1990 with intermediate inquiries in other years.

Many kinds of inquiry collect data on stocks. Provisional summary results were published in *British Business* [QRL.66], and final results from the full and intermediate inquiries in *Business Monitor SDA25: Retailing* [QRL.140] for years up to 1980 and from 1986; and in *Business Monitor SDO25: Retailing* [QRL.143] for 1982 and 1984. The results of the full inquiry in 1986 were published in 1988, and include data on stocks held both at the beginning and at the end of the year by large grocery retailers; other grocery retailers; dairymen; butchers and poulterers; fishmongers; greengrocers and fruiterers; and bread and flour confectioners. In *Business Monitor SDA25* [QRL.140] and the two issues of *Business Monitor SDO25* [QRL.143] for 1982 and 1984, stocks held by food retailers are further analysed by form of organisation; by number of business outlets; by value of turnover; and by number of persons engaged.

Business Monitor SDA26: Wholesaling [QRL.141] presents the results of the annual wholesaling inquiry. Summary figures used to be first published in *British Business* [QRL.66]. The results of the 1986 inquiry were published in 1988, and data were provided on stocks held by businesses classified to "wholesaling of food and drink" (VAT trade codes 8101, 8102 and 8109, excluding slaughterhouses) for the beginning and end of all years from 1980. Reported stocks at the end of one year differ from those at the start of the next, due to the selection of different samples and the change in the reporting year for some businesses. Beginning and end-year stocks held by companies classified to Group 617 "Wholesale distribution of food, drink and tobacco" are also provided for the years from 1980.

Business Monitor SDA28: Catering and Allied Trades [QRL.142] presents the results of the annual catering inquiry. Again summary figures were first published in *British Business* [QRL.66]. The results of the 1986 inquiry were published in 1988, and included estimates of stocks at the beginning and end of all years from 1980. These figures are provided separately for various types of catering establishment, classified by VAT trade code, but do not refer to food stocks alone.

2.9.5 *Regional Coverage*

The *Report on the Census of Production and Construction in Northern Ireland* [QRL.419] provides statistics for the province on the value of stocks and work-in-progress at the end of the year, and the increase during the year. The aggregate total is supplemented by disaggregated figures for stocks of goods on hand for sale; on stocks of materials, stores and fuel; and on work in progress. Data are provided for Class 41/42 in aggregate, and for the various collections of industry Groups specified in section 2.1.2.

2.9.6 *Comments*

From the MAFF point of view, physical measures of stocks play an important part in the derivation of supply balance sheets (see section 2.11 for further details). Data on stocks, as well as on production and trade, are used to provide estimates of "resources" and "domestic uses". These terms are defined as follows:

resources = usable production + imports

domestic uses = resources – exports + stock change

The further deductions of losses, utilisation for animal feed and industrial purposes yield a figure for implied human consumption. Balance sheets are prepared not only for most basic agricultural products, but also for some important processed products (e.g. wheat flour and starch). Hence MAFF collect information both on stocks of raw materials and on stocks of finished goods for consumption. This distinction should perhaps be made more clearly in the notes and footnotes of the *Monthly Digest of Statistics* [QRL.362] and the *Annual Abstract of Statistics* [QRL.37].

The BSO coverage in the annual Production Monitors and in *Business Monitor PA1002* [QRL.93] is at the same time more wide ranging, more standardised and put together in a neater fashion. However, the data on stocks are expressed in value terms and do not focus on individual food items. The BSO sources are thus of more use for assessing the financial implications of changes in stocks, rather than for identifying any physical changes. Moreover, the stock turnover ratios presented are subject to the usual reservations on the use of financial ratios (see section 2.13). Particularly in the Food industries, the level of stocks held by a firm will depend *inter alia* on the nature of the products, perishability, and the industrial applications of food science. The industry ratios cited only provide suitable standards of comparison if the firm in question has the same product mix as the industry.

The wholesaling, retailing and catering inquiries exclude Northern Ireland, but do present monetary estimates of stocks at various points in the food chain. *British Business* [QRL.66] provided convenient summaries until it ceased publication in September 1989. The inquiries are, however, of limited use from the point of view of this Review as none of them distinguish stocks of food from stocks of other products. All three inquiries are conducted primarily for National Accounts purposes, and hence the emphasis is essentially financial.

Finally, it should be noted that the sources above can only provide a partial assessment of food stocks in the United Kingdom, since they do not take account of stocks in transit or held in the home. Perhaps the National Food Survey (see section 2.10.1) could be extended to provide information on the values and quantities of foods stored in the home.

2.10 Consumption

In this section, we do not intend to detail all the multifarious statistical sources on food consumption but it is important to highlight the major references. We therefore consider in some detail the National Food Survey and the Family Expenditure Survey, and discuss the preparation of expenditure estimates in the UK National Accounts. Moreover, we provide a short guide to sources of statistics on catering and meals outside the home, even though this subject is largely outside the purview of this Review.

2.10.1 *The National Food Survey*

2.10.1.1 History

The National Food Survey (NFS) is now a continuous sampling inquiry into the domestic food consumption and expenditure of private households in Great Britain. The overall responsibility for the NFS lies with MAFF but advice is provided by the National Food Survey committee on the conduct of the survey. The selection of the sample lies with the Social Survey Division of the Office of Population Censuses and Surveys (OPCS) which supervises, and contracts out, the fieldwork and coding of the survey to a commercial agency (from 1960–1990 the British Market Research Bureau Ltd. and from 1991 Social and Community Planning Research). The results of the survey are published annually in *Household Food Consumption and Expenditure: Annual Report of the National Food Survey Committee* [QRL.267].

The NFS was initiated by the Ministry of Food in 1940. The original objective was to assess levels of nutrition of defined working class households during World War II. The very first report, *The Urban Working Class Household Diet 1940–1949* [QRL.509], measured consumption of, and expenditure on, the following principal food groups: milk; cheese; meat (including bacon); fish (including canned); eggs (including dried); fats (including butter, margarine and cooking fats); sugar; preserves; potatoes (including chips); other roots; other vegetables (including canned); fruit (including canned, dried and nuts); and cereals. The second report *Studies in Urban Household Diets 1944–1949* [QRL.469] covered essentially the same food components, but included a more specific section on beverages.

As with many war-time initiatives, the NFS was perpetuated in peacetime to continue the assessment of food policies and was moreover expanded to cover further socio-economic groups. The inquiry was further refined in 1950 and operated under the aegis of the Ministry of Food until 1953 since when the annual report has been issued by MAFF. From 1950 to 1964 the title was *Domestic Food Consumption and Expenditure* [QRL.178] but, from 1965 to the present day, the report has been entitled *Household Food Consumption and Expenditure* [QRL.267].

2.10.1.2 Coverage

The coverage of the NFS has become more comprehensive over time. The 1986 Survey reported the responses of 6925 households (from a total of 13491 contacted) from the mainland of Great Britain (including the Isle of Wight, but not the Scilly Isles nor the islands of Scotland). It was published in December 1987 and detailed results (for 1986 unless otherwise stated) were provided as follows:

- quarterly and annual national averages of household consumption, and average annual purchases, of certain individual foods,
- household food consumption of main food groups, analysed by income of head of household,
- household food expenditure on main food groups, analysed by income of head of household,
- household food expenditure on main food groups, analysed by household composition,
- household food consumption of selected food items, analysed according to household composition groups within income groups,

- consumption of main food groups for households in which the head of household was unemployed, 1983–1988,
- expenditure on selected food items analysed by age of housewife,
- expenditure on selected food items analysed by housing tenure,
- consumption of selected food items analysed by ownership of deep freezer,
- household consumption and expenditure on selected food items, analysed by regions of England, plus Wales and Scotland,
- estimates of income elasticities of expenditure, and of quantity purchased, for selected household foods,
- estimates of price elasticities of demand for selected household foods,
- estimates of price and cross-price elasticities of demand for certain foods, 1979–1986.

Consumption figures are expressed in ounces per person per week; expenditure estimates in pence per person per week. In addition to the data listed above, comparable historical statistics for 1984 and 1985 are also provided, together with a commentary, on consumption and expenditure for milk, cream and cheese; meat, fish and eggs; fats; sugar and preserves; vegetables and fruit; bread, cereals and cereal products; beverages and miscellaneous foods; and soft drinks. In general, the number of foods considered in each analysis varies — reference to further breakdowns of the main food groups will be made in the following chapters. Nutritional results are also provided *inter alia* on the contribution of certain foods to energy intake, and household intakes of major nutrients. These data, however, have far less prominence than the economic statistics.

The description so far of the Survey results lists the major part of an extensive coverage. Each Report also contains special analyses, and periodically the NFS has drawn on past data to describe longer-term trends in the consumption of food. The 1986 Report, for instance, contained analyses of 'changes since 1960 in the household composition of cereal products' and the 'employment status of the head of the household'. The 1985 Report provided broad trends for the main food groups back to 1965, and reviewed trends in the consumption of each of the three categories of canned, frozen and other convenience foods.

From 1985, *Household Food Consumption and Expenditure* [QRL.267] has been published in a new format with main tables accompanied by text, illustrative bar charts, and supplementary tables. Much statistical information, which had previously been presented in the main report, is now provided in the separate *National Food Survey: Compendium of Results* [QRL.373]. The compendium contains detailed statistics of average consumption, expenditure and nutritional value of foods recorded by the National Food Survey. Analyses are presented by region and type of area; by income group; by household composition; by age of housewife; by housing tenure; and by ownership of deep freezer. Special analyses are also provided in the 1986 issue of meals eaten outside the home; mid-day meals eaten outside the home by children aged 5–14 years; and purchases, expenditure and prices of soft drinks. The *Compendium of Results* [QRL.373] also provides details of the classification of foodstuffs in the NFS. Each foodstuff separately identified is listed together with its code number, definition, and whether the food is classed as seasonal (S), canned convenience (CC), frozen convenience (CF), or other convenience (CO). Thus, for example:

Food code number:	198
Description:	Instant potato
Seasonal or convenience food:	CO
Definition:	e.g. "Smash", "Yeoman"

Three levels of analysis may be identified in *Household Food Consumption and Expenditure* [QRL.267] and the *Compendium of Results* [QRL.373], viz: analyses of main food groups; analyses of individual foods as defined by the food code numbers; and analyses of selected food items. In general, data on the main food groups and selected food items are used to illustrate the text of *Household Food Consumption and Expenditure* [QRL.267], while statistics on individual food codes are found in the supplementary tables. Detailed analyses are now located in the *Compendium of Results* [QRL.373].

2.10.1.3 Methodology and appraisal

The methodology and structure of the Survey is carefully outlined in each Report, noting any major changes in coverage and presentation. A more detailed description of the methodology, and an appraisal, can be found in the paper by P.J. Lund [B.106] given at the 1982 Statistics Users' Conference on the Distributive Trades and in the summary by Slater [B.164].

Each household which participates in the Survey does so voluntarily for one week only. Information is obtained continuously throughout the year by regularly changing the households surveyed. The sole informant in each household (the housewife or whoever is principally responsible for domestic arrangements) keeps a record, with guidance from an interviewer, of all the food entering the home each day that is intended for human consumption — pet food and meals out are excluded. Details are also noted of the number of meals served, the quantity and cost of food bought, and food placed in and withdrawn from the deep freezer, and many other items.

In 1986, the data were collected by a three-stage stratified random sample. The primary sampling units were a selection of 52 local authority districts. At the second stage, postal sectors were selected within each district and, at the final stage, 18 delivery points were selected from each postal sector. The delivery points were drawn from the Small Users Postcode Address File (PAF). The sampling frame was changed to the PAF in 1984. Prior to that, it had been based on the Electoral Registers. It is argued that the PAF provides better coverage of the population than the Electoral Registers and, moreover, enables the sample to be drawn more economically by computer.

The National Food Survey is the major regular source for consumption and expenditure data on food, demand analyses and nutritional information. But even though unique in many ways, it is not totally comprehensive. First, excluded from the Survey are a few items which individual members often buy for themselves without these purchases necessarily coming to the attention of the housewife; these are chocolates, sugar confectionery, and soft and alcoholic drinks. Second, no information is collected on the cost and composition of meals outside the home, although exceptionally the quantity of school milk consumed by children is recorded. The NFS does, however, record the number of meals eaten outside the home (not from the household supply) so that adjustments can be made to enable more valid comparisons of the nutritional results. Moreover, these figures are analysed by region; by income group; by household composition; by age of housewife; by housing tenure; and by ownership of deep freezer. Third, the Survey does include take-away meals brought home, even if it excludes all food bought and consumed away from home. At the time of writing, it did not collect information on food purchased in hotels and restaurants or as snack meals for consumption outside the home. Fourth, the Survey records quantities entering the household and not the amount actually consumed. Data on consumption must thus be inferred from the expectation that, averaged over sufficient households, the average quantities entering the household should equate with consumption. Consumption is interpreted in the widest possible sense to include waste food discarded or fed to pets. Provided that purchasing habits and economy in food usage are consistent, then consumption can be inferred provided also that there is no general accumulation of household food stocks (on expectation of a price rise, for instance) or general depletion. Finally, some important new developments are noted in the Addenda to this volume.

The National Food Survey does respond and monitor new preoccupations such as consumption by unemployed families and the increasing diversity of processed foods. It is published as an annual Report, usually about one year after the year of the Survey. NFS analyses can be purchased directly from MAFF both to obtain information in greater detail, and in advance of publication of the Annual Report. Standard analyses include further details of selected food codes, and quarterly national averages available about ten weeks after the end of each survey period. *Ad hoc* analyses of 10 per cent of the sample to provide more detail can be requested and purchased from MAFF. Requests should be met more speedily from 1988 with the transfer of survey data to a data base. Basic data from 1979 are available for academic research through the Economic and Social Research Council (ESRC) Data Archive at the University of Essex, Wivenhoe, Colchester. Finally, as has been noted in section 2.10.1.2, *Household Food Consumption and Expenditure* [QRL.267] has been published in a new format since 1985 and much of the detailed statistical analysis from the NFS is now presented in the separate *Compendium of Results* [QRL.373]. These changes are not well documented, however, and it would be desirable if the availability of the *Compendium of Results* [QRL.373] could be noted prominently in the preface to *Household Food Consumption and Expenditure* [QRL.267].

2.10.1.4 Other sources publishing data from the National Food Survey

MAFF Statistics: Food Facts [QRL.319], are a series of press notices from the MAFF providing up-to-date information on the NFS, together with data on UK supplies of food and drink, nutritional information etc. The notices report quarterly estimates of average household consumption of, and total household food expenditure on, about 30 food items, or groups of foods, together with a commentary. The commentary, though not the statistics, was later published in *British Business* [QRL.66]. More detailed information is available on a subscription basis through the NFS branch of MAFF.

The *Annual Abstract of Statistics* [QRL.37] provides annual estimates of household food consumption of about 50 foods in Great Britain. Eleven years' data are listed.

Social Trends [QRL.456] reports index numbers of consumption in the home of 22 selected foods — data are provided for selected years over the past two decades. Moreover, figures are also presented on household expenditure on food analysed by household type, and by income of head of household. *Regional Trends* [QRL.401] draws from the NFS to present data on the consumption of, and expenditure on, a variety of foods, viz: liquid and processed milk and cream; cheese; butter; margarine; eggs; meat and meat products; fish; fresh and other fruit; potatoes; other vegetables and vegetable products; bread; flour; cakes and biscuits; sugar and preserves; coffee; and tea. Figures — two year averages — are provided for the regions of England, Wales, Scotland, and Great Britain in total.

2.10.2 *The Family Expenditure Survey*

2.10.2.1 History

All types of private households in the United Kingdom are covered by the Great Britain Family Expenditure Survey and the Northern Ireland Family Expenditure Survey. The Department of Employment has overall responsibilty for the Survey, and for processing and publishing the results in *Family Expenditure Survey* [QRL.204]. Except in Northern Ireland, sampling, fieldwork, and the coding of the completed records are carried out by the Office of Population Censuses and Surveys (OPCS), Social Survey Division. Northern Ireland households are selected at random from the sample of addresses drawn from the larger scale Northern Ireland main survey for which the interviewing is undertaken by the Policy, Planning and Research Unit of the Department of Finance and Personnel. The two surveys, however, use exactly the same forms.

The Family Expenditure Survey (FES) originated from a recommendation of the Cost of Living Advisory Committee (now the Retail Prices Index Advisory Committee — RPIAC) that an inquiry should take place into the expenditure of private households as a source for the weighting pattern of the Index of Retail Prices. A large-scale Household Expenditure Survey was accordingly undertaken in 1953–54, and the results of this were used for reweighting the Index in 1956. It was first published as *Report of an Enquiry into Household Expenditure 1953–1954* [QRL.405]. The FES subsequently began as a continuous survey in 1957, and the coverage has broadened over the years.

2.10.2.2 Coverage

The FES represents a unique and reliable source of household data on income, expenditure and other aspects of household finances; and provides a perspective of the developments and changes in household circumstances over the last three decades. As regards the products of food processing and manufacture, the FES identifies, and assigns a reference number (between 12 and 43), to 32 separate food items (see Appendix D). Reference number 43 relates to "meals bought away from the home" — an item which has limited coverage in the NFS. The 1986 edition of *Family Expenditure Survey* [QRL.204] was published in December 1987 and contained the following results (for 1986 unless otherwise stated):

- average weekly household expenditure on the 32 separate foods, analysed by level of household income,

- average weekly household expenditure on food (refs. 12–43 combined), analysed by level of disposable household income,
- expenditure on food as a percentage of total household expenditure, 1953/54–1986 (selected years),
- average weekly expenditure of one adult households on the 32 separate foods, analysed by level of household income and by sex and age,
- average weekly expenditure of households without children on the 32 separate foods, analysed by level of household income,
- average weekly expenditure of households with children on the 32 separate foods, analysed by level of household income,
- average weekly expenditure on food of non-retired households with married women,
- average weekly household expenditure on food, analysed by different administrative areas,
- average weekly household expenditure on food, analysed by tenure of household,
- average weekly household expenditure on food, analysed by occupation of head of household,
- average weekly household expenditure on food, analysed by employment status of head of household,
- average weekly household expenditure on food, analysed by number of workers in household and by level of household income,
- average weekly household expenditure on food, analysed by level of income for self-employed and part-time employees,
- average weekly household expenditure on food, analysed by age of head of household,
- quantiles of the distribution of weekly household expenditure on food,
- average weekly household expenditure on the 32 separate foods, analysed by the regions of England, Wales, Scotland, Northern Ireland, and the United Kingdom for the two-year period 1985–86,
- average weekly household expenditure on food, analysed by the regions of England, Scotland and the United Kingdom.

The data are subject to sampling variation, and estimates of expenditure on food are often accompanied by their percentage standard errors.

2.10.2.3 Methodology and appraisal

In 1986, the Great Britain FES changed its sample design for the first time since 1957. Along with other continuous surveys carried out by the OPCS, the FES moved from using the Electoral Registers to using the small users' Postcode Address File (PAF). 672 postal sectors were randomly selected as the primary sampling units, after being arranged in strata comprising standard regions, area type, proportion of owner-occupiers, and proportion of renters. 17 addresses were then visited per primary sampling unit. The Northern Ireland sampling frame is drawn from Rating and Valuation lists. In total, 12,624 addresses were selected in the United Kingdom, and the number of cooperating households amounted to 7045. Fieldwork is arranged so that interviews are spread evenly over the year thereby ensuring that seasonal expenditure changes are covered. Households at the selected addresses are visited in turn and asked to provide the interviewers with information about the household, about incomes, about certain payments which recur fairly regularly, and to maintain detailed expenditure records for fourteen consecutive days.

The methodology of the FES is explained in the introduction to the annual report on the *Family Expenditure Survey* [QRL.204], in the *Family Expenditure Survey Handbook* [B.94] and, more simply, in *Family Expenditure — A Plain Man's Guide to the FES* [B.269] published in 1982, a revised version of which was prepared in 1986 [B.270]. One noted weakness is that the Survey is thought to understate expenditure on confectionery, soft drinks and ice-cream. This is due to the fact that the purchase of these items by children from pocket money will usually be recorded simply as pocket money, since children under 16 are not required to keep expenditure records.

2.10.2.4 Other sources publishing data from the Family Expenditure Survey

A data base from the 1986 Survey is lodged with the Data Archive of the Economic and Social Research Council (ESRC) at the University of Essex, Wivenhoe, Colchester. Extracts, and comparable data from earlier years, are available on request. Moreover, the Department of Employment will supply further details and analyses on request, using the new Scientific Information and Retrieval (SIR) Database Management System now adopted to process the FES data.

The annual report of the *Family Expenditure Survey* [QRL.204] provides an extensive list of publications which contain analyses based on FES data. For example, quarterly expenditure data from the Survey are published as they become available in the *Employment Gazette* [QRL.186]. Quarterly (and annual) results from 1986 appear in the December 1987 issue. The tables show average weekly household and personal spending at current and constant prices, together with the composition of expenditure by commodity group on a quarterly basis for the most recent three years, and on an annual basis for the most recent five years.

Social Trends [QRL.456] reports figures on the pattern of household expenditure (including food), analysed by household type and income level. *Regional Trends* [QRL.401] reproduces FES data on average weekly household expenditure of food, analysed by the regions of England, Wales, Scotland, Northern Ireland, and the United Kingdom in total. Further regional data are given in the various publications for Wales, Scotland and Northern Ireland outlined in section 2.2.2.

2.10.3 *The National Accounts*

The *United Kingdom National Accounts* [QRL.506] provide data on consumers' expenditure, in both current and 1985 prices. This is done for food "commodity" and then disaggregated by "function" where the following items of expenditure are identified: bread and cereals; meat and bacon; fish; milk, cheese and eggs; oils and fats; fruit; potatoes; vegetables; sugar; preserves and confectionery; coffee, tea and cocoa; soft drinks; and other manufactured food. Data are provided for the latest eleven years. Aggregative data on consumers' expenditure are also given at current and at 1985 prices.

Extensive use is made of the National Food Survey in the preparation of the expenditure estimates. The survey quantities are however adjusted upwards in respect of some food items, for example, cakes, biscuits, fresh fruit and nuts, where retail purchases by other members of the household occur for consumption outside the home. About 86 per cent of household expenditure on food is based entirely on the NFS results of quantities and prices. A further 5 per cent is based on the NFS prices only, for example, potato crisps and soft drinks. The remaining 9 per cent is based on supply data provided by manufacturers' associations: the major items in this category are chocolate and sugar confectionery, and ice-cream, the retail prices of which are also provided by the manufacturers. Further details are provided in *United Kingdom National Accounts: Sources and Methods, Third Edition* [B.395].

In the methodological notes at the back of *United Kingdom National Accounts* [QRL.506], estimates are also shown of expenditure on food, covering, in addition to household expenditure, all expenditure on food by both commercial and non-commercial catering establishments. These figures are derived in the course of calculating household consumption from total supplies (i.e. output adjusted for trade), after which the utilisation of food in catering is deduced. The estimates cover all expenditure on food for civilian consumption, including expenditure on food by public authorities for hospitals, prisons, homes for old people etc, and for school meals, welfare foods and milk provided under National Milk Schemes. Excluded is the cost of issues of food to HM Forces. Eleven years' data are provided, in both current and constant 1985 prices.

The data from the *United Kingdom National Accounts* [QRL.506] are reproduced in the *Annual Abstract of Statistics* [QRL.37]. Quarterly data on consumers' expenditure on food are presented in the *Monthly Digest of Statistics* [QRL.362]. Series are provided in both current prices, and constant 1985 prices — the latter both seasonally adjusted and unadjusted. Annual data are also published in current prices and constant 1985 prices. *Economic Trends* [QRL.181] reports seasonally adjusted data of real consumers' expenditure on food at constant prices. Four years' annual, and five years' quarterly, figures are published. *Social Trends* [QRL.456] carries an index of expenditure on food at constant 1985 prices, and figures on the relative proportion of food to total consumers' expenditure at current prices. Data are provided for the latest eight years. And *Regional Trends* [QRL.401] draws from the National Accounts to present data on consumers' expenditure on "Food, drink and tobacco" for the regions of England, Wales, Scotland, Northern Ireland, and the United Kingdom in total. The latest three years' data are provided, together with comparable figures for ten years previously.

2.10.4 *Catering and Meals Outside the Home*

Many people have observed that catering continues to represent a major problem for the statistical sources on food consumption, not least Slater [B.164]. Dawson *et al* [B.43] estimate that expenditure on food outside the home could account for as much as 17 per cent of total food expenditure. Yet catering is largely ignored in the NFS. The FES provides data on "meals bought away from the home", and this covers state school meals, canteen meals and all other meals out, whether eaten on or off the premises. And the *United Kingdom National Accounts* [QRL.506] include estimates of expenditure on food covering expenditure by households, commercial and non-commercial catering establishments together (the data for "catering" which are cited separately include expenditure on both meals and accommodation). The *Annual Review of Agriculture* [QRL.51] also shows consumers' expenditure on food, plus the ratio of such expenditure to total consumers' expenditure. The data include caterers' expenditure on food, and figures are provided for the latest five years.

Business Monitor SDA28: Catering and Allied Trades [QRL.142] presents the results of the annual catering inquiry for Great Britain. The catering inquiry forms part of a family of annual distribution and service inquiries conducted by the BSO. They are done primarily for National Accounts purposes. The coverage of the 1985 inquiry (published in 1987) equated to MLH884–888 of SIC(1968) and included restaurants, cafes, take-away food shops, hotels, holiday camps, public houses, clubs, and catering contractors. Units engaged in catering as a subsidiary activity are not generally included, e.g. a canteen in a factory, meal service in a hospital. In terms of SIC(1980), the inquiry covers Class 66.

The commodity analyses of catering sales report the sales of meals and refreshments and food and non-alcoholic drink by type of catering establishment. The commodity analyses of catering purchases separate out food and non-alcoholic drink by type of catering establishment. However, these data on catering purchases and sales of food are only collected in the periodic benchmark inquiries. The results of the 1982 benchmark inquiry were incorporated in both the 1985 and 1986 editions of *Business Monitor SDA28* [QRL.142]. The next such inquiry was conducted in respect of 1988 — the results were published in 1990. Thus some inferences about the importance of food catering in the economy can be made, supplementing the information about expenditure on meals bought away from home covered for the many cross-classifications in the *Family Expenditure Survey* [QRL.204].

2.10.5 *Comments*

There are four major sources of information on the consumption of food in the United Kingdom, viz: the National Food Survey, the Family Expenditure Survey, the UK National Accounts, and the annual catering inquiry. Each has been outlined above, and the relationships between them have been discussed. The following points should be noted. First, the information available on catering is quite inadequate and this necessarily affects the precision of any estimates of total food consumption. Even *Business Monitor SDA28* [QRL.142] covers only establishments where catering is the primary activity, and omits any consideration of establishments such as factory canteens. The NFS did not cover meals eaten outside the home at the time of writing, although important changes with regard to this are noted in the Addenda to this volume. Both the FES and the National Accounts, in contrast, make estimates of expenditure on such meals. The estimates in the National Accounts are the most comprehensive but are, however, inferred from supply data rather than being measured directly. Second, the NFS and the catering inquiry only cover Great Britain, whereas the FES and the National Accounts both refer to the United Kingdom. Third, the FES and the National Accounts both concentrate on food expenditure, whereas the NFS also considers food consumption. Only aggregate data are provided in the National Accounts; the FES quotes expenditure per household per week; and the NFS provides data on both expenditure and consumption per person per week. Fourth, although the NFS is purportedly the most complete work on food expenditure, it is by no means comprehensive. A single reference work which brought together the main features of the NFS, the FES, the National Accounts, and the annual catering inquiry, and discussed their methodologies, their coverage, and their histories, would be extremely welcome. We have, however, tried to repair this gap here, in some small measure.

2.11 Supplies and Disposals

Great interest was shown in the collection of statistical data on food supplies both during World War I and World War II. *British Food Control* [B.18] is a masterly account by Sir William H. Beveridge of the evolution of policy in World War I. This account is based upon his experience first of all as an official at the Board of Trade and his role in its administration then through his work in the Ministry of Food from its establishment in December 1916. It is an earlier but less famous Beveridge Report which reproduces statistical tables which detail food stocks, net imports, consumption data, retail prices etc. plus descriptions of the control schemes used. The whole scheme drew heavily upon Sir Edward Gonner's labour, who as Director of Intelligence in the Ministry, prepared more than 80 statistical tables.

The wide-ranging system of controls to regulate food consumption and distribution during World War II is comprehensively explained by R.J. Hammond in the relevant three volumes in the "History of the Second World War, United Kingdom Civil Series": Volume 1 *The Growth of Policy* [B.63], Volume 2 *Studies in Administration and Control* [B.64] and the later Volume 3 also entitled *Studies in Administration and Control* [B.65]. These are exhaustive accounts of the system used for the various vital commodities through from procurement to processing. Appendix tables furnish lavish statistics, the most important of which are summarised in the *Statistical Digest of the War* [B.66].

These controls, operated during and after the war by the Ministry of Food, were largely dismantled during 1953 and 1954. Rationing came to an end in the middle of 1954 and, in 1955, the Ministry of Food was merged with the Ministry of Agriculture and Fisheries to form the Ministry of Agriculture, Fisheries and Food (MAFF). Nevertheless, statistics on food supplies were still produced, as was explained by W.D. Stedman Jones in his article on "Food statistics" [B.167] in a forerunner to this Review. Stedman Jones claimed that food statistics fell naturally into three compartments:

- data on supplies available, whether from indigeneous production or imports,
- disposal of the available supplies into human consumption, animal feed, non-feed uses and exports,
- data on the place of food in the national economy.

The statistical information collected by the Ministry of Food during World War II thus set the pattern for much of the current work undertaken by MAFF — see section 2.11.1 for details.

Detailed comments have been provided on statistical sources for output, domestic inputs, input-output, imports, exports, stocks, and consumption in previous sections in this chapter. Each perspective may be evaluated separately, but they may also be considered together to provide insights on available supplies, and to present supply balance sheets and self-sufficiency ratios for the United Kingdom. The resulting picture is a composite one and requires statistics on agricultural output, food processing, and distribution to be drawn from a variety of different agencies (e.g. MAFF, BSO, CSO, HM Customs and Excise etc.). Moreover, it should be noted that a variety of different terms and concepts are often used in discussions of the overall situation. Supplies, disposals, offtake, resources, domestic uses, and self-sufficiency are but some of the terms that are used to refer to related concepts. More detailed definitions will be provided as and when necessary.

2.11.1 *Domestic Supplies of Manufactured Food Products*

Until 1969, data on supplies from the UK Food industries came from various short-period inquiries conducted by the Ministry of Agriculture, Fisheries and Food (MAFF). These inquiries were supplemented by further information from the Censuses of Production conducted by the Census Office of the Board of Trade. From 1969, the inquiries have been supplemented by the Quarterly Sales Inquiries — see section 2.1.1.2 — conducted by the Business Statistics Office (BSO) and, from 1970, by the new Annual Censuses of Production — see section 2.1.1.1. Following the *Review of Government Statistical Services: Report to the Prime Minister* [B.368] by Sir Derek Rayner in December 1980, it was decided to reduce the number of short-period inquiries on the Food industries. Each industry would be covered by only one inquiry, which might be conducted by MAFF, by the BSO, or by a trade association. John Slater [B.164] lists most of the following inquiries undertaken (for most of the 1980s) for the various Groups which comprise the food and feed processing industries:

Group 411
Monthly survey of vegetable oil crushers' returns
Monthly survey of refiners' returns
Monthly survey of the utilisation of refined oils
Quarterly Sales Inquiry for margarine and compound fats
Quarterly Sales Inquiry for organic oils and fats

Group 412
Weekly and monthly slaughterhouse inquiry
Weekly survey of pigs slaughtered
Monthly survey of throughput and stocks of slaughtered poultry
Quarterly Sales Inquiry for bacon curing and meat products
Quarterly Sales Inquiry for poultry and poultry products
Quarterly Sales Inquiry for animal by-products

Group 413
Monthly survey of cheese stocks
Monthly survey of production and stocks of condensed milk and milk powder
Quarterly Sales Inquiry for milk and milk products

Group 414
Quarterly survey of canned and bottled fruit and vegetables
Quarterly Sales Inquiry for fruit and vegetable products

Group 415
Quarterly Sales Inquiry for fish products

Group 416
Monthly and annual surveys of returns from flour millers
Monthly survey of returns from oatmeal millers

Group 418
Monthly survey of the production of glucose and starch
Quarterly Sales Inquiry for starch

Group 419
Quarterly Sales Inquiry for bread and flour confectionery
Quarterly Sales Inquiry for biscuits and crispbread
Monthly survey of members of Cake and Biscuit Alliance (CBA) now the BCCCA

Group 421
Annual survey of stocks of cocoa beans and cocoa products
Quarterly Sales Inquiry for ice-cream
Monthly survey of sales of chocolate and sugar confectionery

Group 422
Monthly and annual surveys of compounders' returns
Biannual survey of livestock rations
Monthly survey of pet food

Group 423
Quarterly survey of the production of potato crisps and snack foods
Quarterly inquiry of processed potato products
Quarterly survey of coffee production and stock usage
Monthly survey of cereal breakfast foods
Quarterly Sales Inquiry of miscellaneous foods

The results of the quarterly BSO sales inquiries are published as Business Monitors in the PQ series — see section 2.1.1.2. The MAFF short-period inquiries are not part of an integrated system, but they generally concern physical production. The results are first published in MAFF Statistical notices — e.g. *MAFF Statistics: Production of Canned and Bottled Fruit and Vegetables in the UK* [QRL.325] — and later in the *Monthly Digest of Statistics* [QRL.362] and up to 1988 in *Output and Utilisation of Farm Produce in the United Kingdom* [QRL.382] — see section 2.11.3. In addition, mention should be made of the monthly MAFF survey of public cold stores, the results of which are published in the statistical notice, *MAFF Statistics:*

Stocks of Selected Dairy Products, Meat and Meat Products, Poultry, Game, Soft Fruit and Vegetables in Public Cold Stores [QRL.335]. The commodities covered by this survey should be evident from the title of the notice.

Further details of the MAFF and BSO inquiries will be presented where appropriate in the following chapters. The primary purpose of the inquiries is to provide an overview of industrial activity, weights for production and price indices, and aggregate estimates for national accounts. Data from all these inquiries are, moreover, used in deriving estimates of food supplies available for consumption. More direct measures of food consumption are provided by the National Food Survey — see section 2.10.1 — and by the Family Expenditure Survey — see section 2.10.2.

2.11.2 *Supply Balance Sheets*

For many years, MAFF have compiled supply balance sheets for most basic agricultural products and for some important processed products. Latterly, EUROSTAT have issued standardised balance sheet questionnaires to all Member States for completion on the basis of methodology agreed in the *ad hoc* Working Group of the Agricultural Statistics Committee. Estimates of resources, and of domestic uses, are derived by MAFF for these balance sheets using data on production, trade and stocks, viz:

resources = usable production + imports

domestic uses = resources – exports + stock changes

Fixed conversion factors are used to transform raw material to product weight. As far as possible, these conversion factors are those agreed by the European Community, except where these are considered inappropriate for the particular conditions of the United Kingdom. Moreover, efforts are made to update conversion coefficients to reflect changing conditions although, except where radical new processes are introduced, such coefficients are likely to change only slowly over time. Adjustments also have to be made for trade flows, requiring the conversion of processed imports and exports to raw material equivalents, and for stock changes in the estimation of total supplies. Statistics are available on stocks in intervention and public cold stores, but little data exist on other commercial stocks or on the amount of wastage as supplies pass through the food chain. The final figures in each balance sheet should thus be interpreted as an estimate of supplies available for consumption, rather than as measures of actual consumption. Balance sheets for the following products are prepared by the MAFF:

- meat
- fats and oils of land animals
- fish
- fats and oils of marine animals
- milk and milk products
- eggs
- cereals
- potatoes
- vegetables and fruit
- sugar and molasses

- oleaginous seeds and fruit
- vegetable fats and oils
- oilcakes
- prepared oils and fats
- feeding stuffs
- wine
- dried pulses.

The data for the United Kingdom, and for other Member States of the EC, are stored in the EUROSTAT CRONOS data bank in Luxembourg, and can be accessed commercially through CISI Wharton. Summary balance sheets are published each year in the *Annual Review of Agriculture* [QRL.51]. The successor publication of [QRL.51], *Agriculture in the United Kingdom*, furnishes supply and utilisation data for many commodities. More detailed balance sheets for the main commodities are published in the two quarterly EUROSTAT publications, *Crop Production* [QRL.167] and *Animal Production* [QRL.36] as well as in *Agriculture: Statistical Yearbook* [QRL.34]. Further details are provided in the paper by John Slater [B.164] and in the chapters on individual industries in this Review.

2.11.3 *Disposals*

Data on "disposals" are published in the *Monthly Digest of Statistics* [QRL.362], and in the *Annual Abstract of Statistics* [QRL.37]. Disposals are estimated from home production and imports, adjusted for changes in the known stocks held in warehouses, cold stores etc. by wholesalers, importers, manufacturers and the government. Disposals of food in the United Kingdom include use in the manufacture of other food (e.g. sugar in jam, biscuits and sweets), the flow into consumption and ingredients used in manufactured products which are exported. The *Monthly Digest of Statistics* [QRL.362] carries a series of tables in the Agriculture and Food section on production, disposals and stocks of principal foods and feeding stuffs. Disposals are expressed in physical terms (usually thousand tonnes). Monthly averages, or totals for four or five week periods, are given for the most recent two years, and averaged over the past six years. The treatment of individual products varies and will be discussed further in the corresponding sections in the chapters on individual industry Groups. The data presented are a useful summary from the many MAFF and BSO sources listed in section 2.11.1. The *Annual Abstract of Statistics* [QRL.37] summarises disposals of a wide range of foods and animal feeding stuffs for the latest eleven years. The relevant table is entitled "disposals" but the term is not fully explained. The footnotes merit careful study to elicit further detail, as the precise treatment of individual products tends to vary. For example, the *Annual Abstract of Statistics* [QRL.37] remarks that the disposals figure for sugar includes the sugar used in the manufacture of foods subsequently exported, but excludes the sugar in imported manufactured foods.

Output and Utilisation of Farm Produce in the United Kingdom [QRL.382] provides estimates of total UK supplies and utilisation of the following up to 1987: wheat; barley; oats; cereals; meat; potatoes; sugar beet; apples; pears; cauliflowers; tomatoes; milk; hen and egg products; duck eggs.

2.11.4 *Self-sufficiency*
MAFF also estimates the level of UK self-sufficiency in food. The measure of self-sufficiency used is the value of total home production of food expressed as a proportion of the value of food consumed in the United Kingdom. It thus supplements the measures of physical self-sufficiency that are prepared for individual commodities for the EUROSTAT supply balance sheets — see section 2.11.2. The measure used covers only food and it does not attempt to assess the position for agricultural products. Food products used for non-food uses, such as brewing, distilling and pet foods, are excluded as well as items such as wool, cotton and hides.

The definition of self-sufficiency is rather more subtle than that suggested by the broad explanation above. Crops grown from imported seed, and cattle fattened on imported feed, are but two instances where care must be taken in any calculation. Moreover, there are also problems of valuation and classification. For the self-sufficiency measure to be meaningful, all the items included should be valued at the same point in the economic process. Thus all food is valued at farm-gate prices — i.e. at the prices of the food prior to processing and distribution — which betrays the fact that the calculation is aimed at monitoring the development of UK agriculture. As regards classification, a further problem lies in deciding how much agricultural production and trade should be considered as human food. It is difficult, for example, to distinguish wheat destined for human food from that utilised for animal feedingstuffs.

Self-sufficiency ratios are prepared by the MAFF for calendar years and the results are calculated in both current and constant prices. Also calculated are ratios of the costs of processing and distributing all food in the United Kingdom as a percentage of total expenditure. The results are published in the *MAFF Statistics: Food Facts* [QRL.319] series, in the *Annual Review of Agriculture* [QRL.51] and its successor publication *Agriculture in the United Kingdom* and in the *Annual Abstract of Statistics* [QRL.37].

Other occasional publications have also addressed the question of self-sufficiency. "The nation's food: 40 years of change" [B.2] carried statistics on supplies, consumption, expenditure and the contribution of UK farmers to the nation's food supplies. "United Kingdom self sufficiency in food, 1970–78" [B.128] provided adjustments to the definition of the United Kingdom's self-sufficiency in food and agricultural products, outlined problems of measurement and classification, and gave results for self-sufficiency (as well as production and consumption) for the period 1970 to 1978.

The connection between raw material inputs and self-sufficiency may also be seen in the White Paper of 1985 entitled *Food From Our Own Resources* [B.280]. It was observed that the size of the processing industry for many commodities was constrained by the level of home production of basic materials, and encouraged the substitution of home for imported inputs. Similar themes were pursued in another White Paper, *Farming and the Nation* [B.271] published in 1979. A statistical assessment of the demand for food was based upon previous years' MAFF data of food supplies moving into consumption, and estimates of future population, income and expenditure trends, and eating habits etc. Supply was taken to depend on price and availability of food imports, self-sufficiency in the major agricultural commodities, farm factors of production, world commodity prospects, and finally marketing and processing.

2.11.5 *Comments*

This section has drawn heavily on two papers by John Slater [B.164] and Arthur Barnett [B.12] which were presented at the 1986 Statistics Users' Conference on Food Statistics. These papers provide excellent background information, and the interested reader would be well advised to consult them directly.

One observation from the brief summary of self-sufficiency is that emphasis has traditionally been placed on agriculture as distinct from food processing. Increased production of the raw materials from the farm has been seen as the key to increased UK food processing, and the latter has been accorded very little statistical attention in the White Papers cited above. Yet, as Barnett [B.12] points out, agriculture accounted for about two per cent of GDP whereas the Food industries accounted for some 3.2 per cent and employed some six hundred thousand people. *Food From Our Own Resources* [B.280] carries the statistically unsupported statement that "70 per cent of food consumed in the UK has been processed to a greater or lesser extent". And *Farming and the Nation* [B.271] noted that food and drink manufacturing accounted for about 12 per cent of total manufacturing at the time, but paid scant attention to food processing as distinct from farm output. The neglect of the food manufacturing industries is thus both unfortunate and unwarranted in this connection.

2.12 Prices

In a market economy, the price system is an information-economising device. The range of food-price information is vast. Consumers seek instantaneous information on market prices. Firms at the various stages of processing, wholesaling, distribution, and retailing, need detailed information as well. The prices of foodstuffs are a major concern for most governments.

A comprehensive review of the information on prices should aim to give the prices of the many raw material inputs, both home-produced and imported, into the food manufacturing process. Then the prices of the output could be traced through the various stages in the food chain where mark-ups appear, finally ending with the selling price to the consumer.

In this Review, we are also interested in sources both of historical data on prices, and of changes in food prices relative to other observed prices. Discussion of both the producer price index and the retail price index is thus important.

Considerable resources are devoted to producing price information. Price searchers, price makers, and price takers seek to establish market clearing prices, but non-market clearing prices are also observed. Queues form if prices are too low and stocks accumulate if prices are too high. Information is continuously updated and established for both current and futures prices. Hence, much price information is officially provided since such knowledge is a vital public good. Government agencies furnish much information in, for example the *Employment Gazette* [QRL.186]. *British Business* [QRL.66], up to September 1989, and its predecessors *Trade and Industry* and the *Board of Trade Journal* were also other official sources. But abundant primary data also flow from commercial sources and the trade press.

2.12.1 *Agricultural and Commodity Prices*

2.12.1.1 Official sources

G.H. Peters describes and appraises the many Ministry of Agriculture, Fisheries and Food (MAFF), and other, sources in detail in his companion Review, *Agriculture* [B.144], in this series. We summarise the major references here since agricultural output prices relate to processors' input prices, as well as to prices paid by merchants and consumers. We concentrate here on sources which detail the prices of a wide range of agricultural outputs. Specialist publications such as *United Kingdom Dairy Facts and Figures* [QRL.503], the *Sea Fisheries Statistical Tables* [QRL.451], and *Fruit and Tropical Products* [QRL.245] and other publications are considered in the following chapters.

Agricultural Statistics: United Kingdom [QRL.32] has a lengthy prices section. Average monthly and annual prices paid to growers are provided for wheat, barley and oats, distinguishing the milled components. A similar treatment, but for England and Wales, is presented for ware potatoes; beans; cattle and pigs; sheep and lambs; store cattle; milking cows; rearing calves; store sheep and store pigs; and autumn hill sheep. The price cited for sugar beet is the average annual price delivered to the factory. Hen egg prices refer to the United Kingdom. Poultry and rabbit prices, fruit prices, and vegetables prices, are for selected wholesale markets in England, with separate treatment of imported goods. Similar data are provided in the single issue of *Agricultural Statistics: England* [QRL.29], and in its predecessor *Agricultural Statistics: England and Wales* [QRL.30].

A guide to the current market situation for many different products is provided in the three parts of the weekly *Agricultural Market Report* [QRL.25], [QRL.26], [QRL.27]. The titles indicate the nature of the products for which average weekly prices are given:

Agricultural Market Report Part I: Prices and Quantities Sold of Selected Cereals, Livestock and Other Agricultural Products [QRL.25] covers average prices of the previous week, the current week, and the comparable week one year ago.

Agricultural Market Report Part II: National Average Wholesale Prices of Home Grown and Imported Horticultural Produce [QRL.26] gives prices for the current and previous week.

Agricultural Market Report Part III: Prices of Home Grown Vegetables By Grade in Six Major Markets in England and Wales [QRL.27] gives the range and most usual prices for class of produce at the end of the previous week.

The *Annual Review of Agriculture* [QRL.51] summarises a variety of commodity price trends, drawing from data collected by the Agricultural departments. The information is for the latest four years and a forecast year as well. This table of price trends aims to give indications of weighted average prices at the first point of sale (e.g. ex-farm prices for wheat, barley, oats and rye; farm-gate prices for potatoes; producer prices for sugar beet; wholesale market prices for apples, pears, tomatoes and cauliflowers; wholesale prices for broilers etc.). Prices normally relate to the United Kingdom, but the accompanying notes merit careful consultation since there are a number of deviations. The *Annual Abstract of Statistics* [QRL.37] furnishes the same information, but for a longer run, though the information is somewhat dated by the time of publication. The 1988 edition, for example, provides twelve annual observations, but the most recent figures given were for 1986.

Separate statistical sources exist for the component parts of the United Kingdom as follows:

Scotland.
The *Economic Report on Scottish Agriculture* [QRL.180] carries average annual prices for the current year (estimated), and for the previous two years, for the following: wheat; barley; oats; potatoes; cattle; calves; sheep; pigs; poultry; beef; sheepmeat; pig meat; poultrymeat; milk and eggs. Further monthly, and average annual, price data appear for home grown grains; fruit and vegetables; milking cows; store stock; and fat stock. Its predecessor, *Agricultural Statistics: Scotland* [QRL.31], had similar coverage in its prices section. The Department of Agriculture and Fisheries for Scotland (DAFS) also produces an annual report, *Agriculture in Scotland* [QRL.33], which provides a statistical review including significant price changes. Finally, up to 1980, the *Weekly Agricultural Market Report* [QRL.511] gave average weekly prices for selected products at the end of the week, the comparable week one year earlier, and the previous week.

Northern Ireland.
The *Statistical Review of Northern Ireland Agriculture* [QRL.460] yields average producer prices for five years (the latest figure is provisional) for cattle; sheep; pigs; milk; eggs; broilers; barley; oats; and potatoes. Further average annual data on market prices of breeding and store livestock and poultry are given. The average producer prices are repeated in the Department of Agriculture for Northern Ireland's (DANI) annual report *Northern Ireland Agriculture* [QRL.376], and for a ten-year run in the *Northern Ireland Annual Abstract of Statistics* [QRL.377]. The *Report on the Agricultural Statistics of Northern Ireland* [QRL.416] collated data on average annual prices. The ninth report related to the period 1966/67–1973/74, and previous reports covered earlier periods.

The current market situation for poultry, eggs, livestock, potatoes, cereals etc. is given in the weekly *Agricultural Market Report* [QRL.24]. Fruit and vegetables are covered in the separate weekly *Horticultural Market Report* [QRL.265]. The data in both [QRL.24] and [QRL.265] are for weekly prices. Finally, the *Quarterly Agricultural Market Report* [QRL.396] gives quarterly price information for the products featured in the *Agricultural Market Report* [QRL.24].

Wales.
Farm Incomes in Wales [QRL.211] reports average annual prices and/or values for the main crops, livestock and livestock products (e,g, milk and eggs). *Welsh Agricultural Statistics* [QRL.515] carries a range of data including monthly and yearly livestock prices. *Welsh Agricultural Statistics Supplement* [QRL.516] also gives data on livestock prices.

Thus the series of inquiries coordinated by MAFF, DAFS, DANI and the Welsh Office provide a range of annual, monthly and weekly price information for points early in the food chain. However, these agricultural output prices should only be considered as rough estimates of, rather than precise figures for, the actual prices paid for the commodities before further processing. Caution must often be exercised in the country coverage. The same applies to the historical coverage in the short agricultural prices section of *A Century of Agricultural Statistics: Great Britain 1866–1966* [QRL.1]. Certain products can be traced back for long periods in [QRL.1]. For example, wheat prices at Exeter are recorded from 1316–24 to 1800–20. Corn returns in England and Wales (wheat, barley, oats) are given from 1771 up to 1966 and average prices of fat cattle per live cwt. from 1899 to 1966.

2.12.1.2 Commercial sources

Many inputs for food processing stem from agricultural sources at home and abroad. Prices, both spot and futures, are often determined on the world's commodity markets. David Nicholas has written *Commodities Futures Trading: A Guide to Information Sources and Computerised Services* [B.134], which provides a good description of the many commodity statistical sources. The *Guide to World Commodity Markets Physical, Futures and Options Trading* [B.26] highlights selected world markets including cocoa; coffee; grains; meat; soyabeans; sugar; and tea, with statistical illustrations of prices, production etc. Part 1 analyses aspects of futures trading, Part 2 covers the commodities, and Part 3 has a very useful world directory of commodity markets.

London commodity markets have been active since at least Roman times with many changes over the years. May 1987 saw the inauguration of the newly-christened London Futures and Option Exchange (London FOX), which succeeded the London Commodity Exchange (LCE). The latter had been formed in 1974 as a non-profit making company controlled by the Terminal Market Association. The exchange's change of name accompanied the physical move from Mark Lane in the City of London to Commodity Quay in St. Katharine Dock. The new exchange has a lineage stretching back to 1571 when Sir Thomas Gresham opened his Bourse in the City to provide the merchant community with a focal point for their many activities.

Many of the commodity spot and futures prices which concern us here are usually reported in the daily press. We highlight here the coverage of the *Financial Times* [QRL.218] although it is well known that other quality dailies, both British and foreign, provide similar ranges of data. The *Financial Times* [QRL.218] gives details of cocoa, coffee, sugar, grains, potatoes, pigs and soyabean meal for London; London FOX traded options in coffee and cocoa; cocoa, coffee, sugar etc. for New York; and soyabeans, oats, maize, wheat, live cattle, live hogs and pork bellies for Chicago.

Also on a daily basis is *The Public Ledger & Daily Freight Register* [QRL.392] which provides a wide range of information on daily and futures prices described in more detail in the specialist chapters. We note here the general coverage of the grains markets; oilseeds and oils; the produce markets (sugar, coffee, cocoa etc.); and less obvious areas such as edible nuts, honey and spices. Besides collecting information from the markets, the collation method involves a telephone survey of contacts and then the calculation of the average prices of the many trading deals. On Saturdays, the more detailed *The Public Ledger's Commodity Week* [QRL.394] is published by the same organisation. This carries a statistical summary of weekly price trends for the following groups: grains/pulses; oil cakes/meals; oilseeds/oils; produce; spices; nut/kernels; and essential oils. The current week's prices are compared both with those of the previous week, and those of the previous year. Weekly surveys are made of the many prices in the listed fruit trade. The provision prices of the many kinds of butter and cheese are included. Thus, *The Public Ledger's Commodity Week* [QRL.394] repeats and enlarges on the daily *The Public Ledger & Daily Freight Register* [QRL.392].

The Public Ledger & Daily Freight Register [QRL.392] claims to be the first daily commercial newspaper for London, and was first issued on 12th January 1760. But a more recent development by the publishers (Turret Wheatland) is *The Public Ledger Commodity Yearbook* [QRL.393] which began in 1980. It covers grains and feeds in Section 1, oilseeds and oil in Section 2, and the produce markets (coffee, cocoa, sugar, tea, spices, edible nuts, honey, dried fruit) in Section 3. Section 4 is devoted to dairy produce (butter, cheese, milk powder). It usually has a market review which gives long-term data on production, stocks, exports, imports etc. and carries graphs showing the historical relationship to current price movements. The data tend to be annual and the approach is to look at all market statistics which have been important in price determination.

Annual statistical reviews and long-run data also appear in the *ICCH Commodities and Financial Futures Yearbook* [QRL.269], published by Landell Mills Commodities Studies Ltd. in association with the International Commodities Clearing House Ltd. The market reviews of cattle; cocoa; coffee; grains; oilseeds, oils and fats; potatoes; soyabeans; sugar etc. in the agricultural commodities section includes some data for spot and futures prices. The commentary in this compendium is valuable.

The *CRB Commodity Yearbook* [QRL.166] is published by the Commodity Research Bureau, and reviews supply/demand trends influencing price determination. It usually has average spot prices for each month, for a run of the past twelve years. Its emphasis tends to be on the United States, but it is noted here since many of the market prices (e.g. cocoa, coffee, tea) impinge on UK processors. The commodities are arranged alphabetically from alcohol to zinc. The statistical tables are thrice yearly updated in the *Commodity Yearbook Statistical Abstract* [QRL.157]. Section 1 contains 400 or so tables corresponding to the monthly tables in the *CRB Commodity Yearbook* [QRL.166]. Section 2 recasts annual tables which have been subject to significant changes. And Section 3 updates the charts of cash (spot) prices of selected leading commodities. The more continuous *Daily Commodity Computer Trend Analyser* [QRL.169] is mailed to subscribers shortly after the markets close every trading day.

Compared with the *CRB Commodity Year Book* [QRL.166] which has been running since 1939, the fourth edition of the *ICCH Commodities and Financial Futures Yearbook* [QRL.269] had not appeared at the time of assembling this section. And although Turret Wheatland provide a multiplicity of daily, weekly and annual publications, the time-lag before the appearance of *The Public Ledger Commodity Yearbook* [QRL.393] is longer than for the *CRB Commodity Yearbook* [QRL.166].

Probably more familiar than these yearbooks is *Farmers Weekly* [QRL.212], which collects a wide range of information in its markets review. For instance, spot and forward prices paid the previous Monday are given for grain (wheat, barley and oats) and oilseed rape, by localities, and similarly for compounding peas and beans. These are sets of prices paid by merchants etc. to farmers. The prices for home-grown grain are given by locality, and futures grain prices summarised. A wide variety of potato prices, from average producer price to futures, are featured. Auction prices in England and Wales for cattle, sheep and pigs by the numerous auction marts are given. Home-produced and imported sugar beet are also featured. Farm prices of eggs, wholesaling selling prices of home-grown vegetables, producer prices for potatoes, and poultry wholesale selling prices etc. are given. The original sources of the material are quoted, viz: MAFF, the Meat and Livestock Commission, the Home Grown Cereals Authority, the Baltic Exchange, the Potato Marketing Board, and Farmers Weekly itself, etc. All the prices concern farmers, growers, agricultural merchants and processors.

The active nature of the soft commodities markets give rise to the plethora of specialist sources discussed in the equivalent sections of some of the ensuing chapters of this volume. With such dynamic and fluid markets, change and innovation are continual. The initiation of London FOX is discussed in the 3 July 1987 issue of *British Business* [QRL.66]. The structure of London's commodity exchanges are summarised in the April 1987 issue of *Euromoney* [B.255].

2.12.2 *Retail Prices*

2.12.2.1 Recorded prices

Each month, the *Employment Gazette* [QRL.186] publishes the average retail prices of selected items of food on one day in the month, usually two months previously. The food items are grouped under the following headings: beef (home-killed); lamb (home-killed); lamb (imported); pork (home-killed); bacon; ham (not shoulder); sausages; pork luncheon meat; corned beef; chicken (roasting); fresh and smoked fish; canned (red) salmon; bread; flour; butter; margarine; lard; cheese; eggs; milk; tea; coffee; sugar; fresh vegetables; and fresh fruit. These average prices are derived from the collection of some 130,000 price quotations for the 600 separate items included in the General Index of Retail Prices (RPI). The survey is undertaken mainly by Department of Employment staff covering more than 180 areas of the United Kingdom. The number of quotations, the average prices, and the range of prices within which at least four fifths of the recorded prices fall, are given. They relate to a single day each month — always a Tuesday — about the middle of the month. These average prices are subject to sampling errors, which means that the average price given in the table may differ from the true average which would have been calculated if it had been possible to obtain quotations from the entire population of retail outlets in the country. There is a 68 per cent chance that the difference will be less than the standard error, and the chance that the difference will be more than double the standard error is about five per cent. At the time of writing, standard errors were last given on page S55 of the February 1985 issue of the *Employment Gazette* [QRL.186], but up to that time standard errors were published once a year.

These prices constitute a limited sample of all food prices, and they refer to but one day in the month. Yet details are provided for both processed and unprocessed foods, and are published for a substantial range of foods. Past time series can be built up using the *Employment Gazette* [QRL.186]. However, *British Labour Statistics Historical Abstract 1866–1968* [QRL.67] conveniently summarises average retail prices of certain articles of food from information supplied for the "cost of living index", which preceded the RPI. Average prices at one point in the month are given for selected years from 1914–1968. This type of information was continued in the *British Labour Statistics Yearbook* [QRL.68], with data for each month of the year and the standard error for January until December 1976.

A different source of price information is the National Food Survey, fully discussed in section 2.10.1 (see also section 2.12.4). Since 1985, the average prices paid for the wide range of foods surveyed during the year have been listed in the supplementary tables to the (new format) *Household Food Consumption and Expenditure* [QRL.267]. Data are given for the past three years. Average price is sometimes referred to as "average unit value". This is defined as the aggregate expenditure by the households in the sample on an item in the Survey classification of foods, divided by the aggregate quantity of that item purchased by those households. A selection of income elasticities (of expenditure and quantity), own-price elasticities, and cross-price elasticities of demand for selected foods, are presented in the demand analyses section. Prior to 1985, more extensive price information detail was published in the (old format) *Household Food Consumption and Expenditure* [QRL.267]. Quarterly, as well as annual, national average prices were given for the year in question, and estimates provided of the standard errors of the annual national averages. The quarterly and annual national average prices for individual foods are now to be found in the *Compendium of Results* [QRL.373].

2.12.2.2 Recommended prices

Prices are continuously signalled through the press, radio, television, teletext etc. and, of course, the very displays, lists and price tags in the shops. The role of the trade press is catalogued in the individual subject chapters. Whilst it is not possible to give an exhaustive list of all sources, we highlight here publications which provide a substantial amount of price information.

The Grocer Price List [QRL.253] gives both trade and retail prices, based on the detailed information supplied by manufacturers, importers, sole agents etc. for the smallest quantity they supply. The price lists are issued with *The Grocer* [QRL.252] on the first Saturday in each month. Price changes notified between issues are published in *The Grocer* [QRL.252] under "Price Changes". The price list is aimed at small retailers and, moreover, forms another way of advertising for the suppliers. Sometimes one encounters the term POA (Price On Application), which means that *The Grocer Price List* [QRL.253] does not publish a price, but that it will be supplied to the retailer by the manufacturer.

The Grocer [QRL.252] itself regularly provides wholesale price information for the interested buyers in the grocery and catering trades. The data are presented in the Meat and Produce and Market Prices tables. The first gives quotatations of the average wholesale prices (including a 15 per cent and 20 per cent distribution charge) for varieties of meat, poultry and game, fresh fish, potatoes, fruit, vegetables and salad. The second reports market prices under the heading of the UK Provision Trade Federation. They are intended as a guide to the prices which can be obtained on the open market. All prices are naturally subject to regional variation and discounting. The coverage includes the many types of butter, bacon, lard, eggs, cheese and sugar. Home and foreign supplies are distinguished where applicable.

The Grocer Buff List predated *The Grocer Price List* [QRL.253]. Issued with *The Grocer* [QRL.252] the first Saturday of each month, it performed a similar service. It gave both trade and retail prices for the month ahead for the smallest quantities available. Such lists were but guides, since for larger orders, "more advantageous terms are usually available".

Shaws Guide to Fair Retail Prices [QRL.453] is published monthly, aiming to suggest the maximum retail prices to be charged, based on minimum wholesale quantities. The service is mainly for subscribing customers like the small village shop, retailers etc. But the prices guide the consumers as well as retailers. When manufacturers do not recommend fair selling prices, they are sometimes suggested by the editors with the help of manufacturers. The prices so indicated are in italics. The suggested prices reckon to show a fair profit on minimum quantities supplied on trade terms, and should normally be the maximum charged in the United Kingdom.

Obviously, the prices in both *The Grocer Price List* [QRL.253] and *Shaws Guide to Fair Retail Prices* [QRL.453] may differ from those charged by the multiples, as these will vary with the daily pricing policies of the stores, often dependent upon internal memoranda from Head Office. Indeed, given the concern expressed about the prices of key lines in [QRL.453] due to the price cutting tactics of multiples, *Shaws Guide to Fair Retail Prices* [QRL.453] now publishes a "Typical Multiple Price" on the final page. It may well be that in most circumstances the small retailer will not be able to match the multiples. But the retailer is at least given an indication of the prices he needs to be looking at if he wishes to compete on price.

2.12.3 *The Retail Prices Index*

The Retail Prices Index (RPI) is compiled by the Department of Employment every month. The results are published monthly in the *Employment Gazette* [QRL.186]. The information found there is listed here, with particular attention paid to food, before we discuss the methodology of the Index and catalogue other publications which quote the RPI.

The Index was re-referenced in 1987 to make January 13th 1987 = 100 following the recommendations of the Retail Prices Index Advisory Committee (RPIAC). Details of all changes following the RPIAC report can be found in the April 1987 edition of the *Employment Gazette* [QRL.186]. Moreover, with effect from February 1987, the structure of the published components has been recast. "Catering" is now the term used to identify the previous category of "meals bought and consumed outside the home". In some cases, however, no direct comparison of the new component with the old is possible. The relationship between the old and new index structure is shown in the September 1986 edition of the *Employment Gazette* [QRL.186].

2.12.3.1 Coverage in the Employment Gazette

The *Employment Gazette* [QRL.186] provides the following coverage of the Retail Prices Index:

- A summary of movements in the all-items index, and in the index excluding seasonal foods. Seasonal food is defined as items of food, the prices of which show significant seasonal variations. These are fresh fruit and vegetables, fresh fish, eggs, and home-killed lamb. Figures are presented for the percentage price change over the previous month, the previous six months, and the previous twelve months. A commentary on the reasons for changes in the indices is appended.
- Detailed figures for various groups, sub-groups and sections. Separate index numbers are provided for "all items", "all items excluding food", "seasonal food", "food excluding seasonal" and "food". "Food" is broken down into 25 separate sections (e.g. fish), and catering into three sections. Index numbers, together with the percentage changes over the past month and twelve months, are provided.
- Detailed figures for various groups, sub-groups and sections. Separate figures are provided *inter alia* for "all items"; "all items excluding seasonal food"; "all items excluding food"; "seasonal food"; "food excluding seasonal food"; "food"; and "catering". Separate indices are also presented for thirty food items which comprise the overall "food" index. Similarly, separate indices are provided for "restaurant meals"; "canteen meals"; and "take-aways and snacks", under the heading of "catering". In each case, the index numbers for the month in question, together with the percentage change over the previous month, and the previous twelve months, are provided.
- Long time series of the indices for "food", "seasonal food", "non-seasonal food" and "catering". Monthly data are provided for the latest two years, January data for the previous eleven years, and annual averages and weights for fourteen years.
- Percentage changes on a year earlier for the main sub-groups including "food" and "catering". Monthly data are provided, together with comparable January figures for the previous fourteen years.
- Annual indices for "food" and "catering" for one-person pensioner households, and two-person pensioner households. Five years' data are presented.

The RPI relates to prices in the United Kingdom. The March issue of the *Employment Gazette* [QRL.186] usually carries a special feature which summarises the changes in the preceding year, detailing the movements of prices within the major groups of food with further subdivisions.

2.12.3.2 Methodology

Details of the methodology and coverage are explained in special features in the *Employment Gazette* [QRL.186], such as that in the August 1987 issue. Most of the statistics in the *Employment Gazette* [QRL.186] attempt to measure monthly changes in the prices of the basket of retail goods and services. The main index covers the "typical" household, which excludes both pensioner households mainly dependent on state benefits, and at the time of writing the four per cent of households with the highest incomes.

The present RPI has its origins in the official "cost of living index", started in 1914, but it is now much more elaborate. The calculations of the monthly indices in respect of a Tuesday near the middle of each month are based upon the 130,000 price quotations of about 600 indicator items which are representative of, but cannot be inclusive of, all foods. The RPI basket is divided into about 80 sections of expenditure which are combined into eleven groups of interest, one of which is food. Some things are more important than others in terms of the money spent on them, and allowance is made for this in the weighting system of the index. For example, a given percentage increase in the price of bread has about four times the effect of a similar increase in the price of butter. Expenditure patterns change over time and, since 1962, the weights have been amended at the beginning of every year, on the basis of the results from the Family Expenditure Survey of the previous June. Details of the annual revision of weights are usually given in the March issue of the *Employment Gazette* [QRL.186], and the weights for the more recent pensioner indices in the April issue. *Retail Prices: Indices 1914–1986* [QRL.434] usefully contains a compact summary of the changes in weights for Food and its many listed items from 1974 to 1986.

The Index is evidently under constant review. However, at the time of writing, a full explanation of the methodology has not appeared since the *Method of Construction and Calculation of the Index of Retail Prices* [B.333] was published in 1967. But the methodology was clearly explained in the October 1975 issue of the *Employment Gazette* [QRL.186], in this "Non-statistical guide to the RPI", and also in the August 1987 issue (as noted above).

The Retail Prices Index Advisory Committee (RPIAC) has produced ten reports since it was first established as the Cost of Living Advisory Committee in 1946. The membership of the Committee is intended to represent all interested parties in the community. It is now convened by the Secretary of State for Employment. The February 1978 issue of the *Employment Gazette* [QRL.186] summarised the technical improvements following their deliberations. The latest report in 1986, *Methodological Issues Affecting the Retail Prices Index* [B.334], recommended that *Method of Construction and Calculation of the Index of Retail Prices* [B.333] should be fully revised to give a thorough and up-to-date account of methodology and coverage.

Changes in the arrangements for the collection of price data must aim to keep pace with switches in consumption patterns. The first stage in the index calculation links the movement in prices in the current year since January to movements in previous years, back to the reference date, at which the index is taken as equal to 100. The reference date has been changed on several occasions, having been successively June 1947, January 1956, January 1962, January 1974 and now January 1987. The annual revision of weights gives the chance of adding to the list of price indicators, such as the additions in recent years of muesli and various convenience foods. It must also consider changes in retail distribution (for instance, discount trading, freezer shops and super stores). The difficulties of interpreting price index numbers are well documented in most of the references above, and in statistics textbooks, but the data do show the changing trends over time. *Retail Prices: Indices 1914–1986* [QRL.434] carries long series of monthly data for Group I (Food) and Group XI (Meals bought and consumed outside the home) from 1956–1986 (January 1956 = 100). The more disaggregated groups, subgroups and sections are similarly given for 1978–1986 (1974 = 100).

2.12.3.3 Other sources publishing the Retail Prices Index

The results from the work of the Department of Employment are disseminated in many other official sources. *British Business* [QRL.66] used to show the previous month's figures, a comparison with the preceding month and the percentage changes over the month and the year. The treatment was for the main commodity groups which include food; seasonal food; non-seasonal food; and catering. The *Monthly Digest of Statistics* [QRL.362] publishes separate index numbers for food and catering monthly for the latest two years, and annual averages for the preceding seven years. The weights for the current year are enumerated. More detailed figures for various groups, sub-groups and sections carry results for the latest seven months, and include the group and sub-group weights. The Business Monitor PQ series reproduce recent retail price indices relevant to the particular industry covered.

The *Annual Abstract of Statistics* [QRL.37] carries the indices for main groups, and thus separately includes food and meals bought and consumed outside the home. Data are provided for March, June, September and December of the latest year, plus annual averages and weights for the previous thirteen years. Earlier averages and weights for the previous base year are given. The *Economic Trends: Annual Supplement* [QRL.182] carries a long time series for the General Index of Retail Prices back to 1948, and citing the index for food. *Economic Trends* [QRL.181] contains the quarterly index for food back to 1963.

Social Trends [QRL.456] reports the average annual percentage change in the General (all items) Index, and in the indices for "food", and "meals bought and consumed outside the home". Even the 1988 issue had yet to adopt the term "catering", which gives an idea of the lag in compilation of this particular source. Nevertheless, the 1988 issue does provide data for 1961–71, 1971–1976, 1976–1980, and then each year from 1980–81 to 1985–86. It is interesting to note the reduction in the weight given to food in the General Index from 350 (out of 1000) in 1961, to 185 in 1986. "Meals bought and consumed outside the home" was not identified as a separate item until 1968. The same publication also contains some interesting data on the length of time it is necessary to work in order to pay for selected (mostly food) commodities and services in various years between 1971 and 1986. The figures are derived for a "typical" married couple with only the husband working, and are calculated from Department of Employment and HM Treasury data. Such calculations provide some idea of changes in the slippery multi-faceted concept of the "standard of living".

The *British Labour Statistics Historical Abstract 1886–1968* [QRL.67] contains fourteen tables on prices, mirroring much of the information already described in the *Employment Gazette* [QRL.186]. The *British Labour Statistics Yearbook* [QRL.68] carried on very much in similar vein from 1969 until 1975. *Statistics on Incomes, Prices, Employment and Production* [QRL.464], published from April 1962 until June 1969, also has group and sub-group coverage.

The *Isle of Man Digest of Economic and Social Statistics* [QRL.295] carries group and sub-group indices and weights in monthly terms with specific reference to the Isle of Man.

2.12.4 *Price Index Numbers in the National Food Survey*

Since the introduction of its new format in 1985, *Household Food Consumption and Expenditure* [QRL.267] has published little data on prices, except for a bar chart relating changes in average expenditure, food prices and the real value of food purchased, between the Survey year and the previous year. Separate charts are provided for convenience foods; seasonal foods; all other foods; and total foods. More detailed information is, however, available in the separate *National Food Survey: Compendium of Results* [QRL.373], as discussed in section 2.10.1.2. The 1986 edition, for example, published in December 1987, provides the following comparative indices:

- indices of prices for main food groups, 1981–1986
- indices of food prices analysed by region and type of area, 1986
- indices of food prices analysed by income group, 1986
- indices of food prices analysed by household composition, 1986
- indices of food prices analysed by age of housewife, 1986
- indices of food prices analysed by housing tenure, 1986
- indices of food prices analysed by ownership of deep freezer, 1986.

Prior to 1985, this information was published in the main report on *Household Food Consumption and Expenditure* [QRL.267]. Furthermore, annual indices of average deflated prices, purchases and demand were compared for the full list of Survey foods, and for broad food groups. These indices related to the most recent six years compared with the average for the whole period which was set at 100.

A price index of the Fisher "Ideal" type is used in the NFS. This index is the geometric mean of two indices with weights appropriate to the earlier and later periods respectively, or in the case of non-temporal comparisons (e.g. regional, income group), with weights appropriate to the group under consideration and the national average respectively. The use of a Fisher index in the National Food Survey should be contrasted with the use of a chain-linked Laspeyres index for the Retail Prices Index with weights revised each year.

2.12.5 *Other Price Index Numbers*

Producer price index numbers (which replaced the former wholesale price indices in August 1983) are available on a monthly basis. Since October 1989, the primary publication source has been *Business Monitor MM22 : Producer Price Indices* (see the Addenda to this volume for publication details). Previously, up to September 1989, the primary source was *British Business* [QRL.66].

Producer price index numbers are base-weighted indices resting on the "basket of goods" concept. Regular five-yearly rebasings are carried out in order to reflect the changing pattern of industry's sales and purchases in the index weights. Further details are provided in the 19th August 1988 issue of *British Business* [QRL.66], and the methodology is summarised in section 2.12.5.3. First, however, we detail the coverage of both input and output price index numbers.

2.12.5.1 Producer price index numbers: input prices

Price index numbers of materials and fuels purchases by detailed sectors of industry are published monthly in *Business Monitor MM22*. Separate indices are provided for each Activity Heading of Class 41/42. Indices for the latest two months are always provisional. Besides the monthly data for the most recent twelve months or more, an annual average is computed for the previous year. *Business Monitor MM22* also contains monthly and annual data for all manufacturing and selected broad sectors, the latter featuring the food manufacturing industries. Separate figures are given for material and fuel.

The *Monthly Digest of Statistics* [QRL.362] provides monthly and annual averages for the latest five years on the price index numbers of materials and fuel purchases for the food manufacturing (Groups 411–423) industries in aggregate. Annual data for the latest six years are published in the *Annual Abstract of Statistics* [QRL.37] for the food manufacturing industries, although separate indices are given for "materials" and "fuels" purchased. And producer price indices for materials and fuel purchases are often published for Activity Headings in the appropriate Business Monitors in the PQ series - see relevant chapters for details.

2.12.5.2 Producer price index numbers: output prices

Business Monitor MM22 also carries monthly and annual data for price index numbers of output (home sales) for all manufacturing and selected broad sectors, including the food manufacturing industries. *Business Monitor MM22* also furnishes the monthly and annual averages for the price index numbers of products manufactured in the United Kingdom (home sales) by detailed sectors of industry i.e. each Activity Heading of Class 41/42.

The *Annual Abstract of Statistics* [QRL.37] publishes the producer price index numbers of commodities produced in the United Kingdom (home sales) for the Activity Headings within food manufacturing in the SIC(1980), drawing on the same BSO sources. Annual data for the latest six years are provided. The *Monthly Digest of Statistics* [QRL.362] provides index numbers of producer prices for the output of Class 41/42 and for the output of the food manufacturing industries (Groups 411–423). Monthly and annual data are given. And indices are also provided in the relevant Business Monitors in the PQ series — see appropriate chapters for details.

2.12.5.3 Methodology

The methodology of construction of the index numbers discussed in sections 2.12.5.1 and 2.12.5.2 is set out in detail in *Wholesale Price Index: Principles and Procedure* [B.397]. The use of the word "wholesale" is rather misleading, since the index does not refer to wholesalers' selling prices but to an earlier stage in the marketing process. One of the reasons for the change in title from "wholesale price index" to "producer price index" in August 1983 was that the old title wrongly suggested that prices are measured at the wholesale stage rather than what are clearly prices at the factory gate. The 15th April 1983 issue of *British Business* [QRL.66] carried an article which describes the change of name, and also details the more fundamental changes involved, and the reclassification from SIC(1968) to SIC(1980). The price index in its current format was introduced in the 1950's, and used 1948 as the base year. Subsequently, the base year has been changed in 1954, 1963, 1968, 1974, 1979 and 1984 to coincide with the years in which a Purchases Inquiry (see section 2.1.1.4) was undertaken. At the time of writing, reference year for prices is 1985. Indices in the current series on a SIC (1980) basis are available back to January 1984 on request.

The BSO will give guidance on the correlation between indices in the old — SIC(1968) — and new — SIC(1980) — systems. Long runs of data must be interpreted with caution, both because of the changes in classification schemes and because of changes in weighting patterns arising from the periodic rebasings.

The input indices are industry based, with the weights used to combine the price quotations based upon purchases made by those establishments classified to the sector concerned in the SIC. Data are also collected for other sectors of UK industry, and for imports. The method of index calculation roughly takes the quantities bought in the base year, values them at the price levels pertaining in both the current period and the reference year, and divides the former by the latter. It should be made clear that the term "base year" refers to the period (at the time of writing 1984) to which the quantity weights pertain. The term "reference year" is different, and designates the year (at the time of writing 1985 = 100) from which the price changes are measured. This fits in with the national accounts system. The output indices are Laspeyres indices, based upon a fixed set of weights. Publication of indices rebased on 1984, with 1985 = 100, began in August 1988, as was signalled in the May 1988 issue of *British Business* [QRL.66].

The price quotations which form the basic data for all the price indices are supplied voluntarily, mainly by manufacturers but with some from trade associations, importers, the trade press etc. The majority are collected and processed by the DTI, but MAFF collects those for food, passing the data on to the DTI for incorporation into the aggregate indices. Further details, and the methodology and interpretation, are set out in *Wholesale Price Index: Principles and Procedure* [B.397].

It should be noted here that the emergence of new products and the measurement of quality change cannot be adequately incorporated in these statistical indices, which reflect, but cannot match, the complexity of the real world.

Finally, we should emphasise again that these indices (since October 1989) are published in the monthly *Business Monitor MM22* which followed the coverage in *British Business* [QRL.66]. Since *Business Monitor MM22* is devoted to this topic alone, it is evidently more convenient for users. But interested researchers now need to study the key to index reference numbers before they turn to the tables in *Business Monitor MM22* unless, of course, they have in their memories the reference number which corresponds to their sector of interest.

2.12.5.4 Price index numbers for current cost accounting

UK price inflation in the 1960's ran at a compound annual rate of three per cent but, by the early 1970's, increases in the RPI had reached ten per cent, and quickly rose to a peak of 26.5 per cent in 1975. The effect on companies' reported profits, and hence tax liabilities, was traumatic. As a result, the Government set up the Sandilands Committee to inquire into the need for, and a method of, accounting for inflation. The Committee recommended a system of value accounting which was labelled "current cost accounting". This system involves the valuation of assets in the Balance Sheet at their "value to the business" rather than at their "historic cost", and some notion of price changes were thus required in order to derive the former from the latter.

The first issue of *Price Index Numbers for Current Cost Accounting* [QRL.390] was compiled by the Government Statistical Service, and was published in April 1976.

Subsequent issues were published by the CSO until December 1979, and thereafter by the Department of Industry until 1981. Many issues of [QRL.390] gave full descriptions of the purposes of compilation and methodology. At that time, responsibility for compilation was transferred to the BSO and, from April 1980, the index numbers have been published monthly in *Business Monitor MM17: Price Index Numbers for Current Cost Accounting (Monthly Supplement)* [QRL.84]. The current coverage for the Food industries is as follows:

- a monthly price index of plant and machinery bought as fixed assets by the Food (AH4115–4239) industries,
- a monthly price index of stocks held by the Food (AH4115–4239, except AH4121) industries.

Two compilations of long time series also exist. *Business Monitor MO18: Price Index Numbers for Current Cost Accounting, Summary Volume 1974–1982* [QRL.87] was published in 1983, and *Business Monitor MO18: Price Index Numbers for Current Cost Accounting, Summary Volume 1983–1987* [QRL.88] was published in 1988.

2.12.6 *Export and Import Prices*

The *Business Monitor MM17: Overseas Trade Statistics of the United Kingdom* [QRL.85] carries data on the values, as well as the quantities, of most commodities covered by the SITC. Yet it does not provide explicit price data. Unit value index numbers for many commodities are published in the *Monthly Review of External Trade Statistics* [QRL.364], and this coverage is discussed in section 2.8.2.4.

In general, however, sources of statistics on import and export prices tend to be specific to particular industries/commodities, and will hence be discussed where applicable in the following chapters. For example, we note in section 8.12.1 that the *Weekly Bulletin* [QRL.512] quotes data on UK delivered and export prices of grain, and imported grain asking prices. In section 7.12.6 we refer to the *European Supplies Bulletin* [QRL.189] which gives the average prices for the imports and exports of fish products.

2.12.7 *Prices and Government Regulation*

There have been numerous investigations which are not only rich sources of price information but also of many other economic dimensions. These *ad hoc* publications are considered in section 2.16, and a list of the relevant reports of the Monopolies Commission, the Monopolies and Mergers Commission, the Price Commission (Investigation Reports), the Price Commission (Main Reports), and the National Board for Prices and Incomes, will be found there. However, the discussion of the reports relevant to each industry will be featured in the chapter for that industry. For example, the Price Commission report on *Tea Prices* [B.435] will be discussed in Chapter 12.

2.12.8 *Comments*

This section necessarily commenced with a review of agricultural prices. Some of these were prices paid by consumers in markets and some indicated prices paid by processors for primary inputs. Overlapping with agriculture are the many sources of commodity prices on domestic and world markets, including spot, forward and futures prices. The original sources of the data are the Commodity Exchanges themselves. The International Commodities Clearing House Limited, and London FOX are two examples. Much of the trading, and many of the prices, are instantaneously disseminated on line, as noted by Nicholas [B.134]. The constant flow of innovation in information technology is often incorporated by the exchanges. A price-reporting system is thus manifest with the ability to access data from the London exchanges and other world markets.

The sources on producer price indices, and price index numbers for current cost accounting are obviously more directly related to the processor, and have been described in section 2.12.5. The treatment of retail prices, and retail price indices, is discussed extensively in sections 2.12.2 and 2.12.3. The official concern with the indices may however be contrasted with the data on prices themselves which are covered in much more detail by the commercial sources. Up-to-date dissemination of both prices, and price changes, is carried out by radio, and on-line through Prestel, Datastream etc. Tracing prices through the entire food chain from the importer/farmer/fisherman via the processor, merchant, wholesaler, retailer etc. is often a complex process, which has sometimes been disentangled by various official investigations referred to in section 2.12.7. Despite the multiplicity of price data, margins cannot always be unscrambled.

Considerable resources are devoted to the continual signalling of prices at all stages. Yet the list price may co-exist with quantity discounts and price shading. Prices at some stages of distribution may be kept secret to outsiders, and the pricing mechanism is sometimes another means of advertising the product. Nor can price information be treated alone without its fraternal twin of quantity. That is why the Clearing Houses are as much concerned with market turnover statistics, and data on quantities of lots traded, to show a healthy market. For example, the 1st April 1988 edition of *Farmers Weekly* [QRL.212] showed the June and August futures prices for live pigs. However, the quantity figures for lots traded in the week suggest that one should not be fooled into thinking that an active market always exists.

2.13 Financial Information

A grand array of accountants and auditors are responsible for the primary information contained in the relevant company Annual Reports and Accounts. Microfiche copies of these accounts are available for purchase at the various branches of Companies House — see Appendix B for addresses. This information is subsequently reproduced, transformed and analysed in a wide range of both official and commercial sources. Paul Norkett's *Guide to Company Information in Great Britain* [B.137] is a useful reference which lists and describes many of these sources, which will also be further discussed in sections 2.13.2, 2.13.3 and 2.13.4. First, however, it is necessary to provide a brief description of the legal and accounting framework which circumscribes the disclosure of company financial information.

2.13.1 *The Legal and Accounting Framework*
The availability and scope of the financial information contained in the Annual Reports are circumscribed by the disclosure requirements of company law, the various accounting standards and, for listed companies, the regulations of the Stock Exchange. Prior to 1948, for instance, there was no legal requirement for the publication of detailed profit and loss accounts. The Companies Act 1948, however, required UK companies for the first time to publish not only detailed profit and loss accounts, but also group accounts in consolidated or other form. Disclosure requirements have subsequently been amended, and generally increased, by the Companies Acts of 1967, 1976, 1980 and 1981 before company law was consolidated by the Companies Act 1985. The main features of these Acts were as follows.

The 1967 Act abolished the category of "exempt private company" created by the 1948 Act, with the result that *all* limited companies were thereafter required to file copies of their profit and loss accounts and balance sheets, together with other documents including the directors' and auditors' reports, with their Annual Return to the Registrar of Companies. These documents were then available for public reference. The 1976 Act dealt *inter alia* with the introduction of accounting reference periods, and the shortening of the period which might elapse between the end of a company's financial year and the preparation and filing of accounts. The 1980 Act was intended to meet the requirements of the EEC Second Directive on the classification of capital of public and private companies. The 1981 Act allowed small and medium-sized companies to file accounts (with the Registrar of Companies) which were exempt from the full legal requirements for published accounts. Medium-sized companies were permitted to submit a modified profit and loss account, which did not need to include details of turnover and gross profit margins. Small companies were permitted to file only an abridged balance sheet. No profit and loss account or directors' report was required. Notwithstanding these exceptions, companies must still present unmodified accounts to their shareholders. Moreover, public companies, whatever their size, are ineligible for these exemptions. The accountancy profession, in the main, strongly opposed these limitations in the standards of reporting as it feared the consequences of the publication of such drastically reduced information. Of the 914,000 companies registered in Great Britain at the end of 1987/88 only about 6,600 were public companies. This was about 0.7 per cent of the effective register so that there is likely to be a lack of information in respect of many companies when the enabling legislation is finally implemented. This numerical illustration is taken from the 1987–1988 edition of *Companies* [QRL.158].

The 1981 Act also implemented the provisions of the EEC Fourth Directive which sought to harmonise accounting practices, and the format and content of annual accounts in the Member States. Companies may now choose between four formats for the profit and loss account, and two formats for the balance sheet. The legislation enabled by these various Acts was eventually rationalised by the Companies Act 1985 which came into effect on 1st July 1985. A full account may be found in Coopers & Lybrand's *Form and Contents of Company Accounts — Manual Part 3: Comprehensive Coverage of Disclosure Requirements of the Companies Act 1985, SSAPs and the Listing Agreement* [B.286]. Details may also be found in Renshall and Aldis [B.155], in Farmer [B.49], and in *The International Stock Exchange Official Yearbook* [QRL.290].

The first Statement of Standard Accounting Practice (SSAP) was issued by the Accounting Standards Committee in January 1971. It has been followed by many others — up to SSAP24 at the end of 1989. The aim of these standards is to restrict the choice of accounting treatment so that published financial statements are presented in such a way that they may be both easily understood and compared. Members of the respective accountancy bodies are expected to observe the standards, and any significant departures should be disclosed and explained in the accounts. Failure to observe the standards exposes the members to enquiry and sanction. Given the continual developments, the annual *Accounting Standards* [B.194] is a convenient way of keeping an eye on current practices.

2.13.2 *Department of Trade and Industry Analyses*

Each year, the Department of Trade and Industry (DTI) carries out an analysis of the accounts of a representative sample of (currently) about 3500 UK companies, and the results are published in *Business Monitor MA3: Company Finance* [QRL.81]. In addition, the first of the approximately half-yearly issues of *Business Monitor MO3: Finance of Top Companies* [QRL.89] was published in May 1988. The second appeared in December 1988. This new Monitor contains results based on the accounts of the 500 largest companies in the base year of the sample used for *Business Monitor MA3* [QRL.81]. The results in *Business Monitor MO3* [QRL.89] are in the same format as those in *Business Monitor MA3* [QRL.81], but the level of industry detail does not descend below "manufacturing", hence no separate figures are provided for the Food industries.

2.13.2.1 Coverage

The nineteenth edition of *Business Monitor MA3* [QRL.81] was published in 1988, and provides the following analyses of "large" companies classified to the Food (Groups 411–423) industries:

- balance sheet information at end of 1983, 1984 and 1985 accounting years
- income and appropriation account information for 1983, 1984 and 1985 accounting years
- sources and uses of funds information for 1983, 1984 and 1985 accounting years
- ratios of net income to average net assets for 1982–86
- ratios of gross trading profit to turnover for 1982–86
- ratios of current assets less stock to current liabilities for 1982–86.

The "large" companies all had capital employed in 1981 of £3 million or more. Definitions of the terms and other financial concepts are provided in the introduction to *Business Monitor MA3* [QRL.81]. Previous editions have carried rather more industrial detail. For example, the sixteenth issue provided analyses not only of "large" companies, but also of "medium and small" companies in the Food industries.

The Companies Act 1948 brought about enormous improvements in the standards of accounts, and thus generated a fertile source of financial information. The *Economist* [QRL.183] and the *Financial Times* [QRL.218] both made early use of this improved flow of information, but the first major analysis of company accounts was provided by the National Institute of Economic and Social Research (NIESR).

Company Income and Finance 1949–1953 [QRL.159] was published in 1956, and presented a detailed analysis of the accounts of 3000 public companies quoted on the UK Stock Exchange. Subsequent analyses were provided for 1954 onwards by the Board of Trade (BoT) and its successor Departments. These were published to 1961 in *Economic Trends* [QRL.181], and from 1960 to 1966 in *Statistics on Incomes, Prices, Employment and Production* [QRL.464]. Thereafter, general financial analysis has been provided first in *Business Monitor M3: Company Finance* [QRL.79] and latterly in *Business Monitor MA3: Company Finance* [QRL.81].

Some comparability over the years is possible but, in a dynamic world, some reservations should be expressed. As noted in section 2.13.1, the disclosure requirements on UK companies have been changed over the years. Changes in the coverage of *Business Monitor M3* [QRL.79] and *Business Monitor MA3* [QRL.81] have followed accordingly, though often with a substantial delay. The small companies required to file accounts after the 1967 Act were not incorporated into the DTI analysis until 1982 when the twelfth issue of *Business Monitor MA3* [QRL.81] appeared. Furthermore, the format changes required by the 1981 Act were predicted not to appear until the twentieth issue came out in 1989. Such tardiness does have the incidental merit of imparting continuity to the data over long periods! Efforts at standardisation mean that some comparability of turnover, gross trading profit etc. is possible. But the detailed examination of the many company reports is evidently still vital. SIC(1968) was replaced by SIC(1980) as the basis of classification in the fourteenth issue, published in 1983. Moreover, the construction of the DTI sample has also been subject to modification.

2.13.2.2 Methodology

A distinction between listed and unlisted companies was made in *Business Monitor M3* [QRL.79], and *Business Monitor MA3* [QRL.81] until the eleventh issue for 1977. Two different sampling frames were developed and used for 1977–1984, which limits the strict comparisons which may be drawn with previous results. The first sampling frame was of the largest 1500 industrial and commercial companies registered in Great Britain. The background and methodology are concisely described by S.J. Penneck in "The top 1500 industrial and commercial companies" [B.140]. The 1975 accounts of some 4000 companies were examined, before a selection was made of the top 1500 on the basis of capital employed. This exercise was replete with difficulties, and the following points must be stressed. GB registered companies ultimately owned by overseas registered parents were included, but subsidiaries of UK registered parents were excluded from the analysis. In an effort to eliminate double counting, the concentration was on consolidated group accounts together with the accounts of recognizably independent companies. But this meant that many large companies in the sample were conglomerates, which were still classified to an industry group on the basis of turnover. The general rule was to classify a company to an industry if 40 per cent of its activity was in that industry, lowering this limit if the remaining activities were widely spread over industries. For instance, Allied Lyons plc and Imperial Group plc both happen to make crisps but the former was classified to "Drink" and the latter to "Tobacco". Reckitt and Colman is a manufacturer of food flavourings, but since it is involved in many other activities this company was classified to "Mixed Manufacturing".

The second sampling frame was described by Clive Lewis in "Constructing a sampling frame of industrial and commercial companies" [B.103]. This work on the financial structure and performance of medium sized and smaller companies was partly impelled by the findings of three commissions of inquiry in their reports. The first was the Bolton Committee which produced *Small Firms: Report of the Committee of Inquiry on Small Firms* [B.375] which was published in 1971. The second was the Royal Commission on the Distribution of Income & Wealth (the Diamond Commission) which issued *Report no.1: Initial Report on the Standing Reference* [B.361] in 1974. Thirdly and more recently in 1980 the Wilson Committee issued the *Report* [B.358] which reviewed the functioning of financial institutions. The Wilson Committee also produced in 1979 *The Financing of Small Firms: Interim Report of the Committee to Review the Functioning of the Financial Institutions* [B.275]. Consequently a 1 in 20 sample was taken of 35,000 companies registered at Companies House. The sample included companies registered in Scotland, but not those registered in Northern Ireland. The procedure is subject to similar criticisms as those levelled at the first sampling frame, but the disaggregated results for the food industry should be more broadly representative given the dispersion in the size of the firms covered.

The old sample was based on the 1975 accounting year, and at the time of writing has been replaced by a new sample based on the 1981 accounting year. The sample is divided into two distinct strata. The first stratum relates to "large" companies, which are defined as the largest 2000 companies which filed accounts in both 1981 and 1982. The second stratum is based on a sample of about 1500 smaller companies, which constitutes a 1 in 300 representative selection of all other GB registered companies. The coverage and methodology of the new sample are described by John Knight in "Top companies in the DTI company accounts analysis" [B.97], and by John Knight and Graham Jenkinson in "Smaller companies in the DTI company accounts analysis" [B.98]. Any changes in coverage are usually detailed in *Statistical News* [B.381].

An attempt to establish some kind of continuity has been made by A. Goudie and G. Meeks in *Company Finance and Performance: Aggregated Financial Accounts for Individual British Industries 1948–1982* [QRL.6]. The standardised data therein are based entirely on the NIESR/BoT/DTI combined dataset. Tapes of the transformed data are available from Dr Meeks at the Department of Applied Economics (DAE) in Cambridge. The DTI has also sent a tape of the Company Accounts Analysis main data file, based on the old sample, for 1977 to 1984 to the ESRC Data Archive at the University of Essex where it has been made available to the public. A tape of the main data file for 1982 to 1985, based on large companies in the new sample, has also been sent to the Archive for access by the public.

The DAE transformation of the BoT/DTI data set for 1970 to 1981, plus the DTI data set from 1982 (new sample), forms the British contribution to a bank of company financial data now in an advanced stage of development by the Commission for the European Communities. The data bank — broken down by industry groups including Food — initially covers the United Kingdom, France, West Germany, Italy, Holland, the United States and Japan. Other Community members will eventually be added. The data bank is known as "La Banque de Données Harmonisées sur les Comptes d'Enterprises" or (BACH) for short.

2.13.3 *Other Official Sources*
The various PA Monitors for individual industries present monetary data on many economic dimensions. Annual data are provided on sales, gross and net output, wages and salaries, the purchases of raw materials, the costs of non-industrial services, gross value added at factor cost, stocks and work-in-progress etc. for the relevant Groups and Activity Headings. *Business Monitor PA1002* [QRL.93] reflects this coverage except that details of purchases and non-industrial services are not given at the Activity Heading level.

The many operating ratios are given by Groups and Activity Headings in the PA Monitors and by Groups in *Business Monitor PA1002* [QRL.93]. Cross-classifications by employment size for wages and salaries, sales, gross and net output, gross value added at factor cost, net capital expenditure and total stocks and work-in-progress at year end are given in the PA Monitors. The regional distributions of net capital expenditure, net output and gross value added at factor cost are also presented. The regional distribution is by Class only for these latter three components in *Business Monitor PA1002* [QRL.93].

But apart from the sources so far noted, there is an interesting paucity of financial information at the Activity Heading, Group and even Class level in what many would regard as authoritative financial sources. Neither *Inland Revenue Statistics* [QRL.278] nor *Financial Statistics* [QRL.217] descend below the level of manufacturing in their industry picture of profit. The *Annual Abstract of Statistics* [QRL.37] reproduces the income and finance data from *Business Monitor MA3* [QRL.81], but only for large companies in aggregate. Data on acquisitions and mergers are provided for the Food industries for the latest eight years — see also section 2.2.5. The figures relate to expenditure by the industry Group of the acquiring company, and the number of companies acquired. A merger (which takes place when two companies combine to form a new company) is reckoned as the acquisition of the smaller company by the larger, and is valued at the market value of the smaller company's share in the newly formed company.

The conglomerate nature of the Food industries obviously presents a difficulty, and this precludes a meaningful summary of key measures such as return on capital, profits etc. for each Activity Heading being inserted in *Business Monitor PA1002* [QRL.93] and the individual Monitors in the PA series. Another contributory reason for this lack of detailed information may be the macroeconomic emphasis on the financing and profitability of British industry, as reflected in the coverage in the *Bank of England Quarterly Bulletin* [QRL.58]. It should be noted, however, that the issues of September 1985, September 1986, November 1987 and November 1988 all carry recent articles on the performance of large companies. The September 1985 issue contains a useful index of articles in this quarterly publication for the years from 1960 to 1985.

The November 1988 issue provides figures for the return on capital employed, and the return on trading assets from 1974 to 1987 for companies in food manufacturing, and also food retailing. The statistics are derived by the Bank from the published accounts of a changing sample of over 1700 of the largest UK companies, mainly listed but, since 1980, including some 400 unquoted companies and around 50 Unlisted Securities Market (USM) companies. These accounts have been made available in computerised form by Datastream Limited (see section 2.13.4.4). These companies represent some three quarters of total assets and income, though they only account for a small proportion by number of the total population of companies.

The data given in the *Bank of England Quarterly Bulletin* [QRL.58] are important for recording trends over a number of years. They have been used by the Office of Fair Trading in *Competition and Retailing* [B.231], and by Slater [B.165] to compare trends in food manufacturing, food retailing and all industrial groups. However, the articles in the *Bank of England Quarterly Bulletin* [QRL.58] continually make cautionary comments about interpretation which may be summarised as follows. First, the data are provisional since delay in submission of accounts means results are based on about two thirds of the companies in the Datastream data base. Second, the Datastream statistics cover both the domestic and overseas activities of large UK companies. Third, unlisted companies have only been included in the data base since 1980. Fourth, rates of return calculated on current cost, rather than historic cost, have been discontinued since the September 1986 issue. Rates of return based on current costs are more meaningful, but the requisite data were not available as compliance with SSAP16 fell from 70 per cent of all companies analysed in 1981, to one per cent in 1985. Finally, the absolute values estimated from Datastream sources tend to be somewhat higher than the *Business Monitor MA3* [QRL.81] results. This probably reflects both definitional and sample differences. An article by Norman Williams in the December 1979 issue of the *Bank of England Quarterly Bulletin* [QRL.58] critically evaluates *Business Monitor MA3* [QRL.81] as a source of financial information. Recorded and real pre-tax rates of returns on equity, and on total trading assets, from 1961 to 1977 are presented for "Food, drink and tobacco".

Each quarter *British Business* [QRL.66] used to publish an industrial breakdown to Class level of company insolvencies in England and Wales. Data were provided for the latest five years and separately expressed as a percentage of total industry insolvency. A separate table gave industry analyses of bankruptcies and deeds of arrangements in annual terms for the self-employed within the Food, drink and tobacco sector. This illustration of the coverage is taken from the 28th October 1988 issue of *British Business* [QRL.66], but the statistics presented have varied in the past, dependent on the prevailing legislation.

Companies [QRL.158] gives a Class breakdown of liquidations notified during the year and previous year, separating compulsory from creditors' voluntary liquidations. It yields totals, both for England and Wales together and Scotland.

Insolvency General Annual Report [QRL.286] analyses bankruptcies and company liquidations by industry. Bankruptcies and deeds of arrangements for England and Wales are enumerated separately from company liquidations, divided into compulsory liquidations and creditors' voluntary liquidations. The company liquidations data are presented for Scotland too. This latter publication reflects the operations of the Insolvency Act 1986 which brought the administration of corporate and personal insolvencies closer together. The preceding *Bankruptcy General Annual Report* [QRL.59] had presented industrial analyses of assets and liabilities in its annual industrial picture of receiving orders and deeds of arrangement. These were the assets and liabilities after insolvency and did not relate to the businesses when they were going concerns.

An early account of the methodology of collecting insolvency statistics for England and Wales was given in the March 1975 (issue 257) of *Economic Trends* [QRL.181].

The Official Receivers reported receiving and administration orders to the Insolvency Service in the DTI as they occurred. They also notified winding up orders for compulsory liquidations. The Companies Registration Office provides a quarterly industrial analysis of creditors' voluntary liquidations. The industrial analysis is not precise because of the difficulty of classifying the main activities of certain businesses. But the statistics for the broad classes may be regarded as fairly reliable.

The primary legislation under which insolvencies, bankruptcies and liquidations are administered is complex and subject to change. See the 22nd April 1988 issue of *British Business* [QRL.66] for brief notes on the DTI revision of the compilation and publication of insolvency statistics for instance. But currently available data with accompanying notes are regularly published in *Companies* [QRL.158] and *Insolvency General Annual Report* [QRL.286] and used to appear in *British Business* [QRL.66]. Most companies which go into liquidation are very small. It can be seen from *Insolvency General Annual Report* [QRL.286] that the numbers have been more significant for food retailing, than for Food, drink and tobacco manufacturing.

2.13.4 *Commercial Sources*

The commercial sector is an important and fast developing source of financial information. A useful situation report is given in the July 1988 issue of *Business Information Review* [B.210] under the title "The 1980's revolution in company information". Even this report will, however, be out-of-date by the time of publication of this Review, given the continual stream of new developments.

In this section we discuss the various commercial publications etc. according to whether they are sources which concentrate on the Food industries, sources which cover the Food industries as part of a wider review of all industries, stockbrokers' reports, or computer data bases.

2.13.4.1 Specialist sources on the Food industries

The *Food Trades Directory & Food Buyer's Yearbook* [B.285], and *Binsted's Directory of Food Trade Marks and Brand Names* [B.203], are useful in identifying firms, brand names and addresses. Other publications combine secondary information on finance and profits, with a profile of the industry. Jordan's *Britain's Food Processing Industry* [B.150] classifies the major food companies to industry Groups in SIC(1980), and names the processes and products covered. The text concludes with summary financial data on 96 companies to provide the analytical framework for assessing financial performance. The top 30 are ranked by turnover, by net tangible assets, by pre-tax profits etc.

Euromonitor Publications are responsible for *The Euromonitor Food Report* [QRL.530] which aims to include all major food companies, and contains an alphabetical list of some 200, drawn from Companies House and company reports. Information is given on the ultimate holding company, the parent company/division, and subsidiaries. Data on turnover and pre-tax profits are presented, together with market overviews culled from many sources.

The Institute of Grocery Distribution (IGD) is a trade association which produces two volumes pertinent to the financial analysis of the Food industries as well as other statistical information, notably the *Food Industry Statistics Digest* [QRL.237]. *Food Company Profiles* [QRL.234] looks at a number of grocery retailers, food manufacturers, mixed businesses, and mixed retailers. It provides an alphabetical index, and shows the relationships between subsidiaries, associates and the parent company. Recent financial results highlight turnover and pre-tax profits. This is complemented by *Food Company Performances* [QRL.233] which gives much more data on basic financial performance over a five year period. A glossary of accounting conventions is provided, and substantial information is given under the broad headings of sales and profits, balance sheet details, and ratio analyses. Key items reported include the return on capital employed, net margins, liquidity, stock turnover, credit period and dividend cover. The work is done by the IGD Trade Economics Department, using information from their data base. These volumes have appeared as Volume 1 and Volume 2 in the past. *Food Company Performances* [QRL.233] tends to be annual and *Food Company Profiles* [QRL.234] the more occasional. Continual revision and updating takes place according to changing business developments. Commercial charges are made for these reports. The IGD price discriminates between company members, individual members, and non-members.

The driving force behind the work of the Inter-Company Comparisons (ICC) Information Group is the desire for continuous company financial information. This cannot be satisfied by the occasional source, hence they provide a growing number of publications based on substantial company samples and analyses of publicly available information. The publications fall into four groups:

- Financial Survey and Company Directory reports
- Business Ratio reports
- Industrial Performance Analysis
- Key Note reports.

The series of "Financial Survey and Company Directory" reports concentrates on comparing the main financial indicators of turnover, pre-tax profits, directors' remuneration, total assets, current assets, current liabilities, return on capital employed and profit margins. The following sixteen surveys relate to the Food industries:

- *Agricultural Growers & Merchants — London/South* [QRL.564]
- *Agricultural Growers & Merchants — Midlands/North* [QRL.565]
- *Animal & Pet Food Manufacturers and Distributors* [QRL.566]
- *Bakery Products Manufacturers* [QRL.567]
- *Confectionery & Ice-cream Manufacturers* [QRL.568]
- *Fish Trawling, Processing & Merchanting* [QRL.569]
- *Food Processors — England and Wales* [QRL.570]
- *Food Processors — Scotland* [QRL.571]
- *Frozen Food Processors, Distributors and Centres* [QRL.572]
- *Fruit, Flower & Vegetable Merchants — London/South* [QRL.573]
- *Fruit, Flower & Vegetable Merchants — Midlands/North* [QRL.574]
- *Grocery Wholesalers & Supermarkets* [QRL.575]
- *Horticultural Growers & Merchants* [QRL.576]
- *Meat, Egg & Poultry Processors* [QRL.577]
- *Meat & Poultry — Scotland* [QRL.578]

- *Tobacco & Confectionery Wholesalers* [QRL.579]

The "Business Ratio" reports" contain a greater degree of financial analysis. The reports are updated annually, and the following cover aspects of the Food industries:

- *Bakeries* [QRL.544]
- *Cash & Carry* [QRL.545]
- *The Catering Industry* [QRL.546]
- *Compound Animal Food Stuffs* [QRL.547]
- *Confectionery Manufacturers* [QRL.548]
- *Dairy Products* [QRL.549]
- *Food Ingredients* [QRL.550]
- *Food Processors (Intermediate)* [QRL.551]
- *Food Processors (Major)* [QRL.552]
- *Frozen Food Distributors* [QRL.553]
- *Frozen Food Producers* [QRL.554]
- *Fruit & Flower Wholesalers* [QRL.555]
- *Fruit, Flower & Vegetable Merchants* [QRL.556]
- *Grocery Wholesalers* [QRL.557]
- *Horticulture: Growers & Gardeners* [QRL.558]
- *Meat Processors* [QRL.559]
- *Meat Wholesalers* [QRL.560]
- *Pet Foods* [QRL.561]
- *Poultry Processors* [QRL.562]
- *Supermarkets* [QRL.563]

As an example of the coverage, the 1987 edition of *Food Processors (Major)* [QRL.552] analyses 75 of the major UK food manufacturers, and provides an alphabetical listing comparing financial performance over the three years ending October 1986. It also contains individual company portraits. In the introductory commentary, the ten largest companies in terms of sales are analysed with respect to their returns on capital, profit margins, stock turnover, liquidity and profit per employee. The ten companies with the highest margins are also ranked. The following list of of ratios is indicative of the detailed treatment provided in this source:

- return on capital employed
- return on assets
- profit margin
- asset utilisation
- fixed asset productivity
- stock turnover
- average collection period
- export ratio
- current ratio
- quick ratio
- borrowing ratio
- equity gearing
- income gearing
- average employee remuneration
- profit per employee

- sales per employee
- capital employed per employee
- fixed assets per employee
- return on shareholders' funds
- return on investment.

Companies are ranked in order of their performance, and the percentage changes between years are calculated. The 1987 edition of *Food Processors (Intermediate)* [QRL.551] furnishes similar information for 116 intermediate food companies. The 1987 edition of *Frozen Food Producers* [QRL.554] profiles 74 of the leading companies classified as the producers of frozen vegetables; frozen fish and shellfish; frozen meat; frozen desserts; ice-cream; and general foods. The 1987 edition of *Food Ingredients* [QRL.550] covers 105 leading companies involved in the production, extraction and distribution of flavourings, additives or improvers essential to modern foods. These range from everyday pepper, salt and sugar through to food dyes and chemically produced additives.

Industrial Performance Analysis: A Financial Analysis of UK Industry and Commerce [QRL.273] is annually published as a single volume, with analyses based on a fixed sample of some 12,000 public and private companies over a three year period representing the whole of British industry. Food manufacturing, and food and drink distribution, are two of the 25 sectors which are classified and ranked (in the 1987/88 edition) by eighteen key areas of performance. Each of these 25 major industrial sectors is further subdivided into constituent sub-sectors whose performances are analysed with reference to key ratios, and to variables from the profit and loss account and the balance sheet. The sub-sectors for food manufacturing are bakeries; compound animal feeding stuff manufacturers; confectionery manufacturers; dairy produce; frozen food producers; meat processors; and poultry processors. The analysis is thus by industrial sector, and sub-sector, rather than by company.

The "Key Note" reports contain market research information on industry structure, although financial appraisal of the major companies is also incorporated. The following twenty reports relate to the Food industries:

- *Bread Bakers* [QRL.580]
- *Breakfast Cereals* [QRL.581]
- *Canned Foods* [QRL.582]
- *Confectionery* [QRL.583]
- *Contract Catering* [QRL.584]
- *Ethnic Foods* [QRL.585]
- *Fast Food Outlets* [QRL.586]
- *Flour Confectionery* [QRL.587]
- *Food Flavourings & Ingredients* [QRL.588]
- *Frozen Foods* [QRL.589]
- *Fruit & Vegetables* [QRL.590]
- *Health Foods* [QRL.591]
- *Hot Drinks* [QRL.592]
- *Meat & Meat Products* [QRL.593]
- *Milk & Dairy Products* [QRL.594]
- *Pet Foods* [QRL.595]

- *Slimming Products* [QRL.596]
- *Sauces & Spreads* [QRL.597]
- *Snack Foods* [QRL.598]
- *Sugar* [QRL.599]

Some comment is called for on the work of the Inter-Company Comparisons (ICC) Publications Group. First, ICC does not produce primary data, though it does give convenient summaries and analyses. Second, ICC warn that "because data cannot always be verified, it is possible that some errors or omissions may occur. Details supplied by the ICC Information Groups should only be used as an aid, to assist the making of business decisions, not as the sole basis of taking such decisions". Third, the single volume *Industrial Performance Analysis* [QRL.273] does not identify companies. Fourth, the subdivisions used in the Key Note reports are not identical to the sectors used in the Business Ratio reports. Thus complete coverage would require purchasing all four groups of publications which is not often economic given the considerable duplication. However, the diversity of information is impressive, the information is updated in successive editions, and the 24 hour on-line company search service from the ICC data base (covering over 70,000 companies) is a progressive development.

2.13.4.2 General sources covering the Food industries

There are many reference sources which enable the names of food companies to be identified prior to seeking further information. Some of these sources also yield financial profiles at the same time.

- *Who Owns Whom* [B.396] enables parent companies to be identified, and subsidiaries to be catalogued.
- *The International Stock Exchange Official Yearbook* [QRL.290] (up to 1986–87 *The Stock Exchange Official Yearbook*) lists companies and public corporations in alphabetical order, and also gives market synopses. Capital structure, turnover, and pre-tax profit are usually presented in the summary financial data.
- *Kompass: Register of British Industry and Commerce* [QRL.301] carries a mass of information. Volumes I and II cover products and services; volume III provides company information; and volume IV gives financial data on the companies identified.
- *The Hambro Company Guide* [QRL.255] is published quarterly, and various food companies may be identified in it. Financial data from company accounts includes turnover, pre-tax profit, retained profit, earnings and dividends per share, intangible assets, fixed assets, fixed investments, stocks, debtors etc.
- *Key British Enterprises* [B.323] is a directory with an alphabetical list of companies. It reports the company, the trade names of products, SIC codes etc.
- *The Times 1000* [QRL.486] is compiled annually by Extel Statistical Services from the financial results of over 7000 companies in the United Kingdom and overseas. Statistical profiles are provided of many food companies. Rankings are presented in terms of turnover, capital employed, net profit before interest

and tax, number of employees, equity market capitalisation, position for the previous year etc. The main activity is listed, though this is often a somewhat arbitrary description. In 1987/88, for example, Unilever was described as a food products, detergents group, and Unigate was profiled as dairymen and food manufacturers etc. The largest acquisitions and mergers are tabled and ranked according to acquiring company, acquired company, and the total value of consideration for equity not already owned. New entrants and leavers are also detailed. The treatment has been broadened to world coverage. Reasonable historical profiles may be traced back to 1966.

- *Business* [QRL.73] magazine regularly publishes data on the "Business 500". The top 500 companies are profiled and ranked by pre-tax profit as a percentage of turnover, pre-tax profit per employee, sales per employee etc. The figures from the most recent financial year are compared with those for 1979. The top ten food companies are named, and ranked by pre-tax profit per employee, and sales per employee.
- The *UK's 10000 Largest Companies* [QRL.500] ranks the top 500 by profit margin, amongst other variables.
- The *Handbook of Market Leaders* [QRL.256] reports information on those companies who are included in the Financial Times All-Share index. Statistics on profit and loss, capital employed, profits etc. accompany the ordinary share section. Net asset value, cash flow, earnings, dividends, and substantial shareholdings (defined to be more than 10 per cent of the equity) are given.
- The *A-Z of UK Brand Leaders* [QRL.55] gives trading addresses and main activities, holding companies, principal subsidiaries, a three year trend for turnover and pre-tax profits, and brand leaders in particular market sectors.
- *Macmillan's Unquoted Companies* [QRL.314] presents a financial profile of Britain's top 10,000 unquoted companies. Profits and margins are included in the alphabetical listing. The industrial category index helpfully gives company names classified by SIC(1980) Activity Heading.
- Jordan's *The Top 2000 Britain's Privately-owned Companies* [QRL.487] and Jordan's *The Second 2000 Britain's Privately-owned Companies* [QRL.452] furnish a range of data covering many items from the balance sheet, profit and loss account, and statement of sources and applications of funds.
- Jordan's *Scotland's Top 500 Companies* [QRL.445] extracts information from data on public display at Companies House in Edinburgh, and provides company names, main business activities, and summarised profit and loss accounts and balance sheets.
- The 1987 edition of *Foreign Owned Company Performance in the UK* [QRL.241] includes an industrial analysis of the role of multinationals in the UK Food industry. 56 foreign firms are compared with 657 UK-owned companies on profit and loss, balance sheet and key ratios. The directory of companies by country of ownership provides the usual ICC summary ratios.

Thus there is an abundant array of information. Many of these titles are in specialist business libraries but most reference libraries should hold at least a few of these.

Individually less bulky, but dependent upon efficient filing, are the cards produced by Extel Financial Ltd. *Extel Financial UK Listed Companies Service: Extel UK*

Quoted [QRL.192] supply annual (white) cards on some 3000 companies which both summarise the commercial background and give a wide range of financial information. The news cards (buff) provide continued and cumulative updates and give share prices, dividends yields, earnings yields, price/earnings ratios etc. together with the latest commercial and financial information. *Extel Financial Unquoted Companies Service: Extel UK Unquoted* [QRL.194] supply both annual and news cards (both pink) which cover these companies. *Extel Financial Unlisted Securities Market Service : Extel UK Unlisted Securities Market* [QRL.193] supplies both annual and news cards (both green).

McCarthy Information Ltd. provide a somewhat complementary service to Extel Financial Ltd., focusing more on company news. Financial data are provided as well. *McCarthy UK Quoted* [QRL.347] supply buff and white cards for this sector by named companies. *McCarthy UK Unquoted* [QRL.348] furnish pink news cards. Details of pre-tax profits, stated earnings per share, capitalisation, financial history etc. are often featured. McCarthy Information Ltd. draws upon over 60 leading newspapers and financial journals. *McCarthy Industry* [B.328] with the blue cards, is a press cutting service for industrial news found in many business libraries. It is mentioned here because information filed alphabetically under the headings of basic foodstuffs, coffee, fish and fish meal, milk and cream etc. are useful for starting on, or updating, information on the Food industries.

2.13.4.3 Stockbrokers' reports

Daily information on share prices, high and low prices for the year, price changes on the previous day, net dividend cover, gross yields, and price/earnings ratios may be found in the *Financial Times* [QRL.218] and other quality newspapers. Company financial profiles based on these data are compiled by specialist food industry analysts working for the various stockbrokers. The following are cited as representative examples of the coverage provided:

- Barclays de Zoete Wedd Research publish *UK Food Manufacturing Weekly Review* [QRL.497] which profiles the share performance of companies in the Food industries. Pre-tax profits, earnings per share, price/earnings ratios, net dividend and gross yields etc. are typically given. Estimated pre-tax profits, dividends etc. are forecast in anticipation of company results. Indeed Barclays de Zoete Wedd provide a variety of information. This ranges from individual company notes, updates, sector notes and the more detailed reviews of food manufacturing as a whole. Predicted figures for pre-tax profits, net dividends etc. are often presented for the coming half year. Past data are frequently provided for comparison. The various standard financial ratios are often calculated. Market developments which may affect the Food industries are detailed.
- County NatWest WoodMac produce the quarterly *Focus on Food Manufacturing* [QRL.229] which begins with spreadsheet summary information on pre-tax profits, price/earnings ratios, dividends yields etc. for alphabetically ordered quoted food companies. Sections on sector performance, sector analysis and brand values precede the detailed company financial profiles, forecasts and latest news.
- Henderson Crosthwaite (HC) give more frequent coverage in their *Consumer Brief* [QRL.162] which runs to about twenty issues a year. Both an historic

and prospective earnings summary for named food manufacturing companies (as well as food retailing and distribution firms) are featured. The historic brief gives prices, net dividends, yields, pre-tax profits, price/earnings ratios etc. The prospective brief gives the consensus and range of expected earnings and the price/earnings ratios for the year ahead compared with the HC forecast. [QRL.162] also carries statistically supported company profiles. The detailed but occasional *Consumer Brief Spotlight* [QRL.163] appears when circumstances warrant.

- Scrimgeour Vickers & Co are responsible for *United Kingdom Research: Food Manufacturing Monthly* [QRL.507] which gives both forecasts and recent results for food manufacturing companies. The summary of forecasts profiles profit before tax, earnings and dividends per share etc. and gives a view of the market factors likely to affect the prices of major stocks. An account of the sector performance describes possible predators and victims. Substantial financial data and geographical profit analyses are provided. The day by day sector diary reflects major economic events influencing companies in the food sector the previous month. The sector calender records recent and forthcoming results for named companies.

The above list is an illustrative sample of what was available in 1988 and 1989. It is by no means exhaustive, and the analysts responsible are not necessarily the most successful. Reports often wax and wane according to the changing interests of the brokerage firms, the demands of their clients and the job transfers of food analysts. The number of reports and newsletters increases when a take-over battle, for instance, is in progress. Although some reports are sent to reference libraries, others are often prepared mainly for clients. These latter reports may be confidential and unavailable to the general public. Sometimes a charge is made for them.

Nevertheless it is possible to accumulate a list of the broking houses involved from the following references. The compilation *Stockbrokers' Research Information Service 1988* [B.79] gives a useful list of the many sources, firms responsible, names of analysts, telephone numbers etc., based on information supplied by stockbrokers in Spring 1988. This indicates the wide variety produced at that time, ranging from daily briefs and regular reports to the occasional substantial reviews of companies and industrial sectors. On-line availability is catalogued for the first time in this latest study and international coverage noted. The previous *Stockbrokers' Research and Information Services 1984* [B.80] was the result of a similar exercise which gave the name of analysts, the firms responsible etc. prior to "Big Bang" which has had a considerable influence on the structure of stockbroking firms. Even if there is continual change in stockbrokers' research and information services, it is an important part of the provision of financial information. Developments have been monitored by the library staff of Templeton College, Oxford since 1977. [B.79] and [B.80] are made available to readers and can be supplied to interested parties on request. Probably future market demand will lead to a further updating of what is available.

Briton's Index of Investment Research Analysts in the UK [B.34] updates the information on stockbrokers specialising in food manufacturing, and also provides telephone numbers. It is published three times a year and is the successor to *Crawford's Investment Research 1986–1987.*

Nelson's Official Research Guide [B.340] is compiled monthly. It lists research reports by originating firm, company, analyst, and date and also gives the number of pages. There is a research firm directory, and a section on research reports classified by originating firm and industry group. The groups separately identified are: food; food/confectionery and soft drinks; food/meat; and dairying food/packaging goods.

The *ICC Directory of Stockbrokers' Reports* [B.310] has a monthly update of the reports, newsletters, reviews etc. provided by the participating firms. An on-line data base is available for the food manufacturing sector, so that the full text of the reports can be supplied. The *ICC Directory* [B.310] bases its emergence on the grounds that "even though stockbrokers are recognised as a major source of high quality business information, their research is not readily available and finding out what has been published is difficult". Its success will depend upon the number of subscribers.

Nevertheless a combination of *Stockbrokers' Research Information Service 1988* [B.79], *Briton's Index* [B.34], *Nelson's* [B.340] and the *ICC Directory* [B.310] probably gives most of what is available.

Finally, the *Extel Ranking of UK Investment Analysts* [B.263], which is published annually, presents another useful list of food analysts and their broking houses in the supplementary food manufacturing section. Twenty-three organisations were ranked in 1988 and further details are provided in section 2.13.5. For the present, it should be noted that some reviews are obtainable free on request, some are automatically provided to business libraries, some are sent only to clients, and others are sent only on payment of a fee. The market for company financial information is thus highly developed. Access to the data needed is probably available eventually to those who are determined enough to get it, but it has been part of our aim in this section to render this task somewhat easier.

2.13.4.4 Computer data bases

The ability to access financial information from a growing electronic fount of centrally stored information should be mentioned, because many of the printed sources are derived from them.

- *TOPIC* [QRL.489] is the name of the real time system established by the London Stock Exchange as its own international electronic stock market.
- *Datastream* [QRL.173] provides computer-based information, and computation services, both on-line and in printed form, supported by continually updated data bases. The return on capital figures cited in the *Bank of England Quarterly Bulletin* [QRL.58] — see section 2.13.3 — are based on data made available in computerised form by Datastream.
- The *ICC Company Information Database* [QRL.268] consists of a company directory derived from Companies House, and ICC financial data. It contains detailed profit and loss, balance sheet and financial ratio analyses. The *ICC Directory of Stockbrokers' Reports* [B.310] has an on-line data base showing the full text of selected stockbrokers' reports, as mentioned in section 2.13.4.3. *ICC Directory of Companies* [B.309] is also a data base.
- *Jordan Watch* [QRL.296] has also established on-line access to information on (some 950,000) British companies. For the most frequently requested companies, further data on profit and loss, balance sheet items, financial ratios etc. are also available. As with ICC, the data base is used as a source for many printed publications.

- Extel's *Exstat* [QRL.191] contains the accounts of many British quoted and unquoted companies. Besides other statistical services, nearly all the data in the *Times 1000* [QRL.486] are derived from this regular monitoring of the financial results of well over 7000 companies in the United Kingdom and overseas.
- Extel launched the well-known US data base *COMPUSTAT* [QRL.160] in the United Kingdom from the beginning of 1989. The UK version of COMPUSTAT contains about 4500 companies, and at that time was one of the very few data bases with a good international spread of company data.

The *Guide to Company Information in Great Britain* [B.137] gives a description of much of what is available. Moreover, the 1986 article by Brendan Walsh entitled "An overview of on-line data bases" [B.180] is a further concise account and evaluation of these burgeoning sources. *On-line Information: A Comprehensive Business Users' Guide* [B.181] is more detailed. *On-line Business Sourcebook* [B.55] is an evaluative guide to business data bases which is completely updated twice a year. Besides listing and evaluating general business information services, the product and market data chapter lists specialist Food and Agriculture data bases. These include Coffeeline, mentioned in Chapter 13, and the Foodline data bases available from the Leatherhead Food Research Association.

It must be emphasised that ICC, Jordan, Extel and Datastream are data base producers. Datastar, Dialog and Prestel are data base hosts, specialising in providing the computer facilities on which data bases are stored, thus bringing together the large volumes of data. Then there are the brokers of data base information. The British Library, the Financial Times Information Service, the Warwick Statistical Service, and the London Business School are four examples of such information retailers.

2.13.5 *Comments*

The primary sources of information are the company reports and the companies themselves. Most of this information is, however, collated in a wide variety of official and commercial sources, and it is these that the serious investigator will probably first consult. The commercial sources tend to provide information for individual companies, whereas the official publications, such as *Business Monitor MA3* [QRL.81] and the *Bank of England Quarterly Bulletin* [QRL.58], concentrate more on the Food industries in aggregate. It should again be emphasised that many of the major food companies are conglomerates, and that this makes any industrial analysis difficult. Nevertheless the ICC Business Ratio Reports and the individual Business Monitors in the PA series do attempt to provide industry detail.

Although some attention is paid to profit in official statistics, it features more prominently in the output of the commercial intelligence organisations. The reliability of reported profit data has been debated by many investigators, not least because of the vagaries of British company law and accountancy practice. We do not propose to discuss this considerable subject in this Review, but we may note the point made by G. Meeks in his book *Disappointing Marriage: A Study of the Gains from Merger* [B.123]. He suggested that the statistics drawn from companies' published accounts were unlikely to be bettered by other analysts, for they were based on the independent labours of many thousands of accountants, auditors and other financial specialists.

The market for company financial information is very highly developed and is continually evolving. Much of this information is sought in the pursuit of profit and growth, and sources which fail to provide a timely and up-to-date service may not themselves survive. Moreover, the acquisition of accurate information is a costly exercise, hence there is a need for an independent assessment of the various sources. Thus, a publication like the *Extel Ranking of UK Investment Analysts* [B.263] is of interest. Extel sent a questionnaire to over 230 fund managers in 1988 and asked them to rank analysts and their reports on the following criteria: depth of knowledge, quality of written material, frequency of follow up, and the accuracy of the earnings' forecasts. Sixty market sectors are covered, and the top three (sometimes four) analysts are identified for food manufacturing. A more detailed breakdown is available on payment of a further charge, and this ranks all twenty-three organisations at that time involved in the food manufacturing sector, viz:

1	Henderson Crosthwaite
2	Warburg Securities
3	James Capel
4	Hoare Govett
5	Citicorp-Scrimgeour Vickers
6	Phillips & Drew
7	Barclays de Zoete Wedd
8	Kleinwort-Grieveson Securities
9	County NatWest Wood Mac
10	Saloman Brothers
11	Laurence Prust
12	Williams de Broe
13	Shearson Lehman Hutton Securities
14	Robert Fleming Securities
15=	Gerrard Vivian Gray
15=	Kitkat & Aitken
15=	Panmure Gordon
15=	Cazenove
19	SBCI Savory Milln
20=	Smith New Court Research
20=	Prudential-Bache
20=	Gilbert Eliott
23	McCaughan Dyson Capel Cure

Continental Illinois began this exercise in 1974, and it has been continued since 1985 under the aegis of Extel. The analysts cited in section 2.13.4.3 were in the upper and middle regions of this league table.

Thus commercial and official sources tend to concentrate on different segments of a large and growing market for financial information. Official sources devote their efforts to providing, as a public but not free service, a statistical background of fairly aggregate data (at the industry level or above). The aim is to provide consistent data over a period of years, but there are significant time lags in publication. On the other hand, the commercial sources focus on information for which their customers are prepared to pay. The emphasis is more on the individual company, or small groups of companies, and the information is processed and sold as soon as possible after it is available.

Both official and commercial sources are seeking to make their products more cost-effective by developing the services they offer. The provision of electronic data bases may mean high costs (see Walsh [B.180]) but time savings may also result. Time and money will both be saved if a five minute computer search identifies material which would otherwise have taken hours to locate and copy. As regards the official sources, at least, it is unlikely that conventional printed sources of information will be completely displaced (at least for a long time to come - if ever).

2.14 Advertising and Market Research

Advertising and market research are both integral parts of the overall marketing process, hence they are treated together in this section. Nevertheless, quite distinct statistical sources exist for each subject, and these will be discussed separately in sections 2.14.1 and 2.14.2.

2.14.1 *Advertising*

The major sources of data on advertising expenditure are the various subscription services provided by Media Expenditure Analysis Limited (MEAL), and these will be discussed in section 2.14.1.1. Other sources include the Advertising Association, the Independent Television Companies Association, the Association of Independent Radio Contractors, the Institute of Practitioners in Advertising, the Business Statistics Office, and the Post Office, and these will be considered in section 2.14.1.2.

2.14.1.1 Media Expenditure Analysis

MEAL is a commercial organisation which provides data (to those who are prepared to pay for it) on which companies advertised what products, at what times, at what rates, and at what costs. The most general, and best known, of the standard publications is the *Tri-Media Digest of Brands and Advertisers* [QRL.493] which gives information on the advertising expenditures of competing firms and brands. Each brand is attributed to one of 372 product groups, which in turn are classified by 22 categories. The Food category covers 54 product groups designated by the letter (F) followed by a two-digit number. These groups are now listed for they show the advertisers' perception and classification of the many products of the Food industries.

F02 Baby food
F04 Biscuits
F06 Bread and bakeries
F08 Butter
F10 Cakes and fruit pies
F12 Cake and pastry mixes
F14 Canned fish

F53 Fresh and fresh-frozen fish
F54 Fresh fruit and vegetables
F56 Frozen confectionery
F58 Frozen ready-to-eat meals
F66 Frozen vegetables
F68 Health drinks
F70 Ice-cream and lollies

F16 Canned fruit
F18 Canned meat and poultry
F20 Canned and processed peas
F22 Canned vegetables and pasta
F24 Cereal (requiring preparation)
F26 Cereal (ready to eat) and supplements
F28 Cheese
F30 Chewing gum
F32 Chocolate confectionery
F36 Coffee and coffee extracts
F38 Condiments
F40 Crispbreads and slimming breads
F42 Convenience desserts
F43 Dehydrated and ready-to-eat foods
F44 Dried fruit
F45 Rice and pasta
F46 Eggs
F50 Flour and baking powder
F51 Food drinks
F52 Fresh and fresh-frozen meat and poultry
F72 Jams, preserves and mincemeat
F74 Junkets and jellies
F75 Margarine
F76 Meat and fish pastes
F78 Meat pies, sausages, bacon
F80 Meat and vegetable extracts
F81 Milk and milk products (except cream)
F82 Sweet toppings (including cream)
F83 Pie fillings
F84 Potato crisps and snacks
F85 Ready-to-eat meals, canned and dried
F86 Sauces, pickles, salad cream
F88 Soups, canned
F89 Soups, packet
F90 Suet, cooking fats, vegetable oils
F92 Sugar
F93 Sugar confectionery
F94 Tea
F96 Food speciality and range
F98 Yoghurt

The *Tri-Media Digest* [QRL.493] gives the brand name, the advertising agency, expenditure for the latest quarter, expenditure for the separate months of that quarter, and the moving annual total. Shares taken by each of the three media — i.e. the press, television, radio — are given as percentages of the moving annual total. Expenditure totals for each medium are then derived for each product group. The expenditure threshold at the time of writing is £60,000 per annum. Any brands with less than this are combined in the "all other brands" total. A useful product index is included.

The *Tri-Media Digest* [QRL.493] has featured television and the press from its first appearance in 1968 (when it was published monthly). Coverage of radio was added from the third quarter of 1986. The data are gathered by monitoring television and radio advertisements, and the advertisements in national newspapers, magazines and regional newspapers. An attempt is made to be exhaustive as possible. Outlets and publications are added when they satisfy the minimum circulation criteria.

It must be stressed that data collected are based on published rates for advertising, as specified on rate cards and summarised in *BRAD (British Rate and Data)* [QRL.64]. *BRAD* [QRL.64] also carries circulation data for newspapers and periodicals etc. However, the published rates for radio and television, in particular, do not always correspond to the rates actually paid. For instance, television spots may be at a premium in December and at a discount in January or February. Obviously, there is a fixed supply of peak advertising time. Rationing would be one solution, but instead there is an auctioning procedure which often results in a market clearing price which is not the same as that on the rate card. Hence MEAL data are also published in "corrected" form, as discussed in section 2.14.1.2

MEAL also provides a range of other services to subscribers. The following standard expenditure reports are available:

- advertisement analysis
- brand expenditure by press groups
- brand expenditure by television regions
- brand expenditure by area
- brand expenditure by medium (press and TV)
- brand expenditure by medium (press; TV & radio)
- brand expenditure on radio
- press advertisement service.

In addition, the on-line MEALINK data base includes all brands in MEAL's top 200 product groups using either television, the national press, consumer magazines or regional press and gives expenditure for individual months within the previous twelve month period. MEAL on Donovan Data Systems (DDS) holds both advertisement records and summarised data.

The *Account List File* [QRL.13] is a monthly update on the work of the advertising agencies. It is mentioned because of its industry/product index, and its client/brand index. The information on each agency gives the name of the client firm, the assignment, the executives responsible, and MEAL expenditure data for the previous year.

The *Tri-Media Digest* [QRL.493] is undoubtedly the standard reference but food brands also feature in *Top Spenders* [QRL.488]. The top 1000 Brands are shown in rank order by total expenditure, and the split between television, newspapers, magazines and radio spending is provided for each brand. The top 50 product groups receive similar annual treatment, and monthly figures on television, press, radio and total expenditure are presented for each group during the previous twelve months. *Ten Year Trends: A Summary of Display Advertising Expenditure* [QRL.482] gives data on display advertising expenditure at rate card costs for each of the MEAL categories and product groups. Ten years' figures are provided for expenditure in total, in the press and on television.

The range of services has increased since the time that the *Tri-Media Digest* [QRL.493] emerged in 1968 as a monthly publication to rival the existing *Advertising Statistical Review* [QRL.19] — the last issue of which was published in March 1970. This latter source dated back to the 1930's, and was published by Legion — the name being as easily recognised then as is that of MEAL now. The coverage, methodology, frequency of publication, and indeed title changed over the years, but the publication provided a useful monitoring service of actual media advertising expenditure on food brands and other products.

Campaign [QRL.145] is a widely marketed weekly publication which annually produces data on the top 100 spenders, as compiled by MEAL. The information given for the named companies includes total expenditure for the latest two years, with a separate breakdown of expenditure on television, the press and radio. The name of the holding company is given, the brand listed, the agencies cited, and the ranking for the previous year recorded. The prominence of food companies in these regular surveys of top spenders is easily confirmed.

For many years MEAL, like Legion before it, dominated. But market forces have recently led to the emergence of a challenger, viz: the *Media Register Monthly*

Summary [QRL.354]. This provides the total expenditure on press and television for the latest month, plus the moving annual total for the same components. Overall totals are given for the previous two months. The brand and agency involved are named. There is a convenient brand index. The material is organised into 34 category headings, and 480 product groups of which no less than 56 are food products. The data are gathered through the monitoring of television commercials, and advertisements in newspapers and magazines etc. The expenditure threshold for brands appearing in the *Monthly Summary* [QRL.354] at the time of writing is £40,000 over the last twelve months. Any brands spending less than £40,000 are combined and shown as "sub-threshold" brands at the end of each product group.

The Food Forecast [QRL.236] contains special reports on food advertising using MEAL data. Rankings, using corrected MEAL data, of the top 100 brands advertising in the food industry for the latest available months are provided giving the generic brand, the product name, and the corrected MEAL expenditure. A further ranking for all generic brands is made with figures for the percentages of total food advertising. Rankings, using corrected MEAL data, of the brands for the most significant MEAL sub-categories are given. An eight year run of data for generic brands within each major MEAL sub-category is also provided. These data are based on unadjusted MEAL figures for the years before 1986 and, uniquely for the food industry, on corrected MEAL figures since 1986. The latter figures use Advertising Association adjustment factors to estimate the actual prices paid. Total spending in each MEAL sub-category is presented in both corrected and unadjusted form for all years.

2.14.1.2 Other sources

Statistics on advertising stem not only from MEAL, but also from the Advertising Association, the Independent Television Companies Association, the Association of Independent Radio Contractors, the Institute of Practitioners in Advertising, the Business Statistics Office, and the Post Office. MEAL is nevertheless dominant in the provision of product by product, and brand by brand, information. However, the Advertising Association (AA) does provide some useful additional refinements in many of their publications, viz: the quarterly *Forecast of Advertising Expenditure* [QRL.240], the *Quarterly Survey of Advertising Expenditure* [QRL.400], the *Advertising Statistics Yearbook* [QRL.20], and the *International Journal of Advertising* [QRL.287].

Forecast of Advertising Expenditure [QRL.240] both reproduces and adjusts MEAL data. Indeed it basically reports two types of data: survey data from the Advertising Association and corrected data from MEAL. As discussed in the previous section, MEAL basically counts the number of advertisements on television and in the press etc., and multiplies these by the card rates published in *BRAD* [QRL.64] to provide the unadjusted estimates. The rates paid in reality are, however, set by auction. Now the Advertising Association compiles statistics from annual and quarterly surveys of the media, the advertisers and advertising agencies. Thus corrected MEAL data are obtained using an adjustment which allows for media discounting, by comparing the MEAL data by media category with the equivalent Advertising Association data. For instance, MEAL television estimates are adjusted in the light of the monthly revenue of the Independent Television Companies Association (ITCA). The revenue of TV-AM is however excluded. The adjustments are only approximate, and details differ both between and within media types, and over time. The ensuing data are, nevertheless, an improvement on the unadjusted estimates.

Quarterly and annual corrected figures are analysed by product category (e.g. Food) in both current and constant prices. Data are provided for the latest five quarters, and six years. In addition, the corrected figures are analysed separately for television and the press at current prices, and twelve months' data on total expenditure are also given. Data for the more detailed product groups within the category of Food are presented in unadjusted form for nine quarters. There is some variation in treatment between product groups. One important characteristic of *Forecast of Advertising Expenditure* [QRL.240] is the provision of expenditure forecasts for seven broad sectors of market demand. Food is consolidated with drink, pharmaceuticals, tobacco, toiletries and cosmetics in the "consumables" sector. Forecasts of corrected expenditure are given up to eight quarters ahead in both current and constant 1980 prices, together with the percentage change over the previous year, or the corresponding quarter of the previous year. Historical comparisons for "consumables" are provided for the latest five years.

The *Quarterly Survey of Advertising Expenditure* [QRL.400], and its predecessor in title the *Quarterly Review of Advertising Expenditure* also present data on food advertising expenditures corrected for Press and TV discounting. Figures on current expenditure, annual percentage change, seasonally adjusted expenditure, the moving annual total, and the annual percentage change in the moving annual total are presented in both current and constant prices. Annual data are provided for the latest six years; quarterly data for the latest four years. There is about a four month publication lag. Corrected data have been presented since the 1985 issue of *Forecast of Advertising Expenditure* [QRL.240].

The various MEAL publications are unavailable in public libraries. However, the work of the Advertising Association is disseminated in a variety of ways and in many publications. Thus, the *Advertising Statistics Yearbook* [QRL.20] is useful in that it pulls together a range of information. The coverage in the various issues since 1983 is reasonably consistent, but there are inevitable changes from time to time. Corrected MEAL data by product category (e.g. food), and unadjusted data for the more detailed product groups, are reproduced from *Forecast of Advertising Expenditure* [QRL.240]. The data are, of course, available earlier in the latter publication. Advertising/sales ratios used to be presented for many product groups (including many foods) in the *Advertising Statistics Yearbook* [QRL.20]. This practice was, however, discontinued in the 1987 issue because of the obvious difficulties of obtaining accurate figures for both the numerator and denominator of the ratio. But the ratios were reintroduced in the 1988 edition.

The *Marketing Pocket Book* [QRL.346] is a compact compendium which has been issued since 1962. The contents vary according to what is ready for inclusion, but typical coverage would include the following: corrected MEAL expenditure data (press and television) by product category (e.g. food); an index of the same; data on the advertising expenditure of the top holding companies, and the top 100 advertisers, as presented in *Campaign* [QRL.145].

The *International Journal of Advertising* [QRL.287] and its many predecessors in title — the *Journal of Advertising* [QRL.297], the *Advertising Magazine* [QRL.17],

Advertising [QRL.15] and *Advertising Quarterly* [QRL.18] — have traditionally reported the results of the Advertising Association Expenditure Survey in the second or third issue every year. Estimates of corrected media expenditure for food can be traced back to 1968 from these postal surveys of media owners, advertising agencies and advertisers etc., and these results may be compared with those generated by MEAL. These annual figures for food exclude the generic advertising of the British Egg Authority, the Cheese Information Service, the Milk Marketing Boards, the National Dairy Council etc. which are classified to the nationalised industries sector. The methodology is clearly explained in the annual article. A typical example of this useful reproduction and interpretation of MEAL AA data is the article by M.J. Waterson in the April–June 1983 issue of the *International Journal of Advertising* [QRL.287]. Waterson cites manufacturers' estimated consumer advertising for food during the period 1970 to 1981. The same author also computes advertising/sales ratios for food from 1969 to 1980 in the January–March issue of the *International Journal of Advertising* [QRL.287]. However, it should be emphasised that the absolute values of the ratios for food are not very revealing, since the divisor of total consumers' expenditure on food includes a vast range of products, some of which are not advertised at all. The official figures on "sales", taken from *United Kingdom National Accounts* [QRL.506], are always subject to revision. Notwithstanding these cautionary remarks, the ratios are nevertheless of some help in showing long-term trends.

The results of earlier work by the Advertising Association are contained in *Advertising Expenditure* [QRL.16], which summarised the four yearly surveys for 1948, 1952, 1956 and 1960. A product/category breakdown was not a feature of the coverage. The data for 1948 did, however, include figures for press advertising on food. The information for 1960 included a breakdown of advertising expenditure in the press, on television, and on British Transport Commission sites, by commodity groups. The earlier *Statistics of Advertising* [QRL.462], published in 1946, carried the most commodity detail, even if predominantly for the year 1935 and a selection of results from 1934 to 1938. The figures for advertising expenditure on commodities, including food, were classified according to press display, outdoor, radio and a total was also given. Early sales/advertising ratios for 1935 for various food products were obtained. An analysis was given of advertising expenditure on food according to press display, outdoor, radio, film, direct mail, window display, and advertising departments etc. A further analysis of expenditures on a number of food commodities was provided for 1935. A similar exercise for a more restricted number of foods was undertaken for radio advertising for 1938. Full details on methodology and sources are furnished in all these early studies.

2.14.1.3 Comments

According to the *Advertising Statistics Yearbook* [QRL.20], advertising expenditure in 1988 amounted to 1.71 per cent of GNP at factor cost. A commonly accepted definition of advertising is that it covers any activity designed to spread information with a view to promoting the sales of marketable goods and services. The *Tri-Media Digest* [QRL.493] concentrates on television, press and radio advertising, but does not cover the totality of advertising activity. The activities of salesmen, the provision of free samples and free demonstrations, the offer of premium merchandise etc. are not necessarily always included in the advertising budgets of business firms. Statistical enquiry should ideally cover all expenditures on sales promotion, but this is hardly possible. Any empirical work which compares advertising intensity according to industry and according to market concentration and which considers the role of advertising in competition and uses computed advertising/sales ratios, must be evaluated with these and many points in mind. Reference may be made to Chapter 6 of Roger Clarke's book entitled *Industrial Economics* [B.37] where such data are used and empirical evidence applied to assessing the role of advertising.

There is an abundance of private sources of advertising data, compared with the current paucity of official BSO data. The interest in advertising rates etc. has led to much information being provided in the *Tri-Media Digest* [QRL.493] and the *Media Register* [QRL.354] etc. Unfortunately, this also means restricted access to the information, unless people are prepared to pay for the privilege. However, the work of the Advertising Association (AA), and in particular the contents of the *Advertising Statistics Yearbook* [QRL.20] and the *Marketing Pocket Book* [QRL.346], render the information much more accessible, as does the existence of *Campaign* [QRL.145].

It is also worth remarking that the propensity to vary the coverage, and to change the titles of existing publications, are as much features of the private as of the public sector. The coverage of the advertising/sales ratio is an example of the former. The four changes of title of the current *International Journal of Advertising* [QRL.287] is a prime example of the latter.

The question of coverage, particularly of the *Tri-Media Digest* [QRL.493], should be noted. As the brochure on *MEAL Standard and On-line Services* [B.329] shows, the monitoring of television, selected radio contractors, newspapers and magazines amounts to more than 250,000 individual advertisements per month, and attempts to be as exhaustive as possible. New magazines are added as they are identified as satisfying the criterion of a minimum circulation of 50,000 copies. But the media sectors of cinema, directories and posters are not covered. Nevertheless, information on the latter is collected by the organisation responsible for the *Media Register* [QRL.354] and separately produced for clients. Similarly the growing media fragmentation of advertising with the use of Oracle, Prestel, videos, projection television, cable television, taxicabs, sports sponsorships, freesheets, direct mail, parking meters, milk bottles etc. evidently surrounds us and needs to be taken into account.

The substantive issue of the divergence between rates actually paid and those reported in *BRAD* [QRL.64] published rates has already been discussed in section 2.14.1.1. It should again be emphasised that the corrected MEAL data are still approximate. The adjustments are only undertaken for product categories (e.g. food) in the light of press and television advertising, but corrected data are not usually available for the 54 separate product groups.

It is worth remarking on the existence of the *Tri-Media Digest* [QRL.493] as a quasi-monopoly for many years. However, the emergence of the *Media Register* [QRL.354] may stimulate an increase in the amount of information available. Whereas the *Tri-Media Digest* [QRL.493] is only available quarterly, the *Media Register* [QRL.354] is published monthly. The *Tri-Media Digest* [QRL.493] has, at the time of writing, an expenditure threshold of £60,000, whereas that for the *Media*

Register [QRL.354] is only £40,000. The *Tri-Media Digest* [QRL.493] can, however, provide a much longer run of historical data, and other ancillary services. Both these publications cover food products, along with other products. The specialist publication, *The Food Forecast* [QRL.236], covers food only and provides corrected MEAL data for the various food product groups and, for 1986, corrected MEAL data for generic brand names.

2.14.2 *Market Research*

A large number of organisations produce reports on various food (and other) markets. In general, these organisations draw most of their data from official statistical inquiries (e.g. the Census of Production, the National Food Survey), and so should not be regarded as primary sources. Hence, we have not detailed these reports in the other sections of this chapter. The reports are, however, useful both in providing descriptions of the markets in question and in pulling together data from diverse sources to present a broad statistical picture, often with commentary. For this reason, it was felt worthwhile to list some of the major organisations preparing market research reports, and to catalogue those reports that relate specifically to the Food industries.

The organisations cited are the Economist Intelligence Unit, Mintel Publications Ltd., Euromonitor Publications Ltd., Marketing Strategies for Industry (UK) Ltd., Market Assessment Publications Ltd., and Key Note Publications Ltd. The first three produce regular journals — *Retail Business* [QRL.432], *Market Intelligence* [QRL.339] and *Market Research: Great Britain* [QRL.343] — which carry reviews of selected markets in each issue. Euromonitor, together with the last three companies, all produce regular (usually annual) reports on specified sectors. Finally, we also discuss the work of the Confederation of British Industry and the Leatherhead Food Research Association of which the latter has a market research as well as a scientific research function.

2.14.2.1 Sources

Retail Business [QRL.432] is published monthly by the Economist Intelligence Unit and carries reports on UK consumer goods markets and retail sectors. Many of these reports feature segments of the Food industries. The data provided usually include details of market size, production, trade patterns, sources of supply, brand shares and distribution. Much of the analysis is based upon published statistics — figures on advertising expenditures, for instance, are usually drawn from the *Tri-Media Digest* [QRL.493]. Such data are often supplemented by information from interviews, trade estimates and commissioned surveys. *Retail Business* [QRL.432] has been published monthly since March 1958, so the various reports may be used to provide some historical perspective, as well as current information on individual product markets in the food trade. A subject index to past reports is available on request from the Economist Intelligence Unit and is periodically issued for the reports. Thus the means of updating information is easy to trace and past surveys can be identified conveniently.

Market Intelligence [QRL.339] is published monthly by Mintel Publications. This well-known source has developed since it was first published in 1972, and it now offers subscribers six reports each month. Mintel claim that the data base covers 90 per cent of consumer disposable income in various areas. Significant coverage is given both to processed foods and fresh foods. The text is illustrated by tables which typically assist in depicting market size and trends, the supply structure, advertising and promotion, packaging, distribution and the consumer. Much of the data is taken from published sources, but these are usually suitably acknowledged.

The monthly *Market Research: Great Britain* [QRL.343] is provided by Euromonitor. A characteristic pattern is to give a statistically illustrated commentary on market overview and size, production and distribution, overseas trade, consumption and prices, packaging and advertising, brands and manufacturers, consumer profiles and outlook. First published in 1971, this source uses both commissioned market research and trade interviews to supplement statistics drawn and transformed from government sources.

Euromonitor are also responsible for the following regular consumer market surveys:

- *The Bakery Products Report* [QRL.523]
- *Catering Equipment in the UK* [QRL.524]
- *Chilled Foods and Ready Meals* [QRL.525]
- *The Convenience Food Report* [QRL.526]
- *The Convenience and Prepared Foods Report* [QRL.527]
- *The Dairy Products Report* [QRL.528]
- *Delicatessen Foods in the UK* [QRL.529]
- *The Euromonitor Food Report* [QRL.530]
- *The Fish and Fish Products Report* [QRL.531]
- *Food Multiples in the UK, 1980–1990* [QRL.532]
- *Food Specialists* [QRL.533]
- *The Fruit and Vegetables Report* [QRL.534]
- *Healthy Foods and Healthy Eating* [QRL.535]
- *The Hot Drinks Report* [QRL.536]
- *Hypermarkets and Superstores Retailing in the UK* [QRL.537]
- *The Meat and Poultry Report* [QRL.538]
- *The Slimming Foods Report* [QRL.539]
- *The Snack Foods Report* [QRL.540]
- *Specialist Food Retailing in the UK, 1980–1990* [QRL.541]
- *Specialist Health Foods in the United Kingdom* [QRL.542]
- *Specialist Health, Slimming and Dietetic Foods* [QRL.543]

The reports are periodically updated, and the interested researcher should ensure that the latest issue is consulted.

Marketing Strategies for Industry (UK) Ltd. produce a similar though rather more lengthy range of surveys:

- *Animal Foods* [QRL.617]
- *Baby Products* [QRL.618]
- *Bag Snacks* [QRL.619]
- *Biscuits* [QRL.620]
- *Breakfast Cereals* [QRL.621]
- *Cakes and Pastries* [QRL.622]
- *Canned Foods* [QRL.623]

- *Catering* [QRL.624]
- *Cereal Bars* [QRL.625]
- *Cheese* [QRL.626]
- *Chocolate Confectionery* [QRL.627]
- *Convenience Stores* [QRL.628]
- *Cooking Additives* [QRL.629]
- *Delicatessen Foods* [QRL.630]
- *Delivered Grocery Wholesaling* [QRL.631]
- *Ethnic Foods* [QRL.632]
- *Fast Food* [QRL.633]
- *Fish and Fish Products* [QRL.634]
- *Fish Retailing* [QRL.635]
- *Freezer Centres* [QRL.636]
- *Frozen Food* [QRL.637]
- *Fruit and Vegetables* [QRL.638]
- *Fruit Juices* [QRL.639]
- *Fruit* [QRL.640]
- *Hot Beverages* [QRL.641]
- *Meat and Meat Products: UK* [QRL.642]
- *Pasta and Pasta Products* [QRL.643]
- *Pet Foods* [QRL.644]
- *Preserved Milk* [QRL.645]
- *Ready Meals: A Market Opportunity for Food Producers and Packaging Companies* [QRL.646]
- *Sauces and Pickles* [QRL.647]
- *Short Life Dairy Products* [QRL.648]
- *Snack Foods* [QRL.649]
- *Sugar Confectionery* [QRL.650]
- *Sweet and Savoury Spreads* [QRL.651]
- *Vegetables* [QRL.652]
- *Yellow Fats* [QRL.653]

These desk-researched reports are generated from the MSI data base.The introduction typically sketches in the market in question followed by information on production and market size, international trade (exports and imports etc.) and market shares.

Market Assessment Publications produce annual market sector reports from a data base built up since 1980. The reports have a brief, standard format and provide information on market definition, UK production, foreign trade, market segmentation and future outlook. The section on market segmentation is often useful, giving details of product type, pack size, price, manufacturers, and brand shares etc. The following seventeen reports refer to the Food industries:

- *Bakery & Cereal Products* [QRL.600]
- *Canned Foods* [QRL.601]
- *Chilled Foods* [QRL.602]
- *Confectionery* [QRL.603]
- *Dairy Products* [QRL.604]
- *Dressings & Sauces* [QRL.605]

- *Fish & Fish Products* [QRL.606]
- *Frozen Foods* [QRL.607]
- *Fruit & Vegetables* [QRL.608]
- *Health & Diet Foods* [QRL.609]
- *Hot Drinks* [QRL.610]
- *Meat & Meat Products* [QRL.611]
- *Pet Products* [QRL.612]
- *Seasonings & Flavourings* [QRL.613]
- *Snack Foods* [QRL.614]
- *Sweet & Savoury Spreads* [QRL.615]
- *Sweets & Desserts* [QRL.616]

The data are drawn from existing published sources, supplemented by consumer purchasing and profile data from specially commissioned National Opinion Poll surveys, and an in-house interviewing programme of manufacturers and retailers.

Key Note Publications publish the various Key Note reports which provide industry sector overviews. The following nineteen reports cover the Food industries, and they are usually updated every eighteen months:

- *Bread Bakers* [QRL.580]
- *Breakfast Cereals* [QRL.581]
- *Canned Foods* [QRL.582]
- *Confectionery* [QRL.583]
- *Contract Catering* [QRL.584]
- *Ethnic Foods* [QRL.585]
- *Fast Food Outlets* [QRL.586]
- *Flour Confectionery* [QRL.587]
- *Food Flavourings & Ingredients* [QRL.588]
- *Frozen Foods* [QRL.589]
- *Fruit & Vegetables* [QRL.590]
- *Health Foods* [QRL.591]
- *Hot Drinks* [QRL.592]
- *Meat & Meat Products* [QRL.593]
- *Milk & Dairy Products* [QRL.594]
- *Pet Foods* [QRL.595]
- *Slimming Products* [QRL.596]
- *Sauces & Spreads* [QRL.597]
- *Snack Foods* [QRL.598]

Statistics illustrate industry structure, market background, recent developments, future prospects and cover consumer profile data. They note the correspondence with SIC(1980), and list further sources of information including trade associations, periodicals, directories and statistical sources. The major companies within each sector are profiled along with salient financial ratios. As part of the ICC stable, these Key Note reports are also discussed in section 2.13.4.1 where more detail on the private provision of financial data is given.

We must also mention the rather different market research carried out for manufacturing by its own association. The *CBI Industrial Trends Survey* [QRL.147] is a well known quarterly inquiry which studies the prospects for the manufacturing industries. The same sample of manufacturing firms is used and the same degree of individual industry detail is prepared. Then in [QRL.147], along with data for other industries, quarterly trends for "Food" are published. The abbreviated monthly enquiry summarises prospects for the more aggregated "Food, drink and tobacco".

The questions asked are not strictly quantitative but seek answers to the directions of recent and imminent trends: the general business situation, export prospects, envisaged capital expenditure, output capacity, order books, employment, output volume, stocks volume, average costs, average prices etc.

From its inception in 1958 until 1971, [QRL.147] was published three times a year in February, June and October. Since June 1971 the Survey has been conducted on a quarterly basis, with publication of the results around the end of January, April, July and October. Results are usually published within two weeks of the closing date for replies and four weeks after the questionnaire first reaches respondents. As such, the results may be regarded as an up-to-date indicator of manufacturing industry and give inklings of movements which may be shown later in the various series of official statistics on output, capital investment, exports, stocks etc.

Finally, we discuss some of the work of the Leatherhead Food Research Association, fully described in the April 1989 issue of *Business Information Review* [B.210]. *Food Market Updates* [QRL.238] are regular two-monthly reports on the various sectors of the UK food and drink markets, researched by the Market Intelligence Service. These reports are sometimes drawn upon in the ensuing chapters. Other services include special reports, new products review and the on-line market information service known as the Food Market Awareness Databank (FOMAD).

2.14.2.2 Comments

First, most of the major organisations are noted in 2.14.2.1, but this list is not completely exhaustive. We have simply focused on those that are most relevant for the Food industries. Various publications catalogue what is available. *A Guide to Marketing Research in the UK* [B.297] gives useful lists and descriptions. The *A-Z of UK Marketing Information Sources* [B.202] has separate chapters on private research publishers and *ad hoc* research companies, and also provides an index of sources and of products. The *Yearbook* of the Market Research Society includes an alphabetical list of organisations and individuals providing market research services. The Findex *Directory of Market Research Reports, Studies and Surveys* [B.239] is an annual US compilation. It also includes non-US publishers in its food section. The *Macmillan Directory of Business Information Sources* [B.175] lists specific food product reports under the Activity Headings of SIC(1980). *Sources of Unofficial UK Statistics* [B.130] profiles some, though not all, organisations. It has a useful index which enables the identification of publications and organisations.

Second, we note the use of market research publications to provide descriptions of industrial structure in the following chapters. Academic books, and reports by the National Board for Prices and Incomes (NBPI), the Monopolies and Mergers Commission (MMC) etc. are generally more authoritative and comprehensive. However, the information therein is generally in need of updating, and the various market research reports are useful in this regard. Moreover, readers are frequently interested in particular companies, and some indication of their market shares is often required. Neither companies' names nor their market shares are provided in the PQ Business Monitors. In contrast, Mintel has an on-line service and most commercial organisations respond in one way or another to the need for up-to-date profiles and data.

Third, the very existence of the many market research organisations reflects an economic need. Such organisations provide concise, readable commentary backed by statistics drawn from a variety of sources, and inevitably charge a price for the service. The information is often presented outside the confines of particular SIC(1980) headings, or sometimes encompasses a range of different industries. *The Hot Drinks Report* [QRL.536] by Euromonitor covers the UK market for tea, coffee and food drinks, and is an example of the latter. The November 1986 issue of *Market Intelligence* [QRL.339] contains a review of the growing pasta market and is an instance of the former.

Finally, promotional brochures for the reports show the competition in terms of price, market segment and coverage, original research, on-line services and updating facilities etc. All the reports, however, typically rely on official data which is supplemented by trade inquiries, commissioned research etc. Any evaluation of the statistical reliability of the trade estimates etc. would require more information on their methodology than is available. This contrasts with the careful explanations of sources and methods given in the majority of official publications. In the last analysis, of course, any evaluation of these private sector reports is undertaken by the market, and unsatisfactory reports should soon become extinct.

2.15 Research and Development

Much attention is paid to the scientific fact of invention and the economic reality of innovation. J.A. Schumpeter in his famous book entitled *The Theory of Economic Development* [B.159] stressed the importance of "innovation" which was broadly defined as the introduction of new methods, new products, new sources of supply and new forms of industrial organisation. It could even be argued that research and development (R&D) should be considered together with advertising and market research. Perceived limitations on expanding the overall market, and brand competition in existing lines, partly explain new product development.

The whole subject of R&D is surveyed by Young, Bosworth and Wilson [B.190] in a companion volume in this Series. Here we restrict our discussion to sources of statistics on formally organised research and development. The Department of Trade and Industry (DTI) carries out two official surveys of R&D in the United Kingdom, and these are described by Bowles in the August 1984 [B.22] and August 1986 [B.23] issues of *Economic Trends* [QRL.181]. The first survey covers spending by industry in the field of science and technology only. The second survey is an annual inquiry addressed to all government departments which aims to measure their spending on R&D in science and technology, and in the social sciences and humanities. These will be discussed in sections 2.15.1 and 2.15.2 respectively. Private sector activity is naturally affected by public funded R&D, hence these two sets of statistics sometimes overlap. Specialist sources relating to the Food industries are discussed in section 2.15.4.

Bowles [B.24] describes the latest developments in the August 1988 issue of *Economic Trends* [QRL.181]. The inquiry addressed to all government departments is still annual. The other inquiry now covers a selection of the larger enterprise groups performing R&D in industry. These annual surveys are anchored to the quadrennial benchmark surveys, the most recent (at the time of assembling this section) being in 1985.

2.15.1 *Industrial Research and Development*

Details of the major benchmark surveys of industrial R&D are published in *Business Monitor MO14: Industrial Research and Development Expenditure and Employment* [QRL.86]. The latest issue was published in 1991 and contained the results of the survey for 1989. Previous benchmark surveys had been carried out by the DTI in 1975, 1978, 1981 and 1985. An additional sample survey was carried out for 1983. Benchmark surveys have occurred every four years with, in the intervening years, a sample survey of significant spenders being conducted annually. The results of these annual surveys, and provisional results for the benchmark surveys, used to be published in *British Business* [QRL.66].

The inquiry by the DTI is addressed to enterprises classified to the production and construction registers maintained by the BSO and also to public corporations, private research laboratories and industrial research associations. Private enterprises with more than 200 employees according to the VAT-based register (3030 enterprises in 1985, 2600 in 1981) are asked if they intended to incur any R&D expenditure during the survey year. Survey forms are then sent out to positive respondents and to those organisations which had not replied. Compliance was required under the Statistics of Trade Act 1947. All public corporations known to engage in scientific R&D were surveyed. And all industrial research associations were approached, and R&D performed by these bodies was included in the results.

Definitions of the various categories of R&D are required before data may be collected and analysed. Guidelines on standard practice for surveys undertaken by member countries are set out in international agreements formulated under the auspices of the OECD. The *Measurement of Scientific and Technical Activities* [B.331] — the so-called Frascati Manual — provides the following definition which covers the work of science and technology, the social sciences, and the humanities, although only the first of these is covered in *Business Monitor MO14* [QRL.86]. R&D is defined in the *Frascati Manual* [B.331] as "creative work undertaken on a systematic basis in order to increase the stock of knowledge of man, culture and society and the use of this stock of knowledge to devise new applications".

The data are collected under three (hopefully) mutually exclusive categories. First, basic research is defined as work undertaken for the advancement of scientific knowledge without a specific practical application in view. Second, applied research is undertaken with either a general or a particular application in view. Third, development utilises the results of basic and applied research directed to the introduction of useful materials, processes, products, devices and systems or the improvement of existing ones. These distinctions are not clearcut, but the fundamental aspect of R&D activity is the presence of some novelty or innovation.

In the early surveys, firms were asked to include all people who spent more than half their working week on R&D. The 1978 survey, however, began the collection of statistics on a "full-time equivalent" basis, though this has made little difference to the employment results. The surveys were carried out on the basis of SIC(1968) for 1975 to 1978, and on the basis of SIC(1980) from 1981 onwards. Thus limited comparisons may be made before and after the introduction of SIC(1980). Moreover, until 1978, the surveys concentrated on R&D carried out, or financed by, industry. The 1981 and subsequent surveys have analysed R&D expenditure and employment, and the sources of funds. From 1983, surveys have sought details of R&D contracted out, as well as undertaken in-house. An area of double counting was thus removed. There is thus effectively a break in the series between 1978 and 1981.

The data in *Business Monitor MO14* [QRL.86] and formerly in *British Business* [QRL.66] are presented for "product groups". Product groups cover products commonly associated in production and usually similar in nature or manner of production. Since establishments in manufacturing industry are basically defined in terms of their principal products, these product groups usually correspond quite closely to industry groups. Product group 32 refers to "food and drink", and corresponds to AH4115–4283. Product group 33 refers to "tobacco". Prior to the 1985 survey, "Food, drink and tobacco" had been treated together. The classification using SIC(1980) must be regarded as approximate, however, since the allocation of R&D to an individual product group is not always straightforward and a single research and development programme may include a range of products. Comparisons over time may be affected by changes in the allocation of research programmes to product groups. The following data are provided for the "Food and drink" product group in the 1985 issue of *Business Monitor MO14* [QRL.86]:

- Sources of finance for R&D within industry in the United Kingdom in 1985. Separate figures are provided for finance from private industry; overseas; the UK Government; and the Ministry of Defence.
- Intramural expenditure (expenditure performed in the enterprises' own laboratories) on R&D in 1985. Separate figures are provided for capital and current expenditure. The former is further broken down into expenditure on land and buildings, and on plant and machinery. The latter is broken down into expenditure on salaries and wages; on materials and equipment; and other expenditure.
- An analysis by type of work of current expenditure on R&D within industry in 1985. Separate figures are provided for expenditure on basic research, applied research, and development.
- Intensity measures. Intramural expenditure on R&D in 1983 and 1985 is expressed as a percentage of sales, net output, and gross value added.
- An occupational grouping of employment on R&D in 1985. Separate figures are provided for scientists and engineers; technicians, laboratory assistants and draughtsmen; and administrative, clerical and other employees.

The 5th February 1988 issue of *British Business* [QRL.66] carries the results of the 1986 sample survey. The sample included 74 enterprises which together accounted for 75 per cent of total expenditure on R&D in 1985. The only statistics provided that relate specifically to "food and drink" are the figures on intramural expenditure. The results for the 1986 survey were obtained by comparing, for the sample, the aggregate expenditure for each product group in 1986 with the corresponding expenditure in 1985. The resulting ratio was then applied to the population estimate for the product group from the benchmark survey in 1985. Once a level of intramural expenditure had thus been estimated for the product groups in 1986, results for the other parameters were adjusted to allow for the differing weighting patterns of the samples for 1985 and 1986.

2.15.2 *Government Funding of Research and Development*

Central government is a significant provider of funds for R&D. Mention has already been made of the annual DTI survey addressed to all government departments. Associated with this survey is the *Annual Review of Government Funded Research and Development* [QRL.52]. The data therein are not analysed by industry but rather by department — e.g. the Ministry of Agriculture, Fisheries and Food (MAFF) — or by research agency — e.g the Agriculture and Food Research Council (AFRC). The following description of coverage is taken from the issue of [QRL.52] published in July 1988.

The *Annual Review* [QRL.52] is in two parts. Part 1 sets out an overall view of United Kingdom R&D, while Part 2 gives a more detailed view of the R&D programmes of individual government departments and agencies. The overall editorial direction is provided by the Cabinet Office. Part 1 contains the following four sections:

- Government resources provided for R&D — a summary of government spending on R&D, broken down by department, primary purpose, type of research, and the manpower employed intramurally on government funded R&D.
- R&D performed in UK industry — the results of the latest industry survey (see section 2.15.1 for sources providing more detail).
- Total R&D in the United Kingdom — a view of gross domestic expenditure on R&D.
- International comparisons of R&D — sets out United Kingdom R&D activity within the context of the European Community and the OECD.

In Part 2, each government department or agency prepares a descriptive text to accompany its statistics. The statistics include at least two basic tables. The first table contains a detailed breakdown of the summary figures that were used in Part 1. This illustrates the subject areas of interest to the department analysed by the primary purpose for the R&D. For example, the MAFF section contains data *inter alia* on food science, crops, livestock, and fisheries. The second table provides a summary of how the R&D is spent.

Much of the data in the *Annual Review* [QRL.52] is reproduced in *Economic Trends* [QRL.181]. The August 1988 issue contains statistics on expenditure and employment on R&D in the United Kingdom for 1986/87 together with estimates for future years. Gross central government expenditure on R&D in science and technology is enumerated separately from R&D in social science and humanities. Similar data are provided for net central government expenditure, after deduction of receipts. Figures on gross expenditure, broken down into basic research; applied research; and development, are also provided for intramural R&D in science and technology. Net expenditure is analysed by EC objectives for R&D spending (e.g. nutrition and food hygiene, animal products, fishing and fish farming, crops, agricultural production and technology). Finally, figures on central government employment (scientists and engineers; technicians; other — including administrative staff; and social scientists) in R&D are also given.

2.15.3 *Historical Data*

Interest in the potential of the nation's scientific and technological resources has given rise to periodic inquiries over the years. *Estimates of Resources Devoted to Scientific and Engineering Research and Development in British Manufacturing Industry, 1955* [QRL.187] was the result of an inquiry conducted under the aegis of what was then the Department of Scientific and Industrial Research (DSIR). This set the scene for many subsequent inquiries in its provision of data on employment and expenditure. The commentary is accompanied by illustrative tables comparing "Food, drink and tobacco" with other product groups. Moreover, the main tables give much more disaggregated data. Figures for persons employed on R&D, and for R&D expenditure, are given for the following product groups from SIC(1948): biscuits (152); sugar and glucose (155); cocoa, chocolate and sugar confectionery (156); preserving of fruit and vegetables (157); other food industries (150, 151, 153); and for Food, drink and tobacco (XIII) in aggregate. "Other food industries" include grain milling, bread and flour confectionery, wholesale slaughtering, and bacon curing and sausages. Further employment data were provided for scientists, engineers, and other employees, with a separate enumeration of full-time workers. The subsequent volume, *Industrial Research and Development Expenditure 1958* [QRL.276] provided briefer commentary and a more limited range of data on employment and expenditure for broad industry Orders only.

The three issues of *Statistics of Science and Technology* [QRL.463] were published in 1967, 1968 and 1970, and brought together a range of data on science and technology. They give information on sources of finance by industrial sector (industry, government, overseas and other); current expenditure by type of research, and by type of expenditure; and capital expenditure on land and buildings, and on plant and equipment. The triennial manpower surveys of 1962, 1965 and 1968 enumerated the the numbers of engineers, technologists and scientists for each industry in Great Britain.

A degree of continuity was maintained by the publication of *Research and Development Expenditure* [QRL.431] in 1973, and of *Research and Development Expenditure and Employment* [QRL.430] in 1976. The Department of Trade and Industry (DTI) became responsible for the provision of statistics on the industrial sector, and these data comprised distinct sections in these two CSO publications. Sources of finance; current expenditure analysed both by type of expenditure, and by type of work; capital expenditure; and an overview are included in both issues. The latter, moreover, includes occupational analyses, contrasting the number of scientists and engineers; technicians, laboratory assistants and draughtsmen; administrative and clerical staff; and others; in private industry with those in public corporations and research associations. The central government section in *Research and Development Expenditure and Employment* [QRL.431] provides very similar coverage to that found latterly in *Economic Trends* [QRL.181].

Thus a fairly comprehensive historical picture may be built up for the years after 1955. Changes in coverage and methodology may be deduced by reading the notes and commentaries accompanying the two DSIR publications [QRL.187] and [QRL.276], the three issues of [QRL.463], the two CSO publications [QRL.430] and [QRL.431], the *Annual Review of Government Funded Research and Development* [QRL.52] and the various editions of *Business Monitor MO14* [QRL.86].

2.15.4 *Specialist Reports on the Food Industries*

Statistics on food R&D funded by MAFF and the AFRC are published in the *Annual Review of Government Funded Research and Development* [QRL.52], as discussed in section 2.15.2. MAFF also publish an annual *Report on Research and Development* [QRL.415]. The statistical content varies between editions, but food R&D is generally identified separately from R&D on agriculture, fisheries etc. In particular, statistics are provided on:

- the distribution of MAFF funded R&D on various types of project in agriculture, food science, and fisheries. R&D on food science, food quality and food processing are separately enumerated, and analysed as activity undertaken in-house; commissioned with the AFRC; or commissioned with other contractors,
- the distribution of government funded R&D in food science. Separate figures are provided for R&D by MAFF (in-house); MAFF commissioned with the AFRC, NERC, RAs, others; AFRC (science vote); DAFS (in-house); DAFS (institutes and colleges); DANI (in-house); and the total,
- the funding of the national programme of food R&D, analysed by government department; MAFF (in-house); MAFF commissioned with the AFRC; MAFF (other); AFRC (science vote); DAFS; DANI.

In addition, the activities and expenditure of the four major research organisations concerned with food are discussed, viz: the British Food Manufacturing Industries Research Association (BFMIRA); the Flour Milling and Baking Research Association (FMBRA); the Campden Food Preservation Research Association (CFPRA); and the British Industrial Biological Research Association (BIBRA). It may be noted that the amount of statistical detail provided on food R&D has grown with the increased significance of industrial food processing.

The *AFRC Annual Report* [QRL.21] provides details of grants for university research, which includes programmes of research in food science as well as other academic disciplines. Further data and discussion are found in the *Corporate Plan* [QRL.165] of the Agricultural and Food Research Council. Examples are provided of the costs and quantifiable benefits of research. Under food research are listed the area of interest, the approximate annual cost, the estimated annual benefit, and a comment on the economic/scientific impact.

There are also a variety of occasional publications which carry discussions of, and sometimes statistics on, R&D expenditure. In 1982, the Advisory Council for Applied Research and Development (ACARD) published a report on *The Food Industry and Technology* [B.281]. This report provided historical background on the evolution of the UK Food industries, and detail on their present scale. It also presented information *inter alia* on the relationship between Agriculture and the Food industries, the UK balance of trade in food products, consumer buying patterns, food distribution and retailing, and some overseas comparisons. There were also sections on R&D, and future technological change, which reproduced some data from the MAFF *Report on Research and Development* [QRL.415]. Finally, there was discussion of the management of government R&D on food, and of technology transfer to the Food industries.

The issue of the effective transfer of technology to the food and drink industries was taken up in a report prepared by the National Economic Development Office (NEDO) in 1985 on behalf of the Food and Drink Manufacturing Economic Development Committee. This report on *Technology Transfer in the UK Food and Drink Industry* [B.388] provided information on the sources from which the Food industries obtained their science and technology. It discussed the importance of science and technology, considered the constraints on the transfer of technology, and presented some data taken from DTI and MAFF sources.

Finally, mention should be made of the occasional reports published by the Joint Consultative Organisation for Research and Development in Agriculture and Food. The March 1984 paper on the *Determination of Research Priorities for the Agriculture and Food Industries* [B.237] presents a concise discussion of the priorities for R&D, and the role of both public and private financial support. The paper is accompanied by illustrative statistical tables, and estimates of MAFF/AFRC/DAFS research expenditure for 1982. The expenditure estimates are disaggregated into: cereals and cereal products; meat and meat products; dairy products; vegetables and vegetable products; and fruit and fruit products taken together with wine, cider and perry. Data from various sources are combined to yield a more detailed industrial breakdown than is usually found.

2.15.5 *Comments*

It is often difficult in practice to distinguish between basic research, applied research, and development. Even the most fundamental research may eventually have practical applications, and the development of simple applications may yield certain insights into basic processes. This presents a problem for the statistical categorisation of R&D expenditure, though it is not easy to see how the problem might be resolved. This, and other such issues were discussed in the Green Paper, *A Framework for Government Research and Development* [B.288], known as "the Rothschild Report" and the subsequent (1972) White Paper, *Framework for Government Research and Development* [B.289]. The principal objective to which these two reports were addressed was the maximisation of research and organisational efficiency for work supported from public funds.

The statistical evidence appears to suggest that R&D expenditure is undertaken primarily by large companies. The innovative nature of small firms was discussed in 1985 in *The UK Food Processing Industry: Opportunities for Change* [B.391], but more statistical data on their activities would be welcome. It is unfortunate that enterprises with less than 200 employees have been excluded since 1981 from the DTI surveys of industrial R&D although it can be said that an "enterprise" may contain any number of companies each of which may employ less than 200. It is also unfortunate that there should be such a substantial time lag in the publication of the results of this survey — the data from the 1985 survey were not published in full until late 1988. A further concern is that no data are available specifically on expenditure carried out by companies in the Food industries. Rather the data relate to "product groups" — as defined in section 2.15.1 — or to the work of particular official bodies. It is certainly true that a single R&D programme may cover a range of products, and that research of benefit to the Food industries may be carried out by companies in other industries. However, an industrial breakdown of R&D expenditure would be desirable in some form given the interest in the Food industries.

There are many and obvious linkages between publicly-funded and privately-funded research and development. Yet, as the House of Lords Select Committee on Science and Technology noted in its report on *Civil Research and Development* [B.226]:

"The available data on industrial R&D are less complete and up-to-date than those on public R&D. This is partly because private R&D decisions are made by a multitude of corporate bodies rather than by a few departments and councils. It is also because private bodies do not in general collect and publish information on their R&D efforts to the same extent as public bodies. The statistical information relating to industrial R&D needs to be significantly upgraded. The DTI's full quadrennial survey with partial surveys biennially may be an improvement on the previous triennial surveys but it still remains an imperfect base for accurate policy making. By contrast the Annual Review has in recent years greatly improved the statistical information relating to public R&D and the Committee would like to see the Government promote similar developments in regard to private R&D, preferably in cooperation with the CBI and other trade bodies."

The Select Committee also recommended that companies should declare their R&D expenditure in their annual reports, and called for a statutory requirement given the ineffectiveness of DTI efforts to get voluntary disclosure. *Civil Research and Development: Government Response to the First Report of the House of Lords Select Committee on Science and Technology* [B.225] did not rule out legislation. But it expressed the hope that the accountancy institutions would adopt the revised SSAP (Statement of Standard Accounting Practice) 13 requiring companies to disclose the amount spent on R&D in their annual reports, and that this would be the best way to generate more detailed information. In fact, under revised companies legislation, companies are now *required* to publish expenditure on R&D in their annual reports.

It is understandable that commercial firms should be unwilling to reveal details of their research expenditure in their annual reports, as this information would then be available to competitors. If the effort of completing forms is a lesser evil, then it may be less ambitious, but more reasonable, to suggest a finer coverage in the DTI inquiry, at least so that the Food industries may be separately identified. Such a solution would not, of course, provide data on "learning by doing". Nor would it capture the unrecorded requests by companies for R&D staff to carry out routine checks of problems in the production process etc., rather than do "high-tech" work. Nor does it take account of the possibility that R&D in one sphere may have spin-offs in a quite different sphere — R&D in the chemical industry may influence the Food industries, and R&D in chemistry, physics and engineering may aid food science. But it would, at least, give a broad indication of trends in industrial R&D for the Food industries.

2.16 Official Investigations

Ad hoc official investigations, whether as a facet of price control or competition policy, are by no means new. Inquiries, with the consequent generation of statistical data, abound during the paternalism of Tudor times and well before that. Ample testimony to this is given in many of the extracts in the classic *English Economic History: Select Documents* [B.19] collected together by Bland, Brown and Tawney. A later collection edited by Fisher and Jurica [B.53] confirms this. Fluctuations in the price of bread and corn have often been the focus of official concern but price ceilings were sometimes applied to a wider range of foods. It was felt, at times, that loyal subjects "cannot gain with their labours and salary sufficient pay for their convenient victuals and sustenance unless speedy remedy be provided on their behalf".

More recently, successive governments have established a series of investigative bodies which have generated statistical data as part of their work. The National Board for Prices and Incomes and the Price Commission were concerned with inflation in the first instance. Other, more long-standing official bodies have had an interest in economic structure, and a concern with excessive market power. This is reflected in the Monopolies and Restrictive Practices Commission Reports, the registered agreements following the passing of the Restrictive Trade Practices Act 1956, and in selected Monopolies Commission reports. The titles of many of these official bodies, and their reports, suggest a concentration on price and competition policy. But more than just data on prices and structure are generated. Wages and salaries, price-cost margins, details of market share etc. are all considered. Thus these reports are valuable sources of statistical data and economic background for many of the dimensions of the Food industries discussed in this Review. We describe and codify the reports here for convenience and accessibility, and give some guidance to the modes of operation of the responsible bodies. Specific reports will be referred to again as sources in many of the chapters on particular industries, and will be listed again there.

2.16.1 *Reports of the National Board for Prices and Incomes, 1965–1971*

The National Board for Prices and Incomes (NBPI) was originally established as a Royal Commission on 8th June 1965, but was reconstructed on a statutory basis in 1966. The Prices and Incomes Act gave it power to call witnesses and require evidence. It was first placed under the aegis of the Department of Economic Affairs and later, from April 1968, under the Department of Employment and Production, now the Department of Employment. In the period up to 1970, the NBPI had responsibility to ensure that price increases, in the particular cases referred to it by the Labour government, should not be made unless they were justified by unavoidable increases in costs. In November 1970, the new Heath administration announced that the NBPI would be abolished. The actual demise took place on 1st March 1971.

The NBPI published 170 reports from its inception in April 1965 to its abolition in March 1971. The *Fifth and Final General Report: July 1969 to March 1971* [B.272] carries an analytical overview of its work, describing its mode of operation and outlining its work on prices, incomes and efficiency assessments. The separate Report no.170 *Fifth and Final General Report: July 1969 to March 1971 (Supplement)* [B.273] conveniently carries a summary of all these reports, and we list below those relating to the Food industries. The coverage and methodology are discussed in further detail in the following chapters.

Published Reports of the National Board for Prices and Incomes

(reports relating to the Food industries)

Report no.3	(Session 1964/65) *Prices of Bread and Flour* [B.408]
Report no.9	(Session 1965/66) *Wages in the Bakery Industry (First Report)* [B.416]
Report no.17	(Session 1966/67) *Wages in the Bakery Industry (Final Report)* [B.415]
Report no.23	(Session 1966/67) *Productivity and Pay during the Period of Severe Restraint* [B.410]
Report no.31	(Session 1966/67) *Distribution Costs of Fresh Fruit and Vegetables* [B.402]
Report no.33	(Session 1966/67) *The Remuneration of Milk Distributors (Interim Report)* [B.412]
Report no.46	(Session 1967/68) *The Remuneration of Milk Distributors (Final Report)* [B.411]
Report no.53	(Session 1967/68) *Flour Prices* [B.404]
Report no.55	(Session 1967–68) *Distributors' Margins in Relation to Manufacturers' Recommended Prices* [B.403]
Report no.75	(Session 1967/68) *Costs and Prices of the Chocolate and Sugar Confectionery Industry* [B.400]
Report no.126	(Session 1968/69) *Smithfield Market* [B.413]
Report no.140	(Session 1969/70) *Pay and Conditions of Workers in the Milk Industry* [B.407]
Report no.144	(Session 1969/70) *Bread Prices and Pay in the Baking Industry (First Report)* [B.398]
Report no.147	(Session 1969/70) *Margarine and Compound Cooking Fats* [B.406]
Report no.151	(Session 1969/70) *Bread Prices and Pay in the Baking Industry (Second Report)* [B.399]
Report no.154	(Session 1970/71) *Tea Prices* [B.414]
Report no.160	(Session 1970/71) *Costs, Prices and Profitability in the Ice-cream Manufacturing Industry* [B.401]
Report no.165	(Session 1970/71) *Prices, Profits and Costs in Food Distribution* [B.409]
Report no.169	(Session 1970/71) *General Problems of Low Pay* [B.405]

A detailed independent study of the methodology and coverage, commissioned by the NBPI, was written by Allan Fels and entitled *The British Prices and Incomes Board* [B.51]. The many NBPI investigations include much already available statistical detail, but this is supplemented by further statistical surveys. The latter are also appraised by R.F. Burch [B.29] in an article with the title "Statistical surveys conducted by the National Board of Prices and Incomes" in the May 1971 issue of *Statistical News* [B.381]. Aubrey Jones, who was the Board's Chairman, discussed the work of the Board in a wider context in *New Inflation: The Politics of Prices and Incomes* [B.92].

The NBPI only dealt with cases referred to it. It was an official body, constituted independently of the government, and its membership was broadly based. The NBPI could only report on its findings to the government which would then act or not, as it thought fit. It investigated and reported remarkably quickly, within 3 to 4 months as a rule. The NBPI used existing sources of information from available official and commercial sources, supplemented by case studies and statistical surveys.

Maunder [B.118] neatly summarises the reports concerning food processing, noting the prominence of references on flour milling and bread. Indeed Aubrey Jones [B.92] recalled that the most passionate discussions within the NBPI concerned the prices of bread and beer. Detailed information was also generated on bread, chocolate and sugar confectionery, margarine and compound cooking fats, tea, and ice-cream in particular.

The Food industries are considered in aggregate in a few instances. *Distributors' Margins* [B.403] surveys the mark-up on processed foods (canned foods, frozen foods, breakfast foods, biscuits, tea, chocolate and sugar confectionery). The data were elicited by interview, following a reference made by the Government, with the aim of ensuring that price increases attributable to the 1967 devaluation were not in fact being overstated. *Prices, Profits and Costs in Food Distribution* [B.409] covered the grocery, fresh meat and fresh fruit and vegetable trades. *General Problems of Low Pay* [B.405] carries a statistical ranking, in order of lowest earnings for men manual workers, for the many components of the Food industries. Another table gives the percentage distribution of male and female full-time manual workers within the lowest decile of hourly earnings. Data are provided for "Food, drink and tobacco" for September 1968 and April 1970. The latter bears out Fels' [B.51] observation that the reports generated a considerable amount of data on incomes.

The NBPI's view, reflected in its refusal to split into a Prices Division and Incomes Division, was that there was a need to deal with the whole spectrum of related issues of prices, costs, productivity and incomes, whether in references concerning incomes or in those concerning prices. Fels [B.51] notes that the NBPI pioneered the regular conduct of detailed earnings surveys on an industry basis in Great Britain, and thus suggested both the idea and method of the New Earnings Survey, introduced in September 1968. *Costs and Prices of the Chocolate and Sugar Confectionery Industry* [B.400], *Margarine and Compound Cooking Fats* [B.406], *Tea Prices* [B.414], and *Costs, Prices and Profitability in the Ice-cream Manufacturing Industry* [B.401] are all examples of wide-ranging investigations which tended to become more detailed later in the life of the NBPI. Information on market structure, market share, raw material costs, labour costs, production costs, marketing and advertising costs, prices etc. tended to be acquired to satisfy a certain preoccupation of the NBPI that price increases should not be encouraged unless justified by unavoidable increases in costs.

2.16.2 *The First Price Commission under the Counter Inflation Act 1973*
The abolition of the NBPI in 1971 symbolised the faith of the new Conservative Government in the competitive forces of a free market economy, tempered by voluntary restraint. At the beginning of 1973, however, a White Paper on *The Programme for Controlling Inflation: The Second Stage. A Draft Bill* [B.356] was published stating that "inflation is the biggest single threat to prosperity and the improvement of our standard of living". It was preceded by the Government's inability, in the Autumn of 1972, to reach a voluntary agreement with the CBI and the TUC on its policy to maintain growth, improve the conditions of the low paid, and moderate the rate of cost and price inflation. It was followed by the Counter Inflation Act 1973 which established two statutory agencies — the Price Commission and the Pay Board — with the functions of operating a Price Code and Pay Code respectively.

The Price Commission's earlier work is discussed by L.H. Lightman in "Price controls in the United Kingdom 1973–78: natural development or radical change" [B.104], and by Sir Arthur Cockfield (its Chairman) in "The Price Commission and price control" [B.38]. It made 33 reports or references under the Counter Inflation Act, from its inception in 1973 through to 1978. The importance of food is seen in the following list.

Published Reports on References under the Counter Inflation Act 1973

(reports relating to references involving the Food industries)

Report no.1	(Session 1974) *The Marketing of Eggs* [B.422]
Report no.2	(1974) *Prices, Margins and Channels of Distribution for Fruit and Vegetables (Interim Report)* [B.429]
Report no.4	(1975) *Prices and Distribution of Bananas* [B.427]
Report no.5	(1975) *Prices, Margins and Channels of Distribution for Fruit and Vegetables (Final Report)* [B.428]
Report no.7	(1975) *Prices and Margins in Meat Distribution* [B.431]
Report no.8	(1975) *Prices of Commonly-purchased Diabetic Foods* [B.424]
Report no.10	(1975) *Food Prices in Outlying Areas* [B.421]
Report no.11	(1975) *Prices and Margins in Poultry Distribution* [B.432]
Report no.13	(1975) *Bread Prices and Costs in Northern Ireland and Great Britain* [B.417]
Report no.14	(1976) *Prices and Margins in the Distribution of Fish* [B.430]
Report no.24 [a]	(1977) *Metrication and Retail Prices First Report: Granulated Sugar, Biscuits, Dried Vegetables and Salt* [B.423]
Report no.25	(1977) *Recommended Retail Prices* [B.433]
Report no.29	(1977) *Coffee; Prices, Costs and Margins* [B.419]
Report no.32	(Session 1977/1978) *Tea Prices* [B.435]

Enforcement of the system of price control rested in the first instance on the idea of "prenotification". Large companies had to give prior notice of intended price increases to the Price Commission, which could challenge them if the increases did not comply with the Price Code. Initially, only the larger companies (about 200 in all) had to prenotify, but this requirement was later extended to medium-sized companies. Companies below the prenotification level had to keep records which could be inspected. A second element of the Price Code was the set of criteria for acceptable price increases. This was founded on the principle that prices should only be allowed to rise to the extent that unavoidable increases in costs per unit of output had to be met. Pay increases beyond those permitted by the Price Code, or heavy advertising expenditures, were not admissable. The third element was the control of companies' profit margins, which were to be limited so as not to exceed the average of the best two years out of the last five. These principles, with adjustments from time to time, operated for over four years from April 1973 to July 1977. They have been outlined here at some length to emphasise that the Reports often involved much more than the examination of price trends. At its peak in March 1975, the Price Commission was staffed by 746 people — see the *Report for the Period 1 June to 31 July 1977* [B.360].

It might appear that fresh foods, rather than processed foods, dominated the Commission's work given the two reports on fruit and vegetables and the studies of eggs, bananas, meat, poultry and fish. However, these reports frequently provide valuable summaries of the entire food sectors from raw material suppliers to processors and distributors. The three processing industries specifically examined were bread making, tea and coffee. The work often utilised existing statistical sources, involved the help of firms of chartered accountants, and used interviews and surveys, as exemplified by *Food Prices in Outlying Areas* [B.421]. Thus, these references involving food companies/products yield much more than just price data.

2.16.3 *The Second Price Commission under the Price Commission Act 1977*

The first Price Commission was mainly intended to administer a rigid Price Code based on allowable costs and reference period profit margins. The Price Commission Act 1977 was recast with the intention of adopting a more flexible and selective approach in meeting the government's price policy objectives. A new Price Commission was established. Large manufacturing and service companies were still required to notify in advance their intention to raise prices. At its discretion, the Price Commission could then investigate the case presented to it and publish a report. The criteria in considering the cases were set out in the Act and were at the outset much more comprehensive in their microeconomic focus than those used by the first Price Commission. The criteria of the 1977 Act included the necessity to recover costs, but also to minimise them. Profits needed to be sufficient to defray the cost of capital and cover risk taking, yet provide funds for innovations and technical improvements etc. Lightman [B.104], and Maunder's paper *The food and drink industries and the second Price Commission (1977–1979)* [B.119], provide good summaries.

The duty of the Price Commission was to come to a decision within a period of 28 days as to whether a prenotified price increase could be justified. If the Price Commission thought a price increase was not justifiable, a formal Investigation would be made within a short period of time (three months) whilst prices were frozen, unless profits fell below a certain minimum level. In addition, the Secretary of State for Prices and Consumer Protection was also free to ask the Price

Commission to scrutinise firms in more detail. Hence the decision could be taken to refer an entire industry, or a sector of the economy, to the Price Commission. In this latter instance, a less rapid Examination would be undertaken, usually taking six months or longer. Again the Price Commission could recommend that prices be frozen — even for more than 12 months.

Both Price Commissions reflected an interventionist philosophy and the second Price Commission was firmly founded on the concept of social accountability — i.e. that even if price increases were justified, companies should, from time to time, explain their pricing decisions to a body acting on behalf of the public and the consumer. The announcement to abolish the Price Commission was one of the first decisions made by the new Conservative government twelve days after their election in May 1979.

In its short lifetime, the Price Commission provided 44 Investigation Reports and 19 Examination Reports, besides completing 2 sectoral studies left over from the first Commission. Various sectors of the Food industries figure prominently as the following lists show:

Investigation Reports under Section 6 of the Price Commission Act 1977

(investigations relating to the Food industries)

Report no.6	(Session 1977/78) *Tate and Lyle Refineries Ltd. — Sugar and Syrup Products* [B.434]
Report no.10	(Session 1977/78) *Cadbury Schweppes Foods Ltd. — Grocery Products* [B.418]
Report no.12	(Session 1977/78) *Weetabix Ltd. — Cereal and Muesli Products* [B.437]
Report no.20	(Session 1977/78) *CPC (United Kingdom) Ltd. — Increases in the Prices of Maize, Starch, Glucose, Syrup, Starch-derived and Glucose-derived Products* [B.420]
Report no.36	(Session 1978/79) *United Biscuits (UK) Ltd. — Biscuits, Crisps, Nuts and Savoury Snacks* [B.436]

Examination Reports under Section 11 of the Price Commission Act 1977

(examinations relating to the Food industries)

Report no.1	(Session 1977/78) *Prices, Costs and Margins in the Importation and Distribution of Bacon* [B.425]
Report no.3	(Session 1977/78) *Prices, Costs and Margins in the Production and Distribution of Compound Feeding Stuffs for Cattle, Pigs and Poultry* [B.426]

The Investigation Reports had to be completed within three months. In practice, this meant that the actual inquiry had to be done in about eight weeks. The financial appraisals were usually carried out by a firm of accountants selected by the Price Commission. The short report on *Tate and Lyle Refineries Ltd.* [B.434] is discussed in more detail in Chapter 9, and shows the importance of the price of raw cane sugar. The lengthier reports on *Cadbury Schweppes Foods Ltd.* [B.418], and *United Biscuits (UK) Ltd.* [B.436] are referred to in Chapter 10 and Chapter 8 respectively. These Investigations showed the role of discounts and rebates to the large retail chains. This became a pressing concern of a later study by the Monopolies and Merger Commission in 1981 — see section 2.16.4.4 for details. The Investigation of *Weetabix Ltd.* [B.437] demonstrated a concern with profits, efficiency and marketing, and its contents are assessed in Chapter 8. *CPC (United Kingdom) Ltd.* [B.420] is discussed in Chapter 11 as it concerns the price of maize. The Examination Report on Bacon [B.425] carried some data on prices, costs and margins, as will be outlined in Chapter 4.

Hence the information which emerged from the Price Commission stemmed from the need to document various elements of competitive behaviour. The Commission focused more on accounting information to assess efficiency, but rather less on wages, costs and working practices, as compared to many of the earlier NBPI studies. However, there is little doubt that, during its short lifetime, the Price Commission had an important effect on the competitive environment.

2.16.4 *Monopolies, Mergers and Restrictive Practices Inquiries*

We turn now to the work of longer standing bodies which, in the course of dealing with the many aspects of competition policy, have given rise to a large body of data relating to the Food industries.

The Monopolies and Restrictive Practices (Inquiry and Control) Act 1948 set up the Monopolies and Restrictive Practices Commission, (referred to, in brief, as the "Monopolies Commission"). Its remit was to decide whether the existence and/or practices of particular statutory monopolies were against "the public interest". The Commission initially dealt with restrictive practices as well. This changed after the Restrictive Trade Practices Act 1956 which established the Restrictive Practices Court. Whereas the original Monopolies Commission was pragmatic in its approach, and had wide discretion in evolving practical criteria, the 1956 Act established a general presumption that restrictive agreements between firms were contrary to the public interest, but the parties in question could try to prove otherwise by using one of the standard exemptions or "gateways". In 1964, the Resale Prices Act established a similar presumption that resale price maintenance was against the public interest (subject to exemptions in cases brought before it) and the Court was charged with balancing the benefits against the costs.

In the following year, the Monopolies and Mergers Act 1965 explicitly emphasised the control of mergers and whether proposed mergers were likely to create a monopoly which would be against the public interest or not. Merger inquiries were undertaken by the Monopolies Commission. Where there was an unfavourable report, the Act permitted the government to prohibit proposed mergers, to impose conditions on a merger, or to dissolve completed mergers. In 1973, the Fair Trading Act consolidated the existing law and established a Director General of Fair Trading responsible for the regulation of monopolies, mergers and restrictive practices. With consumer protection also in mind, the public interest was redefined to include the desirability of maintaining and promoting competition. The now renamed Monopolies and Mergers Commission (MMC) retained significant discretion in interpreting the public interest since it was required to consider "all matters which appear to... be relevant".

The 1973 Act is an important component of policy, along with the original Restrictive Trade Practices Act which was updated in 1968, 1973, and consolidated in 1976 and 1977. The Resale Price Maintenance Act 1976 updated the earlier 1964 Act. Finally the Competition Act 1980, which abolished the second Price Commission, added further provisions for control of anti-competitive practices which restrict, distort or prevent competition. These may be subject to a preliminary investigation by the Director General of Fair Trading. If he finds anti-competitive practices exist, he can refer the firm to the MMC if satisfactory undertakings are not forthcoming. At the second stage, the Secretary of State for Trade and Industry can then make an order prohibiting or modifying the practice after this MMC inquiry. Alternatively the Director General of Fair Trading may seek an undertaking from the firm in question.

This brief canter through post-World War II legislation is necessary because the relevant bodies, and their reports, frequently change their names. Law follows custom, needs and circumstances, particularly when there has been an increased concentration of economic power. There is a vast literature on competition policy. Many textbooks include useful brief surveys of UK competition policy and law. Peter Maunder et al in *Economics Explained* [B.121] provides a concise historical review and description up to the 1980 Competition Act. The chapter in [B.121] is a clear description, replete with appropriate illustrations. The same author also wrote an earlier paper in 1970 "The UK food processing and distribution trades: an appraisal of public policies" [B.114] which discussed the work of the Restrictive Practices Court, the issues of retail price maintenance as well as the role of the Monopolies Commission given the concern with market power in this sector.

Prest and Coppock's *The UK Economy* [B.3], edited by M.J. Artis, is another informative reference as are the previous editions of this well-known text. Peter Johnson's *British Industry; An Economic Introduction* [B.91], and Keith Hartley's *Problems of Economic Policy* [B.73], are useful. Roger Clarke has written two separate chapters on Restrictive Trade Practices Policy, and Monopolies and Mergers Policy, in *Industrial Economics* [B.37]. These textbooks, among others, summarise much of the legislation and cases. However it is necessary to consult, for instance, the annual report *Monopolies and Mergers Commission* [B.336] to keep abreast of the latest developments.

The *Annual Report of the Director General of Fair Trading* [QRL.48] clearly explains the administration of competition policy and consumer affairs, and reports on the work of the MMC. The Director General (Sir Gordon Borrie) is the author of "Competition, mergers and price fixing" [B.20] which can be said to give an inside view. E. Victor Morgan summarises and critically assesses its work for a forty year time span in *Monopolies, Mergers and Restrictive Practices: UK Competition Policy 1948–1987* [B.129].

2.16.4.1 Reports of the Monopolies and Restrictive Practices Commission, 1950–1957

Twenty one reports were published by the Commission under the framework of the Monopolies and Restrictive Practices (Inquiry and Control) Act 1948. Only one report, Report no.19 (Session 1956/57) entitled *Report on the Supply of Tea* [B.452], relates to the Food industries. It carries an examination of the structure of the industry, with many statistical details of exports, imports, auction and retail prices (1952–1956), price changes of retailers, and sales and profits of tea producers (1949–1955). It is further discussed in Chapter 12.

2.16.4.2 Restrictive Trade Practices

The Restrictive Trade Practices Act 1956 had a broad influence on the Food industries, affecting monopolies and resale price maintenance as well as restrictive practices. In particular, the influence on tea blenders and baking is outlined by Maunder [B.118]. The effectiveness of the legislation is further studied in *Competition in British Industry: Restrictive Practices Legislation in Theory and Practice* [B.172]. The accompanying volume *Competition in British Industry: Case Studies of the Effects of Restrictive Practices Legislation* [B.171] includes a case study on bread, together with trade estimates of the market shares and brand names of the major bread firms in 1971. A diagrammatic comparison of price indices of bread, food and all retail prices is also provided.

More recent general summaries are given by Borrie [B.20]. The Director General of Fair Trading took over the functions of the Registrar of Restrictive Trading Agreements following the Fair Trading Act 1973. Previously, the reports to Parliament of the Registrar had catalogued the cases: see, for example, *Restrictive Trading Agreements: Report of the Registrar, 1 July 1969 to 30 June 1972* [B.366]. Latterly, the *Annual Report of the Director General of Fair Trading* [QRL.48] has given an annual summary of activities, appending Directives under section 21(2) of the 1976 Act.

2.16.4.3 Reports of the Monopolies Commission, 1958–1974

The Monopolies and Restrictive Practices Commission was renamed the Monopolies Commission under the Restrictive Trade Practices Act 1956, and the Monopolies and Mergers Act 1965 extended the Commission's investigatory powers to mergers. Of the 54 reports published by the Monopolies Commission, the following seven refer to, and/or are important for, the Food industries.

Published Reports of the Monopolies Commission

(reports relating to the Food industries)

(Session 1966/67)	*Ross Group Limited and Associated Fisheries Limited. Report on the Proposed Merger* [B.453]
(Session 1966/67)	*Infant Milk Foods. A Report on the Supply of Infant Milk Foods* [B.446]
(Session 1968/69)	*Recommended Resale Prices. A Report on the General Effect of the Practice of Recommending or Otherwise Suggesting Prices to be Charged on the Resale of Goods* [B.451]
(Session 1968/69)	*Unilever Limited and Allied Breweries Limited: A Report on the Proposed Merger and General Observations on Mergers* [B.456]

(Session 1970/71)	*Starch, Glucoses and Modified Starches. Report on the Supply of Starch, Glucoses and Modified Starches* [B.454]
(Session 1972/73)	*Breakfast Cereals. A Report on the Supply of Ready Cooked Breakfast Cereal Foods* [B.439]
(Session 1972/73)	*Parallel Pricing. Report on the General Effect on the Public Interest of the Practice of Parallel Pricing* [B.450]

Of general interest for the Food industries is the report on *Recommended Resale Prices* [B.451]. Appendix 3 carries a price survey which compared the price behaviour of items with, and without, recommended prices. About 5000 questionnaires were sent to firms with fewer than ten shops, and approximately 1000 were sent to the head offices of organisations with ten or more shops. A statistical comparison was made: brands like Bird's Eye Fish Fingers were placed in the "recommended price" category, and brands like Instant Quaker Oats in the "non-recommended price" category. The data included recommended prices with overall mean and mode, and non-recommended prices from *Shaws Guide to Fair Retail Prices* [QRL.453], again with overall mean and mode. The analyses of recommended and non-recommended prices were enumerated separately for unaffiliated independent outlets, voluntary group members, cooperative retail societies and multiples. In contrast, the report on *Parallel Pricing* [B.450] carried a more theoretical discussion on the subject of price leadership and market power, but included an appendix of products thought to be subject to parallel pricing. These included bread, cereals, fresh milk, canned evaporated milk, dried milk, sugar, bacon and powdered milk. The report on the *Supply of Infant Milk Foods* [B.446] is discussed in Chapter 5. The report on *Ross Group Limited and Associated Fisheries Limited* [B.453] provides some background for Chapter 7, and the report on the *Supply of Starch, Glucoses and Modified Starches* [B.454] relates to Chapter 11. Report [B.456] includes general observations on mergers, but the later report [B.439] on *Breakfast Cereals* carries more specific details on prices, profits etc., and is further discussed in Chapter 8.

The Commission showed concern with both the theoretical and the practical aspects of economic power, finding data on supplies, trading agreements, prices, pricing policies and profits. Maunder [B.118] provides a summary discussion, and points to the Monopolies Commission as a surrogate for the disbanded NBPI, particularly in the case of the report on *Breakfast Cereals* [B.439]. The paucity of references concerning the Food industries in the 1950's is balanced by increased interest in the late 1960's, and *a fortiori* the 1970's.

2.16.4.4 Reports of the Monopolies and Mergers Commission, 1974–1988

The Monopolies Commission was renamed the Monopolies and Mergers Commission (MMC) under the Fair Trading Act 1973, which also established the Office of Fair Trading and its Director General to oversee UK competition policy. The same Act redefined a statutory monopoly as one involving the supply of one quarter of a market by a single firm, instead of, one third, as was formerly the case. It permitted (as did the 1948 Act) the investigation of complex monopolies where several firms have a combined 25 per cent market share and restriction of competition is evinced.

The Competition Act 1980, as mentioned in section 2.16.4, added another potential dimension to the work of the MMC. It introduced a way of dealing with anti-competitive practices without the need for a full scale monopoly reference. An anti-competitive practice is defined as "a course of conduct which ··· has or is intended to have the effect of restricting, distorting or preventing competition". The Act gives the Director General of Fair Trading power to investigate possible anti-competitive practices. If he finds that such a practice does exist, he may refer the case to the MMC or seek undertakings that the firm in question will cease the practice. In the event of a reference, the MMC seeks to apply the same public interest test as is applied to a monopoly situation as set out in Section 84 of the Fair Trading Act 1973. The MMC is in fact permitted to take into account any factors it judges relevant in determining the public interest. However five specific factors are listed: effective competition; consumer interests; innovation and new entry; the balanced distribution of industry and employment; and the international competitive position of UK producers.

Thus the province of the MMC now combines unitary monopolies, mergers, restrictive practices in the professions and anti-competitive practices as defined in the 1980 Competition Act. From our point of view, of the 134 reports between 1974 and 1988, the following twelve are related to the Food industries:

Published Reports of the Monopolies and Mergers Commission

(reports relating to the Food industries)

(Session 1974/75)	*NFU Development Trust Limited and FMC Limited. Report on the Proposed Merger* [B.449]
(Session 1975/76)	*Frozen Foodstuffs. A Report on the Supply in the United Kingdom of Frozen Foodstuffs for Human Consumption* [B.444]
(Session 1976/77)	*Flour and Bread. A Report on the Supply in the United Kingdom of Wheat Flour and of Bread Made from Wheat Flour* [B.443]
(Session 1976/77)	*Cat and Dog Foods. A Report on the Supply in the United Kingdom of Cat and Dog Foods* [B.440]
(Session 1978/79)	*Ice-cream and Water Ices. A Report on the Supply in the United Kingdom of Ice-cream and Water Ices* [B.445]
(Session 1980/81)	*S and W Berisford Limited and British Sugar Corporation Limited. A Report on the Proposed Merger* [B.438]
(Session 1980/81)	*Discounts to Retailers. Report on the General Effect on the Public Interest of the Practice of Charging Some Retailers Lower Prices than Others or Providing Special Benefits to Some Retailers where the Difference Cannot be Attributed to Savings in the Suppliers' Costs* [B.441]
(Session 1981/82)	*Nabisco Brands Inc. and Huntley and Palmer Foods plc: A Report on the Proposed Merger* [B.448]
(Session 1982/83)	*Linfood Holdings plc and Fitch Lovell plc: A Report on the Proposed Merger* [B.447]
(Session 1985/86)	*White Salt: A Report on the Supply of White Salt in the United Kingdom by Producers of Such Salt* [B.457]
(Session 1985/86)	*Elders IXL Ltd. and Allied Lyons plc: A Report on the Proposed Merger* [B.442]

(Session 1987/88) *Tate and Lyle plc and Ferruzzi Finanziaria SpA and S and W Berisford plc: A Report on the Existing and Proposed Mergers* [B.455]

Of these, the report [B.444] on frozen foodstuffs is an extensive work which covers the development and organisation of the frozen food industry, cutting across several SIC industries. It gives a statistical profile of the reference goods — vegetables, confectionery and fruit, meat (including poultry) and fish — within the companies of Birds Eye Foods Ltd., Imperial Foods Ltd., and Findus Ltd. Data on Unilever's total supply of these goods for 1973–74 are presented. Various statistics on market share, sales of major categories to households (1964–1973), the growth of household demand for frozen foods (1967–1973), retail prices and price comparisons, returns on capital, costs, advertising, profits etc. are derived. In contrast, [B.449] is confined to the marketing and distribution of fatstock and meat in the United Kingdom.

Of those that can be clearly identified with a more particular industry, the report [B.443] on wheat flour and bread is dealt with in Chapter 8. The report [B.448] on the merger between Nabisco, and Huntley and Palmer is drawn on in Chapters 8 and 11. The copious report on *Ice-cream and Water Ices* [B.445] is particularly germane to Chapter 10. Both Report [B.438], and [B.455], are extensively drawn upon in Chapter 9 as most valuable sources in the analysis of the statistics of the sugar market. [B.447] considered broad processing, wholesaling and retailing links operating in the food trade. The report on *White Salt* [B.457] was concerned with the duopoly in the salt market, which is discussed further in Chapter 11.

These reports are frequently extensive and are cited as they supplement published data with statistical evidence from the parties involved. For example, *Elders IXL Ltd. and Allied Lyons plc* [B.442] has relevance for tea, coffee (both instant and ground), biscuits, cakes and ice-cream, as well as alcoholic drinks. Approximate market sizes are presented for each product, and estimates of market share derived for the most popular brands supplied by other firms and compared with those of Allied Lyons.

We stressed in the introduction the importance of the concept of the food chain, and the links between raw material suppliers, processors, wholesalers and retailers etc. in the Food sector. The MMC is not only a source of statistics on mergers etc. within the food processing industries, but has also investigated the balance of power between food manufacturers and food retailers. If the consensus had been of a growing concentration in food manufacturing (see for example W.P.J. Maunder [B.117]), there is now growing countervailing power in the hands of the multiples. *Discounts to Retailers* [B.441] was a primary source in this heated statistical debate. Basic statistics are presented of the cost to twelve manufacturers of special terms to their top ten retail customers, and details are given of the special terms received by the three largest multiple chains. Concentration figures for the top three, and top five, UK manufacturers for 1977 are derived from Business Monitor and product surveys. Further questionnaires seek to elicit data on quantity discounts, buying and selling prices, and the costs of supplying different customers, and to contrast the views of food manufacturers, wholesalers and retailers. An appendix draws on *Business Monitor MA3* [QRL.81], plus sources from the Food and Drink Industries Council, to compare returns on capital employed from 1965–1977 on both historic cost and current cost bases. Returns for food manufacturing are compared with those for all UK manufacturing, and with those for retail distribution. Profit margins for food manufacturers are derived, and the flow of funds, and capital formation, for the three sectors are detailed for selected years.

Discounts to Retailers [B.441] is discussed here for many reasons. First, it carries concise summaries of the various Price Commission and MMC reports (many of them food related) which documented the practice of discounting. Second, it clearly demonstrates the importance of the linkages in the food chain. Third, its provision of a wide-ranging, if contentious, economic and statistical picture of the interaction between food manufacturing and food retailing inspired many succeeding publications and highlights the continued need for statistical information to make judgements. Indeed, since the publication of *Discounts to Retailers* [B.441] the Office of Fair Trading (OFT) and other government departments have continued to receive representation from food manufacturers and small retailers about the discounts and other special terms obtained by the multiple stores. As a result, the Director General of Fair Trading decided to carry out a fact-finding exercise to update *Discounts to Retailers* [B.441], and this resulted in the 1985 publication of *Competition and Retailing* [B.231]. This drew upon a wide range of published data from both official and commercial sources, such as those cited in this Review, for example:

- data on consumers' food expenditure from *Economic Trends Annual Supplement* [QRL.182],
- information on returns on capital employed, and net profit margins, for food manufacturing and retailing from the *Bank of England Quarterly Bulletin* [QRL.58] and *Datastream* [QRL.173] sources,
- R&D information from *Business Monitor MO14* [QRL.86],
- estimated media expenditure on food from the *Advertising Statistics Yearbook* [QRL.20] etc.

Primary data were generated by fieldwork to investigate the buying and selling of a range of products among different categories of retailer, and the relationship between buying and selling prices (i.e. gross margins). The controversial conclusion of *Discounts to Retailers* [B.441] was that, for national brands, lower selling prices were associated with lower buying prices, and that multiple retailers bought and sold at lower prices than other categories of retailer. This stimulated a literature of its own, typified by the collection of conference papers edited by Burns [B.32]. The basic point here is that judgements are made both on the basis of existing statistics, and on data generated specifically in the course of the investigation.

2.16.4.5 Comments on Monopolies Investigations

A description of the scope, procedures and work of these investigations is set out in the booklet *Monopolies and Mergers Commission* [B.336]. A section of the *Annual Report of the Director General of Fair Trading* [QRL.48] reports references outstanding, references received, and references reported on, and any relevant legislative changes. Prior to the Fair Trading Act 1973, details were provided in annual reports to Parliament. For example, *Fair Trading Act 1973: Report by the Secretary of State for Trade and Industry for the Period 1 January 1973 to 31 October 1973* [B.268] was the last such report, and provided information on the work during the year and also presented a review back to 1948.

The MMC now publishes its own annual report entitled *Monopolies and Mergers Commission* [B.336] which describes the *modus operandi* of the full-time Chairman, the appointed part-time members and the Commission staff. Available data are supplemented by statistical inquiry. Merger inquiries have initial periods of not more than six months although recent practice has been to limit inquiries to three months. Extensions of up to three months may be requested. Broader monopoly references may extend to 24 months.

Nothing comparable to the work of Fels [B.51] on the NPBI exists for the MMC, even though there is an impressive literature on competition policy in general. However, E. Victor Morgan [B.129] assembled a concise summary. Donald Hay and John Vickers later encapsulated the present system and discussed suggested changes in their article entitled "The reform of UK competition policy" [B.76] in the August 1988 issue of the *National Institute Economic Review*

Evidently, the MMC has considerable potential to generate data from its proceedings. It has the power to require the attendance of witnesses and to demand the production of documents similar to procedures in a court of law in a civil action. These powers permit the MMC, among other things, to inspect companies' accounts and minutes of board and committee meetings. In practice, however, the MMC usually receives sufficient compliance from companies without the need to invoke its full legal powers. Shortly after a reference is made, the Commission meets the management of the companies involved for informal discussions which often coincides with visits to the factories. Interested parties are also invited to submit evidence and the Commission's staff prepare a questionnaire. This usually includes detailed questions on the history, ownership and management structure of the company; agreements with suppliers or distributors; features of the product; output prices, costs and profits over a period of a least five years; technology; trends in efficiency and productivity; investment and innovation; labour relations and exports etc. Hence these reports can generate much data on many of the dimensions considered in this Review.

Depending on the length of the inquiry, providing answers to the questionnaire evidently involve the management of companies and their legal and economic advisers in a good deal of work and may extend over many months. Meanwhile, the Commission's accountants can inspect the company's accounts, and in cooperation with accounting staff, extract the required figures. In monopoly inquiries, once the information is submitted, the commission prepares a formal "public interest letter" and its three Annexes. Annexe 1 summarises the detailed survey of the industry, the products and the activities of the company concerned. Annexe 2 lists the public interest issues to be discussed at the hearing. Annexe 3 lists the complaints received by the Commission and invites comments. After the company has made written comments, there is a "public interest hearing". The company can comment on factual sections of the draft report and can request that confidential information should not be published. So it is not surprising that it has often taken 18 months or more to present the report to the Secretary of State and, by him, to Parliament. More recently, the time scales have been reduced.

Partly because nothing comparable to the work of Fels [B.51] on the NBPI exists for the MMC, the methodology of many of the MMC Reports are discussed in this Review in the industry chapters where relevant, along with details of the report in question. General references, like *Discounts to Retailers* [B.441], have tended to be few and far between and have been discussed in this chapter.

2.16.5 *Comments*

This chapter has catalogued the voluminous existence of many statistical sources, both official and commercial. The various bodies identified in this section have supplemented these regular sources with a range of *ad hoc* official investigations. These investigations have drawn together existing data and have attempted to fill identified gaps by various methods, including questionnaire surveys, formal evidence from interested parties and balance sheet investigations by consultants etc.

A definite tradition was built up during the lifetime of the NPBI, notably the inquiries into earnings and the investigation of the related issues of prices, costs, productivity and income. The Price Commission, during its two existences, tended to report quickly and was more than just a source of price information as has been made clear.

The longer standing work on monopolies, mergers and restrictive practices since 1948 outlined in section 2.16.4 requires some further comments. Its work on economic structure, concentration and competition is highly relevant to the interconnected Food sector of the economy, whether on a particular market (*Tate, Ferruzzi, Berisford* [B.455]) or on a general reference like *Discounts to Retailers* [B.441].

A major review of both mergers and restrictive trade practices was announced in June 1986. The conclusions were published in the Department of Trade and Industry (DTI) document *Mergers Policy* [B.332] and in a major Green paper entitled *Review of Restrictive Trade Practices Policy* [B.369] published in 1988. The proposals for change in *Mergers Policy* [B.332] have concentrated on making merger control more speedy and flexible. The many objections that merger policy is too permissive were rejected. Satisfaction with the existing basis for policy was expressed together with a reaffirmation of emphasis on the competition criterion at the referral stage. This was an official and by no means an unanimous view. The remit of the review panel in *Mergers Policy* [B.332] did not extend to monopoly and anti-competitive practices policy, thus procedural issues and the reaffirmation of the primary criterion for referrals were highlighted and fundamental policy questions given much less attention.

From our point of view, the MMC now shoulders a great deal of the work which was carried out by previous bodies like the NBPI and the Price Commission. It is thus the major official source of *ad hoc* information. If there were a shift in the burden of proof in merger inquiries and the Secretary of State referred more frequently, the amount of statistical data generated by these inquiries would indeed increase in the future. The long standing Monopolies Commission work on economic structure, concentration and competition is highly relevant for industrial economics. It has furnished valuable information and data on the the Food industries, as well as on other sectors, which are not easily available elsewhere. Would that it could be done on a regular basis rather than as an occasional *ad hoc* exercise!

2.17 Improvements and Comments

This chapter has featured discussion of a wide range of statistical sources. Detailed comments on those sources have been provided at the end of most sections and there is little point in repeating them at this stage. Specific comments on each of the following chapters are provided in the seventeenth section: thus section 7.17, for example, highlights Improvements and Comments with respect to "Fish Processing".

However, a number of general comments may be made here. First, much of the statistical information that might be required is available in a small number of publications, viz:

Output	*Business Monitor PA1002: Summary Volume* [QRL.93] and other Monitors in the Production series
Current Inputs	*Agricultural Statistics: United Kingdom* [QRL.32] *Agriculture in the United Kingdom* *Business Monitor PO1008: Purchases Inquiry* [QRL.116] *Input-output Tables for the United Kingdom* [QRL.284]
Labour	*Employment Gazette* [QRL.186]
Capital	*Business Monitor PA1002: Summary Volume* [QRL.93] and other Monitors in the Production series
Exports and Imports	*Business Monitor MM20: Overseas Trade Statistics of the United Kingdom* [QRL.85]
Overseas Investment	*Business Monitor MA4: Overseas Transactions* [QRL.82]
Stocks	*Business Monitor PA1002: Summary Volume* [QRL.93] and other Monitors in the Production series
Consumption	*Household Food Consumption and Expenditure* [QRL.267] *National Food Survey: Compendium of Results* [QRL.373] *Family Expenditure Survey* [QRL.204]
Supplies and Disposals	MAFF Statistical Notices *Agriculture in the United Kingdom* *Monthly Digest of Statistics* [QRL.362]
Prices	*British Business* [QRL.66] *Employment Gazette* [QRL.186] *Agricultural Statistics: United Kingdom* [QRL.32]
Financial Information	*Business Monitor MA3: Company Finance* [QRL.81] Various commercial sources
Advertising	*Tri-Media Digest of Brands and Advertisers* [QRL.493]
Market Research	*Retail Business* [QRL.432] *Market Intelligence* [QRL.339]
Research and Development	*Business Monitor MO14: Industrial Research and Development Expenditure and Employment* [QRL.86] *Annual Review of Government Funded Research and Development* [QRL.52]

Time and effort might still be needed to locate copies of even these few publications, hence the existence of various compendia of statistical information. Thus the *Annual Abstract of Statistics* [QRL.37], the *Monthly Digest of Statistics* [QRL.362] and *Economic Trends* [QRL.181] should be noted for their wide-ranging coverage. The same applies to *British Business* [QRL.66] until it was discontinued in September 1989 and may well apply to its two successors: *Business Bulletins* [QRL.75] and

Business Briefing [QRL.74]. Some degree of detail must necessarily be sacrificed in order to give summaries of the most salient of statistical series.

Second, much of the information in the sources cited in this chapter is collected and also published separately on an industry basis. Often publication takes place rather quicker, and the coverage is rather more comprehensive. These industry sources will be discussed in the following chapters, wherein will also be described the structures of the various Food industries, and the trade associations and other organisations which operate within the industries. These organisations are often the best sources of up-to-date statistical data and other more qualitative information.

Third, if the UK statistical compendia demonstrate a sizeable time lag before publication, then their European and international counterparts tend to appear even later. The collation, processing, analysis, and publication of official statistical data takes considerable time and, in many instances, the use of unofficial sources may well prove more rewarding.

Finally, after considering each food industry separately in Chapters 3–12, we summarise the salient issues and provide a concluding overview in Chapter 13.

CHAPTER 3

ORGANIC OILS AND FATS

The information in this chapter relates to the organic oils and fats industry, Group 411 in the *CSO Standard Industrial Classification Revised 1980* [B.232]. Other more general sources, which provide statistics on other industry Groups as well, are covered in Chapter 2 and should be consulted as required. The contents of this chapter are as follows:

3.1 Introduction

Industry Group 411 covers the following Activity Headings:

4115 Margarine and compound cooking fats.
4116 Processing organic oils and fats (other than crude animal fat production).
1. Crude oils from fish and other marine animals.
2. Crude oils, cakes and meals from oil seeds and nuts.
3. Treated vegetable, marine and animal oils and fats.
Refining, hydrogenating or similarly treating vegetable, marine and animal oils and fats.

For an alphabetical list of the activities covered by Group 411, see the CSO *Indexes to the Standard Industrial Classification Revised 1980* [B.317].

Oils and fats are chemically very similar, the difference between them being that oils are liquids at normal temperatures (i.e. around 20 degC), whereas fats are normally solids or plastic semi-solids at similar temperatures. Edible fats and oils are known chemically as "glycerides", and are composed of the elements carbon, hydrogen and oxygen — hence the use of the term "organic". All glyceride molecules consist of glycerol to which are attached three fatty acid molecules. It is the nature of these latter molecules that determine the characteristics of the fat or oil.

Edible fats and oils occur widely in most animal and plant foods. In animals, fat is often found as a protective layer around vital organs, as well as being dispersed between layers of muscle and occurring beneath the skin. Animal fat is thus one of the by-products of the slaughtering of animals — see Chapter 4 — for human consumption. The main sources are beef, sheepmeat, and pigmeat. Fish oils are obtained by the extraction of oil from the whole fish. The fish most suitable are those with a high fat content, and these are mainly pelagic (surface feeding) fish such as herring, pilchard, sardines and anchovies.

Vegetable oils are derived from the seeds of plants which grow in many parts of the world, but mainly in the tropical and sub-tropical regions. Much of the trade in groundnuts, and groundnut oil, is supplied by countries in West Africa. Soya bean oil is a by-product of soya meal production. The soya bean when crushed yields a large amount of meal, which is particularly valuable for feeding to livestock, and also a relatively small proportion of oil. Cottonseed is an important source of oil in all cotton producing countries. In general, however, most cottonseed oil is retained in the country of production for domestic use, and only a small proportion of total world supply enters international trade. The main source of supply for both soya bean oil and cottonseed oil is the United States. In Europe, production of soya bean oil is confined almost exclusively to Italy, France and Spain. Rapeseed cultivation has expanded greatly in the United Kingdom and Europe since the 1960's largely as a result of subsidies provided by the European Community — see section 3.3. Rapeseed oil from the UK crop now accounts for some 30 per cent of all oils used in margarine. Olive oil is produced in the countries of the Mediterranean Basin, and is exported mainly by Italy, Spain and Greece. It is produced from the ripened fruit of the olive tree.

In addition to the above edible, or "soft", oils there are a number of other vegetable oils which are processed by industry Group 411. Palm oil, palm kernel oil and coconut oil — sometimes known as the "hard" oils — are used both for certain varieties of margarine and other foods; and for soap manufacture, synthetic detergents and certain other chemical preparations. The oil palm is mostly grown in Nigeria, the Congo, Malaysia and Indonesia. The oil palm fruit consists of an outer skin, an inner layer of fibrous pulp from which comes the palm oil, and a nut of which the inner kernel is rich in the more valuable palm kernel oil. The white flesh — the meat — of the coconut may be eaten raw, processed into products such as dessicated coconut, or dried in the sun or in kilns. It is known as copra when dried, and it is in this state that it is exported to countries which extract and refine the oil. The main sources of supply are the Philippines, Malaysia and Sri Lanka. Finally we mention a third group of "industrial" oils, such as linseed, tung and castor oil. These oils are used in the manufacture of soaps, paints, lubricants, plastics and chemicals. Limited amounts of linseed are grown in the European Community; most of this is produced in France with some additional production in Belgium and the Netherlands.

Margarine was invented in the nineteenth century by a Frenchman, Mège Mouriès, during a competition organized by the French Government to find a substitute for butter. The main ingredients of present-day margarine are vegetable oil, hydrogenated fish oil and/or animal oils and fats balanced together with water containing added milk or whey proteins in an emulsion, and partially crystallised. By UK law, the final product must not contain less than 80 per cent fat, or more than 16 per cent water. Low-fat spreads (40 per cent fat) and other products with fat contents ranging from 60–75 per cent are legally not margarine. Manufacturers in the United Kingdom draw on a wide range of oils — e.g. palm oil, palm kernel oil, sunflower oil, rapeseed oil, soya bean oil, tallow and fish oil — and most margarine is made from a blend of these. The choice of blend varies according to the supply and cost of the raw ingredients, the required properties (melting point, plasticity etc.) of the margarine, and the need to meet labelling claims (e.g. "only vegetable oils", "high in polyunsaturates"). It should be noted that the wide selection of oils and fats available to the manufacturer allows an element of control over raw material costs.

In the United States, the situation is slightly different as it is largely the oil from the indigenous crops of soya bean and cottonseed which is used for margarine.

Compound cooking fats are blends of oils and/or fats chilled and texturised in a similar way to margarine, except that no water is added. They are also known as "shortenings". Lard was the original shortening, and is the term given to the processed fat of pigs. Lard has however lost favour mainly because the advancement of food technology has made the hydrogenation of oils possible. Shortenings are used mainly in the manufacture of pastry and flour confectionery — see Chapter 8.

Activity Heading 4115 in the SIC(1980) corresponds to MLH229.1 "Margarine" in the SIC(1968). Activity Heading 4116 in the SIC(1980) corresponds fairly closely to MLH221 "Vegetable and animal oils and fats" in the SIC(1968). The manufacture of dripping, suet and edible tallow, premier-jus, also stearine and other animal oils and greases previously classified to MLH221, are now classified to AH4126.1 in SIC(1980) — see Chapter 4.

3.2 Industry Structure

The manufacture of fats, oils and margarine is a complicated process — see Figure 3.1 — that involves a number of stages. It is rare that raw, unprocessed oil or fat would be used without being treated in some way. The oils and fats first have to be refined until they are pure, and completely free of taste, smell and colour. The refining process consists of five stages: degumming, neutralisation, bleaching, filtration, and deodorizing, at the end of which the oil is ready for edible purposes. The processed oils may then be used directly as domestic, catering and industrial frying oils, or as main ingredients in the manufacture of biscuits, bakery products, snack foods, soups, sauces, ice-cream, confectionery, and other foods.

The manufacture of margarine entails a further six main processing stages: hydrogenation, final refining, the blending of oils and fats, the production of the aqueous phase, the addition of any special ingredients, and emulsification. Different types of margarine are made by varying the ingredients at various stages. The manufacture of shortenings is very similar, except that no water is added.

The only oilseed crop produced in the United Kingdom in any quantity is rapeseed, of which about 1 million tonnes were crushed in 1987. Rapeseed is a most important crop in British agriculture, and provides over 60 per cent of the seeds crushed in the United Kingdom — see Figure 3.2. Soya beans imported from North and South America account for a further 20 per cent, and the remainder is made up of sunflower seed from America and Europe, palm kernels from West Africa, maize germ (a by-product of the UK starch industry — see Chapter 11), and small amounts of copra and other imports. Castor seeds and linseed are imported and crushed to provide oil for technical uses.

The crude vegetable oil produced from the crush, together with imported crude oils, animal fats and marine oils, gave rise to almost 1.2 million tonnes of refined, deodorised oil in 1987. Rapeseed supplied over 20 per cent of this total — see Figure 3.3 — followed by palm oil and soya bean oil. The share of vegetable oils in the total has increased in recent years because of the trend away from animal fats, and they now account for over 80 per cent of refined edible oil production. Imports of

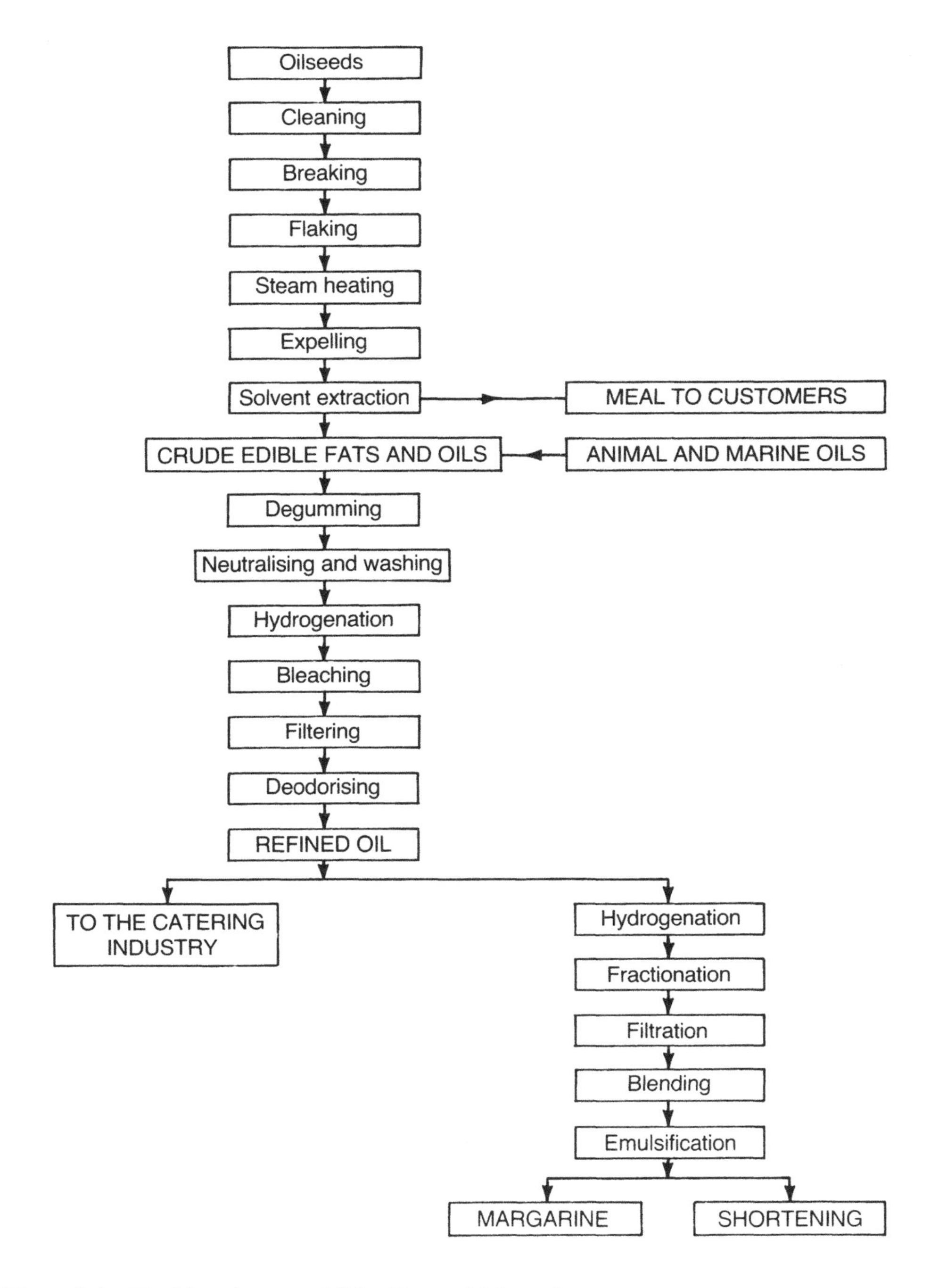

Figure 3.1 The Manufacture of Oils, Fats and Margarine.
Source: Adapted from *Seed Crushing and Oil Processing in the UK* (Seed Crushers' and Oil Processors' Association) and other sources.

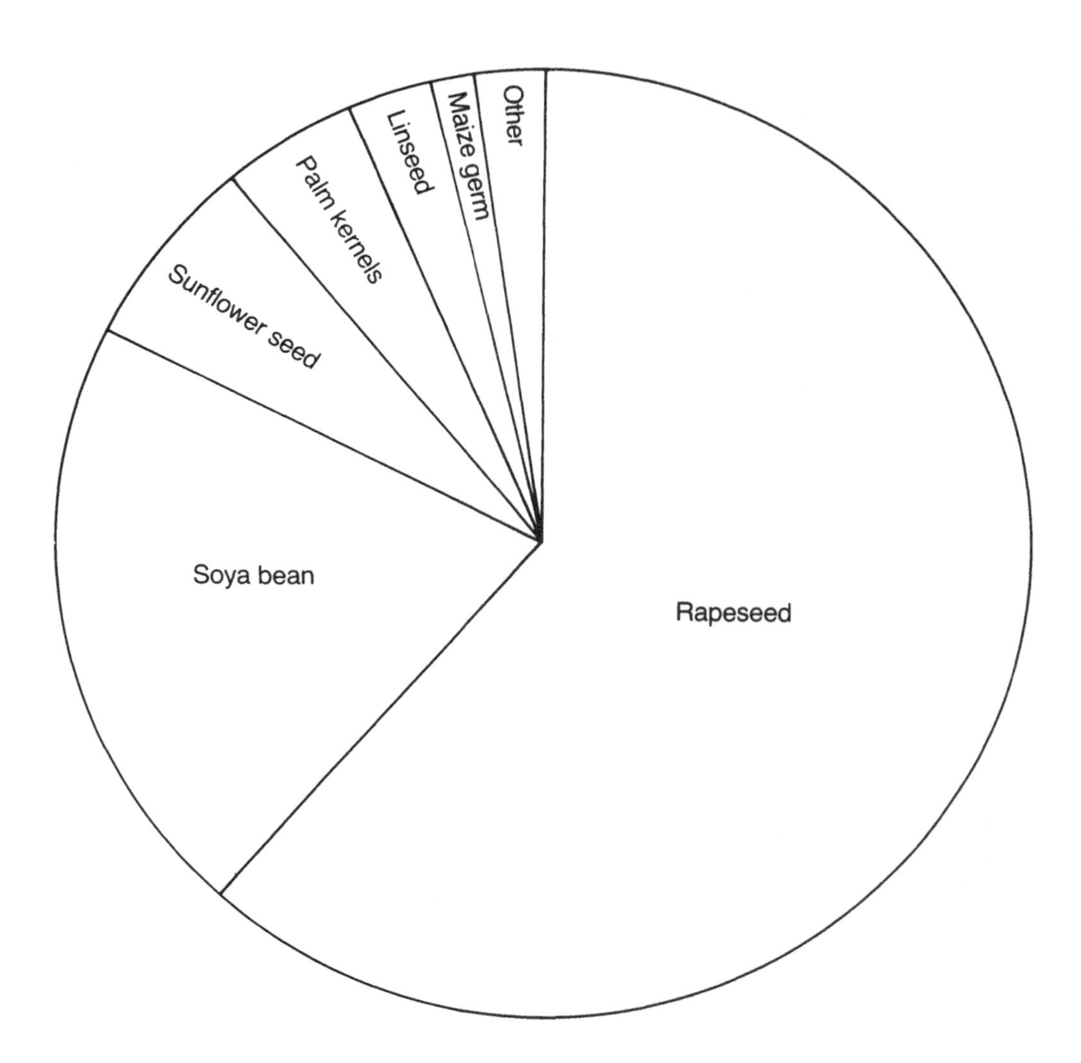

Figure 3.2 Oilseeds Crushed in the United Kingdom, 1987 (53 weeks ended January 2nd 1988).
Source: *MAFF Statistics: Oilseed and Nuts Crushed in the United Kingdom and the Crude Vegetable Oils, Oilcake and Meal Produced* [QRL322]. Ministry of Agriculture, Fisheries and Food. © Crown Copyright.

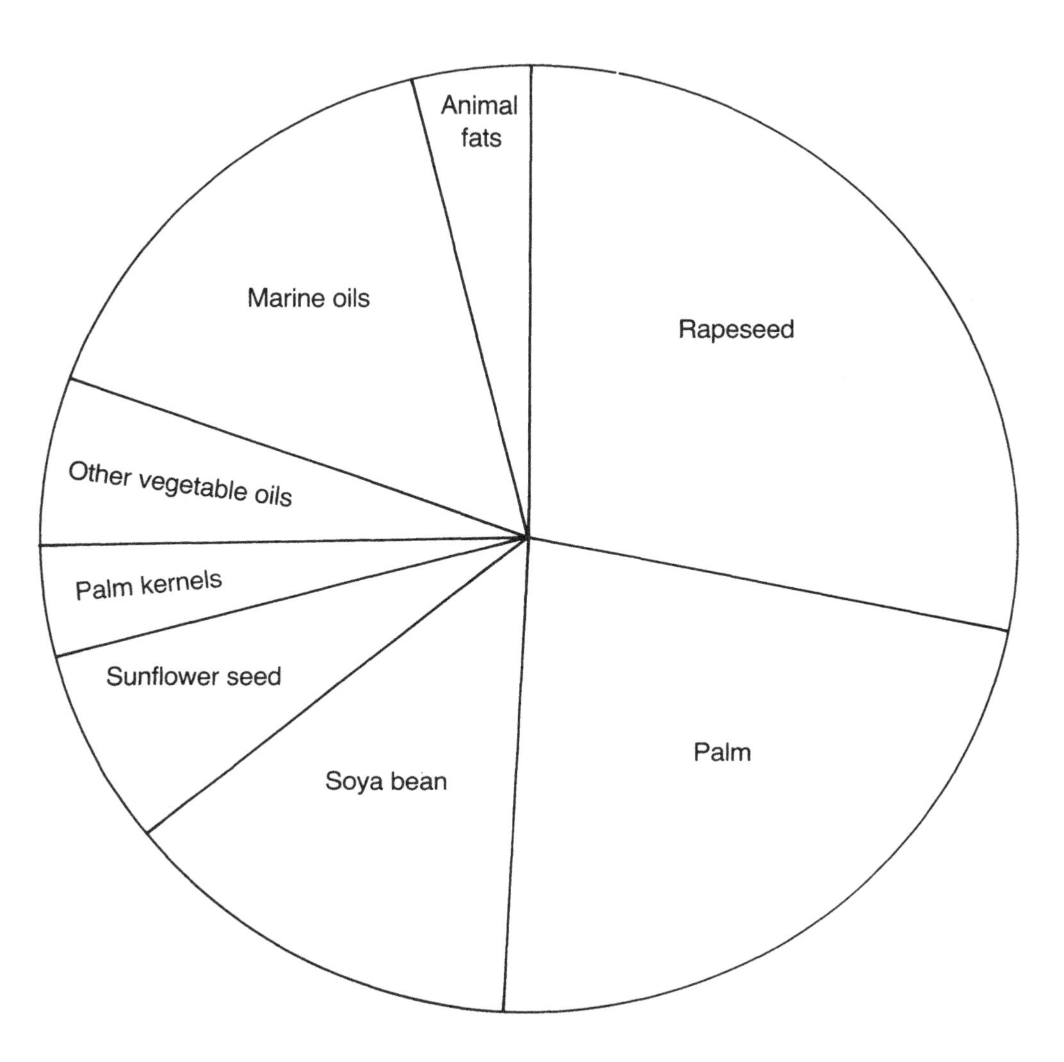

Figure 3.3 UK Production of Processed Edible Oils, 1987 (53 weeks ended January 2nd 1988). Source: *Maff Statistics: Production of Refined, Deodorised Vegetable, Marine Oils and Animal Fats in the United Kingdom* [QRL 328]. Ministry of Agriculture, Fisheries and Food. © Crown Copyright.

refined oil account for about 10 per cent of the domestic market. Oilcakes and meal produced by seed crushing are high in protein, and are a valuable source for animal feedingstuffs. Roughly one quarter of the high protein meal consumed on British farms is produced in this way.

Rees [B.154] reports that the earliest references to oil-milling in England occur in 1377, though the cultivation of oilseeds is certainly of much greater antiquity than this. Rapeseed was for many years an important agricultural crop in England, especially in East Anglia where the soil and drainage conditions were most suitable for its cultivation. Rapeseed was exported, mostly to Amsterdam and Rotterdam, between about 1590 and 1650. It was used in the manufacture of cloth and as a fuel for lamps, with the residual oil-cake being used as cattle food. The need for the produce, however, gradually declined with the advent of gas lighting.

The modern revival in the use of edible oils began with the discovery of hydrogenation in the late nineteenth century. In the period leading up to the First World War, large oilseed-crushing plants were established at principal ports in the United Kingdom as a result of the increase in the demand for margarine and soap on the part of Britain's rapidly growing population. The oil crushers formed a trade association as early as 1863, the main object of which was to establish a standard upon which linseed should be bought. The Linseed Association subsequently provided standards for admixture, fixed charges and fees, in connection with which they introduced standard contracts for the trade. The Association became the Incorporated Oil Seeds Association in 1881. Ninety years later, in 1971, the Incorporated Oil Seeds Association consolidated its activities with those of three other associations responsible for overlooking trade in oilseeds, viz: the London Oil and Tallow Trades Association (founded in 1910), the London Copra Association (1913), and the Seed, Oil, Cake and General Produce Association (1935). The Federation of Oils, Seeds, and Fats Associations (FOSFA) was born. The Federation is basically a contract-issuing body. These contracts help to regulate the trade and allow the purchase and sale of the commodities although the companies may be situated on opposite sides of the globe. FOSFA also provides administrative machinery for the settlement of disputes, and maintains and develops technical standards.

In the United Kingdom, the seed crushing and oil processing industry itself in concentrated in three main areas — the North West of England, London and Hull — and comprises seven seed crushers and ten oil processors. The following companies at the time of writing are involved: Acatos & Hutcheson plc/Pura Foods Ltd; Anglia Oils Ltd; Bibby Edible Oils Ltd; Samuel Banner & Co. Ltd; BOCM Silcock Ltd; Cargill UK Ltd; Chambers & Fargus plc; Louis Dreyfus Industries Ltd; Loders & Nucoline Ltd; Pauls Agriculture Ltd; Proctor & Gamble Ltd; John L. Seaton & Co. Ltd; Unimills Ltd; Van den Berghs & Jurgens Ltd (a subsidiary of Unilever plc). All are members of the Seed Crushers' and Oil Processors' Association (SCOPA).

Margarine and compound cooking fats are made both for the domestic market, packed ready for retail sale and marketed under well-known brand names (e.g. Flora, Krona, Blue Band etc. for margarine and Trex, Cookeen, White Cap, White Flora etc. for cooking fats). They are also made for trade use. In the latter form, they go to caterers and institutions, and as raw materials in the manufacture of other foodstuffs. A large and increasing proportion of production is sold to supermarkets and other major retailers as "own-label" products which are packed under their own brand names. Margarine is part of the so-called "yellow fats" market together with butter (see Chapter 5) and low-fat spreads (e.g. St Ivel Gold, Delight and Outline). Compound cooking fats, together with lard, form a "white fats" market. The various companies involved are represented by the Margarine & Shortening Manufacturers Association. The largest domestic manufacturer of margarine in Van den Berghs & Jurgens, and they also figure as one of the two major companies in the blended cooking fats and oils market — the other is Pura Foods. Smaller companies with a presence in the market include Proctor & Gamble; Cargill; Barmford Brothers; Bevelynn; Carbonell; Percy Dalton; A. Donantonio; Manley Ratcliffe; and John Morrell.

As regards the classification of SIC(1980), Activity Heading 4116 encompasses the complete processing of the oils and fats. AH4116.1 covers the production of crude oils from fish and other marine animals, AH4116.2 covers the crushing of the various types of oilseed, and AH4116.3 covers the subsequent refining of the crude oils. AH4115 relates to the manufacture of margarine and compound cooking fats.

3.3 The European Community

The European Community operates a number of regimes which are relevant to the products of industry Group 411. The 1966 Regulation on the establishment of a common organisation of the market in oils and fats covers colza, rape and sunflower seed, and olive oil. Olive oil is, however, a very different crop and has a completely separate regime which is outlined in section 3.3.4. The regime for colza, rape and sunflower seed is outlined in section 3.3.1, and those for soya beans and linseed in sections 3.3.2 and 3.3.3 respectively. Production of these latter two crops is of little importance in the United Kingdom, but brief descriptions of the regimes are provided nevertheless. More detail is available in *The Common Agricultural Policy of the European Community* [B.52], by Rosemary Fennell.

3.3.1 *Colza, Rape and Sunflower*

The EEC Regulation referred to in section 3.3 theoretically covers all oilseeds, but discussion may in practice be reduced to colza, rape and sunflower seeds. Colza and rape are similar plants, and the two may be considered as one. Moreover, the regimes applying to rape/colza and sunflower seeds are essentially the same, although support prices are not set at the same levels.

The basic regime rests on a "target" price which represents the internal wholesale price which should be obtainable given normal marketing circumstances. Target prices are set each year for colza/rape and sunflower, together with rather lower intervention prices. The difference between the two reflects a marketing margin, and the cost of transporting seed from the production to the consumption areas. In 1986, the regime was amended so as to introduce higher target and intervention prices for certain varieties of colza and rape seed. This measure was introduced as an incentive to producers, as the Community wishes to support only these varieties from 1991 onwards. The regime was further amended in 1987 to limit intervention to the months of October — May, and to introduce a "buying-in" price equal to 94 per cent of the intervention price.

Oilseeds enter the Community levy and duty-free. The world price is usually considerably lower than the target price, so a production subsidy — a deficiency payment — representing the difference between the two is paid to the crusher. This subsidy enables the crusher to pay the high support price while remaining competitive. Maximum guarantee quantities were introduced in 1982 in order to dampen down the recent expansion of production of oilseeds in the Community. The quantities are set each year based on production in a reference period and on expected demand. If anticipated production at the start of the market year exceeds the maximum set for the year, the target price is lowered by a percentage equal to the difference between the two quantities. The amount of production subsidy to the crusher is thus automatically lowered, and so too is the amount the crusher can pay the grower. The intervention and buying-in prices are affected in similar manner.

Export refunds are also available on the above oilseeds — they represent the approximate difference between the internal Community market price and the (lower) average world price. Vegetable oils may also be made available as food aid.

The *Intervention Board for Agricultural Produce: Annual Report* [QRL.293] provides details of UK intervention prices, purchases and sales of rape seed.

3.3.2 *Soya Beans*

The European Community has only a small crop of soya beans, and production is confined almost exclusively to Italy, France and Spain. Soya bean production is subject to a special regime, based on a fixed "guide" price. When the guide price is above the world price (as is usually the case), a deficiency payment is granted to the first-stage buyer of the beans. In addition, maximum guarantee quantities — calculated as outlined in section 3.3.1 — have applied to soya beans from the 1987/88 marketing year. No export refunds are available, and there are no restrictions on imports.

3.3.3 *Linseed*

The EC crop of linseeds is even smaller than that of soya beans. Most production is in France, though additional quantities are produced in Belgium and the Netherlands. The linseed regime is also based on a fixed guide price. A subsidy is, however, paid to the growers, and this is intended to bridge the gap between the guide price and the lower world price. The subsidy is based on indicative (i.e. average) yields which vary according to different zones of the Community rather than on actual yields. No export refunds are available, nor are there any restrictions on imports.

3.3.4 *Olive Oil*

The olive oil regime is covered by the same Regulation as that for colza, rape and sunflower seeds described in section 3.3.1. The regime covers not only olive oil but also olives; residues containing oil having the characteristics of olive oil; and oil cake and other residues resulting from the extraction of olive oil.

The internal market support mechanism is based on five elements: a representative market price (RMP); an intervention price; production aid; a production target price (PTP); and consumption aid — see Figure 3.4. The RMP is set each year at a level which permits olive oil to compete with cheaper, substitute oils. The intervention price is derived by deducting the production aid from the PTP and making allowance for market fluctuations and the cost of transporting the oil from the production to the consumption areas. The consumption aid is a further subsidy, but to consumers so that they only pay the RMP for olive oil.

In addition, a threshold price is also set each year so that imports sell in the Community at the same level as the RMP. Most imports, however, come in under preferential arrangements at a reduced levy. Levies are also applied to olives, and to the various olive oil residues. Olive oil used in the manufacture of preserved fish and vegetables benefits either from suspension of the import levy or from a production refund. Export refunds are based on a tendering system.

3.4 Output

3.4.1 *Output, Sales and Value Added*

3.4.1.1 Ministry of Agriculture, Fisheries and Food inquiries

Much of the available data on the output of industry Group 411 is collected and first published by MAFF in one of three statistical information notices. *MAFF Statistics: Oilseeds and Nuts Crushed, Crude Vegetable Oils, Oilcake and Meal Produced in the United Kingdom* [QRL.322] contains the results from the monthly vegetable oil crushers' returns to MAFF. Quarterly figures are presented of supplies crushed; crude oil produced from crush; and oilcake and meal production for the following oilseeds and nuts: castor seed; copra; linseed; maize germ; palm kernels; rape; soya beans; sunflower; and other oilseeds and nuts. *MAFF Statistics: Production of Refined, Deodorised Vegetable, Marine Oils and Animal Fats in the United Kingdom* [QRL.328] contains the results of the monthly refiners' returns to MAFF. Monthly data are presented on the production of the following oils and fats: coconut oil; cottonseed oil; groundnut oil; maize germ oil; palm oil; palm kernel oil; rapeseed oil; soya bean oil; sunflower oil; other vegetable oil; marine oils; lard; and other animal fats. *MAFF Statistics: Margarine, Other Table Spreads and Solid Cooking Fat Produced in the United Kingdom and the Refined Oils and Animal Fats Used in their Production* [QRL.321] provides monthly figures on the production of margarine (soft vitaminised; other vitaminised; non-vitaminised); other table spreads; and solid cooking fat (bulk; and packet).

These data are later reproduced in a number of publications. The *Monthly Digest of Statistics* [QRL.362] provides monthly data on the volume of crushed oilseeds and nuts; on the crude oil produced therefrom; and on the production of margarine, solid cooking fat, and other table spreads. Butter contained in butter-blended margarine is included in the production of margarine. The *Annual Abstract of Statistics* [QRL.37] publishes annual data on the following: oilseeds and nuts processed; crude oil

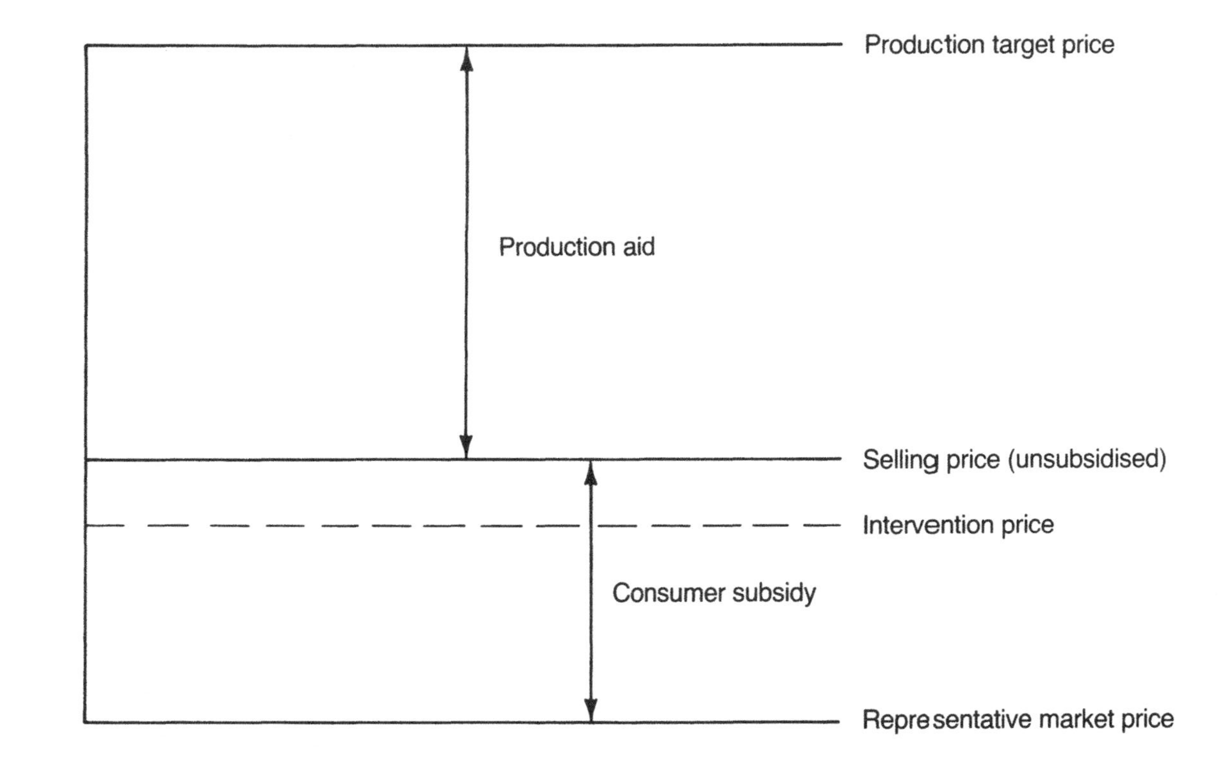

Figure 3.4 The EC Internal Support Regime for Olive Oil.
Source: Fennell, R. *The Common Agricultural Policy of the European Community: Its Institutions and Administrative Organisation* [B52] second edition P.73.

produced (including production of maize oil); oilcake and meal produced (excluding castor meal, cocoa cake and meal); production of margarine; and production of compound fat. Also provided are estimates of supplies per head of population of the following products: margarine; lard and compound cooking fat; and other edible oils and fats.

3.4.1.2 Business Statistics Office inquiries

Business Monitor PQ4115: Margarine and Compound Cooking Fats [QRL.128] publishes quarterly figures for sales for all establishments classified to AH4115, and also quarterly figures of sales of the principal products up to mid-1989. Quarterly figures of sales by UK manufacturers, in both volume and value terms, of the following products are provided: vitaminised margarine for domestic use; vitaminised and non-vitaminised margarine for trade use; compound fat (including shortening) for domestic use; compound fat (including shortening) for trade use. Sales of purchased lard, margarine, compound cooking fat and other fats, which have undergone no process other than packing and the addition of flavouring are included separately under "merchanted goods". A quarterly index of output, which measures changes in the volume of industrial activity, is also given for the Activity Heading.

Business Monitor PQ4116: Organic Oils and Fats [QRL.129] published quarterly figures of sales for all establishments classified to AH4116, and also quarterly figures of sales of the principal products up to mid-1989. Quarterly sales by UK manufacturers, in both volume and value terms, of the following products are provided: unrefined vegetable and seed oils (hydrogenated and unhydrogenated); refined vegetable and seed oils (hydrogenated and unhydrogenated); unrefined fish and marine animal oils; refined fish and marine animal oils; refined inedible animal oils, fats and greases (excluding tallow); acid oils (excluding fatty acids); oil seed cake and meal (including extracted meals); edible emulsifiers. A quarterly index of output for the Activity Heading is also given.

Finally *Business Monitor PA411: Organic Oils and Fats* [QRL.105] provides annual data on total sales, gross and net output for all UK establishments classified to the industry Group. Analysis is also provided of output by size of employment of the establishment, and by standard regions of the United Kingdom.

3.4.2 *Index Numbers of Output*

Business Monitor PQ4115 [QRL.128] carried an index of output for AH4115, and comparable figures for "Food" and "All manufacturing industries". Similar data for AH4116 are provided in *Business Monitor PQ4116* [QRL.129]. Both annual data, and seasonally adjusted quarterly data are presented. The figures for both the "AH4115" and "AH4116" series do not include stock adjustments to correct mixed sales and production data to true production index numbers, nor do they include bias adjustments. Consequently, they are not comparable with the aggregates published in the *Monthly Digest of Statistics* [QRL.362].

3.5 Current Inputs other than Labour

As mentioned in section 3.2, the only oilseed crop produced in the United Kingdom in any quantity is rapeseed. Supplies of other oilseeds are, however, imported — see section 3.8 — into the United Kingdom where they undergo crushing, refining etc.

3.5.1 *Domestic Inputs*

Data on the domestic production of rapeseed are presented in *MAFF Statistics: Agricultural Returns for England, Wales, Regions and Counties* [QRL.316] and *MAFF Statistics: Agricultural Returns for the United Kingdom* [QRL.317]. They used to be later reproduced in *Output and Utilisation of Farm Produce in the United Kingdom* [QRL.382] until this source was discontinued in 1988. Supplies of fats and oils of land and marine animals are by-products of the meat and fish industries respectively. Statistical sources relating to the output of these industries are discussed in sections 4.4 and 7.4 respectively. A final problem to bear in mind is that the industry Group covers a number of different processing stages, and that the later stages use the output of the earlier stages as inputs. Thus, the crude oil produced from the crushed oilseeds and nuts is an input to the production of refined oils: these oils in turn may be used in the production of margarine, other table spreads, and compound cooking fats. Hence reference should be made here to the three MAFF statistical notices already cited in section 3.4 — *MAFF Statistics: Oilseeds and Nuts Crushed, Crude Vegetable Oils, Oilcake and Meal Produced in the United Kingdom* [QRL.322], *MAFF Statistics: Production of Refined, Deodorised Vegetable, Marine Oils and Animal Fats in the United Kingdom* [QRL.328], and *MAFF Statistics: Margarine, Other Table Spreads and Solid Cooking Fat Produced in the United Kingdom and the Refined Oils and Animal Fats Used in Their Production* [QRL.321]. The latter presents monthly data on the following oils and fats used in the production of (a) margarine and other table spreads, and (b) solid cooking fat: coconut oil; groundnut oil; maize germ oil; palm oil; palm kernel oil; rapeseed oil; soya bean oil; sunflower oil; other vegetable oils; marine oils; lard; butter (as butter fat equivalent); and other animal fats.

The most comprehensive analysis of inputs is provided by the Purchases Inquiry — see section 2.1.1.4. The results of the 1984 Inquiry were published in 1987 as *Business Monitor PO1008: Purchases Inquiry* [QRL.116], and contained considerable detail for both AH4115 and AH4116. The inquiry collects information about the commodity detail of industry's purchases of materials and fuel. Thus, for example, purchases of the following materials are separately identified for AH4116: refined vegetable and seed oils and fats; unrefined vegetable and seed oils and fats; refined and unrefined marine animal (including fish) oils and fats; refined and unrefined terrestrial animal oils and fats; soya beans; other seed oils, nuts and kernels; oil seed cake, meal and extracted meals; organic chemicals; and inorganic chemicals. The pattern of commodity purchases returned in the Purchases Inquiry are scaled up to agree with the annual levels in the Census of Production. Information is also given on the effective percentage response rate in terms of employment for each industry.

The Purchases Inquiry is quinquennial; the results of the 1989 Inquiry are to be published in 1992. The results of the 1979 Inquiry were published in *Business Monitor PA1002.1: 1979 Census of Production and Purchases Inquiry* [QRL.94].

Results for the 1974 Inquiry were in a different form, being analyses of returns received without grossing. The statistics for each industry were published in the 1974/75 PA Monitor for that industry.

3.5.2 *Input-output Analysis*

Details of the input-output tables for the United Kingdom have been provided in section 2.5.2. Here we simply present brief comments on the level of detail accorded to the oils and fats industry. "Oils and fats" (AH4115 and AH4116) was identified amongst the industry/commodity groups in the *Input-output Tables for the United Kingdom 1984* [QRL.284]. The same group was also identified in the 1979 tables published in *Business Monitor PA1004* [QRL.101]. The 1974 tables were, however, based on SIC(1968) and the corresponding group was thus "Oils and fats" (MLH221). Information on coverage in previous input-output tables may be found in the references cited in section 2.5.2.

3.6 Labour

Detailed results of the September 1984 Census of Employment for Great Britain were published in the January 1987 edition of the *Employment Gazette* [QRL.186]. The numbers of male employees (full-time and part-time) and female employees (full-time and part-time) in employment in Group 411, AH4115 and AH4116 were separately enumerated. An analysis of total employees in employment by region was also provided. The September 1987 issue of the *Employment Gazette* [QRL.186] presented comparable results for the United Kingdom, incorporating figures from the 1984 Census of Employment for Northern Ireland provided by the Department of Economic Development. No regional analysis was provided, though data for the province could be derived by subtraction of the GB totals from those for the United Kingdom. Monthly figures of employees (male and female) in employment are only provided for "Meat and meat products, organic oils and fats" (Groups 411 and 412 combined) in the *Employment Gazette* [QRL.186].

Business Monitor PA411 [QRL.105] provides annual data on total employment (including working proprietors) and labour costs for the industry Group as a whole. Employment is also analysed by the standard regions of England, plus Wales, Scotland and Northern Ireland; and by size of establishments classified to the industry.

3.7 Capital

3.7.1 *Capital Expenditure*

Business Monitor PA411 [QRL.105] provides a breakdown of gross annual capital expenditure by type of asset — land and buildings; plant and machinery; and vehicles. Annual data on net capital expenditure are also provided for the Group as a whole, analysed by the standard regions of England, plus Wales, Scotland and

Northern Ireland, and also analysed by size of establishments classified to the industry. Moreover, detail is provided of capital expenditure for all establishments classified to each Activity Heading within the industry.

3.7.2 *Suppliers of Machinery*

An alternative perspective on the capital input to Group 411 is provided by the data published in *Business Monitor PQ3244: Food, Drink and Tobacco Processing Machinery; Packaging and Bottling Machinery* [QRL.127]. Statistics are provided therein on quarterly sales of "oil (other than mineral oil) or fat machinery for the food industry, including parts". Moreover, data are presented on imports of the following: "presses for the animal or vegetable fats industries", "other machines and mechanical appliances for the animal or vegetable fats industries", "machinery and apparatus for filtering or purifying edible oils and fats", and "parts of machinery and apparatus for filtering or purifying edible oils and fats".

As a result of the *Review of DTI Statistics* [B.367] — see sections 13.2 and 13.3 — this sales inquiry was not retained within the quarterly system of inquiries after the second quarter of 1989. Statistical data thereafter will be published less frequently and in less product detail.

3.7.3 *Company Reports*

The net book value of tangible fixed assets owned by each company in the industry (see section 3.2 for some of the larger companies), and their authorised future expenditure, will be detailed in their respective Annual Reports.

3.8 International Transactions

3.8.1 *HM Customs and Excise Records*

Data on products pertaining to industry Group 411 may be classified to one of five Divisions of the Standard International Trade Classification (Revision 3), viz: Division 09 "Miscellaneous edible products and preparations"; Division 22 "Oil seeds and oleaginous fruit"; Division 41 "Animal oils and fats"; Division 42 "Fixed vegetable fats and oils; crude, refined or fractionated"; and Division 43 "Animal and vegetable oils and fats, processed, and waxes of animal or vegetable origin". In *Business Monitor MM20: Overseas Trade Statistics of the United Kingdom* [QRL.85], these Divisions are further broken down into detailed headings. These headings are too numerous to list here in full, but it is important to note the main headings given the reliance of the domestic industry on imported supplies. The descriptions of some of the headings have been shortened to economise on space.

091. Margarine; edible mixtures or preparations of animal or vegetable fats or oils, other than of heading 431.20
091.01 Margarine (excluding liquid margarine)
091.09 Edible mixtures or preparations of animal or vegetable fats/oils or of fractions of different fats/oils, other than of heading 431.20

222. Oil seeds and oleaginous fruits of a kind used for the extraction of 'soft' fixed vegetable oils (excluding flours and meals)
222.1 Groundnuts (peanuts), not roasted or otherwise cooked, whether or not shelled or broken
222.2 Soya beans
222.3 Cotton seeds
222.4 Sunflower seeds
222.5 Sesame (sesamum) seeds
222.6 Rape, colza and mustard seeds
222.7 Safflower seeds

223. Oil seeds and oleaginous fruits, whole or broken, used for the extraction of other fixed vegetable oils (including flours and meals, not elsewhere specified)
223.1 Copra
223.2 Palm nuts and palm kernels
223.4 Linseed
223.5 Castor oil seeds
223.7 Oil seeds and oleaginous fruits, not elsewhere specified
223.9 Flours and meals of oil seeds/oleaginous fruits (excluding mustard flour) defatted/wholly/partially re-fatted

411.1 Fats, oils and their fractions, of fish or marine mammals, whether or not refined, but not chemically modified
411.2 Lard; other pig fat and poultry fat, rendered, whether or not pressed or solvent-extracted
411.3 Animal fats and greases, not elsewhere specified

421. Fixed vegetable fats and oils, 'soft', crude, refined or fractionated
421.1 Soya bean oil and its fractions
421.2 Cotton seed oil and its fractions
421.3 Groundnut (peanut) oil and its fractions
421.4 Olive oil and other oil obtained from olives
421.5 Sunflower seed or safflower oil and their fractions
421.6 Maize (corn) oil and its fractions
421.7 Rape, colza or mustard oil and their fractions
421.8 Sesame (sesamum) oil and its fractions

422. Fixed vegetable fats and oils, crude, refined or fractionated, other than 'soft'
422.1 Linseed oil and its fractions
422.2 Palm oil and its fractions
422.3 Coconut (copra) oil and its fractions
422.4 Palm kernel or babassu oil and their fractions
422.5 Castor oil and its fractions
422.9 Other fixed vegetable fats, crude, refined or fractionated, other than 'soft'

431. Animal or vegetable fats and oils, processed waxes, and inedible mixtures or preparations of animal, vegetable fats or oils, not elsewhere specified

Monthly data in *Business Monitor MM20* [QRL.85] are provided in both volume and value terms for a range of importing and exporting countries. Further details of the extensive statistical coverage are presented in section 2.8.2.1. The statistics have been compiled from the declarations which are made to HM Customs and Excise, and which are subject to confirmation by Customs officials. The figures are usually published about one month after the month to which they relate. Details of the HM Customs and Excise tariff/trade code numbers relating to AH4115 and AH4116 used to be found in *Business Monitor PQ4115* [QRL.128] and *Business Monitor PQ4116* [QRL.129] respectively up to the second quarter of 1989.

Business Monitor PQ4115 [QRL.128] provided quarterly figures, up to the second quarter of 1989, in both volume and value terms on imports and exports of margarine; and imitation lard and other prepared edible fats. *Business Monitor PQ4116* [QRL.129] provided, up to the second quarter of 1989, quarterly figures in both volume and value terms on imports and exports of the following:

- oil cake and other residues (except dregs) resulting from the extraction of vegetable oils
- flours or meals of oil seeds or oleaginous fruit non-defatted (excluding mustard flour)
- oils and fats of fish and marine mammals
- fixed vegetable oils and fats
- animal or vegetable oils or fats wholly or partly hydrogenated or solidified or hardened by any other process whether or not refined, but not further prepared
- spermaceti, crude pressed or refined, whether or not coloured
- animal and vegetable oils and fats boiled, oxidised, dehydrated, sulphurised, blown or polymerised by heat in vacuum or inert gas, or otherwise modified.

The level of detail was far more restricted than in *Business Monitor MM20* [QRL.85].

The Commonwealth Secretariat publish biannual figures on the volume of imports from various countries in *Fruit and Tropical Products* [QRL.245] for the following: oilseeds and oils; groundnuts; groundnut oil; soya bean; soya bean oil; cottonseed oil; rapeseed; rapeseed oil; sunflower seed; sunflower seed oil; copra and coconut; palm kernels; palm kernel oil; palm oil; linseed; linseed oil; castor oil; and tung oil. It also provides import prices for selected oilseeds and oils.

3.8.2 *Industry Analyses of Trade*

In contrast to these analyses by type of product, *Business Monitor MQ10: Overseas Trade Analysed in Terms of Industries* [QRL.90] provides quarterly data on exports and imports for Activity Headings 4115 and 4116, as well as for the industry Group as a whole. These figures are also used in *Business Monitor MQ12: Import Penetration and Export Sales Ratios for Manufacturing Industry* [QRL.91] to provide export/sales and import penetration ratios for both Activity Headings and for the industry Group up to the second quarter of 1989 — see section 2.8.2.3 for details of the coverage.

3.9 Stocks

The *Monthly Digest of Statistics* [QRL.362] provides end-month data on stocks of oilseeds and nuts; vegetable oil; and marine oil. The stocks figures include the quantities of oilseeds and nuts, vegetable oils and marine oils respectively held by seed crushers, hardeners, and refiners of oil and manufacturers of margarine and compound fat. All figures are expressed in terms of crude oil equivalent. The *Annual Abstract of Statistics* [QRL.37] publishes data on stocks at end-December of the following: oilcake and meal (excluding castor meal, cocoa cake and meal); oilseeds and nuts; vegetable oil; and marine oil. *Business Monitor PA411* [QRL.105] gives financial data on stocks and work-in-progress for all UK establishments classified to the industry Group at end-December, and also analysis of these data by size of establishment. Moreover, data on stocks and work-in-progress are also provided for each of the Activity Headings.

3.10 Consumption

3.10.1 *The National Food Survey*

The National Food Survey collects consumption data on a variety of products manufactured by industry Group 411, viz:

Food code number	Description
136	Soft margarine
137	Other margarine
138	Total margarine (codes 136 and 137)
139	Lard and compound cooking fat
143	Vegetable and salad oils
145	Reduced fat spreads
146	Low fat spreads
147	Other fats
148	All other fats (codes 145–147)

It should be noted that much of the output of industry Group 411 is used in the manufacture of other food items (e.g. compound cooking fats are used in the making of cakes and pastry) and so is not "consumed" directly. Detailed statistics are published for the various food items listed above in the *National Food Survey: Compendium of Results* [QRL.373]. Annual average figures of both per capita weekly consumption and expenditure are provided for the following main food groups: margarine (138); lard and compound cooking fat (139); other fats (143, 148); and fats (135–148) including butter (135). Moreover, data on margarine (138); lard and compound cooking fat (139); and other fats (143, 148) are analysed by region and type of area; by income group; by household composition; by household composition and income group; by age of housewife; by housing tenure; and by ownership of deep freezer. In addition, indices of expenditure, and of the real value of purchases, on margarine (138), and other fats (139–148) are presented for the latest six years and quarterly and annual national average household expenditure on all the food items listed above are calculated.

The main report on the Survey, *Household Food Consumption and Expenditure* [QRL.267], carries a more limited range of statistical data, as has been discussed in section 2.10.1.2. Commentary is, however, provided with many of the main statistical tables, and data for previous years are often presented for comparison. The income elasticity of expenditure on fats (131–148 i.e. including butter) is calculated.

3.10.2 *The Family Expenditure Survey*

The *Family Expenditure Survey* [QRL.204] provides analyses of the expenditure of various types of households on margarine, and on lard, cooking fats and other fats, at different levels of household income, and by sex and age. It also publishes average figures for weekly expenditure analysed by region.

3.10.3 *The National Accounts*

The *United Kingdom National Accounts* [QRL.506] carries annual data, in both current and constant prices, of household expenditure on "oils and fats". The data are reproduced in the *Annual Abstract of Statistics* [QRL.37].

3.11 Supplies and Disposals

A historical picture may be found in the article by W.D. Stedman Jones [B.167] which includes a section devoted to statistics on "oils and fats". The Economics and Statistics Department of Lever Brothers and Unilever Limited had also contributed a statistical review of "Oils and Fats" [B.346] in the earlier (1952) first volume of *The Sources and Nature of the Statistics of the United Kingdom* [B.95].

MAFF prepare supply balance sheets for the fats and oils of land animals; the fats and oils of marine animals; oleaginous seeds and fruit; vegetable fats and oils; oilcakes; and prepared fats and oils, which are sent to the Statistical Office of the European Communities (EUROSTAT). The balance sheet for the fats and oils of land animals covers the fats derived from beef, pork, lamb, and poultry. Production figures are estimated from the meat balance sheet — see section 4.11 — using national coefficients for the fat content of carcases. The balance sheet for the fats and oils of marine animals covers the fats derived from marine mammals and fish. The production figures for fish fats are obtained from the International Fish Meal Association. The balance sheet for oleaginous seeds and fruit covers rape and other seeds. The figures on production and usage of these seeds are estimated from the monthly MAFF survey of seed crushers, results of which are first published in *MAFF Statistics: Oilseeds and Nuts Crushed, Crude Vegetable Oils, Oilcake and Meal Produced in the United Kingdom* [QRL.322]. The balance sheet for vegetable fats and oils covers the oils derived from rape, sunflower, soya, palm, and other seeds. The data on production and stocks of these oils are derived from the monthly MAFF survey of vegetable oil crushers and refiners, results of which are first published in *MAFF Statistics: Production of Refined, Deodorised Vegetable, Marine Oils and Animal Fats in the United Kingdom* [QRL.328]. The balance sheet for oilcake uses information on utilisation provided by animal feedingstuffs production returns. Finally, the balance sheet for prepared oils and fats covers margarine and other prepared fats. The data are forthcoming from the monthly MAFF survey of oil and fat refiners and margarine producers, the results of which are first published in *MAFF Statistics: Margarine, Other Table Spreads and Solid Cooking Fat Produced in the United Kingdom and the Refined Oils and Animal Fats Used in Their Production* [QRL.321]. These supply balance sheet data are stored in the CRONOS databank — see section 2.11 — and are subequently published in the quarterly EUROSTAT publications, *Animal Production* [QRL.36] and *Crop Production* [QRL.167].

The data from the MAFF surveys also appear in the *Monthly Digest of Statistics* [QRL.362], which provides monthly average figures of disposals of vegetable oil, and usage of marine oil for the manufacture of margarine, solid cooking fat and other table spreads. The crude oil equivalent of the refined oils used in the manufacture of margarine and compound fat and other foods is included in the disposals of vegetable oils, together with the crude oils used as such for soap and other industrial purposes. Exported supplies are included in the disposals. The crude oil equivalent of the refined marine oils used in the production of margarine and compound fat is recorded as the usage of marine oils. Between 1954 and 1959 inclusive, disposals, as usage was then known, only referred to whole oil. The *Annual Abstract of Statistics* [QRL.37] publishes annual figures on disposals of vegetable oil; marine oil for the manufacture of margarine and compound fat; and oilcake and meal.

3.12 Prices

3.12.1 *Commodity Prices*

The *Public Ledger & Daily Freight Register* [QRL.392] published by Turret-Wheatland Ltd. provides daily price information on the following oilseeds and vegetable oils markets:

Oilseeds:	linseed; sesameseed; rapeseed; soyabeans; sunflowerseed; copra; and palm kernels.
Crude oils/fats:	castor oil; tungoil; cottonseed oil; linseed oil; coconut oil; palm kernel oil; palm oil; rapeseed oil; soyabean oil; sunflowerseed oil; groundnut oil; lard; and fish oil.
UK Processed oils:	rapeseed oil; soyabean oil; palm oil; groundnut oil; maize oil; coconut oil.
UK Edible oils:	soyabean oil; rapeseed oil; sunflowerseed oil; palm kernel oil; coconut oil; palm oil; fish oil; animal tallow.
UK Crude oils:	rapeseed oil; soyabean oil; sunflowerseed oil; groundnut oil; palm oil; palm kernel oil; coconut oil; fish oil.

On Saturdays, the Public Ledger appears as *The Public Ledger's Commodity Week* [QRL.394] and this includes weekly price information for the following oilseeds and nuts: Canadian linseed; rapeseed; Sudanese sesame; US soyabeans; Philippine copra; Nigerian palm kernels; Brazilian castor oil; any-origin linseed oil; S. American tung oil; Philippine coconut oil; Malaysian palm kernel oil; Malay/Sumatran palm oil; any-origin groundnut oil; Dutch soya oil; any-origin sunseed oil; fish oil; EEC refiners lard; and English tallow Grade 2.

The newsletter *Oil World* [QRL.380] published by ISTA Mielke GmbH gives weekly information on lowest representative asking prices for the nearest forward shipment in bulk of various oilseeds, crude oils and fats. *Fruit and Tropical Products* [QRL.245], published twice yearly by the Commonwealth Secretariat, provides import prices for the following selected vegetable oilseeds and oils: groundnuts; soya beans; rapeseed; copra; palm kernels; groundnut oil; soyabean oil; sunflower oil; olive oil; palm oil; coconut oil; palm kernel oil; linseed oil; castor oil; and tung oil.

3.12.2 *Retail Prices*

3.12.2.1 Recorded prices

The *Employment Gazette* [QRL.186] gives average retail prices on one day a month for the following: 500g tub of soft margarine; 250g of low fat spread; 250g of lard. The figures are derived from prices collected in more than 180 areas of the United Kingdom. An indication of variations in price is given by showing the ranges within which at least four-fifths of the recorded prices fall. Quarterly and annual national average prices are given in the *Compendium of Results* [QRL.373] for the following: soft margarine; other margarine; total margarine; lard and compound cooking fat; vegetable and salad oils; reduced fat spreads; low fat spreads; other fats.

3.12.2.2 Recommended prices

The prices quoted in *Shaws Guide to Fair Retail Prices* [QRL.453] are for the guidance of consumers and retailers. The amount of brand detail is considerable, and only broad product categories will be listed here for the sake of economy. Recommended retail prices are published on the first day of every month for the following: cooking fats; cooking oil; lard; margarine; olives; and olive oil. When manufacturers do not recommend fair selling prices, they are suggested by the editor with help from the manufacturers. Suggested prices show a fair profit on minimum quantities supplied on trade terms. Typical prices — referred to as KVI (known value item) prices — of key lines in multiple stores are also quoted as a guide, e.g. Mazola oil, Krona margarine.

The Grocer [QRL.252] publishes weekly market prices, subject to regional variation and discounting, on numerous types of lard. In addition, on the first Saturday in each month, *The Grocer Price List* [QRL.253] is published. Recommended prices are quoted for cooking fats; cooking oils; lard; and margarine. Prices are supplied by manufacturers, importers or sole agents, and are for the smallest quantity they supply. Again the amount of brand detail is considerable.

3.12.3 *The Retail Prices Index*
The *Employment Gazette* [QRL.186] carries monthly retail price indices for "oils and fats", and also indicates the percentage change over the previous year. The structure of the published components was recast with effect from February 1987. Previously separate indices had been available for margarine; and for lard and other cooking fats. The relationship between the old and the new index structure was shown in the September 1986 issue of the *Employment Gazette* [QRL.186].

The *Monthly Digest of Statistics* [QRL.362] is an alternative source. *Retail Prices: Indices 1914–1986* [QRL.434] contains group and sub-group indices and weights back to 1974, group indices back to 1956, and all items back to 1947. Quarterly indices, again derived from Department of Employment data, were presented for "oils and fats" in *Business Monitor PQ4115* [QRL.128] up to mid-1989.

3.12.4 *Price Index Numbers in the National Food Survey*
The National Food Survey is another useful source of retail price information. The *Compendium of Results* [QRL.373] presents annual price indices for the following main food groups: margarine (138); other fats (139–148); and fats (135–148) including butter (135).

3.12.5 *Producer Price Index Numbers*
The series of Producer Price Indices are considered in general terms in section 2.12.5. Details of the price indices for the inputs and outputs for the organic oils and fats sector are given below.

3.12.5.1 Producer price index numbers: input prices
Business Monitor MM22: Producer Prices Indices carries the producer price index numbers of materials and fuels purchased for AH4115 and AH4116 giving both monthly and annual data. The monthly data are given for the current and previous years, with the figures for the latest two months provisional. An annual average for the previous year is also presented. *Business Monitor MM22* was published for the first time in October 1989 and continued the coverage in *British Business* [QRL.66].

Business Monitor MM22 also provides a producer price index for the following commodities wholly or mainly imported into the United Kingdom: US soya beans; Philippine copra; West African oils; Dutch soyabean oils; groundnut oil; sunflower seed oil; other fixed vegetable oils; crude palm oil; Philippine coconut oil and Malaysian palm kernel oil. *Business Monitor MM22* gives these data in monthly and annual terms. The *Annual Abstract of Statistics* [QRL.37] presents them in annual form.

Business Monitor PQ4115 [QRL.128] provided quarterly and annual indices of materials purchased up to mid-1989. Under this heading appeared refined vegetable and seed oils and imported oils from MAFF sources. *Business Monitor PQ4116* [QRL.129] provided the producer price index of materials purchased in annual and quarterly terms for imported oil seeds from MAFF sources, again up to mid-1989. However, *MAFF Statistics; Agricultural Price Indices* [QRL.315] provides a monthly producer price index for oilseed rape.

3.12.5.2 Producer price index numbers: output prices

Business Monitor MM22 contains the producer price index numbers of products manufactured in the United Kingdom (home sales) for AH4115 and AH4116. The monthly data are provided for the current and previous year, with the figures for the latest two months provisional. An annual average for the previous year is also presented. *Business Monitor MM22* was published for the first time in October 1989 and continued the coverage in *British Business* [QRL.66]. The *Annual Abstract of Statistics* [QRL.37] gives the annual average for AH4115 and AH4116 for a six-year run for products manufactured in the United Kingdom (home sales).

Business Monitor PQ4115 [QRL.128] provided producer price indices of goods produced in quarterly and annual terms. The following products were identified: margarine (for domestic use); compound fat (for trade use). The data are derived from MAFF sources and compared with the figures for food manufacturing industries (home sales) and all manufactured products (home sales). *Business Monitor PQ4116* [QRL.129] separately identified and compared refined vegetable and seed oils with the same MAFF and DTI series.

3.12.6 *Intervention Prices*

The *Intervention Board for Agricultural Produce: Annual Report* [QRL.293] provides details of UK intervention prices of rapeseed.

3.13 Financial Information

Margarine and Compound Cooking Fats [B.406] by the National Board for Prices and Incomes provides much informative data on trends in costs, prices and profitability in the industry, though the figures are now somewhat dated. *Business Monitor PA411* [QRL.105] publishes annual data on output, wages and salaries, the purchase of materials and the cost of non-industrial services, and gross value added for all UK establishments classified to the industry. Annual data on output and costs, together with various operating ratios, for the two constituent Activity Headings are also provided. Moreover, there are analyses of labour costs by size of establishment; and of net output and gross value added at factor cost by region. Finally, the Annual Reports of the companies cited in section 3.2 will give the usual data and analysis of revenues, costs and profits.

3.14 Advertising and Market Research

Much of the output of industry Group 411 is used as an input in the manufacture of other foods — see section 3.2 for details — and only a few products find their way directly to the consumer. Advertising and market research are largely restricted to these products. Margarine, butter and low-fat spreads form a "yellow fats" market; compound cooking fats and lard form a "white fats" market.

3.14.1 *Advertising*
The *Tri-Media Digest of Brands and Advertisers* [QRL.493] is the standard reference for information on advertising expenditure of competing firms and brands. Data are provided therein — see section 2.14.1.1 for details — on the following product groups relevant to industry Group 411: margarine (F75); suet, cooking fats, vegetable oils (F90). An alternative source is *The Media Register* [QRL.354], which gives details of monthly press and television advertising expenditure for cooking oils and fats (FOO 22); and margarine (FOO 58).

3.14.2 *Market Research*
Both the "yellow fats" and the "white fats" markets have been the subject of occasional reviews carried out by Mintel Publications and Euromonitor Publications. *Market Intelligence* [QRL.339] carries recent reviews of "Dairy spreads within the yellow fats market" (July 1988); and "Cooking fats and oils" (August 1988). *Market Research: Great Britain* [QRL.343] contains analyses of "Oils" (April 1985); "Yellow fats" (November 1986); and "White fats and cooking oil" (May 1988). It should be emphasised that many other organisations also publish market research reports, and so the above does not constitute an exhaustive list. For example, Marketing Strategies for Industry provide an annual review of *Yellow Fats* [QRL.653]. Moreover, all such reports tend to be market-oriented, rather than industry-oriented unlike many of the statistical sources in this Review. Thus butter and margarine are typically considered together in market research reports, although the former is a product of industry Group 413 and the latter a product of industry Group 411.

3.15 Research and Development

There are no generally available sources of statistical information on research and development in the industry. The major companies, notably Unilever, undertake R&D as do MAFF, and some data are now available in company reports.

3.16 Official Investigations

The National Board for Prices and Incomes was requested by the Government in February 1970 to examine and report on the question of costs, prices and profitability in the margarine and compound cooking fats (shortenings) industry. This request was in response to significant increases in selling prices by the leading manufacturers. The Board's report entitled *Margarine and Compound Cooking Fats* [B.406] was submitted in May 1970 and provides both general information on the industry and much statistical data. The report is now, however, somewhat dated.

3.17 Improvements and Comments

Since many of the inputs to industry Group 411 are oilseeds and crude oils imported from abroad, *Business Monitor MM20* [QRL.85] is clearly an important statistical source. Price information on oils, fats and seeds is readily available in a number of commercial publications. Much of the data on the subsequent crushing of the seeds, the refining of the crude oils, and the utilisation of the processed oils are generated by the three MAFF surveys described in sections 3.4 and 3.11.

Finally, mention should be made of a number of secondary sources which provide statistical information on oilseeds and oils, often with commentary, both for the United Kingdom and other countries. The *Oil World Statistics Update* [QRL.381] is a continuously updated publication from ISTA Mielke GmbH. It provides monthly international data on supplies, stocks, production, imports, exports and domestic disappearance. *Agra Europe* [QRL.22] has been issued weekly since 1983. It covers European and world developments affecting the production and marketing of fats and oils, among other commodities. The data on fats and oils are taken from *Oil World* [QRL.380]. The *Annual Review of Oilseeds, Oils and Oilcakes and Other Commodities* [QRL.53] contains reviews of the markets for butter and lard; tallow and greases; cottonseed and cottonseed oil; copra and coconut oil; castor seed and oil; fish oils and whale oil; groundnuts and groundnut oil; linseed and linseed oil; olive oil; palm oil; palm kernels and palm kernel oil; rapeseed and rapeseed oil; mustard seed; sesame seed; soyabeans and soyabean oil; sunflower seed and oil; and tung oil. The Economist Intelligence Unit publish *World Commodity Outlook: Food, Feedstuffs and Beverages* [QRL.520] every year. The 1988 edition has sections on oilseeds and oils; soyabeans; sunflowerseed; cottonseed; groundnuts; rapeseed; copra; palm oil and palm kernels. And *Primary Commodities: Market Developments and Outlook* [QRL.391] and the *CRB Commodity Year Book* [QRL.166] are two further examples — there are many others — of international statistical compendia. It should be noted, however, that the focus in all these volumes is on the untreated commodities which are the inputs to industry Group 411, rather than on the processed oils and fats which constitute the output.

CHAPTER 4

SLAUGHTERING OF ANIMALS AND PRODUCTION OF MEAT AND BY-PRODUCTS

The information in this chapter relates to the slaughtering of animals and production of meat and by-products industry, Group 412 in the *CSO Standard Industrial Classification Revised 1980* [B.232]. Other more general sources, which provide statistics on other industry Groups as well, are covered in Chapter 2 and should be consulted as required. The contents of this chapter are as follows:

4.1 Introduction

Industry Group 412 covers the following Activity Headings:

4121 Slaughterhouses.
Slaughtering of animals for meat for human consumption. Further processing such as removal of bones, offal, glands, etc. or the temporary preservation of hides and skins when undertaken in the slaughterhouse is included. Also included in this heading is the preparation of cuts of fresh meat or edible offals (including subsequent chilling or freezing) in establishments not classifiable to Division 6 (the distribution industry). Slaughtering, etc. of poultry is classified to heading 4123. The processing of animal by-products outside slaughterhouses and the slaughtering or processing of animals unfit for human consumption is classified to heading 4126.

4122 Bacon curing and meat processing.
1. Bacon and ham.
Production of bacon, ham and processed pigmeat products. Pre-cooking or putting into sealed packs is included but canned products are classified to sub-division 3 of this heading.
2. Frozen meat products.
Freezing of prepared meat products e.g. complete meat-based meals, meat pies and puddings, pastes, sausagemeat, etc.
3. Other processed and preserved meats.

4123 Poultry slaughter and processing.
1. Poultry slaughter.
Slaughtering poultry and game birds. Dressing and further preparation (e.g. quartering, chilling or freezing) in the same establishment is included. Similar work done in establishments not slaughtering birds themselves is classified to sub-division 2 of this heading.
2. Poultry meat products.
Processing of poultry meat products (including dressing and quartering fowl in establishments not engaged in slaughtering) such as preparing meals based on poultry, pastes, breasts, etc. either fresh or packeted, canned or frozen. Products containing mixed ingredients of poultry and other meats are classified to heading 4122.

4126 Animal by-product processing.
1. Fats and greases.
Recovery and rendering of fats and greases from terrestrial animals. Hydrogenation of fats is classified to heading 4116.3. Fat splitting and other chemical treatment are classified to heading 2563.
2. Processed guts and offals.
Processing and preparing guts and offals (including bones and blood) such as the manufacture of sausage skins, tripe, dressing, etc.
3. Slaughtering other than for human consumption and other processing of animal by-products.
Production of animal by-products including bone products. Meat meal, hides and skins, inedible poultry by-products, processing fallen animals and slaughter other than for human consumption are included.

For an alphabetical list of all the activities classified to Group 412, see the CSO *Indexes to the Standard Industrial Classification Revised 1980* [B.317]. Many of these activities were previously classified under MLH214 "Bacon curing, meat and fish products" in SIC(1968). Two major changes (in addition to a number of minor ones) have taken place in the SIC(1980) classification.

- "Slaughtering" is now included in Group 412, and thus within the Food industries in SIC(1980), whereas it had been classified with "wholesale distribution" (MLH810.2) in SIC(1968).
- "Fish processing" used to be classified to MLH214 in SIC(1968), but is now classified to the separate Group 415 — see Chapter 7.

Further details may be found in *Standard Industrial Classification Revised 1980: Reconciliation with Standard Industrial Classification 1968* [B.379].

A number of Business Monitors based on the SIC(1980) contain statistical information on the industry Group. *Business Monitor PA412: Slaughtering of Animals and Production of Meat and By-products* [QRL.106] provides annual data for the Group as a whole. Each of the Activity Headings (except AH4121) was, up to mid-1989, the subject of a quarterly Business Monitor, viz:

- *Business Monitor PQ4122: Bacon Curing and Meat Products* [QRL.130]
- *Business Monitor PQ4123: Poultry and Poultry Products* [QRL.131]
- *Business Monitor PQ4126: Animal By-products* [QRL.132]

which contain rather more detailed information. The first issues of *Business Monitor*

PQ4122 [QRL.130] and *Business Monitor PQ4126* [QRL.132] were published for the first quarter of 1983; the first issue of *Business Monitor PQ4123* [QRL.131] was published in the second quarter of 1983. All these initial issues contained data for 1981 and 1982 re-analysed according to the SIC(1980). Following the *Review of DTI Statistics* [B.367] only *Business Monitor PQ4122: Bacon Curing and Meat Products* [QRL.130] now remains. The data in these quarterly publications may be compared with earlier data published in *Business Monitor PQ214: Bacon Curing, Meat and Fish Products* [QRL.120], and also (in the case of animal by-products) in *Business Monitor PQ221: Vegetable and Animal Oils and Fats* [QRL.125].

The main products of the industry Group are thus beef; lamb; pork; bacon and ham; and poultry; together with associated meat products. Sales of offal and by-products provide additional income to that received for carcase meat. The nature of offal varies widely and the end-use of the by-products can be divided roughly into six areas:

- the edible offal market — includes items such as heart, liver, kidneys and tongue commonly consumed by humans,
- the pet food market — makes use of items not passed for human consumption or those surplus to human requirements,
- the market for casings — intestines processed for use as sausage skins and surgical sutures,
- the pharmaceutical industry — use of by-products such as glands (e.g. the pancreas for the production of insulin) and hormones,
- sales of hides and skins — purchased by the leather industry for tanning,
- the rendering industry — the remaining items are rendered into meat and bone meal, edible and industrial fats, fertilisers and extracted proteins.

The output of the industry Group does not, therefore, just comprise food.

4.2 Industry Structure

The industry Group is not homogeneous and may perhaps be best discussed in three parts according to their main products: beef, lamb and pork; bacon; and poultry. It should be appreciated that the division is somewhat arbitrary as there is much functional overlap — e.g. between pork and bacon. Details of the various companies operating within the Group may be gleaned from the ICC "Financial Survey and Company Directory" of *Meat, Egg & Poultry Processors* [QRL.577] and *Meat & Poultry — Scotland* [QRL.578]. Various market research publications also cover the industry — these are detailed in section 4.14.2.

4.2.1 *Beef, Lamb and Pork*

One of the recommendations of the Verdon-Smith Report in 1964 [B.362] — see section 4.16 for details — was the establishment of the Meat and Livestock Commission (MLC), which was set up in 1968. The Commission has since developed a wide range of advisory activities associated with the marketing of carcase (and other) meat and, in particular, it collates and publishes a wide range of statistical information. In particular, the MLC issues two invaluable publications which provide a wealth of statistical information on the meat industry, viz. *UK Market Review* [QRL.498] and *International Meat Market Review* [QRL.289], formerly the *International Market Review* [QRL.288]. Both are published twice a year. The Commission also acts as an agent for the Agriculture Departments and the Intervention Board for Agricultural Produce in operating market support schemes (see section 4.3 for details). The Livestock Marketing Commission for Northern Ireland publishes an *Annual Report* [QRL.40] which provides discussion of market conditions, together with several statistical appendices.

The marketing chain for beef, lamb and pork is shown in Figure 4.1. Many of the large abattoirs are owned by vertically integrated meat companies such as Union International and Hillsdown Holdings. Others are owned by large, sometimes international, enterprises that have diverse interests, e.g. Berisfords, Northern Foods, Anglo Beef Processors, Sainsbury, Swift, Borthwick. The remaining large abattoirs are owned by private companies (only a few of which operate more than one) together with a small number of farmer-owned cooperatives and one or two that are owned and operated by local authorities.

All of these plants, with one or two exceptions, operate as meat wholesalers. Moreover, many of these large plants will also have meat cutting and processing, vacuum packing and boxing facilities. Besides the wholesalers who have slaughtering facilities, there are others who wholesale meat but obtain their meat supplies from other abattoirs. Some may be specialist importers and commodity traders such as Armour Foods, Edward Billington (Meats), Danish Bacon Co., and Towers.

Some meat wholesalers are still (or have subsidiary companies or depots) located near the remaining central meat markets in some major cities (notably Smithfield) but these markets are relatively unimportant today as centres of meat distribution. All meat wholesalers have five broad categories of customer (listed in descending order of importance by turnover): retail butchers, supermarkets (now almost comparable turnover to butchers), meat product manufacturers, commercial and institutional caterers, and other wholesalers. Wholesalers trade both carcases, primal cuts and more fully-prepared or portion-controlled cuts of meat to these broad categories of customer. The exact nature of this trade will differ depending on the type of outlet.

The Slaughtering Industry in Great Britain [QRL.454] is the primary source of data on the slaughtering industry. It is published biennially by the MLC and contains statistical data on slaughterhouse numbers, type of ownership, size distribution and concentration. Additional information may be found in *Livestock Slaughtering in Britain: A Changing Industry* [B.70] and *Structural Change in the Retail Distribution System for Meat in Great Britain* [B.138].

4.2.2 *Bacon*

The following account of the bacon industry is largely based on the Price Commission report, *Prices, Costs and Margins in the Importation and Distribution of Bacon* [B.425] — see section 4.16 for details.

Bacon is made from pork by curing it with salt and other materials. Brine is usually injected into the meat which is then left in this solution for four to five days. Most bacon is "Wiltshire cured" as "sides". (A "side" of bacon is half the pig, minus

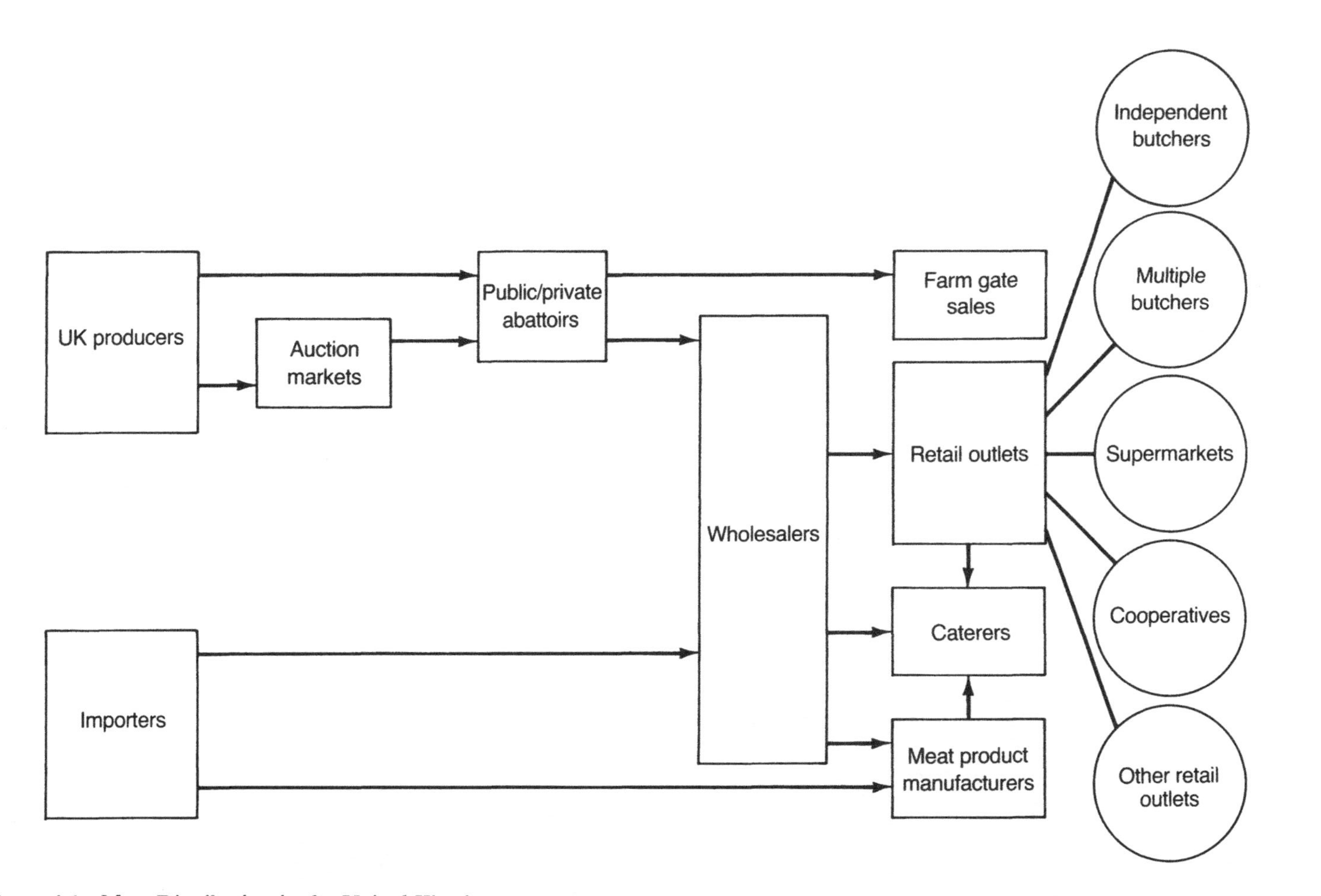

Figure 4.1 Meat Distribution in the United Kingdom.
Source: Meat and Livestock Commission.

the backbone and the head, cut lengthways.) An increasing proportion is cured as pieces. Other methods of curing include "Ayrshire cure", where the fat is removed before curing, and "sweet cure" where sugar, maple syrup or another sweetener is added to the brine. Bacon may also be smoked which imparts a distinctive flavour as well as a golden colour to the rind and helps the bacon to keep better. Before bacon is smoked, it is known as "green" bacon. Pig carcases are graded for quality before selection for Wiltshire curing.

The marketing pattern for bacon is illustrated in Figure 4.2. Considerable functional overlap and common ownership exist, and the classification of each type of enterprise is not always clearcut. The greatest variety of function is shown by UK curers who supply a large proportion of their bacon in the form of sides to caterers and multiple retailers. Curers also supply independent retailers and wholesalers; and may supply sides and distribute various pigmeat products such as bacon, sausages and pies by van sales. A few curers have their own retail shops, and some curers sell through agents.

Imported bacon is handled by importing principals or agents and is mainly sold, as sides in containers, to multiple retailers and wholesalers. Some goes to processors, who then produce vacuum packed joints and rashers. Denmark is the largest supplier of imported bacon, though the Netherlands has emerged as a rival. The handling of bacon is of varying importance to wholesalers. To some, the business is small; to others, it is rather more important. One large company surveyed by the Price Commission accounted for over half the sales of bacon by wholesalers in their sample. Wholesalers may carry out various operations on a side of bacon and may offer a comprehensive service on bacon to the customer, who is usually an independent retailer. Retailers usually sell bacon as just one of a number of products. Bacon can be bought from all the usual grocery outlets — supermarkets, multiple chains, independent grocers etc. — and also from butchers. Some curers, as already mentioned, own their own shops.

4.2.3 *Poultry*

The major reference source for this section is the Price Commission report *Prices and Margins in Poultry Distribution* [B.432] — see section 4.16 for details.

Chickens account for the major part of UK poultry production, and turkeys for most of the balance. Duck, geese etc. are of relatively minor importance in terms of the industry as a whole. One may thus distinguish five main types of poultry produced for the retail trade:

- frozen "oven-ready" chickens which have been killed, plucked, eviscerated and finally frozen by producers,
- fresh chickens which have been killed and plucked by the producer but which are usually offered for sale with their heads, feet and innards,
- fresh "oven-ready" chickens,
- frozen "oven-ready" turkeys which have been processed in much the same way as frozen chickens,
- fresh turkeys which are prepared for sale in the same way as fresh chickens.

In addition, there is a small, but increasing trade in "chilled" chickens and turkeys. These are supplied by some producers to supermarkets and multiple grocers. These

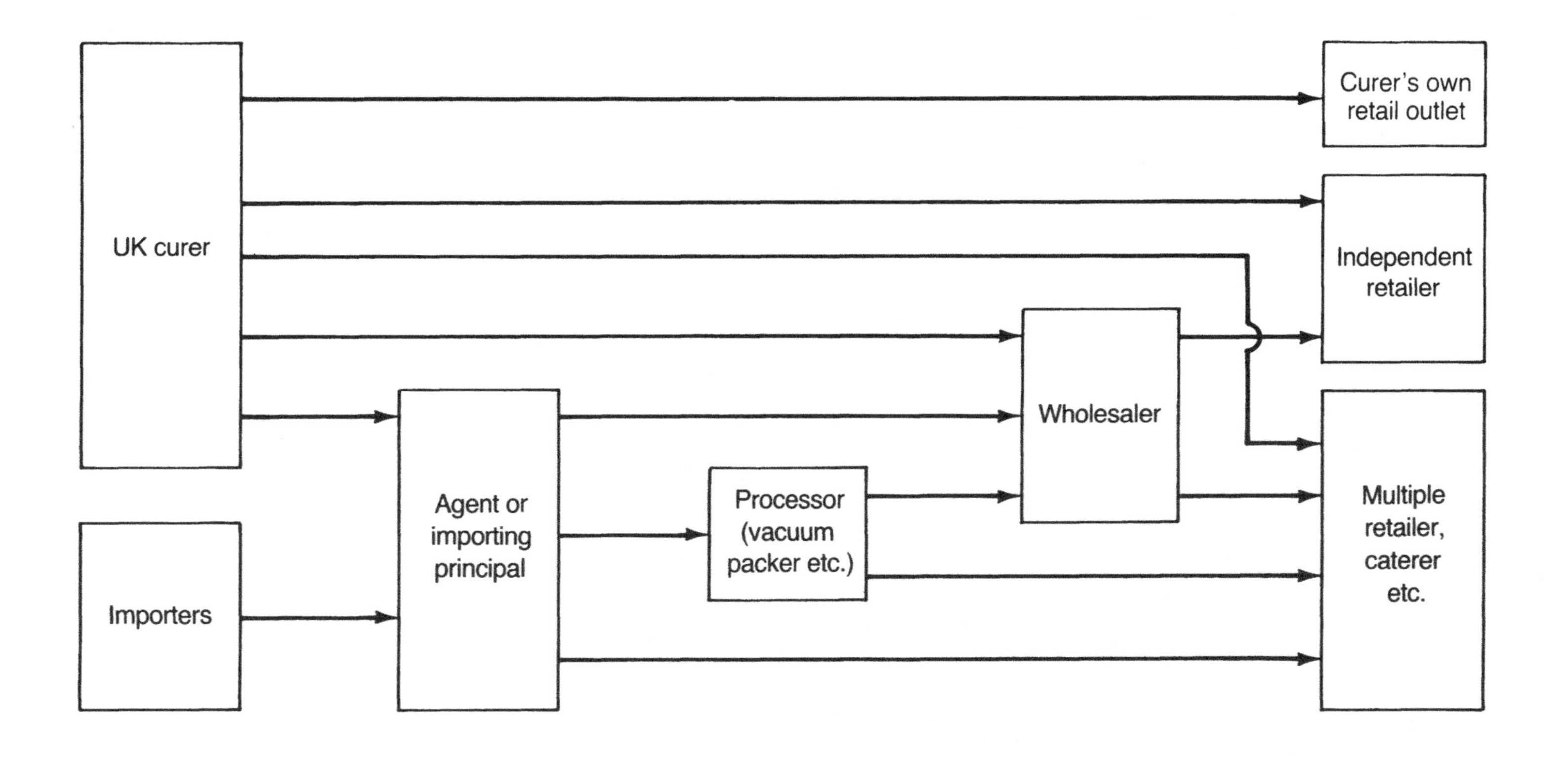

Figure 4.2 Bacon Distribution in the United Kingdom.
Source: *Prices, Costs and Margins in the Importation and Distribution of Bacon* [B425], P.6. Price Commission Examination Report no. 1.

birds are initially processed in much the same way as the frozen variety, but at the stage of "preservation" they are only "chilled". The "chilling" process retains more of the characteristics of the fresh bird, but limits shelf-life to about two weeks.

Methods of production and distribution of poultry are, in general, quite different from those for meat. Meat animals are raised by farmers who are mainly small or medium scale producers. The meat is mainly sold to specialist butchers, who again are mainly small or medium size traders, and most of whom are independent.

In contrast, the poultry trade is dominated by a few large producers whose methods are more akin to manufacture than to farming. About seven or eight companies are responsible for 70 per cent of chicken production. Two companies (Buxted, Bernard Matthews) account for 50–60 per cent of turkey production. These firms are very capital intensive; many are fully integrated, producing their own feed requirements and breeding stock, and also owning their own hatcheries, rearing units and processing plant, distribution centres and transport fleets. The smaller firms (of which there might be 30–40 of any significance in chicken production) are often less integrated, buying in their chicks or eggs and feeding supplies, for example, or sending out chicks for rearing on contract. Poultry is sold more through supermarkets and grocers than through grocers. Butchers only account for about half the volume of sales through grocery outlets, and for a much smaller proportion of frozen poultry.

The counterpart to the Meat and Livestock Commission for the poultry industry is the British Poultry Federation. The Federation does collect statistical information from its members, but this is only distributed within the industry to those who provided data in the first instance. Such a confidential approach is feasible because of the small number of producers, and it has the advantage that the information is not disseminated to buyers, importers and other such interested parties.

4.3 The European Community

The *European Handbook* [QRL.188] is a loose-leaf subsciption service provided by the MLC, and updated continually as circumstances change. It comes in two volumes, the first of which contains detailed rules and regulations of all EC meat and livestock regimes. The description of the regimes also refers to the effects of the CAP on the supply of beef, sheepmeat and pigmeat. The second volume is entirely statistical, and draws together common time series produced by EUROSTAT, OECD, and the Food and Agriculture Organisation (FAO). It provides data *inter alia* on structures, meat balances, prices, trade, and monetary factors/historical exchange rates. Another useful reference giving details of all regimes (including meat and poultry) is *The Common Agricultural Policy of the European Community* [B.52] by Rosemary Fennell. Brief details of the regimes for beef and veal, sheepmeat, pigmeat, and poultry are given in the following sections.

One major effect of EC membership has been the imposition of agri-monetary arrangements, most particularly Monetary Compensation Amounts (MCA), import levies, and export refunds. Details are published weekly in the *European Weekly Market Survey* [QRL.190].

4.3.1 *Beef and Veal*

The United Kingdom adopted the Common Agricultural Policy for beef and veal in February 1973. Two months later, the fatstock guarantee scheme for cattle was terminated after having been in existence since after the War. In its place, the Community has provided for the support of domestic UK prices by means of intervention buying and various premium payments to producers.

Each year, the Council of Ministers sets a "guide" price for adult cattle. This price is fixed taking account of past experience, future trends in the production and consumption of beef and veal, and the situation in the market for milk and dairy products. If the average wholesale price falls below 90 per cent of this guide price, then the intervention arrangements become operative. The price paid for intervention beef — the "buying-in" price — varies according to the grade of the carcase. Buying-in prices are set by the Commission each month, but may be altered if required by the market situation.

The need to freeze beef to preserve it drastically lowers its value and limits the subsequent uses to which it may be put. When the United Kingdom first joined the EC, its meat industry was much less well developed than in many other Member States, and its factories had neither the facilities for, not the experience of, operating large-scale cutting, freezing and processing activities. Accordingly, the United Kingdom persuaded the EC to adopt a system of direct payments to operate in conjunction with intervention buying. The scheme involves the payment of a "variable premium" on adult cattle, other than cows, of EC origin which are slaughtered in the United Kingdom. This is a Community scheme, but it operates only in the United Kingdom and is not available to other Member States. If intervention also occurs, the "buying-in" price is reduced by the amount of the variable premium being paid at the time.

In addition to the above measures, the Community also provides protection for domestic producers of beef through customs duties and levies. The detailed arrangements are quite complicated, and are actually little used in practice as virtually all imports of beef enter the Community under concessionary terms. Subsidies on exports are also available.

4.3.2 *Sheepmeat*

Goatmeat comes under the same regime as does sheepmeat. However, goat rearing is an extremely small enterprise outside the Mediterranean areas of the Community and UK production may safely be ignored in this Review. The comments below, therefore, relate to the regime for sheepmeat alone.

Prior to 1980, the Community had no common agricultural policy for sheepmeat. Production conditions were so dissimilar in the main producer Member States — France and the United Kingdom — that it was not easy to devise a suitable scheme. The present regime is centred on a seasonally adjusted "basic" price, which is fixed annually for fresh and chilled sheep carcases. The price is set taking account of the situation in the market for sheepmeat for the current year, future trends in the production and consumption of sheepmeat, and the market situation in other livestock sectors. The annual premium paid to producers is determined in part by this basic price but also by the price established in representative markets in the various regions of the Community. The premium takes the form of a deficiency payment payable to sheepmeat producers to offset their income loss from the market.

Intervention in the sheepmeat market can take two forms: private storage aid and purchase by an intervention agency of fresh carcases or half-carcases. In practice, the technical limitations on the freezing of sheepmeat (as with beef and veal) mean that little use is made of this support mechanism. In Great Britain (though not in Northern Ireland) a slaughter premium is paid according to the difference between the representative market price and 85 per cent of the basic price. The payment of a slaughter premium excludes the use of intervention by "buying-in". A levy — the "clawback" — equal to the slaughter premium is paid on some products which are subsequently exported from Great Britain.

Imports are subject to customs duty. Moreover, the Community has voluntary restraint agreements (VRA) with all major suppliers. Suppliers limit their exports to the EC to a given quantity each year in return for a low rate of duty. In return, the Community agrees not to allow subsidised exports over and above traditional export levels. Quotas are allocated unilaterally by the EC to other suppliers with whom VRAs have not been concluded.

4.3.3 *Pigmeat*

The fatstock guarantee scheme for pigs ended in mid-1975 when the United Kingdom adopted the CAP for pigs. The regime for pigmeat is based on the notion of pigs as "processed cereals". Control of the cereal market — see section 8.3 — should thus involve a degree of stability in pig production.

A "basic" price is set each year for carcases or half-carcases of a standard quality. The price is set taking into account the costs of pigmeat production, and the need to avoid the creation of structural surpluses. Differences between this basic price and the weekly market (or "reference") price provide the trigger mechanism for market support. This support may take the form of buying-in, or of aids for private storage, though the former is much less frequently used than the latter. Moreover, the Commission is not obliged to introduce intervention measures and there have historically been long periods during which prices were below the trigger level but no market support was provided.

Imports of pigs and pigmeat from third countries are regulated by means of a "sluice-gate" price for carcases. This price is set quarterly and represents the calculated costs of producing pigs abroad. It acts as a minimum import price, to which is added a levy which includes the additional costs of cereals etc. used to produce pigmeat in the Community plus seven per cent of the average sluice-gate price. If the frontier price falls below the sluice-gate price, a supplementary levy may be charged on the imports equal to the difference between the frontier price and the sluice-gate price (see Figure 4.3).

The regime is administered more flexibly than that for beef, with consequent improvements in both production levels and stability. Pig production is, nevertheless, cyclical in nature and this tends to generate quite marked supply fluctuations in the short-run. Farmers' profit levels thus also tend to fluctuate. It had been hoped that the common market would eradicate the cyclical nature of the industry, but it

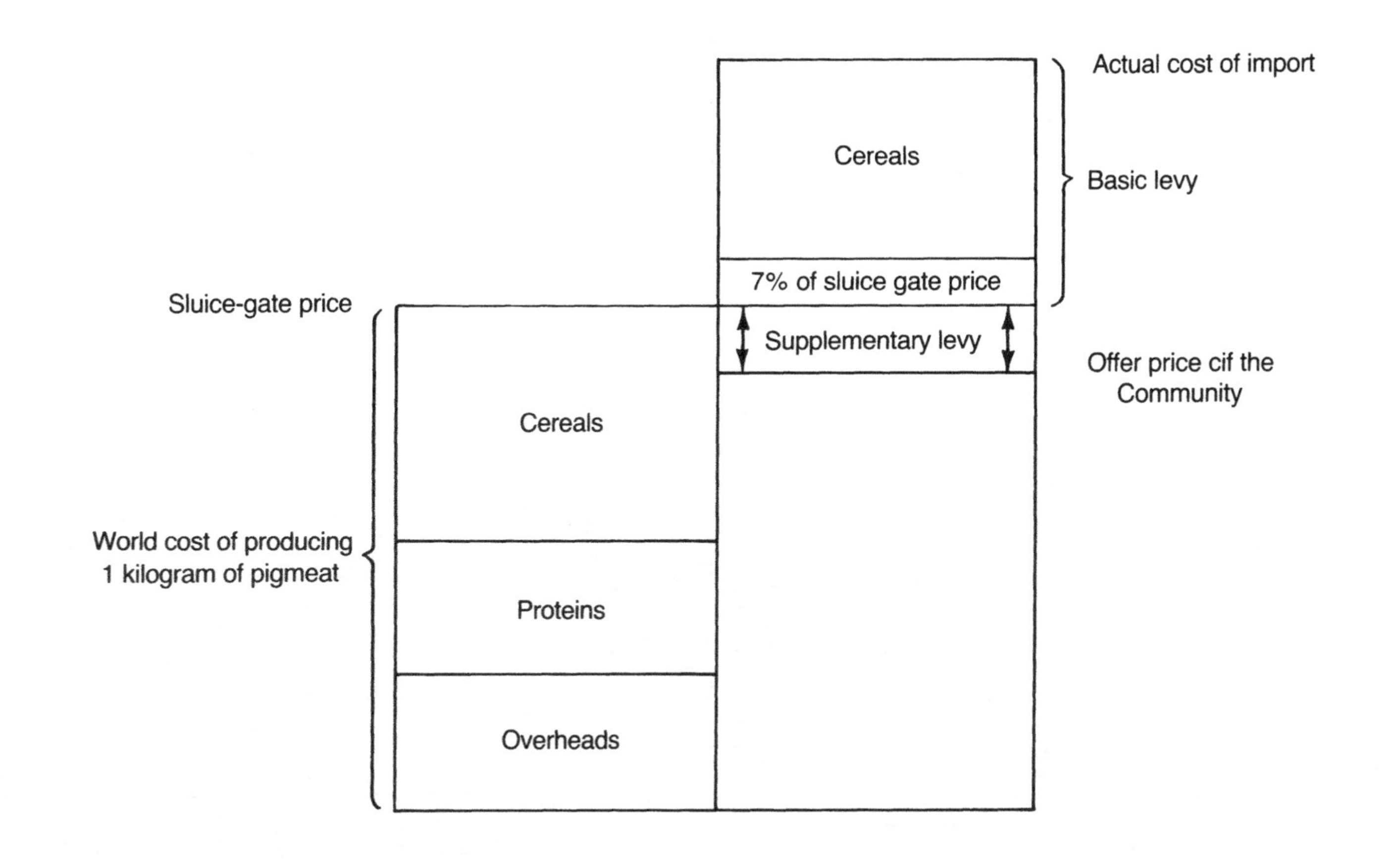

Figure 4.3 Operation of the Import Mechanism for Pigmeat.
Source: Fennell, R. *The Common Agricultural Policy of the European Community: Its Institutions and Administrative Organisation* [B52] P.149.

appears that it has only reduced the peaks and troughs. In general, the regime works fairly well and the market price has tended to remain fairly close to the basic price. For further details, see *The Complete Book of Meat* [B.58].

4.3.4 *Poultry*
There is no overall Community support mechanism for poultry. Prices are allowed to move freely with the industry being expected to take corrective action should prices rise or fall unduly. Community preference is ensured by a system of sluice-gate prices, variable levies and customs duties. The sluice-gate prices are calculated in the same manner, and for the same periods, as for pigmeat. Supplementary levies have to be paid on imports not observing the sluice-gate price as a minimum entry price. Export refunds are also available. The main effects of EC membership have been the introduction of more stringent hygiene legislation and the imposition of regulations regarding maximum water content.

4.4 Output

4.4.1 *Output, Sales and Value Added*

There are at least two measures of output in industry Group 413 that may be of interest. First, there are the numbers of animals slaughtered. Second, there is the subsequent production of meat and meat products. Each will be discussed in turn below. It should be noted that poultry is normally considered separately from cattle, sheep and pigs in the published statistics, reflecting the separate classification in the SIC(1980).

4.4.1.1 Slaughterings
MAFF publish weekly estimates on animals slaughtered in the United Kingdom in *MAFF Statistics: United Kingdom Weekly Slaughtering Statistics* [QRL.337]. Data are provided on the number of head slaughtered of the following animals: steers and heifers; cows and bulls; calves; ewes and rams; other sheep and lambs; sows and boars; other pigs used wholly for bacon; other pigs used partly for bacon; and other pigs — other uses. The estimates are derived from information supplied by representative slaughterhouses and MAFF stress that they are liable to a degree of sampling error. Too much should not be read into changes from one week to another. MAFF also collect monthly and quarterly data on slaughterings from rather wider samples, and these returns are aggregated and published in the *Monthly Digest of Statistics* [QRL.362] and, twice yearly, in the MLC booklet *UK Market Review* [QRL.498]. The figures refer to animals slaughtered in the United Kingdom, including imported fat animals. From July 1954, they are derived from returns recording slaughterings in public and licensed slaughterhouses, including bacon factories. Unrecorded domestic slaughter and slaughter in knackeries are excluded. MLC slaughtering statistics are also contained in the biennial MLC publication *The Slaughtering Industry in Great Britain* [QRL.454]. Annual data are published in the

Annual Abstract of Statistics [QRL.37], and the annual estimated slaughtering of cattle; sheep and lambs; and pigs is recorded in *Output and Utilisation of Farm Produce in the United Kingdom* [QRL.382] up to 1988. *MAFF Statistics: Summary of Returns Made by Bacon Factories in Great Britain* [QRL.336] publishes weekly figures on the slaughter of sows and boars; and other pigs.

The *Annual Abstract of Statistics* [QRL.37] also provides annual data on the number of poultry slaughtered, and *Output and Utilisation of Farm Produce* [QRL.382] published annual data on estimated slaughterings of fowls; duck; geese; and turkeys up to 1988. These data are derived from quarterly census returns on poultry populations, together with monthly returns from hatcheries of placings of day-old chicks and turkey poults for rearing as table birds, and information supplied by packing stations on monthly output of pre-packed and other dressed poultry. Details of the output of pre-packed and other dressed poultry from poultry packing stations in England and Wales are issued quarterly by MAFF in the form of a press notice *MAFF Statistics: Pre-packed and Other Dressed Poultry — Packing Station Throughput of Chickens, Large Roasting Fowls and Boiling Fowls* [QRL.324]. The figures are derived from a voluntary survey with returns being requested from all known packing stations. The statistics measure the throughput of packing stations but do not represent the total output of table poultry in England and Wales. Additional quantities of poultry are marketed direct by producers to wholesale markets and consumers. Moreover, MAFF also publish a press notice *MAFF Statistics: Hatching Eggs and Placings by Hatcheries in the United Kingdom* [QRL.320] which gives monthly data on chicks placed for table poultry production in England and Wales; Scotland; Northern Ireland; and the United Kingdom: and on turkey poults leaving incubation houses in England and Wales; and the United Kingdom.

4.4.1.2 Production of meat

The *Monthly Digest of Statistics* [QRL.362] provides monthly data on the production of various types of meat: beef and veal; mutton and lamb; pork; and offal. From July 1954, the figures represent the estimated production of carcase meat (including trimmings from bacon pigs) and offal from slaughterings, as defined above, and from information available on dressed carcase weights. Pigmeat used for the production of bacon and ham is excluded from the figure for pork above. Data on the production of bacon and ham; and canned meat are published separately. Production figures for bacon and ham relate to the output of curing factories from both home-killed and imported carcases; production by pig clubs or other domestic producers is excluded. Weekly data on bacon and ham production are published in *MAFF Statistics: Summary of Returns Made by Bacon Factories in Great Britain* [QRL.336]. Separate figures are provided for Wiltshire style bacon (dry cured, tank cured sides, and tank cured cuts); Hams and gammons; Rolls (Ayrshire etc.); and other bacon. Figures for production of canned meat relate to all types of canned and bottled meat and meat products. Meat extracts and essences, soups and pastes are, however, excluded. From 1975, the figures are derived from quarterly inquiries undertaken by the Business Statistics Office (BSO).

The data above are also published twice yearly in *UK Market Review* [QRL.498] and the Commonwealth Secretariat publish figures twice yearly on annual meat production of beef and veal; mutton and lamb; pigmeat; and canned meat in *Meat and Dairy Products* [QRL.349]. Quarterly data on home-fed production of beef and veal; mutton and lamb; pork; bacon and ham; and poultry meat are published quarterly in *MAFF Statistics: Quarterly Supplies and Offtake in the United Kingdom — Meat* [QRL.330]. The *Annual Abstract of Statistics* [QRL.37] provides annual data on the production of home-killed meat (including meat subsequently canned) for beef; veal; mutton and lamb; pork; offal; bacon and ham; and poultry meat. Estimates of the production of poultry meat are on the basis of dressed carcase weights (oven ready).

Finally we must consider the various Business Monitors. *Business Monitor PA412* [QRL.106] provides annual data on total sales, gross and net output for all UK establishments classified to the industry Group, together with output figures for each of the four Activity Headings, viz. AH4121, AH4122, AH4123 and AH4126. Prior to 1984, figures were only provided for AH4122 and AH4123.

The quarterly Business Monitors provide rather more detailed information. *Business Monitor PQ4122* [QRL.130] publishes quarterly figures of sales for all UK establishments classified to AH4122, and also quarterly figures of sales of the principal products. Quarterly sales by UK manufacturers in both volume and value terms of the following bacon and meat products (and others) are provided: bacon and ham; meat puddings, pies and sausage rolls; sausage meat; sausages; ready meat meals; slicing meats; savoury pies, pasties and puddings. Sales are defined as deliveries on sale for home and abroad. Forward sales are excluded. Values are net selling values, i.e. value added tax, trade discounts and commissions are excluded. Moreover, quarterly figures in both volume and value terms of production of bacon and meat products by UK manufacturers are provided for preserved meat; meat paste; frozen meat (raw and canned); and meat products.

Business Monitor PQ4123 [QRL.131] publishes quarterly figures of sales of all establishments classified to AH4123, and also quarterly figures for sales of principal products. Quarterly sales by UK manufacturers in both volume and value terms of the following poultry and poultry products (and others) are provided: fresh chicken, turkey and other poultry; frozen chicken, turkey and other poultry; cooked poultry products; ready poultry meals; and poultry paste. Moreover, quarterly figures in volume terms of production of certain poultry products by UK manufacturers are provided for frozen chicken; frozen turkey; and frozen poultry products.

Business Monitor PQ4126 [QRL.132] publishes quarterly figures of sales and output of all establishments classified to AH4126, and also quarterly figures of sales of principal products. Quarterly sales by UK manufacturers in both volume and value terms of the following animal by-products (and others) are provided: animal oils, fats and greases; offals and by-products; bladders, casings and sausage skins; feeding stuffs.

There is no quarterly Business Monitor for AH4121 "Slaughterhouses", though it seems likely that the BSO has the necessary data. It needs to be noted that the foregoing account represents the statistical coverage of the PQ series up to the second quarter of 1989 for now only *Business Monitor PQ4122: Bacon Curing and Meat Products* [QRL.130] remains.

4.4.2 *Index Numbers of Output*
Business Monitor PQ4122 [QRL.130], *Business Monitor PQ4123* [QRL.131] and *Business Monitor PQ4126* [QRL.132] carry indices of output for AH4122, AH4123 and AH4126 respectively. Both annual data, and seasonally adjusted quarterly data are presented, and comparable indices are presented for "Food" and "All manufacturing industries". The figures for the "AH4122", "AH4123" and "AH4126" series do not include stock adjustments to correct mixed sales and production data to true production index numbers, nor do they include bias adjustments. Consequently, they are not comparable with the aggregates published in the *Monthly Digest of Statistics* [QRL.362].

4.5 Current Inputs other than Labour

In the context of Group 412, it is difficult to define what exactly constitutes the inputs, and the output, of the industry. Eggs, fat livestock for slaughter, and imported meat and livestock from abroad, certainly constitute inputs. But slaughtered livestock and poultry which are the output of AH4121 and AH4123.1 are also inputs to other sectors of the industry.

4.5.1 *Domestic Inputs*
In light of the remarks above, reference should be made again — see section 4.4 — to the statutory MAFF surveys of slaughterhouses and bacon factories. The slaughterhouse survey collects data on slaughterhouse throughput of a number of bovine, ovine and porcine categories. Barnett [B.12] reports that the largest slaughterhouses (280 in number) make weekly returns, medium-sized slaughterhouses (220) make monthly returns, and the remainder (360) make quarterly returns. Data on pigs slaughtered are also forthcoming from the bacon factories survey (125 respondents). These statistics, together with those from the slaughterhouses which make weekly returns, are used to estimate the total slaughter in England and Wales. These figures are then combined with estimates from Scotland and Northern Ireland to derive weekly estimates for the United Kingdom, which are then published in *MAFF Statistics: United Kingdom Weekly Slaughtering Statistics* [QRL.337]. *MAFF Statistics: Summary of Returns Made by Bacon Factories in Great Britain* [QRL.336] provides weekly figures on the number of pig carcases used wholly, and partly, for bacon and ham production.

MAFF also publish *Agricultural Market Report Part I: Prices and Quantities Sold of Selected Cereals, Livestock and Other Agricultural Products* [QRL.25] which provides weekly data on the number of fat cattle; sheep; and pigs sold. The Commonwealth Secretariat publish data in *Meat and Dairy Products* [QRL.349] on the number of cattle; and sheep and lambs in the United Kingdom in June and December; and the number of pigs in April, June, August and December. And *UK Market Review* [QRL.498] provides annual data on the number of various types and weights of pigs.

As regards poultry, reference should be made to two MAFF surveys which have already been discussed in section 4.4. The survey on the production and marketing of hatching eggs and chicks is a statutory survey of 106 registered hatcheries in England and Wales. It collects monthly information on the number of eggs put into incubation for fowls (egg strains); fowls (meat strains); geese; ducks; turkeys; and guinea fowl; and the number of chicks of these poultry placed in the same period. Separate figures are given for breeding, multiplying and commercial stock. Hatcheries whose capacities are less than 1000 eggs are exempt from the survey. The results of the survey, together with data for the rest of the United Kingdom, are published each month in *MAFF Statistics: Hatching Eggs and Placings by Hatcheries in the United Kingdom* [QRL.320] and, subsequently (up to 1988), in *Output and Utilisation of Farm Produce* [QRL.382]. Sources of statistics on eggs are discussed further in *Agriculture* [B.144] by G.H. Peters.

The survey of throughput and stocks of dead poultry is a voluntary survey of large poultry packing stations in England and Wales. The survey collects data on slaughterings of chickens (in five weight bands); large roasting fowls; boiling fowls; and turkeys; together with weights of poultry in cold store. The survey is conducted with a view to assessing poultrymeat production in England and Wales and the results are published monthly in *MAFF Statistics: Pre-packed and Other Dressed Poultry — Packing Station Throughput of Chickens, Large Roasting Fowls and Boiling Fowls* [QRL.324]. The data were subsequently reproduced in *Output and Utilisation of Farm Produce* [QRL.428] up to 1988.

The most comprehensive analysis of inputs is provided by the Purchases Inquiry — see section 2.1.1.4. The results of the 1984 Inquiry were published in 1987 as *Business Monitor PO1008: Purchases Inquiry* [QRL.116], and contained considerable detail for both AH4122 and AH4123. Unfortunately, both AH4121 and AH4126 were among the few Activity Headings excluded from the 1984 Inquiry. The inquiry collects information about the commodity detail of industry's purchases of materials and fuel. The level of detail is such that the interdependencies of many food industries may be highlighted. Thus, for example, the amount of "fresh vegetables and fruit" purchased by AH4122 may be identified. The pattern of commodity purchases returned in the Purchases Inquiry are scaled up to agree with the annual levels in the Census of Production. Information is also given on the effective percentage response rate for each industry.

The Purchases Inquiry is quinquennial; the results of the 1989 Inquiry are to be published in 1992. The results of the 1979 Inquiry were published in *Business Monitor PA1002.1: 1979 Census of Production and Purchases Inquiry* [QRL.94]. Results for the 1974 Inquiry were in a different form, being analyses of returns received without grossing. The statistics for each industry were published in the 1974/75 PA Monitor for that industry.

Feedstuffs are not, strictly speaking, an input to industry Group 412. Nevertheless, the following reports do provide some useful information on the industry and so deserve mention: *Prices, Costs and Margins in the Production and Distribution of Compound Feeding Stuff for Cattle, Pigs and Poultry* [B.426], and *Special Report from the Agriculture Committee: The Effect of Feedstuff Prices on the UK Pig and Poultry Industries* [B.378].

4.5.2 *Input-output Analysis*

Details of the input-output tables for the United Kingdom have been provided in section 2.5.2. Here we simply present brief comments on the level of detail accorded to the meat industry. "Slaughtering and meat processing" (AH4121, AH4122, AH4123 and AH4126) was identified amongst the industry/commodity groups in the *Input-output Tables for the United Kingdom 1984* [QRL.284]. The same group was also identified in the 1979 tables published in *Business Monitor PA1004* [QRL.101]. The 1974 tables were, however, based on SIC(1968) and the corresponding group was thus "Meat and fish products" (MLH214). Information on coverage in previous input-output tables may be found in the references cited in section 2.5.2.

4.6 Labour

Detailed results of the September 1984 Census of Employment for Great Britain were published in the January 1987 edition of the *Employment Gazette* [QRL.186]. The number of male employees (full-time and part-time) and female employees (full-time and part-time) in employment in Group 412, AH4121, AH4122, AH4123 and AH4126 were separately enumerated. An analysis of total employees in employment by region was also provided. The September 1987 issue of the *Employment Gazette* [QRL.186] presented comparable results for the United Kingdom, incorporating figures from the 1984 Census of Employment for Northern Ireland provided by the Department of Economic Development. No regional analysis was provided, though data for the province could be derived by subtraction of the GB totals from those for the United Kingdom. Monthly figures of employees (male and female) in employment are only provided for "meat and meat products, organic oils and fats" (Groups 411 and 412 combined) in the *Employment Gazette* [QRL.186].

The *New Earnings Survey* [QRL.375] collects statistics on earnings and hours of full-time employees on adult rates in Great Britain. The level of industrial detail varies in the different analyses, but Group 412 is separately identified in some of the tables published in "Part C: Analyses by Industry". Analyses in a form not published may, however, be supplied on request by the Department of Employment provided they are considered reliable enough for release.

Business Monitor PA412 [QRL.106] provides annual data on total employment (including working proprietors) and labour costs for the industry Group as a whole. Employment is also analysed by the standard regions of England, plus Wales, Scotland and Northern Ireland; and by size of establishments classified to the industry. *Business Monitor PQ4122* [QRL.130] provides quarterly figures on employment for all establishments classified to AH4122. Comparable data are unfortunately not published in *Business Monitor PQ4123* [QRL.131] and *Business Monitor PQ4126* [QRL.132].

4.7 Capital

4.7.1 *Capital Expenditure*

Business Monitor PA412 [QRL.106] provides a breakdown of gross annual capital expenditure by type of asset — land and buildings, plant and machinery, and vehicles. Annual data on net capital expenditure is also provided for the Group as a whole, analysed by the standard regions of England, plus Wales, Scotland and Northern Ireland, and also analysed by size of establishments classified to the industry. Moreover, detail is provided of capital expenditure for all establishments classified to each Activity Heading within the industry.

4.7.2 *Suppliers of Machinery*

An alternative perspective on the capital input to Group 412 is provided by the data published in *Business Monitor PQ3244: Food, Drink and Tobacco Processing Machinery; Packaging and Bottling Machinery* [QRL.127]. Statistics are provided therein on quarterly sales of "slaughterhouse and meat processing machinery (including parts)". Moreover, data are presented on imports of "machinery for the preparation of meat". As a result of the *Review of DTI Statistics* [B.367] — see sections 13.2 and 13.3 — this sales inquiry was not retained within the quarterly system of inquiries after the second quarter of 1989. Statistical data thereafter will be published less frequently and in less product detail.

4.7.3 *Company Reports*

The net book value of tangible fixed assets owned by each company in the industry (see section 4.2 for some of the larger companies), and their authorised future expenditure, will be detailed in their respective Annual Reports.

4.8 International Transactions

4.8.1 *HM Customs and Excise Records*

The products of industry Group 412 are classified to a number of different Divisions in the Standard International Trade Classification (Revision 3), viz: "Meat and meat products" (Division 01); "Animal oils and fats" (Division 41); and "Animal and vegetable oils and fats, processed, and waxes of animal or vegetable origin; inedible mixtures or preparations of animal or vegetable fats and oils not elsewhere specified" (Division 43). In addition, imports of fat livestock for slaughter will be classified to "Live animals chiefly for food" (Division 00). The Divisions are further broken down in *Business Monitor MM20: Overseas Trade Statistics of the United Kingdom* [QRL.85], and data provided for a number of detailed headings. These headings are too numerous to list in full, and the following is but a selection of the main headings under Division 01:

011. Meat of bovine animals, fresh, chilled or frozen
012. Other meat and edible meat offal, fresh, chilled or frozen (excluding meat and meat offal unfit for human consumption)
012.1 Meat of sheep or goats, fresh, chilled or frozen
012.2 Meat of swine, fresh, chilled or frozen
012.3 Meat and edible offal of the poultry of heading 001.40, fresh, chilled or frozen

012.4 Meat of horses, asses, mules or hinnies, fresh, chilled or frozen
012.5 Edible offal of bovine animals, swine, sheep, goats, horses, asses, mules or hinnies, fresh, chilled or frozen
012.9 Meat and edible meat offal, fresh, chilled or frozen, not elsewhere specified
016. Meat and edible meat offal, salted, in brine, dried or smoked; edible flours and meals of meat or meat offal
016.1 Bacon, ham and other dried, salted or smoked meat of swine
016.8 Meat and edible meat offal, other than meat of swine, salted, in brine, dried or smoked; edible flours and meals of meat or meat offal
017. Meat and edible meat offal, prepared or preserved

Monthly data in *Business Monitor MM20* [QRL.85] are provided in both volume and value terms for a range of importing and exporting countries. Further details of the extensive statistical coverage are presented in section 2.8.2.1. The statistics have been compiled from the declarations which are made to HM Customs and Excise, and which are subject to confirmation by Customs officials. The figures are usually published about one month after the month to which they relate.

It should be noted that many of the products classified to the above Divisions in SITC(R3) are not products of industry Group 412. Details of the HM Customs and Excise tariff/trade code numbers corresponding to AH4122, AH4123, and AH4126 may be found in *Business Monitor PQ4122* [QRL.130], *Business Monitor PQ4123* [QRL.131], and *Business Monitor PQ4126* [QRL.132] respectively. *Business Monitor PQ4122* [QRL.130] also provides quarterly import and export data for the following groups of products: bacon, ham and other dried, salted or smoked pigmeat; sausages; other meat and edible offals (excluding poultry), dried, salted or smoked; other prepared or preserved meat or meat offal; meat and fish extracts, meat juices; edible products of animal origin not elsewhere specified or included. Similarly, *Business Monitor PQ4123* [QRL.131] provided quarterly import and export data for the following groups: poultry killed or dressed (including poultry cuts) and edible offals (except liver), fresh, chilled or frozen; poultry liver, fresh, chilled, frozen, salted or in brine; other prepared or preserved offal or meat of poultry. And *Business Monitor PQ4126* [QRL.132] provided quarterly import and export data on: bladders, casings and sausage skins that have been subjected to processing or preserving treatment; lard and other pig-fat and poultry fat, rendered or solvent extracted; other animal oils, fats and greases; bones and horn-cores, unworked, defatted, simply prepared (but not cut to shape), treated with acid or degeletanised, powder and waste of these products; miscellaneous animal by-products (e.g. feathers, unworked bristles etc.).

4.8.2 *Industry Analyses of Trade*

In contrast to these analyses by type of product, *Business Monitor MQ10: Overseas Trade Analysed in Terms of Industries* [QRL.90] provides quarterly data on exports and imports for each Activity Heading and for the industry Group as a whole. These figures are also used in *Business Monitor MQ12: Import Penetration and Export Sales Ratios for Manufacturing Industries* [QRL.91] to provide export/sales, and import penetration ratios again for each Activity Heading (except AH4121) and for industry Group 412 up to the second quarter of 1989 — see section 2.8.2.3 for details of the coverage.

4.8.3 *Industry Sources*

The Meat and Livestock Commission publish both quarterly and annual data collated directly from Customs Returns in *UK Market Review* [QRL.498] on exports of beef and veal; mutton and lamb; pork; bacon and ham; edible offal of beef, pork and lamb; prepared and preserved meat or offal; and poultry (fowls, ducks, turkeys and other) with some analysis by country of destination. Similarly, data on imports of beef and veal; mutton and lamb; pork; bacon and ham; edible offal; prepared and preserved meat or offal; and poultrymeat are presented with some analysis of country of supply. Moreover, the same publication also gives quarterly and annual data on imports of the following livestock: cattle; sheep; and pigs, as does the Commonwealth Secretariat publication, *Meat and Dairy Products* [QRL.349]. *Meat and Dairy Products* [QRL.349] also provides annual figures on exports and imports to and from various countries of beef; veal; mutton; lamb; bacon and ham; pork; poultrymeat; offal; pigmeat; other offal; and meat preparations (canned beef, hams, poultrymeat, poultry liver, sausage, meat extracts).

Weekly data on imported fresh, and frozen, pigmeat used in bacon and ham production are published weekly in *MAFF Statistics: Summary of Returns Made by Bacon Factories in Great Britain* [QRL.336]. *MAFF Statistics: Prospective Arrival Dates of Vessels Carrying Carcase Meat and Offal from Australia, New Zealand and South America* [QRL.329] provides, as its name implies, arrival dates together with the vessel's name, where it is from, the port of arrival and how much of the cargo is frozen, and how much is chilled.

4.9 Stocks

MAFF Statistics: Stocks of Selected Dairy Products, Meat and Meat Products, Poultry, Game, Soft Fruit and Vegetables in Public Cold Stores [QRL.335] provides end-month figures of stocks of beef and veal; lamb and mutton; pork; offal; prepared meat products; poultry and game; and rabbits held in public cold stores in the United Kingdom. No information is available on stocks of these commodities held in cold stores reserved for private concerns. These range from small fishmongers', poulterers' and butchers' stores to larger ones belonging to distributors, manufacturers etc. and the stocks held in these may be considerable.

The *Monthly Digest of Statistics* [QRL.362] also provides monthly data on imported and home produced stocks of beef and veal; mutton and lamb; pork; and offal in cold storage. Prior to July 1983, the figures represented the stocks of imported meat only held in public cold stores surveyed by MAFF. In July 1983 the coverage of the survey was extended and, in addition to an increase in the number of respondents, it now applies to stocks of meat from both imported and home-produced sources. As a result, there is a discontinuity in stock levels recorded from July 1983. Prior to January 1984, meat stored below -10 degC (14 degF) was excluded. Stocks held in cold stores reserved for private concerns or in undischarged cargoes are not included. Similar data are published annually for the end of December only in the *Annual Abstract of Statistics* [QRL.37]. *MAFF Statistics: Quarterly Supplies and Offtake in the United Kingdom — Meat* [QRL.330] gives quarterly figures for stocks of beef and veal; mutton and lamb; pork; bacon and ham; and poultrymeat in cold store.

The *Intervention Board for Agricultural Produce: Annual Report* [QRL.293] publishes data on monthly intervention purchases and sales of beef, and on aided private storage stocks of beef and pigmeat in the United Kingdom.

Business Monitor PA412 [QRL.106] gives financial data on stocks and work-in-progress for all UK establishments classified to the industry Group at end December, and also analysis of these data by the size of establishment. Moreover, these data on stocks and work-in-progress are also provided for each of the four Activity Headings.

4.10 Consumption

4.10.1 *The National Food Survey*

The National Food Survey collects consumption data on a wide variety of meats and meat products manufactured by industry Group 412, viz:

Food code number	Description
25	Beef: joints (including sides) on the bone
26	Beef: joints (boned)
27	Beef steak (less expensive)
28	Beef steak (more expensive)
29	Beef, minced
30	All other beef and veal
31	Total beef and veal (codes 25–30)
32	Mutton
33	Lamb joints (including sides)
34	Lamb chops (including cutlets and fillets)
35	All other lamb
36	Total mutton and lamb (codes 32–35)
37	Pork joints (including sides)
38	Pork chops
39	Pork fillets and steaks
40	All other pork
41	Total pork (codes 37–40)
42	Ox liver
43	Lambs liver
44	Pigs liver
45	Other liver

46	Total liver (codes 42–45)
51	Offals, other than liver
52	Bacon and ham, uncooked, joints (including sides and steaks cut from the joint)
53	Bacon and ham, uncooked, rashers, vacuum-packed
54	Bacon and ham, uncooked, rashers, not vacuum packed
55	Total bacon and ham, uncooked (codes 52–54)
58	Bacon and ham, cooked, including canned
59	Cooked poultry, not purchased in cans
62	Corned meat
66	Other cooked meat, not purchased in cans
71	Other canned meat and canned meat products
73	Broiler chicken, uncooked, including frozen
74	Chicken, uncooked, other than broiler
75	Turkey, uncooked
76	All uncooked poultry other than chicken or turkey
77	Total uncooked poultry, including frozen (codes 74–76)
78	Rabbit and other meat
79	Sausages, uncooked, pork
80	Sausages, uncooked, beef
81	Meat pies, ready-to-eat
82	Sausage rolls, ready-to-eat
83	Total meat pies, and sausage rolls, ready-to-eat (codes 81–82)
86	Frozen burgers
87	Other frozen convenience foods
88	Total frozen convenience meats or frozen convenience meat products (codes 86–87)
89	Delicatessen-type sausages
90	Meat pastes and spreads
91	Meat pies, pasties and puddings
92	Ready meals
93	Other meat products not classified elsewhere
94	Total other meat products (codes 89–93)

Detailed statistics are published on these various foods in the *National Food Survey: Compendium of Results* [QRL.373]. Annual average figures of both per capita weekly consumption and expenditure are provided for the following main food groups: beef and veal (31); mutton and lamb (36); pork (41); total carcase meat (31–41); bacon and ham, uncooked (55); poultry, uncooked (73, 77); other meat and meat products (46–51, 58–71, 78–80, 83, 88, 94); and total meat (31–94). Moreover, these data are analysed by region and type of area; by income group; by household composition; by household composition and income group; by age of housewife; by housing tenure; and by ownership of deep freezer. Indices of expenditure, and of the real value of purchases, are presented for the latest six years. Quarterly and annual national average household expenditure on the following food items are calculated: beef and veal; mutton and lamb; pork; total carcase meat; liver; offals, other than liver; bacon and ham, uncooked; bacon and ham, cooked, including canned; cooked poultry, not purchased in cans; corned meat; other cooked meat, not purchased in cans; other canned meat and canned meat products; broiler chicken, uncooked, including frozen; other poultry, uncooked, including frozen; rabbit and other meat; sausages, uncooked, pork; sausages, uncooked, beef; meat pies and sausage rolls, ready-to-eat; frozen convenience foods or frozen convenience meat products; other meat products; total meat and meat products. Supplementary data are also provided on many other individual food items (e.g. frozen burgers).

The main report on the Survey, *Household Food Consumption and Expenditure* [QRL.267], carries a more limited range of statistical data, as has been discussed in section 2.10.1.2. Commentary is, however, provided with many of the main statistical tables, and data for previous years are often presented for comparison. Income elasticities of expenditure are calculated for beef and veal; mutton and lamb; and pork. Some of the data from the NFS are reproduced in *UK Market Review* [QRL.498] and in *Meat Demand Trends* [QRL.351]. The latter also includes indices of household expenditure on a selection of meat and meat products based on AGB/TCA consumer panel data supplied to the Meat Promotion Executive of the Meat and Livestock Commission.

4.10.2 *The Family Expenditure Survey*

The *Family Expenditure Survey* [QRL.204] provides analyses of the expenditure of various types of household on beef and veal; mutton and lamb; pork; bacon and ham (uncooked); cooked ham (including canned); and other poultry and undefined meat, at different levels of household income, and by sex and age. It also publishes average figures for weekly expenditure analysed by region.

4.10.3 *The National Accounts*

The *United Kingdom National Accounts* [QRL.506] carries annual data, in both current and constant prices, of household expenditure on "meat and bacon". The data are reproduced in the *Annual Abstract of Statistics* [QRL.37].

4.11 Supplies and Disposals

A historical picture may be found in the article by W.D. Stedman Jones [B.167] which includes sections devoted to statistics on "meat" and "bacon and ham". More recently, MAFF compile quarterly supply balance sheets for carcase meat which are published in *MAFF Statistics: Quarterly Supplies and Offtake in the United Kingdom — Meat* [QRL.330]. Information is provided on home production, overseas trade, stocks and offtake and separate tables are presented for beef and veal; mutton and lamb; pork; bacon and ham; poultrymeat; and all carcase meat, bacon, ham, and poultrymeat together. The figures do not, however, include meat offals or trade in preserved or manufactured meat products. Offtake is defined as home-fed production and imports less exports and stock adjustment.

The *Monthly Digest of Statistics* [QRL.362] provides monthly figures on disposals of bacon and ham. Disposals include supplies of home-produced or imported bacon and ham moving into consumption and also such supplies as are used for canning in the United Kingdom. They do not include any imported canned bacon and ham. The *Annual Abstract of Statistics* [QRL.37] publishes annual figures of disposals not only of bacon and ham but also of poultrymeat; and of fresh and frozen beef and veal; mutton and lamb; pork; and offal.

MAFF also prepare supply balance sheets for meat, and for fats and oils of land animals, which are sent to the Statistical Office of the European Communities (EUROSTAT). The commodities covered in the former balance sheet are beef; veal; pork; lamb and mutton; poultry; other meat; and offal. The production figures are taken from MAFF slaughterhouse and poultry throughput surveys — see sections 4.4 and 4.5 for details. National coefficients are used to convert trade in meat products back to carcase equivalent, but these coefficients generally match those used by EUROSTAT. The commodities covered in the latter balance sheet are the fats derived from beef; pork; lamb; and poultry. The production figures are estimated from the meat balance sheets using national coefficients for the fat content of carcases. The supply balance sheet data are stored in the CRONOS databank — see section 2.11 — and are subsequently published in the quarterly EUROSTAT publication, *Animal Production* [QRL.36].

4.12 Prices

4.12.1 *Meat and Live Animal Prices*

There is a wealth of statistical sources which provide detailed price information on the meat and poultry industries both for live, and for dead, animals. The most up-to-date information is published weekly in the MLC publication *UK Weekly Market Survey* [QRL.499], the *Meat Trades Journal* [QRL.353] and in *Agricultural Market Report Part I* [QRL.25].

The *Meat Trades Journal* [QRL.353] is published by Northwood Publications and is the principal trade journal for the fresh meat trade. To attempt a full description of all the listed price data would take too much space, so only a selection of the main tables are mentioned below:

- Weekly average (and range of) prices of various cuts of beef; lamb; pigs; sausages; New Zealand lamb for the following areas: England and Wales; London; Birmingham; Liverpool; Manchester; Sheffield; South-west Scotland; Glasgow. The source for these figures is the MLC's sample of retail outlets.
- Daily average prices of prime cattle; prime sheep; prime ewes at selected markets in the MLC sample of markets.
- Daily wholesale Smithfield prices for beef; veal; lamb; and pork.
- Average weekly Smithfield poultry prices for the following: chickens; ducklings; turkeys; geese; rabbits; hares; grouse; partridges; and pheasants.
- Weekly retail poultry prices.
- Weekly catering wholesale prices.
- Wholesale boxed beef prices.
- Wholesale bacon prices.
- Cattle cash futures.

- Bacon pig prices.
- Deadweight prices of steers; heifers; and young bulls.
- Sheep premium.
- Average prices for different categories of prime cattle at the five representative markets in Ireland.
- Export clawback.
- Beef premium.

The coverage is comprehensive. All of the information on the cattle, sheep and pig markets is provided by the Meat and Livestock Commission. It should be noted that Smithfield market has taken on the character of a residual market in recent years as the wholesaling (primary and secondary) function is being moved back to the slaughtering sector. In response to this, the MLC now publish a wholesale price report in their *UK Weekly Market Survey* [QRL.499], together with all the information (and more) listed above. A monthly supplement to the *UK Weekly Market Survey* [QRL.499] contains offal prices (ex-abattoir) for the three major species.

The *UK Market Review* [QRL.498], published twice yearly, contains the following monthly price information:

- cattle prices and premium payments,
- deadweight cattle prices,
- store cattle prices,
- rearing calf prices,
- sheep prices and variable premium payments,
- store sheep prices,
- deadweight pig prices in Great Britain,
- liveweight pig prices,
- United Kingdom average all pigs price,
- contract bacon pig (Harris Crown) prices,
- Walls' contract heavy hog prices,
- store pig prices,
- regional group weaner prices,
- wholesale meat and bacon prices,
- offal and by-product prices,
- retail prices of beef, lamb and pork (various cuts),
- retail prices of bacon and ham and chicken,
- retail price indices for all meat and bacon,
- feed prices.

The *Agricultural Market Report Part I* [QRL.25] is rather more limited in its scope. Average weekly prices are provided for fat cattle; fat sheep; and fat pigs. The prices are calculated from reports received by the MLC from representative markets in England and Wales. The averages are based on prices in the auction ring and do not include any premium payments. Prices of the following types of poultry are also provided for selected wholesale markets: chickens, hens, ducks, geese, and turkeys — plucked but uneviscerated; chickens, ducks, and turkeys — oven ready; rabbits. All of the above price information is also available on a daily basis on a videotex system operated by Prestel and ICI Agvisor (the information is provided by the MLC). Weekly sample auction prices in Northern Ireland are published by the Livestock Marketing Commission for Northern Ireland in *The Bulletin* [QRL.71].

4.12.2 *Retail Prices*

4.12.2.1 Recorded prices

The *Employment Gazette* [QRL.186] gives average retail prices on one day a month for the following items: home-killed beef (various cuts); home-killed lamb (various cuts); imported lamb (various cuts); home-killed pork (various cuts); bacon (various types); ham (not shoulder); pork and beef sausages; pork luncheon meat; corned beef; frozen, oven-ready roasting chicken; fresh or chilled oven-ready roasting chicken. The figures are derived from prices collected for the purposes of the General Index of Retail Prices in more than 180 areas of the United Kingdom. An indication of variations in price is given by showing the ranges within which at least four-fifths of the recorded prices fell. The Livestock Marketing Commission for Northern Ireland provides a monthly publication, *Meat Retailer* [QRL.352], which contains representative retail prices for beef, lamb, pork and chicken in the province.

Quarterly and annual national average prices are given in the *Compendium of Results* [QRL.373] for the following: beef and veal; mutton and lamb; pork; liver; offals, other than liver; bacon and ham, uncooked; bacon and ham, cooked, including canned; cooked poultry, not purchased in cans; corned meat; other cooked meat, not purchased in cans; other canned meat and canned meat products; broiler chicken, uncooked, including frozen; other poultry, uncooked, including frozen; rabbit and other meat; sausages, uncooked, pork; sausages, uncooked, beef; meat pies and sausage rolls, ready-to-eat; frozen convenience meats or frozen convenience meat products; other meat products. Greater detail on many of these products is also provided in a supplementary table.

4.12.2.2 Recommended prices

The prices quoted in *Shaws Guide to Fair Retail Prices* [QRL.453] are for the guidance of consumers and retailers. The amount of brand detail is considerable, and only broad product categories will be listed here for the sake of brevity. Recommended retail prices are published on the first day of every month for the following: bacon; meat pies and sausages; meat and vegetable extracts and stock cubes; meats (canned); meats (prepacked sliced). When manufacturers do not recommend fair selling prices, they are suggested by the editor with help from the manufacturers. Suggested prices show a fair profit on minimum quantities supplied on trade terms.

The Grocer [QRL.252] publishes average weekly wholesale prices for the following: beef (bone in); beef boneless; steaks; pork chops; lamb chops; lamb cutlets (French trimmed); pork; bacon; veal; lamb; offal; poultry and game. These prices apply nationally for caterers purchasing 500 meals or more a day, and are also a guide to grocery buyers. Weekly market prices, subject to regional variation and discounting, are also presented for numerous cuts of bacon. In addition, on the first Saturday in each month, *The Grocer Price List* [QRL.253] is published. Recommended prices are quoted for bacon; meat and vegetable extracts; meats (bottled); meats (canned); meats (open pack); pastes, fish and meat; patés; pies (meat); and sausages. Prices are supplied by manufacturers, importers or sole agents, and are for the smallest quantity they supply. Again the amount of brand detail is considerable.

4.12.3 *The Retail Prices Index*

The *Employment Gazette* [QRL.186] carries monthly retail price indices for beef; lamb; home-killed lamb; pork; bacon; poultry; and other meat. Percentage changes are indicated over the previous year. The structure of the published components was recast with effect from February 1987. Previously separate indices had been available for beef; lamb; pork; bacon; ham (cooked); and other meat and meat products. The relationship between the old and the new index structure was shown in the September 1986 issue of the *Employment Gazette* [QRL.186].

The *Monthly Digest of Statistics* [QRL.362] is an alternative source. *Retail Prices: Indices 1914–1986* [QRL.434] contains group and sub-group indices and weights back to 1974, group indices back to 1956, and all items back to 1947. Quarterly indices, again derived from Department of Employment data, are presented for "bacon" and "other meat" in *Business Monitor PQ4122* [QRL.130], and for "poultry" in *Business Monitor PQ4123* [QRL.131].

4.12.4 *Price Index Numbers in the National Food Survey*

The National Food Survey is another useful source of consumer price information. The *Compendium of Results* [QRL.373] presents annual price indices for the following main food groups: beef and veal (31); mutton and lamb (36); pork (41); carcase meat (31–41); bacon and ham, uncooked (55); poultry, uncooked (73, 77); other meat and meat products (41, 51, 58–71, 78–88, 94); and all meat (31–94).

4.12.5 *Producer Price Index Numbers*

The series of producer price indices are considered in general terms in section 2.12.5. Details of the price indices for the inputs and outputs of the slaughtering of animals and production of meat and by-products sectors are given below.

4.12.5.1 Producer price index numbers: input prices

Business Monitor MM22: Producer Price Indices carries the producer price index numbers of materials and fuels purchased for AH4122 and AH4123, giving both monthly and annual data. The monthly data are given for the current and previous years, with the figures for the latest two months provisional. An annual average for the previous year is also presented. *Business Monitor M22* was published for the first time in October 1989 and continued the coverage in *British Business* [QRL.66].

Business Monitor PQ4122 [QRL.130] reproduces quarterly and annual MAFF data on producer price indices for the following purchased materials: imported bacon; imported meat; pigs for bacon factories. Moreover, it also provides quarterly price indices for the following produced goods, again from MAFF data: beef; lamb; pork; bacon and ham; meat puddings and pies; sausages; and other processed meats. *Business Monitor PQ4123* [QRL.131] published a quarterly producer price index of poultrymeat products. No input price indices were published in *Business Monitor PQ4126* [QRL.132]. [QRL.131] and QRL.132] ceased coverage after the second quarter of 1989.

The monthly publication *MAFF Statistics: Agricultural Price Indices* [QRL.315] presents indices of producer prices of agricultural products, and indices of purchase prices of the means of agricultural production, both for the United Kingdom. The indices represent the UK's contribution to the aggregate indices compiled for the Community by EUROSTAT. Both monthly and annual indices of producer prices are provided for the following: clean cattle; fat cows; pigs (excluding sows); sows; sheep over one year old; lambs; sheep under one year old; ewes; chickens; other poultry; and, in aggregate, animals (for slaughter and export). Both monthly and annual indices of purchase prices are provided for the following: compound feed for calves; compound feed for cattle; compound feed for pigs; compound feed for poultry; and other compound feedingstuffs — sheep.

4.12.5.2 Producer price index numbers: output prices

Business Monitor MM22 contains the producer price index numbers of products manufactured in the United Kingdom (home sales) for AH4122 and AH4123. The monthly data are provided for the current and previous year, with the figures for the latest two months provisional. An annual average for the previous year is also presented. *Business Monitor MM22* was published for the first time in October 1989 and continued the coverage in *British Business* [QRL.66]. The *Annual Abstract of Statistics* [QRL.37] gives the annual averages for AH4122 and AH4123 for a six-year run for products manufactured in the United Kingdom (home sales).

Business Monitor PQ4122 [QRL.130] provides quarterly and annual price indices for the following produced goods from MAFF data; beef, lamb, pork, bacon and ham; meat pudding and pies; sausages and other processed meats. The data are compared with the figures for food manufacturing industries (home sales) and all manufactured products (home sales) derived from the Department of Trade and Industry sources. *Business Monitor PQ4123* [QRL.131] published up to the second quarter of 1989 a quarterly and annual producer price index for poultrymeat products, drawing the comparisons with food manufacturing industries (home sales) and all manufactured products (home sales). *Business Monitor PQ4126* [QRL.132] published up to the second quarter of 1989 a quarterly and annual producer price index for animal by-products in the summary table.

4.12.6 *Intervention Prices*

The *Report of the Intervention Board* [QRL.293] gives UK intervention prices for beef, and weekly data on the UK beef variable premium.

4.13 Financial Information

The various Price Commission reports detailed in section 4.16 all provide useful statistical information on the financial well-being of the industry, but they are all somewhat dated. *Prices and Margins in Meat Distribution* [B.431] and *Prices and Margins in Poultry Distribution* [B.432] were both published in 1975. *Prices, Costs and Margins in the Importation and Distribution of Bacon* [B.425] was published in 1978. More recently, the MLC published a newsletter on *Operating Costs and Margins in the Slaughtering Industry* [B.348] in 1985. This contained data on costs, margins, profits and capital employed together with some analysis of financial ratios. Useful information on yields, costs and margins is published periodically in the MLC pamphlet *Meat and Marketing Technical Notes* [QRL.350].

Business Monitor PA412 [QRL.106] publishes annual data on output, wages and salaries, the purchase of materials and the cost of non-industrial services, and gross value added for all UK establishments classified to the industry. Annual data on output and costs, together with various operating ratios, for the four constituent Activity Headings — AH4121, AH4122, AH4123 and AH4126 — are also provided. Moreover, there are analyses of labour costs by size of establishment; and of net output and gross value added at factor cost by region.

Financial information on the various companies operating in the industry is available in their Annual Reports, and collated and analysed in the following reviews. The ICC Information Group publish annual Business Ratio reports on *Meat Processors* [QRL.559], *Poultry Processors* [QRL.562], and also on *Meat Wholesalers* [QRL.560]. There is also the Key Note report on *Meat & Meat Products* [QRL.593].

4.14 Advertising and Market Research

4.14.1 *Advertising*

The *Tri-Media Digest of Brands and Advertisers* [QRL.493] is the standard reference for information on the advertising expenditure of competing firms and brands. Data are provided therein — see section 2.14.1.1 for details — on the following product groups relevant to industry Group 412: canned meat and poultry (F18); fresh and fresh-frozen meat and poultry (F52); meat and fish pastes (F78); meat pies, sausages, bacon (F78); and meat and vegetable extracts (F80). An alternative source is *The Media Register* [QRL.354], which gives details of monthly press and television advertising expenditure for bacon (FOO 03); canned meat and poultry (FOO 11); fresh and frozen meats (FOO 35); fresh and frozen poultry (FOO 36); meat pies (FOO 56); sausages (FOO 67); spreads, patés and slicing meats (FOO 72).

4.14.2 *Market Research*

The MLC issue a publication three times a year called *Meat Demand Trends* [QRL.351]. This contains extensive analysis of the market for meat in the United Kingdom and also includes the following statistical tables:

- consumers' expenditure on food, and meat and bacon, in the United Kingdom (at current prices; and at constant prices, seasonally adjusted),
- estimated consumers' expenditure on meat and other protein foods at current prices,
- indices of household expenditure on meat in Great Britain,
- indices of household expenditure on meat products in Great Britain,
- sales of bacon and meat products by UK manufacturers,
- meat expenditure indicators,
- estimated supplies of meat in the United Kingdom,
- indices of household meat purchases by quantity in Great Britain,

- livestock prices,
- indices of manufacturers' wholesale prices of materials purchased and bacon, meat and fish products sold,
- indices of retail prices of meat, other food items and the General Index of Retail Prices,
- indices of deflated retail prices for meat and other food items,
- retail prices of meat cuts in England and Wales.

Much of the historical data is derived from sources already cited, hence detailed descriptions of the statistics quoted are not provided here.

The MLC publish forecasts of UK slaughterings and meat production for the coming year in *UK Market Review* [QRL.498]. They also provide forecasts of meat retailers' likely costs and returns for the coming year in *Trading Outlook for Meat Retailers* [QRL.492]. Three other publications which are of interest are *Market Outlook — Cattle* [QRL.340], *Market Outlook — Pigs* [QRL.341] and *Market Outlook — Sheep* [QRL.342].

The British Chicken Information Service publish an annual *Review of the British Retail Chicken Market* [QRL.439]. This provides data on sales of chicken compared to red meat, and the share of chicken in the total meat market. It also looks at price trends, provides a comparison of fresh and frozen chicken sales, and, from 1986, details developments in the processed chicken market. Finally, an analysis is provided of retail outlets for chicken.

Two MAFF publications which provide statistical information on the meat market are: *Report of the Study Group on the Development of Value-added Products from Pigmeat* [B.364] and *Marketing Studies Report on Outlets for Lamb in Processing and Catering* [B.326].

Finally we mention the occasional reviews carried out by various independent market research organisations. For example, *Retail Business* [QRL.432] carried reviews on "Meat (part 1): Beef and veal" in issue 354 (August 1987); "Meat (part 2): Pork" in issue 355 (September 1987); "Meat (part 3): Lamb and mutton" in issue 356 (October 1987); "Meat (part 4): Bacon and ham" in issue 357 (November 1987); "Meat (part 5): Poultry" in issue 358 (December 1987); "Meat (part 6): Overview and prospects" in issue 359 (January 1988); "Frozen food (part 2)" in issue 363 (May 1988); and "Canned meat" in issue 368 (October 1988). Reports published in *Market Intelligence* [QRL.339] include "Savoury spreads" (February 1987); "Sausages and meat pies" (February 1988); "Fresh meat and bacon" (September 1988); "Delicatessen foods" (November 1988); and "Poultry" (January 1989). And *Market Research: Great Britain* [QRL.343] contains analyses of the markets for "Cooked meats and poultry" (April 1987); "Canned meat" (December 1987); and "Frozen meat products" (November 1988). Market Assessment Publications produce annual market sector reports on *Meat & Meat Products* [QRL.611], and Marketing Strategies for Industry publish *Meat and Meat Products: UK* [QRL.642]. Euromonitor provide *The Meat and Poultry Report* [QRL.538], and there is a section on "Cooked meats and poultry" in *Chilled Foods and Ready Meals* [QRL.525]. It should be emphasised that many other organisations also publish market research reports, and so the above does not constitute an exhaustive list. Moreover, all such reports tend to be market-oriented, rather than industry-oriented, unlike many of the statistical sources covered in this Review.

4.15 Research and Development

The Meat and Livestock Commission carry out research aimed at achieving greater technical efficiency in the industry, such as by improving the design and construction of slaughterhouses. To this end they publish a periodical entitled *Meat and Marketing Technical Notes* [QRL.350], and a series of "Marketing and Meat Trade Technical Bulletins".

4.16 Official Investigations

Historically, there have been a number of official publications which provide details of the structure and development of the meat industry. In 1962, a Committee of Enquiry into Fatstock and Carcase Meat Marketing and Distribution was appointed to investigate the structure of the distributive meat trade, its functions and the margins achieved by importers, wholesalers and retailers. The Verdon-Smith Report [B.362], as it has become known, has since served as a standard reference work on the meat trade. In 1970, the National Board for Prices and Incomes was asked by the government to examine and to report on prices, profits and costs (including labour costs) in food distribution. The report [B.409] was published in 1971 and contained information on butchers' margins and profit levels in the period 1967 to 1969. Then, in 1975, the Price Commission published their report on *Prices and Margins in Meat Distribution* [B.431]. That report outlines the main features of the meat trade in the United Kingdom and trends in prices, supplies and consumption, illustrates the build-up of meat prices, identifies the pricing practices of the meat trade and contains a detailed analysis of costs, margins and profits in meat distribution.

The report on *Prices and Margins in Poultry Distribution* [B.432] sets out the findings of the Price Commission following its study of the prices, margins and channels of distribution for poultry. The objective of the study was to establish the facts about the channels through which poultry is distributed from farm gate or point of import to the consumer; to identify the gross and net percentage margins at each stage of distribution; and to compare these margins, in both percentage and cash terms, with those existing in previous years.

The inquiry on *Prices, Costs and Margins in the Importation and Distribution of Bacon* [B.425] was limited to the distribution and importation of bacon. It was not concerned with such matters as the EC's Common Agricultural Policy, the costs of slaughtering pigs or the cost of curing them. It started from the point at which either British bacon had been cured or imported bacon had entered the United Kingdom. Examination was confined to uncooked bacon, excluding such products as cooked ham, breakfast slices and 'baconburgers'. Sales to the catering trade, or to institutions, were also not considered.

More recently (1986), the National Economic Development Office (NEDO) have published the results of a comparative study of *The Pig Production and Marketing Systems of Denmark, the Netherlands and the United Kingdom* [B.352]. The study sought to identify the precise factors that contribute to the competitive export strengths of Denmark and the Netherlands and paid particular attention to their marketing successes. The report identified the comparative strengths and weaknesses of the UK pig chain, and made suggestions as to how home and export market shares might be increased. The conclusions of this international study were reproduced in a subsequent (1986) NEDO publication, *UK Pig Production and Marketing* [B.393]. The broad recommendations were that the UK industry should increase its marketing effort, take up specific product opportunities identified in the report, and devote more resources to product development and training. In 1986, the Agriculture EDC published a report on *The Adoption of Technology in Agriculture: Poultry Broiler Production* [B.195].

Finally brief mention only is made of the NBPI report on *Smithfield Market* [B.413] published in 1969, *Prices, Costs and Margins in the Production and Distribution of Compound Feeding Stuff for Cattle, Pigs and Poultry* [B.426] published in 1978, and the *Special Report from the Agriculture Committee: The Effect of Feedstuff Prices on the UK Pig and Poultry Industries* [B.378] published in 1983.

4.17 Improvements and Comments

The meat industry is well served by the various publications provided by the Meat and Livestock Commission and MAFF. Coverage of AH4121 could be improved by the publication of a Business Monitor in the PQ series. The data must certainly be available, and it must simply be a question of collation. As regards Northern Ireland, data such as that published in the National Food Survey for Great Britain would be most useful. The Livestock Marketing Commission for Northern Ireland have carried out a study on beef and lamb consumption in the province, but cost means that the research will not be continued.

In contrast to the meat industry, the poultry industry is not well served by statistical publications (no doubt the result of there being only a few large firms in the industry), and data on game are sparse and inadequate. More readily-available statistical information would be welcome.

CHAPTER 5

PREPARATION OF MILK AND MILK PRODUCTS

The information in this chapter relates to the preparation of milk and milk products industry, Group 413 in the *CSO Standard Industrial Classification Revised 1980* [**B**.232]. Other more general sources, which provide statistics on other industry Groups as well, are covered in Chapter 2 and should be consulted as required. The contents of this chapter are as follows:

5.1 Introduction

Industry Group 413 covers the following Activity Heading:

4130 Preparation of milk and milk products.
1. Liquid milk and cream.
Heat treating, pasteurizing and homogenizing liquid milk and cream for wholesale and retail distribution.
2. Butter and cheese.
3. Other milk products.
Production of condensed, evaporated and preserved milk and cream products and of desserts and infant and dietetic foods with a milk base.

For an alphabetical list of the activities covered by Group 413, see the CSO *Indexes to the Standard Industrial Classification Revised 1980* [B.317]. The main products of the industry Group are liquid milk and cream, butter and cheese, and various condensed, evaporated and preserved milk and cream products. Activity Heading 4130.3 covers the production of evaporated milk; malted milk; and sweetened skimmed whey; and the manufacture of condensed milk; desserts with a milk base; dietetic food with a milk base; dried milk; milk based infant food; milk based invalid food; lactose; milk powder; preserved cream; and yogurt.

The separation of cream and the manufacture of butter give rise to quantities of liquid skimmed milk. A substantial part of this is then used to manufacture skimmed milk powders for use in the food processing and catering industries, besides being an ingredient in the manufacture of compound feedingstuffs for animals. Manufacturers use them in bread, flour confectionery, dry cake mixes, margarine, chocolate and sugar confectionery, ice-cream mixes, soup powders, cooked meat products and as an egg albumen substitute. In institutions and canteens, skimmed milk powder may be used in the preparation of tea, coffee, cocoa, cakes, custards, puddings and sauces. Increasing quantities of liquid skimmed milk are now also being marketed directly, or in the form of admixtures with whole milk as low-fat milks.

Group 413 in the SIC(1980) corresponds closely to MLH215 "Milk and milk products" in SIC(1968) except that the latter included ice-cream which is now classified under Group 421 "Ice-cream, cocoa, chocolate and sugar confectionery" — see Chapter 10. The manufacture of desserts with a milk base were previously classified to MLH229.2, but are now covered by AH4130.3.

5.2 Industry Structure

The marketing of milk in the United Kingdom is largely regulated by the UK Milk Marketing Boards — a system whose basic essentials have been in existence for over fifty years. There are five Boards — the Milk Marketing Board of England and Wales, the Scottish Milk Marketing Board, the Aberdeen and District Milk Marketing Board, the North of Scotland Milk Marketing Board, and the Milk Marketing Board for Northern Ireland — which together cover the whole of the United Kingdom except the Isle of Man, the Isles of Scilly, the Channel Islands and a number of islands off the coast of Scotland.

A farmer who intends to produce milk for sale must first obtain the authority of the appropriate government department, and then apply to the relevant area Board to be registered as a producer. A registered producer is then required, unless exempt, to sell milk solely to the Board or through its agency. Each Board has a statutory obligation to buy and find a market for all milk offered for sale by its registered producers, provided the milk complies with certain quality standards. The money received for this milk is pooled along with any other income such as profit from commercial activities. After deductions for transport, advertising and administration, the money is distributed to each producer according to the volume of milk consigned. The Boards are thus essentially co-operatives of dairy farmers. The powers of the Boards, however, relate only to milk sold in liquid form from the farm: a producer who uses his milk on the farm to produce cream, butter, cheese etc. can sell this produce completely outside the provisions of the Milk Marketing Schemes. Furthermore, under EC legislation, producers are entitled to withhold milk from the Boards for the purpose of exporting it or, if the price paid to the producer by the Board falls below a certain level, converting it into skim milk powder and butter for sale into intervention — see section 5.3.

In England and Wales (see Figure 5.1), registered milk producers may function as wholesale producers, producer retailers or producer processors, or any combination of the three. "Wholesale producer" is the term used to describe milk producers who sell milk to the Board on a wholesale contract. This milk is sent by the Board either to manufacturing creameries or to processing dairies for heat treating and bottling. Most processing dairies sell their milk direct to the consumer, but some also sell it wholesale to non-processing retailers for sale to the consumer. A "producer retailer" is a producer who retails part or all of his milk production, either to households or to caterers, hospitals and other institutions. A "producer processor" is similar to a producer retailer, but sells his milk to shops. All those producers functioning as producer processors are also producer retailers.

The arrangements in Northern Ireland and Scotland are similar but some of the terminology is slightly different. In Northern Ireland (see Figure 5.2), producers who sell their milk in liquid form directly or indirectly to retail outlets such as shops are termed "farm pasteurisers". In the Scottish and Aberdeen Board areas, they are called "producer wholesalers". In the Scottish and Aberdeen Board areas, producers who sell to the Board on a wholesale contract are known as "ordinary producers". The pattern of milk flow in Scotland is outlined in Figure 5.3.

The five Boards come together under the aegis of the Federation of United Kingdom Milk Marketing Boards which, among other functions, produces a number

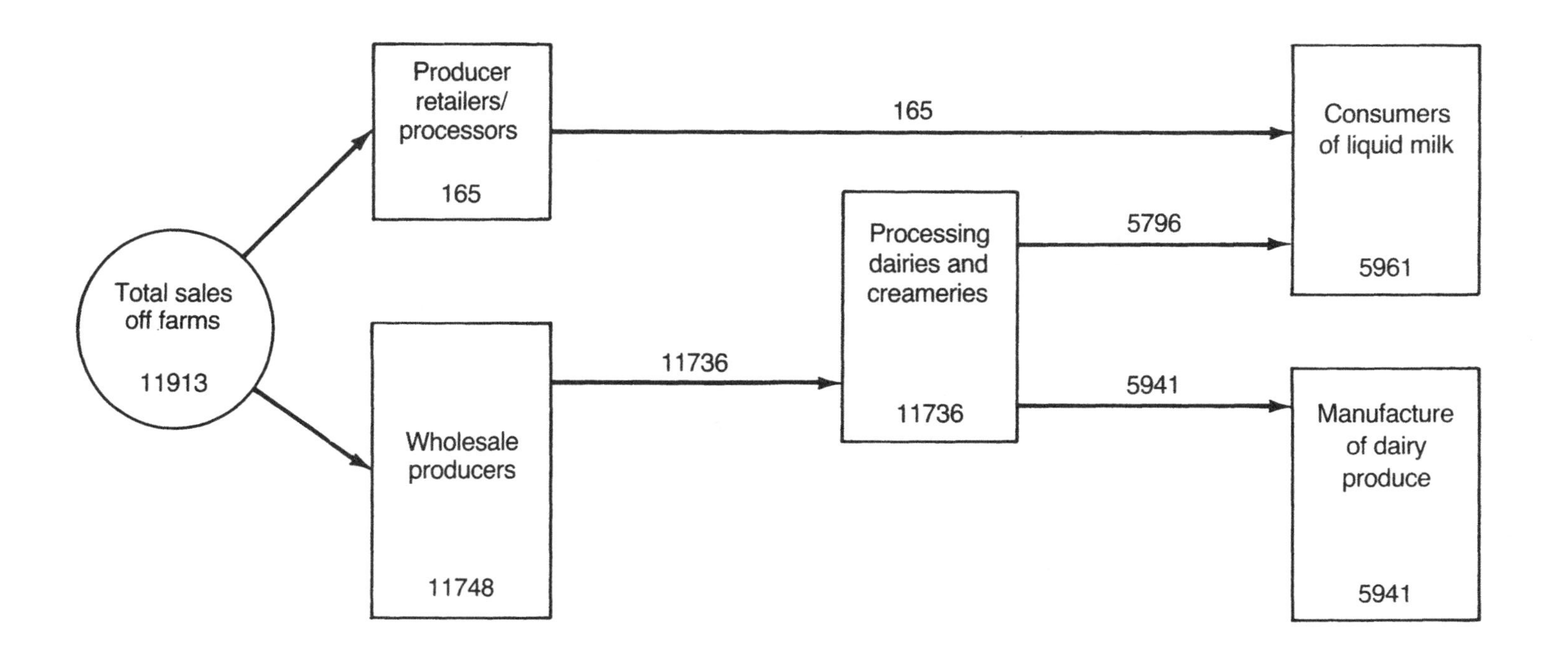

Figure 5.1 Milk Flow in England and Wales.
Source: *United Kingdom Dairy Facts & Figures 1988* [QRL503] P.141.

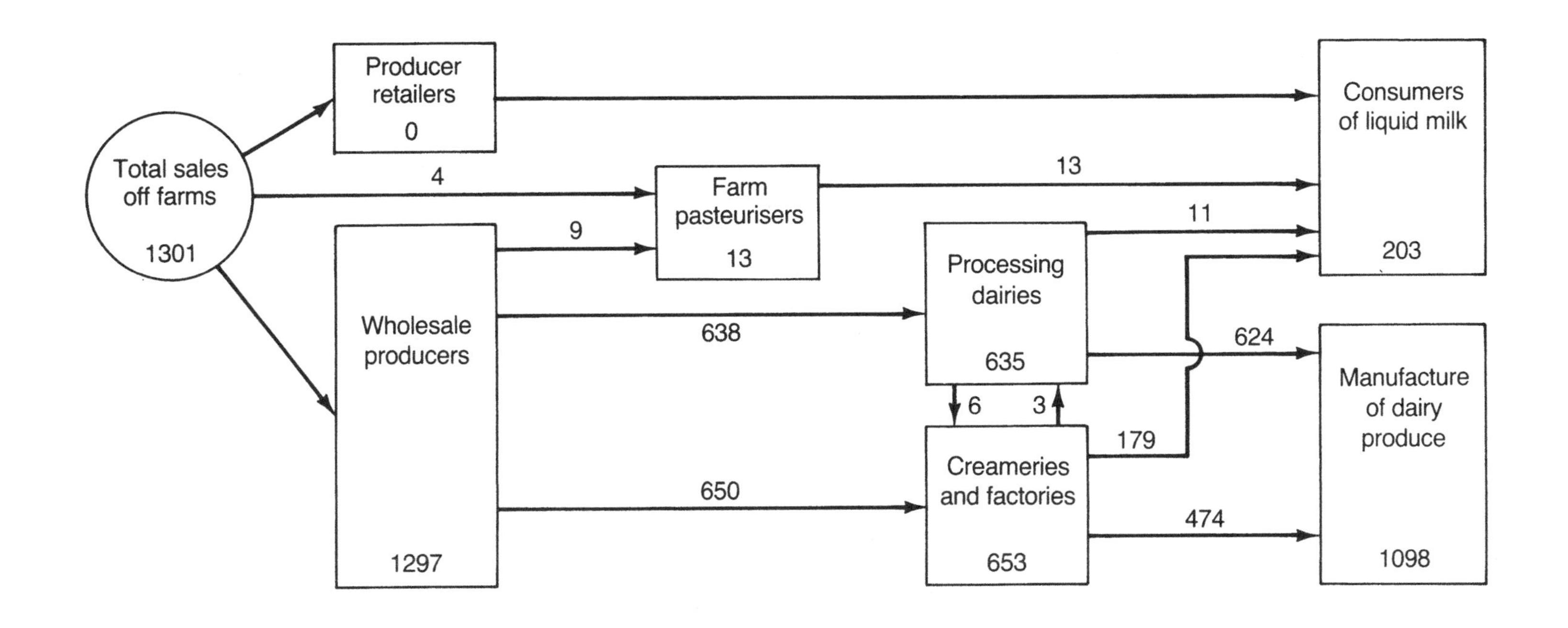

Figure 5.2 Milk Flow in Northern Ireland.
Source: *United Kingdom Dairy Facts & Figures 1988* [QRL503] P.143.

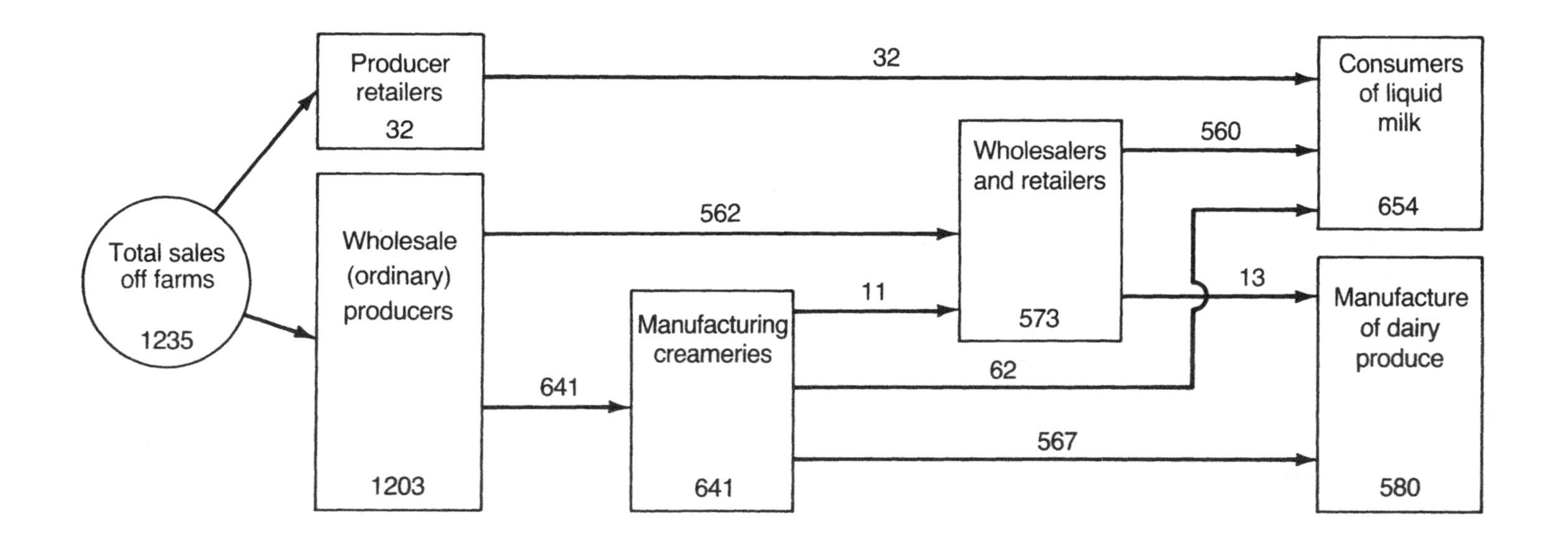

Figure 5.3 Milk Flow in Scotland.
Source: *United Kingdom Dairy Facts & Figures 1988* [QRL503] P.142.

of statistical publications which are of interest. First and foremost, there are the invaluable *United Kingdom Dairy Facts & Figures* [QRL.503] published annually since 1963, and its companion volume *EEC Dairy Facts & Figures* [QRL.184] published annually since 1971. The former, in particular, contains a wealth of statistical information and is by far the most important single source on all aspects of the industry. The main statistics in these two volumes are summarised in three booklets/folding cards entitled *Key Milk Figures in England and Wales* [QRL.298], *Key Milk Figures in Scotland* [QRL.300] and *Key Milk Figures in Northern Ireland* [QRL.299], but these do not provide anywhere near as much detail. Moreover, each Board also produces an Annual Report and Accounts, which contain much annotated statistical information, and a monthly journal which provides up-to-date figures on production, sales, prices etc. The titles of the respective journals are as follows:

England and Wales	*Milk Producer* [QRL.358]
Scotland	*Milk Bulletin* [QRL.355]
Aberdeen and District	*Milk News* [QRL.357]
North of Scotland	*Milk Topics* [QRL.360]
Northern Ireland	*Topics* [QRL.490]

The Milk Marketing Boards act as the unique selling agents to the 'Buyers' of milk. The 'Buyers' — the processors, manufacturers and distributors of dairy produce — are represented by their own organisations: the Dairy Trade Federation, the Scottish Dairy Trade Federation and the Northern Ireland Dairy Trade Federation. Each Trade Federation also produces its own Annual Report and Accounts, as well as other sources of statistical information. The prices of all milk sold by each Board are subject to negotiation at a Joint Committee, comprising representatives of that Board and the 'Buyers' of milk in that area. Milk produced outside the areas covered by the Milk Marketing Schemes is sold subject to direct negotiation between the producer and the buyer.

The Federation of United Kingdom Milk Marketing Boards is affiliated to the various Dairy Trade Federations for the purposes of representation in ASSILEC, the EEC organisation for the dairy trade. Moreover, as a member of the Federation of Agricultural Co-operatives (UK) Ltd., the Federation of the Boards represents that body at milk specialist meetings of COGECA, the EEC organisation representing agricultural co-operatives.

The National Dairy Council is an organisation jointly funded by the Dairy Trade Federation and the Milk Marketing Board of England and Wales. It represents the whole of the dairy industry in England and Wales, and is responsible for the generic publicity and advertising of fresh milk, fresh cream and other products, and English and Welsh cheese. It conducts its activities for English and Welsh cheese through the English Country Cheese Council. The Scottish Dairy Council and the Dairy Council for Northern Ireland perform similar functions.

Finally, mention should be made of two organisations concerned with the marketing of butter. Prior to 1970, English butter was marketed under various companies' brand names, and this diffusion of effort allowed the New Zealanders, the Danes, and the Irish to achieve market domination with their brands Anchor,

Lurpak and Kerrygold respectively. In 1970, the English Butter Marketing Company was formed to promote the sales of a national brand of English butter — Country Life — which is made by ten manufacturers and packed at more than twenty creameries throughout the country. The ten member companies of the EBMC are: Milk Marketing Board; Unigate Foods; Express Dairy Foods; Co-operative Wholesale Society; Associated Fresh Foods; Dale Farm Foods; Greater Nottingham Co-operative Society; Healds Dairies; Plymouth and South Devon Co-op; and United Co-operative Dairies. The Butter Information Council is an international organisation representing the milk producers of the United Kingdom, Republic of Ireland, the Netherlands, Denmark, France and New Zealand. The objective of the Council is to promote the consumption of butter in the United Kingdom through advertising in the media, the provision of educational material for schools and colleges, point of sale material for caterers, and information on fats to the medical profession. It also provides a general information and public relations service.

There are many books on the historical development of the industry of which the following are just a selection. *The United Kingdom Dairy Industry* [B.42] presents a broad outline of the UK dairy industry, its problems and achievements, over the period 1930–1960. *Drinka Pinta* [B.90] is a record of the history of the National Milk Publicity Council from 1920 to 1970. *Milk to Market* [B.9] provides a history of the Milk Marketing Board of England and Wales to 1973. And *Strategy for the UK Dairy Industry* [B.382] assessed some of the opportunities and constraints facing the industry in 1978. The latter, in particular, provides plenty of statistical information, and all give many useful references.

5.3 The European Community

Government support for the dairy sector has traditionally taken the form of a guaranteed price for milk produced, against a standard quantity. This system endured until the accession of the United Kingdom to the European Community in 1973. The next five years were a transitional period during which all existing methods of price support were dismantled. From the 1st January 1978, milk for manufacture had to be sold at a price negotiated between the Boards and the 'Buyers', but the government continued to fix the Boards' selling price of milk for the liquid market as well as the retail price and thereby the liquid processors' and distributors' margins.

The government lifted control of the retail price of liquid milk in Scotland in September 1981, and in England and Wales and Northern Ireland on 1st January 1985. The price of liquid milk in each area has subsequently been agreed by a Joint Committee comprising representatives from the Milk Marketing Board and the milk purchasers. The selling price for milk will vary for each product and may fluctuate during the year.

Meanwhile, on 2nd April 1984, the European Community introduced a supplementary levy to curb the rate of increase in milk output. The scheme is based on quotas imposed at Member State, Board, dairy and/or farm level, with punitive superlevy payments for production beyond fixed levels. This has resulted in an immediate and drastic reduction in milk output in the United Kingdom, and also in a reduction in the use of off-farm inputs from supplying industries.

Although the prices of milk and dairy products are no longer under any form of government control, the European Community operates a system of price support which seeks to establish a "target price". According to the legislation, this "target price" is:

> ···"that price which it is aimed to obtain for the aggregate of producers' milk sales, on the Community market and on external markets, during the milk year."
> (Regulation (EEC)804/68. Article 3(2))

Recent policy steps have weakened the mechanisms for achieving the aim, but basically the system works as follows. The "target price" is determined by the Council of Agricultural Ministers for the whole Community in common currency terms. An intervention system then operates whereby intervention agencies remove from the market any amounts of butter and skimmed milk powder surplus to requirements with the objective of producing a "floor" price. Furthermore, variable levies are imposed on imports from non-EEC countries to prevent such products exerting downward pressure on the market price. Subsidies are also paid to encourage milk products to be exported, fed to stock or consumed within the Community in greater quantities (e.g. school milk, butter).

The intervention price for skimmed milk powder was aligned across the Community at the time of UK accession but it was not until five years later, on 1st January 1978, that a common intervention price for butter was applied in the United Kingdom. The Treaty of Accession also permitted the import of given quantities of butter and Cheddar cheese at minimum guaranteed prices during a five-year transitional period. The agreement for butter was subsequently extended in 1976, 1981 and 1984. The guarantee arrangements for Cheddar cheese were not extended at the end of 1977, but the issue was discussed as part of the 1978–79 round of multilateral trade negotiations under GATT. Special arrangements were subsequently agreed, with effect from 1st January 1980, for Community imports of cheese from New Zealand, Australia and Canada.

Further detail and discussion about the impact of EC membership may be found in *United Kingdom Dairy Facts & Figures* [QRL.503], in the article by Guy Wilkinson [B.186] entitled "The UK dairy industry and the EEC", and in *The Common Agricultural Policy of the European Community* [B.52] by Rosemary Fennell. One very tangible influence is that EC Directives now require the completion of weekly, monthly, quarterly, and annual returns on milk and milk products, including an annual balance sheet showing production, imports, exports, stocks, and domestic uses. These returns are completed by MAFF, with the assistance of the Milk Marketing Boards, and the information is subsequently published by EUROSTAT — see section 2.11 for details.

5.4 Output

As indicated in section 5.3, a quota system has applied to all production of milk and milk products in the European Community since 2nd April 1984. The UK dairy quota is divided by the Ministry of Agriculture between the areas covered by the five Milk Marketing Boards and those islands within the United Kingdom not covered by the Schemes. Individual producer quotas are also imposed. Any Member State within the Community which produces in excess of its quota is liable to a superlevy payment. Details of the dairy quotas for each country in the Community are provided in both *EEC Dairy Facts & Figures* [QRL.184] and *United Kingdom Dairy Facts & Figures* [QRL.503].

The quota applies to all milk produced in the United Kingdom, whether the milk is sold to the relevant Board or used on the farm in the production of cream, butter or cheese, and whether the milk is produced in areas covered by the Milk Marketing Schemes or not. *United Kingdom Dairy Facts & Figures* [QRL.503] provides figures for sales of milk to the Boards in each of the Board regions, broken down by county in England and Wales, and Northern Ireland, and by area in Scotland. Data are also provided on the subsequent utilisation of milk for the various products, e.g. as liquid milk or in the manufacture of butter, cheese, fresh and sterilised cream, condensed milk, whole milk powder and other products. Many of these figures will have previously been published in the Boards' individual journals (see section 5.2). Each Board is responsible for compiling its own data in an effort to update *United Kingdom Dairy Facts & Figures* [QRL.503], but the editing of the book is carried out by the Milk Marketing Board of England and Wales at its headquarters in Thames Ditton. Milk consumed by farm households or used on farms for butter and cream production and calf rearing is excluded. Moreover, milk produced outside the Board areas is not included in these statistics. Provisional monthly data on total production and utilisation in each Board area are provided in the respective journals — [QRL.358], [QRL.355], [QRL.357], [QRL.360] and [QRL.490] — with only a two-month publication delay. MAFF estimates the total quantity of milk produced in the United Kingdom using the MMB's figures of sales through the Boards together with the addition of estimates of sales outside the Schemes and of use on farms (as feed for stock, consumption in farm households or for milk products). These annual estimates were published in *Output and Utilisation of Farm Produce in the United Kingdom* [QRL.382] up to 1988.

It is therefore difficult in the context of the milk and milk products industry to define what exactly constitutes the output, and the inputs, of the industry. As has been explained above, much of the milk processed in the United Kingdom is used in the manufacture of butter, cheese, cream and other products. The industry is thus generating many of its own inputs.

The *Monthly Digest of Statistics* [QRL.362] presents monthly MAFF data on sales of milk through the Milk Marketing Schemes, and also separate figures for sales of liquid milk and milk for manufacture. Production figures are provided for butter; cheese; condensed and evaporated milk (excluding skim concentrates and condensed milk used in the manufacture of chocolate crumb); full-cream milk powder; and skimmed milk powder (excluding buttermilk and whey powder). The figures for butter relate to the output of home creameries, and those for cheese relate to all home-produced cheese other than the small quantities produced on farms outside the Milk Marketing Schemes. Figures for processed cheese are not included as it is re-manufacture of home-produced and imported cheese. The *Annual Abstract of Statistics* [QRL.37] provides annual data on output of milk and milk products in both current and constant prices, and also figures on the volume of milk sales and certain milk products. *Business Monitor PA413: Preparation of Milk and Milk*

Products [QRL.107] gives annual data on total sales, gross and net output for the industry Group as a whole, with no breakdown between products. Prior to 1980 (4th quarter), more detailed data, analysed by product, was available for MLH215 — see section 5.1 — on a quarterly basis in *Business Monitor PQ215 Milk and Milk Products* [QRL.121], publication of which has now ceased. A "topping-up" inquiry — see section 2.1.1.3 — on quarterly product sales in AH4130 was carried out in 1986, and the results were published in the latter part of the year. Quarterly data on the production of various types of condensed milk and milk powder are published in *MAFF Statistics: Production of Processed Milk in the United Kingdom* [QRL.327]. The figures for condensed milk exclude milk used directly for the manufacture of chocolate crumb and also skim concentrate produced for use in the manufacture of, for example, margarine and ice-cream mixes. The statistical notice is published about six weeks after the end of the quarter to which it relates, and covers the production of all known manufacturers in the United Kingdom.

5.5 Current Inputs other than Labour

5.5.1 *Domestic Inputs*

As has already been discussed in section 5.4, it is difficult to define what exactly constitutes the inputs, and the output, of the milk and milk products industry. Certainly, untreated milk off farms constitutes an input, though much of the milk subsequently processed should also be considered as an input in the manufacture of butter, cheese etc. Every month, each of the five Milk Marketing Boards supplies MAFF with provisional estimates for the previous month, together with updated estimated for earlier months, of (a) total sales of milk off farms and (b) the breakdown of these sales into the quantities going for liquid consumption and for the manufacture of each of the various milk products. Details are published in the Boards' journals — [QRL.358], [QRL.355], [QRL.357], [QRL.360] and [QRL.490] — and in the *Monthly Digest of Statistics* [QRL.362]. A more complete analysis of milk supplies and utilisation is eventually published in *United Kingdom Dairy Facts & Figures* [QRL.503].

The milk produced on farms constitutes part of the agricultural output of such farms. Statistics on milk production may thus also be found in agricultural sources, details of which may be found in the companion volume by G.H. Peters to this Review, *Agriculture* [B.144]. Hence, only a very cursory discussion is provided here. Data on the number of dairy and beef cows in the United Kingdom, analysed by county in England and Wales and Northern Ireland, and by area in Scotland are provided in *United Kingdom Dairy Facts & Figures* [QRL.503] reproduced from the results of the regular census carried out by MAFF. The cow population is also broken down by herd and farm size. *Farm Incomes in the United Kingdom* [QRL.210] contains annual data on livestock numbers on "dairy farms" for England, Wales, Scotland and Northern Ireland separately. "Dairy farms" are defined as those where the dairy enterprise accounts for over one third and commonly over two-thirds of total SGM (Standard Gross Margin) and is the largest enterprise group.

The most comprehensive analysis of inputs is provided by the Purchases Inquiry — see section 2.1.1.4. The results of the 1984 Inquiry were published in 1987 as

Business Monitor PO1008: Purchases Inquiry [QRL.116], and contained considerable detail for AH4130. The inquiry collects information about the commodity detail of industry's purchases of materials and fuel, and the level of detail is such that the interdependencies of many of the Food industries may be highlighted. Thus, for example, the amount of "fruit juice" purchased by AH4130 may be identified. The pattern of commodity purchases returned in the Purchases Inquiry are scaled up to agree with the annual levels in the Census of Production. Information is also given on the effective percentage response rate in terms of employment for each industry.

The Purchases Inquiry is quinquennial; the results of the 1989 Inquiry are to be published in 1992. The results of the 1979 Inquiry were published in *Business Monitor PA1002.1: 1979 Census of Production and Purchases Inquiry* [QRL.94] Results for the 1974 Inquiry were in a different form, being analyses of returns received without grossing. The statistics for each industry were published in the 1974/75 PA Monitor for that industry.

5.5.2 *Input-output Analysis*

Details of the input-output tables for the United Kingdom have been provided in section 2.5.2. Here we simply present brief comments on the level of detail accorded to the milk and milk products industry. "Milk and milk products" (AH4130) was identified amongst the industry/commodity groups in the *Input-output Tables for the United Kingdom 1984* [QRL.284]. The same group was also identified in the 1979 tables published in *Business Monitor PA1004* [QRL.101]. The 1974 tables were, however, based on SIC(1968) and the corresponding group was thus "Milk and milk products" (MLH215). Information on coverage in previous input-output tables may be found in the references cited in section 2.5.2.

5.6 Labour

Detailed results of the September 1984 Census of Employment for Great Britain were published in the January 1987 edition of the *Employment Gazette* [QRL.186]. The numbers of male employees (full-time and part-time) and female employees (full-time and part-time) in employment in AH4130 were separately enumerated. An analysis of total employees in employment by region was also provided. The September 1987 issue of the *Employment Gazette* [QRL.186] presented comparable results for the United Kingdom, incorporating figures from the 1984 Census of Employment for Northern Ireland provided by the Department of Economic Development. No regional analysis was provided, though data for the province could be derived by subtraction of the GB totals from those for the United Kingdom. Monthly figures of employees in employment are no longer provided in the *Employment Gazette* [QRL.186].

Business Monitor PA413 [QRL.107] provides annual data on total employment (including working proprietors) and labour costs for the industry Group as a whole. Employment is also analysed by the standard regions of England, plus Wales, Scotland and Northern Ireland; and by size of establishments classified to the industry.

The Dairy Trade Federation produce annual data on employment in manufacturing, processing and retailing in the dairy industry in England and Wales.

The data are published on a folding card entitled *The Dairy Industry* [QRL.172] and have been gathered in the course of a manpower survey carried out by the Industrial Relations Department of the Federation. The survey breaks down the workforce by work sector, category of employee and sex, and detailed results are available from the Federation on request. *Farm Incomes in the United Kingdom* [QRL.210] contains annual data on the labour input in "dairy farms" (see section 5.5 for definition), both including and excluding farmers and their spouses, for England, Wales, Scotland and Northern Ireland separately.

Pay in the milk industry is negotiated through the Milk product/milk processing and distribution NJNC: England and Wales. Detailed analyses of earnings and hours under this collective agreement are provided in "Part A: Streamlined analyses and key analyses by agreement" and "Part B: Report, summary analyses and other analyses by agreement" of the *New Earnings Survey* [QRL.375]. In addition, "Part C: Analyses by industry" contains statistics on earnings and hours of full-time employees on adult rates in Great Britain. The level of industrial detail varies in the different analyses, but "Preparation of Milk and Milk Products" is separately identified in some of the published tables. Analyses in a form not published may, however, be supplied by the Department of Employment provided they are considered reliable enough for release.

The annual cost of the labour input into milk production is estimated in *United Kingdom Dairy Facts & Figures* [QRL.503]. The same publication also provides data on minimum agricultural weekly wage rates for adult workers, and the weekly average total earnings and hours of hired, regular whole-time adult male dairy cowmen in England and Wales, Scotland and Great Britain. Minimum agricultural wage rates are determined by the Agricultural Wages Boards for England and Wales, Scotland and Northern Ireland and are first published in Orders issued by them. Data on the number of producers registered with each Milk Marketing Board appear monthly in their respective journals — [QRL.358], [QRL.355], [QRL.357], [QRL.360] and [QRL.490] — and annually, analysed by category and by area, in *United Kingdom Dairy Facts & Figures* [QRL.503].

A somewhat dated, though still interesting, report was prepared in 1970 by the National Board for Prices and Incomes (NBPI) and entitled *Pay and Conditions of Workers in the Milk Industry* [B.407]. It provides much statistical information on pay and conditions in the industry (see section 5.16 for further details). Two earlier NBPI reports which may also be of interest are *The Remuneration of Milk Distributors (Interim Report)* [B.412] and *The Remuneration of Milk Distributors (Final Report)* [B.411].

5.7 Capital

5.7.1 *Capital Expenditure*

Business Monitor PA413 [QRL.107] provides a breakdown of gross capital expenditure by type of asset — land and buildings, plant and machinery, vehicles. Annual data on net capital expenditure are also provided for the Group as a whole, analysed by the standard regions of England, plus Wales, Scotland and Northern

Ireland, and also analysed by size of establishments classified to the industry. *United Kingdom Dairy Facts & Figures* [QRL.503] provides quarterly data on sales of agricultural land in England and Wales using information notified to local Valuation Offices of the Inland Revenue. There is a delay (probably between six and nine months) between the date on which a sale is agreed and the date the transaction is notified to the Inland Revenue and included in the series.

5.7.2 *Suppliers of Machinery*

An alternative perspective on the capital input to Group 413 is provided by the data published in *Business Monitor PQ3244: Food, Drink and Tobacco Processing Machinery; Packaging and Bottling Machinery* [QRL.127]. Statistics are provided therein on quarterly sales of "dairy machinery and plant (including milk pasteurisation plant and cheese presses but excluding milk bottle feeding machinery, cream containing machines and milking machines" and "parts of dairy machinery and plant". Moreover, data are presented on imports of the following: "cream separators and milk clarifiers", "parts of cream separators and milk clarifiers", and "dairy machinery other than milking machines".

As a result of the *Review of DTI Statistics* [B.367] — see sections 13.2 and 13.3 — this sales inquiry was not retained within the quarterly system of inquiries after the second quarter of 1989. Statistical data thereafter will be published less frequently and in less product detail.

5.7.3 *Company Reports*

The net book value of tangible fixed assets owned by each Board, and their authorised future expenditure, are detailed in their respective Annual Reports. Similar information is available for the Trade Federations and the dairy produce manufacturers in their Annual Reports.

5.8 International Transactions

5.8.1 *HM Customs and Excise Records*

"Dairy products and birds' eggs" comprise Division 02 in the Standard International Trade Classification (Revision 3). In the *Business Monitor MM20: Overseas Trade Statistics of the United Kingdom* [QRL.85], the Division is further broken down into the following headings:

022. Milk and cream and milk products other than butter or cheese
022.1 Milk (including skimmed milk) and cream, not concentrated or sweetened
022.11 Milk of a fat content, by weight, not exceeding one per cent
022.12 Milk and cream of a fat content, by weight, exceeding one per cent but not exceeding six per cent
022.13 Cream of a fat content, by weight, exceeding six per cent

022.2 Milk and cream, concentrated or sweetened
022.21 Milk, in solid form, of a fat content, by weight, not exceeding 1.5 per cent
022.22 Milk and cream, in solid form, of a fat content, by weight, exceeding 1.5 per cent
022.23 Milk and cream, not in solid form, not containing sugar or other sweetening matter
022.24 Milk and cream, not in solid form, containing added sugar or other sweetening matter
022.3 Yogurt; buttermilk, curdled, fermented, or acidified milk and cream; ice-cream
022.31 Yogurt, concentrated/containing added sugar or other sweetener/flavoured or containing added fruit or cocoa
022.32 Buttermilk, curdled milk and cream, kephir and other fermented or acidified milk or cream
022.33 Ice-cream and other edible ice whether or not containing cocoa
022.4 Whey; products consisting of natural milk constituents not elsewhere specified
022.41 Whey
022.49 Products consisting of natural milk constituents not elsewhere specified
023. Butter and other fats and oils derived from milk
024. Cheese and curd
024.1 Grated and powdered cheese, of all kinds
024.2 Processed cheese, not grated or powdered
024.3 Blue-veined cheese
024.9 Other cheese; curd
024.91 Fresh cheese (including whey cheese) not fermented, and curd
024.99 Cheese not elsewhere specified
025. Birds'eggs, and egg yolks, fresh, dried or otherwise preserved, sweetened or not; egg albumin.

Note that headings 022.33 and 025 relate to products which are not manufactured by industry Group 413. Monthly import and export figures for each of these headings, in both volume and value terms, are presented for a range of exporting and importing countries respectively. Further details of the extensive statistical coverage in *Business Monitor MM20* [QRL.85] are provided in section 2.8.2.1. The statistics have been compiled from the declarations which are made to HM Customs and Excise, and which are subject to confirmation by Customs officials. The figures are usually published about one month after the month to which they relate.

Exports and re-exports of milk products (butter, butter oil, cheese, condensed milk, chocolate crumb and milk powder) are published in *United Kingdom Dairy Facts & Figures* [QRL.503] from data provided directly by HM Customs and Excise. The same publication also details imports of the following milk and milk products: liquid milk; butter; butter oil; cheese; condensed milk; chocolate crumb; milk powder; whey powder; cream and yogurt. As indicated in section 5.3, special arrangements apply to the imports of butter and cheese from New Zealand, Australia, and Canada. Details are provided in *EEC Dairy Facts & Figures*

[QRL.184]. *Meat and Dairy Products* [QRL.349], published twice yearly by the Commonwealth Secretariat, gives annual volume figures of exports of various dairy products to all the major countries not only in the Commonwealth, but also in Europe and the rest of the world. The dairy products listed are butter; butter oil; Cheddar cheese; Emmentaler, Gruyère and Sbrinz; Blue Vein; processed cheese; Danbo, Edam, Fontal, Fontina, Fynbo, Gouda, Havarti, Mariboe and Samsoe; Brie and Camembert; other cheese; condensed milk; milk powder, whole and cream; skimmed; partly skimmed; preserved whey; casein and derivatives. Similar coverage is provided for imports from all the most important countries of origin.

5.8.2 *Industry Analyses of Trade*

In contrast to these analyses by type of product, *Business Monitor MQ10: Overseas Trade Analysed in Terms of Industries* [QRL.90] provides quarterly data on exports and imports for AH4130.1, AH4130.2, and AH4130.3, as well as for the industry Group as a whole. These figures are also used in *Business Monitor MQ12: Import Penetration and Export Sales Ratios for Manufacturing Industry* [QRL.91] to provide export/sales, and import penetration ratios for industry Group 413 up to the second quarter of 1989 — see section 2.8.2.3 for details of the coverage.

5.9 Stocks

Each month, MAFF carries out a survey of production and stocks of all known manufacturers of condensed milk and milk powder. The data so collected on stocks of condensed and evaporated milk; full-cream milk powder; and skimmed milk powder are published in the *Monthly Digest of Statistics* [QRL.362]. The same publication also presents data on stocks of butter and cheese. The Ministry carries out a monthly survey of cheese stocks in the United Kingdom, in which it contacts all known manufacturers, factors and importers of cheese. Total butter stocks represent quantities estimated using data from a MAFF survey of public cold stores, from the Intervention Board for Agricultural Produce, and from the New Zealand Dairy Board. Stocks in private stores, or in undischarged cargoes, are excluded. From July 1983, the scope of the survey was extended with a resultant discontinuity in the recording of stock levels.

The *Intervention Board for Agricultural Produce: Annual Report* [QRL.293] provides figures on monthly intervention purchases and sales of butter and skimmed milk powder together with the monthly use in the United Kingdom of denatured skimmed milk powder in animal feed, the monthly use of liquid skimmed milk for stockfeeding, and monthly quantities of skimmed milk manufactured into caseins and caseinates. The report also gives monthly data on intervention stocks of butter, aided private storage stocks of butter and intervention stocks of skimmed milk powder in the United Kingdom. Data on intervention stocks of butter and skimmed milk powder are also published in *United Kingdom Dairy Facts & Figures* [QRL.503] by courtesy of the Intervention Board. The MAFF data on beginning, and end-year, stocks are also presented for butter; cheese; whole milk powder; skimmed milk powder; sweetened condensed milk; and unsweetened condensed milk.

Finally, *Business Monitor PA413* [QRL.107] gives financial data on stocks and work-in-progress for all UK establishments classified to the industry Group at end

December, and analysis of this data by size of establishment.

5.10 Consumption

5.10.1 *The National Food Survey*

The National Food Survey collects consumption data on a wide variety of milk products manufactured by industry Group 413, viz:

Food code number	Description
1	UHT, liquid milk, full price
2	Sterilised milk, full price
3	Other liquid milk, full price
4	Milk, liquid, full price (codes 1–3)
5	Milk, liquid, welfare
6	Milk, liquid, school
8	Other milk
9	Milk, condensed
11	Milk, dried, branded
12	Milk, instant
13	Yoghurt
16	Skimmed milks
17	Cream
18	Cheese, natural, hard, Cheddar and Cheddar type
19	Cheese, natural, hard, other UK varieties or foreign equivalents
20	Cheese, natural, hard, Edam and other continental
21	Cheese, natural, soft
22	Total natural cheese (codes 18–21)
23	Cheese, processed
131	Butter — New Zealand
132	Butter — Danish
133	Butter — UK
134	All other butter
135	Total butter (codes 131–134)

Detailed statistics are published on these various foods in the *National Food Survey: Compendium of Results* [QRL.373]. Annual average figures of both per capita weekly consumption and expenditure are provided for the following main food groups: liquid wholemilk, full price (4); welfare and school milk (5,6); condensed milk (9); dried and other milk (8,11–13); skimmed milks (16); cream (17); total milk and cream (4–17); natural cheese (22); processed cheese (23); total cheese (22,23); butter (135). Moreover, these data are analysed by region and type of area; by income group; by household composition; by household composition and income group; by age of housewife; by housing tenure; and by ownership of deep freezer. In addition, indices of expenditure, and of the real value of purchases, on liquid wholemilk (4), other milk and cream (8–17), total milk and cream (4–17); cheese (22,23), and butter (135) are presented for the latest six years. Further, quarterly and annual national average household expenditure on the following food items are calculated: liquid wholemilk, full price; welfare milk; school milk; condensed milk; other milk; dried milk, branded; instant milk; yoghurt; skimmed milks; cream; natural cheese; processed cheese; and butter.

The main report on the Survey, *Household Food Consumption and Expenditure* [QRL.267], carries a more limited range of statistical data, as has been discussed in section 2.10.1.2. Commentary is, however, provided with many of the main statistical tables and data for previous years are often presented for comparison. Income elasticities of expenditure are calculated for liquid wholemilk and for cheese.

5.10.2 *The Family Expenditure Survey*

The *Family Expenditure Survey* [QRL.204] provides analyses of the expenditure of various types of households on butter; fresh milk; milk products including cream; and cheese at different levels of household income, and by sex and age. It also publishes average figures for weekly expenditure analysed by region. *United Kingdom Dairy Facts & Figures* [QRL.503] cites annual MAFF statistics on consumption per head, and average household expenditure on selected dairy products.

5.10.3 *The National Accounts*

The *United Kingdom National Accounts* [QRL.506] carries annual data, in both current and constant prices, of household expenditure on "milk, cheese and eggs". The data are reproduced in the *Annual Abstract of Statistics* [QRL.37].

5.11 Supplies and Disposals

In the United Kingdom, about half of the milk sold off farms is destined for liquid consumption. The remainder is used in the manufacture of various dairy products — see section 5.1 for details and Figures 5.1, 5.2 and 5.3 for illustrative data. Every month, each of the five Milk Marketing Boards supplies MAFF with provisional estimates for the previous month, and updated estimates for earlier months, of (a) total sales of milk off farms and (b) the breakdown of these sales into the quantities going for liquid consumption and for manufacture into each of the various milk products. These monthly figures on disposals through the Milk Marketing Schemes, and production figures for butter; cheese; condensed and evaporated milk; full-cream milk powder; and skimmed milk powder are then published in the *Monthly Digest of Statistics* [QRL.362]. The figures for butter relate to the output of home creameries, and those for cheese relate to all home-produced cheese other than the small quantities produced on farms outside the Schemes. Figures for processed cheese are not included as it is re-manufacture of home-produced and imported cheese. The data are later published in *United Kingdom Dairy Facts & Figures* [QRL.503].

Annual figures on production and utilisation of milk were provided in *Output and Utilisation of Farm Produce in the United Kingdom* [QRL.382] up to 1988. Sales from Milk Marketing Board Schemes, and utilisation under the Farmhouse Cheesemakers' Schemes (which ended on 28th February 1987), are as recorded by the Milk Marketing Boards. Estimates of milk consumption on farms and sales off farms outside the MMB Schemes are based on farm survey data.

United Kingdom Dairy Facts & Figures [QRL.503] presents annual data on UK supplies and "disappearance" of the following milk products: butter; cheese; whole milk powder; fresh cream; sterilised cream; skimmed milk powder; whole sweetened condensed milk; and whole unsweetened condensed milk. Self-sufficiency ratios for the United Kingdom are also calculated for the following products: butterfat from milk; solids, not fat, from milk; butter; cheese; fresh cream; sterilised cream; skimmed milk powder; sweetened condensed milk; and unsweetened condensed milk. Self-sufficiency is defined for the individual products as equivalent to production divided by domestic disappearance. Self-sufficiency in "butterfat" and "solids not fat" is defined as the total availability of butterfat/solids not fat from UK-produced milk divided by total domestic disappearance of butterfat/solids not fat in all liquid milk and dairy products. No account is taken of estimates of farm use. Moreover, no ratio is calculated for whole milk powder due to data problems.

Finally, MAFF also prepare a supply balance sheet for milk and milk products which is sent to the Statistical Office of the European Communities (EUROSTAT). The commodities covered are milk for drinking; cream; evaporated and concentrated milk; milk powder; butter; and cheese, including processed cheese. The Milk Marketing Boards provide the information on the production and utilisation of milk. Extra data on stocks is generated by the monthly MAFF surveys of cheese and milk powder stocks — see section 5.9 for details. The Intervention Board for Agricultural Produce supplies figures on the usage of milk products for animal feed.

5.12 Prices

5.12.1 *Prices for Untreated Milk*

Under the Milk Marketing Schemes, all money paid for milk by dairies and creameries is pooled and then distributed to each producer in proportion to the amount of milk supplied. In principle, therefore, all producers are treated on an equal basis with each being offered the same price for their milk. The major exception to this general rule is that the Boards have introduced a variety of incentive schemes over the years in order to reward those producers who supply milk of above average quality.

The methods of arriving at the prices to be returned to the wholesale producers differ in detail between each Board but are broadly similar in principle. Except in England and Wales, each Board sets a provisional schedule at the beginning of each milk year of monthly "pool" or "base" prices for milk sent to them, which relate to milk of a specific quality. This schedule of producer prices is reviewed at monthly Board meetings, and may be amended for any updated estimates. These "pool" prices are published in the respective Board journals — [QRL.358], [QRL.355],

[QRL.357], [QRL.360] and [QRL.490] — and in *United Kingdom Dairy Facts & Figures* [QRL.503]. The actual prices paid to individual producers in a particular month will be subject to premiums or deductions depending on whether the quality of the milk consigned is above or below the specific quality. The price will also be adjusted on the basis of hygienic quality and any antibiotics failure. Details of these incentives are also presented in the above publications.

The England and Wales Board operates a system under which the value of wholesale producers' milk is expressed solely in terms of its constituent solids (butterfat, protein and lactose). Price adjustments for hygienic quality and antibiotic failures are then applied in a comparable manner to those for other Boards. In addition, the producers' price is also subject to a scale of seasonal price differentials which is intended to encourage production in those months when overall milk supplies are at their seasonal low. Details are provided in *Milk Producer* [QRL.358] and in *United Kingdom Dairy Facts & Figures* [QRL.503].

Average annual net prices paid to wholesale producers (including the various adjustments) in each Board area, and average monthly prices (excluding co-responsibility levy, superlevy and special service payments) are published in *United Kingdom Dairy Facts & Figures* [QRL.503]. Special service payments relate to the supply of specially designated types (e.g. kosher) of milk. Comparisons of producer prices between Boards should be made with caution as they may not necessarily be calculated on the same basis. A monthly producer price index for milk is provided in *MAFF Statistics: Agricultural Price Indices* [QRL.315].

The prices of all milk sold by the Boards are subject to negotiation at the Joint Committees — see section 5.2. Amongst other factors, the negotiations take into account changes in the "target price" (see section 5.3), changes in product yields, changes in manufacturing and marketing costs, the priority of milk supply required and the prevailing market prices for the different milk products. The result of these negotiations is a range of prices for milk according to the products made from it. Data on the average prices received by each Board for the sale of milk for a variety of products are published in *United Kingdom Dairy Facts & Figures* [QRL.503]. The funds from these sales form the "pool" from which producers receive payment.

5.12.2 *Retail Prices*

5.12.2.1 Recorded prices

The *Employment Gazette* [QRL.186] gives average retail prices on one day a month for the following items: pasteurised milk; skimmed milk; home-produced butter; New Zealand butter; Danish butter; and Cheddar-type cheese. The figures are derived from prices collected for the purposes of the General Index of Retail Prices in more than 180 areas of the United Kingdom. An indication of variations in price is given by showing the ranges within which at least four-fifths of the recorded prices fell. Quarterly and annual national average prices are given in the *Compendium of Results* [QRL.373] for the following: liquid wholemilk, full price; other milk nes; condensed milk; dried milk, branded; yogurt; skimmed milks; cream; natural cheese; processed cheese; and butter. Greater detail on many of these products is also provided in a supplementary table.

5.12.2.2 Recommended prices

The prices quoted in *Shaws Guide to Fair Retail Prices* [QRL.453] are for the guidance of consumers and retailers. The amount of product detail is considerable, and only broad product categories will be listed here for sake of economy. Recommended retail prices are published on the first day of every month for the following: butter; cheese/cheese spreads; cream (canned & fresh); cream (long life); milk (condensed); milk (skimmed sweetened); milk (evaporated); milk (flavoured); milk (long life); milk drinks; milk powder; milk products; milk puddings (creamed); milk shakes; yogurt. When manufacturers do not recommend fair selling prices, they are suggested by the editor with help from the manufacturers. Suggested prices show a fair profit on minimum quantities supplied on trade terms. Typical prices — referred to as KVI (known value item) prices — of key lines in multiple stores are also quoted as a guide, e.g. Carnation milk.

The Grocer [QRL.252] publishes weekly market prices, subject to regional variation and discounting, on numerous types of butter and cheese. In addition, on the first Saturday in each month, *The Grocer Price List* [QRL.253] is published. Recommended prices are quoted for cheese; cream; milk (condensed); milk (powder); milk (products); and yogurt. Prices are supplied by manufacturers, importers or sole agents, and are for the smallest quantities they supply. Again the amount of brand detail is considerable.

5.12.3 *The Retail Prices Index*

The *Employment Gazette* [QRL.186] carries monthly retail price indices for butter; cheese; fresh milk and milk products. Percentage changes over the previous year are indicated. The structure of the published components was recast with effect from February 1987. Previously separate indices had been available for butter; cheese; fresh milk; and canned, dried etc. milk. The relationship between the old and the new index structure was shown in the September 1986 issue of the *Employment Gazette* [QRL.186].

The *Monthly Digest of Statistics* [QRL.362] is an alternative source. *Retail Prices: Indices 1914–1986* [QRL.434] contains group and sub-group indices and weights back to 1974, group indices back to 1956, and all items back to 1947.

5.12.4 *Price Index Numbers in the National Food Survey*

The National Food Survey is another useful source of price information. The *Compendium of Results* [QRL.373] presents annual price indices for the following main food groups: liquid wholemilk (4); other milk and cream (8–17); milk and cream (4–17); cheese (22,23); and butter (135).

5.12.5 *Producer Price Index Numbers*

The series of Producer Price Indices are considered in general terms in section 2.12.5. Details of the price indices for the inputs and outputs for the preparation of milk and milk products are given below.

5.12.5.1 Producer price index numbers: input prices
Business Monitor MM22: Producer Price Indices carries the producer price index numbers of materials and fuels purchased for AH4130 giving both monthly and annual data. The monthly data are given for the current and previous years, with the figures for the latest two months provisional. An annual average for the previous year is also presented. *Business Monitor MM22* was published for the first time in October 1989 and continued the coverage in *British Business* [QRL.66]

A monthly producer price index for milk is provided in *MAFF Statistics: Agricultural Price Indices* [QRL.315]

5.12.5.2 Producer price index numbers: output prices
Business Monitor MM22 contains the producer price index numbers of products manufactured in the United Kingdom (home sales) for AH4130. the monthly data are provided for the current and previous year, with the figures for the latest two months provisional. An annual average for the previous year is also presented. *Business Monitor MM22* was published for the first time in October 1989 and continued the coverage in *British Business* [QRL.66]. The annual *Abstract of Statistics* [QRL.37] gives the annual averages for AH4130 for a six-year run for products manufactured in the United Kingdom (home sales).

5.12.6 *Intervention Prices*
United Kingdom Dairy Facts & Figures [QRL.503] gives the common "target price" for milk, intervention prices for butter and skimmed milk powder, and consumer subsidies on butter, skimmed milk and skimmed milk powder. UK intervention prices for butter and skimmed milk powder are also published in the *Report of the Intervention Board* [QRL.293], and in the Boards' journals — [QRL.358], [QRL.355], [QRL.357], [QRL.360] and [QRL.490].

5.13 Financial Information

Farm Incomes in the United Kingdom [QRL.210] contains the results of the annual Farm Management Survey for "dairy farms" (see section 5.5 for definition). Annual figures are provided on input costs (feed, fertiliser, labour, machinery, depreciation, land and buildings), output revenue and net farm income for farms in England, Wales, Scotland and Northern Ireland. A balance sheet analysis of assets and liabilities of all UK dairy farms is also given.

United Kingdom Dairy Facts & Figures [QRL.503] provides a breakdown of the costs and returns of milk production in England and Wales, and Northern Ireland. The statistics for England and Wales are derived from a continuing study of milk production costs under the National Investigation into the Economics of Milk Production (see section 5.16). The 1988 issue carries data from the 1987/88 survey.

The statistics for Scotland are derived from the Scottish Milk Net Margin Investigation. Differences in methodology applied to the costing of certain items mean that the results are not directly comparable with those for England and Wales.

The figures for Northern Ireland are supplied from the Farm Management Survey conducted by DANI and again are not comparable with those for Scotland, or England and Wales.

Business Monitor PA413 [QRL.107] provides annual data on output, wages and salaries, the purchase of materials and the cost of non-industrial services, and gross value added for all UK establishments classified to the industry. Moreover, there are analyses of labour costs by size of establishment and of net output and gross value added at factor cost by region.

Financial information on the various Milk Marketing Boards, Trade Federations and dairy produce manufacturers is available in their Annual Reports. The ICC Information Group publish an annual Business Ratio report on *Dairy Products* [QRL.549]. There is also a Key Note report on *Milk & Dairy Products* [QRL.594].

Finally, the NBPI carried out a survey on *Pay and Conditions of Workers in the Milk Industry* [B.407] in 1970. The survey of pay and conditions examined the state of the industry with a view to higher efficiency and productivity and contains much interesting, though somewhat dated, financial information (see section 5.16 for further details). Two earlier NBPI reports which may be of interest are *The Remuneration of Milk Distributors (Interim Report)* [B.412] and *The Remuneration of Milk Distributors (Final Report)* [B.411].

5.14 Advertising and Market Research

5.14.1 *Advertising*

An overview of the role of advertising in the UK Dairy Market, with particular reference to the period since accession to the EC, is provided by Hessner and Mellor [B.77]. They concluded that the role of advertising has altered significantly and it is now used not only to expand revenue in the liquid market, but also to reduce the level of the storage and disposal costs in the dairy sector. In practice, the Milk Marketing Boards undertake sales promotion and advertising both independently and on behalf of milk producers as well as on a joint basis with manufacturers and distributors of milk and milk products through the Milk Publicity and Dairy Councils. *United Kingdom Dairy Facts & Figures* [QRL.503] gives details of the Milk Boards' annual expenditure on advertising and sales promotion in England and Wales, Scotland and Northern Ireland, and of advertising expenditure on home and imported milk; cream; cheese; and butter.

The *Tri-Media Digest of Brands and Advertisers* [QRL.493] is the standard reference work for information on the advertising expenditure of competing firms and brands. Data are provided therein — see section 2.14.1.1 for details — on the following product groups relevant to industry Group 413: butter (F08); cheese (F28); milk and milk products, except cream (F81); sweet toppings, including cream (F82); and yogurt (F98). An alternative source is *The Media Register* [QRL.354], which gives details of monthly press and television advertising expenditure for butter (FOO 25); cream (and substitutes (FOO 26); cheese (FOO 27); milk and milk products (FOO 28); and yoghurt (FOO 29).

5.14.2 *Market Research*

The various dairy industry organisations also undertake a considerable amount of market research which provide statistical data about the industry. The three Milk Marketing Boards in Scotland periodically monitor the pattern of milk retailing in Scotland and the results of a study conducted at the end of August and beginning of September 1983 were published in *The Household Market for Milk in Scotland 1983* [B.307]. This has now been superseded by the 1986 study [B.308] which was published in April 1987. Data are provided *inter alia* on the demographic breakdown of milk purchasing levels, the source of milk purchases, milk packaging, milk prices and the frequency of purchase of UHT milk. A similar study was carried out in the summer of 1985 to find out the pattern of cream retailing in Scotland and these results are published in *The Household Market for Cream in Scotland 1985* [B.306]. Data include a demographic breakdown of cream purchasing levels, sales by type of cream, total volumes of fresh and UHT cream purchased by size of container, frequency of purchase, cream prices, cream uses and the reasons given for some households for not buying cream. A complementary study was also undertaken into the catering market for milk and cream and the results published in *The Catering Market for Milk and Cream in Scotland 1984–85* [B.221]. Data are presented on both the value and volume of milk and cream purchased by type of outlet, and the uses to which the milk and cream were put.

The three Milk Marketing Boards in Scotland have been conducting full censuses of all registered milk producers since 1964 with the most recent surveys having been undertaken at regular three-year intervals. The 1987 census covered all farms held by milk producers registered with the Boards and which were producing milk at the time of the investigation. The results are published in *The Structure of Scottish Milk Production at 1987* [B.383]. Data are provided on a wide range of topics including the size distribution of dairy farms, the number of dairy farm workers and an analysis of bulk feed used on farms.

In England and Wales, the Dairy Trade Federation have completed three surveys. The first — the *Annual Milk Bottle Trippage and Packaging Survey* [B.199] — measures the number of times a returnable milk bottle is used to carry milk and also splits the liquid milk market between various pack types. The second is the *Flavoured Drink Market Survey* [B.277] whose aim is to find the total market volume and split according to pack size, heat treatment and fat content. Third, there is the *Dairy Industry Manpower Survey* [B.236] which provides data on the milk industry workforce broken down by work sector, category of employee and sex. These surveys are available primarily to dairymen and related institutions but also to anyone outside the industry requesting specific details.

In June 1985, the National Dairy Council carried out a survey into how housewives buy milk and dairy produce from the milkman, and other related topics. The results of the survey are published in *The Doorstep Delivery Service '85* [B.242] which contains data on milk purchasing and consumption, and consumers' attitudes toward, and requirements from, the delivery service.

Agra Europe (London) Ltd. provide a number of publications relating to the industry, though none qualify as sources of primary statistical data. *Preserved Milk* [QRL.388] is published monthly, and carries detailed coverage of the preserved milk (whole, skim, whey, condensed and casein) market, including graphs and tables on

European and world production, stocks, exports, imports and prices. The data are also available on the Agra Europe data base. *Milk Products* [QRL.359] is a report on EEC butter, cheese and milk production and markets, with graphs and tables covering the principal dairying nations of Europe and the world. At least ten issues are published each year. In addition, Agra Europe have published a number of occasional special reports and briefings: *EEC Dairy Policy: The Failure of Quotas* [B.248] in November 1986; *EEC Dairy Market: Prospects for Autumn and Winter 1987/88* [B.246] in August 1987; *EEC Dairy Market Report 1987* [B.247] in December 1987; *The Effect of Milk Quotas on Community Agriculture* [B.253] in October 1987; *EEC and World Dairy Markets 1988* [B.245] in June 1988; and *The UK Dairy Industry and EEC Legislation: A Commentary on EEC Regulations and Court Proceedings* [B.390] in October 1988.

Finally, we mention the occasional reviews carried out by various market research organisations. *Retail Business* [QRL.432] carries reviews on "Butter, margarine and spreads" in issue 370 (December 1988); on "Cream" in issue 368 (October 1988); on "Milk" in issues 365 and 366 (July and August 1988); and on "Yogurt" in issue 337 (March 1986). Reports published in *Market Intelligence* [QRL.339] include "Delicatessen foods" (November 1988); "Dairy spreads within the yellow fats market" (July 1988); "Cheese" (March 1988); "Milk and cream" (January 1988); and "Convenience desserts" (May 1987). *Market Research: Great Britain* [QRL.343] contains analyses of the markets for "Milk" (February 1988); "Butter" (January 1988); and "Pre-packed cheeses" (May 1987). Euromonitor also publish a market sector survey entitled *The Dairy Products Report* [QRL.528]. Market Assessment Publications produce annual sector reports on *Dairy Products* [QRL.604] and *Sweets & Desserts* [QRL.616], while Marketing Strategies for Industry publish annual reviews of *Cheese* [QRL.626], *Preserved Milk* [QRL.645], *Short-life Dairy Products* [QRL.648] and *Yellow Fats* [QRL.653]. The occasional series of *Food Market Updates* [QRL.238], published by the Leatherhead Food Research Association, includes number 21 on "Dairy products in the UK" (March 1987). This contains data and commentary on butter; cheese; cream; dairy desserts; dairy spreads; ice-cream; milks; and yogurt. Also included is a list of selected references from the Association's market information data base (FOMAD). The data base is available on-line to subscribing companies. It should be emphasised that many other organisations also publish market research reports, and so the above does not constitute an exhaustive list. Moreover, all such reports tend to be market-orientated, rather than industry-orientated, unlike many of the statistical sources covered in this Review. Finally, it should be noted that this list constitutes much of what was available at the time of writing and that there are additions with the passage of time.

5.15 Research and Development

The Milk Marketing Boards offer recording services and, in England and Wales, a consultancy service to individual farmers in all aspects of farm management. The England and Wales Board has a veterinary laboratory in Worcester. And all the Boards operate schemes for the regular analysis of the composition of producers' milk. This analysis is carried out at six Central Testing laboratories established by the Boards. Details of all these facilities are outlined in *United Kingdom Dairy Facts & Figures* [QRL.503].

5.16 Official Investigations

Mention should be made of occasional reports from the National Economic Development Office. *The Dairy Industry: General Issues Affecting the Industry* [B.233] was published in 1987. It considers consumer attitudes, the influences bearing upon consumers, and some of the technical, scientific and policy background to the diet and health debate to which the dairy industry has been exposed. A detailed analysis of the dairy industry's market position and future prospects is provided in *The Dairy Industry: Supply and Demand to 1990* [B.235]. The report analyses likely trends to 1990 and considers the economic, social and commercial environment; the supply of milk from UK farms; UK demand for milk and dairy products; and major issues confronting the dairy industry. The report was published in 1987, and was the successor to *The Dairy Industry: Supply and Demand to 1988* [B.234], published in 1984.

During its short existence, the National Board for Prices and Incomes (NBPI) — see section 2.16.1 — published three reports of relevance to the milk and milk products industry. Report no.33, *The Remuneration of Milk Distributors (Interim Report)* [B.412], and Report no.46, *The Remuneration of Milk Distributors (Final Report)* [B.411], were both published in 1967. In 1970, the NBPI published a report on *Pay and Conditions of Workers in the Milk Industry* [B.407], which examined the state of the industry with a view to higher efficiency and productivity. The Board carried out an extensive survey of pay and conditions, covering the major integrated dairy concerns, processing dairies and milk products manufacturers. Returns were received from 282 organisations and data were provided for 8000 individual workers, some ten per cent of the labour force. Tables (supported by a commentary) show the structure of the industry and the labour force, arrangements for determining wage rates, conditions of employment and averages and distributions of hours worked (including the days of the week), earnings (including various components) and length of service. The analyses are given by size of organisation, location, activity and occupation, for men and women, adults and juveniles. and for full-time and part-time workers. Mention should also be made of the 1967 Monopolies Commission report on the *Supply of Infant Milk Foods* [B.446].

Milk production on the farm falls in the domain of agriculture rather than food manufacture, and thus will not be discussed in detail in this Review. Nevertheless, mention should be made of the National Investigation into the Economics of Milk Production (England and Wales), which is sponsored jointly by the Milk Marketing Board in England and Wales and MAFF. Reports are published periodically by MAFF — see, for example, *Milk Costs 1986/87* [B.335] — and contain much statistical information on costs, returns and margins in the industry. Detailed information on the Scottish Milk Production Net Margins Investigation is available from the Department of Agriculture for Scotland (DAFS). G.H. Peters discusses sources of statistics on milk production in his companion Review in this series, *Agriculture* [B.144].

5.17 Improvements and Comments

The industry is well served for statistical information by the various publications provided by the five Milk Marketing Boards, and the other dairy industry organisations. Moreover, this information is readily available to the public and is not generally restricted to members. In particular *United Kingdom Dairy Facts & Figures* [QRL.503] contains a wealth of information on just about every aspect of the industry and provides an ideal introduction to the novice researcher.

However, there is a serious deficiency of information on products. This point was emphasised by R.E. Williams and J.J. Bienkowski in their paper at the 1986 Statistics Users' Conference on Agricultural and Food Statistics entitled "Statistical sources — milk and milk products" [B.187]. They maintain that no resources have been devoted either by government or the industry to the direct collection of statistics on the production of milk products. Virtually all the statistics in this area are derived or inferred from commercial transactions, e.g. from the data on milk utilisation accruing to the Boards from the way the prices for the milk they sell are calculated. They also point out that, because the industry does not at present have adequate data on low-fat milk sales, the figures that are available on milk utilisation are becoming increasingly inadequate for the calculation of supply balances and product consumption.

The consequent shortcomings in the basic statistical information are of major concern to those in the industry as well as to government. The problem can only be resolved through the co-operation of all sectors and unfortunately this could take some time to emerge. There is then the question of who will meet the additional costs of collecting the information.

CHAPTER 6

PROCESSING OF FRUIT AND VEGETABLES

The information in this chapter relates to the processing of fruit and vegetables industry, Group 414 in the CSO *Standard Industrial Classification Revised 1980* [B.232]. Other more general sources, which provide statistics on other industry Groups as well, are covered in Chapter 2 and should be consulted as required. The contents of this chapter are as follows:

6.1 Introduction

Industry Group 414 covers the following Activity Heading:

4147 Processing of fruit and vegetables.
1. Freezing.
Quick freezing of fruit and vegetables.
2. Pickling and preserving in salt or oil.
3. Jam, marmalade and table jellies.
4. Canning, bottling, drying, etc.

For an alphabetical list of the activities covered by Group 414, see Table 6.1 and the CSO *Indexes to the Standard Industrial Classification Revised 1980* [B.317].

Group 414 corresponds closely to MLH218 "Fruit and vegetable products" under SIC(1968). The following activities, however, were classified to MLH218 but now appear under Group 423 "Miscellaneous foods":

Table 6.1: Activities Classified under Group 414

SIC(1980) AH		SIC(1968) MLH
4147.1	Freezing of fruit and vegetables	
	Fruit quick freezing	218.2
	Quick freezing of fruit and vegetables	218.2
	Vegetable quick freezing	218.2
4147.2	Pickling and preserving of fruit and vegetables in salt or oil	
	Chutney (pickle) manufacturing	218.3
	Fruit pickling	218.3
	Gherkin pickling	218.3
	Olive preserving in salt or brine	218.3
	Piccalilli production	218.3
	Pickle (including beetroot and onion) manufacturing	218.3
	Pickling of fruit	218.3
	Pickling of vegetables	218.3
	Vegetable pickling	218.3
4147.3	Jam, marmalade and table jellies	
	Candied peel manufacturing	218.1
	Crystallised fruit manufacturing	218.1
	Fruit jelly (preserve) manufacturing	218.1
	Fruit pulp manufacturing	218.1
	Homogenised fruit and vegetable manufacturing	218.3
	Jam manufacturing	218.1
	Jelly (table) manufacturing	218.1
	Jelly powder manufacturing	218.1
	Marmalade manufacturing	218.1
	Mincemeat manufacturing	218.1
	Strained fruit manufacturing	218.3
	Strained vegetable manufacturing	218.3
	Table jelly manufacturing	218.1
4147.4	Canning, bottling, drying, etc. of fruit and vegetables	
	Bottling of fruit and vegetables	218.3
	Canning of fruit and vegetables	218.3
	Dehydrating fruit for human consumption	218.3
	Dehydrating of vegetables for human consumption	218.3
	Dried fruit (except field dried) manufacturing	218.3
	Dried fruit cleaning	218.3
	Dried vegetable (except field dried) manufacturing	218.3
	Heat treatment of fruit and vegetables	218.3
	Potato flour manufacturing	218.3
	Vegetable dehydrating, for human consumption	218.3

- Potato crisps and other snack products
- Broths, soups, sauces and other relishes
- Spaghetti canning
- Honey processing and packing
- Dried herbs (except field dried) manufacturing
- Hop extract manufacturing
- Vinegar (malt, spirit, wine, acetic acid) manufacturing
- Wine vinegar manufacturing.

Full details may be found in *Standard Industrial Classification Revised 1980: Reconciliation with Standard Industrial Classification 1968* [B.379].

Business Monitor PA414: Processing of Fruit and Vegetables [QRL.108] currently provides the annual data for the Group as a whole, collecting together the census information on output and costs, capital expenditure, stocks and work-in-progress and operating ratios. Data on employment, wages and salaries, output, capital expenditure, stocks and work-in-progress etc. are cross-classified by employment size. The regional distribution of employment, capital expenditure, output etc. is shown. *Business Monitor PQ4147: Fruit and Vegetable Products* [QRL.133] gives the quarterly data on sales, production, exports and imports etc. up to the second quarter of 1989.

There were a number of differences in the past from the current coverage of this sector, the most important of which are now noted. The time series in the *Historical Record of the Census of Production 1907–1970* [QRL.264] only goes back to 1975 for MLH218 in the SIC(1968). Coverage included (for the years 1935, 1949 and 1950) condiments, other than vinegar, classified to the "starch and miscellaneous foods industry" in SIC(1968). Prior to 1963, it included vegetable juices which were then classified to the "soft drinks industry" MLH232. Prior to 1954 it excluded tinned and bottled soups, curd, honey, macaroni, spaghetti etc. which were consigned to the "Miscellaneous foods trades". This is confirmed by examining *The Report on the Census of Production for 1951* [QRL.422] — see Volume 8 Trade K "Preserved Fruit and Vegetables" and Volume 9 Trade G "Miscellaneous Preserved Foods".

The *First Census of Production of the United Kingdom (1907)* [QRL.219] indeed took "Cocoa, confectionery and fruit preserving" trades together and located dried and preserved vegetables in the "Preserved Meat, Poultry and Fish, Pickle, Sauce and Baking-Powder Trades". Not all the revisions in coverage are detailed in the *Historical Record* [QRL.264] so that the individual Census of Production volumes merit close inspection. However the major recent changes have been the transfers already noted under the SIC(1980) into "Miscellaneous foods". The many changes are emphasised again in section 11.1 of Chapter 11.

6.2 Industry Structure

As with most foods, processed fruit and vegetable products have important links with both the sources of supply and retail outlets. The coverage of *Business Monitor PQ4147* [QRL.133] listed in section 6.4 shows the varied nature of both the products and processes included in this Group, even if the included products are less heterogeneous than "Miscellaneous foods". The structure is now discussed under four sub-sections:

6.2.1 Jam, marmalade and table jellies
6.2.2 Freezing of fruit and vegetables
6.2.3 Canning, bottling, drying etc. of fruit and vegetables
6.2.4 Pickling and preserving of fruit and vegetables; pickles and chutney.

Many of the major companies straddle all four sub-sections and indeed some operate in other Groups of the Food industries.

6.2.1 *Jam, Marmalade and Table Jellies*

The processing industry involves the boiling of preserved fruit (preserved by freezing or with sulphite) with sugar in a sealed vat. The major technological advance has been the use of vacuum cooking by Chivers Hartley which allows processing to take place at a lower temperature hence causing less damage to the fruit. But the production of preserves has a fairly simple basis and is still performed at home in many British households.

An overall market summary was given in the review of "Jams, marmalade and fruit curds" in the November 1985 issue of *Retail Business* [QRL.432]. Two manufacturers dominated at that time: Chivers Hartley (Premier Brands) and Robertson (RHM Avana). Own-label and high quality products are of growing importance. Strawberry jam is the most popular flavour, followed by raspberry, blackcurrant, blackberry and apricot. There are some mixed fruit jams.

The decline in popularity of jams is attributed to concern about sugar content but also the diminished consumption of afternoon tea and high tea. A trend is to use fresh and frozen fruit as distinct from fruit preserved with sulphite. Pure fruit jams imported from Eastern European countries may reflect this tendency. Jams are also categorised according to a 1981 EC Preserves Directive into standard jam, extra jam (more fruit) and reduced sugar jam. The large manufacturers have a range of ten to fifteen standard jams and a smaller number of extra jams. Own-labels are of some importance as well.

The marmalade market is usually divided into four sectors: the most popular thin cut; medium cut; thick cut; and lime (mainly thin cut). The decline in demand, partly attributable to the diminishing popularity of the traditional English breakfast, does mean severe competition in an over supplied market. Robertson's Golden and Silver Shred leads the thin cut marmalade sector. Chivers Olde English is the most prominent thick cut brand. Chivers Hartley is the preserves arm of Premier Brands (since May 1989 part of Hillsdown Holdings) which also produces canned fruit and vegetables.

6.2.2 *Freezing of Fruit and Vegetables*

The freezing of fruit and vegetables is an important component of the frozen food industry. However, it must be noted that the major generalist companies as exemplified by Birds Eye Walls (Unilever), Ross Foods (United Biscuits Frozen Foods), Findus (Nestlé) and Hillsdown Holdings etc. also operate significantly in other SIC(1980) areas: notably "Frozen meat products" (AH4122.2), "Fish processing" (AH4150), "Ice-cream" (AH4213) and the various products classified to "Miscellaneous foods" (AH4239).

Frozen Foodstuffs, A Report on the Supply in the United Kingdom of Frozen Foodstuffs for Human Consumption [B.444] from the Monopolies and Mergers

Commission (MMC) in 1976 contains a description of the development of the frozen foods industry. It was mainly a post World War Two phenomenon, building upon the earlier small-scale quick freezing by fish merchanting companies such as Associated Fisheries Ltd. and H. Smethurst (Fish Curers) Ltd. in the 1930's. The freezing, which was initially for the catering trade, included the freezing of vegetables by Smedley's Ltd. Then Birds Eye, after World War Two, led the way into the manufacture of consumer-size packs of frozen foods for national distribution through the retail trade. The considerable capital outlay on cold stores, refrigerated transport and refrigerated food cabinets in retail outlets was a precondition of its success. Ross Foods and Findus followed these patterns.

The steady growth in the frozen vegetable market means that a high proportion of both the green pea acreage and green bean acreage goes for freezing. The major companies exercise close control over the crop, often supplying the seed, determining planting and harvesting times, approving fertilizers and insecticides and encouraging technical innovation in strains of seeds and harvesting methods.

Peas and beans dominate the frozen vegetable market. Products also include brussels sprouts, cauliflowers, mange-tout, ratatouille, frozen vegetables in sauce, vegetables in rice mixes, the frozen vegetable meal etc. Chips and other potato products are often seen as other distinct segments. McCain (McCain Foods Canada) is a household name prominent in frozen chips. But the potato market is broader than this, given the existence of potato croquettes, jacket potatoes, frozen mashed potatoes etc. and even real mash. There also exists a host of other companies listed by the Potato Marketing Board (PMB) as producers of processed potato products.

The organisation of the frozen vegetable industry is complex and subject to change. The range of products in *Business Monitor PQ4147* [QRL.133] is less detailed than what can be gleaned from market research publications. Consequently, these can be used to keep up to date with information on industry structure. We list some of these below:

- *Fruit & Vegetables* [QRL.608] by Market Assessment Publications.
- *Frozen Foods* [QRL.607] by Market Assessment Publications.
- "Frozen food (Part 1)" in the April 1988 issue of *Retail Business* [QRL.432].
- "Frozen food (Part 2)" in the May 1988 issue of *Retail Business* [QRL.432].
- The Key Note report on *Frozen Foods* [QRL.589].
- "Frozen foods" in the August 1987 issue of *Market Intelligence* [QRL.339].
- *Fruit and Vegetables* [QRL.638] by Marketing Strategies for Industry.
- *Frozen Food* [QRL.637] by Marketing Strategies for Industry.

The opportunity for new suppliers of frozen foods is enhanced by the growth in importance of supermarket chains and the demands of home freezer owners. Firms have developed own-brand labels as the multiple retailers have become involved in the processing end as well as in distribution and marketing. The development and growth of companies like Christian Salvesen and Frigoscandia feeds back to the grower groups wishing to freeze and distribute own products rather than only grow on contract for the major processors. In fact there exists an approximate dichotomy between the major manufacturers with their own storage, depot and distribution facilities etc. and the many small and medium-size companies using the services of the national frozen food distributors.

Paragraph 40 of the 1976 MMC report *Supplies of Frozen Foodstuffs* [B.444] remarked that the quantity of fruit for freezing was miniscule compared with vegetables. Frozen fruit is still the smallest sector in the frozen foods market. Competition from home fresh produce, imported fresh produce, imported frozen fruit and canned produce etc. is evidently strong. Once defrosted, the fruit tend to lose flavour. About half of the volume sales are accounted for by raspberries and the remainder split among apples in sliced form, strawberries, blackberries, melon balls, fruit salad, blueberries, rhubarb, gooseberries, black currants and cherries. Fruit mixes (raspberries and black currants for instance) are quite popular. Birds Eye, Ross and Findus all withdrew from the market in 1985 which was left to Smedley's (Hillsdown Holdings), Scotfresh and Shearing Foods of which the latter appears at the time of writing to be the largest frozen fruit packer in the United Kingdom. However the majority of its frozen fruit goes into fruit pulp for manufacturing jams and pies/puddings. In sum, statistical coverage of the frozen fruit sector is sparse.

6.2.3 *Canning, Bottling, Drying etc. of Fruit and Vegetables*

The canning of fruit and vegetables is another significant component of food processing which used to be covered in *Business Monitor PQ4147* [QRL.133]. There is again an overlap with other products since the canned foods sector can be regarded as a market in its own right. It accounts for the following main areas of consumer demand: canned meat, canned fish, canned vegetables, baked beans, canned pasta, canned tomatoes, canned soup, canned fruit, fruit pie fillings and sponge puddings. We deal here with canned vegetables, canned tomatoes, canned fruit and fruit pie fillings.

The market perception is to include processed peas, carrots, green beans, vegetable mixes, potatoes and mushrooms etc. together under canned vegetables. Many major firms offer a range of products e.g. Lockwoods and Smedley's (Hillsdown), Batchelors Foods (Unilever) in processed peas etc. plus many other household names and own-label. The canned vegetable sector as a whole competes with frozen vegetables, dehydrated produce and fresh vegetables.

Baked beans are a canned vegetable in terms of food technology but viewed as a separate market category since they are uniquely available in canned form alone. The major supplier is Heinz, followed in brand shares by own-label then Crosse & Blackwell (Nestlé). Measurement is somewhat complicated since after the original product of canned haricot beans in tomato sauce, baked beans is often mixed with other foods. Baked beans with sauces ranks as the second largest area of sale. Canned tomatoes are largely imported. Napolina Ltd. and Princes Buitoni Ltd. are the most discernible organisations. Canned tomatoes are third in order of importance in the retail market after baked beans and processed peas. Canned fruit is largely imported. UK canning of seasonal fruits is small. Of over fifty varieties, peaches, pineapples, pears and fruit cocktails predominate. Del Monte (formerly R.J. Reynolds Nabisco USA) is the market leader. Princes Buitoni (Italy) has a significant share. *Business Monitor MM20: Overseas Trade Statistics of the United Kingdom* [QRL.85] show Italy and Greece as important suppliers with Australia and South Africa less significant now. Fruit pie fillings are sold primarily in cans, although products in jars and packets are also available. Morton (Hillsdown), Pickerings (Heinz) and Batchelors (Unilever) are the dominant brand names although the combined forces of own-label products take the largest share of sales.

The range of products in *Business Monitor PQ4147* [QRL.133] is again fleshed out by the following market research publications:

- "Canned fruit and vegetables" in the June 1988 issue of *Market Intelligence* [QRL.339].
- *Canned Foods* [QRL.601] by Market Assessment Publications.
- The Key Note report on *Canned Foods* [QRL.582].
- *Canned Foods* [QRL.623] by Marketing Strategies for Industry.
- "Canned vegetables" in the September 1985 issue of *Retail Business* [QRL.432].
- "Canned fruit" in the July 1985 issue of *Retail Business* [QRL.432].

6.2.4 *Pickling and Preserving of Fruit and Vegetables; Pickles and Chutney*

Pickles consist of vegetables preserved in vinegar or a vinegar-based sauce. They may be divided into two major categories: sweet and sour. The major types of sour pickle are pickled onions, pickled beetroot and piccalilli. Chutney is not always classified as a pickle although it competes with sweet pickle. The major ingredient is normally mangoes (though tomatoes, apples, apricots and peaches are used, flavoured with spices and onions and preserved in vinegar).

The market place usually views pickle and onions, which is placed in AH4147.2 of SIC(1980), as part of a nexus which includes mustards, salad creams and sauces. Salad dressings, tomato sauces, vinegars and condiments etc. may be regarded as significant components of the same market segment. Again there is an overlap in SIC(1980) with "Miscellaneous foods" which covers many of these products. These are all put together in the market research reports as the following list suggests:

- *Sauces and Pickles* [QRL.647] by Marketing Strategies for Industry.
- The Key Note report on *Sauces and Spreads* [QRL.597].
- *Dressings and Sauces* [QRL.605] by Market Assessment Publications.
- "Pickles, sauces and salad dressings" in the August 1982 issue of *Retail Business* [QRL.432].

There are many products and companies but three organisations and their brands stand out. Crosse & Blackwell (Nestlé) claim leadership in the sweet pickle market with the Branston brand. Brooke Bond Oxo (Unilever) produces Hayward which has a significant part of sour pickle sales. Heinz is involved in both the sweet and sour pickle sector. It markets five different flavours of the Ploughman's (sweet pickle) brand: original, tangy, tomato, piccalilli and mild mustard and actively promotes sour pickle products such as its Pickled Onions and Silverskin. Sharwoods (Rank Hovis McDougall) is the dominant brand in the mango chutney sector. Own-labels account for a significant portion of total sales.

6.2.5 *Comments*

A few remarks now need to be made about information on industry structure. Firstly, it has been necessary to draw upon many market research organisations. Their reports cut across the information in *Business Monitor PQ4147* [QRL.133] and *Business Monitor PQ4239: Miscellaneous Foods* [QRL.139]. Secondly, statistics on market shares for important brands and some background on the ownership structure are needed to fill out the limited official data on market shares and concentration. Thirdly, the competition between different kinds of processes: frozen, canned, fresh etc. must be clarified. Fourthly, there is overlap within the Food industries. The companies present in the four subsectors discussed here are also operating in the many segments of "Miscellaneous foods". An obvious example is Heinz, the market leader in baked beans, in canned soup, baby meals, tomato sauce, and canned sponge puddings. This company also has a strong presence in pie fillings and pickles.

Nor is the picture a static one. The review of "Dried food" in the May 1988 issue of *Market Intelligence* [QRL.339] discusses another market which includes fruits, potatoes and vegetables as well as snacks and complete meals. The 1988 report on *Chilled Foods* [QRL.602] by Market Assessment Publications summarises the range of products sold prepacked from the chilled cabinet.

Finally, it needs to be stressed that the summaries in the preceding sections on market structure and the companies involved therein largely relate to the situation in 1988–89. This is obviously subject to change. Yet the reader should now have both the knowledge of the sources, and consequently the means of updating information on market structure, despite the kaleidoscopic changes both in brand names and company ownership. The judicious use of some market research reports, the *Food Trades Directory and Food Buyer's Yearbook* [B.285] and *Who Owns Whom* [B.396] is advised.

6.3 The European Community

6.3.1 *The Economic Influence of the Community*

The beginnings of the fruit and vegetable regime owed much to Italy's insistence in exchange for her acceptance of the Community's cereal policies in the 1960's. The regime has become more significant with Community enlargement and the membership of more Mediterranean countries (Spain, Portugal, Greece). It has also affected processing via the conditions of the supply of raw materials with, for instance, Dutch competition in tomato supply and French provision of apples.

The European Community (EC) market policy for fruit and vegetables affects both the internal market and foreign trade for both fresh and processed products. *Secondary Legislation of the European Communities Subject Edition Volume 28 Fruit and Vegetables* [B.371] includes Council Regulation (EEC) No.1035/72 which outlines the support measures for fresh fruit and vegetables, encompassing both internal market regulations and foreign trade regulations. Council Regulation (EEC) No.516/77 [B.342] is the basic initial reference on the common organisation of the market in products processed from fruit and vegetables. Council Regulation (EEC) No.1152/78 [B.343] is an important amendment impelled by the extension of membership to the Mediterranean regions.

Reference prices are set for fresh fruit and vegetable products: for example there were eighteen of these designated in 1989. These are in effect minimum import prices with penalties on importing nations which do not respect the reference prices. Producer groups are encouraged to control supplies, common quality standards are important and systems of market withdrawal, border protection and export refunds are significant.

More directly for the processing side, Council Regulation (EEC) No.1152/78 introduced the following schemes. Provided processors entered into a contract with agricultural producers to buy specified quantities at minimum prices, they are eligible for processing aids to help them sell their produce competitively with third country suppliers. Initially the scheme applied to five products but support costs rose as more products were added. These products include tomato concentrates; peeled whole tomatoes; tomato juice; peaches in syrup; dried plums; peeled sliced tomatoes; peeled frozen tomatoes; tomato flakes; William pears in syrup; sweet and sour cherries in syrup; dried figs, sultanas and currants. Given that Regulation (EEC) No.1152/78 led to some over-production, border protection by ad valorem duties is now a characteristic feature (no more so than for canned fruit with high sugar content where extra duty applies). Further, a system of import certificates exists to monitor the level of imports of "sensitive products" (e.g. canned mushrooms, frozen raspberries and strawberries). A surveillance system applies to Eastern European imports (notably jams) via import documentation. Finally export refunds are available on sugar used in processed products exported to third countries.

Given the importance of sugar as an input, the various input levies and export rebates on sugar and sugar content which counterbalance the difference between world and EC prices are also relevant. Describing the economic influence of the Community on the processing side is like shooting at a moving target, but there are many useful references which we now briefly note.

The Food and Farm Policies of the European Community [B.71] summarises both the agricultural and processing side of the fruit and vegetable regime.

The House of Lords Select Committee report on the European Communities in Session 1980/1981 on *Fruit and Vegetables* [B.292] describes the regime as in [B.71] but in more detail. It collected together illustrative statistics on the effects of EC membership on imports of fresh fruit and vegetables and export refunds paid etc. It contained submissions from interested parties (e.g. the Food Manufacturers' Federation on tomato extract).

EEC Enlargement in the Fruit and Vegetable Sector with Special Reference to Spain and the United Kingdom [B.81] published in November 1983 and more recently (1986) *Horticultural Trade of the Expanded European Community: Implications for Mediterranean Countries* [B.10] include overviews of EC market policy. These are detailed studies of the prospects for many of both fresh and processed products. The latter covers some twenty fruit and vegetable products and studied the possible effects of extending membership to Greece, Portugal, Spain and Tunisia.

As already noted in section 2.3.3.6, *CAP Monitor* [B.220] provides updated summaries of the regimes. The weekly *Agra Europe* [QRL.22] records any developments in the past week. *Agra Europe Special Report no.35: European Fruit and Vegetable Markets and Trade* [B.260] was produced in April 1987 and reviews production, consumption and trade for the major European markets. The United Kingdom is treated as one of the principal Western European importers. *Agra Europe Special Report no.32: EEC Fruit and Vegetable Policy in an International Context* [B.291] appeared in November 1986. It was a detailed description of internal market support measures and external support arrangements. It contained illustrative statistical material and separate sections on potatoes and the Iberian enlargement. It included an assessment of how far the Common Agricultural Policy (CAP) was protective for fruit and vegetables.

Prior to European entry the Economic Development Committee for Agriculture undertook a number of studies to assess the possible impact of Community membership. These were subsequently published by the National Economic Development Office (NEDO) in 1972 and 1973, covering the following areas:

Apples: UK Farming and the Common Market [B.201]
Potatoes: UK Farming and the Common Market [B.354]
Pears: UK Farming and the Common Market [B.350]
Outdoor Vegetables: UK Farming and the Common Market [B.349]
Soft Fruit: UK Farming and the Common Market [B.376].

These reports considered processing as well as agricultural production. They characteristically summarised processing methods. Statistical tables and appendices were assembled from many primary sources to cover consumption, production, prices, imports, exports, tariffs and quotas, common external tariffs etc. Thus the prospect of accession to the European Community had the effect of provoking these studies which summarised the producer-processor nexus. The level of detail was however limited in comparison with the earlier *Horticulture in Britain. Part I: Vegetables* [B.304] and *Horticulture in Britain. Part II: Fruit and Flowers* [B.305] which are more fully discussed in section 6.5.1.1.

6.3.2 *EUROSTAT and Community Statistics*

EUROSTAT publications assemble a good deal of data but generally more on horticulture than on processing. *Crop Production* [QRL.167] covers land use; areas, yields and production but also includes supply balance sheets for potatoes; potato starch; fresh tomatoes; processed tomatoes; pears; fresh peaches; processed peaches; fresh fruits; dried fruits; etc. These physical analyses of usable production, exports and imports etc. identify processing and industrial uses where relevant.

The Agricultural Situation in the Community [QRL.28] includes in its annual agricultural outlook not only intervention activity in the markets for fresh fruit and vegetable products but also a review of the processed products which receive production aid. The extensive coverage of the statistical data and tables (supply balance sheets, prices etc) includes annual information on quantities of fruit and vegetables bought in. These are also expressed as percentages of harvested production for the United Kingdom and other members.

6.3.3 *The Influence of the Community on the Collection of UK Statistics*

The *Intervention Board for Agricultural Produce: Annual Report* [QRL.293] includes physical data on the withdrawal of certain fresh fruit and vegetables from the market. These withdrawals were made in accordance with the compensation arrangements agreed with the producers' organisations which market the produce and which are recognised by the United Kingdom Agricultural Departments. Both the annual quantities and amounts of compensation paid are given, featuring mainly apples, pears and cauliflowers. In addition, the analyses by sector of UK expenditure borne by the European Agricultural Guidance and Guarantee Fund (EAGGF) summarises the total compensation for withdrawn produce. The costs of export refunds for processed fruit and vegetables are also included which is much more substantial than for fresh fruit and vegetables. Figures for the latest two years are given. Fortnightly rates of aid (in £ per tonne) and monthly quantities are separately recorded for peas and field beans used for human consumption.

Basic Horticultural Statistics for the United Kingdom [QRL.61] records the quantities withdrawn from the market for the last eight years. These intervention arrangements apply to all apples, cauliflowers, pears and tomatoes.

Fruit and Tropical Products [QRL.245] devotes a separate section to trade in fresh/processed fruit in the Community as well as the treatment of exports and imports noted in section 6.8. Annual data on physical imports and exports of the countries are recorded. The divisions are as follows: fresh fruit; processed fruit (i.e. canned and bottled fruit); juices and dried fruit. The totals and separate figures for canned and bottled peaches; pears; pineapples; and other fruit in syrup; are distinct from the total without sugar.

The main influences of the Community on methods of statistical collection are surveyed in section 2.3.3. Evidently, many elements of CAP market management require, and result in, additional information flows. The regulation of external trade includes the issue of import and export licences which gives rise to data on the number of licences applied for, the specific quantity of the product involved etc. Many of the mechanisms are summarised in the *Report of the Intervention Board* [QRL.293].

6.4 Output

6.4.1 *Output, Sales and Value Added*

6.4.1.1 Business Statistics Office inquiries

The annual *Business Monitor PA414* [QRL.108] and *Business Monitor PA1002: Summary Volume* [QRL.93] both provide the four major output measures for this Activity Heading, viz: total sales and work done; gross output; net output and gross value added at factor cost. The coverage is fully set out in section 2.4.1.1.

The quarterly *Business Monitor PQ4147* [QRL.133] used to give commodity sales in value, and often volume, and production figures in volume terms. It is useful to list the main products now covered in the quarterly inquiries in order of appearance. Thus the inquiry encompassed up to the second quarter of 1989:

a) Marmalade, jam, mincemeat, fruit curd, fruit pulp (apple and others), apples (peeled), table jellies and frozen fruit and fruit products (including purée and fruit pies). The latter are split into strawberries, raspberries and other fruit and fruit products.
b) The frozen vegetables and vegetable products itemise green peas, green beans, broad beans, brussels sprouts, potatoes and potato products and other vegetables.
c) Fruit and fruit products are treated according to whether canned and bottled (excluding fruit pulp and pie fillings), fruit pie fillings and dried fruits.
d) Vegetables and vegetable products are itemised according to whether preserved in airtight containers (excluding homogenised baby foods), dehydrated vegetables (potatoes and other) and vegetables, including olives, preserved in salted brine, heat treated and dried vegetables, including dried herbs. Fresh prepared vegetables (potatoes and other) are also treated separately.
e) The various pickle products are piccalilli, sweet pickle, beetroot, red cabbage, pickled onions, mixed pickles, other pickles, chutney and unclassified sales.

Sales of principal products classified to other industries are subtracted from the total sales of principal products of this Activity Heading. Sales by units classified to AH4147 but not in the scope of the Quarterly Sales Inquiries are added in, as are sales of merchanted goods, waste products etc. to obtain the figure for total sales and work done by units classified to AH4147. The data are both quarterly and annual. Sales data are expressed in value terms only for all of (e) and for table jellies and dehydrated vegetables. Units involved have a minimum employment of 35. The quarterly Monitors are also discussed in sections 2.1.1.2 and 2.4.1.1.

The *Historical Record* [QRL.264] records the sales of the following: marmalade and jams; vegetables; pickles; sauces and relishes etc. for various census years from 1907 to 1968 and also gives past time series for gross and net output. However, the variation in coverage and links with "Miscellaneous foods" as noted in section 6.1 must be borne in mind.

6.4.1.2 Ministry of Agriculture, Fisheries and Food inquiries

MAFF Statistics: Production of Canned and Bottled Fruit and Vegetables in the UK [QRL.325] reports the results of the Ministry of Agriculture, Fisheries and Food (MAFF) quarterly survey for the latest available quarter, plus comparative figures for earlier quarters and the previous yearly total. Statistics are given in tonnes of net can content from information voluntarily provided by the major canning and bottling companies in the United Kingdom. The fruit section includes strawberries, raspberries, plums, rhubarb, prunes and other fruit products. The vegetable products separately itemised are: baked beans, red kidney beans, cut/sliced beans, garden peas, processed peas, other pulses, carrots, pasta products (see AH4239), potatoes, mushrooms, vegetable mixes and other vegetable products. Global totals are separately given for fruit and vegetables.

The MAFF survey forms the basis for the statistics published in the *Monthly Digest of Statistics* [QRL.362] and the *Annual Abstract of Statistics* [QRL.37]. The *Monthly Digest of Statistics* [QRL.362] gives production data in thousand tonnes for canned and bottled fruit as distinct from canned vegetables. The former includes fruit canned or bottled in the United Kingdom but also fruits such as peaches, pears and pineapples which are imported, either fresh or in containers, and canned in the United Kingdom. The *Monthly Digest of Statistics* [QRL.362] also shows production data in thousand tonnes for jam and marmalade taken together produced and delivered by manufacturers. From 1975 figures have been derived from the BSO quarterly enquiries. All these data are expressed in monthly averages for the time periods recorded. The *Annual Abstract of Statistics* [QRL.37] gives production in thousand tonnes for canned and bottled fruit, canned vegetables and marmalade and jam for the latest eleven years from the MAFF sources.

6.4.2 *Index Numbers of Output*

Business Monitor PQ4147 [QRL.133] carried the index of output of the production industries for "Fruit and vegetable" products (1980 = 100) until the second quarter of 1989. The figures did not include a stock adjustment to correct mixed sales and production data to true production index numbers. The data are generally for the latest seven quarters (seasonally adjusted) and the last six years.

6.5 Current Inputs other than Labour

6.5.1 *Domestic Inputs*

6.5.1.1 Ministry of Agriculture, Fisheries and Food inquiries

Major current inputs to processing flow evidently from domestic agricultural production and imports. It is again appropriate to consider the chain from agricultural output to the inputs and outputs of processors.

Both *Horticulture in Britain. Part I: Vegetables* [B.304] and *Horticulture in Britain. Part II: Fruit and Flowers* [B.305] are unrivalled in their coverage. The Ministry of Food was closely concerned from an early stage of World War Two with the various branches of the food processing industry because the allocation of materials and food to manufacturers depended on regular information on the relationship between the quantities of the different commodity inputs and the consequent processed outputs. These volumes codified the growing amount of statistical knowledge concerning horticulture. They succeeded in showing in a logical fashion the pattern of horticultural production in the United Kingdom. Each volume describes the structure of agricultural production, production areas, sources of supplies, processing techniques and uses of the raw material in processing and output too. Sections are devoted to every main type of vegetable and fruit. Statistics are drawn together from agricultural production to processed output both in the text and appendices. Thus for peas, for instance, it is possible to see the statistical breakdown of the proportion of peas grown for marketing green peas, for canning or for quick freezing. These volumes are thus full amply backed statistical accounts of the further processing of fruit and vegetables. They were published in 1967 and 1970 respectively. They are not only of historical interest but are also unique representations of this agri-industrial sector.

The purpose of the annual *Basic Horticultural Statistics for the United Kingdom* [QRL.61] is to provide comprehensive national statistics on the horticultural crops grown in the United Kingdom plus some statistics on potatoes. This source gives a ten year run of figures on cropped areas of the United Kingdom, gross yield for the crop year (tonnes per hectare), gross production for the crop year (thousand tonnes), output marketed for the crop year (thousand tonnes), and value of output marketed for both crop and calendar year. The many types of fruit and vegetables are covered in the separate fruit and field vegetable sections. Similar data are given for protected vegetables and potatoes. The focus of this abundant source is on agricultural data, compiled from information provided by the Horticultural Crop Intelligence Committees (HCICs) and the annual June, October and December censuses. More continuous information is available in *Report on Crops and Supplies of Vegetables in England and Wales* [QRL.413] and *Report on Crops and Supplies of Fruit in England and Wales* [QRL.412] which from April 1988 became the successors of the single *Report on Crops and Supplies of Fruit and Vegetables in England and Wales* [QRL.411]. These monthly crop reports reflect the situation on seasonal yields, gross production, wastage, and the quantities marketed during the current season on a regional basis. Monthly data are given plus comparative data for the corresponding period the previous year.

Agricultural Statistics: United Kingdom [QRL.32] is another annual MAFF source which contains a separate horticultural section which includes data on the area of horticultural land. The annual data for brussels sprouts, beetroot and green peas distinguish the area of land used for direct market sales of produce and for providing inputs for further processing in England. The potato data includes production area, yield per acre and production in the United Kingdom and other countries. The English counties' information shows the importance of Lincolnshire and Humberside in providing vegetable inputs and of Kent for commercial orchards.

Output and Utilisation of Farm Produce in the United Kingdom [QRL.382] repeat the data for fruit and vegetables on cropped area, gross yield, gross production, output marketed and value of output marketed. Annual data on area, yield and production of potatoes are also featured. However, [QRL.382] was last published in 1988 and contained data for 1987.

Both *Potato Statistics in Great Britain* [QRL.387] and *Potato Marketing Board Annual Report and Accounts* [QRL.384] include statistics on area, yield and total production. The latter also gives annual data on the number of potato processing plants in Great Britain by product group (crisped, frozen and chilled, canned and dried). The Potato Marketing Board (PMB) evidently provides a good deal of data and not only agricultural. *Potato Processing in Great Britain* [QRL.385] gives the estimated tonnage of raw potatoes used for processing in the United Kingdom for a number of seasons. Separate numbers are given for canned/other; crisped; dehydrated; frozen or chilled; all broken down into home-grown and imported.

Both the *Annual Abstract of Statistics* [QRL.37] and the *Monthly Digest of Statistics* [QRL.362] assemble much data from the Agricultural Departments. The *Annual Abstract of Statistics* [QRL.37] carries data on fruit, vegetables and potato output at current and constant prices. Information on land use by acre and estimated quantity of crops are further detailed. Annual data on land use by area; yields; and production for a selection of field vegetables, protected crops and fruit are summarised in the *Monthly Digest of Statistics* [QRL.362]. Peas, green for processing (shelled weight), are separately itemised in both sources.

6.5.1.2 Business Statistics Office inquiries

Business Monitor PO1008: Purchases Inquiry [QRL.116] always lists the values of the materials for use in production. Fresh vegetable and fruit inputs dominate but other food inputs such as meat, sugars and other food industry products e.g. glucose, starch etc. are given as well as the organic and inorganic chemicals. *Business Monitor PA1002.1: Purchases Inquiry* [QRL.94] gives the results of the 1979 Inquiry, showing the values for the many material inputs used in production. Quantities are shown for potatoes, peas, carrots, dried peas and dried white beans. *Business Monitor PA414* [QRL.108] follows the standard treatment of the annual Production Monitors (see section 2.5.1.2).

6.5.1.3 Regional coverage

The *Economic Report on Scottish Agriculture* [QRL.180] gives annual data on the value of output of vegetables, fruit and potatoes. The land-use-by-area information on vegetables and soft fruit includes data for peas and beans described as for canning, freezing or harvesting dry. Some data are repeated in the commentary in

Agriculture in Scotland [QRL.33]. *The Statistical Review of Northern Ireland Agriculture* [QRL.460] gives annual data on the value of output of vegetables, fruit and potatoes. Values and quantities of mushrooms and apples are separately treated. *Northern Ireland Agriculture* [QRL.376] reports the annual data on output values and quantities and land use by area. *Welsh Agricultural Statistics* [QRL.515] reports land-use-by-area data for fruit, vegetables and potatoes plus UK country comparisons.

6.5.2 *Input-output Analysis*

The coverage of the input-output tables is fully discussed in section 2.5.2. Inputs provided by agriculture evidently flow into fruit and vegetable processing but in the tables for 1979 and 1984 "Fruit and vegetable processing" (AH4147) is rolled up with "Fish processing" (AH4150). Previous tables had even less detail since fruit and vegetable processing was subsumed under "other food".

The *Input-output tables for Northern Ireland: 1963* [QRL.279] identified fruit and vegetable products.

6.6 Labour

A substantial amount of labour force information is extensively discussed for the Food industries overall in section 2.6. We summarise here only the most salient treatments for this Group.

The *Employment Gazette* [QRL.186] contains data on employment in the processing of fruit and vegetables in the two annual articles which summarise the results from the Census of Employment for Great Britain and the United Kingdom respectively. The first gives male/female figures divided into the full-time/part-time Activity Heading breakdown plus the analyses for the twelve standard regions of Great Britain for total employment including Scotland and Wales. The second gives the male/female and full-time/part-time breakdown for the United Kingdom. The usual annual article in the *Employment Gazette* [QRL.186] carries the data for the United Kingdom of the average hours worked and average earnings per hour for the male/female, part-time/full-time cross-classifications, separating manual employees on adult rates from manual employees on other rates for this Group.

Business Monitor PA414 [QRL.108] publishes annual statistics for total employment in the United Kingdom for all establishments classified to the industry. Both the country and the standard regions of England breakdown are given for total employment. The size distribution is done for total employment (including working proprietors; operatives; and administrative, technical and clerical staff). *Business Monitor PA414* [QRL.108] contains data on wages and salaries. Both total and per capita figures are given separately for operatives; and for administrative, technical and clerical; plus the size distributions. The operating ratios table in *Business Monitor PA414* [QRL.108] permits some idea of productivity and labour costs to be inferred from the general net output per head measures, wages and salaries as a percentage of gross value added etc. for the usual five year run. Much of this information is duplicated in the summary tables in *Business Monitor PA1002* [QRL.93].

Of the many volumes of the latest Census of Population, *Census 1981: Economic Activity: Great Britain* [QRL.148] contains tables which specify the total in employment by sex, whether full-time/part-time and cross-classified by type of employees (managers, manual, non-manual etc.) for AH4147 besides yielding the numbers of self-employed for each Activity Heading by sex. Similar data for Scotland are also collected and published in the *Census 1981: Scotland Economic Activity (10% Sample)* [QRL.149].

6.7 Capital

6.7.1 *Capital Expenditure*

Business Monitor PA414 [QRL.108] gives the breakdown by gross capital expenditure by type of asset: land and buildings, plant and machinery and vehicles (all subdivided into acquisitions and disposals) for a five-year period. A total for annual net capital expenditure is given and analysed by employment size of enterprise. Cross-classifications are made for the standard regions of England, Wales, Scotland and Northern Ireland. Net capital expenditure per head and net capital expenditure as a percentage of gross value added are included in the operating ratios table. These data are largely reproduced in *Business Monitor PA1002* [QRL.93] which is the summary volume whose contents are described in section 2.7.1.1.

Previous census data were comparable with SIC(1980). But the Census of Production reports for 1958, 1963 and 1968 included capital expenditure information for further subdivisions within the industry: marmalade, jams etc; frozen fruit and vegetables; canned or bottled fruit and vegetables; vegetable products, soups etc. canned or bottled; pickle; vinegar; potato crisps etc.

6.7.2 *Suppliers of Machinery*

Business Monitor PQ3244 [QRL.127] reported sales of machinery for preparing vegetables, labelling machinery, bottles, cans, boxes etc. which are some indication of capital inputs. The same can be said about imports of other machinery for the working of dried leguminous vegetables and for the preparation of fish, fruit and vegetables etc.

6.7.3 *Occasional Investigations*

S.J. Prais [B.147] derived comparisons of productivity in fruit and vegetable processing in Britain, Germany and the United States. More specifically, the 1976 MMC Report on *Supplies of Frozen Foodstuffs* [B.444] included some Birds Eye data on capital productivity. Changes in fluctuating costs per ton of sales in current and constant terms were shown for 1960, 1970 and 1974 for peas, green beans and potato products separately expressed in £ per ton. It needs to be explained that "fluctuating costs" was a Birds Eye management term to separate "other fluctuating costs" from raw material costs. A considerable effort was made in Chapter 5 of [B.444] to make a statistical assessment of efficiency and Birds Eye supplied much data to show increases in both capital and labour productivity.

6.8 International Transactions

This section deals mainly with exports and imports and may be consulted along with the more detailed section 2.8.

6.8.1 *HM Customs and Excise Records*

The primary data source for imports and exports is the monthly *Business Monitor MM20: Overseas Trade Statistics of the United Kingdom* [QRL.85]. "Vegetables and fruit" is the title of Division 05 in the SITC(R3). The many nine digit level products are contained in the *Business Monitor MA21: Guide to the Classification for Overseas Trade Statistics* [B.213]. Processed imports and exports can be distinguished from other fruit and vegetable imports by use of the index to [QRL.85] or [B.213]. Vegetables may be classified under dried; frozen; prepared or preserved by vinegar or acetic acid; provisionally prepared; otherwise prepared or preserved etc. Fruit can be categorised under drained, glacé or crystallised; dried; frozen; jams and jellies; marmalade; prepared or preserved by vinegar or acetic acid; provisionally preserved; purée and pastes; otherwise prepared or preserved etc. There is considerable commodity detail.

Business Monitor PQ4147 [QRL.133] summarises the value in aggregate of the total exports and imports for this Activity Heading for the latest eight quarters and the past six years up to the second quarter of 1989. Both exports and imports are disaggregated in value and volume terms for the latest five quarters and last two years. The breakdown is the same for exports and imports, and covers about sixteen categories: jam, fruit jellies, marmalade etc.; quick frozen fruit; provisionally preserved fruit; canned and bottled fruit; dried fruit; glacé and crystallised etc.; peel of melons and citrus fruit etc.; quick frozen vegetables; vegetables provisionally preserved etc.; canned vegetables; dried vegetables; fruit and vegetables preserved in vinegar etc.; maize precooked etc.; flours of vegetables and fruits; flour, meal and flakes of potato; other. The original source for the data are HM Customs and Excise. The HM Customs and Excise tariff/trade code numbers are provided for these overseas trade headings.

Other derivative sources are more aggregative. *United Kingdom Trade with European Countries* [QRL.508] and the succeeding *UK External Trade: Area x Commodity Analysis* [QRL.494] give annual data for Division 05 (in value terms) for exports, imports, exports less imports and the percentage of exports over imports, when meaningful, by specified country, with the European Community etc.

The *Monthly Digest of Statistics* [QRL.362] gives the latest two years, last two quarters and three-monthly value figures for Division 05, comparing the cumulative values from the beginning of the year with the same period in the previous year. The *Annual Abstract of Statistics* [QRL.37] reports the eleven-year value figures for Division 05 for exports and imports.

6.8.2 *Industry Analyses of Trade*

Business Monitor MQ10: Overseas Trade Analysed in Terms of Industries [QRL.90] and the earlier *Business Monitor M10* [QRL.77] of the same title, provide quarterly and annual data in terms of value for imports and exports for this Group. *Business Monitor MQ12: Import Penetration and Export Sales Ratios for Manufacturing Industry* [QRL.91] and the preceding *Business Monitor M12* [QRL.78] of the same title rework the statistics to provide the import penetration and export performance ratios. The overall methodology and coverage are discussed fully in section 2.8.2.3.

6.8.3 *Industry Sources*

The annual *Basic Horticultural Statistics for the United Kingdom* [QRL.61] focuses mainly on the imports and exports of fresh fruit, fresh vegetables and potatoes. These are all relevant inputs into processing (see section 6.5.1.1). The annual quantity data for the imports of fresh fruit distinguish the imports of strawberries, either frozen or provisionally preserved, separately from the imports of the many fresh fruit categories. The vegetable imports, exports and re-exports data separate dried peas, dried beans and all other dried vegetables in quantity and value terms. The imports and exports tables for potatoes detail the quantities of processed potatoes in raw equivalent tonnage. The values are expressed as the processed product value. The original sources are mainly HM Customs and Excise and MAFF.

The bi-annual *Fruit and Tropical Products* [QRL.245] carries both quantity and value data for the imports of fresh and preserved vegetables and for the imports of canned and bottled fruit. Supplying countries are identified and details are given for the latest six months, the comparable period the previous year and numbers for the previous two years. The section on preserved vegetables identifies vegetables in solution (onions and others); frozen vegetables (potatoes and others); dried vegetables (onions and total); canned vegetables (tomatoes and others); plus aggregates for all kinds of preserved vegetables. The products identified as preserved in syrup are: peaches; pears; apricots; mixed fruits; pineapples; grapefruit; oranges; other kinds. The fruits preserved without sugar are: oranges; cherries; strawberries; apricots; apples; pineapples; other fruits; crystallised, candied and drained. Frozen fruit is separately treated. The original sources are again HM Customs and Excise and the MAFF.

Potato Statistics in Great Britain [QRL.387] gives annual data for the imports of raw potatoes into Great Britain (thousand tonnes) and imports of processed potatoes into the United Kingdom (thousand tonnes of product). The divisions are for canned; crisped; dehydrated and frozen; with the main supplying countries listed. Results are given for the latest five years and a further table is supplied in thousand tonnes of raw-equivalent. The ratios used to convert raw potato to processed product are given. This publication also carries historical data for Great Britain from 1960 onwards which summarises both imports and exports in thousand tonnes. The main crop, processed (raw-equivalent) and seed categories are each distinguished. These latter data are the same as those in the *Historical Data Summary* [QRL.263] sheets. *Potato Processing in Great Britain* [QRL.385] gives both exports and imports of processed potato products. These data are all converted into raw potato equivalent for the categories of : canned/other; dehydrated; crisped; and frozen and chilled plus a global total. *Potato Statistics Bulletin* [QRL.386] also carries annual imports data including information for the processed potatoes divisions in raw equivalent terms. Imports into Great Britain and shipments from Northern Ireland also specify new, Ware, and seed potatoes by source. The *Potato Marketing Board: Annual Report and Accounts* [QRL.384] carries data for processed potatoes imports into Great Britain (in raw-equivalent terms). It gives a statistically illustrated description of trends in exports. Distictions between raw and processed products are thus carefully drawn in these PMB publications.

6.9 Stocks

6.9.1 *Ministry of Agriculture, Fisheries and Food Inquiries*

Various data on stocks are summarised in the *Monthly Digest of Statistics* [QRL.362]. The information on stocks of potatoes are based on returns from the PMB and the Department of Agriculture, Northern Ireland (DANI). The data on canned and bottled fruit and canned vegetables relate to manufacturers' stocks only and emerge as part of the MAFF quarterly survey of canned and bottled fruit and vegetables. The results are found in *MAFF Statistics: Production of Canned and Bottled Fruit and Vegetables in the UK* [QRL.325].

6.9.2 *Business Statistics Office Inquiries*

Stocks and work-in-progress for the processing of fruit and vegetables are shown in *Business Monitor PA414* [QRL.108] giving changes over a five-year period in value terms and the value at the end of the year. The three-part disaggregation into materials, stores and fuel; work-in-progress; and goods-on-hand for sale is made. The employment size distribution is carried out for the total figure at year-end. Computations for the latest five years for the ratio of gross output to stocks are located in the operating ratios table. Similar information can be found in the summary tables in *Business Monitor PA1002* [QRL.93]. A full catalogue of the BSO inquiries is found in section 2.9.2.

Business Monitor SDO25: Retailing [QRL.143], formerly *Business Monitor SDA25: Retailing* [QRL.140], carries data on the value of stocks held by food retailers at the beginning and the end of the year. Greengrocers and fruiterers are separately identified. Evidently the stocks of processed, as distinct from fresh, produce are subsumed in the totals for large grocery retailers etc.

As noted in section 2.9, *Business Monitor SDA28: Catering and Allied Trades* [QRL.142] measures the values of beginning and end-of-year stocks at various establishments, identifying catering contractors etc. among other outlets.

Stocks exist from the agricultural raw material right through to the shelves of the home. Stocks of canned, bottled, frozen etc. products are in the hands of the manufacturer, wholesaler, grocer etc. Frozen products are held in cold stores by manufacturers, intermediaries, specialist distributors etc. Stockholding is substantial and but a limited picture can be given by the use of both MAFF and BSO sources.

6.10 Consumption

6.10.1 *The National Food Survey*

Household Food Consumption and Expenditure [QRL.267] carries considerable product detail in the quarterly and annual estimates of both average household consumption and expenditure. The sugar and preserves segment gives separate details on marmalade, but jams, jellies and fruit curds are treated together. The vegetables category contains both the different kinds of vegetables and the distinctions between canned, bottled, dried and frozen products. Separate totals are given for processed vegetables placed into fifteen product categories, distinct from the data on fresh vegetables. The main processed products (canned peaches, pears and pineapples; other canned or bottled fruits; dried fruit and dried fruit products; frozen fruit and frozen fruit products); are similarly separately identified from the fresh fruits. Pickles and sauces are treated together in the miscellaneous categories. Thus the consumption of many of the products in AH4147 may be identified. A further statistical analysis according to income group is performed by main food groups which includes sugar and preserves (little product detail); vegetables (with the frozen, processed and fresh distinctions); and fruit and other foods of the miscellaneous grouping which subsumes the pickles. The *National Food Survey: Compendium of Results* [QRL.373] presents the results for annual average consumption per week for main food groups according to region and type of area; cross-classified according to household income; analysed according to household composition; and cross-classified according to age of housewife, housing tenure and comparing households which are freezer-owning with other households. Before 1985, these data were covered in the tables and appendices of *Household Food Consumption and Expenditure* [QRL.267].

The *Annual Abstract of Statistics* [QRL.37] gives some of the *Household Food Consumption and Expenditure* [QRL.267] information in its eleven year run of estimated household food consumption by all households in Great Britain in ounces per person per week. Preserves; canned tomatoes; canned peas; canned beans; canned fruit; and pickles and sauces; are itemised. Other fresh vegetables and frozen vegetables are put together. Other vegetables and vegetable products and other fruit and fruit products are two items identified in the index numbers of consumption in the home of selected foods found in *Social Trends* [QRL.456]. Fresh and other fruit, potatoes, other vegetables and vegetable products, sugar and preserves are included as main foods in the *Regional Trends* [QRL.401] coverage of household consumption, and expenditure on, main foods.

6.10.2 *The Family Expenditure Survey*

A detailed description of the *Family Expenditure Survey* [QRL.204] is given in section 2.10.2. The coverage for this Group is limited. Potatoes; other and undefined vegetables; fruit; syrup, honey, jam, marmalade etc.; other food, foods not defined; — all include products from this Group. These data are cross-classified by levels of household income; for one-adult households by level of household income, sex and age; by levels of household income for households with and without children; and according to region. No distinction is made among fresh and processed produce although their positioning can be seen in the Commodity and service annex to the Survey.

6.10.3 *The National Accounts*

The *United Kingdom National Accounts* [QRL.506] provide data on consumers' expenditure on fruit, potatoes, vegetables and preserves and confectionery. See section 2.10.3 for further details.

6.11 Supplies and Disposals

The term disposal requires careful attention. It is discussed in the *Monthly Digest of Statistics Supplement: Definitions and Explanatory Notes* [B.337]. Inter-related concepts are also reviewed in section 2.11.

The *Annual Review of Agriculture* [QRL.51] and its successor *Agriculture in the United Kingdom* (see section 2.5.1.1 and Addenda) pull together a good deal of data on supplies and disposals.

To begin with, we deal with potatoes which have their own table. Firstly, chats, waste and retained stockfeed and seed for home crop and exports are subtracted from total production to derive the figure for output available for human consumption. Then supplies from the Channel Islands are added in, as are the imports of raw potatoes (both early and maincrop) and processed potatoes. Further adjustments are made for exports of raw and processed potatoes which are subtracted to give the total new supply for human consumption in the United Kingdom for the calendar year (expressed in thousand tonnes). United Kingdom output is also shown as a percentage of total new supply. With regard to disposals, the data are broken down according to human consumption and compensation and stockfeed buying programmes. Finally, the figure for potatoes unsold (including seed) at 31 December is also given.

Physical data for apples (excluding cider apples), pears (excluding Perry pears), cauliflowers and tomatoes are detailed in the "Supplies of certain horticultural crops" table in [QRL.51] and in the "Selected horticultural crops" table in the succeeding publication *Agriculture in the United Kingdom.* Imports are added to the data for output of the respective crops and exports subtracted, to arrive at the figure for total new supply marketed. United Kingdom output as a percentage of total new supply marketed is also given. Figures for closing stocks and total disposals in the calendar year are presented for apples and pears but not for cauliflowers and tomatoes. Hence [QRL.51] and *Agriculture in the United Kingdom* provide a good deal of data on supplies and disposals, for a range of products.

Output and Utilisation [QRL.382] also contains estimates of total production and supplies (in thousand tonnes) together with a final figure for production of potatoes as a percentage of raw supplies for use in the United Kingdom. Estimates of total supplies and output from the current home crop for apples, pears, cauliflowers and tomatoes were also carried, as well as figures for output as a percentage of total new supplies for use in the United Kingdom. However, as noted in Sections 2.5.1.1 and 6.5.1.1, [QRL.382] last appeared in 1988 with data up to 1987. These data have been subsequently incorporated in the *Annual Review of Agriculture* [QRL.51] and the successor publication *Agriculture in the United Kingdom.*

Northern Ireland Agriculture [QRL.376] analyses potato crop production, utilisation in production in Northern Ireland and disposals.

Particular attention is paid to potatoes in the work of the PMB. *Potato Statistics in Great Britain* [QRL.387] summarises supplies and disposals in thousand tonnes. Total supplies are estimated by adding the current crop to home crop from the previous season and imports (including processed raw equivalent) to yield the total. Disposals into human consumption, exports, seed for the next crop, carry over to the next season and wastage are computed. The *Potato Statistics Bulletin* [QRL.386] gives monthly figures for potatoes moving into consumption in Great Britain from all sources. *Potato Processing in Great Britain* [QRL.385] gives annual data for the many types: raw, canned etc. and compares domestic with non-domestic human consumption. Indeed, *A Flow Chart for Potatoes in Great Britain* [QRL.228], uniquely presents magnitudes through the whole chain. Home and imported resources are traced right through into raw and product usage in the home and by the caterer. A full, yet compact, picture of all supplies and disposals is thus drawn.

In fact many of the results, notably in *Output and Utilisation* [QRL.382] the *Annual Review of Agriculture* [QRL.51] and now *Agriculture in the United Kingdom* reflect the MAFF balance sheet calculations for potatoes and vegetables and fruit from the original data obtained from the agricultural censuses, the Horticultural Crop Intelligence Committees, MAFF short-period inquiries to potato processors and the PMB etc.

Some of the results are also distilled in the *Annual Abstract of Statistics* [QRL.37]. The ten-year run of estimated food and drink supplies per head for fruit and vegetables includes canned and bottled fruit; imported dried fruit; potatoes (including products); imported canned tomatoes (including juice and purée); other canned vegetables and pulses (including dried beans and dried peas for canning). Total disposals for potatoes are given (excluding seed and chats). The statistical aggregate of home-grown and imported potatoes for human consumption represents the availability of this commodity for food in the United Kingdom. The *Monthly Digest of Statistics* [QRL.362] identifies the movement into human consumption in the United Kingdom of potatoes from home crop, excluding the potatoes processed for export.

6.12 Prices

6.12.1 *Agricultural and Commodity Prices*

6.12.1.1 Official sources

MAFF provide a variety of statistics on horticultural prices. Much price data relates to fresh produce but the prices of these commodities may be related to the prices of many of the processed products as well.

Basic Horticultural Statistics for the United Kingdom [QRL.61] gives the average farm-gate prices in the United Kingdom for the latest ten crop-years (the last provisional) for a number of fruit and vegetables. The fruit are grouped under dessert apples, culinary apples, pears, plums, cherries and soft fruit (strawberries, raspberries, blackcurrants and other soft fruit). Field vegetables are grouped under roots and onions, brassicas, legumes and others (asparagus, celery, leeks, lettuce, rhubarb and watercress).

The three parts of the Agricultural Market Reports, issued weekly on Fridays, give statistics on the current market situation. *Agricultural Market Report Part I: Prices and Quantities Sold of Selected Cereals, Livestock and Other Agricultural Products* [QRL.25] gives price data on Ware potato sales for the current and previous weeks plus comparisons for one year ago. *Agricultural Market Report Part II: National Average Wholesale Prices of Home Grown and Imported Horticultural Produce* [QRL.26] shows national average wholesale prices of home grown and imported fruit, vegetables, flowers, potatoes and flowering pot plants. The markets represented are Birmingham, Bristol, Leeds, Liverpool, London (New Covent Garden) and Manchester, each being weighted according to estimated throughput. Much detail is given for the many sorts of fruit, vegetables and potatoes, according to class (i.e. grade) and named variety. Price data for the current week specify the most usual prices and the lower and upper ranges. Comparisons for the most usual prices are made for the last week and year. Thirdly, *Agricultural Market Report Part III: Prices of Home Grown Fruit and Vegetables by Grade in Six Major Markets in England and Wales* [QRL.27] specifies prices according to the grades of class I, class II and unclassed for the many types of fruit, vegetable and potato products. Both the range and the most usual prices are given for the week ending according to each of the six market centres listed above.

The *Report on Crops and Supplies of Vegetables in England and Wales* [QRL.413] and the *Report on Crops and Supplies of Fruit in England and Wales* [QRL.412] monitor the national average wholesale market prices of home-grown produce in monthly terms.

The various PMB publications give a good deal of price data. *Potato Statistics in Great Britain* [QRL.387] reports guaranteed and average prices paid to producers in Great Britain by month for a five-year run. Average GB maincrop and early price (lifted on or before 31st July) are given in annual terms along with the average UK maincrop price and guaranteed price. The *Potato Marketing Board: Annual Report and Accounts* [QRL.384] yields the average farmgate price for the crop in Great Britain for the last five years, with the latest observation provisional. It also gives a statistically-illustrated analysis of the course of producer prices and market stabilisation etc. for the previous year. The *Historical Data Summary* [QRL.263] records UK guaranteed and average prices in annual terms back to 1960, repeating the summary information on the last page of *Potato Statistics in Great Britain* [QRL.387].

Agricultural Statistics: United Kingdom [QRL.32] assembles the range of data on the many categories of fruit and vegetables. The information is given monthly for the year in question for selected wholesale markets in England based on the same market sources as the Agricultural Market Reports [QRL.25], [QRL.26] and [QRL.27]. Monthly potato prices at the selected wholesale markets in England are also reported separately from the prices paid to growers in England and Wales for early and maincrop potatoes.

The *Economic Report on Scottish Agriculture* [QRL.180] gives yearly data on the average market prices of potatoes (1st earlies, ware and seed). It also records the average of weekly wholesale prices of Scottish grown fruit and vegetable produce as at Glasgow market for the months of the year in question. The *Statistical Review of Northern Ireland Agriculture* [QRL.460] presents average producer prices of potatoes in annual terms and the average annual (farmgate) prices of mushrooms and apples.

The *Annual Review of Agriculture* [QRL.51] includes some information in its calendar year summary of commodity price trends with a four-year annual run plus yearly forecast. Included are the farmgate price of potatoes paid by registered merchants to growers for early and main crop potatoes in the United Kingdom. Wholesale market prices for apples, pears, tomatoes and cauliflowers are also given. These series used to be the weighted average of wholesale prices for England and Wales but from 1982 onward relate to England only. As so often, the footnotes merit careful scrutiny to check the precise detail of coverage in [QRL.51].

6.12.1.2 Commercial sources

The *Public Ledger & Daily Freight Register* [QRL.392] records main crop potato futures and turnover in lots traded and the futures prices of other inputs (e.g. sugar futures) pertinent for this Group. *The Public Ledger's Commodity Week* [QRL.394] summarises these prices for the past weeks in the commodity prices guide. *The Public Ledger's Commodity Week* [QRL.394] records main crop potato futures and the futures prices of other inputs (e.g. sugar futures) relevant for this Group. *Farmers Weekly* [QRL.212] is another source for potato futures prices.

The weekly *Fruit Trades Journal* [QRL.246] gives the Covent Garden wholesale market prices on the Tuesday of the week in question for the many types of fruit and vegetables plus speciality lines. It also summarises the average wholesale market prices from other market centres, i.e. Belfast, Birmingham, Bristol, Glasgow, Hull, Leeds, Liverpool, Manchester, Nottingham, Sheffield, Southampton etc. Prices quoted represent an average range. MAFF average wholesale price data for the previous week are reproduced.

The *Grower* [QRL.254] carries price information in its market monitor section. Auction prices for selected fruit and vegetables are shown for the main named centres (Evesham, Worcester, Spalding, Wisbech etc.). The average to top wholesale prices are given for a number of market centres. The most usual wholesale market prices are compared with the corresponding week of the previous year. Both the *Fruit Trades Journal* [QRL.246] and the *Grower* [QRL.254] rely on the MAFF Agricultural Market Reports [QRL.26] and [QRL.27] for this wholesale price information. But [QRL.246] and [QRL.254] are mentioned here because they are regularly available to the trade on a weekly basis.

6.12.2 *Retail Prices*

6.12.2.1 Recorded prices

The *Employment Gazette* [QRL.186] only gives average retail prices on one day of the month for fresh vegetables and fruit.

However, *Household Food Consumption and Expenditure* [QRL.267] has more information. In its pre-1985 format, it gave the quarterly and annual average prices for the many sub-divisions of sugar and preserves; vegetables; and fruit; discussed in section 6.10.1. Distinctions are made among fresh and processed products and among canned, frozen and dehydrated items. Since 1985, the average annual prices paid in pence per lb. are given for a three-year period. It is now the *Compendium of Results* [QRL.373] which carries the quarterly and annual average prices for the many products identified in the food codes.

6.12.2.2 Recommended prices

The weekly publication *The Grocer* [QRL.252] includes average wholesale prices for various types of potatoes, fruit and vegetables in its Meat and Produce section. The prices quoted include a 15–20 per cent distribution charge. They are intended to serve as a national guide for caterers and grocery buyers. Most of the prices quoted are for fresh produce but the potatoes section includes "prepared chipped" and "prepared whole large". *The Grocer Price List* [QRL.253], supplied with *The Grocer* [QRL.252] on the first Saturday of each month, has more prices data on processed foods. The extensive sections on pickles, chutney and relishes; frozen foods; canned and bottled fruit; jellies; preserves, treacle and syrups; canned and bottled vegetables etc. usually give information on trade prices of supplying manufacturers, importers, agents etc.

Shaws Guide to Fair Retail Prices [QRL.453] appears monthly. It aims to give the maximum retail prices to be charged for various foods based on minimum wholesale quantities. There are many sections for the numerous products of this Group: baked beans; frozen foods; canned foods; canned and bottled fruits; dried and dehydrated fruit; jam and marmalades; pickles; soup powders and cubes; canned soups; canned tomatoes; canned vegetables; dehydrated vegetables; etc. all figure in the alphabetical listing.

6.12.3 *The Retail Prices Index*

This is published monthly in the *Employment Gazette* [QRL.186] distinguishing sugar and preserves, potatoes (unprocessed separately), vegetables (fresh vegetables separately) and fruit (fresh fruit on its own). The index, at the time of writing, is based on January 1987 and the percentage change over a twelve-month period is given. The *Monthly Digest of Statistics* [QRL.362] details the figures for the latest seven months and shows the respective weights.

The commodity detail in the *Employment Gazette* [QRL.186] was greater up to March 1987. Under the sugar heading, preserves and confectionery, jam, marmalade and syrup (as well as sugar and sweets and chocolate) could be separately identified. Vegetables were categorised as fresh, canned and frozen; separated into potatoes and others. Fresh, dried and canned fruit were distinguished separately.

Business Monitor PQ4147 [QRL.133] formerly summarised the retail prices index for past quarters and years. The series is compared with the all food and all items index.

6.12.4 *Price Index Numbers in the National Food Survey*

In its pre-1985 format, *Household Food Consumption and Expenditure* [QRL.267] gave indices of expenditure, prices, real value of food purchased and the total real value of consumption. Preserves were treated together and other fruit and vegetables distinguished from fresh produce. Some products were also subsumed in the convenience foods section. However, further product detail down to each food code was found in the annual indices of average deflated prices of purchases and demand. The calculation of these indices is explained in section 1.12.4.

Since 1985, some index number information is located in the *Compendium of Results* [QRL.373]. This applies to the annual data (1980 = 100 in 1989) for the indices of prices for the main food groups and the indices of the real value of purchases and the total real value of consumption. But the individual food code details of the annual indices of average deflated prices (average for whole period = 100) are not published so that the data for canned potato; frozen peas; canned peaches, pears and pineapples; and many others are not listed.

6.12.5 *Producer Price Index Numbers*

The series of producer price indices are considered in general terms in section 2.12.5. Details of the price indices for the inputs and outputs of the fruit and vegetable processing sector are given below.

6.12.5.1 Producer price index: input prices

Business Monitor MM22: Producer Price Indices carries the producer price index numbers of materials and fuels purchases for AH4147 giving both monthly and annual data. The monthly data are given for the current and previous years, with the figures for the latest two months provisional. An annual average for the previous year is also presented. *Business Monitor MM22* was published for the first time in October 1989 and continued the coverage in *British Business* [QRL.66].

Business Monitor PQ4147 [QRL.133] gave the producer price indices of materials purchased, usually for the latest available five quarters and past two years. These materials are separately enumerated for five classes of inputs: refined vegetable and seed oils; sugar, refined, bulk; dried fruits; imported peas and beans; home produced potatoes for processing.

6.12.5.2 Producer price index: output prices

Business Monitor MM22 contains the producer price index numbers of products manufactured in the United Kingdom (home sales) for AH4147. The monthly data are provided for the current and previous year, with the figures for the latest two months provisional. An annual average for the previous year is also presented. *Business Monitor MM22* was published for the first time in October 1989 and continued the coverage in *British Business* [QRL.66]. The *Annual Abstract of Statistics* [QRL.37] gives the annual averages for AH4147 for a six-year run for products manufactured in the United Kingdom (home sales).

Business Monitor PQ4147 [QRL.133] gave the producer price indices of goods produced for the latest five quarters (the latest provisional) and for the past two years. There is separate treatment for the following: frozen foods and vegetables; pickles; jam and marmalade; canned fruit and canned vegetables. The data are derived from MAFF sources and compared with the figures for food manufacturing industries (home sales) and all manufactured products (home sales).

6.12.6 *Prices and Government Regulation*

Price information has appeared in official investigations, notably in the 1981 MMC report on *Discount to Retailers* [B.441]. Baked beans received special attention as one of the four original items in the product survey. Questionnaires were sent to 151 companies in January 1978. The statistically-illustrated summary outlined the relationship between trade price lists issued by companies and quantity discounts, recommended retail prices etc. Baked beans are also featured in the separate area price survey which involved 900 pairs of observations for 10 products for 170 retail outlets in Bromley, Dewsbury, and Stirling during the two weeks preceding 14th April 1979. The results published gave average selling prices, buying prices, gross margins and standard deviations for the four major multiples, other multiples, independents and cooperatives. The follow-up report in June 1985 by the Office of Fair Trading, *Competition and Retailing* [B.231], described another area-price survey which explored the relationship between buying and selling prices across different categories of retailers. This study was larger in scope both from the point of view of products and geographical coverage. Baked beans were again featured but orange marmalade and tinned fruit (pear halves) were also included. Comparisons with 1981 were made but no hard statistical data reported.

The MMC report in 1976 on *Supplies of Frozen Foodstuffs* [B.444] contained a variety of price information. Comparative prices for selected products of Birds Eye, Findus and Ross Foods were made available as at 1 September 1975. Stockist prices per dozen and recommended retail prices per pack were listed for peas, brussels sprouts, crinkle cut chips and sliced green beans. Changes in recommended retail prices of beans and peas were also supplied by these companies for the period November 1971 to July 1975. A Birds Eye retail prices index for vegetables (January 1971 to July 1975) was graphically contrasted with the retail prices index for groups of food products taken from the *Employment Gazette* [QRL.186].

The Price Commission's report in 1975 on *Food Prices in Outlying Areas* [B.421] covered frozen garden peas, canned peas, canned peas in tomato sauce, canned peaches, marmalade and strawberry jam among the price comparisons made of average prices and price ranges in outlying and central areas. Other earlier investigations analysed price factors and showed a concern with distribution margins. The National Board for Prices and Incomes in its 1968 report on *Distributors' Margins in Relation to Manufacturers' Recommended Prices* [B.403] drew on a survey of 160 manufacturers to elicit the extent of mark-up after the 1967 devaluation. At this time, in contrast to later, it was remarked that "retail price cutting is common except frozen food".

The Price Commission was responsible for several other investigations of significance. The interim report in 1974 on *Prices, Margins and Channels of Distribution for Fruit and Vegetables* [B.429] and the final report in 1975 on *Prices, Margins and Channels of Distribution for Fruit and Vegetables* [B.428] both concentrated on fresh food, carrying average retail prices for fresh fruit and vegetables. In 1975 *Prices and Distribution of Bananas* [B.427] contained a thorough discussion of the banana trade starting with imports and continuing right through the distribution network. Costs and margins and the structure of prices and margins in the wholesale trade in the United Kingdom were described.

6.13 Financial Information

6.13.1 *Company and Market Research Reports*

As outlined in section 2.10.2, the primary data flow from the companies themselves. Information is collected together in the many publications listed in that section.

It may be stressed here that the ICC Business Ratio report on *Frozen Food Producers* [QRL.554] — 1988 edition — covers all the financial ratios outlined in Chapter 2. Information on return on capital, profit margins, asset utilisation etc. is found by named company. The sections on frozen vegetable producers and general frozen food producers are of particular interest for this chapter. Summary details of net profit before tax, capital employed, rates of return and profit margins etc. are also found in the individual company data card section. The analyses in the ICC Business Ratio report on *Frozen Food Distributors* [QRL.553] are similarly organised. Financial profiles of named companies active in bulk processing and distribution are given. The Key Note Report on *Frozen Foods* [QRL.589] in 1987 gives financial appraisals of major manufacturers like Birds Eye Walls, Ross, Findus and McCain. Various profit measures are presented for a three-year period (including profit growth year on year) separate from data on turnover and liquidity. The coverage here is of AH4122.2 and AH4150 of SIC(1980) as well as AH4147.1. Separate attention is given to vegetables etc. only in the industry structure sector, but the financial information is aggregated for the companies as a whole.

Similar remarks about the lack of disaggregation can be made about company accounts of the major firms. Hillsdown Holdings plc produces its *Report and Accounts* [QRL.403] which gives sector commentaries. But the five-year statements of profit before and after tax etc. are presented for the group as a whole only. At best, divisional shares for percentage of turnover and profit are computed for food processing and distribution. *Unilever Annual Report* [QRL.501] is also aggregative. The value of turnover and operating profit are only broken down into food and drinks and frozen foods and ice-cream.

6.13.2 *Occasional Investigations*

Prices, profits and efficiency were part of the discussion in the 1976 MMC report on *Supplies of Frozen Foodstuffs* [B.444]. This assessment isolated gross profit as a percentage of net sales value for Birds Eye Foods with specific breakdowns for vegetables in 1964, 1967 and 1971–1974. Another table on the return on capital employed for the same years for the same company is not broken down for vegetables alone. Indeed, many of the results reflect the fact that vegetable processing etc. are but part of the multi-product operations of these frozen convenience-food processors.

Similar comments apply to the data on the percentage return on capital employed of Cadbury Schweppes and its subsidiaries for the twelve months ended 4.1.75, 1.1.76

and 1.1.77 in the 1978 Price Commission report on *Cadbury Schweppes Foods Ltd. — Grocery Products* [B.418]. This report is discussed more fully in Chapter 10 but is mentioned here since preserves, mince and puddings (Chivers, Hartleys, Moorhouse), jellies and desserts (Chivers and Glenville) and canned fruit and vegetables (Hartleys) were part of the reference activities.

6.14 Advertising and Market Research

6.14.1 *Advertising*

Detailed product, brand and company data are reflected in the *Tri-Media Digest of Brands and Advertisers* [QRL.493] produced by Media Expenditure Analysis Limited (MEAL). Several of the food categories give competitive advertising expenditure on the many processed fruit and vegetable products as follows:

- (F16) Canned fruit
- (F20) Canned and processed peas
- (F22) Canned vegetables and pasta.
- (F66) Frozen vegetables
- (F72) Jams, preserves and mincemeat
- (F74) Junkets and jellies
- (F86) Sauces, pickles, salad cream.

These first three product categories correspond quite closely with AH4147.4, except that pasta overlaps with AH4239. Group F22 carries the significant data on baked beans as well as canned tomatoes. The important F66 section partly relates to AH4147.1, and includes the data on frozen peas, oven chips etc. F72 and F74 correspond closely to AH4147.3. Details on pickles which belong to AH4147.2 are separately identified from the sauces and salad cream which are classified into AH4239.

The monthly publication, *The Media Register* [QRL.354] has categories which again show the AH4147/4239 overlap. The relevant subdivisions are:

- (FOO 12) Canned — fruit
- (FOO 13) Canned — vegetables and pasta
- (FOO 32) Dried fruit and mincemeat
- (FOO 40) Frozen vegetables
- (FOO 42) Frozen fruit
- (FOO 54) Jams and preserves
- (FOO 59) Pickles, salad dressings and relishes.

Coverage obviously changes with the introduction of new brands. The ready-to-eat meals categories in both the *Tri-Media Digest* [QRL.493] and *The Media Register* [QRL.354] include vegetable products.

Baked bean products etc. are featured in the top 100 brands advertising in the Food industries as ranked by adjusted MEAL expenditure data included in *The Food Forecast* [QRL.236]. Separate rankings are given by generic brand and product name for the frozen vegetables and for the sauces/pickles/salad cream sub-categories.

6.14.2 *Market Research*

The Food Forecast [QRL.236] typifies the links between advertising and market research. MEAL brand data for expenditure for the past nine years (unadjusted) and the latest quarter (adjusted) are given for the many products included in the preserves and relishes; tinned fruit and vegetables; and frozen food sections. Brand shares, judged by the pattern of expenditure of housewives and regional analyses of usage by housewives, are given. Jam and marmalade, pickles and sauces, pickles and chutney, tinned fruit, tinned vegetables, frozen peas, frozen vegetables and frozen fish are shown.

The major companies often cover advertising and other market research data. These reports are usually available on request from the companies themselves. *Birds Eye Frozen Foods: Annual Report* [QRL.63] includes market shares data on the sales of frozen green vegetables and frozen potato products. *The Frozen Food Consumer Market Bulletin* [QRL.242] reviews the vegetable market as well as other frozen foods, comparing market segmentation by value and volume for vegetables as against fish, meat and desserts. *Frozen Food Retail Market Report* [QRL.243] was also produced by Ross and includes other vegetables (besides peas) and potato products in the ten top value growth markets.

The November 1985 issue of *Retail Business* [QRL.432] contains a review of "Jams, marmalade and fruit curd" which details market size, production and trade, manufacturers and brands, consumer profiles, distribution, prices and margins, packaging and prospects besides reproducing MEAL data on advertising.

The April 1988 and May 1988 issues of *Retail Business* [QRL.432] provide market overviews for frozen foods, including green vegetable sales by type and trends in potato products. The October 1987 edition of *Frozen Foods* [QRL.607], by Market Assessment Publications, gives market size, production, foreign trade, market segmentation, competitive structure, consumer profiles, retail outlet analyses, market forecasts etc. as well as MEAL data, for frozen chips; potato products; and frozen vegetables separately. The January 1988 edition of [QRL.607] adds frozen fruit to the segments already studied. The 1987 edition of the Key Note report on *Canned Foods* [QRL.582] also shows the composition of the market and included the share of vegetables as a percentage of frozen foods. The major company profiles etc. were also sketched in. The August 1987 issue of *Market Intelligence* [QRL.339] showed market size, own label volume etc. as well as repeating MEAL media spending.

The September 1985 and July 1985 issues of *Retail Business* [QRL.432] portray the "Canned vegetable" and "Canned fruit" markets respectively. *Canned Foods* [QRL.601] by Market Assessment Publications thoroughly reviews canned fruit, fruit pie fillings, canned vegetables, baked beans and canned tomatoes for the usual categories. The 1987 review of *Canned Foods* [QRL.582] by Key Note lists products and companies. It considers the threat to this sector from frozen and chilled frozen foods and imported products. The June 1988 issue of *Market Intelligence* [QRL.339] depicts the supply structure and assesses the future, besides carrying advertising and promotion data.

The August 1982 issue of *Retail Business* [QRL.432] describes the pickles, sauces and salad dressings sectors. *Dressings & Sauces* [QRL.605] by Market Assessment Publications gives descriptions of the markets for mustards, pickles and chutney, salad cream, sauces and three submarkets of salad dressings, tomato sauce and vinegar. It identifies the connections between AH4147 and AH4249 besides giving data on market size etc. for pickles and chutney which are of direct concern here. Both the 1987 Key Note report on *Sauces and Spreads* [QRL.597], and the 1988 report by Marketing Strategies for Industry entitled *Sauces and Pickles* [QRL.647] give more recent, if less detailed, statistics on production, market shares, trade, consumption and sales, market structure, advertising and promotion etc.

These market research publications give perceptions of market structure (see section 6.2) as well as collecting together various data on advertising, market shares etc.

The Retail Market for Jam and Marmalade [QRL.433] displays information on these markets, drawing on Chivers Hartley's own estimates and Audits of Great Britain's Television Consumer Audit (AGB/TCA) and the AGB/TCA Consumer Panel. Annual figures of value and volume plus percentage changes are given for a seven-year run. The jam market is then split into standard jam, extra jam and reduced sugar jam sectors following the legal definitions of the 1981 EEC Preserves Directive. Marmalade is segmented into the thin-cut (non-lime) marmalade sector, thin-cut lime marmalade sector, medium-cut marmalade sector and thick-cut marmalade sector. Market shares for leading manufacturers and brands are given for the total markets and all these segments.

6.15 Research and Development

Much R&D work goes hand in hand with product development. However hard statistical information is difficult to come by except when expenditure and employment are occasionally recorded in the various annual reports of the companies involved (but see the Addenda for further developments).

The MAFF Food Science Division performs work as a public good both on general projects and specific research on quality. This includes fruit and vegetable processing as one of the commodity groups.

As noted in section 2.15, the Agriculture and Food Research Council (AFRC) coordinate a good deal of R&D. In particular, the *Horticulture: Institute of Horticultural Research Annual Report* [B.303] reports on the activities of the Glasshouse Crops Research Institute (Littlehampton), the East Malling Research Station (Maidstone), the National Vegetable Research Station (Wellesbourne) and the Department of Hop Research at Wye College. The AFRC Institute of Horticultural Research was formed in 1986 as an umbrella organisation. Before that, information giving an overview of research activities on fruit could be gleaned from the *East Malling Research Station Annual Report* [B.243].

Information on R&D tends to be more technical and agricultural than industrial. But the *AFRC Institute of Food Research Annual Report* [B.196] describes research in food processing and provides a list of projects. The *Potato Marketing Board Survey of Potato Research in the United Kingdom* [B.353] has a short section on university and research institute scientific research projects besides the much greater detail of work on physiology and biochemistry, diseases, pests, agronomy, harvesting and handling and storage.

Industry-funded research organisations carry out research both for business and the government. The activities of the Campden Food Preservation Research Association are described in the *Annual Report of the Campden Food Preservation Research Association* [B.200]. Descriptions of work on canning microbiology, and quick freezing etc. are given. Data on annual research expenditure in the annual accounts are also provided. The British Food Manufacturing Industries Research Association, Leatherhead, is of less specific interest. But the Processors and Growers Research Organisation (PGRO), Peterborough, is the main centre for R&D on peas and beans. This includes the suitability of varieties for different forms of processing. Descriptions are available in the *PGRO Annual Report* [B.351].

Given the continual innovation in product development, data are sparse except for the statistics in company reports. Thus we have provided here more a guide to organisations and sources which may provide statistical information. Indeed, trade publications like *Frozen and Chilled Foods* [B.290] and the *Food Trade Review: for Food Manufacturers, Processors and Packers* [B.284] provide monthly articles on the latest developments. Finally, the December 31st issue of the *Grower* [QRL.254] in 1988 carried an exhaustive list of research centres and organizations.

6.16 Official Investigations

The following list of official publications have been discussed in varying detail in the text. Some of them, notably the 1976 MMC work *Supplies of Frozen Foodstuffs* [B.444] covered many dimensions.

Reports of the National Board for Prices and Incomes

Report no.31	(Session 1966/67) *Distribution Costs of Fresh Fruit and Vegetables* [B.402]
Report no.55	(Session 1967/68) *Distributors' Margins in Relation to Manufacturers' Recommended Prices* [B.403]
Report no.165	(Session 1970/71) *Prices, Profits and Costs in Food Distribution* [B.409]

Reports of the Price Commission under the Counter Inflation Act 1973

Report no.2	(1974) *Prices, Margins and Channels of Distribution for Fruit and Vegetables (Interim Report)* [B.429]
Report no.4	(1975) *Prices and Distribution of Bananas* [B.427]
Report no.5	(1975) *Prices, Margins and Channels of Distribution for Fruit and Vegetables (Final Report)* [B.428]
Report no.10	(1975) *Food Prices in Outlying Areas* [B.421]

Reports of the Monopolies and Mergers Commission

(Session 1975/76)	*A Report on the Supply in the United Kingdom of Frozen Foodstuffs for Human Consumption* [B.444]
(Session 1980/81)	*Discounts to Retailers* [B.441]

In addition, the Office of Fair Trading published a report on *Competition and Retailing* [B.231] in 1985 which is also discussed at length in section 2.16.4.4 of Chapter 2.

6.17 Improvements and Comments

The "Processing of fruit and vegetable sector" (Group 414) encompasses very many heteregeous products, even if the variety is rather less than that of the "Miscellaneous foods" sector (Group 423). The transfer of products between these two Groups as a result of revisions to the SIC were noted in section 6.1 and are also considered in Chapter 11. It is important to take such changes into account if consistent coverage of a sector or group of products over time is sought.

The links with the agricultural raw materials are important. Here we are well served by statistical information. Of particular note is the work of the PMB in its various statistical publications. *A Flow Chart of Potatoes in Great Britain* [QRL.228] provides a concise statistical picture of the movements from raw material to processed product. It would be ideal if this could be done for every commodity!

As it is, the coverage of the agricultural inputs is more complete than the treatment of the processed outputs. *Basic Horticultural Statistics for the United Kingdom* [QRL.61] is an instance of a MAFF publication which draws together a lot of information in one place.

The linkages of agriculture with processing have been appreciated in the past. Two outstanding contributions were *Horticulture in Britain. Part I: Vegetables* [B.304] and *Horticulture in Britain. Part II: Fruit and Flowers* [B.305]. But these two detailed descriptions are now dated and we would welcome the updating of such complete pictures of these sectors.

There are in fact three distinct sets of sources: firstly those covering raw materials as agricultural outputs, secondly the BSO treatment of the processors and thirdly the work of the market research organisations which delineate the market nearer the consumer. All these must be consulted if we want to trace through the statistics for any chosen commodity. Often this is not a straightforward matter because the market can perceive processing according to type of process (canned, bottled, frozen) as much as type of product. And then many of the major companies involved in this sector are present in Group 423 "Miscellaneous foods" besides other Groups covered in this Review.

Finally, it is important to note that many production and processing activities do not seem to be measured at all. There is the reality of the many home-grown inputs both from allotments and vegetable gardens. As for processing, there is a significant amount of home processing; the making of jams and marmalade, pickles and preserves are cases in point. The user of statistics interested in this sector of the Food industries must therefore bear these and other complications in mind.

CHAPTER 7

FISH PROCESSING

The information in this chapter relates to the fish processing industries, Group 415 in the *CSO Standard Industrial Classification Revised 1980* [B.232]. Other more general sources, which provide statistics on other industry Groups as well, are covered in Chapter 2 and should be consulted as required. The contents of this chapter are as follows:

7.1 Introduction

Industry Group 415 covers the following Activity Heading:

4150 Fish Processing.

1. Freezing.
Freezing of fish and other marine animals, including fresh and salt water fish, crustacea and molluscs.
2. Other processing and preserving.

For an alphabetical list of the activities covered by Group 415, see Table 7.1 or the CSO *Indexes to the Standard Industrial Classification Revised 1980* [B.317]. The activities of Group 415 were subsumed under MLH214 "Bacon curing, meat and fish products" in SIC(1968). Further details may be found in *Standard Industrial Classification Revised 1980: Reconciliation with Standard Industrial Classification 1968* [B.379].

Table 7.1 Activities Classified under Group 415.

SIC(1980) AH		SIC(1968) MLH
4150.1	Fish: freezing	
	Crustaceans (freezing of)	214.1
	Fish cake (frozen) manufacturing	214.2
	Fish finger (frozen) manufacturing	214.2
	Fish product quick freezing	214.1
	Fish quick freezing	214.1
	Shellfish freezing	214.1
4150.2	Fish: other processing and preserving	
	Canning of fish	214.2
	Fish cake (fresh) manufacturing	214.2
	Fish curing (other than by distributors)	214.2
	Fish drying	214.2
	Fish paste manufacturing	214.2
	Fish processing (not freezing)	214.2
	Fish salting	214.2
	Kipper manufacturing	214.2
	Potted shrimp manufacturing	214.2
	Shellfish preserving (not freezing)	214.2
	Shrimp preserving (not freezing)	214.2

It is more satisfactory that such a distinctive activity as fish processing is again classified separately in SIC(1980).

Business Monitor PA415: Fish Processing [QRL.109] currently provides the annual data for the Group as a whole, collecting together the census information on output and costs, capital expenditure, stocks and work-in-progress and operating ratios. Data on employment, wages and salaries, output, capital expenditure, stocks and work in progress etc. are cross-classified by employment size and a regional distribution of employment, capital expenditure, output etc. is shown. *Business Monitor PQ4150: Fish Products* [QRL.134] gives the quarterly data on sales, production, exports and imports etc. up to the second quarter of 1989.

The long time series in the *Historical Record of the Census of Production 1907–1970* [QRL.264] are usually aggregated into "Bacon curing, meat and fish products" which was MLH214 in the SIC(1968). But the earliest *First Census of Production of the United Kingdom (1907)* [QRL.219] treated the fish curing trade as an entity. The returns were for cured, smoked and salted fish, with quantities and values for herrings, including kippers, bloaters and reds, pilchards, haddocks and other sorts of fish. Canned fish at that time was included under the grouping of the "preserved meat, poultry, and fish, pickle, sauce and baking powder trades".

Fish curing was kept on its own. The data were for a long time broken down for England and Wales, Scotland and Great Britain. "Preserved fish and fish pastes etc." were separated off and, from 1935 to 1950, were assigned to the "starch and miscellaneous foods" industry. *The Report on the Census of Production for 1958* [QRL.424] grouped "Bacon curing, meat and fish products" together for the first time. It brought together what had been the separate treatment of "fish curing" (industry 9B), "bacon curing and sausage" (industry 8D) and "preserved meat" (industry 8E) in *The Report on the Census of Production for 1954* [QRL.423]. This continued through the years of the SIC(1968) until the SIC(1980) once more put fish on its own under the new heading of "Fish processing".

Technological and economic change have led to the various revisions in coverage which are outlined here. The revisions are summarised in the *Historical Record* [QRL.264] and are only fully appreciated when all the census volumes are inspected. This is illustrated in the contrast between the fish curing trades in the *First Census of Production of the United Kingdom (1907)* [QRL.219] and the coverage of fish processing in *Business Monitor PQ4150* [QRL.134] up to 1989.

7.2 Industry Structure

7.2.1 *Fish Processing*

Fish processing is but a part of the important and complex nexus which goes back to the sources of supply. The connections with supplies and distribution are inevitable, and indeed the fishing industry has been of prime national interest long before the 1549 Statute which made Fridays and Saturdays Fish Days (besides days in Lent). In 1563, Wednesdays were also added and the law enforced with great stringency. According to the 1960 *Report of the Committee of Inquiry into the Fishing Industry* [B.363] — the Fleck Report — the objective was not only to encourage consumption but also to maintain the fishing trades as a great school of seamanship.

Understandably, references are more abundant with respect to the fishing industry than fish processing on its own. However, these abundant references which concentrate mainly on the fishing industry often include descriptions of fish processing. The Fleck Report [B.363] relates processing to the fishing industry in 1960. It provides statistical illustration to emphasise new developments and to forecast future changes in economic structure. This reference itself draws attention to the fact that the industry had seven reports following various inquiries between the years 1926 and 1952. The Fleck Report [B.363] indeed predicted the growth of quick freezing and the universality of pre-packaged, advertised and distributed processed products.

Another particularly rich source of information, and the first complete official survey since the Fleck Report [B.363], is the 1978 report on *The Fishing Industry* [B.276] from the Expenditure Committee of the House of Commons. This report encompassed three volumes of text together with maps, oral evidence and statistical data sources. It may lack the logical coherence of the Fleck Report [B.363] but valuable supplementary statistical and economic information was frequently provided for the Committee.

An earlier (1976–77) progress report from the Expenditure Committee, *Inquiry into the Fishing Industry* [B.320], is another source which shows that processing is just part of a complex industry. The report covered the following aspects: the problems of fishing protection; fishing limits and developments in the European Economic Community; catching operations, both inshore and deep sea; building, surveying and maintaining fishing vessels; the processing, marketing and distribution of fish and fish products; fish stocks; the problems of conservation; the potential of fish farming; and the employment patterns and economic significance of the industry both in local and national terms.

The 1976 report by the Price Commission on *Prices and Margins in the Distribution of Fish* [B.430] also provides useful background and data. The illustrative diagram (Figure 7.1) shows the place of the processors in the distribution network for fish, and is adapted from this report. A simple version is found in Aitken [B.1], which also emphasises the significance of the food chain concept. Finally, we must not omit the residues which go for fish meal to pet food manufacturers and which are used as fertilizers. The report by the Price Commission [B.430] included these in the statistical breakdown for 1972 and 1975 of sales of port merchants. The proportion of total sales was given for each of the following categories: wholesalers at other ports, inland market wholesalers, associated companies, retailers (direct), fish friers (direct), caterers and institutions, and fish meal and pet food companies.

7.2.2 *Market Perceptions*

A good starting point is to note that the preservation of such a highly perishable commodity as fish has always been vital to the industry and to society, although techniques have inevitably changed over time. Processing itself has at least three aims: to facilitate the transportation over distance without deterioration; to enable glut supplies to be carried over to days of scantier fish landings; and to give special flavour and convenience — the Fleck Report [B.363], Barker and Yudkin [B.11]. The traditional techniques of salting, smoking and canning used to absorb glut landings, prolong keeping quality and provide distinctive flavour yet are now insignificant in fish product sales compared with the sales of fresh, frozen and prepared fish. Quick freezing at sea and the fish processors' many filleted frozen products now dominate. Supply gluts, particularly for pelagic species, are more often than not absorbed by Eastern Bloc factory vessels commonly known as klondykers. The term "klondyking" refers to direct sales at sea to factory vessels or foreign containers for immediate export without landing.

The fish processing sector itself is heterogeneous both in its products and structure. It includes companies of varying size and nature with roles ranging from fish brokerage to added-value processing. The primary processing includes the

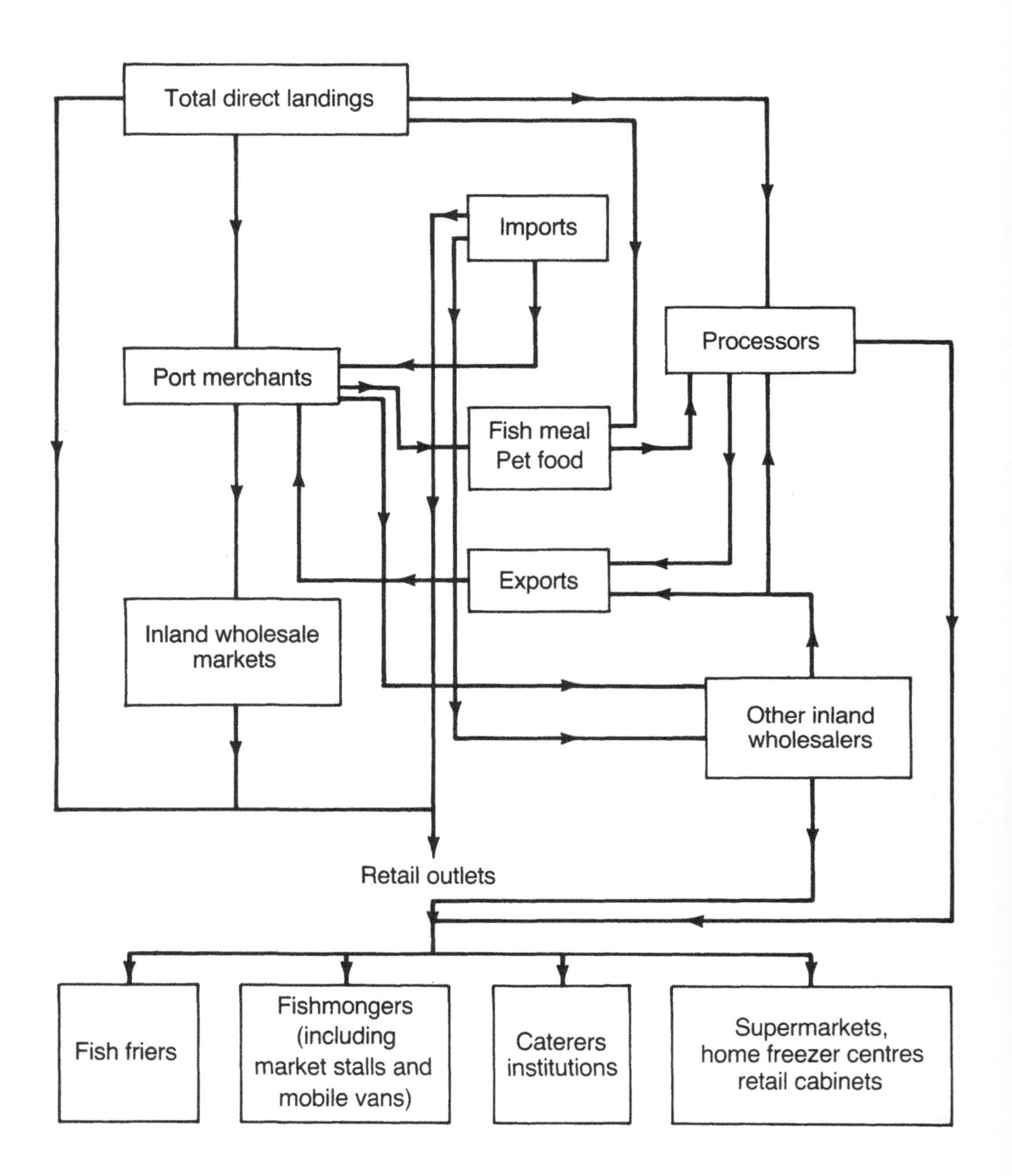

Figure 7.1 The Distribution Network for Fish.
Source: *Prices and Margins in the Distribution of Fish*. [B430], P.8. Price Commission Report no. 14, 1976.

preparation of fresh fish for sales which involves gutting, heading, finning, skinning and filleting. The secondary processes incorporate the frozen fish product which undergoes additional stages from the quick freezing of individual or block frozen fillets and the value-added processing of smoking, marinading, canning, breading and battering, controlled atmospheric and vacuum packaging etc. A third distinction is shellfish processing. Companies' output may be spread over these three activities for the many different species. The relationships are again complicated since many may be engaged in multiple activities in the chain from fish brokerage to processing. Yet again the large companies in particular may be involved in the supply of frozen foods as well as fish: for example, vegetables, confectionery or fruit, meat (including poultry etc.), and so on. The 1976 report by the MMC titled *Frozen Foodstuffs. A Report on the Supply in the United Kingdom of Frozen Foodstuffs for Human Consumption* [B.444] includes an outline of the growth and competitive structure of the frozen food industry, of which fish is an important component.

The Sea Fish Industry Authority (SFIA) suggests that the main distinctive groups may be identified as follows: whole fish, fresh/chilled fillets, frozen fillets, processed fish, smoked fillets, ready-packed, canned, rough salted, marinated and spiced, and shellfish. This is largely a process-based classification where the fish processors are often engaged in a combination of these activities, as well as being involved in the many stages of the distribution chain and in many other food products.

An ideal would be to take the market for each species but this would be an intricate and lengthy task. A clear alternative is to note the market overviews which incorporate some of the more prominent features of supply and demand. Here we mention the description in the January 1988 issue of *Fish & Fish Products* [QRL.606] by Market Assessment Publications. The report is further discussed in section 7.14.

Currently one of the most visible consumer markets is that of processed fish products, and prepared frozen fish which are retailed in consumer packs. This frozen fish segment is dominated by three large generalist firms: Birds Eye Foods Ltd. (Unilever), Findus Ltd (Nestlé), and Ross Foods and Youngs Seafood. The latter are known as Ross/Youngs, and is part of the United Biscuits frozen food interests acquired from the Hanson Trust. Commercial links are maintained from trawler to retail outlets. In contrast to these prominent multinational corporations, there exist smaller specialist producers which often use the nationwide distribution systems of frozen food distributors such as Christian Salvesen and Frigoscandia. Charles Alexander is another major national distribution company.

A second market segment is fresh fish which covers all types of wet fish whether sold whole, filleted or otherwise prepared for the consumer, but not including fresh shellfish. A third segment is canned and bottled fish, defined as the market for all styles of fish products sold packed in cans or, to a lesser extent, bottles and jars. These products (salmon, tuna, mackerel, sardines etc.) are largely imported, and sometimes re-exported. Many domestic and foreign companies are involved: John West Foods (Unilever), which are strong in salmon, and Del Monte, in pilchards, are but two examples. Discussion is provided in the report on *Canned Foods* [QRL.601] by Market Assessment Publications, and in the report on "Canned fish" in the April 1985 issue of *Retail Business* [QRL.432]. Fourth, we can identify shellfish as a market. Since these are sold fresh, frozen and canned/bottled etc., the overlap with the preceding three market segments must be noted. Finally, given the complexities of this entire sector, we note three papers which draw together much industry information and data. They are:

- *Marketing in a dynamic environment; an overview of UK fish processing* [B.191]
- *Fish marketing in the UK* [B.59]
- *New developments in the marketing of fish* [B.40].

7.2.3 *Fish Farming*

Attention is drawn to the growing importance of fish farming. We mention it here even though it is not included in the SIC(1980). Salmon is mostly farmed in the Highlands and Western Isles of Scotland. The data for Scotland have been collected since 1979 and are contained in *Salmon and Trout Farming in Scotland* [QRL.444] which is available on request from the Department of Agriculture and Fisheries for Scotland (DAFS). The data are separately classified for rainbow trout, Atlantic salmon smolts, and Atlantic salmon. Details of the number of companies, employment, broodstock, system of production and total production (tonnes etc.) are recorded. The initiative stemmed from the DAFS Disease Diagnostic unit and the response rate following telephone communication, site visit etc. is very high.

The *Report on the Sea and Inland Fisheries of Northern Ireland* [QRL.429] has, since 1971, usually given the value, the production of, and employment on commercial fish farms in the province. These involve trout, salmon, oysters etc. Separate tables are appended giving the tonnes of oysters sold, estimated value from commercial oyster farms, and fish sold from the Department's fish farm.

Trout is farmed not only in Scotland but also in England and Wales, particularly in Yorkshire and Wessex. Data on England and Wales are generally found only in MAFF commissioned work. *Rainbow Trout: Production and Marketing* [QRL.8] is the result of a postal survey carried out in the Autumn of 1979. It contains extensive data on trout production, trout marketing, trout consumption and distribution, and examines attitudes towards trout, viz:

- Production data: these include production in tonnes per annum for England and Wales together, for Scotland and a total for Great Britain. Estimated production for non-respondents is given. The figures are disaggregated according to the regions and a size distribution attempted for England and Wales, Scotland and Great Britain.
- Marketing data: a cross-classification of table trout according to type of market outlets (farm gate, local hotels and restaurants etc.) is performed for 1979. The type of trout sold (frozen, smoked etc.) is also given and the pattern of monthly sales presented.
- Consumption and distribution data: the distribution system is described. Consumption and prices are estimated from existing sources. Production and hence consumption figures exclude the sports' catch. The distribution of table trout according to market outlets for the regions is obtained for 1979.

Fish Farming in the United Kingdom [QRL.9] provides plenty of data for the United Kingdom as a whole, and covers trout production for the United Kingdom, salmon production in Scotland, and the output of mussels in the United Kingdom. The results presented are mainly derived from a postal survey. The work was published in 1984 and contains data up to 1982. Much of the annual production data for England and Wales, and Scotland in *Rainbow Trout: Production and Marketing* [QRL.8] are updated but separate information is provided for Northern Ireland and aggregate UK figures derived.

Summaries for the other farmed species are appended in [QRL.9] together with the production statistics for salmon in Scotland, and mussels in the United Kingdom. A table ranks the value of the output of UK farmed fish in 1982. Hence the data regularly collected by DAFS are supplemented by MAFF commissioned work.

7.2.4 *General Statistical Sources*

An SFIA occasional paper *Sources of Statistics Pertaining to the British Fishing Industry* [B.377] produced in 1981 summarised international sources, then national sources. The sections are as follows: landings, values and trade; processing; marketing; prices; consumption; employment; miscellaneous publications. More recently, a working paper by the Marine Resources Research Unit of Portsmouth Polytechnic entitled *A Bibliography of Statistical Sources on UK Fisheries* [B.143] gives an alphabetical listing and description of forty nine statistical sources published from 1980 onwards. There are separate sections on national and international sources respectively. A concise subject index refers to the numbers of the sources under the following headings: landings, values and trade; processing; marketing; prices; consumption; employment; general.

Fish Processing in the UK: An Economic Analysis [QRL.3] is a specific investigation into the sea fish processing industry in the United Kingdom based on data jointly collected by staff from SFIA and Arthur Young. It gives a detailed statistical portrait of many economic dimensions beginning with company corporate structure and the age and regional structure of firms engaged in fish processing, including their size ranges. Employment data cover location, age and sex and sectoral employment (i.e. whether primary, secondary or shellfish processing). Purchases of raw materials and supplies data are given and sales output figures covered according to sector, species and outlets. Financial information incorporates hourly wage rates; sales, costs and margins by sectors; gross and net value added by sector; returns to capital by sector etc. The results of responses to interviews rank the views of fish processors on the business difficulties in supply of species, raw materials costs, competition, distribution etc.

This extremely comprehensive report sharpened the distinction between primary and secondary processors, drew out the regional contrasts, and provided more cost data than the regular BSO exercises. It carries 46 statistical tables in the text plus appendices. As previously mentioned, statistical material on the fish processing industry is far less abundant than data on the fishing industry. Hence *Fish Processing in the UK* [QRL.3] is important in that it provides a direct treatment of the processing industry and was undertaken precisely because of the lack of generally available information.

A valuable source of information which collects together much statistical data is the *Annual Report and Accounts: Sea Fish Industry Authority* [QRL.45]. The SFIA assists developments in the fishing industry and promotes the marketing and consumption of fish. The SFIA encompasses the Fishery Economics Research Unit

(FERU) which provides both regular and occasional information on the statistics and economics of the fish nexus. The *Annual Report and Accounts: Sea Fish Industry Authority* [QRL.45] carries data on the fishing fleet, supplies and production, household consumption and international trade.

The *Sea Fish Diary* [QRL.450] summarises data on landings, fishermen, and consumption and has a useful list of the many trade associations. Of these the UK Association of Frozen Food Producers, and the Association of Fish Meal Manufacturers are here listed as possible sources of further information.

The *Herring Industry Board: Annual Report and Accounts* [QRL.262] used to give a full picture of supplies, values of landings according to seasons and ports, imports of fresh and frozen herring, disposals of total landings, herring curing strength and production of cured herring for both Summer and Autumn. Comparisons were made with the previous year. The *White Fish Authority: Annual Report and Accounts* [QRL.518] showed imports, processing, usage and exports of white fish from the various sources. The Herring Industry Board and the White Fish Authority were merged in 1981 and renamed the Sea Fish Industry Authority.

7.3 The European Community

7.3.1 *The Economic Influence of the Community*

The Common Fisheries Policy (CFP) was agreed in 1983 after protracted negotiations since 1966. Its adoption was enshrined in Council Regulation (EEC) No.170/83 [B.345].

The agreed policy was a compromise between the continental and island Member States over access and quotas. The United Kingdom, for example, possesses rich fishing grounds. France, in contrast, meets a strong home demand for fish by mainly using historical access rights to foreign fishing grounds. The CFP attempts to provide a coherent policy with respect to three main areas. First, it is intended to conserve fishing stocks through enforcing national fishing quotas. Second, the Community aims to stabilise fish prices in a manner similar to the stabilisation of agricultural product prices. Third, the structural aspects seek to help fishing communities adjust to the use of modern fishing methods.

Although the impact of EC membership is more evident with respect to the prime resource, it is evident that the size of the fish catch, prices paid, restructuring grants etc. all affect the processing side. Council Regulation (EEC) No.3796/81 [B.344] was specifically related to the common organisation of the market in fishery products. It provides for common marketing standards for fish, the establishment of producers' organisations to coordinate marketing, the fixing of common prices, financial compensation for the withdrawal or carry-over of unsold fish, and arrangements for trade with third countries in fishery products. Secondary legislation has been based on this regulation: the fixing of guide prices and special premiums, suspension of import duties on fish required for processing and the fixing of export refunds etc.

Several books summarise the tortuous negotiations which evolved as first the United Kingdom, and then Denmark, were opposed to the other Member States. *European Integration and the Common Fisheries Policy* [B.101] gives a careful account of the problems of integration. *In Search of a Common Fisheries Policy* [B.50] was written by two officials from the Commission of the European Communities. *The Common Fisheries Policy of the European Community* [B.188] is a comprehensive study, with appraisals of the fishing industries of Western Europe as background, and includes appendices giving maps of fishing rights within British coastal zones, extracts of the basic CFP legislation and a good bibliography. *The European Communities' Common Fisheries Policy: A Critique* [B.45] is a short and more controversial summary. This suggests that a system of private property rights in fishing grounds is more likely to satisfy both fishermen and consumers by leading to greater catches of fish.

The Fifth Report from the Expenditure Committee [B.276], published in 1978, discussed the CFP and contained a background paper by Mrs Birnie of Edinburgh University. The House of Lords Select Committee on the European Communities reviewed the British position in a 1979–80 report on *EEC Fisheries Policy* [B.250]. This carried background statistics on fish landings, quota of fishing fleets etc.

EEC Regulation 355/77: A Programme for the Fisheries Sector in England and Wales 1985–1989 [B.251] was a 1987 MAFF publication which reviewed the investment needs of the processing and marketing sectors, and publicised the financial aid available under Regulation (EEC) No.355/77 to aid rationalisation and modernisation. An economic and statistical by-product was this industry review and collection of statistical tables (landings, imports and exports etc.). A specific analysis was carried out of applications submitted, applications successful and payments.

An occasional SFIA report providing a *Comparison of Government Support to Agriculture and the Fish Catching Sector* [B.230] was published in 1984 and discussed the CFP. It summarised direct expenditure on fishing including market regulation under the CFP, production grants and subsidies, support for capital and other improvements and support for fisheries in special areas etc.

Finally, the CFP has led to publications which carry supporting commentary and statistics. *Agra Europe Eurofish Report: A Fortnightly Review* [QRL.23] provides specialist information, particularly on the total allowable catches (TAC) and quotas. It gives Brussels briefings, data on supplies and prices and summarises the most recent legislation. There is a useful Eurofish Report Index to this regular publication. Also of note was the special (1981) report on *EEC Fisheries: Problems and Prospects for a Common Policy* [B.249]. This detailed, statistically-backed, review profiled fleets, catches, processing and trade in the countries of the Community.

7.3.2 *EUROSTAT and Community Statistics*

Much of the data are collected from Member States using standardised reporting forms. For its work in fishery statistics, EUROSTAT collaborates closely with the other international fishery organisations through the Coordinating Working Party on Atlantic Fishery Statistics (CWP). EUROSTAT uses the same definitions and classifications as are proposed by the CWP and used by these other organisations.

The contents of the EUROSTAT *Fisheries Statistical Yearbook* [QRL.225] and *Quantity and Value of Landings in the EC* [QRL.395] will be described in sections 7.5.1.6 and 7.8.3. We note here that the *Fisheries Statistical Yearbook* [QRL.225] succeeded, from 1986, the *Yearbook of Fishery Statistics*. These single annual volumes replaced the two previous annual volumes which were *Fisheries: Catches by Region* [QRL.223] and *Fisheries: Fishery Products and Fishing Fleet* [QRL.224]. More detailed information may be obtained on request from EUROSTAT, or by consultation of EUROSTAT's CRONOS data base on the Euronet-Diane computer network.

7.3.3 *The Influence of the Community on the Collection of UK Statistics*

The *Intervention Board for Agricultural Produce: Annual Report* [QRL.293] reports on the amount of compensation paid for the withdrawal from the human consumption market of species of fish sold through the producer organisations recognised by the United Kingdom Fisheries' Departments. Amounts of compensation paid are given and the quantity of each species withdrawn from the market enumerated for the year in question.

The major influences of the Community on the methods of statistical collection are surveyed in section 2.3.3. But it is worth noting in this section that the huge growth in statistical requirements arising from the CFP (especially in respect of quota management) has inevitably meant that the publication of domestic statistics has received lower priority within the limited resources available. Hence the long delays in the appearance of the *Sea Fisheries Statistical Tables* [QRL.451] may be partly attributable to the more immediate needs of the CFP.

Indeed, such is the urgent need for catches and landings data for quota management, that they are frequently communicated direct to DG14 (the Directorate General in Belgium) rather than EUROSTAT. Since the CFP was agreed in 1983, the collection and availability of statistics have improved in many ways. The installation of micro computers in the fishing ports was accelerated. Data are entered directly each day and down-loaded nightly to the central system at Lowestoft. This is quicker than the previous completion and collation of forms. Second, log books and landings declarations under Council Regulation (EEC) No.2057/82 are mandatory, rather than voluntary as was previously the case in England and Wales. Third, retrieval is much speedier. Statistics are communicated within the EC such that quota swaps are made of the different species between partner countries.

7.4 Output

7.4.1 *Output, Sales and Value Added*

7.4.1.1 Business Statistics Office inquiries

The annual *Business Monitor PA415: Fish Processing* [QRL.109] and *Business Monitor PA1002: Summary Volume* [QRL.93] both provide the four major output measures for this industry Group, viz: total sales and work done; gross output; net output and gross value added at factor cost. The coverage is fully set out in section 2.4.1.1. The quarterly *Business Monitor PQ4150: Fish Products* [QRL.134] gives commodity sales in value, and sometimes volume, and production figures in volume terms up to mid-1989. The sales and production data are itemised as follows:

- fish pastes in cans, bottles, jars etc.,

- fish, cured, smoked or salted; which separately includes smoked white fish, wet or dry salted white fish and herrings including kippers, (whole and fillets), bloaters, red herrings and salt (pickle) cured,
- fish cakes, puddings and ready meals excluding frozen. The sales data for these are given in value and in volume (tons weight) terms,
- preserved fish in cans, bottles, jars etc. The sales data for these are also given in value and volume (tons weight) terms,
- frozen fish and fish products: these important categories are divided into raw, fresh or smoked (further subdivided into whole fish and fillets, including portions of fillet and other boned fish), ready meals, part processed (e.g. breaded, battered, crumbed, in sauce etc.), shellfish and other.

Sales of principal products classified to other industries are subtracted from the total sales of principal products of this Activity Heading. Sales by units classified to AH4150 of principal products of other industries are added in, as are sales of merchanted goods (which includes chilled or wet fish) and waste products etc. to obtain the figure for total sales and work done by units classified to AH4150. The data are both quarterly and annual. The quarterly Monitors are also discussed in sections 2.1.1.2 and 2.4.1.1.

The *Historical Record* [QRL.264] records the sales of fish and fish products, quick frozen for 1948, 1951, 1954, 1958, 1963 and 1968. However, it is necessary to consult the individual census volumes for changes in treatment over time, carefully studying the introductory notes and actual content. As mentioned in section 7.1, the coverage has varied. For example, the *Final Report on the Fifth Census of Production and the Import Duties Act Inquiry 1935* [QRL.215] included the value of offal output. *The Report on the Census of Production for 1954* [QRL.423] analysed small firms in Great Britain which employed ten or fewer people. This was done separately for net output and sales.

As indicated in section 7.2.1, it is possible to interpret the industry more broadly. *Business Monitor PQ4116: Organic Oils and Fats* [QRL.129] records the quarterly and annual sales of refined fish and marine animal oils (other than lubricating oils) in value and volume terms for the periods covered. The crude, unrefined oil is an output of fish processing. Moreover fish meal is an input into pet food manufacturing and fish residues are used as fertilizer.

7.4.1.2 Ministry of Agriculture, Fisheries and Food inquiries

The *Annual Abstract of Statistics* [QRL.37] yields an eleven-year run of annual data for the volume of production of canned fish. The data are derived from MAFF sources which are further discussed in section 2.4.1.2.

7.4.2 *Index Numbers of Output*

Business Monitor PQ4150 [QRL.134] carries an index of output for "Fish products". This seeks to measure changes in the volume of industrial activity. The figures do not include a stock adjustment to correct mixed sales and production data to true production index numbers, nor do they include a bias adjustment. The data are generally for the latest seven quarters (seasonally adjusted) and the last six years.

7.4.3 *Regional Coverage*

The coverage of the *Report on the Census of Production and Construction in Northern Ireland* [QRL.419] is detailed both in sections 2.1.2 and 2.4.3. Presently, annual data are given for "Meat and fish" combined for the dimensions of total sales and work done, gross output, net output and gross value added at factor cost etc. The former *Digest of Scottish Statistics* [QRL.175] used to give the output data for various fish categories as recorded in section 2.4.3. [QRL.175] was succeeded by the *Scottish Abstract of Statistics* [QRL.446] which does not, however, give these data.

7.4.4 *Occasional Investigations*

Fish Processing in the UK: An Economic Analysis [QRL.3] reports a good deal of data on sales, output and value added for the survey year of 1985. Sales of demersal fish and pelagic fish are given separately by product weight and value broken down into product group (white fish, fresh/chilled fillets etc. as classified by the SFIA and explained in section 7.2.2). The percentage distribution of weight and value within the product group are given. Sales of shellfish are similarly treated except that the product group classification is mostly by species. The value of processors' sales are in addition cross-classified by type of outlet (primary processors, secondary processors, fishmongers, supermarkets etc.) for finfish and shellfish. A regional analysis is carried out for demersal, pelagic and shellfish. Gross output is also presented for the 1985/86 financial year for primary, secondary, shellfish and total for the regions. Value added is similarly treated for regions for the same categories. Both these latter series have a percentage share regional breakdown.

7.5 Current Inputs other than Labour

7.5.1 *Domestic Inputs*

The primary input is the cull of the sea. There is a wealth of data as confirmed by the *Bibliography of Statistical Sources on UK Fisheries 1983* [B.143]. This section will be somewhat lengthy, since considerable efforts are made to enumerate fish resources and landings.

The MAFF/DAFS *Fish Stock Record* [QRL.221] shows the concern with both biological and economic aspects of fishery management. This periodic publication carries data on total allowable catches (TAC) for species by weight and fishing area. It relates "advised TAC" to "adopted TAC" and landings. It attempts to forecast fish catch and arrive at maximum sustainable yields. The advice of the International Council for Exploration of the Sea (ICES) is summarised in tabular, graphic and diagrammatic form. The 1978 report of the Expenditure Committee on the *The Fishing Industry* [B.276] contains valuable maps which identify the major species by breeding grounds and movements. The earlier (1976–77) progress report on the *Inquiry into the Fishing Industry* [B.320] has a focus on resources and catching operations which is also important for the Common Fisheries Policy — see section 7.3.

The collection and coordination of fisheries' statistics is a major exercise which is carried out by the MAFF (Ministry of Agriculture, Fisheries and Food), DAFS

(Department of Agriculture and Fisheries for Scotland) and DANI (Department of Agriculture for Northern Ireland). Initial data on landings are obtained from sales notes completed at the first auction of the fish. Statistical information on fishing efforts and grounds is obtained from the EC log book completed by the skipper. Microprocessors have been installed at the main harbours in England and Northern Ireland for the computerised collection of sea fisheries data linked into the MAFF system at Lowestoft. Similar equipment is now installed by DAFS in Scottish ports.

7.5.1.1 United Kingdom

It should be explained at the outset that there are three major classifications for fish:

Demersal (deep sea fish) e.g. cod, haddock, plaice

Pelagic (surface feeding) e.g. herring, mackerel

Fresh water e.g. salmon, trout

Two main groups exist for shellfish:

Crustaceans e.g. crabs, lobsters, prawns

Molluscs e.g. mussels, cockles, oysters

The *Sea Fisheries Statistical Tables* [QRL.451] are designed to provide a detailed picture of the UK fishing industry. Both the quantities and values of fresh and frozen fish by species landed in the United Kingdom by British vessels and foreign vessels are given for the latest available year. Sub-totals are obtained for pelagic fish (found mainly in coastal waters near the surface), demersal fish (species living on or near the sea bed) and shellfish before a grand total is provided for all fish. Fresh and frozen landings are taken together but there is a separate breakdown for the countries of the United Kingdom and a comparative British and foreign vessel analysis before the United Kingdom total. Historical time series back to 1938 are provided for the main species. Further details of landings at major ports (England and Wales) and districts (Scotland) by British vessels are given. Landings by foreign fishing vessels at British fishing ports are shown. Breakdowns of British landings by region of capture, by main vessel length group, and by distant-water vessels are summarised. Information on landings of fish frozen at sea is presented for a six-year run in terms of weight (tonnes) for the main species for the United Kingdom from freezer trawlers based in England and Wales. The quantities of whole, headless or filleted-at-sea fish landed by British and foreign vessels are shown in terms of equivalent standard weight for the most common form of presentation (head on, gutted for most species). The explanatory notes merit careful study. The arbitrary one tonne = 15,748 oysters is used for England and Wales. Shellfish totals especially are not precise, but may be used to discern trends. It should also be noted that the average annual values of fish series based on landings by British vessels in selected years from 1938 reflect the realisation for first-hand sales of fish to all outlets, i.e. for human consumption and also for other users such as fish meal and animal feedings stuffs.

Given the enormous amount of data in the *Sea Fisheries Statistical Tables* [QRL.451], the *Annual Abstract of Statistics* [QRL.37] carries a useful summary table which gives the landed weight and value of fish of British taking for the United Kingdom for the latest six years. Totals for all fish, wet fish (demersal and pelagic), and shellfish are given separately. The species breakdown within demersal, pelagic and shellfish are included.

There is a time lag before the *Sea Fisheries Statistical Tables* [QRL.451] appear. For instance, at present (1991), the latest available edition was published in 1989 but gave figures mainly for 1988. Thus it is worth drawing attention to the *Monthly Return of Sea Fisheries Statistics: England and Wales* [QRL.363]. This gives the monthly, and cumulative, weight and value data for the current year relating to landings of fish by British and foreign vesssels in England and Wales by species, broken down into demersal, pelagic and shellfish varieties. A monthly and cumulative UK summary is now also given by selected major species, plus species type totals. There is a countrywide coverage of the major ports in England and Wales, with details of British vessels' landings. These and other data are obtainable on application to the Fisheries Statistics Unit of the MAFF at Nobel House, 17, Smith Square, London SW1P 3JR. The latter also performs a similar service in respect of landings in Scotland.

7.5.1.2 Scotland

The separate publication *Scottish Sea Fisheries Statistical Tables* [QRL.449] reflects the importance of fish for the Scottish economy. These Scottish tables date back to 1937 and are currently produced by the Fisheries and Economics Statistics Unit of DAFS. The weight and value by fish group (demersal, pelagic and shellfish), and by the major individual species, are given for the countries of the United Kingdom, distinguishing UK and foreign vessels for the latest five years. A total is derived, and the percentage of landings in Scotland in relation to the UK total is obtained for the main groups and the overall total. The weight of each species landed, the value and the average value (£/tonne) are all provided for an eight-year run. Considerable detail of fish landings for the many species, groups and totals is given in value and volume for each district of Scotland and the many ports. Analyses by methods of fishing down to species is carried out and these data provided for each Scottish port. There are also tables which furnish volume (tonnes) and value data for the major species by month for the latest available five years and value of landings per month for the latest year by the major fishing method. Further data on fishing effort (e.g. hours fishing etc.) and landings in Scotland by species by United Kingdom vessels from specified ICES areas are also reported. [QRL.449], like [QRL.451], is the result of much hard work on the reporting and collation of statistical returns.

The Scottish Abstract of Statistics [QRL.446] reports fish landings in Scotland for the past nine years in volume, separately itemised for UK vessels and foreign vesssels. Both the weight and value of landings for demersal, pelagic and shellfish are given for each district for the latest years. A chart contrasts the value distributed according to main species for Scotland, with England and Wales.

The *Scottish Sea Fisheries Statistical Tables* [QRL.449] are published with a time-lag similar to the *Sea Fisheries Statistical Tables* [QRL.451]. At present (1991), the latest edition was published in 1989 and provided figures mainly for 1988. But the *Monthly Summary of Sea Fisheries Statistics* [QRL.368] gives a more up-to-date picture and is obtainable from the Fisheries Economics and Statistics Unit (FESU). Individual species by weight and value of UK and foreign landings are provided with the many sea areas, weight, size of vessel, method of fishing, fishing effort and weight. The major species are analysed for landings by district, weight and value. The latest statistics are often provisional but are subsequently revised.

Hence the *Monthly Return* [QRL.363] and the *Monthly Summary* [QRL.368] have thus more timely if somewhat more provisional, data than the *Sea Fisheries Statistical Tables* [QRL.451] and the *Scottish Sea Fisheries Statistical Tables* [QRL.449].

7.5.1.3 Northern Ireland

Recent information on landings into Northern Ireland are available on request from DANI in Belfast, which is also responsible for the *Report on the Sea and Inland Fisheries of Northern Ireland* [QRL.429]. The statistical tables include live weight and estimated value of different species of fish landed in Northern Ireland in the latest two years as the essential raw material inputs. Pelagic, demersal and shellfish are itemised by species and totals obtained for wet fish, shellfish and all fish. Annual data are also provided for live weight and estimated value by port and by main species. Estimates for landings by Northern Ireland vessels outside Northern Ireland (in total, in Scotland, in England and Wales and in the Isle of Man) are given. The text also gives a valuable summary of processing, marketing and production activities linked with the sea and inland fisheries for the province. The illustrative statistics in the 1986 report, for instance, showed that Northern Ireland scampi processors accounted for about 15 per cent of the total scampi market in the United Kingdom and the Irish Republic.

Since we have tended to separate the sources for the United Kingdom, Scotland, Northern Ireland and Wales, it needs to be noted from the *Report on the Sea and Inland Fisheries of Northern Ireland* [QRL.429] that inter-regional trade is not unimportant. The Northern Ireland fish processors, located in and around the County Down ports, also obtain their inputs from Scotland and the Irish Republic in order to maintain continuity of throughput.

The processors also act as brokers, for they buy and sell whole fish to and from other processors and wholesale markets in Great Britain and the Irish Republic. Most of the fish sold in processed form can be as fillets, frozen blocks, battered frozen fillets, fish fingers and frozen fillets etc. going to secondary wholesalers in Belfast, Glasgow, Manchester, Dublin and Grimsby. But the industry is primarily directed towards the sale of whole fish which is either rough salted in barrels for export or iced and transported for further processing to the Irish Republic and Great Britain.

Whilst the *Report on the Sea and Inland Fisheries of Northern Ireland* [QRL.429] is annual and dates back to 1922, the separate publication *Northern Ireland Agriculture* [QRL.376] dates back to 1921. It also carries a sizeable section on fisheries which reviews developments during the year. Its statistical contents largely duplicate the *Report on the Sea and Inland Fisheries* [QRL.429] but with less detail. The table on live weight and estimated value of different species of fish landed in Northern Ireland is repeated and a selection of the annual value of landings in Northern Ireland and regional landings elsewhere in the United Kingdom by Northern Ireland vessels is given.

7.5.1.4 Wales

The quantity and value of landings in Wales of fish of British taking is broken down by species for the past five years and two earlier ten-year periods in the *Digest of*

Welsh Statistics [QRL.177] from MAFF sources.

7.5.1.5 Isle of Man

The *Isle of Man Digest of Economic and Social Statistics* [QRL.295] carries a commentary on the significance of fisheries which is traditionally one of the Island's basic industries. The first-hand values of fish landed there are recorded together with the weight, for an eleven-year run. Herring landings according to type and boat (drift, ring and trawl) have a separate treatment back to 1957. The value in the Isle of Man and elsewhere back to 1951 is itemised.

7.5.1.6 International data

A mass of data is generated worldwide to measure the availability and the exploitation of this resource. We mention below sources which also cover the United Kingdom.

The EUROSTAT publication *Fisheries Statistical Yearbook* [QRL.225] includes the United Kingdom in its annual data in liveweight of catches by region, species group and principal species. The quarterly EUROSTAT publication *Quantity and Value of Landings in the EC* [QRL.395] provides annual and monthly data on the quantity and value of landings by species in England and Wales, Scotland and Northern Ireland from MAFF, DAFS and DANI sources.

The *FAO Yearbook: Fishery Statistics: Catches and Landings* [QRL.208] covers nominal catches (canned) in metric tonnes with respect to all fishing areas, inland waters and marine fishing area. Considerable species data are summarised. The *Review of Fisheries in OECD Member Countries* [QRL.438] reproduces landings in the United Kingdom by UK vessels in quantity and value for major species from the MAFF sources. It is mentioned here because it has a useful statistically illustrated review of developments in the chain from fish catching to fish processing for the latest year.

7.5.1.7 Industry sources

The Sea Fish Industry Authority (SFIA) collate data in a number of their publications. The *Annual Report and Accounts: Sea Fish Industry Authority* [QRL.45] gives the quantity, value and source of sea fish landed in the United Kingdom, plus a separate and percentage share calculation for England and Wales, Scotland and Northern Ireland. Demersal and pelagic species are further subdivided for landings by British vessels. Landings of sea fish in the United Kingdom are given by British vessels by region of capture (excluding shellfish). The quantity, value and source of shellfish landed in the United Kingdom are treated similarly to sea fish.

European Supplies Bulletin [QRL.189] usually appears quarterly. It includes landings of demersal, pelagic and shellfish varieties cumulated for the year up to the latest available month and compared to the same period the previous year. The *Supplies Bulletin: United Kingdom Supplies and Prices of Fish and Fish Products* [QRL.475] repeats data from MAFF, DAFS and DANI which summarise the weight and values of landings by British vessels in the United Kingdom and countries for demersal, pelagic and shellfish and disaggregated into the separate species. The data were cumulated from the beginning of the year until the *Supplies Bulletin* [QRL.475] ceased publication in 1987.

Prior to the merger of the Herring Industry Board and the White Fish Authority to form the Sea Fish Industry Authority, much statistical data were incorporated in the *Herring Industry Board: Annual Report and Accounts* [QRL.262], which ran from 1937 to 1981, and the *White Fish Authority: Annual Report and Accounts* [QRL.518]. The former usually gave (up to 1977) the volume of landings by ports and areas. The latter usually incorporated data on the quantity and value of white fish landed in the United Kingdom. Further analyses of demersal and pelagic by vessel groups were appended plus a breakdown by main species. Data on landings and shellfish by British vessels were also included.

7.5.1.8 Port statistics

Port Statistics [QRL.383] include a twelve year run of landings of fish in thousand tonnes by place of landing and economic region of the United Kingdom. Scottish districts and English and Welsh fishing ports are separately itemised prior to the grand total for Great Britain. This information was also featured in the previous *Digest of Port Statistics* [QRL.174] which had an additional breakdown by main species. MAFF and DAFS are the original sources.

7.5.1.9 Business Statistics Office inquiries

The standard treatment is described in section 2.5.1.2, but we briefly note here some additional details relevant to this chapter. *Business Monitor PO1008: Purchases Inquiry* [QRL.116] always lists the values, and sometimes the quantities, (in 1984 of white fish, herrings, salmon, shellfish etc.) of the materials for use in production. The fish inputs obviously dominate but other food ingredients (wheat flours and meal and other cereal products, meat, oils and fats and other food industry products such as starch, other flours and meal, dextrin, seasonings, herbs, spices, egg products etc.) are given. This confirms that some of the inputs into fish processing are part of the output of other segments of the Food industries. The organisation of the 1979 Inquiry in *Business Monitor PA1002.1: Purchases Inquiry* [QRL.94] is similar but with somewhat finer detail in the materials for use in production sections (e.g. details of land, fresh fruit and vegetable, gelatine inputs etc.). *Business Monitor PA415: Fish Processing* [QRL.109] follows the standard treatment of the annual Production Monitors.

7.5.2 *Input-output Analysis*

The coverage of the input-output tables is fully discussed in section 2.5.2. However, we note here that the input-output tables for 1979 and 1984 place “fish processing” (AH4150) together with “fruit and vegetable processing” (AH4147). The input-output tables for 1974 combined “meat and fish products” together under the SIC(1968) classification, so again little useful statistical interdependence can be inferred. Very little interrelationship can be traced with the primary raw materials since “Forestry and fishing” are classified together as an industry/commodity group.

The *Scottish Input-output Tables for 1979* [QRL.448] do recognise the importance of this sector for Scotland because both fishing and fish products are given separate commodity headings based on SIC(1980). Thus the purchases by the fish products groups can be located in the commodity-by-commodity domestic flows matrix. Further data on UK and the rest of the world interconnections are given and some comparison made with 1973. But this is of limited importance since the *Input-output Tables for Scotland: 1973* [QRL.280] were prepared according to SIC(1968).

More insight can be gained from the discussion of the links between primary and secondary processors in *Fish Processing in the UK: An Economic Analysis* [QRL.3]. The illustrative statistics include primary, secondary and shellfish processors material throughput for 1985 in tonnes LWE (landed weight equivalent) broken down by regions of the United Kingdom.

The *Scottish Sea Fisheries Statistical Tables* [QRL.449] are also more specifically related to fish processing. The volume of the raw materials by types of fish (herring, pout, mackerel etc.) used in the production of fishery by-products (fishmeal, fish oil, pet food/animal feed) are shown for the latest five years.

7.6 Labour

A substantial amount of labour force information is discussed for the Food industries overall in section 2.6. We summarise here only the most salient treatments for fish processing.

7.6.1 *Official Sources*

The *Employment Gazette* [QRL.186] contains data on employment in fish processing in two annual articles which summarise the results from the Census of Employment for Great Britain and the United Kingdom respectively. The first gives a male/female and full-time/part-time Activity Heading breakdown plus the analysis for the twelve standard regions of Great Britain for total employment including Scotland and Wales. The second gives the male/female and full-time/part-time Activity Heading breakdown for the United Kingdom. The usual annual article in the *Employment Gazette* [QRL.186] carries the data for the United Kingdom of the average hours worked and average earnings per hour for the male/female, part-time/full-time cross-classifications, separating manual employees on adult rates from manual employees on other rates for fish processing.

Business Monitor PA415 [QRL.109] publishes annual statistics for total employment in the United Kingdom for all establishments classified to the industry Group. Both the country and standard regions of England breakdown are shown for total employment. A size distribution is given for total employment (including working proprietors); operatives; and administrative, technical and clerical staff. *Business Monitor PA415* [QRL.109] also contains data on wages and salaries. Both total and per capita figures are given separately for operatives and administrative, technical and clerical staff together with the size distributions. The operating ratios tables in *Business Monitor PA415* [QRL.109] permit some indication of production and labour costs from the gross and net output per head measures, wages and salaries as a percentage of gross value added etc. for the usual five year run. Much of this is duplicated in the summary tables in *Business Monitor PA1002* [QRL.93]. Naturally the coverage was aggregated into "bacon curing, meat and fish" together from 1958 until SIC(1980) put "fish" on its own again although the earlier years before 1958 presented data for employment etc. in "fish curing".

Census 1981: Economic Activity: Great Britain [QRL.148] contains tables which specify the total in employment by sex, whether full-time/part-time and cross-classified them by type of employees (managers, manual, non-manual etc.) for AH4150. [QRL.148] also gave the numbers of self-employed for each Activity Heading by sex. Similar data for Scotland are also collected and published in the *Census 1981: Scotland Economic Activity (10% Sample)* [QRL.149].

7.6.2 *Occasional Investigations*

Fish Processing in the UK: An Economic Analysis [QRL.3] surveys the many dimensions of employment structure (e.g. location, age, sex and wages etc.). It is a valuable supplement, given the limitations of official statistics. It contains a regional picture of employment in fish processing cross-classified by sex for managerial and clerical, full-time manual and part-time manual employees, plus tables for each type of employee and with the overall UK total. A breakdown for primary, secondary and shellfish processing is given by sex for managerial and clerical, manual labour, manual part-time and total full-time equivalent employees. The age and sex of staff engaged in both full-time manual labour and part-time manual labour is illustrated across the regions of the United Kingdom.

The same publication, [QRL.3], also provides a variety of data on labour costs etc. The proportion of wages and salaries in total costs for primary, secondary and shellfish are shown. The manual wage-paying mechanism by these sectors (whether piece, hourly, weekly, other rates) is given. Hourly wage rates are detailed by region for manual workers (male/female, drivers, supervisors and utility workers). Managerial salary ranges are recorded according to company size. Much labour cost information is also contained in *Financial Results Reported in Fish Processing, 1985* [QRL.2] which was part of the same FERU/SFIA inquiry. Wages and salaries information in total, as a percentage of sales, per employee and per working day are expressed by turnover band for primary processors, secondary processors, fresh fillet producers, frozen fish producers, fish smokers, fish brokers and pelagic fish producers. A similar treatment for shellfish processors whether scampi, scallop or crab producers was also published. Firms were classified to a given class according to their predominant activity.

Both *Fish Processing in the UK: An Economic Analysis* [QRL.3] and *Financial Results Reported in Fish Processing, 1985* [QRL.2] are invaluable sources. However, the data usually refer to the specific years 1985 and 1986. James A. Young [B.191] draws attention to earlier surveys. We must always be dependent on the occasional surveys to supplement official statistics.

The MMC report on *Supplies of Frozen Foodstuffs* [B.444] yields Birds Eye's net output per employee from 1970–1973 in 1970 values. Up-to-date information on productivity, wages and salaries etc. can sometimes be found in the Annual Reports of companies.

Finally, given that it may be argued that fish is in some way processed at sea, the data in the *Sea Fisheries Statistical Tables* [QRL.451] should be mentioned here. The number of fishermen both regularly and partially employed in England and Wales, Scotland and Northern Ireland, together with the UK total, is given as at 31st December for selected years from 1938 to the latest available year. Separate information is available for the latest year by region for regularly and partially employed fishermen plus crofters, in the *Scottish Sea Fisheries Statistical Tables* [QRL.449].

7.7 Capital

7.7.1 *Capital Expenditure*

Business Monitor PA415 [QRL.109] gives a breakdown of gross capital expenditure by type of asset: land and buildings, plant and machinery, and vehicles (all subdivided into acquisitions and disposals) for the five-year period. Annual net capital expenditure is then given and the employment size distribution and the cross-classifications for the standard regions of England, Wales, Scotland and Northern Ireland performed. Net capital expenditure per head and net capital expenditure as a percentage of gross value added are included in the operating ratios table. These data are largely reproduced in *Business Monitor PA1002* [QRL.93].

Previous census of production information typically was different. The census of 1954 gave capital expenditure for fish curing. The census of production reports for 1958, 1963 and 1968 included capital expenditure sub-totals for the fish subdivisions despite the 1958 revision of the SIC which put together bacon curing, meat and fish.

7.7.2 *Suppliers of Machinery*

Business Monitor PQ3244 [QRL.127] gives a somewhat indirect dimension of some capital inputs. Some of the reported sales of bottles, cans, boxes, labelling machinery etc. end up at fish processing firms. The same goes for the imports of other machinery for the preparation of fish, fruit and vegetables and parts of machinery used in the bakery, confectionery, chocolate, macaroni etc. and sugar industries and for the preparation of meat, fish, fruit and vegetables.

7.7.3 *Company Reports and Occasional Investigations*

Details of the net book value of tangible fixed assets, capital employed and projected capital expenditure plans are usually included in the annual reports of individual companies. But given the conglomerate and multinational nature of many of the groups, a source such as the *Unilever Annual Report* [QRL.501] provides more an overview of activities than a detailed statistical breakdown of capital structure and performance of fish processing within Birds Eye.

Fish Processing in the UK: An Economic Analysis [QRL.3] carries more data specific to fish processing firms. Balance sheet values for fixed and working capital are obtained by sector (primary, secondary, shellfish) for the 1985/86 financial year.

The composition of fixed capital is given by sector and distributed across land, buildings and plant; machinery and vehicles with a percentage breakdown by sector. The book value of fixed and working capital invested per business and per employee are each computed by size of company for these sectors as signals of capital intensity. The derivative *Financial Results Reported in Fish Processing, 1985* [QRL.2] also carries more data on fixed capital, working capital and total assets according to sector and to main type of processing (frozen fish, pelagic fish, fish smokers, fish brokers, ranked by turnover). There is evidently an overlap with section 7.13 and some of these sources are also discussed in that section as well.

7.8 International Transactions

7.8.1 *HM Customs and Excise Records*

The primary data source is the monthly *Business Monitor MM20: Overseas Trade Statistics of the United Kingdom* [QRL.85]. "Fish, (not marine mammals), crustaceans, molluscs and aquatic invertebrates and preparations thereof" is the title of Division 03 in the SITC(R3). The full list of commodity headings is too extensive to reproduce here, but are contained in *Business Monitor MA21: Guide to the Classification for Overseas Trade Statistics* [B.213]. The classification embraces both raw fish by species and the various types of species of processed products. The categories of frozen fish fillets; fish, dried, salted or in brine; smoked fish; caviar and caviar substitutes prepared from fish eggs etc. are a selection of what may be broadly regarded as processed products.

Business Monitor PQ4150 [QRL.134] summarises the value in aggregate for the Activity Heading of exports and imports for the latest eight quarters and the past six years. Both exports and imports are disaggregated in value and volume terms for the latest five quarters and last two years. The breakdown is the same for exports and imports and is as follows: dried, salted, in brine or smoked fish; frozen fillets; other frozen fish; prepared or preserved fish not elsewhere specified; frozen, salted in brine, or dried crustacea and molluscs; prepared or preserved (e.g. in cans) crustacea and molluscs; fish waste. The original source for the data is HM Customs and Excise.

Other derivative sources are more aggregative. *United Kingdom Trade with European Countries* [QRL.508] gives annual data in terms of value for Division 03 of exports, imports, exports less imports and the percentage of exports over imports (where meaningful) by specified country, the European Community etc. The succeeding *UK External Trade: Area x Commodity Analysis* [QRL.494] performs a similar service.

The *Monthly Digest of Statistics* [QRL.362] gives the latest two years, the last two quarters, and three monthly value figures for Division 03, comparing the cumulative values from the beginning of the year with the same period in the previous year. The *Annual Abstract of Statistics* [QRL.37] reports the eleven-year value figures for Division 03 for exports and imports.

7.8.2 *Industry Analyses of Trade*

Business Monitor MQ10; Overseas Trade Analysed in Terms of Industries [QRL.90] and the earlier *Business Monitor M10* [QRL.77] of the same title provide quarterly and annual data in terms of value for imports and exports for fish processing. *Business Monitor MQ12: Import Penetration and Export Sales Ratios for Manufacturing Industry* [QRL.91] and the preceding *Business Monitor M12* [QRL.78] of the same title rework the statistics to provide the import penetration and export performance ratios up to the second quarter of 1989. The overall methodology and coverage are fully discussed in section 2.8.2.3.

7.8.3 *European and International Sources*

Regular coverage of imports and exports are described in section 2.8.2.5, but we show here the treatment in international fish publications.

The EUROSTAT *Fisheries Statistical Yearbook* [QRL.225] carries annual data by product weight and value (ECU) for imports and exports. Both totals and intra-EC trade are given for overall fishery products and the following divisions: fresh, chilled or frozen fish; salted, dried or smoked fish; molluscs and crustaceans, fresh, frozen, dried, salted etc; fish preparations and conserves; mollusc and crustacean preparations and conserves; fish oils; and fish meal. Coverage is given for the last six years and an arithmetic mean for the previous years. The *FAO Yearbook: Fishery Statistics: Commodities* [QRL.209] has a host of annual value and quantity of imports and exports data with similar but not identical divisions to the EUROSTAT *Fisheries Statistical Yearbook* [QRL.225]. The *Review of Fisheries in OECD Member Countries* [QRL.438] reproduces annual value and quantity data for imports and exports by major products and by country. Fresh and chilled; frozen (excluding fillets); frozen fillets; salted, dried or smoked; and canned are the subdivisions for the two years recorded.

7.8.4 *Industry Sources*

The *Sea Fisheries Statistical Tables* [QRL.451] summarise the international trade of the United Kingdom with the EEC, EFTA and all other countries. The data are based on figures supplied by HM Customs and Excise. They are presented in a more digestible form for people interested in the fish processing industry than in *Business Monitor MM20* [QRL.85]. The contents of the tables may be summarised as follows:

- Imports of fish and fish preparations: quantity and value by Customs Statistical Classification.
- Imports of fish and fish preparations: value by main categories and countries of consignment.
- Imports of fish and marine mammal products: quantity and value by types of product (meals and flours, oils and whale meat) and countries of consignment.
- Exports of fish and fish preparations: quantity and value by main categories and countries of destination.
- Exports of fish and marine mammal products: quantity and value by types of product (oils and meals) and countries of destination.

All these data are presented for the latest available two years.

There are thus more data on imports than exports in the *Sea Fisheries Statistical Tables* [QRL.451]. The Customs Statistical Classification has a prior division into demersal, pelagic and shellfish. Demersal and pelagic are further subdivided into fresh, including chilled; frozen fillets; other frozen; salted, in brine, dried or smoked; prepared and preserved. Then the main species are enumerated and many of the main product types identified, e.g. frozen fillets; coated with batter or breadcrumbs. The treatment of shellfish is less detailed but similarly organised. Main categories means the prior division is as above with some sub-categories for the most important types of processing and main species involved. The exporting countries are listed for sources of imported fish and the countries of destination shown for the exports. Exports include re-exports which are not separately identified. The main categories identify demersal and pelagic whether fresh, chilled or frozen; semi-preserved; prepared and preserved with overall totals. All forms of shellfish and total fish and fish preparations are the other two categories.

Trade Bulletin: United Kingdom Imports and Exports of Fish and Fish Products [QRL.491] is a monthly publication with about twenty tables related to imports and exports in terms of quantity and value of fish. Both imports and exports are presented according to fish and fishery products for human consumption, fish and fishery products not previously specified, freshwater fish and fish and fishery products by country of origin. The imports section has an additional table for frozen fish from non-EC countries. There is considerable detail for the many species in the human consumption tables under the main segments of fresh or chilled white fish (excluding shellfish; frozen white fish (excluding shellfish); cured white fish (excluding shellfish); shellfish; and fish and shellfish preparations. The species are also further cross-classified e.g. fresh or chilled, frozen and cured under fresh or chilled white fish. The data are presented for the current month and the comparable month the previous year and accumulated comparative data from the beginning of the year. Given the number of tables, both the monthly summary tables and cumulative summary tables are useful, providing details of exports, imports, their percentage changes and the trade balance, with comparative figures for the same periods the previous year for the main segments. The tables are easy to read and have considerable species and product detail including, for example, the quantity and average price of industrial blocks of cod etc. imported from non EC countries.

The *Annual Report and Accounts: the Sea Fish Industry Authority* [QRL.45] carries yearly data on the quantity, value and source of sea fish landed in the UK tables which can be used to compare the contribution of imports to British landings plus percentage changes from year to year. It also carries further summaries of imports and exports in the international trade in sea fish sections. The weight and value of imports, year to year and the percentage changes, are given for cod; haddock; saithe; plaice; herrings; mackerel; other wet fish etc. according to whether fresh and chilled, frozen etc. The sea fish exports summary is less detailed, contrasting wet fish and shell fish. The primary source is again HM Customs and Excise. The previous *Herring Industry Board: Annual Report and Accounts* [QRL.262] and the *White Fish Authority: Annual Report and Accounts* [QRL.518] performed similar functions. The former included imports of fresh and frozen herring, and the latter gave imports and exports of white fish.

7.9 Stocks

Stocks and work-in-progress for fish processing are presented in *Business Monitor PA415* [QRL.109] showing changes over a five-year period in value terms and the value at the end of the latest available year. The three-part disaggregation into materials, stores and fuel; work-in-progress; and goods on hand for sale is given, along with an analysis by size of unit (defined in terms of employment). Computations for the latest five years for the ratio of gross output to stocks are given in the operating ratios table. Similar information can be found in the summary tables in *Business Monitor PA1002* [QRL.93]. A full catalogue of the BSO inquiries is given in section 2.9.2.

Business Monitor SDO25: Retailing [QRL.143], formerly *Business Monitor SDA25: Retailing* [QRL.140], carries data on the value of stocks held by food retailers at the beginning and the end of the year. Fishmongers are separately identified, but the stocks of canned and processed fish products are subsumed in the totals for large grocery retailers etc. *Business Monitor SDA28: Catering and Allied Trades* [QRL.142] identifies fish and chip shops with sandwich and snack bars and measures both beginning, and end-of-year, stocks. But stocks of fish etc. exist elsewhere in many of the other categories e.g. catering contractors.

The *Supplies Bulletin* [QRL.475] estimated total frozen stocks of white fish in the United Kingdom in product weight, enabling two-year comparisons to be made. Cross-classifications according to type of stock (sea-frozen, shore-frozen and imported) were made. These and their sub-categories were further classified according to whether uncooked, prepared or cured. The monthly returns on stocks were almost complete in the 1960's, when it was thought that stock changes made a significant contribution to fluctuations in price. But these returns petered out in 1980–1981.

The nature of stocks is evidently multidimensional but the available statistics only relate to a limited number of these dimensions. Of course, fish stocks exist in nature, in the holds of ships, in the distribution chain, whether in cold stores or transit, on the shelves of shops and in freezers and refrigerators in the home and at retailers etc.

7.10 Consumption

7.10.1 *The National Food Survey*

Given the preoccupation with the nutritional value of fish, *Household Food Consumption and Expenditure* [QRL.267] carries considerable product detail in the estimates of quarterly and annual national averages for household consumption and purchases. Detailed results for the individual fish food codes are given in the supplementary tables as follows: white, filleted, fresh; white unfilleted, fresh; white, uncooked, frozen; herrings, filleted, fresh; herrings, unfilleted, fresh; fat, fresh, other than herrings; white, processed; fat, processed, filleted; fat, processed, unfilleted; shellfish; coated fish; canned salmon, other canned or bottled fish; fish products, not frozen; frozen convenience fish products; and finally total fish. The further analyses according to income group, household composition, region and for responding households with head of household unemployed, are considered according to the incorporation of individual items into the main food groups for fish: fresh fish; processed and shell; prepared, including fish products; frozen, including fish products. Thus a conscious effort is made to separate fresh from processed, and filleted from unfilleted etc. in this treatment. However, the consumption data for household composition groups within income groups, and by ownership of deep freezer, and the expenditure data analysed by age of housewife and housing tenure are presented according to the selected food item of fish. Consumption and expenditure data are also presented for fish by region.

Thus there is the tripartite split of fish into the individual fish food codes, main food groups and selected food items. The supplementary tables in *Household Food Consumption and Expenditure* [QRL.267] tend to carry the greater detail, but further data are found in the *Compendium of Results* [QRL.373]. These include further analyses of fish consumption by main food groups according to: region; type of area; household income; household composition within income groups; age of housewife; housing tenure; comparisons of households which are freezer-owning with other households. Before 1985, these data were largely covered in the tables and appendices of *Household Food Consumption and Expenditure* [QRL.267].

Some of the National Food Survey information is repeated in truncated form in the *Annual Abstract of Statistics* [QRL.37] where fish is placed in three categories: fresh and processed fish; canned fish; and frozen fish and fish products. The data are for estimated household food consumption by all households in Great Britain in ounces per person per week for the eleven-year run. Fish and fish products are identified in the indices of average quantities per person per week of consumption in the home of selected foods in Great Britain for a number of years published in *Social Trends* [QRL.456] which also repeats expenditure data on fish cross-classified by household type. Fish is also one of the main foods in the *Regional Trends* [QRL.401] coverage of household consumption of, and expenditure on, main foods.

7.10.2 *The Family Expenditure Survey*

A detailed description of the *Family Expenditure Survey* [QRL.204] is given in section 2.10.2. The expenditure data are confined to "fish" and "fish and chips". These data are cross-classified by levels of household income; for one adult households by levels of household income, sex and age; by levels of household income for households with and without children; and according to region. No distinction is made between fresh and processed fish although the "Commodity or service annex" shows the items included. However meals bought away from home exclude fish and chips which have their own category.

7.10.3 *The National Accounts*

The *United Kingdom National Accounts* [QRL.506] provide data on consumers' expenditure on fish in both current and 1980 prices, as further explained in section 2.10.3.

7.10.4 *Catering and Meals Outside the Home*

Business Monitor SDA28: Catering and Allied Trades [QRL.142] classifies fish and chip shops together with sandwich and snack bars, and other establishments selling food partly or wholly for consumption off the premises. Catering turnover inclusive of VAT and catering purchases show the level of activity.

7.10.5 *Industry Sources*

It is evidently difficult to be precise about consumption data without listing all individual fish species and without describing how far they are processed. The regular official sources give a good deal of data as already indicated but information on consumption is available too in many of the specialist fish sources.

Household Fish Consumption in Great Britain [QRL.266] results from the fieldwork of Attwood Statistics Ltd. with respect to type and species consumed by a balanced continuous sample of over 4000 families in the seven major TV regions of Great Britain. Average household consumption of fish broken down into fresh, frozen, and fresh and frozen is given. Some eighteen tables give further data on fresh fish purchases by outlet etc. showing the relative retailing importance of the multiple retailer, market stall, fishmongers etc. Comparisons are usually made with the consumption recorded in the corresponding quarter of the previous year. The data are pictured in graphs and by maps which show the TV areas. Attwood supply the data to SFIA under contract but retain the copyright. The *Annual Report and Accounts: Sea Fish Industry Authority* [QRL.45] records some of these data in yearly terms. It usually gives the average household consumption by TV region in product weight and value for the latest and previous year plus illustrative pie charts of fresh and frozen fish purchases by outlet.

The major companies themselves often furnish consumption related data in occasional market reviews. The *Birds Eye Frozen Foods Annual Report* [QRL.63] includes annual figures on total market size for coated fish. *Fish: The Ross Report* [QRL.220] presented data on UK fish consumption in ounces per person using information from the National Food Survey to draw up bar chart comparisons from 1970 to 1983. The changing patterns of fish consumption divided up into fresh; canned/bottled; cooked/processed and frozen fish were also portrayed.

In this section, we note the overlap with section 7.11, particularly the *Annual Abstract of Statistics* [QRL.37]. We note also that the *Sea Fisheries Statistical Tables* [QRL.451] report fish supplies moving into human consumption in kilograms per head of population per annum for the United Kingdom for selected years up to the present compared with pre-war. Fresh, frozen and cured fish (wet fillet equivalent) are separated from shellfish (edible weight) and canned fish (imported) before arriving at the total (edible weight).

7.11 Supplies and Disposals

The term "disposals" requires careful attention, as discussed in the *Monthly Digest of Statistics Supplement* [B.337]. Inter-related concepts are also reviewed in section 2.11. The "Fish, oils and fats" table in the *Monthly Digest of Statistics* [QRL.362] gives data for fresh, frozen and cured fish excluding shellfish. UK landings are clearly expressed as fresh landed-weight-equivalent. Total disposals, which include disposals for export, include fresh, frozen and cured fish again expressed in terms of landed weight. Disposals for food in the United Kingdom include fish used for canning (except the canning of pet foods) whether for home consumption or for export. Fish taken by fish meal manufacturers, fish condemned or unsold, and fish used for fish manufacture, are not included. The column headed "filleted weight" is also relevant for section 7.10, for it shows the estimated edible equivalent, on a fresh fish basis, of the fresh, frozen and cured fish intended for human consumption. The three disposals figures are monthly averages expressed quarterly for the monthly data (for the latest four years) and averaged over the previous six years in monthly terms.

The *Annual Abstract of Statistics* [QRL.37] gives figures for the disposals of fresh, frozen and cured fish (landed weight, excluding shellfish, including usage for canning) for the latest eleven years. In another table, it separates the figures for imported canned fish from those for fresh, frozen and cured fish taken together. This is the eleven-year run for estimated supplies per head of population calculated in kilograms per head per year from the MAFF sources.

The *Scottish Sea Fisheries Statistical Tables* [QRL.449] carry a disposals table on Scottish herring, mackerel and sprat catch. Disposals are divided up into home market, klondyked, overland klondyked, pet food, oil and meal, dumped and bait. Home market includes freshing and kippering, curing, redding and marinating, quick freezing and canning. We stress again the term klondyking which refers to the transport of fish caught by British vessels but not landed in British ports. Good examples are the transhipments to fish freezing vessels typified by the Eastern European and Russian factory ships hovering in Loch Broom near Ullapool. The data in thousand tonnes have an overall total for landings and show what happens to the catch for a five-year run.

The *Annual Report and Accounts: Sea Fish Industry Authority* [QRL.45] has tables which treat British landings of fish together with imports (fresh, frozen and cured) to arrive at an overall total which show the weight and value of supplies for the latest two years. These are in the "supplies and production" tables already discussed in section 7.5.1.7, but the main point here is that imports are added to British landings to show total supplies. The *White Fish Authority: Annual Report and Accounts* [QRL.518] draws a comparable statistical picture in the "supplies and production" appendix. The *Herring Industry Board: Annual Report and Accounts* [QRL.262] usually carried, up to the 1977 issue, a table of landings, disposals and realization by ports or areas which showed the various outlets for the many species.

7.12 Prices

7.12.1 *Commodity and Raw Fish Prices*

7.12.1.1 Official sources

The auction prices of fish landings are collected and collated by MAFF, DAFS and DANI. Returns on prices, as well as landings, in England and Wales and Northern Ireland are collated on computer at Lowestoft. A charge is made for *ad hoc* external requests for information involving computer retrievals.

The *Sea Fisheries Statistical Tables* [QRL.451] present the average annual values of the many species of fish (with subtotals for demersal, pelagic and shellfish) for selected years from 1938 onwards based on landings by British vessels. These data are separately given for England and Wales, Scotland, and Great Britain. They are expressed in £ per tonne in an attempt at standardisation. The footnotes with the tables merit study. For example, the average values throughout are based on realisation for first-hand sale of fish to all outlets, i.e. for human consumption and also for other users such as fish meal and animal feeding stuffs. The *Scottish Sea Fisheries Statistical Tables* [QRL.449] similarly present annual data for the average value of each species landed in £ per tonne for fish landings in Scotland by United Kingdom vessels.

7.12.1.2 Commercial sources

Given the commercial interest in prices, the weekly trade magazine *Fish Trader* [QRL.222] has data on prices in its port and market prices section. The daily prices of the many species at Billingsgate, Aberdeen, Fraserburgh, Peterhead, Fleetwood, Lowestoft and Grimsby are given for Wednesday, Thursday and Friday of each week. All prices are expressed in £ per stone unless otherwise stated.

Fishing News [QRL.227] also carries price information in its catches and prices section. Top landings the previous week by volume and value by named ship at various ports are followed by prices of species at various port markets (Peterhead, Fleetwood, Grimsby, Brixham, Newlyn etc.). The average price on merchants' stalls at Billingsgate are also reported with a separate section for frozen fish species.

The Sea Fisheries Inspectorate Scotland is responsible for *Aberdeen District: Whitefish Report* [QRL.12]. Quantities and values are given for whitefish, nephrops and shrimps. These data are for both the week and cumulated for the current year supplemented by remarks on the movement of fishing vessels.

Evidently, markets like Billingsgate and Birmingham report price data as do the fisheries' offices at the ports. The weekly *City of Birmingham Markets Department Report* [QRL.155] is an example. Fish wholesalers' selling prices on Wednesdays are given for a number of species usually by size and type. Plaice, cod, lemon sole, salmon, herring, coley fillet, haddock fillet and dover sole are reported at the time of writing. *Billingsgate Market Report* [QRL.62] is another example of weekly price reporting. The Superintendent's Office of the latter also issues a daily sheet which gives fair average prices (wholesale prices) for the many species in the *Daily Return for Prices of Fish* [QRL.170]. *Supplies Bulletin: United Kingdom Supplies and Prices of Fish or Fish Products* [QRL.475] gives Billingsgate data for the months of the current and previous years expressing the market prices of selected species of fish in pounds per stone. The data are usually expressed according to a variety of imperial weights. The intricacies of such measures are self apparent and were described for earlier in the century by Walter M. Stern [B.168] in his essay in Barker and Yudkin [B.11].

In rather a different connection, the *Public Ledger's Commodity Week* [QRL.394] and the *Public Ledger & Daily Freight Register* [QRL.392] carry the prices of feed ingredients including fish meal.

With the vast array of price data, traders require continuous information. Fishnet AGB Cable Viewdata was a source of information on first-hand sales and prices at twenty ports in the United Kingdom and selected ports in Northern Europe. Denmark, Western Germany, France and Holland were covered as well as the

United Kingdom, but not Spain, Italy, Portugal and Norway. The data were keyed in every day from 5.00 am onwards. This was a subscription service which began in 1983. Thus the catchers, merchants, wholesalers and processors had Viewdata technology enabling them to see auction prices twice daily, and quantities in and prospects for the following day in the primary fish markets. *Fishing News* [QRL.227] used to draw much of its prices at port markets from Fishnet. However, this subscription service was discontinued in 1990. Even though theoretically useful, the costs to participants became too burdensome. This service has hence ceased, although it could be resurrected if the effective demand were again to re-appear. *Fishing News* [QRL.227], at the time of writing, obtains price data over the telephone. Prestel does still cover a range of MAFF data, available daily, with changes made with time-lags of a few hours.

7.12.2 *Retail Prices*

7.12.2.1 Recorded prices

The *Employment Gazette* [QRL.186] gives average retail prices on one day of the month for the following fish products: cod fillets, haddock fillets, smoked whole haddock, plaice fillets, herrings, kippers with bone, and canned (red) salmon, half-size can. This monthly source notes the number of quotations, and the price range within which 80 per cent of quotations fell. These data are given for the months of the current year and previous years in the *Supplies Bulletin: United Kingdom Supplies and Prices of Fish and Fish Products* [QRL.475] detailing the average retail price in pence per pound for cod fillets, haddock fillets and plaice fillets.

Household Food Consumption and Expenditure [QRL.267], in its pre-1985 format, gave quarterly and annual average prices for the many fish subdivisions listed in section 7.10.1. Frozen convenience fish products, canned salmon, other canned or bottled fish etc. all mainly associated with fish processing were separately identified. Since 1985, the average prices paid in pence per pound are given for a three-year period. The *Compendium of Results* [QRL.373] now carries the quarterly and annual average prices for the many fish subdivisions. *Household Fish Consumption in Great Britain* [QRL.266] lists the pence per pound for the sales to households discussed in section 7.10.5. The percentage change in average price is also recorded.

7.12.2.2 Recommended prices

The *Grocer Price List* [QRL.253], issued with *The Grocer* [QRL.252] on the first Saturday of each month, gives much more detail in its aim to suggest prices for the small retailer. The fish coverage includes bottled fish, canned fish and smoked fish. Under "Frozen foods" are listed the prices for a large number of brands of the major manufacturers. Headings inevitably change and, in the earlier issues, fish is subsectioned into canned and bottled, fishfingers (frozen), fish food and fish paste. Usually both retail and wholesale prices of the existing major brands may be identified.

Shaws Guide to Fair Retail Prices [QRL.453] is published monthly and aims to give the maximum retail prices which may be charged for various foods based on minimum wholesale quantities. Fish features in the frozen food section. There are data for canned and bottled fish from anchovies to tuna treated alphabetically. However *Fish Trader* [QRL.222] only states the retail prices for sea fish in pence per pound.

7.12.3 *The Retail Prices Index*

This is published monthly in the *Employment Gazette* [QRL.186] with an overall category for "Fish" of which "fresh fish" is separately identified. The index is (at the time of writing) based on January 1987 and the percentage change over a twelve month period shown for these two categories. The *Monthly Digest of Statistics* [QRL.362] details the figures for the latest seven months showing the respective weights. *Business Monitor PQ4150* [QRL.134] summarised the retail price index for fish products for past quarters and years. The series for processed fish is compared with the "all food" and "all items" indices.

7.12.4 *Price Index Numbers in the National Food Survey*

In its pre-1985 format, the *Household Food Consumption and Expenditure* [QRL.267] gave indices of expenditure, prices, real values of food purchased and the total value of consumption. Separate statistics were given for the following: fish, fresh and processed; fish, convenience; and fish in total. Fish were also subsumed in the convenience and seasonal foods data. Further product detail down to each food code was found in the annual indices of average deflated prices of purchases and demand. These related to the most recent six years expressed as the average for the whole period.

Since 1985, some index number information is located in the *Compendium of Results* [QRL.373]. This applies to the annual data for the indices of prices for the main food groups and the indices of the real value of purchases and the total real value of consumption. But the individual food code details of the annual indices of average deflated prices are not published. Thus the data for processed white fish, canned salmon, frozen convenience fish products and the many other items of the food codes are not published.

7.12.5 *Producer Price Index Numbers*

The series of producer price indices are considered in general terms in section 2.12.5. Details of the price indices for the input and output of the fish processing sector are given below.

7.12.5.1 Producer price index numbers: input prices

Business Monitor MM22: Producer Price Indices carries the producer price index numbers of materials and fuels purchased for AH4150 giving both monthly and annual data. The monthly data are given for the current and previous years, with the figures for the latest two months provisional. An annual average for the previous year is also presented. *Business Monitor MM22* also identifies fish oils and fats (other than fish liver oil) in the monthly and annual data of price index numbers of commodities wholly or mainly imported into the United Kingdom. *Business Monitor MM22* was published for the first time in October 1989 and generally continued the coverage in *British Business* [QRL.66]

Business Monitor PQ4150 [QRL.134] carried the producer price index of materials purchased (which is home-landed fish) from MAFF sources, usually for the latest available five quarters and past two years.

7.12.5.2 Producer price index numbers: output prices

Business Monitor MM22 contains the producer price index numbers of products manufactured in the United Kingdom (home sales) for AH4150. The monthly data are provided for the current and previous year, with the figures for the latest two months provisional. An annual average for the previous year is also presented. *Business Monitor MM22* was published for the first time in October 1989 and continued the coverage in *British Business* [QRL.66]. *The Annual Abstract of Statistics* [QRL.37] gives the annual averages for AH4150 for a six-year run for products manufactured in the United Kingdom (home sales).

Business Monitor PQ4150 [QRL.134] gave the producer price indices of goods produced for the latest five quarters (the latest provisional) and for the past two years. The series for frozen fish are derived from MAFF sources and compared with the figures for food manufacturing industries (home sales) and all manufactured products (home sales) derived from Department of Trade and Industry sources.

7.12.6 *Export and Import Prices*

The average price of the imports and exports of fish and fish products are given in the *European Supplies Bulletin* [QRL.189], with cumulative monthly data for the latest year, the past year and the percentage change in average price. The original source for the United Kingdom is the computer print-out supplied to the SFIA by HM Customs and Excise.

Given some interdependence in world markets, the supplies and prices section of the fortnightly *Agra Europe Eurofish Report* [QRL.23] features a variety of data on catches, quotas and prices etc. Articles and notes are statistically illustrated. An example from the August 18th 1988 issue is the publication of the agreed price per ton, which Scottish and Shetland fishermen have agreed to supply Russian and East European klondykers with herring.

The *Fishery Market News Report* [QRL.226], sometimes known as the Boston Blue Sheet, available from the National Marine Fisheries Service in the United States, gives the prices to primary wholesalers and processors as quoted by producers, importers and brokers. This New England source is mentioned as it gives the prices of various species and as it is sometimes thought that cod block prices have some influence on UK import prices. *Trade Bulletin: United Kingdom Imports and Exports of Fish and Fish Products* [QRL.491] includes the quantity and average price of industrial blocks of cod etc. imported from non-EEC countries.

7.12.7 *Prices and Government Regulation*

Some price information has appeared in official investigations. The 1975 report by the Price Commission on *Food Prices in Outlying Areas* [B.421] included frozen fish fingers, canned red salmon as well as fresh and smoked fish in the prices collected to compare food prices in outlying areas with the more central areas. Another 1976 Price Commission Report on *Prices and Margins in the Distribution of Fish* [B.430] was mainly concerned with fresh fish but yielded a number of quayside, wholesale and retail prices for 1972–1975. The difficulties of definition were tackled and this reference is confined to fish which had not been "incorporated in any processed product and to which no process has been applied except cleaning, sterilizing, breaking down of bulk supplies, packaging, chilling, freezing, curing and cutting up or filleting".

However the 1976 Monopolies and Mergers Commission Report on *Supplies of Frozen Foodstuffs* [B.444] was unambiguously concerned with the processed product. It gave comparative prices of certain products of Birds Eye, Findus and Ross Foods as at September 1975, which compared and contrasted fish fingers, plaice fillets, codfillets, fishcakes etc. The changes in the recommended retail prices of fish fingers were compared over the previous November 1971 to July 1975.

7.13 Financial Information

7.13.1 *Company and Market Research Reports*

As explained in section 2.10.2, the primary data flow from the companies themselves, and are collated in the many publications listed in that section. Companies involved in fish processing may be identified along with others in the *Times 1000* [QRL.486], and the more specific *Britain's Food Processing Industry* [B.150].

The annual ICC Business Ratio report on *Frozen Food Producers* [QRL.554] presents the calculation of all the ratios listed in Chapter 2. These are given for named firms identified as frozen fish and shellfish producers. The dimensions of return on capital, capital employed etc. are found here. Individual company data cards summarise net profit before tax, interest paid etc. for the latest three years. Another annual ICC Business Ratio report on *Frozen Food Distributors* [QRL.553] contains the same ratio information. The company sector usefully identifies principal activities of firms: for example, George Low (Fish Curer) Ltd. — wholesale merchanting of fish. The annual ICC Financial Survey and Company Directory of *Frozen Food Processors, Distributors and Centres* [QRL.572] makes a division between quoted and unquoted companies. Financial information includes turnover; pre-tax profits; profit margin; rate of return on capital employed; current assets; current liabilities. Finally, the Key Note report on *Frozen Foods* [QRL.589] contain company profiles of Birds Eye Foods Ltd., Findus Ltd., Ross/Youngs etc., and give data on profits and their percentage changes over the previous three years. Other data on pre-tax profits, index of profits, profit margin, return on capital, profit growth year on year also appear. Liquidity ratios, stock turnover etc. are recorded as well.

7.13.2 *Occasional Investigations*

Fish Processing in the UK: An Economic Analysis [QRL.3] includes a whole section on economic performance, mainly for the financial year 1985/1986. Financial results are given by sector (primary, secondary and shellfish) which include sales, cost of purchases, gross margin (sales minus cost of purchase), production costs, total costs etc. before arriving at the net profit figure obtained by deducting interest and depreciation from operating profit. Average figures are obtained according to size of business and the return on capital derived by dividing net profits by total assets (fixed and working capital). The derivative *Financial Results Reported in Fish Processing 1985* [QRL.2] gathers together all the financial information according to sector and to main types of processing (frozen fish; pelagic fish; fish smoking; fish brokers etc.) ranked by turnover. These include the financial and cost profile with figures for operating profit, net profit and return on capital.

Data on financial performance and assessments of economic efficiency can be found occasionally in varying detail in official investigations. The 1976 report by the Monopolies and Mergers Commission on *Supplies of Frozen Foodstuffs* [B.444] carried out a detailed examination of Birds Eye Foods Ltd., Imperial Foods Ltd. and Findus Ltd. The assessment of profits and efficiency isolated gross profits as percentages of net sales value for Birds Eye Foods Ltd. with specific breakdowns for 1964, 1967 and 1971–1974 for fish. Another table on the return on capital employed for the same years for the same company is not broken down for fish alone, but the report brings together much of the existing information on sales, costs, organisation etc. of the frozen food industry and its component products.

The 1976 Price Commission report on *Prices and Margins in the Distribution of Fish* [B.430] gives financial data (1972–1975) on prices and margins at many points of the distribution chain for the sample of wholesale port merchants, wholesale inland merchants, independent fishmongers and multiple fish retailers. A separate analysis for frozen fish processors was performed giving the sales, costs and profits on frozen fish of frozen food processors from a Price Commission Survey.

The 1966 report by the Monopolies Commission on *Ross Group Limited and Associated Fisheries Limited* [B.453] provided an overview of the fishing industry, followed by a financial review of these companies (including illustrative figures on profitability etc.) carried out in the light of the proposed merger.

7.14 Advertising and Market Research

7.14.1 *Advertising*

Fish fingers are the products traditionally characterised by heavy advertising. The trend towards healthier eating (low fat, low cholesterol but high protein) is enhanced both by generic advertising for fish and the considerable product differentiation supported by advertising expenditure.

The *Tri-Media Digest of Brands and Advertisers* [QRL.493] is the prominent source as discussed in section 2.14.1. Expenditure on up to twenty or so brands can be included in the Fresh and fresh-frozen fish (F53) category in this active market. Categories F14 Canned fish and F76 Meat and fish pastes also feature fish components in the products advertised. The *Media Register* [QRL.354], available monthly, has comparable categories to the *Tri-Media Digest* [QRL.493] in FOO 37 Fresh and frozen Fish and FOO 10 Canned fish.

Fish finger products are also featured in the top 100 brands advertising in the Food industry as ranked by adjusted MEAL expenditure data included in *The Food Forecast* [QRL.236]. All sources also identify the generic advertising expenditure of the SFIA which is the established development agency for the fishing industry. The SFIA tends to publicise fresh fish, but its various promotional activities as featured in the *Annual Report and Accounts: Sea Fish Industry Authority* [QRL.45] are designed to raise the demand for fish overall.

In another context, the MMC report on *Supplies of Frozen Foodstuffs* [B.444] explored the advertising expenditure which prompted branded products. The statistics for 1971–1972 were obtained directly from the companies but the prime current sources for the brands are evidently the *Tri-Media Digest* [QRL.493] and the *Media Register* [QRL.354].

7.14.2 *Market Research*

The overlap between advertising and market research is typified in the *Food Forecast* [QRL.236]. This both reproduces MEAL brand data for expenditure on fresh and fresh frozen fish for the past nine years (unadjusted) and the latest quarter (adjusted) along with tables showing brand shares for past years of frozen fish fingers and other frozen fish judged by the pattern of expenditure of housewives. Regional analyses for usage by housewives of frozen fish fingers and other frozen fish are also reported.

The major companies also cover advertising and other market data in reports which are usually available free on request. *Birds Eye Frozen Foods Annual Report* [QRL.63] usually devotes a section to fish, giving illustrative advertising expenditures, market sizes and brand performance in coated fish and a percentage comparison of retail outlets for volume sales of frozen coated fish. The *Frozen Food Consumer Market Bulletin* [QRL.242] reviews the fish market amongst other frozen foods, comparing market segmentation by value and volume for fish as against vegetables, meat and desserts. It succeeded *Fish: The Ross Report* [QRL.220] which was last published in 1984. *The Ross Report* [QRL.220] include market shares of fish products within Ross, a five year review of market performance (fish fingers, fish cakes etc.) in 1000 tons and product sales by TV region amongst other information from Ross/NOP/AGB etc. *Frozen Food: Retail Market Report* [QRL.243] is also produced by Ross and shows overall brand performance as well as the ten top added value growth markets which include fish based products.

"Frozen food (Part 1)" in the April 1988 issue of *Retail Business* [QRL.432] and "Frozen food (Part 2)" in the May 1988 issue of *Retail Business* [QRL.432] consider the frozen food market overall and the performance of specific sectors respectively. The former includes market definition; market size (including fish in retail sales of frozen food 1982–6 from Birds Eye/Walls sources), growth factors; regional patterns; the suppliers; retail distribution and prospects. The latter treats fish products under market trends; market shares; advertising (from MEAL); and prices. "Canned fish" in the April 1985 issue of *Retail Business* [QRL.432] collects together data from trade and other sources on: market size and trends; imports and exports; consumption; suppliers and brands (including market shares for salmon, tuna, pilchards and sardines for 1984) by the main producers and own brands; distribution; prices and margins; advertising and promotion; packaging and prospects.

Fish and Fish Products [QRL.606] and *Frozen Foods* [QRL.607] by Market Assessment Publications both provide market sector overviews. The former reviews the segments of frozen fish, fresh fish, canned and bottled fish and shellfish separately. Data include sales by type, competitive structure and consumer profiles of purchasers. The later draws together information on frozen coated fish for the following dimensions: market definition; market size by value; production by value; foreign trade; market segmentation; competitive structure; advertising and promotion; retail outlets; consumer profiles; regional profile and market forecast. *Canned Foods* [QRL.601] and *Chilled Foods* [QRL.602] by Market Assessment Publications follow similar formats and are also useful in assessing industry structure (see section 7.2.2). Two Mintel *Market Intelligence* [QRL.339] reports of September 1987 and September 1984 cover "Fish products" and collect together data on consumption; companies and brands; fish products; consumer portraits; advertising and promotion and prospects for the future etc.

A 1986 report on "Fish and fish products" in *Market Research: Great Britain* [QRL.343] includes the following market overview: supply to the market; the fresh fish market; the frozen fish market; salmon and trout: a special review; the canned fish market; the market for shellfish; future outlook; then other categories which include fish pastes, pâtés and fresh fish cakes.

The Key Note report on *Frozen Foods* [QRL.589] is also discussed in section 7.13.1, and combines AH4122.2, AH4150 and AH4147.1 of SIC(1980). Company financial profiles are supplemented by data on the distribution of consumption expenditure on fish categories and on market shares.

Many of these publications contain other relevant data besides those on advertising and promotion. They often carry descriptions of market structure too. Since many reports are periodically updated, they can be used as preliminary reviews of the current market situation as well.

7.15 Research and Development

Research and development are featured in many parts of the fish processing nexus from fundamental research into the nature of fish (e.g. the work of Torry Research Station) to product development (sometimes described in the Annual Reports of the major companies). The quick growth of the processed fish market and the quick freezing of fish attest to the importance of technical innovation.

Statistical data are sparse. The *Annual Report and Accounts: Sea Fish Industry Authority* [QRL.45] publishes the annual number of its employees in research and consultancy. [QRL.45] features the sources of income and expenditure (including research projects) in the Research and Experiment Account which is an appendix to the annual Income and Expenditure Account. Further data are provided in another appendix entitled the Seafish Industry Development Programme which summarises the government grant and breaks down expenditure on research projects, sales development and training costs. The SFIA carries on the research on both technical and economic fronts formerly under the aegis of the Herring Industry Board and the White Fish Authority.

7.16 Official Investigations

The following publications involve fish processing in varying degrees and have been drawn upon during this chapter:

Reports of the Price Commission under the Counter Inflation Act 1973

Report no.10 (1975) *Food prices in Outlying Areas* [B.421]
Report no.14 (1976) *Prices and Margins in the Distribution of Fish* [B.430]

Reports of the Monopolies Commission

(Session 1966/67) *Ross Group Ltd. and Associated Fisheries Ltd. Report on the Proposed Merger* [B.453]

Reports of the Monopolies and Mergers Commission

(Session 1975/76) *Frozen Foodstuffs. A Report on the Supply in the United Kingdom of Frozen Foodstuffs for Human Consumption* [B.444]

Given the interdependence of fish processing with fisheries in general, there are a considerable number of other important official documents which have been referred to and are listed together here:

(Session 1960/61) The Report of the Committee of Inquiry into the *Fishing Industry* [B.363] — the Fleck Report
(Session 1976/77) *The Third Report from the Expenditure Committee: Inquiry into the Fishing Industry* [B.320]
(Session 1977/78) *The Fifth Report from the Expenditure Committee: The Fishing Industry* [B.276]
(Session 1979/80) *EEC Fisheries Policy* [B.250] by the House of Lords Select Committee on the European Communities

7.17 Improvements and Comments

It must now be apparent that statistical sources on fish processing present both the producer and the user of statistics with a fascinating and substantial task.

First of all, it has been essential to catalogue in section 7.5 the vast amount of data available as the essential input of the fish catch. Given their importance it could be said that the *Sea Fisheries Statistical Tables* [QRL.451] and the *Scottish Sea Fisheries Statistical Tables* [QRL.449] take a lengthy time (more than two years) to emerge. This, however, is partly remedied by the existence of the *Monthly Return of Sea Fisheries Statistics: England and Wales* [QRL.363] and the *Monthly Summary of*

Fisheries Statistics [QRL.368] as well as the availability of data on application to MAFF, DAFS and DANI. The data sources here are very rich due to the historical importance of the fishing industry, the preoccupation with sustaining this renewable resource and the data requirements of the European Community. As noted in section 7.3, these latter can slow down the publication of UK statistics. Thirty-two species are at the time of writing subject to quota by the European Community.

It would be difficult to claim that the statistics in the *Sea Fisheries Statistical Tables* [QRL.451] are exact but catches of the main demersal and pelagic species are statutorily required under EC Council Regulation 2057/82. However, shellfish statistics are still mainly provided on a voluntary basis with small quantities being landed at a large number of minor ports throughout the country.

Second, there is the basic difficulty of defining fish processing itself. The dividing lines may indeed change according to the period studied and the technology. The Price Commission Report on *Prices and Margins in the Distribution of Fish* [B.430] provided a definition for fresh fish as any fish which has not been "incorporated in any processed product and to which no process has been applied except cleaning, sterilizing, breaking down of bulk supplies, packaging, chilling, freezing, canning, cutting up or filletting." A solution may seem to be to take the reverse as the definition of the processed product. Yet the discussion in section 7.2 showed that market perceptions (demand) often differ from the classification of the suppliers. No classification is clearcut because fish products can combine numerous ingredients. Some fish which is packaged and frozen by processors can be retailed by fishmongers in unpackaged and unthawed form. Fish and chip shops use a mixture of what may be regarded as fresh and processed fish.

Third, as regards the Census of Production, the earlier collection of data showed that statisticians thought in a production function framework in the estimates of the various outputs and inputs for the fish curing trade in the very *First Census of Production of the United Kingdom (1907)* [QRL.219]. In a similar fashion, but in a more modern context, it is important to stress that *Business Monitor PA415* [QRL.109] draws together many statistical dimensions in one place given the importance of output, sales, labour input, wages and salaries, stocks, business ratios etc. This Review however, has categorised data together by type rather than by source.

Fourth, given the need to get an overall picture, the inclusion of fish processing under "Bacon curing, meat and fish products" from 1954 to 1980 in the SIC has to be noted. But now under the SIC(1980) the important activity of "Fish processing" is again on its own.

Fifth, the employment "cut off" in *Business Monitor PA415* [QRL.109] excludes many smaller companies. Every firm with more than 100 employees receives a form, those with 20 to 100 are sampled, and those under 20 largely excluded. This was one of the reasons for the initiative of *Fish Processing in the UK: An Economic Analysis* [QRL.3] discussed in section 7.2.4 and other sections. This study directly focused on fish processing. The considerable amounts of data on employment structure, raw material purchases, processed output and financial results etc included the smaller firms. *Business Monitor PQ4150* [QRL.134] did reflect the total sales of those establishments so classified only so far as the grossing-up exercise is done for those with less than 35 employees. But this was not done for the individual products.

Hence such occasional studies as [QRL.3] are invaluable even if this conversely had limited coverage of the large companies. There is a need for such studies to be recast and repeated from time to time — all the more so since *Business Monitor PQ4150: Fish Products* [QRL.134] was discontinued from mid-1989.

Sixth, the processing of fish may be alternatively assigned to the frozen food, canned food or bottled foods sectors. This can mean that the type of industrial organisation reflects the type of processing as much as the product itself. Whence statistical data are often collected for the frozen food market etc. *per se* rather than specifically for fish. An example of this is the financial ratio analyses of the frozen food market done in the ICC Business Ratio report entitled *Frozen Food Producers* [QRL.554]. A similar comment applies to the review of "Frozen foods" in *Market Research: Great Britain* [QRL.343] which also combined SIC(1980) codes. Likewise the Monopolies and Mergers Commission report on the *Supplies of Frozen Foodstuffs* [B.444] involved reference goods which included fish, vegetables, meat (including poultry) and confectionery and fruit. Profitability investigations were aggregated across these groups even if sales, market share and advertising data could have been more easily identifiable. The inevitable overlap is a fact of life. The current compass of *Business Monitor PA415* [QRL.109] combines together food firms like Birds Eye, Findus and Ross/Youngs which produce many products besides fish.

Statistics have usually been enumerated in terms of both weight and value. The essay by Stern [B.168] emphasised the variation of appropriate measures and names of weights for the many species. Price data for simplicity are often expressed in "pence per lb" in official publications. But it can be argued, as Unilever did in their evidence to the MMC in the report on *Supplies of Frozen Foodstuffs* [B.444], that weight rather than value was the more appropriate determinant of a company's share of total supply. It was also argued that weight was the more salient factor contributing to the processors' packaging, storage and distribution capacity and thus determined the structure of costs.

Finally, this chapter could only have done full justice to the number of species and the many users of fish (besides human consumption) if it had turned into a volume on its own. This can be seen by studying the FAO's International Standard Statistical Classification of Fishery Commodities (ISSCFC) which is used in the collation of national details and the layout of tables in the *FAO Yearbook: Fishery Statistics: Commodities* [QRL.209] and the *FAO Yearbook: Fishery Statistics: Catches and Landings* [QRL.208]. The seven groups of species (freshwater; marine; crustaceans; molluscs; diadromous; whales; seals and other aquatic mammals; miscellaneous aquatic animals) may seem manageable enough. But the systematic list of aquatic organisms is formidably long. The alphabetical list comprises a tightly packed list of thirty seven pages! This is not of course to say that UK processors are concerned with all species but it does show the almost infinite variety of this valuable resource. Both these FAO publications are excellently produced volumes with maps and extensive data. All this may suggest that we ideally need market summaries and statistical collections which cover each and every species from the moment of the catch through the chain of distribution and processing. Even though this chapter may have seemed extensive, it may be regarded as but a summary of the fish sector. There is little doubt that "fish" could merit a book on its own!

CHAPTER 8

GRAIN MILLING AND BREAD, BISCUITS AND FLOUR CONFECTIONERY (INCLUDING BREAKFAST CEREALS)

This chapter is not confined to industrial Groups as delineated in the *CSO Standard Industrial Classification Revised 1980* [B.232]. It covers the grain milling industry (Group 416), the bread, biscuits and flour confectionery industry (Group 419) and also breakfast cereals which belong to Group 423 miscellaneous foods. This is a convenient and more logical arrangement and also one, which it is hoped, will be more useful to the reader. Other more general sources, which provide statistics on other industry Groups as well, are covered in Chapter 2 and should be consulted as required. The contents of this chapter are as follows:

8.1 Introduction

Industry Groups 416 and 419 cover the following Activity Headings:

4160 Grain milling.
Milling, flaking and rolling grain and the production of grain products. Splitting and grinding peas, beans, lentils, sago, tapioca, etc. is included. Production of uncooked breakfast cereals (e.g. oatmeal) is included, but ready-to-eat breakfast cereals are classified to heading 4239.8.

4196 Bread and flour confectionery.
The baking of bread and flour confectionery by plant and master bakers. Bakehouses run in conjunction with retail shops are included

here when they can supply separate information or when baking is the main activity of the combined unit.

4197 Biscuits and crispbread.

4239/8 Breakfast cereals.

For an alphabetical list of the activities covered by Groups 416 and 419, see the CSO *Indexes to the Standard Industrial Classification Revised 1980* [B.317]. AH4160 corresponds to MLH211 in SIC(1968); AH4196 corresponds to MLH212, but also includes small bakeries attached to retail shops (previously classified to MLH820.2); AH4197 corresponds to MLH213. Further details may be found in *Standard Industrial Classification Revised 1980: Reconciliation with Standard Industrial Classification 1968* [B.379].

In addition, sources of statistics on ready-to-eat breakfast cereals are also discussed in this chapter, although these products fall under AH4239.8 in SIC(1980). The coverage is thus what we will term the "cereals sector", from the first-stage industry of grain milling to the second-stage industries of bread, biscuits and flour confectionery, and breakfast cereals. Discussion is limited to cereal products for human consumption, and the animal feeding stuffs and brewing and malting industries are excluded. Starch and certain other cereal-based foods are considered separately in Chapter 11.

The industry definitions above are not necessarily coincidental with markets for final or intermediate products, since compromises encompassing "production based" items are often made. Hence AH4160 includes not only the milling, flaking and rolling of grain and the production of grain products, but also the splitting and grinding of peas, beans, lentils, sago, tapioca etc. Flour is the major product, although self-raising flour made from purchased flour, is currently classified under AH4239 "Miscellaneous foods" along with various other farinaceous products. AH4160 includes the production of uncooked breakfast cereals such as oatmeal, while ready-to-eat breakfast cereals appear under AH4239. AH4196 covers essentially the baking activities of plant and master bakers, but these are not always easily distinguished from retailing activities. Hence, current practice is to include bakehouses run in conjunction with retail shops in AH4196 when separate statistics are available or baking is the main activity of the combined unit. Although basically straightforward in definition, AH4197 has practical difficulties of drawing distinctions between its products and those of the chocolate confectionery industry (AH4214.1) which are cereal based. Output of AH4197 also includes cereal fillers used elsewhere.

A further complication is that the cereals sector has a high degree of vertical, as well as horizontal, integration in its industrial structure. Examples include firms integrated across grain milling, plant baking, bread and flour confectionery, retailing, and catering activities.

8.2 Industry Structure

8.2.1 *Historical Reviews of the Industry*

Major reviews of the history of the bread industry were published in 1928 by W. Ashley, *The Bread of Our Forefathers* [B.5], and in 1957 by R. Sheppard and E.

Newton, *The Story of Bread* [B.161]. Two other invaluable sources, both by J. Jeffreys, are "Bread and cereals" [B.87], published in 1950, and "The bread and flour confectionery trade" [B.88], published in 1954.

However, in many respects, *The Bread Industry in the United Kingdom* [B.113] by W.P.J. Maunder, provides the most satisfactory analysis of structure-conduct-performance in the industry as a whole, and gives an excellent guide to its development up to 1969. In addition, a useful summary of the history of the bread and breakfast cereals industries during the twentieth century is contained in the chapter by E.J.T. Collins in *The Making of the Modern British Diet* [B.39]. T.A.B. Corley's contribution to the same volume considers the biscuit industry during the nineteenth century, although a fuller account of the sector is contained in his *Quaker Enterprise in Biscuits: Huntley & Palmers of Reading 1822–1972* [B.41].

A fascinating analysis of the origins of the US food manufacturing industry and its establishment in the United Kingdom is contained in *At Home Abroad* [B.84]; which also provides an excellent account of the genesis of the UK's breakfast cereal industry. More detailed specific accounts are provided by A.F. Marquette, *Brands, Trademarks and Goodwill: The Story of the Quaker Oats Company* [B.108] and by H.P. Pavell, *The Original Has His Signature — W.K. Kellogg* [B.139].

8.2.2 *The Development of the Industry since 1935*

The structure of the grain milling industry has become increasingly concentrated since the First World War. Although in 1935 there were over 2,600 establishments in grain milling, according to the *Final Report on the Fifth Census of Production and the Import Duties Act Inquiry 1935* [QRL.215], three producers accounted for 39 per cent of total output. This relatively high concentration was brought about by the rationalisation of excess capacity in this declining market — see Maunder [B.113] — and by economies of scale, particularly for port-based locations. The flour milling industry was more concentrated still, with three firms producing two-thirds of the industry output in 1944, as estimated by H.V. Edwards in "Flour milling" [B.46]. At the same time, the bread industry had many more establishments, with 24,000 bakers and confectioners in 1935 and a much lower degree of concentration than in flour milling — see "The structure of British industry" [B.100] by H. Leak and A. Maizels.

However, the growth of Allied Bakeries in particular led to the increasing importance of plant bakers — see *Concentration in British Industry* [B.48] by R. Evely and I.M.D. Little. Maunder [B.113] describes how, in the 1950s, the process of forward integration by Ranks — to become Rank Hovis McDougall (RHM) in 1962 — and Spillers from flour milling to baking, and backward integration by Allied Bakeries — renamed Associated British Foods (ABF) in 1962 — produced a highly concentrated structure of three firms in both sectors. This situation continued until 1978, when Spillers withdrew from plant baking — see the MMC Report on *Flour and Bread* [B.443] and "Bread pricing in Great Britain" [B.156] by A.M. Rushton. The process of concentration in flour milling and its structure in the late 1960s are described in detail by D.K. Britton in *Cereals in the United Kingdom* [B.25].

The structure of flour milling in the mid-1980s remained dominated by three companies: Rank Hovis Ltd., Spillers Milling Ltd. (Dalgety), and Allied Mills Ltd.

(ABF), which together made up about 80 per cent of all UK flour production, according to the 1985 version of *Facts and Figures* [QRL.202]. There were at this time also some 48 independent millers. Over 80 per cent of output was used in breadmaking, biscuit and cake manufacture, but a small quantity (about 5 per cent) was sold as household and self-raising flour. RHM's "British Bakeries" and ABF's "Allied Bakeries" accounted for 60 per cent of bread production, with about 35 independent plant bakers supplying a further 10 per cent, and 4,000 master bakers selling through 15–20,000 retail outlets providing most of the remainder. In addition, there has been a rapid growth of in-store bakeries and hot bread shops often using bought-in dough. The major plant bakers produce virtually all the standard, wrapped and sliced bread, but in recent years they have moved into non-standard and speciality loaves, traditionally the province of the master baker. Supermarket own-label bread has increased its share of standard bread significantly.

The cakes and pastries market is now dominated by two major companies, with the story of RHM's Manor Bakeries' entry into the packaged cakes industry being told, for instance, by Maunder [B.116]. The position in the late 1980s is briefly summarised in the 1986 MMC Report on *Elders IXL Ltd. and Allied-Lyons plc* [B.442] which deals more fully with Allied-Lyons' role in the market, and comments on the one-third share of retailer own-label products in packaged cakes.

The biscuit market is again the province of two major firms — United Biscuits and Nabisco Brands — with a significant proportion also accounted for by retailers' own-labels. United Biscuits was created in 1948 from a merger between McVitie and Price Ltd. and Macfarlane, Lang & Co Ltd., adopting the present name in 1966 — see the Price Commission report, *United Biscuits (UK) Ltd. — Biscuits, Crisps, Nuts and Savoury Snacks* [B.436]. Nabisco Brands' position derives from the takeover of Huntley and Palmers Foods plc in 1982 — see the 1982 MMC Report *Nabisco Brands Inc. and Huntley and Palmer Foods plc* [B.448]. Both reports provide brief but helpful analyses of the biscuit market structure, although more recent information relies on market research reports such as *Retail Business* [QRL.432]. Similarly with breakfast cereals, recent structural data are largely obtained from commercial sources. The pre-eminent position of Kelloggs is well-known and has been described historically by the Monopolies Commission in *Breakfast Cereal Foods* [B.439].

Industry structure in all these cereal markets is described to some extent in the relevant PA Business Monitors. The annual Monitors give the number of enterprises and establishments, a size breakdown, and five-firm concentration ratios. These details are available for "grain milling" (Group 416) and, currently, for "bread, biscuits and flour confectionery" (Group 419), but breakfast cereals are subsumed within "starch and miscellaneous foods" (Group 423). The production-oriented definitions used in the Census of Production limit the value of the data for market structure analysis, as noted earlier. The Quarterly Sales Inquiries give the number of establishments in the various markets covered: "bread and flour confectionery" in *Business Monitor PQ4196: Bread and Flour Confectionery* [QRL.136] and "biscuits" in *Business Monitor PQ4197: Biscuits and Crispbread* [QRL.137]. Coverage of [QRL.136] and [QRL.137] was up to the second quarter of 1989. More detailed analysis of product market concentration was given for 1975, 1976 and 1977 in *Business Monitor PO1006: Statistics of Product Concentration of UK Manufacturers* [QRL.115], which covered flour (for bread, biscuits etc.); flour (household and self-raising); cereal breakfast foods; bread; and biscuits.

Few attempts have been made to analyse the local industry in detail, but the 1983 GLC Report on *Flour Milling and Bread Baking in London* [B.278] provides a useful summary of national and local data.

Turning to the European context, comparative structural data are not easily obtained, but a useful study which outlines problems and methodology is *The Structure of Industry in the EEC* [B.57] by K.D. George and T.W. Ward. Average plant size statistics are given for the United Kingdom, German, French and Italian bread industries and corn milling, with also "grain milling" and "bread, biscuits" four-firm and four-plant concentration ratios. A wider survey is contained in the EC Commission publication *Structural Change and Public Policy in the European Food Industry* [B.43] which includes a good deal of structural data from national sources. Mention should also be made of another EC Commission publication *Concentration, Competition and Competitiveness in the Food Industry of the EEC* [B.99] and the annual European Commission *Report on Competition Policy* [QRL.410]. All these publications contain references to the cereals sector.

8.2.3 *General Statistical Sources*

While *Maunder* [B.113] remains the best overview of the bread industry, a number of further general texts may be cited on the cereals sector. The MMC Report on *Flour and Bread* [B.443] provides an excellent summary of the development of the milling and baking industries from 1935 to 1977. Much pioneering work on the economic analysis of the flour and bread industry was carried out by the National Board for Prices and Incomes [B.408], [B.416], [B.415], [B.404], [B.398] and [B.399] — see section 8.16 for details. *Give Us This Day...* [B.152], by W.D. Reekie is largely derivative, but draws together a number of useful sources. A careful analysis of both the "Grain milling" and "Biscuits" industries is contained in the EC Commission publication, *A Study of the Evolution of Concentration in the Food Industry of the United Kingdom. Part II: Product Market Structure* [B.384], which looks at many of the difficulties in the available structural data. The biscuit industry was also usefully reviewed in a report prepared by the NEDO Biscuits Sector Working Group — *Biscuits* [B.208], and an excellent account of the development of the breakfast cereals industry to 1973 appears in the Monopolies Commission Report on *Breakfast Cereal Foods* [B.439]. Finally, overviews of the cereal product sectors are obtained in a number of market research periodicals, of which *Retail Business* [QRL.432] is generally accessible. Details of recent relevant reports are given in section 8.14.2. Occasional, but more comprehensive, surveys are produced by Euromonitor Publications, Key Note Publications, Mintel, A.C. Nielsen, and Marketing Strategies for Industry among others.

8.2.4 *Trade Associations*

A major role in the provision of information in the cereals sector is played by the Home-Grown Cereals Authority (HGCA), which was established by the Cereals Marketing Act 1965, with the general remit to improve the marketing of home-grown cereals in the United Kingdom. The Authority commissioned the *Britton Report* [B.25], the first major survey on cereals marketing since the Ministry of Agriculture and Fisheries' *Report on the Marketing of Wheat, Barley and Oats in England and Wales* [B.365] in 1928. A dated, but still useful, study of the Authority's activities is *Information in the Cereals Market* [B.169] by I.M.T. Stewart. The Authority produces an extensive range of data, which although focused on ex-farm marketing, UK grain trade, and prices, is by no means confined to these topics. The *Weekly Bulletin* [QRL.512] gives a market commentary, and contains detailed statistical tables on spot prices (UK, continental and international), UK trade, tariffs, forward and futures prices, EEC import levies and export refunds, intervention and support prices. The *Weekly Digest* [QRL.513] contains articles with statistical analysis covering, over the year, many of the topics mentioned above. The *Marketing Note* [QRL.345] — a supplement to the *Weekly Bulletin* [QRL.512] — provides longer articles on marketing topics, and an important statistical appendix on cereal supplies and consumption in the United Kingdom which is also reproduced, with its commentary, in the weekly *Press Notice* [QRL.389]. Figures in the appendix are based on MAFF information and published only after consideration by the Authority and its Advisory Committee. The statistics produced in the *Weekly Bulletin* [QRL.512] are also published on a yearly basis in the annual *Cereals Statistics* [QRL.152], along with other useful information.

Amongst trade associations, the Cake and Biscuit Alliance (CBA) has been of importance in providing details of the UK biscuit trade (home deliveries and exports of its member companies, imports) and EEC figures, in its *Annual Report*. These reports also showed the value of home deliveries and exports of cakes, again derived from its member companies' returns to the Alliance. The Alliance gave information on biscuit deliveries, invoice values, average values, export market deliveries and values, on a four-weekly statistical basis to biscuit members who were subscribers to the statistical service. In January 1987, the Cake and Biscuit Alliance joined with the Cocoa, Chocolate and Confectionery Alliance to form the Biscuit, Cake, Chocolate & Confectionery Alliance (BCCCA) and its statistical services are now continued on a similar basis as before. In addition, the 1987 edition of the *Statistical Year Book* [QRL.461] provided a compendium of annual statistics, including those collected by the CBA over the period 1969–1986.

The flour milling industry is represented by the National Association of British and Irish Millers (NABIM) which produces an annual *Facts and Figures* [QRL.202] on industry structure, wheat usage, balance of payments, production, sales and costs. Much of the information is derived from MAFF and HGCA sources. In the past, both NABIM and the Millers' Mutual Association (MMA) collected more detailed information on output and costs which was circulated to members — see the MMC Report on *Flour and Bread* [B.443]. Other UK organisations and bodies provide limited quantities of statistical data, and much that is published is secondary. The Federation of Bakers' *Facts about Bread 1985* for example, reproduces relevant tables from *Household Food Consumption and Expenditure* [QRL.267]. The National Association of Master Bakers, Confectioners and Caterers (NAMBCC) produces the monthly *Bakers Review* [QRL.57] which lists prices of bread and flour confectionery, and has a cost of materials index.

8.3 The European Community

The EC cereals regime was the first to be devised and implemented in detail, and it both set the pattern, and influenced the price levels adopted, in many other support schemes. The price support mechanism for cereals includes whole grains, flour and first-stage processed cereal products, starch and glucose. The buying however, is, directed towards the basic cereal whole grains with differences between, on the one hand, the mechanism for common (soft) wheat, barley, maize and rye and, on the other hand, wheat of breadmaking quality. The Intervention Board for Agricultural Produce (IBAP) receives offers of cereals for intervention purchase, but the market arrangements are undertaken by its executive agent, the Home-Grown Cereals Authority (HGCA). Details of the intervention systems are set out in the HGCA publication, *EEC Marketing Arrangements for Grains and Processed Products* [QRL.185].

Common prices were introduced in the six countries of the original Community on 1st July 1967, but the regime has developed substantially in methodology and complexity since that date. Of the numerous commentaries and analyses, *The Food and Farm Policies of the European Community* [B.71] by S.A. Harris, A. Swinbank and G.A. Wilkinson, is particularly helpful in its clear exposition both of the policies, and of their impact on the food manufacturing industries. More comprehensive still in the cereals context is the *EEC Marketing Arrangements for Grains and Processed Products* [QRL.185] which is continually updated, and incorporates many recent statistics in its examples. Further information is provided by leaflets supplied by the IBAP on, for example, the detailed operations of the internal support systems and external market operations. Day-to-day information on intervention prices, MCAs, export refunds, representative (green) rates of exchange, cereals co-responsibility levy is provided in the IBAP *Notice to Traders* [QRL.379], and Agra Europe's *CAP Monitor* [B.220]. A comprehensive review of the work of IBAP and its expenditure on support is contained in its annual *Intervention Board for Agricultural Produce: Annual Report* [QRL.293] published in June of the following year.

Statistical details of the impact of EC membership on the UK cereals sector can be gained from many sources. The annual HGCA publication, *Cereals Statistics* [QRL.152], is one of the most comprehensive, but a useful discussion of the policy implications for the industry can be found in "The EEC and the UK's cereals processing industry" [B.153] by F.T. Rees. A 1986 study of the common policy on cereals by N.F. Beard, *Against the Grain? The EC Cereals Policy* [B.14] contains detailed statistics of UK, EC and world cereals, albeit without clear referencing.

The cereals' policy has generally stimulated UK production and yields from farms, and hence altered the sources of raw materials for many cereal processors. The apparently increasing self-sufficiency — as shown in successive issues of the *Annual Review of Agriculture* [QRL.51] and from 1988 *Agriculture in the United Kingdom* — has also relied on the enhanced ability of breadmakers in particular to incorporate more UK wheats. This has come from improved 'harder' varieties that are more tolerant of UK climatic conditions, from use of the Chorleywood baking process which allows a higher proportion of 'softer' wheats, and from the use of wheat gluten to 'reinforce' UK wheats for breadmaking. Less reliance on imported wheat has changed the economics of flour milling and the location of mills: large port-based facilities giving way to medium-size establishments nearer areas of home production. Other effects have been the stimulation of UK grain exports, mainly of feed wheat and barley, and the building of suitable port facilities at, for example, Southampton, Hull and Ipswich — see *UK Grain Exports: A Surrender to the Multinationals?* [B.392].

8.4 Output

8.4.1 *Output, Sales and Value Added*

8.4.1.1 Business Statistics Office inquiries

The cereals sector is covered by a number of quarterly Business Monitors in the PQ series up to mid-1989 — see section 2.1.1.2 for general discussion. *Business Monitor PQ4196: Bread and Flour Confectionery* [QRL.136] and *Business Monitor PQ4197: Biscuits and Crispbread* [QRL.137] provide data for AH4196 and AH4197 respectively. The former enumerates both the volume and value of sales by UK manufacturers of white bread and other bread, and the value of flour confectionery in quick-frozen, pre-packed, unwrapped and other forms. Since the first quarter of 1986, it also includes sales of "savoury pies, pasties and puddings" — from *Business Monitor PQ4122: Bacon Curing and Meat Products* [QRL.130]. The latter indicates sales of chocolate covered biscuits; other sweetened biscuits; semi-sweetened biscuits; unsweetened biscuits plain; savoury biscuits; rusks, crispbreads and matzos; and "all other" types. The cereals components of Group 423 may be found itemised in *Business Monitor PQ4239: Miscellaneous Foods* [QRL.139] which gives *inter alia* statistics on sales of "cereal breakfast foods (in packets for retail sales)" and "self-raising flour" made from purchased flour. No quarterly Monitor is however published for AH4160 "Grain milling".

Previous Monitors in the PQ series include *Business Monitor PQ212: Bread and Flour Confectionery* [QRL.118] which ran from the first quarter of 1973 until the fourth quarter of 1982, and which gave similar statistics to its successor *Business Monitor PQ4196* [QRL.136]. *Business Monitor PQ213: Biscuits* [QRL.119] covered the same period, and had much the same content as its successor *Business Monitor PQ4197* [QRL.137]. *Business Monitor PQ211: Grain Milling* [QRL.117] provided information from the second quarter of 1973 until publication ceased at the end of 1980. It gave sales data in both volume and value terms on the following products: wheat flour — bread making (white, brown and wholemeal), biscuit making, cakes, household, self-raising, semolina, meal and groats, other; oats — rolled oats, oat flakes and flour, crushed oats; barley — meal, flour, etc.; maize — meal and flour, flaked maize (human and non-human usage shown separately); rice; cereal breakfast foods — wheat, maize, other; soya meal, flour; split lentils and peas; and waste products. After 1986, sales of cereal breakfast foods were shown initially in *Business Monitor PQ229.2: Starch and Miscellaneous Foods* [QRL.126], and subsequently in *Business Monitor PQ4239* [QRL.139] along with those of self-raising flour made from purchased flour.

The proportion of industry activity covered in the PQ series inquiries has fallen as reporting size thresholds have been increased. In 1981, for *Business Monitor PQ4196*

[QRL.136] and *Business Monitor PQ4197* [QRL.137], the minimum establishment size was raised from 50 to 100 employees and, at the same time, that for *Business Monitor PQ4239* [QRL.139] was increased from 25 to 35 employees. The effect of this increase on *Business Monitor PQ4196* [QRL.136] and *Business Monitor PQ4197* [QRL.137] was to reduce the establishment coverage to 80 per cent and 91 per cent respectively of the employment in these industries. However, the "total sales and work done" figure in these Monitors relates to *all* establishments in the industry, as also in *Business Monitor PA1002: Summary Volume* [QRL.93], which gives sales for all Activity Headings covered by the PQ series, and provides information on the grossing-up methods employed.

AH4160 "Grain milling" and AH4196 "Bread and flour confectionery" were among the industries selected for the Topping-up Inquiry — see section 2.1.1.3 — in 1985. The former was included because the industry had been dropped from the quarterly sales inquiries in 1980. The latter was included because its employment threshold had been raised significantly, and thus coverage had fallen markedly. The results of the topping-up inquiries were published during 1986.

The relevant annual Monitors are *Business Monitor PA416: Grain Milling* [QRL.110] and *Business Monitor PA419: Bread, Biscuits and Flour Confectionery* [QRL.111]. These provide annual data on total sales, gross and net output for all UK establishments classified to the industry Groups. Analyses are also provided of output by size of employment of the establishment, and by standard regions of the United Kingdom.

Finally, a few brief comments are appropriate on the censuses prior to 1970, in particular with regard to their coverage of data on output. A more complete account requires close reading of the *Historical Record of the Census of Production, 1907–1970* [QRL.264] and the various Monitors noted above. Output and, particularly, sales statistics were typically provided in great detail, and this is useful in segregating items not included in later studies. For example, "Grain milling" frequently involved a major part of the animal feedstuffs trade in its production (e.g. in 1935) but, in 1954 and 1958, the output of certain establishments was statistically shared between "grain milling", "animal and poultry foods", and the "vegetable and animal oils and fats" industry. The "Bread and flour confectionery" trade in 1935 and before included those engaged in the manufacture of ice-cream (a separate industry in 1948). A more difficult problem for the industry arose with the classification of baking at a retail stage, particularly given the overlap with the *Census of Distribution and Other Services* [QRL.150] from 1950 onwards. In fact, the Census of Distribution distinguished "Bread and flour confectionery *with* baking" and "Bread and flour confectionery *without* baking" in the 1950 report, and provided a much more detailed analysis than was shown in the Census of Production for that year. The latter only gave companies in this industry that undertook no retailing.

8.4.1.2 Ministry of Agriculture, Fisheries and Food inquiries

Details of the various MAFF inquiries are provided by Slater [B.164] and discussed by Barnett [B.12]. The cereals processing industry at the time of writing is currently subject to four MAFF surveys: Flour millers; Brewers, distillers and maltsters; Oatmillers; and Cereal breakfast foods. The Flour Millers survey collects details of wheat used for milling and the flour produced; that of the Oatmillers obtains information on oats milled for human consumption. The *Monthly Digest of Statistics* [QRL.362] publishes five-yearly and fourteen-monthly statistics on sales of home-grown wheat for food, wheat milled (home-produced and imported), flour produced and disposals (including exports); and on sales of home-grown oats for milling, oats milled, and products of oat-milling. Similarly the *Monthly Digest of Statistics* [QRL.362] also gives annual and monthly levels of breakfast cereal production (the results of the MAFF survey); and also details of biscuit production (from BSO surveys). Coverage and definitions are described in the *Monthly Digest of Statistics Supplement: Definitions and Explanatory Notes* [B.337]. Annual statistics derived from these MAFF surveys are found in the *Annual Abstract of Statistics* [QRL.37], which shows wheat milled (home and imported); flour and offals produced; oats milled and products produced; production of breakfast cereals; and, from BSO data, disposals of home-produced biscuits. All statistics cover a ten-year period. The MAFF booklet, *Output and Utilisation of Farm Produce in the United Kingdom* [QRL.382], published annually up to 1988, contains seven years' of annual data with detailed breakdown of utilisation and output from home crops of wheat, barley and oats. Annual data are now available in *Agriculture in the United Kingdom*.

Regional statistics for Scotland are shown in *Economic Report on Scottish Agriculture* [QRL.180], which includes data on the milling of Scottish grown wheat and oats, and the *Scottish Abstract of Statistics* [QRL.446], which shows the volume of wheat milled and oats processed.

The Home-Grown Cereals Authority also makes use of MAFF surveys in its *Marketing Note* [QRL.345] which gives, on a regular basis, the best available detailed analysis of human and industrial usage of grains and of products produced. For instance, the Note published on 1st December 1986 shows, for the 1984/5 cereal marketing year (August-July), utilisation and output figures including: wheat flour used in breadmaking (white, brown and wholemeal), biscuits, household flour; self-raising flour; cake, other; wheat used for breakfast cereals; oats used in baking, porridge, and for muesli; rye for bread making; as well as details of barley and maize usage, including maize for breakfast cereals. Six-year runs of wheat flour products (by percentage volume) are provided in somewhat less detail, along with a discussion of other grain products. Another Note on "Human and industrial consumption of wheat in the UK" (12th May 1986) gives three-monthly figures for total wheat flour production over a five-year period, as well as a breakdown of production by type as above. The HGCA publication, *Cereals Statistics* [QRL.152] provides monthly statistics, over five-year periods, on usage of grains by UK processors.

8.4.1.3 Industry sources

The statistical services of the BCCCA were mentioned in section 8.2.4. Its *Statistical Year Book* [QRL.461], a subscription source, continues the provision of statistics on cake and biscuit deliveries of its predecessor, the CBA *Annual Report*. This report was particularly detailed in terms of biscuit deliveries analysed by type, and in information on distributor's own-label biscuits. The other BCCCA publication, the *Annual Review* [QRL.49], now provides summary data.

8.4.2 *Index Numbers of Output*

The index of industrial production is published in many places, e.g. the *United Kingdom National Accounts* [QRL.506], the *Annual Abstract of Statistics* [QRL.37] and formerly in *British Business* [QRL.66] as well as in specific articles in *Economic Trends* [QRL.181] and other CSO publications. The level of detail provided on the cereals sector is however limited. Separate indices are provided for industry Group 419 "Bread, biscuits and flour confectionery", but Group 416 is omitted as grain milling is classified as an intermediate good industry, and breakfast cereals are subsumed within Group 423 "Miscellaneous foods".

Some earlier, and otherwise unpublished, data on the index are given by Mordue [B.127]. Statistics for various MLHs are provided for 1970 and 1975 (five-year averages) and 1978, 1979, and 1980 (annual averages).

8.5 Current Inputs other than Labour

8.5.1 *Domestic Inputs*

The most detailed breakdown of industry purchases of inputs comes in the quinquennial Purchases Inquiry conducted by the BSO and published as *Business Monitor PO1008: Purchases Inquiry* [QRL.116]. The results of the 1984 Inquiry were published in 1987 and those of the 1989 Inquiry were published in 1992. AH4160 "Grain milling", AH4196 "Bread and flour confectionery" and AH4197 "Biscuits" were separately distinguished, and purchases of primary and intermediate agricultural and food products shown, along with packaging, fuel and electricity, etc. A previous inquiry — also based on SIC(1980) — covered the year 1979 and the broadly comparable results were published in *Business Monitor PA1002.1: Census of Production and Purchases Inquiry* [QRL.94] in 1984. Details about earlier inquiries are provided in section 2.5.1.2. The annual Production Monitors also give information on purchases for the various industry Groups. Purchases are divided into "materials for use in production, and packaging and fuel" and "goods for merchanting or factoring". Also detailed are the "costs of industrial services received", "the cost of non-industrial services received", and "rates, excluding water rates".

The output of UK agriculture forms a major input to the cereals processing industries, particularly grain milling. Sales of home-grown wheat, barley and oats for food are shown separately in the *Monthly Digest of Statistics* [QRL.362] for the last five years and for the last fourteen months. The *Annual Abstract of Statistics* [QRL.37] provides the following ten-year series: the quantity of cereal crops harvested; sales of home-grown wheat (flour millers' receipts), barley, and oats (oatmeal millers' receipts); and wheat and oats milled. *Output and Utilisation of Farm Produce* [QRL.382], up to its last issue in 1988, shows annual supplies of wheat, barley, oats and mixed corn, with the quantities of wheat and oats milled. Similar statistics in slightly less detail are given in the *Annual Review of Agriculture* [QRL.51] and its successor *Agriculture in the United Kingdom*.

The most comprehensive annual statistics, however, are found in the HGCA *Cereals Statistics* [QRL.152], which gives the UK cereals production over 12 years, and also three-year analysis by county and region. Annual supplies and utilisation figures are given for wheat, barley, oats and mixed cereals, maize and total cereals; and monthly statistics, over five years, are provided for the usage of wheat, barley and maize by processors in the United Kingdom. Analysis of grain usage in the United Kingdom is also published in various issues per year of the HGCA *Marketing Note* [QRL.345]. Annual cereal supplies, and detailed cumulative monthly usage statistics, are indicated in the two appendices to the *Marketing Note* [QRL.345], which is published each week. *Facts and Figures* [QRL.202], published annually by NABIM, includes MAFF and HGCA figures on wheat usage by flourmillers, but also includes its own estimate of wheat from EC sources. Data are given over eight years.

Other sources of information on agricultural production of cereals include *Agricultural Statistics: United Kingdom* [QRL.32] and for particular countries, the *Economic Report on Scottish Agriculture* [QRL.180], the *Scottish Abstract of Statistics* [QRL.446], the *Statistical Review of Northern Ireland Agriculture* [QRL.460], the *Northern Ireland Annual Abstract of Statistics* [QRL.377], and the *Digest of Welsh Statistics* [QRL.177].

8.5.2 *Input-output Analysis*

Details of the input-output tables for the United Kingdom have been provided in section 2.5.2. Here we simply provide brief comments on the level of detail accorded to the cereals sector. The 1954 *Input-output Tables for the United Kingdom 1954* [QRL.281] presented less detail than their successors, but cereal foodstuffs are shown as the only separately identified sector of the Food industries. In the 1968 tables, the revised SIC(1968) allowed the identification of "grain milling" and "other cereal foodstuffs". The introduction of SIC(1980) meant that "grain milling and starch" and "bread, biscuits and flour confectionery" were cited in the 1979 tables. The tables indicate clearly the dependence of grain milling on inputs derived from UK agriculture and, to a decreasing extent, on imports. "Bread, biscuits and flour confectionery" rely in turn on the intermediate products of grain milling for the majority of its inputs, although imports, oils and fats, and sugar also feature significantly.

The *Input-output Tables for Scotland: 1973* [QRL.280] were prepared on the basis of SIC(1968) and distinguish "bakery products" (MLH212 and MLH213). Grain milling is subsumed within "other food products" and the intra-cereals sector dependency is not so clear.

8.6 Labour

8.6.1 *Employment*

The most detailed official statistics on employment in Great Britain come from the Census of Employment with figures based on the SIC(1980) available for 1981, 1984, 1987, 1989 and 1991. The results of the 1984 Survey were published in a key article in the January 1987 issue of the *Employment Gazette* [QRL.186]. The data provide details for "Bread and flour confectionery" (AH4196) and "Biscuits and crispbread" (AH4197), but not for "Grain milling" (AH4160). Although "Miscellaneous foods" (AH4239) is shown, there is no breakdown into sub-divisions such as breakfast cereals. Details of employment are given for all employees, sub-divided into male and female, both also disaggregated into part-time and full-time. A regional analysis of employment, under the Activity Headings, is provided for England by the usual economic regions. UK data is only available for Class 41/42.

The *Employment Gazette* [QRL.186] publishes both monthly and quarterly data, the latter being in a rather less aggregated form. Current monthly statistics on "employees in employment" combine Groups 413–423, and 429; while the quarterly statistics separate out Group 419 to leave Groups 413–418, 420–423, 429 aggregated. Monthly figures are shown over a two-year period, while the quarterly statistics are given for the latest quarter, the preceding one, and a year previous. Early editions of the *Employment Gazette* [QRL.186] generally provided a more detailed breakdown of current employment. For example, the 1983 February publication listed quarterly statistics by MLH, including MLH211, MLH212, MLH213 and MLH229. The SIC(1980) analysis was first presented in the 1984 February issue of the *Employment Gazette* [QRL.186] which showed "Bread, biscuits and flour confectionery" (Group 419). But "Grain milling" was combined with "Starch and miscellaneous foods" and with "Animal feeding stuffs" (i.e. Groups 416/418/422/423). In 1986, the quarterly information was again regrouped, with "Grain milling, bread, biscuits and flour confectionery and starch" (Groups 416/418/419) shown together, while "Animal feeding stuffs and miscellaneous foods" (Groups 422/423) formed another category.

The annual employment situation, taken at June in each year, is also published in the *Annual Abstract of Statistics* [QRL.37] for the same SIC(1980) groupings as are provided in the GB quarterly data in the *Employment Gazette* [QRL.186]. The 1988 *Annual Abstract of Statistics* [QRL.37] picks out "Bread, biscuits and flour confectionery" (Group 419), but combines Groups 413–418, 420–423, and 429. Data are given over five years (1982–1986). The 1987 edition again identified Group 419, and provided aggregate employment figures for Groups 416/418/422/423.

8.6.2 *Labour Costs*

The primary source of data on earnings of employees is the annual *New Earnings Survey* [QRL.375], which provides detailed statistics on industry Group 419 "bread, biscuits and flour confectionery", and on AH4196 "bread and flour confectionery". Part C, the analysis by industry, gives average gross weekly and hourly earnings, average weekly hours, for full-time manual and non-manual males and full-time manual and non-manual females. Increases in earnings over the year are given, for weekly and hourly earnings of the same classes of employees, using matched samples. Ranges of earnings, and decile and quartile analyses are shown, and the detailed make-up of gross weekly earnings, including overtime, PBR, and shift premiums. The same industry detail (Group 419, AH4196) is also provided in Parts A and B of the *New Earnings Survey* [QRL.375] since the bakery industry is subject to a national wage agreement.

Average weekly and hourly earnings and hours worked are also shown in an annual article in the *Employment Gazette* [QRL.186] following the pattern of the

New Earnings Survey results. These data are given for Group 416 "Grain milling" and Group 419 "Bread, biscuis and flour confectionery" within the cereals sector.

Costs of wages and salaries are shown in the annual *Business Monitor PA416* [QRL.110] and *Business Monitor PA419* [QRL.111]. Analyses are presented for operatives, and for administrative, technical and clerical staff, on a total and per head basis, with an associated breakdown of establishment size groups by employment. Within the operating ratios section, wages and salaries are shown as a percentage of gross value added, and also per operative and per administrative, technical and clerical employee.

The analysis of wage costs within the flour and, particularly, the bread industries has been subject to numerous official investigations. The work of the National Board for Prices and Incomes (NBPI) gave rise to five main reports of relevance:

Report no.3	(Session 1965/66) *Prices of Bread and Flour* [B.408]
Report no.9	(Session 1965/66) *Wages in the Bakery Industry (First Report)* [B.416]
Report no.17	(Session 1966/67) *Wages in the Bakery Industry (Final Report)* [B.415]
Report no.144	(Session 1969/70) *Bread Prices and Pay in the Baking Industry (First Report)* [B.398]
Report no.151	(Session 1970/71) *Bread Prices and Pay in the Baking Industry (Second Report)* [B.399]

Together with the 1975 Price Commission report on *Bread Prices and Costs in Northern Ireland and Great Britain* [B.417], these provide a wealth of cost, and particularly labour cost, data on the sector. NBPI Report no.3 [B.408] provides a detailed average breakdown of the cost structures in both flour and baking; the latter subsequently being used as the basis of analysis for the bread section of *Economies of Scale in Manufacturing Industry* [B.148] by C. Pratten. NBPI Report no.9 [B.416] discusses wages in depth. NBPI Report no.17 [B.415] analyses the wage negotiating machinery and labour earnings; while Report no.151 [B.399] gives a detailed breakdown of pay rates and costs in bread production and distribution.

8.6.3 *Labour Productivity*

Some measures of labour productivity in the cereals processing industries may be inferred from the operating ratios published in the relevant annual Production Monitors. A study which draws on the Census statistics over the period 1963–1973 is *Post-war Trends in Employment, Productivity, Output, Labour Costs and Prices by Industry in the UK* [B.189], by R. Wragg and T. Robertson. This identifies "output per head" and "unit wage and salary costs" over the period in grain milling; biscuits; and bread and flour confectionery. Earlier information on the same industries is analysed in "Labour productivity and concentration: food processing industries" [B.13], by D.I. Bateman. Labour productivity analysis is also implicit in the total factor productivity analysis carried out at MLH level by Mordue and Marshall [B.127]. Useful productivity data may also be obtained from the reports of the National Board for Prices and Incomes and the Price Commission referred to in section 8.6.2.

Studies on labour productivity in the biscuits industry, other than those mentioned above, are rather rare but *Productivity and Industrial Structure* [B.147] uses the

Census of Production data in order to compare labour productivity in Britain, Germany and USA.

8.6.4 *Industrial Stoppages*
The annual review on stoppages published in the *Employment Gazette* [QRL.186] refers generally to broad divisions of industry, but identifies separately the working days lost (per 1000 employees) for "grain milling, biscuits, bread and flour confectionery".

8.6.5 *Industrial Accidents*
Coverage in the past did include industrial detail — see section 2.6.15 — but the annual *Health and Safety Statistics* [QRL.261] from the Health and Safety Executive has been recently confined to Class data.

The Health and Safety Executive also published an occasional report on *Food and Packaging Health and Safety, 1977–1982* [B.279], which analysed possible risks to health and safety in various Food industries. Relevant sectors include baking; cake and biscuits; flour and provender milling; and grain handling.

8.7 Capital

8.7.1 *Capital Expenditure*

The Census of Production provides the main industry-based analysis. Statistics are provided in the various annual Production Monitors, and *Business Monitor PA1002* [QRL.93] also presents data for some Activity Headings. Thus figures on total capital expenditure are given for Groups 416 "Grain milling" and 419 "Bread, biscuits and flour confectionery", and for AH4196 "Bread and flour confectionery" and AH4197 "Biscuits". Data on Group 423 are only provided in aggregate. The breakdown of expenditure into sub-headings of "land and buildings", "plant and machinery" and "vehicles" is given net for Groups 416, 419 and 423 in *Business Monitor PA1002* [QRL.93], but broken down into acquisitions and disposals in the individual Monitors. An analysis of net capital expenditure by employment size group is given for the industries, and figures for net capital expenditure per head and net capital expenditure as a percentage of value added are also provided. *Business Monitor PO1008: Purchases Inquiry* [QRL.116] also provides a table of capital expenditure for cereals industries at the Activity Heading level.

8.7.2 *Suppliers of Machinery*
A little indirectly, it was also possible to infer the puchases of certain capital items in the cereals sector from the details of the sales, imports and exports of appropriate machinery in *Business Monitor PQ3244: Food, Drink and Tobacco Processing Machinery* [QRL.127]. The Monitor identifies sales of "Bakery and biscuit ovens, complete"; "Bakery, biscuit and flour confectionery machinery, complete" (with

"dough machinery" and "other"); "machinery for grain milling, grain milling plant, and oil and fats machinery", on a quarterly basis over the five most recent quarters and two most recent years. Trade statistics, derived from *Business Monitor MM20: Overseas Trade Statistics of the United Kingdom* [QRL.85] are quoted, indicating code numbers, and are at least as detailed as the sales data.

8.7.3 *Occasional Investigations*

At the MLH level, Mordue and Marshall [B.127] analysed changes in gross capital over the period 1968–76 for "grain milling" (MLH211), "bread and flour confectionery" (MLH212), and "biscuits" (MLH213); and discussed methodological issues. Mention should be made also of *Productivity and Industrial Structure* [B.147] which, in the chapter on "Manufactured foods", compared the biscuits industries in Britain, Germany and the United States of America, and discussed capital and capital productivity.

8.8 International Transactions

8.8.1 *HM Customs and Excise Records*

"Cereals and cereal preparations" comprise Division 04 in the Standard International Trade Classification (Revision 3). In *Business Monitor MM20: Overseas Trade Statistics of the United Kingdom* [QRL.85], the Division is further broken down into the following main headings:

041. Wheat (including spelt) and meslin, unmilled.
042. Rice.
043. Barley, unmilled.
044. Maize (not including sweet corn), unmilled.
045. Cereals, unmilled (other than wheat, rice, barley and maize).
046. Meal and flour of wheat and flour of meslin.
047. Other cereal meals and flours.
048. Cereal preparations and preparations of flour or starch of fruits or vegetables.

Further details of the extensive statistical coverage in *Business Monitor MM20* [QRL.85] are provided in section 2.8.2.1. The statistics have been compiled from the declarations which are made to HM Customs and Excise, and which are subject to confirmation by Customs officials. The figures are usually published about one month after the month to which they relate.

Details of the HM Customs and Excise tariff/trade code numbers corresponding to AH4196, AH4197 and AH4239 may be found in *Business Monitor PQ4196* [QRL.136], *Business Monitor PQ4197* [QRL.137] and *Business Monitor PQ4239* [QRL.139] respectively. *Business Monitor PQ4197* [QRL.137] also provides quarterly import and export data for a wide range of products. By contrast, the number of items listed in *Business Monitor PQ4196* [QRL.136] is very few, mostly cakes.

Business Monitor PQ4239 [QRL.139] gives quarterly import and export data for "prepared foods by swelling or roasting of cereals or cereal products, from (separately) maize, rice or other cereals".

With the cessation of publication of *Business Monitor PQ211* [QRL.117], data on the traded products of the grain milling industry have to be culled directly from *Business Monitor MM20* [QRL.85], although the HGCA's *Marketing Note* [QRL.345] on human and industrial wheat consumption gives analyses of UK exports of wheat flour, and of wheat gluten. Similar statistics for other grains are provided in appropriate editions of *Marketing Note* [QRL.345]. Finally, with the reduction of the Business Monitor PQ coverage from mid-1989, we are now even more heavily reliant on *Business Monitor MM20* [QRL.85] for for the detailed coverage of *all* products.

8.8.2 *Industry Analyses of Trade*

In contrast to these analyses by type of product, *Business Monitor MQ10: Overseas Trade Analysed in Terms of Industries* [QRL.90] provides quarterly data on exports and imports from Group 416, AH4196, AH4197 and AH4239.8. These figures are also used in *Business Monitor MQ12: Import Penetration and Export Sales Ratios for Manufacturing Industry* [QRL.91] to provide export/sales and import penetration ratios again for the above groupings up to the second quarter of 1989 — see section 2.8.2.3 for details of the coverage and methodology. Mordue [B.126] provides constant-price series for the imports and exports of MLH211/212 and MLH213 for 1975–1980.

8.8.3 *Industry Sources*

With regard to biscuits, the CBA *Annual Report* gave deliveries of biscuits to export markets and imports into the home market, with volume and value (invoice in gross fob) analysed by variety. The invoice value of export market cake deliveries (again gross fob) was also shown. All statistics were derived from Alliance members' returns along with HM Customs and Excise data for biscuits and for cakes. The new BCCCA *Annual Review* [QRL.49] gives only limited current yearly statistics. The main publication, the *Statistical Year Book* [QRL.461] now gives the annual data for biscuits. Its first issue in 1987 gave statistics over the period 1969–1986.

8.9 Stocks

Data on stocks are presented in a variety of publications. Commodity statistics are available in both the *Monthly Digest of Statistics* [QRL.362] and the *Annual Abstract of Statistics* [QRL.37] and cover stocks of wheat and flour, barley, and oats. Stocks of wheat and flour (including flour expressed in terms of wheat) cover those held by flour millers, cereal breakfast foods manufacturers, and importers and dealers. Stocks of oats are those held by main processors, including oatmeal millers, provender millers (Great Britain only) and compound feedingstuffs manufacturers. The data in the *Monthly Digest of Statistics* [QRL.362] span the most recent five years, and most recent fourteen months. The data in the *Annual Abstract of Statistics* [QRL.37] give end-December stock levels over a ten-year period.

More detailed commodity analysis is published in the HGCA *Marketing Note* [QRL.345]. The appendix shows wheat stocks on farm, with processors (flourmillers, distillers, and others), and in intervention stores. Similar analyses are carried out for barley, maize and oats. The monthly cumulative figures for all grains are shown, compared with the same period in the two previous marketing years. The occasional *Marketing Note* [QRL.345] covers details of consumption, published roughly once a year for each grain type and includes levels of stocks for the end of each quarter of the marketing year.

While not strictly part of the cereals processing industry, farm stocks are important for input availability into the grain milling industry (amongst others), and also may be a significant influence on prices. In addition to the HGCA statistics mentioned above, levels of farm stocks of wheat, barley and oats are shown in *MAFF Statistics: Cereal Stocks Survey* [QRL.318] for each end-month and formerly in the *Annual Review of Agriculture* [QRL.51] and *Output and Utilisation* [QRL.382] for the end of December. Changes in farm and other stocks are now reported in *Agriculture in the United Kingdom.*

The HGCA *Weekly Bulletin* [QRL.512] indicates the state of UK cereals intervention for any one week: opening stocks, offers, intake, export sales, home sales, current stocks. The annual *Report of the Intervention Board* [QRL.293] provides details of monthly intervention purchases and sales, and stocks at the end of the month. The costs of the intervention buying of cereals, and receipts for the sales of intervention stocks, are also shown. Intervention stocks of wheat and barley at the end of the calendar year were also contained in *Output and Utilisation* [QRL.382] and are now covered in *Agriculture in the United Kingdom.*

Finally *Business Monitor PA416* [QRL.110] and *Business Monitor PA419* [QRL.111] present financial data on "stocks and work-in-progress", showing changes over a five-year period and end-of-period stock levels. Disaggregated data are provided for: materials, stores and fuel; work-in-progress; and goods on hand for sale. The tables of operating ratios give five years' figures for the ratio of gross output to stocks.

8.10 Consumption

8.10.1 *The National Food Survey*

The National Food Survey collects consumption data on a wide variety of cereal products manufactured by industry Groups 416 and 419, viz:

Food code number	Description
251	Bread, white, large, unsliced
252	Bread, white, large, sliced
253	Bread, white, small, unsliced

254	Bread, white, small, sliced
255	Bread, brown
256	Bread, wholewheat and wholemeal
258	Rolls (excluding starch-reduced rolls)
259	Malt bread and fruit bread
260	Vienna bread and French bread
261	Starch-reduced bread and rolls
262	Other bread
263	Total other bread (codes 258–262)
264	Flour
267	Buns, scones and teacakes
270	Cakes and pastries
271	Crispbread
274	Biscuits, other than chocolate
277	Biscuits, chocolate
281	Oatmeal and oat products
282	Breakfast cereals
285	Canned milk puddings
286	Other puddings
287	Rice
290	Cereal-based invalid foods (including "slimming" foods)
291	Infant cereal foods
292	Frozen cakes and pastries
293	Other frozen convenience cereal foods
294	Total frozen cereal convenience foods (codes 292–293)
295	Canned pasta
296	Pizza
297	Cake, pudding and dessert mixes
298	Other cereal convenience foods
299	Total cereal convenience foods (including canned) not specified elsewhere (codes 295–298)
301	Other cereal foods

(Food codes 290, 291, 295, 296 and 297 are included in this list for reference although the items are products of Group 423 and therefore discussed in Chapter 11.)

Detailed statistics are published on all these various foods in the *National Food Survey: Compendium of Results* [QRL.373]. Annual average figures of both per capita weekly consumption and expenditure are provided for the following main food groups: brown bread (255); white bread (251–254); wholewheat and wholemeal bread (256); other bread (263); total bread (251–263); flour (264); cakes (267–270); biscuits (271–277); oatmeal and oat products (281); breakfast cereals (282); other cereals (285–291, 294, 299, 301); total cereals (251–301). In addition these data are analysed by region and type of area; by income group; by household composition; by household composition and income group; by age of housewife; by housing tenure; and by ownership of deep freezer. Indices of expenditure, and of the real value of purchases, are presented for the latest six years. Quarterly and annual national average household expenditure on some 25 individual cereal items are also calculated.

The main report on the National Food Survey, *Household Food Consumption and Expenditure* [QRL.267], carries a more limited range of statistical data, as has been discussed in section 2.10.1.2. Commentary is, however, provided with many of the main statistical tables and data for previous years are often presented for comparison. Results from the NFS are more immediately available in *MAFF Statistics: Food Facts* [QRL.319] and formerly in *British Business* [QRL.66]. Further details of both the methodology of the NFS and of other publications carrying NFS data, are provided in section 2.10.1.

8.10.2 *The Family Expenditure Survey*

The *Family Expenditure Survey* [QRL.204] provides analyses of the expenditure of various types of household on bread, rolls etc; flour; biscuits, cakes; breakfast and other cereals; at different levels of household income, and by sex and age. It also publishes average figures for weekly expenditure analysed by region. Results for the FES are also published quarterly in the *Employment Gazette* [QRL.186]. For further details, see section 2.10.2.

8.10.3 *The National Accounts*

The annual *United Kingdom National Accounts* [QRL.506] gives tables of UK consumers' aggregate expenditure by function at current and constant prices over an eleven-year period. These tables include household expenditure on food in total, and for broad categories such as "bread and cereals" — see section 2.10.3.

8.10.4 *Industry Sources*

Finally, many market research reports reproduce consumption statistics and include their own trade estimates. These will be catalogued in section 8.14, but it is useful to note the following at this stage. Taylor Nelson and Associates produce biannual reports [QRL.414] on the results of their Family Food Panel. The Flour Advisory Bureau provides details of market research on bread-eating and household characteristics.

8.11 Supplies and Disposals

It is not just the output of UK cereal farms which provides the inputs of the UK cereals processing industry, rather it is the balance of home output, stock changes, and imports and exports of basic cereals. This balance, in turn, is likely to exert considerable influence on cereal raw material prices for industry and the market is also subject to the market interventions allowed for under the EEC common agricultural policy, as discussed in section 8.3. MAFF constructs balance sheets for major commodities, including cereals (wheat — hard and soft, barley, rye and oats, rice) on the basis of the various MAFF farm and processor surveys — see Slater [B.164]. Details are stored in the EUROSTAT CRONOS data bank, and published quarterly by EUROSTAT in *Crop Production* [QRL.167]. Balance sheets of cereals supply and demand are given in the statistical appendix to the HGCA *Marketing Note* [QRL.345]. Provisional figures are shown for the most recent marketing year, and estimates for the current marketing year. An excellent discussion of these statistics is given by Low [B.105]. Mention should be made of the 1983 MAFF report, *The United Kingdom Cereals Market: The Next Five Years* [B.394] which gives a review, with statistical appendices, of developments in the UK market; and also *A Statistical Digest of UK and EC Production, Utilisation and Trade in Cereals* [B.15], by N.F. Beard, which contains a wealth of UK and EC cereal statistics including several balance sheets. Finally no survey of UK cereals supply would be complete without reference again to the *Britton Report* [B.25] and its comprehensive survey of production and utilisation. Although dated (most statistics relate to the mid-1980s), the detail in the study is without parallel.

"Disposals" in the sense used in CSO publications covers the use of home production and imports, adjusted for changes in stocks, which may be sold as intermediate goods, go into consumption, or be exported (see the *Monthly Digest of Statistics: Definitions and Explanatory Notes* [B.337]). As in Chapter 2, it should be noted that a number of publications, notably the *Annual Abstract of Statistics* [QRL.37] and the *Monthly Digest of Statistics* [QRL.362], give details of cereals disposals as such by this definition: for example, flour disposals, and maize disposals (for food and industrial uses).

8.12 Prices

8.12.1 *Agricultural and Commodity Prices*

Inputs, in particular, into grain milling are derived from agricultural sources at home or abroad and brief mention will be made of prices at this level. The most tailor-made sources of information for this industrial sector are those produced by the Home-Grown Cereals Authority. The *Weekly Bulletin* [QRL.512] gives home-grown ex-farm grain spot prices (by country and region), forward prices, with EEC support prices, and also grain futures market prices in London (GAFTA) and Chicago. UK delivered and export prices, Continental and international grain prices, and imported grain asking prices are shown. Tariff arrangements — the MCAs that apply to intra-Community grain trade — are listed, along with EEC exchange rates for agricultural commodities — "green" rates — central and spot rates, and import charges and levies. The HGCA provides a *Daily Telephone Information Service* [QRL.171] which gives regional spot prices and London Futures prices for EEC wheat and barley, and also details of EEC arrangements for MCAs, import levies and export refunds. Occasional commentary on price developments appears in the *Weekly Digest* [QRL.513]. The HGCA annual *Cereals Statistics* [QRL.152] provides extensive tables of weekly, monthly and quarterly forward and spot prices, monthly import prices, export prices and futures prices, and discusses EEC monetary arrangements in detail.

Other important sources of commodity prices include the MAFF weekly *Agricultural Market Report: Part I: Prices and Quantities Sold of Selected Cereals, Livestock and Other Agricultural Products* [QRL.25] which gives growers' average prices (as required under the Corn Returns Act), port, and local spot prices for all major grains. The Northern Ireland *Agricultural Market Report* [QRL.24] and the *Economic Report on Scottish Agriculture* [QRL.180] give similar growers' statistics on their regions. The *Annual Review of Agriculture* [QRL.51] also contains average ex-farm cereal prices. Information from the Corn Returns for England and Wales is published in the official *London Gazette* [B.325].

International information on cereal prices may be obtained from sources in addition to the HGCA *Weekly Bulletin* [QRL.512] mentioned above. The International Commodities Clearing House publication, *ICCH Commodities and Financial Futures Yearbook* [QRL.269] provided spot and futures prices for cereals. The *CRB Commodity Yearbook* [QRL.166] reviews international trends in supply and demand. It is updated three-times a year by means of the *Commodity Yearbook Statistical Abstract* [QRL.157]. A *Daily Commodity Computer Trend Analyser* [QRL.169] is also available to subscribers. The *Public Ledger & Daily Freight Register* [QRL.392] is a daily publication including cereal prices from London market sources.

The *Official Journal of the European Communities* [B.341] is the primary source for CAP prices and other market and trading arrangements. In addition to the HGCA *Daily Telephone Information Service* [QRL.171], the IBAP *Notice to Traders* [QRL.379] gives weekly information on the same areas. The *Intervention Board: Annual Report* [QRL.293] contains series of monthly intervention prices for cereals.

Commodity spot and futures market prices are normally reported in the daily press, particularly the *Financial Times* [QRL.218], in the weekly farming press such as *Farmers Weekly* [QRL.212], on radio, and through on-line information systems such as Datastream and Prestel.

8.12.2 *Retail Prices*

8.12.2.1 Recorded prices

Official data on retail food prices are published monthly in the *Employment Gazette* [QRL.186] based on samples taken throughout the United Kingdom. Average prices are given for white bread, per 800g wrapped and sliced loaf; white bread, per 800g unwrapped loaf; white bread, per 400g loaf, unsliced; brown bread, per 400g loaf, unsliced; brown bread, per 800g loaf, unsliced; and self-raising flour, per 1.5 kg. The number of quotations is noted, and the price range within which 80 per cent of quotations fell.

8.12.2.2 Recommended prices

Commercial sources of retail price levels usually refer to manufacturers' recommended prices, as in *The Grocer Price List* [QRL.253], *The Bakers Review* [QRL.57], or *Shaws Guide to Fair Retail Prices* [QRL.453]. *The Grocer Price List* [QRL.253] carries very limited information on bread, but is extremely detailed on biscuits, breakfast cereals, cakes, flour, and cereal products. However, retail prices are not always given (instead trade wholesale prices will be listed), although sometimes *only* retail prices are shown. The Federation of Bakers also produces average retail price information.

8.12.3 *The Retail Prices Index*

The Retail Prices Index (RPI) is published in a variety of places, but the primary source is again the *Employment Gazette* [QRL.186]. The cereals section includes "bread, flour, cereals, biscuits and cakes", with subdivisions on "bread", "flour", "other cereals", and "biscuits". Indices are calculated monthly in respect of a Tuesday near the middle of each month, and weights for the indices are based on information from the Family Expenditure Survey for the previous year. The indices are given for the particular date chosen, and percentage changes shown over the previous month and twelve months. The *Monthly Digest of Statistics* [QRL.362] reproduces the index over the last seven months with cereals items provided in full detail. The relevant Business Monitors in the PQ series also reproduce recent retail price indices relevant to the particular industry covered.

8.12.4 *Price Index Numbers in the National Food Survey*

A somewhat different source of price information comes from the annual *National Food Survey: Compendium of Results* [QRL.373]. Average prices (in pence per lb) paid for foods in the year surveyed are shown by quarterly and yearly averages. The very fine detail of product classification was mentioned in section 8.10. Price indices are given, in a less detailed form, for the year surveyed, and the preceding one, compared to a single base year. A further set of indices is also provided covering, in fine product detail, the most recent six years, with the index based on the average of the six years.

8.12.5 *Producer Price Index Numbers*

The series of Producer Price Indices are considered in general terms in section 2.12.5. Details of the bread and flour confectionery sector and the biscuits and crispbread sector are given below.

8.12.5.1 Producer price index numbers: input prices

Business Monitor MM22: Producer Price Indices carries the producer price index numbers of materials and fuels purchased for AH4196 and AH4197 giving both monthly and annual data. The monthly data are given for the current and previous years, with the figures for the latest two months provisional. An annual average for the previous year is also presented. *Business Monitor MM22* was published for the first time in October 1989 and continued the coverage in *British Business* [QRL.66].

Business Monitor PQ4196 [QRL.136] gave the producer price index of materials purchased from MAFF sources, usually for the latest available five quarters and past two years. These materials are separately identified for five types of inputs: margarine and compound fat for trade use; sugar, refined bulk; imported butter; dried fruits; all flour. *Business Monitor PQ4197* [QRL.137] gives indices for the following: margarine and compound fat for trade use; refined vegetable and seed oils; sugar, refined, bulk; imported butter; cocoa butter; dried fruit; imported nuts; biscuit flour.

8.12.5.2 Producer price index numbers: output prices
Business Monitor MM22 contains the producer price index numbers of products manufactured in the United Kingdom (home sales) for AH4196 and AH4197. The monthly data are provided for the current and previous year, with the figures for the latest two months provisional. An annual average for the previous year is also presented. *Business Monitor MM22* was published for the first time in October 1989 and continued the coverage in *British Business* [QRL.66]. The *Annual Abstract of Statistics* [QRL.37] gives the annual average for AH4196 and AH4197 for a six-year run for products manufactured in the United Kingdom (home sales).

Business Monitor PQ4196 [QRL.136] gave the producer price indices of goods produced for the latest five quarters and for the past two years. There is separate treatment of bread and flour confectionery which are compared with the figures for food manufacturing industries (home sales) and all manufactured products (home sales). *Business Monitor PQ4197* [QRL.137] performed a similar function for the following products; biscuits, sweetened and semi-sweetened; biscuits, unsweetened, plain; savoury biscuits; chocolate covered biscuits; biscuits and rusks.

8.12.6 *Prices and Government Regulation*
Control over the prices of cereal products, particularly bread, has a long and varied history, going back at least to the Assize of Bread in 1266 which sought to fix the weight and price of bread — see Sheppard and Newton [B.161]. Major studies of more recent pricing issues in the sector include that of Maunder [B.113], who provides a fine analysis of attempts to fix (by bakers), and control (by governments), bread prices from between the two World Wars until 1969. Maunder continues his commentary in [B.115]. Reekie [B.152] takes the discussion along to 1978, and further detail is given by Rushton [B.156].

The 1977 MMC Report on *Flour and Bread* [B.443] outlines the statutory controls, regulations and subsidies which applied to bread and to flour from 1939 to late 1976, and in the process gives many details of prices, both in general and, for example, comparing price movements of the major bakers. The various reports from the NBPI dealing with bread and/or flour prices — [B.408], [B.416], [B.415], [B.404], [B.398] and [B.399] — are listed in section 8.16. All, to a greater or lesser extent, discuss retail (and other) prices and price changes. The Board was concerned that price increases only took place under cost, or return-on-capital-justified circumstances, and its reports give detailed analyses of costs as well as prices. The MMC Report on *Flour and Bread* [B.443] goes on to describe the "voluntary" price arrangements whereby the government was informed of intentions to raise bread prices, and the subsequent counter-inflation legislation under the various stages of the Price Code during the 1970s.

The work of the Price Commission in this period gave rise to only one further report specifically on bread, *Bread Prices and Costs in Northern Ireland and Great Britain* [B.417]. However, two other reports were concerned with cereal products: *Food Prices in Outlying Areas* [B.421] where white and brown bread, biscuits, and flour were surveyed and reported in some detail, especially white bread and flour; and *Metrication and Retail Prices (First Report)* [B.423] which discussed biscuit prices. In addition, two Investigation Reports considered specific companies in the cereals sector: *Weetabix Ltd.* [B.437] and *United Biscuits (UK) Ltd.* [B.436].

Details of the household flour subsidy, and the bread subsidy schemes, are again contained in the MMC Report on *Flour and Bread* [B.443]. At the same time, maximum retail prices of subsidised bread loaves were specified in eleven successive Bread Prices Orders, which operated until May 1979 — see Rushton [B.156]. In 1974, the Price Commission required food distributors to cut gross margins by 10 per cent, and although initially this only applied to large multiples, the requirement was later extended to almost all distributors. The effect was to increase pressure on plant bakeries to grant discounts to retailers which, as explained in *Flour and Bread* [B.443], would have been paid for largely by the bread subsidy schemes. Hence the 1975 Bread Subsidy scheme limited discounts to a maximum of 22.5 per cent. Lists of average discounts granted by major bakers from 1971 until 1975 are again given in *Flour and Bread* [B.443].

The issue of bread prices and discounts was taken up in the 1981 MMC Report on *Discounts to Retailers* [B.441], and in the 1985 follow-up report by the Office of Fair Trading, *Competition and Retailing* [B.231]. The 1981 report, for example, surveyed average selling prices, buying prices, gross margins (and standard deviations) for a range of products including bread (and biscuits). Comparisons were made across different types of retail estabishments: the four major multiples, other multiples, independents, and retail co-operatives. Further discussion of discounts is contained at various points in the text.

Far less intervention has been evidenced in the other main cereal trades' retail pricing methods. The exception was breakfast cereals where Kelloggs, from 1983 until recently, was required to pre-notify the Government of intended retail price increases. This requirement followed the 1973 MMC Report on *Breakfast Cereal Foods* [B.439] which also provided an analysis of the price of Kelloggs' Corn Flakes from 1952 through 1972.

8.13 Financial Information

8.13.1 *Company and Market Research Reports*

The primary sources of much financial information are the public company reports, but there are limitations to the usefulness of much of the data and problems with report availability. Many of the UK quoted companies in the cereals sector are multiproduct and/or multinational, and separate statistics for the appropriate divisions are rarely shown in detail. In addition, reports for foreign-owned or privately-owned companies and other forms of business organisation operating in the sector may not be easily obtained.

A number of commercially available sources list food companies, amongst others, and provide financial data. These are catalogued in section 2.13.4. Note should also be made of the cereal companies quoted in the IGD *Food Companies Profiles* [QRL.234] and *Food Company Performances* [QRL.233]. The reports by the ICC Information Group are also very comprehensive and provide detailed financial statistics on the individual companies as well as sector analysis. Examples include the 1986 Business Ratio report on *Bakeries* [QRL.544], and the 1987 Financial Survey report on *Bakery Products Manufacturers* [QRL.567]. In addition a number of market research and stockbroking companies undertake reviews of the cereals sector, typically based on company reports or financial services sources. Recent examples will be given in section 8.14.

8.13.2 *Business Statistics Office Inquiries*
Financial data are also presented in *Business Monitor PA416* [QRL.110] and *Business Monitor PA419* [QRL.111], but necessarily in somewhat aggregate form.

8.13.3 *Occasional Investigations*
Reports by various investigating bodies frequently provide detailed financial information on the companies in the food industries concerned. Many have been mentioned above (and will be listed in section 8.16), but particularly useful for the cereals sector have been the six reports from the NBPI, viz: [B.408], [B.416], [B.415], [B.404], [B.398] and [B.399]; the 1975 Price Commission report on *Bread Prices and Costs* [B.417]; the 1977 MMC report on *Flour and Bread* [B.443] which contains detailed analysis of the sector and its main companies; and the 1973 Monopolies Commission report on *Breakfast Cereal Foods* [B.439] which studies Kelloggs and the sector as a whole. Reports directed at named companies in the sector include two by the Price Commission, on *Weetabix Ltd.* [B.437] and on *United Biscuits (UK) Ltd.* [B.436], and two by the MMC on *Nabisco Brands Inc. and Huntley and Palmer Foods plc* [B.448] and *Elders IXL Ltd. and Allied-Lyons plc* [B.442]. The reports only provide analysis over limited periods but the data are often detailed and placed in context.

8.14 Advertising and Market Research

8.14.1 *Advertising*

Detailed analyses of product and company advertising are contained in the publications of Media Expenditure Analysis Ltd. (MEAL). The *Tri-Media Digest* [QRL.493] provides brand-level details of expenditure on advertising for all main cereal industry products and firms. The commercial cost and lack of public availability of this information leads to its use in secondary sources, such as the *Advertising Statistics Yearbook* [QRL.20]. This gives details for various product markets in the cereals sector.

Market research reports, referred to in section 8.14.2 and elsewhere, use MEAL data and their own trade estimates of advertising expenditure. Official investigations have also tended to rely on company or MEAL information, which they have occasionally published. The Monopolies Commission report on *Breakfast Cereal Foods* [B.439] gave details of Kelloggs' advertising expenditure and advertising/sales ratios, and further information on the same industry was contained in the Price Commission report on *Weetabix Ltd.* [B.437]. The Price Commission report on *United Biscuits (UK) Ltd.* [B.436] provided limited information on United Biscuits and the biscuit industry, again from MEAL sources.

During the mid-1970s, national advertising of bread was banned under an agreement between the government and the main plant bakers. However, millers and bakers formed the Bread Advisory Group (BAG) which in recent years has spent significant sums on generic bread advertising. Estimates of BAG and company advertising (since 1970) are contained in market research reports, for example, *Retail Business* [QRL.432].

8.14.2 *Market Research*

A number of market research organisations publish reports on the cereals sector. Reference can usefully be made to the *Marketing Surveys Index* [B.327] for a comprehensive listing.

Retail Business [QRL.432] carries reviews on "Cakes and pastries" in issue 361 (March 1988); "Flour" in issue 352 (July 1987); "Biscuits" in issue 360 (February 1988); "Bread" in issue 348 (February 1987); and "Breakfast cereals" in issue 349 (March 1987). These include not only derived data from official sources, but also trade estimates on such items as market value, and company and brand market shares. *Market Research: Great Britain* [QRL.343] contains analysis of the market for "Bakery products" (1986). There are annual Key Note reports on *Bread Bakers* [QRL.580], *Breakfast Cereals* [QRL.581] and *Flour Confectionery* [QRL.587]. Marketing Strategies for Industry provide reports on *Biscuits* [QRL.620], *Breakfast Cereals* [QRL.621], and *Cakes and Pastries* [QRL.622]. *Focus on Food Manufacturing* [QRL.229], published monthly by County Nat West Securities Ltd. provides details *inter alia* of biscuit deliveries by type. And the Centre for Business Research at Manchester Business School published a 1985 report on *The UK Biscuit Market* [B.389].

8.15 Research and Development

Details of companies' research and development expenditures are contained in their Annual Reports. Official investigations have occasionally been particularly concerned with this aspect and have provided statistics. A good example is the MMC Report on *Flour and Bread* [B.443] which gave details of R&D spending by the major plant bakers at the time, i.e. ABF, RHM and Spillers.

The other main area of research expenditure in the sector is the work on the Flour Milling and Baking Research Association (FMBRA), details of which can be found in its annual report. Like other research associations, FMBRA is supported by MAFF as well as companies within the industry, and details of MAFF's R&D activities can be found in their annual *Report on Research and Development* [QRL.415]. Three Research Institutes (RI) are also specifically concerned with food, and they carry out work of relevance to the cereals sector. Details of the activities of the food RIs may be found in the *AFRC Annual Report* [QRL.21]. This also contains details of university research work on food science projects.

8.16 Official Investigations

A number of reports of official investigations concerning the cereals sector have been published. Details have been discussed in relevant parts of the text, and so the reports are simply listed here for convenience.

Reports of the National Board for Prices and Incomes

Report no.3	(Session 1964/65) *Prices of Bread and Flour* [B.408]
Report no.9	(Session 1965/66) *Wages in the Bakery Industry (First Report)* [B.416]
Report no.17	(Session 1966/67) *Wages in the Bakery Industry (Final Report)* [B.415]
Report no.53	(Session 1967/68) *Flour Prices* [B.404]
Report no.144	(Session 1969/70) *Bread Prices and Pay in the Baking Industry (First Report)* [B.398]
Report no.151	(Session 1969/70) *Bread Prices and Pay in the Baking Industry (Second Report)* [B.399]

Reports of the Price Commission under the Counter Inflation Act 1973

Report no.10	(1975) *Food Prices in Outlying Areas* [B.421]
Report no.13	(1975) *Bread Prices and Costs in Northern Ireland and Great Britain* [B.417]
Report no.24 [a]	(1977) *Metrication and Retail Prices (First Report): Granulated Sugar, Biscuits, Dried Vegetables and Salt* [B.423]

Investigation Reports of the Price Commission

Report no.12	(Session 1977/78) *Weetabix Ltd. — Cereal and Muesli Products* [B.437]
Report no.36	(Session 1978/79) *United Biscuits (UK) Ltd. — Biscuits, Crisps, Nuts and Savoury Snacks* [B.436]

Reports of the Monopolies Commission

(Session 1972/73)	*Breakfast Cereals. A Report on the Supply of Ready Cooked Breakfast Cereal Foods* [B.439]
(Session 1972/73)	*Parallel Pricing. A Report on the General Effect on the Public Interest of the Practice of Parallel Pricing* [B.450]

Reports of the Monopolies and Mergers Commission

(Session 1976/77)	*Flour and Bread. A Report on the Supply in the United Kingdom of Wheat Flour and Bread Made from Wheat Flour* [B.443]
(Session 1981/82)	*Discounts to Retailers. A Report on the General Effect on the Public Interest of the Practice of Charging Some Retailers Lower Prices than Others or Providing Special Benefits to Some Retailers Where the Difference Cannot be Attributed to Savings in the Suppliers' Costs* [B.441]
(Session 1981/82)	*Nabisco Brands Inc. and Huntley and Palmer Foods plc: A Report on the Proposed Merger* [B.448]
(Session 1985/86)	*Elders IXL Ltd. and Allied-Lyons plc: A Report on the Proposed Merger* [B.442]

8.17 Improvements and Comments

A good deal has been written about the statistics on the cereals sector, and comments in the *Britton Report* [B.25] and in *Information in the Cereals Market* [B.169] may be still read with interest. The latter, in particular, analyses the role of the Home-Grown Cereals Authority in providing statistical services. The comments on cereal statistics by the HGCA Head of Marketing at the 1986 Statistics' Users Council Agricultural and Food Statistics Conference (Low [B.105]) highlight some of the problems and deficiencies which remain. It was pointed out at the same conference that there is a mismatch that often arises between official statistics, which are *production*, rather than *market*, defined, and the needs of the industrial user of market information. The authors also expressed concern about the employment threshold levels used in the Census of Production, which effectively remove the activities of many smaller food businesses from what were the regular statistical publications, such as the Production Monitors in the PQ series. For AH4196 "Bread and flour confectionery", the shortfall was considerable as indicated by the Topping-up Inquiry undertaken for 1985. The loss of a quarterly PQ Monitor on AH4160 "Grain milling" since 1980 was also unfortunate as is the truncation of the Business Monitor PQ series in mid-1989.

As ever, a major criticism remains the diverse and disparate sources of information on the cereals sector, as in so many other Food industries. A comprehensive compendium of cereals data, along the lines of those produced in the United States, would have great advantages for all users.

CHAPTER 9

SUGAR AND SUGAR BY-PRODUCTS

The information in this chapter relates to the sugar and sugar by-products industries, Group 420 in the *CSO Standard Industrial Classification Revised 1980* [B.232]. Other more general sources, which provide statistics on other industry Groups as well, are covered in Chapter 2 and should be consulted as required. The contents of this chapter are as follows:

9.1 Introduction

Industry Group 420 covers AH4200 "Sugar and sugar by-products", and an alphabetical list of the activities covered is given in Table 9.1 below extracted from the CSO *Indexes to the Standard Industrial Classification Revised 1980* [B.317].

Group 420 in SIC(1980) corresponds to MLH216 "Sugar" in SIC(1968) and in SIC(1958). For the years from 1907 to 1935 and 1949, 1950 and 1951, the Census of Production put glucose with sugar. For instance the 1948 census covered the "Sugar and glucose trade" as MLH155 in SIC(1948). But the manufacture of glucose was included under "Starch and miscellaneous foods" from 1958 and this alternative sweetener is included in Group 423 in SIC(1980) — see Chapter 11.

Business Monitor PA420: Sugar and Sugar By-products [QRL.112] provides annual data on output and costs, capital expenditure, stocks and work-in-progress and

Table 9.1: Activities classified under SIC(1980) Group 420 and SIC(1968) MLH216

SIC(1980)		SIC(1968)
AH4200	Sugar and sugar by-products	MLH216
	Beet pulp manufacturing	
	Beet sugar manufacturing	
	Caramel (not sweets) manufacturing	
	Caster sugar manufacturing	
	Icing sugar manufacturing	
	Invert sugar manufacturing	
	Liquid sugar manufacturing	
	Molasses manufacturing	
	Powdered sugar manufacturing	
	Sugar milling	
	Sugar refining	
	Syrup (sugar) manufacturing	
	Treacle manufacturing	
	White sugar manufacturing	

operating ratios. But due to disclosure difficulties, there is no cross-classification by employment size of employment, wages and salaries, output, capital expenditure, stocks and work-in-progress etc. Thus the sugar coverage is, indeed, sparse compared with other food Activity Headings.

The sensitive nature of the sugar trade, given the virtual duopoly of Tate & Lyle and British Sugar has meant no such disclosure since the limited treatment in the 1976 Census of Production report on sugar. The risk of disclosing information about individual enterprises also means there was no PQ Monitor and the Topping-up Inquiry was not even published for this Group. However, past quarterly data on sales, production, exports and imports etc. can be located in *Business Monitor PQ216: Sugar* [QRL.123] which ran in a similar format from the first quarter of 1973 to the third quarter of 1980.

Far more extensive detail on the industry has been provided in the past. For example, there were thirteen tables in the Industry Report in the *Report on the Census of Production 1968* [QRL.418] which included output and employment and wages and salaries analyses by size of establishment; data on sales of principal products; analyses of purchases by larger establishments in the industry employing 25 or more people and data on transport costs etc. Indeed for the years 1954, 1958, 1963 and 1968, two subdivisions of the industry were given for the analysis of larger establishments employing 25 or more persons. Establishments of the British Sugar Corporation were allocated to the grouping headed "beet sugar" and all other establishments to the "other sugar" group. Thus the analyses for output, sales, purchases, stocks and work-in-progress, employment, wages and salaries, capital expenditure etc. for the larger establishments gave separate totals for beet sugar and other sugar besides an overall total.

The *Historical Record of the Census of Production, 1907–1970* [QRL.264] gives summary data on sales, output, stocks and work-in-progress, employment, wages and salaries etc. for selected years from 1907 to 1970. But there is little doubt that disclosure difficulties have reduced the availability of information from 1968 onwards and we are thus unusually reliant on *ad hoc* sources for basic data.

9.2 Industry Structure

9.2.1 *The Sugar Production Processes and the Dominant Companies*

Sugar is produced from either sugar beet, grown in temperate zones, or from tropical sugar cane. The UK market for sugar is shared between beet and cane in approximately equal proportions. In the United Kingdom, British Sugar is the sole producer of beet sugar, and Tate & Lyle is the major refiner of cane sugar. Tate & Lyle took over Manbré & Garton in 1976. There have been many changes since Philip Lyle described the statistical sources and industry structure in his chapter entitled the *Sugar Industry* [B.107] in the earlier M.G. Kendall volume in 1952.

Cane sugar refineries produce sugar from imported raw cane sugar. The raw cane sugar is produced from sugar cane at factories located in the countries of origin but still contains many impurities. It is transported in bulk-carrying vessels to port refineries where the impurities are removed.

We now consider the production processes for cane sugar in a little more detail aided by Figure 9.1 below.

The initial process of refining cane sugar is usually carried out in the country of origin when "sugar juice" is extracted from the sugar cane and crystallised. This process results in the raw cane sugar which is a light brown sticky solid product which can be handled mechanically for transport by ship to the refineries. This raw cane sugar contains impurities which must be removed before a product considered suitable for human consumption can be produced. But demerara and other natural brown sugars are refined from raw cane sugar.

There are many end-products such as molasses, treacles, inverts and refined syrup, milled sugars, pure cane and brown sugars, pure cane white granulated sugar and pure cane liquid sugars resulting from the processes by which cane sugar refineries produce sugar from imported raw cane sugar. The purpose of refining raw cane sugar is to remove undesirable impurities to leave an end-product of pure natural sucrose. The end-product contains no artificial colourings, preservatives or flavourings of any kind. White refined sugar contains at least 99.95 per cent pure sucrose, whereas brown sugars will contain a small proportion of molasses which impart colour and flavour.

On arrival at a sugar refinery, the sugar consists of brown sugar crystals containing many impurities and covered with a coating of molasses. The outer layers are first softened with warm syrup. This mixture, called 'magma', is passed into centrifugal machines to separate the syrup from the crystals in a process known as affination. Although already washed, there are still some impurities within the raw crystals, so these are now dissolved in water. In the carbonation process the solution is treated with lime and carbon dioxide is bubbled through it. A chalk precipitate results which traps impurities which are then removed in a filter press. The emerging liquor is now a clear amber colour which is then passed over bone charcoal or

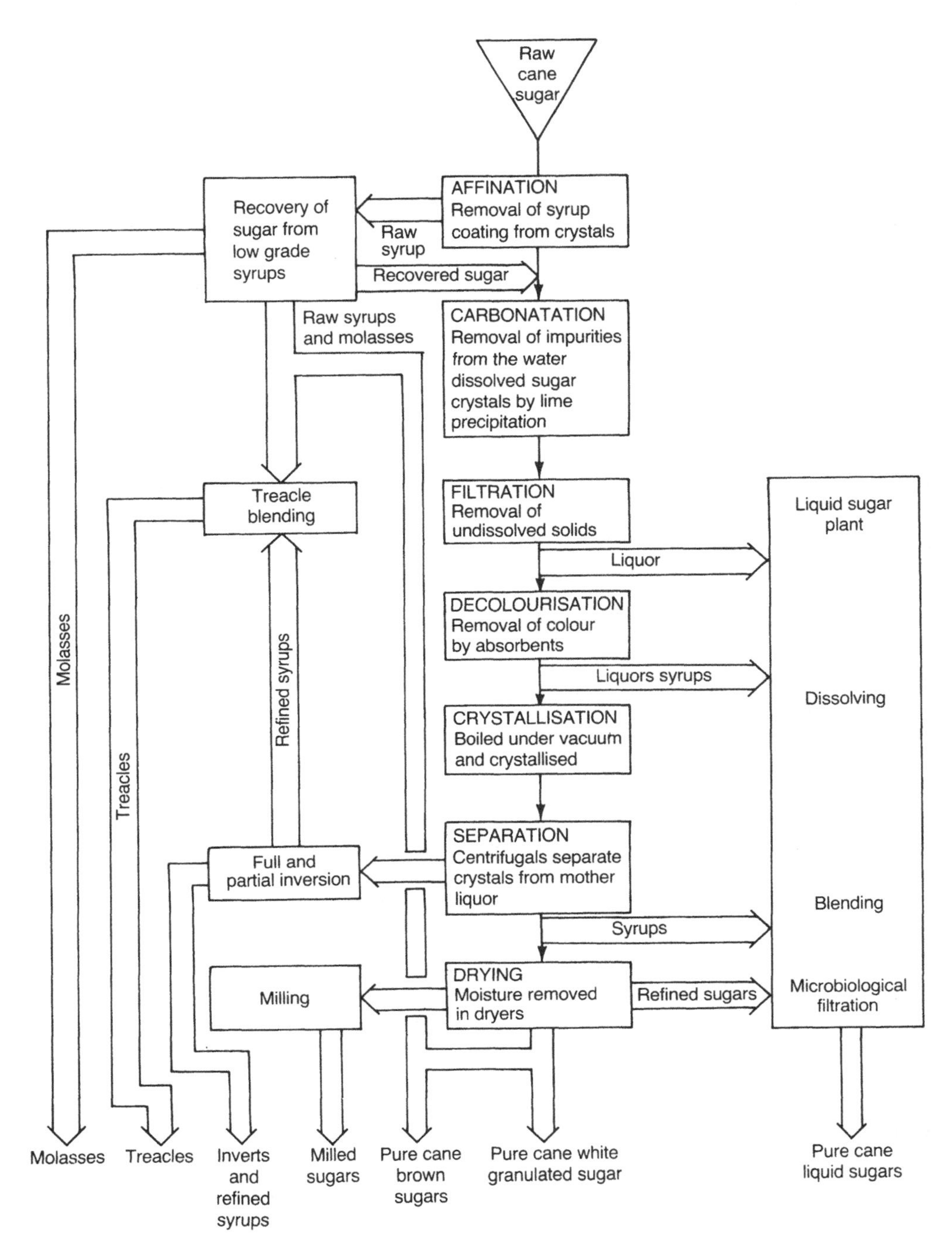

Figure 9.1 The Sugar Refining Process.
Source: *Tate & Lyle plc and Ferruzzi Finanziaria SpA and S & W Berisford plc. A Report on the Existing and Proposed Mergers* [B455], P.251. Monopolies and Mergers Commission Report. 1987.

another decolourising agent such as resin in order to remove virtually all soluble impurities and any non-sweetening colouring matter. The liquor itself becomes clear and colourless — ready for recrystallisation. The liquor is subsequently boiled under vacuum in large enclosed pans. Low boiling temperatures, made possible by the use of a vacuum, are used to avoid forming colour or destroying the sugar by heat. When the liquor in the pan reaches the right thickness, indicating the correct proportion of sugar to water, crystallisation is started by adding a controlled quantity of very small crystals to the liquor. These tiny crystals are known as "seeds" and are the size of grains of icing sugar. When the tiny crystals have grown to the required size, they are separated from the mother liquor in centrifugal machines and dried in granulators.

However, the mother liquor still contains a high level of sugar, so that the boiling and crystallisation process can be repeated up to three times, before the continuous re-heating has caused too much colour to form to allow white sugar of good enough colour to be produced. Liquor no longer able to yield white sugar crystals is either used to produce a range of other sugars and syrups where colour is not so important (e.g. golden syrup), or is boiled and crystallised, together with syrup separated from the raw sugar magma, in the "recovery house". The "recovered" crystalline sugar goes back to the beginning of the refining process and joins the washed raw crystals. The final syrup, from which it is no longer economical or practical to "recover" sugar, is called "refinery molasses". Different sizes of crystals are normally produced by variations in boiling technique and duration. The crystals are graded by screening before packing as either granulated, finest granulated or caster sugar. Icing sugar is made by pulverising crystals in a mill. Cube sugar is made by compressing moist sugar crystals in moulds and then drying.

Finally, Tate & Lyle Sugars' sugar products are supplied in bulk (both dry and liquid) or in bags to industrial consumers, mainly food and drink manufacturers' and as packets to the retail sector which consists of domestic and catering customers. The main product in both sectors is white granulated sugar. Table 9.2 summarises the range of Tate & Lyle Sugars' sugar products, how they are packed and the sectors to which they are supplied.

In the seventeenth and eighteenth centuries, the West Indian islands produced the bulk of the United Kingdom's sugar (see Monopolies and Mergers Commission *A Report on the Proposed Merger of S & W Berisford Limited and British Sugar Corporation Limited* [B.438]). Since accession to the European Community (EC) in 1973, the sources of supply have been widened under the Lomé convention February 1975 and its Sugar Protocol to take in the ex-colonies of France, Belgium and the Netherlands as well. The signatories to the Lomé convention are known as the African, Caribbean and Pacific (ACP) States. The influence of the Common Agricultural Policy (CAP) on the cane producers is further discussed in section 9.3.1. Some other background is also given in the 1978 report of the Price Commission on *Tate and Lyle Refineries Ltd. — Sugar and Syrup Products* [B.434].

Unsuccessful attempts were made to create a beet industry in the United Kingdom in 1832, 1850 and 1868 — see Harris [B.68]. However, the First World War changed the climate of opinion in Britain. The Agricultural Policy Sub-committee of the Cabinet's Reconstruction Committee recommended in 1917 that a British beet industry be established as a way of reducing our dependence on imported supplies.

Table 9.2: Tate & Lyle Sugars' Sugar Products

Product	Packing	Sector supplied
White granulated sugar	Bulk and bags	Industrial
	Packets	Retail
White granulated specialities, caster and vending sugars	Bags	Industrial
	Packets	Retail
Industrial granulated sugar	Bulk and bags	Industrial
Milled specialities and icing sugars	Bags	Industrial
	Packets	Retail
Cubes	Packets	Retail
Brown sugars	Bags	Industrial
	Packets and bags	Retail
Liquid sugars	Bulk	Industrial
Inverts and syrups	Bulk and drums	Industrial
	Tins and jars	Retail
Treacles	Bulk and drums	Industrial
	Tins	Retail

Source: Tate & Lyle from [B.455]

Internal government support assisted the growth of the beet industry. Under the Sugar Industry (Reorganisation) Act 1936, what were then eighteen beet factories (including four in which Tate & Lyle Ltd. had a majority interest) were amalgamated to form the British Sugar Corporation Ltd (BSC). The government took an initial 15 per cent stockholding. Henceforth, up to European Community (EC) accession, the UK market was essentially controlled by government policy. The amount of beet sugar to be produced was specified, the market was geographically split into beet and cane zones and refining margins were controlled. The statutory body, the Sugar Board, acted both as the government agent in providing the necessary funds to BSC to make deficiency payments to farmers and as the agent for purchasing raw cane sugar under the Commonwealth Sugar Agreement (CSA).

As the beet industry is firmly established, a summary of sugar beet agronomy and sugar beet processing now follows. In the United Kingdom, the growing season for sugar beet is approximately eight months, from planting in March/April to lifting from the end of September to December. The sugar yield is heavily dependent both on soil type and on the weather in the growing season. Ideally, a deep, well structured, free draining soil is required together with an adequate level of nutrients. But the sugar yield is influenced to a lesser degree by the grower's ability to control pests, diseases and weed growth. Thus growing techniques are important to produce a healthy crop.

In the United Kingdom, sugar beet is grown as a break crop, breaking the cycle of cereal crops every few years. As a particularly capital intensive crop, successful harvesting requires specialist mechanical harvesters, and considerable crop losses can occur if attention is not paid to accurate machine setting and operation. Furthermore, the processing factories require regular supplies of beet in good condition over a four-month period, which means that the beet harvested in the first half of the "Campaign" may have to be stored by the farmer in clamps before transportation to the processing factories. The term "Campaign" is used to refer to the whole of the lifting and processing period for sugar beet. This normally runs from the end of September to mid/end January in the United Kingdom. Apart from the sugar content in the beet, by-products in the form of beet tops (leaves, stems and crowns) are available for use on the farm as fodder and green manure, and beet pulp is produced at the factory in considerable quantities for use as animal feed.

The delivery of beet to the factory is carefully controlled and monitored. The programmed schedule is designed to maintain factory stocks at a satisfactory level in accordance with production requirements. The storage capacity at the factory is sufficient to allow deliveries to be made ten hours every day, five and a half days per week. On the arrival of each lorry, a sample is taken and analysed for dirt, tare and sugar content in order that payment can be made to the grower for his entire consignment in accordance with the sugar beet contract. The remaining beet in the lorry is unloaded into storage areas to await processing. The process is described below and illustrated in Figure 9.2.

The beets are recovered from storage by water transport systems, passed through equipment to remove stones and trash, and then washed to remove adhering soil and other foreign matter. Next they are elevated to a storage hopper from which they are fed to machines which slice them into thin chevron shaped strips. These strips pass to diffusion plant where the sugar, together with some impurities which are subsequently removed, is extracted with hot water. Raw sugar-laden juice from the diffuser is pumped into tanks to be mixed with a lime suspension and carbon dioxide gas. The quicklime and carbon dioxide required for this process are produced in kilns on the factory site. This treatment precipitates many impurities, which are removed in filters. The juice is treated with further carbon dioxide and soda ash under fine control conditions and then refiltered.

The filtered juice passes to an ion-exchange plant to remove calcium ions and is then treated with sulphur dioxide. It is now known as "thin juice", which is then greatly reduced in bulk in evaporation vessels. The design of the evaporators is such that the vapour leaving one vessel is employed as the heating medium for the next stage, thus giving maximum economy in heat use. The steam employed in this and all other process-heating operations is produced in boilers fired by either coal, oil or gas on the site. The steam is also used to generate all factory power requirements.

The juice is further boiled and concentrated under vacuum. Vapour from the evaporators is used for this purpose so that further fuel economy is achieved. During this stage of the process, small crystals form in the juice and grow to produce a viscous mass. This flows to a battery of centrifugal machines. The baskets of these machines have a fine mesh screen and are rotated at high speed to spin off the syrup portion. The remaining crystals are washed with boiling water to remove the adhering syrup. The pure white sugar now passes to a granulator, where it is dried and cooled ready for bagging or for storage in bulk.

The syrup from the centrifugal machines is recrystallised to produce lower grade sugar, which is reprocessed with juice from the evaporators to manufacture further

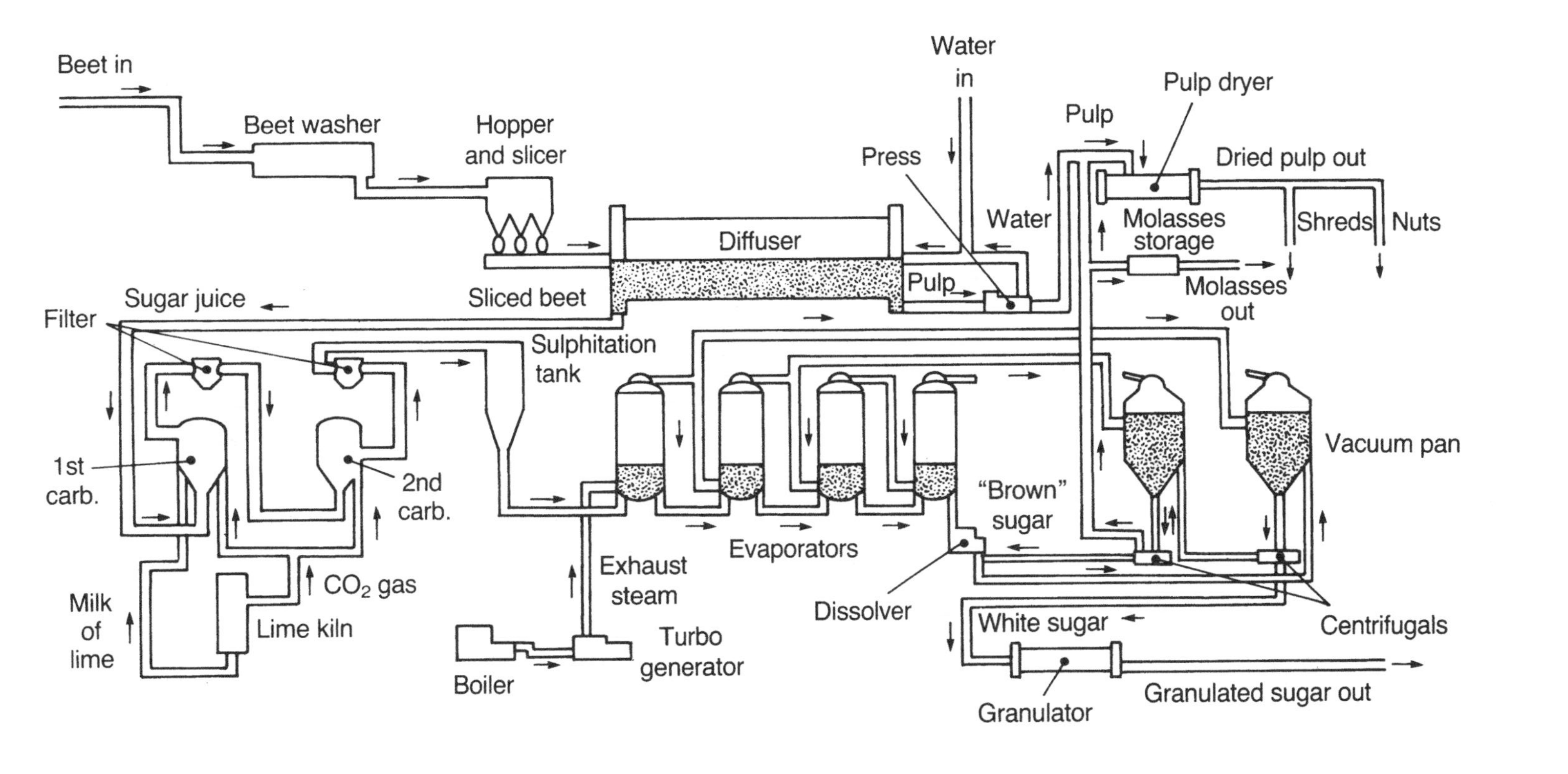

Figure 9.2 A Typical Beet Sugar Factory.
Source: *Tate & Lyle plc and Ferruzzi Finanziaria SpA and S & W Berisford plc: A Report on the Existing and Proposed Mergers*. [B455]. P.243. Monopolies and Mergers Commission Report, 1987.

high-grade products. This process is repeated with the remaining syrup and, following storage and cooling, the mass is separated once more to produce sugar for reprocessing and syrup (which is known as molasses).

For a beet processing factory to work efficiently, beet must be delivered in accordance with a programme schedule to match production requirements and capacity. As a rough guide, according to [B.455], processing 1,000 tonnes of beet produces approximately:

120–140 tonnes of sugar
20 tonnes of molasses which is available for sale
85 tonnes of molassed pulp (sold either as shredded pulp or pulp nuts)
100 tonnes of waste lime.

It uses in this process:

67 tonnes of fuel (oil, coal or natural gas used in main boilers and pulp dryers)
50 tonnes of limestone
4 tonnes of coke (for burning limestone to make lime).

British Sugar's factories begin operations at the end of September or, if the growing season has been delayed, in early October. They operate for up to 120 days. During this period, production is carried on for twenty four hours a day, seven days a week and continues over the Christmas and New Year public holidays.

With EC accession in 1973, the industry became subject to the EC regime as discussed in section 9.3.1. British Sugar, as the sole UK beet sugar producer, is in fact allocated the entire UK quota by the government. Indeed, compared with the beet producers, the cane refineries have found themselves in a weaker competitive position. This is thought to be due to the EC Sugar Regime which affects the margin between institutional input prices and output prices for both beet and cane sugar. As previously mentioned, the two remaining refineries became one when Tate & Lyle took over Manbré & Garton in 1976.

Market power has always been a matter of public concern and after the 1978 report of the Price Commission on *Tate & Lyle* [B.434], there was the 1981 MMC inquiry on *Berisford and British Sugar* [B.438]. This followed the Berisford bid which was partly motivated by the intention of acquiring the BSC manufacturing base to complement its own well established commodity trading activities.

Sugar merchants can be regarded as a third force, acting as intermediaries between producers and importers and industrial and retail customers. Their role is also outlined in the 1981 MMC inquiry on *Berisford and British Sugar* [B.438].

The sugar market is also complicated by the existence of industrial and retail markets where sugar competes with other sweeteners. But the concentrated nature of the market, the changing commercial forces at work and the role of government agencies has led to the multiplicity of sources drawn upon in this section which carry both structural description and many statistical components. The most recent and complete, in addition to the sources so far mentioned, is the detailed MMC report in 1987 on *Tate and Lyle plc and Ferruzzi Finanziaria SpA and S & W Berisford plc: a Report on the Existing and Proposed Mergers* [B.455]. This report concluded that any further concentration of ownership was not in the public interest and furnished abundant portraits of the structure and performance of these influential companies in the sugar sector and beyond.

9.2.2 *The Sugar Market*

The market may be analysed according to whether retail or industrial, according to product type and as part of the entire sweeteners market. The 1987 MMC report on *Tate, Ferruzzi and Berisford* [B.455], and the earlier and shorter Key Note report on *Sugar* [QRL.599], provide descriptions and data. *Sugar* [QRL.599] gives a breakdown for six retail types: granulated; caster sugar with smaller crystals; icing sugar; cube sugar; coffee crystals; preserving sugar.

Tate, Ferruzzi and Berisford [B.455] gives the most detailed statistical descriptions of the sugar market. We can only summarise the most important components of this important source. White granulated sugar, the end product of processing both beet or cane, represents the major part of the market by value. [B.455] gives the estimated share of sugar types in total sugar sales for 1984 and 1985 in percentage terms. White granulated is shown to dominate, and these statistics are broken down according to whether bulk sugar, bagged or retail packed. The sub-total for white granulated is arrived at and succeeded by the percentages for liquid sugar, sucrose-based sugar mixes and speciality sugars.

Some of these sub-markets merit further explanation. Liquid sugars, for example, are used in the food processing industry. The highest quality is made by dissolving white granulated sugar whereas lower grades are made only from cane by blending liquors produced at various stages of the cane sugar refining process. Sucrose-based sweeteners also have specialist applications in food processing.

Tate, Ferruzzi and Berisford [B.455] groups under speciality sugars all dry sugars, other than white granulated, and syrups and treacles as well, giving Tate & Lyle market shares. Speciality sugars include the brown sugars and comprise both Demerara or Barbados imported for sale without being further refined. There are also the "manufactured" brown sugars which consist of white sugar crystals washed with molasses or syrups. This entire sector is influenced by ideas about health and natural food as analysed by Yudkin [B.193].

Sugar is sucrose, the chemical compounds of glucose and fructose. But the UK sugar market must be viewed in conjuction with a range of other sweeteners. Caloric sweeteners are isoglucose (also known as high fructose corn syrup) and similar products and other sweeteners such as sorbitol and mannitol. Low calorie sweeteners include saccharine and aspartame. [B.455] also categorises the market shares by value according to product type cross-classified by sources of supply in an MMC user survey. Here, white granulated, liquid granulated, sweetener mixes and speciality sugars are identified in percentage share terms according to whether they come from British Sugar, Tate & Lyle, direct from merchants, other UK, Community imports or other imports.

In general, white granulated sugar, liquid sugar, sucrose mixer, most of the sugar substitutes and some speciality sugars are sold to the industrial market whilst retail packed, white granulated and speciality sugars go to the domestic market. This distinction between the retail and industrial market is drawn out in [B.455] and is also featured in the 1981 MMC report on *Berisford and British Sugar* [B.438]. The latter carries an important table which shows the proportion of industrial sugar sold to other Food industries. It gives the estimated share of sugar in the total material input from BSC estimates. Industrial sugar is a significant input into other Food industries: chocolate and sugar confectionery; flour and baking products; ice-cream and milk; canned and frozen food; jams and preserves; as categorised in [B.438].

Molasses is a by-product of both beet sugar production and of cane refining and is thus an important subsidiary business. Its uses can be further divided broadly into industrial fermentation processes (yeast, citric acid and alcohol) and as a constituent in animal feeds. The market for molasses is summarised on pp.30–31 of the 1987 MMC report *Tate, Ferruzzi and Berisford* [B.455]. The estimated total market in physical quantities in 1985 is detailed, showing the supplies of beet and cane according to uses (i.e. yeast and citric acid, alcohol, animal feeds etc.). The magnitudes are attributable to United Molasses (Tate & Lyle) and British Sugar. Information was provided directly by the suppliers.

9.2.3 *The Dominant Companies*

Tate & Lyle owes its origins to two nineteenth century sugar refining firms. In 1859 Henry Tate became a partner in a sugar refinery business which became known as Henry Tate and Sons. In 1865 Abram Lyle established Abram Lyle and Sons Ltd. The two firms merged to form Tate & Lyle in 1921. In 1976 Tate & Lyle took over Manbré & Garton Ltd., the other UK major cane refiner. Manbré & Garton had subsidiaries involved in the wet milling of maize for the manufacture of starch products, syrups, sweeteners and caramel colouring. Thus this acquisition extended Tate & Lyle's range of sugar products and derivatives. The main activities of the Tate & Lyle Group continue to be concerned with sugar production and refining and sugar trading; the production, trading and distribution of molasses; the production of cereal sweeteners and starches; and maltings. Indeed, considerable diversification has taken place. Other activities include agribusiness (including production of animal feeds); bulk liquid storage; insurance etc. With its acquisitions in the US and Europe, Tate & Lyle can be regarded as a multinational company with diversified interests in sugar refining, starch production and cereal sweeteners. Turnover and profit before tax both in value and percentage share terms are given for many of its business activities (for 1985) on p.47 of [B.455].

British Sugar plc has been a wholly-owned subsidiary of S & W Berisford since 1982. The company's main activities are the processing of sugar beet and the manufacture and sale of sugar, animal feeds and molasses. S & W Berisford itself is a holding company for an international group of companies with a wide variety of activities. It had its origins in a chemist and grocery business founded by Samuel and William Berisford in the 1850's. The business moved into sugar merchanting under another William Berisford, the grandson of one of the founders. It extended its interests, notably with the acquisition of J.H. Rayner (Mincing Lane) Ltd. The latter had extensive international trading interests in cocoa and coffee as well some business in sugar and metals. S & W Berisford today is one of the world's largest commodity traders.

Of the four main merchants handling sugar in the United Kingdom, Napier Brown and Co. Ltd. is the largest. It purchased Berisford's UK sugar merchanting operation shortly before the Berisford take over of British Sugar in 1982. The second largest, James Budgett and Son Ltd., is a subsidiary of E.D.&F. Man, the world's largest sugar trader. Billington's merchants white sugar in the United Kingdom but also imports speciality sugars on its own account from Mauritius.

British Sugar markets white sugars under Silver Spoon but only small quantities of brown sugar and syrup. Tate & Lyle uses brand names for a range of white and brown sugars and has the famous "golden syrup" (Lyle) and the Fowlers' and Lyle's treacles. Billington's, Whitworth's and Berisford are other brand names in brown sugars but they process and pack, rather than refine. Own-label products are visible but less so than in many of the other food markets. It is more difficult for large retail chains to undercut the prices of established brands.

Finally, it is of some importance to record that the ownership situation changed markedly in January 1991. Associated British Foods, the milling and baking group, bought British Sugar. Be that as it may, and whatever other structural changes may ensue, the sugar market is still firmly identified with the activities of British Sugar and Tate & Lyle.

9.2.4 *Specialist Sources*

The importance of *ad hoc* official sources is apparent. [B.434], [B.438] and [B.455] have been and will be drawn on heavily throughout this chapter both for their explanations of industry structure and as sources of statistics.

Reports issued by the companies take on a significant importance as well. *The British Sugar Report* [QRL.70] collects together annual data on the sugar markets, sales and publicity etc. Both the *British Sugar plc: Annual Report* [QRL.69] and *S & W Berisford plc: Report and Accounts* [QRL.442] give market overviews which carry illustrative statistics. *Tate and Lyle: Annual Report* [QRL.479] does likewise for the Tate & Lyle family of companies.

Section 9.3 shows that the United Kingdom cannot be isolated from EC markets. But it is also important to stress that the United Kingdom is part of the world sugar market. Consequently, some major international and commercial sources are noted here. F.O. Licht's is regarded as the leading international sugar statistical service and is responsible for the *F.O. Licht's International Sugar Report* [QRL.199] and the *F.O. Licht's International Molasses and Alcohol Report* [QRL.198]. The firm was founded in 1861 by Franz Otto Licht, a Prussian revenue officer especially involved with the government beet sugar tax who on his retirement established a statistical office for the beet sugar industry of the German Zollverein. Both F.O. Licht's publications now review world markets. The former has a useful quarterly index where articles concerning company news, consumption, competition and mergers etc. in the United Kingdom as well as other countries can be easily located. The data on prices, sugar balances, non-sucrose sweeteners, the molasses markets etc. will be referred to later in this chapter. Both [QRL.199] and [QRL.198] provide a useful overview of the markets and are usually published thirty six times a year and twenty four times a year respectively. *F.O. Licht's World Sugar Statistics* [QRL.200] is the annual compendium, carrying similar ranges of data.

The Czarnikow Sugar Review [QRL.168], which has been published since 1873, reviews world sugar production and consumption and is also a source of price data. E.D.&F. Man (Sugar) Ltd. issue *The Sugar Situation* [QRL.472] each month. This is a statistically-illustrated market review having a special section on raw sugar and white sugar transactions. *Gill & Duffus Sugar Market Report* [QRL.251] used to be another well-known source, issued six times a year, which summarised world trends. However [QRL.251] was discontinued in September 1989 after the merger of Gill & Duffus with E.D.&F. Man. *LMC Commodity Bulletin: Sugar* [QRL.313] is a review which primarily assesses the supply/demand balance.

Many of the commercial sources combine both primary market information and summarise statistical data from official sources in digestible form, along with their market surveys and predictions. They also draw upon the many statistics issued by the International Sugar Organisation (ISO) of which the United Kingdom as a member of the EC belongs. The monthly *Statistical Bulletin* [QRL.459] provides wide-ranging data on world production, consumption, stocks, exports, imports, net exports, net imports and spot prices. The *Sugar Year Book* [QRL.473] replicates much of these data in this annual publication. However, as noted in section 9.3.3, the contents of [QRL.437] record data for the EC as a whole, since 1973, and no longer separately identify the UK.

9.3 The European Community

9.3.1 *The Economic Influence of the Community*

The European Community sugar regime and the scope for trade within the Community are important influences on the sugar market in the United Kingdom. The United Kingdom's entry to the European Community in 1973 signalled what were to be major changes on both the sources of supply and the nature of competition.

Under the Sugar Act of 1956, the Sugar Board regulated both the UK industry and influenced imports. Deficiency payments were made for the home sugar beet crop. The Sugar Board had the statutory duty to buy at the negotiated price the sugar contracted for under the Commonwealth Sugar Agreement (CSA). As noted in section 9.2.1, the UK market was essentially supervised by Government policy, which placed both cane refiners and BSC under close control with respect to volumes, prices, profit margins and even areas of marketing operations. The *Sugar Board* [QRL.471] in its nineteenth and final annual report contains an annex giving the story of the life of the Sugar Board.

This system of guaranteed prices, deficiency payments and Commonwealth access was terminated in 1973 when the United Kingdom became subject to the scope of the Common Agricultural Policy (CAP) of which the Sugar Regime is a part. The CSA expired in 1974. The Sugar Regime differs from that for all other agricultural products covered by the CAP in that production is regulated both through a system of intervention prices and through national production quotas. The main elements of the regime are:

a) A system of national production quotas restricting the quantity of sugar produced in the Community that it is entitled to support under the CAP.
b) A system of linked institutional prices for white sugar, raw sugar and sugar beet giving a guaranteed minimum price for Community-produced sugar beet used in the manufacture of sugar.
c) A system of production levies designed so that sugar processors and beet growers help meet the cost of disposing of Community production falling within quota, but surplus to consumption.
d) Preferential access for imports of cane sugar from ACP countries up to their quota entitlements. This refers to the Community's commitment to purchase and import sugar under the Lomé convention 1975 and its Sugar Protocol.

e) Free trade within the Community, but with a system of levies and refunds on trade with countries outside the Community designed to insulate the European market from fluctuations in world prices and to allow the disposal on world markets of European production which is surplus to European production.

In addition, we need to explain the quota system in a little more detail. "A" quota is the annual basic white sugar quota laid down for each Member State of the Community for the duration of each periodic Sugar Regime which normally lasts for five years. The producer of "A" quota sugar must pay a levy to the Community authorities. The "B" quota is the annual quantity of sugar determined for each Member State which, together with its "A" quota, constitute its maximum quota. The size of the "B" quota for different countries can be different percentages of their "A" quotas but the producer of "B" quota sugar must pay a levy, considerably higher than that on "A" quota sugar to the Community. Finally, "C" sugar is defined as all beet sugar produced in excess of the "A" and "B" quotas. There is no regulatory limit on "C" sugar production, but such sugar must be exported outside the Community by producers with no guarantee as to its price and no export restitution payment.

This summary of the Sugar Regime is filled out both in *Berisford and British Sugar* [B.438] and in the 1987 MMC report *Tate, Ferruzzi and Berisford* [B.455]. [B.438] and [B.455] go into considerable detail, but it is worth noting that CAP arrangements, in particular the size of production quotas, are subject to change.

A fuller, but earlier, account of the sugar regime is given by Harris, Swinbank and Wilkinson in *The Food and Farm Policies of the European Community* [B.71] and in Graham's paper on "Sugar and sweeteners" in *The EEC and the Food Industries* [B.60]. The Agra Europe publication *CAP Monitor* [B.220] gives a regularly updated account of the details of the CAP and all the commodity regimes, including sugar. This is of some importance because both adjustments to policies and the mechanics of the operations are often made and need to be noted. Indeed when it became apparent that starch manufacturers wanted to move into isoglucose production which for certain uses was preferred to sugar syrups, the Community acted to control production. The separate regime to control isoglucose production was incorporated with that for sugar in 1981.

Finally, MAFF provides a well-organised description in the *EC Sugar Regime* [B.244] which is available from the "Sugar, Oils and Fats" division of the Ministry. Continual updating is always needed and this guide is regularly revised.

9.3.2 *EUROSTAT and Community Statistics*

Much data need to be collated from Member States and indeed, regularly updated to help run the Sugar Regime. *The Agricultural Situation in the Community* [QRL.28] has a review of the marketing year which concisely describes the market situation and outlook. The ensuing statistical tables reflect both those data submitted by Member States and those needed for Community purposes. Statistical information on areas under sugar beet, yield and production of sugar etc. are supplied by Member States. However the annual quantity data on UK sugar production, by quota (in 1000 tonnes white sugar), comes under a different category. Included are the basic quantities of the "A" quota and "B" quota; the production of "A" quota,

"B" quota and "C" sugar; the crops in total and the quantity of sugar carried over. All data are annual. World supply balances, the European share in international trade, European sugar supply balance and average world prices (Paris, London and New York) etc. help give a more complete picture of European and worldwide sugar supply and demand trends.

9.3.3 *The Influence of the Community on the Collection of UK Statistics*

The *Intervention Board for Agricultural Produce: Annual Report* [QRL.293] carries a statistically-backed review of the Sugar Regime. This usually includes a physical enumeration of "A" and "B" quotas and rates of levy for both sugar and isoglucose.

Total payments made to manufacturers and some other stockholders of Community sugar to offset storage costs are given. Production refunds paid on sugar and on certain sugar products used in the manufacture of specified products in the chemical industry are recorded. The statistical tables themselves append the analysis by sector (including sugar) of UK expenditure borne by the European Agricultural Guidance and Guarantee Fund (EAGGF). In practice, despite the elaborate structure of the Sugar Regime, intervention buying very seldom occurs. Thus the data on annual expenditure on export refunds in the *Intervention Board: Annual Report* [QRL.293] reflects the EC's principal mechanism for disposing of its surplus sugar. Sugar used in the chemical industry and notably the annual expenditure on the Sugar Storage Costs Scheme are given. This storage refund is the reimbursement for the costs of holding sugar in store and thus helps to smooth out prices from "Campaign" to "Campaign".

The MMC report on *Tate, Ferruzzi and Berisford* [B.455] in 1987 also reflected the European dimensions. Special MMC studies calculated the British Sugar "A" and "B" quotas as a percentage of the Community total and compared British Sugar and Tate & Lyle production and sales as a proportion of the total Community for 1984/1985. The company profiles of not only British Sugar and Tate & Lyle but also Ferruzzi, Béghin-Say etc. drew upon both national and Community statistical sources.

Membership of the EC has made some difference to UK coverage in international and specialist publications which are also discussed in section 9.2.4. These are usually concerned with world supply and demand, stocks, prices etc. An example of this is the coverage in the *Sugar Year Book* [QRL.473]. Prior to UK membership of the EC, this publication recorded production, imports, net imports, exports, net exports, consumption and stocks etc. for the United Kingdom in the country tables. However, from 1973 onwards, the International Sugar Organisation (ISO) collections record data for the EC rather than the UK which now belongs to the ISO as part of the EC. Since ISO publications are heavily drawn on in the sugar trade, this change in coverage is repeated in the many derivative publications.

The very nature of the Sugar Regime has made some differences to information, available particularly the range of prices. The *Sugar Board* [QRL.471] in its annual report used to review market movements and the Board's operations, with specific data on purchase prices paid under the CSA and the negotiated prices and quota arrangements. A range of illustrative data on world prices, retail prices and the Board's purchases and sales were given.

With the Sugar Regime of the CAP, the coverage of statistical data changed. The EC arrangements are described in a glossary to the 1987 MMC report on *Tate,*

Ferruzzi and Berisford [B.455]. But the MAFF *Sugar and Beet Prices* [QRL.470] is a most concise guide. The intervention price for white sugar, the intervention price for raw sugar, the basic beet price (both "A" quota and "B" quota), threshold prices (white, raw and molasses) and target price (white) are all summarised on this sheet which is available on application from the MAFF Sugar, Oils and Fats division. Prices usually operate with effect from 1 July of each year following annual negotiations. Of the commercial reports which duplicate this information, E.D.&F. Man (Sugar) Limited in *The Sugar Situation* [QRL.472] report these ranges of prices as soon as possible after they are fixed.

We also mention here *Bulletin Statistique du FIRS* [QRL.72] because France has its own intervention board for sugar alone. This monthly bulletin portrays the Community, French and world situations with considerable statistical back-up. The data are consolidated annually in *La Campagne Sucrière* [QRL.303]. Statistical information on UK production, imports, exports, quotas, prices etc. as well as interior community exchange and third country trade are included. The coverage is more complete than that in the *Intervention Board: Annual Report* [QRL.293] which gave information on annual intervention prices up to 1980.

9.4 Output

9.4.1 *Output, Sales and Value Added*

9.4.1.1 Business Statistics Office inquiries

The annual *Business Monitor PA420: Sugar and Sugar By-products* [QRL.112] and *Business Monitor PA1002: Summary Volume* [QRL.93] both provide the four major output measures for this Activity Heading, viz: total sales and work done; gross output; net output and gross value added at factor cost. The coverage is further explained in section 2.4.1.1.

As noted in section 9.1, the product detail was more extensive in the past. In the Censuses of Production for the years 1954, 1958, 1963 and 1968 a distinction was made between "beet sugar" and "other sugar" for the output and sales components. The sales of principal products were also expressed in quantity and value terms for the following range of products: sugar, unrefined; sugar, refined or rendered for icing, fondant etc; syrup and treacle; invert sugar, other than syrup and treacle; molasses; caramel; beet pulp (including wet pulp in terms of dry pulp); other products, including waste products. These data applied to establishments employing 25 or more people. *Business Monitor PQ216: Sugar* [QRL.123] had subsequent quarterly and annual sales data for sugars refined or rendered; sucrose (liquid sugar); sucrose/glucose mixes; molasses (dark). But [QRL.123] ceased in 1980. The *Historical Record* [QRL.264] collated sales data from 1907 to 1968 although for 1924 and earlier years, unrefined sugar was excluded from the totals. The value of net output is summarised up to 1970.

9.4.1.2 Ministry of Agriculture, Fisheries and Food inquiries

The *Annual Abstract of Statistics* [QRL.37] gives an eleven-year run for the production of sugar from home-grown sugar beet (as refined sugar) in physical terms. The data for syrup and treacle and glucose are given in the same table. The *Monthly Digest of Statistics* [QRL.362] gives monthly averages for the production of sugar (as refined) from home-grown sugar beet as recorded by British Sugar and returned to the MAFF. Data are produced on some by-products, taking syrup and treacle together, and glucose separately.

9.4.2 *Index Numbers of Output*

Business Monitor PQ216 [QRL.123] used to carry the index of production for MLH216 under the SIC(1968) for previous quarters and years.

9.4.3 *Company Reports and Occasional Investigations*

Given the paucity of information in the Business Monitor series, we are unusually dependent upon *ad hoc* official investigations. Firstly, the extensive MMC study *Tate, Ferruzzi and Berisford* [B.455] gives a range of information from mainly company sources and MMC surveys and may be recorded as follows:

- Supply of sugar in the United Kingdom (market shares by volume) as between British Sugar deliveries, Tate & Lyle deliveries (including Manbré & Garton for 1972/3) and imports. These data cover selected years from 1972/73 to 1985.
- Supply of sugar in the United Kingdom by value and by percentage share from the same three sources for 1984 and 1985.
- Share of sugar types in total sugar sales by value for 1984 and 1985 (i.e. bulk, bagged, retail packed white granulated; liquid sugar; sucrose based sugar mixes; speciality sugars).
- Deliveries of white granulated sugar by tanker, bags and retail pack for 1985.
- Supply of sugar in the United Kingdom, market share estimates by value and by product type for 1985. This table cross-classifies product type according to the following: white granulated breakdowns; liquid; sweetener mixes; and speciality sugars. The share of British Sugar; Tate & Lyle; direct from merchants; other UK; Community imports; and other imports are shown.

The supplies of molasses to UK users has been already noted in section 9.2.2.

Furthermore, the company profile of British Sugar identified annual data on the percentage and value of the contribution of sugar, molasses and animal feeds to turnover. Sugar sales were analysed according to destination (i.e. domestic retail or industrial and export sales). Industrial and retail sales were further split in volume and turnover according to dry bulk, packets etc. British Sugar volume and turnover sales of molasses and animal feed (including exports) were shown separately.

The profile of Tate & Lyle resulted in a description of the range of sugar products: sales by outlet for 1985/6 whether retail, industrial, British Sugar, European Community non-European exports; and the sales by main product for the same period i.e. industrial (dry bulk, liquid, bags and other) and retail (packets and other).

The earlier 1981 MMC inquiry on *Berisford and British Sugar* [B.438] also carried a good deal of data as follows:

- British Sugar's volume production, white sugar delivered etc. from 1972/3 to 1979/80.
- The market shares of the three sources (British Sugar; Tate & Lyle and Manbré & Garton; imports) in percentage terms for the same years.

- Subdivisions for 1978/79 of the three sources in percentage terms for retail/catering; industrial dry; and industrial liquid.

The role of merchants was also assessed together with supporting annual data as to the quantity of sugar invoiced through merchants by British Sugar, merchants' purchases on own account from British Sugar, total tonnage of refined sugar merchanted by Berisford's Sugar Division and percentage breakdown of "nominal merchanting" and "true merchanting" later cross-classified according to British Sugar and Tate & Lyle.

Tate and Lyle [B.434] included percentage market shares for 1976 and 1977 in the retail sugar market according to product (all sugars, granulated, caster, icing, cubes, soft brown, demerara, syrup and treacle).

Some more recent data are published in the *British Sugar Report* [QRL.70]. Breakdowns of speciality sugars (caster, golden granulated, brown, demerara, icing and others) are given in value terms. Two-yearly sales movements are provided for the product range from granulated sugar to treacle. The total sugar market is split into market shares for Silver Spoon (i.e British Sugar), Tate & Lyle, Billington, Whitworth Holdings and own-label. *British Sugar plc: Annual Report* [QRL.69] published more production-orientated data for the year (the "Campaign") and total sales/value. These annual data are both broken up according to whether "sugar", "animal feed" and "other". *Tate and Lyle: Annual Report* [QRL.479] publishes separate turnover data for sugar production and refining in the United Kingdom. The activities of cereal sweeteners and starches; sugar trading; molasses; and speciality feeds etc. are also specified in the financial statements.

9.5 Current Inputs other than Labour

An important primary input is imported raw cane sugar imports as noted in section 9.8 where *Business Monitor MM20: Overseas Trade Statistics of the United Kingdom* [QRL.85] is discussed. However, the sugar beet output of domestic agriculture is a major input as well, and these sources are now reviewed.

9.5.1 *Domestic Inputs*

9.5.1.1 Ministry of Agriculture, Fisheries and Food inquiries

MAFF Statistics: Agricultural Returns: England and Wales, Regions and Counties [QRL.316] gives sugar beet output (not for stock feeding) by county, region and country. *Agricultural Statistics: United Kingdom* [QRL.32] gives data for England on sugar beet production area, yield per hectare and volume production for the latest five years. The yield and production figures refer to washed and topped beet and production figures are supplied by British Sugar plc.

Output and Utilisation of Farm Produce in the United Kingdom [QRL.382] provided a great deal of annual data for the United Kingdom which specifically related to both agriculture and processing. But [QRL.382] ceased publication in 1988 and the latest data related to 1987. Besides production area, yield and beet production, a figure for percentage sugar content was given. The volume production for sugar was provided, separating raw equivalent from refined equivalent. Figures for molasses were subdivided into two: for distilling, yeast etc.; and for incorporation into pulp. Pulp was divided into two as well: dry, plain molassed; and wet. Production figures were supplied by British Sugar. Production coming out of the factory in the early part of the New Year was regarded as being part of the previous calendar year's production. The mantle of [QRL.382] is in many ways assumed by *Agriculture in the UK*, the successor since 1989 of the *Annual Review of Agriculture* [QRL.51].

The *Annual Review of Agriculture* [QRL.51] is also discussed in section 9.11. Annual figures for yield, beet production, percentage sugar content and percentage sugar extraction rate are produced and an overall production figure for sugar (1000 tonnes refined basis) arrived at. With the figures for imports and exports, the statistics for total new supply and production as a percentage of total new supply in the United Kingdom are presented. From 1989, coverage is continued in *Agriculture in the United Kingdom.*

The *Monthly Digest of Statistics* [QRL.362] also provides the annual data on crop areas, yields per hectare and volume production. It also gives monthly averages for the production of sugar (as refined) from home-grown sugar beet. These data clearly show the period of the "Campaign" with statistics usually available for the months of October through February.

The *Annual Abstract of Statistics* [QRL.37] carries the annual data on sugar beet acreage, quantity harvested and value of output from the Agricultural departments. The annual quantities of production from home-grown sugar beet (as refined sugar) are also given.

9.5.1.2 Business Statistics Office inquiries

Business Monitor PO1008: Purchases Inquiry [QRL.116] does nothing more than record the value of purchases (other than for merchanting or factoring) for 1984. The coverage of the previous Purchases Inquiry for this Group in 1979 was similarly limited as can be seen from *Business Monitor PA1002.1: 1979 Census of Production and Purchases Inquiry* [QRL.94]. The heart of the problem is again disclosure difficulties. In fact the standard treatment in *Business Monitor PA420* [QRL.112] goes further than [QRL.116]. The purchases of materials for use in production, packaging and fuel, and the purchase of goods for merchanting or factoring are shown in value terms and the cost of the various non-industrial services (vehicle hire, rates etc.) are also recorded.

Purchases data are again given separately for beet sugar and other sugar in the Census of Production inquiries for 1954, 1958, 1963 and 1968.

9.5.2 *Input-output Analysis*

The coverage of the input-output tables is fully discussed in section 2.5.2. *Input-output tables for the United Kingdom 1984* [QRL.284] has a special significance for sugar as it is a commodity of final demand, an important input to other Food industries and is imported in both its raw and processed state. Sugar is classified as an industry/commodity group. The use matrix, which shows the commodity analysis of purchases by industry from domestic production in 1984, clearly indicates the importance of sugar output as an input into the other Food industries and elsewhere: particularly confectionery; bread, biscuits and flour confectionery; fruit, vegetables and fish processing; miscellaneous foods; alcoholic drinks and soft drinks etc. This is confirmed by the data in *Business Monitor PO1008* [QRL.116] and *Business Monitor PA1002* [QRL.93] which show the values and sometimes the volume of sugar purchases by other important food industry customers; notably starch; ice-cream, cocoa chocolate and sugar confectionery etc.

In addition, input-output relationships can be inferred from some data in the 1987 MMC report *Tate, Ferruzzi and Berisford* [B.455]. Both British Sugar and Tate & Lyle provide data which enumerate the volume in thousand tonnes white sugar equivalent (WSE) of retail and industrial sales of sugar. Both provide further breakdowns in volume and revenue terms for industrial (dry bulk, liquid, bags) and retail. More directly, the 1981 MMC report on *Berisford and British Sugar* [B.438] gives British Sugar estimates for the uses of industrial sugar. The proportion of industrial sugar sold to a particular industry and the estimated share of sugar in the total material input is found for: chocolate and sugar confectionery; flour and bakery products; ice-cream and milk; canned and frozen food and jams and preserves as noted in section 9.2.2.

9.6 Labour

A substantial amount of labour force information is discussed for the Food industries overall in section 2.6. We summarise here only the most salient treatments for sugar and sugar by-products.

9.6.1 *Official Sources*

The *Employment Gazette* [QRL.186] carries employment data in two annual articles which summarise the results from the Census of Employment for Great Britain and the United Kingdom respectively. The first is in the format of male/female and full-time/part-time Activity Heading breakdowns plus the analysis for employees in employment for the twelve standard regions of Great Britain including Scotland and Wales. The second treats the United Kingdom as a whole for the male/female and full-time/part-time format. It is to be noted for sugar and sugar products that no figure is given for part-time male employment in either case and that the GB figures are identical to the UK figures signalling no activity in Northern Ireland. The annual article in the *Employment Gazette* [QRL.186] also carries the data for the United Kingdom of the average hours worked and average earnings per hour for the male/female, part-time/full-time cross-classification for manual employees at adult rates.

Business Monitor PA420 [QRL.112] includes annual statistics for total employment in the United Kingdom for all establishments classified to the industry. The operating ratio table permits some indication of productivity and labour costs from the gross and net output per head measures, wages and salaries as a percentage of gross value added etc. for the usual five year run. The disclosure difficulties noted in section 9.1 inhibit the usual PA Monitor detail on the size distributions of employment, wages and salaries etc. The size distributions of employment (operative and others) and wages and salaries (operatives and others) and the regional distribution of employment were last given in 1976.

Previous coverage was more detailed, as exemplified in the Census of Production for 1963 and 1968. Size analyses of total numbers employed and of employees and their wages and salaries (operatives and others) were presented as well as a percentage analysis of employees by age and sex. For the larger establishments (employing 25 or more people), employment figures for proprietors, operatives, and other employees were given. Wages and salaries data, both in total and per capita (operatives and others), were separately given for the beet sugar and other sugar subdivisions.

The 1981 Census of Population for Great Britain, *Census 1981: Economic Activity: Great Britain* [QRL.148] specified the total in employment by sex, whether full-time or part-time cross-classified by type of employees (managers, foremen and supervisors (manual and non-manual)) etc. for AH4200. Unlike the annual article in the *Employment Gazette* [QRL.186], full details on part-time employment are given but in the case of "Sugar and sugar by-products" there are no self-employed males and females. Similar data for Scotland are also collected and published in the *Census 1981: Scotland Economic Activity (10% Sample)* [QRL.149].

9.6.2 *Company Reports and Occasional Investigations*

In the light of the paucity of BSO coverage, specialist sources take on an added significance. *British Sugar plc: Annual Report* [QRL.69] gives a global total for the average weekly number of employees, including directors of the group, during the current year and previous year. Other data given include yearly wages and salaries costs, social security costs and other pensions costs, besides the usual size class information in company reports on the emoluments of directors and remuneration of highly paid employees, other than directors. *S & W Berisford plc: Report and Accounts* [QRL.442] also gives employee numbers in British Sugar for the current and previous year. *Tate and Lyle plc: Annual Report* [QRL.479] enumerates the average weekly number of employees in sugar production and refineries in the United Kingdom. This number excludes employees within related companies.

Tate, Ferruzzi and Berisford [B.455] summarises employment data for both Tate & Lyle and British Sugar. For British Sugar in particular, the matter of the period covered is evidently important because employment rises in the "Campaign". Hence the statement that "British Sugar employs 3,900 permanent staff and 1,800 casual employees taken on during the "Campaign"; of these numbers some 4,000 permanent and temporary staff are employed directly in the factories". The year is not specified for these data, but no doubt these figures refer to the position when the evidence to the MMC was submitted. This illustrates the difficulties with the labour figures in *British Sugar plc: Annual Report* [QRL.69] since only various *ad hoc* statements from the company as to casuals employed during the "Campaign", as against permanent employees all year round would, clarify employment patterns. *Tate, Ferruzzi and Berisford* [B.455] also enumerates both total Tate & Lyle employees in the United Kingdom and Tate & Lyle Sugar's employees from 1976 to 1986.

Tate, Ferruzzi and Berisford [B.455] also provides some closer measures of labour productivity than the operating ratio measures in *Business Monitor PA420* [QRL.112] and the earlier work on labour productivity of Bateman [B.13] and Mordue and Marshall [B.127] mentioned in section 2.6.12. Bateman [B.13] in fact analysed beet sugar separately from raw sugar for 1954/58 and 1959/63 given that early Census of Production work split the data this way. Thus the percentage change in labour productivity was calculated.

More recent measures of productivity were provided in [B.455]. The percentage increase in production per employee in beet factories was given between 1978/79 and 1984/85. Calculations were based on the increase in total production (in tonnes WSE) and the fall in the annual average numbers employed from Berisford and British Sugar sources. The MMC were given detailed information on sugar produced per employee beside twelve measures of technical efficiency but only published the changes for the period in percentage terms. This confirms that detailed economic measures of productivity do exist at the level of the firm, even though they are rarely available in the public domain.

9.7 Capital

This section covers data on capital expenditure, details of tangible fixed assets etc. These are separated from other financial information (e.g. profits and return on capital) discussed in section 9.13.

9.7.1 *Capital Expenditure*

Business Monitor PA420 [QRL.112] gives the breakdown of gross capital expenditure by type of asset: land and buildings, plant and machinery and vehicles (all subdivided into acquisitions and disposals for a five-year period). These data are largely reproduced in *Business Monitor PA1002* [QRL.93] whose normal contents are summarised in section 2.7.1.1. But it must be again noted that the coverage of *Business Monitor PA420* [QRL.112] is less detailed for sugar. The analyses of net capital expenditure by size group and standard region have not been given since 1976.

Previous Census of Production inquiries, for instance those of 1963 and 1968, provide the capital expenditure by types of asset breakdown separately for beet sugar and other sugar for establishments employing 25 or more persons.

9.7.2 *Suppliers of Machinery*

More tangentially, *Business Monitor PQ3244: Food. Drink and Tobacco Processing Machinery: Packaging and Bottling Machinery* [QRL.127] used to give the value of imports of machinery for sugar manufacture which represents some capital expenditure. However the data on the sales of sugar-making and refining machinery (excluding centrifuges, including parts) is included in "Grain milling plant".

9.7.3 *Company Reports and Occasional Investigations*

British Sugar plc: Annual Report [QRL.69] summarises the value of tangible assets and the purchase of tangible fixed assets for the latest two years in consolidated balance sheets prepared on a current cost basis. Tangible fixed assets split into freehold land and buildings; plant and machinery (owned and leased); fixtures, fittings, tools and equipment (owned and leased); are given separate valuations at a specific date. Additions, disposals etc are taken into account to arrive at the net book value figure. However, tangible fixed assets are also valued at historic cost. *S & W Berisford plc: Report and Accounts* [QRL.442] produce tangible assets data for the group as a whole. A separate figure (for the latest two years) for capital employed in British Sugar is identified.

Tate and Lyle: Annual Report [QRL.479] presents information for the latest two years on tangible fixed assets and capital expenditure. The tangible fixed assets data for the latest year separately identify the following: land and buildings; bulk liquid storage (including molasses storage); plant and machinery; and assets in course of construction. The accounts are mainly prepared on an historic cost basis as distinct from those of British Sugar and S & W Berisford which are dominantly current cost. The detailed definitions and footnotes in all these annual reports merit careful scrutiny.

Official investigations of the industry have generated much data of interest, drawing together information from the companies for purposes of comparison. The appendices of *Tate, Ferruzzi and Berisford* [B.455] give summarised balance-sheet and sources-and-applications-of-funds data for British Sugar, S & W Berisford and Tate & Lyle. Annual data on tangible fixed assets, capital employed and the purchase of tangible fixed assets can be compared for a number of years (usually 1980–1985) on an historic cost basis. The text gives more specific information including capital expenditure by British Sugar and Tate & Lyle Sugar. The analysis for Tate & Lyle gives capital expenditure for the four locations of Thames, Plaistow, Millwall and Westburn. Comparative data on average capital employed and average net assets (historic cost, plus revaluation of certain fixed assets) are given for British Sugar, S & W Berisford and the Tate & Lyle group.

The earlier *Berisford and British Sugar* [B.438] in 1981 provided data on additions to fixed assets etc in the flow-of-funds statements for both companies. Descriptions of capital investment programmes, statistically illustrated, are a feature of both [B.438] and [B.455].

9.8 International Transactions

This section deals predominantly with exports and imports and may be consulted along with the more detailed section 2.8.

9.8.1 *HM Customs and Excise Records*

The main data source is the monthly *Business Monitor MM20: Overseas Trade Statistics of the United Kingdom* [QRL.85]. The usual details of the volume and value of exports and imports for each month and the monthly cumulative totals etc. are provided.

As usual, the annual *Business Monitor MA21: Guide to the Classification for Overseas Trade Statistics* [B.213] catalogues the detailed commodity treatment of the

SITC(R3). This is important as sugar cane etc. is a primary input (see section 9.5). Division 06 "Sugar, sugar preparations and honey" distinguishes beet from cane and identifies a range of processed products as follows:

061.11 Cane sugar, raw, in solid form, not containing added flavouring or colouring matter.
061.12 Beet sugar, raw, in solid form not containing added flavouring or colouring matter.
061.21 Beet or cane sugar and chemically pure sucrose in solid form, containing added flavouring or colouring matter.
061.29 Beet or cane sugar and chemically pure sucrose in solid form, not elsewhere specified.
061.51 Cane molasses resulting from the extraction or refining of sugar.
061.59 Beet sugar molasses and other molasses (e.g. corn molasses) resulting from the extraction or refining of sugar.
061.6 Natural honey.
061.91 Lactose and lactose syrup.
061.92 Maple sugar and maple syrup.
061.93 Glucose (dextrose) and glucose syrup not containing in the dry state less than 20 per cent by weight of fructose.
061.94 Glucose and glucose syrup, containing, in the dry state, at least 20 per cent but not more than 50 per cent by weight of fructose.
061.95 Pure fructose.
061.96 Other fructose and fructose syrup containing in the dry state more than 50 per cent by weight of fructose.
061.99 Other sugars (including invert sugar), syrups and sugar products of heading 061.90, nes.
062.1 Fruits, nuts, fruit peel and other parts of plants, preserved by sugar and other sweetening matter.
062.21 Chewing gum, whether or not sugar-coated.
062.29 Sugar confectionery, nes.

The index to [QRL.85] or [B.213] is worth consulting. There are finer classifications down to nine digits separating, for instance, raw cane and beet sugar for refining and other. However, we also note that 054.87 sugar beet, fresh or dried, whether or not ground, and 054.88 sugar cane, fresh or dried, whether or not ground, are placed under Division 05 "Vegetables and fruit".

Business Monitor PQ216 [QRL.123] summarised the value and volume in annual and quarterly terms of the major items extracted from the *Overseas Trade Statistics* [QRL.85]. Sugars, beet and cane (including dried sugar beet); refined sugars; molasses; other sugars; flavoured and coloured sugar syrups; beet, pulp, bagasse and other waste of sugar manufacture; were the selected groupings in this PQ Monitor. As noted in section 9.1, this ran only from the first quarter of 1973 to the third quarter of 1980.

United Kingdom Trade with European Countries [QRL.508] and the succeeding *UK External Trade: Area × Commodity Analysis* [QRL.494] have a more aggregative treatment. They give annual data in terms of value for Division 06 for exports (fob), imports (cif), exports less imports and the percentage of exports and imports for specified countries, trading areas etc.

The *Monthly Digest of Statistics* [QRL.362] gives the latest two years, the last two quarters and three monthly value figures for Division 06 etc. and compares the cumulative values from the beginning of the year with the same period in the previous year. The *Annual Abstract of Statistics* [QRL.37] reports the eleven-year value figures for Division 06 etc. for exports and imports.

9.8.2 *Industry Analyses of Trade*

Business Monitor MQ10: Overseas Trade Analysed in Terms of Industries [QRL.90] and its predecessor *Business Monitor M10* [QRL.77] provide quarterly and annual data in terms of value for imports and exports for this Group. *Business Monitor MQ12: Import Penetration and Export Sales Ratios for Manufacturing Industry* [QRL.91] and the preceding *Business Monitor M12* [QRL.78] of the same title present the calculations of the import penetration and export performance ratios. Since sugar is not now covered by the Quarterly Sales Inquiries, sales of principal products have been estimated using the Annual Census of Production, the Index of Production and Producer Price Indices. Thus the results for this Group may be even less precise than for the others we have covered.

9.8.3 *Occasional Investigations*

The coverage of export and import flows is complicated both by Commonwealth links and latterly by membership of the EC (see also section 9.3). The MMC report in 1981 on *Berisford and British Sugar* [B.438] enumerated the volume (in WSE) of CSA cane and Commonwealth "frees" compared with UK beet production and demand for 1956/57, 1966/67, 1970/71, 1971/72 and 1972/73. A further analysis from 1977/78 to 1979/80 combined MAFF sources and this MMC inquiry to give total EC imports into the United Kingdom and Berisford's EC imports both in total and as a proportion to the total etc. for the later years running from 1977/78 to 1979/80. The imports of merchants and brokers were contrasted with Berisford's EC imports. All data are in volume terms.

Tate, Ferruzzi and Berisford [B.455] uses illustrative statistics in this major review of the sugar market. The percentage of imports as compared with British Sugar and Tate & Lyle deliveries are given for 1972/73, 1979/80, 1983, 1984 and 1985. The text also carries illustrative statistics for the following: volume imports into the United Kingdom from other Community countries, the tonnage of white granulated imports into the United Kingdom, (information derived from merchants and MAFF) and some indication of the size of direct consumption speciality sugars from the ACP countries. These data were usually for 1985.

9.9 Stocks

9.9.1 *Ministry of Agriculture, Fisheries and Food Inquiries*

The *Monthly Digest of Statistics* [QRL.362] provides data on end-of-period stocks in physical terms as noted in section 2.9.1. These statistics are summarised from MAFF and BSO sources. Stocks include both imported and home-produced supplies of refined and raw sugar (in terms of refined). The *Annual Abstract of Statistics* [QRL.37] includes sugar in the table of recorded stocks at year-end, including stocks in bond or held by the main processors, as noted in section 2.9.1.

9.9.2 *Business Statistics Office Inquiries*
Stocks and work in progress for "Sugar and sugar by-products" are presented in value terms in *Business Monitor PA420* [QRL.112]. Changes over a five-year period in value terms are shown and the value at the end of the latest available year given. The three-part disaggregation into materials; stores and fuel; work-in-progress and goods on hand for sale; is presented.

The earlier Census of Production data for the years 1954, 1958, 1963 and 1968 gave the change during the year and end-of-year value figures for the "beet sugar" and "other sugar" subdivisions.

Computations for the latest five years for the ratio of gross output to stocks are given in the operating ratios table. Similar information can be found in the summary tables in *Business Monitor PA1002* [QRL.93]. A full catalogue of the BSO inquiries is given in section 2.9.2. Thus the statistics embrace many concepts and the goods on hand for sale figures reflect not only refined sugar but the various by-products classified to this Group.

9.9.3 *Industry Sources*
The concept of stocks is important in assessing both supplies and price hence estimates of stocks are featured in many publications. MAFF is the original fount of the data which are communicated to the European Commission and in turn passed on to the ISO of which the European Community is a member. In what follows, the measures are expressed as raw value in beet terms. This means using conversion factors to convert beet white, cane whites and cane raws into the figures for raw value in beet terms.

The *Statistical Bulletin* [QRL.459] defines stocks "as the sum total of all stocks of sugar held by country or territories in sugar factories, refineries and port facilities and, where this can be ascertained, in warehouses". Both [QRL.459] and the *Sugar Year Book* [QRL.473] identified beginning and closing stocks for the United Kingdom up to 1972. But since then, these statistics are given for the EC as a whole.

F.O. Licht's International Sugar Report [QRL.199] is a well known source and its quarterly supplement *World Sugar Balances* [QRL.521] gives runs of monthly data for many years on opening stocks, end stocks and supplies/deficit stocks expressed as raw values. Stocks are part of the discussions on sugar balances summarised in this chapter in section 9.11.

9.10 Consumption

9.10.1 *The National Food Survey*

Household Food Consumption and Expenditure [QRL.267] gives estimates of the quarterly and annual national averages for household consumption and purchases in the supplementary tables. Sugar is itemised separately from the following products which have high sugar content: syrup and treacle; jams, jellies and fruit curds; marmalade; honey. A global total for sugar and preserves is given. The further analyses according to income group, household composition and for responding households with head of household unemployed, do consider sugar separately from honey, preserves, syrup and treacle (the latter being all put together). In other analyses, however, sugar is not separately specified.

Thus the finest classification sees sugar itemised separately from syrup and treacle. Sugar is still treated separately from other sugar-related items in the main food group results. It is, however, lumped into the category "sugar and preserves" in the treatment of selected food items. Whence the tripartite split noted in section 2.10.1.2 (food codes, main food groups, selected food items) does not give exhaustive detail for sugar, which is not subdivided further (e.g. white granulated, brown etc.). Nor are there indications of sugar content in meals consumed outside the home in catering, canteen and snacks etc. nor in the consumption of cakes, biscuits etc.

National Food Survey: Compendium of Results [QRL.373] incorporates further analyses of consumption by main food groups according to region; type of area; household income; household composition within income groups; age of housewife; housing tenure; and comparisons of households which are freezer-owning with other households. Before 1985, these data were largely covered in the tables and appendices of *Household Food Consumption and Expenditure* [QRL.267].

Some of the *Household Food Consumption and Expenditure* [QRL.267] data are summarised in other sources. The *Annual Abstract of Statistics* [QRL.37] gives estimates of consumption for all households in Great Britain in ounces per person per week for the eleven-year run, treating sugar separately from preserves. *Social Trends* [QRL.456] includes sugar as an item in the "indices of average quantities per person per week of consumption in the home of selected foods in Great Britain" for a number of years. *Regional Trends* [QRL.401] gives the household consumption of, and expenditure on, main foods — thus sugar is treated with preserves. The data are in quantity and pence per person per week expressed as averages for the latest two years and presented for Great Britain, the English standard regions and England, Wales and Scotland separately.

9.10.2 *The Family Expenditure Survey*

A detailed description of the *Family Expenditure Survey* [QRL.204] is given in section 2.10.2. The expenditure data separately itemises sugar from syrup, honey, jam, marmalade etc. These data are cross-classified by levels of household income; for one adult households by levels of income, sex and age; by levels of household income for households with and without children and according to region.

9.10.3 *The National Accounts*

The *United Kingdom National Accounts* [QRL.506] provides consumers' expenditure by function in both current and 1980 prices as further explained in section 2.10.3. Sugar is itemised separately from preserves and confectionery.

9.10.4 *Occasional Investigations*
National consumption statistics are assembled in the work on sugar balances (see section 9.11). The 1981 MMC report *Berisford and British Sugar* [B.438] gives consumption statistics in thousand tonnes WSE for 1977/78 to 1979/80 in the summary of the domestic demand for sugar (net of sugar traded in manufactured foodstuffs) from MAFF sources. *Tate, Ferruzzi and Berisford* [B.455] summarises the production and consumption of sugar for the Community ten, drawing on an MMC study from European Commission data. This shows UK consumption as well as the difference between production and consumption and the difference between "A" and "B2" quota production and consumption.

9.11 Supplies and Disposals

The concepts of domestic supplies, supply balance sheets, disposals and self-sufficiency have been reviewed in section 2.11. We pinpoint the following with respect to sugar noting the connections with section 9.5.1.

The *Annual Review of Agriculture* [QRL.51] (and from 1989, *Agriculture in the United Kingdom*) takes into account domestic production of sugar from beet and imports and exports to arrive at annual and forecast figures for total new supply and production as a percentage of total new supply in the United Kingdom (in terms of 1000 tonnes refined basis). Non- quota sugar brought forward from the previous year counts towards the production quota but not as "new supply" in the current year. The import and export figures include only sugar as such and take no account of the sugar content of processed products. Up to 1987, *Output and Utilisation* [QRL.382] concentrated on the estimated production and utilisation of sugar beet in the United Kingdom as already noted in section 9.5.1.

The *Monthly Digest of Statistics* [QRL.362] gives monthly data for sugar (as refined) both in terms of disposals and for food in the United Kingdom. The disposals figures includes the use of sugar as an input into the processing of other foods (e.g. sugar in jam and biscuits etc.) and are adjusted by the net trade sugar contained in processed products. The *Annual Abstract of Statistics* [QRL.37] gives both the figures for total disposals and for food in the United Kingdom on an annual basis. The latter includes sugar used in the manufacture of other foods subsequently exported but excludes sugar in imported manufactured foods. A separate table carries the estimates of the supply per head of population in kgs per year. These include the sugar content of imported maufactured foods but exclude sugar used in the production of alcoholic drink.

As indicated in section 9.9 on stocks and section 9.12 on prices, there is considerable statistical interest in the relationship between supply and demand and sugar balances. This is reflected in both official and private sector publications as follows. The MAFF co-ordinate data on exports, imports, consumption, opening and closing stocks etc. which are communicated to the European Commission and the ISO. The *Statistical Bulletin* [QRL.459] and the *Sugar Year Book* [QRL.473] estimate annual total supply as beginning-stocks, production and imports. Total distribution is defined as consumption, exports and ending-stocks. These data are provided for the European Community and for the United Kingdom up to 1972. *World Sugar*

Balances [QRL.521] estimates the sugar balance for the United Kingdom and the countries of the world by considering opening stocks, output, imports, "disappear" (ie. consumption etc.), exports and stocks, giving monthly data for many years. *The Czarnikow Sugar Review* [QRL.168] gives more aggregated data for yearly production and consumption and the difference in raw value. The publications of E.D.&F. Man (Sugar) Limited *The Sugar Situation* [QRL.472] and the *World Sugar Situation and Outlook* [QRL.522], serve similar functions, combining statistics of sugar balances with discussions of factors influencing production and consumption in world markets. *F.O. Licht's World Sugar Statistics* [QRL.200] includes world sugar balances by countries in 1000 tonnes raw value. These comprise initial stocks, production, imports, consumption, exports and final stocks.

9.12 Prices

9.12.1 *Agricultural and Commodity Prices*

9.12.1.1 Official sources

Agricultural Statistics: United Kingdom [QRL.32] records the yearly-average prices of sugar beet delivered to factory in £ per tonne. This estimated average price paid to growers in the United Kingdom by British Sugar plc is based on the estimated sugar content of beet which varies from year to year (e.g. 18.1 per cent in 1986).

The *Annual Review of Agriculture* [QRL.51] gives the annual producer price paid by British Sugar plc to growers in £ per tonne. For some years the figure is provisional because it may exclude "C" beet payments and so may be subject to modification for "C" sugar production carried over into the current year. From 1989, the coverage is continued in *Agriculture in the United Kingdom.*

9.12.1.2 Commercial sources

Minimum prices are controlled by the European Community as explained in section 9.3 but there are a range of sources which report the world prices of this internationally traded commodity. Most accessible is the *Financial Times* [QRL.218] which reports futures (raw and white sugar) prices actively traded on the London FOX (Futures and Options Exchange). Many specialist publications report the price traded on international markets, in Paris and New York as well as London.

It must be noted for all sources that prices are usually given according to type of contract. For instance the raw and white sugar contracts in London are respectively the no.6 Contract and the no.5 Contract. White sugar is traded in Paris on the no.2 Contract. New York raw sugar contracts are the no.11 Contract and the no.14 Contract. Details of these different types of contracts may be found in [QRL.199] and [QRL.251]. We now devote a few short paragraphs to the many organisations presently or formerly involved.

F.O. Licht's International Sugar Report [QRL.199] gives daily world spot and futures prices for London raw and white, Paris white, New York, raw and white, Hong Kong and the ISO price. Price premiums and discounts are given for all the contracts.

Gill & Duffus: Sugar Market Report [QRL.251] gave monthly highs and lows for raw sugar market prices in New York (Contract no.11) and London (Contract

No.6). Monthly high and lows were given for white sugar market prices in London (Contract no.5) and in Paris (Contract no.2). [QRL.251], however, ceased to appear after September 1989.

Woodhouse Drake and Carey (Commodities) Limited [QRL.519] was a weekly commentary on the sugar market. The section on the sugar futures markets included sugar futures market values for London raw and white sugar contracts, the New York No.11 Contract and the Paris white sugar market.

The Reuter Sugar Newsletter [QRL.437] gave prices for London Sugar futures including the White Sugar no.5, the London daily sugar price, the ISO daily price and the Tate & Lyle refined export price. It also provided information on the Paris White Sugar Futures market, New York Sugar and the London Sugar Futures Contract no.6. As [QRL.437] was published daily and had a range of commentary as well as price information, it was regarded as an important and timely source. Even though the last issue of [QRL.437] appeared on 30 April 1990, the information is presently available in another form. The previous days' news and prices appear as real time information on both screen and printer for subscribers. Historical data and news are also obtainable from Reuter's sources.

The Czarnikow Sugar Review [QRL.168] has an attachment which includes the London daily price for raws and the daily ISO prices. The text also reports the settlement prices published by the International Commodities Clearing House (ICCH) each Monday for the past four weeks. Raw sugar (no.6) and white sugar (no.5) are included for London and raw sugar (nos.11 and 14) are given for New York.

The Sugar Situation [QRL.472] by E.D.& F. Man, generally more descriptive than statistical, gives raw sugar and white sugar transactional prices with buyer, origin of sugar, quantity and shipment date.

Bulletin Statistique du FIRS [QRL.72] reports the monthly average spot prices for the Paris market (white sugar) and for London and New York (raw sugar). The annual *La Campagne Sucrière* [QRL.303] also reports monthly averages for spot prices.

Evidently, most of these sources provide commentary and data on production, consumption, exports, imports and stocks etc. in order to portray the main market features which influence price determination.

We have focused on the specialist sugar sources in this section. But as an internationally traded commodity, sugar naturally features in the many commodity price guides already noted in section 2.12.1.2. The treatment in *The Public Ledger & Daily Freight Register* [QRL.392] can be reiterated. This covers the London FOX closing prices for raw sugar no.6 Contract, white sugar no.5 Contract together with the turnover in the number of lots. Closing prices in the Paris White Sugar market are recorded and the Indicator Prices section gives London Daily White Prices, London Daily Raw Price, International Sugar Agreement daily price and Tate & Lyle export price. *The Public Ledger's Commodity Week* [QRL.394] features both London and New York in the international futures daily price section for the previous five week-days. It reports the weekly price trend compared with last week and last year for London Daily Price (LDP) raw sugar.

9.12.2 *Retail Prices*

9.12.2.1 Recorded prices

The *Employment Gazette* [QRL.186] gives monthly average retail prices for granulated sugar per kg together with the price range within which 80 per cent of the quotations fell. The number of price quotations taken for this standard item in the United Kingdom is also given.

Household Food Consumption and Expenditure [QRL.267] reports average prices paid for sugar for the last three years. The demand analyses include income and own-price elasticities for sugar and preserves combined. In its old (pre-1985) format, *Household Food Consumption and Expenditure* [QRL.267] carried quarterly, as well as annual average prices, for the year in question.

9.12.2.2 Recommended prices

The Grocer [QRL.252] provides each week a wide range of data on sugar in the market prices section. This includes the list price of British Sugar grocery and catering sugars, bagged sugar and bulk sugars. The information on Tate & Lyle is split into the various domestic and catering products, manufacturing packs and bulk tankers. These data are intended as a guide to the prices at which supplies can be obtained on the open market but are subject to regional variation and sometimes discounting.

The Grocer Price List [QRL.253] usually indicates both trade and retail prices, but given the extensive trade price coverage in *The Grocer* [QRL.252], there is no separate section on sugar. However, the trade and retail prices of various brands of sweeteners and the trade prices of syrup are listed.

Shaws Guide to Fair Retail Prices [QRL.453] gives considerable detail in the Sugar sector of a wide range of products in its guide to fair selling prices. The same can be said about syrup (e.g. Lyle's Golden and Dark, Whitworth's Golden Syrup).

9.12.3 *The Retail Prices Index*

The *Employment Gazette* [QRL.186] includes sugar and preserves as one of the food items in the Retail Prices Index. Percentage changes over the month and previous twelve months are given. The data and the weights are also featured in the *Monthly Digest of Statistics* [QRL.362].

9.12.4 *Price Index Numbers in the National Food Survey*

In its pre-1985 format, *Household Food Consumption and Expenditure* [QRL.267] gave indices of expenditure, prices, real value of food purchased and the total real value of consumption. Sugar is treated on its own as Food Code 150 but is obviously also an input into preserves etc. The annual indices of average deflated prices, purchases and demand also relate to sugar with no further breakdown. These indices relate to the most recent six years expressed as an average of 100.

Since 1985, the index number information is located in the *Compendium of Results* [QRL.373]. This applies to the annual data for the indices of prices for the main food groups, and the indices of the real value of purchases and the total real value of consumption.

9.12.5 *Producer Price Index Numbers*
The series of Producer Price Index Numbers is considered in general terms in section 2.12.5. Details of the price indices for sugar and sugar-by products are given below.

9.12.5.1 Producer price index numbers: input prices
Business Monitor MM22: Producer Price Indices carries the producer price index of materials and fuels purchased for AH4200, carrying both monthly and annual data. The monthly data are given for the current and previous year, with the figures for the latest two months provisional. An annual average for the previous year is also presented. *Business Monitor MM22* was published for the first time in October 1989 and continued the coverage in *British Business* [QRL.66].

9.12.5.2 Producer price index numbers: output prices
Business Monitor MM22 Producer Price Indices contains the producer price index numbers of products manufactured in the United Kingdom (home sales) for AH4200. The monthly data are provided for the current and previous year, with the figures for the latest two months provisional. An annual average for the previous year is also presented. *Business Monitor MM22* continued the coverage of *British Business* [QRL.66]. The *Annual Abstract of Statistics* [QRL.37] gives the annual averages for AH4200 for a five-year run for commodities produced in the United Kingdom (home sales).

9.12.6 *Export and Import Prices*
The Reuter Sugar Newsletter [QRL.437] gave the Tate & Lyle refined export price. *The Public Ledger & Daily Freight Register* [QRL.392] includes the Tate & Lyle export prices in the indicator prices section.

9.12.7 *Prices and Government Regulation*
Some price information has appeared in official investigations. The 1975 Price Commission report on *Food Prices in Outlying Areas* [B.421] included granulated white Tate & Lyle 2lbs sugar in this comparison of food prices in outlying areas with the more central areas. The 1977 Price Commission's *Metrication and Retail Prices (First Report): Granulated Sugar, Biscuits, Dried Vegetables and Salt* [B.423] included both Tate & Lyle and BSC "Silverspoon" in the comparison of prices one month before, during, and four months after, metrication. Appropriate monetary conversions were made.

The price of cane raws, beet raws and world prices are an important background to the 1978 Price Commission Report on *Tate and Lyle* [B.434]. Yearly price comparisons were made from 1974 through to 1978. This investigation touched on the rationalisation of the UK cane sugar industry as well as whether notified price increases were justified.

An increased understanding of pricing mechanisms may be gleaned from the 1981 MMC report on *Berisford and British Sugar* [B.438]. British Sugar's marketing strategy is described and determinants of prices are discussed. In particular, there is the distinction between "true merchanting" and "nominal merchanting". The latter means that the merchant processes the orders, invoices the customers and collects payments. He is given a flat rate per tonne allowance by the refiner. The former means the purchase of sugar by the merchant on his own account from United Kingdom and/or foreign sources before the subsequent resale (after storage, rebagging etc.) to the end user. This report gives an increased understanding of the role of the middlemen. Tonnages and shares of quantities merchanted in the two ways were revealed rather than any price and discount detail given.

Like [B.438], the 1987 MMC report *Tate, Ferruzzi and Berisford* [B.455] gives insights into the complexities of prices, including the European dimensions already discussed in section 9.3. Included are annual figures from 1981/82 to 1985/86 which compared the CAP effective support price (United Kingdom) with the world price from an MMC study. These were followed by comparison of margins for beet refining and ACP sugar cane refining in the United Kingdom. The whole merchanting structure in the United Kingdom is again described, the degree of price competition between British Sugar and Tate & Lyle studied and the influence of imported supplies considered. An assessment of price changes, if a merger were to go through, were attempted. However, hard statistics on the differences between British Sugar and Tate & Lyle prices after taking account of discounts and including delivery are not revealed.

9.13 Financial Information

9.13.1 *Company Reports*

The most evident data sources are the annual company reports. *British Sugar plc: Annual Report* [QRL.69] carries a host of salient figures beginning with annual data on turnover and profit before tax etc. The consolidated statement of profit and loss includes turnover, gross profit, operating profit, earnings per share, retained profit etc. for the current and preceding year. Other financial information is included in the consolidated balance sheet, the consolidated statement of sources and application of funds and the consolidated statement of value added. Additional information includes turnover separately itemised for sugar. The accounts are mainly prepared on the basis of current cost accounting. Summary data are provided for the past five years as published on turnover, profit before tax, profit before tax/turnover etc. as well as a series adjusted to 1987 prices. *S & W Berisford plc Report and Accounts* [QRL.442] is more concerned with group profit and turnover etc. but does provide separate data on food and separate summary data on profit and turnover for British Sugar.

Tate and Lyle: Annual Report [QRL.479] records turnover and profit data for the current and previous year in the group profit and loss account. Other group financial information appears in the balance sheets and statement of sources and application of funds. Turnover and profit before taxation is analysed according to class of business which separately identifies sugar production and refining in the United Kingdom, cereal sweeteners and starches, sugar trading, molasses and speciality feeds and malting etc. The separate section on Tate & Lyle Sugars contrasts the sugar and the sweetener production contributions to group profit.

Precise comparisons of financial variables is complicated because sugar is the major but not the only interest of British Sugar and Tate & Lyle. Furthermore, British Sugar accounts are mainly prepared using current cost accounting whereas Tate & Lyle use the historic cost convention as noted in section 9.7.3. However *British Sugar plc: Annual Report* [QRL.69] carries an alternative series for turnover and profit, capital employed and earnings and dividends (including return on capital employed) based on historic cost financial information.

9.13.2 *Occasional Investigations*

Substantial financial information and analyses have been an integral part of official investigations of the sugar sector. The 1987 MMC report on *Tate, Ferruzzi and Berisford* [B.455] is the most recent and most exhaustive of these. The appendices collect together summarised balance sheets, profit and loss accounts, statements of source and application of funds etc from British Sugar, Berisford and Tate & Lyle accounts besides European data from the Ferruzzi and Béghin-Say group etc. Thus turnover, profit etc. can be compared for a number of years, usually from 1980/81 through 1984/85. The text carries further data including the following:

- Returns on average capital employed and net tangible assets 1980/81 to 1984/85 (historical costs, plus revaluations of certain fixed assets) for British Sugar, Berisford and Tate & Lyle.
- Contributions to British Sugar's turnover by sugar, molasses and animal feeds.
- Turnover and profit before taxation for the Tate & Lyle group identifying sugar production and refining in the United Kingdom, sugar trading, molasses, cereal sweeteners and malting etc. The percentage contribution of each compared to turnover and profit is computed for the latest year.

Much further attention is paid to the beet processing margin and the ACP cane refining margin which were both published on p.10 of [B.455]. But the UK sugar producers' profit margins for bulk dry sugar, bulk liquid sugar and 1 kg packs are not published. The same applies to Tate & Lyle's margin over the UK effective support price and Tate & Lyle Sugar's financial performance. The general perception was that British Sugar's profitability was superior to that of Tate & Lyle in bulk dry sugar etc. although disclosure difficulties prevented the publication of sensitive profit information. The technical discussion in [B.455] in any case emphasised the difficulties of comparing rates of return on capital given the different sets of accounting methods used.

The 1981 MMC report on *Berisford and British Sugar* [B.438] also contains financial information in this MMC investigation of the proposed acquisition of British Sugar by S & W Berisford. Full summaries of turnover and profits etc. and the financial accounts based on historic costs are appended for Berisford (1974/75 to 1978/79) and British Sugar (1974/75 to 1979/80). Information in the text includes financial portraits of British Sugar including the return on average capital employed, profit before taxation etc. The S & W Berisford data include operating profit and a geographical and divisional analysis (i.e. processing, merchanting etc) of turnover and pre-tax profits. Berisford's accounts stemmed from its activities as a more diversified merchanting group of which international sugar trading, rather than processing, was the dominant activity.

Tate and Lyle [B.434] was the 1978 Price Commission report which followed the notified price increases by Tate & Lyle. It included data on capital employed, profit before taxation and percentage returns on capital employed from a study prepared by Price Waterhouse Company for the years ending September 1975 to September 1977.

9.14 Advertising and Market Research

9.14.1 *Advertising*

The advertising expenditure on sugar is not spectacular. Tate & Lyle and British Sugar are well known and the market is mature. Nevertheless the *Tri-Media Digest of Brands and Advertisers* [QRL.493] is the major source as discussed in section 2.14.1. Data are found in the F92 category entitled Sugar. Alternative sweeteners (Sweetex etc) can be located in category R70 under Slimming aids. Advertising campaigns for speciality sugars are reflected in the *Tri-Media Digest* [QRL.493] figures. Advertising is much heavier in the products which are heavily sugar related: e.g. (F70) Ice-cream and lollies; (F72) Jams, preserves and mincemeat; (F32) Chocolate confectionery; (F93) Sugar confectionery etc. Many brand names are featured here.

The monthly publication, *The Media Register* [QRL.354] has an explicit recognition of the interdependence of the sweetener market in its category (FOO 74) Sugar and artificial sweeteners. Here comparative advertising spending on sugar (e.g. Billington sugar) and artificial sweeteners (e.g. Hermesetas Gold Tablets) may be compared. Syrups are covered under (FOO 54) Jams and preserves.

This account does not cover the media commentary, favourable or otherwise, on sugar. British Sugar has been mounting a national campaign (e.g. Silver Spoon). Tate & Lyle have featured the well-known "Mr. Cube". Of the sugar-based products, Tate & Lyle's Golden Syrup and Treacles have been prominent in women's magazines (eg. Woman's Own and Women's Realm) so the level of promotion recorded in *Tri-Media Digest* [QRL.493] etc. may well be an underestimate of the amount of publicity.

9.14.2 *Market Research*

The British Sugar Report [QRL.70] has already been referred to in section 9.2.4. However, it also describes advertising strategy with particular reference to the Silver Spoon brand. The many sugar products which are marketed are listed. The total sugar market is analysed in terms of value. The percentage annual breakdown in market share of Silver Spoon, Tate & Lyle, Billington, Whitworth holdings and own-label is reported from independent research. The sugar market is separately categorised for speciality sugars, subdivided into caster, golden granulated, brown, demerara, icing and others. *The British Sugar Report* [QRL.70] is particularly devoted to the marketing aspects of sugar but both *S & W Berisford plc: Report and Accounts* [QRL.442] and *Tate and Lyle: Annual Report* [QRL.479] review and assess the prospects for sugars and alternative sweeteners.

The July 1987 issue of *Market Intelligence* [QRL.339] addresses the markets for sugar and artificial sweeteners together. This demonstrates the growing perception that these two product groups satisfy the consumer's desire for sweetened foodstuffs. The sugar section reviews market size and trends, companies and brands, consumer profiles and advertising and promotion. The artificial sweeteners section reviews types of sweeteners, market size and trends, companies and brands, distribution, the consumer and advertising and promotion. The latter, in contrast to sugar, is heavily promoted.

The September 1986 issue of *Food Market Updates* [QRL.238] entitled "Sweeteners in the UK" gives a statistically-backed description of this market. Derivative data on sugar dominate. However artificial sweeteners (the table top market), artificial sweeteners as food ingredients (low calorie soft drinks, low calorie beverages, reduced calorie yoghurt) and honey are all considered. The Leatherhead Food Research Association acknowledges sources used and includes its own estimates.

The earlier Key Note report in May 1982 entitled *Sugar* [QRL.599] gave a clear statistically-supported description of industry structure. Market size and trends (including the UK sweetener market shares, uses of industrial sugar etc), market developments and future prospects were given. Financial appraisals and summaries of Tate & Lyle and British Sugar reported accounts were appended.

Given that the sugar market is at best static, market research reports are generally less numerous for sugar than the other sectors covered in this Review. But both [QRL.339] and [QRL.599] contain concise market overviews which carry shorter summaries of market structure than the *ad hoc* studies drawn upon in section 9.2.

9.15 Research and Development

Tate and Lyle: Annual Report [QRL.479] gives a global annual figure for expenditure by this group on R&D. In accordance with group accounting policies, this amount was charged to the profit and loss account. A general description is also given of the research facilities at Reading University (the Philip Lyle Memorial Research Laboratory). The concentration here is on technical services and products and process development for operating businesses as well as strategic research. Sweeteners and sweetener-related product research is of major importance. The 1987 Report comments on the development of sucralose for the speciality sweeteners division. The 1987 MMC report on *Tate, Ferruzzi and Berisford* [B.455] also describes research activities. It reported (paragraph S.22) that an average of £3m annually had been spent during 1976–1986.

British Sugar plc: Annual Report [QRL.69] gives annual figures for expenditure on R&D for the current and preceding year. All such expenditures are charged to the group profit and loss account. *Tate, Ferruzzi and Berisford* [B.455] also gives British

Sugar expenditure on R&D. The statistics from 1980/81 to 1985/86 (estimated) come with some specific comments in the footnotes which illustrate the difficulties in defining and measuring R&D as discussed in section 2.15. The figures given on p.43 range from £1.24m spent for 1980/81 to an estimated £2.45m for 1985/86. These figures exclude most of the expenditure on improving process efficiency (about £0.5m to £0.75m annually) because of the difficulty of distinguishing this from expenditure on the capital investment programme. The figures also exclude expenditure on product development by the Marketing Department as this is not classified as R&D. Finally, some of British Sugar's research activities — for instance at the Agricultural Research Institute, Norwich — are devoted to the improvement of beet varieties and thus basic scientific research applied to agriculture.

Hence the existing data on research spending are probably underestimates of total research activity. Furthermore, they do not include outright acquisition of other companies (eg. in the biotechnology field) evidently an example of direct purchase of R&D.

9.16 Official Investigations

Reference has been made to the following official reports in this chapter. In particular, extensive use has been made of the two MMC reports.

Reports of the Price Commission under the Counter Inflation Act 1973

Report no.10 — (1975) *Food prices in Outlying Areas* [B.421]

Report no.25 — (1977) *Metrication and Retail Prices (First Report): Granulated Sugar, Biscuits, Dried Vegetables and Salt* [B.423]

Investigation Report of the Price Commission

Report no.6 — (Session 1977/78) *Tate and Lyle Refineries Ltd. — Sugar and Syrup Products* [B.434]

Reports of the Monopolies and Mergers Commission

(Session 1980/81) — *S and W Berisford Limited and British Sugar Corporation Limited. A Report on the Proposed Merger* [B.438]

(Session 1987/88) — *Tate and Lyle plc and Ferruzzi Finanziaria Spa and S and W Berisford plc: A Report on the Existing and Proposed Mergers* [B.455]

9.17 Improvements and Comments

The statistical coverage of Group 420 is quite problematic because of the existence of the virtual duopoly of British Sugar and Tate & Lyle. Hence there is a restricted coverage in *Business Monitor PA420* [QRL.112]. There is, for example, no cross-classification by the employment size distribution. Furthermore, the coverage in the Business Monitor PQ series for Sugar ceased long before the general reduction in PQ coverage in mid-1989 following the *Review of DTI Statistics* [B.367]. In addition, and quite exceptionally, the results of the 1985 Topping-up Inquiry are not even made publicly available. As noted in section 9.1 and other sections of this chapter, disclosure was not so inhibited in the past when statistics for "sugar beet" and "other sugars" used to be given separately. Consequently, there is an unusual reliance in this chapter on official *ad hoc* sources and the published accounts of the major companies.

Of the statistics published, there are some notable shortcomings which could be more easily addressed. First, sugar consumption statistics, in for instance *Household Food Consumption and Expenditure* [QRL.267], are worthy of greater disaggregation given the concern about "pure, white and deadly" expressed by Yudkin [B.193] amongst others. Given the importance of brown sugar and the product differentiation into speciality sugars, there could be some additional coverage here as well. *The British Sugar Report* [QRL.70] notes only the value of the speciality sugar market and does not give consumption per head figures.

Secondly, the seasonality of the "Campaign" would render employment data more meaningful for British Sugar if there were available two sets of employment statistics for the peak as distinct from the off-peak months. Thirdly, as noted in section 9.13, British Sugar accounts are mainly prepared using the current cost accounting method whereas Tate & Lyle use the historic cost convention. There is limited movement towards consistency and comparability given that *British Sugar plc: Annual Report* [QRL.69] contained some data based on historic cost. The 1987 MMC report *Tate, Ferruzzi and Berisford* [B.455] was also able to make some comparisons of the financial components. A purist may say that the current cost convention should ideally be used in all circumstances.

The sugar trade is complex, stretching from the agricultural management of sugar beet farms and cane plantations through to the advanced chemistry of sugar and the sugar by-products. Many products are often considered together including sugars, syrup, sugar by-products, treacle manufacturing, molasses etc. And, in a wider context, given that the demand for sugar is declining, the existence of the sweetener market as a whole needs to be addressed. This is attempted in the July 1987 issue of *Market Intelligence* [QRL.339] which looked at the market for sugar and artificial sweeteners overall and in the advertising categories defined in *The Media Register* [QRL.354]. The market can be extended to include the categories of low calorie sweeteners exemplified by saccharine and aspartame as distinct from the calorie sweeteners which include refined sugar and corn sweeteners. It would be valuable if the MAFF could consider the possibility of constructing balance sheets for sweeteners as a whole, comparable with the work undertaken in this area by USDA.

The sugar market excites considerable interest, both internationally as well as nationally. This chapter has shown that the UK market and its statistics cannot be properly understood unless they are considered along with the influences of the EC and in relation to world markets. Thus to follow the movements in stocks, supply/demand balance and price determination, sources like *F.O. Licht's International Sugar Report* [QRL.199] and the specialist commercial sources like *The Reuter Sugar Newsletter* [QRL.437] (since 30 April 1990 available on-line for subscribers) need to be consulted. Consequently, we have seen fit to include the major commercial sources as well as the regular official sources.

Membership of the European Community led to a number of new quantities and prices, admirably summarised in the *EC Sugar Regime* [B.244], and more lengthily described in the 1987 MMC report on *Tate, Ferruzzi and Berisford* [B.455]. There is indeed need for a glossary of terms, for one must watch carefully which definition of sugar is used, whether raw or white, for example. British figures in the *Monthly Digest of Statistics* [QRL.362] for stocks are expressed in terms of white sugar equivalent (WSE) whereas *F.O. Licht's International Sugar Report* [QRL.199] give the data in raw beet equivalent.

Given the paucity of coverage in the work of the BSO, we lean heavily upon the occasional official inquiries and the published accounts of the major companies. As it was, despite the size of the 1987 MMC report on *Tate, Ferruzzi and Berisford* [B.455], there were still shortcomings. Indeed, many statistical tables in this report (e.g. Tate & Lyle's margin over United Kingdom effective support price) omitted details for confidentiality reasons in accordance with section 83(3) of the Fair Trading Act 1973. Furthermore, it is true to say that much expert guidance is needed if the non-specialist reader wants to appreciate the subtlety of the data reported, notably those in [B.455]. This is not to say that the leading companies do not co-operate in providing much statistical information but their efforts must naturally be geared to the protection of their shareholders and, indeed, carefully thought out public relations.

Possible solutions may be to institute periodic official inquiries, selecting particular products from year to year yielding more detailed production figures than at present. Another possibility may be that the Sugar Bureau could expand its services to a more complete coverage of economic and statistical, as well as scientific, information. At present, there is an uneven coverage of statistical information with, for instance, much more data on the London FOX prices than on the output of white granulated sugar.

CHAPTER 10

ICE-CREAM, COCOA, CHOCOLATE AND SUGAR CONFECTIONERY

The information in this chapter relates to the ice-cream, cocoa, chocolate and sugar confectionery industries, Group 421 in the *CSO Standard Industrial Classification Revised 1980* [B.232]. Other more general sources, which provide statistics on other industry Groups as well, are covered in Chapter 2 and should be consulted as required. The contents of this chapter are as follows:

10.1 Introduction

Industry Group 421 covers the following Activity Headings of SIC(1980):

4213 Ice-cream.
4214 Cocoa, chocolate and sugar confectionery.
1. Cocoa and chocolate.
2. Sugar confectionery.

For an alphabetical list of the activities covered by Group 421, see Table 10.1 or the CSO *Indexes to the Standard Industrial Classification Revised 1980* [B.317]. The ice-cream heading includes both dairy and non-dairy products. It seeks to take account of all flavours and sizes, ranging from ice-cream bought as a single unit to products bought in bulk. The various water-ice products include ice lollies and other frozen confections on a stick. The cocoa sub-heading embraces the primary stages of cocoa bean roasting and dressing, together with cocoa butter manufacturing. The sugar confectionery sub-heading gathers together a wide range of sugar-based products. AH4214.1 and AH4214.2 correspond to MLH217.1 and MLH217.2 in SIC(1968). The manufacture of ice-cream was, however, classified to MLH215 "Milk and milk products", and the manufacture of ice-cream powder to MLH229.2 "Starch and miscellaneous foods" in SIC(1968).

Business Monitor PA421: Ice-cream, Cocoa, Chocolate and Sugar Confectionery [QRL.113] currently provides the annual data for the Group as a whole. Census of Production information on output and costs, capital expenditure, stocks and work-in-progress and operating ratios is presented. Data on employment, wages and salaries, output, capital expenditure, stocks and work-in-progress etc. are cross-

Table 10.1: Activities Classified under Group 421

SIC(1980) AH		SIC(1968) MLH
4213	Ice-cream	
	Ice-cream (all flavours) manufacturing	215.3
	Ice-cream powder manufacturing	229.2
	Water ices manufacturing	215.3
4214.1	Cocoa and chocolate	
	Chocolate manufacturing	217.1
	Chocolate confectionery manufacturing	217.1
	Chocolate couverture manufacturing	217.1
	Cocoa bean roasting and dressing	217.1
	Cocoa butter manufacturing	217.1
	Cocoa powder (drinking chocolate etc.) manufacturing	217.1
	Drinking chocolate manufacturing	217.1
	Milk chocolate manufacturing	217.1
	Milk cocoa manufacturing	217.1
4214.2	Sugar confectionery	
	Boiled sugar confectionery manufacturing	217.2
	Boiled sweet manufacturing	217.2
	Butterscotch manufacturing	217.2
	Caramel (sweets) manufacturing	217.2
	Chewing gum manufacturing	217.2
	Clear gum (confectionery) manufacturing	217.2
	Confectioner's novelty manufacturing	217.2
	Fondant manufacturing	217.2
	Jujube manufacturing	217.2
	Liquorice manufacturing	217.2
	Lozenge (not medicated) manufacturing	217.2
	Marshmallow manufacturing	217.2
	Marzipan sweets manufacturing	217.2
	Nougat manufacturing	217.2
	Nut and bean confectionery manufacturing	217.2
	Pastille manufacturing	217.2
	Pomfret (pontefract) cake manufacturing	217.2
	Spice making (in Yorkshire)	217.2
	Toffee manufacturing	217.2
	Turkish delight manufacturing	217.2

classified by employment size. Regional distributions of employment, capital expenditure, output etc. are shown.

Business Monitor PQ4213: Ice-cream [QRL.138] gives the quarterly data on sales, production, exports and imports etc. for AH4213. However, substantial information on the domestic market for cocoa and confectionery products has been, and is, separately collected by the trade association representing the industry. This is the Biscuit, Cake, Chocolate and Confectionery Alliance (BCCCA) formed from the merger in January 1987 of the Cocoa, Chocolate and Confectionery Alliance (CCCA) and the Cake and Biscuit Alliance (CBA). Information used to be published in the *Annual Report* [QRL.41] of the CCCA. The compilation and despatch of statistics for each sector has been continued by the BCCCA. Current data are now contained in the new *Statistical Year Book* [QRL.461] available from the BCCCA. The first issue of [QRL.461] in 1986 summarised the statistics for each year from 1954 to 1986 for the CCCA, and from 1969 to 1986 for the CBA. The work of the trade associations has already been noted by Slater [B.164], and partially explains the non-existence of a separate PQ Monitor for "cocoa and chocolate" and "sugar confectionery".

The separate coverage up to the end of 1980 of quarterly sales data etc. in *Business Monitor PQ217: Cocoa, Chocolate and Sugar Confectionery* [QRL.124] is further discussed in section 10.4. *Business Monitor PQ215: Milk and Milk Products* [QRL.121] included ice-cream up to the end of 1980, before the publication of the separate *Business Monitor PQ215.3: Ice-cream* [QRL.122] which preceded the current *Business Monitor PQ4213: Ice-cream* [QRL.138]. The *Historical Record of the Census of Production, 1907–1970* [QRL.264], and the previous Census of Production volumes should be consulted with regard to the previous historical classification of the above activities. In 1930, for example, ice-cream manufacturing was included in the "Bread and flour confectionery" industry.

10.2 Industry Structure

There are four recognizable economic markets classified to this Group. The structure of the ice-cream manufacturing industry is discussed first, followed by separate summaries for the cocoa industry, the chocolate confectionery industry, and the sugar confectionery industry. Much of the statistical data on these latter three industries is provided by the BCCCA, which seeks to provide the most accurate and reliable statistics possible for its members, based upon carefully-thought-out classification schemes — see sections 10.2.3 and 10.2.4. The major publication is now the *Statistical Year Book* [QRL.461] which was first published for 1986, although some statistical data are still given in the *Annual Review* [QRL.49]. Previously, under the aegis of the CCCA, the *Annual Report* [QRL.41] had a more detailed coverage than the current *Annual Review* [QRL.49].

The data base is essentially the returns that most members submit to the BCCCA for each four-week period. Returns need not be signed and are identified by a secret code number which is strictly confidential between the member and the Alliance officers directly concerned in compiling the industry statistics. Returns are collated into summaries, which are available free to members. The same summaries are available to non-members on an annual subscription basis. Similarly, the *Statistical Year Book* [QRL.461] is free to members and is also available for a fee to non-members. This substantial volume is split into separate sections as follows: biscuits; cakes; chocolate; cocoa; sugar confectionery; trade; and the perspective section. [QRL.461] will be drawn upon during this chapter as will the *Annual Review* [QRL.49] and the *Annual Report* [QRL.41]. Information collected includes delivery/despatch figures (figures for goods moving into distribution at manufacturers' list prices); consumption; imports; exports; prices; raw materials etc. The BCCCA, and the former CCCA publications, are the primary data sources for many other reports, e.g. *Retail Business* [QRL.432] and *Market Intelligence* [QRL.339].

10.2.1 *Ice-cream*

Ice-cream has a long and distinguished history, as explained in *All About Ice-cream* [B.198] and *The History of Ice-cream* [B.302]. Ice-cream undoubtedly evolved from the chilled wines and other iced beverages and foods that graced the tables of potentates of antiquity and the water ices that were popular in the early medieval period. The Roman emperor, Nero, sent fleets of slaves to the mountains to bring snow and ice to cool and freeze the fruit drinks he favoured. As water ices became popular in the early medieval period, it is possible that milk and cream were mixed with other ingredients and were served as frozen desserts.

Indeed, a state banquet given by Charles I was made memorable by the appearance of a new dish which was the frozen dessert or cream-ice concocted by Charles' French chef. The assembled gourmets received it and consumed it with delight. The chef was rewarded with a pension of £500 per annum provided the recipe was kept a secret. But when Charles I was beheaded in 1649, the secret of the "frozen milk" had already been divulged.

Of course, nowadays in the United Kingdom and elsewhere, ice-cream is a food item of mass consumption and not just provided for the privileged few. Three distinct sets of ice-cream manufacturers may be identified. First are the two dominant companies: Birds Eye Wall's Limited and Lyons Maid Limited which between them hold over 50 per cent of the market. Next there are 15–20 manufacturers of medium size. Thirdly there are well over 1000 small, independent, often family-run firms scattered across the United Kingdom, many being highly localised and most with less then 25 employees.

The two leading firms themselves provide statistical information, notably in the *Wall's Report* [QRL.510] and *Ice-cream in the '80s* [QRL.270]. The nature of the market is complex and may be categorised as follows. First, there are impulse, or in-hand products, which are bought and eaten outside. Second, there is bulk take-home ice-cream, which besides the standard product can include "complete desserts". Thirdly, multipacks — cartons of individual impulse items sold to be taken home and eaten at home — have been enjoying substantial growth over recent years. Finally, the provision of catering packs for sale and consumption in hotels, restaurants, snack bars etc. can be noted. An upward trend in ice-cream production is shown in most of the sources. It is well-known that the nature of demand is traditionally seasonal, with peaks in demand a function of periods of warm weather. A significant move to smooth out the peak has been the drive to sell take-home products which provide a base load of demand for the major manufacturers to complement the general provision of impulse in-hand varieties by both the major companies and the many local family firms.

Of the market leaders, the most prominent is Wall's (part of the Unilever group). It had a 39 per cent share of the market followed by Lyons Maid (Allied-Lyons) with 12.5 per cent. Retailers' own brands accounted for 23 per cent and others made up 25.5 per cent. This brief market picture for the year of 1987 is taken from the *Wall's Report* [QRL.510], derived from AGB/Attwood/Wall's work and *Ice-cream in the '80s* [QRL.270] from AGB/Attwood/Lyons Maid information sources. We also note here the market review of "Ice-cream" in the August 1987 issue of *Retail Business* [QRL.432], which uses both official data and trade information. Indeed, many market research organisations monitor the market with special reports on the ice-cream industry. These are further discussed in section 10.14 and may be used to update information on market share.

An earlier and more complete, if partially dated, picture of structure can be found in the Monopolies and Mergers Commission (MMC) publication, *Ice-cream and Water Ices. A Report on the Supply in the United Kingdom of Ice-cream and Water Ices* [B.445]. This confirmed the dominance of Wall's and Lyons Maid, which are both based upon a national distribution network dependent upon refrigeration capacity. The 1970 report by the National Board for Prices and Incomes (NBPI) on *Costs, Prices and Profitability in the Ice-cream Manufacturing Industry* [B.401] gave a most concise summary of the economic structure at that time, including information on financial ownership.

Two trade associations exist to represent the interests of their members. The Ice Cream Federation Ltd. represents the large manufacturers, whereas the Ice Cream Alliance Ltd. acts for the many small manufacturers and distributors. Neither body collects statistics but they do advise on the availability of information sources as well as monitoring government and EC regulations on the composition of ice-cream.

Overall, the market has shown aspects of both concentration, growth and market innovation in recent years. Especially notable has been the interest of the Milk Marketing Board in promoting dairy ice-cream products as distinct from the regular ice-cream which is mainly made from vegetable fats.

10.2.2 *Cocoa*

In 1519 Cortez discovered that cocoa had been cultivated by the Aztecs for at least 3000 years. In 1528 he introduced a chocolate drink to Spain. Cocoa has thus been consumed as a beverage for many centuries. It was not until 1828 that the Dutch manufacturer Conrad J. Van Houten made another discovery. He found that, when ground and pressed, cocoa beans yielded up their fat content or butter. By adding this "butter" to sugar and the original grindings, Van Houten produced an elementary chocolate in the palatable and solid form of cocoa. Later developments in Switzerland included adding milk to the production process. This all helped stimulate the demand for cocoa beans.

The cocoa bean and its derivatives are internationally traded commodities which serve both as the main constituents of cocoa and chocolate drinks and as vital inputs into chocolate and sugar confectionery manufacture. The flow diagram (Figure 10.1) gives a simple illustration of cocoa processing and chocolate production. Essentially the cocoa processors grind the beans and separate them into the cocoa butter used with cocoa paste mainly for making chocolate and cocoa powder. The latter is found in cocoa and chocolate drinks and as an ingredient in ice-cream manufacture and sweets.

Gill & Duffus, as one of the leading trading organisations in the international cocoa market, provides a major service to all sections of the industry from the cocoa

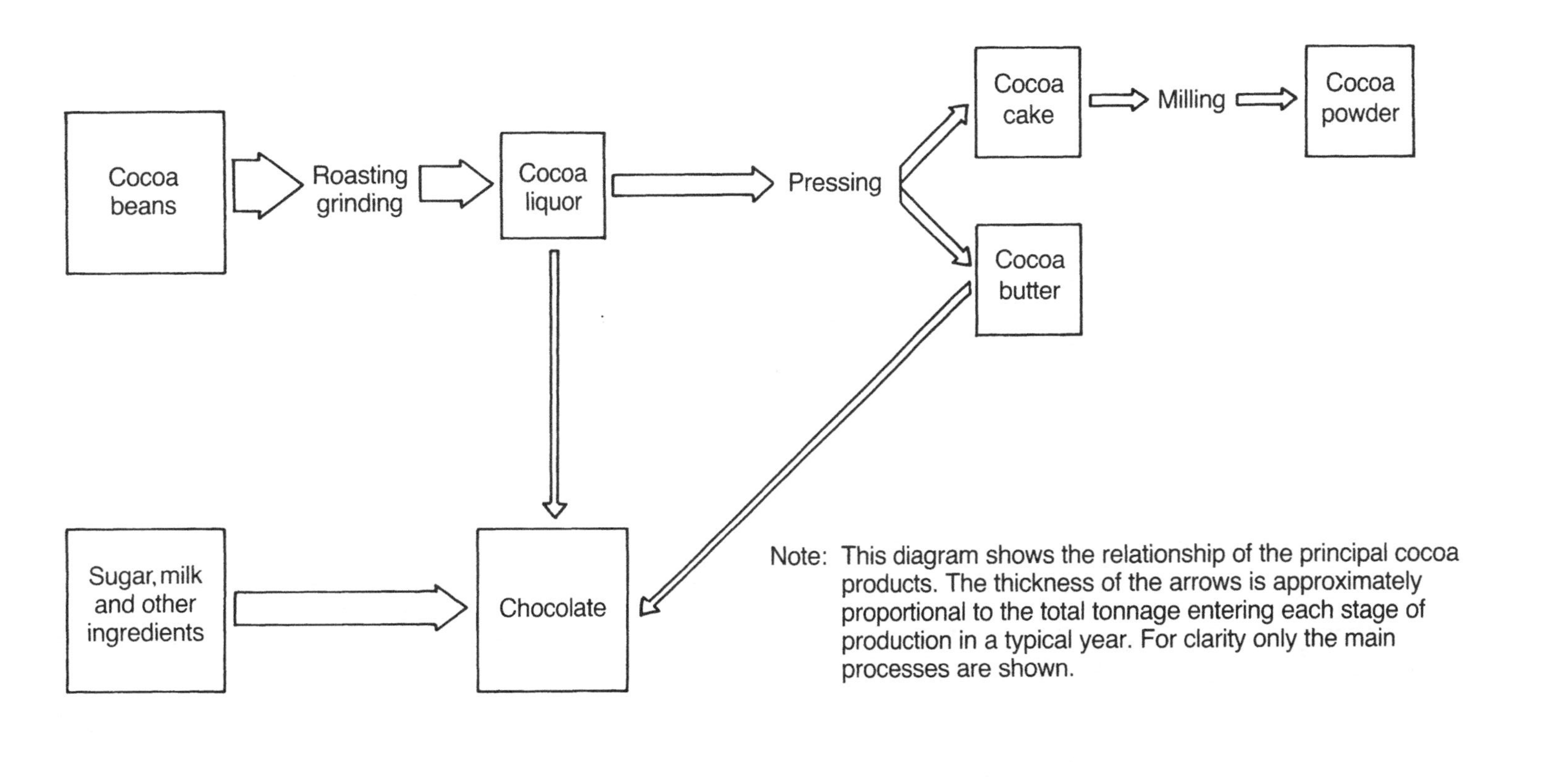

Figure 10.1 Flow Diagram of Cocoa Processing and Chocolate Production.
Source: *Gill & Duffus: Cocoa Statistics* [QRL250].

producer to the cocoa processor. Formed in 1907 to supply edible nuts and other raw materials to the confectionery and baking industry, this company traded in cocoa beans from 1929 and ventured into manufacturing in 1940 through British Cocoa Mills in Hull. Gill & Duffus is hence involved in all aspects of cocoa. In 1985 it became part of the Dalgety Group, one of the world's major food and agriculture companies, and in 1990 was acquired by E.D.& F. Man.

Not surprisingly, a major data source is the *Gill & Duffus: Cocoa Market Report* [QRL.249]. This provides an overview of the world market. The November 1988 issue, for example, carried seventeen statistical tables as well as commentary and diagrams. It is a major source for statistics on the world production of raw cocoa, world grindings, consumption, stocks, supply and demand balances, imports and exports, physical and futures prices etc. as will be seen during the course of this chapter. Furthermore, whilst the *Gill & Duffus: Cocoa Market Report* [QRL.249] is published six times a year, longer time series of the many components are collected together in successive editions of *Gill & Duffus: Cocoa Statistics* [QRL.250] which is issued at intervals.

Further, we draw attention to the market for cocoa powder itself and the closely related drinking chocolate which is a convenience version of cocoa powder plus sugar. These products compete with malted drinks and both cocoa and malted products which are instant (i.e. prepared by the addition of boiling water). The market is sometimes perceived by the trade as "Food drinks" (see the March 1983 report in *Market Intelligence* [QRL.339] for example). But it can also be regarded as part of the "Hot drinks" market as a whole, as discussed in the 1988 Key Note report entitled *Hot Drinks* [QRL.592]. Indeed producers, such as Premier Brands who are responsible for Cadbury's Drinking Chocolate and Cocoa, Rowntree's, and the various own-label producers, tend to delineate their markets in relation to both malted drinks, such as Horlicks and Ovaltine, and the many brands of tea and coffee which are discussed in Chapter 12.

10.2.3 *Chocolate Confectionery*

The trade recognises a split between chocolate-based products and the sugar-based products which are discussed in section 10.2.4. The main statistical source for both sectors is the BCCCA which divides the market for chocolate into nine segments as follows:

- (C1) solid milk or blended chocolate without additions — the classic bar of milk products (e.g. Cadbury's Dairy Milk and Yorkie)
- (C2) solid milk or blended chocolate with additions (e.g. fruit and nut)
- (C3) solid plain chocolate
- (C4) filled bars, tablets etc. with biscuit or wafer centre (e.g. Kit Kat)
- (C5) filled blocks, bars and count lines with other centres (e.g. Mars) ("count lines" refer to items sold by count rather than by weight)
- (C6) chocolate assortments — small pieces with different fillings (e.g. those in boxes such as Dairy Box, Milk Tray, Black Magic and All Gold which are thus "bite" size chocolates)
- (C7) chocolate straight lines — where the fillings are all the same (e.g. Maltesers, Smarties, peppermint creams)
- (C8) chocolate liqueurs — at least half of the chocolates have centres incorporating alcoholic beverages

- (C9) chocolate novelties (e.g. Easter eggs).

Despite the numerous products in the shops, this sector is dominated by the three major groups: Cadbury, Mars, and Rowntree Mackintosh (now owned by Nestlé). Taken together, they account for about 80 per cent of sales volume. UK-based producers have long histories, yet there is a significant multinational interest in the chocolate sector, notably Mars (USA) and Nestlé (Switzerland). At the luxury end of the market alongside specialist domestic firms, we note Lindt (Switzerland), Tobler Suchard (Switzerland) and Ferrero as well-known examples. The survey of "Chocolate confectionery (part 1)" in the November 1986 issue of *Retail Business* [QRL.432] is but one example of market research reports in this area compiled by the private sector.

10.2.4 *Sugar Confectionery*

The BCCCA specifies seven segments for the numerous products in this market. A long list of product types has already been noted in Table 10.1.

- (S1) Boiled sugar — the traditional hard sugar sweet often sold loose from large jars (e.g. fruit drops, acid drops, barley sugar)
- (S2) Toffee and caramel — as well as products labelled coffee, caramel, this includes fudge, eclairs etc.
- (S3) Gums, jellies and pastilles — covers the range of products based on gelling agents (e.g. gums, gelatine, pectins contain starches thus wine gums, fruit pastilles, jelly babies)
- (S4) Liquorice — self explanatory and also includes Pontefract Cake
- (S5) Chewing gum — in all forms, including bubble gum
- (S6) Other (non-medicated) confectionery (e.g. hard mints like Rowntree's Polo and Trebor's range of mints, marzipan confectionery, marshmallows)
- (S7) Medicated confectionery — refers to cough sweets and throat lozenges (e.g. Mars Lockets and Tunes, Lofthouse's Fisherman's Friend).

The sugar confectionery sector is much more fragmented than the chocolate sector although Cadbury, Mars and Rowntree Mackintosh (now Nestlé) operate here too. Bassett Foods, Barker and Dobson, Trebor (especially for mints) are other household names besides the many more sugar confectionery manufacturers which belong to the BCCCA. The market is covered in the December 1986 issue of *Retail Business* [QRL.432] in a special report entitled "Sugar confectionery (part 2)". This report points out that, among other features, the sugar confectionery sector is more limited in total volume and value than the chocolate confectionery sector.

10.2.5 *Comments*

Distinctions are made in the official statistics between the ice-cream manufacturers and the firms operating in the cocoa, chocolate confectionery, and sugar confectionery sectors. These correspond respectively to ice-cream (AH4213) and cocoa, chocolate and sugar confectionery (AH4214). Yet the commercial segmentation is much finer as noted in the treatment in sections 10.2.1, 10.2.2, 10.2.3 and 10.2.4. Despite these subdivisions, the major firms are usually active in many, if not all, market segments.

10.3 The European Community

The European Community (EC) has had a significant influence in both an economic and statistical sense on the cocoa, chocolate and sugar confectionery sector. Background is given in successive issues of the *Annual Report* [QRL.41] and the *Annual Review* [QRL.49]. Useful dossiers of the many developments in the industry, including European aspects, are contained in the booklet called *The Cocoa, Chocolate and Confectionery Alliance 1951–1981* [B.35].

Notable from an economic point of view has been the transformation of the arrangements for the pricing and marketing of many inputs, e.g. sugar and milk, as discussed in other chapters of this Review. Secondly, there is the question of both EC legislation on food additives in the United Kingdom and the debates over the adoption of the standards of composition laid down in the EC Directive on cocoa and chocolate products. Third, there is the issue of VAT rates from BCCCA pressures for the zero rating of confectionery and internal market plans from 1992 when the European Commission proposes rates of 14–20 per cent for the standard band and a reduced band of 4–9 per cent for essentials like food.

The statistical impact includes participation in the Association of the Chocolate, Biscuit and Confectionery Industries of the EEC (CAOBISCO), work on the harmonised system (HS) of product classification in trade statistics and greater prominence to Europe in UK statistical coverage. As a member of CAOBISCO, the UK Trade Association (now the BCCCA) was instrumental in the largely successful efforts of CAOBISCO to draw up a scheme of statistical headings for implementation by the EC within the HS framework. The aim was to give the sort of statistical breakdowns on imports and exports that meet the major needs of the industry throughout the Community. Detailed statistics are vital for monitoring trends and planning the marketing efforts of the companies concerned.

EC membership has also meant the communication of statistical data assembled in *CAOBISCO: Statistical Monograph* [QRL.146] which combines information from national trade associations, EUROSTAT and Gill & Duffus. The many tables identify the United Kingdom in the data on production of cocoa and chocolate products and sugar confectionery; consumption; values of sales; VAT rates and other taxes on CAOBISCO products; raw materials (cocoa and other inputs); and the trade split into intra-EEC trade, external trade, and EC/EFTA trade.

Membership of the European Community has encouraged great prominence to EC statistics in many of the domestic publications. The *Annual Review* [QRL.49] regularly summarises the importance of the EC. It also uses HM Customs and Excise sources to feature the volume and percentage of exports of biscuits, cakes, chocolate and sugar confectionery to other Community countries. The *Annual Report* [QRL.41] carried summary data on chocolate/chocolate confectionery and sugar confectionery in the Community, giving annual data on production, imports, imports from the United Kingdom, exports, exports to the United Kingdom, consumption and consumption per capita.

Finally, it remains to be seen what impact the envisaged completion of the internal market may have after 1992. EC trade figures since January 1988 have been largely collected under criteria hammered out between CAOBISCO and the Community Customs authorities. In particular, there may be problems in compiling meaningful statistics in the absence of information from Customs border posts which at the moment monitor and record trade flows between the Member States. Of course, this problem is of general concern.

Similar remarks may be made about ice-cream. The Ice Cream Federation in particular represents the interests of the industry in the EC context. Questions of permitted additives and food labelling etc. are subject to the various EC Directives and Regulations as well as domestic legislation.

10.4 Output

10.4.1 *Output, Sales and Value Added*

10.4.1.1 Business Statistics Office inquiries

The annual *Business Monitor PA421: Ice-cream, Cocoa, Chocolate and Sugar Confectionery* [QRL.113] and *Business Monitor PA1002: Summary Volume* [QRL.93] both provide the four major output measures for this Group, viz. total sales and work done; gross output; net output; and gross value added at factor cost. The general methodology and coverage are set out in section 2.4.1.1. The data for ice-cream (AH4213) are treated separately from cocoa, chocolate and sugar confectionery (AH4214) on occasion, as for example in 1986. Previously, under SIC(1968), ice-cream was subsumed with milk in *Business Monitor PA215: Milk and Milk Products*. *Business Monitor PA217: Cocoa, Chocolate and Sugar Confectionery* treated these products together.

The quarterly *Business Monitor PQ4213: Ice-cream* [QRL.138] has provided separate commodity sales data in terms of value and volume for the following: bulk; soft ice-cream mix; home packs; water ices; other stick confections; other ice-cream; unclassified sales (including ice-cream mixes) in values only; and dairy ice-cream included in the above headings.

Sales of principal products by units classified to other industries are subtracted from the total sales of principal products of this Activity Heading. Sales by units classified to AH4213 as principal products of other industries are added in, as are merchanted goods and services rendered, in order to obtain the total sales by units classified to AH4213. The data are both quarterly and annual. The quarterly Monitors are also discussed in general in sections 2.1.1.2 and 2.4.1.1. The coverage in *Business Monitor PQ4213* [QRL.138] under SIC(1980) contains product information as comparable as possible with the previous *Business Monitor PQ215.3: Ice-cream* [QRL.122] under SIC(1968) and *Business Monitor PQ215: Milk and Milk Products* [QRL.121].

Under SIC(1968), *Business Monitor PQ217: Cocoa, Chocolate and Sugar Confectionery* [QRL.124] gave coverage up to the fourth quarter of 1980. Separate commodity sales data in terms of value and volume were given for the following: chocolate and chocolate confectionery; sugar confectionery (excluding medicated confectionery); chocolate couverture and similar products; chocolate crumb; cocoa butter; unclassified sales in value only; waste products, residues etc. in value only. The usual adjustments for sales of principal products etc. were made for the quarterly and annual data.

Earlier statistics can be found in the relevant Census of Production volumes. Output figures for milk and milk products and cocoa, chocolate and sugar confectionery can be traced back to 1907 in the *Historical Record* [QRL.264].

10.4.1.2 Industry Sources

The *Statistical Year Book* [QRL.461] gives the volume of despatches of cocoa powders and drinking chocolate in the cocoa section and also carries more statistics in the chocolate and the sugar confectionery sections. Home-trade despatches in value and volume terms are given for both these latter groups. A further breakdown for despatches (values and volumes) are provided for the nine Alliance chocolate types (C1-C9) described in section 10.2.3 and the seven Alliance sugar confectionery types (S1-S7) discussed in section 10.2.4. Distinctions are made between manufacturers' values by type and consumer values (i.e. recommended or estimated selling prices) by type. The *Statistical Year Book* [QRL.461] generally provides a compendium of current BCCCA data, CCCA annual data back to 1954, and CBA data back to 1969. A good deal of information is available, although the data previous to 1971 had fewer separate classifications than the subsequent C1-C9. Product innovation always provides challenges to classification schemes which rarely remain static.

The *Annual Review* [QRL.49] reports annual figures for the latest two years (volumes and values) for despatches for UK consumption for biscuits; cake; chocolate; and sugar confectionery. The *Annual Report* [QRL.41] also contained this information but had a more detailed statistical coverage which included manufacturers' sales of chocolate and cocoa confectionery; sugar confectionery (including medicated confectionery); total (finished confectionery); cocoa powder and drinking chocolate; chocolate couverture.

The *Statistical Bulletin* compares volume results for the latest year for the top ten producers in the world. A total is given plus separate breakdown for chocolate; sugar confectionery; and biscuits and other baked goods. This publication of the International Office of Cocoa, Chocolate and Sugar Confectionery (IOCCC) generally covers around twenty countries in varying amounts of detail and reliability.

The *Annual Abstract of Statistics* [QRL.37] gives separate production figures in thousand tonnes for chocolate confectionery and sugar confectionery, excluding medicated confectionery, for the usual eleven-year run. The *Monthly Digest of Statistics* [QRL.362] records the monthly averages of production for chocolate and sugar confectionery taken together. The figures quoted are for specified months in the current and preceding years and average monthly production over the past six years. The figures in both [QRL.37] and [QRL.362] are derived from statistics collected by the BCCCA.

10.4.2 *Index Numbers of Output*

Business Monitor PQ4213 [QRL.138] carries the index of output of the production industries for ice-cream. The figures for AH4213 do not include a stock adjustment to correct mixed sales and production data to true production index numbers nor do they include a bias adjustment. The data are generally for the latest seven quarters (seasonally adjusted) and the last six years. Seasonal adjustment, particularly important for ice-cream, was not recorded prior to the second quarter 1984 edition of this Monitor.

10.5 Current Inputs other than Labour

10.5.1 *Domestic Inputs*

Some of the main raw materials used for current inputs are imported. There is some overlap here with section 10.8. The imports of cocoa beans are evidently important, as well as the imports of cocoa butter, liquor and powder. Statistical information may be found in a range of publications, whether official, commercial or from the BCCCA.

The *Cocoa Market Report* [QRL.249] gives monthly and annual statistics of imports of butter, liquor and powder for selected countries including the United Kingdom. Annual and quarterly data on world grindings of raw cocoa are also provided. The coverage in *Gill & Duffus: Cocoa Statistics* [QRL.250] is similar. The *Quarterly Bulletin of Cocoa Statistics* [QRL.397] collates a good deal of data which includes quarterly and annual statistics of imports of cocoa beans; cocoa butter; cocoa powder and cake; and cocoa paste/liquor for selected countries including the United Kingdom. Quarterly and annual statistics on grindings of cocoa beans are given by country including the United Kingdom. *Fruit and Tropical Products* [QRL.245] gives quarterly and annual figures of cocoa bean grindings in the United Kingdom amongst other selected countries, plus information (annual and from January to the month indicated) on imports of raw cocoa, cocoa butter, cocoa paste and cocoa powder/cake. The *Statistical Year Book* [QRL.461] has a section on the annual volume of cocoa raw materials imported. The headings of cocoa beans; cocoa pastes — defatted and not defatted; cocoa butter; cocoa powder unsweetened; parts — couverture, crumb, cocoa powder sweeteners; are summarised from *Business Monitor MM20: Overseas Trade Statistics of the United Kingdom* [QRL.85] which is the primary source used by many other publications. The *Monthly Digest of Statistics* [QRL.362] gives monthly average data for the quantity of beans ground from figures compiled by the BCCCA.

It is apparent that many of the raw materials used in production are the output of other Food industries. For ice-cream this includes "Organic oils and fats", "Preparation of milk and milk Products", and "Sugar and sugar by-products". The various constituents can be gleaned directly from the materials for use in production section of *Business Monitor PO1008: Purchases Inquiry* [QRL.116] for 1984 and *Business Monitor PA1002.1: Census of Production and Purchases Inquiry* [QRL.94] for 1979. Whole milk; milk powder; cream, fresh or sterilized; butterfat; refined vegetable oils etc.; refined sugar; all manufactured forms of cocoa, chocolate and sugar confectionery (e.g. chocolate couverture, block or powder etc.); are amongst the items included, always in terms of value and sometimes for quantities as well. AH4214 is similarly treated in these purchases inquiries and the material used in production examined: cocoa beans; chocolate crumb; cocoa butter; milk; refined sugar; starch etc. which are among the many ingredient inputs. Data on packaging materials; food, electricity etc.; replacement parts and consumable tools; are given separately for AH4213 and AH4214 in these purchases inquiries.

Business Monitor PA421 [QRL.113] follows the standard treatment of the annual Production Monitors but does specify the costs for AH4213 and AH4214 separately. Purchases of materials for use in production, packaging and fuel; the various costs of non-industrial services like hire of vehicles, plant and machinery etc. are covered. This treatment is reflected in the summary volume *Business Monitor PA1002* [QRL.93].

Some more specific guidance to the weights of raw materials can be found in the *Statistical Year Book* [QRL.461] from members' returns of the principal ingredients purchased for use in Alliance finished products. These include sugar; syrup/treacle; glucose; biscuit flour; other wheat flour; starch; other cereals; cocoa beans; cocoa butter; oils and fats other than dairy and cocoa butter; eggs; gelling agents etc. Milk and milk products; dried fruit and jam; nuts (e.g. almond); are also detailed.

10.5.2 *Input-output Analysis*

The latest *Input-output Tables for the United Kingdom 1984* [QRL.284] reflect some, but certainly not all, of the interdependencies. AH4213 and AH4214 are included under "Confectionery". *Business Monitor PA1004: Input-output Tables for the United Kingdom 1979* [QRL.101], which adhered to SIC(1968), had ice-cream included with milk and milk products. Cocoa, chocolate and sugar confectionery were put together. The values in the commodity analysis of purchases from domestic production show the significance of sugar inputs in particular.

10.6 Labour

Labour force information for the Food industries overall is discussed in detail in section 2.6. We summarise here only the main sources.

10.6.1 *Official Sources*

The *Employment Gazette* [QRL.186] carries data on employment in two annual articles which summarise the results from the Census of Employment for Great Britain and the United Kingdom respectively. Both cover Group 421 in total, and AH4213 and AH4214 separately. The first gives male/female employment for both full-time/part-time plus the analyses for the twelve standard regions of Great Britain for total employment including Scotland and Wales. The second gives the male/female for part time/full time labour results for the United Kingdom.

The usual annual article in the *Employment Gazette* [QRL.186] carries data for the United Kingdom of the average hours worked and average earnings per week for the male/female, part time/full time classifications, separating manual employees on adult rates from manual employees on other rates. The coverage is for the whole industry Group 421.

Business Monitor PA421 [QRL.113] publishes annual statistics for total employment and net output per head in the United Kingdom for all businesses classified to this Group. A size distribution is given for total employment (including working proprietors); operatives; and administrative, technical and clerical workers. The size distribution is also carried out for labour costs i.e. wages and salaries separately for operatives; administrative, technical and clerical; both expressed in total and per capita terms. AH4213 and AH4214 are occasionally treated separately (e.g. 1986 for total employment and the productivity measure of net output per head). The operating ratios table in *Business Monitor PA421* [QRL.113] permits some indication of productivity and labour costs for AH4213 and AH4214 since the gross and net output per head measures of wages and salaries as a percentage of gross value added etc. are given for the latest year. Much of the data are duplicated in the summary tables in *Business Monitor PA1002* [QRL.93]. Naturally the coverage differed under SIC(1968) as noted in section 10.1.

Employment data from the 1981 Census of Population for Great Britain are given in *Census 1981: Economic Activity: Great Britain* [QRL.148]. This shows the total in employment by sex, whether full-time/part-time and cross-classified by type of employees (managers, manual, non-manual etc.). It also gives the numbers of self-employed by sex. The Census of Population separately identifies AH4213 and AH4214. Similar information for Scotland is collected and published in the *Census 1981: Scotland Economic Activity (10% Sample)* [QRL.149].

10.6.2 *Industry Sources*

The BCCCA *Annual Review* [QRL.49] gives estimates for the previous year of the numbers employed — split into chocolate confectionery; sugar confectionery; biscuits; cake and an overall total. The previous CCCA *Annual Report* [QRL.41] reported the number employed in the production of cocoa; chocolate confectionery; sugar confectionery. The subdivision into male and female employment was made for a ten-year run. Both [QRL.49] and [QRL.41] based their data on the *Employment Gazette* [QRL.186]. In addition, they both comment on labour market issues, particularly training issues relevant to member companies as administered by the Training and Education Committee. Recent issues have surveyed training standards, training costs, trades union involvement in training etc.

The companies themselves show details on employment and labour costs in their Annual Reports. An example is *Rowntree plc: Annual Report and Accounts* [QRL.441] which gives statistics on the average number of employees for the latest two years in the United Kingdom and Ireland, broken down for the main constituent companies plus separate data for international coverage. Information on wages and salaries are also included in the accounts.

10.7 Capital

Business Monitor PA421 [QRL.113] provides details of gross capital expenditure by type of asset: land and buildings; plant and machinery; vehicles; all divided into acquisitions and disposals for the five-year period. Annual net capital expenditure is also given with cross-classifications for the standard regions of England, Wales, Scotland and Northern Ireland. Separate information on capital expenditure was provided for AH4213 and AH4214 in 1986 for land and buildings; plant and machinery; vehicles; all divided into acquisitions and disposals. Net capital expenditure per head and net capital expenditure as a percentage of gross value added are included in the operating ratios table for 1986 for AH4213 and AH4214. Some of the information is duplicated in the summary tables in *Business Monitor*

PA1002 [QRL.93]. Previous coverage differs under the SIC(1968) as noted in section 10.1.

10.8 International Transactions

10.8.1 *HM Customs and Excise Records*

The products of Group 421 fall under various headings in the Standard International Trade Classification (Revision 3). In broad terms, ice-cream comes under Division 02 "Dairy products and birds' eggs"; sugar confectionery comes under Division 06 "Sugar, sugar preparations and honey"; and cocoa, and chocolate confectionery, come under Division 07 "Coffee, tea, cocoa, spices, and manufactures thereof". In *Business Monitor MM20: Overseas Trade Statistics of the United Kingdom* [QRL.85], these Divisions are further broken down into the following main headings:

22.33	Ice-cream and other edible ice whether or not containing cocoa
62.	Sugar confectionery
62.1	Fruit, nuts, fruit peel and other parts of plants, preserved by sugar and other sweetening matter (drained, glacé or crystallized)
62.2	Sugar confectionery (including white chocolate), not containing cocoa
62.21	Chewing gum, whether or not sugar-coated
62.29	Other
72.1	Cocoa beans, whole or broken, raw or roasted
72.2	Cocoa powder not containing added sugar or other sweetening matter
	Cocoa paste, whether or not defatted
72.31	Cocoa paste not defatted (liquor)
72.32	Cocoa paste wholly or partly defatted (cocoa cake)
72.4	Cocoa butter, fat or oil
72.5	Cocoa shells, husks, skins and other cocoa waste
73.	Chocolate and other food preparations containing cocoa, not elsewhere specified
73.1	Cocoa powder containing added sugar or other sweetening matter
73.2	Other food preparations, containing cocoa, in blocks or slabs weighing more than 2kg or in liquid, paste, powder, granular or other bulk forms in containers or immediate packings of a content exceeding 2kg
73.3	Other food preparations containing cocoa, in blocks, slabs or bars
73.9	Food preparations containing cocoa, not elsewhere specified

Further details of the extensive statistical coverage in *Business Monitor MM20: Overseas Trade Statistics of the United Kingdom* [QRL.85] are provided in section 2.8.2.1. The statistics have been compiled from the declarations made to HM Customs and Excise, and which are subject to confirmation by Customs officials. The figures are usually published about one month after the month to which they relate.

Business Monitor PQ4213 [QRL.138] summarises the value and volume of ice-cream (excluding ice-cream powder) exports and imports. Data are provided for the latest five quarters and previous two years and summary value data are given for longer quarterly and annual runs. The original source is HM Customs and Excise. The HM Customs and Excise tariff/trade numbers used in the compilation of this table are listed. *Business Monitor PQ217* [QRL.124] contained summary value and volume data for listed cocoa, chocolate and sugar confectionery products until its publication ceased in the third quarter of 1980.

10.8.2 *Industry Analyses of Trade*

In contrast to analyses by type of product, *Business Monitor MQ10: Overseas Trade Analysed in Terms of Industries* [QRL.90] provides quarterly and annual data on the value of imports and exports for AH4213 and AH4214 as well as for the industry Group as a whole. This coverage dates from the first quarter of 1983 under SIC(1980). The preceding coverage of *Business Monitor MQ10* [QRL.90] and the earlier *Business Monitor M10* [QRL.77] of the same title reflects the SIC(1968) treatment. This identified ice-cream in "Milk and milk products" and combined "Cocoa, chocolate and sugar confectionery" together. *Business Monitor MQ12: Import Penetration and Export Sales Ratios for Manufacturing Industries* [QRL.91] and the preceding *Business Monitor M12* [QRL.78] of the same title rework the statistics to provide the import penetration and export performance ratios. These are provided in *Business Monitor MQ12* [QRL.91] under SIC(1980) for AH4213, AH4214 and industry Group 421 as a whole from the first quarter of 1983 up to the second quarter of 1989. Overall methodology and coverage are explained in section 2.8.2.3.

10.8.3 *Industry Sources*

A good deal of information on international transactions has been described in section 10.5. The data, particularly on imports of raw materials, cover the crucial inputs into the manufacturing processes. Hence we will not repeat here the extensive coverage in the *Cocoa Market Report* [QRL.249], *Cocoa Statistics* [QRL.250], the *Quarterly Bulletin of Cocoa Statistics* [QRL.397] and *Fruit and Tropical Products* [QRL.245].

We do describe the information which is conveniently collected together in the *Statistical Year Book* [QRL.461], especially that of the trade section. In the imports section, the annual volume of cocoa raw materials, UK imports of chocolate confectionery by type and UK imports of sugar confectionery by type are enumerated in separate tables. The exports section covers the volume of exports of raw materials, UK exports of chocolate confectionery by type and UK exports of sugar confectionery by type. This coverage summarises the data according to the HM Customs and Excise Tariff rather than the Alliance classification, viz:

- Cocoa raw materials: cocoa beans; cocoa paste; cocoa butter; cocoa powder — unsweetened; parts — couverture, crumb, cocoa powder sweeteners.
- Chocolate confectionery: unfilled tablets and bars; other unfilled; filled tablets and bars; chocolate liquers; other chocolate confectionery; sugar confectionery containing cocoa; white chocolate; total.

- Sugar confectionery: boiled sugars; toffee/caramel; gums/jellies; liquorice; chewing gums; other; medicated; total; pastes and masses (including liquorice extract); total.

The *Statistical Year Book* [QRL.461] also analyses the volume of competing imports of chocolate and sugar confectionery in total and includes separate figures for exports since the despatches data cover the home trade, exports and a total.

The publications of the BCCCA show a keen interest in exports and imports although coverage tends to vary from year to year according to prevailing interests. The 1988 *Annual Review* [QRL.49] identified the top ten export markets in terms of annual value figures for the latest year split into chocolate; sugar; biscuits; cakes and a total. Imports of Alliance products are similarly treated. The previous *Annual Report* [QRL.41] usually gave annual volume and value figures for exports (e.g. sugar confectionery; chocolate and chocolate confectionery; chocolate couverture and chocolate crumb; cocoa powder and drinking chocolate; cocoa butter; cocoa paste; total: all cross-classified by export markets) and imports of chocolate couverture; chocolate and chocolate confectionery (including white chocolate); chocolate liqueurs; sugar confectionery.

The IOCCC *Statistical Bulletin* is a derivative source for national providers of statistics yet furnishes a range of interesting comparative international data on trade. The top ten importing and exporting countries of finished goods in weight for chocolate; sugar confectionery; biscuits and other baked goods; and a total are ranked for the latest available year. The percentage of production volume represented by exports is given for a number of years for these three product categories. Data on the percentage of the volume of national consumption represented by imports are also provided.

10.9 Stocks

It must be noted that the stock holding of cocoa beans plus the purchases and sales of buffer stocks by the International Cocoa Organisation (ICCO) exercises a significant influence on world cocoa prices. Statistics on stocks play an important part in the balance of supply and demand and are found in many sources.

The *Quarterly Bulletin of Cocoa Statistics* [QRL.397] gives summary data on the world cocoa bean position. These include production quantities (adjusted by subtracting one per cent of gross world crop for loss in weight); grindings; surplus or deficit; and stocks. The cocoa bean year runs from 1 October to 30 September. Stocks at year-end are computed based on the yearly difference between net production and grindings and on the assumption that world stocks at the end of the 1973/74 cocoa year amounted to 325,000 tonnes. The *Cocoa Market Report* [QRL.249] checks the balance of cocoa supply and demand in a table of data back to 1946/47 for the cocoa season October to September. The picture of global availability includes opening stocks; gross world crop; net world crop (an adjustment for weight loss); total availability; seasonal grindings; closing stocks and stock change. Comparable information is contained in *Cocoa Statistics* [QRL.250].

LMC Commodity Bulletin: Cocoa [QRL.311] draws together data on cocoa bean supply/demand balance from the ICCO, Reuters and LMC estimates. Net world supply and world demand are matched to compute changes in stocks. Total stocks at end-period are calculated with ICCO Buffer Stocks separately given. The data are annual and quarterly.

In addition, the review which precedes the cocoa statistics in *Fruit and Tropical Products* [QRL.245], specifies the size of, and changes in, the ICCO buffer stocks. On a more domestic note, *MAFF Statistics: Returns of Stocks of Cocoa Beans and Cocoa Products* [QRL.332] gives the stocks of cocoa beans and cocoa products held by dealers and manufacturers at end-December. The coverage is for the past seven years and includes cocoa beans; cocoa nibs; unsweetened cocoa powder; cocoa paste and liquor; cocoa cake and cocoa butter. The data are in tonnes and a print out can be obtained from MAFF on request. The *Monthly Digest of Statistics* [QRL.362] contained, until February 1988, monthly averages of the stocks of chocolate and sugar confectionery, excluding medicated confectionery. These are stocks held by manufacturers only and the figures were collected by the BCCCA until 1988. These data were presented in annual terms in the *Annual Abstract of Statistics* [QRL.37].

Business Monitor PA421 [QRL.113] gives the financial data on stocks and work-in-progress for this Group. The increase during the year for stocks of materials, stores and fuel taken together is separately given for AH4213 and AH4214 in 1986. The operating ratio of gross output to stocks is computed for the latest year. However, only data for the whole Group are given for the three components of materials, stores and fuel; work-in-progress; goods on hand for sale at end December, change during the year for the last five years and analysis of the total by size of establishment. Group data are reported in the summary tables in *Business Monitor PA1002* [QRL.93].

Business Monitor SDO25: Retailing [QRL.143], formerly *Business Monitor SDA25* [QRL.140], carries data on the values of beginning- and end-year stocks for retailers of confectionery and tobacco and for newsagents. *Business Monitor SDA28: Catering and Allied Trades* [QRL.142], carries beginning- and end-year stocks for restaurants, cafés, snack bars etc. selling food for consumption on the premises only. Thus very little information can be identified on the considerable stocks in retailing and catering.

The data on stocks are thus variable, with the most extensive information existing for cocoa stocks, both internationally and nationally. It is not otherwise easy to find other data; whether for the stocks of ice-cream stored in retail outlets and the home or the separate quantities and values of stocks of chocolate and sugar confectionery held at the various stages of the distribution chain and in the home.

10.10 Consumption

10.10.1 *The National Food Survey*

The National Food Survey only collects consumption data on a restricted number of products manufactured by industry Group 421, because many of them are consumed outside the home. Data are, however, collected on the following items:

Food code number	Description
270	Cakes and pastries (including chocolate cakes)
277	Biscuits, chocolate
312	Cocoa powder and drinking chocolate
332	Ice-cream, mousse
333	All convenience foods not specified elsewhere (includes frozen dairy desserts)

Item 270 also includes cakes and pastries, other than chocolate cakes, which are the products of industry Group 419. Statistics are published in the *National Food Survey: Compendium of Results* [QRL.373]. Annual average figures of both per capita weekly consumption and expenditure are provided for the main food groups but only cocoa and drinking chocolate can be separately identified. The data are analysed by region and type of area; by income group; by household consumption and income group; by age of housewife; by housing tenure and by ownership of deep freezer.

The main report of the Survey, *Household Food Consumption and Expenditure* [QRL.267], also carries some statistical data, particularly in the supplementary tables. The quarterly and annual national averages of consumption of individual foods per capita weekly includes chocolate biscuits; cocoa and drinking chocolate; and ice-cream, mousse. The analyses of consumption and expenditure according to income group identifies cocoa and drinking chocolate, which is also a selected item, with consumption detailed according to household composition groups within income groups. Before 1985, these data were largely covered in the tables and appendices of *Household Food Consumption and Expenditure* [QRL.267].

10.10.2 *The Family Expenditure Survey*

The *Family Expenditure Survey* [QRL.204] provides expenditure data on biscuits, cake etc; sweets and chocolate; cocoa, drinking chocolate, other food drinks; and ice-cream. These analyses are given for various types of household, by sex, by age and by region as explained in section 2.10.2.2. Although the expenditure of households with children is the greatest category, the Survey is thought to underestimate spending by this Group. A significant portion is purchased by children out of their pocket money (see section 2.10.2.3). Much of the demand is also due to many people buying *snacks* outside the home, as distinct from *meals* bought away from home.

10.10.3 *The National Accounts*

The *United Kingdom National Accounts* [QRL.506] provides annual data on consumers' expenditure on preserves and confectionery; coffee, tea and cocoa at both current and 1980 prices. Chocolate and sugar confectionery and cocoa are thus subsumed under these heads. Ice-cream comes within "other manufactured food". As explained in section 2.10.3, upward adjustments are made for food items bought for consumption outside the home. Indeed the data related to chocolate and sugar confectionery and ice-cream are supplied by manufacturers' associations. The reliability gradings in *United Kingdom National Accounts: Sources and Methods. Third Edition* [B.395] are given as grade B, which is the same as for other foods.

10.10.4 *Industry Sources*

The *Statistical Year Book* [QRL.461] carries annual data on per capita United Kingdom consumption for chocolate confectionery and sugar confectionery. These figures are derived from physical estimates of total supplies to the UK market from despatches by UK manufacturers plus estimates of imports of competitive products. The BCCCA then uses these statistics to calculate the UK consumption per capita figures by dividing through by UK population statistics. The results are evidently only approximate but indicate general trends.

Both manufacturers' invoice values and consumer values are reported, representing price times quantity of goods. When both manufacturers' invoice values and the VAT rate are deducted from the estimated consumer values then distributors' margins are arrived at. Even if consumer values are thought to be overestimates in the light of discounting, at least trends over a period have again been shown.

The *Annual Review* [QRL.49] also takes into account home trade despatches and competitive imports to arrive at annual statistics for volume in total and quantity per head per week and value in total and value per head per week for biscuits; chocolate; sugar confectionery. The previous *Annual Report* [QRL.41] yielded similar information to the *Statistical Year Book* [QRL.461].

The *Cocoa Market Report* [QRL.249] presents rather different annual and quarterly statistics for cocoa consumption in metric tonnes for the United Kingdom. Consumption represents cocoa bean grindings adjusted by net imports and exports of cocoa products and chocolate converted into bean equivalent. The standard conversion factors for cocoa butter; cocoa liquor; cocoa powder and cake; chocolate; milk crumb; are given. Cocoa consumption is calculated using Gill & Duffus grindings estimates.

Commercial information takes on an additional importance given the extensive consumption and purchases outside the home of many of the products in this Group. Market research, as well as the work of trade associations like the BCCCA which has already been covered, may be considered here. Market research is further detailed in section 10.14.2.

Ice-cream in the 80's [QRL.270] provides consumption data in the separate market surveys of the in-hand sector and of the dessert and take-home ice-cream sectors. The in-hand sector leaflet shows the percentage of people purchasing ice-cream across age groups; adults and children purchasing behaviour distributed in percentage terms broken down according to adult, child, female, male, girls, boys, and the percentage of people buying in-hand ice-cream across the regions. The products are split into: wrapped impulse; soft ice-cream; scooped ice-cream and the total in-hand market from AGB/Attwood sources. The dessert and take home leaflet concentrates on housewife profiles from National Opinion Poll (NOP) sources. These include percentage of ice-cream buyers according to age, social class, working status and children in household. The take-home market is specifically covered and percentage calculations according to age, social class and working status are made.

Contrasting percentages are also calculated according to whether or not households have children or possess freezers. Evidently the importance in consumption of housewives buying ice-cream in the 25–44 years-old age group with children and freezers in the household is measured by these kinds of data.

Successive issues of the *Wall's Report* [QRL.510] analyse the ice-cream market according to information at hand and current trends. The 1987 *Wall's Report* [QRL.510] reveals a picture of the relative shares of children (under 14) and adults, of impulse ice-cream consumption from 1984 to 1986. The source is largely AGB/ Attwood. Other relevant market information like children's average weekly pocket money is provided.

Confectionery: Sweet Facts [QRL.161] specifies the consumption of confectionery in weight terms (ounces and grams) per head per week for that year.

Cadbury Confectionery Market Review [QRL.144] describes UK consumption expenditure in pence per head per week and gives UK consumption volume in grams per head per week. Chocolate confectionery and sugar confectionery are separately treated in the biennial data for 1980, 1982, 1984 and 1986 published in the 1987 review. International comparisons are made for confectionery consumption overall. The frequency of consumption of chocolate blocks/bars is shown from Cadbury estimates.

Finally, the coverage in *Retail Business* [QRL.432], *Market Intelligence* [QRL.339] etc. noted in section 10.14.2 also incorporates consumption data. These are often derived from the companies themselves, the BCCCA, AGB/Attwood, NOP etc.

10.11 Supplies and Disposals

Supplies per head of the population per year are given for the eleven-year run for cocoa powder in the *Annual Abstract of Statistics* [QRL.37]. Figures for 1980 onwards are not comparable with those for earlier years because of a revised method of estimating supplies for human consumption of offal, cocoa butter and cocoa powder and sugar. These data are from MAFF sources. However, since the 1988 edition of [QRL.37], cocoa and coffee have been combined together. Other aspects of supplies and the connections with stocks are discussed in section 10.9.

As noted in section 2.11.3, disposals are estimated from home production and imports, adjusted for changes in known stocks, including use in the manufacture of other foods and ingredients used in manufactured products which are exported. The *Annual Abstract of Statistics* [QRL.37] includes physical measures of disposals for cocoa beans excluding re-exports and for chocolate and sugar confectionery, excluding medicated confectionery. The *Monthly Digest of Statistics* [QRL.362] carries the monthly averages for disposals of chocolate and sugar confectionery.

The *Statistical Year Book* [QRL.461] gives volume figures for the total supplies to the UK market by adding imports of competing products to despatches as noted in section 10.10.4.

10.12 Prices

10.12.1 *Agricultural and Commodity Prices*

Cocoa is a commodity traded on world markets, notably the London Cocoa Terminal Market; the New York Coffee, Sugar and Cocoa Exchange; the Marché International des Cacaos en Fèves de la Bourse de Commerce de Paris; and the Amsterdam market. As such, much information is available in the daily financial press. For example, the *Financial Times* [QRL.218] reports cocoa futures prices, turnover and ICCO indicator prices.

A major source for a wide range of cocoa prices is the *Cocoa Market Report* [QRL.249] which gives the following information:

a) Physical cocoa prices for "Spot Ghana Amsterdam" and the "Nearest Shipment Position — Ghana London". These data are given daily for the latest six months plus the monthly average. A little additional explanation is perhaps needed. "Spot Ghana Amsterdam" refers to the current market price (in £ per metric ton ex-store) for Ghana cocoa beans in Amsterdam. "Nearest Shipment — Ghana London" relates to Ghana cocoa beans in the London market. Cocoa prices are quoted for March, May, July, September and December. Thus if September is spot then the "nearest shipment position" (in £ per metric ton cif) refers to December prices.

b) London Terminal market — first three futures closing prices. These data are again daily plus the monthly averages for the months in question.

c) New York Terminal market — first three futures settlement prices. Similar periods to the above.

d) Separate tables for the highs/lows in both the London and New York Terminal markets. These data are in monthly terms.

e) Cocoa product prices (as distinct from cocoa beans) i.e. cocoa butter and cocoa powder. These include monthly prices for the current year, quarterly for the previous year and yearly back to 1972 (in the November 1988 issue of [QRL.249] for unit export value in the Netherlands and unit import value in the USA. These unit values per metric ton are obtained by dividing total values by total quantities for the periods in question. Cocoa butter prices are an estimated series for "nearby top four Dutch butter" and ratios are quoted against the London terminal. Cocoa powder prices are for "10 to 12 per cent fat content, alkalised quality". Ratios are quoted against the nearest position in the London terminal.

f) Miscellaneous price series gives monthly (for the latest three months) and annual data (back to 1960 in the November 1988 issue of [QRL.249]) for the following: ICCO Daily Price; Spot Price Ghana, London; Spot Price, Bahia, New York; UK Unit Import Value, Cocoa Beans; and USA Unit Import Value, Cocoa Beans.

These price series are largely replicated in *Cocoa Statistics* [QRL.280] with some long historical comparisons. It needs to be noted that specialist publications like [QRL.249] and [QRL.250] provide a world market review and commentary for those closely involved with the cocoa trade. The text and notes to the tables merit careful study, for valuable background is given to the general reader who needs to understand the terms in the tables. World production is described according to country and geographical area (i.e. Cote d'Ivoire, Ghana, Nigeria, Brazil, Malaysia, rest of the world), world consumption assessed, world stocks estimated and the statistical situation and outlook provided in the commentary.

The markets themselves are the originators of the information. The London Cocoa Terminal Market is part of the London Futures and Option Exchange (London FOX) — before June 1987 the London Commodity Exchange (LCE). Commodity Markets Services (CMS), a subsidiary of London FOX, relays the instantaneous entries on the floor of the exchange, performs a price distribution role for subscribers and passes on information as a vendor to other organisations. The trade slips on the market floor are cleared by the International Commodity Clearing House (ICCH) which issues *Market Turnover Statistics* [QRL.344] which reports the monthly turnover for cocoa futures in 10 tonne lots.

The Reuter Cocoa Newsletter [QRL.435] collects together a range of data along with its world-wide market summaries. These include futures prices in London and Paris, key London FOX turnover figures in lots traded, cocoa options quotes and London Cocoa shipments closing differentials for Ghana cocoa payable against London Terminal prices including spot ex-store and futures prices.

The Public Ledger & Daily Freight Register [QRL.392] records London FOX closing prices, turnover and high/low prices for the latest days' business. It also carries cocoa information in the "Producer prices" section. This yields the following price information: cocoa butter (West African pressed spot); liquor (Brazilian spot) and beans (main crop Ivory Coast spot dock/warehouse). ICCO futures prices and the indicator 10-day average price are also given. *The Public Ledger's Commodity Week* [QRL.394] records the previous week's prices of London and New York cocoa in its international futures table. Weekly price trends for cocoa futures are provided for the week with last-week and last-year comparisons. The monthly price record, high/low/average, is given for the latest three months.

The *Quarterly Bulletin of Cocoa Statistics* [QRL.397] has a rather different focus. It gives the monthly averages of daily and indicator prices of cocoa beans in accordance with Article 26 of the International Cocoa Agreement (ICA) 1986. The daily price for cocoa beans (averaged monthly and annually in the tables) is the average of the quotations of the nearest three active future trading months on the London Cocoa Terminal Market and on the New York Coffee, Sugar and Cocoa Exchange at the time of London close. The indicator price is the average of daily prices over a period of ten consecutive days. This publication also produces monthly averages for many recent years of cocoa bean prices which are of international significance: Spot Ghana and futures in London and futures in New York.

Fruit and Tropical Products [QRL.245] repeats the London and New York cocoa prices. These include Spot Ghana in London and the average daily price in London and New York for three month futures.

Finally, *LMC Commodity Bulletin: Cocoa* [QRL.311] is worthy of note in this section since much statistical data concerning the cocoa world are collected together in this publication. These include the following: quarterly and annual cocoa bean prices in London and New York and the ICCO daily price; quarterly averages of cocoa product prices and ratios (cocoa butter and cocoa powder) and quarterly averages of confectionery ingredient prices and gross margins. These cover cocoa liquor, cocoa butter, white sugar, milk (12.5 per cent solids) for crumb, palm oil, olein and the confectionery consumer price index and estimated gross margin index. Other relevant ingredient prices (wheat, peanuts, almond, desiccated coconut) are also provided.

10.12.2 *Retail Prices*

10.12.2.1 Recorded prices

The *Employment Gazette* [QRL.186] does not include any of the products of this Group in the average retail prices of items collected primarily for the purposes of the General Index of Retail Prices (see section 10.12.3). But, of the official information sources, *Household Food Consumption and Expenditure* [QRL.267] gives average prices paid for chocolate biscuits; cocoa and drinking chocolate; ice-cream, mousse; for the last three years. The *Compendium of Results* [QRL.373] carries the quarterly and annual averages for the last year. In its old format, *Household Food Consumption and Expenditure* [QRL.267] carried quarterly and annual average prices for the year in question.

10.12.2.2 Recommended prices

Much more extensive detail is found in commercial sources. *The Grocer Price List* [QRL.253], issued with *The Grocer* [QRL.252] on the first Saturday of each month, has separate sections on: ice-cream; chocolate and chocolate spreads; cocoa and drinking chocolate; confectionery; cereal bars etc. A large number of brands are listed and sometimes advertised. Suggested prices are for largely retail and trade, specifying the wide variety of weights, size of pack etc.

Shaws Guide to Fair Retail Prices [QRL.453] aims to suggest the maximum retail prices to be charged based on minimum wholesale quantities. Various products can be found within the categories of biscuits, cakes, cooking chocolate, drinking chocolate, frozen foods (for ice-cream) and ice lollies/freeze drinks. It is worth noting that there are so many confectionery products that a separate section is devoted to them. Firms are listed alphabetically followed by price details for the individual brands.

10.12.3 *The Retail Prices Index*

The *Employment Gazette* [QRL.186] General Index of Retail Prices includes sweets and chocolate under "Food". Cocoa is subsumed under coffee and other hot drinks. The coverage is similar in the *Monthly Digest of Statistics* [QRL.362] which gives figures for the latest seven months, showing the respective weights.

However, the specialist source *Statistical Year Book* [QRL.461] produces a price movement series for chocolate confectionery, sugar confectionery and biscuits. Annual average values per tonne in proportion to the average value in 1974 are calculated so that comparisons from 1954 to 1987 can be made. The same tables record the "all items" and "basic foods" index for recent years.

10.12.4 *Price Index Numbers in the National Food Survey*
In its pre-1985 format, *Household Food Consumption and Expenditure* [QRL.267] gave the annual indices of average deflated prices, purchases and demand related to chocolate biscuits; cocoa and drinking chocolate; ice-cream, mousse. Neither the *Compendium of Results* [QRL.373] nor the current *Household Food Consumption and Expenditure* [QRL.267] give detailed coverage.

10.12.5 *Producer Price Index Numbers*
The series of Producer Price Indices are considered in general terms in section 2.12.5. Details of the price indices for the inputs and outputs of the ice-cream and the cocoa, chocolate and sugar confectionery sectors are given below.

10.12.5.1 Producer price index numbers: input prices
Business Monitor MM22: Producer Price Indices carries the producer price index numbers of materials and fuels purchased for AH4213 and AH4214, giving both monthly and annual data. The monthly data are provided for the current and previous years, with the figures for the latest two months provisional. An annual average for the previous year is also presented. *Business Monitor MM22* was published for the first time in October 1989 and continued the coverage in *British Business* [QRL.66].

Under the SIC(1968), *Business Monitor PQ217* [QRL.124] carried data on wholesale price indices of agricultural raw materials purchased to include refined sugar; imported cocoa butter; nuts and cocoa; in quarterly and annual terms from MAFF sources.

10.12.5.2 Producer price index numbers: output prices
Business Monitor MM22 contains the producer price index numbers of products manufactured in the United Kingdom (home sales) for AH4213 and AH4214. The monthly data are provided for the current and previous year, with the figures for the latest two months provisional. An annual average for the previous year is also presented. *Business Monitor MM22* was published for the first time in October 1989 and continued the coverage in *British Business* [QRL.66]. The *Annual Abstract of Statistics* [QRL.37] gives the annual averages for AH4213 and AH4214 for a six-year run for products manufactured in the United Kingdom (home sales).

Under the SIC(1968), *Business Monitor PQ217* [QRL.124] gave the wholesale price indices of goods produced (taken from MAFF sources). Chocolate and sugar confectionery; chocolate and chocolate confectionery; sugar confectionery; were separately identified.

10.13 Financial Information

As explained in section 2.13, the primary data flows from the companies themselves and are collated in the many publications listed in that section. Companies from this

Group can be identified along with others in the *Times 1000* [QRL.486] and the more specific *Britain's Food Processing Industry 1985* [B.150] etc.

The ICC Financial Survey of *Confectionery & Ice-cream Manufacturers* [QRL.568] gives financial and market profiles of both quoted and unquoted companies. Data on turnover; pre-tax profits; directors' remuneration; total assets; current assets; current liabilities; return on capital employed; percentage profit margin etc. can be found here. The company coverage is quite extensive. The alphabetical index gives company name and the page reference. A geographical index subdivides companies by postcode area.

The annual ICC Business Ratio report on *Confectionery Manufacturers* [QRL.548] was in its eleventh edition in 1988. The many ratios, from return on capital employed to return on investment etc., described in section 2.13.4.1, are collected together here. The individual company data cards give the principal activities of about sixty five companies. The companies are assessed alphabetically with summary information on capital employed, rate of return etc. Eleven companies are ranked with respect to the financial ratio in question.

Some financial information is summarised in the Key Note report on *Confectionery* [QRL.583]. This industry sector overview selects nine prominent companies. Financial data under the three main headings of turnover, profits and profitability and liquidity are given.

Most of the information in these reports is of course derived from the accounts filed with the Registrar of Companies. An attempt is made to systematise the information given in various company reports. *Rowntree plc: Annual Report and Accounts* [QRL.441] presents summarised group profit and loss accounts, balance sheets and sources and application of funds. Financial data for Mars can be found at Companies House. As many major manufacturers sell a number of non-confectionery products and as Rowntree used historic, more difficult to locate, costs, whereas Mars used current costs in the reports studied, it is difficult to assess and compare financial profiles, performance and profitability. The same comments can be made about the ICC rankings. A small specialist company could identify its profitability with respect to chocolate manufacture whilst a multiproduct firm would have more difficulty. A company like British Cocoa Mills is very likely to have the highest stock turnover etc. So all financial information needs to be interpreted with respect to the nature of the company and its activities very much in mind.

10.14 Advertising and Market Research

10.14.1 *Advertising*

Many of the products in this Group are characterised by very heavy advertising expenditure, aimed at all ages using the wide variety of media. The *Tri-Media Digest of Brands and Advertisers* [QRL.493] is the major source, as discussed in section 2.14.1. Categories (F30) Chewing gum; (F32) Chocolate confectionery; (F70) Ice-cream and lollies; and (F93) Sugar confectionery, are all directly relevant. Some products and constituents come within (F10) Cakes and fruit pies; (F12) Cake and pastry mixes; and (F56) Frozen confectionery. Expenditure and the many brands involved are detailed.

The monthly *Media Register* [QRL.354] reckons advertising expenditure in this Group to be important enough to give confectionery a category heading of its own which is separate from food. Confectionery is then divided up into the following groups: (CON10) Cereal bars; (CON30) Chocolate — assortment and selflines; (CON40) Chocolate — boxed; (CON50) Chocolate — countlines; (CON60) Chocolate liqueurs and novelties; (CON70) Chocolate — moulded, (CON80) Chocolate — seasonal; and (CON90) Sugar confectionery. (Note that "selflines" means all items are alike and "countlines" refers to items sold by count rather than by weight).

The Food Forecast [QRL.236] includes many products from this Group in its ranking of the top 100 brands advertised in the food industry. Adjusted MEAL expenditure data is used. Chocolate confectionery and sugar confectionery are separately ranked for adjusted MEAL expenditure data. Chocolate confectionery and sugar confectionery are separately ranked for adjusted MEAL expenditure by generic brand and product name.

10.14.2 *Market Research*

The Food Forecast [QRL.236] typifies the link between advertising and market research. MEAL brand data for expenditure on chocolate and sugar confectionery are reproduced for the past nine years (unadjusted) and the latest quarter (adjusted). Brand shares for past years and regional analyses are given. Separate figures for mints; toffee and caramels; sugar confectionery; bars of chocolate; chocolate assortments and other boxed chocolates; are given.

A major effort is made by companies which publish reports carrying market information. We give four examples of this approach below. These reports are usually available on application to the companies themselves.

The *Wall's Report* [QRL.510] covers many market dimensions as reviewed in 10.2.1. The market facts section typically gives the following: volume and value data for the total ice-cream market; ice-cream brand shares for wrapped impulse and take-home; ice-cream sector performance for the different products (wrapped; scooping/soft; multipack; complete desserts; premium ice-cream; standard ice-cream); impulse and take-home ice-cream trade outlet split; wrapped and multipack brand shares and total take-home ice-cream brand shares and market sectors. The data are usually based on AGB/Walls field work. In sum the *Wall's Report* [QRL.510] surveys many aspects of the market from the progress of new product launches to the extent of children's average weekly pocket money. Walls' advertising, both in total and as a percentage of total industry spend, is identified in annual terms from MEAL-TV and Press/Walls sources. This dominance befits a company which appeals to younger consumers by advertising in comics and magazines. A famous example from the past was the character of Tommy Walls along with Dan Dare in the Eagle comic!

Ice-cream in the 80s [QRL.270] provides separate market surveys of the in-hand sector of Britain's ice-cream market. It also carries analyses which covers the rather different segments of dessert and take-home ice-cream. Data on the in-hand sector relate annual volume/value of sales against weather patterns; sales pattern by products; percentage outlets sales by type of outlet according to the summer season; and distribution of purchasers by region and television area. There is considerable information on confectioners, tobacconists and newsagents (CTNs). Data in the separate dessert and take- home ice-cream leaflet cover annual value information; patterns of home freezer ownership and purchases; the take-home market in the regions and analyses by TV area and outlet shares. The data are combined from Lyons Maid, AGB/Attwood and NOP sources.

Confectionery: Sweet Facts [QRL.161] is issued by Rowntree Mackintosh Confectionery. It contains a host of varied market information which includes the following: value data relating the confectionery market to other food and drink sectors; chocolate and sugar market segments contrasted in size and further broken down in terms of value according to BCCCA classifications; league tables of the top 36 brands in terms of value; top selling counter lines and boxed chocolates in CTNs; top selling check-out lines, and boxed chocolates and multipacks in grocers' shops. A good deal of market share information on the major manufacturers nationally, and on their penetration in Scotland, London and South and North and Midlands is given. Estimates were derived from company sources etc.

Cadbury Confectionery Market Review [QRL.144] contains separate sections on the following: market value; volume sales; market status; UK consumption expenditure; UK consumption volume; confectionery consumption world-wide; confectionery eating in Britain; confectionery market support for brands by the three major companies and others; trade sector performance and top UK confectionery brands by value across the three major companies and others.

We have already mentioned some of the reviews carried out by market research organizations in section 10.2. We summarise their coverage here. *Retail Business* [QRL.432] carries reviews on "Ice-cream" in issue 354 (August 1987); on "Chocolate confectionery" in issue 345 (November 1986); and on "Sugar confectionery" in issue 346 (December 1986). The general format cuts across many of the types of data catalogued in this chapter. Market size; production; foreign trade; consumption patterns; manufacturers and brands; distribution; prices and margins; packaging; advertising and promotion; and finally prospects; are all covered. *Market Intelligence* [QRL.339] has issued reports on "Chocolate confectionery" (November 1987); "Chocolate" (September 1985); "Hot beverages" (December 1987); and "Food drinks" (March 1983). The usual treatment portrays market size and trends; market sectors; foreign trade; companies and brands; distribution; packaging; the consumer; advertising and promotion; and finally the future. Of the reports from other organisations, *Market Research: Great Britain* [QRL.343] surveyed "Ice-cream" (July 1988). Market Assessment Publications provide an annual market sector report on *Confectionery* [QRL.603], and Key Note publish a sector overview of *Hot Drinks* [QRL.592].

This selection of reports is by no means exhaustive but the main sources have been identified here and in section 2.14.2. As the explanation in section 10.2 has shown, market structure tends to cut across industry structure as delineated by SIC(1980). Market research reports provide both statistical summaries and some perception of the changing market environment.

10.15 Research and Development

The *Annual Review* [QRL.49] and the previous *Annual Report* [QRL.41] have regular information on scientific and technical developments which concern members of the

BCCCA. These range from cocoa research issues; the concern with additives, colours etc.; to the scientific questions underlying technical R&D, food safety and other issues. This information is more of a descriptive nature and more of interest to research specialists working in the industry and technical institutions. The primary statistical souces of actual expenditure and employment are the company reports and accounts.

The other side of the coin is "near to the market" research. This concerns the close connection of product development and market research. This is a feature of the sources noted in section 10.14.2. There is the considerable product differentiation. This is exemplified by the *Wall's Report* [QRL.510] which describes the growth of multipack and new product lines and the *Cadbury Confectionery Market Review* [QRL.144] with a similar interest in developing market segments.

For ice-cream, additional information on R&D, is sometimes available from the Ice Cream Federation and the Ice Cream Alliance.

10.16 Official Investigations

10.16.1 *Ice-Cream*

In 1970, the National Board for Prices and Incomes (NBPI) published *Costs, Prices and Profitability in the Ice-cream Manufacturing Industry* [B.401]. The report resulted from investigations following price increases under the early warning arrangements. It furnishes historical data relevant for sections 10.2.1, 10.5, 10.9, 10.12, 10.13 and 10.14.

The structure of the industry at that time and a brief history of recent mergers and financial structure are summarised in the Appendix to the report. Given the level of concentration, the report provides a statistically supported picture of the dominance of T.Wall & Sons (Ice-cream) Ltd. and Lyons Maid Ltd. Northern Ireland was excluded from the investigation.

The retail value of the market was broken down according to product mix in value terms (impulse-buying, take-home, catering etc.) and by outlet type (shops, mobile vans, catering etc.) according to estimates from one of the leading manufacturers. Details are given not only of the smaller manufacturers but of how the joint ownership of Total Refrigeration Ltd. (the company which supplied and maintained the important freezer cabinets) enabled T.Wall and Lyons Maid to ensure direct sales to retailers. Quantity discounts given by T.Wall and Lyons Maid are enumerated and their price indices reported from 1969 to June 1970 for a wide variety of products. The pressure of rising costs leading to recent price increases was noted. The cost structure is given for both companies in percentage terms showing the relative importance of edible ingredients; packaging materials; production (labour and overheads); cold storage and distribution; selling, marketing and advertising; refrigeration in retail premises; other. Thus a good deal of economic information besides price was used to arrive at the conclusion that the price increases were justified.

In 1979, the Monopolies and Mergers Commission (MMC) published *A Report on the Supply in the United Kingdom of Ice-cream and Water Ices* [B.445]. The previous

NBPI report [B.401] concluded that there were no excessive profits but *Ice-cream and Water Ices* [B.445] provided a more exhaustive examination of financial and many other industrial features in this monopoly reference. It furnishes data relevant for sections 10.2.1, 10.4, 10.5, 10.6, 10.7, 10.12, 10.13, 10.14 and 10.15. As it covered so many dimensions of the industry, the information given is considered collectively. Here is a selection of what is available:

- Wall's and Glacier estimates in value of the 1976 market (impulse buying, catering, self-service super markets, freezer centres, mobiles, CTNs, seasonal etc.).
- Market shares in 1976 by value (per cent).
- Full profile of T.Wall & Sons (Ice-cream) Ltd. This included data on percentage volume breakdown into five product groups, numbers employed, R&D expenditure, type of outlet serviced with numbers (CTNs, supermarkets, canteens etc.), discounts and bonuses, advertising and promotional expenditures etc. Appendices include full details of price lists as at 2 October 1978; comparison of production hours and target capacity by type of production machine 1972–1976, trading results and detailed return on capital employed data for 1972–1977.
- Full profile of Lyons Maid Ltd. and other subsidiaries of Glacier Foods Ltd. These included data on outlet share, raw material suppliers, numbers employed, R&D expenditure, discounted bonuses, advertising and promotional expenditure etc. Appendices again included full details of price lists as at 2 October 1978, trading results and detailed returns on capital employed data for 1972–1977. The additional discussions of the production and distribution connections, the profiles of the secondary manufacturers, consideration of features from capacity utilisation to advertising intensity, evidence from all interested parties etc. led to the conclusion that a monopoly situation existed.

Thus a wide range of data from official sources generously supplemented by information from this investigation were thus utilised.

10.16.2 *Cocoa, Chocolate and Sugar Confectionery*

During the latter part of 1967, a number of large manufacturers submitted applications for price increases to come into operation at the beginning of 1968 in accordance with the early-warning arrangements under counter-inflationary policy. Although MAFF thought that these proposed increases in the prices of chocolate and sugar confectionery were justified under the criteria set out in successive White Papers on Prices and Incomes, both MAFF and the Secretary of State for Economic Affairs decided that the NBPI should be asked to examine the structure of costs and prices in the industry "with special regard to the industry's capacity to undertake new investment."

The result six months later was the publication of *Costs and Prices of the Chocolate and Sugar Confectionery Industry* [B.400]. The NBPI inquiry involved all the large manufacturers in the industry, and a cross-section of the medium-sized and smaller manufacturers. Detailed information on their prices, sales, costs, wages structure, productivity, cash flow, investment and capital employed were provided.

The report carries statistical data culled from regular official statistical sources and enriched by the NBPI's discussion with what was then the CCCA. The CCCA submitted representations on behalf of the industry as a whole. The following description and comments show that the range of data obtained is relevant to most sections of this chapter:

- Table 1 of the text gives the make-up of consumer sales in 1967 in value and the percentage distribution across manufacturers' sales, distributors' margins and purchase tax from CCCA sources.
- Table 2 of the text gives expenditure on press and television advertising 1962 to 1967. Chocolate and sugar confectionery are compared in value with tobacco and alcohol from what was then the regular source of Legion Information Services Ltd.
- Table 3 of the text reports average rate of return on capital employed of the ten largest companies for 1965, 1966 and 1967 from the NBPI inquiry. This rate of return was defined on net assets at end year balance sheet valuation.

Much of the detailed information on market shares, sales, output per head, costs, profits etc. are found in the Appendicies. These data frequently distinguish between the top four, the next six and the rest of the companies in the market at that time. [B.400] clearly showed how much data had to be collected to make a judgement on an industry where the top four firms made 80 per cent of the chocolates and nearly 25 per cent of the sweets in 1967. Both Fels [B.51] and [B.400] carry good discussions of the methodology used in this exceptional investigation.

Data for many dimensions of this chapter can also be gleaned from *Cadbury Schweppes Foods Ltd. — Grocery Products* [B.418]. This 1978 Price Commission report resulted from the investigation which followed that firm's notification of its intention to increase the price of its general range of food products (excluding canned goods) by a weighted average of 7.42 per cent. This report contains some separate data and information on the chocolate-related products for this multi-product firm. Besides the use of *Shaws Guide to Fair Retail Prices* [QRL.453] for cocoa and drinking chocolate (retail prices for January 1974 to February 1978), the Price Commission compared changes in the prices of cocoa beans, butter and cake from its own study. The chapters on cocoa buying, manufacture in general and in Cadbury Schweppes Foods give some good background on the relationships between ingredient inputs and cocoa-based product outputs, particularly with respect to price relationships.

The Cadbury Schweppes company profile shows the 1976 sales breakdown for products linked with Cadbury chocolate confectionery (i.e. cocoa; drinking chocolate; chocolate spread; bournvita; biscuits — chocolate and plain) compared with major new product developments and other products. The financial performance of Cadbury Schweppes from 1975 to 1977 was summarised for the many components: profit before tax; sales; percentage margin on sales (excluding tax); capital employed and percentage return on capital employed; and cash flow. These data are largely from the published accounts. But there is no separate breakdown of profit etc. in this multi-product food group for its chocolate and related products. This confirms in many ways the uniqueness of the NBPI report on *Costs and Prices of the Chocolate and Sugar Confectionery Industry* [B.400] discussed earlier in this section.

10.17 Improvements and Comments

The first point is an obvious one with respect to SIC(1980) coverage. Grouping together ice-cream with cocoa, sugar confectionery and chocolate confectionery must be more of a demand-side, than a process-based, classification. There is limited commonality of both manufacturers and ingredients. Indeed the work of the BCCCA and the Ice Cream Alliance confirms that the industry has perceptions which differ markedly from official classifications. That said, it is nevertheless true that in some aspects, this Group is well served by statistical sources although the coverage is inevitably variable. The shortcomings of official data on consumption of the many chocolate and sugar confectionery products outside the home in *Household Food Consumption and Expenditure* [QRL.267] has been already noted in section 10.10.1.

In contrast, there are ample data on cocoa commodity prices and trade. The *Cocoa Market Report* [QRL.249], *Cocoa Statistics* [QRL.250] and the *Quarterly Bulletin of Cocoa Statistics* [QRL.397] all collect together information of interest to cocoa producers and cocoa processors.

The BCCCA, and its predecessor the CCCA, have provided a wealth of information since the first *Annual Report* [QRL.41] was published in 1948. The coverage of the *Statistical Year Book* [QRL.461] and the *Annual Review* [QRL.49] have been referred to in many sections of this chapter. The information is collected in the first instance from members and for members. These are primary data which are communicated by member companies to the BCCCA. As such, it must be stressed that the definitions of product classifications change from time to time.

The fruits of most of this work used to be generally available in the *Annual Report* [QRL.41]. But, as noted in section 10.2, since the merger of the CCCA and the CBA, the *Statistical Year Book* [QRL.461] has to be purchased by non-members. The freely-available *Annual Review* [QRL.49] contains much less data than the previous *Annual Report* [QRL.41] which covered most statistical dimensions in its time. This is an understandable development given the costs of collection. Thus a charge is now made for the data which were formerly freely available.

The Ice Cream Alliance and the Ice Cream Federation provide no comparable service to the BCCCA. However, there is separate coverage for ice-cream in the quarterly *Business Monitor PQ4213* [QRL.138] which survived the truncation of the PQ Monitor series in 1989.

Given the extensive work of the BCCCA, we are reliant upon the *Statistical Year Book* [QRL.461] for the coverage of cocoa, chocolate and sugar confectionery rather than the BSO. Here it is worth emphasising that *Business Monitor PA421* [QRL.113] sometimes treats AH4213 and AH4214 separately under SIC(1980). It would be helpful if guides to the separate coverage of these two Activity Headings could be made more precise in the accompanying notes to the Business Monitors. In fact, the summary tables in *Business Monitor PA1002* [QRL.93] do provide yearly runs for employment; wages and salaries; output; net capital expenditure; by the separate Activity Headings.

For financial information, we again depend upon the published accounts of companies. But many of the major manufacturers are multi-product firms. The range of data in the 1968 NBPI report on *Costs and Prices of the Chocolate and Sugar Confectionery Industry* [B.400] fulfilled a useful function more than twenty years ago but nothing compares to this today. Conversely, there is much more information on consumption, advertising and brand performance (see section 10.14.2) from the companies themselves. Perhaps this is only to be expected in an industry which has many products aimed at all age groups.

Finally, there is the problem of the inadequate treatment of small firms in this Group. It is serious, for example, that the BSO coverage in *Business Monitor PQ4213* [QRL.138] largely excludes establishments employing 25 people or less. This may obviously apply to official sources but it may be also be true of trade associations like the BCCCA and the Ice Cream Alliance which can only collect data from members and/or those willing and able to supply it. Insofar as firms choose not to be members, their activities will be hardly recorded. This feature of the sparse coverage of smaller firms is not unique to this Group. However the gaps can only be repaired by regular surveys of their activities.

CHAPTER 11

STARCH AND MISCELLANEOUS FOODS (EXCLUDING TEA, COFFEE AND BREAKFAST CEREALS)

The information in this chapter relates to the starch industry, Group 418, and the miscellaneous foods industries, Group 423, in the *CSO Standard Industrial Classification Revised 1980* [B.232]. It must be noted, however, that tea and coffee are dealt with separately in Chapter 12 and that breakfast cereals are treated along with grain milling and bread, biscuits and flour confectionery in Chapter 8. Other more general sources, which provide statistics on other industry Groups as well, are covered in Chapter 2 and should be consulted as required. The contents of this chapter are as follows:

11.1 Introduction

Industry Groups 418 and 423 cover the following Activity Headings:

4180 Starch.
Manufacture of maize, wheat, potato, and other starches and starch products, including soluble starch, dextrin, glucose, syrups and dextrose.

4239 Miscellaneous Foods.
1. Coffee and coffee substitutes.
2. Tea.
3. Potato crisps and other snack products.
4. Infant and dietetic foods.
Manufacture of infant and dietetic foods including products based on flour but excluding those having a milk base which are classified to

heading 4130. Starch and malt extracts are included.
5. Sweets and puddings, cake mixtures, cornflour products and yeast.
6. Broths, soups, sauces and other relishes.
7. Pasta products (including filled pasta).
8. Breakfast cereals.
Manufacture of ready-to-eat breakfast cereals excluding uncooked products (e.g. oatmeal) which are classified to heading 4160.
9. All other foods, not elsewhere specified.

Table 11.1: Activities Classified Under Groups 418 and 423 of SIC(1980) Compared with SIC(1968)

SIC(1980) AH		SIC(1968) MLH
4180	Starch	
	Arrowroot manufacturing	229.2
	Dextrin manufacturing	229.2
	Dextrose manufacturing	229.2
	Glucose manufacturing	229.2
	Laundry starch manufacturing	229.2
	Maize starch manufacturing	229.2
	Potato starch manufacturing	229.2
	Rice starch manufacturing	229.2
	Soluble starch manufacturing	229.2
	Starch manufacturing	229.2
	Warp starch manufacturing	229.2
	Wheat starch manufacturing	229.2
4239.1	Coffee and coffee substitutes (see Chapter 12)	
4239.2	Tea (see Chapter 12)	
4239.3	Potato crisps and other snack products	
	Potato crisp manufacturing	218.3
	Potato puff manufacturing	218.3
	Potato stick manufacturing	218.3
	Potato straw manufacturing	218.3
	Snack products, puffed or extruded (from farinaceous or proteinaceous material) manufacturing	218.3
4239.4	Infant and dietetic foods, starch and malt extract	
	Diabetic food manufacturing	229.2
	Dietetic food (excluding milk-based) manufacturing	229.2
	Infant food (other than milk-based) manufacturing	229.2
	Invalid food (other than milk-based) manufacturing	229.2
	Malt extract manufacturing	229.2

SIC(1980) AH		SIC(1968) MLH
	Yeast and vegetable extract manufacturing	229.2
4239.5	Sweets and puddings, cake mixtures, cornflower products and yeast	
	Aerating powder manufacturing	229.2
	Baking powder manufacturing	229.2
	Blancmange powder manufacturing	229.2
	Cake mixture manufacturing	229.2
	Canned pudding, including rice pudding, manufacturing	229.2
	Cornflour manufacturing	229.2
	Custard powder manufacturing	229.2
	Fruit pudding (canned) manufacturing	229.2
	Junket powder manufacturing	229.2
	Pudding mixture manufacturing	229.2
	Rice pudding (canned) manufacturing	229.2
	Yeast preparation	229.2
4239.6	Broths, soups, sauces and other relishes	
	Canned broth, containing meat or vegetables or both, manufacturing	218.3
	Canned soup, containing meat or vegetables or both, manufacturing	218.3
	Catsup manufacturing	218.3
	Ketchup manufacturing	218.3
	Mayonnaise manufacturing	218.3
	Mint sauce manufacturing	229.2
	Powdered broth, containing meat or vegetables or both, manufacturing	218.3
	Relish manufacturing	218.3
	Salad cream manufacturing	218.3
	Salad dressing manufacturing	218.3
	Sandwich spread manufacturing	218.3
	Sauce manufacturing	218.3
	Soup manufacturing	218.3
4239.7	Pasta products (including filled pasta)	
	Macaroni manufacturing	229.2
	Noodle manufacturing	229.2
	Ravioli manufacturing	229.2
	Spaghetti manufacturing	229.2
	Spaghetti canning	218.3
	Vermicelli manufacturing	229.2
4239.8	Breakfast cereals (see Chapter 8)	

SIC(1980) AH		SIC(1968) MLH
4239.9	All other foods, not elsewhere specified	
	Almond grinding	229.2
	Chicory root drying manufacturing	229.2
	Curry powder manufacturing	229.2
	Dried egg manufacturing	229.2
	Dried herbs (except field dried) manufacturing	218.3
	Egg drying	229.2
	Egg pickling	229.2
	Egg substitute manufacturing	229.2
	Flaked coconut (including desiccated but not sugared) manufacturing	229.2
	Forcemeat manufacturing	229.2
	Gravy manufacturing	229.2
	Gravy salt (not at salt mine or brine pit) manufacturing	229.2
	Ground pepper manufacturing	229.2
	Ground spice manufacturing	229.2
	Herb tea manufacturing	229.2
	Honey processing and packing	218.1
	Hop extract manufacturing	218.3
	Ice manufacturing	229.2
	Isinglass manufacturing	229.2
4239.9	All other foods, not elsewhere specified	
	Mustard manufacturing	229.2
	Nut food manufacturing	229.2
	Nut shelling, grinding and preparing	229.2
	Peanut butter manufacturing	229.2
	Pepper substitute manufacturing	229.2
	Salt preparation (not at salt mine or brine pit) manufacturing	229.2
	Seasoning manufacturing	229.2
	Spice purifying	229.2
	Stuffing manufacturing	229.2
	Vinegar (malt, spirit, wine, acetic acid) manufacturing	218.3
	Wine vinegar manufacturing	218.3

For an alphabetical list of the activities covered by Groups 418 and 423, see Table 11.1 or CSO *Indexes to the Standard Industrial Classification Revised 1980* [B.317]. Group 418 covers a variety of food and non-food products many of which are starch derivatives, such as glucose, dextrose and dextrin. Group 423 embraces a wide and diverse range of foods and beverages, which are classified into nine sub-headings. For the most part, each of these sub-headings contains a theme — a common process or market — but in the case of the ninth category "all other foods, not elsewhere specified" we necessarily have a collection of mixed items, although perhaps many could be grouped as "food ingredients and seasonings".

Most of the items in these two SIC(1980) Groups were previously classified under MLH229.2 in SIC(1968). The main motive for the changes incorporated in SIC(1980) was to bring the classification more into line with the NACE classification used by the European Community. Anyone who wishes to compare the two classifications should make use of the detailed *Standard Industrial Classification Revised 1980: Reconciliation with Standard Industrial Classification 1968* [B.379]. In addition to the division of MLH229.2 "Starch and miscellaneous foods" into Groups 418 and 423, the following changes were also effected:

Activities included under MLH229.2 but not included in Group 423

SIC(1968)		SIC(1980)
229.2	Rennet (not artificial) manufacturing	4126.3
229.2	Desserts, with a milk base, manufacturing	4130.3
229.2	Ice-cream powder manufacturing	4213

Activities not included under MLH229.2 but included in Group 423

SIC(1968)		SIC(1980)
218.3	Potato crisps and other snack products	4239.3
218.3	Broths, soups, sauces and other relishes	4239.6
218.3	Spaghetti canning	4239.7
211.2	Breakfast cereals	4239.8
218.3	Dried herbs (except field dried) manufacturing	4239.9
218.1	Honey processing and packaging	4239.9
218.3	Hop extract manufacturing	4239.9
218.3	Vinegar manufacturing	4239.9
218.3	Wine vinegar manufacturing	4239.9

Thus "Fruit and vegetable products" (MLH218) has been the 'donor' of several activities to AH4239, rather than to Group 414 "Processing of fruit and vegetables", which might perhaps have been a more natural recipient. In this latter Group, it is worth noting that AH4147.2 "Pickling and preserving of fruit and vegetables in salt or oil" contains many activities that result in similar products to those found in AH4239.6 or AH4239.9. Further discussion of the common markets for such products from different industrial Groups will be provided in subsequent sections. Comments on the definition of "Starch and miscellaneous foods" under earlier SICs may be found in the *Historical Record of the Census of Production 1907–1970* [QRL.264].

Finally, it should be emphasised again that some activities classified to Group 423 are discussed in other chapters in this Review. Breakfast cereals (AH4239.8) have already been covered in Chapter 8. Tea (AH4239.2) and coffee (AH4239.1) are the subject of Chapter 12. Statistics which relate to Group 423 in aggregate are considered in this chapter.

11.2 Industry Structure

Business Monitors in the annual Production series are normally provided for single industry Groups, but data for Groups 418 and 423 are consolidated in *Business*

Monitor PA423: Starch and Miscellaneous Foods [QRL.114]. Two quarterly sales inquiries were however undertaken up to the second quarter of 1989, the results of which were published separately in *Business Monitor PQ4180: Starch* [QRL.135] and *Business Monitor PQ4239: Miscellaneous Foods* [QRL.139]. Both quarterly Monitors were produced in that form since the first quarter of 1983, and both related to establishments of 35 or more employees. Since the first quarter of 1987, however, a change occurred in the reporting arrangements for the sales inquiries which gave more prominence to the company unit in determining the coverage of returns. Most returns were then completed for a *single company*, including any "non-productive" activities; but for a limited number of larger mixed-activity companies, returns remained on an establishment basis. For further details, see the introduction to either of the above Monitors.

Table 11.2: Principal Products of SIC(1980) Groups 418 and 423 and Number of Enterprises, 1987

Product (Group 418)	Enterprises
Group 418	
Maize starch	4
Maize by-products:	
Maize germ and oil	3
Gluten less than 30 per cent protein	**
Gluten more than 30 per cent protein	3
Corn steep liquor	**
Glucose:	
Solid (including powdered)	6
Syrup	4
Wheat gluten	**
Wheat starch	**
Unclassified sales	6
Group 423	
Cereal breakfast foods in packets for retail sale:	
Wheat	8
Maize	4
Other (including mixed)	14
Potato crisps and sticks	10
Snack products made from potato granules, maize and other cereals	14
Honey	5
Sauces:	
Tomato sauce and ketchup	12
Other thick sauces	25
Thin sauces	7
Salad cream and mayonnaise	16
Other sauces and relishes	32
Vinegar	12
Soups:	

Product (Group 423)	Enterprises
Ready to serve	9
Other (including condensed, soup squares and powders)	10
Meat substitutes of vegetable origin	5
Homogenised baby foods	3
Farinaceous preparations for use as foods, excluding proprietary food drinks:	
Starch food powders:	
Blancmange powder and custard powder	12
Pre-packed cornflour	5
Other (including dessert powders (for serving cold) and similar products)	11
Frozen mousse desserts	–
Flour-based pudding mixtures	5
Flour-based cake mixtures, bun pre-mixes and similar products	8
Canned (including rice) puddings, desserts, custards etc. (served hot or cold)	4
Self-raising flour made from purchased flour	4
Aerating (baking) powders	8
Ready meals and other products of vegetable or grain without pastry including frozen meals (excluding canned)	**
Macaroni, spaghetti, vermicelli, noodles and similar pasta products (canned)	7
Macaroni, spaghetti, vermicelli, noodles and similar pasta products (excluding canned)	6
Other farinaceous preparations used as foods	4
Bread improvers, cake extenders and similar products	8
Proprietary foods and food drinks (not specifically medicinal) other than yoghurt and other milk based products	6
Gravy salt and other preparations for gravy making (including stock cubes)	14
Yeast	7
Seasonings, stuffings and forcemeat	14
Vegetable extracts	6
Coffee and coffee and chicory extracts (excluding liquid essences):	
Coffee, roasted and ground (excluding decaffeinated)	9
Coffee and chicory, roasted and ground (excluding decaffeinated)	8
Coffee with fig seasoning (Viennese coffee)	6
Soluble coffees:	
Spray dried (excluding decaffeinated)	7
Freeze dried (excluding decaffeinated)	3
Decaffeinated	3
Liquid essences	–
Tea:	
Blended	15
In bags	15

Product (Group 423)	Enterprises
Mustard	8
Ground pepper and pepper substitute, compound etc.	8
Spices, ground:	
Curry powder	8
Other	9
Egg products (excluding egg substitutes)	5
Peanut butter and the like	3
Nuts, shelled or otherwise prepared:	
Processed (excluding shelled and cleaned):	
Peanuts	11
Cashews	8
Mixed nuts	9
Other	8
Unprocessed, i.e. shelled and cleaned	5
Unclassified sales	46

Sources This information is adapted from data in the 1988 issues (third quarter) of *Business Monitor PQ4180* [QRL.135] and *Business Monitor PQ4239* [QRL.139]

The figures show the number of enterprises contributing to the heading in any one of the four quarters of 1987. An enterprise comprises one or more units under common ownership or control.

– means nil.

** means not available.

Both *Business Monitor PQ4180* [QRL.135] and *Business Monitor PQ4239* [QRL.139] published sales in a fair degree of detail, especially the latter which included some 56 separate categories — see Table 11.2 for more details of the principal products of Groups 418 and 423 and the number of enterprises. It is not, always possible, however, to align these with the SIC(1980) classifications. Further details of sales are given in section 11.4, although it is worth noting two general difficulties regarding the disclosure of data. The first is that some products of AH4239 are only manufactured by small firms with less than 35 employees. Information relating to these sales is thus not shown separately in *Business Monitor PQ4239* [QRL.139], but only in the final aggregate total for the Activity Heading. Ice production seems to be a case in point. The second instance arises when fewer than three firms (with more than 35 employees) are responsible for the whole market output, and thus data on individual firms could be identified from published statistics. Salt would be an example here. Again the relevant data are not published.

Group 423 covers a significant proportion of the activities of the Food industries: 13 per cent of employment; 15 per cent of sales; and, indicative of the capital intensive nature of many of the processes involved, almost one quarter of capital expenditure. These figures are derived from the 1985 edition of *Business Monitor PA1002: Summary Volume* [QRL.93]. However, the range of different activities covered means that statistics relating to the Group as a whole are of limited value in describing the structures of the various industries concerned. For example, data from the Census of Production suggest that Group 423 exhibits a low level of concentration, with a five-firm concentration ratio (CR5) of only 26 per cent in 1985. Previous inquiries — e.g. Watts [B.184] — yield similar results. Yet analysis of specific activities gives an entirely different picture, with concentration levels among the highest in the Food industries: it is simply the aggregation of data in Group 423 that produces the low CR5 level mentioned above. Some indication of the degree of product concentration may be gleaned from *Business Monitor PQ4239* [QRL.139], where the number of enterprises contributing to the inquiry is shown for each food product — see Table 11.2. The only enterprises included in the published statistics will be those with more than 35 employees, and data on concentration will only be published where the market has three or more such enterprises.

Of historical interest are the concentration data published in *Business Monitor PO1006: Statistics of Product Concentration of UK Manufacturers* [QRL.115], which gave CR5 ratios for the years 1975, 1976, and 1977 for the following products: potato crisps, pickles, sauces and relishes; soups (including meat substitutes) and homogenised baby food; maize starch and by-products; farinaceous preparations for use as foods; glucose, yeast, bread improvers and similar products; proprietary foods and food drinks; seasonings, stuffings, gravy salt, spices and other products; nuts, shelled, ground and coconut.

The structures of the following seven product markets will now be described in turn: starch (AH4180); potato crisps and other snack products (AH4239.3); infant and dietetic foods, starch and malt extract (AH4239.4); sweets and puddings, cake mixtures, cornflour products and yeast (AH4239.5); broths, soups, sauces and other relishes (AH4239.6); pasta products (AH4239.7); and all other foods, not elsewhere specified (AH4239.9).

11.2.1 *Starch*

In the United Kingdom, starch is processed from cereal raw materials (principally maize, and also wheat) and is itself an intermediate product used directly and as derivatives in the food, drink and non-food industries. In 1985, it was estimated that 70 per cent of the total usage of starch and starch derivatives in the United Kingdom was in the food and drink industries, with confectionery accounting for nearly one quarter of total usage. The main non-food users were the paper and board, adhesives, pharmaceuticals, textiles, plastics and biotechnology industries — see the 1985 House of Lords report on the *EEC Starch Regime* [B.252].

Starch itself is produced as an ingredient for many foods. It is the principal constituent of custard and blancmange powders; and is used in the manufacture of cakes, biscuits, cake mixes, gravy powders, doughs, packeted puddings, ice-cream, batters, soups and canned meats — see the 1971 Monopolies Commission report on the *Supply of Starch, Glucoses and Modified Starches* [B.454]. Imported maize is the major input, accounting in 1985 for about 85–90 per cent of UK starch production, with a growing wheat starch industry making up the balance. The increasing output of wheat starch is partly due to the developing use of wheat gluten, a co-product, to strengthen UK and other EC soft flours in the bread-making grist and partly due to technical progress and favourable EC arrangements under the CAP — see *EEC Starch Regime* [B.252].

Three firms — CPC (UK) Ltd., Tunnel Refineries (owned by Tate & Lyle since its acquisition of Staley) and Cargill UK Ltd. — account for the entire maize starch industry at the time of writing. In the past, Tate & Lyle were independently involved in several ways, but their previous maize starch and glucose capacity (much of which was acquired in the Manbre0 & Garton take-over in 1976) was closed down in 1980. More companies are concerned with the wheat starch industry, but since the withdrawal of Tate & Lyle from potato starch (farina) manufacture, there has been no production of starch from this source in the United Kingdom.

The major starch product, glucose, is manufactured by the same principal companies from slurry or "wet starch" in a vertically integrated process. Glucose is primarily used in the food and drinks industry, but dextrose is also incorporated in pharmaceutical products. Limitations on the production of isoglucose — High Fructose Corn Syrup (HFCS) — by EC quotas on individual companies have restricted its use as an industrial sweetener. Tunnel Refineries is the only UK isoglucose producer. Modified starches, such as dextrine, are mainly used in the manufacture of adhesives.

General reviews of the UK starch industry are neither common nor frequent. The 1971 Monopolies Commission report on the *Supply of Starch, Glucoses and Modified Starches* [B.454] gives a useful account of the historical development of the industry. The 1978 Price Commission report on *CPC (United Kingdom) Ltd. — Increases in the Prices of Maize, Starch, Glucose, Syrup, Starch-derived and Glucose-derived Products* [B.420] brings information on the principal company slightly up-to-date. While the 1985 House of Lords report on the *EEC Starch Regime* [B.252] is more recent and does give a broad picture of the industry, its primary concern is with the arrangements affecting starch under the Common Agricultural Policy (CAP).

11.2.2 *Potato Crisps and Other Snack Products*

Crisps and snacks constitute a separate market, more perhaps by process and ingredient than by consumers' perception. Potato crisps (and sticks) are defined by manufacturers as "fried slices of raw potato", whereas savoury snacks are reconstituted from cereal or potato flour by extrusion before frying. Consumers may see little difference between potato crisps, and snacks such as reconstituted crisps (e.g. square crisps). Processed nuts — classified to AH4239.9 — are also considered as part of the snack market in one of the main surveys of the industry, the annual *KP Snack Foods Review* [QRL.302]. This gives *inter alia* market structure information covering the major products, producers and brand shares. The total snack market (crisps, savoury snacks, and nuts) is dominated by three companies: Nabisco, United Biscuits and Dalgety. In crisps, Walker's (Nabisco) are the leading brand and hold about one quarter of the market, with Golden Wonder (Dalgety) and KP (United Biscuits) next in brand order. Nabisco also produce Smith's and Tudor crisps, and Nabisco and KP make most retailers' own-label brands. Dalgety also acquired Hunter's snacks and crisps business in 1988. Together the three leaders produce some 85 per cent of UK crisps — *KP Snack Foods Review* [QRL.302]. In savoury snacks, KP and Smith's vie for leadership with around a 30 per cent market share each. Similarly the leading three companies account for more than 85 per cent of the snack market. On the other hand, processed nuts are dominated by a clear market leader (KP) with more than 50 per cent of sales with Nabisco, through Smith's and Planters, the other major producer. Golden Wonder is only very small in this market.

The development of the potato crisp and savoury snack markets has been relatively well documented. The period in the 1960s when Smith's traditional market leadership in crisps was challenged and overtaken by Golden Wonder is traced historically and analysed by Bevan [B.17]. A 1981 publication from the EC Commission, *Potato Products Production and Markets in the European Communities* [B.192] by N.A. Young, contains an account of the early development of the potato-processing industry, its products, processes, and raw material requirements. It reviews the industries in the then nine Member States of the Community, including the United Kingdom. A further analysis of snack and crisp market structures appears in the 1982 MMC publication, *Nabisco Brands Inc. and Huntley and Palmer Foods plc: A Report on the Proposed Merger* [B.448]. Numerous market research reports also cover the field with regular reviews of the markets for crisps, savoury snacks and processed nuts, either considered separately or together as total snacks — see section 11.14 for further details.

11.2.3 *Infant and Dietetic Foods, Starch and Malt Extract*

The infant foods covered by this sub-heading include products based on flour, but exclude those having a milk base which are classified to AH4130 "Preparation of milk and milk products". Rusks are part of AH4197 "Biscuits and crispbread". However, many of the references covering the baby foods market do so as a whole, including baby milk foods, rusks and baby drinks along with baby cereal meals and homogenised foods, which are the subject of this section. A useful summary of the total market is contained in the annual report prepared by Cow & Gate entitled *Babyfoods: Market Report* [QRL.56].

Numerous market research reports exist in this area including the reviews of "Baby foods" in the August and September 1986 issues of *Retail Business* [QRL.432], and the report by Marketing Strategies for Industry on *Baby Products* [QRL.618]. The reports again suggest a market dominated by few companies, with some encompassing the whole range of baby products. The main companies at the time of writing (1988) are: Boots, (since its acquisition of Farley Health Products from Glaxo in 1986), Cow & Gate, (owned by the Dutch firm Nutricia) and Milupa, (a subsidiary of the West German firm, Alttana AG, ultimately owned by Varta AG.). Heinz and Wyeth Laboratories, both US companies, are also major forces in the trade, despite being more specialised. The baby meals sector is led by Heinz, with over one-third value share, while Milupa and Cow & Gate have one-fifth each. Robinsons, a subsidiary of Reckitt & Colman, and Boots (Crookes-Farley) virtually complete the market structure.

Other than the reports mentioned, there are few texts which discuss the baby foods' market in detail. In 1967 the Monopolies Commission reported on the *Supply of Infant Milk Foods* [B.446] with only a brief resume of the other aspects of the baby foods' market which concern us here. The 1975 EC Commission publication, *Study in the Evolution of Concentration in the Food Industry: The United Kingdom. Part I, Part II (Product Market Structure)* [B.384] devoted a brief chapter in Volume

I of Part II to infant foods. This is now mainly of historical interest, although it highlights the extreme difficulty faced by potential new entrants into this highly-branded market. Nestlé, Libbys, Batchelors, Scotts and more recently Gerber (through CPC's established position) have tried to challenge Heinz's leadership, but have subsequently withdrawn.

The dietetic foods category of this section covers a multitude of products. Most easily defined are diabetic foods, which are essentially sugar-free versions of grocery food products, such as preserves, chocolate and confectionery, sweets, jellies and desserts, canned fruits, etc. Diabetic foods are largely sold through chemists and many appear under Boots' own-label, although only pastilles are actually produced by the company. Otherwise major producers such as Cadbury-Schweppes, CPC in the Frank Cooper brand range, and Allied-Lyons are involved along with the most specialised producer, Smith Kendon Ltd., which manufactures confectionery under the Skels label. Market structure is concentrated, and competition limited. Generally this area is less well-defined in cereal products, such as mueslis and biscuits, where sugar-free alternatives are marketed through groceries and form a normal part of their product range. Sugar substitutes may also be consumed for diabetic or other health, including slimming, reasons.

Official statistics are not common or detailed in this area. The 1975 Price Commission report on the *Prices of Commonly-purchased Diabetic Foods* [B.424] provides a dated but comprehensive review which formed in turn the basis for the diabetic foods section in the 1975 EC Commission report [B.384]. The latter, like many of the market research reports in this area, covers a wide range of dietetic and health foods.

Dietetic foods are strictly defined as meal replacements and slimmers' products. However, in practice many other variants of standard items may be discussed: e.g. starch-reduced bread, rolls and crispbreads, muesli, diet and low calorie products, low fat spreads, and so on. Market research reports such as *The Slimming Foods Report* [QRL.539] published in 1983 by Euromonitor, and the Key Note review of *Slimming Products* [QRL.596], include many of these products in their reviews. Official statistics, based on the narrow definition of AH4239.4, cover a market largely dominated by pharmaceutical companies, particularly Unicliffe Ltd. (a subsidiary of Pfizer Inc.) which produces Limmits and Trimetts, and which claims a brand leadership in excess of half the total market. The appetite-suppressant sub-market is led by Ayds, a Cuticura product.

Invalid foods discussed in this section, again other than milk-based, are produced principally by pharmaceutical companies such as Beechams (Bemax), Fisons Pharmaceuticals (Bengers) and Glaxo (Complan). Similar products in origin, but now developed into a wider market, are the proprietary branded food drinks. In this concentrated market, Beechams is the leader with Horlicks. Other major companies are Wander (Ovaltine) and Cadbury-Schweppes (Bournvita). A useful source of information on this market is the *Milk Food Drinks: Market Report* [QRL.356] published by Beecham Bovril Brands.

Detailed information is again limited in official statistics, but comprehensive discussions occur in market research publications, a good example being *Specialist Health, Slimming and Dietetic Foods* [QRL.543] by Euromonitor. Other health food reports, such as by Key Note and Marketing Strategies for Industry cover vitamin and dietary supplements, such as produced by Booker (Healthcare), Boots (Crookes Healthcare) and Hanson (Sevenseas Healthcare). The health food drinks are discussed in only a few market research publications, the report by Market Assessment Publications on *Hot Drinks* [QRL.610] being one example.

This section also covers malt extracts, yeast and vegetable extract, mainly used as cooking aids — flavouring and gravy making — but also as spreads or drinks. Yeast-extract products are dominated by Beecham through Marmite while another brand, Bovril, of the same company contains both yeast and beef extract — it is thus classified to AH4122.3. Market research reports such as "Gravy products" in the November 1985 issue of *Retail Business* [QRL.432] provide details, but the overlapping nature of the market makes structure analysis difficult — see section 11.2.7.

11.2.4 *Sweets and Puddings, Cake Mixtures, Cornflour Products and Yeast*

A major part of this sub-heading is concerned with the manufacture of puddings and desserts, either in canned or other convenience form, or as mixes or powders, including custard and blancmange. In addition, the heading includes the manufacture of cake and pudding mixes, cornflour, aerating or baking powder, and yeast.

Of the canned puddings, rice pudding is the most important in terms of market size, and is included under this sub-heading despite its milk base which would normally lead to its classification under AH4130.3. Ambrosia, made by Beecham, is the clear market leader taking half the volume sales, with Libbys the second largest manufacturer, and there is a substantial retailers' own-label presence. Other sectors of the canned pudding market consist of "fruit pie filling", where Mortons (Beecham), Batchelor (Unilever) and Pickerings (Heinz) are the major brands, and "canned sponge and Christmas puddings", where Heinz again accounts for much of the trade. Market research reports once more provide the most detailed estimates of this market, examples being the Key Note report on *Canned Foods* [QRL.582], *The Convenience Food Report* [QRL.526] by Euromonitor, and the review of *Sweets & Desserts* [QRL.616] by Market Assessment Publications.

In the packaged desserts section, many US firms command the key market position. General Foods' long-established Birds custard powder and instant custard account for more than 50 per cent of sales in these markets. Retailers' own-labels hold about one-third of the custard powder market with CPC's Brown and Polson brand also holding an interest. UK manufacturers include Pearce Duff (Dalgety) and Rowntree Mackintosh (Nestlé), while Beecham's Ambrosia entirely dominates the canned, ready-to-serve custard market. Birds again holds a pre-eminent position in the market for instant whips and toppings (Instant Whip, Angel Delight, Dream Topping), and also in the whole trifle market.

Nabisco (part of R.J. Reynolds) has market leadership in the area of cake mixes (Mary Baker, Romix) and lemon pie fillings (Royal), and strong interests in cheese cake/dessert cake mixes (Royal, Granny Smith's). Greens of Brighton (owned by the US-based Pillsbury) is the major brand in this latter product market. Another puddings market is blancmange, where Brown & Polson (CPC) accounts for one-third of market sales. The same company also dominates a very similar product with a different use: cornflour. Other companies with interests in both products, albeit on a smaller scale, include Pearce Duff (Dalgety), Hazelwood Foods, and Rowntree Mackintosh (Nestle0). Market research reports covering this area include "Packaged desserts" in July 1983 issue of *Retail Business* [QRL.432], *The Convenience Food Report* [QRL.526] by Euromonitor and the review of *Sweets & Desserts* [QRL.616] by Market Assessment Publications.

A cooking aid also covered by this Activity Heading is baking (or aerating) powders. The established leading brand is Borwicks, which is owned by the US-based Pillsbury. British Pepper & Spice (S & W Berisfords), Pearce & Duff (Dalgety), General Foods, Lion and Rowntree Mackintosh (Nestle0) are other firms active in this market.

The final product in this sub-heading is yeast, which is mainly supplied to the bread and flour confectionery industry, but also enters the consumer market. Again we have a concentrated market, some seven firms accounting for the total output. It should be noted that bakers' yeast derived from distillery production is covered by AH4240.1.

11.2.5 *Broths, Soups, Sauces and Other Relishes*

Soups and broths (the distinction is not clear) form a substantial market which can be segmented in various ways. One is between canned soup (ready-to-serve and condensed) and dried (standard and "instant") including soup squares. Moreover, considering the consumers' market one may also distinguish "commodity soups" — basic long established products — chunky or meal-substitute soups, low calorie diet soups, and speciality soups.

Canned soup accounts for more than three-fifths of the total. Heinz remains the clear market leader with almost 60 per cent of canned soup sales, mainly derived through "commodity" products. Campbell's Soups (the US Campbell Soup Company), the only UK producer of condensed soups, and Crosse & Blackwell (Nestle0) compete in the commodity and speciality markets, with retailers' own-labels also significant in both areas. In packet soups, the market is more evenly shared between Batchelor (Unilever) with about one-third of the sales, Knorr (CPC) one-quarter, Crosse & Blackwell one-tenth, and a significant retailers' own-label presence. The instant soup market, on the other hand, is clearly dominated by Batchelor which accounts for over 70 per cent of sales, while Knorr and Crosse & Blackwell retain a limited share. Information on soups is most easily obtained from market research reports, some specific, such as the review of "Soup" in the September 1987 issue of *Retail Business* [QRL.432], and others covering wider markets, for example the Key Note report on *Canned Foods* [QRL.582] and *The Convenience Food Report* [QRL.526] by Euromonitor.

The remainder of this sub-heading is a little more heterogeneous. It consists of two main product ranges: sauces and relishes, and salad cream and mayonnaise. Some of the items — e.g chutneys, pickles, piccalillis — are similar in use to products classified to AH4147.2, and also to condiments, mustards and vinegar covered in AH4239.9. Market research reports occasionally group all these products together.

The tomato sauce and ketchup market has Heinz as leader, with a greater than 50 per cent share. Other manufacturers are HP/Daddies (now part of the French BSN group), Hazelwood Foods, and Crosse & Blackwell, while own-labels take a quarter of the market. Thick brown sauces are dominated by HP, with traditional HP fruity and Daddies collectively exceeding 60 per cent of the market, while Crosse & Blackwell's Branston sauces, Colman's OK, Hazelwood Foods and own-label brands complete the picture. Thin sauces are completely dominated by Lea & Perrin's Worcester sauce, another HP brand. These markets are discussed in market research reports such as the Key Note report on *Sauces & Spreads* [QRL.597] and the 1977 *Retail Business* [QRL.432] report on "Pickles and sauces".

Another important section of this market is canned and other cook-in sauces. The market leader is Homepride, a Dalgety brand, with three-quarters of the canned sauce trade, while other major producers include Campbells, Colmans, Buitoni (Italian firm IBP), Crosse & Blackwell, and Knorr (CPC). The 1986 report by Marketing Strategies for Industry on *Cooking Additives* [QRL.629] considers this area.

Finally, condiment sauces of significance include mint sauce, of which Colmans has a majority share. Other manufacturers include Rayner Burgess, Hazelwood Foods, HP, Lion, Baxters, Manley Ratcliffe and Rowntree Sun Pat. All these producers also make other condiment sauces of various types. The "spreads" part of this sub-heading covers salad creams and mayonnaise. Traditional salad cream is again dominated by Heinz with half the market sales, but retailers' own-label brands take up one-third. Crosse & Blackwell commands a similarly strong position in the low-calorie salad cream market with its Waistline brand exceeding 50 per cent. Mayonnaise producers include both these leaders, plus CPC with their Hellman's brand, Rayner Burgess and Manley Ratcliffe. Other sauces and dressings — Thousand Island, Blue Cheese, Continental varieties — are more evenly shared, but US companies Kraft (30 per cent) and Heinz (20 per cent) are the leaders. Heinz dominates the sandwich spread market completely. The Key Note report on *Sauces & Spreads* [QRL.597], the review of *Sauces & Pickles* [QRL.647] by Marketing Strategies for Industry, and the 1988 review of "Pickles and sauces" in *Retail Business* [QRL.432], are examples of the more detailed information sources.

11.2.6 *Pasta Products (including filled pasta)*

Pasta products are cereals, based on durum wheat, which are processed and dried, canned, chilled or frozen. Canned pasta is the established product, with spaghetti and its variants accounting for two-thirds of the trade. Heinz once more has a commanding share at around 70 per cent, other producers being Buitoni, Crosse & Blackwell, HP, and Napolina.

Dried pasta has been a developing market in recent years in the United Kingdom, supplied by one major UK producer and many imported products. Pasta Foods (Rank Hovis McDougall) covers a wide range of items under the Record label, and also produces other brands such as as Stoneground Wholewheat and retailers' own-label pasta. Imports include the Buitoni (acquired by Nestlé in 1988), Banilla, Cirio, Napolina and Lily brands from Italy, and Helios from Greece. Spaghetti is the most important individual product with about half the dried pasta sales by volume. Pasta Foods and Buitoni share market leadership, but retailers' own-label products account for almost half the total.

Fresh pasta is a relatively small market developed from the catering trade, and covers noodle and ribbon pasta (requiring sauce) and filled pasta such as ravioli and tortellini (no sauce necessary). Specialist producers, such as Pasta Reale, Rossi and Spaghetti House supply this market. Frozen pasta, on the other hand is supplied in the form of ready-made and snack foods by major producers, such as Birds Eye (Unilever), Findus (Nestlé) and McVities (United Biscuits). Golden Wonder (Dalgety) dominate the pasta "snack pot" market.

Information in this market is again derived from market research reports, examples being "Pasta" in the April 1986 issue of *Retail Business* [QRL.432], "Pasta" in the February 1985 edition of *Market Research: Great Britain* [QRL.343], the report on *Pasta and Pasta Products* [QRL.643] by Marketing Strategies for Industry, *The Convenience Food Report* [QRL.526] by Euromonitor, and the Key Note Report on *Canned Foods* [QRL.582].

11.2.7 *All Other Foods, Not Elsewhere Specified*

This sub-heading encompasses all the remaining food products not covered under other headings. It is thus a heterogeneous collection, though many of the products might be loosely described as "food ingredients and seasonings".

Gravy products, including gravy salt, perform specific functions in cooking, but others such as stock cubes, meat and vegetable extracts (the latter discussed in section 11.2.3) also may be used in gravy making and flavouring. Gravy brownings continue to be completely dominated by Bisto (Rank Hovis McDougall) with some 85 per cent of the market, other producers being Burdalls, Goldenfry, Birds (General Foods) and Colmans with its "Gravy Pot" product. Stock cubes have been traditionally the province of Oxo (Brooke Bond Oxo — a Unilever company) which retains a two-thirds market share, but Bovril (Beechams) has gained one-fifth of the trade in recent years, and other interests include Knorr (CPC) and Maggi (Nestlé, imports). Market research reports which discuss this market include "Gravy products" in the June 1980 issue of *Retail Business* [QRL.432], the 1986 report on *Cooking Additives* [QRL.629] by Marketing Strategies for Industry, and *Seasonings & Flavourings* [QRL.613] by Market Assessment Publications.

Pepper, spices and herbs form another section of this market, although again we may divide it into a number of sub-markets. The ground pepper sector is unusually competitive, with retailers' own-labels forming the largest group, accounting for around half the market sales. The leading manufacturer's brand is Lion (CC Spice), with Saxa (RHM), Millstone (British Pepper & Spice — S & W Berisfords) and Schwartz/McCormick as other producers.

In the spice market, curry powder is distinguished as a separate sub-section. Here Sharwood (RHM) is the clear market leader with 70 per cent of sales, Schwartz/McCormick and Lion also being involved. Other herbs and spices, including similarly packed seasonings, are very much dominated by Schwartz/McCormick (60 per cent), but retailers' own-labels provide an important alternative.

In general, this market has companies which are vertically integrated grinders/packers, particularly since the 1984 takeover of Schwartz by the US company McCormick (through the acquisition of its Canadian parent Jenks Brothers (Paterson Jenks)), but others merely pack for retail sale. Schwartz retains overall market leadership as measured by the value of sales; but Lion, with its significant and own-label interests, packs the largest volume. Information on this sub-market is provided by *Retail Business* [QRL.432] in its October 1985 issue on "Pepper, spices and herbs", and by the reviews of *Cooking Additives* [QRL.629] by Marketing Strategies for Industry and the same title by Market Assessment Publications.

A similar market is that of mustard, which has a long-established leader in Colmans with some four-fifths of the trade, although Lion and retailers' own-label products are now a more significant force. Vinegar too is a market with strong leadership, British Vinegar's brands dominating the malt sector through Sarsons, and the speciality sector through Dufrais. Other producers include HP (BSN), Heinz, Hazelwoods and Sharwoods (RHM). The Key Note report on *Sauces & Spreads* [QRL.597] provides recent data.

Salt is a product with many industrial applications and less than 10 per cent of the UK's output is sold, after repacking, for domestic use in cooking or as a condiment. A further 15 per cent of the salt industry's output is used by the Food industries in processing, although this proportion is declining. Only two companies, ICI and British Salt, manufacture salt in the United Kingdom in a roughly equal duopoly of the total market, albeit with specialist sector inequalities in their market shares. The consumer market in salt is dominated by RHM's brands, Saxa and Cerebos, although retailers' own brands are very significant in this commodity. Sea salt competition is small but has been growing, along with substitutes. The 1986 MMC report on *White Salt: A Report on the Supply of White Salt in the United Kingdom by Producers of Such Salt* [B.457] gives a thorough analysis of salt manufacture, but deals only incidentally with the market for the household product. Research reports again are the major source of details of this market, an example being the review of *Seasonings & Flavourings* [QRL.613] by Market Assessment Publications.

Another cooking ingredient market covers stuffing mixes, including forcemeat, which again has a strong market brand leader in Paxo, produced by RHM in a wide range of varieties. The same company also makes Norfolk Sage and Onion stuffing. Knorr Stuffing Mixes (CPC) and retailers' own-labels form the major competition. Marketing Strategies for Industry produce a review of *Cooking Additives* [QRL.629] and Market Assessment Publications provide a similarly titled report.

The remainder of this section attempts to review the rather amorphous group of products not yet discussed, although information may be very limited in some cases. The processed nuts market was considered under section 11.2.2 as a snack food, but market research reports argue that some products, such as almonds and other raw nuts are used as cooking ingredients and treat them separately. However, very little information is published on this sector as such. Peanut butter is regarded as part of the spreads market, and is discussed, for example, in the Key Note report on *Sauces & Spreads* [QRL.597], and in *Sweet and Savoury Spreads* [QRL.651] by Marketing Strategies for Industry. The clear market leader is Sun-Pat, now part of Rowntree Mackintosh (Nestlé), who also produce peanut butter under the Gales label. The same producer is the largest brand in the honey market with about one third of sales, although here retailers' own-labels (mostly made by Manley Ratcliffe) make up over half the trade. The same market research reports cover this market, and there is a specific, if rather dated *Retail Business* [QRL.432] report entitled "Honey" in August 1981.

Other products not discussed in detail but whose manufacture is covered by AH4239.9 include egg products, flaked coconut, herb tea, hop extract, ice, and isinglass.

11.3 The European Community

The most direct influences of the Community on the activities of industry Groups 418 and 423 are provided by the starch and sugar regimes, although policies in other areas, such as maize, durum wheat (for pasta), tomato products, potatoes, and oilseeds, impinge on the markets covered.

The starch regime has been significantly modified in recent years as a result of biotechnical developments enabling a significant expansion of non-food uses of starch (and sugar). The basic scheme of production refunds was designed to lower the prices of imported maize (subject to EC levies) down to comparable levels of other inputs that might be used in starch manufacture, especially petro-chemicals. The fundamentals are discussed in Harris, Swinbank and Wilkinson [B.71]. Detailed analyses and comments are contained in the two House of Lords reports, *Starch and Seeds* [B.380] of 1977/8, and *EEC Starch Regime* [B.252] in 1984/5. For information on the revised system of subsidising starch use by the chemical industry, but phasing out the aids to the Food industries, see the article by S.A. Harris on "The provision of carbohydrates for the European Community's biotechnology and chemical industries" [B.69]. This refers in detail to the various Community documents.

Glucose comes under the provisions of the Starch regime and its production from maize is subsidised in precisely the same way as starch. Isoglucose, known as high fructose corn syrup in the USA, was seen however as a direct competitor with sugar, and hence incorporated in the sugar regime (in 1981). Normal starch and glucose refunds did not apply when the product was used to manufacture isoglucose, investment grants for isoglucose by national governments were banned, and a system of very restrictive production quotas on individual companies introduced — see Harris, Swinbank and Wilkinson [B.71] and the paper by J.W.L. Graham on "Sugar and sweeteners" [B.60].

Fundamental to the starch and sweeteners regime is the cost of the basic ingredient: maize. This is influenced by the EC cereals arrangements, details of which are provided in leaflets produced by the Intervention Board for Agricultural Produce (IBAP). Comprehensive up-to-date information on the regimes is published by the Home-Grown Cereals Authority (HGCA) as *EEC Marketing Arrangements for Grains and Processed Products* [QRL.185]. The same organisation also produces a yearly compendium of data in the annual *Cereal Statistics* [QRL.152]. The IBAP *Notice to Traders* [QRL.379] and the HGCA *Weekly Bulletin* [QRL.512] provide short-term information on intervention prices, MCAs, rates of exchange, export refunds, and levies — see Chapter 8 for further details.

Pasta products are based on durum wheat, for which there is a production aid scheme applicable in "economically disadvantaged areas", mainly in Greece and Italy. A system of target, threshold and intervention prices also applies to durum wheat; details and statistics are again available from IBAP and HGCA publications.

Since this chapter covers many highly-processed foods incorporating a wide range of ingredients, inevitably prices and availability will be influenced by most, if not all, regimes. In particular, issues arise in the importing of raw materials and trading in processed products where, for example, relief may be given to goods exported outside the Community for the high cost of EEC-supported or protected ingredients.

Problems may also arise when minority interests in one Community country gain support measures which affect other EC producers' ingredient supplies and costs.

Rice — particularly long grain rice — is a case in point, and extreme difficulties were encountered in the discriminatory aid given to tomato products. References cited above provide details, and for the latter case see also the EC Commission on *Guidelines for European Agriculture* [B.300], and the 1981 House of Lords report on *Fruit and Vegetables* [B.292].

11.4 Output

11.4.1 *Output, Sales and Value Added*

11.4.1.1 Business Statistics Office inquiries

Business Monitor PQ4180: Starch [QRL.135] and *Business Monitor PQ4239: Miscellaneous Foods* [QRL.139] contain the results of the quarterly sales inquiries relating to Groups 418 and 423. Table 11.2 details the individual items for which data on sales are provided. The minimum employment threshold for businesses covered by these inquiries is 35 persons, although the "total sales" figures include estimates of the (unclassified) output of smaller businesses. *Business Monitor PA1002: Summary Volume* [QRL.93] may be consulted for details of the grossing-up methods employed. Given this employment threshold, both inquiries yield reasonably high levels of coverage: 99 per cent for AH4180 and 93 per cent for AH4239. However, following the *Review of DTI Statistics* [B.367] both *Business Monitor PQ4180* [QRL.135] and *Business Monitor PQ4239* [QRL.139] were not retained within the quarterly system after the second quarter of 1989.

Various changes had previously been effected in the collection and presentation of these sales statistics. Since the first quarter of 1987, reporting arrangements for all quarterly inquiries were altered to give greater prominence to the company unit — see section 11.2. The previous year saw the introduction of a new summary table in the PQ Business Monitors. This provided data on sales from establishments classified to the industry, an output index, and sales of products classified to the industry. Changes were also introduced in the products separately identified. Sales of "peanut butter and the like" were reported from the first quarter of 1987; of "vegetable extracts" from the first quarter of 1986; "*canned* pasta products" were separated from "*uncanned* pasta products" from the first quarter of 1985; "mustard" was separated from "ground pepper etc." from the first quarter of 1984. The first two categories mentioned above were previously incorporated in "unclassified" sales.

Finally, it was noted in section 11.2 that the annual *Business Monitor PA423: Starch and Miscellaneous Foods* [QRL.114] contains aggregate data on Groups 418 and 423 together. This Monitor provides details of various output measures: sales of goods produced, total sales and work done, gross output, net output (in total and per head), gross value added at factor cost (again in total and per head). These measures are analysed by establishment size group (on an employment basis), and the figures also reported in *Business Monitor PA1002* [QRL.93]. *Business Monitor PA423* [QRL.114] also shows various output operating ratios.

11.4.1.2 Ministry of Agriculture, Fisheries and Food inquiries

MAFF carry out a number of short period inquiries, the results of which are published in various MAFF Statistical Information Notices, the *Monthly Digest of*

Statistics [QRL.362], the *Annual Abstract of Statistics* [QRL.37], or *Output and Utilisation of Farm Produce in the United Kingdom* [QRL.382] (the latter up to 1987). These inquiries complement the sales inquiries undertaken by the BSO which were discussed in section 11.4.1.2. Slater [B.164] mentions the monthly MAFF surveys of glucose and starch production, and the quarterly inquiries into the production of potato crisps and snack foods, and of processed potato products.

The quarterly *MAFF Statistics: Potato Crisp and Snack Foods Survey* [QRL.323] groups the products as "Crisps and sticks" and "Snack products". Four quarters' sales are shown, analysed by weight, by private label and manufacturers' brand, and by flavour. The division into these two broad categories coincides with that adopted in the BSO sales inquiries, and with that used in the *KP Snack Foods Review* [QRL.302] which publishes aggregate annual sales data on the broad groups.

Significant differences between the BSO and MAFF statistics in this market have led to industry concern in recent years. The trade association — the Snack, Nut and Crisp Manufacturers' Association Ltd. (SNACMA) — was formed in 1983 by the leading companies in order to provide a source of detailed market statistics compiled from members' returns. The Association's information is not published or generally available to non-members. Output data on processed nuts was included in a MAFF Statistical Information Notice until 1984, but was subsequently discontinued. The *KP Snack Foods Review* [QRL.302] again publishes broad market figures on sales of processed nuts, and the product is also covered in SNACMA's unpublished data.

Output data on the products of these Groups are not generally covered in MAFF Statistical Information Notices, although production of "Pasta products" is revealed in *MAFF Statistics: Production of Canned and Bottled Fruit and Vegetables in the UK* [QRL.325]. Normally the results of the MAFF inquiries are presented in the *Monthly Digest of Statistics* [QRL.362], which includes production of syrup and glucose treacle (derived from starch industries). Data on soups (canned and powdered) are derived from BSO quarterly inquiries. Figures are monthly production averages in thousand tonnes, and cover six calendar years and the fifteen most recent months for which information is available. It should also be noted that the figures for canned vegetables in the same publication include pasta products such as macaroni and spaghetti in tomato sauce. The *Annual Abstract of Statistics* [QRL.37] shows data for the same products on an annual basis over a ten year period.

The former annual publication *Output and Utilisation* [QRL.382] gives figures for output of "starch and glucose" derived from home wheat sources over a seven-year period. This provides only a limited part of the total starch and glucose production since, as noted above, maize starch forms the bulk of UK output.

In addition to the *KP Snack Foods Review* [QRL.302], there are many other estimates of output/sales in this sector derived from industry sources. The market research reports of various companies mentioned in section 11.2 frequently include "trade estimates" of output and sales in varying degrees of detail.

11.4.2 *Index Numbers of Output*

The index of industrial production is published in many places, e.g. the *United Kingdom National Accounts* [QRL.506], *British Business* [QRL.66] (up to September 1989), and the *Annual Abstract of Statistics* [QRL.37]. The level of detail is, however, limited and one aggregate index is provided for "Starch and miscellaneous foods", which includes tea, coffee and breakfast cereals. Some earlier, and otherwise unpublished data on the index are given by Mordue [B.126]. Statistics for various MLHs are provided for 1970 and 1975 (five-year averages) and for 1978, 1979 and 1980 (annual averages).

11.5 Current Inputs other than Labour

11.5.1 *Domestic Inputs*

Group 423 covers such a wide range of products and processes that the coverage of, in particular, raw material inputs is necessarily very broad. The quinquennial *Business Monitor PO1008: Purchases Inquiry* [QRL.116] provides the most detailed analysis, and distinguishes "Starch" (AH4180) and "Miscellaneous foods" (AH4239) in its 1984 edition. Principal categories of raw material purchases shown, for "Starch" are: maize, wheat flours, tapioca; and for "Miscellaneous foods" are: refined vegetable and seed oils and fats, lard; milk and milk products; wheat flours, meal; malt and malt extracts; sugar; nuts; fresh fruit, vegetables; dried and preserved fruit; eggs and egg products; starch; cocoa; tea; coffee; gelatine; meat; meat extracts. Some of these inputs clearly relate to products not covered in this chapter, such as tea and coffee. The inquiry provides data in both value and volume terms. Entries for both AH4180 and AH4239 give details of other purchases such as stationery, packaging, replacement parts, fuel and electricity.

MAFF Statistics: Potato Crisp and Snack Foods Survey [QRL.323] gives an analysis of four quarters' of usage of raw potatoes for potato crisps and sticks. A division of "home grown" and "imported" potatoes is made where information on the latter is available.

At a less detailed level, *Business Monitor PA423* [QRL.114] shows purchases of "materials for use in production, and packaging and fuel" and "purchases of goods for merchanting or factoring", along with "costs of industrial services received", "non-industrial services received", "licensing of motor vehicles" and "payment of rates".

Many of these inputs are the products of UK farming or first-stage food manufacturing and details of the output and/or sales of these sectors appear in numerous sources. The *Monthly Digest of Statistics* [QRL.362], for example, gives production and/or sales of cereals, potatoes, sugar, meat, oil and fats, milk and milk products. The *Annual Abstract of Statistics* [QRL.37] provides data on the quantity of crops harvested, animal production, sales of agricultural produce and livestock, and production of processed food (and animal feedstuffs). Further details are published in *Output and Utilisation* [QRL.382], up to 1987, and the *Annual Review of Agriculture* [QRL.51] and its successor *Agriculture in the United Kingdom*. Additional sources appear in other chapters of this Review and in Peters [B.144].

11.5.2 *Input-output Analysis*

Input-output analysis attempts to demonstrate how the purchases of one UK industry are often the products of another, or are imported from abroad. It thus attempts to highlight the degree of inter-industry dependency. The extent to which this dependency is revealed, however, is determined by the level of industrial detail in this analysis. The introduction of SIC(1980) meant that "Grain milling and starch" (AH4160 and AH4180) and "Miscellaneous foods" (AH4239) were separately cited in *Business Monitor PA1004: Input-output Tables for the United Kingdom 1979* [QRL.101]. The former has a substantial although decreasing dependency on imports, although the statistics fail to indicate the heavy reliance of starch on imported maize.

Previous tables based on SIC(1968) tended to put "Margarine" (MLH229.1) and "Starch and miscellaneous foods" (MLH229.2) together, and are hence difficult to compare with the latest versions.

11.6 Labour

11.6.1 *Employment*

The most detailed official statistics on employment in Great Britain come from the Census of Employment with figures based on the SIC(1980) available for 1981, 1984, 1987, 1989 and 1991. The results of the 1984 Survey were published in a key article in the January 1987 issue of the *Employment Gazette* [QRL.186]. Data are provided for the various Activity Headings, and separate figures are published for "Starch" (AH4180) and "Miscellaneous foods" (AH4239). No detailed breakdown of employment within AH4239 is, however, provided. Details of employment are given for all employees, sub-divided into male and female, both also disaggregated into part-time and full-time. An analysis of employment for each Activity Heading is provided for the usual economic regions of England. UK data is only available in the census for Class 41/42 in aggregate.

The monthly *Employment Gazette* [QRL.186] publishes both monthly and quarterly data, the latter being in a rather less aggregate form. Current (1988) monthly statistics on "employees in employment" combine Groups 413–423 and 429; while Group 419 is treated separately in the quarterly data to leave Groups 413–418, 420–423 and 429 aggregated. Monthly figures are shown over a two-year period, while the quarterly statistics are given for the latest quarter, the previous quarter, and the previous year. The degree of aggregation means that the data provide little useful information on the "Starch" and/or "Miscellaneous foods" industries.

Earlier editions of the *Employment Gazette* [QRL.186] generally provided more detailed analyses of employment. For example, the February 1983 issue listed quarterly statistics by MLH of SIC(1968), with "Margarine" and "Other Food industries" grouped under MLH229. SIC(1980) was first used as the basis of classification in the February 1984 issue. "Starch" (Group 418), "Miscellaneous foods" (423), "Grain milling" (416) and "Animal feedstuffs" (422) were taken together. In 1986, new groupings were introduced for the quarterly statistics. Groups 416, 418 and 419 formed one category, while Groups 422 and 423 formed another.

The annual Census of Production provides labour force details for the main SIC(1980) Groups, and statistics on "Starch and miscellaneous foods" are shown in *Business Monitor PA423* [QRL.114], and in the summary tables of *Business Monitor*

PA1002 [QRL.93]. In addition to total employees (including working proprietors), the census divides the labour force into "operatives" and "administrative, technical and clerical" categories. An analysis of employment by business size is also given. Previous censuses have analysed employment by MLH, and separate data were provided for MLH229.2.

11.6.2 *Earnings and Hours of Work*

The *New Earnings Survey* [QRL.375], taken in October each year, produces the most detailed data on earnings and hours of work of manual employees. "Starch and miscellaneous foods" is shown in the industry analysis which appears in the April issue of *Employment Gazette* [QRL.186] in the year following the survey. Average weekly earnings of manual employees, both on adult and on other rates, are given, with the former broken down into full-time (all, male, female) and part-time (female only), and the latter into full-time (male and female). Hours worked per week on average, and average earnings per hour are also provided for the same groups of workers. Surprisingly, the *New Earnings Survey* [QRL.375] does not distinguish "Miscellaneous foods" as a category either in its "Analysis by industry" (Part C) or in its "Streamlined analysis" (Part A).

The annual Census of Production gives the costs of wages and salaries for "Starch and miscellaneous foods" in *Business Monitor PA423* [QRL.114]. Details are provided on a total and per head basis for the two categories: "operatives", and "administrative, technical and clerical staff"; and analysed by employment size of business. Wages and salaries are also calculated as a proportion of gross value added and shown for the two categories of employees

An important source of unofficial but detailed data on wages and conditions of work is the *UK Food and Drink Industry: Wages and Conditions Survey* [QRL.495]. This "Blue Book", compiled and published annually by the General Municipal, Boilermakers' Union (GMB), previously known as the General, Municipal Boilermakers and Allied Trades Union (GMBATU), summarises numerous aspects of wage rates, bonus payments, overtime rates, sick leave, holiday allowances and other conditions derived from reports of union officials in firms in the Food sector.

11.6.3 *Labour Productivity*

There is limited information on labour productivity within "Starch and miscellaneous foods" since the industry has not been subjected to the scrutiny applied to some other sectors. Perhaps such aggregate data would anyway be questionable in an industry so heterogeneous. However, it is possible to refer to the operating ratios contained in the annual *Business Monitor PA423* [QRL.114], and hence infer some measure of labour productivity. Sadly, some of the work based on census data — e.g. Wragg and Robertson [B.189] — excludes "Miscellaneous foods" from the analysis. Mordue and Marshall [B.127] provide the only direct analysis of labour productivity in this industry as part of their work on total factor productivity in UK food and drink manufacturing. The statistics relate to the period 1968–76, and are data are provided for MLH229 — i.e. "Margarine, starch and other foods".

11.6.4 *Industrial Training*
The various issues of the *Annual Report and Accounts* [QRL.44] of the Food, Drink and Tobacco Training Board outlined the Board's training activities up to 1983, using industrial groupings similar to, but different from, the SIC(1980). "Starch and miscellaneous foods" featured under the category of general food processing.

11.6.5 *Industrial Accidents*
The compendium *Health and Safety Statistics* [QRL.261] accompanies the annual *Health and Safety at Work* [QRL.259]. Currently, fatal and major injuries are analysed by Activity Heading, although reports from 1970–86 used the MLH categories of SIC(1968).

11.6.6 *Comments*
Data on many other aspects of labour force activity are currently not published in sufficient detail to enable "Miscellaneous foods" or its components to be identified separately. This applies to unemployment statistics (classified by previous employment), vacancies and redundancies. Data on stoppages due to industrial disputes have only been published in the *Employment Gazette* [QRL.186] for Class 41/42 in recent years, although data were available for individual MLH until 1981.

There has been rather less analysis of labour costs in Groups 419 and 423 than has been provided for other sectors of the Food industries, e.g. bread and flour confectionery. While there have been reports by the Monopolies Commission, the Price Commission, and House of Lords Select Committees on elements of the "Starch" and "Miscellaneous foods" industries — see section 11.16 — few comment on labour costs in detail, and none provide helpful statistics in the way the National Board for Prices and Incomes (NBPI) provided on wage costs in the baking industry during the second half of the 1960s.

11.7 Capital

11.7.1 *Capital Expenditure*

A major source is again the annual *Business Monitor PA423* [QRL.114] which indicates capital expenditure by firms classified to the "Starch and miscellaneous foods" industries annually for the previous five years. The expenditure is analysed into the following categories: land and buildings (sub-divided into "new building work" and "land and existing buildings"); plant and machinery; and vehicles. For each of these categories, acquisitions, disposals and net expenditure are shown. The summary tables in *Business Monitor PA1002* [QRL.93] give net capital expenditure for Group 423 and, as in *Business Monitor PA423* [QRL.114], there is a breakdown into establishment size categories by employment. Figures for net capital expenditure per head and as a percentage of gross value added appear in the table of operating ratios in *Business Monitor PA423* [QRL.114]. Finally, mention should be made of the quinquennial Purchases Inquiry published as *Business Monitor PO1008* [QRL.116] which provides details of net capital expenditure for "Starch" (AH4180) and "Miscellaneous foods" (AH4239). A regional analysis by Activity Heading is shown both for net capital expenditure and for the operating ratios.

11.7.2 *Occasional Investigations*

The measurement of capital productivity has rarely been attempted at a more disaggregated level than the industry Group. However, Mordue and Marshall [B.127] give indices for MLH229 "Margarine, starch and other foods" over the period 1968–76. In the process, they assess the growth of capital stock in the "industry" and discuss problems in calculation, such as depreciation.

11.8 International Transactions

11.8.1 *HM Customs and Excise Records*

"Coffee, tea, cocoa, spices, and manufactures thereof" comprise Division 07, and "Miscellaneous edible products and preparations" comprise Division 09 in the Standard International Trade Classification (Revision 3). Most of the products of Groups 418 and 423 will be classified to one of these two Divisions, though some may be found under Divisions 01, 02, 03, 04, 05, and 06. Coffee and tea are discussed in Chapter 12. The following headings which are of relevance for this chapter are identified in *Business Monitor MM20: Overseas Trade Statistics of the United Kingdom* [QRL.85]:

048.3	Macaroni, spaghetti and similar products (pasta, uncooked, not stuffed or otherwise prepared)
054.83	Arrowroot, sweet potatoes & similar roots & tubers with high starch or inulin content, fresh or dried; sago pith
061.93	Glucose (dextrose) and glucose syrup, not containing fructose or containing, in the dry state, less than 20 per cent by weight of fructose
061.94	Glucose and glucose syrup, containing, in the dry state, at least 20 per cent but not more than 50 per cent by weight of fructose
075.	Spices
098.4	Sauces and preparations thereof; mixed condiments and seasonings; mustard; vinegar and substitutes from acetic acid
098.5	Soups and broths and preparations thereof
098.6	Yeasts; other single-cell micro-organisms dead (other than vaccines of heading 541.63); prepared baking powders
098.91	Pasta, cooked or stuffed; couscous, whether or not prepared
098.93	Food prepared for infants, for retail sale, or flour, meal, starch or malt extract (with or without cocoa powder)
098.94	Malt extract
098.99	Other food preparations, not elsewhere specified.

Further details of the extensive statistical coverage in *Business Monitor MM20* [QRL.85] are provided in section 2.8.2.1. The statistics have been compiled from the declarations which are made to HM Customs and Excise, and which are subject to confirmation by Customs officials. The figures are usually published about one month after the month to which they relate.

Details of the HM Customs and Excise tariff/trade code numbers corresponding to AH4180 and AH4239 were found up to mid-1989 in *Business Monitor PQ4180* [QRL.135] and *Business Monitor PQ4239* [QRL.139] respectively. *Business Monitor PQ4180* [QRL.135] provided quarterly import and export data for glucoses; dextrins; starches; residues; and wheat gluten. *Business Monitor PQ4239* [QRL.139] gave quarterly import and export data for: prepared cereal foods such as puffed rice, cornflakes, etc. (i) obtained from maize, (ii) obtained from rice, (iii) other; honey; potato products; sauces etc.; vinegar; soups and broths ((a) canned, (b) other); homogenised composite food preparations; preparations of flour, meal, starch or malt extract; egg yolks and shelled eggs; yeasts and baking powders; coffee; tea; mustard; spices; nuts; macaroni, spaghetti; others. Prior to 1983, "Starch and miscellaneous foods" were covered largely by *Business Monitor PQ229.2: Starch and Miscellaneous Foods* [QRL.126].

The very fine detail provided in *Business Monitor MM20* [QRL.85] permits the monitoring of trade flows in highly specific products, but this same detail makes for tedious summation when more commonly defined markets are concerned. Furthermore, these markets do not correspond to the commodity headings, or to the more aggregate Divisions. Hence other publications which reclassify the data are of significance. For example, Food from Britain provides annual details of UK food exports and imports in a more easily recognisable form — *United Kingdom Food and Drink Trade: Annual Statistics* [QRL.505] and *United Kingdom Food and Drink Exports: Priority Markets* [QRL.504]. Examples of products falling in the "Starch and miscellaneous foods" category include sauces, mixed condiments, pasta, mustards, soups/broths, and crisps.

11.8.2 *Industry Analyses of Trade*

In contrast to the analyses by type of product, *Business Monitor MQ10: Overseas Trade Analysed in Terms of Industries* [QRL.90] provides quarterly data on exports and imports from AH4180 and from the nine sub-headings of AH4239 — see Table 11.1 for titles. These figures are also used in *Business Monitor MQ12: Import Penetration and Export Sales Ratios for Manufacturing Industry* [QRL.91] which provided export/sales and import penetration ratios for AH4180 and AH4239 up to the second quarter of 1989 — see section 2.8.2.3 for details of the coverage and methodology. Mordue [B.126] provides constant-price series for the imports and exports of MLH229 for 1975–1980.

11.9 Stocks

Data on stocks are given in the annual *Business Monitor PA423* [QRL.114], and in the summary tables of *Business Monitor PA1002* [QRL.93]. The former shows increases in the value of stocks and work-in-progress annually over five years, and their value at the end of the final year. The data are broken down into "materials, stores and fuel", "work-in-progress" and "goods on hand for sale". Total stocks and work-in-progress at the end of the year are analysed by enterprise size in *Business Monitor PA423* [QRL.114].

Few of the products cited in the *Monthly Digest of Statistics* [QRL.362] directly relate to "Starch and miscellaneous foods" although total stocks of potatoes, some of which will serve as inputs to the snack and crisp industry, do appear. Stocks of tea and raw coffee, which are considered in Chapter 12, are also enumerated. Figures are given for fourteen months and five years. Other stocks — e.g. cereals, sugar, meat, oil seeds and nuts, butter, cheese, condensed and evaporated milk, and milk powder — will be significant for some products in Groups 418 and 423, but the details are too numerous to list. Similar kinds of information, on an annual basis over twelve years, appear in the *Annual Abstract of Statistics* [QRL.37], with a table of end-year stocks of food and feeding stuffs.

11.10 Consumption

11.10.1 *The National Food Survey*

The National Food Survey (NFS) collects consumption data on a wide variety of products manufactured by industry Groups 418 and 423, viz:

Food code number	Description
154	Honey
200	Crisps and other potato products, *not* frozen
290	Cereal-based invalid foods (including "slimmimg" foods)
291	Infant cereal foods
295	Canned pasta
296	Pizza
297	Cake, pudding and dessert mixes
301	Other cereal foods
315	Baby foods, canned or bottled
318	Soups, canned
319	Soups, dehydrated and powdered
323	Spreads and dresings
327	Pickles and sauces
328	Meat and yeast extracts
334	Salt
336	Miscellaneous (expenditure only)
339	Novel protein foods

Detailed statistics are published on these various foods in the *National Food Survey: Compendium of Results* [QRL.373]. Annual average figures of both per capita weekly consumption and expenditure are provided for the following main food groups: honey, preserves, syrup and treacle (151–154); soups, canned, dehydrated and powdered (318, 319); other foods (314, 315, 323–339); and total "miscellaneous" foods (314–339). Moreover, these data are analysed by region and type of area; by income group; by household composition; by household composition and income group; by age of housewife; by housing tenure; and by ownership of deep freezer. Indices of expenditure, and of the real value of purchases, are presented for the latest six years. Quarterly and annual national average household expenditure on the following items are also calculated: honey; crisps and other potato products, not frozen; cereal-based invalid foods (including "slimming" foods); infant cereal foods; baby foods, canned or bottled; soups, canned; soups, dehydrated and powdered; spreads and dressings; pickles and sauces; meat and yeast extracts; salt; miscellaneous; novel protein foods; and total "miscellaneous" foods.

A number of points should be born in mind about the above coverage. First, many of the products of Groups 418 and 423 are not consumed directly by households, but are used as intermediate products in the manufacture of other foods. Second, the overall "Miscellaneous foods" (314–339) heading in the NFS classification does not correspond to the products of Group 423. For example, NFS code 336 covers items like vinegar, gravy mixes and salts, forcemeat, mustard, pepper, flavourings and colourings, yeast, herbs, curry powders and spices. Yet it also contains items such as made-up jellies, and milk shakes (syrup and powder) which are the products of Activity Headings other than AH4239. Moreover, the NFS category "baby foods, canned or bottled" (315) covers all types of baby foods, including dairy-based foods and soups, with the exception of infant foods that are cereal-based which are coded as "infant cereal foods" (291). The manufacture of dairy-based infant foods is classified to AH4130.3 in SIC(1980). Third, many foods produced by AH4239 are classified under headings other than "Miscellaneous foods" within the NFS classification. Thus "infant cereal foods" (291) are classified under "cereals"; "crisps and other potato products" (200) under "vegetables"; and "honey" (154) under "sugar and preserves". Finally, the Survey specifically excludes meals or snacks purchased to eat outside the home. This should be borne in mind when considering the data on, in particular, the consumption of potato crisps and other snack products.

The main report on the Survey, *Household Food Consumption and Expenditure* [QRL.267], carries a more limited range of statistical data, as has been discussed in section 2.10.1.2. Commentary is, however, provided with many of the main statistical tables, and data for previous years are often presented for comparison. Results from the NFS are more immediately available in *MAFF Statistics: Food Facts* [QRL.319] and in *British Business* [QRL.66] (up to 1989). The detail in *Food Facts* [QRL.319] is insufficient to identify miscellaneous foods in aggregate or individually, except for tea and coffee which are discussed in Chapter 12. Further details of both the methodology of the Survey, and of other publications carrying NFS data, are provided in section 2.10.1. *Household Food Consumption and Expenditure* [QRL.267] also carries occasional reports on topics related to the products covered in this chapter. The 1986 edition analysed long-term trends in cereals. The 1987 edition analysed long-term trends in vegetables and fruit, and mention was made of potato products, because of the increasing proportion of total potato consumption accounted for in this form. There was, however, little discussion of snack foods, since it was recognised that a significant part of such consumption takes place outside the home and is therefore excluded from the Survey.

11.10.2 *The Family Expenditure Survey*

The *Family Expenditure Survey* [QRL.204] does not give the same detail on food that is shown in the National Food Survey. Yet it provides a useful alternative source of expenditure data for some items covered in this chapter. Average weekly household expenditure is shown for: potato crisps, sticks etc; non-milk baby, junior and geriatric foods; pickles, sauces, chutneys, mayonnaise; sweet and savoury flavourings, condiments, colourings, decorations, yeast. However this detailed breakdown is not shown in all the tables of analysis (by income group, household composition and income, occupation, employment, age, region), where the category "other food" tends to embrace most items that concern this chapter. A summary of the quarterly expenditure figures for the main categories is also published in the *Employment Gazette* [QRL.186].

11.10.3 *The National Accounts*

Tables of consumers' expenditure "by function" are given in the annual *United Kingdom National Accounts* [QRL.506]. Expenditure in both current price and constant (1980) price terms is shown over a ten-year period. The degree of aggregation is such that only "coffee, tea and cocoa" from "Miscellaneous foods" is separately identified (see Chapter 12), the rest being lumped into "Other manufactured foods". The statistics also appear in annual form in the *Annual Abstract of Statistics* [QRL.37] and as quarterly estimates in both the *Monthly Digest of Statistics* [QRL.362] and *Economic Trends* [QRL.181].

11.10.4 *Supplies Moving into Consumption*

Despite the title "supplies", this information provides a useful complement to the household consumption figures measured by the NFS and the FES, since it aims to estimate basic foodstuffs available for consumption, whether eaten in the home or outside — in restaurants, institutional catering, casually, etc. The finest detail is shown in *MAFF Statistics: Food Facts* [QRL.319] which, although published a little irregularly, provides a continuous set of annual data linking with the pre-Second World War estimates of Angel and Hurdle [B.2]. There are, however, some inevitable definitional adjustments. It is important to emphasise the note accompanying the tables in *Food Facts* [QRL.319]: the estimates will tend to overstate consumption levels because of an unknown wastage factor between farm gate and table. As long as this degree of wastage remains constant, trends will be correctly shown over time.

Particular items of interest to "Starch and miscellaneous foods" found in *Food Facts* [QRL.319] are: starch and other farinaceous foods; glucose; egg products; potato products, with crisps, frozen, canned and dehydrated shown separately (as raw potato equivalent). Breakfast cereals (Chapter 8), tea and coffee (Chapter 12) and cocoa (see Chapter 10) are also shown separately.

11.10.5 *Industry Sources*

Given the limitations of the official information on the consumption of "Starch and miscellaneous foods" products, details may need to be derived from commercial sources. Many of the market research reports mentioned in section 11.2 and elsewhere refer to "trade estimates" of consumer characteristics. This is particularly the case for products not covered in detail in the National Food Survey, such as spices and condiments, vinegar or gravy mixes, or where out-of-home consumption is significant, such as snack foods. In other areas of market research, consumption data appear in reports from major firms reflecting their particular market interests. Examples include branded food drinks with the annual Beecham Bovril Brands *Milk Food Drinks: Market Report* [QRL.356], and infant foods with the Cow & Gate *Baby Foods: Market Report* [QRL.56].

11.11 Supplies and Disposals

Mention has been made in section 11.10.4 of the *MAFF Statistics: Food Facts* [QRL.319] which provides estimates of basic commodities moving into consumption, measured as they enter the food manufacturing and/or distribution system. The notes accompanying the tables indicate that the supplies are generally based on home production plus imports less exports with allowances for items that are used as animal feed, for industrial uses or for food that is stored, for example as intervention stocks.

A related calculation undertaken by MAFF is the construction of supply balance sheets for the main basic agricultural products. These are submitted to EUROSTAT, stored in the CRONOS data bank in Luxembourg, and may be accessed commercially through CISI Wharton — see Slater [B.164]. The only item of direct concern to this chapter is the balance sheet for "Starch", but many of the balance sheets will have indirect relevance given the range of products manufactured under "Miscellaneous foods".

Data on disposals of food appear in the *Monthly Digest of Statistics* [QRL.362], and in the *Annual Abstract of Statistics* [QRL.37], and are similar to supplies in that imports are added to home production, adjusted for stocks. Disposals, however, include deliveries to manufacturers of non-food products and to exporters — see the *Monthly Digest of Statistics Supplement: Definitions and Explanatory Notes* [B.337]. Again few items are of direct relevance to this chapter, although disposals of maize identify a separate category for "food and industrial uses", which must include *inter alia* maize used for starch. This figure is most clearly shown in the *Monthly Digest of Statistics* [QRL.362] where sixteen months and six years' (monthly averages) data are given; but the yearly figure may be calculated from the *Annual Abstract of Statistics* [QRL.37] ten-year series.

11.12 Prices

11.12.1 *Agricultural and Commodity Prices*

The range of commodities used in the processing and manufacture of "Starch and miscellaneous foods" is too wide to allow for any kind of comprehensive reference to raw material prices in this section. However, some major items may be mentioned.

Cereals, particularly maize and to an increasing extent wheat, provide the principal ingredients in the "Starch" industry, and prices are available from many sources as outlined in Chapter 8. Pre-eminent amongst these are the publications of the Home-Grown Cereals Authority (HGCA). The HGCA *Weekly Bulletin* [QRL.512], for example, includes EEC and international grain prices, along with such tariffs or subsidies that may apply. Other important sources of short-term price information include the three MAFF Weekly Agricultural Market Reports [QRL.25], [QRL.26] and [QRL.27] as well as the *Public Ledger & Daily Freight Register* [QRL.392]. The MAFF publication, *Agricultural Statistics: United Kingdom* [QRL.32], gives monthly and annual average prices data for all major cereals and other farm crops.

Additional sources of crop price information include *Potato Statistics in Great Britain* [QRL.387] by the Potato Marketing Board, the *ICCH Commodities and Financial Futures Yearbook* [QRL.269] by the International Commodities Clearing House, the *Annual Review of Oilseeds, Oils and Oilcakes and Other Commodities* [QRL.53] and press reports such as appear in *Farmers Weekly* [QRL.212].

Livestock information is found in the MAFF *Agricultural Market Report Part I: Prices and Quantities Sold of Selected Cereals, Livestock and Other Agricultural Products* [QRL.25], in *Agricultural Statistics: United Kingdom* [QRL.32] and also in the statistical publications of the Meat and Livestock Commission — see Chapter 4 for details. Prices of dairy products are provided in some detail in *United Kingdom Dairy Facts & Figures* [QRL.503]. See Chapter 5.

Horticultural products are featured in the MAFF *Agricultural Market Report: Part II National Average Wholesale Prices of Home Grown and Imported Horticultural Produce* [QRL.26] and *Agricultural Market Report: Part III Prices of Home Grown Vegetables by Grade in Six Major Markets in England and Wales* [QRL.27] and *Agricultural Statistics: United Kingdom* [QRL.32].

Again for livestock and horticultural prices, press reports as in *Farmers Weekly* [QRL.212] are an important source of current market price information. Further details on these and other sources can be found in Peters [B.144] and in appropriate chapters of this Review. The summary in this section merely confirms the heteregeneous nature of the inputs as well as the outputs of the "Starch and miscellaneous foods" sector.

11.12.2 *Retail Prices*

11.12.2.1 Recorded prices

"Starch and miscellaneous foods" as such receive relatively limited coverage in official retail price statistics. The *Employment Gazette* [QRL.186] publishes monthly averages based on retail price quotations taken in retailers around the United Kingdom. However, none of the products considered in this chapter appear in the list (although tea, coffee, and self-raising flour, considered in Chapter 12 and Chapter 8 respectively, do).

11.12.2.2 Recommended prices

Although commercial sources of price information publish a wealth of detail on foodstuffs in the "Miscellaneous foods" category, these prices are normally "list" rather than actual retail market prices. *The Grocer Price List* [QRL.253], for example, quotes trade and/or retail prices *recommended* by manufacturers, importers or sole agents for manufacturers' brands in the following groups: baby foods; blancmange and cornflour; cake, pudding mixtures and convenience desserts; flavours, colours and essences; gelatine; gravy makers and brownings; honey; horseradish sauce and creams; Indian food; meat and vegetable extracts; Mexican food; milk products and yogurt (includes branded food drinks); mint sauce and jellies; mustard; nuts and nut kernels; pasta products; pickles, chutney and relishes; potato crisps and snacks; puddings and suet; salads, salad creams and dressings; salt; sauces and cooking aids; soups; spices, herbs and cooking aids; spreads, pastes and paté; vinegar and non-brewed condiment.

11.12.3 *The Retail Prices Index*

The Retail Prices Index (RPI) is published monthly in the *Employment Gazette* [QRL.186]. With regard to the products covered in this chapter, there are separate indices for potato products including crisps and snacks (from 1987 onwards); and "other foods". The latter covers ice-cream; canned and packeted food, e.g. "ready meals"; soups; jelly; sauces; flavourings and additives. The price indicators used in "other foods" are: ice-cream; selected frozen convenience foods; canned and packet soups; stock cubes; and various sauces, pickles and condiments: all of these concern us in this chapter, but the detail is lost within the index of the broad "other foods" group. The indices shown in the *Employment Gazette* [QRL.186] refer to the latest month available, and percentage changes are calculated over the previous month, and the previous year. The September 1986 issue gives details of the January 1987 rebasing, and the reconcilation of the new with the old series. An annual revision of the "weights" used in the RPI is undertaken on the basis of the latest available results from the Family Expenditure Survey, and is the subject of an annual article in the *Employment Gazette* [QRL.186]. Other publications detailing the RPI indices for items covered in this chapter include the *Monthly Digest of Statistics* [QRL.362], which gives seven months of all indices, and *Business Monitor PQ4239* [QRL.139] up to mid-1989. A full explanation of the RPI is given in section 2.12.3.

11.12.4 *Price Index Numbers in the National Food Survey*

Household Food Consumption and Expenditure [QRL.267] contains various references to retail prices. The more recent issues (from 1985) give annual average prices paid for all the main "Miscellaneous foods" identified in section 11.10.1. The statistics are shown for the three most recent years. In contrast, the pre-1985 reports gave a single year's average prices, with averages also for four quarters. These quarterly averages are now published in the *Compendium of Results* [QRL.373]. Price indices were published in the pre-1985 reports as part of the economic analysis in Appendix B, and again covered those "Miscellaneous foods" identified in the survey. These calculations are still carried out by the MAFF, and may be obtained from them by genuine researchers.

11.12.5 *Producer Price Index Numbers*

The series of Producer Price Indices are considered in general terms in section 2.12.5. Details of the price indices for the inputs and outputs of the "Starch and miscellaneous foods" sectors are given below.

11.12.5.1 Producer price index numbers: input prices

Business Monitor MM22: Producer Price Indices carries the producer price index numbers of materials and fuels purchases for AH4180 and AH4239 giving both monthly and annual data. The monthly data are given for the current and previous years, with the figures for the latest two months provisional. An annual average for the previous year is also presented. *Business Monitor MM22* was published for the first time in October 1989 and continued the coverage in *British Business* [QRL.66]

Producer price index numbers of materials purchased are published in *Business Monitor PQ4231* [QRL.139] up to mid-1989 but not in *Business Monitor PQ4180* [QRL.135]. The indices in the former are collected by MAFF and cover five quarters and two years and the following products are listed: refined vegetable and seed oils; sugar, refined, bulk; imported maize; imported nuts; imported coffee beans; imported tea. The last two products are obviously relevant to Chapter 12. The pre-1984 *Business Monitor PQ229.2* [QRL.126] provided wholesale price indices for imported maize, and for refined sugar, over six quarters and five years.

11.12.5.2 Producer price index numbers: output prices

Business Monitor MM22 contains the producer price index numbers of products manufactured in the United Kingdom (home sales) for AH4180 and AH4239. The monthly data are provided for the current and previous year, with the figures for the latest two months provisional. An annual average for the previous year is also presented. *Business Monitor MM22* was published for the first time in October 1989 and continued the coverage in *British Business* [QRL.66]. The *Annual Abstract of Statistics* [QRL.37] gives the annual average for AH4180 and AH4239 for a six-year run for products manufactured in the United Kingdom (home sales).

A finer breakdown of price indices of goods produced appeared in *Business Monitor PQ4239* [QRL.139] up to mid-1989 from MAFF sources. Indices are provided for potato crisps; infant and dietetic food; cake and pudding mixtures; rice puddings, canned; canned puddings, desserts, custard; soups, canned; sauces; seasonings and stuffings; nuts, prepared; proprietary foods and food drinks; gravy salts and other gravy preparations. Five quarters and two years' of statistics are shown.

11.12.6 *Prices and Government Regulation*

Starch prices appear in the 1971 report of the Monopolies Commission on *Starch, Glucoses and Modified Starches* [B.454] in relation to the discussion of Brown and Polson's marketing policies. The report gives a table of prices supplied by Brown and Polson for its six main products over the period 1960 to 1970. The same company, under its parent's name, was investigated by the Price Commission in 1978 — see the report on *CPC (United Kingdom) Ltd.* [B.420]. The report gave details of maize prices, but none of product prices as such. References to starch prices abound in the 1985 House of Lords Select Committee report on the *EEC Starch Regime* [B.252]

Annex 5 of which contains comprehensive information on the price of starch in the United States, the world market, and the European Community over the period 1979–1983.

There are a number of Price Commission reports on "Miscellaneous foods", and these discuss pricing matters including discounts, allowances and the like. Examples include the 1975 report on the *Prices of Commonly Purchased Diabetic Foods* [B.424], and the 1979 report on *United Biscuits (UK) Ltd. — Biscuits, Crisps, Nuts and Savoury Snacks* [B.436]. The former report gives a table of comparative prices for diabetic and non-diabetic equivalent products, as at May 1975. The table includes prices of chocolate, orange marmalade, canned peaches, pastilles and soft drinks. Products in this area have not featured in any significant way in more general official investigations into prices or been subject to price controls.

11.13 Financial Information

Much of the financial information available on public companies comes from their annual reports, with all the limitations of disclosure that are implied. Further, as the companies become increasingly diversified and multinational, separate identification of "Starch and miscellaneous foods" activities within the United Kingdom becomes harder to achieve. The many commercial services and publications which provide financial information have been listed extensively in section 2.13. The few official investigations into markets covered by this chapter offer relatively limited financial information. The Monopolies Commission report on *Starch, Glucoses and Modified Starches* [B.454] provides very broad statistics on Brown & Polson (CPC), the main company investigated. Details of sales, profit on sales, and profit on capital, in total and broken down into glucoses, total starches and other goods, are given annually for the years 1966–70. The Price Commission report on *CPC (United Kingdom) Ltd.* [B.420] shows pre-tax profits for 1968, annually 1975–78 (forecast), with trading profits and percentage profit on sales given annually for 1973–78 (forecast). Gross margins are provided for the main groups — starch, glucose syrups, starch-derived and glucose-derived products — produced by CPC. *United Biscuits (UK) Ltd.* [B.436] were also subject to investigation by the Price Commission and some financial data are shown for the Foods Division of the company, which covers crisps, nuts and snacks. Trading profits for the Division, and in terms of contribution to turnover and percentage turnover, are given for each of the five years from 1974 to 1978. Financial data in the Price Commission's report on *Diabetic Foods* [B.424] are largely confined to distribution margins for different outlets.

11.14 Advertising and Market Research

11.14.1 *Advertising*

Given the heterogeneous nature of Groups 418 and 423, considerable variations occur as to the importance of advertising for the products concerned. It is nevertheless worth noting that some products exhibit advertising/sales ratios many times the food industry average (approx one per cent). Media Expenditure Analysis Ltd. (MEAL) is the main source of advertising information, and their data are published in the *Tri-Media Digest* [QRL.493]. Detailed statistics of brands and advertisers are included, and are summarised by product market in the *Advertising Statistics Yearbook* [QRL.20]. Alternative sources are the *Media Register* [QRL.354] and *The Food Forecast* [QRL.236].

Relevant markets covered by MEAL data are: baby foods, divided into juices and syrups, main meals, milk products, and rusks; cakes and pastries, which include cake mixes; convenience desserts, including custard, dessert mixes, packet whips and delights; gravy products; low calorie foods, including artificial sweeteners, meal replacements, salad dressings, and soups; meat and vegetable extracts; mustard; nuts, pre-packed; packet meals; pasta, divided into canned, dry, savoury, and frozen; potato crisps; sauces, pickles, salad cream; savoury snacks; soup, both canned and packet; stuffing. Companies active in the area are detailed in the *Advertising Statistics Yearbook* [QRL.20], and in *Campaign* [QRL.145] and *Top Spenders* [QRL.488]. Market research publications in this area occasionally give their own or trade estimates of advertising expenditures where MEAL data is unavailable or in insufficient detail. Examples include the estimates in *Retail Business* [QRL.432], such as in the reports on "Gravy products" and "Packaged desserts", where press and television advertising expenditures are given for individual brands.

11.14.2 *Market Research*

Numerous publications cover, or are relevant to, product markets in "Starch and miscellaneous foods". A most useful guide to market research reports in general is the *Marketing Surveys Index* [B.327], produced by Marketing Strategies for Industry and the Institute of Marketing. Although an annual publication, it is updated monthly and provides a comprehensive listing, with brief abstracts, of market research reports, including some from European organisations. The complicated index system of subject/report/author is tedious but effective.

Reviews in *Retail Business* [QRL.432] and *Market Intelligence* [QRL.339], together with Key Note reports, are available in many public reference libraries. More specialist business libraries keep *Market Research: Great Britain* [QRL.343], and the various reports published by Market Assessment Publications and Marketing Strategies for Industry. It is also possible to find publications by the British Market Research Bureau, Database International, Market Power, as well as reports by organisations such as the Leatherhead Food Research Association, and surveys by individual companies of the markets in which they operate.

The "Starch" industry as such is not covered in this type of publication, since the vast majority of its output is sold on to industrial users for incorporation into confectionery, alcoholic and soft drinks, soups, jams etc., or manufactured into other products (glucoses etc.) in vertically integrated processes. Glucose as a sugar alternative appears in reports on "sweeteners" and other substitutes in "slimming, diet and health food" reports.

Snack products receive extensive coverage in many market research reports on "crisps", "savoury snacks" and "processed nuts", either in total or separately. The annual *KP Snack Foods Review* [QRL.302] is an important firm-generated source in this area. Infant foods are also well served by both market research and company-based information. The former are produced under various appropriate titles: "baby foods", "baby care products", "infant foods" etc.; while the most well-known publication from a major producer is the Cow & Gate *Baby Foods Annual Report* [QRL.56]. Dietetic foods tend to be incorporated in wider surveys of markets involving "slimming aids", "diet products", "health foods" and the like. Health food drinks rarely feature in these, but appear in market research reports covering "hot drinks" and in Beecham Bovril Brands' annual *Milk Food Drinks: Market Report* [QRL.356].

Sweets and puddings, in canned or other convenience forms, tend to be discussed in general publications on "canned foods" or "convenience foods", although specific areas such as "sweets and desserts" or "packaged desserts" are also the subject of reports. "Canned foods" and "convenience foods" reviews also often feature soups, but these too may have specialised reports. Sauces, relishes, salad cream and mayonnaise again tend to feature in reports on the general area of "sauces and spreads", or "pickles and sauces"; while the cook-in sauces appear in reviews of "cooking additives or aids". Pasta products feature in "canned foods" or "convenience foods" reports, although once more there are specific "pasta" and "pasta and pasta products" publications.

Many of the remaining products covered in "Miscellaneous foods" may be grouped as food ingredients and seasonings, and not surprisingly appear in reports on "cooking additives", "seasonings and flavourings", "gravy products" or "pepper, spices and herbs".

11.15 Research and Development

The "Starch" industry has close associations with various other agri-food sectors, such as sugar and cereals, and with the broad field of biotechnology into which significant R&D efforts have been directed in recent years. A good deal of interest in biotechnology has taken place at the European Community level, with reports from the Commission on, for example, *Biotechnology: The Community's Role* [B.204], *Biotechnology in the Community* [B.205], and *Biotechnology in the Community: Stimulating Agro-industrial Development* [B.207]. Similarly, discussion of starch occurs in the 1987 House of Lords Select Committee inquiry *Biotechnology in the Community* [B.206].

Few details on commercially significant biotechnology R&D are generally available, although companies may reveal some information on topics and expenditure in their Annual Reports. In the "Starch" industry as such, the amount of specific information is limited. At a company level, some details on expenditures by Brown & Polson (now CPC (UK) Ltd.) are given in the Monopolies Commission report on *Starch, Glucoses and Modified Starches* [B.454]. The figures relate to 1969, and enumerate separately spending internal to the company and the funding of R&D to be carried on by outside bodies on the firm's behalf. Elsewhere information on R&D is thin. Typically those companies with interests in the "Miscellaneous foods" industries only reveal overall R&D expenditure in their Annual Reports, with insufficient detail to pinpoint particular foods or markets.

11.16 Official Investigations

As indicated in section 11.2, there have been relatively few investigations into the "Starch and miscellaneous foods" sector. This is possibly surprising given the high degree of concentration in specific markets.

Starch has received the most attention, with both an investigation by the Monopolies Commission in 1971, and a report by the Price Commission in 1978. The Monopolies Commission report on the *Supply of Starch, Glucoses and Modified Starches* [B.454] considered the position of Brown and Polson, then part of the American company called Corn Products International Inc. The report describes the industry and its development in some detail, and provides a good deal of data on Brown & Polson, though rather less on other suppliers: Garton, Albion etc. While Brown & Polson's share of the market in the United Kingdom made it clearly monopolistic in the Commission's terms, the presence of low-priced imports prevented exploitation of that position of dominance in 1971. Similar conclusions were reached as a result of the 1978 Price Commission report on *CPC (United Kingdom) Ltd.* [B.420], which was the new company name for Brown & Polson. The Commission noted the effects of the Common Agricultural Policy on CPC's raw material costs, and considered the company's operations to be generally efficient. It did not oppose the suggested price increases. Mention should also be made of the 1985 House of Lords Select Committee report on the *EEC Starch Regime* [B.252]. While this report is mainly concerned with the operation of the CAP in this market, it also gives details of industrial structure, raw material sources and starch utilisation and speculates on future developments.

As regards "Miscellaneous foods", the snack industry was considered by the Monopolies and Mergers Commission in *Nabisco Brands Inc. and Huntley and Palmer Foods plc: A Report on the Proposed Merger* [B.448]. Details are shown for sales of crisps (1975–81) and nuts (1973–81), plus a breakdown of market shares in the crisps, snacks and nuts markets, along with a historical account of the development of the major companies' interests in the markets. The snack foods sector was the subject of a minority note of dissent against the proposed merger. The Price Commission report on *United Biscuits (UK) Ltd.* [B.436] was concerned in part with the increases in prices of crisps, nuts and snacks. It gives brief details of the company's market position in 1978 through its KP brand, in the potato crisp, savoury snack, and processed nut markets. United Biscuits' turnover figures for 1974 and 1978 are also provided for these three markets, sub-divided into retailers' own-label and UBs' brands. The Commission was critical of United Biscuits' price discount policy, and although the price increases requested were allowed, further price rises on the notified products were prohibited for nine months.

The 1975 Price Commission report on *Prices of Commonly-purchased Diabetic Foods* [B.424] provides a very comprehensive breakdown of the diabetic foods market. This market was sub-divided into nine sections: preserves; chocolate and confectionery; pastilles and sweets; jellies and desserts; canned fruits; biscuits; cakes and cake mixes; canned meals; and sugar substitutes. Obviously the main focus of the report is pricing and, although the proposed increases were allowed, the generally high level of prices of diabetic foods relative to comparable standard products was noted, as was the substantial variations between prices of brands of similar diabetic foods.

Other investigations tend to deal only peripherally with the products of this chapter. Baby foods are the subject of the 1967 Monopolies Commission report on *The Supply of Infant Milk Foods* [B.446]. However, the scope of the investigation limits its relevance to the non-milk baby foods covered in this chapter, which are only touched upon in a general introduction to the whole market. The 1986 Monopolies and Mergers Commission report on *White Salt* [B.457] is concerned with salt production for all uses, and hence only to a minor extent with the consumer market which accounts for some ten per cent of output.

The Price Commission report on *Cadbury Schweppes Foods Ltd.* [B.418] contains some mention of malted hot drinks (e.g. Bournvita), although the main focus of the report is on cocoa-based grocery products, including drinking chocolate — see Chapter 10. Other beverages, particularly coffee and tea, which have been subject to investigations are discussed in Chapter 12.

11.17 Improvements and Comments

Inevitably comment must be made concerning the wide range of heterogeneous products encompassed by "Starch and miscellaneous foods", and hence the limited value of statistics which attempt to describe the nature of the market or competition. Reference has already been made to the Census of Production data in this context where, for example, the five-firm concentration ratio suggests a low degree of monopolization, but consideration of the separate product markets yields many cases of market leadership and a very high proportion of sales in a few hands. It is simply the aggregation of markets that lowers the concentration ratio.

Paradoxically, there are also allocations between Group 423 and other Groups that appear to divide markets. For example, the division in the SIC(1980) of non-milk products (in AH4239) and milk-based products (in AH4139) that separates three markets (desserts, dietetic and baby foods) is rarely if ever followed by market researchers. Similarly the markets for sauces and condiments (classified to AH4239) are similar to those for pickles and chutneys (AH4147 "Processing of fruit and vegetables") and are frequently grouped together by researchers.

CHAPTER 12

TEA AND COFFEE

The various activities associated with the blending and manufacture of tea and coffee are classified under Group 423 "Miscellaneous foods" in the *CSO Standard Industrial Classification Revised 1980* [B.232]. Statistical sources for this Group were discussed in Chapter 11, where it was indicated that sources on tea and coffee would be discussed separately as they were so numerous. Other more general sources, which provide statistics on other industry Groups as well, are covered in Chapter 2 and should be consulted as required. The contents of this chapter are as follows:

12.1 Introduction

The information in this chapter relates to the following products within Activity Heading 4239 of SIC(1980):

4239.1 Coffee and coffee substitutes
Coffee bag manufacturing
Coffee blending
Coffee essence and extract manufacturing
Coffee grinding and roasting (not retail)
Coffee/chicory essence and extract manufacturing
Dandelion coffee manufacturing
Decaffeinated coffee manufacturing
Instant coffee manufacturing
Liquid coffee manufacturing

4239.2 Tea
Seasoning manufacturing
Soluble tea manufacturing
Spice purifying manufacturing
Tea bag manufacturing
Tea blending
Tea extract and essence manufacturing

For details of the other Activity Headings within Group 423, see Table 11.1. It should be noted that "herb tea manufacturing" is classified to AH4239.9 "All other foods, not elsewhere specified".

Tea and coffee were previously classified to MLH229 "Food industries not elsewhere specified" in SIC(1968), and were grouped with "Starch and miscellaneous foods" under MLH229.2.

The *Report on the Census of Production 1968* [QRL.418] separated out blended tea. It subdivided coffee into: (i) coffee, roasted and ground (ii) coffee and chicory, roasted and ground, (iii) soluble powder (dry extract). The preceding Census of Production reports for 1954, 1958 and 1963 were confined to coffee, and coffee and chicory extracts and essences. Thus tea blending and coffee roasting and blending were out of the scope of the Census of Production. But it must be noted that in the *Final Report on the Census of Production for 1948* [QRL.214] and in *The Report on the Census of Production for 1951* [QRL.422] there were separate reports for "Tea blending and coffee roasting", which were then regarded as part of the distribution trades. Establishments manufacturing coffee and chicory extracts were included in the report on "Miscellaneous foods". These examples illustrate the variations in coverage over the years. The *Historical Record of the Census of Production, 1907 to 1970* [QRL.264] gives a summary, but inspection of the actual census volumes is recommended if more precision is required.

12.2 Industry Structure

12.2.1 *Coffee*

12.2.1.1 The Organisation of the industry

Coffee has a rich literature. The book by W.H. Ukers entitled *All About Coffee* [B.176] is an early encyclopaedic classic. C.F. Marshall's *The World Coffee Trade: A Guide to the Production, Trading and Consumption of Coffee* [B.111] is a more recent survey. In addition to the regular market research reports noted in this chapter, *Survey of the Coffee Industry in the United Kingdom* [B.386] is another reference. Commissioned by the International Coffee Organisation (ICO), this collected together market descriptions and illustrative statistics from primary and secondary sources plus primary survey inquiries.

It is not within our remit here to give a complete history of the coffee trade, but it is worth noting that coffee originated from Ethiopia around AD1000, was taken to Saudi Arabia in the fifteenth century and spread to Europe in the sixteenth and seventeenth centuries. London and Oxford coffee houses date from the mid-seventeenth century and commercial production from the nineteenth. Coffee features as an important commodity in international trade and indeed is one of the world's most valuable commodities.

A sophisticated network of trade, processing, distribution and sales has been built up. Statistical data are furnished at the many stages of the coffee trade. Figure 12.1, adapted from the 1977 Price Commission report on *Coffee; Prices, Costs and Margins* [B.419], portrays the many economic agents involved at that time. [B.419] gave a concise explanation of the structure of the coffee trade and still has much relevance today. For example, most coffee enters the United Kingdom in the form of

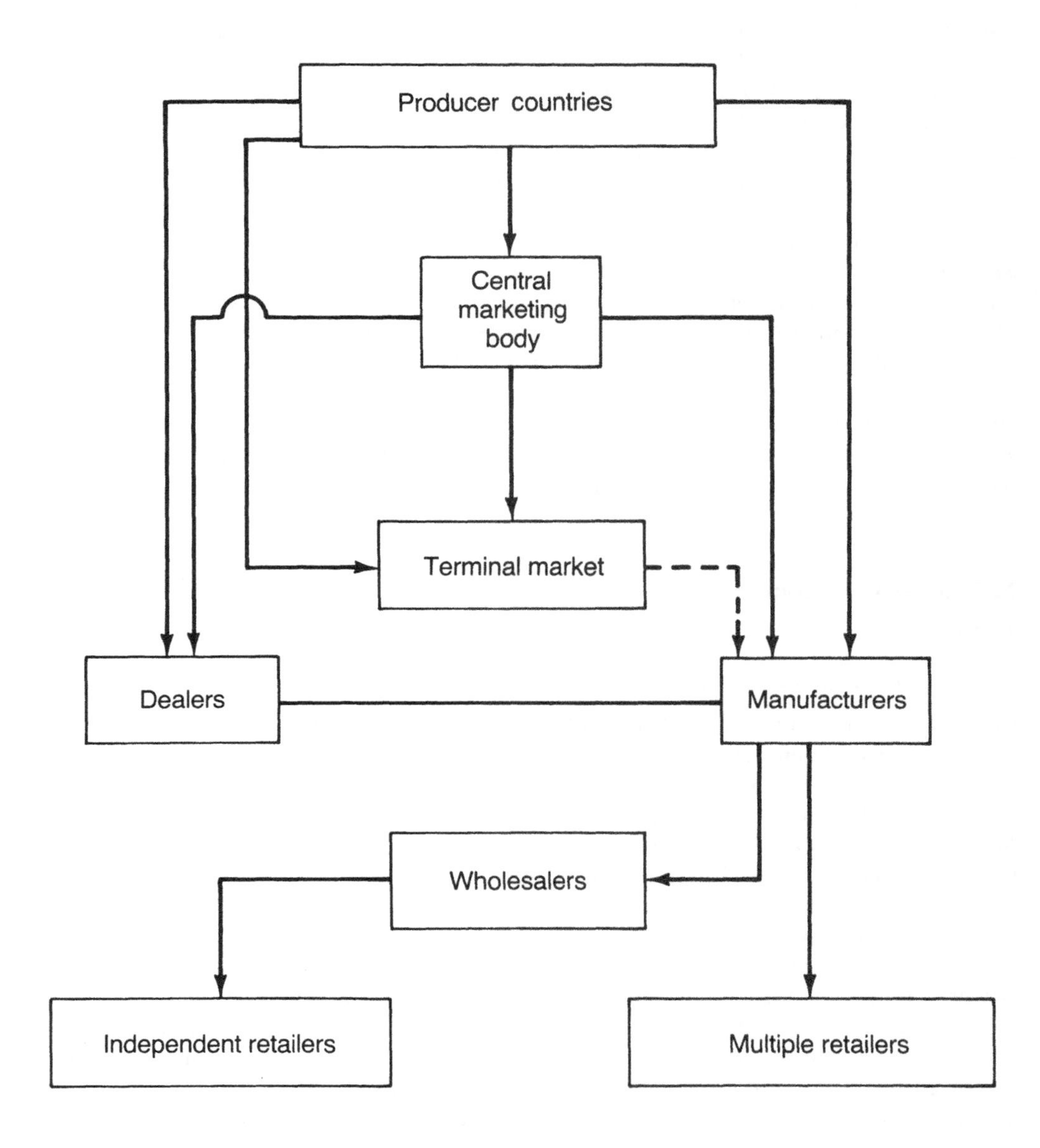

Figure 12.1 Channels of Distribution in the Coffee Trade.
Source: *Coffee: Prices, Costs and Margins* [B419], P.5, Price Commission Report no. 29, 1977.

green beans (i.e. dried but not roasted) before further processing. There are also substantial imports of soluble coffee.

Coffee thrives in tropical regions of moderate altitude. The size of crop is evidently related to the efficiency of general farming practices, but often critically depends on the presence or absence of drought or frost. Coffee Arabica (mild) predominates in Latin America and Coffee Robusta (generally more bitter) dominates in Africa. The four main categories for trading purposes are as follows: Colombian milds, other milds, unwashed Arabicas, and Robustas. After harvesting etc. the coffee bean is separated from the cherry in which it grows. It is packed in sacks for export, either by the producer direct or through a central marketing authority. Some of the crop may be converted into soluble coffee. Manufacturers in the United Kingdom may purchase their supplies direct from producer countries, their marketing authorities, through dealers and may also use the London market for hedging, speculation and arbitrage. After processing, coffee comes to the consumer via a variety of retailing channels (supermarket, coffee shop etc.) and in a number of forms.

The market classifies coffees in about five main ways: roasted beans; ground coffee; soluble (both powder and granules); liquid essence; and decaffeinated. With respect to the first two of these, two firms have dominated the market for roasted and ground coffee. Trade estimates at the time of writing are that Lyons Tetley (a subsidiary of Allied-Lyons) and Kenco Coffee (Kraft General Foods, formerly General Foods) have the major share of some 70 per cent. Yet the upper end of the market has to some extent splintered for there is is a good deal of competition and product innovation at the quality fringes. The purchase by retailers of green beans, which are roasted for subsequent sale as beans, or mixed and ground on their own premises, is an example of this. The extension of the filter-fine market and the increasing share of own-label are among other developments which have encouraged the market leaders to respond with major relaunches, rather akin to the re-entry of the major brewers into real ale. Competition has resulted in a greater demand for the milder Arabicas and, consequently, increased choice and quality. Indeed, there is much room for variety. The blend may be for all purposes (medium strength blends); continental (dark roast after dinner); light roast after dinner; French (coffee and chicory addition); Viennese (coffee and fig mixture); Brazilian (light to medium strength); America (Central American medium roast). This dynamic position at the top end of the market contrasts with the bottom end where the liquid essence of Camp Brand is a monopoly with declining sales.

Nowadays, soluble (or "instant") coffee is the type that most people drink. It was introduced to the UK market in 1939 and became increasingly popular after World War Two. Manufacturers use blends of coffee beans which permit them some latitude in their commodity purchases. Soluble or instant coffee comes in two forms: spray-dried or freeze-dried. Both methods involve the dehydration of brewed, roasted and ground coffee. The brewing is done in large vessels under high pressures and temperatures. The extract is then dried, but it is the different drying processes that cause major differences in taste. In the spray-drying process, the extract is sprayed through hot air. The heat dries off the water but it also takes away some of the aroma and taste. Freeze drying dehydrates in a vacuum below freezing point. This newer and more expensive process retains more of the original flavour. Freeze-dried coffee accounts for a rising share of the instant-coffee output which is sold in both powder and granule forms. Nestlé dominates the instant coffee sector with Nescafé, followed by Kraft General Foods (Maxwell House, Mellow Birds etc.) and Brooke Bond Oxo (part of Unilever) which produces Red Mountain. Manufacturers also supply the important own-label market.

This is a simplified summary of a heterogeneous market described in the many market research reports, typified by the October 1987 issue of *Retail Business* [QRL.432]. Finally, one of the more recent growth areas is decaffeinated coffee sold in the forms of beans, ground coffee, powder and granules. It is too much to expect that official coverage could extend to all varieties of coffee marketed, but *Business Monitor PQ4239: Miscellaneous Foods* [QRL.139] did have separate sales data on decaffeinated coffee amongst the other varieties until it ceased publication in the second quarter of 1989.

12.2.1.2 Industry sources

The International Coffee Organization (ICO) was established in 1963 when the 1962 International Coffee Agreement (ICA) entered into force for a period of five years. The ICO has continued to operate under the provision of subsequent agreements. As at December 1988, according to *ICO Basic Information: Objective, Structure, History and Operation* [B.311], seventy four governments were members. The fifty exporting members accounted for some 99 per cent of the world's production of coffee and twenty two importing countries accounted for some 90 per cent of the world's consumption of coffee. Thus the statistical information which is continually collated serves as an important potential source of information for both the United Kingdom and world markets.

Members provide the data which used to be published in the *Quarterly Statistical Bulletin* [QRL.398] which was the successor to the *Quarterly Statistical Bulletin on Coffee* [QRL.399]. The organisation of the information varied but the emphasis was on the world market where the United Kingdom could be readily identified under the following sections:

- Section I: Supply. This gave gross opening stocks, total production, domestic consumption and thus exportable production.
- Section II: Exports. Here the sources of supply to the United Kingdom were identified.
- Sections III and IV. Imports, re-exports, inventories and consumption were detailed.
- Section V. Contained a wide range of price information.
- Section VI: Values. Much of the quarterly and annual data pertained to quantities so a value section was usually included.

Although some of these data are catalogued, information to the general public has become more restricted. After the July–September 1982 edition of the *Quarterly Statistical Bulletin on Coffee* [QRL.399], the data were mainly made available at the ICO itself. From the middle of 1988, further restrictions were placed on availability at the ICO partly on the grounds of the provisional nature of the data.

Given the value of the world coffee market, other sources of information do exist, which draw heavily on ICO data. *F.O.Licht's International Coffee Report* [QRL.197] aims at a comprehensive coverage of the world market giving news, background, analyses and statistics. It covers production, quotas, exports, imports, prices etc. Statistical illustrations abound but the regular series on prices, exports and imports do not usually feature the United Kingdom. However, the annual index means that statistics specific to the United Kingdom (notably exports, imports and balances) can be conveniently found. *E.D.&F. Man (Coffee) Limited: World Coffee Situation* [QRL.179] is a briefer summary sheet which usually shows ICO indicator prices and other prices. It also includes reviews of producer and consumer markets. *LMC Commodity Bulletin: Coffee* [QRL.312] is a third commentary on this market carrying illustrative statistics on supply and demand, consumption, stocks, prices etc. These specialist research organisations usually combine ICO information and national statistical data with their own estimates.

It should be apparent that the ICO is an important source of statistical data, the availability of which can be checked on application to the ICO Library. For a continually updated bibliography, *Coffeeline* [B.228] is a bibliographical data base created by the ICO. It contains material identified and processed by the Organisation from the beginning of 1973. The aim is to cover the whole field of information on coffee including cultivation, processing, production, consumption and market surveys. Although it does not give day-to-day market information of the type conveyed by daily news services, statistical data are incorporated into *Coffeeline* [B.228] summaries. *Coffeeline* [B.228] is a bibliographic, as distinct from a statistical, data base, but it contains potentially useful material for those interested in the coffee sector. Most of the monthly update of *Coffeeline* [B.228] is listed in the *International Coffee Organization Library Monthly Entries* [B.321].

12.2.2 *Tea*

12.2.2.1 The organisation of the industry

Tea has a considerable literature, as befits the most popular beverage in the United Kingdom apart from water. It accounts for about 45 per cent of all we drink apart from water. It is derived from the natural product Camellia Sinensis which is indigenous to China and parts of India. The definitive and authoritative work on tea is by W.H. Ukers entitled *All About Tea: Volumes I and II* [B.177], with Volume II vital for its extensive index. A more recent publication, which makes use of primary statistics and surveys the global importance of tea, is by Denys Forrest entitled *The World Tea Trade: A Survey of the Production, Distribution and Consumption of Tea* [B.54]. Much background information is attractively and concisely contained in generic publicity material of the Tea Council entitled *File on Tea* [B.274].

Discovered in China more than 5,000 years ago, tea began to reach Britain via the East India Company which was granted its charter by Elizabeth I. The first public sales of tea were reputably held by Thomas Garway of Garaway's Coffee House in 1651. In 1660, a broadsheet issued by Garway extolled the virtues of tea as "wholesome, preserving perfect health until extreme old age, good for clearing the sight". It was further claimed that tea could cure "gripping of the guts, cold, dropsies, scurvys and it could make the body active and lusty".

Despite this apparent publicity, it remained a commodity for the wealthy until the nineteenth century. The 1784 Commutation Act, which reduced the tax on tea from

119 per cent to 12 per cent and the 1832 Act, which repealed the East India Company charter and opened up trading, both helped to stimulate consumption. Falling prices, rising incomes and improved distribution helped to increase the consumption of tea five-fold in the half century to 1900. Plantations spread from India to what was then Ceylon and later to Africa. Large-scale availability was stimulated in the 1850s and 1860s by organised tea clipper races. Its universal provision was enhanced by the growth of grocery chains as outlined by Peter Mathias in his book *The Retailing Revolution* [B.112].

Existing statistical information is generated at the many links of the tea chain from plantations in producing countries through to final consumption. The growers own plantations in India, Sri Lanka, Kenya etc. and the Secretaries and Agents arrange for the tea to be transported to the United Kingdom and elsewhere. Tea awaiting auction is held in warehouses by the warehouse keepers and is sampled by prospective buyers. The London Auction is unique as it remains the only international platform for teas from all over the world. Tea from ten to twelve countries is sometimes being bid for in the same auction. The London Auction is conducted by selling brokers on behalf of the producers on a commission basis. The tea is bought by the buying brokers for the blenders. The blenders may also buy through dealers whose job it is to locate supplies and buy and sell as principals. Thus the blenders buy tea in bulk, blend it, and put it in retail packs. It is then distributed through wholesalers or direct to retailers or to the catering trade. The organisation of the market was clearly explained in the 1978 Price Commission Report on *Tea Prices* [B.435].

The United Kingdom remains the biggest trader of tea in the world. In addition to buying for UK consumption, tea is exported to Europe, North America, Japan and various other countries even to the extent of re-exporting packet tea to India. As a mature market, a choice in supermarkets of 35 to 55 brands is quite normal in the United Kingdom. The September 1987 issue of *Retail Business* [QRL.432] splits the tea market into five sectors as follows:

a) Speciality teas. This growth area of the market consists of pure teas from a specific growing region (e.g. Darjeeling) and teas with a special aroma or flavour (e.g. Earl Grey).
b) High quality premium brands. This flourishing sector is typified by Brooke Bond Choice, Co-op Indian Prince.
c) Popular teas. These are the major grocery brands such as PG Tips, Typhoo, Tetley etc.
d) Value-for-money blends. Secondary cheaper blends are Brooke Bond D, Co-op Rich Leaf etc.
e) Economy teas. These very cheap blends are declining in importance.

If there is room for a number of companies in speciality teas or high quality premium blends, the mass market is largely dominated by the top four of Brooke Bond Oxo; Lyons Tetley; Premier Brands-Typhoo; and the Co-operative Wholesale Society.

Finally, the growth of the tea bag market in the past decade is a major development. This reflects the rising primacy of time-saving over ceremonial as well as changes in packaging technology. In 1908, a New York tea dealer, Thomas Sullivan, began to send out samples to his retail and private customers in small hand sewn silk bags. He later substituted gauze and the tea bag was well established in the United States by the 1920s. The tea bag in the United Kingdom began in the popular tea segment but has now extended to the other groups. Another development, instant tea (Nestea etc.), is minor except in the catering trade.

12.2.2.2 Industry sources

Given the importance of the United Kingdom for the tea trade, statistics on its many dimensions are found together in specialist publications. Of particular note is the work of the International Tea Committee. This organisation was set up in 1933 to administer what was then the International Tea Agreement. Although the International Tea Agreement was discontinued in 1955 (it is thought that the producing/exporting countries are now too numerous to render any commodity agreement effective), the collection of worldwide statistical data is now a notable feature of the work of the International Tea Committee.

The *Annual Bulletin of Statistics* [QRL.38], provides a wide range of annual data from the raw material sources to final consumption. There are sections on cultivation area, production and exports; imports and consumption; imports and re-exports; stocks; auctions and prices, general overview; instant tea; tea duties; and a useful directory of companies in and associated with the tea trade. The separate *Supplement to Annual Bulletin of Statistics* [QRL.474] usually appears later in the year. It gives the latest annual information on production, exports, consumption and supply/absorption. A third publication, the *Monthly Statistical Summary* [QRL.367], is designed to make available with greater speed the more important figures relating to the following: production; exports; imports; stocks; quantities sold; and average prices at the various auction centres. It supplements but does not replace the *Annual Bulletin of Statistics* [QRL.38].

The *Tea Market Report* [QRL.480] is available weekly from the Tea Brokers' Association of London. It includes data on supplies, sales, prices, stocks, imports and weighed teas awaiting sale. It is also referred to in other sections of this chapter.

Tea Statistics Year [QRL.481] is an annual publication of J. Thomas & Co. Private Limited, a Calcutta firm with over 125 years experience of tea auctioning and with correspondents in London. A worldwide picture is drawn of areas under tea; production; sales; exports; consumption; tea duties and taxes in producing countries; and tea import duties in consuming countries. It is mentioned here as it has a separate section on the United Kingdom which gives imports, re-exports and stocks in particular. The *Tea Market Annual Report* [B.387] issued by the same company, is an annual economic review. The reference is to India in particular but important markets and trading centres including the United Kingdom are covered along with statistical illustrations and charts. *Tea Statistics Year* [QRL.481] collects together the data from the International Tea Committee, the Tea Brokers' Association of London and the various tea organisations and associations worldwide. However, the major sources for the United Kingdom are the *Annual Bulletin of Statistics* [QRL.38] and the sister publications of the International Tea Committee. These are the fount of much of the data found in the other collections and commentaries. The International Tea Committee collects together much of the primary data on the United Kingdom and the worldwide tea trade.

12.3 The European Community

Apart from coverage in the various EUROSTAT publications, there is little significant economic and statistical impact of the Community on the tea and coffee trades apart from the general features covered in section 2.3.

12.4 Output

Output data are closely related to the individual sales statistics of the many commodities as formerly published in *Business Monitor PQ4239* [QRL.139] up to the second quarter of 1989. Sales figures for businesses in the scope of the Quarterly Sales Inquiries are given for the latest available five quarters and for the previous two years. The data are presented both in value (£ million) and volume (tonnes) and also give the largest number of enterprises contributing to the heading in any one of the quarters for the latest year. The data are itemised as follows:

Coffee and coffee and chicory extracts (excluding liquid essences)
Coffee, roasted and ground (excluding decaffeinated)
Coffee and chicory, roasted and ground (excluding decaffeinated)
Coffee with fig seasoning (Viennese coffee)
Soluble coffees:
  Spray dried (excluding decaffeinated).
  Freeze dried (excluding decaffeinated).
  Decaffeinated.
Tea:
  Blended
  In bags

Quarterly and annual volume and value sales data under SIC(1968) were given in *Business Monitor PQ229.2: Starch and Miscellaneous Foods* [QRL.126] which ran from the first quarter of 1973 to the fourth quarter of 1982.

The regular data on total sales and work done; gross output; net output and gross value added at factor cost; are of course combined with the many other products in *Business Monitor PA423: Starch and Miscellaneous Foods* [QRL.114]. But more precise output data are collected by MAFF to meet the UK's obligations under the International Coffee Agreement (ICA).

MAFF Statistics: Returns from Manufacturers of Regular Coffee, Coffee Essences and Extracts [QRL.331] is a quarterly MAFF survey. The data relate to the thirteen-week period just ended. The production section is split into three parts. First, the quantity (in cwt) of regular coffee produced is given. Second, the quantity (in cwt) of dry coffee extract, dry soluble coffee powder and dry coffee/chicory extract produced is presented. Third, the quantity (in gallons) of liquid coffee essence and liquid coffee/chicory essence produced is given. The data are obtainable by application to the MAFF but details are not disclosed for individual companies. Since information on usage and stocks are also given, [QRL.331] is referred to again in sections 12.5 and 12.9.

12.5 Current Inputs other than Labour

The main commodities used in tea blending and coffee roasting etc. are imported. There is thus an overlap here with section 12.8. The *Quarterly Statistical Bulletin* [QRL.398] usually yielded annual quantity figures for the imports of green coffee by importing members from all sources. Imports by importing members from each exporting member were also broken down by type of coffee: Colombian milds; other milds; unwashed Arabicas; Robustas. Imports by importing members from non-members were separately shown. Roastings for regular and soluble coffee in importing member countries were also given.

Fruit and Tropical Products [QRL.245] collects together a good deal of data in its coffee section. These include physical data on the imports of raw coffee into the United Kingdom in annual runs from January to the month indicated. The sources of raw coffee imports into selected countries from exporting countries are given for the latest year and quarter.

The *Annual Bulletin of Statistics* [QRL.38] gives exports of tea from producing countries, showing countries of destination. The data are in metric tons and US dollars for the latest six years. A detailed picture can be built up of the suppliers to the United Kingdom. Separate statistics for the United Kingdom are provided for imports, in volume and value, showing countries of origin for the latest six years. Monthly data are given in the *Monthly Statistical Summary* [QRL.367]. All these data are largely reproduced in *Tea Statistics Year* [QRL.481].

Data on the value and quantity of materials used in production are found in *Business Monitor PO1008: Purchases Inquiry* [QRL.116] for 1984 and *Business Monitor PA1002.1: Census of Production and Purchases Inquiry* [QRL.94] for 1979. The value and quantity of coffee beans and tea are given. However, the data for other inputs refer to AH4239 "Miscellaneous foods" in totality.

The MAFF is responsible for the *MAFF Statistics: Return from Manufacturers of Regular Coffee, Coffee Essences and Extracts* [QRL.331], which shows figures for usage of raw coffee (excluding chicory). Separate data are provided for the quantity roasted for regular coffee and the quantity used in the production of liquid coffee essence, liquid coffee/chicory essence, dry coffee extracts, dry soluble coffee powder and dry coffee/chicory extract.

Evidently the inputs of the raw materials depend upon the product under consideration. Raw coffee can be transformed into coffee beans, soluble coffee etc. Teas are blended, packeted and put in tea bags.

12.6 Labour

Statistical information on the many dimensions of labour are largely subsumed within "Starch and miscellaneous foods", for which sources are discussed in section 11.6. Company level information can be found in many of the sources cited in section 2.6, and in so far as tea and coffee processing are identified in the annual reports of companies.

However, employment and labour cost data were provided for the coffee subdivision in the Censuses of Production for 1954, 1958, 1963 and 1968. The "Tea blending" and "Coffee roasting" report in the *Final Report on the Census of Production for 1948* [QRL.214] gave aggregate data and size distribution and standard region analyses for employment and labour costs. There was also detailed coverage for "Tea blending" and "Coffee blending" in *The Report on the Census of Production for 1951* [QRL.422].

12.7 Capital

Statistical information on capital is incorporated within "Starch and miscellaneous foods", for which sources are discussed in section 11.7. Company level information can be located again in many of the sources cited in section 2.7, and in so far as tea and coffee processing are identified in the annual reports of companies.

Some data on capital inputs may be inferred from *Business Monitor PQ3244: Food, Drink and Tobacco Processing Machinery, Packaging and Bottling Machinery* [QRL.127]. This gives the value for the latest five quarters and last two years of machinery for the preparation of tea and coffee up to the second quarter of 1989.

12.8 International Transactions

12.8.1 *HM Customs and Excise Records*

The primary data source is the monthly *Business Monitor MM20: Overseas Trade Statistics of the United Kingdom* [QRL.85]. "Coffee, tea, cocoa, spices and manufactures thereof" is the title of Division 07 of the SITC(R3). The Division is further broken down for coffee and tea as follows:

071	Coffee and coffee substitutes
071.1	Coffee, not roasted, whether or not decaffeinated, coffee husks and skins
071.11	Coffee, not roasted, not decaffeinated
071.12	Coffee, not roasted, decaffeinated
071.13	Coffee husks and skins
071.2	Coffee, roasted
071.3	Coffee extracts, essences and concentrates, coffee-based preparations, coffee substitutes and extracts, essences thereof
071.31	Extracts, essences and concentrates of coffee and preparations with a basis of these products, or with a basis of coffee
071.32	Coffee substitutes containing coffee in any proportion
071.33	Roasted chicory and other roasted coffee substitutes (not containing coffee) and extracts, essences and concentrates thereof
074	Tea and maté
074.11	Green tea (not fermented) in immediate packings of a content not exceeding 3kg
074.12	Other green tea (not fermented)
074.13	Black tea (fermented) and partly fermented tea, in immediate packings of a content not exceeding 3kg

074.14 Other black tea (fermented) and other partly fermented tea
074.3 Maté; extracts, essences and concentrates of tea or maté, and preparations with a basis of tea, maté, or their extracts, essences or concentrates
074.31 Maté
074.32 Extracts, essences and concentrates of tea or maté, and preparations with a basis of tea, maté, or their extracts, essences or concentrates

It is to be noted that some of these headings are relevant to the discussion of current inputs in section 12.5. There is some distinction for raw material inputs from processed products particularly for coffee. Maté (074.31) is not covered in this chapter. Otherwise the monthly import and export figures for each of these headings is given in both volume and value terms for the wide range of exporting and importing countries. Further details of the *Overseas Trade Statistics of the United Kingdom* [QRL.85] are provided in section 2.8.2.1.

Business Monitor PQ4239 [QRL.139] had value and quantity data of exports and imports for the last five quarters and latest two years until it ceased publication in 1989. Coffee, including essences and extracts, and tea and maté are the two sets of distinctions made. The original source of the data is HM Customs and Excise. Tariff/trade code numbers are provided for these headings.

Other derivative sources are more aggregative. *UK External Trade: Area x Commodity Analysis* [QRL.494] gives annual data for Division 07 of exports, imports, exports less imports and the percentage of exports over imports when meaningful by specified country, the European Community etc. The preceding *United Kingdom Trade with European Countries* [QRL.508] performed a similar service.

The *Monthly Digest of Statistics* [QRL.362] gives the latest two years, two quarters and three-monthly value figures for Division 07, comparing the cumulative value from the beginning of the year with the same period in the previous year. The *Annual Abstract of Statistics* [QRL.37] reports the eleven-year value figures for Division 07 for exports and imports.

12.8.2 *Industry Analyses of Trade*

More specific data on the exports and imports of coffee and tea are covered in *Business Monitor MQ10: Overseas Trade Analysed in Terms of Industries* [QRL.90] and the earlier *Business Monitor M10* [QRL.77] of the same title. Quarterly and annual data in terms of value are given for coffee and coffee substitutes and tea.

12.8.3 *Industry Sources*

Both these commodities are widely traded in both raw and processed forms. The data, particularly for inputs of raw materials, are again relevant for section 12.5.

The *Quarterly Statistical Bulletin* [QRL.398], included a mass of information on international coffee flows. Besides aggregate data in value and volume for imports and exports, physical data are given on the imports of roasted coffee and the imports of soluble coffee by importing members from all sources in annual terms. Re-exports of all forms of coffee, of green coffee, of roasted coffee and of soluble coffee are shown. Separate statistics for net imports of processed coffee by importing members from all sources are computed by expressing volumes in green bean equivalent.

Fruit and Tropical Products [QRL.245] summarises the trade in soluble coffee expressed in green bean equivalent. The data are annual and from January to the month indicated for exports/re-exports and imports. The United Kingdom is separately identified among the other countries.

The *Annual Bulletin of Statistics* [QRL.38] collects together a variety of data on tea exports, imports and re-exports. Besides tea imports in value and volume, additional data are provided on tea imports in packets not exceeding 3kg. These show countries of origin and re-exports of tea with countries of destination. The figures exclude re-exports from the United Kingdom to the Channel Islands but include direct re-exports from the Channel Islands to countries other than the United Kingdom. Figures for tea imports for consumption in each country are derived by adjusting imports for re-exports. A long annual series of UK imports, re-exports, net imports and apparent consumption per head is given from 1950 to the present. Monthly data are produced in the *Monthly Statistical Summary* [QRL.367], yielding quantities for the last available month, cumulative totals for the year and comparable statistics for the previous year. The *Supplement to Annual Bulletin of Statistics* [QRL.474] furnishes the annual physical data on tea imports for consumption (imports adjusted for re-exports). *Tea Statistics Year* [QRL.481] reproduces most of these International Tea Committee statistics in its UK section. It also provides specific Indian data on exports of packet teas, tea bags and instant tea to all destinations (values and volumes) in annual terms.

The *Tea Market Report* [QRL.480] provides considerable insight into tea availability. It enumerates packages (landed and offshore) at the end of each week, giving a detailed picture of country, tea garden and average per kilo price. This publication is also discussed in section 12.12.1.

12.9 Stocks

12.9.1 *Coffee*

The specialist sources reflect a wide preoccupation with stocks and changes in stock levels. The *Quarterly Statistical Bulletin* [QRL.398] gives inventories of green coffee at the end of selected quarters for the United Kingdom as well as other importing member countries. Inventories refer to stocks of green coffee held by importers and roasters and exclude any stocks held in free ports. These data are also given in *Fruit and Tropical Products* [QRL.245].

Stocks figure significantly in commentaries on the interrelationships among world demand, consumption, production and stocks as in *F.O.Licht's International Coffee Report* [QRL.197], *E.D.&F. Man (Coffee) Limited: World Coffee Situation* [QRL.179] and *LMC Commodity Bulletin: Coffee* [QRL.312]. The focus here is on the world market as well as the United Kingdom.

There are two surveys carried out by MAFF relating to coffee. The first is the quarterly *MAFF Statistics: Stocks of Raw Coffee in Public Warehouses* [QRL.334]. This first of all provides a figure for stocks in public warehouses. Separate figures are then given for imports not yet landed and stocks in transit to the warehouse defined as stocks in transit overall. All these added together give total stocks. The term "public warehouses" refers to warehouses at the ports but can include warehouses owned by private firms. The important point to note is that these are stocks in the hands of traders as distinct from the processors. The stocks of the processors are covered by the second survey *MAFF Statistics; Return from Manufacturers of Regular Coffee; Coffee Essences and Extracts* [QRL.331] This survey collects figures on stocks (excluding stocks of coffee held on account in public warehouses) which is thus the total stocks of raw coffee at the end of the period held by the processors.

The *Monthly Digest of Statistics* [QRL.362] gives statistics for the monthly averages for end-of-period stocks. Stocks comprise raw coffee in public warehouses, raw coffee in transit to such warehouses and, since 1963, manufacturers' stocks. Hence these are the aggregate statistics of traders' and processors' stocks. Finally, the *Annual Abstract of Statistics* [QRL.37] carries the aggregate stock data at end December in each year.

12.9.2 *Tea*

The Tea Brokers' Association of London summarises physical stock data in the *Stocks and Tea Movements* [QRL.465] weekly sheet. First, the warehouses data show stocks the previous Friday, receipts and deliveries during the week just passed and stock at the end of the week. These statistics are the physical stock taken by the warehouses of all teas whether sold and not collected, teas awaiting sale and even private imports. These are distinct from the second set of data for end-week stock at primary wholesalers which represents packed stock plus work-in-progress. These figures show the tea held by blenders, whether in their premises or held in warehouses. A third set of figures gives the stock of weighed tea awaiting sales, yielding the end of week (Friday) figure in packages. These data are also separately given in the *Tea Market Report* [QRL.480]. All three sets of data record comparisons with the same period the previous year.

These three sets of figures are somewhat confusing, as they stand, to anyone not closely acquainted with the tea trade and merit some additional explanation.

The weekly statistics are provided by the Tea Clearing House (the warehouse keepers) and incorporate data from the Tea Buyers' Association (which represents the primary wholesalers like Brooke Bond Food plc and Lyons Tetley plc etc.). These weekly statistics are as follows:

a) Total stock held (unsold auction, sold uncollected auction and private imports). These are the *first* set of figures referred to in the paragraph above.

b) Teas awaiting sale (unsold auction, subdivided by country of origin, already included in (a) above). These are the *third* set of figures referred to in the paragraph above.

The primary wholesalers' stock returns cover teas held by them already blended and packed, teas awaiting packing plus teas paid for by them but lying in the warehouses of Tea Clearing House members and others. These are the *second* set of figures referred to in the first paragraph of this section and this portion has already been included in (a) above.

Hence these three sets of figures partly cross-refer to each other and cannot be separated. The reason is a commercial one with respect to those making the returns.

It is felt that blenders would not wish their exact stock positions to be available to their competitors and it has habitually been impossible to verify an exact percentage stock holding in each category.

Note that these data on stocks can be regarded only as showing trends, despite the attempt to separate out public and private stocks and to standardise the packages which were converted at 51.256 kilos per package as on Friday 30 December 1988. MAFF now relies on the information from the tea trade itself. Up to the end of 1984 it carried out its own quarterly survey into stocks held by primary wholesalers. When this was added to the figure for stocks of tea in public and private warehouses (collected by the Tea Clearing House), figures for total stocks could be arrived at.

Data on stocks as at the last Friday in the three previous months (compared with the same month in the previous year) are provided in the *Monthly Statistical Summary* [QRL.367], which gives a public/private warehouse figure and a figure for primary wholesalers too. Tea stocks for these two categories are also given in the *Annual Bulletin of Statistics* [QRL.38]. Some information is also featured in *Tea Statistics Year* [QRL.481].

Information on end-of-period stocks (quarterly and annual) for public warehouses and primary wholesalers added together appears in the *Monthly Digest of Statistics* [QRL.362]. The *Annual Abstract of Statistics* [QRL.37] carries these data at end December for the latest twelve years.

It may also be noted that, over and above these industrial and MAFF sources, stock statistics were recorded in the past in the Census of Production. Data on stocks of products on hand for sale were reported in the 1949 and 1951 Census of Production in the "Tea blenders and Coffee roasters" reports ([QRL.420 and [QRL.422]). The 1954, 1958, 1963 and 1968 Census of Production reports gave statistics for coffee stocks only ([QRL.423], [QRL.424], [QRL.417] and [QRL.418]).

Finally, none of the data discussed in this section refer to blended tea awaiting shipment from blenders, nor teas in the retail chain nor in the home. With respect to the latter, we cannot resist the temptation of referring to a famous housewife, Mrs Margaret Thatcher. At midnight on the 24th December 1984, the Indian Government of Mrs Indira Gandhi placed an export ban on tea from India, wishing, amongst other things, to ensure adequate supplies to the indigenous population at election time. In the subsequent four-week period tea prices at the London Auction rose from £1 a kilo to £3.50 a kilo. The ensuing rise in the retail price provoked many adverse comments from consumers. Mrs Margaret Thatcher stated that the prudent housewife who had laid in stocks in advance was protected and that others with less foresight would behave more rationally in the future! We can only guess at the size of household stocks, whether held in the traditional form in tea caddies, in packets or as boxes of tea bags!

12.10 Consumption

12.10.1 *The National Food Survey*

The National Food Survey collects information on a number of tea and coffee products as the following description from the food codes shows:

Food code number	Description
304	Tea — includes tea bags but not instant tea which is put with Miscellaneous in code 336
307	Coffee, bean and ground — includes coffee bags and sachets
308	Coffee, instant — this includes accelerated freeze-dried instant coffee
309	Coffee, essences — quantities are recorded in fluid ounces.

Some statistics are published in the *National Food Survey: Compendium of Results* [QRL.373]. Annual average figures of both per capita weekly consumption and expenditures are provided for the main food groups. These comprise tea; coffee; cocoa and drinking chocolate and branded food drinks under the heading of beverages. Cross-classifications by region and type of area; by income group; by household composition; by household composition within income groups; by age of housewife; by housing tenure and by ownership of deep freezer are provided.

The main report on the Survey, *Household Food Consumption and Expenditure* [QRL.267] carries some statistical data, particularly in the supplementary tables. The quarterly and annual national averages of consumption of individual foods details tea, instant coffee and coffee essences. The analysis of consumption and expenditure according to income group identifies the main food groups. Both consumption and expenditure are analysed according to household composition groups within income groups. Before 1985, these data were largely covered in the tables and appendices of *Household Food Consumption and Expenditure* [QRL.267]. It may be noted that beverages are often taken together in the analyses of consumption patterns. Income elasticities of expenditure are computed for tea and instant coffee. Cross-price elasticities of demand are occasionally presented for tea and coffee. These coefficients are decisively lower than unity which may be surprising for what are commonly regarded as obvious "substitutes".

12.10.2 *The Family Expenditure Survey*

The *Family Expenditure Survey* [QRL.204] gives average weekly expenditure on tea and coffee. These data are cross-classified by levels of household income; for one-adult households or different levels of household income and by sex and age; by levels of household income for households with and without children and according to region.

12.10.3 *The National Accounts*

The *United Kingdom National Accounts* [QRL.506] provide data on consumers' expenditure on coffee, tea and cocoa aggregated together at both current and 1980 prices, as further explained in section 2.10.3.

12.10.4 *Industry Sources*

However, the source which contains the most detailed and continuous information is the *National Drinks Survey* [QRL.372] which can be purchased from the Nestlé company. This survey is a 360-day inquiry which has been running since 1966. It covers the whole consumption field for beverages; whether hot, cold or alcoholic. About 11,000 interviews are carried out to elicit what people drink during daily periods, how much of each drink is consumed and the time and place. This picture of consumption by time of day reflects the habits of all demographic age groups over two years' old and portrays regional variations. The data are analysed by brand for coffee but only generically for tea. Availability to interested commercial parties and the public is subject to Nestlé discretion.

Aggregate data on "Disappearance" in the *Quarterly Statistical Bulletin* [QRL.398] seeks to indicate the volume of coffee entering the consumption channels in importing Member countries. "Disappearance" is measured by deducting re-exports from imports and adjusting the resulting figure for changes in visible inventories, although this method does not take into account changes in "invisible inventories" such as larder and shelf stocks. These data are given by quarter in the *Quarterly Statistical Bulletin* [QRL.398]. The latter also includes quarterly data on physical household purchases for the United Kingdom amongst other importing members. The data on "Disappearance" are repeated in *Fruit and Tropical Products* [QRL.245].

The International Tea Committee is also concerned with aggregate consumption figures. The *Annual Bulletin of Statistics* [QRL.38] features tea imports for consumption in each country, but also deduces statistics for apparent consumption per head and an overall total for a long time series since 1950. The *Monthly Statistical Summary* [QRL.367] and *Supplement to Annual Bulletin of Statistics* [QRL.474] give tea imports for consumption data. The former graphs United Kingdom "Apparent consumption of tea" showing the annual and the two-year moving average. The material in the *Annual Bulletin of Statistics* [QRL.38] is again largely repeated in *Tea Statistics Year* [QRL.481].

12.11 Supplies and Disposals

Supplies per head of the population are given for a twelve-year run for tea and coffee in the *Annual Abstract of Statistics* [QRL.37]. This also includes physical measures of the disposals of raw coffee and tea excluding re-exports. The *Monthly Digest of Statistics* [QRL.362] also carries the monthly averages for the disposals of raw coffee and tea.

Disposals for raw coffee and tea are rather different from the "disposals" explained in section 2.11.3. For tea, disposals are the quantities moving into consumption and exclude exports. For raw coffee, disposals are the total quantities destined for consumption in the United Kingdom but include re-exports of raw beans and exports of processed coffee.

The term supplies can be more broadly interpreted as it relates to imports, re-exports, consumption and stocks as discussed in other sections of this chapter. The data on "Disappearance" in the *Quarterly Statistical Bulletin* [QRL.398] is discussed in section 12.10.4 with respect to coffee. The treatment of "apparent" consumption per head for tea in the *Annual Bulletin of Statistics* [QRL.38] was noted in the same section. Stocks data for both commodities are discussed in section 12.9.

In addition, *F.O.Licht's International Coffee Report* [QRL.197] is always preoccupied with the world coffee balance, looking at production, international trade, ICO quotas etc. *E.D.&F. Man (Coffee) Limited: World Coffee Situation* [QRL.179] shows a similar interest but with less detail. *LMC Commodity Bulletin: Coffee* [QRL.312] carries specific data on ICO members' market balance (million bags, green coffee) in annual and quarterly terms. This shows exports to members, disappearance and changes in stocks. These figures may be compared with ICO members' market demand (million bags, green coffee) in annual and quarterly terms. The United Kingdom is separately shown in these ICO-based data.

12.12 Prices

12.12.1 *Agricultural and Commodity Prices*

12.12.1.1. Coffee

Coffee is an internationally traded commodity. Consequently, a plethora of data on spot and futures prices appear daily in the press. The *Financial Times* [QRL.218], for example, gives the days' close for futures prices, the previous day's prices high/low, plus turnover and ICO indicator prices. New York is also covered. The main trading markets are New York (mainly Robusta suitable for processing into instant coffee), New York (principally Brazilian and other Arabicas), the French markets of le Havre and Marseilles (mostly trading in coffee of West African origins) and Bremen-Hamburg (dealing mainly in fine coffees from Colombia and East Africa). International trading is often heavily influenced by controls on supply and the movements of coffee exercised under the International Coffee Agreement (ICA). Indicator prices are summarised in the *Weekly Report on Prices* [QRL.514] available from the ICO and issued each Thursday. The daily and fifteen-day moving average indicators are detailed plus the weekly change in indicator and other prices at the major trading centres (eg. the London Terminal Market).

It is, of course, common knowledge that the ICA, even where agreed by members, controlled only qotas and prices imperfectly. In fact, producers were supposedly free to sell beyond their quota allocation to non-member consuming countries, as stated under the ICA, but not at lower prices. Prices in the parallel market were often thought to average some 60 per cent of the quota prices. This gave an incentive for "tourist coffee" sold to non-members, to be illegally resold in member countries.

Thus the ICA is by no means a stable association of producers and consumers and periodically breaks down, as it did when agreement on new quota and price arrangements could not be reached on July 3rd 1989. The ICA, at the time of writing, is in force to the extent that member countries meet once yearly to talk about regulations. When ICO quotas (and to some degree prices) are in force, as they have been for periods in the past, the ICO meets twice yearly. The ICA, like many other attempts at commodity cartels, has had a chequered existence and the current situation can be updated by means of the financial press and the ICO itself.

The *Reuter Coffee Newsletter* [QRL.436] provides a statistically illustrated commentary on the latest factors influencing prices at all important trading centres. Occasional data on substitutes (e.g. tea and cocoa) and complements (e.g. sugar) are sometimes provided. Issued on weekdays, it carries London Robusta coffee prices in a similar format to the *Financial Times* [QRL.218], as well as more data on the number of contracts made. There is a full coverage of prices at other trading centres and ICO indicator prices in the statistical appendix which follows the main commentary.

F.O.Licht's International Coffee Report [QRL.197] summarises daily world wide ICO coffee prices and New York spot coffee prices. *E.D.&F. Man (Coffee) Limited: World Coffee Situation* [QRL.179] reports ICO indicator prices. *LMC Commodity Bulletin: Coffee* [QRL.312] carries a table on coffee prices which gives monthly averages for the latest quarters and years. These include market prices (e.g. London Robusta) and retail prices (e.g. UK soluble).

The Public Ledger & Daily Freight Register [QRL.392] repeats the London FOX closing prices for Robusta coffee and gives the ICO indicator prices. *The Public Ledger's Commodity Week* [QRL.394] features both London and New York coffee in the futures prices summary for the days of the week just ended. Both Robusta futures and ICO indicators are included in the commodity price guide. The monthly price record covers the average prices with high and low for the previous three months.

Finally, as indicated in section 12.2.1.2, the *Quarterly Statistical Bulletin* [QRL.398] included a range of price information over and above the daily ICO indicator prices. Data on the unit value of exports and imports, prices to growers in exporting member countries and retail prices of roasted coffee in importing member countries were gathered together.

12.12.1.2 Tea

Although there is no futures market in tea, trading arrangements are varied and sophisticated. The producer has three possible methods of completing the transaction: to sell a proportion of his crop forward, to sell privately on an invoice basis either for shipment or afloat, or to sell in auction either in the country of origin or in the London Auction, both "Landed sale" or "Offshore sale". "Landed sale" refers to landed auctions of tea in warehouses whereas "Offshore sale" relates to tea auctioned whilst in transit from the producers.

A good deal of price information is contained in the weekly *Tea Market Report* [QRL.480]. This yields the price indications for the week, compared with the corresponding week the previous year, for quality, medium and low medium teas. A good deal of detail is included which covers the country and tea garden of origin, the number of packages and weight and average price per kilo for the week just ended. Comparisons are made with the corresponding week in the previous year. Data in similar form on offshore sales are also provided.

The *Annual Bulletin of Statistics* [QRL.38] repeats the monthly price quotations for tea at the London auctions for the latest twelve months with lowest and highest for the year, now divided into quality, medium and low medium. The *Tea Market Report* [QRL.480] is the original source. Other data are monthly average prices of tea sold at London auctions from 1951 to date; the annual average prices of tea sold at London auctions according to region of origin; and annual average prices of tea sold at auctions in producing countries. Quantities sold at London auctions are also provided plus the quantities of tea sold and average prices at London offshore auctions. Price data are also contained in the *Monthly Statistical Summary*

[QRL.367] which gives weekly average prices and quantities at the London and other auctions plus the London offshore auctions.

The Public Ledger & Daily Freight Register [QRL.392] reports tea auction average prices from a number of named countries for the current and previous week and a figure for the auction average. *The Public Ledger's Commodity Week* [QRL.394] includes the London auction average price in both the commodity price guide and the monthly price record of average, high and low prices for the previous three months. These are just straightforward summaries and nowhere near as detailed as the coverage in the *Tea Market Report* [QRL.480].

12.12.2 *Retail Prices*

12.12.2.1 Recorded prices

The *Employment Gazette* [QRL.186] gives average retail prices on one day of the month for the following products: pure, instant coffee per 100g; ground (filter fine) coffee per 1/2lb; loose tea per 125g; tea bags, per 250g. This monthly source notes the number of quotations and the price range within which 80 per cent of the quotations fell.

Household Food Consumption and Expenditure [QRL.267] in its pre-1985 format gave quarterly and annual average prices in the beverage section for tea; coffee, bean and ground; coffee, instant; and coffee essences besides cocoa and drinking chocolate and branded food drinks. Since 1985, the average prices paid for these individual foods are given for a three-year period in the supplementary tables. The *Compendium of Results* [QRL.373] now carries the quarterly and annual average prices for these subdivisions.

12.12.2.2 Recommended prices

The *Grocer Price List* [QRL.253], issued with *The Grocer* [QRL.252] on the first Saturday of each month, gives considerable detail in its aim to suggest prices for the small retailer. There are separate sections for coffee (ground); coffee (instant); and tea. Wholesale prices are always given and retail prices/fair selling prices often suggested. *Shaws Guide to Fair Retail Prices* [QRL.453] aims to suggest the maximum retail price to be charged based on minimum wholesale quantities. The prices of various firms and their brands can be found within the following categories: coffee essence; coffee, ground and beans; coffee, instant; and tea.

12.12.3 *The Retail Prices Index*

This is published monthly in the *Employment Gazette* [QRL.186] grouping coffee and other hot drinks together but separating out tea. The percentage change over a twelve-month period is shown for these two groupings. The *Monthly Digest of Statistics* [QRL.362] details the figure for the latest seven months showing the respective weights.

Business Monitor PQ4239 [QRL.139] summarised, until the second quarter of 1989, the retail price indices for coffee and other hot drinks and tea for past quarters and the last year. These series were compared with the "all food" and "all items" indices.

12.12.4 *Price Index Numbers in the National Food Survey*

In its pre-1985 format, *Household Food Consumption and Expenditure* [QRL.267] gave indices of expenditure, prices, real value of food purchased and the total value of consumption for beverages taken together. Product detail down to the food codes (i.e. coffee, bean and ground; instant coffee; tea; cocoa and drinking chocolate and branded food drinks) was found in the annual indices of average deflated prices, purchases and demand. These related to the most recent six years expressed as the average for the whole period.

Since 1985, some index number information is located in the *Compendium of Results* [QRL.373]. This applies to the annual data for the indices of expenditure, prices and the real value of food purchased for beverages as a main food group. But the individual food code details of the annual indices of average deflated prices etc. are no longer published.

12.12.5 *Producer Price Index Numbers*

The series of Producer Price Indices are considered in general terms in section 2.12.5. However the coverage in *Business Monitor MM22: Producer Price Indices* (since October 1989) only incorporates "Miscellaneous foods", described in section 11.12.5. Past coverage for coffee and tea are considered below.

12.12.5.1 Producer price index numbers: input prices.

Business Monitor PQ4239 [QRL.139] carried, until the second quarter of 1989, the producer price indices of materials purchased for imported tea and imported coffee beans from MAFF sources usually for the latest five quarters (the last provisional) and the last two years. The previous *Business Monitor PQ229.2* [QRL.126] carried the wholesale price indices of agricultural raw materials purchased for coffee and tea, with data back to 1971 in the second issue, when these series were first covered.

12.12.5.2 Producer price index numbers: output prices

Business Monitor PQ4239 [QRL.139] yielded, until the second quarter of 1989, the producer price indices of goods produced usually for the latest five quarters (the latest provisional) and the past two years. There were separate series for soluble coffee; roasted and ground coffee and blended tea from MAFF sources. Comparisons were made with the figures for food manufacturing industries (home sales) and all manufactured products (home sales) from DTI sources. The previous *Business Monitor PQ229.2* [QRL.126] carried the wholesale price indices of goods produced and identified soluble coffee and liquid essence; ground and roasted coffee and blended tea back to 1971 when the series was first covered in the first issue of 1974.

12.12.6 *Export and Import Prices*
Export and import price indices were produced for coffee (including essences and extracts) and tea in the second and third issue only of *Business Monitor PQ229.2* [QRL.126] in 1973 from MAFF sources. The *Quarterly Statistical Bulletin* [QRL.398] showed the unit value of imports (cif) by importing members of the ICO (including the United Kingdom) for the past few quarters.

12.12.7 *Prices and Government Regulation*
Coffee and tea prices feature prominently in many investigations. Given the links with costs, prices and economic structure they are discussed together in section 12.16.

12.13 Financial Information

As outlined in section 2.10.2, the primary data flows from the companies themselves and are collated together in the many publications listed in that section. But given the multi-product nature of many of the companies now involved in tea and coffee processing, sources like the *Times 1000* [QRL.486] and the more specific *Britain's Food Processing Industry* [B.150] are of limited use.

Key Note does carry some financial data in the 1988 edition of the *Hot Drinks* [QRL.592] report. Besides the industry structure information, there are data on profits and profitability and liquidity contained in the financial profiles of the Nestlé Company, Brooke Bond Oxo, General Foods and R. Twining. This information, derived from company reports, is less valuable for General Foods than for R. Twining which at least predominately processes and sells tea.

Much detailed but dated information is featured in the 1970 NBPI report on *Tea Prices* [B.414], the 1977 Price Commission report on *Coffee: Prices, Costs and Margins* [B.419] and the 1978 Price Commission report on *Tea Prices* [B.435]. These, together with other reports, are discussed in more depth in section 12.16. It is worth stressing here how aggregative the financial data have become. This is exemplified in the 1985 Monopolies and Mergers Commission (MMC) report on *Elders IXL Ltd. and Allied-Lyons plc* [B.442]. This compares with the greater product detail in the earlier data in *Tea Prices* [B.435] and *Coffee: Prices, Costs and Margins* [B.419]. The latter yields information on profits, margins etc. from the many segments of the trade, including processors and blenders. The data do reflect a time when food conglomerates were less preponderant.

12.14 Advertising and Market Research

12.14.1 *Advertising*

Advertising on both coffee and tea is substantial and continuous. The *Tri-Media Digest of Brands and Advertisers* [QRL.493] is the basic source as discussed in section 2.14.1. Expenditure on the many brands is covered under Coffee and coffee extracts (F36), and under Tea (F94). There is significant product differentiation at the quality end of the market. There is also the continual promotion of the staple household lines of soluble coffee, tea bags etc. *The Media Register* [QRL.354] gives rival monthly summaries under the categories: Coffee — Fresh (FOO 17); Coffee — Instant (FOO 18); and Tea (FOO 80).

Both coffee and tea brands appear in the top 100 brands advertising in the Food industry as ranked by adjusted MEAL expenditure data included in *The Food Forecast* [QRL.236]. For tea at least, these data underestimate total advertising activity since the Co-operative Wholesale Society does not advertise nationally but mainly promotes within their own shops.

12.14.2 *Market Research*

The connection between advertising and market research is characterised in the *Food Forecast* [QRL.236] whose coverage confirms the importance of tea and coffee as markets in their own right. The separate section on "Beverages" reproduces MEAL brand data for expenditure on coffee and coffee extracts, and tea for the past nine years (unadjusted) and the latest quarter (adjusted). Accompanying tables show brand shares for previous years for instant coffee, tea (by the packet), and tea bags judged by the pattern of expenditure of housewives. Regional analyses for usage are also given.

The October 1987 issue of *Retail Business* [QRL.432] carried a market report on "Coffee". This collected together data and commentary on the dimensions of consumption, foreign trade, sales, market size, distribution, catering, future prospects etc., as well as summarising annual MEAL data on brand advertising expenditure on coffee and coffee extracts. The September 1987 issue of *Retail Business* [QRL.432] performed a similar exercise in its market report on "Tea". Previous special reports in *Retail Business* [QRL.432] have collected together primary data on these markets supplemented by the market commentary and trade estimates.

Many of the market research reports regard coffee and tea as part of the hot drinks market. Market Assessment Publications, in their annual report on *Hot Drinks* [QRL.610], give a market sector overview before treating instant coffee; ground coffee; tea; food beverages; instant food beverages; milk powders; convalescence drinks separately. Data to show sales by types; competitive structure; advertising; retail outlets and consumer profiles are put together.

The December 1987 issue of *Market Intelligence* [QRL.339] contains a review of "Hot beverages", which draws together market data on tea; coffee; and food drinks all preceded by a hot beverages market overview. Information on sales and supply structure; advertising and promotion; distribution; consumption; the consumer and future developments are included. Commercial developments such as the launch of the one-cup tea bags, the growth in freeze-dried coffee sales and the rise in the decaffeinated coffee market are statistically illustrated.

The 1988 edition of the Key Note report on *Hot Drinks* [QRL.592] has already been noted in section 12.13. It deals with the categories of coffee; tea; drinking-chocolate and hot drinks. Industry structure, customer profile, companies and brand share, market size and trends, recent developments and future prospects etc. are described along with the major company profiles.

Marketing Strategies for Industry produce a report on *Hot Beverages* [QRL.641] which includes separate sections on tea; coffee; cocoa and drinking chocolate; malted food drinks and instant food drinks. Illustrative data on market size, production, international trade, regional consumption and market shares were presented.

The Hot Drinks Report [QRL.536], published by Euromonitor in 1984, drew together a multitude of the available statistical tables on coffee; tea; and food drinks. A market overview of all three markets was followed by separate sections which gave background structure, consumer profile, major suppliers, future outlook etc. The text was supported by many statistical tables from official and trade sources. For example the details of annual tea advertising expenditure by manufacturers cited Euromonitor/MEAL estimates which included the generic campaign of advertising expenditure run by the Tea Council. The section on vending (drinks vended by type, estimated volume sales, prices, major suppliers, advertising spending etc.) covers a significant portion of the market.

The Leatherhead Food Research Association also surveyed "Hot beverages in the UK" in the July 1985 edition of *Food Market Updates* [QRL.238]. This yielded hot beverage market coverage by product type, and a range of statistical data. Commentaries on commercial developments, for instance the launch of fruit flavoured tea designed to attract younger consumers, were featured.

12.15 Research and Development

Again, R&D goes hand in hand with advertising and market research. There is very slender statistical information available publicly, if any at all. Teas are blended to suit regional tastes and water supplies. This is a well developed art and science. Such information is within the province of the major tea blenders whether concerned with trying new speciality teas or experimenting with production technology etc. The emergence of the tea-bag, the development of tea vending machines, instant teas and so on are other illustrations of major inventions and innovations. *The Grocer* [QRL.252] occasionally reviews product developments of the participating companies.

Whilst R&D for tea is primarily British, the application of science and technology to coffee-based products is American as well as British. Descriptions of product development are often featured in the annual reports of the companies. At least the *General Foods Corporation: Annual Report Fiscal* [QRL.247] gives annual research expenditure in its supplemental information section but that covers a wide range of products.

12.16 Official Investigations

Tea and coffee have figured prominently in many reports, from the early 1956 Monopolies and Restrictive Practices Commission report on *The Supply of Tea* [B.452] to the discussion in the 1985 MMC report on the proposed merger of *Elders IXL Ltd. and Allied Lyons plc* [B.442]. Most of the investigative bodies have scrutinised either tea or coffee or both. The material in this section is discussed as follows under the sub-headings of the various bodies involved.

12.16.1 *The National Board for Prices and Incomes*
Tea Prices [B.414] was published in 1970 after the NPBI was requested to examine "the costs, prices and profitability of the tea buying, blending, packing and distributing industry". Besides a brief description of the industry, it summarised the market share of the top four retail firms. It drew upon annual statistics on profit in pence per lb and percentage return on capital and examined the relationships between charges, trade prices and costs. The information sources were mainly the companies themselves. The general conclusions were that Brooke Bond was a price leader making significant expenditures on advertising. The NBPI discouraged further price increases.

12.16.2 *The Price Commission*
The 1975 Price Commission report on *Food Prices in Outlying Areas* [B.421] gave data on the variation in the retail prices of 1/4lb Typhoo P.G.Tips for small towns near major cities contrasted with prices in defined outlying areas which ranged from North Scotland to South-West England. Prices were collected from 426 retailers of which 196 were in outlying areas in this study.

The 1977 Price Commission report on *Coffee: Prices, Costs and Margins* [B.419] has already been drawn upon in section 12.2.1.1. It merits further discussion since many statistics on the coffee trade are conveniently drawn together in this study. Following a sharp rise in the price of coffee, each sector of the UK coffee trade was examined. Use was made of both existing primary sources and 417 Price Commission questionnaires which sought information about prices, costs and margins. Perceptions were strengthened by discussions with trade associations, individual manufacturers, dealers, retailers etc.

Primary data included an analysis of market share by type of outlet in 1976. Here the Price Commission augmented Business Monitor data. The statistics confirm that the distribution pattern for coffee among independents, multiples and co-operatives differed little from that for all grocers. Table 5 in the report gives the price and cost build-up for a 4 ounce jar of soluble coffee for the years 1971–1976 and notionally for Spring 1977. This is expressed in pence through the distribution chain including coffee costs, transport costs, dealers' and manufacturers' costs and margins, wholesale margins etc. to the final selling price at the retailers. The breakdown is given at each stage with a cumulative total. The report subsequently examined each stage of distribution. This corresponded very much to the paths outlined in Figure 12.1 above. The following data were given:

- Table 6 showed coffee dealers' gross net profit margins 1974–1976.
- Table 7 reported the turnover, costs and margins for soluble coffee manufacturers for the same period from the Price Commission sample. Direct costs, indirect costs and net profits before tax etc. were given. The percentage changes in these magnitudes for 1974–1976 were also calculated.
- A bar chart presentation of the composition of manufacturers' selling prices compared coffee costs, direct and indirect costs and net profit.
- Table 8 gave capital employed by soluble coffee manufacturers for 1974–1976.

Concern about price variability was also investigated, aided by a price survey undertaken by the Regional Offices of the Price Commission on 3 February 1977.

This covered 248 multiple retailers and co-operatives and 119 independent retailers. From the computation of the average price and price range of six selected brands of soluble and ground coffee, the coefficient of variation was obtained. This showed coffee to be the third most variable of the twelve grocery products selected. Peas and orange squash exhibited more variation.

Coffee: Prices, Costs and Margins [B.419] clearly revealed how the regular sources covered in this chapter, ranging from the BSO to the ICO etc., needed supplementing by Price Commission survey work in order to obtain a statistically more significant grip on the prices, costs and margins relationships at all stages of the distribution chain. Some gaps remained. For instance, the dealers informed the Price Commission that they were unable to distinguish between margins achieved on physical and futures transactions and between margins on UK and foreign deals. Yet this report enjoyed a good measure of success in generating additional statistical information. This was indeed necessary for a more complete picture to be sketched in, given the coverage of existing primary sources.

Tea Prices [B.435] is another example of the work of the Price Commission. It has also been discussed in section 12.2.2.1. It reported in 1978. The concerns at the time were both the sharp changes in the London auction price of tea (September 1976 — December 1977) and how quickly and fully the retail price of tea reflected these movements in the world price. This characteristically lucid and brief study was based on 323 Price Commission questionnaires sent out to firms drawn from many parts of the tea chain. These data again supplemented normal primary sources in this examination of prices, costs and margins. The report featured the following tables of particular interest:

- Table 1. Percentage price breakdown of the retail price of a 1/4lb packet of tea in August 1977 showing margins at all stages including the blenders' or distributors' gross margins.
- Tables 4, 5, 6 and 7 gave net profit margins of UK controlled overseas producers, selling brokers, buying brokers and dealers in annual terms, usually for at least three financial years.
- Table 8 gave financial results of blenders 1974–1977. Direct costs (tea, packaging and labour) were subtracted from sales to arrive at gross margin. Overheads were considered and figures for net profit before tax and gross margin were arrived at.
- Table 9 analysed total capital employed by blenders 1974–1976 broken down into fixed assets and net current assets (tea stock, other).

The study suggested that blenders followed upward movements in world tea prices faster than downward movements and recommended further retail price reductions.

12.16.3 *The Monopolies and Restrictive Practices Commission*

The Supply of Tea [B.452], which has already been discussed in section 2.16.4.1, summarised the structure of the industry as it then was. Statistical data on production and supply, imports and exports of tea, and sales and profits of tea producers (1949–1955) were drawn from both primary sources and *ad hoc* material. The focus on price was again significant. The relationship between the London auction and retail prices of tea are graphed from 31st March 1952 to 1st January

1956. The comparison of retail prices of Brooke Bond, Lyons and Typhoo for various blends at January 1954 and July 1955 were obtained from blenders and packers directly. Both Lyons and Brooke Bond supplied data on the duties and amount of price changes of numerous brands over selected months from 1st March 1954 to 1 July 1955. The conclusion was generally that the tea trade was conducted on keenly competitive lines. This contrasted with the statistical illustrations of price collusion in the text. It also sat uneasily with a verbal statement of classic price collusion made as follows by Brooke Bond. "It had been customary for many years to inform··· J. Lyons & Co. Ltd. by telephone of our intention to change our packet prices up or down and details of such changes have been communicated. Messrs. J. Lyons & Co. have reciprocated when the initiative has been taken by them".

12.16.4 *The Monopolies and Mergers Commission*

The 1985 MMC report on *Elders IXL Ltd. and Allied-Lyons plc* [B.442] contained some specific information on tea, ground coffee and instant coffee. Allied Breweries Ltd. acquired Showerings, Vine Products and Whiteways Ltd. in 1968, and J. Lyons & Company Ltd. in 1978. Allied-Lyons plc carries on its major trading activities through the Beer Division and Wines and Spirits Division as well as the Food Division. Although the company operates in many markets, the following data are provided:

- Table 3.3 shows percentage market shares by sector (including private label suppliers) for 1985 for the firms in the tea, instant coffee and ground coffee markets as well as for biscuits, cakes and ice-cream.
- Table 4.6 gives the approximate size of each of these markets (£m) in 1984. It compares the approximate percentage share for branded products contrasting Allied-Lyons with the largest supplier. Allied-Lyons all products shares are compared with all suppliers of private label. The data are in volume terms for tea, instant coffee and ground coffee but by value for biscuits, cakes and ice-cream.

These data were provided by Allied-Lyons for the MMC. But it is notable that the brief, but useful, statistically-illustrated summaries of the United Kingdom coffee, tea and other food-related markets drew upon trade association estimates and various market surveys by, for example, Mintel, Euromonitor and the Economist Intelligence Unit. These supplement, for instance, the work of MAFF and the CSO. This mirrors the approach of this chapter which has catalogued the statistical information on tea and coffee from disparate official and commercial sources.

12.17 Improvements and Comments

Much of the data on tea and coffee are subsumed under Group 423 "Starch and miscellaneous foods", as noted in Chapter 11. Thus for labour, capital and financial information, in particular, one must rely on company level information. Nevertheless, tea and coffee were important enough to merit separate coverage in the past (see the Censuses of Production for 1948 and 1951). Separate sales data were still given in *Business Monitor PQ4239* [QRL.139] up to the second quarter of 1989 when it ceased publication.

There is considerable interest in both tea and coffee supplies worldwide. These commodities are well served by the various publications of the International Tea Committee and the International Coffee Organisation etc. — see section 12.2. But it is a matter of some regret that the *Quarterly Statistical Bulletin* [QRL.398] of the ICO is no longer available. Elsewhere the coverage varies across sections. There are more data on raw material stocks, international trade, prices and consumption than say on R&D and finance. This is characteristic of many of the products included in this Review.

At least the obstacles to assessing trade flows are less dramatic than they were for tea in the eighteenth century as trenchantly noted by T.S. Ashton in his classic text entitled *An Economic History of England: The 18th Century* [B.6].

> "In 1784, the accountant for the East India Company, who had good reason to know about such matters, estimated that of the tea consumed in Britain, hardly a third had been legally imported: the rest had come in surreptitiously, mainly from the Continent. It was believed that the illicit trade in tea encouraged the smuggling of other things that would not have been brought in 'except, as it were, in the train of a more capital, or more convenient article'. Hence as a measure to reduce smuggling in general, it was decided to lower the import duty on tea from the 119 per cent at which it stood to 12 and a half per cent. Whatever the effect on the contraband trade in other commodities, the volume of tea that passed through the customs house increased vastly: in 1784 the amount entered for home consumption was 4,962,000 lbs; in the following year it was 16,307,000 lbs. Rarely can the accuracy of a statistical estimate have been more decisively confirmed: the accountant must have been delighted."

It can of course be argued that coffee and tea are more stimulants and comforts of life rather than foods and that they should not be featured in a Review of this nature at all. Notwithstanding this, they are included along with other foods in the regular publications like *Household Food Consumption and Expenditure* [QRL.267], the *Annual Abstract of Statistics* [QRL.37] etc. regularly catalogued in this Review. It is thus consistent as well as interesting to cover them here. Perhaps what should be emphasized is that they are both considered as part of the hot drinks market together with cocoa and other food drinks. On the other hand, they are sometimes looked at in conjunction with all beverages, whether hot or cold, whether soft drinks or whether alcoholic drinks.

The abundance of information on raw material supplies and the detailed coverage of these markets has been discussed in section 12.14.2. This is contrasted with the comparative vacuum in recent times on the processing side. Nothing yet updates the 1977 Price Commission report on *Coffee: Prices, Costs and Margins* [B.419] and the 1978 Price Commission report on *Tea Prices* [B.435]. Only a survey of the companies, covered in this chapter, from purchases of the raw materials to point of sale could accomplish this. It would indeed be a detailed task of interest and endeavour for both the academic and business world given the conglomerate nature of the main companies involved in these markets. Indeed, at the time of writing, work is in progress by the MMC on the soluble coffee market and the report will be noted in the Addenda to this volume.

CHAPTER 13

CONCLUDING REMARKS

13.1 Introduction

Our remarks in this chapter are divided into six sections. First, we discuss the implications of the changing attitude of governments towards the collection and provision of statistical data. Second, we comment on the particular effects that these changes have made on the collection of data on the Food industries. Third, we consider the availability of information on the methodologies of the various statistical inquiries cited, and suggest a need for a comprehensive Manual of Methodology. Fourth, we look at the role of commercial and other non-official sources of statistical information. Fifth, we detail the various guides to recently-published statistical sources, and suggest how this Review might itself be updated so as always to provide the latest possible information on statistical developments. Finally, we reflect on the many facets of the material covered in this Review.

13.2 The Government Statistical Service

The Central Statistical Office (CSO) was established in 1941 with the specific purpose of compiling estimates of the national income in connection with the planning of the war economy. It was located in the Cabinet Office since its work involved the drawing together of data from a number of departments. It was said that Winston Churchill was frustrated because he received conflicting numbers from different departments. Yet statistical collection did not become the responsibility of a single office and has since been the work of many government departments. Thus it has been necessary to catalogue the diverse sources from the many agencies in this Review.

If the Ministry of Food was given impetus by war, the Business Statistics Office (BSO) was a child of peace. The paucity of a suitable range of business statistics capable of monitoring satisfactorily changes in the British economy and industrial structure began to be heavily criticised in the 1950s and the 1960s. These criticisms culminated in the *Fourth Report from the Estimates Committee* [B.287] which was a detailed report from the House of Commons Estimates Committee in 1966/67. It corresponded to political interest at the time in indicative planning and Government intervention in industry which perceived the need for an increased range of macroeconomic and microeconomic statistics. Out of this was created the BSO with the responsibility for collecting and publishing statistics and developing what was then referred to as a common register of business.

The BSO began operating at the beginning of 1969 and initially took over the work previously carried out by the former Census Office of the Board of Trade at

Eastcote, whose main functions were to carry out, at five- and ten-year intervals, the large-scale Censuses of Production and Distribution. The demand for more frequent data led to the flowering of statistics under the BSO (located at Newport, South Wales in 1972) and the creation of the Business Monitor series, of which the annual PA Monitors and the quarterly PQ Monitors have been catalogued heavily in this Review.

This climate which favoured the expanded collection of official statistics began to change in the mid-1970s with the rising concern about the costs of public expenditure. In the case of business statistics, the representatives of small firms in particular voiced complaints about the costs which government imposed on them. These of course included the compliance costs of providing statistical information for the various inquiries. The number of staff at the BSO peaked at about 1100 in 1975, and has since fallen by over one-third mainly since 1979, to about 725 in 1985 and to 670 at end-1988. When the BSO became part of the enlarged CSO on 31 July 1989, BSO Newport employed 674 people.

The drive for economy, if not retrenchment, was well under way before the publication in December 1980 of the *Review of Government Statistical Services: Report to the Prime Minister* [B.368] — the Rayner Review — by Sir Derek Rayner. This was followed by the April 1981 White Paper entitled *Government Statistical Services* [B.294] which summarised the proposals and set out the recommendations department by department. In fact, Rayner produced not only the report catalogued here as [B.368], but also twenty-two separate "examinations reports" for different government departments which all contained their own recommendations. Particularly significant for this Review were the detailed reports on the DTI, the CSO, MAFF, HM Customs and Excise and the Department of Employment.

Rayner carried out a rigorous survey and cost-cutting exercise which aimed to save £20 million out of the £100 million spent on the Government Statistical Services in 1979. Rayner took the view that statistics should be provided only when they were useful to government departments. The government was no longer viewed as the universal provider of the stock of statistics. This robust attack on the Government Statistical Services was intended as another dimension of the policy of limiting the role of the state. This approach aroused considerable controversy and is evidently still a subject of public debate since the provision of statistics may be regarded as a public good. The Rayner preoccupation with "getting rid of" paid scant attention to the benefit of statistical information to the public and tax-payer at large, besides the needs of industry, the labour force and academic researchers. Thus Rayner could be regarded as a cost-benefit analysis which paid little attention to the benefits and external economies derived from the provision of information. It also gave little weight to the view that the more informed we are about our activities the more civilised we are, despite the evident costs of both collection and compliance. Indeed firms have split personalities in regard to statistics. Cost-cutting proposals capitalise on the resentment of the time it takes to respond to inquiries yet all business firms need as much information about the market as they can get.

The 1988 Statistics Users' Conference dealt with UK International Trade Statistics against the backcloth of considerable speculation about the sources and availability of visible trade statistics after 1992. But the opening address, given by Mr Francis Maude, who was at that time Parliamentary Under Secretary of State for Corporate

Affairs, in many ways epitomised the high point of the government's non-intervention stance with respect to the collection of official statistics. Indeed, Maude regarded the collection of statistics as a deregulation issue, and reaffirmed the Rayner Doctrine in his observation that the government should be mainly responsible for the provision of statistics for its *own* uses. It should not fulfill the statistical needs of the private sector since the market place would eventually provide. This brought into question the coverage after 1992 of *Business Monitor: Overseas Trade Statistics of the United Kingdom* [QRL.85] as Maude drew a parallel between the EC, after the formation of the Single Market, and the United States of America and questioned the need for *any* EC trade data. These and other issues were summarised in the February 1989 issue of *Statistical News* [B.381].

It is evident that the current system for collecting trade statistics, which is based on HM Customs' administrative needs, could not operate with respect to trade between Member States of the European Community if the main border formalities are eliminated with the completion of the single market. But after consulting its own users and Member States, the European Commission has concluded there would still be a need for comprehensive statistics of trade between Member States. The European Commission has thus prepared proposals for the framework of systems to operate in all Member States. The overall schemes are complex but the aim is to provide linked systems which control the collection of VAT on goods traded between Member States and thus generate intra-EC trade statistics. Such proposals are summarised in the August 1989 and Autumn 1990 issues of *Statistical News* [B.381]. With respect to statistics of trade with countries outside the European Community, these will continue to be collected under the current system.

Under the revised system, many businesses will still have to provide comprehensive information on their trade with firms in other Member States. But it may be possible to sharply reduce the burdens on small and medium-sized traders depending upon what levels of statistical thresholds are determined. The Commission have suggested that they may propose that the largest 20 per cent of traders provide detailed monthly returns. In the UK these traders account for around 96 per cent of the value of intra-EC trade. Such a threshold, it is claimed, would ensure adequate collection of detailed statistics in most industries. The UK continues to try to strike the difficult balance between minimising the burden of supplying information whilst ensuring that information which is needed continues to be available. But in the end these issues will be decided by all Member States under qualified majority voting. Reports on the latest proposals, and in particular for our purposes, on the eventual level of disaggregation can be located in successive numbers of *Statistical News* [B.381] and in the *Business Bulletins* [QRL.75] series entitled "Statistical changes in 1992".

The philosophies and requirements of governments of course change, and indeed, after 1979, contrasted with the more collectivist climate of opinion which prevailed following [B.287] in 1966/67 running through to the late seventies (see pages 565–566). Given the policy from 1979 onwards that intervention in industry be minimised, there was seen in the 1980s to be a reduced need for detailed disaggregated figures. Hence far fewer statistics should be collected by those departments where policy is made. These questions were further considered in the *Review of DTI Statistics* [B.367] published in May 1989 — now commonly referred to as the "Armstrong-Rees Report". This report assessed the entire approach of the DTI and the BSO to statistical data collection. It focused on the purposes for which data collection are required, the compliance cost of providing statistics and the frequency with which data are collected and published. It was consequently proposed to severely truncate the Business Monitor coverage — as further explained in section 13.3.

Whereas it appeared that there would be less detail in business statistics, there was also to be a significant reorganisation of statistical services following another review of economic statistics, *Government Economic Statistics: A Scrutiny Report* [B.293] — the Pickford Review. The Pickford Review [B.293] was the outcome of the efficiency scrutiny led by the Cabinet Office with the brief of examining "the present interdepartmental arrangements for the production of government economic statistics and to make recommendations for achieving cost-effective improvements where necessary".

Consequently, it is now intended that the CSO should live up to its name. Since July 1989, as well as its main job of compiling the national accounts, the enlarged CSO has been in charge of the Retail Prices Index and the Family Expenditure Survey (both the former responsibility of the Department of Employment), and all the statistical series such as on industrial production and investment, previously collected by the Department of Trade and Industry (DTI) and the Business Statistics Office. However, the Department of Employment keeps control over labour statistics, particularly those on unemployment.

Thus the statistical wheel has turned a full circle from its zenith in the early 1970s to its nadir in the late 1980s from the point of view of the research economist and business executive seeking detailed information. It may well be that in the end we shall be saved by EUROSTAT and the statistical requirements of the European Community.

13.3 The Food Industries

This Review has shown that a good deal of data exists on the Food industries even if they are published in many different places. We summarised in section 1.3 the agencies collecting official statistics for most of the period under consideration. It would indeed be most convenient if all relevant data could be located in one statistical collection. An "Annual Abstract of Statistics on the Food Industries" would be the ultimate ideal. If that appears rather ambitious, at least we can claim here to have succeeded in explaining the disparate agencies (from the MAFF to the BSO and further) which are responsible for the collection of official statistics.

This Review has also emphasised that market research agencies and trade associations are also responsible for the collection of statistics. These statistics are both sold on the open market and provided as part of the services for paid-up members. Publications often attempt the dual role of addressing the demands of commercial interests for the latest information on industrial structure and providing detailed statistical returns to the businesses in question. In general, the individual chapters in this Review have catalogued many distinctive specialist publications. Examples are the *Statistical Year Book* [QRL.461] of the Biscuit, Cake, Chocolate and Confectionery Alliance (BCCCA) discussed in Chapter 10 and the *Annual Bulletin of Statistics* [QRL.38] of the International Tea Committee discussed in Chapter 12. Thus there does sometimes exist a dominant source which provides a significant amount of information on the industry in question.

Each section in Chapter 2 contains concluding comments which assess the data available and suggests possible improvements. Every chapter from Chapter 3 to Chapter 12 ends with a section on "Improvements and Comments". Thus it is not intended to duplicate these remarks here. However, some observations are in order, particularly in the light of the recent wide-ranging studies already mentioned in section 13.2

The Rayner Review [B.368] of December 1980 and the Armstrong-Rees Review [B.367] of April 1989 both led to reductions in the coverage of statistical data. Many of these instances have been summarised in the sections on "Improvements and Comments" throughout this Review, and we will not repeat them in detail here. It is sufficient to emphasise that the Rayner Review [B.368] has had a serious effect on the provision of statistics on the Food industries.

The administrative responses to the call to economise may be regarded as fivefold. First, the most straightforward solution is to cut out statistical surveys completely. A second is to stop or cut back proposed developments. A third is to reduce frequency — from quarterly to annual for instance. A fourth device is to stop producing provisional results for major inquiries. Finally, a fifth and probably the most crucial in terms of saving staff and reducing forms, is to take smaller samples which usually includes raising the "cut-off" level below which firms are exempted from statistical inquiries. Most of these methods have been used since 1979 for the Food industries and we list examples below.

a) From the final quarter of 1981, the "cut-off" levels in the Quarterly Sales Inquiries were raised selectively for different industries. Sampling was also used to reduce the burden of form filling. This meant a one-in-four sample of units employing between 20 and 49, a one-in-two for those employing between 50 and 99, and full coverage of all units employing 100 or more.

b) As noted in section 2.1.1.2, six food manufacturing industries were dropped altogether from the Quarterly Sales Inquiries. Thus to collect product sales information from those dropped, and those where the employment threshold was raised, the Topping-up Inquiry noted in section 2.1.1.3 was undertaken.

c) The decision to drop the six food manufacturing industries may be partly explained by the existence of similar inquiries carried out by MAFF or by trade associations such as the BCCCA. A list of such short-period inquiries is provided in section 2.11.1. The reduction of MAFF efforts in "manufactured foods" which duplicated those of the DTI is a reflection of the Rayner Review [B.368]. There were other modifications, such as the elimination of the "jam" inquiry. However, the proposed merger of the National Food Survey (NFS) and the Family Expenditure Survey (FES) did not take place for the reasons explained by R. Barnes and R. Redpath in the May 1982 issue of *Statistical News* [B.381].

d) The monthly inquiries into manufacturers' export prices which had begun in 1975 were discontinued at the beginning of 1980. It was initially intended to extend coverage to a wide range of industries with the aim of compiling a range of export price indices. Hence, and rather surprisingly, there is no export price index which would have been roughly comparable to the long-established wholesale price indices (now renamed producer price indices).

e) One of the most publicised features of the Rayner Review [B.368] was the decision to base unemployment statistics on claimants' declarations of their unemployment at Benefit Offices. Industrial analysis of unemployment ceased in May 1982 as noted in section 2.6.2.

f) Following the Rayner Review [B.368], the Census of Employment became triennial rather than annual. But it has since become a "periodic" sample survey as described in the August 1987 issue of the *Employment Gazette* [QRL.186]. Special feature articles in the April 1991 and the May 1991 issues of the *Gazette* gave the results for the United Kingdom and Great Britain respectively. However, rather finer industrial breakdowns of employment can now be gathered from the PA Business Monitors rather than the Census of Employment which some users may find surprising. Rayner also led to the diminished coverage of *Time Rates of Wages and Hours of Work* [QRL.483] as noted in section 2.6.10.1.

g) A corollary of the slimmer statistical services of the BSO — as noted by Laurie Berman in the 27 February 1981 issue of *British Business* [QRL.66] — is the need to carry out more complete inquiries every five years. This is done to provide the benchmark information required for "grossing up" the Annual Census of Production data and for the National Accounts. It also means that clear explanations of statistical procedures are needed; a point which is also stressed in section 13.4.

The *Review of DTI Statistics* [B.367] has already had an influence on the future availability of statistical data for the Food industries even though it is not clear at present whether all its recommendations will be implemented over the planned three-year period. The authors were clearly directed to follow the Rayner principle that statistics are collected primarily for use within government. The evident aim was to minimise compliance costs by reducing the frequency of all, or some part, of the same inquiries, by reducing the amount of detailed information, by reducing sample size and by streamlining the number of questions on the forms. Several of the proposals affect the extent of Food industries' coverage and are summarised as follows:

a) *Quarterly Sales Inquiry*. The number of products overall for which sales information is collected was to be reduced from 4600 to 2400. Moreover, product detail for most of these would only be collected annually. Thus most firms would only be asked to supply total sales information quarterly, instead of sales by product as previously. Further savings could be made by reducing the sample size from 12,900 to 7500. This already had, by mid-1989, a severe effect on the present inquiries into the Food industries.

b) *Annual Census of Production*. The sample size should be reduced from 16,000 to 13,000. Further economies were envisaged if firms employing less than 100 were not asked to provide an asset breakdown of capital expenditure. It was suggested that questions on the breakdown of employment by type of employee, on various details of sales from different types of work done, and on various expenditure details could be eliminated. Only totals would be requested, apart from in the benchmark censuses.

c) *Purchases Inquiry*. The next full quinquennial purchases inquiry to 10,600 firms was originally planned for 1989. Firms were asked to supply information on purchases of products which typically accounted for 0.5 per cent or more of total purchases for their Activity Heading. It was proposed to raise this "cut-off" to three per cent or $10m since the previous detail was mainly needed in the construction of input-output tables but is not vital to most other users of the inquiry, the interests of the DTI or other departments' interests in the pattern of purchases. A reduction in sample size by 10–20 per cent for many Activity Headings was also envisaged.

These are the three main effects on the various statistical inquiries considered in this Review, but there are also other ramifications and recommendations:

a) The truncation of the Quarterly Sales Inquiry means that the method of construction of the Index of Production will adopt a basis of total sales for most Activity Headings rather than using product sales data.
b) Converting the voluntary quarterly capital expenditure survey to a statutory annual basis is under consideration, although the questions on "land and existing buildings" (see section 2.7) may be dropped if Inland Revenue data should provide a suitable alternative.
c) The amount of detailed information on employment and expenditure both in the annual and four-yearly surveys of R&D may be reduced.
d) Rotational sampling (where firms are included in the sample for four years and then excluded for several years) is under consideration for the Distributive and Service Trades.
e) The triennial benchmark Overseas Assets and Liabilities Inquiry may become quinquennial if the limited assets and liabilities information collected in the annual inquiry provides "satisfactory" results.

The *Review of DTI Statistics* [B.367] and the Rayner Review [B.368] both share the view that data collection involves the companies involved in compliance costs. However, [B.367] did not give details on how compliance costs were estimated. A telephone survey was carried out, interviewing respondents in 436 firms, backed up by more detailed interviews with both firms and trade associations. Furthermore, no attempt to assess the benefits of statistical data was made even though it was estimated that savings for industry in compliance costs amount to $1.7m a year. Presumably, the proposal to charge users for statistics on the BSO Agency status may in the end partially reflect the value of the data, although they will have a diminished value if less are collected.

The final long-term outcome of the *Review of DTI Statistics* [B.367] remains to be seen. However, a clear summary of the picture at the time of writing was given by Roger Norton in the July 14th and July 21st 1989 issues of *British Business* [QRL.66]. Of the PQ Monitors listed in section 2.1.1.2 and extensively catalogued in other chapters of this Review, only *Business Monitor PQ4122: Bacon Curing and Meat Processing* [QRL.130] and *Business Monitor PQ4213: Ice-cream* [QRL.138] remain after the second quarter of 1989.

Yet it is now apparent that a major influence of the European Community is that attempts to cut down on statistical coverage may be limited by EC requirements. The proposals for the Annual Census of Production cannot be implemented, despite being accepted in principle, because the United Kingdom would not then be able to comply with EC Directives. But the omens for the Quarterly Sales Inquiry have been unfavourable, because data have been largely passed on a voluntary basis to EUROSTAT. It was estimated at the time that a further £0.5m a year saving would be made if the requirements of the SOEC could be reduced. We will leave it to the reader to judge whether the estimated compliance cost savings of £1.7m per annum and a potential saving of £0.5m per year outweigh the loss of the benefits of adequate statistical information about the United Kingdom.

13.4 Methodology

This Review has focused on the coverage of statistical inquiries, but has also discussed methodology at length, particularly in Chapter 2. Any overall assessment of statistical sources should clearly consider the subject of methodology, as well as data coverage, data presentation, data quality, the frequency of data collection and revision, and the length of any time lags before publication. Many of the official sources have thorough methodological overviews. Some examples are as follows:

a) *Business Monitor PA1001: Introductory Notes* [B.214] gives an outline of the Census of Production methods. It explains objectives, the classifications used, the reporting unit, the register, the coverage, the questionnaire, the collection of data and the period covered etc. The estimation section explains how non-responders, unsatisfactory returns, and businesses not selected for the census are dealt with. All PA and PQ Business Monitors have briefer notes which focus more on coverage.
b) The *Input-output Tables for the United Kingdom 1984* [QRL.284] has been discussed in section 2.5.2.1. Yet is is worth noting that the 1988 edition carries a fairly detailed presentation of the methodology used.
c) *United Kingdom National Accounts: Sources and Methods. Third Edition* [B.395] is well known. It carries careful definitions yet there is insufficient explanation of how the reliability gradings are derived.
d) *Household Food Consumption and Expenditure* [QRL.267] and the *Family Expenditure Survey* [QRL.204] both carry explanations of methodologies which are fairly accessible.
e) The *Employment Gazette* [QRL.186], *British Business* [QRL.66] and *Statistical News* [B.381] are other examples of publications which contain further clarification and assessment of data collection. A heavier burden may be placed on [QRL.186] and [B.381] now that from September 1989 *British Business* [QRL.66] has been discontinued. Occasional articles of interest, however, also appear in *Economic Trends* [QRL.181].

Thus we could go through many of our references and describe the contents pertaining to methodology as well as to coverage. This would be an extremely lengthy task, yet we think there is a clear need for a Manual of Methodology which would draw together all the technical notes which are presently scattered around the various publications. We see the need for a clear guide to both sampling methods and the underlying theory. This is all the more necessary as sampling has increased, given the drive to economise on the number of units surveyed since the Rayner Review [B.368]. A standard manual, which could be updated from time to time, could be written to explain the methodology of the BSO, MAFF etc. Explanations of the methods used in each department could then be usefully collected together in a single volume.

The need for a clear explanation of statistical procedures is thus already apparent. This need has been reinforced rather than weakened by the general diminution in coverage since 1979 and the future planned cuts described in the *Review of DTI Statistics* [B.367]. Indeed, one of the recommendations in [B.367] is that "more attention should be given to the calculation of sampling errors and users should justify the degree of accuracy they need as this has an important bearing on sample size". It was backed up by the following recommendation that "to the extent our other recommendations free professional resources, some can be redeployed to assist in the development of statistical techniques". However, there are clear limitations to what can be achieved by waving a statistical wand if the amount of initial information and industry detail has been severely pruned.

There exist many good textbooks on economic theory and statistical methods. But as Jackson [B.85] and Simpson [B.163] have argued, there is a clear need to match up the economic and statistical theory with the practice of data collection and data availability. Jackson [B.85] wrote in 1980 at a time when he regarded the teaching of economics to have fallen behind the "information revolution" and the expansion of data in the previous thirty years. He complained of the lack of knowledge both of the sources and applications of "real world" statistics. He cited textbooks to be grieviously at fault "in not giving more systematic information to students as to exactly where up-to-date information can be obtained". He made a valiant if rather turgid attempt to repair this gap in his own 1982 textbook entitled *Introduction to Economics: Theory and Data* [B.86]. Simpson [B.163] pursued a similar line of argument in the less statistically abundant times of 1988, commenting that "there remains an uncritical attitude among academics towards statistics produced by official agencies".

Given these concerns, what new texts are there on methods of statistical investigation? Two editions (1958, 1971) of *Survey Methods in Social Investigation* [B.133] by Moser and Kalton have been subsequently reprinted a number of times. But there does not exist, to our knowledge, any more recent single publication which specifically sets out to give explanations of the many statistical methodologies used in the various government departments (or private agencies) which collect and publish data.

We obviously realise that there are often good explanations which accompany existing publications — the summary of the methodology used in the *Input-output Tables of the United Kingdom 1984* [QRL.284] is a case in point. We also know that both standard texts and specialist journals for statisticians and economists furnish such material as well. Yet we consider that the assembly together of clear and rigorous descriptions of methodologies in one volume would be of considerable benefit. Such a Manual of Methodology which is loose-leafed and which then could be updated would be of immense help to both collectors and users of statistics.

Finally, the remarks of Jackson [B.85] and Simpson [B.163] probably stem from their perceptions that prestige in the economics profession is often related more to the elegant exposition of theory than the collection and interpretation of data. This climate of opinion may now well be changing given the increasing importance which is being attached to applied work. Certainly, the writing of this book has been a hard, unspectacular and unremitting slog. Yet at times it has been satisfying to achieve exactitude and that carries its own type of rigour.

One is always reflecting on how better one could have done a job once it is done. It was not in our remit, and in fact it is largely forbidden, to reproduce any data or give explanations of methodologies used. We were largely confined to the description and critique of the sources themselves and what they contained, against the background of the structure of the Food industries. Doubtless, if we could have written a book which had four prongs: an outline of the industrial structure; a catalogue of the sources themselves; some illustrative statistics; and an analysis of the many methodologies used; then the satisfaction and the achievement would have been the greater. The marrying all together of theoretical constructs and the relevant data (which is what we would ideally have liked to have done) with the structural background and the comprehensive detailing of sources (which we have attempted to do in this review), is in its completeness a veritable Everest of a summit which may be some day surmounted and conquered.

13.5 Commercial Sources

In this Review on the Food industries, we have been most conscious of the fact that many people want to find out statistical information on companies. This has been particularly apparent in our approach to section 2.13 "Financial Information" and section 2.14 "Advertising and Market Research". It has also been necessary in the sections on "Industry Structure" to outline the vital components of the Food industries, with reference to company names. An inevitable consequence of this is the use of market research publications such as *Retail Business* [QRL.432], *Market Intelligence* [QRL.339] and *Market Research: Great Britain* [QRL.343], to mention just three of the most widely available sources.

Financial comment in the Press and all these market research sources are replete with company names which is what the typical user usually seeks. What makes the Business Monitor series so dry in many ways is an inevitable result of the requirements of the Statistics of Trade Act 1947. We quote from *Business Monitor PO1001: Guide to Short Term Statistics of Manufacturers' Sales* [B.216] as follows:

> "No individual estimates or returns, and no information relating to an individual undertaking, obtained under the foregoing provisions of this Act, shall, without the previous consent in writing of the person carrying on the undertaking which is the subject of the estimates, returns or information, be disclosed except:
>
> a) In accordance with directions given by the Minister in charge of the government department in possession of the estimates, returns or information to a government department or to the Import Duties Advisory Committee for the purpose of the exercise by that Department or Committee of any of their functions; or
>
> b) for the purposes of any proceedings for an offence under this Act or any report for those proceedings."

Another illustration can be taken from *Business Monitor PA1001: Introductory Notes*

[B.214] which draws from sub-section 9(5)(b) of the Statistics of Trade Act 1947 as follows:

> "The following provisions shall have effect with respect to any report, summary or other communication to the public of information obtained under the foregoing provisions of this Act:
> 'in compiling any such report, summary or communication the competent authority shall so arrange it as to prevent any particulars published therein from being identified as being particulars relating to any individual person or undertaking except with the previous consent in writing of that person or the person carrying on that undertaking, as the case may be; but this provision shall not prevent the disclosure of the total quantity or value of any articles produced, sold or delivered, so, however, that before disclosing any such total the competent authority shall have regard to any representations made to them by any person who alleges that the disclosure thereof would enable particulars relating to him or to an undertaking carried on by him to be deduced from the total disclosed'."

Thus figures which would be likely to disclose particulars relating to an individual undertaking are not published unless the contributor has given written consent for their publication.

Whilst it is not possible to rival the excitement of the financial press, a possible solution may be to include some brief description of the structure of the industry concerned as an introduction to the PA Business Monitors. Users have already commented that the occasional matching of brand names and companies with the food codes in *National Food Survey: Compendium of Results* [QRL.373] has been a recent welcome development.

There is no doubt that the private sector information services are flourishing because of the need for company-related data. The work of Mort and Siddall [B.130] in cataloguing sources of unofficial UK statistics has already been noted. A summary of Leona Siddall's report entitled *A Survey of United Kingdom Non-official Statistical Sources and Their Role in Business Information* [B.162] was featured in the May 1985 issue of *Statistical News* [B.381].

However, non-official sources are far from perfect. A major criticism which emerged in Siddall's research was that very little detail on the methods used to compile the statistics was given. 65 per cent gave no information at all, only 35 per cent had detailed notes and definitions, and only 18 per cent gave the exact sources of every table or time series included. If we are entering an age when non-official sources are becoming more and more important, given the diminution of official coverage, it is vital that methodologies are explained in both the promotional literature and the publications themselves.

13.6 The Provision of Current Information

The compilation of this Review has been the literary equivalent of painting the Severn Bridge. It has also been the physical equivalent of climbing a particularly difficult mountain when what seemed to be the final ridge to the global summit was superseded by yet another. No sooner has one draft been finished than it is necessary to rewrite earlier sections. New statistical publications are regularly being provided. New editions of existing compendia are published. Some sources are discontinued; others undergo a change of name. Classification schemes are periodically revised. The level of coverage of many statistical inquiries is varied. Three examples from the period during which this Review was prepared will illustrate the problem. In January 1988, the Standard International Trade Classification was revised, for the third time. The following year, in January 1989, the *Overseas Trade Statistics of the United Kingdom* [QRL.85] became part of the Business Monitor stable, and thereafter appeared as *Business Monitor MM20: Overseas Trade Statistics of the United Kingdom* [QRL.85]. Thirdly, the last issue of the weekly *British Business* [QRL.66] made its final appearance in September 1989. It has been since succeeded by two publications. *Business Bulletins* [QRL.75] takes over the provision of disaggregated statistics and *Business Briefing* [QRL.74] gives commentary and news, backed up with more aggregated data. Obviously we have done our best to incorporate all such changes of which we were aware at the time of submission of the manuscript. Yet there will inevitably be further changes before the Review is published, and still more before you — the reader — find a need to consult it.

This raises the important question of how the information collected in this Review may best be updated. We would deny that the above comments mean that the Review should be consigned on publication to the "history" section. We have provided a wealth of information on the historical evolution, changes in name, changes in coverage etc. of selected titles so that the reader can see the development and continuity of much of the work of both the public and private sectors. Many of the sources, moreover, will not change appreciably for a long time. After all, the *Annual Abstract of Statistics* [QRL.37] has survived a good few years. Yet it is true that this Review may only realise its full potential if it can also provide current information on statistical sources. To a certain extent, this can be achieved by listing various guides to the publication of new editions of both official and commercial sources of statistics, and this we do in sections 13.6.1 and 13.6.2. Such guides, however, only list what is available but do not discuss coverage or methodology in any detail. More fundamentally, the provision of such current information means that this Review — like the statistical sources it aims to catalogue — should itself be updated regularly. This might take the form of periodic (annual/biannual) editions of the Review or, preferably, the availability of a continuously updated version on-line. Despite the fact that the Review was processed on the mainframe computer at King's College London, the provision of such an ambitious service may well be beyond the resources of the authors. Nevertheless, we feel that such a service would be invaluable and we hope that some commercial (or perhaps official) organisation will also realise the market possibilities.

13.6.1 *Guides to Official Sources*

A number of guides provide information on recently published official statistical sources. The following may prove useful to the inquisitive researcher:

a) The *CSO Guide to Official Statistics* [B.298] was first published in 1976 in response to a recommendation from the Estimates Committee of the House of Commons. The sixth edition was published in 1990 and the five earlier editions, published in 1976, 1978, 1980, 1982 and 1986, are a guide to coverage in the past. [B.298] is designed to encourage the widest possible use of official statistics and also to provide a comprehensive reference guide for all users of statistics. It is worth remarking, however, that with the compulsory reduction of statistical coverage, noted in this book and emphasised in this chapter, that the 1990 version is noticeably slimmer than its predecessors.

b) *Government Statistics: A Brief Guide to Sources* [B.295] is produced annually by the Press and Information Service of the Central Statistical Office (CSO). This free booklet gives a synoptic review of leading official statistics, department by department, and with current addresses and contact telephone numbers.

c) *Business Monitors* [B.219] is a leaflet which lists the currently available Monitors. All available Monitors have a numerical identification based on the SIC(1980). The listing is catalogued according to Production, Distribution and Occasional Monitors.

Statistical developments and future trends are frequently described in the sources themselves. The *Employment Gazette* [QRL.186] provides a constant flow of notes and articles on proposed changes. *British Business* [QRL.66] has been referred to frequently in this Review. It contained articles on projected changes as well as being a fount of statistics for a long period of time under its many changes of title until its demise in September 1989.

In addition, all the major departments issue Press releases: for example *MAFF Statistics: Food Facts* [QRL.319] is published by MAFF as a series of press notices providing recent information on the NFS.

Finally, the quarterly *Statistical News* [B.381] carries a regular section on recently available statistical series and publications besides carrying articles which range over the coverage, as well as the developments, in statistical sources. *Eurostat News* [B.262] performs a similar service for the EC and it will become more and more important in the future.

13.6.2 *Guides to Commercial Sources*

Most commercial sources are regularly updated although, to the extent that they rely upon official data from the National Food Survey, the Census of Production etc., there should be no presumption that they provide more recent information. Yet, to take one example, financial information on individual companies is collated and published much quicker than in *Business Monitor MA3: Company Finance* [QRL.81]. The following guides are useful in providing details of the vast range of sources available, some of which we have discussed in sections 2.2.1.2, 2.13.4 and 2.14.2.

a) *A Guide to Marketing Research in the UK* [B.297] provides a very full list of sources in its sections on general sources; company directories; company financial data sources; market information; market research companies; advertising data; periodicals and newspapers; and on-line information. Official sources of information, libraries and other information sources are also covered. Key Note produced the first edition to this guide in 1987 and it will no doubt be subsequently updated.

b) Another development is the *Business Information Yearbook* [B.212] first published in 1988 for 1988/89. It reviews the year in business information and has detailed chapters on company and market information. The coverage is both of official and commercial sources, data banks, on-line information etc. If the intention to present an annual survey of the world of business is kept up, then this will prove a valuable guide.

c) *Marketing Surveys Index* [B.327] is a cumulative monthly directory of published market research worldwide. It is the means of identifying recent market research reports, financial reports and on-line information. For instance, the alphabetical index guides the reader to a six-digit reference which briefly describes the publication and gives a reference number which identifies the name, address, telephone number and contact in the company responsible for the latest report.

d) All the major Market Research organisations — see section 2.14.2 — provide regular promotional material for their reports and also give notice of impending reviews in their various publications.

e) Finally, it is worth mentioning the *Monthly Index to the Financial Times* [B.338]. The newspaper carries daily features which interpret business statistics and also publishes occasional in-depth supplements on the Food industry.

13.7 Final Observations

There is some ideal research design that the statistician himself has in mind — that the coverage be representative, whether a sample or a census, that the classification used may be acceptable, that the data collected may be in sufficient quantity and of satisfactory quality, that they can be updated, that they appear quickly and that they are clearly presented.

Given that this is a book on sources of industrial statistics, we have to bear in mind the needs of the ultimate users. The needs of the economist and statistician differ from those of the business consultant. The economist and statistician, for example, may indeed be discontented with the amount of concentration ratio data in *Business Monitor PA1002: Summary Volume* [QRL.93] whereas the business consultant may be quite happy with the market-share information and accompanying commentary in *Retail Business* [QRL.432].

The ultimate perfection may be a single volume on "Sources of Statistics on the Food Industries", together with an accompanying "Manual of Methodology". Such an approach would be of little use to the researcher who wanted to look up a single statistic on weekly per capita consumption of chocolate biscuits!. However, such two-volume solutions already exist, for example:

- The *Monthly Digest of Statistics* [QRL.362] and the *Monthly Digest of Statistics Supplement: Definitions and Explanatory Notes* [B.337].
- The *United Kingdom National Accounts* [QRL.506] and *United Kingdom National Accounts: Sources and Methods. Third Edition* [B.395].
- The *Family Expenditure Survey* [QRL.204] and the *Family Expenditure Survey Handbook* [B.94].

Another approach is not for the producer to operate from some lofty pedestal but to ask the user what he or she wants and provide a user-friendly means of access. The answer may lie to some extent in the written text which accompanies or precedes statistics, an example of which is found in the production of the *Annual Abstract of Statistics* [QRL.37]. Another answer may be in the more digestible visual display which partly explains the new format of *Household Food Consumption and Expenditure* [QRL.267] since 1985. Bar charts and histograms accompany the text together with a selection of statistical tables. Yet this has meant that much data has been relegated to the Appendix and the little publicised *National Food Survey: Compendium of Results* [QRL.373]. Yet another answer may be for rapid communication between users and producers of the statistics which do exist. Access to computerised data bases is clearly one very powerful solution exemplified by EUROSTAT, which makes available the two large data bases of COMEXT and CRONOS through private hosts — see section 2.3. A domestic example is the CSO data bank for the *United Kingdom National Accounts* [QRL.506] — mentioned in section 2.2.1.

Other users of statistics may be more interested in one particular type of data (e.g. data on food consumption statistics) and yet others may be interested in one particular industry (e.g data on fish processing). We have at least tried to accommodate these two categories of users both in the format of the Quick Reference List and in the organisation of this Review into industry chapters. Another class of users may want to find out how the Food industries sit in the industrial structure of the United Kingdom. This explains what we regard to be the jewel in the crown of this particular Review — our Chapter 2 on "General Sources" in this text serves to point the way to finding out about *any* industry.

Whatever the shortcomings which have been noted, whether for the academic researcher or business user, the very size of this Review shows the voluminous nature of the material available. If the Rayner Review [B.368] in 1980, and the Armstrong-Rees Review [B.367] in 1989 mean that domestic provision of statistics will be more restricted in the future, there will still be the steadily-increasing output of EUROSTAT publications with which to contend.

In his 1957 review, W.D. Stedman Jones managed to restrict himself to 30 pages on "Food statistics" [B.167]. Admittedly he confined himself to an introduction, and sections on commodity statistics, food consumption, and production and national expenditure on food. Moreover, his essay was one of a series on "statistics of particular commodities" which was accompanied in the two volumes of the same opus [B.95] and [B.96] by various "general surveys" on the Census of Production and Distribution; Overseas Trade; Agriculture; Labour Statistics; National Income and Related Statistics; Regional Economic Statistics, to name but some of the more pertinent. In comparison, our lack of brevity may be attributed to three main factors. First, we have ranged much more widely in the seventeen sections of each chapter, and covered prices, advertising, R&D etc. Second, we have covered both general sources and specific industry sources in the same Review. Hence, we have made reference to such general statistical sources as *United Kingdom National Accounts* [QRL.506], and the *Input-output Tables for the United Kingdom 1984* [QRL.284]. Finally, we have also covered more specialist "food" publications such as *Household Food Consumption and Expenditure* [QRL.267], and provided even finer industry detail by considering specific industries such as "Fish processing" separately.

The amount of data, both public and commercial, national and international, has also grown since 1957, although reduction and rationalisation has been a feature since about 1979. At least it is some consolation to conclude that there is still a considerable quantity of statistics on the Food industries. We have aimed to record both those sources which are readily available, and those which may be regarded as less popular and even recondite and obscure. Some of them at least will be of fascination to some user somewhere. Immanuel Kant expressed it well in his *Critique of Pure Reason* [B.93]. For all of us "Concepts without content are empty; observations without concepts are blind".

QUICK REFERENCE LIST GUIDE

The purpose of the Quick Reference List is to provide a quick but comprehensive subject guide to the 653 statistical sources cited in this Review. The List presents a simple classification of the principal statistical series published in these sources. Each series is classified according to the type of data it presents — e.g. data on output, on inputs, on prices etc. The full list of the headings and sub-headings used is provided in the Quick Reference List Table of Contents which follows this Description. In general, the headings reflect the organisation of material within the chapters of the text (see the Contents at the beginning of the Review for details and Chapter 1 for discussion). In contrast to the chapters on individual food industries, however, the Quick Reference List does not recognise industrial boundaries, and thus the section on, for example, "output" covers statistical series on output in all food industries. Finally the Quick Reference List Key to Publications gives bibliographic information about the 653 sources cited in the Review. Each source is therein allocated a "QRL number" — for example *Monthly Digest of Statistics* [QRL.362] — which is used to identify the source both within the Quick Reference List and also within the text.

A number of additional points should also be noted:

(1) The Quick Reference List provides a guide to statistical series which are often reproduced, in whole or in part, in more than one publication. QRL numbers are presented for each of these sources in the Quick Reference List, but the text should also be consulted as the authoritative guide as to which source is the most important. A cross-reference to the text is given for each statistical series for this purpose.

(2) General sources are listed first under each heading in the Quick Reference List, followed by pertinent specialist sources. Under "Spot and Futures Prices" for example, *The Public Ledger & Daily Freight Register* [QRL.392] appears as a source of prices for many commodities. However, the many sources for fish prices — the *Sea Fisheries Statistical Tables* [QRL.451], the *Scottish Sea Fisheries Statistical Tables* [QRL.449], *Fish Trader* [QRL.222], *Fishing News* [QRL.227], *Aberdeen District: Whitefish Report* [QRL.12], *City of Birmingham Markets Department Report* [QRL.155], and *Billingsgate Market Report* [QRL.62] etc. merit distinct identification on their own.

(3) In some instances, the lowest level of aggregation for which data are available is the "Food industry" or even the "Food, drink and tobacco manufacturing industries". Statistics on Research and Development, for example, are typically only available at an aggregate level, and hence references to specialist publications for individual industries are minimal. In other instances, the level

of detail provided may be quite considerable, and a full description may only be found in the text. For example, *Household Food Consumption and Expenditure* [QRL.267] and the *Compendium of Results* [QRL.373] are both described in detail in section 2.10.1 and in section 10 of each subsequent chapter. The Quick Reference List, however, simply notes that these publications carry data on consumption and expenditure, and refers the reader to the text.

(4) There is always the problem of duplication both within the text and within the Quick Reference List. We have tended to err on the side of repetition given that a major objective of the Review is the easy location of statistical information. For example, there are frequent citations of *Business Monitor PA1002: Summary Volume* [QRL.93] and the many publications in the Business Monitor PA Series in relation to the many statistical dimensions that they cover: output, purchases of inputs, employees in employment, labour costs, labour productivity, net capital expenditure, stocks and work in progress etc.

(5) Care has been taken both in the text and in the Quick Reference List to specify the geographical area covered by the statistical series. We have also taken into consideration the output of the Statistical Office of the European Communities (EUROSTAT). The principal reason for the inclusion of EUROSTAT sources is that researchers may be interested in collections of statistical series which facilitate inter-country comparisons. Such publications are considered separately from UK sources in section 2.3, but may also be cited where relevant in other sections of the text. For example, the *External Trade Analytical Tables* [QRL.196] may also be found in section 2.8.1 on "International Trade". *Crop Production* [QRL.167] and *Animal Production* [QRL.36] appear both in section 2.3 and in section 2.11 on "Supplies and Disposals".

(6) There are always continual changes in the way official publications are issued, as well as frequent deletions and additions. The picture is not a static one. An example is the metamorphosis of *Overseas Trade Statistics of the United Kingdom* into *Business Monitor MM20: Overseas Trade Statistics of the United Kingdom* [QRL.85] with effect from January 1989. A further example is the discontinued publication of *British Business* [QRL.66] from September 1989, and its replacement by *Business Bulletins* [QRL.75] and *Business Briefing* [QRL.74]. Details of such changes are sometimes provided in the comments attached to each series in the Quick Reference List Key to Publications, but only if space permits. Further detail on past changes is more often presented in the text. Future developments in official statistics are usually signalled through Press Notices from the CSO, DTI and MAFF, and may often be advertised in the publications themselves. *British Business* [QRL.66] carried advance warning of its demise, and details of how it would be replaced. Finally, the news sections of the quarterly *Statistical News* [B.381] are an invaluable and standard reference on past, current and future developments.

(7) The market research reports which are devoted to particular sectors are listed together at the end of the Quick Reference List Key to Publications from [QRL.523] to [QRL.653]. Four other widely used sources — *Retail Business*

[QRL.432], *Market Intelligence* [QRL.339], *Market Research: Great Britain* [QRL.343] and *Food Market Updates* [QRL.238] — carry a variety of reviews in each issue and these sources are listed alphabetically in the Key among the other references which run from [QRL.1] to [QRL.522]. All such reports and reviews are subject to continual change, and guidance on how to keep up-to-date is provided in Chapter 13. It suffices here to mention the updating service of *Marketing Surveys Index* [B.327].

Every effort has been made to design the Quick Reference List as an efficient and effective method of locating key sources. But it must be stressed that the main text provides far more detailed information, whereas the Quick Reference List is simply a sophisticated index. Both provide guides to the statistical sources available, but their functions are different though complementary. A mountaineering analogy is useful. The text may be compared with the late A. Wainwright's famous guides to the Lakeland fells, which sometimes seem to document every step and view. His work was a personal extension of the maps of the Ordnance Survey, providing detailed pictorial illustrations of landmarks and landscapes, together with mappings and painstaking descriptions of the many possible routes. In contrast, the Quick Reference List may be likened to A. Bategelle's succinct mountaineering guides to the Eastern and Western Pyrenees. These slim and compact books, classic in their rigour, waste not a word in delineating the essential features of the routes of several walks and climbs, aided by outline maps and well-chosen photographs. Both approaches have their merits. The preference of readers may vary according to taste and experience. We have tried to present two alternative descriptions of the routes, and we hope that the reader will both enjoy the journey and arrive enlightened at his or her destination.

QUICK REFERENCE LIST TABLE OF CONTENTS

REVIEWS OF UNITED KINGDOM STATISTICAL SOURCES

Edited by M.C. Fleming and W.F. Maunder

PUBLISHED BY CHAPMAN & HALL

Volume XXIII	**Agriculture** G.H. Peters
Volume XXIV	**Local Government** J.M. Gillespie
Volume XXV	**Family Planning** P.F. Selman
Volume XXVI	**International Aspects of UK Economic Activities** P.J. Buckley and R.D. Pearce
Volume XXVII	**Research and Development** D.L. Bosworth and R.A. Wilson
Volume XXVIII	**The Food Industries** J. Mark and R. Strange
Volume XXIX	**Distribution** C.M. Moir and J. Dawson

QUICK REFERENCE LIST

Type of data	Breakdown	Area	Frequency	QRL publication	Text reference
INDUSTRY STRUCTURE					
Industrial Concentration					
Industrial concentration	Group	UK	Annual	[QRL.93]	2.2.5
	MLH	UK	Annual	[QRL.115]	2.2.4. Discontinued – data available for 1963, 1968, 1975, 1976 and 1977
	Bread/flour milling	UK	Annual	[QRL.202]	8.2.2
Mergers and Acquisitions					
Mergers and acquisitions	Food	UK	Quarterly	[QRL.92]	2.2.6
	Summary data	UK	Quarterly	[QRL.66]	2.2.6. Discontinued
	Food	UK	Annual	[QRL.37]	2.2.6
	Activity Heading; company	UK	Monthly	[QRL.14]	2.2.6
	Class	UK	Annual	[QRL.48]	2.2.6
Market Structure — General Coverage					
Market structure	Selected markets	UK	Annual	[QRL.229], [QRL.339], [QRL.343], [QRL.432]	Section 14.2 of each chapter. See section 2 of each chapter for market structure description. These reports should be consulted for specific groups

	Food, canned	UK	Various	[QRL.229], [QRL.339], [QRL.343], [QRL.432], [QRL.582], [QRL.601], [QRL.623]	6.2, 7.2.2, 7.14.2, 11.2.5 and 11.2.6. Overlaps many SIC Industry Groups
	Food, frozen	UK	Various	[QRL.229], [QRL.339], [QRL.343], [QRL.432], [QRL.554], [QRL.572], [QRL.589], [QRL.607], [QRL.637], [QRL.63], [QRL.242], [QRL.220], [QRL.243]	Overlaps many SIC Industry Groups
Market Structure — Specific Product Group Coverage					
All other foods, not elsewhere specified	Various components	UK	Annual	[QRL.597], [QRL.613], [QRL.629], [QRL.651]	11.2.7, 11.14.2. See text for finer product subdivisions of sauces, spreads, seasonings, cooking additives etc.
Broths, soups, sauces and other relishes	Various components	UK	Annual	[QRL.526], [QRL.527], [QRL.582], [QRL.597], [QRL.605], [QRL.629], [QRL.647]	11.2.5, 11.14.2. See text for finer product subdivisions, and section 6.2 for further discussion

Type of data	Breakdown	Area	Frequency	QRL publication	Text reference
Cereals	Various components	UK	Annual	[QRL.202], [QRL.580], [QRL.581], [QRL.587], [QRL.620], [QRL.621], [QRL.622]	8.2.2, 8.2.3, 8.2.4, 8.14.2. See text for finer product subdivisions of bread, biscuits, cakes and pastries, breakfast cereals etc.
Chocolate confectionery	Various components	UK	Annual	[QRL.41], [QRL.49], [QRL.461]	10.2, 10.2.3
Cocoa	Various components	UK	Annual	[QRL.592]	10.2.2, 10.14.2. See text for further discussion
Fish and fish products	Various components	UK	Annual	[QRL.601], [QRL.589], [QRL.606], [QRL.607]	7.2.2, 7.14.2. See text for further discussion
Fruit and vegetables	Various components	UK	Annual	[QRL.582], [QRL.589], [QRL.597], [QRL.601], [QRL.605], [QRL.607], [QRL.608], [QRL.623], [QRL.638], [QRL.647]	6.2, 6.14.2. See text for finer product subdivisions and section 11.2
Infant and dietetic foods, starch and malt extract	Various components	UK	Annual	[QRL.539], [QRL.542], [QRL.543], [QRL.591], [QRL.596], [QRL.610], [QRL.618]	11.2.3, 11.14.2. See text for these finer product subdivisions including slimming and health foods etc.

Meat	Various types of meat	UK	Biannual	[QRL.289], [QRL.498]	4.2.1
Meat and meat products	Various components	UK	Annual	[QRL.525], [QRL.538], [QRL.559], [QRL.562], [QRL.577], [QRL.578], [QRL.593], [QRL.611], [QRL.642]	4.2, 4.14.2. See text for finer product subdivisions
Milk and milk products	Various components	UK	Various	[QRL.238], [QRL.359], [QRL.388], [QRL.528], [QRL.604], [QRL.626], [QRL.645], [QRL.648], [QRL.653]	5.14.2. See text for further subdivisions of milk, cheese, dairy products etc.
Oils and fats	Various components	UK	Annual	[QRL.653]	3.2 and 3.14.2
		World and countries	Annual	[QRL.53], [QRL.166], [QRL.391], [QRL.520]	3.17
		World and countries	Various	[QRL.22], [QRL.381]	3.17
Pasta products	Various components	UK	Annual	[QRL.526], [QRL.527], [QRL.582], [QRL.643]	11.2.6. See text for finer product subdivisions
Potato crisps and other snack products	Various components	UK	Annual	[QRL.302]	11.2.2, 11.14.2. See text for finer product subdivisions
Sugar confectionery	Various components	UK	Annual	[QRL.41], [QRL.49], [QRL.461]	10.2, 10.2.4. See text for further details

Type of data	Breakdown	Area	Frequency	QRL publication	Text reference
Sugar and sugar by-products	Various components	UK	Annual	[QRL.599]	9.2, 9.14.2
Sweets and puddings, cake mixtures, cornflour products and yeast	Various components	UK	Annual	[QRL.526], [QRL.527], [QRL.582], [QRL.616]	11.2.4. See text for finer product subdivisions
EUROPE					
European Community Overview					
European Community overview	Various components	EC and countries	Annual	[QRL.248]	2.3.1
Industry Structure					
Industry structure	Various components	EC and countries	Annual	[QRL.410]	2.3.1
	Various components by NACE Heading and by region	EC and countries	Annual	[QRL.466]	2.3.3.1
	Various components by NACE Heading and size of enterprise	EC and countries	Annual	[QRL.467]	2.3.3.1
	Various components by NACE Heading	EC and countries	Annual	[QRL.468]	2.3.3.1
Output					
Output	Various food products	EC and countries	Quarterly	[QRL.274]	2.3.3.1. See text for further details
Agricultural Data					
Agricultural data	Various components	EC and countries	Annual	[QRL.28]	2.3.1, 6.3.2, 9.3.2. Data are provided on agricultural inputs and outputs, agricultural prices, EAGGF guarantee and guidance expenditure, trade by commodity

Food Consumption and Expenditure					
Food consumption and expenditure	Various food products	EC and countries	Annual	[QRL.203]	2.3.2. Standardised results
Labour					
Labour Force	Aggregate data	EC and countries	Annual	[QRL.310]	2.3.3.4
Labour Costs	Various components	EC and countries	Hourly	[QRL.304], [QRL.305], [QRL.308]	2.3.3.4, 2.6.11
National Accounts					
National Accounts	Various components	EC and countries	Annual	[QRL.370]	2.3.3.3. Data are provided on gross value added, employee compensation, change of value added and employee compensation per head, final consumption of foodstuffs
	Aggregate data	EC and countries	Annual	[QRL.369]	2.3.3.3
Input-output					
Input-output	Industry/Commodity	EC and countries	Annual	[QRL.371]	2.3.3.3
Exports and Imports					
Exports and Imports	By commodity, in both value and quantity	EC and countries	Annual	[QRL.35], [QRL.196]	2.3.3.5, 2.8.2.5
Supply Balance Sheets					
Supply balance sheets	Various commodities	EC and countries	Annual	[QRL.34], [QRL.36], [QRL.167]	2.3.3.7, 2.11.2, 6.3.2

Type of data	Breakdown	Area	Frequency	QRL publication	Text reference
Some Specific Commodity Sources					
Cereals, intervention system; prices, levies etc.	Various	UK	Various	[QRL.152], [QRL.185], [QRL.293], [QRL.379], [QRL.512]	8.3, 11.3
Fish, intervention arrangements; quantities withdrawn, compensation	Various	UK	Annual	[QRL.293]	7.3.3
Fruit and vegetables, intervention arrangements; quantities withdrawn, compensation	Various	UK	Annual	[QRL.28], [QRL.61], [QRL.293]	6.3.2, 6.3.3
Meat industry; some agri-monetary arrangements	Various subsidies, levies etc.	EC and countries	Weekly	[QRL.190]	4.3
Meat, stocks of; intervention purchases, sales and aided private storage	Beef; pigmeat	UK	Annual	[QRL.293]	4.9
Milk and milk products; institutional, threshold and intervention prices	Various products	UK	Effective date	[QRL.503]	5.3
Oilseeds; intervention prices, purchases and sale of rape seed	Various	UK	Annual	[QRL.293]	3.3.1

Sugar; intervention system; physical enumeration of quotas, levy rates etc.	Various types	UK	Annual	[QRL.293]	9.3.3
OUTPUT *General Sources* *Business Statistics Office Inquiries*					
Total sales and work done; gross output; net output; gross value added at factor cost	Group; Group by size (employment) of enterprise	UK and countries	Annual	[QRL.93], [QRL.105] to [QRL.114]	Section 4 of each chapter
Total sales and work done; gross output; net output (historical data)	Order; Order by size (employment) of enterprise	UK/GB	Annual	[QRL.264]	2.1.1.6 and section 4 of each chapter
Total sales and work done; gross output; net output; gross value added at factor cost	Group	Northern Ireland	Annual	[QRL.419]	2.1.2
Gross output; gross value added	Class	Scotland	Annual	[QRL.446]	2.4.3
Gross value added	Class	Scotland	Annual	[QRL.447]	2.4.3
Net output; net output per employee	Class	Wales	Annual	[QRL.517]	2.4.3
Gross value added	Class	UK, countries and regions	Annual	[QRL.401]	2.4.3
Commodity sales and production	Selected products	UK	Quarterly	[QRL.128] to [QRL.139]	Section 4 of each chapter
Commodity sales	Selected products in the Topping-up Inquiry	UK	Occasional	[QRL.285]	2.1.1.3
Gross domestic product	Food industry	UK	Annual	[QRL.506]	2.1.3, 2.4.1.3

Type of data	Breakdown	Area	Frequency	QRL publication	Text reference
Ministry of Agriculture, Fisheries and Food Inquiries					
MAFF — General sources					
Food production	Various processed and agricultural products	UK	Annual	[QRL.37]	2.4.1.2 and section 4 of each chapter
	Various processed and agricultural products	UK	Monthly	[QRL.362]	2.4.1.2 and section 4 of each chapter
	Various processed and agricultural products	Scotland	Annual	[QRL.175]	2.4.1.2
MAFF — Specific commodity sources					
Animals, slaughter of	Various animals	UK	Weekly	[QRL.337]	4.4.1.1 and 4.5.1. Data are also reported in [QRL.37], [QRL.362], [QRL.382], [QRL.498]
Bacon and ham, production of	Various types	GB	Weekly	[QRL.336]	4.4.1.2
Chick placings	Chicks placed; turkey poults leaving incubation houses	UK and countries	Monthly	[QRL.320]	4.4.1.1, 4.5.1
Coffee, production of	Regular coffee; dry coffee extracts etc; liquid coffee essence	UK	Quarterly	[QRL.331]	12.4
Fruit and vegetables (canned), production of	Various products	UK	Quarterly	[QRL.325]	6.4.1.2, 11.4.1.2
Grains, output and utilisation of	Wheat flour; oats; rye; barley; maize	UK	Cereal marketing year	[QRL.345]	8.4.1.2. Shows usage of grains and products produced (bread, biscuits, flour etc.). See text for details
Grains, output and utilisation of	Various grains	UK	Monthly	[QRL.152]	8.4.1.2
Margarine and cooking fats, production of	Various types	UK	Monthly	[QRL.321]	3.4.1.1

Milk (condensed) and milk (powder), production of	Various types	UK	Quarterly	[QRL.327]	5.4
Meat, home-fed production of	Various types of meat	UK	Quarterly	[QRL.330]	4.4.1.2
Oil (crude vegetable), oilcake and meal, production of	Various oilseeds and nuts	UK	Quarterly	[QRL.322]	3.4.1.1
Oilseeds and nuts crushed	Various oilseeds and nuts	UK	Quarterly	[QRL.332]	3.4.1.1
Pigs, slaughter of	Various types of pig	GB	Weekly	[QRL.336]	4.4.1.1
Potato crisps and snack foods, production of	Various products	UK	Quarterly	[QRL.323]	11.4.1.2. See also [QRL.302]
Poultry, output of from packing stations	Various poultry	England and Wales	Quarterly	[QRL.324]	4.4.1.1, 4.5.1
Poultry, slaughter of	Various poultry	UK	Annual	[QRL.37], [QRL.382]	4.4.1.1
Rapeseed, production of	Aggregate data	UK and countries	Annual	[QRL.316], [QRL.317]	3.5.1
Vegetable (refined, deodorised), marine oils and animal fats, production of	Various oils and fats	UK	Monthly	[QRL.328]	3.4.1.1
Index Numbers of Output					
Index numbers of output at constant factor cost	Food industry	UK	Annual	[QRL.37], [QRL.506]	2.4.2
	Food industry	Scotland	Annual	[QRL.447]	2.4.3
	Food industry	Scotland	Annual	[QRL.446]	2.4.3
Index numbers of output	Food; Food, drink and tobacco	UK	Monthly	[QRL.362]	2.4.2. Seasonally adjusted
	Class	UK	Monthly	[QRL.66]	2.4.2. Seasonally adjusted
	Activity Heading	UK	Quarterly	[QRL.128] to [QRL.139]	2.4.2 and section 4 of each chapter
	Groups 413, 419, 421, 422, and 423	UK	Annual	[QRL.37]	2.4.2

Type of data	Breakdown	Area	Frequency	QRL publication	Text reference
Index numbers of production	Food industry	Northern Ireland	Quarterly	[QRL.377]	2.4.3. Seasonally adjusted
	Class	Northern Ireland	Quarterly	[QRL.176]	2.4.3
	Food industry	Scotland	Quarterly	[QRL.447]	2.4.3. Seasonally adjusted
	Class	Wales	Quarterly	[QRL.177], [QRL.517]	2.4.3
Output in Specific Industrial Sectors					
Cocoa powders; drinking chocolate; chocolate; confectionery	Despatch data, in both value and quantity	UK	Annual	[QRL.41], [QRL.49], [QRL.461]	10.2, 10.2.3, 10.2.4, 10.4.1.2
Dairy quotas	Milk Marketing Board	EC and countries	Annual	[QRL.184], [QRL.503]	5.3
Fish farming, output of	Salmon; trout; mussels	UK and countries	Annual	[QRL.8], [QRL.9]	7.2.3
Fish farming, output of	Salmon; trout; oysters	Northern Ireland	Annual	[QRL.429]	7.2.3
Fish farming, output of	Salmon; trout; company	Scotland	Annual	[QRL.444]	7.2.3. See text for further details
Fish processing, sales, output and value added	Weight; value; type of outlet; region	UK	Annual	[QRL.3]	7.4.4
Meat, production of	Various types of meat	UK	Various	[QRL.349], [QRL.498]	4.4.1.2
Milk, sales of to Milk Marketing Boards	Utilisation for various milk products	UK, countries, Board areas, and counties	Annual	[QRL.503]	5.4. Provisional monthly data are provided in [QRL.355], [QRL.357], [QRL.358], [QRL.360], [QRL.490] for each Board area. See text for further details

Milk, total quantity produced	Aggregate data	UK	Annual	[QRL.382]	5.4
Sugar and sugar by-products, sales and production of	Type of sugar	UK	Annual	[QRL.69], [QRL.70], [QRL.479]	9.4.3
CURRENT INPUTS OTHER THAN LABOUR					
Agricultural Output (Inputs for food processing)					
Agricultural output (historical data)	Various products	UK and countries	Annual	[QRL.1]	2.5.1.3
Agricultural output	Various products	England and Wales	Annual	[QRL.316]	2.5.1.1, 9.5.1.1
		Northern Ireland	Annual	[QRL.376], [QRL.377], [QRL.460]	2.5.1.4, 6.5.1.3, 8.5.1
		Scotland	Annual	[QRL.33], [QRL.180], [QRL.446]	2.5.1.4, 6.5.1.3, 8.5.1
		UK	Annual	[QRL.32], [QRL.37], [QRL.50], [QRL.51], [QRL.362]	2.5.1.1, 6.5.1.1, 8.5.1, 9.5.1.1, 11.5.1
		Wales	Annual	[QRL.177], [QRL.515]	2.5.1.4, 6.5.1.3, 8.5.1
Cereals output	Country, region	UK	Monthly; annual	[QRL.152], [QRL.202], [QRL.345]	8.5.1. See text for more precision
Cows (dairy and beef), numbers	Aggregate data	UK, countries and counties	Annual	[QRL.503]	5.5.1
Horticultural crops	Various	UK	Annual	[QRL.32], [QRL.61], [QRL.382]	2.5.1.1, 6.5.1.1, 9.5.1.1
		UK	Monthly	[QRL.411], [QRL.412], [QRL.413]	6.5.1.1

Type of data	Breakdown	Area	Frequency	QRL publication	Text reference
Livestock numbers on dairy farms	Various types of livestock	UK and countries	Annual	[QRL.210]	5.5.1
Potato output	Area, yields	GB	Annual	[QRL.384], [QRL.387]	6.5.1.1
Fish Landings					
Fish landings	Quantity; value; species; port; region of capture; vessel	UK and countries	Annual	[QRL.451]	7.5.1.1. See text for more details
	Weight; value; species	UK	Annual	[QRL.37]	7.5.1.1
	Various	UK and countries	Annual; monthly	[QRL.45], [QRL.189], [QRL.475]	7.5.1.7
	Weight; port	UK and countries	Annual	[QRL.174], [QRL.383]	7.5.1.8
	Various	UK and other countries	Annual; monthly	[QRL.208], [QRL.225], [QRL.395], [QRL.438]	7.3.2, 7.5.1.6. Derivative Eurostat and international sources
	Weight; value; species; port	England and Wales	Monthly	[QRL.363]	7.5.1.1. Also has UK summary data
	Weight; value; vessel	Isle of Man	Annual	[QRL.295]	7.5.1.5
	Weight; value; species	Northern Ireland	Annual	[QRL.376], [QRL.429]	7.5.1.3
	Weight; value; species; port	Scotland	Monthly; annual	[QRL.449]	7.5.1.2. See text for further details
	Weight; value; species	Scotland	Annual	[QRL.446]	7.5.1.2
	Weight; value; species; port	Scotland and UK	Monthly	[QRL.368]	7.5.1.2
	Quantity; value; species	Wales	Annual	[QRL.177]	7.5.1.4
Purchases of Inputs					
Purchases of inputs	Activity Heading; Group	UK	Annual	[QRL.93], [QRL.105] to [QRL.114]	2.5.1.2 and section 5 of each chapter

	Various components by Activity Heading	UK	Annual	[QRL.94], [QRL.116], [QRL.417], [QRL.418], [QRL.425]	2.5.1.2 and section 5 of each chapter
	Chemical products	UK	Annual	[QRL.102], [QRL.103]	2.5.1.2
Specific Commodity Sources					
Bacon and ham production, use of pig carcases	Various components	GB	Weekly	[QRL.336]	4.5.1
Cattle (fat), sheep and pigs, sales of	Animal	UK	Weekly	[QRL.25]	4.5.1
Cocoa, grindings of raw cocoa	Physical data	UK and selected countries	Quarterly	[QRL.245], [QRL.249], [QRL.397]	10.5.1
Coffee, raw coffee usage in processing	Regular coffee; liquid coffee; soluble coffee	UK	Quarterly	[QRL.331]	12.5
Ice-cream, cocoa, chocolate and sugar confectionery, purchase of ingredients	Various	UK	Annual	[QRL.461]	10.5.1. See text for further details
Margarine and cooking fats, use of refined oil in the production of	Various oils and fats	UK	Monthly	[QRL.321]	3.5.1
Potato crisps and stocks, usage of raw potatoes in	Home-grown, imported	UK	Quarterly	[QRL.323]	11.5.1
Potato processing, usage of raw potatoes in	Type	GB	Annual	[QRL.385]	6.5.1.1

Type of data	Breakdown	Area	Frequency	QRL publication	Text reference
Input-output Analysis					
Input-output	Industry; commodity	UK	Annual	[QRL.97] to [QRL.101], [QRL.282], [QRL.283], [QRL.284]	2.5.2.1 and section 5.2 in each chapter. Level of coverage varies – see text for details
	Food, drink and tobacco; cereal foodstuffs	UK	Annual	[QRL.281]	2.5.2.1, 8.5.2
	Food processing	UK	Annual	[QRL.4]	2.5.2.1
	Food industry, plus some disaggregated data	Scotland	Annual	[QRL.280], [QRL.448]	2.5.2.2, 7.5.2
	Food industry; agriculture	Wales	Annual	[QRL.7]	2.5.2.2
	Food industry, plus some disaggregated data	Northern Ireland	Annual	[QRL.279]	2.5.2.2, 6.5.2
Fish processing	Primary – secondary fish processors	UK	Annual	[QRL.3]	7.5.2
	Raw materials used in fishery by-products	Scotland	Annual	[QRL.449]	7.5.2
LABOUR					
Employees in Employment					
Employees in employment	Activity Heading; size of establishment; region	UK	Annual	[QRL.93], [QRL.96], [QRL.105] to [QRL.114], [QRL.264]	2.6.1.2 and section 6 in each chapter
	Class	UK	Monthly	[QRL.362]	2.6.1.1
	Class	UK; GB	Annual	[QRL.37]	2.6.1.1
	Activity Heading; sex; full-time/part-time	UK	Annual	[QRL.186]	2.6.1.1 and section 6 in each chapter
	Group; sex	GB	Monthly	[QRL.186]	2.6.1.1 and section 6 in each chapter
	Group; sex; full-time/part-time	GB	Quarterly	[QRL.186]	2.6.1.1

	Activity heading; sex; full-time/part-time	GB	Annual	[QRL.148]	2.6.1.3
	Activity Heading; sex; full-time/part-time	Northern Ireland	Annual	[QRL.378]	2.6.1.3
	Class; selected Groups	Northern Ireland	Annual	[QRL.419]	2.6.1.4
	Class; sex; full-time/part-time	Northern Ireland	Quarterly	[QRL.377]	2.6.1.4. Derivative source
	Activity Heading; sex; full-time/part-time	Scotland	Annual	[QRL.149]	2.6.1.3
	Activity Heading; Class; sex	Scotland	Annual	[QRL.446]	2.6.1.4
	Class; sex	Wales	Annual	[QRL.177]	2.6.1.4. Class data ceased from 1988 issue
	Class; full-time/part-time	Wales	Annual	[QRL.517]	2.6.1.4
Chocolate confectionery, sugar confectionery, biscuits, cakes, industry total, employment in	BCCCA categories	UK	Annual	[QRL.41], [QRL.49]	10.6.2
Dairy industry, employment in	Manufacturing, processing, retailing	England and Wales	Annual	[QRL.375]	5.6
Fish processing, employment structure in	Type of processing; occupation; sex; region	UK	Annual	[QRL.3]	7.6.2. See text for further details
Fishermen, employment of	Full-time/ part-time	UK and countries	Annual	[QRL.451]	7.6.2
	Full-time/ part-time, crofters	Scotland	Annual	[QRL.449]	7.6.2
Sugar and sugar by-products, employment in	Named companies	UK	Annual	[QRL.69], [QRL.442], [QRL.479]	9.6.2. See text for details. Includes data on all employees, including directors. Has labour costs data
Occupational Analyses					
Occupational analyses	Employment status; Activity Heading; sex	GB	Annual	[QRL.148]	2.6.1.5. More detailed occupational analysis by Class

Type of data	Breakdown	Area	Frequency	QRL publication	Text reference
		Scotland	Annual	[QRL.149]	2.6.1.5. More detailed occupational analysis by Class
	Employment status; Class; sex	Northern Ireland	Annual	[QRL.378]	2.6.1.5
	Operatives and others, by Group	UK	Annual	[QRL.93], [QRL.105] to [QRL.114], [QRL.264]	2.6.1.5 and section 6 of each chapter
	Operatives and others, by Class and selected Group	Northern Ireland	Annual	[QRL.419]	2.6.1.5
	Operatives and others, by Class and sex	GB	Annual	[QRL.186]	2.6.1.5. Summary information also appears in [QRL.37]
Self-employed					
Self-employed	Activity Heading; sex	GB	Annual	[QRL.148]	2.6.1.6, 6.6, 7.6.1, 9.6.1, 10.6.1
	Class; sex	Northern Ireland	Annual	[QRL.378]	2.6.1.6
	Activity Heading; sex	Scotland	Annual	[QRL.149]	2.6.1.6, 6.6, 7.6.1, 9.6.1, 10.6.1
Unemployment					
Unemployment	MLH	UK; GB	Quarterly	[QRL.186]	2.6.2. Industrial analysis ceased in May 1982 – see text for details. Past time series can be found in [QRL.67], [QRL.68], [QRL.464]
	Class; sex; travel	Northern Ireland	Annual	[QRL.377]	2.6.2

Vacancies					
Vacancies	Class	UK	Quarterly	[QRL.186]	2.6.3. Industrial analysis ceased in August 1985 – see text for details. Past time series can be found in [QRL.68] and [QRL.464]
Labour Turnover					
Labour turnover	Class	GB	Four week periods	[QRL.186]	2.6.4
Redundancies					
Redundancies	Class	GB	Quarterly	[QRL.186]	2.6.5
	Class; sex	Northern Ireland	Annual	[QRL.377]	2.6.5. Discontinued from January 1987
Industrial Stoppages					
Industrial stoppages	Class	UK	Annual	[QRL.186]	2.6.6. Annual special feature in [QRL.186] gives more information
	Class	Northern Ireland	Annual	[QRL.377]	2.6.6
	Various	UK; GB	Annual	[QRL.10]	2.6.6
Earnings and Hours of Work					
Earnings and hours of work	Various	GB	Annual	[QRL.186], [QRL.375]	2.6.8.1, 2.6.8.3, 4.6.1, 5.6, 8.6.2, 11.6.2
	Various	UK	Annual	[QRL.186], [QRL.362]	2.6.8.2, 2.6.8.3, 8.6.2, 11.6.2
Earnings and hours of work for full-time manual workers	Class; sex	Northern Ireland	Annual	[QRL.377]	2.6.8.4
Earnings and hours of work for full-time male manual workers	Class	Scotland	Annual	[QRL.446]	2.6.8.4
Earnings and hours of work for male manual workers	Class	Wales	Annual	[QRL.177]	2.6.8.4

Type of data	Breakdown	Area	Frequency	QRL publication	Text reference
Wage Rates and Conditions of Work					
Wage rates and conditions of Work	Basic rates and conditions	UK and countries	Weekly	[QRL.483], [QRL.484], [QRL.485]	2.6.9.1. Reports national collective agreements and Wages Councils. Historical data are provided in [QRL.67] and [QRL.68]
	Industrial agreement; company	UK and countries	Weekly	[QRL.271], [QRL.272], [QRL.275]	2.6.9.2
	Industrial agreement; company	UK and countries	Weekly	[QRL.43], [QRL.60], [QRL.201], [QRL.404], [QRL.495]	2.6.9.2. Mainly union sources
Changes in wage rates and conditions of work	Type of worker	UK and countries	Weekly	[QRL.153]	2.6.9.1
Index of Average Earnings					
Index of average earnings	Class	GB	Monthly	[QRL.37], [QRL.186], [QRL.362]	2.6.7
Index of Wage Rates for Manual Workers					
Index of wage rates for manual workers	Class	UK	Monthly	[QRL.186]	2.6.9.3. Discontinued from April 1984 issue
Salaries and Remuneration Packages					
Salaries and remuneration packages	Company	UK	Weekly; monthly	[QRL.271], [QRL.272], [QRL.275]	2.6.10.2

	Industrial category; company; type of executive and managerial position	UK	Annual	[QRL.154], [QRL.257], [QRL.258], [QRL.361], [QRL.402], [QRL.440], [QRL.443], [QRL.478]	2.6.10.2
		UK	Annual	[QRL.476], [QRL.477]	2.6.10.2. Private "club" surveys
Labour Costs					
Labour costs	Industry; category of labour cost	GB	Annual	[QRL.306], [QRL.307]	2.3.3.4, 2.6.11
	Operatives; administrative, technical and clerical staff	UK	Annual	[QRL.93], [QRL.105] to [QRL.114]	2.6.10.1, 2.6.11 and section 6 in each chapter. Data on wages and salaries per head are provided in the analyses by size of establishment
		Northern Ireland	Annual	[QRL.419]	2.6.10.1, 2.6.11. Data on wages and salaries per head are also provided
	Various components	GB	Annual	[QRL.186]	2.3.3.4, 2.6.11
	Class	UK	Annual	[QRL.305]	2.3.3.4, 2.6.11
Fish processing, labour costs in	Type of processing, wage rates, salary ranges	UK	Various	[QRL.2], [QRL.3]	7.6.2
Labour Productivity					
Labour productivity (index)	Class	UK	Quarterly	[QRL.186]	2.6.12
Labour productivity (net output and gross value added per head)	Group by size of establishment	UK	Annual	[QRL.93], [QRL.105] to [QRL.114]	2.6.12 and section 6 of each chapter
	Group	Northern Ireland	Annual	[QRL.419]	2.6.12

Type of data	Breakdown	Area	Frequency	QRL publication	Text reference
Union Membership					
Union membership	Broad industry	UK	Annual	[QRL.419]	2.6.13
	Union	UK	Annual	[QRL.46]	2.6.13
	Aggregate data	Northern Ireland	Annual	[QRL.409]	2.6.13
Industrial Training					
Industrial training	Various components by product sector	GB	Annual	[QRL.44]	2.6.14. Discontinued after 1983
Industrial Accidents					
Industrial accidents	Fatal injuries; major injuries; incident rates	GB	Annual	[QRL.47], [QRL.259], [QRL.260], [QRL.261], [QRL.277], [QRL.338]	2.6.15
	Disablement; death	GB	Annual	[QRL.455]	2.6.15
CAPITAL *General Sources*					
Fixed assets (tangible, intangible, investments in subsidiaries)	Class	GB	Annual	[QRL.79], [QRL.81]	2.7.2
Gross capital stock in the food industry	Type of asset	UK	Annual	[QRL.506]	2.7.2
Production of machinery for the Food, drink and tobacco manufacturing industries	Various types of machinery	UK	Quarterly	[QRL.127]	2.7.1.4 and section 7.2 in each chapter. Provides indirect data on capital input

Production of machinery for the food, chemical and related industries	Various types of machinery	UK	Annual	[QRL.104]	2.7.1.4. Provides indirect data on capital input
Gross domestic fixed capital formation in the food industry	Type of asset	UK	Annual	[QRL.506]	2.7.1.3
Expenditure on fixed assets (tangible, intangible, acquisitions)	Class	GB	Annual	[QRL.79], [QRL.81]	2.7.1.2. Derived from a sample of company annual accounts
Fixed capital expenditure	Food industry	UK	Quarterly	[QRL.66], [QRL.362]	2.7.1.1
Net capital expenditure	Class	Scotland	Annual	[QRL.446], [QRL.447]	2.7.1.5
		Wales	Annual	[QRL.177]	2.7.1.5
	Land and buildings; plant and machinery; vehicles	Northern Ireland	Annual	[QRL.419]	2.7.1.5
		UK	Annual	[QRL.93], [QRL.105] to [QRL.114], [QRL.264]	2.7.1.1 and section 7 in each chapter
Specific Industry Sources					
Fish Processing, composition of fixed capital in	Processing sector	UK	Annual	[QRL.2], [QRL.3]	7.7.3. See text for detailed description
Sugar and sugar by-products, capital expenditure, fixed assets	Company	UK	Annual	[QRL.69], [QRL.442], [QRL.479]	9.7.3. See text for further description

Type of data	Breakdown	Area	Frequency	QRL publication	Text reference
INTERNATIONAL TRANSACTIONS *Exports and Imports* *Primary General Sources*					
Exports and imports, in both value and quantity	Fine commodity detail by country	UK	Monthly	[QRL.80], [QRL.85]	2.8.2.1 and section 8 of each chapter. See text of sections 2.8 and 2.3.3.5 for full discussion of statistics and classification schemes
Exports and imports	Divisions of SITC(R3)	UK	Quarterly	[QRL.362]	2.8.2.1 and section 8 of each chapter
	Sections and Divisions of SITC(R3)	UK	Annual	[QRL.37]	2.8.2.1 and section 8 of each chapter
	Selected countries	UK	Annual	[QRL.494], [QRL.508]	2.8.2.1, 6.8.1, 7.8.1, 9.8.1, 12.8.1
Exports, imports and visible balance	Food, beverages and tobacco	UK	Annual	[QRL.502]	2.8.2.1
	Food, beverages and tobacco	UK	Monthly	[QRL.364]	2.8.2.1. [QRL.364] contains monthly, quarterly and annual data. Quarterly and annual data are also found in [QRL.366] and [QRL.365]
Exports and imports (Port statistics)	Bulk commodity; port	GB	Annual	[QRL.39], [QRL.174], [QRL.383], [QRL.457], [QRL.458]	2.8.2. [QRL.383] is the source of current data. The other publications generally carried rather greater commodity detail but have now been discontinued
	Food and live animals	Annual	Scotland	[QRL.446], [QRL.447]	2.8.2.2

Volume and unit value index numbers of exports and imports	Various commodity groups	UK	Monthly	[QRL.362], [QRL.364], [QRL.365]	2.8.2.4. See text for details of commodity groups
Derivative General Sources					
Exports, imports and trade balance	Selected food commodities	UK	Monthly	[QRL.496]	2.8.2.1. Other Food from Britain publications provide useful summary data, e.g. [QRL.504] and [QRL.505]
Exports and imports (Derivative EUROSTAT sources)	Commodity by country, in both value and quantity	EC and countries	Annual	[QRL.35], [QRL.196]	2.3.3.5, 2.8.2.5. See text for discussion of changes in classification schemes
	Commodity by country, in value	EC and countries	Monthly	[QRL.195]	2.3.3.5, 2.8.2.5
Exports and imports (Derivative UN sources)	Commodity by country, in both value and quantity	World and countries	Annual	[QRL.156], [QRL.292]	2.8.2.5
Exports and imports (Derivative FAO sources)	Agricultural products by country, in both value and quantity	World and countries	Annual	[QRL.207]	2.8.2.5
	Selected agricultural products by country	World and countries	Quarterly	[QRL.206]	2.8.2.5
Exports and imports (Derivative GATT sources)	Main food products by country	World and countries	Annual	[QRL.291]	2.8.2.5
Industry Analyses					
Industry analysis of exports and imports	Activity Heading; sub-heading	UK	Quarterly	[QRL.77], [QRL.90], [QRL.128] to [QRL.139]	2.8.2.3 and section 8 of each chapter
Import penetration and export sales ratios	Activity Heading	UK	Quarterly	[QRL.78], [QRL.91]	2.8.2.3 and section 8 of each chapter
	Class	UK	Annual	[QRL.66], [QRL.362]	2.8.2.3

Type of data	Breakdown	Area	Frequency	QRL publication	Text reference
Commodity Analyses					
Cocoa, chocolate and sugar confectionery	Various raw materials/BCCCA categories	UK	Annual	[QRL.41], [QRL.49]	8.8.3, 10.8.3. See text for further details
Cocoa and cocoa products	Imports of cocoa butter; cocoa liquor; cocoa powder	UK and selected countries	Monthly	[QRL.249]	10.5.1, 10.8.3. [QRL.397] provides quarterly data, and [QRL.250] provides annual data
	Imports of cocoa beans; cocoa paste; cocoa butter; cocoa powder; couverture; crumb	UK	Annual	[QRL.461]	10.5.1, 10.8.3
Coffee	Exports/imports/re-exports of roasted coffee/soluble coffee etc. by country	UK and other countries	Annual	[QRL.245], [QRL.398]	12.5, 12.8.3. See text for further discussion
Dairy products	Various products by country	UK	Biannual	[QRL.349]	5.8.1
Fish	Quantity; value; type; species	UK	Annual	[QRL.451]	7.8.4. See text for discussion of the considerable detail
	Quantity; value; type; species	UK	Monthly	[QRL.491]	7.8.4. See text for further details
	Quantity; value; source; type; species	UK	Annual	[QRL.45]	7.8.4
	Various products	UK and other countries	Annual	[QRL.209], [QRL.225], [QRL.438]	7.8.3
Fruit and vegetables	Various imports (value/quantity) by country	UK	Six months	[QRL.245]	6.3.3, 6.8.3
Fruit and vegetables, fresh	Various products, in both value and quantity	UK	Annual	[QRL.61]	6.8.3
Grain	Exports of various grains	UK	Monthly	[QRL.345]	8.8.1
Livestock (imports) and meat (exports)	Various types	UK	Quarterly	[QRL.498]	4.8.3
Livestock (imports) and meat and livestock (exports)	Various types	UK	Annual	[QRL.349]	4.8.3

Milk products	Various exports/re-exports	UK	Annual	[QRL.503]	5.8.1
Milk and milk products	Various imports	UK	Annual	[QRL.503]	5.8.1
Oilseeds and oils, imports	Various oilseeds and oils by country of origin	UK	Biannual	[QRL.245]	3.8.1
Pigmeat, imports used in bacon and ham production	Fresh; frozen	GB	Weekly	[QRL.336]	4.8.3
Potato products, processed	Various products	GB	Annual	[QRL.385]	6.8.3. Data are expressed in raw potato equivalent
Potato products, raw and processed	Various product imports	GB	Annual	[QRL.263], [QRL.384], [QRL.386], [QRL.387]	6.8.3
Tea	Imports by country/grade	UK and other countries	Weekly	[QRL.480]	12.8.3
	Exports/imports/ re-exports by country	UK and other countries	Annual	[QRL.38], [QRL.474], [QRL.481]	12.5, 12.8.3. See text for further discussion
		UK and other countries	Monthly	[QRL.367]	12.5, 12.8.3
Overseas Investment, Earnings and Assets					
Direct investment and earnings	Class	UK	Annual	[QRL.82]	2.8.3
External assets and liabilities	Class	UK	Triannual	[QRL.76]	2.8.3
Food Aid					
Food aid	Recipient	UK	Annual	[QRL.65]	2.8.4
		World and countries	Monthly	[QRL.230], [QRL.239]	2.8.4
	Commodity by donor and recipient	World and countries	Annual	[QRL.231]	2.8.4

Type of data	Breakdown	Area	Frequency	QRL publication	Text reference
Unit Values and Prices					
Volume and unit value index numbers of exports and imports	Various commodity groups	UK	Monthly	[QRL.362], [QRL.364], [QRL.365]	2.8.2.4. See text for details of commodity groups
Import prices of oilseeds and oils	Selected oilseeds and oils	UK	Biannual	[QRL.245]	3.8.1, 3.12.1
STOCKS *General Sources*					
Food stocks	Selected commodities	UK	Annual	[QRL.37]	2.9.1 and section 9 of each chapter
		UK	Monthly	[QRL.362]	2.9.1 and section 9 of each chapter
Stocks and work-in-progress in the food industry	Materials and fuel; work-in-progress; goods on hand for sale	UK	Annual	[QRL.506]	2.9.3
Stocks and work-in-progress	Materials, stores and fuel; work-in-progress; goods on hand for sale	UK	Annual	[QRL.93], [QRL.105] to [QRL.114], [QRL.264]	2.9.2 and section 9 of each chapter
		Northern Ireland	Annual	[QRL.419]	2.9.5
Caterers' stocks	Type of catering establishment	UK	Annual	[QRL.66], [QRL.142]	2.9.4, 6.9.2, 7.9, 10.9
Retailers' stocks	Type of food retailer; number of outlets; value of turnover; employment	GB	Annual	[QRL.140], [QRL.143]	2.9.4, 6.9.2, 7.9, 10.9
	Type of food retailer	GB	Annual	[QRL.66]	2.9.4
Wholesalers' stocks	Food and drink industry	UK	Annual	[QRL.66], [QRL.141]	2.9.4

Specific Commodity Sources

Butter and skimmed milk powder, intervention stocks of	Various types	UK	Annual	[QRL.503]	5.9
Cocoa beans	Various components	World	Annual	[QRL.249], [QRL.250], [QRL.311], [QRL.397]	10.9
	ICCO buffer stocks	World	Quarterly	[QRL.245]	10.8.3
Cocoa beans and cocoa products	Cocoa beans; cocoa nibs; unsweetened cocoa powder; cocoa paste and liquor; cocoa cake; cocoa butter	UK	Annual	[QRL.332]	10.9
Coffee, green (held by importers and roasters)	Various components	UK and other countries	Quarterly	[QRL.245], [QRL.399]	12.9.1
Coffee, green	Various components	UK and other countries	Quarterly	[QRL.179], [QRL.197], [QRL.312]	12.9.1
Coffee, raw (in public warehouses and in transit)	Warehouses; in transit	UK	Quarterly	[QRL.334]	12.9.1
Coffee, raw	Total stocks	UK	Quarterly	[QRL.331]	12.9.1
Fish	Type of frozen fish	UK	Monthly	[QRL.475]	7.9. Discontinued in 1981
Fruit, canned and bottled	Selected items of manufacturers' stocks	UK	Quarterly	[QRL.325]	6.9.1
Grain	Commodity	UK	Monthly	[QRL.318], [QRL.345]	8.9. See text for further details
Meat, in public cold stores	Type of meat	UK	Monthly	[QRL.335]	4.9
Meat, aided private storage stocks of	Beef; pigmeat	UK	Annual	[QRL.293]	4.9
Oils (refined, deodorised vegetable, marine) and fats (animal)	Various oils and fats	UK	Monthly	[QRL.321]	3.11

Type of data	Breakdown	Area	Frequency	QRL publication	Text reference
Sugar and sugar products	Commodity	UK	Quarterly	[QRL.199], [QRL.200]	9.9.3, 9.11
Tea	Warehouses; primary wholesalers; weighed teas awaiting sale	UK	Weekly	[QRL.465], [QRL.480]	12.9.2. See text for detailed discussion
	Warehouses; primary wholesalers	UK	Monthly	[QRL.367]	12.9.2
		UK	Annual	[QRL.38], [QRL.481]	12.9.2
CONSUMPTION					
General Consumption Data					
National Food Survey					
Food consumption (Historical data)	Principal food groups	GB	Annual	[QRL.469], [QRL.509]	2.10.1.1
Food consumption	Main food groups; individual foods; selected food items	GB	Annual	[QRL.178], [QRL.267], [QRL.373]	2.10.1.2, 2.10.1.3 and section 10 of each chapter. See text for details of coverage and of further analyses
	Various components	GB	Annual	[QRL.37], [QRL.319], [QRL.401], [QRL.456]	2.10.1.4 and section 10 of each chapter. These sources provide a selection of the results from the National Food Survey
Specific Commodity Sources					
Beverages	Hot; cold; alcoholic by age group; region etc	UK	Annual	[QRL.372]	12.10.4. See text for further details
Cereals	Various cereals	UK	Various	[QRL.414]	8.10.4
Chocolate and sugar confectionery	Quantity; value	UK	Annual	[QRL.41], [QRL.49], [QRL.461]	10.10.4. Despatch data
Cocoa	Various components in bean equivalent	UK and other countries	Quarterly	[QRL.249]	10.10.4. See text for discussion

Coffee, disappearance of	Aggregate data	UK	Quarterly	[QRL.399], [QRL.245]	12.10.4, 12.11. See text for further explanation
Confectionery	Various components	UK	Annual	[QRL.161]	10.10.4
	Quantity; value	UK	Annual	[QRL.144]	10.10.4
Fish	Various types frozen; fresh	GB	Quarterly	[QRL.266]	7.10.5
	Various types fresh; canned and bottled; cooked and processed; frozen	UK	Annual	[QRL.220]	7.10.5
Food drinks (branded)	Various drinks	UK	Annual	[QRL.356]	11.10.5
Ice-cream	Type; age group	UK	Annual	[QRL.270], [QRL.510]	10.10.4
Infant foods	Various foods	UK	Annual	[QRL.56]	11.10.5
Tea	Imports for consumption/Quantity	UK	Annual	[QRL.38], [QRL.367], [QRL.474], [QRL.481]	12.10.4, 12.11
Expenditure Data *National Food Survey*					
Food expenditure (Historical data)	Principal food groups	GB	Annual	[QRL.469], [QRL.509]	2.10.1
Food expenditure	Main food groups; individual foods; selected food items	GB	Annual	[QRL.178], [QRL.267], [QRL.373]	2.10.1 and section 10 of each chapter. See text for details of coverage and of further analyses
Family Expenditure Survey					
Food expenditure	Various components	UK	Annual	[QRL.204]	2.10.2.2, 2.10.2.3 and section 10 of each chapter. See text for further discussion and Appendix D for details of the headings used to identify food expenditure information
	Various components	UK	Monthly; annual	[QRL.186], [QRL.401], [QRL.456]	2.10.2.4

Type of data	Breakdown	Area	Frequency	QRL publication	Text reference
National Accounts Data					
Consumers' expenditure	Commodity; function	UK	Annual	[QRL.37], [QRL.506]	2.10.3 and section 10 of each chapter
Consumers' expenditure on food	Aggregate data	UK	Quarterly	[QRL.181], [QRL.362]	2.10.3
Index numbers of consumers' expenditure on food	Aggregate data	UK	Annual	[QRL.456]	2.10.3
Consumers' expenditure on food, drink and tobacco	Region	UK, countries and regions	Annual	[QRL.401]	2.10.3
Catering and Meals bought away from Home					
Household and total catering expenditure on food	Aggregate data	UK	Annual	[QRL.51], [QRL.506]	2.10.3. See methodological notes at the back of [QRL.506]
Catering sales and purchases of food and non-alcoholic drink	Type of establishment	GB	Annual	[QRL.142]	2.10.4
Meals bought away from home	Various components	UK	Weekly	[QRL.204]	2.10.2.2, 2.10.4
SUPPLIES AND DISPOSALS					
General Sources					
Disposals	Various commodities	UK	Monthly	[QRL.362]	2.11.3 and section 11 of each chapter
	Various commodities	UK	Annual	[QRL.37]	2.11.3 and section 11 of each chapter
Food self-sufficiency	Aggregate data	UK	Annual	[QRL.37], [QRL.51], [QRL.319]	2.11.3

Food supplies moving into human consumption	Aggregate data	UK	Annual	[QRL.37]	Section 11 of each chapter
					2.11.3 and section 11 of each chapter
Specific Commodity Sources					
Chocolate, chocolate confectionery and sugar confectionery, supplies of	Chocolate and chocolate confectionery; sugar confectionery	UK	Annual	[QRL.461]	10.11
Fish, disposals of	Herring; mackerel; sprat by type of market/processing	Scotland	Annual	[QRL.449]	7.11. See text for further discussion
Fish, supplies of	Weight; value	UK	Annual	[QRL.45]	7.11
Fruits and vegetables, supplies of	Various	UK	Annual	[QRL.37], [QRL.382]	6.11
Milk products, supplies and disappearance of	Various products	UK	Annual	[QRL.503]	5.11. Self-sufficiency ratios are also calculated. See text for further details
Potatoes, disposals of	Various types	GB	Annual	[QRL.387]	6.11
	Various types	Northern Ireland	Annual	[QRL.376]	6.11
Potatoes, supplies of	Various	GB	Annual	[QRL.387]	6.11
Supply Balance Sheets					
Supply Balance Sheets	Various commodities	UK	Annual	[QRL.36], [QRL.51], [QRL.167]	2.11.2
Cereals	Various cereals	UK	Annual	[QRL.345]	8.11
Fats and oils, of Land Animals	Various fats and oils	UK	Quarterly	[QRL.36]	3.11
Fats and oils, of Marine Animals	Various fats and oils	UK	Quarterly	[QRL.36]	3.11
Fats and oils, prepared	Various fats and oils	UK	Monthly	[QRL.167], [QRL.321]	3.11
Fats and oils, vegetable	Various oilseeds and nuts	UK	Monthly	[QRL.167], [QRL.328]	3.11
Meat	Various types of meat	UK	Quarterly	[QRL.36]	4.11

Type of data	Breakdown	Area	Frequency	QRL publication	Text reference
Meat, carcase	Various types of meat	UK	Quarterly	[QRL.330]	4.11. Figures exclude meat offals and trade in manufactured meat products
Seeds and fruit, oleaginous	Rape and other seeds	UK	Quarterly	[QRL.167], [QRL.322]	3.11
Supply/demand Balance					
Coffee	Various components	World and countries	Quarterly	[QRL.179], [QRL.197], [QRL.312]	12.11. See text for details of supply/demand balances measures
Sugar	Various components	World and countries	Annual	[QRL.168], [QRL.200], [QRL.472], [QRL.521], [QRL.522]	9.11. See text for details of supply/demand balances measures
PRICES *Agricultural Prices* *General Sources*					
Agricultural prices	Various agricultural commodities	UK	Annual	[QRL.37], [QRL.51]	2.12.1.1, 6.12.1.1, 8.12.1.1, 9.12.1.1
		England and Wales	Monthly	[QRL.29], [QRL.30], [QRL.32]	2.12.1.1, 6.12.1.1, 9.12.1.1, 11.12.1
		Northern Ireland	Annual	[QRL.376], [QRL.377], [QRL.416], [QRL.460]	2.12.1.1, 6.12.1.1
		Northern Ireland	Weekly	[QRL.24]	2.12.1.1, 8.12.1
		Northern Ireland	Quarterly	[QRL.396]	2.12.1.1

		Scotland	Monthly	[QRL.31], [QRL.33], [QRL.180]	2.12.1.1, 6.12.1.1, 8.12.1.1
		Scotland	Weekly	[QRL.511]	2.12.1.1
	Various produce	Wales	Annual	[QRL.211]	2.12.1.1
		Wales	Monthly	[QRL.515], [QRL.516]	2.12.1.1
Historical price data	Various	UK and countries	Annual	[QRL.1]	2.12.1.1
Specific Commodity Sources					
Horticultural products					
Horticultural produce, home-grown and imported	Various produce	England and Wales	Weekly	[QRL.26]	2.12.1.1, 6.12.1.1 11.12.1. See text for further details
Fruit and vegetable produce	Grade	England and Wales	Weekly	[QRL.27]	2.12.1.1, 6.12.1.1, 11.12.1. See text for further details
Fruit and vegetables, average farm-gate prices	Various produce	UK	Annual	[QRL.61]	6.12.1.1
Fruit and vegetables (home-grown), average wholesale prices	Various	England and Wales	Monthly	[QRL.412], [QRL.413]	6.12.1.1
Fruit and vegetables, wholesale prices	Various	England and Wales	Tuesday prices	[QRL.246]	6.12.1.2. See text for market centres
Fruit and vegetables, auction prices	Selected produce	England and Wales	Weekly	[QRL.254]	6.12.1.2. See text for market centres
Fruit and vegetables	Various produce by grade	Northern Ireland	Weekly	[QRL.265]	2.12.1.1
Meat and livestock					
Livestock (fat), average auction prices	Cattle; sheep; pigs; various poultry	England and Wales	Weekly	[QRL.25]	4.12.1
Livestock (fat), sample auction prices	Various animals	Northern Ireland	Weekly	[QRL.71]	4.12.1
Meat and live animals	Various types	UK	Weekly	[QRL.353], [QRL.498]	4.12.1. See text for further details

Type of data	Breakdown	Area	Frequency	QRL publication	Text reference
		UK	Monthly	[QRL.498]	4.12.1
Milk					
Milk ("pool" or base prices), sold to Milk Marketing Boards	Board	UK	Monthly	[QRL.503]	5.12.1. Prices for each individual Board are provided in [QRL.355], [QRL.357], [QRL.358], [QRL.360] and [QRL.490]
Milk prices (average), paid to wholesale producers	Milk Marketing Board	UK	Annual	[QRL.503]	5.12.1
Potatoes					
Agricultural prices	Various types	GB	Annual	[QRL.263], [QRL.384], [QRL.387]	6.12.1.1 See text for further explanation
Guaranteed and average prices	Various types	GB	Monthly	[QRL.387]	6.12.1.1. See text for further explanation
Spot and Futures Prices General Sources					
Spot and futures prices	Main traded commodities	World markets – usually London, New York and Chicago	Daily	[QRL.218]	2.12.1.2. See text for further details
		London and selected world markets	Daily	[QRL.392]	2.12.1.2 and section 12 of each chapter. See text for further details
		London and selected world markets	Weekly	[QRL.394]	2.12.1.2 and section 12 of each chapter. See text for further details

		London and selected world markets	Annual	[QRL.269], [QRL.393]	2.12.1.2. See text for further details
		US and world markets	Various	[QRL.157], [QRL.166], [QRL.169]	2.12.1.2, 8.12.1. See text for further details
	Selected agricultural commodities	UK	Weekly	[QRL.212]	2.12.1.2, 6.12.1.2, 8.12.1, 11.12.1. See text for further details
Specific Commodity Sources					
Cereals and grains					
Cereals and grains	Various	UK	Various	[QRL.152], [QRL.171], [QRL.512], [QRL.513]	8.12.1
Cocoa					
Cocoa	Various	London and other trading centres	Daily	[QRL.245], [QRL.249], [QRL.250], [QRL.435]	10.12.1. See text for further details
Cocoa beans	ICCO indicator prices	World	Daily	[QRL.249], [QRL.250], [QRL.311], [QRL.397]	10.12.1. See text for further details
Cocoa products	Cocoa butter, cocoa powder	UK	Monthly	[QRL.249], [QRL.250], [QRL.311]	10.12.1
Coffee					
Coffee	Various types	London and other trading centres	Daily	[QRL.197], [QRL.436], [QRL.514]	12.12.1.1. [QRL.179] reports ICO indicator prices. [QRL.312] gives monthly averages. [QRL.399] contains a range of prices. See text for full explanation

Type of data	Breakdown	Area	Frequency	QRL publication	Text reference
Oilseeds and nuts					
Forward shipments representative asking prices	Various oilseeds and nuts	World	Weekly	[QRL.380]	3.12.1
Sugar					
Spot and futures prices	Contract	London and other trading centres	Monthly	[QRL.72], [QRL.251], [QRL.303]	9.12.1.2
		London and other trading centres	Daily	[QRL.168], [QRL.199], [QRL.218], [QRL.437]	9.12.1.2. See text for further discussion
Fish Prices					
Fish prices	Species	UK and countries	Annual	[QRL.451]	7.12.1.1
		UK	Monthly	[QRL.475]	7.12.1.2
	Species by port; market	UK	Weekly	[QRL.12], [QRL.62], [QRL.155], [QRL.227]	7.12.1.2
		UK	Daily	[QRL.222]	7.12.1.2. See text for further details
		Scotland	Annual	[QRL.449]	7.12.1.1
Feed ingredient prices, including fish meal	Various ingredients	UK	Weekly	[QRL.392], [QRL.394]	7.12.1.2
Tea Prices					
Tea, auction prices	Grade; country; tea-garden	UK	Weekly	[QRL.367], [QRL.480]	12.12.1.2
Tea prices	Grade	UK	Annual	[QRL.38]	12.12.1.2

Retail, Trade and Wholesale Prices					
General Sources					
Average retail prices	Selected food items in the RPI	UK	Monthly	[QRL.186]	2.12.2.1 and section 12.2 of each chapter. Past data are available in [QRL.67] and [QRL.68]
	Individual foods in the NFS	GB	Quarterly	[QRL.373]	2.12.2.1 and section 12.2 of each chapter
Recommended trade and retail prices	Branded products	UK	Monthly	[QRL.253]	2.12.2.2 and section 12.2 of each chapter. [QRL.252] notifies price changes between issues of [QRL.253]
Recommended retail prices	Branded products	UK	Weekly	[QRL.453]	2.12.1.2 and section 12.2 of each chapter
Average wholesale market prices	Various meat and grocery products/provisions	UK	Weekly	[QRL.252]	2.12.2.2. See text for further details
Specific Commodity Sources					
Fish, retail prices	Cod; haddock; plaice fillets	UK	Annual	[QRL.475]	7.12.2.1
Meat, representative retail prices	Beef; lamb; pork; chicken	Northern Ireland	Monthly	[QRL.352]	4.12.2.1
Milk sales, average prices received by Milk Marketing Boards	Board; milk product	UK	Annual	[QRL.503]	5.12.1
Export and Import Prices					
Fish	Fish; fish products	UK	Monthly	[QRL.189]	7.12.6
	Species	UK and other countries	Various	[QRL.226], [QRL.491]	7.12.6. Prices as quoted by producers, importers and brokers to primary wholesalers. See text for further details
Sugar, refined sugar export price (Tate & Lyle)	Aggregate data	UK	Daily	[QRL.392], [QRL.437]	9.12.6

Type of data	Breakdown	Area	Frequency	QRL publication	Text reference
Price Indices					
Retail Prices Index					
Retail price index numbers	Food items; food groups	UK	Monthly	[QRL.186], [QRL.362]	2.12.3 and section 12.3 of each chapter. [QRL.186] is more detailed than [QRL.362]. Past data may be found in [QRL.434], and in [QRL.67], [QRL.68] and [QRL.464]
	Food items	UK	Quarterly	[QRL.128] to [QRL.139]	2.12.3.3 and section 12.3 of each chapter
	Food; seasonal food; non-seasonal food; catering	UK	Monthly	[QRL.66]	2.12.3.3
	Food	UK	Monthly	[QRL.181]	2.12.3.3
	Food	UK	Quarterly	[QRL.182]	2.12.3.3
	Food; meals bought and consumed away from home	UK	Annual	[QRL.37], [QRL.456]	2.12.3.3
	Food groups; sub-groups	Isle of Man	Monthly	[QRL.295]	2.12.3.3
Price Index Numbers in the National Food Survey					
Price index numbers in the NFS	Food groups	GB	Annual	[QRL.373]	2.12.4 and section 12.4 of each chapter. See text for details of further analyses
Producer Price Index Numbers					
Input prices	Activity Heading	UK	Monthly	[QRL.66], [QRL.37]	2.12.5.1 and section 12.5 of each chapter. See *Business Monitor MM22: Producer Price Indices* which continued [QRL.66] coverage from October 1989
	Food manufacturing	UK	Monthly	[QRL.362]	2.12.5.1

	Various commodities	UK	Quarterly	[QRL.128] to [QRL.139]	2.12.5.1 and section 12.5 of each chapter
Output prices	Activity Heading	UK	Monthly	[QRL.66], [QRL.37]	2.12.5.2 and section 12.5 of each chapter. See *Business Monitor MM22: Producer Price Indices* which continued [QRL.66] coverage from October 1989
		UK	Quarterly	[QRL.128] to [QRL.139]	2.12.5.2 and section 12.5 of each chapter
	Food manufacturing	UK	Monthly	[QRL.362]	2.12.5.2
Producer Price Index Numbers for Current Cost Accounting					
Price index numbers for current cost accounting	Food industries: plant and machinery/stocks	UK	Monthly	[QRL.84], [QRL.87], [QRL.88]	2.12.5.4. Past data available in [QRL.390]
Producer price index for milk	Aggregate index	UK	Monthly	[QRL.315]	5.12.1
Index Numbers for Exports and Imports					
Unit value index numbers	Commodity	UK	Monthly	[QRL.364]	2.12.6. Longer time series are available in [QRL.365] and [QRL.366]
Coffee, unit value	Imports/aggregate data	UK and ICO members	Quarterly	[QRL.398]	12.12.6
Coffee; tea	Exports/Imports	UK	Quarterly	[QRL.126]	12.12.6. Index numbers only provided in second and third issues (1973)
Intervention Prices					
Intervention prices	Various commodities/other linked prices	UK	Annual	[QRL.293], [QRL.379]	2.3.3.6 and section 3 of each chapter. Intervention sales, purchases etc. are also surveyed in [QRL.293]

Type of data	Breakdown	Area	Frequency	QRL publication	Text reference
Sugar regime	Prices; quotas	EC and countries	Annual	[QRL.72], [QRL.293], [QRL.303], [QRL.470]	9.12
Milk and milk products	Various products/other linked prices	UK	Effective date	[QRL.503]	5.3
Price movements of confectionery products	Chocolate confectionery; sugar confectionery	UK	Annual	[QRL.461]	10.12.3
FINANCIAL INFORMATION *Company Accounts – General Sources*					
Company financial data	Various components (profit, turnover etc.) by company	UK	Annual	[QRL.73], [QRL.241], [QRL.255], [QRL.256], [QRL.290], [QRL.301], [QRL.314], [QRL.445], [QRL.452], [QRL.486], [QRL.487], [QRL.500]	2.13.4.2. See text for further details of these company almanacs
		UK	Various	[QRL.162], [QRL.163], [QRL.229], [QRL.497], [QRL.507]	2.13.4.3, 2.13.5. The coverage is subject to frequent change in these stockbrokers' reports

		UK	Periodic update	[QRL.192], [QRL.194], [QRL.347], [QRL.348]	2.13.4.3. [QRL.192] and [QRL.194] have the greater financial coverage, whereas [QRL.347] and [QRL.348] are more oriented towards news
		UK	Various	[QRL.160], [QRL.173], [QRL.191], [QRL.268], [QRL.296], [QRL.489]	2.13.4.4 Computer data bases
Food manufacturing	Various components (data and company profiles) by company	UK	Annual	[QRL.233], [QRL.234], [QRL.530]	2.13.4.1 Compiled from IGD data base
	Various components (profit, turnover etc.) by company	UK	Annual	[QRL.564] to [QRL.579]	2.13.6.1 and section 13 of each chapter. ICC Financial Survey and Company Directory
	Financial indicators, ratios and rankings for named companies	UK	Annual	[QRL.544] to [QRL.563]	2.13.4.1 and section 13 of each chapter. ICC Business Ratio reports
	Various components (profit, turnover etc.)	UK	Annual	[QRL.580] to [QRL.599]	2.13.4.1 and section 13 of each chapter. ICC Key Note reports
	Various components (profit, turnover etc.) by industrial sector and sub-sector	UK	Annual	[QRL.273]	2.13.4.1. See text for details of the sub-sectors identified in food manufacturing. ICC summary
Return on capital employed; return on trading assets	Industry	UK	Annual	[QRL.58]	2.13.3. Derived from published company accounts for the Bank of England

Type of data	Breakdown	Area	Frequency	QRL publication	Text reference
Summary company accounts	Balance sheet; income and appropriation account; sources and uses of funds; ratios by Class	UK	Annual	[QRL.79], [QRL.81]	2.13.1. Past data are available in [QRL.6], [QRL.181] and [QRL.464]. BSO summaries
Census of Production Data					
Monetary data on output and costs	Group; Activity Heading	UK	Annual	[QRL.93], [QRL.105] to [QRL.114]	2.13.3 and section 13 of each chapter
Insolvency Statistics					
Bankruptcies and insolvencies	Class	England and Wales	Annual	[QRL.66]	2.13.3.
Liquidations	Compulsory/voluntary by Class	England and Wales; Scotland	Annual	[QRL.158]	2.13.3
Insolvent companies, assets and liabilities	Industry	England and Wales; Scotland	Annual	[QRL.286]	2.13.3
Specific Industry Data					
Fish processing	Various components by size of business	UK	Annual	[QRL.2], [QRL.3]	7.13.2. See text for further details
Ice-cream, chocolate etc.	Various components by company	UK	Annual	[QRL.441]	10.13
Meat industry, yields, costs and margins	Various components	UK	Occasional	[QRL.350]	4.13
Milk production, costs and returns	Various components	England and Wales, and Northern Ireland	Annual	[QRL.503]	5.13
Milk products	Various components (profit, turnover etc.)	UK	Annual	[QRL.549], [QRL.594]	5.13

Sugar and sugar by-products, company data	Various components (profit, turnover etc.)	UK	Annual	[QRL.69], [QRL.442], [QRL.479]	9.13.1
ADVERTISING *General Sources* *Actual Expenditure*					
Advertising expenditure	Food brand; agency; media	UK	Monthly	[QRL.493]	2.14.1.1 and section 14.1 of each chapter. MEALINK data base is available on-line. See text for further details
	Top 100 advertisers; media	UK	Annual	[QRL.145], [QRL.346]	2.14.1.1, 2.14.1.2
	Top 100 generic brands; product name	UK	Annual	[QRL.236]	2.14.1.1 and section 14.1 of each chapter. [QRL.488] gives details of top 100 brands. See text for further discussion
Corrected MEAL data	Food; media	UK	Quarterly	[QRL.15], [QRL.17], [QRL.18], [QRL.20], [QRL.236], [QRL.240], [QRL.287], [QRL.297], [QRL.400]	2.14.1.2
Historical data	Various components	UK	Various	[QRL.16], [QRL.19], [QRL.462]	2.14.1.1, 2.14.1.2
Advertising/sales Ratios					
Advertising/sales ratios	Food	UK	Annual	[QRL.20], [QRL.287]	2.14.1.2

Type of data	Breakdown	Area	Frequency	QRL publication	Text reference
Forecasts					
Forecasts of advertising expenditure	Food	UK	Quarterly	[QRL.236], [QRL.240]	2.14.1.1, 2.14.1.2
Specific Sources					
Fish processing, generic promotional material	Various components	UK	Annual	[QRL.45]	7.14.1
Milk and milk products, expenditure and promotion	Various components	UK and countries	Annual	[QRL.503]	5.14.1
Other Data					
Agency information	Industry/product; client/brand	UK	Annual	[QRL.13], [QRL.145]	2.14.1.1. [QRL.13] is updated monthly
Rates and circulation	Media	UK	Monthly	[QRL.64]	2.14.1.1
MARKET RESEARCH *Industrial Trends Surveys*					
Market prospects	Various components	UK	Quarterly	[QRL.147]	2.14.2.1
Market Research Sources					
Market research	Various components of market structure and performance	UK	Various	[QRL.523] to [QRL.653]	2.14.2, 2.14.2.1, 2.14.2.2 and section 14.2 of each chapter. See text for further details. See also market structure QRL
Specific Product Sectors					
Baby foods	Various baby foods	UK	Annual	[QRL.56]	11.2.3, 11.14.2
Chicken, market research on	Various components	GB	Annual	[QRL.439]	4.14.2

Confectionery	Various components by brand	UK	Annual	[QRL.144], [QRL.161]	10.14.2. See text for further details
Fish and fish products	Company profiles	UK	Annual	[QRL.220], [QRL.242], [QRL.243], [QRL.244]	7.14.2
Food drinks	Various types	UK	Annual	[QRL.356]	11.2.3, 11.14.2
Frozen food and vegetables,	Company profiles	UK	Annual	[QRL.242], [QRL.243], [QRL.244]	6.14.2
Ice-cream	Various components by brand	UK	Annual	[QRL.270], [QRL.510]	10.2.1, 10.14.2. See text for further details
Jam and marmalade	Company profiles	UK	Annual	[QRL.433]	6.14.2
Meat and meat products	Various components	UK	Various	[QRL.351]	4.14.2. See text for further details
Meat retailers' likely costs and returns, forecasts of	Various components	UK	Annual	[QRL.492]	4.14.2
Meat market trends forecasts	Various components	UK	Quarterly	[QRL.340], [QRL.341], [QRL.342]	4.14.2
Slaughterings and meat production, forecasts	Various components	UK	Annual	[QRL.498]	4.14.2
Snack foods	Various snack foods	UK	Annual	[QRL.302]	11.14.2
Sugar and sugar by-products	Company; brand	UK	Annual	[QRL.69], [QRL.442], [QRL.479]	9.14.2
RESEARCH AND DEVELOPMENT					
General Sources					
Industrial R&D	Source of funds; expenditure; intensity; type of research worker; by product group	UK	Annual	[QRL.86]	2.15.1. "Food and drink" is cited as one product group
	Source of finance by sector; employment by industry; expenditure by type of research	UK	Annual	[QRL.430], [QRL.431], [QRL.463]	2.15.3

Type of data	Breakdown	Area	Frequency	QRL publication	Text reference
	Intramural expenditure/product group	UK	Annual	[QRL.66]	2.15.1
Industrial R&D (Historical data)	Employment and expenditure by product group	UK	Annual	[QRL.187], [QRL.276]	2.15.3. "Food, drink and tobacco" is cited as one product group, but some tables give more disaggregated data
Expenditure and employment, centrally funded	Government Department; Research Council	UK	Annual	[QRL.52], [QRL.181]	2.15.2
Expenditure and employment, government funded	Food industry; Government Department; type of research	UK	Annual	[QRL.52]	2.15.4. Description of R&D activity also provided
Expenditure	Food industry; source of funds; type of research	UK	Annual	[QRL.21], [QRL.165], [QRL.415]	2.15.4
Specific Sources					
Cocoa, chocolate etc.	Various BCCCA interests; expenditure	UK	Annual	[QRL.41], [QRL.49]	10.15
Coffee	Aggregate data; expenditure	World	Annual	[QRL.247]	12.15
Confectionery, chocolate and sugar (product development)	Product line	UK	Annual	[QRL.144]	10.15
Fish processing	Employment; expenditure	UK	Annual	[QRL.45]	7.15
Ice-cream (product development)	Product line	UK	Annual	[QRL.510]	10.15
Sugar	Aggregate data; expenditure	UK	Annual	[QRL.69], [QRL.479]	9.15

QUICK REFERENCE LIST KEY TO PUBLICATIONS

(Listed alphabetically by author, where authors are named, and then alphabetically by title except for reports by market research organisations; the latter are grouped together separately from [QRL.523] onwards).

Reference	Author or Organisation	Title	Publisher	Frequency or date	Remarks
[QRL.1]	Baines, A.H.	*A Century of Agricultural Statistics: Great Britain 1866-1966*	HMSO, London	1968	
[QRL.2]	Banks, Richard	*Financial Results Reported in Fish Processing, 1985*	SFIA, Edinburgh	1988	Available from SFIA, Fishery Economics Research Unit
[QRL.3]	Banks, Richard	*Fish Processing in the UK: An Economic Analysis*	SFIA, Edinburgh	1988	Available from SFIA, Fishery Economics Research Unit
[QRL.4]	Barna, T.	"The interdependence of the British Economy" *Journal of the Royal Statistical Society, Series A (General)* 115, (1), pp.29-81	Royal Statistical Society, London	1952	
[QRL.5]	Burrell, A., Hill, B. and Medland, J.	*Statistical Handbook of UK Agriculture*	Macmillan, London	1984	
[QRL.6]	Goudie, A. and Meeks, G.	*Company Finance and Performance: Aggregate Financial Accounts for Individual British Industries 1948-1982*	Department of Applied Economics, University of Cambridge, Cambridge	1986	
[QRL.7]	Ireson, R. and Tomkins, C.	*Inter-regional Input-output Tables for Wales and the Rest of the United Kingdom: 1968*	Welsh Council, Cardiff	1978	
[QRL.8]	Lewis, M.R.	*Rainbow Trout: Production and Marketing* Department of Agricultural Economics and Management, Miscellaneous study no.68	University of Reading, Reading	1980	

Reference	Author or Organisation	Title	Publisher	Frequency or date	Remarks
[QRL.9]	Lewis, M.R.	*Fish Farming in the United Kingdom* Department of Agricultural Economics and Management, Miscellaneous study no.71	University of Reading, Reading	1984	
[QRL.10]	Smith, C.T.B., Clifton, R., Makeham, P., Creigh, S.W. and Burns, R.V.	*Strikes in Britain* Manpower Paper no.15	HMSO, London	1978	
[QRL.11]	Stewart, I.G.	"Input-output tables for the United Kingdom" *London and Cambridge Economic Bulletin, New Series, The Times Review of Industry*, no.28, pp. vii-ix	Times Newspapers Ltd, London	December 1958	
[QRL.12]	Sea Fisheries Inspectorate Scotland	*Aberdeen District: White Fish Report*	Sea Fisheries Inspectorate, Scotland	Weekly	
[QRL.13]	Black Box Publishers Ltd	*Account List File*	Black Box Publishing Ltd in association with MEAL, London	Monthly	
[QRL.14]	Tudor House Publications	*Acquisitions Monthly*	Tudor House Publications, Tunbridge Wells	Monthly	
[QRL.15]	The Advertising Association	*Advertising*	The Advertising Association, London	Quarterly from Summer 1978 to Winter 1979/80	Preceded by [QRL.18]. Succeeded by [QRL.17]
[QRL.16]	The Advertising Association	*Advertising Expenditure*	The Advertising Association, London	Every four years	1948, 1952, 1956 and 1964
[QRL.17]	The Advertising Association	*Advertising Magazine*	The Advertising Association, London	Quarterly from Spring 1980 to Autumn 1981	Preceded by [QRL.15]. Succeeded by [QRL.297]

[QRL.18]	The Advertising Association	*Advertising Quarterly*	The Advertising Association, London	Quarterly from Autumn 1968 to Spring 1978	Succeeded by [QRL.15]
[QRL.19]	Legion Information Services	*Advertising Statistical Review*	Legion Information Services, London	Monthly until March 1970	Discontinued
[QRL.20]	The Advertising Association	*Advertising Statistics Yearbook*	NTC Publications Ltd, Henley-on-Thames, and The Advertising Association, London	Annual	The 1983 edition was entitled *The Statistical Yearbook*
[QRL.21]	Ministry of Agriculture, Fisheries and Food	*AFRC Annual Report*	Agriculture and Food Research Council, Swindon	Annual	Available from AFRC
[QRL.22]	Agra Europe (London) Ltd	*Agra Europe*	Agra Europe (London) Ltd, Tunbridge Wells	Weekly	
[QRL.23]	Agra Europe (London) Ltd	*Agra Europe Eurofish Report: A Fortnightly Review*	Agra Europe, Tunbridge Wells	Fortnightly	
[QRL.24]	Department of Agriculture for Northern Ireland, Economics and Statistics Division	*Agricultural Market Report*	DANI, Belfast	Weekly from March 1988	Previously *Agricultural Market Report 2* Available from DANI Economics and Statistics Division
[QRL.25]	Ministry of Agriculture, Fisheries and Food	*Agricultural Market Report Part I: Prices and Quantities Sold of Selected Cereals, Livestock and Other Agricultural Products*	MAFF, Guildford	Weekly	Available from MAFF, Branch A (Censuses and Prices)

Reference	Author or Organisation	Title	Publisher	Frequency or date	Remarks
[QRL.26]	Ministry of Agriculture, Fisheries and Food	*Agricultural Market Report Part II: National Average Wholesale Prices and Home Grown and Imported Horticultural Produce*	MAFF, Guildford	Weekly	Available from MAFF, Branch A (Censuses and Prices). Successor to the *Horticultural Supplement*
[QRL.27]	Ministry of Agriculture, Fisheries and Food	*Agricultural Market Report Part III: Prices of Home Grown Vegetables by Grade in Six Major Markets in England and Wales*	MAFF, Guildford	Weekly	Available from MAFF, Branch A (Censuses and Prices). Last issue 28 March 1991
[QRL.28]	Commission of the European Communities	*The Agricultural Situation in the Community*	Office for Official Publications of the European Communities, Luxembourg	Annual since 1966	Published in conjunction with [QRL.248]
[QRL.29]	Ministry of Agriculture, Fisheries and Food	*Agricultural Statistics: England*	HMSO, London	1981	One edition (1978/79). Succeeded by [QRL.32]
[QRL.30]	Ministry of Agriculture, Fisheries and Food	*Agricultural Statistics: England and Wales*	HMSO, London	Annual until 1976/77	
[QRL.31]	Department of Agriculture and Fisheries for Scotland	*Agricultural Statistics: Scotland*	HMSO, Edinburgh	Annual from 1912 to 1975	Succeeded by [QRL.180]

[QRL.32]	Ministry of Agriculture, Fisheries and Food; Department of Agriculture and Fisheries for Scotland; Department of Agriculture for Northern Ireland; Welsh Office	*Agricultural Statistics: United Kingdom*	HMSO, London	Annual	Amalgamated with [QRL.29] from 1980
[QRL.33]	Secretary of State for Scotland	*Agriculture in Scotland*	HMSO, Edinburgh	Annual	Command paper
[QRL.34]	Statistical Office of the European Communities	*Agriculture: Statistical Yearbook*	Office for Official Publications of the European Communities, Luxembourg	Annual since 1986	Previously entitled *Yearbook of Agricultural Statistics*
[QRL.35]	Statistical Office of the European Communities	*Analytical Tables of Foreign Trade*	Office for Official Publications of the European Communities, Luxembourg	Annual	Succeeded by [QRL.196]
[QRL.36]	Statistical Office of the European Communities	*Animal Production*	Office for Official Publications of the European Communities, Luxembourg	Quarterly	
[QRL.37]	Central Statistical Office	*Annual Abstract of Statistics*	HMSO, London	Annual since 1948 (no.84)	Preceded by *Statistical Abstract for the United Kingdom* (no.83 published in 1940)
[QRL.38]	International Tea Committee Ltd	*Annual Bulletin of Statistics*	International Tea Committee, London	Annual since 1960	Preceded by *Bulletin of Statistics* (1946-1960)

Reference	Author or Organisation	Title	Publisher	Frequency or date	Remarks
[QRL.39]	National Ports Council	*Annual Digest of Port Statistics* (two volumes)	National Ports Council, London	Annual from 1973 to 1979	Preceded by [QRL.174]. Succeeded by [QRL.383]
[QRL.40]	Livestock Marketing Commission for Northern Ireland	*Annual Report*	Livestock Marketing Commission for Northern Ireland, Belfast	Annual	
[QRL.41]	The Cocoa, Chocolate and Confectionery Alliance	*Annual Report*	The Cocoa, Chocolate and Confectionery Alliance, London	Annual from 1948 to 1985	Back copies available on request from the BCCCA. Succeeded by [QRL.49]
[QRL.42]	Bakers, Food and Allied Workers' Union	*Annual Report*	BFAWU, Welwyn Garden City	Annual	
[QRL.43]	Union of Shop, Distributive and Allied Workers	*Annual Report*	USDAW, Manchester	Annual	
[QRL.44]	The Food Drink and Tobacco Industry Training Board	*Annual Report and Accounts*	The Food, Drink and Tobacco Industry Training Board, Gloucester	Annual from 1973 to 1983	
[QRL.45]	Sea Fish Industry Authority	*Annual Report and Accounts: Sea Fish Industry Authority*	SFIA, Edinburgh	Annual since 1981	Preceded by [QRL.518] and [QRL.262]
[QRL.46]	Certification Office for Trade Unions and Employers' Associations	*Annual Report of the Certification Officer*	Certification Office for Trade Unions and Employers' Associations, London	Annual since 1976	

[QRL.47]	Department of Employment	*Annual Report of the Chief Inspector of Factories*	HMSO, London	Annual from 1880 to 1974 with minor title variants	Command paper
[QRL.48]	Office of Fair Trading	*Annual Report of the Director General of Fair Trading*	HMSO, London	Annual since 1975	Command paper
[QRL.49]	The Biscuit, Cake, Chocolate and Confectionery Alliance	*Annual Review*	The Biscuit, Cake, Chocolate and Confectionery Alliance, London	Annual since 1987	Preceded by [QRL.41]
[QRL.50]	Command paper	*Annual Review and Determination of Guarantees*	HMSO, London	Annual from 1951 to 1972	Succeeded by [QRL.51]
[QRL.51]	Ministry of Agriculture, Fisheries and Food; Secretary of State for Scotland; Secretary of State for Northern Ireland; and Secretary of State for Wales	*Annual Review of Agriculture*	HMSO, London	Annual	Command paper. Preceded by [QRL.50]. From 1989 succeeded by *Agriculture in the United Kingdom* with slightly different coverage. Issues of both [QRL.51] and the new publication appeared for 1988
[QRL.52]	Cabinet Office	*Annual Review of Government Funded Research and Development*	HMSO, London	Annual	
[QRL.53]	Frank Fehr and Co. Ltd	*Annual Review of Oilseeds, Oils and Oilcakes and Other Commodities*	Frank Fehr and Co. Ltd, London	Annual	
[QRL.54]	British Ports Association	*Annual Statistical Abstract of the UK Ports Industry*	British Ports Association, London	1983	Discontinued

Reference	Author or Organisation	Title	Publisher	Frequency or date	Remarks
[QRL.55]	Euromonitor Publications Ltd	*A-Z of UK Brand Leaders*	Euromonitor Publications Ltd, London	1984	
[QRL.56]	Cow & Gate Ltd	*Baby Foods: Market Report*	Cow & Gate Ltd, Trowbridge	Annual	
[QRL.57]	National Association of Master Bakers, Confectioners and Caterers	*Bakers Review*	NAMBCC, Ware	Monthly	
[QRL.58]	Bank of England	*Bank of England Quarterly Bulletin*	Bank of England, London	Quarterly since 1960	
[QRL.59]	Department of Trade and Industry	*Bankruptcy General Annual Report*	HMSO, London	Annual from 1921 to 1986	Succeeded by [QRL.286]
[QRL.60]	Labour Research Department	*Bargaining Report*	Labour Research Department, London	11 times a year	
[QRL.61]	Ministry of Agriculture, Fisheries and Food	*Basic Horticultural Statistics for the United Kingdom*	HMSO, London	Annual	Available from MAFF, Branch B, Statistics (Agricultural Commodities) Division
[QRL.62]	Billingsgate Market	*Billingsgate Market Report*	Billingsgate Market, London	Weekly	Available from the Billingsgate Market Superintendent's Office
[QRL.63]	Birds Eye Wall's Ltd	*Birds Eye Frozen Foods: Annual Report*	Birds Eye Wall's Ltd, Walton-on-Thames	Annual	
[QRL.64]	British Rate and Data	*BRAD (British Rate and Data)*	Maclean-Hunter, Barnet	Monthly	

[QRL.65]	Overseas Development Administration	*British Aid Statistics: Statistics of UK Economic Aid to Developing Countries*	HMSO, London	Annual since 1968	Available from ODA (Statistics Division)
[QRL.66]	Department of Trade and Industry	*British Business*	DTI, London	Weekly from 21 September 1979 to 29 September 1989	Formerly entitled *Trade and Industry* (21 October 1970 to 14 September 1979) and *The Board of Trade Journal* (1886 to 14 October 1970). After publication ceased in 1989, detailed statistics appear in [QRL.75] from October 1989. Commentary and aggregate statistics are to be found in [QRL.74]
[QRL.67]	Department of Employment and Productivity	*British Labour Statistics Historical Abstract 1886-1968*	HMSO, London	1971	
[QRL.68]	Department of Employment	*British Labour Statistics Yearbook*	HMSO, London	Annual, 1969-1975	
[QRL.69]	British Sugar plc	*British Sugar plc: Annual Report*	British Sugar plc, Peterborough	Annual	
[QRL.70]	British Sugar plc	*The British Sugar Report*	British Sugar plc, Peterborough	Annual	

Reference	Author or Organisation	Title	Publisher	Frequency or date	Remarks
[QRL.71]	Livestock Marketing Commission for Northern Ireland	*The Bulletin*	Livestock Marketing Commission for Northern Ireland, Belfast	Weekly	
[QRL.72]	Le Fonds d'Intervention et de Regularisation du Marché du Sucre	*Bulletin Statistique du FIRS*	FIRS, Paris	Monthly	
[QRL.73]	Business People Publications Ltd	*Business*	Business People Publications Ltd, London	Monthly since March 1986	
[QRL.74]	Association of British Chambers of Commerce	*Business Briefing*	Association of British Chambers of Commerce, London	Weekly	First issue 20th October 1989. Takes over the commentary role of [QRL.66]. Also contains aggregate statistics
[QRL.75]	Central Statistical Office, Business Statistics Office	*Business Bulletins*	BSO, Newport	Varies according to series, but about 100 issues per annum	From October 1989. Continues detailed statistical coverage previously provided in [QRL.66]
[QRL.76]	Department of Trade and Industry, Business Statistics Office	*Business Monitor M04: Census of Overseas Assets*	HMSO, London	Occasional	

[QRL.77]	Department of Trade and Industry, Business Statistics Office	*Business Monitor M10: Overseas Trade Analysed in Terms of Industries*	HMSO, London	Irregular from 1974	Published for years 1974, 1975 and 1976 then 1977 Q1 and Q2, 1977 Q3 and Q4, 1978 Q1, Q2, and Q3. Succeeded by [QRL.90]
[QRL.78]	Department of Trade and Industry, Business Statistics Office	*Business Monitor M12: Import Penetration and Export Sales Ratios for Manufacturing Industry*	HMSO, London	Quarterly	Succeeded by [QRL.91]
[QRL.79]	Department of Trade and Industry, Business Statistics Office	*Business Monitor M3: Company Finance*	HMSO, London	Annual	Succeeded by [QRL.81]
[QRL.80]	Central Statistical Office	*Business Monitor MA20: Overseas Trade Statistics of the United Kingdom*	HMSO, London	Annual since 1990	Preceded by *Overseas Trade Statistics of the United Kingdom*
[QRL.81]	Department of Trade and Industry, Business Statistics Office	*Business Monitor MA3: Company Finance*	HMSO, London	Annual	Preceded by [QRL.79]
[QRL.82]	Department of Trade and Industry, Business Statistics Office	*Business Monitor MA4: Overseas Transactions*	HMSO, London	Annual	Preceded by *Business Monitor M4: Overseas Transactions*
[QRL.83]	Department of Trade and Industry, Business Statistics Office	*Business Monitor MA4 Supplement: Census of Overseas Assets*	HMSO, London	Triennial	Supplement to [QRL.82]
[QRL.84]	Department of Trade and Industry, Business Statistics Office	*Business Monitor MM17: Price Index Numbers for Current Cost Accounting (Monthly Supplement)*	HMSO, London	Monthly since April 1980	Preceded by [QRL.390]

Reference	Author or Organisation	Title	Publisher	Frequency or date	Remarks
[QRL.85]	Department of Trade and Industry	*Business Monitor MM20: Overseas Trade Statistics of the United Kingdom*	HMSO, London	Monthly since January 1989	Preceded by *Overseas Trade Statistics of the United Kingdom*
[QRL.86]	Department of Trade and Industry, Business Statistics Office	*Business Monitor MO14: Industrial Research and Development Expenditure and Employment*	HMSO, London	Occasional	
[QRL.87]	Department of Trade and Industry, Business Statistics Office	*Business Monitor MO18: Price Index Numbers for Current Cost Accounting, Summary Volume 1974-1982*	HMSO, London	1983	
[QRL.88]	Department of Trade and Industry, Business Statistics Office	*Business Monitor MO18: Price Index Numbers for Current Cost Accounting, Summary Volume 1983-1987*	HMSO, London	1988	
[QRL.89]	Department of Trade and Industry, Business Statistics Office	*Business Monitor MO3: Finance of Top Companies*	HMSO, London	Biannual (approx) since 1988	
[QRL.90]	Department of Trade and Industry, Business Statistics Office	*Business Monitor MQ10: Overseas Trade Analysed in Terms of Industries*	HMSO, London	Quarterly from 1979	Preceded by [QRL.77]
[QRL.91]	Department of Trade and Industry, Business Statistics Office	*Business Monitor MQ12: Import Penetration and Export Sales Ratios for Manufacturing Industry*	HMSO, London	Quarterly	Preceded by [QRL.78]

[QRL.92]	Department of Trade and Industry, Business Statistics Office	*Business Monitor MQ7: Acquisitions and Mergers by Industrial and Commercial Companies*	HMSO, London	Quarterly since 1978 Q4	Preceded by *Business Monitor M7: Acquisitions and Mergers of Companies* (until 1975 Q4) and *Business Monitor M7: Acquisitions and Mergers by Industrial and Commercial Companies* (1976 Q1 to 1978 Q3)
[QRL.93]	Department of Trade and Industry, Business Statistics Office	*Business Monitor PA1002: Summary Volume*	HMSO, London	Annual	
[QRL.94]	Department of Trade and Industry, Business Statistics Office	*Business Monitor PA1002.1: 1979 Census of Production and Purchases Inquiry*	HMSO, London	1983	Published with the 1979 Census of Production
[QRL.95]	Department of Trade and Industry, Business Statistics Office	*Business Monitor PA1003: Analyses of United Kingdom Manufacturing (Local) Units by Employment Size*	HMSO, London	Annual from 1971 to 1984	Succeeded by [QRL.96]
[QRL.96]	Department of Trade and Industry, Business Statistics Office	*Business Monitor PA1003: Size Analyses of United Kingdom Businesses*	HMSO, London	Annual since 1985	Preceded by [QRL.95]
[QRL.97]	Central Statistical Office	*Business Monitor PA1004: Input-output Tables for the United Kingdom 1970*	HMSO, London	1974	
[QRL.98]	Central Statistical Office	*Business Monitor PA1004: Input-output Tables for the United Kingdom 1971*	HMSO, London	1975	

Reference	Author or Organisation	Title	Publisher	Frequency or date	Remarks
[QRL.99]	Central Statistical Office	*Business Monitor PA1004: Input-output Tables for the United Kingdom 1972*	HMSO, London	1976	
[QRL.100]	Central Statistical Office	*Business Monitor PA1004: Input-output Tables for the United Kingdom 1974*	HMSO, London	1980	
[QRL.101]	Central Statistical Office	*Business Monitor PA1004: Input-output Tables for the United Kingdom 1979*	HMSO, London	1983	
[QRL.102]	Department of Trade and Industry, Business Statistics Office	*Business Monitor PA251: Basic Industrial Chemicals*	HMSO, London	Annual	
[QRL.103]	Department of Trade and Industry, Business Statistics Office	*Business Monitor PA256: Specialised Chemical Products Mainly for Industrial and Agricultural Purposes*	HMSO, London	Annual	
[QRL.104]	Department of Trade and Industry, Business Statistics Office	*Business Monitor PA324: Machinery for the Food, Chemical and Related Industries, Process Engineering Contractors*	HMSO, London	Annual	
[QRL.105]	Department of Trade and Industry, Business Statistics Office	*Business Monitor PA411: Organic Oils and Fats*	HMSO, London	Annual since 1980	
[QRL.106]	Department of Trade and Industry, Business Statistics Office	*Business Monitor PA412: Slaughtering of Animals and Production of Meat and By-products*	HMSO, London	Annual since 1980	
[QRL.107]	Department of Trade and Industry, Business Statistics Office	*Business Monitor PA413: Preparation of Milk and Milk Products*	HMSO, London	Annual since 1980	
[QRL.108]	Department of Trade and Industry, Business Statistics Office	*Business Monitor PA414: Processing of Fruit and Vegetables*	HMSO, London	Annual since 1980	

[QRL.109]	Department of Trade and Industry, Business Statistics Office	*Business Monitor PA415: Fish Processing*	HMSO, London	Annual since 1980	
[QRL.110]	Department of Trade and Industry, Business Statistics Office	*Business Monitor PA416: Grain Milling*	HMSO, London	Annual since 1980	
[QRL.111]	Department of Trade and Industry, Business Statistics Office	*Business Monitor PA419: Bread, Biscuits and Flour Confectionery*	HMSO, London	Annual since 1980	
[QRL.112]	Department of Trade and Industry, Business Statistics Office	*Business Monitor PA420: Sugar and Sugar By-products*	HMSO, London	Annual since 1980	
[QRL.113]	Department of Trade and Industry, Business Statistics Office	*Business Monitor PA421: Ice-cream, Cocoa, Chocolate and Sugar Confectionery*	HMSO, London	Annual since 1980	
[QRL.114]	Department of Trade and Industry, Business Statistics Office	*Business Monitor PA423: Starch and Miscellaneous Foods*	HMSO, London	Annual since 1980	
[QRL.115]	Business Statistics Office	*Business Monitor PO1006: Statistics of Product Concentration of UK Manufacturers*	HMSO, London	Occasional.	Discontinued. Last issue published in 1980
[QRL.116]	Department of Trade and Industry, Business Statistics Office	*Business Monitor PO1008: Purchases Inquiry 1984*	HMSO, London	1987	
[QRL.117]	Department of Trade and Industry, Business Statistics Office	*Business Monitor PQ211: Grain Milling*	HMSO, London	Quarterly from 1973 Q1 to 1980 Q4	
[QRL.118]	Department of Trade and Industry, Business Statistics Office	*Business Monitor PQ212: Bread and Flour Confectionery*	HMSO, London	Quarterly from 1973 Q1 to 1982 Q4	
[QRL.119]	Department of Trade and Industry, Business Statistics Office	*Business Monitor PQ213: Biscuits*	HMSO, London	Quarterly from 1973 Q1 to 1982 Q4	
[QRL.120]	Department of Trade and Industry, Business Statistics Office	*Business Monitor PQ214: Bacon Curing, Meat and Fish Products*	HMSO, London	Quarterly from 1973 Q1 to 1982 Q4	

Reference	Author or Organisation	Title	Publisher	Frequency or date	Remarks
[QRL.121]	Department of Trade and Industry	*Business Monitor PQ215: Milk and Milk Products*	HMSO, London	Quarterly until 1980	
[QRL.122]	Department of Trade and Industry, Business Statistics Office	*Business Monitor PQ215.3: Ice-cream*	HMSO, London	Quarterly until 1982 Q4	
[QRL.123]	Department of Trade and Industry, Business Statistics Office	*Business Monitor PQ216: Sugar*	HMSO, London	Quarterly from 1973 Q1 to 1980 Q3	
[QRL.124]	Department of Trade and Industry, Business Statistics Office	*Business Monitor PQ217: Cocoa, Chocolate and Sugar Confectionery*	HMSO, London	Quarterly until 1980 Q4	
[QRL.125]	Department of Trade and Industry, Business Statistics Office	*Business Monitor PQ221: Vegetable and Animal Oils and Fats*	HMSO, London	Quarterly from 1977 Q1 to 1982 Q4	
[QRL.126]	Department of Trade and Industry, Business Statistics Office	*Business Monitor PQ229.2: Starch and Miscellaneous Foods*	HMSO, London	Quarterly from 1973 Q1 to 1982 Q4	
[QRL.127]	Department of Trade and Industry, Business Statistics Office	*Business Monitor PQ3244: Food, Drink and Tobacco Processing Machinery; Packaging and Bottling Machinery*	HMSO, London	Quarterly	
[QRL.128]	Department of Trade and Industry, Business Statistics Office	*Business Monitor PQ4115: Margarine and Compound Cooking Fats*	HMSO, London	Quarterly	Discontinued 1989
[QRL.129]	Department of Trade and Industry, Business Statistics Office	*Business Monitor PQ4116: Organic Oils and Fats*	HMSO, London	Quarterly	Discontinued 1989
[QRL.130]	Department of Trade and Industry, Business Statistics Office	*Business Monitor PQ4122: Bacon Curing and Meat Products*	HMSO, London	Quarterly	
[QRL.131]	Department of Trade and Industry, Business Statistics Office	*Business Monitor PQ4123: Poultry and Poultry Products*	HMSO, London	Quarterly	Discontinued 1989

[QRL.132]	Department of Trade and Industry, Business Statistics Office	*Business Monitor PQ4126: Animal By-products*	HMSO, London	Quarterly	Discontinued 1989
[QRL.133]	Department of Trade and Industry, Business Statistics Office	*Business Monitor PQ4147: Fruit and Vegetable Products*	HMSO, London	Quarterly	Discontinued 1989
[QRL.134]	Department of Trade and Industry, Business Statistics Office	*Business Monitor PQ4150: Fish Products*	HMSO, London	Quarterly	Discontinued 1989
[QRL.135]	Department of Trade and Industry, Business Statistics Office	*Business Monitor PQ4180: Starch*	HMSO, London	Quarterly	Discontinued 1989
[QRL.136]	Department of Trade and Industry, Business Statistics Office	*Business Monitor PQ4196: Bread and Flour Confectionery*	HMSO, London	Quarterly	Discontinued 1989
[QRL.137]	Department of Trade and Industry, Business Statistics Office	*Business Monitor PQ4197: Biscuits and Crispbread*	HMSO, London	Quarterly	Discontinued 1989
[QRL.138]	Department of Trade and Industry, Business Statistics Office	*Business Monitor PQ4213: Ice-cream*	HMSO, London	Quarterly	
[QRL.139]	Department of Trade and Industry, Business Statistics Office	*Business Monitor PQ4239: Miscellaneous Foods*	HMSO, London	Quarterly	Discontinued 1989
[QRL.140]	Business Statistics Office, Department of Trade and Industry	*Business Monitor SDA25: Retailing*	HMSO, London	Annual from 1976 to 1980	Succeeded by [QRL.143]
[QRL.141]	Business Statistics Office, Department of Trade and Industry	*Business Monitor SDA26: Wholesaling*	HMSO, London	Annual	
[QRL.142]	Department of Trade and Industry, Business Statistics Office	*Business Monitor SDA28: Catering and Allied Trades*	HMSO, London	Annual	
[QRL.143]	Business Statistics Office, Department of Trade and Industry	*Business Monitor SDO25: Retailing*	HMSO, London	Biennial since 1982	Preceded by [QRL.140]

Reference	Author or Organisation	Title	Publisher	Frequency or date	Remarks
[QRL.144]	Cadbury Ltd	*Cadbury Confectionery Market Review*	Cadbury Ltd, Birmingham	Annual	
[QRL.145]	Marketing Publications Ltd	*Campaign*	Marketing Publications Ltd, London	Weekly since September 1968	
[QRL.146]	Association of the Chocolate, Biscuit and Confectionery Industries of the EEC	*CAOBISCO: Statistical Monograph*	CAOBISCO: Brussels	Annual since 1962	
[QRL.147]	CBI Economic Trends Department	*CBI Industrial Trends Survey*	CBI, London	Quarterly	
[QRL.148]	Office of Population Censuses and Surveys	*Census 1981: Economic Activity: Great Britain*	HMSO, London	1984	
[QRL.149]	Registrar General Scotland	*Census 1981: Scotland Economic Activity (10% Sample)*	HMSO, Edinburgh	1984	
[QRL.150]	Department of Trade and Industry, Business Statistics Office	*Census of Distribution and Other Services*	HMSO, London	Occasional since 1950	Published by the Board of Trade (1950 to 1966) and then by the BSO in the Business Monitor SD series since 1971
[QRL.151]	Board of Trade	*Censuses of Production for 1950, 1949 and 1948. Summary Tables - Part 1*	HMSO, London	1953	Restricted coverage
[QRL.152]	Home-Grown Cereals Authority	*Cereals Statistics*	HGCA, London	Annual	
[QRL.153]	Department of Employment	*Changes in Rates of Wages and Hours of Work*	HMSO, London	Monthly from May 1968 to December 1982	

[QRL.154]	Monks Partnership, Charterhouse	*Charterhouse Top Management Remuneration*	Monks Partnership, Saffron Walden	Annual (October) with March supplement	
[QRL.155]	City of Birmingham Markets Department	*City of Birmingham Markets Department Report*	City of Birmingham Markets Department, Birmingham	Weekly	
[QRL.156]	Statistical Office of the United Nations	*Commodity Trade Statistics*	United Nations, New York	Annual since 1981	
[QRL.157]	Commodity Research Bureau	*Commodity Yearbook Statistical Abstract*	Commodity Research Bureau, New York	Triannual	
[QRL.158]	Department of Trade and Industry	*Companies*	HMSO, London	Annual since 1980	
[QRL.159]	National Institute of Economic and Social Research	*Company Income and Finance 1949-1953*	NIESR, London	1956	
[QRL.160]	Standard and Poor's Corporation, Compustat Services Inc	*COMPUSTAT*	Compustat Services Inc, Engelwood		Data base
[QRL.161]	Rowntree Mackintosh Confectionery	*Confectionery: Sweet Facts*	Rowntree Mackintosh Confectionery, York	Annual	
[QRL.162]	Henderson Crosthwaite	*Consumer Brief*	Henderson Crosthwaite Institutional Brokers Ltd, London	20 issues a year (usually)	
[QRL.163]	Henderson Crosthwaite	*Consumer Brief Spotlight*	Henderson Crosthwaite Institutional Brokers Ltd, London	Occasional	

Reference	Author or Organisation	Title	Publisher	Frequency or date	Remarks
[QRL.164]	Statistical Office of the European Communities	*Consumer Prices in the EC 1980*	Office for Official Publications of the European Communities, Luxembourg	1983	
[QRL.165]	Agriculture and Food Research Council	*Corporate Plan*	Agriculture and Food Research Council, Swindon	Annual	Available from AFRC
[QRL.166]	Commodity Research Bureau	*CRB Commodity Yearbook*	Commodity Research Bureau, New York	Annual since 1939	
[QRL.167]	Statistical Office of the European Communities	*Crop Production*	Office for Official Publications of the European Communities, Luxembourg	Quarterly	
[QRL.168]	Czarnikow Brokers Ltd	*The Czarnikow Sugar Review*	Czarnikow Brokers Ltd, London	Monthly since 1873	On subscription
[QRL.169]	Commodity Research Bureau	*Daily Commodity Computer Trend Analyser*	Commodity Research Bureau, New York	Daily	
[QRL.170]	Billingsgate Market	*Daily Returns of Prices of Fish*	Billingsgate Market, London	Daily	Available from the Billingsgate Market Super-intendent's Office
[QRL.171]	Home-Grown Cereals Authority	*Daily Telephone Information Service*	HGCA, London	Continuous	
[QRL.172]	Dairy Trade Federation	*The Dairy Industry*	Dairy Trade Federation, London	Annual	

[QRL.173]	Datastream International Ltd	*Datastream*	Datastream International Ltd, London		Data base
[QRL.174]	National Ports Council	*Digest of Port Statistics*	National Ports Council, London	Annual from 1966 to 1973	
[QRL.175]	Scottish Home Department	*Digest of Scottish Statistics*	HMSO, Edinburgh	Biannual from 1953 to April 1979	Succeeded by [QRL.446] and [QRL.447]
[QRL.176]	Department of Finance	*Digest of Statistics: Northern Ireland*	HMSO, Belfast	Biannual each March and September from 1954 up to March 1980	Succeeded by [QRL.377]
[QRL.177]	Welsh Office	*Digest of Welsh Statistics*	Welsh Office, Cardiff	Annual since 1954	Available direct from the Welsh Office
[QRL.178]	National Food Survey Committee, Ministry of Agriculture, Fisheries and Food	*Domestic Food Consumption and Expenditure*	HMSO, London	Annual from 1950 to 1964	Succeeded by [QRL.267]
[QRL.179]	E.D.&F Man (Coffee) Ltd	*E.D.&F Man (Coffee) Ltd: World Coffee Situation*	E.D.&F Man (Coffee) Ltd, London	Monthly	
[QRL.180]	Department of Agriculture and Fisheries for Scotland	*Economic Report on Scottish Agriculture*	HMSO, Edinburgh	Annual since 1980	Replaced [QRL.31] and *Scottish Agricultural Economics*. Results for 1979 are published in the 1980 volume
[QRL.181]	Central Statistical Office	*Economic Trends*	HMSO, London	Monthly	
[QRL.182]	Central Statistical Office	*Economic Trends: Annual Supplement*	HMSO, London	Annual	

Reference	Author or Organisation	Title	Publisher	Frequency or date	Remarks
[QRL.183]	The Economist Newspaper Ltd	*The Economist*	The Economist Newspaper, London	Weekly	
[QRL.184]	Federation of United Kingdom Milk Marketing Boards	*EEC Dairy Facts & Figures*	Federation of United Kingdom Milk Marketing Boards, Thames Ditton	Annual	
[QRL.185]	Home-Grown Cereals Authority	*EEC Marketing Arrangements for Grains and Processed Products*	HGCA, London	Continuous updating from 1985	
[QRL.186]	Department of Employment	*Employment Gazette*	HMSO, London	Monthly since January 1979	Preceded by the *Department of Employment Gazette* (Jan 1971 to Dec 1978), the *Employment and Productivity Gazette* (June 1968 to Dec 1970), the *Ministry of Labour Gazette* (June 1922 to May 1968) and the *London Gazette* (May–Dec 1893 to May 1922)
[QRL.187]	Department of Scientific and Industrial Research	*Estimates of Resources Devoted to Scientific and Engineering Research and Development in British Manufacturing Industry, 1955*	HMSO, London	1958	

[QRL.188]	Meat and Livestock Commission	*European Handbook*	MLC, Bletchley	Updated continually		
[QRL.189]	Fishery Economics Research Unit, Sea Fish Industry Authority	*European Supplies Bulletin*	SFIA, Edinburgh	Quarterly (usually)		
[QRL.190]	Meat and Livestock Commission	*European Weekly Market Survey*	MLC, Bletchley	Weekly		
[QRL.191]	Extel Financial Ltd	*Exstat*	Extel Financial Ltd, London			Data base
[QRL.192]	Extel Financial Ltd	*Extel Financial UK Listed Companies Service: Extel UK Quoted*	Extel Financial Ltd, London	Updated daily		
[QRL.193]	Extel Financial Ltd	*Extel Financial Unlisted Securities Market Service: Extel UK Unlisted Securities Market*	Extel Financial Ltd, London	Updated twice weekly		
[QRL.194]	Extel Financial Ltd	*Extel Financial Unquoted Companies Service: Extel UK Unquoted*	Extel Financial Ltd, London	Updated weekly		
[QRL.195]	Statistical Office of the European Communities	*External Trade: Monthly Statistics*	Office for Official Publications of the European Communities, Luxembourg	Monthly		
[QRL.196]	Statistical Office of the European Communities	*External Trade Analytical Tables*	Office for Official Publications of the European Communities, Luxembourg	Annual		Preceded by [QRL.35]
[QRL.197]	F.O. Licht	*F.O. Licht's International Coffee Report*	F.O. Licht, Ratzeburg	Bi-monthly (24 times a year)		
[QRL.198]	F.O. Licht	*F.O. Licht's International Molasses and Alcohol Report*	F.O. Licht, Ratzeburg	Usually 24 issues a year	On subscription	
[QRL.199]	F.O. Licht	*F.O. Licht's International Sugar Report*	F.O. Licht, Ratzeburg	Usually 36 issues a year, or every 10 days		
[QRL.200]	F.O. Licht	*F.O. Licht's World Sugar Statistics (Supplement to International Sugar Economics Yearbook and Directory)*	F.O. Licht, Ratzeburg	Annual	On subscription	

Reference	Author or Organisation	Title	Publisher	Frequency or date	Remarks
[QRL.201]	Labour Research Department	*Fact Service*	Labour Research Department, London	Weekly	
[QRL.202]	National Association of British and Irish Millers	*Facts and Figures*	NABIM, London	Annual	
[QRL.203]	Statistical Office of the European Communities	*Family Budgets: Comparative Tables: Germany, France, Italy, United Kingdom*	Office for Official Publications of the European Communities, Luxembourg	1984	Compiled from harmonized national surveys
[QRL.204]	Department of Employment	*Family Expenditure Survey*	HMSO, London	Annual	1957-1959 and 1960-1961 are covered together. Earlier data can be found in [QRL.405]. From 1990 entitled *Family Spending*
[QRL.205]	Food and Agricultural Organisation of the United Nations	*FAO Monthly Bulletin of Statistics*	FAO, Rome	Monthly until 1988	Succeeded by [QRL.206]
[QRL.206]	Food and Agricultural Organisation of the United Nations	*FAO Quarterly Bulletin of Statistics*	FAO, Rome	Quarterly since 1989	Preceded by [QRL.205] from 1978 to 1988
[QRL.207]	Food and Agricultural Organisation of the United Nations	*FAO Trade Commerce*	FAO, Rome	Annual	Preceded by *FAO Trade Yearbook* (1976 to 1986)

[QRL.208]	Food and Agriculture Organisation of the United Nations	*FAO Yearbook: Fishery Statistics: Catches and Landings*	FAO, Rome	Annual	Available from HMSO
[QRL.209]	Food and Agriculture Organisation of the United Nations	*FAO Yearbook: Fishery Statistics: Commodities*	FAO, Rome	Annual	Available from HMSO
[QRL.210]	Ministry of Agriculture, Fisheries and Food	*Farm Incomes in the United Kingdom*	HMSO, London	Annual	
[QRL.211]	Welsh Office	*Farm Incomes in Wales*	Welsh Office, Cardiff	Annual since 1987	Preceded by *Farm Accounts in Wales*
[QRL.212]	Reed Business Publishing	*Farmers Weekly*	Reed Business Publishing, Haywards Heath	Weekly	
[QRL.213]	Board of Trade	*Final Report of the Third Census of Production of the United Kingdom (1924)*	HMSO, London	1931	Five volumes. Includes Second Census of Production 1912. Parliamentary paper
[QRL.214]	Board of Trade	*Final Report on the Census of Production for 1948*	HMSO, London	1952	Five volumes
[QRL.215]	Board of Trade	*Final Report on the Fifth Census of Production and the Import Duties Act Inquiry 1935*	HMSO, London	1938	Three volumes. Parliamentary paper
[QRL.216]	Board of Trade	*Final Report on the Fourth Census of Production (1930)*	HMSO, London	1933	Five volumes. Parliamentary paper
[QRL.217]	Central Statistical Office	*Financial Statistics*	HMSO, London	Monthly	
[QRL.218]	Financial Times Ltd	*Financial Times*	Financial Times Ltd, London	Daily	
[QRL.219]	Board of Trade, Labour Department	*First Census of Production of the United Kingdom (1907)*	HMSO, London	1913	Extracted from the Parliamentary Paper Cd6320

Reference	Author or Organisation	Title	Publisher	Frequency or date	Remarks
[QRL.220]	Ross Foods Ltd	*Fish: The Ross Report*	Ross Foods Ltd, Grimsby	1984	Succeeded by [QRL.242]
[QRL.221]	Ministry of Agriculture, Fisheries and Food, Department of Agriculture and Fisheries for Scotland	*Fish Stock Record*	HMSO, London	Occasional	
[QRL.222]	FMJ International Publications	*Fish Trader*	FMJ International Publications Ltd, Redhill	Weekly	Preceded by the *Fish Trades Gazette*, established in 1883
[QRL.223]	Statistical Office of the European Communities	*Fisheries: Catches by Region*	Office for Official Publications of the European Communities, Luxembourg	Annual until 1983	Succeeded by [QRL.225]
[QRL.224]	Statistical Office of the European Communities	*Fisheries: Fishery Products and Fishing Fleet*	Office for Official Publications of the European Communities, Luxembourg	Annual until 1983	Succeeded by [QRL.225]
[QRL.225]	Statistical Office of the European Communities	*Fisheries Statistical Yearbook*	Office for Official Publications of the European Communities, Luxembourg	Annual since 1984	Available from HMSO. Entitled the *Yearbook of Fishery Statistics* before 1986. Replaced the two annual volumes [QRL.223] and [QRL.224]

[QRL.226]	National Marine Fisheries Service	*Fishery Market News Report*	National Marine Fisheries Service, Boston	Daily	Sometimes known as the "Boston Blue Sheet"
[QRL.227]	AGB Heighway Ltd	*Fishing News*	AGB Heighway Ltd, London	Weekly	
[QRL.228]	Potato Marketing Board	*A Flow Chart for Potatoes in Great Britain*	Potato Marketing Board, Oxford		A leaflet. Available from Potato Marketing Board (Statistics Department)
[QRL.229]	County NatWest WoodMac	*Focus on Food Manufacturing*	County NatWest Securities Ltd, London	Quarterly	
[QRL.230]	Food and Agriculture Organisation of the United Nations	*Food Aid Bulletin*	FAO, Rome	Occasional	
[QRL.231]	Food and Agriculture Organisation of the United Nations	*Food Aid in Figures*	FAO, Rome	Annual since 1983	
[QRL.232]	National Economic Development Office	*Food and Drink Statistics Data Bank*	National Economic Development Office, London	Annual	Ceased publication in 1988
[QRL.233]	Institute of Grocery Distribution	*Food Company Performances*	IGD, Letchmore Heath	Annual	Preceded by *Companies in the Food Industry. Volume II: Performance*

Reference	Author or Organisation	Title	Publisher	Frequency or date	Remarks
[QRL.234]	Institute of Grocery Distribution	*Food Company Profiles*	IGD, Letchmore Heath	Occasional	Preceded by *Companies in the Food Industry. Volume I: Profiles*
[QRL.235]	Food from Britain	*Food Focus Volumes I and II*	Food from Britain, London	Annual	Formerly entitled (1986) *British Food Facts and Figures*
[QRL.236]	Industry Forecasts Ltd	*The Food Forecast*	Industry Forecasts Ltd, Henley-on-Thames	Quarterly	
[QRL.237]	Institute of Grocery Distribution	*The Food Industry Statistics Digest*	Institute of Grocery Distribution, Letchmore Heath	Updated monthly	
[QRL.238]	Leatherhead Food Research Association	*Food Market Updates*	Leatherhead Food Research Association, Leatherhead	Twice monthly	
[QRL.239]	Food and Agricultural Organisation of the United Nations	*Food Outlook*	FAO, Rome	Monthly	
[QRL.240]	The Advertising Association, Media Expenditure Analysis Ltd	*Forecast of Advertising Expenditure*	The Advertising Association, London	Quarterly	
[QRL.241]	ICC Information Group Ltd	*Foreign-owned Company Performance in the UK*	ICC Information Group Ltd, London	1987	

[QRL.242]	Ross Foods Ltd	*Frozen Food Consumer Market Bulletin*	Ross Foods Ltd, Grimsby	1985	Preceded by [QRL.220]. Succeeded by [QRL.243]
[QRL.243]	Ross Foods Ltd	*Frozen Food Retail Market Report*	Ross Foods Ltd, Grimsby	1986	Preceded by [QRL.242]
[QRL.244]	Birds Eye	*Frozen Foods: Birds Eye Report*	Birds Eye Wall's Ltd, Walton-on-Thames	Annual (usually)	Preceded by the *Frozen Foods Annual Report*
[QRL.245]	Commonwealth Secretariat	*Fruit and Tropical Products*	Commonwealth Secretariat, London	Biannual since December 1978	
[QRL.246]	Lockwood Press Ltd	*Fruit Trades Journal*	Lockwood Press Ltd, London	Weekly	
[QRL.247]	General Foods Corporation	*General Foods Corporation: Annual Report Fiscal*	General Foods Corporation, New York	Annual	
[QRL.248]	Commission of the European Communities	*General Report on the Activities of the European Communities*	Office for Official Publications of the European Communities, Luxembourg	Annual since 1967	Early reports identify the European Coal and Steel Community, the European Economic Community and the European Atomic Energy Authority as "responsible bodies"
[QRL.249]	Gill & Duffus plc	*Gill & Duffus: Cocoa Market Report*	Gill & Duffus Group plc, London	Usually three times a year	

Reference	Author or Organisation	Title	Publisher	Frequency or date	Remarks
[QRL.250]	Gill & Duffus plc	*Gill & Duffus: Cocoa Statistics*	Gill & Duffus Group plc, London	Occasional	Merged with [QRL.249] since 1990
[QRL.251]	Gill & Duffus plc	*Gill & Duffus: Sugar Market Report*	Gill & Duffus Group plc, London	Usually 6 times a year	Discontinued September 1989
[QRL.252]	William Reed Ltd	*The Grocer*	William Reed Ltd, London	Weekly	
[QRL.253]	William Reed Ltd	*The Grocer Price List*	William Reed Ltd, London	Monthly	Issued with [QRL.252] on the first Saturday of each month. Preceded by *The Grocer Buff List*
[QRL.254]	Grower Publications	*Grower*	Grower Publications, London	Weekly	
[QRL.255]	Hemmington Scott Publishing Ltd	*The Hambro Company Guide*	Hemmington Scott Publishing Ltd, London	Quarterly	
[QRL.256]	Extel Financial Ltd	*Handbook of Market Leaders*	Extel Financial Ltd, London	Biannual	
[QRL.257]	Hay Management Consultants	*Hay Remuneration Comparison*	Hay Management Consultants, London	Annual with quarterly updates	
[QRL.258]	Hay Management Consultants	*Hay Survey of Employee Benefits*	Hay Management Consultants, London	Annual	
[QRL.259]	Health and Safety Executive	*Health and Safety at Work: Report by HM Chief Inspector of Factories*	HMSO, London	Annual since 1985	

[QRL.260]	Health and Safety Commission	*Health and Safety Commission Report*	HMSO, London	Annual since 1974	
[QRL.261]	Health and Safety Executive	*Health and Safety Statistics*	HMSO, London	Annual since 1975	
[QRL.262]	Herring Industry Board	*Herring Industry Board: Annual Report and Accounts*	Herring Industry Board, Edinburgh	Annual from 1936 to 1981	Published by HMSO as a Cmnd paper up to 1971. The Herring Industry Board has now merged with the White Fish Authority to form the Sea Fish Industry Authority
[QRL.263]	Potato Marketing Board	*Historical Data Summary*	Potato Marketing Board, Oxford	Annual	A leaflet. Available from Potato Marketing Board (Statistics Department)
[QRL.264]	Business Statistics Office	*Historical Record of the Census of Production 1907 to 1970*	HMSO, London	1978	Out of print. Available at BSO Library, Newport
[QRL.265]	Department of Agriculture for Northern Ireland, Economics and Statistics Division	*Horticultural Market Report*	DANI, Belfast	Weekly since March 1988	Preceded by *Agricultural Market Report 1*. Available from DANI Economics and Statistics Division

Reference	Author or Organisation	Title	Publisher	Frequency or date	Remarks
[QRL.266]	Attwood Statistics for Sea Fish Industry Authority	*Household Fish Consumption in Great Britain*	SFIA, Edinburgh	Quarterly (usually)	
[QRL.267]	National Food Survey Committee, Ministry of Agriculture, Fisheries and Food	*Household Food Consumption and Expenditure: Annual Report of the National Food Survey Committee*	HMSO, London	Annual since 1965	From 1985 to be consulted with [QRL.373]. Preceded by [QRL.178] between 1954 and 1964, and other titles
[QRL.268]	ICC Information Group Ltd	*ICC Company Information Data base*	ICC Information Group, London		Data base
[QRL.269]	Landell Mills Commodity Studies Ltd, International Commodities Clearing House Ltd	*ICCH Commodities and Financial Futures Yearbook*	Landell Mills Commodities Studies Ltd, Oxford	1982	
[QRL.270]	Lyons Maid Ltd	*Ice-cream in the '80s*	Lyons Maid Ltd, Greenford	Annual from 1982 to 1984, then occasional	
[QRL.271]	Incomes Data Services Ltd	*IDS Report*	Incomes Data Services Ltd, London	Twice monthly	
[QRL.272]	Incomes Data Services Ltd	*IDS Study*	Incomes Data Services Ltd, London	Twice monthly	
[QRL.273]	ICC Information Group Ltd	*Industrial Performance Analysis: A Financial Analysis of UK Industry and Commerce*	ICC Information Group Ltd, London	Annual	

[QRL.274]	Statistical Office of the European Communities	*Industrial Production: Quarterly Statistics*	Office for Official Publications of the European Communities, Luxembourg	Quarterly	Previously entitled the *Quarterly Bulletin of Industrial Production*, which succeeded the annual *Industrial Production*
[QRL.275]	Industrial Relations Services	*Industrial Relations Review and Report*	Eclipse Publications, London	Twice monthly	
[QRL.276]	Department of Scientific and Industrial Research	*Industrial Research and Development Expenditure 1958*	HMSO, London	1960	
[QRL.277]	Health and Safety Executive	*Industries and Services*	HMSO, London	1977	Sole issue containing data for 1975
[QRL.278]	Board of Inland Revenue	*Inland Revenue Statistics*	HMSO, London	Annual since 1970	
[QRL.279]	Ministry of Finance	*Input-output Tables for Northern Ireland: 1963*	HMSO, Belfast	1973	
[QRL.280]	The Fraser of Allander Institute; Scottish Council (Development and Industry); IBM UK Science Centre	*Input-output Tables for Scotland: 1973*	Scottish Academic Press, Edinburgh and London	1978	
[QRL.281]	Central Statistical Office	*Input-output Tables for the United Kingdom 1954 Studies in Official Statistics no.8*	HMSO, London	1961	
[QRL.282]	Central Statistical Office	*Input-output Tables for the United Kingdom 1963 Studies in Official Statistics no.16*	HMSO, London	1970	
[QRL.283]	Central Statistical office	*Input-output Tables for the United Kingdom 1968 Studies in Official Statistics no.22*	HMSO, London	1973	

Reference	Author or Organisation	Title	Publisher	Frequency or date	Remarks
[QRL.284]	Central Statistical Office	*Input-output Tables for the United Kingdom 1984*	HMSO, London	1988	
[QRL.285]	Business Statistics Office	*Inquiry into Sales of Industry 1985: Introductory Notes and Results Tables for the 1985 Topping-up Inquiry into Product Sales in Selected Manufacturing Industries*	BSO, Newport	1985	Available from the Library at the BSO
[QRL.286]	Department of Trade and Industry	*Insolvency General Annual Report*	HMSO, London	Annual since 1987	Preceded by [QRL.59]
[QRL.287]	The Advertising Association	*International Journal of Advertising*	Cassell, London	Quarterly since January-March 1983	Preceded by [QRL.297]
[QRL.288]	Meat and Livestock Commission	*International Market Review*	MLC, Bletchley	Biannual	Succeeded by [QRL.289]
[QRL.289]	Meat and Livestock Commission	*International Meat Market Review*	MLC, Bletchley	Biannual	Preceded by [QRL.288]
[QRL.290]	The International Stock Exchange of the United Kingdom	*The International Stock Exchange Official Yearbook*	Macmillan, London	Annual	Preceded by *The Stock Exchange Official Yearbook* until 1986/87
[QRL.291]	General Agreement on Tariffs and Trade	*International Trade*	GATT, Geneva	Annual	
[QRL.292]	Statistical Office of the United Nations	*International Trade Statistics Yearbook*	United Nations, New York	Annual since 1986	Preceded by *Yearbook of International Trade Statistics*
[QRL.293]	Intervention Board for Agricultural Produce	*Intervention Board for Agricultural Produce: Annual Report*	HMSO, London	Annual since 1973	Command paper. Has appeared under various titles

[QRL.294]	International Office of Cocoa, Chocolate and Sugar Confectinery	*IOCCC: Statistical Bulletin*	IOCCC, Brussels	Annual	
[QRL.295]	Isle of Man Government	*Isle of Man Digest of Economic and Social Statistics*	Isle of Man Government, Douglas	Occasional	
[QRL.296]	Jordan & Sons Ltd	*Jordan Watch*	Jordan & Sons Ltd, London		Data base
[QRL.297]	The Advertising Association	*Journal of Advertising*	Holt, Rinehart and Winston, Eastbourne	Quarterly from January-March 1982 to October-December 1982	Preceded by [QRL.17]. Succeeded by [QRL.287]
[QRL.298]	The Milk Marketing Board of England and Wales	*Key Milk Figures in England and Wales*	Milk Marketing Board of England and Wales, Thames Ditton	Annual	
[QRL.299]	The Milk Marketing Board for Northern Ireland	*Key Milk Figures in Northern Ireland*	Milk Marketing Board for Northern Ireland, Belfast	Annual	
[QRL.300]	The Three Milk Marketing Boards in Scotland	*Key Milk Figures in Scotland*	The Scottish Milk Marketing Board, Paisley	Annual	
[QRL.301]	Reed Information Services in association with the Confederation of British Industry	*Kompass: Register of British Industry and Commerce. Volumes I to IV*	Kompass Publishers, East Grinstead	Annual since 1962	
[QRL.302]	KP Foods	*KP Snack Foods Review*	KP Foods, Middlesex	Annual	KP Foods is a division of United Biscuits (UK) Ltd
[QRL.303]	Le Fonds d'Intervention et de Regularisation du Marché du Sucre	*La Campagne Sucrière*	FIRS, Paris	Annual	

Reference	Author or Organisation	Title	Publisher	Frequency or date	Remarks
[QRL.304]	Statistical Office of the European Communities	*Labour Costs*	Office for Official Publications of the European Communities, Luxembourg		Microfiche
[QRL.305]	Statistical Office of the European Communities	*Labour Costs. Volume 1: Principal Results; Volume 2: Results by Size Classes and by Regions*	Office for Official Publications of the European Communities, Luxembourg	Triennial	Results available for 1978, 1981, 1984, and 1987. From 1988, survey became quadrennial
[QRL.306]	Department of Employment	*Labour Costs in Great Britain 1968*	HMSO, London	1971	
[QRL.307]	Department of Employment and Productivity	*Labour Costs in Great Britain in 1964*	HMSO, London	1968	
[QRL.308]	Statistical Office of the European Communities	*Labour Costs in Industry 1972-1975* 4 volumes	Office for Official Publications of the European Communities, Luxembourg	1977	
[QRL.309]	Office of Population Censuses and Surveys	*Labour Force Survey*	HMSO, London	Annual since 1983	Biennial before 1983
[QRL.310]	Statistical Office of the European Communities	*Labour Force Survey: Results*	Office for Official Publications of the European Communities, Luxembourg	Annual since 1984	Previously the *Labour Force Sample Survey* 1973-83
[QRL.311]	Landell Mills Commodities Studies Ltd	*LMC Commodity Bulletin: Cocoa*	Landell Mills Commodities Studies Ltd, Oxford	Monthly	

[QRL.312]	Landell Mills Commodities Studies Ltd	*LMC Commodity Bulletin: Coffee*	Landell Mills Commodities Studies Ltd, Oxford	Monthly	
[QRL.313]	Landell Mills Commodities Studies Ltd	*LMC Commodity Bulletin: Sugar*	Landell Mills Commodities Studies Ltd, Oxford	Monthly	
[QRL.314]	Macmillan Publishers Ltd	*Macmillan's Unquoted Companies*	Macmillan Publishers Ltd, Basingstoke	Annual	First edition (1985); second edition (1986/87)
[QRL.315]	Ministry of Agriculture, Fisheries and Food	*MAFF Statistics: Agricultural Price Indices*	MAFF, London	Monthly	
[QRL.316]	Ministry of Agriculture, Fisheries and Food	*MAFF Statistics: Agricultural Returns: England, Wales, Regions and Counties*	MAFF, London	Annual	
[QRL.317]	Ministry of Agriculture, Fisheries and Food	*MAFF Statistics: Agricultural Returns for the United Kingdom*	MAFF, London	Annual	
[QRL.318]	Ministry of Agriculture, Fisheries and Food	*MAFF Statistics: Cereal Stocks Survey*	MAFF, London	Quarterly	
[QRL.319]	Ministry of Agriculture, Fisheries and Food	*MAFF Statistics: Food Facts*	MAFF, London		Specific results on National Food Survey. Available quarterly on application to MAFF
[QRL.320]	Ministry of Agriculture, Fisheries and Food	*MAFF Statistics: Hatching Eggs and Placings by Hatcheries in the United Kingdom*	MAFF, London	Monthly	
[QRL.321]	Ministry of Agriculture, Fisheries and Food	*MAFF Statistics: Margarine, Other Table Spreads and Solid Cooking Fat Produced in the United Kingdom and the Refined Oils and Animals Fats Used in Their Production*	MAFF, London	Monthly	

Reference	Author or Organisation	Title	Publisher	Frequency or date	Remarks
[QRL.322]	Ministry of Agriculture, Fisheries and Food	*MAFF Statistics: Oilseeds and Nuts Crushed, Crude Vegetable Oils, Oilcake and Meal Produced in the United Kingdom*	MAFF, London	Quarterly	
[QRL.323]	Ministry of Agriculture, Fisheries and Food	*MAFF Statistics: Potato Crisp and Snack Foods Survey*	MAFF, London	Quarterly	
[QRL.324]	Ministry of Agriculture, Fisheries and Food	*MAFF Statistics: Pre-packed and Other Dressed Poultry — Packing Station Throughput of Chickens, Large Roasting Fowls and Boiling Fowls*	MAFF, London	Quarterly	
[QRL.325]	Ministry of Agriculture, Fisheries and Food	*MAFF Statistics: Production of Canned and Bottled Fruit and Vegetables in the UK*	MAFF, London	Quarterly	Available from MAFF, Branch B, Statistics (Agricultural Commodities) Division
[QRL.326]	Ministry of Agriculture, Fisheries and Food	*MAFF Statistics: Production of Compounds and Other Processed Feedingstuffs in Great Britain*	MAFF, London	Monthly	
[QRL.327]	Ministry of Agriculture, Fisheries and Food	*MAFF Statistics: Production of Processed Milk in the United Kingdom*	MAFF, London	Quarterly	
[QRL.328]	Ministry of Agriculture, Fisheries and Food	*MAFF Statistics: Production of Refined, Deodorised Vegetable, Marine Oils and Animal Fats in the United Kingdom*	MAFF, London	Monthly	
[QRL.329]	Ministry of Agriculture, Fisheries and Food	*MAFF Statistics: Prospective Arrival Dates of Vessels Carrying Carcase Meat and Offal from Australia, New Zealand and South America*	MAFF, London	Weekly	

[QRL.330]	Ministry of Agriculture, Fisheries and Food	*MAFF Statistics: Quarterly Supplies and Offtake in the United Kingdom - Meat*	MAFF, London	Quarterly
[QRL.331]	Ministry of Agriculture, Fisheries and Food	*MAFF Statistics: Returns from Manufacturers of Regular Coffee, Coffee Essences and Extracts*	MAFF, London	Quarterly
[QRL.332]	Ministry of Agriculture, Fisheries and Food	*MAFF Statistics: Returns of Cocoa Beans and Cocoa Products*	MAFF, London	Annual
[QRL.333]	Ministry of Agriculture, Fisheries and Food	*MAFF Statistics: Sample Survey into the Composition of Main Compound Feed Rations*	MAFF, London	Every six months
[QRL.334]	Ministry of Agriculture, Fisheries and Food	*MAFF Statistics: Stocks of Raw Coffee in Public Warehouses*	MAFF, London	Quarterly
[QRL.335]	Ministry of Agriculture, Fisheries and Food	*MAFF Statistics: Stocks of Selected Dairy Products, Meat and Meat Products, Poultry, Game, Soft Fruit and Vegetables in Public Cold Stores*	MAFF, London	Monthly
[QRL.336]	Ministry of Agriculture, Fisheries and Food	*MAFF Statistics: Summary of Returns Made by Bacon Factories in Great Britain*	MAFF, London	Weekly
[QRL.337]	Ministry of Agriculture, Fisheries and Food	*MAFF Statistics: United Kingdom Weekly Slaughtering Statistics*	MAFF, London	Weekly
[QRL.338]	Health and Safety Executive	*Manufacturing and Service Industries Report*	HMSO, London	Annual from 1976 to 1984
[QRL.339]	Mintel Publications Ltd	*Market Intelligence*	Mintel Publications Ltd, London	Monthly
[QRL.340]	Meat and Livestock Commission	*Market Outlook - Cattle*	MLC, Bletchley	Quarterly
[QRL.341]	Meat and Livestock Commission	*Market Outlook - Pigs*	MLC, Bletchley	Quarterly
[QRL.342]	Meat and Livestock Commission	*Market Outlook - Sheep*	MLC, Bletchley	Three times a year
[QRL.343]	Euromonitor Publications Ltd	*Market Research: Great Britain*	Euromonitor Publications Ltd, London	Monthly

Reference	Author or Organisation	Title	Publisher	Frequency or date	Remarks
[QRL.344]	International Commodities Clearing House Ltd	*Market Turnover Statistics*	International Commodities Clearing House Ltd, London	Monthly	
[QRL.345]	Home-Grown Cereals Authority	*Marketing Note*	HGCA, London	Weekly	
[QRL.346]	The Advertising Association	*Marketing Pocket Book*	The Advertising Association, London	Annual since 1989	Published biennially (usually) by Young and Rubicam (1962-1979), then by The Advertising Association (1982, 1984, 1986 and 1988)
[QRL.347]	McCarthy Information Ltd	*McCarthy UK Quoted*	McCarthy Information Ltd, Warminster	Daily	
[QRL.348]	McCarthy Information Ltd	*McCarthy UK Unquoted*	McCarthy Information Ltd, Warminster	Weekly	
[QRL.349]	Commonwealth Secretariat	*Meat and Dairy Products*	Commonwealth Secretariat, London	Biannual	
[QRL.350]	Meat and Livestock Commission	*Meat and Marketing Technical Notes*	MLC, Bletchley	Three times a year	
[QRL.351]	Meat and Livestock Commission	*Meat Demand Trends*	MLC, Bletchley	Three times a year	

[QRL.352]	Livestock Marketing Commission for Northern Ireland	*Meat Retailer*	Livestock Marketing Commission for Northern Ireland, Belfast	Monthly
[QRL.353]	Northwood Publications Ltd	*Meat Trades Journal*	Northwood Publications, London	Weekly
[QRL.354]	The Media Register	*The Media Register Monthly Summary*	The Media Register, London	Monthly
[QRL.355]	The Scottish Milk Marketing Board	*Milk Bulletin*	The Scottish Milk Marketing Board, Paisley	Monthly
[QRL.356]	Beecham Bovril Brands	*Milk Food Drinks: Market Report*	Beecham Bovril Brands, Middlesex	Annual
[QRL.357]	The Aberdeen and District Milk Marketing Board	*Milk News*	The Aberdeen and District Milk Marketing Board, Aberdeen	Monthly
[QRL.358]	The Milk Marketing Board of England and Wales	*Milk Producer*	The Milk Marketing Board of England and Wales, Thames Ditton	Monthly
[QRL.359]	Agra Europe (London) Ltd	*Milk Products*	Agra Europe (London) Ltd, Tunbridge Wells	Ten times a year
[QRL.360]	The North of Scotland Milk Marketing Board	*Milk Topics*	The North of Scotland Milk Marketing Board, Inverness	Monthly
[QRL.361]	Monks Partnership	*Monks Guide to Board and Senior Management in Companies up to £20m Turnover*	Monks Partnership, Saffron Walden	Annual
[QRL.362]	Central Statistical Office	*Monthly Digest of Statistics*	HMSO, London	Monthly

Reference	Author or Organisation	Title	Publisher	Frequency or date	Remarks
[QRL.363]	Ministry of Agriculture, Fisheries and Food	*Monthly Return of Sea Fisheries Statistics: England and Wales*	MAFF, London	Monthly	Available from MAFF Fisheries Statistics Unit
[QRL.364]	Department of Trade and Industry	*Monthly Review of External Trade Statistics*	DTI, London	Monthly	Suspended December 1987 but likely to be reinstated. Contact DTI for details
[QRL.365]	Department of Trade and Industry	*Monthly Review of External Trade Statistics: Annual Supplement*	DTI, London	Annual	See also [QRL.366]
[QRL.366]	Department of Trade and Industry	*Monthly Review of External Trade Statistics: Mid-year Supplement*	DTI, London		See also [QRL.365]
[QRL.367]	International Tea Committee Ltd	*Monthly Statistical Summary*	International Tea Committee, London	Monthly since 1955	Past data from 1936 under different titles
[QRL.368]	Department of Agriculture and Fisheries for Scotland	*Monthly Summary of Sea Fisheries Statistics*	DAFS, Edinburgh	Monthly	Available from FESU
[QRL.369]	Statistical Office of the European Communities	*National Accounts ESA: Aggregates*	Office for Official Publications of the European Communities, Luxembourg	Annual	Provides data for a number of years. The 1987 edition covers 1970-1986
[QRL.370]	Statistical Office of the European Communities	*National Accounts ESA: Detailed Tables by Branch*	Office for Official Publications of the European Communities, Luxembourg	Irregular	Has covered 1970-1987, 1970-1986, 1960-1985 and 1955-1965

[QRL.371]	Statistical Office of the European Communities	*National Accounts ESA: Input-output Tables*	Office for Official Publications of the European Communities, Luxembourg	Irregular	The 1980 edition was published in 1986 and the 1977 edition was published in 1983
[QRL.372]	Nestlé	*National Drinks Survey*	Nestlé, Croydon	Annual since 1966	Available from Marketing Research Department, Nestlé
[QRL.373]	National Food Survey Committee, Ministry of Agriculture, Fisheries and Food	*National Food Survey: Compendium of Results*	MAFF, London	Annual since 1985	Available from National Food Survey Branch, MAFF
[QRL.374]	Central Statistical Office	*National Income and Expenditure*	HMSO, London	Annual until 1983	Succeeded by [QRL.506]
[QRL.375]	Department of Employment	*New Earnings Survey*	HMSO, London	Annual	In six parts
[QRL.376]	Department of Agriculture for Northern Ireland	*Northern Ireland Agriculture*	HMSO, Belfast	Annual	
[QRL.377]	Policy, Planning and Research Unit, Department of Finance and Personnel	*Northern Ireland Annual Abstract of Statistics*	Policy Planning and Research Unit, Belfast	Annual since 1982	Available direct from the Policy, Planning and Research Unit
[QRL.378]	Department of Health and Social Services, Registrar General Northern Ireland	*The Northern Ireland Census 1981: Economic Activity Report*	HMSO, Belfast	1983	
[QRL.379]	Intervention Board for Agricultural Produce	*Notice to Traders*	Intervention Board for Agricultural Produce, Reading	Occasional	
[QRL.380]	ISTA Mielke GmbH	*Oil World*	ISTA Mielke GmbH, Hamburg	Weekly	
[QRL.381]	ISTA Mielke GmbH	*Oil World Statistics Update*	ISTA Mielke GmbH, Hamburg	Continuous update	

Reference	Author or Organisation	Title	Publisher	Frequency or date	Remarks
[QRL.382]	Ministry of Agriculture, Fisheries and Food	*Output and Utilisation of Farm Produce in the United Kingdom*	HMSO, London	Annual	Discontinued 1988. Some data now appear in *Agriculture in the United Kingdom*
[QRL.383]	Department of Transport, British Ports Federation	*Port Statistics*	Department of Transport, British Ports Federation, London	Annual since 1981	
[QRL.384]	Potato Marketing Board	*Potato Marketing Board: Annual Report and Accounts*	Potato Marketing Board, London	Annual	
[QRL.385]	Potato Marketing Board	*Potato Processing in Great Britain*	Potato Marketing Board, Oxford	Annual	Available from Potato Marketing Board (Statistics Department)
[QRL.386]	Potato Marketing Board	*Potato Statistics Bulletin*	Potato Marketing Board, Oxford	Annual	A leaflet. Available from Potato Marketing Board (Statistics Department)
[QRL.387]	Potato Marketing Board	*Potato Statistics in Great Britain*	Potato Marketing Board, Oxford	Annual	Available from Potato Marketing Board (Statistics Department)

[QRL.388]	Agra Europe (London) Ltd	*Preserved Milk*	Agra Europe (London) Ltd, Tunbridge Wells	Monthly	
[QRL.389]	Home-Grown Cereals Authority	*Press Notice*	HGCA, London	Weekly	
[QRL.390]	Central Statistical Office	*Price Index Numbers for Current Cost Accounting*	HMSO, London	Triannual from April 1976 to April 1980	Final issues in April 1980 and April 1981. Succeeded by [QRL.84]
[QRL.391]	Commodities Division of the Research Department, International Monetary Fund	*Primary Commodities: Market Developments and Outlook*	IMF, Washington	Occasional	
[QRL.392]	Turret-Wheatland Ltd, Commodity Division	*The Public Ledger & Daily Freight Register*	Turret-Wheatland Ltd, Watford	Daily since 12 January 1760	
[QRL.393]	Turret-Wheatland Ltd, Commodity Division	*The Public Ledger Commodity Yearbook*	Turret-Wheatland Ltd, Watford	Annual since 1982	
[QRL.394]	Turret-Wheatland Ltd, Commodity Division	*The Public Ledger's Commodity Week*	Turret-Wheatland Ltd, Watford	Saturdays with [QRL.392]	
[QRL.395]	Statistical Office of the European Communities	*Quantity and Value of Landings in the EC*	Office for Official Publications of the European Communities, Luxembourg	Quarterly	
[QRL.396]	Department of Agriculture for Northern Ireland, Economics and Statistics Division	*Quarterly Agricultural Market Report*	DANI, Belfast	Quarterly	Available from DANI Economics and Statistics Division
[QRL.397]	International Cocoa Organisation	*Quarterly Bulletin of Cocoa Statistics*	ICCO, London	Quarterly	
[QRL.398]	International Coffee Organisation	*Quarterly Statistical Bulletin*	ICO, London	Quarterly since 1982	Restricted information from middle 1988. Preceded by [QRL.399]

Reference	Author or Organisation	Title	Publisher	Frequency or date	Remarks
[QRL.399]	International Coffee Organisation (ICO)	*Quarterly Statistical Bulletin on Coffee*	ICO, London	Quarterly from 1971 to 1982	Succeeded by [QRL.398]
[QRL.400]	The Advertising Association, Media Expenditure Analysis Ltd	*Quarterly Survey of Advertising Expenditure*	The Advertising Association, London	Quarterly since April 1987	Preceded by *Quarterly Review of Advertising Expenditure* (June 1984 - January 1987)
[QRL.401]	Central Statistical Office	*Regional Trends*	HMSO, London	Annual since 1981	Preceded by *Regional Statistics* (1979-80) and by the *Abstract of Regional Statistics* (1965-1979)
[QRL.402]	Remuneration Economics Ltd	*Remuneration Economics: Survey of Financial Functions*	Remuneration Economics Ltd, Kingston-upon-Thames	Annual	
[QRL.403]	Hillsdown Holdings plc	*Report and Accounts*	Hillsdown Holdings, London	Annual	
[QRL.404]	Transport and General Workers Union	*Report and Accounts*	TGWU, London	Annual	
[QRL.405]	Ministry of Labour and National Service	*Report of an Enquiry into Household Expenditure 1953-1954*	HMSO, London	1957	

[QRL.406]	Registry of Friendly Societies	*Report of the Chief Registrar*	HMSO, London	Annual since 1979	Preceded by the *Report of the Chief Registrar of Friendly Societies* and [QRL.407]
[QRL.407]	Registry of Trade Unions and Employers' Associations	*Report of the Chief Registrar of Trade Unions and Employers' Associations*	HMSO, London	Annual from 1971 to 1973	
[QRL.408]	Her Majesty's Customs and Excise	*Report of the Commissioners of Her Majesty's Customs and Excise for the Year Ended*	HMSO, London	Annual since 1909	Command paper
[QRL.409]	Department of Economic Development	*Report of the Registrar of Friendly Societies: Northern Ireland*	HMSO, Belfast	Annual since 1922	
[QRL.410]	Commission of the European Communities	*Report on Competition Policy*	Office for Official Publications of the European Communities, Luxembourg	Annual since 1972	Published in conjunction with [QRL.248]
[QRL.411]	Ministry of Agriculture, Fisheries and Food	*Report on Crops and Supplies of Fruit and Vegetables in England and Wales*	MAFF, London	Monthly until April 1988	Available from MAFF, Branch B, Statistics (Agricultural Commodities) Division
[QRL.412]	Ministry of Agriculture, Fisheries and Food	*Report on Crops and Supplies of Fruit in England and Wales*	MAFF, London	Monthly since April 1988	Available from MAFF, Branch B, Statistics (Agricultural Commodities) Division

Reference	Author or Organisation	Title	Publisher	Frequency or date	Remarks
[QRL.413]	Ministry of Agriculture, Fisheries and Food	*Report on Crops and Supplies of Vegetables in England and Wales*	MAFF, London	Monthly since April 1988	Available from MAFF, Branch B, Statistics (Agricultural Commodities) Division
[QRL.414]	Taylor Nelson & Associates	*Report on Family Food Panel*	Taylor Nelson & Associates, Epsom	Biannual	
[QRL.415]	Ministry of Agriculture, Fisheries and Food	*Report on Research and Development*	MAFF, London	Annual	
[QRL.416]	Department of Agriculture for Northern Ireland	*Report on the Agricultural Statistics of Northern Ireland*	HMSO, Belfast	Occasional	
[QRL.417]	Board of Trade	*Report on the Census of Production 1963*	HMSO, London	1970	Three volumes plus summary tables
[QRL.418]	Department of Trade and Industry, Business Statistics Office	*Report on the Census of Production 1968*	HMSO, London	1973	Four volumes
[QRL.419]	Department of Economic Development, Northern Ireland	*Report on the Census of Production and Construction in Northern Ireland*	HMSO, Belfast	Annual	
[QRL.420]	Board of Trade	*The Report on the Census of Production for 1949*	HMSO, London	1952	One volume
[QRL.421]	Board of Trade	*The Report on the Census of Production for 1950*	HMSO, London	1953	One volume
[QRL.422]	Board of Trade	*The Report on the Census of Production for 1951*	HMSO, London	1955	Twelve volumes plus summary tables

[QRL.423]	Board of Trade	*The Report on the Census of Production for 1954*	HMSO, London	1957	Twelve volumes plus summary tables
[QRL.424]	Board of Trade	*The Report on the Census of Production for 1958*	HMSO, London	1960-61	Three volumes
[QRL.425]	Department of Trade and Industry, Business Statistics Office	*Report on the Censuses of Production 1974 and 1975*	HMSO, London	1978	Slimline inquiry
[QRL.426]	Board of Trade	*The Report on the Censuses of Production for 1952 and 1953*	HMSO, London	1956	Slimline inquiry
[QRL.427]	Board of Trade	*The Report on the Censuses of Production for 1959, 1960, 1961 and 1962*	HMSO, London	1964	Slimline inquiry
[QRL.428]	Department of Trade and Industry	*The Report on the Censuses of Production for 1964, 1965, 1966 and 1967*	HMSO, London	1971	Slimline inquiry
[QRL.429]	Department of Agriculture for Northern Ireland	*Report on the Sea and Inland Fisheries of Northern Ireland*	HMSO, Belfast	Annual since 1922	
[QRL.430]	Central Statistical Office	*Research and Development: Expenditure and Employment Studies in Official Statistics no.27*	HMSO, London	1976	
[QRL.431]	Central Statistical Office	*Research and Development Expenditure Studies in Official Statistics no.21*	HMSO, London	1973	
[QRL.432]	Economist Intelligence Unit	*Retail Business*	Economist Intelligence Unit, London	Monthly	
[QRL.433]	Chivers Hartley	*The Retail Market for Jam and Marmalade*	Chivers Hartley, Cambridge	1986	Available from the Sales Information Executive, Chivers Hartley
[QRL.434]	Department of Employment	*Retail Prices: Indices 1914-1986*	HMSO, London	1987	
[QRL.435]	Reuters Ltd	*The Reuter Cocoa Newsletter*	Reuters Ltd, London	Daily	

Reference	Author or Organisation	Title	Publisher	Frequency or date	Remarks
[QRL.436]	Reuters Ltd	*The Reuter Coffee Newsletter*	Reuters Ltd, London	Daily	Formerly available on subscription. From 1990 on data base
[QRL.437]	Reuters Ltd	*The Reuter Sugar Newsletter*	Reuters Ltd, London	Daily	Formerly available on subscription. From 1990 on data base
[QRL.438]	Organisation for Economic Cooperation and Development	*Review of Fisheries in OECD Member Countries*	OECD, Paris	Annual	Available from HMSO
[QRL.439]	British Chicken Information Service	*Review of the British Retail Chicken Market*	British Chicken Information Service, London	Annual	
[QRL.440]	The Reward Group	*Reward: The Management Salary Survey*	The Reward Group, Stone	Biannual in March and September since September 1987	Preceded by the *Reward Salary and Living Cost Report*. May be consulted in the Library at the Department of Employment.
[QRL.441]	Rowntree plc	*Rowntree plc: Annual Report and Accounts*	Rowntree, York	Annual	
[QRL.442]	S&W Berisford plc	*S&W Berisford plc: Report and Accounts*	S&W Berisford, London	Annual	
[QRL.443]	Monks Partnership	*Sales and Marketing Remuneration in Fast Moving Consumer Goods*	Monks Partnership, Saffron Walden	Annual until 1988	

[QRL.444]	Department of Agriculture and Fisheries for Scotland	*Salmon and Trout Farming in Scotland: Report of DAFS Annual Survey*	DAFS, Edinburgh	Annual since 1979	Available from DAFS, Fisheries Economics and Statistics Unit
[QRL.445]	Jordan & Sons Ltd	*Scotland's Top 500 Companies*	Jordan & Sons Ltd, London	Annual	
[QRL.446]	Scottish Office	*Scottish Abstract of Statistics*	HMSO, Edinburgh	Annual since 1971	Together with [QRL.447], it replaced [QRL.175]
[QRL.447]	Scottish Office	*Scottish Economic Bulletin*	HMSO, Edinburgh	Biannual since 1971	Together with [QRL.446], it replaced [QRL.175]
[QRL.448]	Scottish Office	*Scottish Input-output Tables for 1979. Volumes 1-4*	Economics and Statistics Unit of the Industry Department for Scotland, Edinburgh	1984	
[QRL.449]	Department of Agriculture and Fisheries for Scotland (Fisheries Economics and Statistics Unit)	*Scottish Sea Fisheries Statistical Tables*	Government Statistical Service, Edinburgh	Annual since 1923	
[QRL.450]	Sea Fish Industry Authority	*Sea Fish Diary*	SFIA, Edinburgh	Annual	
[QRL.451]	Ministry of Agriculture, Fisheries and Food	*Sea Fisheries Statistical Tables*	HMSO, London	Annual since 1886	
[QRL.452]	Jordan & Sons Ltd	*The Second 2000 Britain's Privately Owned Companies*	Jordan & Sons Ltd, London	Annual	
[QRL.453]	Shaws Price Guides Ltd	*Shaws Guide to Fair Retail Prices*	Shaws Price Guides Ltd, Abingdon	Monthly	
[QRL.454]	Meat and Livestock Commission	*The Slaughtering Industry in Great Britain*	MLC, Bletchley	Biennial	

Reference	Author or Organisation	Title	Publisher	Frequency or date	Remarks
[QRL.455]	Department of Health and Social Security	*Social Security Statistics*	HMSO, London	Annual since 1972	1980 issue incorporates data for 1979
[QRL.456]	Central Statistical Office	*Social Trends*	HMSO, London	Annual since 1970	
[QRL.457]	British Ports Association	*Statistical Abstract of the UK Ports Industry*	British Ports Association, London	Annual	Discontinued
[QRL.458]	British Ports Association	*Statistical Abstract of the UK Ports Industry*	British Ports Association, London	Quarterly	Discontinued
[QRL.459]	International Sugar Organization	*Statistical Bulletin*	International Sugar Organization, London	Monthly since 1937	UK coverage to 1972
[QRL.460]	Department of Agriculture for Northern Ireland, Economics and Statistics Division	*Statistical Review of Northern Ireland Agriculture*	DANI, Belfast	Annual since 1973/74	
[QRL.461]	The Biscuit, Cake, Chocolate and Confectionery Alliance	*Statistical Year Book*	BCCCA, London	Annual since 1986	Available on subscription from the BCCCA
[QRL.462]	National Institute of Economic and Social Research	*Statistics of Advertising*	NIESR, London	1946	
[QRL.463]	Department of Education and Science, Ministry of Technology	*Statistics of Science and Technology*	HMSO, London	Annual	Three issues (1967, 1968 and 1970)
[QRL.464]	Ministry of Labour, Department of Employment and Productivity	*Statistics on Incomes, Prices, Employment and Production*	HMSO, London	Quarterly from April 1962 to June 1969	

[QRL.465]	The Tea Brokers' Association of London	*Stocks and Tea Movements*	The Tea Brokers' Association of London, London	Weekly (every Friday)	
[QRL.466]	Statistical Office of the European Communities	*Structure and Activity of Industry: Data by Regions*	Office for Official Publications of the European Communities, Luxembourg	Occasional	
[QRL.467]	Statistical Office of the European Communities	*Structure and Activity of Industry: Data by Size of Enterprises*	Statistical Office of the European Communities, Luxembourg	Annual	
[QRL.468]	Statistical Office of the European Communities	*Structure and Activity of Industry: Main Results*	Office for Official Publications of the European Communities, Luxembourg	Annual since 1979/80	
[QRL.469]	National Food Survey Committee, Ministry of Agriculture, Fisheries and Food	*Studies in Urban Household Diets 1944-1949: The 2nd Report of the National Food Survey Committee*	HMSO, London	1956	
[QRL.470]	Ministry of Agriculture, Fisheries and Food	*Sugar and Beet Prices*	MAFF, London	Annual	Available from MAFF (Sugar, Oils and Fats Division)
[QRL.471]	Sugar Board	*Sugar Board*	HMSO, London	Annual from 1956 to 1976	
[QRL.472]	E.D.&F. Man (Sugar) Ltd	*The Sugar Situation*	E.D.&F. Man (Sugar) Ltd, London	Monthly	On subscription
[QRL.473]	International Sugar Organization	*Sugar Year Book*	International Sugar Organization, London	Annual since 1946	UK coverage to 1972

Reference	Author or Organisation	Title	Publisher	Frequency or date	Remarks
[QRL.474]	International Tea Committee Ltd	*Supplement to Annual Bulletin of Statistics*	International Tea Committee, London	Annual since 1987	Entitled *Annual Bulletin of Statistics Supplementary Tables* (1984-86)
[QRL.475]	Fishery Economics Research Unit, Sea Fish Industry Authority	*Supplies Bulletin: United Kingdom Supplies and Prices of Fish and Fish Products*	SFIA, Edinburgh	Quarterly (usually) until 1987	Available from SFIA
[QRL.476]	Hewitt Associates	*Survey of Executive Compensation Among Consumer Packaged Goods Companies in the United Kingdom*	Hewitt Associates, St. Albans	Occasional (usually annual)	
[QRL.477]	Hewitt Associates	*Survey of Remuneration in Levels of Senior UK Managers and Headquarters and Operating Unit Levels*	Hewitt Associates, St. Albans	Occasional (usually annual)	
[QRL.478]	Salary Research, P/ E Inbucon Ltd	*Survey of UK Executive Salaries and Benefits*	P/E Inbucon Ltd, Egham	Annual since 1962	
[QRL.479]	Tate & Lyle	*Tate & Lyle: Annual Report*	Tate & Lyle, London	Annual	
[QRL.480]	The Tea Brokers' Association of London	*Tea Market Report*	The Tea Brokers' Association of London, London	Weekly (every Friday)	
[QRL.481]	J. Thomas & Co Private Ltd	*Tea Statistics Year*	J. Thomas & Co Private Ltd, Calcutta	Annual	
[QRL.482]	Media Expenditure Analysis Ltd	*Ten Year Trends: A Summary of Display Advertising Expenditures*	Media Expenditure Analysis Ltd, London	Annual since 1973	

[QRL.483]	Department of Employment (Statistics A1)	*Time Rates of Wages and Hours of Work*	Department of Employment, Watford	Monthly since January 1983	A loose leaf folder available from Statistics A1 which has replaced both [QRL.153] and [QRL.484]
[QRL.484]	Department of Employment	*Time Rates of Wages and Hours of Work*	HMSO, London	Annual from 1946 to 1982	Entitled *Time Rates of Wages and Hours of Labour* from 1946 to 1959
[QRL.485]	Department of Employment (Statistics A1)	*Time Rates of Wages and Hours of Work*	Department of Employment, Watford	Annual	Derived from monthly publication [QRL.483], and continues the annual series previously found in [QRL.484]
[QRL.486]	Times Books Ltd	*Times 1000*	Times Books Ltd, London	Annual since 1970-71	Preceded by the *Times 300* (1966-1967) and the *Times 500* (1968-1971)
[QRL.487]	Jordan & Sons Ltd	*The Top 2000 Britain's Privately Owned Companies*	Jordan & Sons Ltd, London	Annual	
[QRL.488]	Media Expenditure Analysis Ltd	*Top Spenders*	Media Expenditure Analysis Ltd, London	Annual	
[QRL.489]	The International Stock Exchange	*TOPIC*	Datastream International Ltd, London		Data base

Reference	Author or Organisation	Title	Publisher	Frequency or date	Remarks
[QRL.490]	The Milk Marketing Board for Northern Ireland	*Topics*	The Milk Marketing Board for Northern Ireland, Belfast	Monthly	
[QRL.491]	Sea Fish Industry Authority	*Trade Bulletin: United Kingdom Imports and Exports of Fish and Fish Products*	SFIA, Edinburgh	Monthly	
[QRL.492]	Meat and Livestock Commission	*Trading Outlook for Meat Retailers*	MLC, Bletchley	Biannual	
[QRL.493]	Media Expenditure Analysis Ltd	*Tri-Media Digest of Brands and Advertisers*	Media Expenditure Analysis Ltd, London	Quarterly since 1968	
[QRL.494]	Department of Trade and Industry	*UK External Trade: Area x Commodity Analysis*	Department of Trade and Industry, London	Quarterly from December 1984	Preceded by [QRL.508]
[QRL.495]	General, Municipal and Boilermakers' Union	*UK Food and Drink Industry Wages and Conditions Survey*	GMB, Esher	Annual	
[QRL.496]	Food From Britain	*UK Food and Drink Trade Statistics*	Food from Britain, London	Monthly	
[QRL.497]	Barclays de Zoete Wedd Research	*UK Food Manufacturing Weekly Review*	Barclays de Zoete Wedd, London	Occasional	
[QRL.498]	Meat and Livestock Commission	*UK Market Review*	MLC, Bletchley	Biannual	
[QRL.499]	Meat and Livestock Commission	*UK Weekly Market Survey*	MLC, Bletchley	Weekly	
[QRL.500]	ELC International	*UK's 10000 Largest Companies*	ELC International, London	Annual since 1985	
[QRL.501]	Unilever plc	*Unilever Annual Report*	Unilever, London	Annual	
[QRL.502]	Central Statistical Office	*United Kingdom Balance of Payments*	HMSO, London	Annual since 1946	Known as the CSO "Pink Book"

[QRL.503]	The Federation of United Kingdom Milk Marketing Boards	*United Kingdom Dairy Facts & Figures*	The Federation of United Kingdom Milk Marketing Boards, Thames Ditton	Annual since 1963	Available from the Head Office of each area Milk Marketing Board
[QRL.504]	Food from Britain	*United Kingdom Food and Drink Exports: Priority Markets*	Food from Britain, London	Annual	
[QRL.505]	Food from Britain	*United Kingdom Food and Drink Trade: Annual Statistics*	Food from Britain, London	Annual	
[QRL.506]	Central Statistical Office	*United Kingdom National Accounts*	HMSO, London	Annual since 1984	Preceded by [QRL.374]
[QRL.507]	Scrimgeour Vickers & Co	*United Kingdom Research: Food Manufacturing Monthly*	Scrimgeour Vickers & Co, London	Occasional	
[QRL.508]	Department of Trade and Industry	*United Kingdom Trade with European Countries*	Department of Trade and Industry, London	Quarterly until March 1985	Succeeded by [QRL.494]
[QRL.509]	National Food Survey Committee, Ministry of Food	*Urban Working-class Household Diet 1940-1949*	HMSO, London	1951	
[QRL.510]	Birds Eye Wall's Ltd	*Wall's Report*	Birds Eye Wall's Ltd, Walton- on-Thames	Annual	
[QRL.511]	Department of Agriculture and Fisheries for Scotland, Economics and Statistics Unit	*Weekly Agricultural Market Report*	DAFS, Edinburgh	Weekly	
[QRL.512]	Home-Grown Cereals Authority	*Weekly Bulletin*	HGCA, London	Weekly	
[QRL.513]	Home-Grown Cereals Authority	*Weekly Digest*	HGCA, London	Weekly	
[QRL.514]	International Coffee Organisation	*Weekly Report on Prices*	International Coffee Organisation, London	Weekly (Thursday)	
[QRL.515]	Welsh Office	*Welsh Agricultural Statistics*	Welsh Office, Cardiff	Annual since 1979	

Reference	Author or Organisation	Title	Publisher	Frequency or date	Remarks
[QRL.516]	Welsh Office	*Welsh Agricultural Statistics Supplement*	Welsh Office, Cardiff	Occasional	Issued as supplement to [QRL.515]
[QRL.517]	Welsh Office	*Welsh Economic Trends*	Welsh Office, Cardiff	Annual since 1974	Available direct from the Welsh Office
[QRL.518]	White Fish Authority	*White Fish Authority: Annual Report and Accounts*	White Fish Authority, Edinburgh	Annual from 1952 to 1981	The White Fish Authority has now merged with the Herring Industry Board to form the Sea Fish Industry Authority
[QRL.519]	Woodhouse, Drake and Carey Ltd	*Woodhouse, Drake and Carey (Commodities) Ltd*	Woodhouse, Drake and Carey Ltd, London	Weekly	Discontinued
[QRL.520]	Economist Intelligence Unit	*World Commodity Outlook: Food, Feedstuffs and Beverages*	Economist Intelligence Unit, London	Annual	
[QRL.521]	F.O. Licht	*World Sugar Balances* Supplement with F.O. Licht's *International Sugar Report*	F.O. Licht, Ratzeburg	Irregular - three or four issues a year	
[QRL.522]	E.D.&F. Man (Sugar) Ltd	*World Sugar Situation and Outlook*	E.D.&F. Man (Sugar) Ltd, London	3 times a year	

Reports by Market Research Organisations
(Listed alphabetically by name of organisation and then by title).
See also references [QRL.238], [QRL.339], [QRL.343] and [QRL.432] which also refer to market research reports.

[QRL.523]	Euromonitor Publications Ltd	*The Bakery Products Report*	Euromonitor Publications Ltd, London	Occasional
[QRL.524]	Euromonitor Publications Ltd	*Catering Equipment in the UK*	Euromonitor Publications Ltd, London	Occasional
[QRL.525]	Euromonitor Publications Ltd	*Chilled Foods and Ready Meals*	Euromonitor Publications Ltd, London	Occasional
[QRL.526]	Euromonitor Publications Ltd	*The Convenience Food Report*	Euromonitor Publications Ltd, London	Occasional
[QRL.527]	Euromonitor Publications Ltd	*The Convenience and Prepared Foods Report*	Euromonitor Publications Ltd, London	Occasional
[QRL.528]	Euromonitor Publications Ltd	*The Dairy Products Report*	Euromonitor Publications Ltd, London	Occasional
[QRL.529]	Euromonitor Publications Ltd	*Delicatessen Foods in the UK*	Euromonitor Publications Ltd, London	Occasional
[QRL.530]	Euromonitor Publications Ltd	*The Euromonitor Food Report*	Euromonitor Publications Ltd, London	Occasional
[QRL.531]	Euromonitor Publications Ltd	*The Fish and Fish Products Report*	Euromonitor Publications Ltd, London	Occasional
[QRL.532]	Euromonitor Publications Ltd	*Food Multiples in the UK*	Euromonitor Publications Ltd, London	Occasional

Reference	Author or Organisation	Title	Publisher	Frequency or date	Remarks
[QRL.533]	Euromonitor Publications Ltd	*Food Specialists*	Euromonitor Publications Ltd, London	Occasional	
[QRL.534]	Euromonitor Publications Ltd	*The Fruit and Vegetables Report*	Euromonitor Publications Ltd, London	Occasional	
[QRL.535]	Euromonitor Publications Ltd	*Healthy Foods and Healthy Eating*	Euromonitor Publications Ltd, London	Occasional	
[QRL.536]	Euromonitor Publications Ltd	*The Hot Drinks Report*	Euromonitor Publications Ltd, London	Occasional	
[QRL.537]	Euromonitor Publications Ltd	*Hypermarkets and Superstores Retailing in the UK*	Euromonitor Publications Ltd, London	Occasional	
[QRL.538]	Euromonitor Publications Ltd	*The Meat and Poultry Report*	Euromonitor Publications Ltd, London	Occasional	
[QRL.539]	Euromonitor Publications Ltd	*The Slimming Foods Report*	Euromonitor Publications Ltd, London	Occasional	
[QRL.540]	Euromonitor Publications Ltd	*The Snack Foods Report*	Euromonitor Publications Ltd, London	Occasional	
[QRL.541]	Euromonitor Publications Ltd	*Specialist Food Retailing in the UK*	Euromonitor Publications Ltd, London	Occasional	
[QRL.542]	Euromonitor Publications Ltd	*Specialist Health Foods in the United Kingdom*	Euromonitor Publications Ltd, London	Occasional	
[QRL.543]	Euromonitor Publications Ltd	*Specialist Health, Slimming and Dietetic Foods*	Euromonitor Publications Ltd, London	Occasional	

[QRL.544]	ICC Information Group Ltd	*Bakeries*	ICC Information Group Ltd, London	Annual
[QRL.545]	ICC Information Group Ltd	*Cash & Carry*	ICC Information Group Ltd, London	Annual
[QRL.546]	ICC Information Group Ltd	*The Catering Industry*	ICC Information Group Ltd, London	Annual
[QRL.547]	ICC Information Group Ltd	*Compound Animal Feed Stuffs*	ICC Information Group Ltd, London	Annual
[QRL.548]	ICC Information Group Ltd	*Confectionery Manufacturers*	ICC Information Group Ltd, London	Annual
[QRL.549]	ICC Information Group Ltd	*Dairy Products*	ICC Information Group Ltd, London	Annual
[QRL.550]	ICC Information Group Ltd	*Food Ingredients*	ICC Information Group Ltd, London	Annual
[QRL.551]	ICC Information Group Ltd	*Food Processors (Intermediate)*	ICC Information Group Ltd, London	Annual
[QRL.552]	ICC Information Group Ltd	*Food Processors (Major)*	ICC Information Group Ltd, London	Annual
[QRL.553]	ICC Information Group Ltd	*Frozen Food Distributors*	ICC Information Group Ltd, London	Annual
[QRL.554]	ICC Information Group Ltd	*Frozen Food Producers*	ICC Information Group Ltd, London	Annual
[QRL.555]	ICC Information Group Ltd	*Fruit and Flower Wholesalers*	ICC Information Group Ltd, London	Annual

Reference	Author or Organisation	Title	Publisher	Frequency or date	Remarks
[QRL.556]	ICC Information Group Ltd	*Fruit, Flower & Vegetable Merchants*	ICC Information Group Ltd, London	Annual	
[QRL.557]	ICC Information Group Ltd	*Grocery Wholesalers*	ICC Information Group Ltd, London	Annual	
[QRL.558]	ICC Information Group Ltd	*Horticulture: Growers & Gardeners*	ICC Information Group Ltd, London	Annual	
[QRL.559]	ICC Information Group Ltd	*Meat Processors*	ICC Information Group Ltd, London	Annual	
[QRL.560]	ICC Information Group Ltd	*Meat Wholesalers*	ICC Information Group Ltd, London	Annual	
[QRL.561]	ICC Information Group Ltd	*Pet Foods*	ICC Information Group Ltd, London	Annual	
[QRL.562]	ICC Information Group Ltd	*Poultry Processors*	ICC Information Group Ltd, London	Annual	
[QRL.563]	ICC Information Group Ltd	*Supermarkets*	ICC Information Group Ltd, London	Annual	
[QRL.564]	ICC Information Group Ltd	*Agricultural Growers & Merchants - London/South*	ICC Information Group Ltd, London	Occasional	
[QRL.565]	ICC Information Group Ltd	*Agricultural Growers & Merchants - Midlands/North*	ICC Information Group Ltd, London	Occasional	
[QRL.566]	ICC Information Group Ltd	*Animal & Pet Food Manufacturers and Distributors*	ICC Information Group Ltd, London	Occasional	

[QRL.567]	ICC Information Group Ltd	*Bakery Products Manufacturers*	ICC Information Group Ltd, London	Occasional
[QRL.568]	ICC Information Group Ltd	*Confectionery & Ice-cream Manufacturers*	ICC Information Group Ltd, London	Occasional
[QRL.569]	ICC Information Group Ltd	*Fish Trawling, Processing and Merchanting*	ICC Information Group Ltd, London	Occasional
[QRL.570]	ICC Information Group Ltd	*Food Processors - England and Wales*	ICC Information Group Ltd, London	Occasional
[QRL.571]	ICC Information Group Ltd	*Food Processors - Scotland*	ICC Information Group Ltd, London	Occasional
[QRL.572]	ICC Information Group Ltd	*Frozen Food Processors, Distributors and Centres*	ICC Information Group Ltd, London	Occasional
[QRL.573]	ICC Information Group Ltd	*Fruit, Flower & Vegetable Merchants - London/South*	ICC Information Group Ltd, London	Occasional
[QRL.574]	ICC Information Group Ltd	*Fruit, Flower & Vegetable Merchants - Midlands/North*	ICC Information Group Ltd, London	Occasional
[QRL.575]	ICC Information Group Ltd	*Grocery Wholesalers & Supermarkets*	ICC Information Group Ltd, London	Occasional
[QRL.576]	ICC Information Group Ltd	*Horticultural Growers & Merchants*	ICC Information Group Ltd, London	Occasional
[QRL.577]	ICC Information Group Ltd	*Meat, Egg & Poultry Processors*	ICC Information Group Ltd, London	Occasional
[QRL.578]	ICC Information Group Ltd	*Meat & Poultry - Scotland*	ICC Information Group Ltd, London	Occasional

Reference	Author or Organisation	Title	Publisher	Frequency or date	Remarks
[QRL.579]	ICC Information Group Ltd,	*Tobacco & Confectionery Wholesalers*	ICC Information Group Ltd, London	Occasional	
[QRL.580]	Key Note Publications Ltd	*Bread Bakers*	Key Note Publications Ltd, London	Occasional	
[QRL.581]	Key Note Publications Ltd	*Breakfast Cereals*	Key Note Publications Ltd, London	Occasional	
[QRL.582]	Key Note Publications Ltd	*Canned Foods*	Key Note Publications Ltd, London	Occasional	
[QRL.583]	Key Note Publications Ltd	*Confectionery*	Key Note Publications Ltd, London	Occasional	
[QRL.584]	Key Note Publications Ltd	*Contract Catering*	Key Note Publications Ltd, London	Occasional	
[QRL.585]	Key Note Publications Ltd	*Ethnic Foods*	Key Note Publications Ltd, London	Occasional	
[QRL.586]	Key Note Publications Ltd	*Fast Food Outlets*	Key Note Publications Ltd, London	Occasional	
[QRL.587]	Key Note Publications Ltd	*Flour Confectionery*	Key Note Publications Ltd, London	Occasional	
[QRL.588]	Key Note Publications Ltd	*Food Flavourings & Ingredients*	Key Note Publications Ltd, London	Occasional	
[QRL.589]	Key Note Publications Ltd	*Frozen Foods*	Key Note Publications Ltd, London	Occasional	

[QRL.590]	Key Note Publications Ltd	*Fruit & Vegetables*	Key Note Publications Ltd, London	Occasional
[QRL.591]	Key Note Publications Ltd	*Health Foods*	Key Note Publications Ltd, London	Occasional
[QRL.592]	Key Note Publications Ltd	*Hot Drinks*	Key Note Publications Ltd, London	Occasional
[QRL.593]	Key Note Publications Ltd	*Meat & Meat Products*	Key Note Publications Ltd, London	Occasional
[QRL.594]	Key Note Publications Ltd	*Milk & Dairy Products*	Key Note Publications Ltd, London	Occasional
[QRL.595]	Key Note Publications Ltd	*Pet Foods*	Key Note Publications Ltd, London	Occasional
[QRL.596]	Key Note Publications Ltd	*Slimming Products*	Key Note Publications Ltd, London	Occasional
[QRL.597]	Key Note Publications Ltd	*Sauces & Spreads*	Key Note Publications Ltd, London	Occasional
[QRL.598]	Key Note Publications Ltd	*Snack Foods*	Key Note Publications Ltd, London	Occasional
[QRL.599]	Key Note Publications Ltd	*Sugar*	Key Note Publications Ltd, London	Occasional
[QRL.600]	Market Assessment Publications Ltd	*Bakery & Cereal Products*	Market Assessment Publications Ltd, London	Annual

Reference	Author or Organisation	Title	Publisher	Frequency or date	Remarks
[QRL.601]	Market Assessment Publications Ltd	*Canned Foods*	Market Assessment Publications Ltd, London	Annual	
[QRL.602]	Market Assessment Publications Ltd	*Chilled Foods*	Market Assessment Publications Ltd, London	Annual	
[QRL.603]	Market Assessment Publications Ltd	*Confectionery*	Market Assessment Publications Ltd, London	Annual	
[QRL.604]	Market Assessment Publications Ltd	*Dairy Products*	Market Assessment Publications Ltd, London	Annual	
[QRL.605]	Market Assessment Publications Ltd	*Dressings & Sauces*	Market Assessment Publications Ltd, London	Annual	
[QRL.606]	Market Assessment Publications Ltd	*Fish & Fish Products*	Market Assessment Publications Ltd, London	Annual	
[QRL.607]	Market Assessment Publications Ltd	*Frozen Foods*	Market Assessment Publications Ltd, London	Annual	
[QRL.608]	Market Assessment Publications Ltd	*Fruit & Vegetables*	Market Assessment Publications Ltd, London	Annual	

[QRL.609]	Market Assessment Publications Ltd	*Health & Diet Foods*	Market Assessment Publications Ltd, London	Annual
[QRL.610]	Market Assessment Publications Ltd	*Hot Drinks*	Market Assessment Publications Ltd, London	Annual
[QRL.611]	Market Assessment Publications Ltd	*Meat & Meat Products*	Market Assessment Publications Ltd, London	Annual
[QRL.612]	Market Assessment Publications Ltd	*Pet Products*	Market Assessment Publications Ltd, London	Annual
[QRL.613]	Market Assessment Publications Ltd	*Seasonings & Flavourings*	Market Assessment Publications Ltd, London	Annual
[QRL.614]	Market Assessment Publications Ltd	*Snack Foods*	Market Assessment Publications Ltd, London	Annual
[QRL.615]	Market Assessment Publications Ltd	*Sweet & Savoury Spreads*	Market Assessment Publications Ltd, London	Annual
[QRL.616]	Market Assessment Publications Ltd	*Sweets & Desserts*	Market Assessment Publications Ltd, London	Annual
[QRL.617]	Marketing Strategies for Industry (UK) Ltd	*Animal Foods*	Marketing Strategies for Industry (UK) Ltd, Mitcham	Annual

Reference	Author or Organisation	Title	Publisher	Frequency or date	Remarks
[QRL.618]	Marketing Strategies for Industry (UK) Ltd	*Baby Products*	Marketing Strategies for Industry (UK) Ltd, Mitcham	Occasional	
[QRL.619]	Marketing Strategies for Industry (UK) Ltd	*Bag Snacks*	Marketing Strategies for Industry (UK) Ltd, Mitcham	Occasional	
[QRL.620]	Marketing Strategies for Industry (UK) Ltd	*Biscuits*	Marketing Strategies for Industry (UK) Ltd, Mitcham	Occasional	
[QRL.621]	Marketing Strategies for Industry (UK) Ltd	*Breakfast Cereals*	Marketing Strategies for Industry (UK) Ltd, Mitcham	Occasional	
[QRL.622]	Marketing Strategies for Industry (UK) Ltd	*Cakes and Pastries*	Marketing Strategies for Industry (UK) Ltd, Mitcham	Occasional	
[QRL.623]	Marketing Strategies for Industry (UK) Ltd	*Canned Foods*	Marketing Strategies for Industry (UK) Ltd, Mitcham	Occasional	
[QRL.624]	Marketing Strategies for Industry (UK) Ltd	*Catering*	Marketing Strategies for Industry (UK) Ltd, Mitcham	Occasional	
[QRL.625]	Marketing Strategies for Industry (UK) Ltd	*Cereal Bars*	Marketing Strategies for Industry (UK) Ltd, Mitcham	Occasional	

[QRL.626]	Marketing Strategies for Industry (UK) Ltd	*Cheese*	Marketing Strategies for Industry (UK) Ltd, Mitcham	Occasional
[QRL.627]	Marketing Strategies for Industry (UK) Ltd	*Chocolate Confectionery*	Marketing Strategies for Industry (UK) Ltd, Mitcham	Occasional
[QRL.628]	Marketing Strategies for Industry (UK) Ltd.	*Convenience Stores*	Marketing Strategies for Industry (UK) Ltd, Mitcham	Occasional
[QRL.629]	Marketing Strategies for Industry (UK) Ltd	*Cooking Additives*	Marketing Strategies for Industry (UK) Ltd, Mitcham	Occasional
[QRL.630]	Marketing Strategies for Industry (UK) Ltd	*Delicatessen Foods*	Marketing Strategies for Industry (UK) Ltd, Mitcham	Occasional
[QRL.631]	Marketing Strategies for Industry (UK) Ltd	*Delivered Grocery Wholesaling*	Marketing Strategies for Industry (UK) Ltd, Mitcham	Occasional
[QRL.632]	Marketing Strategies for Industry (UK) Ltd	*Ethnic Foods*	Marketing Strategies for Industry (UK) Ltd, Mitcham	Occasional
[QRL.633]	Marketing Strategies for Industry (UK) Ltd	*Fast Food*	Marketing Strategies for Industry (UK) Ltd, Mitcham	Occasional
[QRL.634]	Marketing Strategies for Industry (UK) Ltd	*Fish and Fish Products*	Marketing Strategies for Industry (UK) Ltd, Mitcham	Occasional

Reference	Author or Organisation	Title	Publisher	Frequency or date	Remarks
[QRL.635]	Marketing Strategies for Industry (UK) Ltd	*Fish Retailing*	Marketing Strategies for Industry (UK) Ltd, Mitcham	Occasional	
[QRL.636]	Marketing Strategies for Industry (UK) Ltd	*Freezer Centres*	Marketing Strategies for Industry (UK) Ltd, Mitcham	Occasional	
[QRL.637]	Marketing Strategies for Industry (UK) Ltd	*Frozen Food*	Marketing Strategies for Industry (UK) Ltd, Mitcham	Occasional	
[QRL.638]	Marketing Strategies for Industry (UK) Ltd	*Fruit and Vegetables*	Marketing Strategies for Industry (UK) Ltd, Mitcham	Occasional	
[QRL.639]	Marketing Strategies for Industry (UK) Ltd	*Fruit Juices*	Marketing Strategies for Industry (UK) Ltd, Mitcham	Occasional	
[QRL.640]	Marketing Strategies for Industry (UK) Ltd	*Fruit*	Marketing Strategies for Industry (UK) Ltd, Mitcham	Occasional	
[QRL.641]	Marketing Strategies for Industry (UK) Ltd	*Hot Beverages*	Marketing Strategies for Industry (UK) Ltd, Mitcham	Occasional	
[QRL.642]	Marketing Strategies for Industry (UK) Ltd	*Meat and Meat Products, UK*	Marketing Strategies for Industry (UK) Ltd, Mitcham	Occasional	

[QRL.643]	Marketing Strategies for Industry (UK) Ltd	*Pasta and Pasta Products*	Marketing Strategies for Industry (UK) Ltd, Mitcham	Occasional
[QRL.644]	Marketing Strategies for Industry (UK) Ltd	*Pet Foods*	Marketing Strategies for Industry (UK) Ltd, Mitcham	Occasional
[QRL.645]	Marketing Strategies for Industry (UK) Ltd	*Preserved Milk*	Marketing Strategies for Industry (UK) Ltd, Mitcham	Occasional
[QRL.646]	Marketing Strategies for Industry (UK) Ltd	*Ready Meals, a Market Opportunity for Food Producers and Packaging Companies*	Marketing Strategies for Industry (UK) Ltd, Mitcham	Occasional
[QRL.647]	Marketing Strategies for Industry (UK) Ltd	*Sauces and Pickles*	Marketing Strategies for Industry (UK) Ltd, Mitcham	Occasional
[QRL.648]	Marketing Strategies for Industry (UK) Ltd	*Short Life Dairy Products*	Marketing Strategies for Industry (UK) Ltd, Mitcham	Occasional
[QRL.649]	Marketing Strategies for Industry (UK) Ltd	*Snack Foods*	Marketing Strategies for Industry (UK) Ltd, Mitcham	Occasional
[QRL.650]	Marketing Strategies for Industry (UK) Ltd	*Sugar Confectionery*	Marketing Strategies for Industry (UK) Ltd, Mitcham	Occasional
[QRL.651]	Marketing Strategies for Industry (UK) Ltd	*Sweet and Savoury Spreads*	Marketing Strategies for Industry (UK) Ltd, Mitcham	Occasional

Reference	Author or Organisation	Title	Publisher	Frequency or date	Remarks
[QRL.652]	Marketing Strategies for Industry (UK) Ltd.	*Vegetables*	Marketing Strategies for Industry (UK) Ltd, Mitcham	Occasional	
[QRL.653]	Marketing Strategies for Industry (UK) Ltd	*Yellow Fats*	Marketing Strategies for Industry (UK) Ltd, Mitcham	Occasional	

BIBLIOGRAPHY

(Arranged alphabetically by author for named authors first and then alphabetically by title except for reports of the National Board for Prices and Incomes, the Price Commissions and the Monopolies and Mergers Commission: these are grouped together *separately* at the end).

[B.1] Aitken, A. *Fish Handling and Processing*. second edition. Torry Research Station, Aberdeen, 1982.

[B.2] Angel, L.J. and Hurdle, G.E. "The nation's food: 40 years of change". *Economic Trends*, no.294, April 1978.

[B.3] Artis, M.J. *Prest and Coppock's The UK Economy: A Manual of Applied Economics*. eleventh edition. Weidenfeld and Nicolson, London, 1986.

[B.4] Ashby, A.W. "Britain's food manufacturing industry". *Journal of Agricultural Economics*, vol.29, no.3, September 1978.

[B.5] Ashley, W. *The Bread of Our Forefathers*. Clarendon Press, Oxford, 1928.

[B.6] Ashton, T.S. *An Economic History of England: The 18th Century*. Methuen, London, 1955.

[B.7] Bain, G.S. and Price, R.J. "Union growth and employment trends in the United Kingdom 1964-1970". *British Journal of Industrial Relations*, vol 10, no.3, November 1972.

[B.8] Bain, G.S. and Price, R.J. *Profiles of Union Growth: A Comparative Statistical Portrait of Eight Countries. Warwick Studies in Industrial Relations*. Blackwell, Oxford, 1980.

[B.9] Baker, Stanley. *Milk to Market: Forty Years of Milk Marketing*. Heinemann, London, 1973.

[B.10] Bale, M.D. (ed). *Horticultural Trade of the Expanded European Community: Implications for Mediterranean Countries. A World Bank Symposium*. International Bank for Reconstruction and Development, Washington, 1986.

[B.11] Barker, T.C. and Yudkin, J. *Fish in Britain: Trends in its Supply, Distribution and Consumption during the Past Two Centuries. Queen Elizabeth College, Department of Nutrition Occasional Paper*. University of London, London, 1971.

[B.12] Barnett, A. "Review of MAFF statistics", in Statistics Users' Council, *The Proceedings of the Agricultural and Food Statistics Conference (November 10th 1986)*. IMAC Research, Esher, March 1987.

[B.13] Bateman, D.I. "Labour productivity and concentration in the food processing industries". *Journal of Agricultural Economics*, vol.21, no.3, September 1970.

[B.14] Beard, N.F. *Against the Grain? The EC Cereals Policy*. Centre for Agricultural Strategy, University of Reading, Reading, 1986.

[B.15] Beard, N.F. *A Statistical Digest of UK and EC Production, Utilisation and Trade in Cereals*. University of Nottingham, Department of Economics, Discussion Paper no.50. University of Nottingham, Nottingham, March 1986.

[B.16] Berman, L.S. "Developments in statistics at the Department of Trade and Industry". *Statistical News*, no.22, August 1973.

[B.17] Bevan, A. "The UK potato crisp industry 1968-1972: a study of new entry competition". *Journal of Industrial Economics*, vol.22, June 1974.

[B.18] Beveridge, Sir W.H. *British Food Control. The Economic and Social History of the World War, British Series*. Oxford University Press, London, 1928.

[B.19] Bland, A.E., Brown, P.A. and Tawney R.H. (eds). *English Economic History: Select Documents*. G.Bell and Sons Ltd., London, 1914.

[B.20] Borrie, Sir G. "Competition, mergers and price fixing". *Lloyds Bank Review*, no.164, April 1987.

[B.21] Bowditch, R.A. "Developments in British official statistics". *Statistical News*, no.47, November 1979.

[B.22] Bowles, J.R. "Research and development in the United Kingdom in 1981". *Economic Trends*, no.370, August 1984.

[B.23] Bowles, J.R. "Central government expenditure on research and development in 1984". *Economic Trends*, no.394, August 1986.

[B.24] Bowles, J.R. "Research and development in the UK in 1986". *Economic Trends*, no.418, August 1988.

[B.25] Britton, D.K. *Cereals in the United Kingdom*. Pergamon Press, Oxford, 1969.

[B.26] Buckley, J. (ed). *Guide to World Commodity Markets: Physical, Futures and Options Trading*. fifth edition. Kogan Page, London, 1986.

[B.27] Buckley, P.J. and Pearce, R. *International Aspects of UK Economic Activities. Reviews of United Kingdom Statistical Sources, vol.26*. Chapman and Hall, London, 1991.

[B.28] Bulmer-Thomas, V. *Input-output Analysis in Developing Countries: Sources, Methods and Applications*. Wiley, Chichester, 1982.

[B.29] Burch, A.F. "Statistical surveys conducted by the National Board of Prices and Incomes". *Statistical News*, no. 13, May 1971.

[B.30] Burns, J. "The UK food chain with particular reference to the inter-relations between manufacturers and distributors". *Journal of Agricultural Economics*, vol.44, no.3, 1983.

[B.31] Burns, J., McInerney, J. and Swinbank, A. (eds). *The Food Industry: Economics and Policies*. Heinemann, London, 1983.

[B.32] Burns, J. and Swinbank, A. (eds). *Competition Policy in the Food Industries. Department of Agricultural Economics and Management, University of Reading, Food Economics Study no.4*. University of Reading, Reading, 1988.

[B.33] Buxton, N.K. and Mackay, D.I. *British Employment Statistics*. Blackwell, Oxford, 1977.

[B.34] Caulton, V. *Briton's Index of Investment Research Analysts in the UK*. Briton's and Caulton Publishing and Media Services, Canterbury (annual since 1988).

[B.35] Chapman, J.E. *The Cocoa, Chocolate and Confectionery Alliance 1951-1981*. CCCA, London, 1982.

[B.36] Clarke, G. "Life with Eurostat: a personal view". *Statistical News*, no.67, November 1984.

[B.37] Clarke, R. *Industrial Economics*. Blackwell, Oxford, 1985.

[B.38] Cockfield, A. "The Price Commission and the price control". *The Three Banks Review*, no.117, March 1978.

[B.39] Collins, E.J.T. "The consumer revolution and the growth of factory food", in Oddy, D.J. and Miller, D.S. (eds), *The Making of the Modern British Diet*. Croom Helm, London, 1976.

[B.40] Connell, J.J. "New developments in the marketing of fish". *Food Marketing*, vol.3, no.1, 1987. (Marketing in the Food Chain: Conference Proceedings Part II).

[B.41] Corley, T.A.B. *Quaker Enterprise in Biscuits: Huntley and Palmers of Reading 1822-1972*. Hutchinson, London, 1972.

[B.42] Crossley, E.L. (ed). *The United Kingdom Dairy Industry*. United Kingdom Dairy Association, London, 1959.

[B.43] Dawson, J.A., Shaw, S.A., Burt, S. and Rana, J. *Structural Change and Public Policy in The European Food Industry. FAST Occasional Papers no.125*. Directorate General for Science Research and Development, Commission of the European Communities, Brussels, 1986.

[B.44] Dean, A. *Wages and Earnings. Reviews of United Kingdom Statistical Sources, vol.13*. Pergamon Press, Oxford, 1980.

[B.45] Dnes, A.W. *The European Communities' Common Fisheries Policy: A Critique. Hume paper no.4*. The David Hume Institute, Glencorse, 1986.

[B.46] Edwards, H.V. "Flour Milling", in M.P. Fogarty (ed). *Further Studies in Industrial Organisation*. Methuen, London, 1948.

[B.47] Elis-Williams, D. "Seasonal adjustment of the overseas trade figures". *Economic Trends*, no.328, February 1981.

[B.48] Evely, R. and Little, I.M.D. *Concentration in British Industry: An Empirical Study of the Structure of Industrial Production. NIESR Economic and Social Studies no.16*. Cambridge University Press, Cambridge, 1960.

[B.49] Farmer, E.R. *Making Sense of Company Reports*. Van Nostrand Reinhold, Wokingham, 1986.

[B.50] Farrell, J. and Elles, J. *In Search of a Common Fisheries Policy*. Gower, Aldershot, 1984.

[B.51] Fels, A. *The British Prices and Incomes Board. University of Cambridge, Department of Applied Economics, Occasional Paper 29*. Cambridge University Press, Cambridge, 1972.

[B.52] Fennell, R. *The Common Agricultural Policy of the European Community: Its Institutions and Administrative Organisation*. second edition. BSP Professional, Oxford, 1987.

[B.53] Fisher, H.E.S. and Jurica, A.R.J. (eds). *Documents in English Economic History: England from 1000 to 1760*. G. Bell and Sons Ltd., London, 1977.

[B.54] Forrest, D. *The World Tea Trade: A Survey of the Production, Distribution and Consumption of Tea*. Woodhead-Faulkner Ltd., Cambridge, 1985.

[B.55] Foster, P. and Foster, A. *Online Business Source Book*. Headland Press, Cleveland, 1988.

[B.56] Garside, W.R. *The Measurement of Unemployment (Methods and Sources in Great Britain 1850-1979)*. Blackwell, Oxford, 1980.

[B.57] George, K.D. and Ward, T. *The Structure of Industry in the EEC. Department of Applied Economics, University of Cambridge, Occasional Paper 43*. Cambridge University Press, Cambridge, 1975.

[B.58] Gerrard, F. and Mallion, F.J. (eds). *The Complete Book of Meat*. Virtue & Co. Ltd., Coulsdon, 1980.

[B.59] Goulding, I. "Fish marketing in the UK", in Beharrell, B. and Goulding, I. (eds). *Marketing Problems in the Food Chain. Papers Presented at a Conference at Sheffield City Polytechnic, September 1984*. Sheffield City Polytechnic, Sheffield, 1986.

[B.60] Graham, J.W.L. "Sugar and sweeteners", in Swinbank, A. and Burns, J. (eds). *The EEC and the Food Industries. Department of Agricultural Economics and Management, University of Reading, Food Economics Study no.1*. University of Reading, Reading, 1984.

[B.61] Griffin, T. "Revised estimates of the consumption and stocks of fixed capital". *Economic Trends*, no.264, October 1975.

[B.62] Griffin, T. "The stock of fixed assets in the United Kingdom: how to make best use of the statistics". *Economic Trends*, no.276, October 1976.

[B.63] Hammond, R.J. *Food I. The Growth of Policy. History of the Second World War, United Kingdom Civil Series*. HMSO and Longmans Green and Co. Ltd., London, 1951.

[B.64] Hammond, R.J. *Food II. Studies in Administration and Control. History of the Second World War, United Kingdom Civil Series*. HMSO and Longmans Green and Co. Ltd., London, 1956.

[B.65] Hammond, R.J. *Food III. Studies in Administration and Control. History of the Second World War, United Kingdom Civil Series*. HMSO and Longmans Green and Co. Ltd., London, 1962.

[B.66] Hancock, W.K. (ed). *Statistical Digest of the War. History of the Second World War, United Kingdom Civil Series*. HMSO and Longmans Green and Co. Ltd., London, 1951.

[B.67] Hannah, L. and Kay, J.A. *Concentration in Modern Industry: Theory, Measurement and the UK Experience*. Macmillan, London, 1977.

[B.68] Harris, S. *The UK Sugar Economy*. Paper presented at the Thirtieth Congress of the International Confederation of European Beet Growers, 1984. Unpublished paper, available from the author.

[B.69] Harris, S. "The provision of carbohydrates for the European Community's biotechnology and chemical industries". *Journal of Agricultural Economics*, vol.33, no.3, September 1987.

[B.70] Harris, S. and Pickard, D.H. *Livestock Slaughtering in Britain: A Changing Industry*. Centre for European Agricultural Studies, Wye College, Ashford, 1979.

[B.71] Harris, S., Swinbank, A. and Wilkinson, G. *The Food and Farm Policies of the European Community*. Wiley, London, 1983.

[B.72] Hart, P.E., Utton, M.A. and Walshe, G. *Mergers and Concentration in British Industry. NIESR Occasional Paper no.26*. Cambridge University Press, Cambridge, 1973.

[B.73] Hartley, K. *Problems of Economic Policy. Economics and Society Series no.3*. Allen & Unwin, London, 1977.

[B.74] Harvey, D.R. (ed). *The Future of the Agriculture & Food System*. University of Reading, Reading, 1987.

[B.75] Harvey, J. *Statistics Europe: Sources for Social, Economic and Market Research*. fifth edition. CBD Research Ltd., Beckenham, 1987.

[B.76] Hay, D. and Vickers, J. "The reform of UK competition policy". *National Institute Economic Review*, no. 125, August 1988.

[B.77] Hessner, C. and Mellor, C.J. "An empirical analysis of the relationship between advertising and sales: a case study of the liquid milk market". *Journal of Agricultural Economics*, vol.38, no.2, May 1986.

[B.78] Hewer, A. "Manufacturing industry in the seventies: an assessment of import penetration and export performance". *Economic Trends*, no.320, June 1980.

[B.79] Hilton, K.P. and Ayres-McAuley, N. *Stockbrokers' Research and Information Services 1988*. fifth edition. Templeton College, Oxford, 1988.

[B.80] Hilton, K.P. and Watson, J.G. *Stockbrokers' Research and Information Services 1984*. Oxford Centre for Management Studies, Oxford, 1984.

[B.81] Hinton, L. *EEC Enlargement in the Fruit and Vegetable Sector: With Special Reference to Spain and the United Kingdom*. Cambridge University Press, Cambridge, 1983.

[B.82] Hopkins, M. (ed). *European Communities Information: Its Use and Users*. Mansell, London, 1985.

[B.83] Horsman, E.G. "Britain and value-added taxation". *Lloyds Bank Review*, no.103, January 1972.

[B.84] Horst, T. *At Home Abroad*. MIT Press, Boston, 1964.

[B.85] Jackson, D. "Economics education and the real world". *Lloyds Bank Review*, no.138, October 1980.

[B.86] Jackson, D. *Introduction to Economics: Theory and Data*. Macmillan, London, 1982.

[B.87] Jefferys, J. "Bread and cereals", in *The Distribution of Consumer Goods. NIESR Economic and Social Studies no.9*. Cambridge University Press, Cambridge, 1950.

[B.88] Jefferys, J. "The bread and flour confectionery trade", in *Retail Trading in Britain: A Study of Trends in Retailing with Special Reference to the Development of Cooperative Multiple Shop and Department Store Methods of Trading. NIESR Economic and Social Studies no.13*. Cambridge University Press, Cambridge, 1954.

[B.89] Jeffries, J. *A Guide to the Official Publications of the European Communities*. second edition. Mansell, London, 1981.

[B.90] Jenkins, A. *Drinka Pinta: The Story of Milk and the Industry that Serves it*. Heinemann, London, 1970.

[B.91] Johnson, P.S. *British Industry: An Economic Introduction*. Blackwell, Oxford, 1985.

[B.92] Jones, A. *New Inflation: The Politics of Prices and Incomes*. Deutsch, London, 1973.

[B.93] Kant, I. *Critique of Pure Reason*. Macmillan, London, 1961.

[B.94] Kemsley, W.F.F. *Family Expenditure Survey Handbook: Sampling, Fieldwork, Coding Procedures and Related Methodological Experiments*. HMSO, London, 1980.

[B.95] Kendall, M.G. (ed). *The Sources and Nature of the Statistics of the United Kingdom, volume 1.* Oliver and Boyd, London, 1952.

[B.96] Kendall, M.G. (ed). *The Sources and Nature of the Statistics of the United Kingdom, volume 2.* Oliver and Boyd, London, 1957.

[B.97] Knight, J. "Top companies in the DTI company accounts analysis". *Statistical News,* no.76, February 1987.

[B.98] Knight, J, and Jenkinson, G. "Smaller companies in the DTI company accounts analysis". *Statistical News,* no. 77, May 1987.

[B.99] Kostaradpoulou, A.E. *Concentration, Competition and Competitiveness in the Food Industry of the EEC.* Commission of the European Communities, Brussels, 1983.

[B.100] Leak, H. and Maizels, A. "The structure of British industry". *Journal of the Royal Statistical Society,* vol.108, parts I-II, 1945.

[B.101] Leigh, M. *European Integration and the Common Fisheries Policy.* Croom Helm, London, 1983.

[B.102] Leontief, W. *Input-output Economics.* Oxford University Press, New York, 1966,

[B.103] Lewis, C. "Constructing a sampling frame of industrial and commercial companies". *Statistical News,* no. 44, February 1979.

[B.104] Lightman, L.H. "Price controls in the United Kingdom 1973-78: natural development or radical change". *Journal of Agricultural Economics,* vol.29, no.3, September 1978.

[B.105] Low, E. "UK cereal market statistics", in *Agricultural and Food Statistics.* IMAC Research, Esher, 1987.

[B.106] Lund, P.J. "The National Food Survey", paper presented at the *Statistics Users' Conference on the Distributive Trades.* NEDO, London, 1983.

[B.107] Lyle, P. "Sugar industry", in Kendall, M.G. (ed). *The Sources and Nature of the Statistics of the United Kingdom, volume 1.* Oliver and Boyd, London, 1952.

[B.108] Marquette, A.F. *Brands, Trademarks and Goodwill: The Story of the Quaker Oats Company.* McGraw-Hill, New York, 1967.

[B.109] Marsden, D. and Redlbacher, L. *A Guide to Current Sources of Wage Statistics in the European Community.* Office for Official Publications of the European Communities, Luxembourg, 1984.

[B.110] Marsh, J.S. and Swanney, P.T. *Agriculture and the European Community.* Allen & Unwin, London, 1980.

[B.111] Marshall, C.F. *The World Coffee Trade: A Guide to the Production, Trading and Consumption of Coffee.* Woodhead-Faulkner Ltd., Cambridge, 1983.

[B.112] Mathias, P. *The Retailing Revolution.* Longmans Green & Co. Ltd., London, 1967.

[B.113] Maunder, W.P.J. *The Bread Industry in the United Kingdom.* University of Nottingham and Loughborough University, Loughborough, 1969.

[B.114] Maunder, W.P.J. "The UK food processing and distribution trades: an appraisal of public policies". *Journal of Agricultural Economics,* vol.21, no.3, September 1970.

[B.115] Maunder, W.P.J. "Competition in British industry", in Swann, D., O'Brien, D.P., Maunder, W.P.J. and Howe, W.S. *Case Studies of the Effects of Restrictive Practices Legislation.* Loughborough University, Loughborough, 1973.

[B.116] Maunder, W.P.J. "Competition from new entrants: packaged cakes", in Barker, P.J., Blois, K.J., Howe, W.S., Maunder, W.P.J. and Tighe, M.J. *Case Studies in the Competitive Process.* Heinemann, London, 1976.

[B.117] Maunder, W.P.J. "Food manufacture", in Johnson, P.S. (ed). *The Structure of British Industry.* Granada, St. Albans, 1980.

[B.118] Maunder, W.P.J. "Competition policy in the food industry", in Burns, J., McInerney, J. and Swinbank, A. (eds). *The Food Industry: Economics and Policies.* Heinemann, London, 1983.

[B.119] Maunder, W.P.J. "The food and drink industries and the second Price Commission (1977-1979)". *Journal of Agricultural Economics,* vol.35, no.3, September 1984.

[B.120] Maunder, W.P.J. "Food manufacture", in Johnson, P.S. (ed). *The Structure of British Industry.* second edition. Allen & Unwin, London, 1988.

[B.121] Maunder, W.P.J., Myers, D., Wall, N. and LeRoy Miller, R. *Economics Explained.* Collins Educational, London, 1987.

[B.122] Maurice, R. (ed). *National Accounts Statistics: Sources and Methods. Studies in Official Statistics no.13*. HMSO, London, 1968.

[B.123] Meeks, G. *Disappointing Marriage: A Study of the Gains from Merger. Department of Applied Economics, University of Cambridge, Occasional Paper 51*. Cambridge University Press, Cambridge, 1977.

[B.124] Millard, P. *Trade Associations and Professional Bodies of the United Kingdom*, eighth edition. Pergamon, Oxford, 1987.

[B.125] Moir, C. and Dawson, J. *Distribution. Reviews of United Kingdom Statistical Sources, vol.28*. Chapman and Hall, London, 1992.

[B.126] Mordue, R.E. "The food sector in the context of the UK economy", in Burns, J., McInerney, J. and Swinbank, A. (eds). *The Food Industry: Economics and Policies*. Heinemann, London, 1983.

[B.127] Mordue, R.E. and Marshall, J.D. "Changes in total factor productivity in UK food and drink manufacturing". *Journal of Agricultural Economics*, vol.30, no.2, May 1979.

[B.128] Mordue, R.E. and Parrett, J. "United Kingdom self sufficiency in food, 1970-78". *Economic Trends*, no.312, October 1979.

[B.129] Morgan, E.V. *Monopolies, Mergers and Restrictive Practices: UK Competition Policy 1948-87. The David Hume Institute, Hume Paper no.7*. The David Hume Institute, Edinburgh, 1987.

[B.130] Mort, D. and Siddall, L. *Sources of Unofficial UK Statistics*. Gower, Aldershot, 1985.

[B.131] Moser, C.A. and Beesley, I.B. "United Kingdom official statistics and the European Communities". *Statistical News*, no.22, August 1973.

[B.132] Moser, C.A. and Beesley, I.B. "United Kingdom official statistics and the European Communities". *Journal of the Royal Statistical Society*, Series A (General), vol.136, part 4, 1973.

[B.133] Moser, C.A. and Kalton, G. *Survey Methods in Social Investigation*. Heinemann, London, 1971.

[B.134] Nicholas, D. *Commodities Futures Trading: A Guide to Information Sources and Computerised Services*. Mansell, London, 1985.

[B.135] Nichols, J.R. *The Impact of the EEC on the UK Food Industry (Effects on the Strategy of UK Food, Drink and Tobacco Manufacturing Companies)*. Milton Publications, Farnborough, 1978.

[B.136] Nichols, J.R. *Case Studies on the Effects of the EEC on the UK Food and Drink Industry*. Bath University Press, Bath, 1979.

[B.137] Norkett, P. *Guide to Company Information in Great Britain*. Longman Group Ltd., Harlow, 1986.

[B.138] Palmer, C.M. *Structural Change in the Retail Distribution System for Meat in Great Britain*. MLC, Bletchley, 1979.

[B.139] Pavell, H.P. *The Original has his Signature — W. K. Kellogg*. Prentice-Hall, New York, 1956.

[B.140] Penneck, S.J. "The top 1500 industrial and commercial companies". *Statistical News*, no.43, November 1978.

[B.141] Perry, J.A. "The rebased estimate of the index of the output of the production industries". *Economic Trends*, no.360, October 1983.

[B.142] Perry, J.A. "The development of a new register of businesses". *Statistical News*, no.70, August 1985.

[B.143] Peters, G.A. *A Bibliography of Statistical Sources on UK Fisheries. Portsmouth Polytechnic, Marine Resources Research Unit, Research Paper Series no.50*. Portsmouth Polytechnic, Portsmouth, 1987.

[B.144] Peters, G.H. *Agriculture. Reviews of United Kingdom Statistical Sources, vol.23*. Chapman and Hall, London, 1988.

[B.145] Polley, J.A. "Index of industrial production for Scotland: reclassification and rebasing". *Scottish Economic Bulletin*, no.29, July 1984.

[B.146] Prais, S.J. *The Evolution of Giant Firms in Britain. NIESR Economic and Social Studies no.30*. Cambridge University Press, Cambridge, 1976.

[B.147] Prais, S.J. *Productivity and Industrial Structure: A Statistical Study of Manufacturing Industry in Britain, Germany and the United States. NIESR Economic and Social Studies no.33.* Cambridge University Press, Cambridge, 1981.
[B.148] Pratten, C. *Economies of Scale in Manufacturing Industry. University of Cambridge, Department of Applied Economics Occasional Papers no.28.* Cambridge University Press, Cambridge, 1971.
[B.149] Price, R.J. and Bain, G.S. "Union growth in Britain: retrospect and prospects". *British Journal of Industrial Relations*, vol.21, no.1, March 1983.
[B.150] Price, R.P. *Britain's Food Processing Industry.* Jordan & Sons Ltd., London, April 1985.
[B.151] Ramsey, A. *Eurostat Index.* Capital Planning Information Ltd., Stamford, 1986.
[B.152] Reekie, W.D. *Give Us This Day. Hobart Paper 79.* Institute of Economic Affairs, Lancing, 1978.
[B.153] Rees, F.T. "The EEC and the UK's cereals processing industry", in Swinbank, A. and Burns, J. (eds). *The EEC and the Food Industries. University of Reading, Department of Agricultural Economics and Management, Food Economics Study no.1.* University of Reading, Reading, 1984.
[B.154] Rees, G.L. assisted by Craig, R.S. and Jones, D.R. "The vegetable oil, oil-seed and oil-cake market", in *Britain's Commodity Markets.* Paul Elek Books, London, 1972.
[B.155] Renshall, M. and Aldis, J. *Companies Act 1985: A Guide to the Accounting and Reporting Requirements.* Institute of Chartered Accountants in England and Wales, London, 1987.
[B.156] Rushton, A.M. "Bread pricing in Great Britain", in *Price Formation Processes and the Changing Nature of Food Systems.* OECD, Paris, 1980.
[B.157] Sawyer, M.C. *The Economics of Industries and Firms.* second edition. Croom Helm, Beckenham, 1985.
[B.158] Sawyer, M.C. and Aaronovitch, S. *Big Business: Theoretical and Empirical Aspects of Concentration and Mergers in the UK.* Macmillan, London, 1975.
[B.159] Schumpeter, J. *The Theory of Economic Development.* Harvard University Press, Cambridge, 1934.
[B.160] Sellwood, R. "New statistical series analysing commodities imported and exported according to the industries of which they are the principal products". *Economic Trends*, no.265, February 1975.
[B.161] Sheppard, R. and Newton, E. *The Story of Bread.* Routledge and Kegan Paul, London, 1957.
[B.162] Siddall, D. *A Survey of United Kingdom Non-official Statistical Sources and Their Role in Business Information. British Library R&D Report 5821.* University of Warwick, Coventry, August 1984.
[B.163] Simpson, D. "What economists need to know". *The Royal Bank of Scotland Review*, no.160, December 1988.
[B.164] Slater, J.M. "Statistics of food supplies and consumption", in *Statistics Users' Council, The Proceedings of the Agricultural and Food Statistics Conference (November 10th 1986).* IMAC Research, Esher, 1987.
[B.165] Slater, J.M. "The food sector in the UK", in Burns, J. and Swinbank, A. (eds). *Competition Policy in the Food Industries. University of Reading, Department of Agricultural Economics and Management, Food Economics Study no.4.* University of Reading, Reading, 1988.
[B.166] Sohn, I. *Readings in Input-output Analysis.* Oxford University Press, New York, 1986.
[B.167] Stedman Jones, W.D. "Food statistics", in Kendall, M.G. (ed). *The Sources and Nature of the Statistics of the United Kingdom, volume 2.* Oliver and Boyd, London, 1957.
[B.168] Stern, W.M. "The sea fish supply in Billingsgate from the nineteenth century to the second world war", in Barker, T.C. and Yudkin, J. (eds). *Fish in Britain: Trends in its Supply, Distribution and Consumption during the Past Two Centuries. Queen Elizabeth College, Department of Nutrition Occasional Paper.* University of London, London, 1971.

[B.169] Stewart, I.M.T. *Information in the Cereals Market*. Hutchinson, London, 1970.

[B.170] Swann, D. *The Economics of the Common Market*. sixth edition. Penguin, London, 1988.

[B.171] Swann, D., O'Brien, D.P., Maunder, W.P.J. and Howe, W.S. *Competition in British Industry: Case Studies of the Effects of Restrictive Practices Legislation*. Loughborough University, Loughborough, 1973.

[B.172] Swann, D., O'Brien, D.P., Maunder, W.P.J. and Howe, W.S. *Competition in British Industry: Restrictive Practices Legislation in Theory and Practice*. Allen & Unwin Ltd., London, 1974.

[B.173] Swinbank, A. and Burns, J. (eds). *The EEC and the Food Industries. Department of Agricultural Economics and Management, University of Reading, Food Economics Study no.1*. University of Reading, Reading, 1984.

[B.174] Thomson, I.R. *The Documentation of the European Communities*. Mansell, London, 1989.

[B.175] Tudor, J. *Macmillan Directory of Business Information Sources*. Macmillan, London, 1987.

[B.176] Ukers, W.H. *All About Coffee*. second edition. The Tea and Coffee Trade Journal Company, New York, 1935.

[B.177] Ukers, W.H. *All About Tea*. two volumes. The Tea and Coffee Trade Journal Company, New York, 1935.

[B.178] Utton, M.A. *Diversification and Competition. NIESR Occasional Paper no.31*. Cambridge University Press, Cambridge, 1979.

[B.179] Vernon, K.D.C. (ed). *Information Sources in Management and Business*. Butterworths, London, 1984.

[B.180] Walsh, B. "An overview of on-line databases". *Accountancy*, vol.97, issue 1110, February 1986.

[B.181] Walsh, B., Butcher, B. and Freund, A. *On-line Information: A Comprehensive Business-users' Guide*. Blackwell, Oxford, 1987.

[B.182] Walsh, K., Izatt, A. and Pearson, R. *The UK Labour Market: The IMS Guide to Information*. Kogan Page, London, 1984.

[B.183] Walsh, K. and Pearson, R. *How to Analyse the Labour Market*. Gower, Aldershot, 1984.

[B.184] Watts, B.G.A. "Structural adjustment in the United Kingdom food manufacturing industry over the past twenty years". Paper presented at a symposium on *The Adjustment and the Challenges Facing the Food Industries in the 1980's*. OECD, Paris, 1982.

[B.185] Wells, J.D. and Imber, J.C. "The home and export performance of United Kingdom industries". *Economic Trends*, no.286, August 1977.

[B.186] Wilkinson, G. "The UK dairy industry and the EEC", in Swinbank, A. and Burns, J. (eds). *The EEC and the Food Industries. University of Reading, Department of Agricultural Economics and Management, Food Economics Study no.1*. University of Reading, Reading, 1984.

[B.187] Williams, R.E. and Bienkowski, J.J. "Statistical sources — milk and milk products". Unpublished paper, available from the Milk Marketing Board for England and Wales.

[B.188] Wise, M. *The Common Fisheries Policy of the European Community*. Methuen, London, 1984.

[B.189] Wragg, R. and Robertson, J. *Post-war Trends in Employment, Productivity, Output, Labour Costs and Prices by Industry in the United Kingdom. Department of Employment Research Paper no.3*. Department of Employment, London, June 1978.

[B.190] Young, A., Bosworth, D.L. and Wilson, R. *Research and Development. Reviews of United Kingdom Statistical Sources. vol.27*. Chapman and Hall, London (forthcoming).

[B.191] Young, J.A. "Marketing in a dynamic environment: an overview of UK fish processing". *Food Marketing*, vol.3, no.1, 1987. (Marketing in the Food Chain: Conference Proceedings Part II).

[B.192] Young, N.A. "Potato products: production and markets in the European Communities". *European Commission, Information on Agriculture Series no.75*. Office for Official Publications of the European Communities, Luxembourg, 1981.
[B.193] Yudkin, J. *Pure, White and Deadly*. revised and expanded edition. Viking, London, 1986.
[B.194] The Institute of Chartered Accountants in England and Wales. *Accounting Standards*. The Institute of Chartered Accountants in England and Wales, London (annual).
[B.195] Agriculture Economic Development Committee, National Economic Development Office. *The Adoption of Technology in Agriculture: Poultry Broiler Production*. NEDO, London, 1986.
[B.196] Agriculture and Food Research Council. *AFRC Institute of Food Research Annual Report*. AFRC, Swindon (annual since 1987).
[B.197] Ministry of Agriculture, Fisheries and Food. *Agricultural and Food Statistics: A Guide To Official Sources. Studies in Official Statistics no.23*. HMSO, London, 1974.
[B.198] Ice Cream Federation Ltd. *All About Ice Cream*. Ice Cream Federation Ltd., London (undated).
[B.199] Dairy Trade Federation. *Annual Milk Bottle Trippage and Packaging Survey*. Dairy Trade Federation, London (annual).
[B.200] Campden Food and Drink Research Association. *Annual Report of the Campden Food Preservation Research Association*. Campden Food Preservation Research Association, Chipping Campden (annual).
[B.201] Economic Development Committee for Agriculture, National Economic Development Office. *Apples: UK Farming and the Common Market*. NEDO, London, 1972.
[B.202] Euromonitor Publications Ltd. *A-Z of UK Marketing Information Sources*. first edition. The Market Research Society, London, 1984.
[B.203] Food Trades Press Ltd. *Binsted's Directory of Food Trade Marks and Brand Names*. seventh edition. Food Trade Press Ltd., Orpington, 1986.
[B.204] Commission of the European Communities. *Biotechnology: The Community's Role. COM(83)328*. Commission of the European Communities, Brussels, 1983.
[B.205] Commission of the European Communities. *Biotechnology in the Community. COM(83)672*. Commission of the European Communities, Brussels, 1983.
[B.206] House of Lords Select Committee on the European Communities. *Biotechnology in the Community*. HL145. (Session 1987/88). HMSO, London, 1987.
[B.207] Commission of the European Communities. *Biotechnology in the Community: Stimulating Agro-industrial Development*. COM(86)221. Commission of the European Communities, Brussels, 1986.
[B.208] Food and Drink Manufacturing Economic Development Committee, National Economic Development Office. *Biscuits*. NEDO, London, 1978.
[B.209] London School of Economics. *British Journal of Industrial Relations*. Blackwell, Oxford (triannual since 1963).
[B.210] Headland Press. *Business Information Review*. Headland Press, Cleveland (quarterly).
[B.211] Headland Press. *Business Information Sourcebook*. Headland Press, Cleveland (1985 and updates).
[B.212] Headland Press. *Business Information Yearbook*. Headland Press, Cleveland (annual).
[B.213] HM Customs and Excise (Statistical Office). *Business Monitor MA21: Guide to the Classification for Overseas Trade Statistics*. HMSO, London (annual).
[B.214] Business Statistics Office. *Business Monitor PA1001: Introductory Notes*. HMSO, London (annual).
[B.215] Department of Trade and Industry, Business Statistics Office. *Business Monitor PO1000: Index of Commodities*. HMSO, London, 1983.
[B.216] Business Statistics Office. *Business Monitor PO1001: Guide to Short-term Statistics of Manufacturers' Sales*. HMSO, London, 1984.
[B.217] Business Statistics Office. *Business Monitor PO1007: Classified List of Manufacturing Businesses 1984*. HMSO, London, 1984.
[B.218] Central Statistical Office. *Business Monitor PO1007: The UK Directory of Manufacturing Businesses 1989*. HMSO, London, 1989.

[B.219] Business Statistics Office. *Business Monitors*. HMSO, London, 1988 (updated occasionally).

[B.220] Agra Europe (London) Ltd. *CAP Monitor*. Agra Europe (London) Ltd., Tunbridge Wells (updated continually).

[B.221] The Milk Marketing Boards in Scotland and the West of Scotland Agricultural College. *The Catering Market for Milk and Cream in Scotland 1984-85*. The Scottish Milk Marketing Board, Paisley, 1985.

[B.222] Office of Population Censuses and Surveys. *Census 1981: Definition, Great Britain*. HMSO, London, 1981.

[B.223] Office of Population Censuses and Surveys. *Census 1981: User Guide*. OPCS, Titchfield, 1981-1985.

[B.224] Office of Population Censuses and Surveys. *Census 1981: User Guide Catalogue*. OPCS, Titchfield, 1982.

[B.225] Command Paper. *Civil Research and Development: Government Response to the First Report of the House of Lords Select Committee on Science and Technology*. Cm 185. (Session 1987/88). HMSO, London, 1987.

[B.226] House of Lords Select Committee on Science and Technology. *Civil Research and Development*. HL20 I, II, III. (Session 1986/87). HMSO, London, 1986.

[B.227] Office of Population Censuses and Surveys. *Classification of Occupations and Coding Index 1980*. HMSO, London, 1980.

[B.228] International Coffee Organisation. *Coffeeline*. ICO, London (data base).

[B.229] Statistical Office of the European Communities. *Common Nomenclature of Industrial Products: NIPRO*. Statistical Office of the European Communities, Luxembourg, 1976.

[B.230] Sea Fish Industry Authority. *Comparison of Government Support to Agriculture and the Fish Catching Sector. FERU Occasional Paper Series no.3*. SFIA, Edinburgh, 1984.

[B.231] Office of Fair Trading. *Competition and Retailing*. Office of Fair Trading, London, 1985.

[B.232] Central Statistical Office. *CSO Standard Industrial Classification Revised 1980*. HMSO, London, 1979.

[B.233] National Economic Development Office. *The Dairy Industry: General Issues Affecting the Industry*. HMSO, London, 1987.

[B.234] National Economic Development Office. *The Dairy Industry: Supply and Demand to 1988*. NEDO, London, 1984.

[B.235] National Economic Development Office. *The Dairy Industry: Supply and Demand to 1990*. NEDO, London, 1987.

[B.236] Dairy Trade Federation. *Dairy Industry Manpower Survey*. Dairy Trade Federation, London, 1985.

[B.237] Joint Consultative Organisation for Research and Development in Agriculture and Food. *Determination of Research Priorities for the Agricultural and Food Industries*. JCO Consultative Board, London, 1984.

[B.238] Department of Employment. *Directory of Employees' Associations, Trade Unions, Joint Organisations etc*. HMSO, London, 1987.

[B.239] Findex. *The Directory of Market Research Reports, Studies and Surveys*. eighth edition. Cambridge Information Group Directories Inc., Bethesda, 1988.

[B.240] Incomes Data Services Ltd. *Directory of Salary Surveys*. Incomes Data Services Ltd., London (annual).

[B.241] Office for Official Publications of the European Communities. *Documents*. Office for Official Publications of the European Communities, Luxembourg (monthly, quarterly and annual).

[B.242] National Dairy Council. *The Doorstep Delivery Service '85*. National Dairy Council, London, 1985.

[B.243] East Malling Research Station. *East Malling Research Station Annual Report*. East Malling Research Station, Maidstone (annual up to 1986).

[B.244] Ministry of Agriculture, Fisheries and Food (Sugar, Oils and Fats Division). *EC Sugar Regime*. MAFF, London, September 1988.
[B.245] Agra Europe (London) Ltd. *EEC and World Dairy Markets 1988*. Agra Europe (London) Ltd., Tunbridge Wells, 1988.
[B.246] Agra Europe (London) Ltd. *EEC Dairy Market - Prospects for Autumn and Winter 1987/88*. Agra Europe (London) Ltd., Tunbridge Wells, 1987.
[B.247] Agra Europe (London) Ltd. *EEC Dairy Market Report 1987*. Agra Europe (London) Ltd., Tunbridge Wells, 1987.
[B.248] Agra Europe (London) Ltd. *EEC Dairy Policy: The Failure of Quotas*. Agra Europe (London) Ltd., Tunbridge Wells, 1986.
[B.249] Agra Europe (London) Ltd. *EEC Fisheries: Problems and Prospects for a Common Policy. Special Report no.11*. Agra Europe (London) Ltd., Tunbridge Wells, 1981.
[B.250] House of Lords Select Committee on the European Communities. *EEC Fisheries Policy*. HL351. (Session 1979/80). HMSO, London, 1980.
[B.251] Ministry of Agriculture, Fisheries and Food. *EEC Regulation 355/77: A Programme for the Fisheries Sector in England and Wales 1985-1987*. MAFF, London, 1987.
[B.252] House of Lords Select Committee on the European Communities. *EEC Starch Regime*. HL176. (Session 1984/85). HMSO, London, 1985.
[B.253] Agra Europe (London) Ltd. *The Effect of Milk Quotas on Community Agriculture*. Agra Europe (London) Ltd., Tunbridge Wells, 1987.
[B.254] Department of Employment. *Employment Statistics: Sources and Definitions*. Department of Employment, London, 1985.
[B.255] Euromoney Publications plc. *Euromoney*. Euromoney Publications plc, London (monthly).
[B.256] European Documentation Centre of the University of Wales. *European Access*. Chadwyck-Healey Ltd., Cambridge, (six times a year since 1985).
[B.257] Office for Official Publications of the European Communities. *The European Community as a Publisher*. Office for Official Publications of the European Communities, Luxembourg (annual).
[B.258] Commission of the European Communities. *European File*. Office for Official Publications of the European Communities, Luxembourg (occasional since 1979).
[B.259] Newman Books Ltd. *European Food Trades Directory. Formerly Food Trades Directory and Food Buyers' Yearbook*. Newman Books Ltd., London, biennial.
[B.260] Agra Europe (London) Ltd. *European Fruit and Vegetable Markets and Trade. Agra Europe Special Report no.35*. Agra Europe (London) Ltd., Tunbridge Wells, April 1987.
[B.261] Statistical Office of the European Communities. *Eurostat Catalogue: Publications and Electronics Services*. Office for Official Publications of the European Communities, Luxembourg, 1988.
[B.262] Statistical Office of the European Communities. *Eurostat News*. Office for Official Publications of the European Communities, Luxembourg (quarterly since 1976).
[B.263] Extel Financial Ltd. *Extel Ranking of UK Investment Analysts*. Extel Financial Ltd., London (annual).
[B.264] Statistical Office of the European Communities. *External Trade Analytical Tables: Glossarium*. Office for the Official Publications of the European Communities, Luxembourg (annual).
[B.265] Statistical Office of the European Communities. *External Trade Monthly Statistics: Glossarium*. Office for the Official Publications of the European Communities, Luxembourg (annual).
[B.266] Statistical Office of the European Communities. *External Trade Nomenclature of Goods: Correlation Tables Nimexe 1988 to CN 1987*. Office for Official Publications of the European Communities, Luxembourg, 1988.
[B.267] Statistical Office of the European Communities. *External Trade Statistics: User's Guide*. second edition. Office for the Official Publications of the European Communities, Luxembourg, 1985.

[B.268] Secretary of State for Trade and Industry. *Fair Trading Act 1973: Report by the Secretary of State for Trade and Industry for the Period l January 1973 to 31 October 1973 on the Operation of the Monopolies and Mergers Acts 1948 and 1965*. HC175. (Session 1973/74). HMSO, London, 1974.

[B.269] Department of Employment (Statistics A6). *Family Expenditure: A Plain Man's Guide to the Family Expenditure Survey*. Department of Employment, London, July 1982.

[B.270] Department of Employment (Statistics A6). *Family Expenditure: A Plain Man's Guide to the Family Expenditure Survey*. Department of Employment, London, July 1986.

[B.271] Ministry of Agriculture, Fisheries and Food. *Farming and the Nation*. Cmnd 7458. (Session 1978/79). HMSO, London, February 1979.

[B.272] National Board for Prices and Incomes. *Fifth and Final General Report: July 1969 to March 1971*. Cmnd 4649. (Session 1970/71). HMSO, London, 1971.

[B.273] National Board for Prices and Incomes. *Fifth and Final General Report: July 1969 to March 1971 (Supplement)*. Cmnd 4649-I. (Session 1970/71). HMSO, London, 1971.

[B.274] The Tea Council Information Service. *File on Tea*. The Tea Council Information Service, London, 1987.

[B.275] Committee to Review the Functioning of the Financial Institutions. (The Wilson Committee). *The Financing of Small Firms: Interim Report of the Committee to Review the Functioning of Financial Institutions*. Cmnd 7503. (Session 1978/79). HMSO, London, 1979.

[B.276] House of Commons Expenditure Committee (Trade and Industry Sub-committee). *The Fishing Industry*. HC356, HC356-ii, HC356-iii, Volume I, Volume II and Volume III. (Fifth Report from the Expenditure Committee). (Session 1977/78). HMSO, London, 1978.

[B.277] Dairy Trade Federation. *Flavoured Drink Market Survey*. Dairy Trade Federation, London, 1985.

[B.278] GLC Economic Policy Group. *Flour Milling and Bread Baking in London. Strategy Document no.15*. GLC, London, September 1983.

[B.279] Health and Safety Executive. *Food and Packaging Health and Safety*. HMSO, London, 1984.

[B.280] Ministry of Agriculture, Fisheries and Food. *Food from Our Own Resources*. Cmnd 6020. (Session 1974/75). HMSO, London, April 1975.

[B.281] Cabinet Office, Advisory Council for Applied Research and Development. *The Food Industry and Technology*. HMSO, London, 1987.

[B.282] Newman Books Ltd. *Food Industry Directory 1989-90*. Newman Books Ltd., London, 1989.

[B.283] Economic Development Committee for Food Manufacturing, National Economic Development Office. *Food Statistics: A Guide to the Major Official and Unofficial UK Sources*. NEDO, London, 1968.

[B.284] Food Trade Press Ltd. *Food Trade Review: For Food Manufacturers, Processors and Packers*. Food Trade Press Ltd., Orpington (monthly).

[B.285] Newman Books Ltd. *Food Trades Directory and Food Buyer's Yearbook (Incorporating Food Processing Industry Directory)*. twentieth revised edition. Newman Books Ltd., London, 1987.

[B.286] Coopers and Lybrand *Form and Content of Company Accounts — Manual Part 3: Comprehensive Coverage of Disclosure Requirements of the Companies Act 1985, SSAPs and the Listing Agreement*. Financial Training Services, London, 1986.

[B.287] House of Commons Estimates Committee. *Fourth Report from the Estimates Committee: Government Statistical Services*. HC246. (Session 1966/67). HMSO, London, 1967.

[B.288] Command Paper. *A Framework for Government Research and Development. (The Rothschild Report)*. Cmnd 4814. (Session 1971/72). HMSO, London, 1971.

[B.289] Command Paper. *Framework for Government Research and Development*. Cmnd 5046. (Session 1971/72). HMSO, London, 1972.

[B.290] Retail Journals Ltd. *Frozen and Chilled Foods*. Retail Journals Ltd., Redhill (monthly).

[B.291] Agra Europe (London) Ltd. *Fruit and Vegetable Policy in an International Context. Agra Europe Special Report no.32.* Agra Europe (London) Ltd., Tunbridge Wells, November 1986.
[B.292] House of Lords Select Committee on the European Communities. *Fruit and Vegetables. Twenty Second Report.* HL147. (Session 1980/81). HMSO, London, 1981.
[B.293] Cabinet Office. *Government Economic Statistics: A Scrutiny Report. (The Pickford Report).* HMSO, London, April 1989.
[B.294] Command Paper. *Government Statistical Services.* Cmnd 8236. (Session 1980/81). HMSO, London, April 1981.
[B.295] Central Statistical Office. *Government Statistics: A Brief Guide to Sources.* Central Statistical Office, London (annual).
[B.296] Office of Population Censuses and Surveys. *Guide to Census Reports: Great Britain 1801-1966.* HMSO, London, 1977.
[B.297] Key Note Publications Ltd. *A Guide to Marketing Research in the UK.* first edition. Key Note Publications Ltd., London, 1987.
[B.298] Central Statistical Office. *Guide to Official Statistics no.5.* HMSO, London, 1986.
[B.299] HM Customs and Excise (Statistical Office). *Guide to the Classification for Overseas Trade Statistics: Correlation Tables.* HMSO, London, 1988.
[B.300] Commission of the European Communities. *Guidelines for European Agriculture.* COM(81)608. Commission of the European Communities, Brussels, 1981.
[B.301] Customs Cooperation Council. *Harmonized Commodity Description and Coding System: Explanatory Notes.* Customs Cooperation Council, Brussels, 1986.
[B.302] International Association of Ice Cream Manufacturers. *The History of Ice Cream.* International Association of Ice Cream Manufacturers, Washington (undated).
[B.303] Agriculture and Food Research Council. *Horticulture: Institute of Horticultural Research Annual Report.* Institute of Horticultural Research, East Malling (annual).
[B.304] Ministry of Agriculture, Fisheries and Food. *Horticulture in Britain. Part I: Vegetables.* HMSO, London, 1967.
[B.305] Ministry of Agriculture, Fisheries and Food. *Horticulture in Britain. Part II: Fruit and Flowers.* HMSO, London, 1970.
[B.306] The Milk Marketing Boards in Scotland. *The Household Market for Cream in Scotland 1985.* The Scottish Milk Marketing Board, Paisley, 1985.
[B.307] The Milk Marketing Boards in Scotland. *The Household Market for Milk in Scotland 1983.* The Scottish Milk Marketing Board, Paisley, 1984.
[B.308] The Milk Marketing Boards in Scotland. *The Household Market for Milk in Scotland 1986.* The Scottish Milk Marketing Board, Paisley, 1987.
[B.309] ICC Information Group Ltd. *ICC Directory of Companies.* ICC Information Group Ltd., London (data base).
[B.310] ICC Information Group Ltd. *ICC Directory of Stockbrokers Reports.* ICC Information Group Ltd., London, annual (and monthly updates).
[B.311] International Coffee Organisation. *ICO Basic Information: Objectives, Structure, History and Operation.* ICO, London, December 1988.
[B.312] Food and Drink Manufacturing Economic Development Committee, National Economic Development Council. *Improving Productivity in the Food and Drink Manufacturing Industries: The Case for a Joint Approach.* NEDC, London, 1982.
[B.313] Incomes Data Services Ltd. *Incomes Data Index.* Incomes Data Services Ltd., London (annual).
[B.314] Central Statistical Office. *The Index of Industrial Production: Method of Compilation. Studies in Official Statistics no.7.* HMSO, London, 1959.
[B.315] Central Statistical Office. *The Index of Industrial Production. Studies in Official Statistics no.2.* HMSO, London, 1952.
[B.316] Central Statistical Office. *The Index of Industrial Production and Other Output Measures. Studies in Official Statistics no.17.* HMSO, London, 1970.
[B.317] Central Statistical Office. *Indexes to the Standard Industrial Classification Revised 1980.* HMSO, London, 1981.

[B.318] Industrial Relations Services. *Industrial Relations Review and Report Index*. Eclipse Publications Ltd., London (annual).
[B.319] United Nations. *Input-output Tables and Analysis. Studies in Methods, Series F, no.14, rev 1*. United Nations, New York, 1973.
[B.320] House of Commons Expenditure Committee (Trade and Industry Sub-committee). *Inquiry into the Fishing Industry: Progress Report*. HC255. (Session 1976/77). HMSO, London, 1977.
[B.321] International Coffee Organisation. *International Coffee Organisation Library: Monthly Entries*. ICO, London (monthly).
[B.322] Statistical Office of the European Communities. *Introductory Course for Officials of the National Statistical Services*. EUROSTAT, Luxembourg, 1987.
[B.323] Dun and Bradstreet Ltd. *Key British Enterprises*. Dun and Bradstreet Ltd., London (annual).
[B.324] Statistical Office of the European Communities. *Labour Force Sample Survey: Methods and Definitions*. Office for Official Publications of the European Communities, Luxembourg, 1988.
[B.325] Official Government Notices. *London Gazette*. HMSO, London (daily).
[B.326] Ministry of Agriculture, Fisheries and Food. *Marketing Studies Report on Outlets for Lamb in Processing and Catering*. MAFF, London, 1985.
[B.327] Marketing Strategies for Industry (UK) Ltd. and the Institute of Marketing. *Marketing Surveys Index*. Marketing Strategies for Industry (UK) Ltd., Mitcham (monthly).
[B.328] McCarthy Information Ltd. *McCarthy Industry*. McCarthy Information Ltd., Warminster, press cuttings.
[B.329] Media Expenditure Analysis Ltd. *MEAL Standard and Online Services*. Media Expenditure Analysis Ltd., London (updated regularly).
[B.330] Central Statistical Office. *The Measurement of Changes in Production: The Index of Industrial Production and the Output-based Measures of Gross Domestic Product. Studies in Official Statistics no.25*. HMSO, London, 1976.
[B.331] Organisation for Economic Cooperation and Development. *Measurement of Scientific and Technical Activities. (The Frascati Manual)*. OECD, Paris, 1981.
[B.332] Department of Trade and Industry. *Mergers Policy*. HMSO, London, 1988.
[B.333] Ministry of Labour. *Method of Construction and Calculation of the Index of Retail Prices. Studies in Official Statistics no.6*. HMSO, London, 1967.
[B.334] Retail Prices Index Advisory Committee. *Methodological Issues Affecting the Retail Prices Index*. Cmnd 9848. (Session 1985/86). HMSO, London, July 1986.
[B.335] Milk Marketing Board for England and Wales. *Milk Costs 1986/87*. Milk Marketing Board for England and Wales, Thames Ditton, 1987.
[B.336] Monopolies and Mergers Commission. *Monopolies and Mergers Commission*. HMSO, London (annual).
[B.337] Central Statistical Office. *Monthly Digest of Statistics Supplement: Definitions and Explanatory Notes*. HMSO, London (annual).
[B.338] Research Publications Ltd. *Monthly Index to the Financial Times*. Research Publications, Reading (monthly).
[B.339] Central Statistical Office. *The National Accounts — A Short Guide. Studies in Official Statistics no.36*. HMSO, London, 1981.
[B.340] W.R. Nelson & Co. *Nelson's Official Research Guide*. W.R. Nelson & Co., New York (annual).
[B.341] European Parliament. *Official Journal of the European Communities*. Office for Official Publications of the European Communities, Luxembourg (daily).
[B.342] European Parliament. *Official Journal of the European Communities, vol.20, no.L73*. Office for Official Publications of the European Communities, Luxembourg, 21 March 1977.
[B.343] European Parliament. *Official Journal of the European Communities, vol.21, no.L144*. Office for Official Publications of the European Communities, Luxembourg, 31 May 1978.

[B.344] European Parliament. *Official Journal of the European Communities, vol.24, no.L379*. Office for Official Publications of the European Communities, Luxembourg, 31 December 1981.
[B.345] European Parliament *Official Journal of the European Communities, vol.26, no.L24*. Office for Official Publications of the European Communities, Luxembourg, 27 January 1983.
[B.346] Economics and Statistics Department of Lever Brothers and Unilever Limited. "Oils and fats", in Kendall, M.G. (ed). *The Sources and Nature of the Statistics of the United Kingdom, volume 1*. Oliver and Boyd, London, 1952.
[B.347] Office of Population Censuses and Surveys. *OPCS Census Guide 3: 1981 Census: Britain's Workforce*. HMSO, London, 1985.
[B.348] Meat and Livestock Commission. *Operating Costs and Margins in the Slaughtering Industry*. MLC, Bletchley, 1985.
[B.349] Economic Development Committee for Agriculture, National Economic Development Office. *Outdoor Vegetables: UK Farming and the Common Market*. NEDO, London, 1973.
[B.350] Economic Development Committee for Agriculture, National Economic Development Office. *Pears: UK Farming and the Common Market*. NEDO, London, 1977.
[B.351] Processors and Growers' Research Organisation. *PGRO Annual Report*. PGRO, Peterborough (annual).
[B.352] National Economic Development Office. *The Pig Production and Marketing Systems of Denmark, the Netherlands and the United Kingdom*. NEDO, London, 1986.
[B.353] Potato Marketing Board. *Potato Marketing Board Survey of Potato Research in the United Kingdom*. Potato Marketing Board, Oxford (occasional).
[B.354] Economic Development Committee for Agriculture, National Economic Development Office. *Potatoes: UK Farming and the Common Market*. NEDO, London, 1977.
[B.355] Food and Drink Manufacturing Economic Development Committee, National Economic Development Council. *Productivity Growth in the UK Food and Drink Manufacturing Industries*. NEDC, London, 1978.
[B.356] Command Paper. *The Programme for Controlling Inflation: The Second Stage. A Draft Bill*. Cmnd 5206. (Session 1972/73). HMSO, London, 1973.
[B.357] Office for Official Publications of the European Communities. *Publications of the European Communities*. Office for Official Publications of the European Communities, Luxembourg (quarterly).
[B.358] Committee to Review the Functioning of the Financial Institutions. (The Wilson Committee). *Report and Appendices*. Cmnd 7937. (Session 1972/73). HMSO, London, 1980.
[B.359] Price Commission. *Report for the Period December 1 1975 to February 29 1976*. HC314. (Session 1975/76). HMSO, London, 1976.
[B.360] Price Commission. *Report for the Period 1 June to 31 July 1977*. Cmnd 6950. (Session 1976/77). HMSO, London, 1977.
[B.361] Royal Commission on the Distribution of Income and Wealth (The Diamond Commission). *Report no.1. Initial Report on the Standing Reference*. Cmnd 6171. (Session 1974/75). HMSO, London, 1974.
[B.362] Secretary of State for the Home Department, the Minister of Agriculture, Fisheries and Food, and the Secretary of State for Scotland. *Report of the Committee of Enquiry into Fatstock and Carcase Meat Marketing and Distribution. (The Verdon-Smith Report)*. Cmnd 2282. (Session 1963/64). HMSO, London, 1964.
[B.363] Command Paper. *Report of the Committee of Inquiry into the Fishing Industry. (The Fleck Report)*. Cmnd 1266. (Session 1960/61). HMSO, London, 1960.
[B.364] Ministry of Agriculture, Fisheries and Food. *Report of the Study Group on the Development of Value-added Products from Pigmeat*. MAFF, London, 1986.
[B.365] Ministry of Agriculture, Fisheries and Food. *Report on the Marketing of Wheat, Barley and Oats in England and Wales. Economic Series no.11*. HMSO, London, 1928.
[B.366] Secretary of State for Trade and Industry. *Restrictive Trading Agreements: Report of the Registrar 1 July 1969 to 30 June 1972*. Cmnd 5195. (Session 1972/73). HMSO,

London, 1973.
[B.367] Department of Trade and Industry. *Review of DTI Statistics. (The Armstrong-Rees Report).* DTI, London, May 1989.
[B.368] Government Statistical Services. *Review of Government Statistical Services: Report to the Prime Minister. (The Rayner Report).* HMSO, London, December 1980.
[B.369] Department of Trade and Industry. *Review of Restrictive Trade Practices Policy.* Cm 331. (Session 1987/88). HMSO, London, 1988.
[B.370] Food and Drink Manufacturing Economic Development Committee, National Economic Development Office. *Review of the Food and Drink Manufacturing Industry.* NEDO, London, 1986.
[B.371] Statutory Publications Office. *Secondary Legislation of the European Communities. Volume 28: Fruit and Vegetables.* HMSO, London, 1973.
[B.372] Central Statistical Office. *Series and Weights Used in the Index of Output of the Production Industries — 1980 Base. Occasional Paper no.18.* HMSO, London, 1983.
[B.373] Central Statistical Office. *Series and Weights Used in the Output-based Estimates of Gross Domestic Product at Factor Cost (1980=100). Occasional Paper no.20.* HMSO, London, 1984.
[B.374] Centre of European Agricultural Studies. *The Single European Market and the Food and Drink Industry: Political Myth or Market Opportunity.* Centre of European Agricultural Studies, Wye, 1988.
[B.375] Committee of Inquiry on Small Firms. *Small Firms: Report of the Committee of Inquiry on Small Firms. The Bolton Committee.* Cmnd 4811. (Session 1971/72). HMSO, London, 1971.
[B.376] Economic Development Committee for Agriculture, National Economic Development Office. *Soft Fruit: UK Farming and the Common Market.* NEDO, London, 1973.
[B.377] Sea Fish Industry Authority. *Sources of Statistics Pertaining to the British Fishing Industry. FERU Occasional Paper Series no.3.* SFIA, Edinburgh, 1981.
[B.378] Ministry of Agriculture, Fisheries and Food. *Special Report from the Agriculture Committee: The Effect of Feedstuff Prices on the UK Pig and Poultry Industries.* HC539-I. (Session 1983/84). HMSO, London, 1984.
[B.379] Central Statistical Office. *Standard Industrial Classification Revised 1980: Reconciliation with Standard Industrial Classification 1968.* CSO, London, 1980.
[B.380] House of Lords Select Committee on the European Communities. *Starch and Seeds.* HL48. (Session 1977/78). HMSO, London, 1977.
[B.381] Central Statistical Office. *Statistical News.* HMSO, London (quarterly).
[B.382] Centre for Agricultural Strategy. *Strategy for the UK Dairy Industry.* Centre for Agricultural Strategy, Reading, 1978.
[B.383] The Three Milk Marketing Boards in Scotland. *The Structure of Scottish Milk Production at 1987.* The Scottish Milk Marketing Board, Paisley, 1985.
[B.384] Commission of the European Communities. *A Study of the Evolution of Concentration in the Food Industry of the United Kingdom. Part I, Part II (Product Market Structure).* Commission of the European Communities, Brussels, 1975.
[B.385] Central Statistical Office. *Supplementary Analysis of Series Used in the Index of the Output of the Production Industries — 1980 Base.* HMSO, London, 1984.
[B.386] Acumen Marketing Group (for the International Coffee Organisation). *Survey of the Coffee Industry in the United Kingdom. Two volumes.* Acumen Marketing Group, London, 1982.
[B.387] J. Thomas & Co. Private Ltd. *Tea Market Annual Report.* J. Thomas & Co. Private Ltd., Calcutta (annual).
[B.388] Food and Drink Manufacturing Economic Development Committee, National Economic Development Office. *Technology Transfer in the UK Food and Drink Industry.* NEDO, London, 1985.
[B.389] Manchester Business School. *The UK Biscuit Market.* Manchester Business School, Manchester, 1985.
[B.390] Agra Europe (London) Ltd. *The UK Dairy Industry and EEC Legislation: A Commentary on EEC Regulations and Court Proceedings.* Agra Europe (London)

Ltd., Tunbridge Wells, 1988.
[B.391] Technical Change Centre. *The UK Food Processing Industry: Opportunities for Change*. Technical Change Centre, London, 1985.
[B.392] Agra Europe (London) Ltd. *UK Grain Exports — A Surrender to the Multinationals? Agra Europe Special Report no. 22*. Agra Europe (London) Ltd., Tunbridge Wells, 1984.
[B.393] National Economic Development Office. *UK Pig Production and Marketing*. NEDO, London, 1986.
[B.394] Ministry of Agriculture, Fisheries and Food. *The United Kingdom Cereals Market: The Next Five Years*. MAFF, London, 1983.
[B.395] Central Statistical Office. *United Kingdom National Accounts: Sources and Methods. Studies in Official Statistics no.37,* third edition. HMSO, London, 1985.
[B.396] Dun and Bradstreet Ltd. *Who Owns Whom: United Kingdom and Republic of Ireland. Two volumes*. Dun and Bradstreet Ltd., London (annual).
[B.397] Central Statistical Office. *Wholesale Price Index: Principles and Procedures. Studies in Official Statistics no.32*. HMSO, London, 1980.

Reports of the National Board for Prices and Incomes

[B.398] *Bread Prices and Pay in the Baking Industry (First Report)*. NPBI Report no.144. Cmnd 4239. (Session 1969/70). HMSO, London, 1970.
[B.399] *Bread Prices and Pay in the Baking Industry (Second Report)*. NPBI Report no.151. Cmnd 4428. (Session 1970/71). HMSO, London, 1970.
[B.400] *Costs and Prices of the Chocolate and Sugar Confectionery Industry*. NPBI Report no.75. Cmnd 3694. (Session 1967/68), HMSO, London, 1968.
[B.401] *Costs, Prices and Profitability in the Ice-cream Manufacturing Industry*. NPBI Report no.160. Cmnd 4548. (Session 1970/71). HMSO, London, 1970
[B.402] *Distribution Costs of Fresh Fruit and Vegetables*. NPBI Report no.31. Cmnd 3265. (Session 1966/67). HMSO, London, 1967.
[B.403] *Distributors' Margins in Relation to Manufacturers' Recommended Prices*. NPBI Report no.55. Cmnd 3546. (Session 1967/68). HMSO, London, 1968.
[B.404] *Flour Prices*. NPBI Report no.53. Cmnd 3522. (Session 1967/68). HMSO, London, 1968.
[B.405] *General Problems of Low Pay*. NPBI Report no.169. Cmnd 4648. (Session 1970/71). HMSO, London, 1971.
[B.406] *Margarine and Compound Cooking Fats*. NPBI Report no.147. Cmnd 4368. (Session 1969/70). HMSO, London, 1970.
[B.407] *Pay and Conditions of Workers in the Milk Industry*. NPBI Report no.140. Cmnd 4267. (Session 1969/70). HMSO, London, 1970.
[B.408] *Prices of Bread and Flour*. NPBI Report no.3. Cmnd 2760. (Session 1965/66). HMSO, London, 1965.
[B.409] *Prices, Profits and Costs in Food Distribution*. NPBI Report no.165. Cmnd 4645. (Session 1970/71). HMSO London, 1971.
[B.410] *Productivity and Pay during the Period of Severe Restraint*. NPBI Report no.23. Cmnd 3167. (Session 1966/67). HMSO, London, 1966.
[B.411] *The Remuneration of Milk Distributors (Final Report)*. NBPI Report no.46. Cmnd 3477. (Session 1967/68). HMSO, London, 1967.
[B.412] *The Remuneration of Milk Distributors (Interim Report)*. NBPI Report no.33. Cmnd 3294. (Session 1966/67). HMSO, London, 1967.
[B.413] *Smithfield Market*. NPBI Report no.126. Cmnd 4171. (Session 1968/69). HMSO, London, 1969.
[B.414] *Tea Prices*. NBPI Report no. 154. Cmnd 4456. (Session 1970/71). HMSO, London, 1970.
[B.415] *Wages in the Bakery Industry (Final Report)*. NBPI Report no.17. Cmnd 3019. (Session 1966/67). HMSO, London, 1966.

[B.416] *Wages in the Bakery Industry (First Report)*. NBPI Report no.9. Cmnd 2878. (Session 1965/66). HMSO, London, 1966.

Reports of the Prices Commissions

[B.417] *Bread Prices and Costs in Northern Ireland and Great Britain*. Price Commission Report no.13. HMSO, London, 1976.
[B.418] *Cadbury Schweppes Food Ltd. — Grocery Products*. Price Commission Investigation Report no.10. HC293. (Session 1977/78). HMSO, London, 1978.
[B.419] *Coffee; Prices, Costs and Margins*. Price Commission Report no.29. HMSO, London, 1977.
[B.420] *CPC (United Kingdom) Ltd. — Increases in the Prices of Maize Starch, Glucose, Syrup, and Starch-derived and Glucose-derived Products*. Price Commission Investigation Report no.20. HC613. (Session 1977/78). HMSO, London, 1978.
[B.421] *Food Prices in Outlying Areas*. Price Commission Report no.10. HMSO, London, 1975
[B.422] *The Marketing of Eggs*. Price Commission Report no.1. HC329. (Session 1974). HMSO, London, 1974.
[B.423] *Metrication and Retail Prices (First Report): Granulated Sugar, Biscuits, Dried Vegetables and Salt*. Price Commission Report no.24 [a]. HMSO, London, 1977.
[B.424] *Prices of Commonly-purchased Diabetic Foods*. Price Commission Report no.8. HMSO, London, 1975.
[B.425] *Prices; Costs and Margins in the Importation and Distribution of Bacon*. Price Commission Examination Report no.1. HC229. (Session 1977/78). HMSO, London, 1978.
[B.426] *Prices, Costs and Margins in the Production and Distribution of Compound Feeding Stuffs for Cattle, Pigs and Poultry*. Price Commission Examination Report no.3. HC338. (Session 1977/78). HMSO, London, 1978.
[B.427] *Prices and Distribution of Bananas*. Price Commission Report no.4. HMSO, London, 1975.
[B.428] *Prices, Margins and Channels of Distribution for Fruit and Vegetables (Final Report)*. Price Commission Report no.5. HMSO, London, 1975.
[B.429] *Prices, Margins and Channels of Distribution for Fruit and Vegetables (Interim Report)*. Price Commission Report no.2. HMSO, London, 1974.
[B.430] *Prices and Margins in the Distribution of Fish*. Price Commission Report no.14. HMSO, London, 1976.
[B.431] *Prices and Margins in Meat Distribution*. Price Commission Report no.7. HMSO, London, 1975.
[B.432] *Prices and Margins in Poultry Distribution*. Price Commission Report no.11. HMSO, London, 1975.
[B.433] *Recommended Retail Prices*. Price Commission Report no.25. HMSO, London, 1977.
[B.434] *Tate & Lyle Refineries Ltd. — Sugar and Syrup Products*. Price Commission Investigation Report no.6. HC224. (Session 1977/78). HMSO, London, 1978.
[B.435] *Tea Prices*. Price Commission Report no.32. HMSO, London, 1978.
[B.436] *United Biscuits (UK) Ltd. — Biscuits, Crisps Nuts and Savoury Snacks*. Price Commission Investigation Report no.36. HC347. (Session 1987/79). HMSO, London, 1979.
[B.437] *Weetabix Ltd. — Cereal and Muesli Products*. Price Commission Investigation Report no.12. HC336. (Session 1977/78). HMSO, London, 1978.

Reports of the Monopolies and Mergers Commissions, former Monopolies Commission and former Monopolies and Restrictive Practices Commission.

[B.438] *S & W Berisford Limited and British Sugar Corporation Limited. A Report on the Proposed Merger*. Monopolies and Mergers Commission Report. HC241. (Session

1980/81). HMSO, London, 1981.

[B.439] *Breakfast Cereals. A Report on the Supply of Ready Cooked Breakfast Cereal Foods.* Monopolies Commission Report. HC2. (Session 1972/73). HMSO, London, 1973.

[B.440] *Cat and Dog Foods. A Report on the Supply in the United Kingdom of Cat and Dog Foods.* Monopolies and Mergers Commission Report. HC447. (Session 1976/77). HMSO, London, 1977.

[B.441] *Discounts to Retailers. Report on the General Effect on the Public Interest of the Practice of Charging Some Retailers Lower Prices than Others or Providing Special Benefits to Some Retailers Where the Difference Cannot be Attributed to Savings in the Suppliers' Costs.* Monopolies and Mergers Commission Report. HC311. (Session 1980/81). HMSO, London, 1981.

[B.442] *Elders IXL Ltd. and Allied-Lyons plc: A Report on the Proposed Merger.* Monopolies and Mergers Commission Report. Cmnd 9892. (Session 1985/86). HMSO, London, 1986.

[B.443] *Flour and Bread. A Report on the Supply in the United Kingdom of Wheat Flour and of Bread Made from Wheat Flour.* Monopolies and Mergers Commission Report. HC412. (Session 1976/77). HMSO, London, 1977.

[B.444] *Frozen Foodstuffs. A Report on the Supply in the United Kingdom of Frozen Foodstuffs for Human Consumption.* Monopolies and Mergers Commission Report. HC674. (Session 1975/76). HMSO, London, 1976.

[B.445] *Ice-cream and Water Ices. A Report on the Supply in the United Kingdom of Ice-cream and Water Ices.* Monopolies and Mergers Commission Report. Cmnd 7632. (Session 1979/80). HMSO, London, 1979.

[B.446] *Infant Milk Foods. A Report on the Supply of Infant Milk Foods.* Monopolies Commission Report. HC319. (Session 1966/67). HMSO, London, 1967.

[B.447] *Linfood Holdings plc and Fitch Lovell plc: A Report on the Proposed Merger.* Monopolies and Mergers Commission Report. Cmnd 8874. (Session 1982/83). HMSO, London, 1983.

[B.448] *Nabisco Brands Inc. and Huntley and Palmer Foods plc: A Report on the Proposed Merger.* Monopolies and Mergers Commission Report. Cmnd 8680. (Session 1981/82). HMSO, London, 1982.

[B.449] *NFU Development Trust Limited and FMC Limited. Report on the Proposed Merger.* Monopolies and Mergers Commission Report. HC441. (Session 1974/75). HMSO, London, 1975.

[B.450] *Parallel Pricing. Report on the General Effect on the Public Interest of the Practice of Parallel Pricing.* Monopolies Commission Report. Cmnd 5330. (Session 1972/73). HMSO, London, 1973.

[B.451] *Recommended Resale Prices. A Report on the General Effect on the Public Interest of the Practice of Recommending or Otherwise Suggesting Prices to be Charged on the Resale of Goods.* Monopolies Commission Report. HC100. (Session 1968/69). HMSO, London, 1969.

[B.452] *Report on the Supply of Tea.* Monopolies and Restrictive Commission Report. HC15. (Session 1956/57). HMSO, London, 1956.

[B.453] *Ross Group Limited and Associated Fisheries Limited. Report on the Proposed Merger.* Monopolies Commission Report. HC42. (Session 1966/67). HMSO, London, 1966.

[B.454] *Starch, Glucoses and Modified Starches. Report on the Supply of Starch, Glucoses and Modified Starches.* Monopolies Commission Report. HC615. (Session 1970/71). HMSO, London, 1971.

[B.455] *Tate and Lyle plc and Ferruzzi Finanziaria SpA and S and W Berisford plc: A Report on the Existing and Proposed Mergers.* Monopolies and Mergers Commission Report. Cm 89 (Session 1987/88). HMSO, London, 1987.

[B.456] *Unilever Limited and Allied Breweries Limited: A Report on the Proposed Merger and General Observations on Mergers.* Monopolies Commission Report. HC297. (Session 1968/69). HMSO, London, 1969.

[B.457] *White Salt: A Report on the Supply of White Salt in the United Kingdom by Producers of Such Salt*. Monopolies and Mergers Commission Report. Cmnd 9778. (Session 1985/86). HMSO, London, 1986.

APPENDIX A: Reconciliation of Standard Industrial Classification (1980) with Standard Industrial Classification (1968) for Classes 41 and 42: "Food, drink and tobacco manufacturing Industries"

Group	Activity Heading	Heading	MLH or Sub-division 1968	Heading or Part Covered	Remarks
411		Organic oils and fats (other than crude animal fats)			
	4115	Margarine and compound cooking fats	229/1	Margarine	
	4116	Processing organic oils and fats (other than crude animal fats)			
	4116/1	Crude oils from fish and other marine animals	221 pt.	The production of crude oil and fats from fish and other marine animals	
	4116/2	Crude oils, cakes and meals from oilseeds and nuts	221 pt.	The production of crude oil from oilseeds and nuts; including the production of oilseed cakes and meals	
	4116/3	Treated vegetable, marine and animal oils and fats	221 pt.	The refining and hydrogenation (hardening) of vegetable and marine oils, including olive oil, whale oils and fish liver oils, and technical tallow	The manufacture of dripping, suet and edible tallow, premier-jus, also stearine and other animal oils and greases are classified to heading 4126/1
412		Slaughter of animals and production of meat			
	4121	Slaughterhouses	810/2 pt.	Wholesale slaughtering of animals for human consumption and their subsequent processing in the slaughterhouse	Slaughtering etc. of poultry is classified to heading 4123. The processing of animal by-products outside slaughterhouses, slaughtering or processing of animals unfit for human consumption are classified to heading 4126

Group	Activity Heading	Heading	MLH or Sub-division 1968	Heading or Part Covered	Remarks
			214/2 pt.	Meat chilling or freezing for human consumption only	
	4122	Bacon curing and meat processing			
	4122/1	Bacon and ham	214/2 pt.	Production of bacon, ham and processing pigment products only	Pre-cooking or putting into sealed packs is included but canned products are classified to heading 4122/3
	4122/2	Frozen meat products	214/1 pt.	Freezing of prepared meat products e.g. complete meat based meals, pies, puddings, sausage rolls etc.	Fish and fish product freezing is classified to heading 4150/1. Poultry and poultry meat product freezing is classified to 4123/1 and 4123/2 respectively
	4122/3	Other processed and preserved meats	214/2 pt.	Canning and otherwise preserving meat (other than by quick freezing). Making sausages, meat pies, pasties and puddings; meat extracts, essences and pastes	Production at distributive establishments is classified to division 6
	4123	Poultry slaughter and processing			
	4123/1	Poultry slaughter	214/1 pt.	Slaughtering, dressing, and further preparation of game birds; chicken cuts (chilled, fresh and frozen) production in slaughterhouses	
			214/2 pt.	Poultry dressing only (in slaughterhouses)	
	4123/2	Poultry and meat products	214/1 pt.	Chicken ready-to-eat meals manufacturing only	Including dressing and quartering fowl in establishments not engaged in slaughtering
			214/2 pt.	Processing of poultry meat products such as pastes, breasts, etc., either fresh or packeted, canned or frozen	Products containing mixed ingredients of poultry and other meats are classified to heading 4122

	4126	Animal by-product processing			
	4126/1	Fats and greases	221 pt.	The manufacture of dripping, suet, tallow, premier-jus, oleo-stearine and other animal oils and greases only	Hydrogenation of fats is classified to heading 4116/3. Fat splitting and other chemical treatment is classified to heading 2563
	4126/2	Processed guts and offals	214/2 pt.	Bladder processing, sausage casing production, processed edible offals production, tripe dressing etc.	Includes the processing of bones and blood
	4126/3	Slaughtering other than for human consumption and other processing of animal by-products	221 pt.	Animal by-products of bone such as bone meal and bone flour; meat meal; bone boiling, crushing and degreasing	Bone oil manufacturing is classified to 4126/1 and bone glue manufacturing to 2562
			899/7 pt.	Animal by-products from knackers e.g. hooves, hides and unrendered and crude fat	
			214/2 pt.	Bile processing only	
			229/2 pt.	Rennet (not artificial) manufacturing only	
413	4130	Preparation of milk and milk products			
	4130/1	Liquid milk and cream	215/1	Heat treatment of milk	
			215/2 pt.	Manufacturing fresh and preserved cream only	
	4130/2	Butter and cheese	215/2 pt.	Manufacturing butter and cheese etc. only	
	4130/3	Other milk products	215/2 pt.	Making condensed, evaporated and dried milk and infant and invalid food with a milk base etc.	
			229/2 pt.	Desserts with a milk base manufacturing only	
414	4147	Processing of fruit and vegetables			
	4147/1	Freezing	218/2	Quick freezing of fruit and vegetables	
	4147/2	Pickling and preserving in salt or oil	218/3 pt.	Preserving fruit and vegetables by pickling and preserving in salt or oil	

Group	Activity Heading	Heading	MLH or Sub-division 1968	Heading or Part Covered	Remarks
	4147/3	Jam, marmalade and table jellies	218/1	Jam, marmalade, jellies etc.	Honey processing and packing is classified to heading 4239/9
			218/3 pt.	Strained fruit and vegetable manufacturing and homogenized fruit and vegetable manufacturing only	
	4147/4	Canning, bottling, drying etc.	218/3 pt.	Preserving fruit and vegetables by canning, bottling, drying (except field drying), dehydrating; processing fruit and vegetables by heat treatment	
415	4150	Fish processing			
	4150/1	Freezing	214/1 pt.	Quick freezing of fish and fish products only	Including crustacean and molluscs
			214/2 pt.	Fish finger (frozen) manufacturing only	
	4150/2	Other processing and preserving	214/2 pt.	Fish canning, curing, drying, salting and any other fish processing which does not involve freezing; the manufacture of fresh fish cake, fish paste, kippers, potted shrimp; shrimp and shellfish preserving	
416	4160	Grain milling	211	Grain milling	Production of uncooked breakfast cereals (e.g. oatmeal is included, but ready-to-eat breakfast cereals are classified to heading 4239/8)
418	4180	Starch	229/2 pt.	Manufacturing starch and starch products such as glucose, dextrose and soluble starch	
419		Bread, biscuits and flour confectionery			

	4196	Bread and flour confectionery	212	Bread and flour confectionery	Bakehouses run in conjunction with retail shops are included here when they can supply separate statistical information or when baking is the main activity of the combined unit
	4261/3	Fruit wines	239/2 pt.	Apple and fruit wine manufacturing	Including wine made from fresh grapes
427	4270	Brewing and malting			
	4270/1	Beer and other brewing products	231 pt.	Brewing beer	
	4270/2	Malt and malt products	231 pt.	Malting barley	
428	4283	Soft drinks			
	4283/1	Mineral waters and soft drinks (carbonated and still)	232	Soft drinks	Fruit and vegetable juices are classified to heading 4283/2
	4283/2	Fruit and vegetable juices (concentrated and unconcentrated)	232 pt.	Fruit and vegetable juices only	
429	4290	Tobacco industry	240	Tobacco	

Source: Central Statistical Office *Standard Industrial Classification Revised 1980: Reconciliation with Standard Industrial Classification 1968*, pp.31-36. [B.379]

APPENDIX B: Names and Addresses of Trade Associations, Trades Unions, and Other Professional Organisations Connected with the Food Industries

Aberdeen and District Milk Marketing Board,
PO Box 117, Twin Spires, Bucksburn, Aberdeen AB9 8AH.

The Advertising Association,
Abford House, 15 Wilton Road, London SW1V 1NJ.

AGB Heighway Ltd.,
Alexandra House, 81-89 Farringdon Road, London EC1 M30L.

Agra Europe (London) Ltd.,
25 Frant Road, Tunbridge Wells, Kent TN2 5JT.

Agriculture and Food Research Council,
The Research Centre, Farnsby Street, Swindon SN1 5AT, Wilts.

Association of the Chocolate, Biscuit and Confectionery Industries of the EEC,
1 rue Defacqz (Bte 7), 1050 Brussels, Belgium.

Association of Professional, Executive, Clerical and Computer Staff,
22 Worple Road, London SW19 4DF.

Bacon and Meat Manufacturers' Association,
18 Cornwall Terrace, London NW1 4QP.

Bakers, Food and Allied Workers' Union,
Stanborough House, Great North Road, Stanborough, Welwyn Garden City, Herts AL8 7TA.

Baltic Futures Exchange,
Baltic Exchange Chambers, 24-28 St. Mary Axe, London EC3A 8EP.

Barclays de Zoete Wedd Ltd.,
2 Swan Lane, London EC4R 3TS.

Berisford International,
1 Prescot Street, London E1 8AY.

Billingsgate Market Superintendents' Office,
41, Billingsgate Market, 87 West India Dock, London E14 8ST.

Birds Eye Wall's Ltd.,
Walton Court, Station Avenue, Walton-on-Thames, Surrey KT12 1NT.

Birmingham City Markets,
Manor House, 40 Moat Lane, Digbeth, Birmingham B5 5BD.

Biscuit, Cake, Chocolate and Confectionery Alliance,
11 Green Street, London W1V 3RF.

British Chicken Information Service,
Bury House, 126/128 Cromwell Road, Kensington, London SW7 4ET.

British Food Manufacturing Industries Research Association,
(Leatherhead Food RA),
Randalls Road, Leatherhead, Surrey KT22 7RY.

British Frozen Food Federation,
Honeypot Lane, Colsterworth, Grantham, Lincs NG33 5LX.

British Fruit and Vegetable Canners' Association,
6 Catherine Street, London WC2B 5JJ.

British Ports Federation,
Commonwealth House, 1-19 New Oxford Street, London WC1A 1DZ.

British Poultry Federation Ltd.,
High Holborn House, 52-54 High Holborn, London WC1V 6SX.

British Soluble Coffee Manufacturers' Association,
6 Catherine Street, London WC2B 5JJ.

British Sugar PLC,
PO Box 26, Oundle Road, Peterborough PE2 9QU.

Business People Publications Ltd.,
234 King's Road, London SW3 5UA.

Business Statistics Office,
Cardiff Road, Newport, Gwent NP9 1XG.

Butter Information Council,
Tubs Hill House, London Road, Sevenoaks, Kent TN13 1BL.

Cadbury Ltd.,
PO Box 12. Bournville, Birmingham, B30 2LU.

Campden Food Preservation Research Association,
Chipping Camden, Glos GL55 6LP.

Central Statistical Office,
Cardiff Road, Newport, Gwent NP9 1XG

Certification Office for Trade Unions and Employers Associations,
27 Wilton Street, London SW1X 7AZ.

Chivers Hartley,
The Orchard, Histon, Cambridge CB4 4NR.

Commodity Research Bureau,
75 Montgomery Street, Jersey City, NJ 07302, United States of America.

Commonwealth Secretariat,
Marlborough House, Pall Mall, London SW1Y 5HX.

Companies House,
55-71 City Road, London EC1Y 1BB.

Companies Registration Office,
IDH House, Chichester Street, Belfast BT1 4JX.

Compustat Services Inc., Standard and Poor's Corporation,
7400 South Alton Court, Englewood, Colorado 80112 2394,
United States of America.

Confederation of British Industry,
Centre Point, New Oxford Street, London WC1A 1DU.

County Natwest Securities Ltd.,
(incorporating Wood Mackenzie & Co. Ltd.)
Drapers Gardens, 12 Throgmorton Avenue, London EC2P 2ES.

Czarnikow Brokers Ltd.,
66 Mark Lane, London EC3D 3EH.

The Dairy Council for Northern Ireland,
456 Antrim Road, Belfast BT15 5GB.

Dairy Trade Federation,
19 Cornwall Terrace, London NW1 4QP.

Datastream International Ltd.,
Monmouth House, 58-64 City Road, London EC1Y 2AL.

Department of Agriculture and Fisheries for Scotland,
Chesser House, 500 Gorgie Road, Edinburgh EH11 3AW.

Department of Agriculture for Northern Ireland (Economics and Statistics Division),
Room 817, Dundonald House, Upper Newtownards Road, Belfast BY4 3SF.

Department of Employment,
Caxton House, Tothill Street, London SW1H 9NF.

Department of Employment (Statistics A1),
Orphanage Road, Watford, Hertfordshire WD1 1PJ.

Department of Trade and Industry,
1 Victoria Street, London SW1H 0ET.

Dun and Bradstreet,
Holmers Farm Way, High Wycombe, Bucks HB12 4UL.

Eclipse Publications
18-20 Highbury Place, London N5 1QP.

Economist Intelligence Unit,
40 Duke Street, London W1A 1DW.

Electrical, Electronic, Telecommunications and Plumbing Union,
Hayes Court, West Common Road, Bromley BR2 7AU.

English Butter Marketing Company Ltd.,
Giggs Hill Green, Thames Ditton, Surrey KT7 0EA.

Euromoney Publications PLC,
Whitefriars House, 6 Carmelite Street, London EC4V 5EX.

Euromonitor Publications Ltd.,
87-88 Turnmill Street, London EC1M 5QU.

Extel Financial Ltd.,
Fitzroy House, 13-17 Epworth Street, London EC2A 4DL.

Federation of Bakers,
20 Bedford Square, London WC1B 5HF.

Federation of Oils, Seeds and Fats Associations Ltd.,
Baltic Exchange Chambers, 24 St. Mary Axe, London EC3A 8ER.

Fisheries Economics and Statistics Unit,
Department of Agriculture and Fisheries for Scotland,
Room 405, Chesser House, 500 Gorgie Road, Edinburgh EH11 3AW.

FMJ International,
Queensway Houses, 2 Queensway, Redhill, Surrey RH1 1QS.

Fonds d'Intervention de Regularisation du Marché du Sucre,
120 Boulevard de Courcelles, 75017 Paris, France.

Food and Drink Federation,
6 Catherine Street, London WC2B 5JJ.

Food from Britain,
301-344 Market Towers, New Covent Garden Market, London SW8 5NQ.

Food Trade Press Ltd.,
Station House, Hortons Way, Westerham, Kent TN16 1BZ.

Frank Fehr and Co. Ltd.,
Prince Rupert House, 64 Queen Street, London EC4R 1ER.

General Foods Corporation,
250 North Street, White Plains, NY 10625, United States of America.

General Municipal and Boilermakers' and Allied Trades Union,
Thorne House, Ruxley Ridge, Claygate, Esher, Surrey KT10 0TL.

The Grain and Feed Trade Association,
Baltic Exchange Chambers, 24/28 St. Mary Axe, London EC3A 8EP.

Grower Publications Ltd.,
50 Doughty Street, London WC1N 2LS.

Hay Management Consultants Ltd.,
52 Grosvenor Gardens, London SW1W 0AU.

Hemmington Scott Publishing,
City Innovation Centre, 26-31 Whiskin Street, London EC1R 0BP.

Henderson Crosthwaite Institutional Brokers Ltd.,
32 St. Mary-At-Hill, London EC3P 3AT.

Hewitt Associates,
Romeland House, Romeland Hill, St. Albans, Herts AL3 4EZ.

Hillsdown Holdings Ltd.,
32 Hampstead High Street, London NW3 1QD.

Home-Grown Cereals Authority,
Hamlyn House, Highgate Hill, London N19 5PR.

ICC Information Group Ltd.,
28-42 Banner Street, London EC1Y 8QE.

Ice Cream Alliance Ltd.,
90-94 Gray's Inn Road, London WC1X 8AH.

Ice Cream Federation,
1 Green Street, London W1Y 3RG.

Incomes Data Services Ltd.,
193 St. John Street, London EC1V 4LS.

Industry Forecasts Ltd.,
PO Box 69, Henley-on-Thames, Oxon RG9 2BZ.

Institute of Grocery Distribution,
Letchmore Heath, Watford, Herts WD2 8DQ.

International Cocoa Organisation,
22 Berners Street, London W1P 3DG.

International Coffee Organisation,
22 Berners Street, London W1P 4DD.

International Office of Cocoa, Chocolate and Sugar Confectionery,
172 Avenue de Cortenberg, 1040 Brussels, Belgium.

International Sugar Organisation,
28 Haymarket, London SW1Y 4SP.

International Tea Committee,
Sir John Lyon House, 5 High Timber Street, London EC4V 3NH.

ISTA Mielke GmbH,
2100 Hamburg 90, POB 90 08 03, West Germany.

Jordan and Sons Ltd.,
Jordan House, 47 Brunswick Place, London N1 6EE.

Key Note Publications Ltd.,
28-42 Banner Street, London EC1Y 8QE.

Labour Research Department,
78 Blackfriars Road, London SE1 8HF.

Landell Mills Commodities Studies Ltd.,
14-16 George Street, Oxford OX1 2AF.

F.O. Licht,
Zuckerwirtschaftlischer Verlag und Marktforschung GmbH64,
PO Box 1220, D-2418, Ratzeburg, Germany.

Livestock Marketing Commission for Northern Ireland,
Newforge Lane, Belfast BT9 5PP.

Lockwood Press Ltd.,
430-438 Market Towers, New Covent Garden Market, London SW8 5NN.

London Futures and Options Exchange,
1 Commodity Quay, St. Katharines Dock, London El 9AX.

Lyons Maid Ltd.,
Bridge Park, Oldfield Lane North, Greenford, Middlesex UB6 0BA.

Maclean Hunter Ltd.,
Maclean Hunter House, Chalk Lane, Cockfosters Road, Barnet, Herts EN4 0BU.

Macmillan Publishers Ltd.,
Houndmills, Basingstoke, Hampshire RG21 2XS.

MAFF Publications,
London SE99 7TP.

E.D. & F. Man Ltd.,
Sugar Quay, Lower Thames Street, London EC3R 6DU.

Margarine and Shortening Manufacturers' Association,
6 Catherine Street, London WC2B 5JJ.

Market Assessment Publications Ltd.,
2 Duncan Terrace, London N1 8BZ.

Marketing Magazine Haymarket Publishing,
30 Lancaster Gate, London W2 3LP.

Marketing Strategies for Industry (UK) Ltd.,
32 Mill Green Road, Mitcham, Surrev CR4 4HY.

McCarthy Information Ltd.,
Manor House, Ash Walk, Warminster, Wiltshire BA12 8PY.

Meat and Livestock Commission,
PO Box 44, Queensway House: Bletchley MK2 2EF.

Media Expenditure Analysis Limited,
63 St. Martins Lane, London WC2 4JT.

The Media Register,
1 Langley Court, London WC2E 9JY.

The Milk Marketing Board for Northern Ireland,
456 Antrim Road, Belfast BT15 5GD.

The Milk Marketing Board of England and Wales,
Thames Ditton, Surrey KT7 0EL.

Ministry of Agriculture, Fisheries and Food,
Whitehall Place, London SW1A 2HH.

Ministry of Agriculture, Fisheries and Food,
Branch A (Censuses and Prices),
Room A509, Government Buildings, Epsom Road, Guildford, Surrey GU1 2LD.

Ministry of Agriculture, Fisheries and Food,
Branch B, Statistics (Agricultural Commodities) Division,
Ergon/Nobel House, 17 Smith Square, London SW1P 3JR.

Ministry of Agriculture, Fisheries and Food,
(Fisheries Statistics Unit),
Room 423, Nobel House, 17 Smith Square, London SW1P 3JR.

Mintel Publications Ltd.,
7 Arundel Street, London WC2R 3DR.

Monks Partnership
Debden Green, Saffron Walden, Essex CB11 3LX.

National Association of British and Irish Millers,
21 Arlington Street, London SW1A 1RN.

National Association of Master Bakers, Confectioners and Caterers,
21 Baldock Street, Ware, Herts SG12 9DH.

National Dairy Council,
John Princes Street, London W1M 0AP.

National Economic Development Office,
Millbank Tower, Millbank, London SW1P 4QX.

National Federation of Meat Traders,
1 Belgrove, Tunbridge Wells, Kent TN1 1YW.

National Food Survey Branch,
Ministry of Agriculture, Fisheries and Food,
Room 419, Whitehall Place (West Block), London SW1A 2HH.

National Institute of Economic and Social Research,
2 Dean Trench Street, London SW1P 3HE.

National Marine Fisheries Service,
(United States Department of Commerce, National Oceanic and Atmospheric Administration), 408 Atlantic Avenue, Room 141, Boston, MA 02210-2203, United States of America.

Nestlé,
St. George's House, Croydon, CR9 1NR.

Northern Ireland Dairy Trade Federation,
123-137 York Street, Belfast BT15 1AB.

The North of Scotland Milk Marketing Board,
Claymore House, 29 Ardconnel Terrace, Inverness IV2 3AF.

Northwood Publications Ltd.,
Theba House, 49-50 Hatton Garden, London EC1N 8XS.

NTC Publications Ltd.,
PO Box 69, 22-24 Bell Street, Henley-on-Thames, Oxon RG9 2B7.

Overseas Development Administration (Statistics Division),
Abercrombie House, East Kilbride G75 8ED.

P.E. International Ltd.,
Park House, Wick Road, Egham, Surrey TW20 0HW.

Pet Food Manufacturers' Association,
6 Catherine Street, London WC2B 5JJ.

Potato Marketing Board,
50 Hans Crescent, Knightsbridge, London SW1X 0NB.

Potato Marketing Board (Statistics Department),
Broad Field House, 4 Between Towns Road, Cowley, Oxford OX4 3NA.

Reed Business Publishing,
Oakfield House, Perrymant Road, Haywards Heath, Sussex RH16 3DH.

Registrar of Companies,
102 George Street, Edinburgh EH2 3DJ.

Registrar of Companies,
Companies House, Crown Way, Cardiff CF4 3UZ.

Remuneration Economics Ltd.,
51 Portland Road, Kingston-upon-Thames, Surrey KT1 2SH.

Reuters Ltd.,
85 Fleet Street, London EC4P 4AJ.

The Reward Group,
Reward House, Diamond Way, Stone Business Park, Stone, Staffordshire ST15 0SD.

Ross Foods Ltd.,
Ross House, Grimsby, South Humberside DN31 3SW.

Rowntree Mackintosh Ltd.,
York YO1 1XY.

The Scottish Dairy Council,
266 Clyde Street, Glasgow Gl 4QS.

Scottish Dairy Trade Federation,
24 Blythswood Square, Glasgow G2 4QS.

The Scottish Milk Marketing Board,
Underwood Road, Paisley PA3 1TJ.

Scrimgeour Vickers Asset Management,
Regis House, King William Street, London EC4R 9AD.

Sea Fish Industry Authority,
Sea Fisheries House, 10 Young Street, Edinburgh EH2 4JQ.

Seed Crushers' and Oil Processors' Association,
6 Catherine Street, London WC2B 5JJ.

Shaws Price Guides Ltd.,
PO Box 32, Abingdon, Oxfordshire OX14 3LJ.

Snack, Nut and Crisp Manufacturers Association Ltd.,
Swiss Centre, 10 Wardour Street, London W1V 3HG.

Statistical Office of the European Communities,
Bâtiment Jean Monnet, Rue Alcide de Gaspari, L-2920 Luxembourg-Kirchberg.

Statistics Users' Council,
Lancaster House, More Lane, Esher, Surrey KT10 8AP.

Sugar Bureau,
120 Rodney House, Dolphin Square, London SW1V 3LS.

Tate & Lyle PLC,
Sugar Quay, Lower Thames Street, London EC32 6DQ.

Taylor Nelson Research Ltd.,
44-46 Upper High Street, Epsom, Surrey KT17 4QS.

Tea Brokers' Association of London,
Sir John Lyon House, 5 High Timber Street, London EC4V 3NH.

Tea Buyers' Association,
69 Cannon Street, London EC4N 5AB.

Tea Clearing House,
Sir John Lyon House, 5 High Timber Street, London EC4V 3NH.

Tea Council,
Sir John Lyon House, 5 High Timber Street, London EC4V 3NH.

J. Thomas & Co. Private Ltd.,
11 R.N. Mukherjee Road, PO Box No. 69, Calcutta 70000, India.

Torry Research Station,
135 Abbey Road, Aberdeen AB9 8DG.

Trades Union Congress,
Congress House, 23-28 Great Russell Street, London WC1B 3LS.

Transport and General Workers' Union,
Transport House, Smith Square, London SW1P 9JB.

Turret-Wheatland Ltd.,
Commodity Division, 12 Greycaine Road. Bushey Mill Lane, Watford. Herts WD2 4JP.

Union of Shop Distributive and Allied Workers,
Oakley, 188 Wilmslow Road, Fallowfield, Manchester M14 6LJ.

United Kingdom Association of Frozen Food Producers,
1 Green Street, London W1Y 3RG.

William Reed Ltd.
5 Southwark Street, London SE1 1PO.

APPENDIX C: Statistical Inquiries Relating to the Food and Feed Processing Industries

Inquiry	Sponsoring Department	Data Collected
Group 411: Organic Oils and Fats		
Monthly vegetable oil crushers' return	MAFF	Crushing, production and stocks of different oilseed types
Monthly refiners' returns	MAFF	Stocks and production of different oils in various stages of refining
Monthly utilisation of refined oils	MAFF	Quantities of various oils used in manufacture of margarine, other spreads and cooking fat, Production of margarine etc.
Quarterly margarine and compound fats inquiry (PQ4115)*	BSO	Sales of margarine and compound cooking fat for trade and domestic use
Quarterly organic oils and fats inquiry (PQ4116)*	BSO	Sales of vegetable oils and oilcake; various other items
Group 412: Meat and Meat Production		
Weekly and monthly slaughterhouse surveys	MAFF	Number and weight of animals slaughtered by animal type
Weekly survey of pigs slaughtered	MAFF	Number of pigs slaughtered, numbers used for bacon and ham and weight of bacon and ham produced
Monthly throughput and stocks of slaughtered poultry*	MAFF	Slaughtering and stocks of different types of poultry
Quarterly bacon curing and meat products inquiry (PQ4122)*	BSO	Sales of various types of preserved and frozen meat & meat products; production of some meat products
Quarterly poultry and poultry products inquiry (PQ4123)*	BSO	Sales and production of various types of poultry and poultry products
Quarterly animal by-products inquiry (PQ4126)*	BSO	Sales of animal by-products, e.g. tallow, offals, meat and bone meal
Group 414: Processing of Fruit and Vegetables		
Quarterly survey of canned and bottled fruit and vegetables	MAFF	Production and stocks of the major products of the fruit and vegetable canning industry
Quarterly fruit and vegetable products inquiry (PQ4147)*	BSO	Sales of main products, e.g. jam, frozen products and pickles Production of certain items

Inquiry	Sponsoring Department	Data Collected
Annual analysis by variety of jam products (discontinued)	MAFF	Production of different types of jam
Group 415: Fish Products		
Quarterly fish products inquiry (PQ4150)*	BSO	Sales of fish pastes, cured fish, frozen fish and fish products, Production of certain preserved and frozen fish and fish products
Group 416: Grain Milling		
Monthly and annual returns from flour millers	MAFF	Volumes of wheat milled, flour produced and stocks
Monthly return from oatmeal millers	MAFF	Volumes of oats milled and stocks
Group 418: Starch		
Monthly production of glucose and starch*	MAFF	Raw materials used in the production of glucose and starch
Quarterly starch inquiry (PQ4180)*	BSO	Sales of maize starch, other starch, by-products and glucose
Group 419: Bread, Biscuits and Flour Confectionery		
Quarterly bread and flour confectionery inquiry (PQ4196)*	BSO	Sales of bread and flour confectionery
Quarterly biscuits and crispbread inquiry (PQ4197)*	BSO	Sales of biscuits
Monthly Cake and Biscuit Alliance surveys of Alliance members	CBA	Sales of biscuits and deliveries of cakes
Group 421: Ice-cream, Cocoa, Chocolate and Sugar Confectionery		
Annual cocoa beans and cocoa products stocks returns	MAFF	Stocks of cocoa beans, nibs, powder, paste, cake and butter
Quarterly ice-cream inquiry (PQ4213)*	BSO	Sales of ice-cream
Monthly surveys by the CCCA	CCCA	Sales by value and quantity of chocolate and sugar confectionery, Deliveries to home (i.e. UK) trade
Group 422: Animal Feedingstuffs		
Monthly and annual compounders return	MAFF	Quantities of compound animal feed manufactured and raw materials used
Twice-yearly livestock ration survey*	MAFF	Composition of main livestock feed rations
Monthly pet food survey*	BSO	Quantities of canned and other pet food produced
Group 423: Miscellaneous Foods		
Quarterly production of potato crisps and snack foods	MAFF	Production of potato and maize-based snack products, Usage of potatoes

Inquiry	Sponsoring Department	Data Collected
Quarterly inquiry of processed potato products	MAFF	Production of processed potato products and usage of raw potatoes in their manufacture
Quarterly coffee production and stocks usage	MAFF	Coffee production, usage of raw coffee and stocks
Monthly cereal breakfast foods survey	MAFF	Production, receipts and stocks of raw materials used in manufacture of cereal breakfast foods
Quarterly miscellaneous foods inquiry (PQ4239)*	BSO	Sales of various foods, e.g. breakfast cereals, crisps, sauces, soups, farinaceous preparations, coffee, tea and nuts, Production of soups, sauces and meat substitutes.

Notes

(1) This list corresponds to those inquiries which were undertaken up to 1989. Most of the quarterly inquiries undertaken by the Business Statistics Office (BSO), and published as part of the Business Monitor PQ series, were discontinued from the third quarter of 1989 — see Chapter 13 for details. The only exceptions are *Business Monitor PQ4122: Bacon Curing and Meat Products* [QRL.130] and *Business Monitor PQ4213: Ice-cream* [QRL.138].

(2) The Biscuit, Cake, Chocolate and Confectionery Alliance (BCCCA) was formed in January 1987 from the merger of the Cocoa, Chocolate and Confectionery Alliance (CCCA) and the Cake and Biscuit Alliance (CBA). The compilation and despatch of the statistics is now the responsibility of the BCCCA.

(3) Details of the inquiries for Group 422 are included for completeness even though sources of statistics on this Group are not explicitly covered in this Review.

(4) Surveys denoted (*) are sample surveys; all others cover the total population.

Source: John M. Slater, "Statistics of food supplies and consumption." [B.164].

APPENDIX D: Headings used for Identifying Expenditure Information in the Family Expenditure Survey

Reference number	
Food (bought from large supermarket chains)	
10A	Bread, milk loaves, rolls etc.
11A	Flour, plain and self-raising
12A	Biscuits, cakes etc.
13A	Breakfast and other cereals
14A	Beef and veal
15A	Mutton and lamb
16A	Pork
17A	Bacon and ham (uncooked)
18A	Ham, cooked (including canned)
19A	Poultry, other and undefined meat
20A	Fish (including shellfish)
21A	Fish and chips, fried fish, fish cakes
22A	Butter
23A	Margarine
24A	Lard, cooking fats, vegetable fats and oils
25A	Milk, fresh
26A	Milk products including cream
27A	Cheese, including processed cheese
28A	Eggs
29A	Potatoes, potato products
30A	Other and undefined vegetables
31A	Fruit, nuts etc.
32A	Sugar
33A	Syrup, honey, lemon curd, jam, marmalade etc.
34A	Sweets and chocolates
35A	Tea
36A	Coffee
37A	Cocoa, drinking chocolate, other food drinks
38A	Soft drinks, e.g. squashes cordials, crystals, powders
39A	Ice-cream, iced lollies
40A	Other food, foods not defined
Food (not bought from large supermarket chains)	
10B–40B	Headings as above for 10A–40A
41	Meals bought away from home

Source: *Family Expenditure Survey* [QRL.204].

ADDENDA

These Addenda refer to *major* changes and developments that have taken place between the completion of the main text in March 1989 and the final proof reading stage in March 1992. The material is cross-referenced to the section of the main text which is affected. Additional publication references are given at the end of the Addenda arranged in two lists: one for statistical publications and one for bibliographic references which are prefixed "ADS" and "ADB" respectively. In addition, a review of sources available in machine-readable form, including on-line data bases, is included at the end of these Addenda. It should be noted that the material in 2.5.1.1 updates some of *Agriculture* [B.144] by George Peters which is volume 23 in this series.

Chapter 2 General Statistical Sources for the Food Industries

2.1.1 *Business Statistics Office Inquiries*

Responsibility for these inquiries now rests with the CSO. Major changes have taken place following the publication of the *Review of DTI Statistics* [B.367] in May 1989 (the "Armstrong-Rees" Report). The frequency of most of the sales inquiries has been reduced from quarterly to annual. Currently only 31 quarterly inquiries survive. This situation may well change in the future (for further information, contact the CSO Library, New Government Buildings, Cardiff Road, Newport, Gwent NP9 1XG). For the Food industries the remaining quarterly sales inquiries include the following:

- *Business Monitor PQ4122: Bacon Curing and Meat Products* [QRL.130]
- *Business Monitor PQ4213: Ice-cream* [QRL.138]

The former PQ Monitors for other sectors have been replaced by "PAS" Monitors as follows:

- *Business Monitor PAS4115: Margarine and Compound Cooking Fats* [ADS.6]
- *Business Monitor PAS4116: Organic Oils and Fats* [ADS.7]
- *Business Monitor PAS4123: Poultry and Poultry Products* [ADS.8]
- *Business Monitor PAS4147: Fruit and Vegetable Products* [ADS.9]
- *Business Monitor PAS4150: Fish Products* [ADS.10]
- *Business Monitor PAS4180: Starch* [ADS.11]
- *Business Monitor PAS4196: Bread and Flour Confectionery* [ADS.12]
- *Business Monitor PAS4197: Biscuits and Crispbread* [ADS.13]
- *Business Monitor PAS4239: Miscellaneous Foods* [ADS.14]

These PAS Monitors typically give the following:

Summary tables for total sales, output etc.
Annual sales data (value and, in most cases, volume) for product subdivisions
Annual exports and imports for product subdivisions
Tariff/trade code numbers corresponding to export/import headings
Index of output of the production industries
Producer price indices of materials purchased and of goods produced
Retail price indices.

Details of methodology and coverage are given in the notes at the beginning of each PAS Monitor and filled out in the 1991 publication of *Business Monitor PO1000: Index to Commodities and Business Monitor Titles* [ADB.20]. This publication also contains an alphabetical product index to Business Monitor publications and a full list of Business Monitor titles. The leaflet, *Business Monitors* [B.219] also has a list.

Following the *Review of DTI Statistics* [B.367], the publication outlets were also reviewed. Since 1989, the CSO have issued "Business Bulletins", denoted since 1 April 1991 as "CSO Bulletins". These bulletins do not followed a set pattern but have been used to publish statistics as soon as possible and to relay statistical data and commentaries on statistical developments, often in an *ad hoc* fashion, as circumstances demand. Many of these bulletins are referred to in these Addenda.

CSO Bulletin: Inquiry into Sales of Industry [ADS.24] publishes the results of the inquiry into sales of selected industries during 1990. [ADS.24] gives commodity sales in value (and sometimes volume) for 1985 and 1990 for disaggregated products of the following Activity Headings in the Food industries:

AH4126 Animal by-products
AH4130 Preparation of milk and milk products
AH4160 Grain milling
AH4214 Cocoa, chocolate and sugar confectionery
AH4221 Compound animal feed
AH4222 Pet foods and non compound animal feeds.

The background to this is that for a small number of industries there have been no regular product inquiries since 1981, but all of the above except AH4126, were included in the Topping-up Inquiry carried out in 1985 (see section 2.1.1.3). It has been further decided that all the above should be covered by periodic inquiries normally to be held at not more than five-yearly intervals.

2.1.1.5 Register analyses

Business Monitor PO1007A: UK Directory of Manufacturing Businesses 1990 Supplement [ADB.21] was published as a supplement to *Business Monitor PO1007: The UK Directory of Manufacturing Businesses* [B.218]. This supplement added 3,551 names and addresses to the 14,436 already published and the 1991 *Business Monitor PO1007A* [ADB.21] has since made further additions.

Registers themselves are valuable as a possible source for further statistical inquiries and special analyses may be provided by the CSO. Further details are available from the CSO Librarian, Newport. [ADB.21] gives the names and addresses of units in alphabetical order with respect to the Activity Headings of SIC(1980). As a live register, the food firms listed in [ADB.21] show the numbers added since the publication of [B.218].

2.1.1.6 Historical data

The following collections of historical data contain some Food industries coverage.

Mitchell, B.R. and Deane, P. *Abstract of Historical Statistics* [ADS.2]

Mitchell, B.R. and Jones, H.G. *Second Abstract of British Historical Statistics* [ADS.4]

Mitchell B.R. *British Historical Statistics* [ADS.3].

2.2.1 *Guides to Sources*

The following works may also be noted.

- P.A. Sheard *A Guide to the British Food Manufacturing Industry* [ADB.13]. This collects together information submitted by companies. Section I covers industry statistics, giving marketing data, the top 100 food companies, acquisitions and mergers and companies taken into receivership. The information on acquisitions and mergers is valuable since it names the acquiring companies, details the deals and enumerates the money spent. Section 2 contains company information and Section 3 company addresses. The fourth edition is planned to cover developments from January 1991 to December 1992.
- *United Kingdom: Food Manufacturers and Processors* [ADB.39] is a reference guide which surveys food companies, giving the names and addresses of companies in alphabetical order by country.
- *Food and Drink from Britain: Buyers' Guide* [ADB.32] gives the names and addresses of companies in the company index, has a product section (names and addresses of companies by product), gives brand names and summarises information services.
- *Frozen and Chilled Foods Yearbook* [ADB.33] is another alphabetical directory detailing companies and their addresses by product group.
- *Agri-facts: A Handbook of UK and EEC Agricultural and Food Statistics* [ADS.1] is mainly agricultural despite its title. The food section covers mainly consumption, reproducing data from *Social Trends* [QRL.456] and *United Kingdom National Accounts* [QRL.506]
- *A Hundred Years of British Food and Farming: A Statistical Survey* [ADB.8] again emphasises agriculture more than food but has interesting commentaries and food consumption and expenditure data.
- *Compendium of Marketing Information Sources* [ADB.22] is mentioned here because it attempts to cover both official and unofficial statistics. It has sections on libraries and information services, abstracts and indexes; on-line data bases and databanks; official sources; non-official sources; market research agencies; company information; indexes. It was published in 1989, is now somewhat dated but no doubt will be updated.

2.2.2 *General Statistical Sources*

Key Data [ADS.32] aims to present basic statistics of the main economic and social areas in compact form. The contents have varied from time to time but there are separate sections on "Agriculture" and "Industry".

Because of its presence in most public libraries, we also mention *Britain: An Official Handbook* [ADB.18] which contains a succinct summary of the Food industries, with illustrative statistical tables and data.

2.2.3 *Descriptions of Economic Structure*

The Food Industries are discussed along with agriculture as being bound together in the food chain (see also Section 1.1) which extends from the production and processing of agricultural inputs through to food retailing and catering.

Neil Ward [ADB.17] uses data from the *Annual Review of Agriculture* [QRL.51], *Business Monitor PA1002: Summary Volume* [QRL.93] and *United Kingdom National Accounts* [QRL.506] to provide a useful summary of the entire sector. Furthermore, a unique table gives the corporate structure of the UK food chain in 1987, detailing total sales, concentration and the key corporations with nationality and percentage market share. Agricultural machinery, animal feedstuffs, fertilizer, agrochemicals, agriculture, food manufacturing and food retailing are all treated separately.

V.N. Balasubramanyam and D.T. Nguyen [ADB.2] make use of *Business Monitor PA1002: Summary Volume* [QRL.93] to update the earlier papers of A.W. Ashby, W.S. Howe and J.A. Burns in Burns, J., McInerney, J. and Swinbank, A. *The Food Industry: Economics and Policies* [B.31]. [ADB.2] provides more recent data on the domestic market for food and drink, details factor proportions in the UK food, drink and manufacturing industries, gives value added per employee, wage rates and total factor productivity for food manufacturing industries, calculates the growth in total factor productivity and summarises profitability measures of the UK food and drink industries. The period is mostly 1979–1986 and the treatment is disaggregated according to SIC(1980), except for the global food manufacturing profitability figures from 1982/83. Both Ward [ADB.17] and V.N. Balasubramanyam and D.T. Nguyen [ADB.2] are secondary but are recent and concise references. They make good use of primary statistical sources to portray salient structural characteristics.

Of the many books on the economics of agriculture, we note the text of Berkeley Hill and Derek Ray entitled *Economics for Agriculture: Food, Farming and the Rural Economy* [ADB.5]. It integrates the food industry and agriculture with discriminating use of data sources. The chapters on "The consumer end of the food chain", "The farmer and the food industry in the food chain" and "The role of international trade in the food chain" are of value to the food economist.

Finally, John Sutton draws upon many official and commercial sources in a most interesting fashion in his book entitled *Sunk Costs and Market Structure: Price Competition, Advertising and the Evolution of Concentration* [ADB.16]. He uses data from the food and drink sectors of six prominent economies: the UK, the US, Japan, Germany (the Federal Republic), France and Italy. His main objective is to explain determinants of concentration by both econometric tests and industry case histories. The book has extensive data illustrations, descriptions of food industry structure and appendices on the following Food industries: salt; sugar; flour; bread; processed pork products; canned vegetables; prepared soups; margarine; cereal markets; confectionery industries; biscuits; coffee; pet foods and baby foods; beer etc.

2.2.4 *Numbers of Firms and Legal Units*

Tables in *CSO Bulletin: Size Analysis of UK Businesses* [ADS.26] preview the more detailed size analyses to be published later in the year in *Business Monitor PA1003:*

Size Analyses of United Kingdom Businesses [QRL.96]. There is coverage for SIC Class 41/42, giving employment size data for local units in manufacturing industry.

2.2.6 *Mergers and Acquisitions*

CSO Bulletin: Acquisitions and Mergers [ADS.17] has now replaced *Business Monitor MQ7: Acquisitions and Mergers by Industrial and Commercial Companies* [QRL.92]. In fact [ADS.17] and [QRL.92] ran in tandem for a while. From the second quarter of 1990 [ADS.17] was expanded to give identical coverage with [QRL.92] prior to replacing it completely from the third quarter of 1990. Expenditure on acquisitions of independent companies and mergers within the United Kingdom is given, classified by industry of acquiring company. Annual and quarterly data on the number acquiring, the number acquired and the value in £m with respect to the food industry are given. The sales of subsidiaries between company groups within the United Kingdom is, however, reported by industry groups of the acquiring company according to the more aggregative "Food, drink and tobacco" industry.

2.3 The European Community

These remarks relate mainly to section 2.3. But, in the light of UK EC links, other sections of the text are affected, particularly section 2.2 Industry Structure and section 2.8 International Transactions. Given the likelihood of change, it should be remarked that most developments are signalled in *Statistical News* [B.381] and *Eurostat News* [B.262]. In addition, the CSO has also produced periodic issues of the *CSO Bulletin: Statistical Changes in 1992* [ADB.24].

Two important features which influence future work, and which are very much connected with our membership of the European Community, are as follows. Firstly, the SIC is to be revised in line with NACE Rev 1, operative from 1 January 1993. These proposed developments are discussed in an article by Ken Mears [ADB.9] in the Spring 1991 issue of *Statistical News* [B.381]. Secondly, the pervasive influence of Europe is shown in the EUROSTAT scheme of harmonised European products sales statistics. This is known as PRODCOM i.e. the PROducts of the European COMmunity. Further details are outlined in the EUROSTAT document *PRODCOM: Description of the EUROSTAT Project for Comprehensive Community Production Statistics* [ADB.37]. The aim, with the emergence of the single market, is to prepare business statistics which give European results with the same degree of accuracy and reliability as the best national statistics. A second purpose is to correlate the product data with trade data. This is why the common classification for the national surveys of industrial production are to be based ultimately on the Community external trade classification, the Combined Nomenclature (CN). The first PRODCOM inquiries will be conducted in respect of 1992.

2.3.2 *EUROSTAT and Community Statistics*

We note an additional number of guides to Europe and European information sources to those already described in section 2.3.2.

- Anne Ramsay: *European Communities Information* [ADB.12]. This is a most useful brief summary of EC information, confined to basic material but an excellent starting point.

- Anne Ramsay: *EUROJARGON* [ADB.11]. An invaluable guide to EC acronyms, directives and sobriquets.
- *Guide to European Company Information on EC Countries* [ADB.35]. This publication concentrates on company sources. It lists pan-European directories, on-line hosts, data bases, CD-ROMS and diskettes, other services, before summarizing information on the EC12 in comparable format.
- *The European Directory of Marketing Information Sources* [ADB.29]. The second edition covers seventeen major Western European countries including all EFTA countries and all the member countries of the EC. It has sections on the following: Official sources and publications; Libraries and information services; Leading market research companies; Leading consumer research publications; Information data bases and data banks; Abstracts and indexes; Major businesses and marketing journals; Major business and marketing associations; European business contacts; Socio-economic profiles. Each country is treated under these sections.
- *The European Directory of Non-official Statistical Sources* [ADB.30]. This covers pan-European sources, Denmark, Greece, Norway, Sweden, West Germany, Austria, Finland, Italy, Portugal, Switzerland, Belgium, France, Netherlands, Spain and the United Kingdom. The approach is similar to *Sources of Unofficial UK Statistics* [B.130] with the alphabetical listing of sources and a useful subject index. For instance it is possible under "foods" to locate the relevant trade association. This is important for a country like France where statistics produced by the major trade associations form the basis of industrial production data.
- *European Directory of Consumer Market Reports and Surveys* [ADB.28] identifies recent reports on Western European consumer markets. It has six sections: General reports; Food, drink and tobacco; Grocery; Non-food consumer durables; Services and leisure; Directory of publishers and reports. We note it here since Food, drink and tobacco features prominently. There is both a general index and geographic subject index.
- *European Business Intelligence Briefing* [ADB.27] is a monthly newsletter which analyses sources of European companies, market and product information.

2.4.2 *Index Numbers of Output*

Series and Weights and Supplementary Analysis of Series used in the Index of Output of the Production Industries 1985 Base [ADB.38] was published to explain the rebasing of the index of production from September 1988 and gives full details of weights (at a disaggregated level) and their sources. The methodology is explained in an article by S.D. Kingaby [ADB.6] entitled "The rebased index of production" in the February 1989 issue of *Economic Trends* [QRL.181]. The annex of [ADB.6] gives the index of output of the production industries 1985 = 100 for food from 1977 to 1987.

2.5.1.1 Ministry of Agriculture, Fisheries and Food inquiries

It was noted in the text that *Agriculture in the United Kingdom* [ADS.5] is the successor to the *Annual Review of Agriculture* [QRL.51]. For 1988, the last issue of

[QRL.51] and the first issue of *Agriculture in the United Kingdom* [ADS.5] both appeared. Furthermore, *Agriculture in the United Kingdom* [ADS.5] now includes much of the information formerly presented in another discontinued publication *Output and Utilisation of Farm Produce in the United Kingdom* [QRL.382].

Changes in coverage are described in the Preface to [ADS.5], but since in fact *Agriculture in the United Kingdom* [ADS.5] is germane to many sections of this volume (as were [QRL.51] and [QRL.382]), we briefly summarise the coverage of the 1990 version of [ADS.5] relevant to this volume.

- Agriculture and food in the national economy. This includes annual summary data on imports, exports, UK self-sufficiency, consumers' expenditure on food and retail price indices etc.
- Producer prices for agricultural products.
- Commodity tables. These combine production and supplies and utilisation data formerly in [QRL.51] and [QRL.382] for a range of commodities, livestock and livestock products.
- Public expenditure on agriculture. Three tables give a range of data important for section 2.3.3.6, notably statistics on intervention prices and stocks. Sometimes the coverage is relevant for section 3 of the industry chapters on the European Community.

Agriculture in the United Kingdom [ADS.5] thus shows the overlap between the United Kingdom agricultural industry and the Food industries. The data in each section are prefaced by a short annual review.

Furthermore, there have been some recent changes in the coverage of the *Annual Abstract of Statistics* [QRL.37]. Firstly, from the 1992 issue, the table which gave the annual physical data on the estimated food and drink supplies per head of the population has been deleted. Secondly, from the 1991 issue onwards, the information on the cost of food processing and distribution in the United Kingdom no longer appears. Thirdly, the data on United Kingdom self-sufficiency survived in 1991 but was deleted in 1992. This reduced coverage of [QRL.37] is to be regretted for [QRL.37] is a more accessible and better known source than *Agriculture in the United Kingdom* [ADS.5] which is not easily available in public libraries.

2.5.2 *Input-output Analysis*

Further insight into the methodology of input-output analyses as applied to the agricultural and Food sector is provided by Robin Lynch in [ADB.10] in a paper entitled "The agricultural sector in the compilation of United Kingdom input-output tables". In particular, he explains how the Purchases Inquiry and the results of surveys such as the National Food Survey and the Family Expenditure Survey are used to estimate food demand.

Lynch's paper, in fact, forms part of a book edited by Peter Midmore entitled *Input- output Models in the Agricultural Sector* [ADB.10] which collects together other papers of interest as follows. J.R.S. McDonald, A.S. Rayner and J.M. Bates make extensive use of input-output tables from 1954 to 1984 in their paper on "Productivity growth and structural change in agriculture and the UK food chain: 1954–1984". They seek to estimate productivity growth at all stages of the food chain including intermediate transactions. Results are given for "Food processing"

1954–1963 and 1963–1974 and for "Food" 1979–1984. They clearly show the growing relative importance of the food processing sector and the declining relative importance of the agricultural and distribution sector in the estimates of distribution of consumer food expenditure between these three sectors.

Barker in [ADB.10] covered a shorter time period in his "Sources of structural change in the UK agriculture and food industries 1979–1984" but sought to account for structural change by tracing back the changes from final demand through the input-output structure of intermediate demand to production or imports. Errington in [ADB.10] illustrates the increasing tendency of the food processing and distribution network to add value to agricultural outputs. Leat and Chambers in [ADB.10] describe the construction of an input-output model of agriculture and Food industries in the Grampian region of North-East Scotland. Midmore himself [ADB.10] discusses the weaknesses of input-output analysis as a technique used to explain intersectoral economic relationships.

We are all reliant on the data sources *per se* which must always take some time to emerge. Although input-output tables are normally published for every five years, *Input-output Tables for the United Kingdom 1985* [ADS.31] also appeared because the national accounts were rebased in 1985. But it should be stressed that 1984 is the benchmark year and work is at present concentrated towards the production of the 1989 tables.

2.6 Labour

Labour Market Quarterly Report [ADS.34] is compiled by the Employment Department. It provides summary labour market statistics and commentary, drawing mainly from the *Employment Gazette* [QRL.186].

Employment News [ADS.30] is a free monthly newspaper with summary data published by the Employment Department.

2.6.1.1 Department of Employment inquiries

From 1992, the Labour Force Survey is being carried out quarterly. Results for the first quarter of 1992 are scheduled to be published in September 1992. For more information, contact Statistical Services Division C2, Employment Department, Caxton House, Tothill Street, London SW1H 9NF. More detailed results can be obtained from the ESRC Data Archive at the University of Essex and from Quantime (the Labour Force Survey data base).

The 1993 Census of Employment will be the first full-scale census since 1981. The Census of Employment is now taken every two years.

2.6.1.2 Business Statistics inquiries

Tables in *CSO Bulletin: Size Analysis of UK Businesses* [ADS.26] give employment size data for SIC Class 41/42, previewing [QRL.96].

2.6.14 *Industrial Training*
Training Statistics [ADS.43] now gathers together the available statistics in one publication. The percentage of establishments providing training in Class 41/42 are given, based on the Skill Needs in Great Britain Survey. Data on training from the Labour Force Survey are also presented.

2.8 International Transactions

Changes in the system for collecting trade statistics have already been discussed in section 13.2 and are further described in *CSO Bulletin: Methodological Issues re Trade Statistics* [ADB.23].

The August 1991 issue of the *CSO Bulletin: Statistical Changes in 1992* [ADB.24] gives a summary of the new system for collecting statistics of trade between EC member states to be introduced from 1 January 1993. This new system, known as Intrastat, links the generation of intra-EC trade statistics with the control of VAT collection on goods traded between member states. All VAT registered businesses will be required to complete two additional boxes on their VAT returns: one giving the total value of supplies (exports) to other member states and the other giving the total value of acquisitions (imports) from other member states. This system will succeed the present Customs declaration (from the Single Administrative Document) which is to be abolished after 1992. The system for recording trade with other countries, based on Customs declarations, will continue unchanged.

2.8.3 *International Capital Movements*
CSO Bulletin: Overseas Earnings from Royalties [ADS.25] gives receipts and payments for Class 41/42.

2.9.2 *Business Statistics Inquiries*
CSO Bulletin: Capital Expenditure and Stockbuilding [ADS.18] gives quarterly data on stock changes for Class 41/42.

2.9.4 *Stocks at Wholesalers, Retailers and Caterers*
CSO Bulletin: Distributive and Service Trades [ADS.20] gives results later available in *Business Monitor SDA25: Retailing* [QRL.140], *Business Monitor SDA26: Wholesaling* [QRL.141] and *Business Monitor SDA28: Catering and Allied Trades* [QRL.142].

2.10.1 *The National Food Survey*
An interesting collection of papers was presented at a symposium held in London in December 1990 to mark fifty years of the NFS — probably the longest running continuous survey of household food consumption in the world. The papers, published under the title *Fifty Years of the National Food Survey 1940–1990*

[ADB.14], edited by Dr J.M. Slater, reflect on past and current work as well as reporting on proposed future changes. The sections cover Food policy and the NFS, Historical perspectives of the NFS, NFS and the national diet, The value of the National Food Survey, and Planned changes to the NFS. An appendix neatly summarises the structure of the NFS.

We draw attention here to Yeomans' paper in [ADB.14] which reports on the NFS Committee's review of certain aspects of the NFS, carried out with the purpose of improving the coverage. The purpose is to reduce some of the shortcomings as noted in 2.10.1.3 of this text. Consequently, from 1992, the NFS is being expanded to collect information on food bought and eaten away from home. Given that it is estimated that expenditure on food bought and eaten outside the home has risen from about 20 per cent of expenditure on food in 1980 to about 30 per cent in 1990, this will go some way to filling an important gap in economic and nutritional data. A second major change from 1992 is that confectionery and alcohol are now being covered in the NFS. Soft drinks date are integrated into the main analyses. Particulars of soft drinks bought for household supply have been recorded from 1975 but this information was excluded from the main analyses because of the likelihood of bias from under recording. In sum, [ADB.14] is a remarkable collection of papers which merits extended study. Furthermore, the 1990 edition of *Household Food Consumption and Expenditure* [QRL.267] carries special analyses of data covering the fifty-year period 1940–1990.

Finally, the changes in methodology and coverage are noted in the 1992 issue of [QRL.267] itself. Readers may need reminding that data are available even if not published in [QRL.267]. We have referred to the *National Food Survey: Compendium of Results* [QRL.373] in the main part of this volume. But we also note in these Addenda that the publication *National Food Survey: Estimates of Household Food Consumption and Expenditure 1991* [ADB.36] summarises what additional data are available together with a price list and an order form.

2.10.2 *The Family Expenditure Survey*

CSO Bulletin: Family Expenditure Survey [ADS.21] gives a selection of data from the FES.

2.10.4 *Catering and Meals Outside the Home*

CSO Bulletin: Distributive and Service Trades [ADS.20] report some results from the annual catering inquiry for Great Britain later available in *Business Monitor SDA28: Catering and Allied Trades* [QRL.142].

2.11.4 *Self-sufficiency*

See section 2.5.1.1 of these Addenda for details of the elimination of supplies and self-sufficiency information in the *Annual Abstract of Statistics* [QRL.37].

2.13 Financial Information.

CSO Bulletin: Company Finance [ADS.19] has been discontinued but *Business Monitor MA3: Company Finance* [QRL.81] should be published in 1992 at least. The CSO has decided to phase out the Company Accounts Analysis (CAA) in its present form because of differences between company accounting concepts and those utilised in the national accounts.

CSO Bulletin: Finance of Top Companies [ADS.22] has been discontinued. It contained some data from *Business Monitor MO3: Finance of Large Companies* [QRL.89] which has also been discontinued. Company accounts for large company groups contain a large, growing and indistinguishable element of the activities of overseas subsidiaries and branches which detracts from any potential use of CAA data within the CSO as an input into the national accounts. The existing register used for CAA will, however, be maintained. A restricted set of statistics will continue to be extracted from published accounts.

2.14.2 *Market Research*

Checkout [ADS.15] has emerged as another monthly journal containing news, articles and statistics on the food and drink market. The statistical data it contains enable interested parties to keep up with market developments. For example, issue twelve volume three of December 1991 of [ADS.15] gives the Checkout/Nielsen chart on the top 100 grocery brands, reporting product sales, brand owner, last year's rank, marketing managers and advertising spent (MEAL data) which includes well-known food products.

2.15 Research and Development

CSO Bulletin: Industrial Research and Development [ADS.23] gave provisional results of the CSO large scale (benchmark) survey of expenditure and employment in research and development (R&D) performed in UK industry in 1989. This preceded the final results published later in *Business Monitor MO14: Industrial Research and Development Expenditure and Employment* [QRL.86]. But [ADS.23] did not have results for food and drink later covered in [QRL.86].

However, a spur to company reporting of statistics on R&D has been given by the Enterprise Initiative of the Department of Trade and Industry. An innovation pack is now available from the Innovation Unit and statistical coverage has now improved. *Company Reporting: The Independent's UK R&D Scoreboard* [ADS.16] was first published for 1991 and forms part of this innovation pack. The tables also appeared in the 10th June 1991 issue of the *Independent* newspaper. They take advantage of the requirement that companies must now include R&D expenditure in their annual reports and give the following information:

(1) Ranking of UK companies by R&D spend.

This table gives alphabetical coverage of companies including those in the Food sector. Data are presented for current spend, percentage change, R&D per employee and industry rank. These are compared with sales, percentage change in sales, sales per employee, R&D as a percentage of sales and rank. Profit (loss), percentage change, R&D as percentage of profit and ranks are also produced.

(2) Top ten UK companies by R&D spend.
This table gives the same dimensions for the top ten.

(3) International comparisons of R&D spend by top 100 R&D spenders.

For the Food sector, the industry comparison for the same components is made between the UK and Japan.

The definition of R&D used is set out in the accounting standard SSAP13. The authors have included R&D spending charged against profits and any spending which has been capitalised in the year.

It is intended that the bodies responsible, Company Reporting and Sheffield University Management School, will make this an annual report and it is hoped will extend food industry and other coverage to smaller companies. [ADS.16] is a welcome development for it was previously difficult to find any figures for the food industry and individual companies.

2.16.4.4 Reports of the Monopolies and Mergers Commission 1989–1991.
Three reports provide background information and data on various segments of the Food industries. The reports are:

Hillsdown Holdings plc and Pittard Garner plc: A Report on the Proposed Merger [ADB.40] in April 1989.

Tate and Lyle plc and British Sugar plc: A Report on the Proposed Merger [ADB.42] in February 1991.

Soluble Coffee: A Report on the Supply of Soluble Coffee for Retail Sale within the United Kingdom [ADB.41] in March 1991.

The report on *Hillsdown Holdings plc and Pittard Garner plc* [ADB.40] provides useful information on Hillsdown's activities in fresh meat and bacon, poultry, eggs and animal feeds and food processing and distribution.

Tate and Lyle plc and British Sugar plc [ADB.42] reported in 1991 following the decision of Berisford International plc to put its subsidiary British Sugar plc up for sale. Although not as extensive as the earlier *Tate and Lyle plc and Ferruzzi Finanziaria SpA and S and W Berisford plc: A Report on the Existing and Proposed Mergers* [B.455], it provides a concise overview of the United Kingdom sugar market. It yields turnover and profit data on the Tate & Lyle group, analysed according to business activity, but details are omitted for Tate & Lyle Sugars for disclosure reasons. Various data on supplies of sugar beet, production facilities, employment etc. as well as financial results are given for British Sugar. It is usually possible to get a statistical picture of these firms up to 1990. The report also reviews the EC sugar market. The details on the EC sugar market include statistical illustrations on the production and consumption of sugar in the EC12, the total Community sugar balance, the numbers of sugar companies in the EC and, for the two UK producers, the shares of industrial sugar sales by individual food and other industry sectors.

Soluble Coffee: A Report on the Supply of Soluble Coffee for Retail Sale within the United Kingdom [ADB.41] was published in 1991. The background to this first investigation on the soluble coffee market since the 1977 Price Commission report on *Coffee, Prices, Costs and Margins* [B.419] was that in 1989 The Nestlé Company Ltd. supplied some 48 per cent of the volume and 56 per cent of the value of soluble coffee for retail sale. [ADB.41] provides a plethora of statistical information on the market for soluble coffee, market shares, the principal suppliers, prices, profitability of the principal suppliers and returns on capital employed. [ADB.41] is a thoroughly interesting inquiry which draws on a variety of data up to 1989/90 to help come to the conclusion that Nestlé was not abusing its market position.

Chapter 3 Organic Oils and Fats

The PQ Monitors have been replaced by two PAS Monitors for this Group:
Business Monitor PAS4115 : Margarine and Compound Cooking Fats [ADS.6]
Business Monitor PAS4116: Organic Oils and Fats [ADS.7].

Chapter 4 Slaughtering of Animals and Production of Meat and By-products

Business Monitor PQ4122: Bacon Curing and Meat Production [QRL.130] survives. There is now also one PAS Monitor for this Group:
Business Monitor PAS4123: Poultry and Poultry Products [ADS.8]

CSO Bulletin: Inquiry into Sales of Industry [ADS.24] gives disaggregated sales data for AH4126, AH4221 and AH4222. See section 2.1.1 of these Addenda.

Chapter 5 Milk and Milk Products

We noted in section 5.17 the serious data deficiency on many milk-related products. However *CSO Bulletin: Inquiry into Sales of Industry* [ADS.24] gives disaggregated sales data for AH4130. See section 2.1.1 of these Addenda.

Review of the Fresh Chilled Dairy Products Market [ADS.37] carries some further information. Data are usually available on the following: value and volume of total fresh chilled dairy products (yogurt, cottage cheese etc.); product category percentages by value; consumer trends in UK and Europe including per capita consumption of yogurt; statistical profiles by product of the yogurts and desserts markets; the frozen yogurt and yogurt drinks markets; the cottage cheese, salads and cream markets; predictions for the next year.

Chapter 6 Processing of Fruit and Vegetables

The PAS Monitor *Business Monitor PAS4147: Fruit and Vegetable Products* [ADS.9] replaces the former PQ Monitor.

6.2.1 *Jam, Marmalade and Table Jellies.*
The Sweet Spreads Market [ADS.41] covers jam, marmalade, honey, peanut butter, syrup and treacle, lemon and fruit curds and chocolate. Annual data on retail sales

in both money and percentage terms are given. Jam and marmalade are thus separately compared with other sweet spreads.

6.2.3 *Canning, Bottling, Drying etc. of Fruit and Vegetables*

Market Facts: Canned Fruit and Fruit Juice [ADS.35] is compiled from industry and market research sources by the Del Monte company. It contains data both on the entire market and individual products.

It gives a market size comparison in value for canned fruit compared with yoghurt, chilled desserts etc. Total canned fruits, fruit in syrup and fruit in juice are profiled according to market size, brand shares and a regional consumption index. The same is done for the individual products of pineapple, peaches, pears, fruit cocktail and ambient desserts. For canned fruit, the main products (pears, peaches, pineapple etc.) are treated similarly by fruit type composition, in-syrup and in-juice. [ADS.35] also contains statistical data on the fruit juice market.

6.2.4 *Pickling and Preserving of Fruit and Vegetables; Pickles and Chutney*

Sauce Supremacy: Condiments in Perspective [ADS.38] gives the condiments market sector shares percentage values for the various products: e.g. tomato ketchup, pickle, salad dressings, mayonnaise, mustard, chutney, brown sauce, apple sauce etc. Manufacturers' shares are also given. The UK bottled sauces and tomato ketchup markets are separately profiled.

6.14.2 *Market Research*

See [ADS.35] in 6.2.3 above for data on canned fruit and fruit juice.

Chapter 7 Fish Processing

Business Monitor PAS4150: Fish Products [ADS.10] replaces the former PQ Monitor.

Fisheries Economics Newsletter [ADB.31] carries articles, news items and abstracts for those interested in fisheries economics and aquaculture.

Statistical Sources on Fish Processing — Past and Present [ADB.7] is an expansion and adaptation of Chapter 7 of this volume prepared as a monograph for the SFIA by John Mark and Roger Strange. It draws together statistical sources on both fisheries and fish processing in a comprehensive fashion.

7.5 *Current Inputs other than Labour*

KEY Indicators [ADS.33] reproduces data on fish landings and supplies.

7.8 *International Transactions*

KEY Indicators [ADS.33] gives import and export data by species.

7.10.4 *Catering and Meals Outside the Home*
KEY Indicators [ADS.33] includes caterers' purchases by species/product and the share of catering market by outlet.

7.10.5 *Industry Sources*
KEY Indicators [ADS.33] portrays household purchases in Great Britain in value and volume terms by species. Market shares by type of outlet are given for both fresh and frozen fish. [ADS.33] also contains demographic analyses of purchasing patterns.

7.12.3 *The Retail Prices Index*
KEY Indicators [ADS.33] shows the index for all fish compared with all items; all food; and beef.

Chapter 8 Grain Milling and Bread, Biscuits and Flour Confectionery (including Breakfast Cereals).

CSO Bulletin: Inquiry into Sales of Industry [ADS.24] gives disaggregated sales data for AH4160. See section 2.1.1 of these Addenda.

Chapter 9 Sugar and Sugar by-Products

A book by George C. Abbott simply titled *Sugar* [ADB.1] contains statistical illustrations relevant to many sections of this chapter. It gives an account of the organisation and structure of production, the marketing of sugar, international control measures and sugar policy in major markets, including the domestic markets of the UK, Common Market and the US. A major preoccupation throughout is international sugar policy.

The sugar market is also described in *Tate and Lyle plc and British Sugar plc: A Report on the Proposed Merger* [ADB.42] — see Addenda section 2.16.4.4 above.

Chapter 10 Ice-cream, Cocoa, Chocolate and Sugar Confectionery

CSO Bulletin: Inquiry into Sales of Industry [ADS.24] gives disaggregated sales data for AH4214. See section 2.1.1 of these Addenda.

10.8.3 *Industry Sources*
The IOCCC *Statistical Bulletin* [ADS.39] gives data on consumption, production and international trade. The main objective is to make international comparisons with respect to the products of the chocolate, sugar confectionery and biscuit industries. Statistics are given from the top ten importing and exporting countries.

10.14.2 *Market Research*

Sweet Success: Review of UK Confectionery Market [ADS.42] is popularly known as the *Trebor Bassett Sweet Market Report*. It gives a detailed overview of the market, based upon data collected by Nielsen Retail Audit, Gordon Simmons Research Ltd., Media Register, the OPCS, the Institute of Petroleum, BCCCA and Trebor Bassett Ltd. itself. It portrays the sweet market by volume and value; profiled by age, type of sweet, type of packaging and company shares. It carries considerable detail on the top twenty selling sweets by retail outlet categorised by multiple CTN, independent CTN, multiple groceries; cooperatives; independent grocers; other retail outlets (filling stations, off-licences etc.). It looks to the future in its analyses of developing brands. A statistical appendix records the top selling roll sweets, the top selling half-pound bag sweets and the comparative size (by value) of confectionery compared with some other UK food markets (eg. bread, biscuits, cereals etc.). Adult purchases and eating habits are compared with those of children. Cross-country comparisons of per capita consumption of chocolate and sweets are drawn.

The SweetMate Report [ADS.40] analyses the bagged confectionery market, drawing from various market research sources. This report is divided into three parts; the confectionery market, the bagged confectionery market and outlets for bagged confectionery. The split between chocolate and sugar confectionery, the products breakdown, the dominant companies involved, consumer profiles and the various outlets are scrutinised.

Wall's Pocket Money Monitor [ADS.44] is based upon a Gallup survey and has become the major authority on the spending power of Britain's children. First produced in 1975, it is now (1992) in its seventeenth year. It is particularly germane to the products of this Group as it reports the percentages of childrens' pocket money spent on sweets and ice-cream as well as crisps etc.

Chapter 11 Starch and Miscellaneous Foods

There are now two PAS Monitors for this Group:

Business Monitor PAS4180: Starch [ADS.11]

Business Monitor PAS4239: Miscellaneous Foods [ADS.14].

11.2.2 *Potato Crisps and other Snack Products*

The *Edible Nut Market Report* [ADS.28] is produced twice yearly by Man-Producten Rotterdam. It gives a statistically-backed commentary on the world markets for the following: groundnuts; cashews; almonds; brazils; hazelnuts. Various data are provided on world production and crops by exporting countries and imports by the major consumers. Physical quantities are often reported. e.g. UK annual imports of almonds in metric tons. Edible nut kernel prices are given in quarterly terms for all these nuts both in local currencies and sterling equivalent.

[ADS.28] succeeded the Gill & Duffus publication: the *Edible Nut Market Report* [ADS.27] which had a similar but not identical coverage. Gill & Duffus also produced the annual *Edible Nut Statistics* [ADS.29]. This publication may be continued by the Research and Planning Department of Man-Producten.

11.2.7 *All Other Foods, Not Elsewhere Specified*
The *Pepper Report* [ADS.36] is also produced by Man-Producten. It gives a statistical picture of supply by exporting country. Demand is shown by importing country including the UK. The data are normally annual but the average spot prices for white and black pepper in the USA are in monthly terms.

The Sweet Spreads Market [ADS.41], referred to in section 6.2.1 of these Addenda, also features trends in peanut butter and honey sales, patterns of consumption and advertising. Brand names are referred to.

Chapter 12 Tea and Coffee

A Monopolies and Mergers Commission Report: *Soluble Coffee: A Report on the Supply of Soluble Coffee for Retail Sale within the United Kingdom* [ADB.41] was published in March 1991. For details see Addenda section 2.16.4.4 above.

12.12.1.1 Coffee
The *Weekly Report on Prices* [ADS.45] is issued by the ICO. It gives the prices and numbers of open contracts for robustas on the London Terminal Market and indicator prices. This information is published for the previous five market days, previous four weeks ending Thursdays, previous three months and previous three years. Other tables gives price information on world markets. Future, spot and indicator prices for many types of coffee are covered, often by geographical origin. New York, Bremen/Hamburg, Le Havre/Marseilles are included as well as London. Graphs are appended to show price histories in response to various circumstances from the 1985 drought in Brazil to the suspension of quotas by the ICO.

New Developments in Electronic Media

There is little doubt that the new technology is changing the landscape of business information. This affects the food and other industries. Given the growing inclination to seek specific business information on-line as well as from hard copy statistical publications and business directories, we now summarise the main developments. We list first the most useful directories:

Directory of On-line Data bases [ADB.25]
Directory of Portable Data bases [ADB.26]
Brit-line Directory of British Data bases [ADB.19]
The On-line Business Sourcebook [ADB.3]

Data bases collect together company information, where companies in the Food industries may be identified. *The On-line Business Sourcebook* [ADB.3] gives a particularly useful analysis, showing the range of coverage including company directories, company accounts, mergers and acquisitions, prices, market research, industrial economics and finance, international trade etc. *Portable Business Data bases* [ADB.4] performs a complementary service with the same content headings for business data bases available on floppy disc and CD-ROMS.

The Instant Guide to Company Information On-line Europe [ADB.15] is another response to the expansion in company data base information. It covers both pan-European data bases and company data bases for 16 European countries including the United Kingdom, plus an A–Z of data bases and an A–Z of hosts.

Generally, the CD-Roms/on-line data bases e.g. ICC/Jordans for the UK, can do sector analyses based on SIC codes. Sources such as Extel Microview/Micro Exstat integrate financial information with financial news to track equities and portfolios. *General Business File* [ADB.34], with US and international company coverage, brings together multiple information sources in a single integrated reference tool and may be regarded as a good example of the latest state of the art.

Secondly, we note the Foodline data bases produced and available from the Leatherhead Food Research Association.

FOMAD (Food Market Awareness Data base) is updated weekly and provides coverage of published information on food and drink markets worldwide. Information can be derived from statistical publications which is useful, but secondary data on market sizes, market shares, consumption, advertising spending, retail and packaging trends are also of interest.

FLAIRS (Food Launch Awareness in the Retail Sector) is a databank which covers new food and drink products on the UK market updated weekly. Information on brand name, product type, manufacturer, novel features, launch date, country of origin and test market area is available. This databank is divided into two libraries: FLAIRS NOVEL and FLAIRS UK. The former gives information on novel products launched world-wide, whether in the areas of concept, ingredients, or flavour and packaging. The latter gives news of all food and drink products launched or relaunched on the UK retail market that have been recorded in the trade or marketing press.

Thirdly, the statistical coverage of the CSO's Data bank service offers regularly updated macroeconomic and related statistical data in computer-readable form. Data sets are available on magnetic tape or floppy disc (readable in LOTUS or SMART). Further information is obtainable from The Data bank Manager, Central Statistical Office, Room 52A/4, Government Offices, Great George St., London SW1R 3AU.

Finally, the ESRC Data Archive contains raw data from many official inquiries. A catalogue and further information are available from the Director, ESRC Data Archive, University of Essex, Colchester CO4 3SQ.

Final Remarks

Writing these Addenda has *not* been like completing a leisurely victory lap after running a particularly taxing Marathon. It has been more akin to sprinting round the whole course again! The statistical landscape is always changing, but we have sought to note the major new features as we sped by.

Additional References

(These lists are arranged in the same way as the QRL Key and Bibliography — i.e. publications with a named author are listed alphabetically by author first. Other publications follow and are arranged alphabetically by title. There are two lists, one covering statistical sources and one giving other references).

Statistical Publications

[ADS.1] Burrell, A. Hill, B. and Medland, J. *Agri-facts: A Handbook of UK and EEC Agricultural and Food Statistics.* Harvester Wheatsheaf, Hemel Hempstead, 1990.

[ADS.2] Mitchell, B.R. and Deane, P. *Abstract of British Historical Statistics.* Cambridge University Press, Cambridge, 1962.

[ADS.3] Mitchell, B.R. *British Historical Statistics.* Cambridge University Press, Cambridge, 1988.

[ADS.4] Mitchell, B.R. and Jones, H.G. *Second Abstract of British Historical Statistics.* Cambridge University Press, Cambridge, 1971.

[ADS.5] Ministry of Agriculture, Fisheries and Food. *Agriculture in the United Kingdom.* HMSO, London, Annual.

[ADS.6] Central Statistical Office. *Business Monitor PAS4115: Margarine and Compound Cooking Fats.* HMSO, London, Annual.

[ADS.7] Central Statistical Office. *Business Monitor PAS4116: Organic Oils and Fats.* HMSO, London, Annual.

[ADS.8] Central Statistical Office. *Business Monitor PAS4123: Poultry and Poultry Products.* HMSO, London, Annual.

[ADS.9] Central Statistical Office. *Business Monitor PAS4147: Fruit and Vegetable Products.* HMSO, London, Annual.

[ADS.10] Central Statistical Office. *Business Monitor PAS4150: Fish Products.* HMSO, London, Annual.

[ADS.11] Central Statistical Office. *Business Monitor PAS4180: Starch.* HMSO, London, Annual.

[ADS.12] Central Statistical Office. *Business Monitor PAS4196: Bread and Flour Confectionery.* HMSO, London, Annual.

[ADS.13] Central Statistical Office. *Business Monitor PAS4197: Biscuits and Crispbread.* HMSO, London, Annual.

[ADS.14] Central Statistical Office. *Business Monitor PAS4239: Miscellaneous Foods.* HMSO, London, Annual.

[ADS.15] Blakebeck Magazines Ltd. *Checkout.* Blakebeck Magazines Ltd., London, Monthly.

[ADS.16] Company Reporting Ltd. *Company Reporting: The Independent's UK R&D Scoreboard.* Company Reporting Ltd., Edinburgh, 1991.

[ADS.17] Central Statistical Office. *CSO Bulletin: Acquisitions and Mergers within the UK.* CSO, Newport, Quarterly.

[ADS.18] Central Statistical Office. *Capital Expenditure and Stock Building.* CSO, Newport, Quarterly.

[ADS.19] Central Statistical Office. *CSO Bulletin: Company Finance.* CSO, Newport, Discontinued.

[ADS.20] Central Statistical Office. *CSO Bulletin: Distributive and Service Trades.* CSO, Newport, Annual.

[ADS.21] Central Statistical Office. *CSO Bulletin: Family Expenditure Survey.* CSO, Newport, Annual.

[ADS.22] Central Statistical Office. *CSO Bulletin: Finance of Large Companies.* CSO, Newport, Discontinued.

[ADS.23] Central Statistical Office. *CSO Bulletin: Industrial Research and Development*. CSO, Newport, Annual.
[ADS.24] Central Statistical Office. *CSO Bulletin: Inquiry into Sales of Industry*. CSO, Newport, Quinquennial.
[ADS.25] Central Statistical Office. *CSO Bulletin: Overseas Earnings from Royalties*. CSO, Newport, Annual.
[ADS.26] Central Statistical Office. *CSO Bulletin: Size Analyses of UK Businesses*. CSO, Newport, Annual.
[ADS.27] Gill & Duffus. *Edible Nut Market Report*. Gill & Duffus plc, London, Quarterly to 1990.
[ADS.28] Man-Producten Rotterdam B.V. *Edible Nut Market Report*. Man-Producten Rotterdam B.V., Biannual.
[ADS.29] Gill & Duffus. *Edible Nut Statistics*. Gill & Duffus plc, London, Annual to 1990.
[ADS.30] Employment Department. *Employment News*. Employment Department Group, London, Monthly.
[ADS.31] Central Statistical Office. *Input-output Tables for the United Kingdom 1985*. Working paper of the Central Statistical Office, London, June 1989.
[ADS.32] Central Statistical Office. *Key Data*. HMSO, London, Annual from 1986.
[ADS.33] Sea Fish Industry Authority. *Key Indicators*. Sea Fish Industry Authority, Edinburgh, Occasional.
[ADS.34] Employment Department. *Labour Market Quarterly Report*. Employment Department Skill and Enterprise Network, Sheffield, Occasional.
[ADS.35] Del Monte. *Market Facts: Canned Fruit and Fruit Juice*. Del Monte, Staines, Annual.
[ADS.36] Man-Producten Rotterdam B.V. *Pepper Report*. Man-Producten Rotterdam B.V., Annual.
[ADS.37] Eden Vale. *Review of the Fresh Chilled Dairy Products Market*. Eden Vale, South Ruislip, Annual.
[ADS.38] H.J. Heinz Company Ltd. *Sauce Supremacy: Condiments in Perspective*. H.J. Heinz Company Ltd., Hayes, 1992.
[ADS.39] International Office of Cocoa, Chocolate and Sugar Confectionery. *Statistical Bulletin*. IOCCC, Brussels, Annual.
[ADS.40] SweetMate Ltd. *The SweetMate Report*. SweetMate Ltd., Hayes, 1992.
[ADS.41] The Nestlé Company Ltd. *The Sweet Spreads Market*. The Nestlé Company Ltd., Croydon, 1990.
[ADS.42] Trebor Bassett. *Sweet Success: Review of the UK Confectionery Market*. Trebor Bassett Ltd., Denham, Annual.
[ADS.43] Employment Department. *Training Statistics*. HMSO, London, Annual.
[ADS.44] Birds Eye Wall's Ltd. *Wall's Pocket Money Monitor*. Birds Eye Wall's Ltd., Walton-on-Thames, Annual.
[ADS.45] International Coffee Organisation. *Weekly Report on Prices*. International Coffee Organisation, London, Weekly.

Other References

[ADB.1] Abbott, G. *Sugar*. Routledge, London, 1990.

[ADB.2] Balasubramanyam, V.N. and Nguyen, D.T. "Structure and performance of the UK food and drink industries". *Journal of Agricultural Economics*. vol.42, no.1, January 1991.

[ADB.3] Foster, P. *The On-line Business Sourcebook*. Headland Press, Cleveland, Four times a year.

[ADB.4] Foster, P. *Portable Business Data bases*. Business Research Guide no.9. Headland Press, Cleveland, 1991.

[ADB.5] Hill, B. and Ray, D. *Economics for Agriculture: Food, Farming and the Rural Economy*. Macmillan Education Ltd., Basingstoke and London, 1991.

[ADB.6] Kingaby, S.D. "The rebased index of production". *Economic Trends*. no.24, February 1989.

[ADB.7] Mark, J. and Strange, R. *Statistical Sources on Fish Processing — Past and Present*. Sea Fish Industry Authority Occasional Paper Series no.2, Sea Fish Industry Authority, Edinburgh, 1991.

[ADB.8] Marks, H.F., in Britton, D.K. (ed). *A Hundred Years of British Food and Farming: A Statistical Survey*. Taylor and Francis, London, 1989.

[ADB.9] Mears, Ken. "The first revision of the European classification of economic activities: NACE Rev 1". *Statistical News*. no.92, Spring 1991.

[ADB.10] Midmore, P. (ed). *Input-output Models in the Agriculture Sector*. Avebury, Aldershot, 1991.

[ADB.11] Ramsay, A. *Eurojargon: A Dictionary of EC Acronyms, Abbreviations and Sobriquets*. third edition. Capital Planning Information Ltd., Stamford, 1991.

[ADB.12] Ramsay, A. *European Communities Information*. The Association of Assistant Librarians, London, 1990.

[ADB.13] Sheard, P.R. *A Guide to the British Food Manufacturing Industry*. third edition. Nova Press, Frome, 1991.

[ADB.14] Slater, J.M. (ed). *Fifty Years of the National Food Survey 1940–1990*. HMSO, London, 1991.

[ADB.15] Spencer, N. (ed). *The Instant Guide to Company Information On-line Europe*. The British Library Board, London, 1991.

[ADB.16] Sutton, J. *Sunk Costs and Market Structure: Price Competition, Advertising and the Evolution of Concentration*. The MIT Press, Cambridge, Massachusetts and London, England, 1991.

[ADB.17] Ward, N. "A preliminary analysis of the UK food chain". *Food Policy*. vol.15, no.5, October 1990.

[ADB.18] Foreign and Commonwealth Office. *Britain: An Official Handbook*. HMSO, London, Annual.

[ADB.19] British Institute of Management. *Brit-line: Directory of British Data bases*. McGraw Hill, Maidenhead, 1989.

[ADB.20] Central Statistical Office. *Business Monitor PO1000: Index to Commodities and Business Monitor Titles*. HMSO, London, 1991.

[ADB.21] Central Statistical Office. *Business Monitor PO1007A: UK Directory of Manufacturing Businesses 1990 Supplement*. HMSO, London, 1990.

[ADB.22] Euromonitor Ltd. *Compendium of Marketing Information Sources*. first edition. Euromonitor Publications plc, London, 1989.

[ADB.23] Central Statistical Office. *CSO Bulletin: Methodological Issues re Trade Statistics*. CSO, Newport, Adhoc.

[ADB.24] Central Statistical Office. *CSO Bulletin: Statistical Changes in 1992*. CSO, Newport, Adhoc.

[ADB.25] Cuadra/Gale. *Directory of On-line Data bases*. Gale Research International Ltd., Detroit and London, Two main issues and two up-dates yearly.

[ADB.26] Cuadra/Elsevier. *Directory of Portable Data bases*. Cuadra/Elsevier, New York, Bi-annual.

[ADB.27] Headland Press. *European Business Intelligence Briefing*. Headland Press, Cleveland, Monthly.

[ADB.28] Euromonitor Publications Ltd. *European Directory of Consumer Market Reports and Surveys*. first edition. Euromonitor Publications plc, London, 1991.

[ADB.29] Euromonitor Publications Ltd. *The European Directory of Marketing Information Sources*. second edition. Euromonitor Publications plc, London, 1991.

[ADB.30] Euromonitor Publications Ltd. *The European Directory of Non-official Statistical Sources*. first edition. Euromonitor Publications plc, London, 1988.

[ADB.31] Sea Fish Industry Authority. *Fisheries Economics Newsletter*. Sea Fish Industry Authority, Edinburgh, Monthly.

[ADB.32] Food from Britain. *Food and Drink from Britain: Buyers' Guide*. Food from Britain, London, 1990.

[ADB.33] Hazelwood Frozen Foods Ltd. *Frozen and Chilled Foods Yearbook*. Hazelwood Frozen Foods Ltd., Clwyd, Annual.

[ADB.34] Information Access Company. *General Business File*. Information Access Company, Foster City, California, USA.

[ADB.35] London Business School Information Service. *Guide to European Company Information on EC Countries*. fourth edition. London Business School Information Service, London, 1990.

[ADB.36] Ministry of Agriculture, Fisheries and Food. *National Food Survey: Estimates of Household Food Consumption and Expenditure, 1991*. National Food Survey Branch, London, 1991.

[ADB.37] Statistical Office of the European Communities. *PRODCOM: Description of the Eurostat Project for Comprehensive Community Production Statistics*. Statistical Office of the European Communities, Luxembourg, September 1989.

[ADB.38] Central Statistical Office. *Series and Weights and Supplementary Analysis of Series used in the Index of Output of the Production Industries 1985 Base. Occasional Paper no.22*. HMSO, London, April 1989.

[ADB.39] Marketing Data Europe Ltd. *United Kingdom: Food Manufacturers and Processors*. Marketing Data Europe Ltd., London, 1989.

Reports of the Monopolies and Mergers Commissions

[ADB.40] Monopolies and Mergers Commission. *Hillsdown Holdings plc and Pittard Garner plc: A Report on the Proposed Merger*. Monopolies and Mergers Commission Report. Cm 665. (Session 1988/89). HMSO, London, 1989.

[ADB.41] Monopolies and Mergers Commission. *Soluble Coffee: A Report on the Supply of Soluble Coffee for Retail Sale within the United Kingdom*. Monopolies and Mergers Commission Report. Cm 1459 (Session 1990/91). HMSO, London, March 1991.

[ADB.42] Monopolies and Mergers Commission. *Tate and Lyle plc and British Sugar plc: A Report on the Proposed Merger*. Monopolies and Mergers Commission Report. Cm 1435 (Session 1990/91). HMSO, London, 1991.

SUBJECT INDEX

For Product Safety Concerns and Information please contact our EU representative GPSR@taylorandfrancis.com Taylor & Francis Verlag GmbH, Kaufingerstraße 24, 80331 München, Germany

Printed and bound by CPI Group (UK) Ltd, Croydon, CR0 4YY
08/05/2025
01864495-0003